Cheshire and Burn's Modern Law of Real Property

NICK TULLOCH

LMH

First Edition	September	1925
Second Edition	September	1927
Third Edition	February	1933
Fourth Edition	July	1944
Second Impression	August	1945
Third Impression	January	1947
Fourth Impression	December	1947
Sixth Edition	September	1949
Second Impression	July	1952
Seventh Edition	September	1954
Second Impression	September	1956
Eighth Edition	March	1958
Second Impression	January	1961
Ninth Edition	March	1962
Second Impression	February	1964
Third Impression	August	1966
Tenth Edition	May	1967
Second Impression	April	1970
Eleventh Edition	April	1972
Second Impression	May	1974
Twelfth Edition	May	1976
Thirteenth Edition	August	1982
Second Impression	August	1983
Third Impression	January	1987
Fourteenth Edition	June	1988
Fifteenth Edition	July	1994

Cheshire and Burn's

MODERN LAW OF REAL PROPERTY

Fifteenth Edition

E H Burn BCL, MA

Barrister and Honorary Bencher of Lincoln's Inn;
Professor of Law in The City University;
Emeritus Student of Christ Church, Oxford

London, Dublin, Edinburgh
Butterworths
1994

United Kingdom	Butterworth & Co (Publishers) Ltd, Halsbury House, 35 Chancery Lane, LONDON WC2A 1EL and 4 Hill Street, EDINBURGH EH2 3JZ
Australia	Butterworths, SYDNEY, MELBOURNE, BRISBANE, ADELAIDE, PERTH, CANBERRA and HOBART
Canada	Butterworths Canada Ltd, TORONTO and VANCOUVER
Ireland	Butterworth (Ireland) Ltd, DUBLIN
Malaysia	Malayan Law Journal Sdn Bhd, KUALA LUMPUR
New Zealand	Butterworths of New Zealand Ltd, WELLINGTON and AUCKLAND
Puerto Rico	Butterworth of Puerto Rico, Inc, SAN JUAN
Singapore	Butterworths Asia, SINGAPORE
South Africa	Butterworth Publishers (Pty) Ltd, DURBAN
USA	Butterworth Legal Publishers, CARLSBAD, California; and SALEM, New Hampshire

A CIP Catalogue record for this book is available from the British Library.

ISBN 0 406 02977 6

Typeset in Great Britain by William Clowes Limited, Beccles and London
Printed in Great Britain by The Bath Press, Avon

Preface to the Fifteenth Edition

Since the last edition of this book in 1988 more water has flowed under the bridge. There has been a steady stream of cases and statutes and a spate of recommendations from the Law Commission.

The House of Lords has decided the relevant date for the determination of an overriding interest under section 70(1)(g) of the Land Registration Act 1925; shed further light on the meaning of actual occupation in that paragraph (so too have decisions of the Court of Appeal and first instance); reaffirmed the ancient requirement (of some 500 years) of certainty of duration in a lease and the rule (of some 100 years) that the burden of a positive covenant does not run with freehold land (nor does section 79 of the Law of Property Act 1925 reverse *Austerberry v Corporation of Oldham*). The House has re-examined the distinction between a lease and a licence in the context of multiple occupation and pretence; and given strict guidance to an institutional mortgagee where a wife has been induced to stand as surety for her husband's debt by his undue influence or misrepresentation. It has also widened the effect of peaceable re-entry by a landlord on relief against forfeiture for breach of covenant in a lease; and eliminated the intrusion of *scintilla temporis* into the area of mortgages.

The Privy Council has examined the requirements for a scheme of development; and applied the test of unconscionability to the enforcement of an estoppel licence.

The Court of Appeal, on the other hand, has elaborated the principles of rectification in the Land Registration Act 1925; sanctioned a lock-out agreement so as to prevent gazumping; considered the distinction between a lease and a licence in the context of a shifting population and in that of joint and several liability for the payment of rent; emphasised that the implication of a yearly tenancy from the payment of rent on an annual basis is only a presumption; relied on the contractual nature of a lease so as to enable a tenant to avoid forfeiture for breach of a covenant short of frustration (likewise, at first instance, to enable a tenant to repudiate a lease for breach of covenant by the landlord); provided modern instances of ancient rules in easements, including the rights to park a motor car and to use a way as a fire-escape and as a route for a supermarket trolley; decided that 175 years' non-user of a right of way did not amount to its abandonment; characterised the duty of a mortgagee to a mortgagor or his guarantor when exercising the remedy of sale as sounding in their special relationship and not in negligence (there has been a similar retreat from *Cuckmere* twice in the Privy Council); come to the aid of a mortgagor with a negative equity by permitting him to sell against the wishes of the mortgagee; and simplified the meaning of adverse possession (*Leigh v Jack* is no more).

Important decisions at first instance include the purposive and welcome interpretation of section 2 of the Law of Property (Miscellaneous Provisions) Act 1989 on the new formalities required for contracts for the disposition of land.

Legislation since the last edition is again of primary importance in the field of landlord and tenant. The Housing Act 1988 has phased out the outmoded Rent Act 1977 and substituted more realistic tenancies—assured and assured shorthold; and the Leasehold Reform, Housing and Urban Development Act 1993 has conferred rights to collective enfranchisement and lease renewal on tenants of flats and initiated changes in public sector housing. In other areas planning law has been consolidated by the Town and Country Planning Act 1990 and refined by the Planning and Compensation Act 1991; and new formalities for contracts for the disposition of land and for deeds and their execution have been substituted by the Law of Property (Miscellaneous Provisions) Act 1989. There are also passing references to three Acts of 1991 with the commendably short titles of Badgers (twice) and Deer (once).

There has been continued and continuous activity by the Law Commission. Fifteen Reports have appeared since the last edition. Of these five are substantial: Land Registration, accompanied by a draft Bill designed to produce "a modern, and we hope, a simpler version of the 1925 Act" (welcome especially since at last the Act was finally extended to the whole of England and Wales in 1990); new schemes for Trusts of Land and for Land Mortgages; Part II of the Landlord and Tenant Act 1954; Duration of Liability of Parties to Leases; and, as a final instalment to the reform of the law of covenants, there are recommendations for the removal of obsolete restrictive covenants. The Law Commission has also published seven Working Papers (their title was changed to Consultation Papers in 1991). Of these, two are of major importance; Responsibility for State and Condition of Property and The Rules against Perpetuities and Excessive Accumulations. (One of the options is to abolish both of these rules, which have so bedevilled the law of future interests and so bewildered those who try to understand them.)

This new material, and much else besides, has been incorporated into the fifteenth edition, and has necessitated substantial rewriting of the text. I am again most grateful to all those friends and critics who have given me their help and advice.

I would particularly like to thank Keith Davies, Professor of Law in the University of Reading, for revising Planning Law; Jill Martin, Professor of Law, King's College, London for revising Security of Tenure and Control of Rent; and Marilyn Kennedy-McGregor, Barrister of Gray's Inn and of Lincoln's Inn, and John Cartwright, Student of Christ Church, Oxford, and my former colleague there, who read the proofs and revised his index. For their many valuable suggestions of form and substance I am most grateful.

Finally, I wish to thank the publishers for undertaking the compilation of the Table of Cases, Statutes and Statutory Instruments, and for their ready and expert help at all times.

This edition purports to state the law as it was on 1 January 1994, but more recent developments have been incorporated where space permitted.

E.H.B

ST HUGH'S COLLEGE
OXFORD
20 May 1994

Preface to the First Edition

My classical friends assure me that the principles which every author should observe were laid down for all time by Horace. Compose, submit the result line by line to Maecius, consult the judgment of two friends, and preserve to yourself a *locus poenitentiae* by withholding publication for nine years. Such rules are no doubt of inestimable value, but unfortunately the real property legislation of the last few years has been too rapid to permit of an author profiting by the wisdom of Horace in the particular matter of delay. Despite his awful warning,

nescit vox missa reverti,

which never seemed so impressive to me as it does now on the eve of publication, I felt, in view of the representations of colleagues and pupils, that some attempt should be made to publish with as little delay as possible an account of the new system of real property law.

As the lack of adequate time is the only excuse that I can offer for the shortcomings of this book, it may be in point to indicate why I have thought it advisable to publish as soon as possible. The old system of real property law was described with such lucidity and fullness in several works of repute that it would have been presumptuous to offer another book had the law remained unaltered. It is, however, to be profoundly modified on 1 January 1926. The process of modification was begun by the Law of Property Act 1922. This was originally designed to come into operation on 1 January 1925, but a closer examination of the Act showed that it would not lead to a simplification of the law, especially in the matter of accessibility, unless it were cast into a different form. Its greatest defect was that while it introduced a number of new rules and brought about a number of abolitions, both in the existing common law and the existing statutes, it did not repeal and re-enact the latter in a manner calculated to render the search for the law the simple task it should be. To avoid, therefore, what might have been chaos, the legislature set to work in 1924 to consolidate a great part of the statute law bearing on real property, and to incorporate the principles and alteration of the Act of 1922 in the consolidating statutes. Such of the provisions of the Act of 1922 as were not of a merely transitional character were repealed and re-enacted in the consolidating statutes, while the date at which the transitional provisions were to come into operation was postponed to 1 January 1926. Six consolidating bills were drafted and appeared in print during the late summer of 1924, but it was not until April 1925, that they were passed by Parliament.

The position was, then that only in April 1925, did the new legal rules which, for the moment at any rate, are destined to regulate rights of property in the land, become known, and though they were postponed from coming into operation until 1 January 1926, the result was that a student had but eight months within which to master the new system. Examinations wait for no man, and when it is remembered that the King's Printer's copies of the new Acts cover more than six hundred pages, it will be realised that the prospect with which a student was faced was not a happy one.

When it was known in January 1924, what the intentions of the legislature were, I therefore felt justified in attempting to prepare a book which would not merely record the changes, but would present the law as a composite whole. Despite the short time available, I felt that something was required, before the new era dawned in January 1926, to enable students to envisage a legal system which is, in many respects, widely different from that described in existing books. The present book represents an attempt to supply the want. It has many defects, but it is hoped that they are defects which can be readily eradicated should sufficient support be forthcoming to justify the publication of a second edition.

One of these defects is a somewhat excessive length, though something may be said in palliation of what, to a student, is perhaps the worst vice known to the law. In the first place the number of pages has been greatly increased owing to the manner in which the text has been set out. The subject is complicated, and the design has been to space the text out and to add numerous headings and identations, so that the subject matter may easily catch the eye of a reader. Secondly, the book contains a number of repetitions which are due partly to the speed at which it has been written and partly to the intervals which, owing to other calls upon my time, have separated the composition of its various parts. Thirdly, it must be admitted that the bulk of real property law is greater now than it formerly was. At the beginning of my labours I was imbued with the idea that the task of a student had been lightened. So much had disappeared. The old rules relating to remainders, the old canons of descent, the rule in Shelley's Case, copyholds, gavelkind— they were all gone, and one's first impression was that the amount of law which a book on real property need deal with had been diminished. This will be true in twenty or thirty years' time, but unfortunately it is far from the truth at the present moment. Quite apart from the fact that a knowledge of the old law remains necessary for the purpose of investigating title, it is also a fact that a great many of the new rules can neither be understood nor explained unless the former rules are known. The Administration of Estates Act 1925, for instance, abolishes curtesy, but the Law of Property Act 1925 retains it in the case of entailed interests.

So much may be said by way of excuse. The Horatian requirement of time has been lacking, but not the other essentials. The role of Maecius has been filled by Mr. T. K. Brighouse MA, a former colleague of mine in the University College of Wales, Aberystwyth, who, though not a lawyer, has been an experienced and valuable critic on the literary side. Despite what must be a distinctly repellent subject to a layman, he has read every word of this book at least twice, and has not only saved me from some of the worst mistakes of a naturally defective style, but has advised and procured alterations in many passages where my proposed treatment would have obscured the lucidity of statement. The extent of my obligation to him is immeasurable.

On the legal side, the help I have received has been equally considerable. The main task has fallen on Mr. P. H. L. Brough of the Equity Bar, who has sacrificed a great deal of his time to reading and advising on the manuscript before it has been submitted to others. Moreover, he has given me the benefit of his practical experience in the initial stages of the book by helping to arrange the form in which some of the more difficult parts of the new legislation might be set out. His clearness of vision and his natural aptitude for realising the object of an obscure enactment have been of inestimable value to me.

I owe a debt of deep gratitude to Sir John Miles BCL, MA, Fellow and Tutor of Merton College, Oxford, who besides encouraging me to begin the preparation of this book, has always been anxious at the sacrifice of his own time to afford me the benefit of his mature knowledge and sound advice.

To Profesor J. D. I. Hughes BCL, MA, of Leeds University, to Mr. Ernest A. Steele LLB, of Halifax, and to Mr. L. E. Salt MA, Fellow and Bursar of Pembroke College, Oxford, I am under a deep obligation. They have each done me the honour of reading the whole of the book in proof form, and when I recall the number of their suggestions and criticisms to which I have paid heed, I realise the extent of my indebtedness to them. Their unselfish labours have prevented the appearance of innumerable sins, both of omission and commission, and their judgment has frequently kept me from straying into an unwise method of treatment.

Mr. Harold Potter LLB, of Birmingham University, and Mr. John Snow MA, of New College, Oxford, have very kindly read the chapter on conveyancing and have suggested several practical improvements which have been of the utmost value to me. It is, however, only fair to Mr. Potter to say that he would have elaborated the introductory note to Book III in a manner which would have greatly increased its usefulness and value, had not his proposals unfortunately reached me too late to permit of their inclusion.

The above is an inadequate acknowledgment of the services which have been rendered to me, but at the same time it must be recorded that none of the gentlemen who have so willingly extended me their aid is responsible in the slightest degree for the mistakes and failings which no doubt will be found to characterise this book. For these I am wholly responsible, while only partially responsible for anything which may be worthy of approval.

Lastly, I must acknowledge the help, of a different character, but no less valuable, which I have received from my wife. From the moment when this book was begun she abandoned a great part of her leisure and, having mastered for the occasion the unattractive art of typing, converted an almost illegible manuscript into a form which made the task of all those who had to deal with it a task of ease instead of a burden.

G. C. C.

OXFORD
September 1925

Contents

PART I INTRODUCTION TO THE MODERN LAW

PART II ESTATES AND INTERESTS IN LAND

A. THE ESTATE IN FEE SIMPLE ABSOLUTE IN POSSESSION

B. INTERESTS ARISING UNDER A STRICT SETTLEMENT OR TRUST FOR SALE

C. COMMERCIAL INTERESTS

I Interests conferring a right to the land itself

II Interests conferring a right enforceable against the land of another

PART III THE TRANSFER AND EXTINCTION OF ESTATES AND INTERESTS

A. TRANSFER INTER VIVOS BY ESTATE OWNERS

B. TRANSFER ON DEATH

C. EXTINCTION OF ESTATES AND INTERESTS

D. INCAPACITIES AND DISABILITIES WITH REGARD TO THE HOLDING AND TRANSFER OF ESTATES AND INTERESTS

PART IV PLANNING LAW

Table of statutes

References in this Table to *Statutes* are to Halsbury's Statutes of England (Fourth Edition) showing the volume and page at which the annotated text of an Act may be found.

Table of statutory instruments

List of Cases

Abbreviations

OJLS	Oxford Journal of Legal Studies
SJ	Solicitors' Journal
U of WALR	University of Western Australia Law Review
Yale LJ	Yale Law Journal

Bibliography

Aldridge	*Boundaries, Walls and Fences*, 7th edn., by T. M. Aldridge (1992)
	Leasehold Law, by T. M. Aldridge (1980)
Annand and Cain	*Enquiries before Contract*, by R. Annand and B. Cain (1986)
	Remedies under the Contract, by R. Annand and B. Cain (1988)
Annand and Whish	*The Contract*, by R. Annand and R. Whish (1987)
Arden and Partington	*Housing Law*, by A. Arden and M. Partington (1983)
	Quiet Enjoyment, by A. Arden and M. Partington, 3rd edn., revised (1990)
Ashburner	*Ashburner's Principles of Equity*, 2nd edn., by D. Browne (1933)
Bacon	*Bacon's New Abridgement of the Law*, 7th edn., by Sir Henry Gwillim and C. E. Dodd (1832)
Bailey	*The Law of Wills*, by S. J. Bailey, 7th edn. (1973)
Barnsley	*Conveyancing Law and Practice*, by D. G. Barnsley, 3rd edn. (1988)
	Barnsley's Land Options, 2nd edn., by R. Castle (1992)
Behan	*The Use of Land as Affected by Covenants*, by J. C. V. Behan (1924)
Berstein and Reynolds	*Handbook of Rent Review*, by R. Bernstein and K. Reynolds (1981)
Blackstone	*Commentaries on the Laws of England*, by Sir William Blackstone, 15th edn., by E. Christian (1809)
Bonfield	*Marriage Settlements, 1601–1740*, by L. Bonfield (1983)
Brand	*Encyclopedia of the Law of Compulsory Purchase and Compensation*, by C. M. Brand (1960)
Bromley	*Family Law*, by P. M. Bromley and N. V. Lowe, 7th edn. (1987)
Brunyate	*Limitation of Actions in Equity*, by J. B. Brunyate (1932)
Bullen and Leake and Jacob	*Precedents of Pleadings*, 12th edn., by I. H. Jacob (1975)
Burnett	*The Elements of Conveyancing*, by J. F. R. Burnett, 8th edn. (1952)
Burton	*An Elementary Compendium of the Law of Real Property*, by W. H. Burton, 8th edn., by E. F. Cooper (1856)
Challis	*Challis's Law of Real Property*, 3rd edn., by C. Sweet (1911)
Cherry	*The New Property Acts. Series of Lectures with Questions and Answers*, by Sir Benjamin Cherry (1926)
Cheshire Fifoot and Furmston	*Cheshire Fifoot and Furmston's Law of Contract*, 12th edn., by M. P. Furmston (1991)
Cheshire and North	*Cheshire and North, Private International Law*, 12th edn., by P. M. North and J. J. Fawcett (1992)
Clarke and Adams	*Rent Reviews and Variable Rents*, by D. N. Clarke and J. E. Adams, 2nd edn. (1984)

Clayden	*The Law and History of Commons and Village Greens*, by P. Clayden (1985)
Co. Litt.	*Coke's Commentary upon Littleton*, 19th edn., with notes by F. Hargrave and C. Butler (1832)
Comyns	*A Digest of the Laws of England*, by Sir John Comyns (1822)
Coote	*Coote's Treatise on the Law of Mortgages*, 9th edn., by R. L. Ramsbotham (1927)
Cousins	*The Law of Mortgages*, by E. F. Cousins (1989)
Crabb	*Leases Covenants and Consents*, by L. Crabb (1991)
Cretney	*Enduring Powers of Attorney*, by S. M. Cretney, 3rd edn. (1991)
Cretney and Masson	*Principles of Family Law*, by S. M. Cretney and J. M. Masson, 5th edn. (1990)
Cruise	*Cruise's Digest of the Laws of England*, 4th edn., by H. H. White (1835)
Dart	*Dart's Vendors and Purchasers of Real Estate*, 8th edn., by E. P. Hewitt and M. R. C. Overton (1929)
Davies	*Law of Compulsory Purchase and Compensation*, by K. Davies, 4th edn. (1984)
Dawson and Pearce	*Licences Relating to the Occupation or Use of Land*, by I. J. Dawson and R. A. Pearce (1979)
Denyer-Green	*Law of Compulsory Purchase and Compensation*, by D. Denyer-Green, 3rd edn. (1989)
Digby	*An Introduction to the History of the Law of Real Property*, 5th edn., by K. E. Digby and W. M. Harrison (1897)
Easton	*The Law of Rentcharges (commonly called chief rents) mainly from a conveyancing standpoint*, 2nd edn., by H. C. Easton (1931)
Ellis	*Rights to Light*, by P. Ellis (1992)
Elphinstone	*Introduction to Conveyancing*, by Sir Howard Elphinstone, 7th edn., by F. T. Maw (1918)
Elphinstone	*Covenants affecting Land*, by Sir Lancelot Elphinstone (1946)
Emmet	*Emmet's Notes on Perusing Titles and on Practical Conveyancing*, 19th edn., by J. T. Farrand (1986)
Encyclopaedia	*The Encyclopaedia of Forms and Precedents*, 4th edn. (1964)
English and Saville	*Strict Settlement*, by B. English and J. Saville (1985)
Evans and Smith	*Evans: The Law of Landlord and Tenant*, 4th edn., by P. F. Smith (1993)
Fairest	*Mortgages*, by P. B. Fairest, 2nd edn. (1980)
Farrand	*Contract and Conveyance*, by J. T. Farrand, 2nd edn. (1973); 4th edn. (1983)
Farwell	*Farwell on Powers*, 3rd edn., by C. J. W. Farwell and F. K. Archer (1916)
Fearne	*An Essay on the Learning of Contingent Remainders and Executory Devises*, by Charles Fearne, 10th edn., with notes by C. Butler, with *An Original View of Executory Interests in Real and Personal Property*, by Josiah W. Smith (1844)
Finn	*Essays in Equity*, by P. D. Finn (1985)
Fisher and Lightwood	*Fisher and Lightwood's Law of Mortgage*, 10th edn., by E. L. G. Tyler (1988)
Foa	*Foa's General Law of Landlord and Tenant*, 8th edn., by H. Heathcote-Williams (1957)
Freedman and Shapiro	*Service Charges. Law and Practice*, by S. Freedman and E. Shapiro (1989)
Fry	*A Treatise on the Specific Performance of Contracts*, by Sir Charles Fry, 6th edn., by G. R. Northcote (1921)

Gadsden	*The Law of Commons*, by G. D. Gadsden (1988)
Gale	*Gale on Easements*, 15th edn., by S. G. Maurice (1986)
Garner	*Local Land Charges*, by J. F. Garner, 11th edn. (1992)
George	*The Sale of Flats*, 5th edn., by E. F. George and A. George (1984)
Gibson	*Gibson's Conveyancing*, 21st edn., by R. A. Donell, P. R. Dean, R. G. Holbrook, C. K. Liddle and J. A. Treleaven (1980)
Gilbert	*A Treatise on Rents*, by Sir Jeffrey Gilbert (1758)
	Gilbert on Uses and Trusts, 3rd edn., by E. B. Sugden (1811)
Goff and Jones	*The Law of Restitution*, by Lord Goff of Chieveley and G. Jones, 4th edn. (1993)
Goode	*Consumer Credit Legislation*, by R. M. Goode (1985)
Gordon	*The Law relating to Mobile Homes and Caravans*, by R. J. F. Gordon (1985)
Grant	*Encyclopedia of Planning Law and Practice* ed. by M. Grant
Gray	*The Rule against Perpetuities*, by J. C. Gray, 4th edn., by R. Gray (1942)
Gray	*Copyhold, Equity and the Common Law*, by C. M. Gray (1963)
Greenwood	Butterworth's Planning Law Handbook, 3rd edn., by B. Greenwood (1992)
Guest and Lloyd	*Encyclopedia of Consumer Credit Law*, by A. G. Guest and M. G. Lloyd (1975)
Hague	*Leasehold Enfranchisement*, by N. T. Hague, 2nd edn. (1987)
Hall	*A Treatise of the Law relating to Profits à prendre and Rights of Common*, by J. E. Hall (1871)
Halsbury	*Halsbury's Laws of England*, 4th edn. (1973–1987)
H & M	*Hanbury and Martin, Modern Equity*, 14th edn., by J. E. Martin (1993)
Hargreaves	*An Introduction to the Principles of Land Law*, 4th edn., by G. A. Grove and J. F. Garner (1963)
Harris	*Variation of Trusts*, by J. W. Harris (1975)
Harris and Ryan	*An Outline of the Law Relating to Common Land and Public Access to the Countryside*, by B. Harris and G. Ryan (1967)
Harvey	*Settlements of Land*, by B. W. Harvey (1973)
Hawkins and Ryder	*Hawkins and Ryder on the Construction of Wills*, ed. by E. C. Ryder (1965)
Hayes	*An Introduction to Conveyancing*, by William Hayes, 5th edn. (1840)
Hayton	*Registered Land*, by D. J. Hayton, 3rd edn. (1981)
Heap	*An Outline of Planning Law*, by Sir Desmond Heap, 10th edn. (1991)
Heywood and Massey	*Court of Protection Practice*, 12th edn., by N. A. Whitehorn (1991)
Hill	*Treasure Trove in Law and Practice from the Earliest Time to the Present Day*, by Sir George Hill (1936)
Hill and Redman	*Hill and Redman's Landlord and Tenant*, 17th edn., by M. Barnes (1982)
Holdsworth	*A History of English Law*, by Sir William Holdsworth
	An Historical Introduction to the Land Law, by Sir William Holdsworth (1927)
Holyoak and Allen	*Civil Liability for Defective Premises*, by J. H. Holyoak and D. K. Allen (1982)
Hughes	*Public Sector Housing*, 2nd edn., by D. H. Hughes (1987)

Ing	*Bona Vacantia*, by N. D. Ing (1971)
Jackson	*The Law of Easements and Profits*, by P. Jackson (1978)
Jarman	*Jarman on Wills*, 8th edn., by R. W. Jennings and J. C. Harper (1951)
Jones and Goodhart	*Specific Performance*, by G. Jones and W. Goodhart (1986)
Kenny	*Sweet and Maxwell's Conveyancing Practice*, by P. Kenny, C. Burke and A. M. Kenny (1993)
Lawson and Rudden	*The Law of Property*, 2nd edn., by F. H. Lawson and B. Rudden (1982)
Leake	*A Digest of the Law of Uses and Profits of Land*, by S. M. Leake (1888)
Lewison	*Interpretation of Contracts*, by K. Lewison (1989)
Lightwood	*A Treatise on Possession of Land*, by J. M. Lightwood (1894)
Litt	*Littleton's Tenures* (1481). See Co. Litt.
Maclean	*Trusts and Powers*, by D. M. Maclean (1989)
McAuslan	*Land, Law and Planning: Cases, Materials and Text*, by P. McAuslan (1975)
McGee	*Limitation Periods*, by A. McGee (1990)
McNair	*The Law of the Air*, by Sir Arnold McNair, 3rd edn., by M. R. E. Kerr and A. H. M. Evans (1964)
Maitland	*The Collected Papers of Frederick William Maitland*, ed. by H. A. L. Fisher (1911)
	The Constitutional History of England, by F. W. Maitland (1908)
	Equity, by F. W. Maitland, revised by John Brunyate (1936)
	Forms of Action at Common Law, by F. W. Maitland, ed. by A. H. Chaytor and W. J. Whittaker (1936)
Martin	*Residential Security*, by J. E. Martin (1989)
Martyn	*Family Provision: Law and Practice*, 2nd edn., by J. G. R. Martyn (1985)
Maudsley	*The Modern Law of Perpetuities*, by R. H. Maudsley (1979)
M & B	*Maudsley and Burn's Land Law: Cases and Materials*, 6th edn., by E. H. Burn (1992)
	Maudsley and Burn's Trusts and Trustees: Cases and Materials, 4th edn., by E. H. Burn (1988)
Maurice	*Family Provision on Death*, by S. G. Maurice, 6th edn. (1987)
Megarry	*The Rent Acts*, by Sir Robert Megarry, 11th edn. (1988)
Megarry and Wade	*The Law of Real Property*, by Sir Robert Megarry and H. W. R. Wade; 5th edn. (1984)
Mellows	*The Law of Succession*, by A. R. Mellows, 5th edn. by C. V. Margrave-Jones (1993)
Miller	*The Machinery of Succession*, by J. G. Miller (1977)
Morris and Leach	*The Rule against Perpetuities*, by J. H. C. Morris and W. Barton Leach, 2nd end., (1962), with supplement (1964)
Norton	*Norton on Deeds*, 2nd edn., by R. J. A. Morrison and H. J. Goolden (1928)
Oakley	*Constructive Trusts*, 2nd edn., by A. J. Oakley (1987)
Oswald	*Common Land and Commons Registration Act 1965*, by R. Oswald (1989)
Parry and Clark	*Parry and Clark on the Law of Succession*, 9th edn., by J. B. Clark (1988)
Pawlowski	*The Forfeiture of Leases*, by M. Pawlowski (1993)
Platt	*A Practical Treatise on the Law of Covenants*, by Thomas Platt (1829)
	A Treatise on the Law of Leases, by Thomas Platt (1847)

Plucknett	*A Concise History of the Common Law*, by T. F. T. Plucknett, 5th edn. (1956)
	Legislation of Edward I, by T. F. T. Plucknett (1949)
Pollock	*The Land Laws*, by Sir Frederick Pollock, 3rd edn., (1896)
Pollock and Maitland	*The History of English Law before the time of Edward I*, by Sir Frederick Pollock and F. W. Maitland, 2nd edn., (1898), revised with introduction and bibliography by S. F. Milsom (1968)
Pollock and Wright	*An Essay on Possession in the Common Law*, by F. Pollock and R. S. Wright (1888)
Preston	*An Elementary Treatise on Estates*, by Richard Preston, 2nd edn. (1820–1827)
	An Essay in a Course of Lectures on Abstracts of Title, by Richard Preston, 2nd edn. (1823–1824)
Preston and Newsom	*Preston and Newsom on Limitation of Actions*, 3rd edn., by G. H. Newsom and L. Abel-Smith (1953)
	Preston and Newsom on Limitation of Actions, 4th edn., by S. Weeks (1989)
	Preston and Newsom's Restrictive Covenants affecting Freehold Land, 8th edn., by G. L. Newsom (1991)
Prideaux	*Prideaux's Forms and Precedents in Conveyancing*, 25th edn., vol. 1 by T. K. Wigan and I. M. Phillips; vol. 2 by V. G. H. Hallett, A. P. McNabb and T. A. Blanco White; vol. 3 by I. M. Phillips, E. H. Scamell and V. G. H. Hallett (1958–1959)
Prime and Scanlan	*Limitation Periods*, by T. Prime and G. Scanlan (1990)
Redmond-Cooper	*Limitation of Actions* by R. Redmond-Cooper (1992)
Robinson	*Law of Game, Salmon and Freshwater Fishing in Scotland*, by S. S. Robinson (1990)
Rodgers	*Housing—The New Law. A Guide to the Housing Act 1988*, by C. P. Rodgers (1989)
Ross	*Inheritance Act Claims: Law and Practice*, by S. Ross (1993)
Rossdale	*Probate and the Administration of Estates*, by P. S. A. Rossdale (1989)
Round	*Feudal England*, by J. H. Round (1895)
Rudall	*Party Walls*, by A. R. Rudall, 3rd edn. (1922)
Rudden and Moseley	*An Outline of the Law of Mortgages (Nokes)*, by B. Rudden and H. Moseley (1967)
Ruoff and Pryer	*Land Registration Handbook Forms and Practice*, by T. B. F. Ruoff and E. J. Pryer (1990)
Ruoff and Roper	*The Law and Practice of Registered Conveyancing*, by T. B. F. Ruoff, R. B. Roper, E. J. Pryer, C. West and R. Fearnley (1991)
Ruoff	*Rentcharges in Registered Conveyancing*, by T. B. F. Ruoff (1961)
	Searching without Tears. The Land Charges Computer, by T. B. F. Ruoff (1974)
Sanders	*Sanders on Uses and Trusts*, 5th edn., by G. W. Sanders and J. Warner (1844)
Sara	*Boundaries and Easements*, by C. Sara (1991)
Scriven	*A Treatise on the Law of Copyholds*, by J. Scriven, 7th edn., by A. Brown (1896)
Scrutton	*Land in Fetters*, by T. E. Scrutton (1886)
Sheppard	*Sheppard's Touchstone of Common Assurances*, 8th edn., by E. G. Atherley (1826)
Sherriff	*Service Charges in Leases: A Practical Guide*, by G. Sherriff (1989)

Sherrin and Bonehill	*The Law and Practice of Intestate Succession*, by C. H. Sherrin and R. C. Bonehill (1987)
Silverman	*Searches and Enquiries*, by F. Silverman, 2nd edn. (1992)
	Standard Conditions of Sale, by F. Silverman, 4th edn. (1992)
	The Law Society's Conveyancing Handbook, by F. Silverman (1993)
Simes	*Public Policy and the Dead Hand*, by Lewis M. Simes (1955)
Simpson	*A History of the Land Law*, 2nd edn., by A. W. B. Simpson (1986)
Smith	*Smith's Leading Cases*, 13th edn., by Sir Thomas Chitty, A. T. Denning and C. P. Harvey (1929)
Snell	*Snell's Principles of Equity*, 29th edn., by P. V. Baker and P. St. J. Langan (1990)
Speaight and Stone	*The Law of Defective Premises*, by A. Speaight and G. Stone (1982)
Spencer Bower and Turner	*The Law relating to Estoppel by Representation*, 3rd edn., by Sir Alexander Turner (1977)
Spencer Bower, Turner and Sutton	*The Law Relating to Actionable Non-Disclosure and Other Breaches of Duty in Relations of Confidence, Influence and Advantage*, 2nd edn. by Sir Alexander Turner and R. J. Sutton (1990)
Storey	*Conveyancing*, by I. R. Storey, 4th edn. (1993)
Sugden	*A Practical Treatise of Powers*, by Edward Sugden, 9th edn. (1861)
	The Law of Vendors and Purchasers of Estates, by Edward Sugden, 14th edn. (1862)
Telling and Duxbury	*Planning Law and Procedure*, by A. E. Telling and R. M. C. Duxbury, 9th edn. (1993)
Theobald	*Theobald on Wills*, 15th edn., by J. G. Ross Martyn and J. B. Clark (1993)
Thompson	*Co-ownership*, by M. P. Thompson (1988)
	Investigation and Proof of Title by M. P. Thompson (1991)
Treitel	*The Law of Contract*, by G. H. Treitel, 8th edn. (1991)
Tudor	*Tudor's Leading Cases on Real Property, Conveyancing, and the Construction of Wills and Deeds*, 4th edn., by T. H. Carson and H. B. Bompas (1898)
Turner	*The Equity of Redemption*, by R. W. Turner (1931)
Tyler	*Tyler's Family Provision*, 2nd edn., by R. D. Oughton (1984)
Underhill and Hayton	*Underhill Law relating to Trusts and Trustees*, 14th edn. by D. J. Hayton (1987)
Vaizey	*A Treatise on the Law of Settlements of Property*, by J. S. Vaizey (1987)
Viner	*A General Abridgment of Law and Equity*, by Charles Viner, 2nd edn. (1791)
Vinogradoff	*Villainage in England*, by P. Vinogradoff (1892)
Waldock	*The Law of Mortgages*, by C. H. M. Waldock, 2nd edn. (1950)
Walker	*Charging Orders Against Land*, by G. C. P. Walker (1992)
Watt	*Agricultural Holdings*, by J. Muir Watt, 13th edn. (1988)
Webber	*Possession Proceedings*, 3rd edn. by G. Webber (1990)
	Possession of Business Premises, by G. Webber (1992)
West	*West's Law of Dilapidations*, edited by P. F. Smith, 9th edn. (1988)
White and Tudor	*White and Tudor's Leading Cases in Equity*, 9th Edn., by E. P. Hewitt and J. B. Richardson (1928)
Wilkinson	*The Standard Conditions of Sale of Land*, by H. W. Wilkinson, 4th revised edn. (1990)

Williams	*A Treatise on the Law of Vendor and Purchaser of Real Estate and Chattels Real*, 4th edn., by T. Cyprian Williams and J. M. Lightwood (1936)
	The Contract of Sale of Land as affected by the Legislation of 1925, by T. Cyprian Williams (1930)
Williams	*Williams' [W. J. Williams] Contract of Sale of Land and Title to Land*, 4th edn., by G. Battersby (1975)
	Williams' [W. J. Williams] Law Relating to Wills, 6th edn., by C. H. Sherrin, R. F. D. Barlow and R. A. Wallington (1987)
Williams	*The Statute of Frauds, Section Four, in the Light of its Judicial Interpretation*, by James Williams (1932)
Williams	*Handbook of Dilapidations*, by D. Williams, P. Freedman, E. Shapiro and J. Thom (1992)
Williams, Mortimer and Sunnocks	*Williams, Mortimer and Sunnocks on Executors, Administrators and Probate*, ed. by J. H. G. Sunnocks and J. G. Ross Martyn (1993) (being the 17th edn. of Williams [Sir Edward Vaughan Williams] on Executors and the 5th edn. of Mortimer on Probate.*
Wisdom	*Aspects of Water Law*, by A. S. Wisdom (1981)
	Wisdom's Law of Watercourses, 5th edn. by W. Howarth (1992)
Wolstenholme and Cherry	*Wolstenholme and Cherry's Conveyancing Statutes*, 12th edn., by Sir Benjamin Cherry, D. H. Parry and J. R. P. Maxwell (1932)
	Wolstenholme and Cherry's Conveyancing Statutes, 13th edn., by J. T. Farrand (1972)
Wontner	*Wontner's Guide to Land Registry Practice*, 18th edn., by P. J. Timothy (1991)
Woodfall	*Woodfall's Law of Landlord and Tenant*, 28th edn., ed. by K. Lewison and K. M. Garnett
Woolrych	*A Treatise on the Law of Rights of Common*, 2nd edn., by H. W. Woolrych (1850)
Wurtzburg and Mills	*Wurtzburg and Mills Building Society Law*, 15th edn., ed. by T. Lloyd, E. Ovey and M. Waters (1990)
Yates and Hawkins	*Landlord and Tenant*, by D. Yates and A. J. Hawkins, 2nd edn. (1986)

Part I

Introduction to the modern law

SUMMARY

Chapter 1

The pattern of development

SUMMARY

A. ORIGIN OF MODERN LAND LAW

Modern English land law[1] is based on the reforms enacted in a series of statutes which were passed in 1925 and came into force on 1 January 1926. These were:

> Settled Land Act;
> Trustee Act;
> Law of Property Act;
> Land Registration Act;
> Land Charges Act;
> Administration of Estates Act.

Since 1925 there has been continuous legislative activity, especially in the fields of landlord and tenant and the public control of the use of land; and the system of registration of title to land has in large part superseded earlier methods of conveyancing. But the principles of modern land law are contained in the 1925 legislation. An understanding of those principles is essential to the understanding of the modern law; at the same time, some understanding of the land law as it developed from medieval times to 1926 is essential to the understanding of the 1925 legislation.

(a) Feudal basis

In this development over a period of nearly a thousand years, the land law is a mirror of one aspect of English life; it is a body of law which, while based on a feudal system imposed by the Norman Conquest, has adapted itself to a succession of political and social upheavals, culminating in the welfare state of the twentieth century. It was the public importance of the land law in the feudal society of its origin which eventually brought its troubles. When the country settled down after the upheaval of the Norman Conquest, the social bond which, both on the public and on the private side of life, united men together in a political whole was the land. Broadly speaking, land constituted the sole form of wealth, and it was through its agency that the everyday needs of the governing and the governed classes were satisfied. The result of this

---

1 This includes Wales, but not Scotland or Northern Ireland. For the inter-relation between English and Irish land law, see Wylie, *Irish Land Law* (2nd edn), chapter 1.

was that from an early date a complicated system of law, founded on custom and developed by the decisions of the courts, began to grow up, and we may call it for convenience the common law system.

(b) Legislative reforms of early nineteenth century

In its origin this system was eminently suitable for a society that was based and centred on the land, and appropriate to the simple notions prevailing in a feudal population, but in several respects it gradually came to outlive the reason for its existence. It tended to become static. Rules that were in harmony with their early environment lived on long after they had become anachronisms. Law will wither unless it expands to keep pace with the progressive ideas of an advancing community, but in this particular context the rigidity and formalism of the common lawyers retarded the process, and, though equity intervened to great effect in several directions, the few reforms attempted by the legislation before the first quarter of the nineteenth century served to complicate rather than to simplify the law. Statutory reform, however, began in earnest after the report of the Real Property Commissioners in 1829. Although the commissioners began their report by saying that this department of English law "appears to come almost as near to perfection as can be expected in any human institutions,"[2] they nevertheless went on to express their opinion that the modes by which interests in land were created, transferred and secured had become unnecessarily defective and that they demanded substantial alteration. The result of this view was that on their recommendation a number of statutes were passed between 1832 and 1827 which swept away many impediments to the smooth operation of the law. The chief of these were:

> Prescription Act 1832;
> Fines and Recoveries Act 1833;
> Real Property Limitation Act 1833;
> Dower Act 1833;
> Inheritance Act 1833;
> Wills Act 1837.

B. LEGISLATION OF 1925

(a) Main object

Between 1837 and 1922 the legislature became more and more active in the sphere of real property law, but most of the enactments were directed towards the simplification of conveyancing and the extension of the landowner's powers of enjoyment. No comprehensive effort was made to smooth the path by abolishing the substantive defects that had settled on the main body of the law like barnacles on the hull of a ship. Then came the war of 1914–1918, and with it a general desire to set the social life of the nation in order. One of the results of this desire was to give an impetus to land legislation, and it will be as well to state at the outset the main idea which lay at the back of the legislation that resulted. It was nothing more than a desire to render the sale of land as rapid and simple a matter as is the sale of goods or of stocks and

2 Real Property Commissioners' First Report, p. 6.

shares.[3] A layman knows that if he desires to transfer to another the ownership of a chattel, such as a motor car or a picture, the normal requirement is the making of a contract which names the parties, records their intention, describes the article to be sold and states the price to be paid. The moment that such a contract is concluded, the ownership of the article, in the absence of a contrary intention, passes to the buyer. At first sight it is difficult to appreciate why the same simple expedient cannot be adopted in the case of land, and not unnaturally a layman grows impatient of the long and expensive investigation attendant upon the conveyance of a piece of land.

But the difference is inevitable, and the reason is that in the great majority of cases the possessor of personal goods is their absolute owner, and therefore able to pass a title which will confer upon their deliveree an equally full and unincumbered ownership. If A is in possession of a piano, it is probable that he is its owner, and in most cases a buyer is safe in paying its value and taking delivery of possession. No doubt the maxim of the law is *nemo dat quod non habet*, and if it should happen that A, instead of being the owner, is a thief or is merely holding the piano under a hire purchase agreement, then a buyer from him will not acquire ownership. But the fact remains that despite risks of this nature a buyer is generally justified in assuming that the possessor of goods is also the owner, and as a rule there is no need to go to trouble and expense in order to ascertain whether some person other than the possessor has any interest in them. It is a legitimate risk to take. But for a purchaser of land to be content with the word of the vendor and with the appearance of ownership that flows from his possession would be an act of sheer folly.

Land and goods are and must ever be on a different plane. Land is fixed, permanent and vital to the needs of society, and a subject-matter in which rights may be granted to persons other than the ostensible owner. A is in possession of land and is obviously exercising all the powers of enjoyment and management which amount to the popular idea of ownership, but none the less it is by no means certain that he is in fact entitled to dispose of the interest that he may have agreed to sell. He may be in possession under a lease for any period from one to 999 years or more, or he may have a life interest under a family settlement; and even if he holds the fee simple—the largest interest known to the law and one that approximates to the absolute ownership of goods—it is likely that he or his predecessors have granted to third parties rights, such as mortgages, restrictive covenants and rights of way, which continue to be enforceable against the land regardless of any transfer to which it may have been subjected. So long as third parties can in this way have enforceable rights against land which outwardly appears to belong absolutely to the possessor, it is difficult, in the absence of compulsory registration of title, to devise a system under which conveyances of land can be conducted with the facility of sales of goods; and even then it will always be necessary for a purchaser to make careful searches and inquiries in order to see that there are no third party rights which will bind the land after it has been transferred to him.

We may start, then, with the assumption that no effort of legislative genius

---

3 See Birkenhead, *Points of View*, vol. ii. p. 34, discussing LPA 1922. As Lord Chancellor, he was responsible for the passage of this Act and, subsequently, the whole of the 1925 legislation through the House of Lords.

can, from the point of view of simplicity and rapidity, put conveyances of land on an equal footing with sales of goods. But when the question of reforming the law came before Parliament in 1922, the result of 900 years of development from a feudal origin was that the law of real property contained so many antiquated rules and useless technicalities that additional and unnecessary impediments had arisen to hinder the facile transfer of land. The real property law as it existed in 1922 might justly be described as an archaic feudalistic system which, though originally evolved to satisfy the needs of a society based and centred on the land, had by considerable ingenuity been twisted and distorted into a shape more or less suitable to a commercial society dominated by money. The movement of progressive societies has been from land to money, or rather to trade, and a legal system which acquired its main features at a time when land constituted the major part of the country's wealth can scarcely be described as suitable to an industrial community. To borrow the words of Bagehot directed to a different subject, the 1922 real property law might be likened to "an old man who still wears with attached fondness clothes in the fashion of his youth; what you see of him is the same; what you do not see is wholly altered".

To take any structure, whether it be a system of law, a constitution or a house, and for a period of 600 years to patch it here and there in order to adapt it to new conditions, cannot fail to lead to complications of a bewildering character.

(b) Law of Property Act 1922. Assimilation of real and personal property

Confirmed in the views just mentioned, the legislature began in 1922 to reform the law on a far more ambitious scale than had been attempted in the earlier legislative changes, for, though the main purpose was to simplify conveyancing, yet this was pursued not merely by a simplification of the machinery of land transfer, but also by a free use of the pruning knife. In the official view, reforms were needed as a prelude to the simplification and extension of the system of registration of title.[4]

The first Act to be passed was the Law of Property Act 1922, which was described in its preamble as

> An Act to assimilate and amend the law of Real and Personal Estate, to abolish copyhold and other special tenures, to amend the law relating to commonable lands and of intestacy, and to amend the Wills Act, 1837, the Settled Land Acts, 1882 to 1890, the Conveyancing Acts, 1881 to 1911, the Trustee Act, 1893 and the Land Transfer Acts, 1875 and 1897.

The all-important fact that emerges from this descriptive title is that one main object was to "assimilate . . . the law of real and personal estate".

We shall see as we proceed that a comparison of the law relating to real and personal property respectively is, from the point of view of convenience and reason, very much to the advantage of the latter. Part I of the Act put the two forms of property as nearly as possible upon the same footing, a result

---

4 Wolstenholme and Cherry, *Conveyancing Statutes* (12th edn), vol. i. p. clxvi. See the speech of Sir Leslie Scott, who was Solicitor-General, introducing the Bill into the House of Commons (1922) 154 HC Debates (5th Series) 90; reproduced with annotations by B. B. Benas in Scott, *The New Law of Property Explained* (1925); and the valuable six *Lectures* by Sir Benjamin Cherry on *The New Property Acts* (1926), and especially his series of Questions and Answers at pp. 104 et seq. See also Anderson, *Lawyers and the Making of English Land Law 1832–1940* (1992).

which was obtained partly by abolishing the chief differences that formerly existed between the two, and partly by eliminating many of the technical anachronisms that had grown up in the land laws. In addition, the law of personal property, which thus became the dominating system, was itself amended in several particulars.

(c) Legislation of 1925. Consolidating Acts

The date at which the Act of 1922 was appointed to come into operation, however, was postponed, for the changes it made were sufficiently drastic to necessitate the re-drafting and consolidation of the real property statute law from the year 1285. The Law of Property (Amendment) Act 1924 was therefore passed to facilitate the task of consolidation, and then all but the transitional provisions of this Act and of the Act of 1922 were absorbed into the six statutes, passed in 1925, which are set out at the beginning of this chapter.[5]

These statutes are all consolidating Acts. Where the Acts of 1922 and 1924 make no change in the old law, there is a presumption that the Acts of 1925 did not change it. But where the Acts of 1922 and 1924 do make some change, there is only a presumption that the Acts of 1925 did not change the changes made by those two Acts.[6]

The practical result at the present day is that the whole law of real property is contained partly in these statutes, partly in older statutes, partly in subsequent legislation, such as the various Landlord and Tenant Acts, the Town and Country Planning Acts and the Rent Acts, and partly in the mass of judge-made rules so far as these, which still form the bulk of the law, have not been abolished or modified by statute.

C. TRIPARTITE HISTORICAL DIVISION

Real property law, like most of the other branches of our jurisprudence, falls into three divisions, which are due to the order of its historical development:

First of all we get the purely common law system, which was designed to meet the needs of a feudal society.

Secondly in order of time we have the equitable system which, though not comprehensive, was gradually evolved in certain directions with a view to adapting the common law rules to a society moved by different ideals and possessing a more commercial outlook on life.

And finally we come to the various legislative enactments by which the

---

5 For a detailed commentary, see the six volumes of Wolstenholme and Cherry, *Conveyancing Statutes* (13th edn 1972, edited by J. T. Farrand). Previous editions are valuable, as these contain the commentaries of Wolstenholme (who was responsible for drafting CA 1881 and SLA 1882) and Cherry (the property statutes of 1922 and 1925).

6 *Beswick v Beswick* [1968] AC 58, [1967] 2 All ER 1197; cf. *Maunsell v Olins* [1975] AC 373 at 392–3, [1975] 1 All ER 16 at 26–27; *Farrell v Alexander* [1977] AC 59 at 72, 82, 96, [1976] 2 All ER 721 at 725, 733, 743; *Johnson v Moreton* [1980] AC 37 at 56, [1978] 3 All ER 37 at 46. See also *Grey v IRC* [1960] AC 1, [1959] 3 All ER 603; *Lloyds Bank Ltd v Marcan* [1973] 1 WLR 339 at 344, [1973] 2 All ER 359 at 367; affd [1973] 1 WLR 1387, [1973] 3 All ER 754; *Re Dodwell & Co Ltd's Trust* [1979] Ch 301 at 308, [1978] 3 All ER 738 at 741; *R v Heron* [1982] 1 WLR 451 at 459, [1982] 1 All ER 993 at 998; Wolstenholme and Cherry, vol. 1, p. 31; (1959) 75 LQR 307 (R.E.M.).

judge-made law of land was rendered more adequate to the needs of society.

We will now sketch in its barest outline the common law system, then describe at somewhat greater length certain conceptions that were introduced into the law by the Chancellor in the exercise of his equitable jurisdiction, and finally discuss the legislative changes of 1925.

Chapter 2

The common law system

SUMMARY

SECTION I THE DOCTRINE OF TENURE[1]

A. FEUDALISM IN EUROPE

(1) DEVELOPMENT OF CONTINENTAL FEUDALISM

The outstanding feature of the English land law and one that explains many of its peculiarities is that, at least from the time of the Norman Conquest, it fell into line with the continental systems and became and remained for several centuries intensely feudalistic. *Feudalism* itself is a word of some vagueness and ambiguity, and one that was certainly unknown to the peoples to whom it is applied. It is often thought to represent the history of Western Europe from the eighth to the fourteenth century,[2] and, like the modern use of the word *capitalism*, to describe the social characteristics of the period.[3] To a lawyer, however, it represents:

> A state of society in which the main social bond is the relation between lord and man, a relation implying on the lord's part protection and defence; on the man's part protection, service and reverence, the service including service in arms. This personal relation is inseparably involved in a proprietary relation, the tenure of land—the man holds of the lord, the man's service is a burden on the land, the lord has important rights in the land.[4]

Thus it is the negation of independence. It implies subordination, it means that one man is deliberately made inferior to another.

In pre-feudal days the land of Europe was owned absolutely, though subject to custom, by persons who were grouped together in village communities,

---

1 For the history of this doctrine, see Simpson, *A History of the Land Law* (2nd edn), pp. 1 et seq.
2 Pollock and Maitland, *History of English Law* (2nd edn), vol. i. p. 67.
3 Plucknett, *Concise History of the Common Law* (5th edn), p. 506.
4 Maitland, *Constitutional History of England*, p. 143.

and it therefore becomes a matter of interest to discover why it was that a great part of the world lapsed from a state of comparative freedom into one of servility, why landownership disappeared and land tenure took its place. The change represented a retrogressive step in the history of man, but in Europe it was one of the necessary consequences of the disruption of the Roman Empire by the Barbarian invaders. The overthrow of that Empire caused chaos and disorganisation in Europe and produced conditions in which it was necessary for private persons to procure for themselves a higher degree of protection than could be furnished by their own unaided efforts. In those days interference with personal freedom or with the ownership of property might come from several different quarters, such as a revolt of peasants, the arrogance of a powerful neighbour, the extortion of a government or the hostility of some tribe. The only method of obtaining security was mutual support, and so men deliberately subordinated themselves to the strong hand of some magnate versed in the arts of war, and were compensated for the diminution of personal independence and the loss of landownership by acquiring the protection afforded by the forces of which he disposed. This process involved both a personal and a proprietary subordination, but it is only on the latter that we need dwell.

One of the effects of the feudalization of Europe was that from a legal aspect land became the exclusive bond of union between men. Individual or communal landownership was destroyed. The ownership of the whole of the land in any given district was vested in the overlord, and the persons who had formerly owned it in their own right now held it from the overlord. In return for the land which they held they were bound to render services, chiefly of a military nature, to the overlord, while the latter in his turn was bound to protect his tenants. Feudalism implied a reciprocity of rights and duties. The lord gained in dignity and became entitled to personal services, while the tenant obtained security.

This conversion from ownership to tenure began in the lower ranks of society, but quickly spread upwards until it finally embraced the greater part of the land of Western Europe. Various reasons contributed to this extension. The general anarchy of the times, the lack of a central government sufficiently strong to ensure a well-ordered and peaceful existence, and the natural ambition of magnates to increase the extent of their possessions induced even the large landowners to put themselves and their land under the protection of someone greater than themselves.

This development took place under the Franks, and in the time of the Carolingians a still further impetus was given to the movement, for the government itself—if such a term can be applied to those times—was obliged to resort to the principle of feudalism. Administration had to be carried on somehow and taxes were difficult to collect. The solution was to farm out Crown lands to great men who paid a sum of money to the government and who in return became lords of the lands (which were called benefices) and of the persons who dwelt thereon. A little later, when military pressure from the east and the south made it imperative that society should be organized on a basis that would afford protection to the State, the device of granting benefices in return for military services, a device that was gradually failing owing to the scarcity of Crown lands, was widened in scope by an act of confiscation.

The Church had become the greatest landowner in Europe. Charles Martel, who was Mayor of the Frankish Empire in the first part of the eighth century, deliberately carried out wholesale seizures of Church property, but in AD 751 some sort of amicable arrangement was made whereby vast tracts of Church lands were granted by the ecclesiastical corporations to laymen at the request of the King. The Church ownership of the lands was recognized by the payment of an ,uneconomic rent to the corporations, while the tenants—and this was the significance of the transaction—became liable by virtue of their holdings to render services to the King.[5] Thus did the net of feudalism spread everywhere. In this way life and government were made to depend upon the land.[6]

(2) THE MANOR

This can be seen by an examination of that unit of society which is called the manor. The grant of benefices led to the creation of great estates or manors vested in the grantees from the Crown. Topographically a manor denoted a certain area of land consisting of a number of houses, strips of arable and pasture land and waste lands, all of which were within the domain of the lord of the manor. The waste, in proportion to the cultivated land, formed by far the greater part of the manor, a fact which serves to explain the inclosures of later centuries. But we shall miss the significance of this system unless we realize that the manor was both a social and an administrative unit through the agency of which a whole country was governed. Each manor was, as it were, a small government in itself.

The central government required soldiers and money, but instead of approaching its subjects directly it looked no further than the lord of the manor. His obligation vis-à-vis the government was to supply a fully equipped fighting force, and the right which he obtained in return was that of holding his manor or group of manors immune from the legal and administrative control of the government. Thus, when the power of a central government was on the wane, it became customary to grant immunities to powerful men, which meant nothing more nor less than that the functions of government were handed over to feudal lords. As Vinogradoff has said:

> As in the later Empire, the government is obliged to have recourse to great landlords in order to carry out its functions of police, justice, military and fiscal authority. Great estates had become extra-territorial already under Roman rule in the fourth and fifth centuries, and it would be superfluous to point out how much more the governments of the barbarians stood in need of the help of great landowners.[7]

One of the most important features of the administrative side of a Continental manor was the lord's right of jurisdiction. As the royal writ did not run within the territorial limits of a manor, the lord set up local courts of his own, and it was only in the manorial court of the defendant that a plaintiff was entitled to sue. Thus, to use the expressive language of Stubbs,[8] there was

> a graduated system of jurisdiction based on land tenure, in which every lord judged, taxed, and commanded the class next below him, . . . in which private war, private coinage, private prisons took the place of the imperial institutions of government.

5 Vinogradoff, *Cambridge Medieval History*, vol. ii. p. 646.
6 See generally, *Encyclopaedia Britannica*, sub nom. Feudalism.
7 Vinogradoff, ibid., p. 651.
8 *Constitutional History*, vol. i. p. 292.

(3) CHARACTERISTICS OF FEUDALISM

By way of summary we may say that the characteristics of feudalism are the relation of lord and vassal; the principle that every person interested in land is a mere holder thereof, a tenant and not an owner; the condition that this tenure shall continue to exist only so long as the tenant performs the particular services imposed upon him at the beginning of the tenure; and lastly, the recognition of a reciprocity of rights and duties. The foundation of the whole system is the fief—that is to say, the land which the inferior holds as tenant of the superior. The word *fief* becomes *feudum* in Latin, and *feud*, and later *fee* in English.

B. FEUDALISM IN ENGLAND

(1) DEVELOPMENT OF ENGLISH FEUDALISM

We now come to consider the effect which this Continental feudalism had upon the land law of England. As the scope of this book makes it undesirable to elaborate particular questions of legal history, it is not proposed to discuss the extent to which feudalism existed in England prior to the Conquest. That a system was in vogue which bore similarities to Continental feudalism cannot be doubted, but the only fact that we need notice here is that the Normans applied their own ideas to the conditions prevalent in this country, and succeeded in establishing an English variety of feudalism which, though differing in many respects from that of the Continent, became a striking and universal feature of the land law. The policy of William the Conqueror left England, whatever it may have been before, a highly feudalized state. He took the line that, since the English landowners had denied his right to the Crown of England and had compelled him to assert it by force, their landed possessions became his to dispose of as he chose.[9] What he did was not so much to seize land and parcel it out among his Norman followers, as to allow all Englishmen who recognized him as King to redeem by money payments the estates which by right of conquest had momentarily passed to him.

This process of confiscation and redistribution flowed on evenly, and though it cannot be said that the redistributions amounted to direct feudal grants, there is no doubt that they came to be regarded as such when the idea of Norman feudalism took hold of men's minds. As Stubbs says:

> After each effort the royal hand was laid on more heavily; more and more land changed owners, and with the change of owners the title changed. The complicated and unintelligible irregularities of the Anglo-Saxon tenures were exchanged for the simple and uniform feudal theory. The 1500 tenants in chief of Domesday take the place of the countless landowners of King Edward's day . . . It is enough for our purpose to ascertain that a universal assimilation of title followed the general changes of ownership. The King of Domesday is the supreme landlord; all the land of the nation, the old folkland, has become the King's, and all private land is held mediately or immediately of him; all holders are bound to their lords by homage and fealty, either actually demanded or understood to be demandable, in every case of transfer by inheritance or otherwise.[10]

---

9 Stenton, *William the Conqueror*, pp. 494–5.
10 Stubbs, *Constitutional History*, vol. i. pp. 296–7.

This English feudalism differed from the Continental variety in that all freemen were bound by the Salisbury Oath of 1086 to swear allegiance directly to the King instead of to the immediate lord from whom they held their lands; and again in the fact that William, instead of setting up great territorial jurisdictions, organized administration in such a way that he governed the country through sheriffs who were directly responsible to him. Though the Frankish system of tenure displaced the Anglo-Saxon system, the establishment of a feudal mode of government was deliberately avoided. But in respect of tenure the result was much the same as on the Continent. By a certain date, which we need not attempt to define, the doctrine of land tenure became universal in England.

(2) LAND TENURE

Every acre of land in the country was held of the King. As Pollock and Maitland have said:

> The person whom we may call the owner, the person who has the right to use and abuse the land, to cultivate it or leave it uncultivated, to keep all others off it, holds the land of the King either immediately or mediately.[11]

(a) Seignories

If a tenant held immediately of the King, he was said to hold of him in chief or *in capite*. But the position might be less simple. Instead of a tenant holding directly of the King he might hold mediately, as for instance where C held of B who held of A who held of the King. C, who stood at the bottom of the scale, and who to a layman would look more like an owner than anybody else, was called the *tenant in demesne—tenet terram in dominico suo*. The persons between him and the King were called *mesne lords*, and their lordships were called *seignories*. A held the land, not in *demesne* but in service, since he was entitled to the services of B, and B was in a similar position, since he was entitled to the services of C. The services due from these tenants would not necessarily be of the same nature, for A might hold of the King by military service, B of A in return for a money rent, and C of B in return for some personal service. In such a case each grantee owed to his immediate grantor the service that he had agreed to render, and from this point of view the service was called *intrinsec*. Services were not merely personal, but charged on the tenement, so that if A failed in the performance of his military duties the King could distrain upon the land in the hands of C, as could A if B fell into arrears with the rent. B could agree to perform the military service in place of A, but no private arrangement of this kind could free the land from the burden. From this point of view the service was called *forinsec*, i.e. foreign to any bargain between other parties.[12] Of course, if, for example, A failed to perform his military service and the King proceeded against the land in C's occupation, the latter had a remedy against A, called the writ of *mesne*. A tenant came under an obligation, confirmed by the oath of fealty, to serve his lord faithfully, and the price of infidelity in this respect was the forfeiture of his fief. In particular, forfeiture ensued if he did anything to the

11 *History of English Law* (2nd edn), vol. ii. p. 232.
12 Pollock and Maitland, *History of English Law* (2nd edn), vol. i. p. 237.

disinherison of his lord, as, for example, if he deliberately failed to defend an action for the recovery of land brought against him by a third party.[13]

Perhaps the most striking fact about English feudalism was the universality of this doctrine of land tenure. On the Continent tenure applied only to those who held lands in return for military services,[14] but in England it applied to every holder whatever the nature of the duties that he had agreed to perform might be. Moreover a movement began by which the number of mesne lordships was increased to a bewildering extent. As each year passed, more and more sub-tenancies were created. A, who held of the King, would transfer his land or part of it to B, and B to C, and so on, but each transfer, instead of being an out and out grant by which the transferor got rid of his entire interest, would operate as a grant of land to be held by each transferee as tenant of his immediate transferor. As a result "innumerable petty lords sprang up between the great barons and the immediate tenant of the soil".[15]

(b) Subinfeudation

This process, which was termed subinfeudation, was carried to such lengths that Maitland was able to discover a case where there were as many as eight sub-tenancies in the same piece of land. One explanation of this reluctance to part with one's entire interest was the economic significance of land in the centuries immediately succeeding the Conquest. Apart from cattle, land was practically the only form of wealth. Money was scarce, and something had to take its place as a medium of exchange. This can be illustrated by the recompense usually given for services rendered.

Domestic servants in a manor were paid by a crude method of profit-sharing. As Vinogradoff has stated:

> The swine-herd of Glastonbury Abbey, for instance, received one sucking-pig a year, the interior parts of the best pig and the tails of all the others which were slaughtered in the abbey. The chief scullion had a right to all remnants of viands—but not of game—to the feathers and the bowels of geese.[16]

But the form which payment took in the case of labourers on the manorial estate, and also in the case of servants who rendered non-domestic services for a great lord, was a grant of land to be held only so long as the services were properly performed. Thus it was through one of the forms of tenure, known as tenure by sergeanty, that most of the wants of men were satisfied. The persons who severally acted as president of a lord's court, carried his letters, fed his hounds, cared for his horses and found him in bows and arrows, generally held land as tenants in sergeanty of the lord.[17] They would continue to hold the land as long as they served faithfully, and no longer.

(c) Statute Quia Emptores 1290

In other words, the importance of land as a means of payment made it advisable for tenants to keep as tenacious a hold upon it as possible, and, when a transfer was contemplated, to subinfeudate rather than dispose of it

13 For a discussion of this defunct principle, see the judgment of DENNING LJ in *Warner v Sampson* [1959] 1 QB 297 at 312–6, [1959] 1 All ER 120 at 123–6.
14 Holdsworth, *History of English Law*, vol. ii. p. 199.
15 Hayes, *Introduction to Conveyancing*, vol. i. p. 9.
16 Vinogradoff, *Villainage in England*, pp. 321–2.
17 Pollock and Maitland, *History of English Law* (2nd edn), vol. i. p. 285.

outright. But, for reasons into which we need not enter,[18] the practice of subinfeudation was obnoxious to the great lords, and was finally prohibited in 1290 by the Statute *Quia Emptores*.[19]

(i) Effect This important statute altered the law in two respects:

First, it set at rest a controversy by enacting that every free man should be at liberty to alienate the whole or part of his land without the consent of his lord. If part only were conveyed, the services were to be apportioned.

Secondly, it enacted that every alienee should hold the land of the same lord of whom the alienor previously held. The effect of this was to prevent the creation of new tenancies. The alienor dropped out, the alienee stepped into his shoes for all purposes, and thus instead of a new sub-tenancy there was the substitution of one tenant for another. If, therefore, the existence of a mesne lordship is proved at the present day, it follows that it must have been created before 1290, or created by the Crown thereafter.

(ii) Limits The statute, however, extended only to land held for a fee simple estate, i.e. the largest interest known to the law,[20] and it has never prevented the creation of a new tenure by the grant of a lesser estate, such as a fee tail or a life interest.

The statute did not bind the Crown. This had two consequences.

In the first place, the privilege of unrestricted alienation did not avail tenants *in capite*. In their case the consent of the Crown remained necessary and in practice this was given only on the payment of a fine.[1]

Secondly, the Crown was unaffected by the abolition of subinfeudation and was therefore still able to create new tenancies in respect of the fee simple.

(iii) Importance *Quia Emptores* was indeed a landmark in the history of real property. Its chief virtue was that it led to the gradual disappearance of the numerous petty lordships that had arisen between the Crown and the tenant in *demesne*. Blackacre might no doubt have been held before 1290 by B of A, but if in course of time it passed into the hands of a succession of alienees, each one being substituted for his predecessor, it would utlimately become extremely difficult to prove the existence of A's original lordship. Thus, there was a constant tendency for seignories to become vested in the Crown, and to this extent the law was simplified.

C. FORMS OF TENURE

A feature of English feudalism, and one that complicated the law of land, was that there was not one common kind of tenure. We have seen how in early days, if a man wanted work of a regular nature done for him, he would generally get it done in exchange for land granted by him to the workman. Considering the diversity of personal needs which require to be satisfied, it is obvious that the services due from tenants would vary considerably in nature, importance and dignity. One tenant had to fight; another to look after a household, or to provide arms, or to pray for the soul of his overlord, or to do such agricultural work as might be demanded of him. There were

18 See Challis, *Law of Real Property* (3rd edn), pp. 18–19.
19 Holdsworth, *History of English Law*, vol. iii. p. 79.
20 The meaning of "fee simple" will appear later; pp. 31, 155.
 1 Challis, pp. 14, 15. Such fines were abolished by the Tenures Abolition Act 1660.

vast differences between the possible services. It was considered an
honourable thing to fight, but not to plough, and thus there gradually arose
different forms of tenure based upon the differences in the nature of the
services. The following table shows the state of affairs in the time of Edward I,
when the tenures had become stabilized.

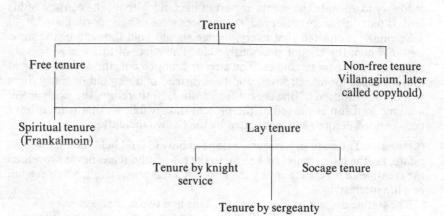

(1) KNIGHT SERVICE [2]

(a) Nature of knight service

The most important of the regular tenures in early days was knight service,
or the tenure by which a man was obliged to render military services in return
for the land that he held. Soon after the Conquest a process set in whereby
the military needs of the country were satisfied in this manner. All the land
of the country was held directly of the King, and it was a practically universal
rule that the tenants in chief—that is, those men who held directly of the
King as distinct from sub-tenants who owed their position to the practice of
subinfeudation—held by knight service. Each tenant in chief had to produce
for forty days in each year a definite number of fully armed horsemen. The
number required in any particular case did not depend upon the extent of the
tenant's land, but was arbitrarily fixed when the grant of the land was made,
and, as the unit of the feudal host was a constabularia consisting of ten
knights, it appears always to have been some multiple of 5 or 10.[3] For about
a hundred years after the Conquest the army—to the strength of about 5000
knights—was actually raised in this way, but it was soon discovered that
such a short service as forty days scarcely promoted the success of military
operations, and the King began in about 1166 to exact money payments
called scutage from the tenants in chief instead of requiring the production
of the fixed quota of knights. But by the time of Edward I even scutage had
become useless as a means of providing an army, and it can be said that
thenceforth the tenure ceased to be military in the sense that it no longer
served to supply forces for the defence of the realm.[4]

What at first sight seems remarkable is that knight service, instead of
falling into oblivion after it had ceased to fulfil its original function, continued

2 See Holdsworth, *History of English Law,* vol. iii. pp. 37–46.
3 Round, *Feudal England,* pp. 259–60.
4 Pollock and Maitland, *History of English Law* (2nd edn), vol. i. p. 252.

to develop, and ended by hardening into a legal system far stricter and more onerous than it had hitherto been. The explanation of this inopportune survival was that, quite apart from the duty of military service, the tenure carried with it certain feudal incidents which had such a high financial value for the lords of whom the lands were held that to foster and develop it became a matter of great personal interest. Subinfeudation led to the extension of knight service, and though the military sub-tenant had neither to fight nor to pay scutage, yet, being a military tenant, he was subject to a number of onerous claims from which he would have been free had his tenure been one of the other forms. As the matter is now merely of antiquarian interest, we must confine ourselves to the barest statement of the most valuable of the rights enforceable against a military tenant, namely:

(b) Incidents of knight service

(i) Relief The lord was entitled to the payment of a certain sum, called a relief, when a new tenant succeeded to the land on the death of the old tenant. Payment of the relief entitled the heir to immediate possession, but this was not so where the land was held of the King. In this case the official escheator took possession and held an inquest as to who was next heir. It was only when the heir had done homage and paid the relief that he was entitled to enter the land. This royal privilege of first possession was called *primer seisin*.[5]

(ii) Aids The lord was entitled to demand in three special cases that his tenants should pay him a certain sum of money called an aid. The three cases arose when the lord was imprisoned and required a ransom; when he desired to make his eldest son a knight; and when he was obliged to supply his eldest daughter with a dowry on her marriage.

(iii) Escheat propter delictum tenentis The commission by the tenant of a felony caused the land to escheat, that is to pass to the lord of whom it was held. Felony originally meant a breach of that faith and trust which ought to exist between lord and vassal, e.g. where the tenant laid violent hands on his lord. At an early date, however, felony lost its exclusively feudal signification and came to mean in effect any serious crime such as murder. The result of this was to benefit the lords, and though it would seem incompatible with the interests of the Crown as custodian of the public peace that the land of a murderer or a thief should pass to a subject, the right of escheat was expressly confirmed by Magna Carta in 1215, subject to the proviso that the land should be held by the Crown for a year and a day. Forfeiture of the land was now said to occur because the felon's blood was attainted or corrupted.[6]

(iv) Escheat propter defectum sanguinis This type of escheat was the right of the lord to take the land of his tenant who died intestate without leaving heirs.

(v) Wardship The most profitable right of the lord was that of wardship. If an existing tenant died leaving as his heir a male under 21 or a female under 14, the lord was entitled to the wardship of the heir, and as a consequence

---

5 Pollock and Maitland, *History of English Law* (2nd edn), vol. i. p. 311.
6 Ibid., p. 303; Digby, *History of the Law of Real Property*, p. 132; Holdsworth, *History of English Law*, vol. iii. p. 67.

was free to make what use he liked of the lands during the minority without any obligation to render an account of his stewardship. Upon reaching the prescribed age the ward might sue for *livery* or *ousterlemain*, i.e. might enforce delivery of the land. For this privilege half a year's profits had to be paid, though relief was not exigible.

(vi) Marriage Another privilege which the lord enjoyed in respect of infant tenants was the right of marriage. As Blackstone has said:

> While the infant was in ward, the guardian had the power of tendering him or her a suitable match, without disparagement or inequality; which if the infants refused, they forfeited the value of the marriage, *valorem maritagii*, to their guardian; that is, so much as a jury would assess, or anyone would bona fide give to the guardian for such an alliance; and if the infants married themselves without the guardian's consent, they forfeited double the value, *duplicem valorem maritagii*.[7]

(2) TENURE BY SERGEANTY[8]

Tenure by sergeanty was in early times, and from an economic point of view, of considerable importance, but it soon ceased to be anything more than a peculiarly dignified method of holding land. All tenures imply service of one kind or another, but the characteristic of sergeanty was that it required the tenant to perform services of an essentially personal nature. It was that particular form of landholding which was designed to supply the necessities of life. In the first place the great officials of the realm were sergeants, and as such might be required:

> to carry the banner of the king, or his lance, or to lead his army, or to be his marshall, or to carry his sword before him at his coronation, or to be his sewer at his coronation or his carver or his butler, or to be one of his chamberlains at the receipt of his exchequer or to do other like services.[9]

Duties of this nature came to be regarded as conferring honour and dignity, and for this reason outlasted the tenure itself, but they did not exhaust the forms of personal services that might be demanded from sergeants. A great lord would require that his accounts should be kept, his letters carried, his estates managed, armour provided, his food cooked, and so on, and he would in most cases grant lands to various sergeants to be held by them so long as the duties were faithfully performed. However, as time went on, it was realized that this was scarcely a convenient method of supplying the needs of life, and tenure by sergeanty began to decay as early as the fourteenth century. It died out altogether except in the case of those great men who performed honourable services for the King, or of humbler persons whose duty it might be to perform some small military duty, such as to supply transport. Moreover, the idea took root, and was fixed law by Littleton's day, that the tenure could exist only between the King and his immediate tenants in chief. The tenure of the great men who performed what were regarded as honourable services came to be called *grand sergeanty*, while that of the lesser military tenants was termed *petit sergeanty*. Grand sergeanty came to be similar to knight service, while petit sergeanty, after the time of Littleton, was practically equivalent to socage.[10]

7 Blackstone, vol. ii. p. 70.
8 Holdsworth, *History of English Law*, vol. iii. pp. 46 et seq.
9 Littleton, s. 153.
10 Holdsworth, *History of English Law*, vol. iii. p. 51.

(3) FRANKALMOIN

Frankalmoin was the tenure by which a man made provision for the repose of his soul, and it arose where lands were granted to an ecclesiastical body on the understanding that as tenant it would say prayers and masses for the souls of the grantor and his heirs. For various reasons the tenure fell into desuetude.[11]

(4) TENURES ABOLITION ACT 1660

It is not necessary to describe these tenures further, because in 1660 a considerable simplification of the forms of landholding was effected by the legislature. The Tenures Abolition Act, which was passed in that year, practically destroyed all the *free* lay tenures except socage. Tenure by knight service was destroyed altogether, and sergeanty was allowed to continue only in a limited form. Formerly it had rendered the tenant liable to onerous duties similar to those that might be exacted from a knight service tenant, but the effect of the Act was to abolish it as a separate tenure, and, where it existed, only to leave the privilege of performing those honorary services which, as we have seen, were peculiar to the higher ranks of sergeants. In other words, sergeanty was converted into socage,[12] the exceptional feature of the converted land being that the tenant might in some cases substantiate his right to perform certain honorary and dignified services.

Although frankalmoin was not formally abolished by the Act of 1660, it was seldom encountered in practice.

The Act of 1660 was, then, a move in the right direction, since it simplified the system of landholding by practically reducing the former tenures to two, that is to say, to socage and copyhold, though the simplification was not quite so complete as this, owing to the retention of divergent customary methods of holding land known as gavelkind, ancient demesne and borough-English.[13] Yet, even apart from these peculiar cases it is obvious that the existence from 1660 to 1925 of two separate and quite different methods by which a man might hold land, tended to increase the complexities of conveyancing and to render real property law unnecessarily difficult.

We must now briefly describe the two tenures of socage and copyhold which held the field until the legislation of 1925 abolished the latter.

(5) SOCAGE[14]

As distinguished from knight service, socage was that species of tenure which represented the new aspect that the economic life of the country gradually assumed. It was essentially non-military and free from the worst features of knight service. At first it could not be defined in positive terms, but was described negatively as being that form of tenure which was neither spiritual, military, sergeanty nor villeinage.

---

11 The chief reason for the decline of frankalmoin tenure was that upon alienation of the land, even to another ecclesiastical body, or upon escheat of the lordship to a superior lord, the tenure was converted into socage. Moreover, no fresh grant in frankalmoin, except by the Crown, has been possible since *Quia Emptores*; Challis, *Law of Real Property* (3rd edn), p. 11. Ecclesiastical bodies more frequently held land by one of the other tenures: Maitland, *Constitutional History of England*, p. 25.

12 Challis, *Law of Real Property* (3rd edn), p. 9.

13 P. 24, post.

14 Holdsworth, *History of English Law*, vol. iii. pp. 51 et seq.

(a) Origin

In early days the services due in respect of the land varied considerably. The tenant might pay a nominal rent sufficient to record the fact that the lands were held of the lord, or a substantial rent equal to the economic value of the land, while sometimes his obligation would extend to the performance of agricultural services. Originally, no doubt, the *socmanni*, as they were called, belonged to the lower orders of society, but the tendency was for this mode of landholding to extend upwards, since it was free from the worst of the feudal burdens incidental to knight service, and to escape those even the greater landowners were willing to sacrifice something of their dignity.

(b) Commutation of services

The next step was that it became usual to commute services, whatever these might have been, into money payments, and though these, when they were originally fixed, no doubt represented the economic value of the land, yet with the gradual fall in the value of money they became in course of time so insignificant in amount as scarcely to merit the trouble of collection.[15] Thus at the present day it is practically impossible to prove that A holds of B in socage tenure, for the payment of rent which would have revealed the existence of the tenure has in most cases not been made for centuries. B does not lose much, for the rent is generally of little pecuniary value, and the only other event which might have benefited him before the doctrine of escheat was abolished as from 1 January 1926—namely, the death of the tenant intestate and without heirs, whereby the land would pass to B by escheat—is normally of rare occurrence. Of course the land must be held of somebody, and the rule is that, where no private person can prove his lordship, it is deemed to be held of the Crown.

So socage became the great residuary tenure. It included every tenure which was not knight service, sergeanty, frankalmoin or villeinage, and its outstanding characteristic came to be that it involved some service which was absolutely certain and fixed, and which in the vast majority of cases took the form of a money payment.[16] Though subject to aids and to relief, it was free from the onerous rights of wardship and marriage that characterized knight service. The guardian of an infant socage tenant was the nearest relative who was incapable of inheriting the land. It was enacted by the Statute of Marlborough 1267 that a guardian in socage must account for the profits of the land at the end of his stewardship, and must not give or sell the ward in marriage.

(6) COPYHOLD[17]

The other tenure to which as late as 1925 English land might be subject was copyhold, the modern name for the old villeinage. Although this tenure was abolished as from 1 January 1926, something must be said about its origin and peculiar characteristics.

---

15 Pollock and Maitland, *History of English Law* (2nd edn), vol. i. p. 291.
16 Littleton, s. 117.
17 Holdsworth, *History of English Law*, vol. iii. pp. 491 et seq; vol. vii. pp. 296 et seq; Simpson, *A History of the Land Law* (2nd edn), pp. 155 et seq; Scriven, *Law of Copyholds* (7th edn); Gray, *Copyhold, Equity and the Common Law* (1963).

(a) Origin

We see in this tenure a system of land holding which represented in modern times customs far older than feudalism, and which dated back to the primitive method of agriculture called the open field system. In remote days the actual tillers of the English soil were almost certainly members of free village communities who owned in common the land that they farmed; but after the Conquest, although they still continued to follow those precepts and habits of agriculture that had been customary for generations, they were gradually absorbed into the feudal system. An overlord had appeared, a new concept in the shape of the manor had been established, and by imperceptible degrees the humble tillers found themselves part of the manorial organisation; no longer free owners, but instead subservient to an overlord upon whose will, according to the strict letter of the law, they were absolutely dependent. Blackstone thought that the modern copyholders were merely serfs who by continual encroachments on their superiors had gradually established a customary right to estates which strictly speaking had always been held at the will of the lords,[18] but in fact the truth is the exact reverse, for the lords had gradually induced the belief that only by their will were these ancient owners permitted to enjoy their customary rights and estates.[19]

(b) The manor

To understand the character of copyhold tenure we must refer once more to the feudal manor which was the unit of society in mediaeval England.

A typical manor consisted of:

1. the land belonging to the lord, which was called his demesne;
2. the land held of the lord by free tenants whether in socage or knight service;
3. the land held of the lord by persons called villein tenants;
4. rights of jurisdiction exercisable by the lord over the free tenants in the Court Baron, and over the villeins in the Court Customary;
5. waste land on which the tenants were entitled to pasture their cattle.

(i) Farm system The first point that emerges about the villeins is that it was they who cultivated the lord's demesne, a practice which originated in what has been termed the farm system. "Farm" in Anglo-Saxon times meant food, and the system in vogue was for the tenant, in return for his holding, to produce a farm—that is, enough food to sustain his lord for some given period, say a night, a week or a fortnight.[20]

(ii) Labour service system In the thirteenth century this primitive system gave way to the labour service system,[1] which meant that the villein tenant came under an obligation, often specified in the greatest detail,[2] to cultivate by his own labour his lord's demesne. But the mere obligation to perform agricultural services does not alone suffice to distinguish a villein from a socage tenant, since it was by no means impossible for a socage tenant to be subject to the same liability. What, then, was the test of villein tenure?

18 Blackstone, vol. ii. p. 95.
19 See Pollock, *The Land Laws*, pp. 43–52, 208–9.
20 Vinogradoff, *Villainage in England*, pp. 301–2.
1 Ibid., p. 304.
2 See, for example, Pollock and Maitland, *History of English Law* (2nd edn), vol. i. p. 366.

(c) Test of villein tenure

One fact which might be thought at first sight to provide this test is that the villeins received no protection in the King's courts. If they were unjustifiably ejected by the lord, they could recover neither possession nor damages in the royal courts, for in the view of the latter they were nothing more than tenants at the will of the lord.[3] But though superficially the tenure seemed precarious to the last degree, it was saved from being so in actual fact because the tenants were entitled to protection from the lord's manorial court, where those rules which had been hallowed by immemorial custom within the manor were recognized and enforced. These manorial customs gradually grew into legal systems under which the rights and the duties of the tenants were defined, and the everyday events of marriage, succession, alienation and the like were regulated.[4] But the lack of a remedy in the royal courts was not a sufficient test of villeinage or no villeinage since it also affected an ordinary tenant for years.

That test is to be found, however, in the nature of the services rendered by a tenant. If a man was bound to perform agricultural services it could not be said that he was necessarily a villein tenant, but if he did not know from day to day *what* kind of work would be assigned to him, then he was looked upon as a villein tenant. In other words, the test was the uncertainty of the nature of the work. As Pollock and Maitland have said:

> When they go to bed on Sunday night they do not know what Monday's work will be; it may be threshing, ditching, carrying; they cannot tell. This seems the point that is seized by law and that general opinion of which law is the exponent: any considerable uncertainty as to the amount or the kind of the agricultural services makes the tenure unfree. The tenure is unfree, not because the tenant holds at the will of the lord, in the sense of being removable at a moment's notice, but because his services, though in many respects minutely defined by custom, cannot be altogether defined without frequent reference to the lord's will.[5]

So then in the thirteenth century villeinage was that tenure in which the return made by the tenant for his holding was the performance on his lord's demesne of agricultural services uncertain in nature.

(d) Money payment system

In the fourteenth and fifteenth centuries this labour service system gave way to a money payment system under which the tenant in villeinage paid a rent to his lord instead of giving personal services, and the lord cultivated his demesne by hired labour.[6] This was an example of the general movement from natural husbandry to the money system, which was fostered in England by several causes, such as the growth of the woollen trade with Flanders and the great increase of trade with the Continent as a result of the English occupation of Normandy and Aquitaine.[7]

---

3 Pollock and Maitland, *History of English Law* (2nd edn), vol. i. p. 360.
4 Vinogradoff, *Villainage in England*, p. 172.
5 Pollock and Maitland, *History of English Law* (2nd edn), vol. i. p. 371.
6 Holdsworth, *History of English Law*, vol. iii. p. 204.
7 Vinogradoff, *Villainage in England*, p. 180.

(e) Villein tenure becomes copyhold

The result of the change as regards villeinage was to benefit the tenant, because the rents remained stabilized despite the gradual fall in monetary values. This transition from labour services to money payments corresponded with the transition in nomenclature from villeinage to copyhold tenure.

> With the completion of the transition from praedial services to money rents, tenure in villeinage may be said to have come to an end . . . The essence of villein tenure had consisted in the uncertainty of the tenant's services, and when the old agricultural services were commuted for a fixed money payment, this uncertainty passed away.[8]

The derivation of the word "copyhold" is this: the copyhold tenant, like his predecessor the villein, held at the will of the lord; but yet at the same time he held on the conditions which had become fixed by the customs of his particular manor. The lord's will could not be exercised capriciously, but only in conformity with custom. He still held a court, and that court kept records of all transactions affecting the lands. These records were called the rolls of the court. When, for instance, a tenant sold his interest to a third party, the circumstances of the sale would be recorded, and the buyer would receive a copy of the court rolls in so far as they affected his holding.[9] Inasmuch as he held his estate by copy of court roll, he came to be called a copyholder.

The change from villeinage to copyhold was of far-reaching importance to the tenant. He was rid of all traces of servility; he acquired an interest which in essentials was on all-fours with interests in land held by socage tenure, and above all he obtained recognition and protection from the King's courts. This protection was assured by the end of the fifteenth century. Coke summed up the position in expressive language:

> But now copyholders stand upon a sure ground, now they weigh not their lord's displeasure, they shake not at every sudden blast of wind, they eat, drink and sleep securely; only having a special care of the main chance, viz., to perform carefully what duties and services soever their tenure doth exact, and custom doth require: then let lord frown, the copyholder cares not, knowing himself safe, and not within any danger. For if the lord's anger grow to expulsion, the law hath provided several weapons of remedy; for it is at his election, either to sue a *subpoena* or an action of trespass against the lord. Time hath dealt very favourably with copyholders in divers respects.[10]

(f) Defects of copyhold tenure

Despite the possibility of enfranchisement, a process by which copyhold might be converted into socage tenure, a great proportion of English land, even in 1925, was still copyhold. The tenure was distinguished by several defects. For instance, the customs, which represented the local law governing land of this tenure, varied considerably from manor to manor, so that it was impossible to determine the law applicable to a disputed matter without an examination of the manorial records; the form of conveyance was far different from that required in the case of socage; copyhold and socage lands

8 Page, *The End of Villeinage*, p. 83, cited Holdsworth, vol. iii. p. 206.
9 A system of registration of title thus existed long before LRA 1925. But, as we shall see, this system lapsed with the abolition of copyhold.
10 *Compleat Copyholder*, s. 9.

were often intermixed in so confusing a fashion as to make it difficult to discriminate between them, a dilemma from which the only escape in the event of a sale was the execution of two conveyances, one appropriate for copyhold, the other for a socage holding; certain rights of the land were so burdensome to the tenant that they caused strife and ill-will; and finally, it was impossible for either the lord or the tenant, without the assent of the other, to exploit the minerals under the land.

This bare summary of the history of copyhold tenure should be enough to show that from about the beginning of the seventeenth century it was nothing more nor less than an outmoded and exceedingly inconvenient form of ordinary tenure. It served no particular social need and it certainly impeded a simplified system of conveyancing because of its frequent diversity from socage tenure. It has been rightly described as "an anachronism and a nuisance".[11]

(7) CUSTOMARY METHODS OF LANDHOLDING

In addition to these regular tenures there also existed in certain districts a few customary methods of landholding under which land was subject in various respects to a number of abnormal incidents. Instances are gavelkind, borough-English and ancient demesne.

(a) Gavelkind

Gavelkind is a word which denotes the customs that have applied since the Conquest to socage land situated in Kent.[12] Such land was in certain particulars subject to different legal rules from those obtaining in other parts of the country. Thus,

  (i)   the land descended upon intestacy to all the sons equally;
  (ii) a husband who survived his wife was entitled until his re-marriage to
        a life estate in one-half of her land although issue of the marriage
        might not have been born;[13]
  (iii) a widow was entitled until her re-marriage to dower in one-half of her
        husband's land;
  (iv) an infant could alienate his land by the form of conveyance known as
        a feoffment when he reached 15 years of age; and
  (v)   the land was devisable.

(b) Borough-English

Borough-English was a custom, found in certain parts of the country, under which the land descended to the youngest son to the exclusion of all the other children.[14]

(c) Ancient demesne

Ancient demesne land was land held by freehold tenants in any manor which had belonged to the Crown in the time of Edward the Confessor or William

---

11 Underhill, *Century of Law Reform*, p. 310.
12 Pollock and Maitland, *History of English Law* (2nd edn), vol. ii. pp. 271 et seq; Blackstone, vol. ii. p. 84; Challis, *Law of Real Property* (3rd edn), p. 14.
13 *Re Howlett* [1949] Ch 767, [1949] 2 All ER 490.
14 Littleton, ss. 165, 211; Blackstone, vol. ii. p. 83.

the Conqueror.[15] The tenants in ancient demesne were subject to certain restraints and entitled to certain immunities.[16]

(8) SUMMARY OF TENURES IN 1925

If we now take stock of the feudal tenures as they existed in 1925 we shall find the position to have been as follows: the greater part of English land was held by socage tenure, a considerable part was subject to copyhold tenure, while the remainder was held either in grand sergeanty or in frankalmoin, or was affected by the peculiar customs of gavelkind, borough-English or ancient demesne. Here was room for at least one form of simplification, and we shall see later[17] that the Law of Property Acts 1922 and 1925 seized the opportunity. They converted copyhold and ancient demesne into socage tenure; they abolished gavelkind, borough-English, and all other customary modes of descent; and they purported to abolish frankalmoin.[18] The honorary services incident to sergeanty were retained. Escheat *propter defectum sanguinis*, which was the right of a lord to take the land of his tenant who had died intestate without leaving heirs, was abolished and replaced by a right in the Crown to take the land as *bona vacantia* in the same way that it takes goods.

The result is that though the general theory of tenure is still a part of English law in the sense that all land is held of a superior and is incapable of absolute ownership, yet the law of tenure is both simpler and of less significance than it was before 1926. It is simpler because there is now only one form of tenure—namely, socage. It is of less significance because all the tenurial incidents (including escheat) which might in exceptional cases have brought profit to a mesne lord have been abolished, so that there is no inducement for a private person to prove that he is the lord of land. We can, in fact, now describe the theory of tenure, despite the great part that it has played in the history of English law, as a conception of merely academic interest. It no longer restricts the tenant in his free enjoyment of the land.

SECTION II THE DOCTRINE OF THE ESTATE[19]

A. SEISIN. POSSESSION NOT OWNERSHIP

Tenure signifies the relation between lord and tenant, and what it implies is that the person whom we should naturally call the owner does not own the land, but merely holds it as tenant of the Crown or of some other feudal superior. But if he is not owner of the land, what is the nature of the interest that he holds? In statutes, in judicial decisions and in common speech he is always described as a "landowner", but we may well ask what it is that he owns.

It may be said at once that the doctrine of tenure as developed in England made it difficult, if not impossible, to regard either him or his lord as the

15 Co. Fourth Inst. 269; Blackstone, vol. ii. p. 99; Holdsworth, *History of English Law*, vol. iii. pp. 263–9; Challis, *Law of Real Property* (3rd edn), p. 29; *Merttens v Hill* [1901] 1 Ch 842.
16 Real Property Commissioners, Third Report, pp. 12 et seq; *Merttens v Hill*, supra; *Iveagh v Martin* [1961] 1 QB 232, [1960] 2 All ER 668.
17 P. 79, post.
18 As to frankalmoin, see p. 81, post.
19 Holdsworth, *History of English Law*, vol. iii. pp. 101–37; Pollock and Maitland, *History of English Law* (2nd edn), vol. ii. pp. 2–29; Hargreaves, *Introduction to Land Law* (4th edn), pp. 19–25, 42–54; Simpson, *A History of the Land Law* (2nd edn), pp. 47 et seq.

owner of the land itself. The land could not be owned by the tenant, since it was recoverable by the lord if the tenurial services were not faithfully performed; it could not be owned by the lord, since he had no claim to it as long as the tenant fulfilled his duties.[20]

Quite apart from this practical difficulty, however, the truth is that English law has never applied the conception of ownership to land. "Ownership" is a word of many meanings, but in the present context we can take it to signify a title to a subject-matter, whether movable or immovable, that is good against the whole world. The holder of the title, such as the owner of a motor car, has a real as opposed to a personal right—he is the absolute owner. This position is illustrated by the Roman doctrine of *dominium*, under which the *dominus* was entitled to the absolute and exclusive right of property in the land. Nothing less in the way of ownership was recognized. A man had either absolute ownership or no ownership at all. Possession was regarded as fundamentally different—*nihil commune habet proprietas cum possessione*[1]—and, though it was adequately protected, the remedies available were personal, not real.

In sharp contrast to this attitude, English law, in analysing the relation of the tenant to the land, has directed its attention not to ownership, but to possession, or, as it is called in the case of land, *seisin*. All titles to land are ultimately based upon possession in the sense that the title of the man seised prevails against all who can show no better right to seisin. Seisin is a root of title, and it may be said without undue exaggeration that so far as land is concerned there is in England no law of ownership, but only a law of possession.

> ... "Seisin" ... is an enjoyment of property based upon title, and is not essentially distinguishable from right. In other words, the sharp distinction between property and possession made in Roman law did not obtain in English law; seisin is not the Roman possession and right is not the Roman ownership. Both of these conceptions are represented in English law only by seisin, and it was the essence of the conception of seisin that some seisins might be better than others.[2]

This unfailing emphasis upon the concrete and obvious fact of possession will be apparent if we consider for a moment the following three topics: the remedies that lie for the recovery of land, the position of a tenant who is wrongfully dispossessed, and the long established mechanism of conveyancing.

(a) Possessory nature of early actions for recovery of land

The English actions for the recovery of land, called in early days *real actions*, have consistently and continuously turned upon the right to possession. Moreover, their object throughout has been not to enquire whether the title to possession set up by the defendant is an absolute title good against all persons, but whether it is relatively better than any title that the plaintiff can establish. English land law is committed to the doctrine of relative titles to possession. Thus, the issue raised in the most ancient and solemn remedy, the *writ of right*, was not whether the demandant (plaintiff) could prove an absolute title good against third parties, but whether he or the tenant

---

20 Hargreaves, p. 44.
 1 *Digest of Justinian*, 41.2.12.1.
 2 Plucknett, *Concise History of the Common Law* (5th edn), p. 358.

(defendant) could establish the earlier and therefore the better seisin.[3] Similarly, the possessory assizes, simpler remedies introduced by Henry II to supplement the writ of right and to rectify a recent invasion of possession, merely considered the specific question whether the demandant or his ancestor had been unjustly disseised of his free tenement by the defendant. The assize of *novel disseisin*, i.e. recent dispossession, enabled A to recover land from B on proof that he had been ejected by B. The assize of *mort d'ancestor* availed him if he could show that X, his ancestor, had died seised of his land, and that the defendant had entered upon the land on X's death.

The sole question in these actions was one of fact relating to seisin. Did B disseise A? Did B take the seisin held by A's ancestor?[4] If so, the court ordered restoration of the seisin, but it did not adjudge that A held an absolute title good against all adversaries. If the defendant wished to litigate the question of title further, he would be driven to issue a writ of right.[5]

At a later date the various *writs of entry* met the case where the disseisin of which the demandant complained was not so immediate, as, for example, where B, after disseising the demandant, had granted the land to Y, who had granted it to the defendant. These actions, no less than the possessory assizes, merely decided whether the better right to seisin lay in the demandant or in the defendant.

Finally, it must be observed that this mediaeval principle of relativity of titles dominated the later action of ejectment and still dominates the modern action for the recovery of land as it is now called.[6] All that the plaintiff need do is to prove that he has a better right to possession than the defendant, not that he has a better right than anybody else. If, for instance, he is ejected by the defendant, he will recover by virtue of his prior possession, notwithstanding that a still better right may reside in some third person.[7]

(b) Effect of loss of seisin on proprietary rights

The effects that flow from a disseisin of the tenant afford a further illustration of the crucial part played by possession in English law. It was established at an early date that the seisin wrongfully taken by the disseisor was the commencement of a fresh title and that it gave him a real though tortious interest, valid against all but the disseisee and his successors in title.

> Possession being once admitted to be a root of title, every possession must create a title which, as against all subsequent intruders, has all the incidents and advantages of a true title.[8]

The disseisor has full beneficial rights over the land. He holds a fee simple estate which is transmissible either *inter vivos* or by will, and which the disseisee cannot defeat unless he takes proceedings within twelve years after the wrongful entry.[9] Moreover, although the disseisee had a right of action

3 Lightwood, *Possession of Land*, pp. 73–4; Plucknett, *Concise History of the Common Law* (5th edn), p. 358; Simpson, *A History of the Land Law* (2nd edn), pp. 37 et seq.
4 Holdsworth, *History of English Law*, vol. iii. p. 90; Maitland, *Forms of Action*, p. 28.
5 Plucknett, *Concise History of the Common Law* (5th edn), p. 359.
6 (1940) 56 LQR 376 (A. D. Hargreaves), replied to by Holdsworth in 56 LQR 479–82.
7 *Asher v Whitlock* (1865) LR 1 QB 1; M & B p. 203.
8 Pollock and Wright, *Possession in the Common Law*, p. 95.
9 Limitation Act 1980, pp. 887 et seq, post.

to recover the land, for a long period in our legal history his lack of possession confronted him with serious and ever-increasing difficulties as against the disseisor and his successors in title. In mediaeval days and for long afterwards, the effect of the disseisin was to deprive him of most of his beneficial rights over the land until he had vindicated his claim to seisin in the appropriate real action. His former rights were reduced to a right of entry, a reduction that entailed certain important consequences.

Thus, the disseisee lost the power of alienation, for, being dispossessed, he was unable to make the delivery of seisin essential for a conveyance of land, and a right of entry could neither be devised until 1837,[10] nor be conveyed *inter vivos* until 1845.[11]

Circumstances might well occur which would deprive him of his right of entry and leave him with a mere right of action—a *chose in action* that was equally inalienable, though it would descend to his heirs.[12] For instance, where the disseisor died while still in possession, the land passed to his heir by operation of law with the result that the interest held by him was no longer regarded as tortious. The right of entry was said to be "tolled", i.e. taken away, by descent cast.[13]

Again, if the disseisee failed to recover seisin, his widow had no right to dower;[14] if he died heirless, the land did not in all cases escheat to his lord;[15] and if he died leaving an infant heir, his lord was not entitled to wardship.[16]

The position may be summarized in the words of Holdsworth:

> The person seised has all the rights of an owner; the person disseised has the right to get seisin by entry or action; but, till he has got it, he has none of the rights as an owner. In other words, the common law recognizes, not *dominium* and *possessio*, but seisin only.[17]

(c) Possession root of title for conveyancing purposes

The third illustration of the emphasis laid by English land law upon possession, not upon ownership, is afforded by the practice of conveyancers. A vendor must prove to the satisfaction of the purchaser, not only that he is entitled to the land which he has agreed to sell, but also that his title is not subject to adverse claims vested in third parties. He can scarcely be expected to prove that he has a title good against the whole world, for, since land is permanent and indestructible, it may well be that there exists a competing and better title created many years ago and still existing.

English land law has no doctrine akin to that of Roman law by which possession for a definite but short period had the positive effect of investing the possessor with *dominium*. As one writer has observed, the absolute ownership of a perishable chattel, such as a motor car, is a comparatively easy matter to prove, but "if we were to insist upon the same fulness of ownership with regard to land we should have to trace back our title to the

---

10 Wills Act 1837, s. 3.
11 Real Property Act 1845, s. 6.
12 Hayes, *Introduction to Conveyancing*, vol. i. p. 231.
13 The doctrine of descent cast was abolished by the Real Property Limitation Act 1833, s. 39.
14 Maitland, *Collected Papers*, vol. i. p. 366.
15 Ibid., pp. 368–9.
16 Ibid., p. 369. On the subject generally, see Holdsworth, *History of English Law*, vol. iii. pp. 91–2.
17 Holdsworth, *History of English Law*, vol. iii. p. 95.

original grant of Paradise to Adam".[18] What the vendor can do, however, and what he does in practice is to rely upon the fundamental principle that seisin is evidence of his title to the land.

> With very few exceptions, there is only one way in which an apparent owner of English land who is minded to deal with it can show his right so to do; and that way is to show that he and those through whom he claims have possessed the land for a time sufficient to exclude any reasonable probability of a superior adverse claim.[19]

What, then, emerges so far is that land cannot be the subject-matter of ownership, though the person in whom its seisin is vested is entitled to exercise proprietary rights in respect of it. But again the question recurs—what is the nature of the interest held by the person seised? Is there nothing that he can be said to own? The answer made by English law is unique. The person entitled to seisin owns an abstract entity, call an *estate*, which is interposed between him and the land.[20] "The English lawyer . . . first detaches the ownership from the land itself, and then attaches it to an imaginary thing which he calls an estate."[1]

B. FEATURES OF DOCTRINE OF ESTATE

The estate represents the extent of the right to seisin. Thus the correct description of a tenant entitled to immediate seisin for his life is that he is *seised of Blackacre for an estate for life*. This estate entitles its owner to exercise proprietary rights over the land for the prescribed period, subject to observance of the tenurial duties, and it may be disposed of as freely as any other subject-matter of ownership. This doctrine, as will be explained later,[2] is not confined to the case where a man is entitled to immediate seisin. If he is definitely entitled to it at some future time, he is equally the owner of an estate.

Two phenomena of great significance have emerged during the development of this doctrine by the common law.

First, estates vary in size according to the time for which they are to endure. On this basis they are classified as estates of freehold and estates less than freehold.

Secondly, several different persons may simultaneously own distinct and separate estates in the same piece of land.

These matters will now be discussed in more detail.

(1) ESTATES CLASSIFIED ACCORDING TO DURATION

The main classification of estates depends upon their quantification and their quantification depends upon their duration. The estate will vary in size according to the time for which it is to continue. "Proprietary rights in land

---

18 Hargreaves, *Introduction to Land Law* (4th edn), p. 42.
19 Pollock and Wright, *Possession in the Common Law*, pp. 94–5.
20 Lawson, *Rational Strength of English Law*, p. 87.
 1 Markby, *Elements of English Law*, s. 330.
 2 P. 32, post.

are, we may say, projected upon the plane of time."[3] Thus a person may be entitled to seisin for ever or for a lesser period.

(a) Meaning of freehold estate

Estates are sub-classified into those of freehold and those of less than freehold. Into which of these categories they fell depended in the earliest days upon the quality of the tenure by which the estate owner held his land. A tenant in knight service, sergeanty, socage or frankalmoin was called a "freeholder," since the services due from him were free from servile incidents." He was said to have a frank tenement or freehold estate to distinguish him from a villein tenant.[4] Such was the original meaning of the expression "freehold estate".

But one of the characteristics of these free tenants was that the time for which they were entitled to hold the land was not fixed and certain. They invariably held either for life or for some other space of time dependent upon an event that might not happen within a lifetime, and it was this uncertainty of duration, not the quality of the services to be rendered, that gradually came to be regarded as the essential feature of a freehold estate.[5] Thus, even at the present day, an estate is freehold if its duration is uncertain; it is less than freehold if the time of its termination is fixed or capable of being fixed. The life tenant is a freeholder, but not so the tenant holding under a lease for a definite period, even though he holds for as long a period as 999 years.[6]

(b) Freeholds and non-freeholds distinguished in respect of seisin

Freehold and non-freehold estates were further distinguished in respect of seisin. At first the word "seisin" was used to denote possession both of land and of chattels, but this usage did not last long and by the fifteenth century a man was said to be seised of land, but possessed of chattels. Later the subject-matter of seisin became even further restricted. The real actions that lay for the recovery of land, the possessory assizes and the writs of entry, were available only to freeholders, i.e. to tenants in fee simple, in tail and for life. These actions, as we have seen, were based entirely upon seisin and since they availed only freeholders it is not unnatural that the word "seisin" was reserved exclusively to describe the possession of a freehold estate. Since mediaeval days it has been correct, for instance, to describe a tenant for life as seised, but a tenant for years as possessed, of the land.

(c) Tabular illustration

On the basis of duration common law has classified estates in the manner set out in the following table.

---

3 Pollock and Maitland, *History of English Law* (2nd law), vol. ii. p. 10. Compare the language used in the course of argument in *Walsingham's Case* (1579) 2 Plowd 547 at 555: "The land itself is one thing, and the estate in the land is another thing, for an estate in the land is a time in the land, or land for a time, and there are diversities of estates, which are no more than diversities of time, for he who has a fee simple in land has a time in the land without end or the land for time without end."
4 Ibid., vol. ii. p. 78; Holdsworth, *History of English Law*, vol. ii. p. 351.
5 Co Litt 43*b*.
6 See, generally, *Preston on Estates*, vol. i. c. 1.

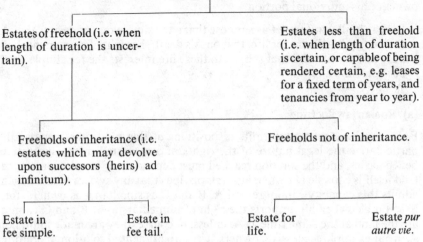

Estates classified according to their duration.

Estates of freehold (i.e. when length of duration is uncertain).

Estates less than freehold (i.e. when length of duration is certain, or capable of being rendered certain, e.g. leases for a fixed term of years, and tenancies from year to year).

Freeholds of inheritance (i.e. estates which may devolve upon successors (heirs) ad infinitum).

Freeholds not of inheritance.

Estate in fee simple.

Estate in fee tail.

Estate for life.

Estate *pur autre vie.*

(d) Freehold estates

As regards duration, the three freehold estates may be distinguished as follows:

(i) Fee simple The fee simple[7] is the largest estate in point of duration, for, being one that is granted to a man *and his heirs*, it will last as long as the person entitled to it for the time being dies leaving an heir, and therefore it may last for ever in the sense that it may never pass to the Crown so long as there is an heir. The word *fee* denotes its inheritability, and the word *simple* indicates that it is inheritable by the general heirs of the owner for the time being whether they be ascendants, descendants or collateral.

(ii) Fee tail The fee tail,[8] which is the only other estate of inheritance, is less in quantum than the fee simple since it is inheritable only by the specified descendants of the original grantee and never by his ascendants, and also because it is descendible only to his lineal issue and not to his collateral relatives. Thus it is inferior to the fee simple in the sense that it has not as great a capacity for perpetual existence. The classic formula for its creation is—to A and the *heirs of his body*.

(iii) Life estate The life estate[9] includes an estate which A holds for his own life and also one that he holds during the lifetime of B, this second species being called an estate *pur autre vie.*

(2) APPORTIONMENT OF FEE SIMPLE

The second phenomenon mentioned above is that the fee simple, which entitles the tenant to use the land for an infinite time, is regarded by English law as an aggregate out of which any number of smaller *and simultaneous* estates may be carved.[10] The entire subject-matter of enjoyment is

7 See chapter 8, p. 155, post.
8 See chapter 11, p. 245, post.
9 See chapter 12, p. 265, post.
10 Digby, *History of the Law of Real Property*, p. 270.

apportionable among a number of persons, each of whom is the present owner of his individual portion.

By way of illustration let us suppose that a fee simple owner desires that A shall enjoy Blackacre for life, that on A's death the right of enjoyment shall pass to B for life and that subject to these life interests the fee simple shall be vested in C.

(a) Roman law doctrine

Every legal system that permits dispositions of this kind must necessarily particularize the legal nature of the rights, if any, vested in the successive beneficiaries, and the solution reached must depend upon whether or not the land itself is capable of ownership. It is obvious that any system of law which admits this capacity cannot regard A, B and C as simultaneous owners, for, in so far as ownership imports the right of immediate user, B and C cannot use the land at the same time as A, unless, of course, they are made joint, not as in our example successive, owners. The jurisprudential solution, therefore, if the land itself is the subject of ownership, is to insist that it can be the subject only of absolute ownership, and that where, as in the above example, there is a limitation to a succession of persons the entire and absolute ownership shall pass from one beneficiary to another upon the happening of the prescribed events. This is what is called *substitution*. Under this doctrine, if land is limited to A, then to B and then to C, the legal result is that these persons in their turn become owners of the property, each taking by substitution for the one who preceded him; each in his turn being complete owner; but each taking nothing until his turn comes.[11]

B, for instance, is not even a limited owner of the land during the life of A, but on the death of the latter he becomes the absolute owner of the land for a limited time. Until his turn comes he has no proprietary interest that he can alienate or otherwise dispose of.

This is the solution of Roman law and of certain modern legal systems which regard *dominium* as the exclusive and unlimited right to the land itself, not merely to its user.

By Roman law, A, the owner, might indeed let the land to X by *locatio conductio* or grant it to him for life by way of *usufruct*, but his ownership was affected by neither transaction. In the former case, X, if evicted, had merely a contractual right enforceable against A alone; in the latter, he acquired only a *jus in re aliena*, i.e. a right to use for his life land the ownership of which remained vested in A.

(b) English law doctrine

English law, however, having divorced ownership from the land itself and attached it to an imaginary thing called an *estate*, which entitles the owner to use the land for a longer or a shorter period of time, has been able to take a bolder course. Having decided that estates may vary in size according to their duration, it goes a step further and concedes that any estate, whether its duration is long or short and whether it confers a right to immediate or to future seisin, is capable of a present existing ownership.

11 See Markby, *Elements of Law*, s. 330.

(c) Consequences of English law doctrine

Two results flow from this view.

(i) Different degrees of estate ownership First, there may be different degrees or gradations of estate ownership. The tenant in tail and the tenant for life, no less than the tenant in fee simple, are owners of their estates. As compared with the tenant in fee simple, they must, indeed, be described as *limited* owners, since their estates have not the same capacity of infinite duration. None the less they are owners, and their ownership differs from that of the tenant in fee simply only in degree—in quantity. There is no difference in kind or quality.[12]

The same remedies for the recovery of the land and the same powers of dealing with the estate by way of alienation are available, irrespective of the size of the estate. The different freehold estates, in other words, represent various grades in the hierarchy of ownership.

(ii) Futurity of right to seisin not incompatible with present ownership The second result of the English doctrine is that an estate may be the subject of a present existing ownership, even though the right of the owner to seisin is postponed to a future time. This is explicable in elementary terms.

An estate is the right to possess and use the land for the period of time for which it has been granted. In the case of the fee simple the period is infinite, since the estate is capable of perpetual existence. The entire ownership, in other words, resides in the person holding the fee simple, since he and his successors are entitled to use the land for ever. But time is divisible, and this right of perpetual user may be divided into successive periods of limited duration or, as one writer put it, into successive intervals of time.[13] One slice of the perpetual time, one slice of the entire ownership, may be given to A, another to B, and so on. Therefore, if the fee simple owner makes a grant

to A for life, then to B for life and then to C in tail,

each grantee receives at once a portion of the one uniform subject-matter, namely the right to use the land. A, B and C each hold a distinct and separate share of the identical thing. The only difference between them lies in the periods for which the user is to be enjoyed. Moreover, there is no futurity about the *ownership* of B and C. Upon the execution of the grant they become the immediate and absolute owners of an estate. It is not the right of ownership, but the right to actual seisin of the land that is future. Indeed, by virtue of their power of disposition they may exchange their property for money and so make it immediately available.[14]

(d) Advantages of English law doctrine

In conclusion, it may be said that this doctrine of the estate has given an elasticity to the English law of land that is not found in countries outside the area of the common law.[15] This is particularly true in respect of settlements, i.e. dispositions of property designed to provide for a succession of persons, such as the present and future members of a family. The desire to do this has

12 Pollock and Maitland, *History of English Law* (2nd edn), vol. ii. p. 7.
13 (1857) 1 Jurid Soc p. 537 (S. M. Leake).
14 Ibid., p. 538.
15 It has been described by a distinguished writer as "one of the most brilliant feats of the English mind": Lawson, *Rational Strength of English Law*, p. 97.

dominated English real property law throughout its long history; for land, with its virtue of permanency, is an ideal source of endowment and its use for this purpose has been favoured by the courts. The aims of a settlor will be more effectively attained if he is permitted to vest a definite right of ownership in certain persons upon the occurrence of certain prescribed events in the future, as for example by directing that if a son is born to the present tenant of Blackacre, he shall, on reaching his majority, immediately acquire a definite proprietary interest, even though the present tenant is still alive. If the land itself is the subject-matter of ownership, the simultaneous existence of two or more owners, unless they are to take jointly, is, as we have seen, impossible, and therefore in countries where that concept of ownership prevails the power to create successive interests stretching into the future is necessarily restricted. But once admit that what is owned is an imaginary thing called an estate, then it immediately becomes possible to frame elaborate and subtle schemes for the passing of the beneficial enjoyment of the land to one person after another in certain prescribed eventualities. There is room "to deal with ownership in a more fanciful way than if it were attached to the soil."[16]

C. LEASEHOLD INTEREST. TERM OF YEARS[17]

We will now conclude with a short description of the leasehold interest or term of years which, quantitatively considered, is the smallest proprietary interest recognised by English law.

(a) Not a freehold estate

This interest, generally referred to as a term of years, arises where land has been demised, i.e. leased, for a definite number of years. It thus lacks the requirement of an uncertain duration, and though the period for which it is to last may be very great, as for instance 999 years, yet it is not a freehold estate, and in the eye of the law is a smaller interest than a life estate.

(b) Not real property

Moreover it is not even real property. At an early period English law arrived at the general principle that, while land could be recovered specifically by a dispossessed tenant from a man who had ejected him, yet a person who was deprived of personal chattels could not enforce their actual recovery, but had to content himself with compensation in the shape of pecuniary damages. Broadly speaking, actions fell into two classes. The *real actions* lay for the restitution of some object, and the *personal actions* for the recovery of damages. As land was the only object of which restitution *in specie* could be enforced, it followed that it formed the only subject matter of a real action, and it is not surprising to find the ancient lawyers seizing upon this fact and defining land as real property. Property which could be recovered in a real action was itself called real property, and thus it resulted that real property consisted solely of interests in land.

16 Markby, *Elements of Law*, s. 330.
17 Holdsworth, *History of English Law*, vol. iii. pp. 213–7; vol. vii. pp. 238–96; Simpson, *A History of the Land Law* (2nd edn), pp. 71–77, 92–95, 247–256.

But not every interest in land could be specifically recovered, for, as we have seen, the real actions were available only to freeholders, i.e. only to tenants who were seised of the land. A tenant for years was possessed, not seised, and if dispossessed he could originally bring only a personal action for the recovery of damages against the grantor of his term. It is true that by the close of the Middle Ages a remedy had been introduced whereby he might recover the term itself, but nevertheless he was still regarded, and has ever since been regarded, as a non-freeholder. The doctrine of seisin was never extended to his interest, and the *possessory assizes* and the *writ of right*, which were the real actions properly so called, were never made available to him. He continued to hold merely personal property because originally his sole remedy was to bring a personal action.

At first sight this refusal of the law to regard a leaseholder's interest as real property is curious. It was not due to the unimportance or insignificance of terms of years. Such interests were on the contrary exceedingly valuable. The cause of their segregation, the reason why they were dissociated from the real actions and from feudal doctrine, was probably none other than economic pressure.[18]

At a time when investments in the modern sense of the term were unknown, one of the few methods by which a man might increase his income was to purchase a beneficial lease and take the profits of the land as interest on the money expended. Again, one of the ordinary methods of exacting security for a debt was for the debtor to lease his lands at a nominal rent to the creditor, so that the latter could obtain interest at the agreed rate out of the profits of the land without coming into conflict with the usury laws.[19] Another familiar form of investment was to purchase a wardship, which was the right to administer for one's own benefit the lands of an infant tenant in knight service. But if terms of years and wardships were to be effective investments, it was necessary that they should not be regarded as freehold estates in land carrying seisin, or, in more general terms, it was convenient to exclude them from the domain of strict real property law. There were several considerations that made this line of action advisable, but none was more potent than the fact that freehold estates as distinct from chattels could not be left by will. It may have been a matter of sound policy that an estate in lands should inevitably descend to the heir of the deceased tenant, but it would be poor comfort to tell a man who had invested his money in the purchase of a term of years that he had lost the right of bequeathing his money because he had converted it into land. After showing that as early as 1200 there was a large speculative traffic in wardships, Pollock and Maitland say:

> And then as to the term of years, we believe that in the twelfth century and later, this stands often, if not generally, in the same economic category. It is a beneficial lease bought for a sum of ready money; it is an investment of capital, and therefore for testamentary purposes it is *quasi catallum*.[20]

18 Pollock and Maitland, *History of English Law* (2nd edn), vol. ii. pp. 113 et seq; Plucknett, *Concise History of the Common Law* (5th edn), pp. 571–3.
19 Holdsworth, *History of English Law*, vol. iii. pp. 128, 215.
20 Pollock and Maitland, *History of English Law* (2nd edn), vol. ii. p. 117.

D. CLASSIFICATION OF PROPERTY

(a) Real and personal property

The position reached by the common law was that estates of freehold represented real property law in the strict sense of that term, and as such were subject to all the consequences of feudal tenure; while on the other hand leaseholds (together with some other rights in land) were personal property and not so subject, and for this reason were neither affected by the incidents of feudalism, nor governed by the same legal rules as freeholds.

(b) Chattels real and personal

This position soon gave rise to a difficulty, for a term of years, no matter how it might be treated by the technique of the law, was obviously a valuable interest in land, and one which it was appropriate to bring within the province of the land laws. To sever its connection with the law of land merely because it was outside the scope of the real actions would have been absurd, and so the law was obliged to surmount the difficulty by the invention of a new terminology.

It was already a commonplace that the subject-matter of proprietary interests was either real property or chattels. Chattels were personal property, since they were not specifically recoverable in a real action. Leaseholds were thus subject to the law of chattels, but since they lacked the attribute of movability the obvious solution was to regard them as a *tertium quid*— interests partly real and partly personal. Thus it was that personal property was sub-divided into chattels real and chattels personal.

> Chattels real, saith Sir Edward Coke, are such as concern or savour of the realty; as terms for years of land, wardships in chivalry, . . . the next presentation to a church, estates by statute merchant, statute staple,[1] *elegit*[2] or the like. And these are called real chattels, as being interests issuing out of or annexed to real estates; of which they have one quality, viz. immobility, which denominates them *real*, but want the other, viz. a sufficient legal indeterminate duration, and this want it is that constitutes them *chattels*.[3]

Thus there are two classes of chattels known to English law—chattels real as described by Coke, and chattels personal, which originally were confined to movable things, but which are now taken to comprise many forms of wealth, such as negotiable instruments, copyright, patents, trade marks, shares in a company and so on.

(c) Summary

We see, therefore, that the Law of Property as a whole falls into the following three divisions:

The *law of property* strictly so called, i.e. the rules that govern freehold interests in land—the fee simple, the entailed interest and the life interest;

---

1 A tenancy by statute merchant or statute staple arose when a merchant creditor by taking advantage of the Statutes Merchant and Staple (Edward I and III) obtained seisin of his debtor's lands; see Digby, *History of the Law of Real Property*, p. 282.

2 A writ of execution by which a judgment creditor might obtain seisin of his debtor's lands. It was abolished by Supreme Court Act 1981, s. 141.

3 Blackstone, vol. ii. p. 386.

The *law of chattels real*, i.e. the rules that govern leaseholds;
The *law of pure personalty*.

Of these three departments of law the first and the last stand furthest apart, for the law of real property has been constructed on feudal principles, while the law of pure personalty has drawn its inspiration from a variety of non-feudal sources, such as Roman and Canon law and the customs of merchants. Midway between the two comes the law of chattels real, which Blackstone describes as having a "mongrel amphibious nature", since it has derived its rules partly from real property law and partly from the law of pure personalty. The tendency, however, for several centuries has been to bring freeholds into conformity with chattels real, and the process of assimilation has been carried to such lengths, especially by the legislation of 1925, that we now have substantially a common and uniform system of law for real property and chattels real.[4] But, as we shall see, in spite of this assimilation, leaseholds today still remain personal as opposed to real property.[5]

4 Pp. 84, et seq, post.
5 P. 358, post.

Chapter 3

Modification of the common law by equity

SUMMARY

Our task is to show how equity modified and tempered the feudal principles of the common law by its introduction of the "use" and the consequent establishment of the trust concept, which is probably the most outstanding characteristic of English law. It is this concept that has produced the peculiarly English distinction between the legal and the equitable estate that forms the basis of modern conveyancing.

SECTION I DISADVANTAGES INCIDENTAL TO THE COMMON LAW TENURES

To understand the origin of uses it is necessary to examine the position of a tenant of land under the common law. That his position was not without its troubles can be realized by a glance at some of the disabilities and burdens which weighed upon him, several of which were due to the important part played by seisin in the feudal system. The feature of that system was its immaturity, as regards both the interests which might be created in land and the methods by which the interests could be dealt with. Possession is an obvious fact, and in early days it was the dominating fact upon which most of the repressive rules that came into being were founded.

Two fundamental principles which in themselves were sufficient to establish the importance of seisin were that the feudal services which in the early history of tenure were of such consequence to the lord were enforceable against the person seised and only against him; and again that it was only against the same person that an action for the recovery of land could be brought. It was necessary that there should always be some person capable of meeting adverse claims and preserving the seisin for successors.[1] The effect of not knowing who was actually seised of land would be the loss of public and private rights therein,[2] and therefore two inviolable rules that became established were that there must never be an abeyance of seisin, or in other words that there must be an uninterrupted tenancy of the freehold; and that every transfer of a freehold estate must be effected by an open and public delivery of seisin. Any disposition that would cloud the title to the seisin was forbidden at common law.

The following were some of the fetters laid on the free enjoyment of a freehold estate at common law:

A. CONVEYANCES WERE REQUIRED TO BE PUBLIC AND FORMAL

In a feudal society it was imperative that there should be no uncertainty as to the identity of the freehold tenant of any piece of land. A question might arise regarding the title to the land or the right of a lord to enforce the feudal dues to which he was entitled, and as both these matters could be settled only if it was known who was seised, common law ordained that every transfer of a freehold estate must be effected by an open and public delivery of seisin, either upon or within view of the land conveyed. The merit of this was that in the event of a dispute the actual freehold tenant would be well known to the neighbourhood. The method itself was called *feoffment with livery of seisin*, but the operative part of the transaction was the delivery, and a charter of feoffment, which only served to authenticate the transaction, was not strictly necessary.[3]

There were other kinds of common law assurances, but it may be said of them all that they were open and notorious, though, when the feudal vigour began to abate, they gradually ceased to bear this characteristic.[4] It often happens that a man, instead of publishing his dealings with land to the world at large, prefers to resort to some transaction which is secret and free from ceremony, but at common law this was a desire that was unattainable, at any rate in the early days.

B. THE TYPES OF INTERESTS WERE STRICTLY LIMITED

As it was essential that the seisin should not be in abeyance for an instant, but should always be vested in a freehold tenant, it followed that every conveyance of freehold had to be made to take immediate effect, so that the seisin passed at once to the grantee. This meant that many dispositions which a tenant might legitimately desire to make were rendered impossible. For instance, a gift of a freehold interest which was to vest in the donee if and when he attained 21 years of age was void, since such a gift had to be completed by delivery of seisin, and if seisin were delivered at once, it would, having been parted with by the donor, be vested in nobody until the donee

---

1 See Co Litt 342*b*, Butler's note (1).
2 Challis, *Law of Real Property* (3rd edn), p. 100.
3 Co Litt 271*b*, note 1.
4 Hayes, *Introduction to Conveyancing*, vol. i. pp. 29–30. For the history of the subject, see Holdsworth, *History of English Law*, vol. iii. pp. 220–46; vol. vii. pp. 353 et seq.

attained 21. If a grant were made to A for life and after his death to B when he attained 21, the grant to the latter failed unless he had reached that age at the death of A, because otherwise an abeyance of seisin would have occurred. Again, under a grant to A for life and after his death to the future children of B, only children who were in existence at A's death could take, for to allow later children to come in would have broken still another general principle, namely, that a transfer of a freehold interest had to be carried out by a public transaction.

Thus it is clear that the concentration of the common law upon the simple fact of possession led to extreme simplicity in the interests that might be created, and restricted within narrow bounds the limitation of future interests.[5]

C. A TENANT AT COMMON LAW COULD NOT DEVISE HIS FREEHOLD ESTATE

Whatever may have been the rule in Anglo-Saxon days, one of the effects of the introduction of feudal tenure into this country was to abolish the right of leaving freeholds by will, except in a few particular localities and boroughs. To have allowed such wills would not only have diminished the lord's right of taking the land by escheat and have been a hardship to the heir, but it would have run counter to a feudal policy which demanded that every transfer should be notorious and public.[6]

D. A TENANT AT COMMON LAW WAS LIABLE TO CERTAIN ONEROUS FEUDAL INCIDENTS[7]

This is no place to elaborate the burdensome nature of the tenurial dues that have already been briefly described. It must suffice to cite an expressive passage in which Blackstone sums up the position of one who held his lands in knight service:

In the meantime the families of all our nobility and gentry groaned under the intolerable burthens, which (in consequence of the fiction adopted after the Conquest) were introduced and laid upon them by the subtlety and finesse of the Norman lawyers. For, besides the scutages to which they were liable in defect of personal attendance, which however were assessed by themselves in parliament, they might be called upon by the king or lord paramount for aids, whenever his eldest son was to be knighted or his eldest daughter married; not to forget the ransom of his own person. The heir, on the death of his ancestor, if of full age, was plundered of the first emoluments arising from his inheritance, by the way of relief and primer seisin; and, if under age, of the whole of his estate during infancy. And then, as Sir Thomas Smith very feelingly complains, "when he came to his own, after he was out of wardship, his woods decayed, houses fallen down, stock wasted and gone, lands let forth and ploughed to be barren," to reduce him still farther, he was yet to pay half a year's profit as a fine for suing out his livery; and also the price or value of his marriage, if he refused such wife as his lord and guardian had bartered for, and imposed upon him; or twice that value, if he married another woman. Add to this, the untimely and expensive honour of knighthood; to make his poverty more completely splendid. And when by these deductions his fortune was so shattered and ruined that perhaps he was obliged to sell his patrimony, he

5 Pp. 275, et seq, post.
6 Holdsworth, *History of English Law,* vol. iii. pp. 75–6.
7 See pp. 16–8, ante.

had not even that poor privilege allowed him, without paying an exorbitant fine for a licence of alienation.[8]

There were additional disadvantages that resulted directly from the important part played by the feudal services. Thus, for instance, several of the feudal dues consisted of payments which were made by the newcomer upon the death of a tenant, and, as these would never be enforceable if the lands were granted to a body which never died, the rule soon became established that lands, granted to an association such as a monastery without the licence of the King and the lord paramount, were forfeited. Such a grant was called a *grant in mortmain*, and statutes were passed from time to time maintaining the rule as to forfeiture.[9]

Enough has now been said to show that the position of a freehold tenant at common law, as regards freedom of disposition, was not enviable. To quote Hayes:

> Large deductions must, therefore, be made from the praise lavished on the ancient common law, when its provisions are said to have promoted security of enjoyment, simplicity of title and notoriety of transfer. As civilization advanced, it proved less and less sufficient to attain those favourite objects of its founders, while it was manifestly ill-adapted to meet the growing demands of freedom and commerce. The rules of ownership and modes of assurance which we have endeavoured to explain, composed an unbending and oppressive code, utterly inadequate to the extended view and complicated interests of an intelligent and wealthy community. The progress of society called for a more pliant and liberal policy.[10]

SECTION II DISADVANTAGES OF COMMON LAW TENURES AVOIDED BY THE DEVICE OF PUTTING LANDS IN USE

History shows us that whenever a grievance presses hardly on the greater part of the population, it is not long before a remedy is discovered, and it was certainly not long before a "more pliant and liberal policy" was introduced with regard to the rights and powers of landowners in general. But the new policy did not come from the common law. It was the sole work of the Chancellor, who made it possible by means of the protection which he gave in his court of equity to the new conception called the *use* of lands. It was due to this alone that a tenant was enabled to retain the ordinary advantages of landholding which were assured to him by the common law while escaping some of the worst disabilities of that system.

A. ORIGIN AND EFFECT OF PUTTING LANDS IN USE

(1) ORIGIN OF THE USE

The word "use" is derived not from the Latin *usus* but from *opus*.[11] Maitland has shown us that before Domesday it was a common practice for one man

8 Blackstone, vol. ii. p. 76.
9 Ibid., vol. ii. p. 268; p. 936, post.
10 Hayes, *Introduction to Conveyancing*, vol. i. pp. 30–1.
11 Maitland, *Collected Papers*, vol. ii. p. 403; Pollock and Maitland, *History of English Law* (2nd edn), vol. ii. p. 228. For the origin and history of uses, see Holdsworth, *History of English Law*, vol. iv. pp. 407 et seq; (1965) 81 LQR 562 (J. L. Barton); Simpson, *A History of the Land Law* (2nd edn), pp. 173 et seq.

to deal with land *ad opus*—on behalf of—another, as, for instance, where the sheriff seized lands *ad opus domini Regis*, where a knight about to go to the Crusades conveyed his property to a friend on behalf of his wife and children, or where the vendor of an unfree tenement surrendered it to the lord to hold on behalf of the purchaser.[12] The word *opus*, which was in such connections commonly adopted, became gradually transformed into *oes, ues*, and thence into *use*. Now, if one person could deal with land on behalf of or to the use of another for a particular purpose, the question that inevitably occurred to men was why one person should not in a *general* way be allowed to hold land to the use of another. This, as a matter of fact, is exactly what was done in course of time. The tenant A would transfer his land by a common law conveyance to B, who undertook to hold it on behalf of, or, adopting the correct expression, to the use of, A. In such a case B was called the *feoffee to uses*, that is, the person to whom the feoffment had on certain conditions been made; while A went by the name of the *cestui que use*, which meant the person on whose behalf the land was held.

The practice did not spring into life all at once, and Maitland believed that 1230 was the earliest time at which one man was holding land permanently and generally to the use of another.

> In the second quarter of the thirteenth century came hither the Franciscan friars. The rule of their order prescribes the most perfect poverty: they are not to have any wealth at all. . . . Still, despite this high ideal, it becomes plain that they must have at least some dormitory to sleep in. They have come as missionaries to the towns. The device is adopted of having land conveyed to the borough community to the use of the friars.[13]

By the fourteenth century this device had become more extensive and there is evidence that it was a common practice for a landholder to convey his land to two or more friends *ad opus suum*—to his own use[14]—or to the use of a third person.

(2) LEGAL EFFECT OF PUTTING LANDS IN USE

(a) *Cestui que use* lost his rights at common law

The important point to observe is the legal effect of this practice. It was to cut off the *cestui que use* in the eyes of the *common law* from all connection with the land. By an assurance operating at common law he had conveyed his estate to the feoffees to uses, and was therefore deprived of all common law rights over the land. He was nothing, feoffees were everything; he had exchanged an actual estate for an intangible right, for instead of keeping seisin he had decided to rely upon the confidence that he had reposed in the feoffees.

> If, therefore, B (the feoffee) refused to account to his *cestui que use* A for the profits, or wrongfully conveyed the estate to another, this was merely a breach of confidence on the part of B, for which the common law gave no redress; much less did that law acknowledge any right in A to the possession or enjoyment of the land. The ordinary judicature knew no other proprietor than B; to him, and to him alone, attached the privileges and liabilities of a landholder; for he it was, to whom the possession was

12 Maitland, supra.
13 Maitland, *Equity*, p. 25; and see *Collected Papers*, vol. ii. p. 408. A Papal Bull ordained in 1279 that a use was not property.
14 Ibid., pp. 25–6.

legally delivered. To have regarded A in any other light than that of a mere stranger to the soil would have been to subvert a system raised upon investiture and tenure. It was accordingly decided at a very early period[15] that the common law judges had no jurisdiction whatever in regard to the use.[16]

If the feoffees failed or refused to carry out the directions imposed upon them,[17] or if they deliberately alienated the land for their own purposes,[18] there was no common law action by which they could be rendered liable, and as a *cestui que use* who was let into possession of the land was regarded as a mere tenant at will of the feoffees to uses, he could be turned out by the latter at any moment, and in the event of contumacy could be sued in trespass.[19]

(b) Uses protected by Chancellor

This absence of all remedy seems at first sight to stultify the practice of putting lands in use, and it would have been fatal had no alternative means been discovered for protecting the *cestui que use*. But an adequate form of protection was ready to hand. From about the year 1400 the Chancellor, in the first blush of his growing jurisdiction, stepped in and interceded on behalf of the *cestui que use*. He could not interfere with the jurisdiction of the common law courts by proceeding in a direct fashion against the land itself, because the absolute title to the land was vested in the feoffees by operation of the immutable principles enforced in those courts, but his role was to see that men acted honestly according to the precepts of good morality, and, in accordance with the principle that equity acts *in personam*, he did not hesitate to proceed against feoffees who disregarded the moral rights of the *cestui que use*. He was in a stronger position than the common law courts, for not only could he order a person to perform some definite act under pain of attachment, but his power of viva voce examination enabled him to discover breaches of good faith.

> The spectacle of feoffees retaining for themselves land which they had received upon the faith of their dealing with it for the benefit of others was too repugnant to the sense of justice of the community to be endured. The common law could give no remedy, for by its principles the feoffee was the absolute owner of the land. A statute might have vested, as the Statute of Uses a century later did vest, the legal title in the *cestui que use*. But in the absence of a statute the only remedy for the injustice of disloyal feoffees to uses was to compel them to convey the title to the *cestui que use* or hold it for his benefit. Accordingly the right of the *cestui que use* was worked out by enforcing the doctrine of personal obedience.[20]

In other words, the wrong which an unfaithful feoffee committed was breach of contract, but it was a breach for which at that time no remedy lay in the ordinary courts, since the general principle of the enforceability of contracts was still undeveloped. Further, it was common for a use to be declared in favour of a third party, and even if the modern doctrine of contract had been perfected, the rules as to privity of contract would have precluded the grant of a remedy to the *cestui que use*.

---

15 4 Edw. 4.
16 Hayes, *Introduction to Conveyancing*, vol. i. p. 33.
17 3 Rot Parl 511, No. 112, cited Ames (1907–8) 21 HLR, p. 265; *Select Essays in Anglo-American Legal History*, vol. ii. p. 741.
18 Sanders, *Uses and Trusts*, vol. i. p. 67.
19 *Preston on Estates*, vol. i. p. 145.
20 Ames, *Select Essays in Anglo-American Legal History*, vol. ii. p. 741.

B. CREATION OF THE DISTINCTION BETWEEN THE LEGAL AND THE EQUITABLE ESTATE

We have seen that from the year 1400 the Chancellor began to build up a comprehensive jurisdiction over uses, but it is especially important to observe that his intervention in this field led to the introduction into English law of what is generally described as a duality of land ownership. He did not deny that the *feoffee* was entitled at common law to the exclusion of the *cestui que use*, since the land had been conveyed to him by a conveyance effective at common law. That fact was inescapable, but what the Chancellor insisted upon was that the *feoffee* should scrupulously observe the directions imposed upon him by the *feoffor*. The feoffment had not been made to him for his own benefit.

In other words, while the *feoffee* was regarded as owner by the common law, the *cestui que use* was considered to be the true owner by equity: the former had the legal ownership, the latter the equitable ownership of the same piece of land. Thus we get the essentially English distinction between the legal and the equitable estate—the legal estate recognized and protected by the common law courts, and the equitable estate recognized and protected only by the Chancellor. This is what is meant by *duality of ownership*. Starting with the assumption that A had conveyed land to B to be held to the use of A, or to the use of C, Hayes, writing in 1840, described the position that arose:[1]

> But, under the auspices of an ecclesiastical chancellor, the use, though alien to the soil, took root in our civil jurisprudence, and attained to a degree of influence and importance which at length almost superseded the ancient polity. Means were soon devised for compelling B, the owner in point of law, to keep good faith towards A or C, the owner in point of conscience. The king, in his Court of Chancery, assumed jurisdiction to extort a disclosure upon oath of the nature and extent of the confidence reposed in B, and to enforce a strict discharge of the duties of his trust. Hence Equity arose. From this period, when the right of A (or C) became cognizable in the Court of Chancery, we may speak of him as the equitable or beneficial owner, and of B as the legal owner. But in order to preserve a clear perception of the twofold character of the system, we must keep steadily in view the fact that B had still the *real* right, to be enforced, on one side of Westminster Hall, by judgment of law *in rem*, which went at once to the possession of the land itself; while A (or C) had nothing more than a mere right *in personam*, to be enforced on the other side of the Hall, by subpoena, directed against the individual trustee. The Chancery, in assuming jurisdiction over the use, left untouched and inviolate the ownership at the common law. It exercised no direct control over the land, but only coerced and imprisoned the person of the legal owner who obstinately resisted its authority. It usurped none of the powers or functions of a court of law, but, leaving to the latter the redress of wrongs done to the realty, confined its jurisdiction to matters of trust and confidence, which could not be reached by the arm of ordinary justice.

C. ADVANTAGES OF PUTTING LANDS IN USE

Before we proceed any further it is desirable to notice how some of the worst burdens incidental to tenure at common law might be avoided by the device of a use.

1 Hayes, *Introduction to Conveyancing*, vol. i. pp. 33–4.

There were at least six substantial advantages that might accrue to the *cestui que use*.

(1) LANDS BECAME DEVISABLE

That very natural desire that the power of testamentary disposition, which already applied to goods and chattels, should be extended to land, contributed more largely than any other factor to the rapid establishment of the use. The obligation of the feoffees to administer the legal estate according to the wishes of the *cestui que use* was not confined to the lifetime of the latter, and from an early date it was the usual practice for the beneficial owner to specify what the destination of the use should be after his death. In this indirect way, by making a testamentary disposition of the equitable as distinct from the legal estate, men were accustomed to provide for their younger sons, daughters and other relatives, to ensure the payment of their debts and to make charitable gifts.[2]

(2) CONVEYANCES OF LAND FACILITATED[3]

The common law principle that a conveyance should be open and notorious could easily be evaded by means of the use, for just as the *cestui que use* could direct what dispositions of the land should be made after his death, so he could give similar directions that would be operative during his life. A transfer of the use required no formality; the one essential was that the intention of its owner should be clearly manifested. Moreover, the system of conveyancing was radically affected as the result of an equitable doctrine which applied even where land had not deliberately been put in use. This was that a mere contract to sell a legal estate raised a use in favour of the purchaser immediately on payment of the purchase money. Such a contract was called a *bargain and sale*, and though at first it passed merely an equitable estate to the purchaser, it gained a far wider operation after the Statute of Uses in 1535 and developed into the normal method of conveying *legal* estates.[4]

---

2 Holdsworth, *History of English Law*, vol. iv. pp. 438–9.

3 Ibid., pp. 424–7.

4 For the history of the matter, see Holdsworth, *History of English Law*, vol. vii. pp. 356–60. The process of development may be briefly described as follows:
(1) A, having bargained and sold land to B for a fee simple estate and having received the purchase money, was implicitly seised to the use of B.
(2) The Statute of Uses provided that when A stood seised to the use of B, the latter should acquire the *legal* estate (p. 49, post). Had this been the only enactment, therefore, a bargain and sale after the statute would have provided a secret method of conveying *legal* estates.
(3) The Statute of Enrolments, however, passed at the same time, enacted that no estate of *inheritance or freehold* should pass, nor should any use be raised, by a bargain and sale, unless the bargain and sale was made by deed and enrolled in one of the King's Courts of Record.
(4) The last statute applied only to sales of freehold or inheritable estates. Therefore a bargain and sale of a leasehold might be made privately without enrolment. This fact was quickly appreciated (certainly before 1620), and it became usual to transfer a fee simple as follows: A bargained and sold Blackacre to B *for one year*. On payment of the purchase money A became seised to the use of B. The Statute of Uses operated upon this state of affairs and passed the legal possession to B, leaving the reversion in A. Next day A executed a deed of *release* which extinguished his reversion and consequently enlarged B's leasehold into the fee simple. This form of conveyance, which was called a *lease and release*, remained the normal method of conveyance until 1841, when it was enacted that a release alone should be as effectual as a lease and release. A simple deed of grant was substituted for a release in 1845.

(3) SETTLEMENTS OF LAND FACILITATED

We have already mentioned,[5] and indeed shall have occasion to explain more fully later,[6] that the power of a landowner at common law to create future interests was so severely restricted that only the simplest forms of settlements of a legal estate were possible. This stringency was relaxed upon the introduction of uses. The use, to which the restrictive rules of common law were wholly inapplicable, conferred upon its owner an almost unrestrained liberty to specify who the future beneficiaries should be, upon what events their interests should arise, and in what order the interests should take effect. The equitable estate was, in fact, a pliable instrument, a subject-matter that could be moulded by its owner into such forms as might appear desirable to him. Thus arose what were called shifting and springing uses.[7]

(4) AVOIDANCE OF FEUDAL BURDENS

The most oppressive of the feudal burdens to which a tenant was liable at common law[8] were those that became exigible at his death, namely, wardship, marriage, reliefs and primer seisin. No relief from these would be gained by the appointment of a sole feoffee to uses, for the latter, in his capacity as tenant at law, would be caught in the feudal net and *his* death would entitle the lord to exact such dues as might be demandable. The usual practice, therefore, was to enfeoff, not one, but several, persons as joint tenants. The rule of joint tenancy is that the share of a tenant who dies does not pass to his heir but accrues to the surviving tenants.[9] He leaves nothing for which his heir can be made to pay a relief, he leaves nobody over whom the lord can claim the right of wardship or of marriage. The one essential, therefore, was to ensure that the number of feoffees never fell below two. The death of the *cestui que use* himself, despite his position as the true beneficial owner, created no right to feudal dues, since they were the consequence of tenure, and the use "being the creature of conscience, the offspring of moral obligation, could not be the subject of tenure".[10] "The lord could not look behind the feoffees; they were his tenants: it was nothing to him that they were allowing another person to enjoy land which by law was theirs."[11]

(5) AVOIDANCE OF FORFEITURE AND ESCHEAT

Land held by tenure at common law was forfeited to the Crown if the tenant committed high treason, and upon his conviction or outlawry for felony it passed to the Crown for a year and a day and then escheated to the lord.[12] These unpleasant consequences, however, were avoided, if a tenant, before

See (1988) 104 LQR 617 (J. M. Kaye), arguing that the object of the Statute of Enrolments was not to prevent secret conveyancing, but that "it was foreseen that, without it, the Statute of Uses would have had some unfortunate effects upon security of titles."
5 P. 40, ante.
6 Pp. 276–80, post.
7 Pp. 280–1, post.
8 Pp. 17–8, ante.
9 P. 215, post.
10 Hayes, *Introduction to Conveyancing*, vol. i. p. 34.
11 Maitland, *Equity*, p. 27.
12 See Challis, *Law of Real Property* (3rd edn), pp. 33 et seq.

embarking upon some doubtful enterprise, had the prescience to vest his lands in a few confidential friends. The delinquent might possibly suffer the extreme penalty, but at least his family would not be destitute.

(6) EVASION OF THE MORTMAIN STATUTES

We have noticed that, since those feudal dues that became exigible at the death of a tenant would be lost to the lord if land came into the hands of a body that might never die, such as a corporation, a series of Acts, generally called the Mortmain Statutes, were passed from an early date providing that land granted to a corporation without the licence of the King and lord paramount should be forfeited.[13] Uses, however, provided an obvious means of evading this prohibition, and, until the practice was finally stopped in 1392,[14] it was a common plan for a donor to enfeoff a number of persons to hold to the use of a monastery or other corporation.

D. INFLUENCE OF COMMON LAW DOCTRINES ON THE USE

We should next notice how the Chancellor dealt with this new form of ownership called the use or equitable estate. It was his own creation. He had invented something hitherto unknown to the law. He was free to do what he liked with his own. In the quaint language of an old judge, the use was as clay in the hands of the potter,[15] and, as the owner of a use was in theory allowed to give any imaginable directions as to its enjoyment, the Chancellor might have allowed it to be moulded into forms entirely subversive of common law principles. There were, in fact, several forms of landed interests, unattainable at common law, which he did permit to be carved out of the use, but they were mostly confined to the realm of future interests. Thus, for instance, the dispositions mentioned on page 40, which would have been void at common law, were open to a landowner if he was content to create them by way of use.

It may be said in general, indeed, that in framing rules for the governance of the use the Chancellor refused to be bound, or to let the development of the use be hampered, by any of the common law rules connected with tenure. And yet it was certainly not his policy to encourage wide deviations from the established tenets of law. The exact contrary was the case. Having begun by affording an adequate protection to the use, he then to some extent allowed the fact that its basis rested on personal confidence to fade into the background, and proceeded to regard it as a kind of interest in land, "a sort of immaterialized piece of land", in which actual estates might be created just as they might be created at common law.[16]

In other words, the general policy of the Chancellor in his development of the use was to adopt the accepted rules of common law. When necessary he was prepared to depart from those rules on the ground of convenience, but he usually took them as his guide. It can, indeed, be said.

> that there scarcely is a rule of law or equity of more ancient origin, or which admits of fewer exceptions, than the rule that Equity followeth the law.[17]

13 P. 936, post.
14 15 Ric. 2, c. 5.
15 *Brent's Case* (1583) 2 Leon 14 at 16, per MANWOOD J.
16 Maitland, *Equity*, p. 31.
17 Butler's note to Co Litt 250*b*, xvi.

Thus upon the death of the *cestui que use*, Equity applied the common law rules of descent; the common law rights of a husband to the wife's property after her death were extended to the equitable interest, though a wife was not dowable out of her husband's equitable estates until 1833; and estates, similar in extent to those possible at law, might be created in the use. As Butler noted:

> There is the same division in Equity as there is at law, of estates of freehold and inheritance, of estates of freehold only, and of estates less than freehold; of estates in possession, remainder or reversion; and of estates several and of estates undivided.[18]

To sum up this part of the discussion we may say that a use of lands existed where the legal estate was vested in A in such circumstances that he was subject to a trust enforceable in equity to convey the legal estate to such persons, and in the meantime to apply the rents and profits in such manner, as the *cestui que use* should direct; and, failing directions, should hold the land and pay the profits to the use of the *cestui que use* himself.[19]

E. THE LATER HISTORY OF USES AND THE RISE OF THE MODERN TRUST ESTATE

What, then, is the essential difference between the legal and the equitable estate? It is clear at first sight that the legal estate carries the bare technical ownership, while its equitable counterpart gives the *cestui que use* beneficial ownership. One is the nut, the other the kernel. If land is conveyed to

A and his heirs to the use of B and his heirs,

there is no doubt that A is the true *legal* owner. But it is an unprofitable ownership, for unless he succeeds in some fraudulent enterprise he will be compelled to deal with the land as B desires. In truth, the difference goes much deeper than this, but before stating wherein it lies we should say something of the subsequent history of uses.

(1) STATUTE OF USES 1535

(a) Object of Statute

The equitable estate, which was the greatest achievement of the Chancellor, was not allowed to pursue its course of development undisturbed. It was assailed by the legislature under Henry VIII, who, with a view to the "extirping and extinguishment of all such subtle practised feoffments, fines, recoveries, abuses", procured the passing of the Statute of Uses in 1535.[20] Many reasons were alleged in justification of this statute, but the real object of the King's action was to restore to something like their ancient buoyancy and dimensions those feudal dues of which the collection had been rendered so much less fruitful by the practice of conveying land to uses. The simplest remedy was to abolish uses altogether, and this the King tried to do. In 1532 a Bill was presented to Parliament in an attempt to limit the consequences of uses. This met with strong opposition, however, and Henry warned the

18 Butler's note to Co Litt 250*b*, xvi.
19 Sugden's *Gilbert on Uses*, p. 1; Fearne, *Contingent Remainders*, p. 291, note *h*.
20 27 Hen 8, c. 10.

Commons in March 1532 that he would "search out the extremity of the law". This he did by obtaining, in the case of *Lord Dacre* in 1535, a decision that any devise of lands by a tenant in chief who died leaving an heir under age was *ipso facto* fraudulent. Parliament, thus faced with a fait accompli which undermined the title of many tenants in chief, was prevailed upon to pass the Statute of Uses.[1]

The Act contained a very long preamble, the general object of which was to denigrate as grievances the advantages which uses conferred upon the landowning class as a whole, while keeping in the background the real purpose of the statute, which was to replenish the royal coffers. The preamble made the statute look as if it were a highly popular measure, but Maitland put the matter in its true historical setting when he said:

> A long preamble states the evil effects of the system [of uses], and legal writers of a later day have regarded the words of this preamble as though they stated a generally admitted evil. As a matter of historical fact this is not true. The Statute of Uses was forced upon an extremely unwilling parliament by an extremely strong-willed King. It was very unpopular and was one of the excuses, if not one of the causes, of the great Catholic Rebellion known as the Pilgrimage of Grace. It was at once seen that it would deprive men of that testamentary power, that power of purchasing the repose of their souls, which they had long enjoyed. The King was the one person who had all to gain and nothing to lose by the abolition of uses.[2]

(b) Effect of Statute

The statute was passed, however, and its effect was to abolish the distinction between the legal and the equitable estate in the case of the passive use, that is to say where the feoffees stood seised to the use of B and were the mere passive instruments for carrying out the directions of B. A conveyance to

> A and his heirs to the use of B and his heirs,

which before the statute would have carried only the equitable estate to B, operated after 1535 to pass the legal estate to him. This was so because the statute provided in effect that, when any person was seised of lands to the use of any other person, the *cestui que use* should be deemed to have lawful seisin of the land to the extent of his interest in the use, and the seisin that prior to the statute would have been in the feoffee to uses, A, should be deemed to be in the *cestui que use*, B. In other words, the statute brought about two results:

> First, to adopt a technical expression it *executed the use*, that is to say, it turned B's former equitable estate into a legal estate carrying common law seisin; and
> Secondly, the common law seisin, which would normally have been vested in A as a consequence of the conveyance, was taken away from him entirely.[3]

A was a mere nonentity, and as a general rule nothing was to be gained by conveying to A to the use of B instead of making a direct conveyance at common law to B, since in both cases B was seised of the legal estate, and by

---

1 (1967) 82 EHR 673 (E. W. Ives); Bean, *The Decline of English Feudalism*, chapter 6. For an earlier view of the origins of the Statute, see Holdsworth, *History of English Law*, vol. iv. pp. 450–61; (1912–13) 26 HLR, pp. 108–27.
2 Maitland, *Equity*, p. 34; and see Froude, *History of England*, vol. iii. pp. 91, 105, 158.
3 Fearne, *Contingent Remainders*, p. 273, Butler's note.

reason of that fact was in both cases subject to the dues, burdens and incapacities that had always affected an estate at common law.

(c) Advantages and disadvantages of Statute

The advantages of the statute lay with the common lawyers and with the King, its disadvantages with the general class of landowners. The common lawyers profited because they acquired a profitable jurisdiction over the uses that had been turned into legal estates. The King profited because the conversion of uses into legal estates involved the abolition of the power to devise lands, and this, in itself, increased very considerably the value of the tenurial incidents.[4]

The statute was a real grievance in many ways. For one thing the common belief was that it prevented wills of land, and, though this was a misapprehension,[5] it caused such irritation[6] that it was found necessary in 1540 to pass the Statute of Wills which permitted a tenant to devise all his socage lands and two-thirds of his lands held in knight service.

It would seem then, if we proceeded no further with the history of uses, as if Lord COKE was right when he said that

> the makers of the statute at last resolved, that uses were so subtle and perverse, that they could by no policy or provision be governed or reformed; and therefore, as a skilful gardener will not cut away the leaves of the weeds, but extirpate them by the roots, and as a wise householder will not cover or stir up the fire which is secretly kindled in his house, but utterly put it out; so the makers of the said statute did not intend to provide a remedy and reformation by the continuance or preservation, but by the extinction and extirpation of uses; and because uses were so subtle and ungovernable, they have with an indissoluble knot coupled and married them to the land, which of all the elements is the most ponderous and immovable.[7]

(d) Uses not executed by Statute

This, however, was to go too far, for the Act did not entirely abolish uses. There were at least two cases in which the grantees to uses retained the legal estate and were still compelled by the Chancellor to fulfil the intention of the grantor.

(i) Uses of leaseholds First, since the statute applied only where a feoffee was seised to the use of another, it was necessarily inoperative where a term of years, as distinct from a freehold estate, was given to A to the use of B, for A was possessed, not seised, of the subject-matter.

(ii) Active uses Secondly, the exclusion of the statute was admitted where an active duty was imposed upon the feoffees to uses, as for instance where they were directed to collect the rents and profits and to pay them to B. In these circumstances it was recognized that the legal estate must remain with the feoffees, for otherwise they could not justify their right to the rents.

In both these instances, the conscience of the feoffees to uses was affected and they came under a moral duty to deal with the legal estate on behalf of the beneficiary—in the one case to transfer the term to him, in the other to

4 Holdsworth, *History of English Law*, vol. iv. pp. 463–4.
5 See (1944) 7 CLJ 354 (R. E. Megarry).
6 Froude, *History of England*, vol. iii. p. 89.
7 *Chudleigh's Case* (1594) 1 Co Rep 124*a*.

secure the rents for him—and it was a duty that was enforceable only by the Chancellor. As regards terminology, however, it became usual to describe the person whose conscience was affected in these cases as being under a *trust* to carry out the directions of the grantor.[8] The uses were not those which the statute could execute, yet they were trusts which in conscience ought to be performed.[9] The statutory abolition of the passive use, of course, was in no way affected by this exercise of the Chancellor's jurisdiction. It long remained true that if the fee simple were granted to A to the use of B, A was divested of the legal estate and deprived of his former functions. Nevertheless, the principle that a moral duty must be performed was developed with such insistence that the passive use was ultimately restored in the shape of the passive trust, for the courts of equity gradually extended the circumstances in which the person upon whom the statute conferred the legal estate was bound in conscience to hold it in trust for some other person in accordance with the intention of the grantor.[10]

(e) The use upon a use

A striking example of this enduring concern of Chancery with the problem of conscience is furnished by the ancient rule that there could be no use upon a use. The rule established before the statute was that if land were conveyed to

A and his heirs to the use of B and his heirs to the use of C and his heirs.

it was only the use in favour of B that took effect. He acquired the equitable estate, and the second use in favour of C was ruled out as being repugnant to the first.[11] This was confirmed at common law soon after the statute in *Jane Tyrrel's Case*,[12] the result of which was that B, not A, acquired the legal estate and the limitation in favour of C was still nugatory. The repugnancy of his use with that of B was, of course, apparent, for as was said in another case,

The use is only a liberty to take the profits, but two cannot severally take the profits of the same land, therefore there cannot be an use upon an use.[13]

(2) DEVELOPMENT OF MODERN TRUST

(a) Passive use finally restored

Although it was equally apparent, as Blackstone remarks,[14] that B was never intended by the parties to have any beneficial interest in the land, the

---

8 Plucknett, *Concise History of the Common Law* (5th edn), pp. 598–9.
9 Blackstone, vol. ii. p. 336.
10 Plucknett, *Concise History of the Common Law* (5th edn), p. 599.
11 (1532) Bro Ab, Feoff. al Uses, 40; cited Ames, *Select Essays in Anglo-American Legal History*, vol. ii. p. 748.
12 (1557) 2 Dyer 155a; Digby, *History of the Law of Real Property*, p. 375.
    Jane bargained and sold land (p. 46, ante) to her son, G, and his heirs, upon the understanding that G was to hold to the use of Jane for life and thereafter to the use of himself in tail. The purchase money was paid, and therefore by implication of law Jane was seised to the use of G. The statute operated upon this use, and gave G the legal fee simple. But further uses had been declared, namely, to Jane for life and then to G in tail, and the question was whether these were valid or not. It was held that they were void.
13 *Daw v Newborough* (1716) 1 Com 242; cited Ames, vol. ii. p. 748.
14 Vol. ii. p. 336.

Chancery court at first came to the same conclusion and repudiated the second use.[15] Ultimately, however, and certainly by 1700, it reversed this view and restored the passive use by holding that B must be regarded as holding the legal estate in trust for C. It was against conscience for one man to retain what was clearly intended for another. The exact stages by which this result was reached are not discernible. It was long thought that *Sambach v Dalston* (or *Darston*)[16] in 1634 was the decisive authority, but research has shown that this is to go too far.[17] The importance of that decision was the refusal of the court to ignore the grantor's intention. In the actual circumstances of the case he intended to benefit not only C, but also an infant after the death of C and therefore the court directed B to make such dispositions of the land as would fulfil the whole of the grantor's design. This direction, however, did not involve the restoration of the passive use or any recognition of the modern passive trust, for B's obligation was to divest himself of the legal estate, not to retain it and hold it on behalf of C.[18]

(b) Rise of modern passive trust

Eventually, however, a change in the political situation facilitated the restoration of the passive use. The passive use had been abolished in 1535 for the sole reason that the King laid the loss of his feudal revenue at its door. But towards the end of the seventeenth century a complete revolution had occurred in the political sphere. Owing to the abolition of the military tenures in 1660 and to the gradual fall in the value of money, the feudal dues had become of little consequence and, indeed, the royal finances had been put on a more satisfactory footing. This fact, coupled with an almost universal desire for the old liberty of action, enabled the Chancellor once more to recognize the former distinction between the legal and the equitable estate whenever the intention was that B should hold land on behalf of C. The device eventually adopted by conveyancers to make this intention effective was merely to limit a use upon a use.[19] Thus, if it was desired to create an equitable estate in favour of C, instead of adopting the pre-statute method of a conveyance to A to the use of C, all that was necessary was to add a second use and make the conveyance run to A to the use of B to the use of C. The effect of this was that the statute divested A of his interest and passed the legal estate to B, with the result that, since the second use was not executed by the statute, C was left with a mere equitable estate corresponding with the equitable estate that existed in the pre-statute days under the name of the use.

(c) Creation and terminology

Thus the old distinction was retained in spite of the statute, but both the method of creating the distinction and the terminology adopted to describe

15 *Girland v Sharp* (1595) Cro Eliz 382; Digby, *History of the Law of Real Property*, p. 375.
16 (1635) Toth 188; Nelson 30, sub nom. *Morris, Lambeth et Margery v Darston.*
17 (1958) 74 LQR 550 (J. E. Strathdene); Simpson, *A History of the Land Law* (2nd edn), p. 202; see further (1957) CLJ 72 (D. E. C. Yale); (1966) 82 LQR 215 (J. L. Barton), arguing that "the trust of freehold was an accepted institution at any rate in the latter part of the sixteenth century"; and this is supported by two recently discovered manuscripts: (1977) 93 LQR 33 (J. H. Baker).
18 Plucknett, *Concise History of the Common Law* (5th edn), pp. 601–2.
19 Ibid., p. 602.

it were changed. The first use in favour of B, which was executed by the statute, was still called a use, but the second one in favour of C, on which the statute did not operate, was for greater clearness always designated a "trust".[20]

The practice ultimately adopted was to leave A out altogether and to create the equitable estate by conveying the land

> unto and to the use of B and his heirs in trust for C and his heirs.

The effect of this was that B, called the *trustee*, acquired the legal estate by virtue of the common law; but he also obtained the use, and though he was deemed to take the legal estate at common law and not under the statute, for there was no other person seised to this use,[1] yet, since a use had been declared in his favour, the rule that there could be no use upon a use prevented the statute from operating upon the second use and passing the legal estate to C.[2]

Thus, despite the complacent optimism of Lord COKE, the old distinction between the legal and the equitable estate was fully restored by at any rate the early eighteenth century. In 1738, Lord HARDWICKE stated the position in these words:

> Yet [after 1535] the judges still adhered to the doctrine, that there could be no such thing as *an use upon an use*, but where the first use was declared, there it was executed, and must rest for that estate: therefore, on a limitation to A and his heirs, to the use of B and his heirs, in trust for D, B's estate was held there to be executed by the statute, and D took nothing.
>
> Of this construction equity took hold, and said that the intention was to be supported. It is plain B was not intended to take, his conscience was affected. To this the reason of mankind assented, and it has stood on this foot ever since, and by this means a statute made upon great consideration, introduced in a solemn and pompous manner, by this strict construction, has had no other effect than to add at most three words to a conveyance.[3]

The last remark of the Lord Chancellor, however, though picturesque and arresting, was scarcely accurate, for, as we shall see, the statute had a vital and a lasting effect in so far as it enabled a class of future interests (springing and shifting uses), hitherto unknown to the common law, to be carved out of the legal estate.[4]

F. THE ESSENTIAL DIFFERENCE BETWEEN THE LEGAL AND THE EQUITABLE ESTATE

The position with regard to equitable estates remained as indicated above until 1 January 1926. If, that is to say, it was desired to create a trust estate,

---

20 Hayes, *Introduction to Conveyancing*, vol. i. p. 54. See Holdsworth, *History of English Law*, vol. v. pp. 307–9; vol. vi. pp. 641–4.

 1 "The statute ought to be expounded that when the party seised to the use and the *cestui que use* is one person, he never taketh by the statute, except there be a direct impossibility for the use to take effect by the common law": Bacon, *Uses*, 47.

 2 *Samme's Case* (1609) 13 Co Rep 54; *Doe d Lloyd v Passingham* (1827) 6 B & C 305; *Orme's Case* (1872) LR 8 CP 281; *Hadfield's Case* (1873) LR 8 CP 306; *Cooper v Kynock* (1872) 7 Ch App 398; *Sanders on Uses and Trusts* (5th edn), vol. i. p. 89; Hargreaves, *Introduction to Land Law* (4th edn), pp. 96–8.

 3 *Hopkins v Hopkins* (1738) 1 Atk 581 at 591.

 4 Pp. 280–2, post.

all that was necessary was to convey land *unto and to the use of* trustees in fee simple, in trust for the *cestui que trust*—or beneficiary, as we will designate him in the future.

The questions that now require answering are:

1. What is the nature of trust estates, and
2. What is the exact point of difference between them and legal estates?

(1) NATURE OF THE TRUST ESTATE

In the first place it may be said in a general way that the uses which continued, after and in spite of the statute, to have their old effect were simply the same original uses appearing under the different name of trusts.[5] But this is not the whole story. As Lord MANSFIELD said in *Burgess v Wheate*.[6]

> An use and a trust may essentially be looked upon as two names for the same thing; but the opposition consists in the difference of the practice of the Court of Chancery.

As is inevitable in the development of any legal conception equitable interests became much more elaborate and were adapted to many more purposes than in the days before the Statute of Uses. Lord Keeper HENLEY said in the same case:[7]

> Geometry was the same in the time of Euclid as in that of Sir Isaac Newton, though he applied the principles and rules to effect greater discoveries and more important demonstrations ... An use, say the older books, was neither *jus in re*, nor *ad rem*, but a confidence resting in privity of person and estate, without remedy but in a court of equity. What else is a trust? What other definition can be given of it? No other is attempted. But it is said since the existence of trusts (since the statute), equity has modelled them into the shape and quality of real estates, much more than it did in earlier times when they were called uses. It has made tenants by the curtesy, permitted tenants in tail to suffer common recoveries etc. And why? Because equity follows the law. And between *cestui que trust* and those claiming by, from and under him, it is equity that he should be considered as formally possessed of that estate of which he is and appears substantial owner. But this is only the effect of the equitable jurisdiction's growing to maturity, and was an accident that to a degree accompanied uses as well as trusts. Lord Bacon observes that they grew to strength and credit by degrees and as the Chancery grew more eminent.

Thus uses required that the feoffee to uses should have the fee simple estate, but trusts could be declared upon the estates of tenants in tail, for life or for years; uses were generally passive, that is, the feoffee was a dormant instrument compelled by equity to obey the directions of the *cestui que use*, but later development allowed the creation of special trusts under which the trustee might be directed to perform such duties as the sale of land, the accumulation of profits, the management of estates and so on. Again, the use applied only to land, but the subject-matter of trusts has expanded to such a degree that at the present day it includes, not only every conceivable kind of property, but even objects unconnected with property. The trust, for instance, has enabled unincorporated associations, such as clubs, trade unions and nonconformist bodies, which, owing to the indefinite and fluctuating character of their personnel, are not persons in the legal sense, both to own property and to fulfil the objects of their formation. The ownership of premises cannot reside in an unincorporated club, but it may be vested in a

5 *Lloyd v Spillet* (1741) 2 Atk 148, per Lord HARDWICKE.
6 (1757–9) 1 Eden 177 at 217.
7 Ibid., at 248.

few persons, who, in the capacity of trustees, will not only have a legally protected ownership but will be amenable to the jurisdiction of the court if they fail to administer the property on behalf of the members and in accordance with the rules.[8] Then again the trust is not the only form of equitable interest known to the law. The interest that arises in favour of a person who has made a valid contract for the purchase of land or a valid contract for a lease; the right which an owner possesses to enforce certain restrictive covenants; the interest in land retained by a person before 1926 who mortgaged the land in return for a loan of money—these are all equitable interests and exhibit the one great characteristic that distinguishes them from legal estates.[9]

(2) DIFFERENCE BETWEEN LEGAL AND EQUITABLE ESTATE

That brings us to the second point. What is that characteristic, or, in other words, what is the difference between the legal and the equitable estate?

As we have said, the difference is not adequately defined by the statement that the legal estate confers an empty title, while the equitable estate amounts to beneficial ownership of the land. The fundamental distinction is this:

> A legal estate is a right *in rem*, an equitable estate a right *in personam*, that is to say, the former confers a right enforceable against the whole world, the latter one which can be enforced only against a limited number of persons.

(a) Legal estate

If A is entitled to the legal estate in Blackacre, then as a general rule it is true to say that, apart from some voluntary act of his own, he cannot be deprived of his rights in the land by the fraud of some third person. If, for instance, the owner of a fee simple grants a legal term of years in the land to A and then sells and conveys the fee simple to X, fraudulently concealing the existence of the lease, the rights of A as the owner of a legal estate are entirely unaffected by the transaction.

Exactly the same principle applies to all legal as distinct from equitable interests. For instance, a landowner may allow his neighbour to enjoy some right over his land such as a right of way. If the right which is so enjoyed exhibits certain characteristics (to be described in a later chapter),[10] it is known as an easement, and an easement is capable of being a legal interest, and if so, is permanently enforceable against all subsequent owners of the land over which it is exercisable. That land may very well be bought by a person who does not know of the right and has no reason to know of it, but nevertheless it will be binding upon him. The person entitled to enjoy the right has a legal interest which can be enforced against all persons whether they know of it or not.

(b) Equitable estate

So then the legal estate, or in fact any legal interest however small, is binding against all people, no matter how they have obtained what seem to be

---

8 See Maitland, *Collected Papers*, vol. iii. pp. 271–84 (*The Unincorporate Body*); pp. 321–404 (*Trust and Corporation*).
9 Pp. 65–6, post.
10 Chapter 18, pp. 517 et seq, post.

absolute and unrestricted rights over the land. But the rights conferred upon the owner of an equitable estate are not and never have been so extensive as this, though they are enforceable against so many people that they come to look very like *jura in rem*. The general principle is that they are enforceable only against those persons who, owing to the circumstances in which they have acquired the land, ought in conscience to be held responsible. This principle derives from the consistent refusal of the Chancellor to enforce the use against a person who acquired the land from the feoffee to uses unless he was affected by the confidence that had been reposed in the original feoffee.

> As the use had its beginning in personal confidence, so its continuance, as a binding obligation on the legal owner of the land, was measured by the continuance of that confidence.[11]

The number of persons who were deemed to be affected by this confidence gradually grew in number.

(c) Extension of enforceability of equitable estate

The starting point was of course that the trustee himself, or the *feoffee to uses* as he was originally called, was permanently bound to observe the trust. The first extension of this was made in 1465, when it was held that a person who bought the land from the trustee with notice of the conditions upon which the land was held was bound by the trust.[12] The next stage, reached in 1522, was that all those who came to the trustee's estate by way of succession, such as his heir or doweress, were held responsible for carrying out the trust.[13] The law, which had reached this point at the time when the Statute of Uses was passed, was adopted and carried further by the courts when equitable estates reappeared under the name of trusts. Thus it was decided by *Chudleigh's Case* in 1595[14] that a voluntary alienee from the trustee, that is to say, a person who had acquired the estate without giving valuable consideration for it, was bound by the trust even though he had no notice of its existence. Therefore a trust was enforceable both against a man who bought the land *with notice* of the trust, and against one who received it by way of gift but without notice. Again, at some date after 1660,[15] trusts were made enforceable against creditors of the trustee who had seized the trust estate with a view to obtaining satisfaction for the debts due to them.

The one person, therefore, whose conscience was unaffected and against whom the equitable estate became unenforceable was the purchaser for value of the legal estate *without notice* of the rights of the *cestui que use*. If the feoffee to uses fraudulently sold and conveyed the land to an unsuspecting purchaser, the equity of the *cestui que use* was gone so far as the land was concerned and he could not claim relief against the purchaser. Nevertheless his equity remained in full force against the fraudulent trustee.

> The *very* land was irrecoverably gone, but the use remained; and while the conscience of the person *to* whom the possession had passed was unaffected, the

---

11 Hayes, *Introduction to Conveyancing*, vol. i. p. 42. See also Sanders, *Uses and Trusts*, vol. i. pp. 55–6.
12 YB 5 Ed IV, Mich pl 16, fo. 7. For the whole of this subject, see the account given by Jenks in his *Modern Land Law*, pp. 141 et seq.
13 YB 14 Hen VIII, Mich pl 5 fo. 8, cited Jenks; Maitland, *Equity*, p. 117.
14 1 Co Rep 113b at 122b; *Mansell v Mansell* (1732) 2 P Wms 678.
15 See Maitland, *Equity*, p. 112.

person *from* whom it had passed was still liable, as before, to fulfil the equities tacitly included in the use.[16]

(d) Summary

We are now in a position to summarize the essential difference between the legal and equitable estate. We have said that a legal interest is enforceable against all the world, while an equitable interest can be enforced only against a limited number of persons. To be more precise, if an equitable interest in Blackacre is created in favour of X, the following are the persons who, if they subsequently acquire an interest in land, will take that interest subject to X's right:

1.   a person who acquires Blackacre as the heir, devisee or personal representative of the trustee;
2.   a person who has acquired the legal estate in Blackacre *without the payment of valuable consideration*, even though he has no notice of the equitable interest;
3.   a creditor of the trustee, whether with or without notice of the trust; or
4.   a person who has given valueable consideration for the legal estate in Blackacre, but who is affected by notice of the equitable interest.

An equitable interest such as a trust is, then, if we put the matter with strict regard to historical accuracy, one that can be enforced only against those particular persons, but a definition which is almost equally accurate[17] is that an equitable interest is one that is enforceable against the whole world *except a bona fide purchaser for valuable consideration of the legal estate which is subject to the equitable interest, provided that, when the purchaser acquired the legal estate, he had no notice of the equitable interest.* In the case of such a person there is no reason why equity should not allow the common law to run its normal course. Equity follows the law, and will not interfere with the law unless there is some very strong equitable ground for doing so. Where a person has paid for the interest which is secure at law, and moreover has acted honestly and diligently there is no equitable reason for postponing him to somebody who from the point of view of equity is in no stronger position, and from the point of view of law is in a far inferior position.

The position was put very forcibly by JAMES LJ in *Pilcher v Rawlins*:[18]

I propose simply to apply myself to the case of a purchaser for valuable consideration, without notice, obtaining, upon the occasion of his purchase, and by means of his purchase deed, some legal estate, some legal right, some legal advantage; and, according to my view of the established law of this court, such a purchaser's plea of a purchase for valuable consideration without notice is an absolute, unqualified, unanswerable defence, and an unanswerable plea to the jurisdiction of this court. Such a purchaser, when he has once put in that plea, may be interrogated and tested to any extent as to the valuable consideration which he has given in order to shew the *bona fides* or *mala fides* of his purchase, and also the presence or the absence of notice; but when once he has gone through that ordeal, and has satisfied the terms of the plea of purchase for valuable consideration without notice, then this court has no jurisdiction whatever to do anything more

16 Hayes, *Introduction to Conveyancing*, vol. i. p. 43.
17 But see Maitland, *Equity*, pp. 120–21.
18 (1872) 7 Ch App 259 at 268; M & B p. 28; p. 65, post.

than to let him depart in possession of that legal estate, that legal right, that legal advantage which he has obtained whatever it may be. In such a case the purchaser is entitled to hold that which, without breach of duty, he has had conveyed to him.

Apparently, the only exception to this immunity enjoyed by the purchaser for value without notice arises where in fact the vendor's only title to convey the fee simple is that he is tenant for life under a settlement, but he fraudulently conceals the existence of the settlement.[19]

(3) THE DOCTRINE OF THE BONA FIDE PURCHASER FOR VALUE OF THE LEGAL ESTATE WITHOUT NOTICE

There thus emerges the doctrine of the bona fide purchaser for value of the legal estate without notice. Maitland has called such a purchaser "Equity's darling".[20] This doctrine is a cardinal principle of the land law, and, although it has been shorn of much of its importance by subsequent legislation, it still remains a basis of the law and is used as a residuary principle to solve problems of the enforceability of third party rights for which statute makes no provision. We must now look at the details of the doctrine.

(a) Purchaser for value

The purchaser must have given consideration in money or money's worth[1] or marriage. Otherwise he is a donee and is bound by the equitable interest whether he has notice of it or not. The consideration need not be adequate, and may even be nominal.[2] Money's worth extends to all forms of non-monetary consideration, such as other land or chattels or stocks and shares. Marriage is limited to a future marriage; a promise in consideration of a future marriage, called an ante-nuptial agreement, is deemed to have been made for value,[3] but a promise made in consideration of a past marriage, called a post-nuptial agreement, is not.

A purchaser is not limited to a person who acquires the fee simple, but includes a mortgagee[4] or lessee.

(b) Legal estate

The purchaser must normally show that he has acquired a legal estate in the land. The doctrine is based on the maxim that where the equities are equal the law prevails; and as between the beneficiary's equitable interest and the innocent purchaser's legal estate, the equities are equal, and the purchaser's legal estate prevails.

On the other hand, the purchaser of an equitable interest in land takes the land subject to existing equitable interests in the same land whether he has

---

19 *Weston v Henshaw* [1950] Ch 510; M & B p. 311; see, however, *Re Morgan's Lease* [1972] Ch 1, [1971] 2 All ER 235; M & B p. 312; p. 816, post.
20 See Maitland, *Collected Papers*, vol. iii. p. 350.
1 *Thorndike v Hunt* (1859) 3 De GF & J 563.
2 *Bassett v Nosworthy* (1673) Cas temp Finch 102; *Midland Bank Trust Co Ltd v Green* [1981] AC 513, [1981] 1 All ER 153; M & B p. 40.
3 *A-G v Jacobs Smith* [1895] 2 QB 341.
4 *Caunce v Caunce* [1969] 1 WLR 286, [1969] 1 All ER 722; M & B p. 274; *Kingsnorth Finance Co Ltd v Tizard* [1986] 1 WLR 783, [1986] 2 All ER; M & B p. 144; p. 63, post.

notice of them or not.[5] The competition here is between two equitable interests and the rule is that the first in time prevails. *Qui prior est tempore potior est jure.*[6]

The purchaser for value of an equitable interest without notice, however, takes free of an *equity* or a *mere equity*. An equitable interest is distinguishable from what is generally called an *equity* or a *mere equity*. This is a concept that defies precise definition, but it includes a right to enforce an equitable remedy, such as specific performance, or to set aside or rectify a conveyance for fraud, undue influence, mistake and similar reasons.[7]

The defence of the purchaser for value without notice thus avails the purchaser of an equitable interest against the owner of an earlier equity, but not against the owner of an earlier equitable interest.

(c) Without notice

(i) Actual notice A purchaser of the land for valuable consideration from the trustee was not liable to carry out the trusts provided that he had no notice of them when he acquired the legal estate, but it is obvious that, unless a careful watch had been kept on the conduct of such a purchaser, he would have taken care not to have notice. The definition of notice was therefore made elastic. If a purchaser was diligent enough and acted in a reasonable and sensible manner, making all those investigations which the purchaser of land normally did make, then he was affected only by actual notice of trusts. If, however, he omitted to make the usual investigations then he might be affected by constructive notice.

(ii) Constructive notice It has always been regarded as difficult to frame a satisfactory definition of constructive notice,[8] but it is generally taken to include two different things:[9]

1. The notice which is implied when a purchaser omits to investigate the vendor's title properly or to make reasonable inquiries as to deeds or facts which come to his knowledge.
2. The notice which is imputed to a purchaser by reason of the fact that his solicitor or other legal agent has actual or implied notice of some fact. This is generally called "imputed notice".[10]

Now the question is: what ought a prudent, careful man to do when he is purchasing an estate? The answer will afford us an insight into the equitable doctrine of notice, and at the same time will show us in what circumstances

---

5 It has, however, been held that, if B, an equitable incumbrancer for value without notice of A's prior equitable incumbrance, gets in the legal estate, he takes precedence over A, even if he then has notice; *Bailey v Barnes* [1894] 1 Ch 25; cf. *McCarthy and Stone Ltd v Julian S Hodge & Co Ltd* [1971] 1 WLR 1547, [1971] 2 All ER 973; M & B p. 51.

6 *Phillips v Phillips* (1861) 4 De GF & J 208 at 215; *Cave v Cave* (1880) 15 Ch D 639. But see pp. 729–31, post for the modification of this principle by LPA 1925, s. 137 (1).

7 *Phillips v Phillips*, supra, at 218, per Lord WESTBURY; *National Provincial Bank Ltd v Ainsworth* [1965] AC 1175 at 1238, [1965] 2 All ER 472 at 488, per Lord UPJOHN; at 1252–3, at 497, per Lord WILBERFORCE; (1955) 71 LQR 480 (R. E. Megarry); *Shiloh Spinners Ltd v Harding* [1973] AC 691 at 721, [1973] 1 All ER 90 at 99, per Lord WILBERFORCE. See generally Hanbury & Maudsley, *Modern Equity* (13th edn), chapter 28.

8 Sugden, *Law of Vendors and Purchasers*, p. 755.

9 White and Tudor, *Leading Cases in Equity* (9th edn), vol. ii. p. 172.

10 *Kingsnorth Finance Co Ltd v Tizard* [1986] 1 WLR 783, [1986] 2 All ER 54; M & B p. 144. See also *Sharpe v Foy* (1868) 4 Ch App 35; *Re Cousins* (1886) 31 Ch D 671.

a purchaser takes an estate free from any trust or other equitable interests to which it may be subject.

It is not necessary to go back further than the Conveyancing Act 1882 (now re-enacted by the Law of Property Act 1925[11]), which contained a section designed to protect purchasers against a doctrine that had been refined to the point of unfairness. The Act provides that no purchaser is to be affected by notice of any instrument, fact or thing unless he actually knows of it, or unless he would have known of it had such inquiries and inspections been made, as ought reasonably to have been made by him, or unless his solicitor, while carrying out that particular transaction, actually obtains knowledge of that instrument, etc., or would have obtained it had he made reasonable inquiries and inspections. What it comes to, then, is that a purchaser is deemed to have notice of anything which he has failed to discover either because he did not investigate the title properly, or because he did not inquire for deeds relating to the land, or because he did not inspect it.

We will take these three cases separately:

1. *Notice from not investigating title* For centuries it has been regarded as essential that a man who is purchasing land should investigate the title of his vendor, that is to say, should require the vendor to "prove his title" by producing evidence to show that the interest which he has contracted to sell is vested in him, and that it is unincumbered by rights and interests enforceable against the land by third parties. Under the system of unregistered conveyancing,[12] proof of the title[13] takes the form of requiring the vendor to set out the history of the land in what is called an *abstract of title* with a view to showing how the interest he has contracted to sell became vested in him, so as to prove that for a given number of years he and his predecessors have rightfully exercised dominion over the land consistent with that interest. The old rule both at law and in equity was that, if a vendor could adduce evidence of acts of ownership for a period of not less than sixty years, he had satisfied the obligation which lay upon him, and, unless anything appeared to the contrary, had proved a title which the purchaser was bound to accept. But there was no rigid rule about the length of this period, for it was useless to trace the title for sixty years unless the result was to show that the vendor was entitled to convey that interest which he had agreed to sell.[14] For instance, a vendor might very well show sixty years' possession in himself, but if this possession was held under a long lease, something more was obviously required to substantiate a right to sell the fee simple. The vendor's proof must always begin with a "good root of title", i.e. with some instrument transferring the interest that the purchaser now seeks to obtain.

The Vendor and Purchaser Act 1874 provided that in an open contract of sale, that is, where no express stipulation had been entered into fixing a precise date from which title should be traced, forty years should be substituted for the old period of sixty years. Thus under the law as it existed in 1925 a vendor who failed to persuade the purchaser to accept a shorter title was obliged to adduce evidence of acts of ownership stretching over a period of at least forty years. This obligation was satisfied by the vendor

---

11 S. 199 (1) (ii); p. 725, post.
12 For registered conveyancing, see pp. 97 et seq, post.
13 For a fuller account of investigation of title, see pp. 750 et seq, post.
14 Williams, *Vendor and Purchaser* (1st edn), p. 76.

showing what conveyances of the estate—whether *inter vivos* or as a result of death—had been effected, for, to take a simple illustration, if documents could be produced showing that forty-five years earlier X had bought the estate for valuable consideration and then left it by will to the vendor, it was pretty clear that the latter could make a good title.

> If, then, on the sale of a freehold in fee, the vendor produces the title-deeds for the last forty years, and these show that the fee simple in the land sold has been conveyed to him, free from incumbrances, and if there be satisfactory evidence that the deeds produced relate to the land sold, and the vendor be in possession of the land and of the deeds, he has shown a good title to the land.[15]

The general obligations of a vendor are the same under the modern law, except that the period for which title must be traced under an open contract, reduced from forty to thirty years in 1925,[16] has been further reduced to fifteen years.[17]

The first duty of the vendor is to prepare an abstract of title, that is, a statement of the material parts of all deeds and other instruments by which the property has been disposed of during the period in question, and also of all facts, such as births, deaths and marriages, which affect the ownership of the land. But in addition to producing this abstract the vendor is required to verify its contents by producing either the actual documents abstracted or the best possible evidence of the contents of those which he is not in a position to produce, and by proving facts, such as births and deaths, which are material to the title.

We can now understand what is meant by constructive notice. One object of investigating title is to discover whether the land is subject to rights vested in persons other than the vendor, and the equitable doctrine of notice ordains that a purchaser is bound by any right which he would have discovered had he made the ordinary investigations as sketched above. Moreover, if the vendor has imposed conditions requiring a purchaser to accept a title shorter than the statutory period, the doctrine of notice is extended to rights which would have been disclosed had title been shown for the full period.[18]

In general, then, it may be said that a purchaser will be bound by equitable interests of which he may in fact be ignorant but whose existence he would have discovered had he acted as a prudent man of business, placed in similar circumstances, would have acted.[19]

2. *Notice from not inquiring for deeds* As we have just seen, the system of unregistered conveyancing requires that a person who is buying land should examine the vendor's deeds, in order both to ascertain whether a good title can be made and to ensure that no third person possesses rights enforceable against the land. It follows from this that, if a purchaser makes no inquiries for the title-deeds, and allows them to remain in the possession of a third person, he will be deemed to have notice of any equitable claims which the possessor of the deeds may have against the land.[20] If, however, he makes inquiry but fails to secure their production, his liability for any equity that

15 Williams, *Vendor and Purchaser* (1st edn), p. 84.
16 LPA 1925, s. 44 (1).
17 LPA 1969, s. 23 in respect of contracts made on or after 1 January 1970. See Law Commission Interim Report on Root of Title to Freehold Land (1967) (Law Com. No. 9).
18 *Re Cox and Neve's Contract* [1891] 2 Ch 109 at 117–18.
19 *Bailey v Barnes* [1894] 1 Ch 25 at 35.
20 *Walker v Linom* [1907] 2 Ch 104; M & B p. 796.

they would have disclosed depends upon whether or not his failure was due to his own gross negligence. If he is satisfied with an unreasonable excuse for their non-production, he is liable[1]; but if the excuse is reasonable, he may successfully shelter behind the plea of purchaser of the legal estate for valuable consideration without notice.[2]

3. *Notice from not inspecting land* A purchaser should inspect the land and make such inquiries as a reasonable purchaser would make; what those inquiries are depends on the circumstances of each individual case.[3] He will have constructive notice of any rights which are reasonably discoverable.[4] In particular he should make inquiries of any tenant or other person in occupation of the land, since the occupation of a person is constructive notice to a purchaser of the interest of that person; not only indeed of his interest, but of his other rights.[5] "A tenant's occupation is notice of all that tenant's rights,[6] but not of his lessor's title or rights."[7] This is known as the rule in *Hunt v Luck* and it was further elaborated in that case by VAUGHAN WILLIAMS LJ as follows:[8]

> If a purchaser or a mortgagee has notice that the vendor or mortgagor is not in possession of the property, he must make inquiries of the person in possession—of the tenant who is in possession—and find out from him what his rights are, and, if he does not choose to do that, then whatever title he acquires as purchaser or mortgagee will be subject to the title or right of the tenant in possession.

If, however, the person in occupation of the land deliberately puts the inquirer off the scent by withholding information about his interest, he will

---

1 *Oliver v Hinton* [1899] 2 Ch 264 at 274; M & B p. 791.
2 *Hewitt v Loosemore* (1851) 9 Hare 449; M & B p. 790. On the subject generally, see pp. 709 et seq, post especially p. 711, n. 17.
3 *Midland Bank Ltd v Farmpride Hatcheries Ltd* (1980) 260 EG 493 at 498, per OLIVER LJ; M & B p. 30.
4 *Hervey v Smith* (1856) 22 Beav 299 (purchaser of house held to have constructive notice of equitable easement to use two chimneys for the passage of smoke from the mere fact of there being fourteen chimney pots on top of the chimney stack and only twelve flues in the house); *Kingsnorth Finance Co Ltd v Tizard* [1986] 1 WLR 783, [1986] 2 All ER 54; M & B, p. 144; p. 749 post (mortgagee held to have constructive notice of mortgagor's wife's equitable interest in matrimonial home due to (a) his agent's inspection at a time prearranged with the mortgagor (b) his failure to make further inquiries after his agent (i) found evidence of occupation by twin 15 year old children of the mortgagor and (ii) was informed by the mortgagor, who had described himself as single on the mortgage application form, that he was separated from his wife who was residing nearby). The decision is criticised in [1986] Conv 283 (M. P. Thompson); (1986) 136 NLJ 771 (P. Luxton); [1986] All ER Rev 181 (P. J. Clarke). See also *Northern Bank Ltd v Henry* [1981] Ir 1; *Barclays Bank plc v O'Brien* [1993] 3 WLR 786, [1993] 4 All ER 417, p. 682 post (bank's constructive notice of wife's suretyship agreement induced by undue influence of husband).
5 *Barnhart v Greenshields* (1853) 9 Moo PCC 18. But not of an equity to rectification of a tenancy agreement which the tenant may have against the vendor: *Smith v Jones* [1954] 1 WLR 1089, [1954] 2 All ER 823; M & B p. 49.
6 E.g., an option to purchase: *Daniels v Davison* (1809) 16 Ves 249.
7 *Hunt v Luck* [1901] 1 Ch 45 at 51 per FARWELL J; approved by CA [1902] 1 Ch 428 at 432. The principle is preserved by LPA 1925, s. 14: *City of London Building Society v Flegg* [1988] AC 54 at 80, [1987] 3 All ER 435 at 445, per Lord OLIVER OF AYLMERTON; p. 898 post.
8 *Hunt v Luck*, supra, at 433.

be estopped from relying on the defence that the inquirer had constructive notice arising from the occupation.[9]

Finally, it is now clear that the rule operates to give a purchaser or mortgagee constructive notice of the interest of a person in occupation, if the vendor or mortgagor is also in occupation.[10]

(d) Bona fide

This requirement is not synonymous with absence of notice. As Lord WILBERFORCE said in *Midland Bank Trust Co Ltd v Green*[11]

> The character in the law known as the bona fide (good faith) purchaser for value without notice was the creation of equity. In order to affect a purchaser for value of a legal estate with some equity or equitable interest, equity fastened upon his conscience and the composite expression was used to epitomise the circumstances in which equity would or rather would not do so. I think that it would generally be true to say that the words "in good faith" related to the existence of notice. Equity in other words, required not only absence of notice, but genuine and honest absence of notice. As the law developed, this requirement became crystallised in the doctrine of constructive notice which assumed a statutory form in the Conveyancing Act 1882, section 3. But it would be a mistake to suppose that the requirement of good faith extended only to the matter of notice, or that when notice came to be regulated by statute, the requirement of good faith became obsolete. Equity still retained its interest in and power over the purchaser's conscience. The classic judgment of JAMES LJ in *Pilcher v Rawlins*[12] is clear authority that it did: good faith there is stated as a separate test which may have to be passed even though absence of notice is proved. And there are references in cases subsequent to 1882 which confirm the proposition that honesty or bona fides remained something which might be inquired into.[13]

(e) Purchaser with notice from purchaser without notice

A bona fide purchaser for value of a legal estate without notice, who takes free from equitable interests, may nevertheless pass a good title to a purchaser

---

9 *Midland Bank Ltd v Farmpride Hatcheries Ltd*, supra (where a company mortgaged its property to a bank, a contractual licensee who was in occupation of a house under a licence from the company, of which he and his wife were in complete control, was held to be estopped from relying on the doctrine; he had "set up a smoke-screen designed to hide even the possible existence of some interest in himself which could derogate from the interest of the company ostensibly conferred by the mortgage", per SHAW LJ at 497); OLIVER and BUCKLEY LJJ held that the bank did not have constructive notice, because the licensee was not only in control of the company but also had been negotiating as agent on his principal's behalf. "He does not thereby make any representation that his principal has an indefeasible title to the property offered as security ... but he does at least represent that he has his principal's authority to offer the property free from any undisclosed adverse interest of his own" (per OLIVER LJ at 498). His failure to disclose that interest entitled the bank to assume that there was no such interest. See (1982) 132 NLJ 68 (H. W. Wilkinson).

The issues of the binding effect of a licence on a third party (p. 589, post) and of the lifting of the veil of corporate personality were not raised. See (1982) 132 NLJ 68 (H. W. Wilkinson); [1982] Conv 67 (R. E. Annand); (1982) 79 LSG 464 (H. Lawless and J. Alder). Cf in registered land, the proviso to LRA 1925, s. 70 (1) (*g*); p. 103, post.

10 *Kingsnorth Finance Co Ltd v Tizard*, supra, not following *Caunce v Caunce* [1969] 1 WLR 286, [1969] 1 All ER 722; cf the position in registered land: *Hodgson v Marks* [1971] Ch 892 at 934–5, [1971] 2 All ER 684 at 690, and *Williams & Glyn's Bank Ltd v Boland* [1981] AC 487, [1980] 2 All ER 408; M & B p. 122; p. 793, post.

11 [1981] AC 513 at 528, [1981] 1 All ER 153 at 157; p. 760, post.

12 (1872) 7 Ch App 259 at 269; p. 58, ante.

13 *Berwick & Co v Price* [1905] 1 Ch 632 at 639; *Taylor v London and County Banking Co* [1901] 2 Ch 231 at 256; *Oliver v Hinton* [1899] 2 Ch 264 at 273.

who *has* notice of them.[14] Otherwise the owner of the equitable interest, by proclaiming his right, could make it difficult for the purchaser without notice to sell the land which he had purchased. There is an exception to this rule; where a trustee who is bound by equitable interests sells the trust property in breach of trust to a purchaser without notice, and then re-acquires the property, he will again hold it subject to the equitable interests. He cannot take advantage of the purchaser's immunity under the doctrine.[15]

(f) Effect on equitable estate

In brief, then, an equitable estate is not so safe as a legal estate. An equitable owner may find himself, without any fault or negligence on his part, postponed to a third person who has obtained the legal estate in the same land, and his remedy will be reduced to that of recovering the value of the estate from the fraudulent or negligent trustee. The facts of *Pilcher v Rawlins*[16] will serve to illustrate this proposition.

Pilcher, who was the sole surviving trustee of £8,373, which he held in trust for X for life and after his death for X's children, lent the money to Rawlins on a legal mortgage of Blackacre. This was a perfectly legitimate transaction, the effect of which was to vest the legal estate of Blackacre in Pilcher as trustee on the same trusts for X, so that until the mortgage was redeemed by Rawlins, Pilcher acquired the legal and X the equitable estate of the lands.

Rawlins then arranged to grant a legal mortgage of Blackacre to Z in return for a loan of £10,000. As things stood this was impossible because a legal mortgage before 1926 necessitated the transfer to the lender of the legal fee simple, and this was vested in Pilcher. Pilcher, however, decided to abet Rawlins in the fraudulent scheme. First of all Rawlins (who was a solicitor) prepared an abstract of title to Blackacre which stopped short of and excluded the mortgage to Pilcher and thus made it appear that the legal fee simple was still vested in himself. Of course it was not, but at this point Pilcher came into the plot by re-conveying his legal estate in Blackacre to Rawlins in consideration of a repayment of X's trust moneys. This repayment was never in fact made, but Rawlins, having thus attained the legal estate, was enabled to transfer it to Z, who paid over the £10,000. The deed of re-conveyance was suppressed. When the fraud was discovered, the question was, which of the two innocent parties, X or Z, had the better right to Blackacre.

It was held that, as Z had acted reasonably and honestly, the legal interest which had passed to him must prevail over the mere equitable interest vested in X. Pilcher was the sole trustee and as such had the legal estate and the title-deeds. That being so, the effect of his reconveyance was to give the legal estate to Rawlins, and, as the whole mortgage transaction was concealed, there was no document to put Z on inquiry.

G. OTHER FORMS OF EQUITABLE INTERESTS

Throughout the preceding account we have principally considered one form of equitable interest, the trust, but though this is the most important species,

---

14 *Wilkes v Spooner* [1911] 2 KB 473; M & B p. 29.
15 *Bovey v Smith* (1682) 1 Vern 84; *Lowther v Carlton* (1741) 2 Atk 242; *Sweet v Southcote* (1786) 2 Bro CC 66; *Re Stapleford Colliery Co* (1880) 14 Ch D 432.
16 (1872) 7 Ch App 259; M & B p. 28.

we must observe that it is not the only one. The trust, already described, is an interest which corresponds with a legal interest in the sense that just as there may be a legal fee simple, entailed interest or life interest, so also may there be equitable counterparts possessing the same incidents, for equity follows the law.[17] But other equitable interests may exist which have no analogy at common law. The more important of these, which will require a more detailed discussion later, are the following:

(i) Estate contract This arises where the owner of a legal estate either agrees to convey it to the other contracting party or to create a legal estate out of it in favour of that other. Thus, if A, the owner of the fee simple absolute in Blackacre, agrees to sell it to B or to create a term of years absolute out of it in favour of B, the equitable interest in the land as measured by the terms of the contract passes at once to B, although the legal estate remains with A until an actual conveyance or lease has been executed.[18]

(ii) Restrictive covenant i.e. a covenant by which the use of the covenantor's land is restricted for the benefit of the covenantee's adjoining land, e.g. where it is agreed that it shall not be used for the purpose of trade. The effect of such a covenant, if the necessary conditions are satisfied,[19] is that the covenantee acquires an equitable interest in the burdened land in the sense that he is entitled to an injunction preventing a breach of the agreement by the covenantor or by his successors in title except a bona fide purchaser for value of the legal estate without notice of the covenant.

(iii) Equity of redemption i.e. the right of a mortgagor to redeem the mortgaged property upon payment of all that is due by way of capital or interest.[20]

(iv) Equitable charge This arises, where, without the transfer of any definite estate, land is designated as security for the payment of a sum of money.[1] In such a case, the chargee acquires an equitable interest that entitles him to take proceedings for the sale of the land.[2]

(v) Equitable lien This is similar in effect to the equitable charge, and most generally arises when the vendor conveys the land to the purchaser before he has been paid. If so, he becomes entitled by operation of law to an equitable lien on the land for the amount of the unpaid purchase money which is enforceable by a sale under the direction of the court.[3]

(vi) Licence by estoppel This right, which emerged during the 20th century, arises, for example, where A encourages B to occupy A's land, and B, relying on this encouragement to his detriment, then occupies A's land. A is estopped (i.e. prevented) from insisting on his strict legal rights where it would be unconscionable for him to do so. B has an equitable interest which is enforceable against A and his successors in title except a bona fide purchaser for value of the legal estate without notice.[4]

---

17 We shall see later (pp. 91–2, post) that by the legislation of 1925 it is now impossible for entailed and life interests to subsist as *legal* as distinct from equitable estates.
18 P. 759, post.
19 Pp. 614 et seq, post.
20 P. 660, post.
 1 Land can be similarly charged at law. See pp. 667, 670, post.
 2 P. 708, post.
 3 P. 125, post.
 4 P. 595, post.

Chapter 4

Settlements[1]

SUMMARY

An owner of property may need to do more than to own it during his lifetime and then to pass it on to someone else when he dies. He may desire to create successive interests, as, for example, by giving it in his will to his widow for her life, with a remainder to the children; or by providing on a son's marriage a life interest for the son, and after the son's death for the daughter-in-law, and after her death for their children. He may even wish to found a family dynasty.

Any historical survey must begin with this latter type of settlement which has been a feature of English social life for many centuries. It was the desire of the aristocracy to order the future destiny of their land and to prevent its sale out of the family which has decisively affected the form and substance of real property law. A fee simple owner makes what is called a *settlement* by which he retains the benefit of ownership during his own life, but withholds the entire ownership in the shape of the fee simple from his descendants for as long as possible by reducing them, one after the other, to the position of mere limited owners. The English doctrine of estates is ideally adapted to the achievement of this object. The fee simple of infinite duration is divisible into shorter periods of time each of which may be allotted successively to a number of persons, with the result that while these periods are running there is no person able to dispose of the entire ownership.

SECTION I THE STRICT SETTLEMENT

A. FORM OF SETTLEMENT

(1) SETTLEMENT

Settlements in one form or another have been common since at any rate the early thirteenth century,[2] and indeed for some 200 years after the statute *De*

---

1 Simpson, *A History of the Land Law* (2nd edn), pp. 233–241; Harvey, *Settlements of Land* (1973); Bonfield, *Marriage Settlements 1601–1740* (1983); English and Saville, *Strict Settlement* (1983), which contains details of several dynastic settlements of land; and essays in Rubin and Sugarman, *Law, Economy and Society* (1984) pp. 1–123 (D. Sugarman and G. R. Rubin), 124–167 (M. R. Chesterman), 168–191 (E. Spring) and 209–210 (B. English); Spring, *Strict Settlement, Role in History* (1989) EHR 454.
2 By gifts to a person and a special class of heirs; p. 245, post.

Donis Conditionalibus in 1285,[3] it was possible to grant an estate tail that would perforce descend from heir to heir and would permanently remain inconvertible into a fee simple. Although by the end of the fifteenth century means had been contrived to cut short such an impolitic tying-up of the land, by allowing any tenant in tail in possession and of full age to bar the entail and so to acquire the fee simple,[4] the urge to keep the land in the family for as long as the law would permit still persisted, and by the time of the Restoration the general form of the *strict settlement* had been established. It is desirable to appreciate its general design even at this early stage in the book if the significance of much of the existing legislation is to be grasped. Suppose, for instance, that a fee simple owner, A, a widower, has decided to use the land as a source of endowment for his only son B, who is about to be married, and for B's issue. In such a case the practice for several centuries was for A to execute a deed of settlement by which he limits the land to himself for life; then to B for life and then, after making provision for B's widow and younger children, to the first and every other son of B successively in tail.

Under such a settlement the desire of A to keep the land in the family is at least partly achieved, for no one will be able to acquire complete control over the land before the eldest son of B, who may bar the entail and so convert it into a fee simple as soon as he attains his majority. To create a fee simple absolute, however, the disentailment must either be effected by him after he has become entitled in possession on the deaths of A and B or, if he desires to act earlier, it must be effected with the collaboration of the present possessor. There is no difficulty, therefore, if he waits until the successive life tenants, A and B, are dead, for in that case he is tenant in tail in possession and free to act independently. But even while, say, B is tenant for life in possession, he may join as party to the disentailment and thus enable his son to acquire the fee simple absolute.

(2) RESETTLEMENT

This collaboration of life tenant in possession and tenant in tail in remainder—usually of father and son—has consistently been utilized by conveyancers as part of the scheme to prolong the retention of the land in the family. That scheme will, of course, succeed automatically if the eldest son or other heir in each generation refrains throughout his life from barring the entail, for in that event the entailed interest will descend in due course to his own heir. But the danger is that he will bar the entail when he becomes entitled in possession and will then acquire and sell the fee simple. Hence the long established practice of making what is called a *resettlement* by which the eldest son, on the attainment of his majority, is in most cases persuaded to bar the entail with the concurrence of his father and then voluntarily to settle the fee simple thus acquired upon himself for a mere life interest with a further limitation in favour of his own sons successively in tail. This ensures that the land will remain in the family for yet another generation. If, therefore, a resettlement is effected in each generation, the land is held by a succession of limited owners and there is nobody who can claim to be owner of the fee simple.[5]

3 P. 246, post. For the effect of this statute, see Plucknett, *Legislation of Edward I*, pp. 125–35.
4 P. 247, post, common recovery.
5 For a clear account, see Elphinstone, *Introduction to Conveyancing* (7th edn), pp. 638 et seq.

(3) EFFECT OF STATUTE OF USES 1535

Settlements, as we have said, are of respectable antiquity, but at common law the opportunities of carving up the *legal* fee simple so as to anticipate events that might affect the family in the future were severely restricted, for limitations only of the simplest nature were allowed. The Chancellor, on the other hand, had never imposed restrictions upon limitations of the *equitable* estate. The use might be moulded into any form congenial to its creator and adapted to solve the riddles of the future. The Statute of Uses 1535, therefore, played an important part in the evolution of the strict settlement, an evolution that was complete towards the end of the seventeenth century. The flexibility of the use was imparted to the legal estate by the statute. What was impossible at common law might now be achieved by a single assurance, either a grant to uses or a will. The simple expedient of vesting the legal estate in feoffees with a declaration of the uses to which they were to hold, entitled the beneficiaries to legal interests in the land, as and when their rights matured.

(a) Grant of fee simple defeasible by later events

The opportunities of a settlor were now greater. For instance, common law did not permit a man to convey a freehold estate to himself, nor did it recognize any estate limited to take effect after the grant of a fee simple.[6]

Neither of these rules, however, affected the use and they ceased to affect the legal estate into which the use was converted by the Statute of Uses, if the limitation was made by a grant to uses or by will. The normal method of creating a marriage settlement was for the settlor to grant his fee simple to feoffees to the use of himself in fee simple until the intended marriage, and thereafter to the use of himself for life with remainder to such uses in favour of his wife and issue as his fancy might dictate. Thus, after the statute he acquired a determinable fee simple during the interval between the settlement and the marriage, but on his marriage it was displaced in favour of the subsequent limitations, which were themselves legal.[7]

(b) Springing and shifting uses

Again, at common law a freehold estate could not be given to a man to begin at some future date,[8] nor was it permissible to annex to a grant a condition that the freehold should shift from the donee to another person upon the happening of a prescribed event.[9]

Yet, the Chancellor had always protected such limitations of the equitable estate and therefore when uses were statutorily converted into legal estates, a limitation to feoffees to the use of X when he married (springing use) or to the use of Y for life, but if he became insolvent then to the use of Z for life (shifting use), operated to vest a legal estate in X and Z upon the occurrence of the prescribed events.

(c) Powers of appointment

Another innovation of the Chancellor that greatly increased the pliability of settlements was the *power of appointment*. The normal procedure upon the

6 P. 280, post.
7 Digby, *History of the Law of Real Property*, pp. 357–8.
8 P. 280, post.
9 P. 280, post.

creation of a use was for the feoffor to declare then and there the exact uses to which the land should be held. But such a definitive declaration was not essential. The feoffor might reserve to himself or to a third person a power to declare in the future what uses should arise or to revoke existing uses and substitute new ones in their place. The donee of such a power, who might be a stranger having no proprietary interest, present or future, in the land, was thus enabled before the Statute of Uses to give fresh directions as to the enjoyment of the equitable estate. If, for example, in place of an existing use in favour of A for life, he *appointed* to the use of B in tail, the original feoffees immediately stood seised to the use of B who consequently acquired an equitable estate tail. If the appointment were made after the statute, B would take a legal estate tail.

Thus, through the machinery of powers, an appointor was able to dispose of an estate that he did not own, and the legal ownership might at his instance be freely shifted and modified to suit exigencies occurring after the date of the settlement.

B. DISADVANTAGES OF SETTLEMENT

A settlement of land, though it afforded a convenient means of providing for descendants and, when followed by periodic resettlements, of keeping the land in the family, suffered from three particular disadvantages. It tended to render land inalienable, it might have an adverse effect upon the prosperity of the family and it complicated conveyancing.

(1) INALIENABILITY OF THE LAND

The first of these dangers was inherent in the pliability that the legal estate had inherited from the use. It soon became obvious that, unless some limit of time was imposed upon the power to create future interests, an astute employment of a series of springing and shifting clauses might well render the fee simple inalienable for an unreasonable period. Thus, the general employment in settlements of such devices to create a series of merely limited interests, enduring far into the future, would have starved the market of land to the detriment of the community. The courts have always fought against the creation of inalienable interests and have held them void.[10] Further, they have developed what is now called the *rule against perpetuities*, which looks to the date at which a contingent interest will vest, if it vests at all, and hold it to be void as a perpetuity if the date is too remote. This rule, which will require detailed treatment later,[11] allows a settlor to provide that an estate will shift to a person or spring up in his favour upon the occurrence of a prescribed contingency, but it ordains that the estate shall be void unless the contingency, if it ever happens at all, will necessarily happen not later than twenty-one years from the death of some person or persons alive when the settlement takes effect.

10 P. 343, post.
11 Pp. 286 et seq, post.

(2) IMPOVERISHMENT OF THE LAND

(a) Effect of settlement on power of alienation

The chief defect inherent in a system of strict settlements and of periodic re-settlements is that at no point of time is there any beneficiary competent to exercise many of the powers of a fee simple owner, unless indeed a right to do so is reserved by the settlement or granted by some statute. The person who under this system has every appearance of being owner is the life tenant in possession, but since his beneficial interest must necessarily determine with his death it follows that any interest granted by him must also determine at that moment. A conveyance by him purporting to pass the fee simple will at common law pass to the grantee nothing more than an estate *pur autre vie*, and a lease for any number of years will automatically determine on his death unless saved by statute or permitted by the settlement. The grave effects resulting from this limited power of alienation in the days when the strict settlement was the foundation of landed society can easily be realized. Given a system whereby it is usual for a fee simple owner, in view of his approaching marriage, to limit the land to himself for life and then to his eldest son in tail, and given further the inclination to resettle the land in each generation on the eldest son for life, with remainder in tail to *his* eldest son, a moment's reflection will show what a prejudicial effect such a perpetual series of life tenants, each devoid of the power to convey the fee simple estate, must have not only on the supply of land available for purposes of trade, but also on the prosperity of the settled land itself.

The common practice, by which the eldest son under a strict settlement was persuaded on reaching his majority to convert his estate tail into a fee simple and then to resettle the fee simple upon himself for a mere life estate with remainder to his own issue in tail, was stigmatized as follows by a critic some years ago:[12]

> It is commonly supposed that a son acts with his eyes open and with a special eye to the contingencies of the future and of family life. But what are the real facts of the case? Before the future owner of the land has come into possession, before he has any experience of his property, or of what is best to be done, or what he can do with regard to it, before the exigencies of the future or his own real position are known to him, before the character, number and wants of his children are learned, or the claims of parental affection and duty can make themselves felt, while still very much at the mercy of a predecessor desirous of posthumous greatness and power, he enters into an irrevocable disposition by which he parts with the rights of a proprietor over his future property for ever, and settles its devolution, burdened with charges, upon an unborn heir.

Under such a system there never exists, apart from statute, a beneficial owner capable of selling or dealing with the fee simple. In the words of Sir Frederick Pollock:

> The lord of this mansion is named by all men its owner; it is said to belong to him; the park, the demesne, the farms are called his. But we shall be almost safe in assuming that he is not the full and free owner of any part of it. He is a "limited owner", having an interest only for his own life. He might have become the full owner . . . if he had possessed the means of waiting, the independence of thought and will to break with the tradition of his order and the bias of his education, and the energy to persevere in his dissent against the counsels and feelings of his family.

12 Cliffe Leslie, *Fraser's Magazine*, Feb. 1867, cited Scrutton, *Land in Fetters*, p. 135.

But he had every inducement to let things go their accustomed way. Those whom he had always trusted told him, and probably with sincere belief, that the accustomed way was the best for the family, for the land, for the tenants and for the country. And there could be no doubt that it was at the time the most agreeable to himself.[13]

(b) Economic disadvantages

It is clear, in fact, that an uncontrolled system of settlements and re-settlements is an evil—both social and economic—to any country which tolerates it, though it was not one that was apparent to the lawyers of the early nineteenth century. Thus we find the Real Property Commissioners in their report of 1829 stating:

> The owner of the soil is, we think, vested with exactly the dominion and power of disposition over it required for the public good, and landed property in England is admirably made to answer all the purposes to which it is applicable. Settlements bestow on the present possessor of an estate the benefits of ownership, and secure the property to his posterity . . . In England families are preserved and purchasers always find a supply of land in the market.

This language is specious. It is true in the sense that settled land could usually be sold in fee simple, because a settlement might contain, and a well-drawn settlement would contain, powers enabling the tenant for life to deal with the land by way of sale, lease, mortgage and so on.[14] If he took advantage of such a power and for instance sold the land to X, the fact that he was a mere life tenant was no obstacle to the transfer of the fee simple, for the feoffees had been directed by the settlement to hold to such uses as might be appointed by the donee of the power and therefore they now held to the use of the appointee X. Thus under the Statute of Uses, X acquired a legal fee simple. But although the land could be rendered manageable and saleable by this device, it happened only too often that powers were either omitted altogether or were too restricted in character. Speaking broadly, land was kept in families only at the expense of removing it from commerce and too often starving it of money necessary for its development and improvement. No doubt the evil was not so great under the rural conditions prevalent until the early nineteenth century, but it became urgent when the vast spread of industrialism produced a demand for coal and other minerals, and converted England from an agricultural to a trading community. To appreciate the nature of the problem it is only necessary to examine the position of a life tenant of settled land in, say, 1835. This was admirably summed up by Underhill:[15]

> Unless the will or settlement . . . contained express powers (which was frequently not the case) a tenant for life could neither sell, exchange, nor partition the settled property, however desirable it might be. If the estate consisted of a large tract of poor country, fruitful in dignity but scanty in rent, and specially if the portions of younger children charged on it were heavy, he too often found it a *damnosa hereditas*; the rents, after payment of interest on the portions, leaving a mere pittance for the unfortunate life tenant to live on, and quite disabling him from making improvements, or even keeping the property in a decent state of repair.

13 *Land Laws*, p. 9.
14 For a seventeenth-century precedent, see Holdsworth, *History of English Law*, vol. vii. p. 547.
15 *Century of Law Reform*, pp. 284–5.

Nay more, if he did spend money in improvements, the money was sunk in the estate to the detriment of his younger children. He could not pull down the mansion-house, however old or inconvenient it might be, nor even, strictly, make any substantial alteration in it. Unless expressly made unimpeachable for waste, he could not open new mines. But in addition to these disabilities, what pressed still more hardly upon him, and on the development of the estate generally, was his inability to make long leases.[16] Consequently when valuable minerals lay beneath a settled property, or the growth of the neighbouring town made it ripe for building sites (the rents for which would greatly exceed the agricultural rent) nothing could lawfully be done. The tenant for life could not open mines himself, even if he had the necessary capital for working them; nor, even if unimpeachable for waste, could he grant leases of them to others for a term which would repay the lessees for the necessary expenditure in pits and plant; nor could he grant building leases or sell for building purposes at fee farm rents. In some settlements powers were expressly inserted, enabling the trustees to grant such leases and to sell, exchange and partition. But frequently, especially in wills, such powers were omitted, and in such cases the only means of doing justice to the land was to apply for a private Act of Parliament authorizing the trustees or life tenant to sell, exchange, partition or lease. But such Acts were expensive luxuries, only open to the rich, and beyond the means of most country gentlemen of moderate means.

C. STATUTORY REFORM

(1) BEFORE 1882

When, however, the modern industrial era set in, the legislature took the matter in hand, and in a tentative manner began to pass a series of public Acts of Parliament which enabled settled land to be dealt with in a manner likely to enhance its prosperity. A start was made in the 1840s with statutes which empowered tenants for life to borrow money for the purpose of carrying out permanent drainage improvements and to charge the loan on the inheritance. Then the Improvement of Land Act 1864 enabled a tenant for life to raise money with the consent of the Ministry of Agriculture in order to execute certain specified improvements, and to charge the loan on the corpus of the property.[17] Further examples were the Limited Owners Residences Acts 1870 and 1871, which allowed money to be raised for completing or adding to a mansion-house; and the Limited Owners Reservoirs Act 1877, which sanctioned the same method for the construction of permanent waterworks.

But in 1856 the much more important Settled Estates Act had been passed which contained the germ of all the future legislation on the subject. Its object was to facilitate leases and sales of settled estates, and after being amended by several statutes in the succeeding generation, it was replaced in 1877 by the Settled Estates Act of that year. This allowed the Chancery Division of the High Court to sanction the sale, exchange or partition of the settled land, and the grant of leases of 21 years for an agricultural or occupation lease, 40 years for a mining lease, and 99 years for a building lease. It also allowed the tenant for life without resorting to the court to make a valid lease up to a period of 21 years. So this Act made great strides towards permitting all opportunities for the proper development of the land to be

16 A tenant *in tail*, however, was empowered by the Fines and Recoveries Act 1833, s. 41, to grant a lease for a term not exceeding 21 years.
17 P. 650, post.

seized, but its weakness was that, except in the case of short leases, its enabling powers could not be exercised without an order of the court. It had in truth facilitated dealings, since it substituted an order of the court for a private Act of Parliament, but it stopped short of placing the powers unreservedly in the hands of the tenant for life.

About this time an agitation sprang up for the total abolition of life estates and the restriction of grants to the creation of a fee simple, the argument being that settlements, besides making conveyances difficult and costly, deprived a father of a much-needed power of control over his eldest son, and prevented an estate from being thrown on the market when its poverty made such a course desirable. For better or for worse the argument did not prevail. It was realized that settlements enabled a fair and reasonable provision to be made for all the members of a family, and therefore, while the general features of the time-honoured system were retained, a plan was evolved to prevent settled land from becoming an inert mass through lack of capital or of adequate powers of management.[18]

(2) SETTLED LAND ACT 1882

The principle adopted by Lord CAIRNS and incorporated in the famous Settled Land Act of 1882 was to put the entire management of the land into the hands of the tenant for life for the time being, and to give him, at his own sole discretion and without asking the permission of the court or the trustees of the settlement, wide powers of selling, leasing, mortgaging and otherwise dealing with the property. These powers were independent of, and could not be restrained by, the settlement itself, but they were subject to certain statutory provisions designed to protect the interests of all persons entitled under the settlement, and to prevent the tenant for life from acquiring more than a life interest in the income or profits.

The objects of the Act were lucidly explained by CHITTY LJ in the following words:[19]

> The object is to render land a marketable article, notwithstanding the settlement. Its main purpose is the welfare of the land itself, and of all interested therein, including the tenants and not merely the persons taking under the settlement. The Act of 1882 had a much wider scope than the Settled Estates Acts. The scheme adopted is to facilitate the striking off from the land of the fetters imposed by settlement; and this is accomplished by conferring on *tenants for life in possession*, and others considered to stand in a like relation to the land, large powers of dealing with the land by way of sale, exchange, lease and otherwise, and by jealously guarding those powers from attempts to defeat them or to hamper their exercise. At the same time the rights of persons claiming under the settlement are carefully preserved in the case of a sale by shifting the settlement from the land to the purchase money which has to be paid into court or into the hands of trustees.

The Act of 1882 was amended in small particulars by further statutes passed in 1884, 1887, 1889, and 1890, but its policy has stood the test of time, and though it has now been repealed and replaced by the Settled Land Act 1925, its general principles still continue to govern the rights and the liabilities of a tenant for life under a strict settlement.

18 Underhill, *Century of Law Reform*, pp. 287–90.
19 *Re Mundy and Roper's Contract* [1899] 1 Ch 275 at 288.

(a) The legal title

The third disadvantage of a settlement—its aggravation of the complexity of conveyancing—became evident when a tenant for life, by virtue of a power conferred upon him, had agreed to sell the fee simple to a purchaser. In this event, he would prove the title down to the date of the settlement in the normal fashion by tracing the history of the land back to a good root of title, in order to show that the fee simple was owned by the original settlor. So far there was nothing abnormal, but at this point arose the difficulty that the vendor himself did not own the estate that he had contracted to sell. His case would be, of course, that as tenant for life under a settlement he possessed a power, conferred upon him either by the settlement itself or after 1882 by the Settled Land Act, to convey the fee simple. The general rule on this matter is that the exercise of a power, whether it is given by act of parties or by statute, is void unless all the conditions imposed by the instrument or statute from which it derives are literally observed. If attention is concentrated on a sale after 1882, the governing factors in this respect were that the Act of that year empowered a tenant for life under a settlement to convey a good title to the fee simple, provided that the purchase money was paid to the trustees. In other words, before the statutory power of sale or any other statutory power was validly exercisable, it was essential that, *within the meaning of the Act,*

the instrument under which the vendor held was a "settlement";
the vendor himself was a "tenant for life" or one of the persons to whom the statutory powers were given;
the trustees were properly appointed.

In order, therefore, to verify that these conditions were satisfied, it was necessary for the original deed of settlement and, in fact, several further deeds if there had been one or more resettlements, to be abstracted by the vendor and investigated by the purchaser. Thus, in order to satisfy himself that a good title would be made, the purchaser was confronted with the formidable task of scrutinizing a series of transactions and documents stretching back perhaps for very many years.

(b) Overreaching of beneficial interests

In contrast to this complication which beset a purchaser of settled land, his position vis-à-vis the beneficial interests under the settlement was simple. This was due to the doctrine of overreaching: it originated in conveyancing practice and was adopted by the Settled Land Act 1882. The Act provides that if the purchaser pays the purchase money to at least two trustees or into Court (and *not* to the tenant for life) the interests of the beneficiaries under the settlement shall be transferred from the land to the purchase money.[20] Thus the purchaser by virtue of the Act takes the land free from the beneficial interests; and he does this even though he has notice of them and even though the interests may be legal. The conveyancing advantage to the purchaser is obvious. So far as the beneficiaries are concerned, they lose their opportunity of enjoying the land qua land, but, instead, they have equivalent interests in the purchase money. A beneficial interest in a fund of £50,000 is just as valuable as the same interest in land worth £50,000; more valuable, if

---

20 SLA 1882, ss. 20, 22 (5), 39 (1).

the money is invested more profitably; less valuable, if the land was a better investment. The question is one of choice of investment of the family capital.

SECTION II THE TRUST FOR SALE

So far we have concentrated attention upon the strict settlement. An entirely different way of applying the principle of the settlement to land was by means of a trust for sale, a method that has been common in wills for some 500 years and in deeds since the early nineteenth century.[1] It has now almost superseded the strict settlement.

If it were used to create a family settlement *inter vivos* as described in Section I, the transaction would fall into two parts and, though not strictly necessary, would usually be effected by two separate deeds. If, for instance, it precedes the marriage of the settlor:

> The first deed in its opening clause conveys the fee simple to the trustees upon trust (with the consent of the husband until the intended marriage, and after the marriage with the consent of the husband and wife, or of the survivor, and after the death of the survivor at the discretion of the trustees) to sell the said fee simple.
> The second clause of the deed directs the trustees to hold the money arising from the sale and the rents and profits accruing prior to the sale upon such trusts as are declared by a deed already engrossed and made between the same parties and on the same date as the present deed.[2]

According to the equitable doctrine of conversion the effect of the execution of this deed is that in the eyes of equity the land is notionally converted into money, for that doctrine, based on the principle that equity looks on that as done which ought to be done, insists that an imperative direction to turn land into money shall impress the land with the quality of money no matter how long the sale may be postponed.[3] The important point to notice, therefore, is that a trust for sale relating to the fee simple and containing a succession of beneficial limitations is a settlement of personalty, not of realty.

The second deed sets out the beneficial trusts of the personalty into which the realty has already been notionally converted. It will usually provide in the first place that the income, whether arising from the invested purchase money or from the rents and profits prior to the sale, shall be held in trust for the husband during his life and after his death in trust for his wife if she survives him. Secondly, it will provide that after the death of the husband and wife the capital shall be divided among the children or remoter issue of the marriage in such shares as the husband and wife or the survivor shall appoint, and, failing appointment, among the children equally.[4]

The investigation of title upon a sale by the trustees raises none of the difficulties that, as we have already seen, formerly attended a sale by a tenant for life under a strict settlement. The legal fee simple is vested in the trustees for sale and it is from them that the purchaser takes his title. His main concern is to ascertain that the settlor was entitled to the fee simple that was conveyed to the trustees for sale. As far as the interests of the beneficiaries are concerned, the purchaser takes free from them if he pays the purchase

---

1 (1929) 3 CLJ, p. 63 (J. M. Lightwood).
2 See Burnett, *Elements of Conveyancing* (8th edn), pp. 455–6.
3 *Fletcher v Ashburner* (1779) 1 Bro CC 497. The reverse is also true.
4 Burnett, *Elements of Conveyancing* (8th edn), pp. 456–8.

money to at least two trustees.[5] In contrast to the position under the strict settlement, overreaching under the trust for sale is automatic: no statutory intervention is necessary. The legal estate is held by the trustees for sale on trust to sell, and the beneficial interests are imposed upon the proceeds of sale or upon the rents and profits until sale. They are not upon the land. The only trust upon the land is the trust to sell. Where therefore the trustees for sale sell the land in performance of their duty to sell, the land which the purchaser takes is unaffected by any trusts; the trusts are and always have been imposed upon the purchase money. Nevertheless, section 2(1) of the Law of Property Act 1925 makes statutory provision for overreaching.

Furthermore, the purchaser is not responsible for the proper application of the money, provided that he pays it to at least two trustees.[5] The beneficiaries must now look to the trustees and to them alone. This was not always so. In earlier days it was considered that the purchaser, since he had notice of the existence of beneficial limitations, was bound to see that the money was applied in accordance with the trust,[6] and it therefore became the usual practice to insert a clause in the first deed authorizing the trustees to give the purchaser a receipt exonerating him from liability in this respect. This has been made unnecessary, however, by a series of statutes dating from 1859,[7] which are now represented by the following:

The receipt in writing of a trustee for any money . . . payable to him under any trust or power shall be a sufficient discharge to the person paying . . . the same and shall effectually exonerate him from seeing to the application or being answerable for any loss or misapplication thereof.[8]

SECTION III SUMMARY OF THE TWO METHODS OF SETTLING LAND

Before 1926 there had been evolved two methods of settling land; the strict settlement, in which the purchaser took his title from the tenant for life under the Settled Land Act 1882, and the trust for sale in which he took it from the trustees for sale. In both he might overreach the interests of the beneficiaries, even though he had notice of them. As to which was used depended on the object of the settlor. The strict settlement was appropriate where "land was settled with the object of founding a family or continuing the possession of family estates in the line of primogeniture";[9] here the tenant for life would reside on the land and himself exercise control over it. On the other hand the trust for sale was convenient where the property settled was not to be kept in the family, but was to be treated as an investment and as a source of income for the beneficiaries. It was especially useful where the fund settled was a mixture of personalty and realty and where the ultimate object was the division of land among children equally. As we shall see, the dominant factor today has become that of taxation.[10]

5 Or to a trust corporation: LPA 1925, ss. 2(1) (ii), 27(2); LP(A)A 1926, Sch.
6 Vaizey, *The Law of Settlements of Property*, pp. 1409–12.
7 LP(A)A 1859, s. 23; Conveyancing Act 1881, s. 36; Trustee Act 1893, s. 20.
8 Trustee Act 1925, s. 14 (1).
9 (1929) 3 CLJ, p. 63 (J. M. Lightwood).
10 P. 209, post.

Finally we may notice that in 1925, the legislature, impressed by the advantages that the trust for sale imparted to the practice of conveyancing, made it the basis of several of the reforms introduced in that year. In particular, it was by extending the machinery and principle of the trust for sale that the law relating to concurrent interests[11] was strikingly simplified.

11 Pp. 213, et seq, post.

Chapter 5

The simplification of the law in 1925

SUMMARY

Even as late as the conclusion of the war of 1914 there were many features of the land law which seemed unnecessarily cumbrous and antiquated to a generation that, for the moment at any rate, considered itself destined to effect a general simplification of life. There was certainly much in the fundamentals of the subject that would seem strange to an impartial critic. Thus land was the subject of tenure, not of ownership, but instead of there being one common form of tenure with incidents of universal application, there were the two distinct forms of socage and copyhold, with various divergent offshoots such as gavelkind and borough-English. This division of tenures, which led to differences in the ordinary incidents of ownership and in the modes of conveyance, was complicated by a cross-division under which estates were classified as being either freehold or leasehold. The main object of the legislation of 1925 was the simplification of conveyancing, and the committee that was appointed to suggest alterations was instructed by its terms of reference "to consider the present position of land transfer, and to advise what action should be taken to *facilitate and cheapen the transfer of land.*" It was found, however, that a necessary preliminary to the attainment of this object was the simplification of the law of real property. It is scarcely possible to modernize a system of transfer if the subject-matter of the transfer is itself governed by antiquated rules. An analysis of the legislation of 1925, therefore, requires us to consider how it simplified, first the law of real property, and then the system of conveyancing.

SECTION I SIMPLIFICATION OF THE LAW OF REAL PROPERTY

In 1925 land was subject, not to one system, but to three systems of law. This surprising result was caused by the distinction between freeholds and chattels real,[1] and by the existence of two forms of tenure—socage and copyhold.

1 Pp. 35–7, ante.

The law of real property strictly so-called, which governed freehold interests in land, was still different in several respects from that which governed chattels real. Furthermore, whether the interest enjoyed by a proprietor was a freehold or a chattel real, the land affected would be held either by socage or by copyhold tenure. This was an added complication, since in several important respects the rules governing socage and copyhold lands were divergent. There was thus a law of freeholds, a law of leaseholds and a law of copyholds. The obvious solution, therefore, and the one adopted by the legislature, was first to institute one common form of tenure by the abolition of copyhold; then to assimilate as far as practicable the law of real property and of chattels real; finally, to abolish certain anachronisms of the common law—irritating survivals that were inimical to a simplified legal system. We will consider these three improvements separately.

A. THE REDUCTION OF TENURES TO ONE COMMON FORM

(1) HISTORY OF SIMPLIFICATION OF TENURES

The account that we have already given of tenure shows that for a long period there has been a gradual but continuous reduction in the number of possible tenures. This process was far advanced before 1926, but in that year uniformity was at last attained.

Seven hundred years ago the law on this subject was complicated. In the time of Edward I there were four distinct and important varieties of tenure, distinguished from each other by the different kinds of services due and each exhibiting fundamental differences in the substantive rules of law to which they were subject.[2] This led to the growth of a mass of confused and intricate law, and it was only by slow degrees that simplification began to emerge.

(a) Statute *Quia Emptores* 1290

The Statute *Quia Emptores*, though it was not concerned with the actual reduction of the several varieties, at least stemmed the increasing confusion, since it forbade the creation of any further tenures within each variety. The introduction of the doctrine of *uses* led indirectly to a decline in the importance of tenures, for the relationship of lord and tenant would lose much of its value and significance if it was freed from those tenurial incidents the avoidance of which was one of the chief inducements to put land in use.

(b) Statute of Uses 1535

The Statute of Uses, on the other hand, was a retrograde step in the process of simplification, though it was only for a time that it restored the importance of tenures. Before another century had passed the King no longer looked to the feudal incidents for a revenue, while the country as a whole evinced a desire to regain the advantages which had disappeared with the abolition of uses, and to be rid of the burdensome incidents that were a feature of the law of tenures.

2 Pp. 15 et seq, ante.

(c) Tenures Abolition Act 1660

In fact, even before the ultimate re-establishment of uses in the seventeenth century the first direct simplification of tenures was effected by the Tenures Abolition Act in 1660. The effect of this Act was the reduction of tenures to socage, copyhold and frankalmoin, though the honorary incidents of grand sergeanty were retained, and various customary modes of holding land, such as gavelkind, borough-English and ancient demesne, continued to exist in certain parts of the country. In effect only two important tenures remained—namely, socage and copyhold.

(d) Conveyancing complicated by copyhold

The position, then, long before 1926, showed a vast improvement upon that of the time of Edward I, but, as we have already seen, the continued existence of copyhold as a distinct tenure not only disturbed the simplicity of conveyancing, but also tended to embarrass the full exploitation of the land.[3] Not only did the form of conveyance vary according as the land was socage or copyhold, but, what was a far more serious blemish, such legal incidents as the mode of descent and the types of interest created often differed from those recognized by the general law. In this respect, indeed, there was not even a system of law common to all copyholds, for the actual customs upon which the legal incidents were dependent frequently varied from manor to manor. There was thus room for reform in this particular field of law, and the opportunity was seized by the legislature.

(2) ABOLITION OF ALL TENURES EXCEPT SOCAGE

All previous modes of descent, whether operating by the general law or by the custom of gavelkind or borough-English or by any other custom of any county, locality or manor, were abrogated.[4] Escheat[5] *propter defectum sanguinis* was discarded and replaced by the right of the Crown to take as *bona vacantia* the interest of a tenant who died intestate and heirless.[6] The honorary services incident to tenure by sergeanty, where they still existed, were expressly reserved, but the tenure itself had already disappeared.[7] An attempt was also made to abolish frankalmoin, though whether it succeeded is doubtful. The Statute of 1660, which by its first section abolished knight service, provided in s. 7 that nothing in the first section was to affect frankalmoin. The Administration of Estates Act 1925, instead of abolishing frankalmoin by express language, merely repealed s. 7 of the Statute of 1660.[8] This repeal, however, would appear to be fruitless, for even if the seventh section had been omitted from the Statute, frankalmoin would have been unaffected by an enactment that merely abolished knight service. The matter is indeed of little importance, for no land can be held by frankalmoin at the present day unless it has been continuously so held by the same ecclesiastical tenant since before *Quia Emptores* 1290.[9] Finally, and at long last, the

---

3 P. 23, ante.
4 AEA 1925, s. 45 (1) (a).
5 Pp. 17, 25, ante.
6 AEA 1925, s. 45 (1) (d).
7 LPA 1922, s. 136.
8 Sch. 2.
9 P. 19, n. 11, ante.

decisive step was taken of abolishing copyhold tenure. As from 1 January 1926, every parcel of copyhold land was enfranchised and converted into freehold land held by socage tenure.[10]

(3) EXTINGUISHMENT OF MANORIAL INCIDENTS

It was realized, of course, that copyhold tenure could not be dismissed in this peremptory manner, for certain manorial incidents had long been associated with it, and to extinguish without compensation such of those as possessed a money value would obviously be unjust to the beneficiary, whether lord or copyholder. The solution adopted was based upon a tripartite classification of these incidents.

(a) Extinguished at once

The first class, consisting of those that had become anachronisms were extinguished immediately subject to a single payment of compensation.[11]

(b) Continued until 1950

The second class consisted of those incidents that still possessed a money value. These were temporarily saved,[12] but it was provided that they should be extinguished upon the payment of compensation, the amount of which was to be determined either by agreement or by the Minister of Agriculture and Fisheries at the instance of either party. The final date of extinction was to be 31 December 1935, though if by then no agreement upon the amount of compensation had been reached either party might apply to the Minister requiring the amount to be determined, provided that the application was made before 31 December 1940. Owing to the war, this was later extended to 1 November 1950.[13]

(c) Continued indefinitely

The following incidents, falling within the third class, were permanently saved and they continue to attach to the land, unless the parties agree to their extinction upon payment of compensation.[14]

    (a) Any commonable rights to which the tenant is entitled;[15]
    (b) Any right of the lord or the tenant to mines, minerals, gravel pits or quarries, whether in or under the land;[16]
    (c) Any rights of the lord in respect of fairs, markets or sporting;

10 LPA 1922, Part V, ss. 128–137, and Sch. 2 as amended by LP(A)A 1924, s. 2 and Sch. 2; LPA 1922, s. 189.
11 Ibid., Sch. 12, para. 1; forfeiture for an alienation without the lord's licence; liability of the copyholder to customary suits and to do fealty; customary modes of descent or any custom relating to dower (p. 874, post), curtesy (p. 250, post) or freebench (Blackstone, vol. ii. p. 337).
12 Ibid., s. 128 (2): *rents*; fines payable to the lord in certain circumstances; *reliefs* payable to the lord upon descent of the land; *heriots*, the right of the lord to seize the best beast or best chattel upon the tenant's decease; *forfeitures* for a variety of acts by the tenant; the right of the lord to fell *timber* trees.
13 S.I. 1949 No. 836.
14 LPA 1922, s. 138 (12).
15 Ibid., Sch. 12, para. 4, p. 564, post.
16 Ibid., Sch. 12, para. 5.

(d) Any liability for the construction, maintenance, cleansing or repair of any dykes, ditches, canals, sea or river walls, bridges, levels, ways, etc.[17]

Lordships of manors continue to exist; they represent mesne tenure between the Crown and the freeholders. In addition to potential manorial rights, the owner is entitled to be called "Lord of the Manor" and has the right to the manorial records, which may date from before the Norman Conquest.[18]

(4) UNIMPORTANCE OF DOCTRINE OF TENURE

Thus, after some 900 years of development the doctrine of tenure still characterizes the English law of real property. Land is still incapable of ownership by a subject. Every acre is held by a tenant, not owned, though by a gradual process of elimination the various forms of tenure that complicated the law in former days have at last been reduced to the one type—socage. But what are the practical effects of the doctrine? Are the rights that the English tenant in fee simple enjoys any less valuable, for instance, than those of an absolute owner of land in the State of New York where all feudal tenures have been expressly abolished? Is tenure a mere name, a reminder only of the pomp and splendour of former days? The truth is, of course, that it is a mere historical survival that now has little practical effect. To have styled the tenant a landowner some centuries ago would have been inaccurate, since his very right to retain the land was conditional on his performance of the tenurial liabilities. But in course of time these liabilities have almost entirely disappeared, and it is only on the rarest occasion that anything of value can now be claimed by virtue of tenure. Until 1926, indeed, a lord, if he were still able to establish his lordship, might be fortunate enough to derive an unearned increment under the doctrine of escheat, but he lost even this vague *spes successionis* when the Administration of Estates Act 1925 provided that the land of a tenant who dies intestate without leaving near relatives shall pass to the Crown.[19] The feudal doctrine of tenure has no doubt impressed an indelible mark upon the framework of the law, but it no longer affects the tenant's rights of enjoyment, though the modern tendency to stress the rights of the community at large has resulted in the imposition of restrictions upon him that were unknown to earlier ages. The living results of feudalism must be sought, not in the realm of tenures, but in that classification of estates which is a peculiarity of English law. Apart from this "wonderful calculus of estates", as Maitland expressed it, perhaps the sole feudal incident that is a living force at the present day consists of those rights of common which the

---

17 LPA 1922, Sch. 12, para. 6.
18 In 1985 twenty-nine Lordships were sold at public auction; the highest price paid was £21,200 for the Lordship of Codicote in Hertfordshire. This included a right to hold a fair in the manor on the Vigil and Feast of St. James and the two following days: (1985) 274 EG 15.
19 Ss. 45, 46 (1) (vi). Escheat may, however, still exist if a trustee in bankruptcy of a landowner disclaims the land: *British General Insurance Co Ltd v A-G* [1945] LJNCCR 113; (1946) 62 LQR 223 (R. E. Megarry), or if a corporation (other than a company incorporated under the Companies Acts) holding real property is dissolved: *Re Sir Thomas Spencer Wells* [1933] Ch 29 at 54; *Re Strathblaine Estates Ltd* [1948] Ch 228. See too (1954) 70 LQR 25 (D. W. Elliott); *Re Lowes' Will Trusts* [1973] 1 WLR 882 at 884, [1973] 2 All ER 1136 at 1137, where RUSSELL LJ said: "By a happy chance [escheat to the Crown of realty *propter defectum sanguinis*] has arisen from the past in connection with the Phoenix Inn in Stratford-on-Avon".

successors of the copyhold lord and tenant may still hold in the manorial waste. To quote Maitland again:

> Everyone knows that this doctrine [of tenure], however indispensable as an explanation for some of the subtleties of real property law, is, in fact, untrue. "The first thing the student has to do is to get rid of the idea of absolute ownership." So says Mr. Williams[20]; but we may add, with equal truth, that the second thing he has to do is to learn how, by slow degrees, the statement that there is no absolute ownership of land has been deprived of most of its important consequences.[1]

If this was true in 1880 when Maitland wrote, how unsubstantial must the doctrine of tenure be after the abolition of copyholds in 1925.

Finally, it should be observed that although the substance has gone, the form remains. To quote MEGARRY J:

> Hundreds of ... phrases and concepts which permeate our law will have to be remembered if reforming zeal ever proposes to sweep away the theoretical structure of tenures and estates upon which English land law rests.[2]

B. THE ASSIMILATION OF REAL AND PERSONAL PROPERTY LAW

Originally, as we have seen, there were wide distinctions between the law of real and of personal property, but there has been a tendency ever since an early age to make both these departments of the law subject to the same legal rules, and in the main the rules that have been adopted are those that govern personal property. Thus the legislation of 1925 attempted to complete a process of assimilation that was already far advanced. We shall perhaps gain a greater clearness of view if we first consider in what particulars a common body of legal rules had been created before 1926, and then review the contents of the statutes designed to procure as complete a unification as possible.

(1) MATTERS IN WHICH ASSIMILATION HAD BEEN EFFECTED PRIOR TO 1926

(a) Remedies for dispossession

The original rule that leaseholds, unlike freeholds, were not specifically recoverable[3] ceased to be true towards the middle of the fifteenth century, by which time the action *de ejectione firmae* was available to the termor or lessee. The actions that lay for recovery of land were still, indeed, different according as the demandant's interest was freehold or leasehold, but complete assimilation in this particular was attained in the seventeenth century, by which time the *de ejectione firmae* had been borrowed from the law of chattels real and, under the name of the action of ejectment, had been adapted to the recovery of freeholds.[4]

20 Williams, *The Law of Real Property* (12th edn), p. 17.
1 Maitland, *Collected Papers*, vol. i. p. 196. See also Challis, *Law of Real Property* (3rd edn), p. 3.
2 *Lowe (Inspector of Taxes) v JW Ashmore Ltd* [1971] Ch 545 at 554, [1971] 1 All ER 1057 at 1068.
3 P. 34, ante.
4 Holdsworth, *History of English Law*, vol. vii. pp. 4 et seq.

(b) Power of testamentary disposition

It was always possible to bequeath leaseholds and other forms of personal property, but the feudal law would not admit a will of freeholds. A partial power of testamentary disposition over real property was obtained, however, in 1540, when the Statute of Wills permitted tenants to devise all their socage lands and two-thirds of their land held in knight service. This testamentary power was completed by the Tenures Abolition Act of 1660,[5] which converted knight service tenure into free and common socage.

(c) Availability of property for creditors

While at an early date leaseholds and other forms of personal property belonging to a deceased debtor constituted assets available for all creditors, the general rule was that a fee simple estate passed directly to the heir or devisee of a deceased tenant and could not be seized by his creditors. Gradual inroads upon this immunity of real property were, however, made by statute and by equity, and assimilation was almost attained in 1833, when the Administration of Estates Act made all land belonging to a deceased debtor available as assets for the one class of creditors—namely, simple contract creditors—who had not already obtained a remedy against freeholds. There was, however, still a difference in respect of remedies, for to render personal property available a creditor had to proceed against the personal representatives, while to satisfy his claim against real property, which did not vest in the personal representatives, he had to bring a suit in equity for administration. Assimilation on this point came with the Land Transfer Act 1897, which provided that realty should vest in the personal representatives, as had always been the practice with personalty.

The law that regulated the right of a creditor to seize the land of his *living* debtor was also assimilated before 1926. At common law all the chattels, real and personal, of a judgment debtor might be seized, but there was no right to satisfaction out of his freeholds. The Statute of Westminster 1285 made half the debtor's land available for creditors, and this was extended to the whole of the land by the Judgments Act of 1838.

(2) MATTERS IN WHICH ASSIMILATION WAS EFFECTED BY THE LEGISLATION OF 1925

The process of assimilation was carried further by the legislation of 1925 in the following respects.

(a) Size and nature of estates and interests

Before 1926 there was a fundamental distinction between realty and personalty with regard to the interests that might be created.

In the case of real property it has been possible for many centuries to create not only legal and equitable estates of different sizes—namely, the fee simple, the estate tail and the life estate—but also to split the full fee simple up into a series of partial and successive legal or equitable interests, as for example by a grant to A for life, then to B in tail, and then to C in fee simple.

The position with regard to personal property was different. Pure personalty (goods and money) and chattels real (such as an unexpired lease for 20 years)

5 Car. 2, c. 24.

were *at common law* the subjects of absolute ownership only. They were outside the doctrine of estates altogether and they could not be divided into successive interests. A grant of an existing term of years to A for life or in tail made A at common law the owner of the entire term. A gift for an hour was a gift for ever. The position *in equity* was slightly different, for to a limited extent equity did permit successive interests to be created in personalty if the device of a grant to trustees was adopted. If the owner of a leasehold for 30 years granted it to trustees

upon trust for A for life and then upon trust for B for life,

A did not become absolute owner of the whole term as he would have done at common law, but held merely for life, while on his death B similarly became entitled to a life estate. The interests of both A and B were of course equitable. There was one method, however, though it was seldom used, by which even at common law an effective life estate might be given in personalty—namely, by will. Without adopting the instrument of a trust a testator might make a direct bequest of a leasehold

to A for life with a further gift to B for life,

and the bequests would be upheld. But it is important to observe that before 1926 it was impossible to create an estate tail in leaseholds either by a direct bequest or through the instrumentality of trustees. A term of years, not being an estate of inheritance, could not be entailed.[6]

(i) Summary of pre-1926 law A summary of the law is, then, that in real property there might be legal or equitable fees simple, estates tail or life interests, either alone or in succession, but that in personal property there was normally only absolute ownership, though there might be equitable and, exceptionally, legal life interests.

(ii) Assimilation by Law of Property Act 1925 Assimilation, as regards both the size of the interests creatable and their nature when created, was, however, effected as from 1 January 1926 by the Law of Property Act 1925. In the first place this provides that personalty may be entailed.[7] The result is that the nature of the subject-matter no longer affects the quantitative interest that may be carved out of it. In realty there may be a fee simple estate, in personalty absolute ownership; while in both cases either entailed interests or life interests may validly be created. Secondly, as we shall see later,[8] entailed and life interests, whether in real or in personal property, can no longer exist as legal estates, but must always be equitable. Moreover, it is no longer possible to have a future *legal* estate in freeholds.

(b) Descent on intestacy

Perhaps the most striking difference between realty and personalty in 1925 lay in the rules that regulated their descent or distribution upon the death of the owner intestate. The old canons of descent, based upon feudal doctrines as amended by statute, governed the descent of fee simple and entailed estates, while the Statutes of Distribution contained a different set of rules prescribing what relatives were entitled to share the leaseholds and personal

6 *Leventhorpe v Ashbie* (1635) 1 Roll Abr 831.
7 LPA, s. 130 (1); p. 258, post.
8 Ibid., s. 1 (1), (2), (3); p. 91, post.

chattels of the deceased. Both these systems, together with various customary modes of descent, have been abolished and new distributive rules have been introduced which apply to both real and personal property.[9] The old canons of descent have, however, been retained for entailed interests.

(c) Order in which assets were applied for payment of debts

It is essential that definite rules shall prescribe the order in which the beneficiaries under a will must be deprived of their interests for the benefit of the unpaid creditors of the testator. The rules before 1926 on this matter represented another difference between real and personal property, for they required the exhaustion of the general personal estate before recourse was had to the realty. They were replaced by new provisions in the Administration of Estates Act 1925 which, from this point of view, have put realty and personalty on the same footing.[10]

(d) Necessity for words of limitation

A conveyance which was intended to pass the whole fee simple had under the old law to contain technical words of limitation, namely, to A and *his heirs* or to A *in fee simple*, otherwise it operated to pass only a life estate. Such words were not necessary in the case of a transfer of leaseholds; a simple grant to A, without more, was sufficient to transfer the whole interest of the grantor. Assimilation on this point, however, was effected by the Law of Property Act 1925,[11] which provides that a conveyance of freehold land without words of limitation shall pass the whole interest held by the grantor unless a contrary intention appears in the conveyance.

(e) Method of creating legal mortgages

The method of creating a legal mortgage of the fee simple before 1926 was by a conveyance of the legal fee simple to the mortgagee with a proviso that he should re-convey the estate upon repayment of the loan; but where the subject-matter of the mortgage was a leasehold interest, the almost universal practice was for the mortgagor to grant a sub-lease of the property to the mortgagee. This particular difference between freeholds and leaseholds has now disappeared, for the practice of conveying the fee simple is forbidden, and it is enacted that a legal mortgage of freeholds must be made by the grant of a lease or its equivalent.[12]

(f) Application of rule in *Dearle v Hall*

If successive assignments or mortgages of an *equitable* interest in property were made before 1926, the order in which the several assignees or mortgagees were entitled to repayment out of the property depended upon the nature of the property. If it was land, whether freehold or leasehold, they ranked for payment according to the order of time in which they had taken their assignment or mortgage; but if it was pure personalty, the rule in *Dearle v*

9 AEA 1925, ss. 45, 46, as amended by IEA 1952 and Family Provision Act 1966; pp. 875 et seq, post.
10 Ibid., s. 34 (3), Sch. 1, Part II.
11 S. 60 (1); p. 158, post.
12 Pp. 663 et seq, post.

Hall[13] applied, and the priorities were governed by the order of time in which the assignments or mortgages had been notified to the trustees of the personalty. This rule now applies to equitable interests in land, so that a later assignee who is the first to notify the estate owner of the land affected ranks prior to an earlier assignment of which he had no notice when he took his own assignment.[14]

(3) REMAINING DIFFERENCES BETWEEN REALTY AND PERSONALTY

The above review of those differences between realty and personalty that were eradicated by the legislation of 1925 shows that the law relating to the two forms of property has been assimilated as far as is possible. Certain differences must, of course, inevitably persist. For instance, easements and profits may subsist in land, but not in pure personalty; time under the Limitation Act 1980 varies according as the subject-matter is realty or personalty; the forms of alienation are different; so is the procedure on alienation, for investigation of title, though not usual in the case of personalty, is essential upon the transfer of an interest in land; but it would seem that most of the divergences must always in the nature of things continue to exist, since they result inevitably from the physical difference between the two forms of property.

C. THE ABOLITION OF CERTAIN ANACHRONISMS

A subsidiary part of the simplification of land transfer was the abolition of certain real property rules and doctrines which, though they had originally been introduced to preserve principles of importance in feudal days, were nothing more than obstructive anachronisms in 1925. The abolitions and alterations of this character effected by the various Acts will be described later, and we shall therefore content ourselves for the moment with a mere enumeration of those that are the most important:

 (i) the abolition of the rule in *Shelley's Case*;[15]
 (ii) the indirect abolition of the old contingent remainder rules;[16]
 (iii) the abolition of the rule in *Whitby v Mitchell*;[17]
 (iv) the almost complete abolition of the old canons of descent;[18]
 (v) the final abolition of the doctrine of *Dumpor's Case* so far as it related to leases;[19]
 (vi) the reversal of the rule that husband and wife were always two persons for the purposes of the acquisition of land;[20]

13 *Dearle v Hall* (1828) 3 Russ 1; M&B p. 798.
14 LPA 1925, s. 137; pp. 716 et seq, post.
15 P. 256, post.
16 P. 279, post.
17 P. 285, post.
18 P. 875, post.
19 P. 419, post.
20 P. 928, post.

(vii) the abolition of special occupancy.[1]

SECTION II SIMPLIFICATION OF CONVEYANCING: THE CULT OF THE ESTATE OWNER

There are two systems of conveyancing in England and Wales today; the unregistered system, under which title to land is deduced from past transactions relating to the property, and the registered system, where the title is recorded on a national register and is guaranteed by the state. The registered system under the Land Registration Act 1925 has gradually superseded the unregistered system and since 1990 has been made compulsory over the whole of England and Wales; compulsory in the sense that dealings in land must now be carried out under the new and not the old system of conveyancing.[2] A detailed discussion of both systems will be found in Part III.[3] In this section we are concerned with a general outline of the two systems, and with a comparison of their main features from the point of view of a purchaser.

A. UNREGISTERED CONVEYANCING

Under the system of unregistered conveyancing, a purchaser must make inquiries and bear the responsibility of satisfying himself on two matters—first, that the vendor is entitled to convey the estate which he has contracted to sell, secondly, that there are no incumbrances in favour of third parties that will continue to affect the land after the conveyance.

The legislation of 1925 made no fundamental alteration in the practice relating to the former matter,[4] but devoted its main attention to the question of incumbrances. In the normal case there will be no undisclosed incumbrances, but nevertheless the doctrine of constructive notice exists and a purchaser dare not do otherwise than institute an expensive inquiry. The danger is obvious. Land is different from such subjects of ownership as goods, since more often than not it is affected by rights vested in parties other than the ostensible owner.

A may appear to be absolute unincumbered tenant in fee simple of Blackacre, but investigation may disclose that B has an easement of way over the land, that C has a right to prevent the erection of buildings upon it, or that D, having lent £10,000 to A, has taken a mortgage upon Blackacre as security for repayment of the loan.

The power to create rights of this description in favour of third parties, and enforceable primarily against the land itself rather than against its owner, is a valuable, in fact an inevitable, feature of our social life. For the sake of brevity, we will describe them in future as third party rights.

1 P. 26, n. 19, post.
2 Pp. 97 et seq.
3 Pp. 747 et seq.
4 P. 61 et seq, ante.

(1) CLASSIFICATION OF THIRD PARTY RIGHTS

In some cases (as for instance in the case of easements and restrictive covenants), third party rights are a necessary local complement of land-ownership; in others they originate in the financial requirements of owners; while in others (as for instance in the rights given to children by a settlement), they are due to the social traditions of family life. They may be conveniently divided into two cases:

first, those arising either under a settlement or a trust for sale, as for instance financial provisions made for a widow and after her death for the children of the marriage;
secondly, those arising under some other transaction connected with the landowner's activities as a landowner or business man. Examples of this second class are easements, profits, restrictive covenants, estate contracts, mortgages and annuities.

But whatever their origin or character, it is obvious that the possibility of their existence and the risk that they may continue to bind the land after its sale, must cause a purchaser to walk warily and with no undue haste.

(2) EXTENT TO WHICH A PURCHASER WAS BOUND BY THIRD PARTY RIGHTS
   BEFORE 1926

The extent to which a purchaser is affected by third party rights depends upon the fundamental distinction between the legal and the equitable estate.[5] A bona fide purchaser for value of the legal fee simple which is subject to third party rights is absolutely bound by them if they amount to legal estates or interests, the question of his actual knowledge or ignorance of their existence being irrelevant. On the other hand, he is not bound by rights that are merely equitable in nature, unless he has actual or constructive notice of their existence. Thus:

An easement in perpetuity or a lease for a definite number of years will be enforceable against even an innocent purchaser because each is a legal interest, i.e. a right *in rem* enforceable against the whole world. On the other hand, if a fee simple owner has made an estate contract with X (e.g. has agreed to sell him the legal fee simple or to grant him a lease), or if he has subjected the land to a restrictive covenant in favour of Y (as for instance by covenanting that he will erect no business premises), the rights thus vested in X and Y, since they are merely equitable in nature, will not bind a subsequent purchaser for value who takes a conveyance of the legal estate from the fee simple owner, unless he is affected with notice.

The outstanding facts then, are that a purchaser has more to fear from legal than from equitable third party rights, and conversely that the third party himself is less secure with an equitable than a legal right.

(3) OUTLINE OF STATUTORY CHANGES BY LEGISLATION OF 1925

The following is a bare sketch of how the legislation attempted to simplify the problem of third party rights.

5   P. 54 et seq, ante.

(a) It drastically curtailed the category of legal estates and legal third party rights. The result is that after 1925 most third party rights are equitable.
(b) It made the legal estate the basis of conveyancing. The principal effect of this is that the legal estate can be conveyed only by its owner, not as frequently occurred under the former law by a person who had no estate in the land at all.[6]
(c) The existing system by which in certain circumstances the conveyance of a legal estate by way of sale overreached equitable third party rights, i.e. encumbered the purchase money instead of the land with their payment and relieved the purchaser of the duty to investigate them, was extended. In the result,

  (i) these rights are cleared off the land altogether if they can equally well be satisfied out of the purchase money; but
  (ii) if this is not possible, then they can be registered as *land charges* in a public register, so that their owners are protected and a purchaser is warned.

This sketch now requires a little elaboration.

(a) Reduction in number of legal estates

Before 1926 any recognized interest in land, regarded quantitatively, might be either legal or equitable. The Law of Property Act 1925, however, reduced the possible legal estates to the fee simple absolute in possession in the case of freeholds, and the term of years absolute in the case of leaseholds.

The person in whom such an estate is vested is called the *estate owner*. All other estates, interests and charges in or over the land can exist only as equitable interests,[7] with the exception of those interests permitted to exist at law by section 1 (2) of the Act.[8]

In the case of freeholds, for instance, the:

determinable fee simple,[9]
entailed interest,[10]
life interest,[11]
future interest of whatever size,[12]

can subsist only in equity, not at law. Each one must be created behind a trust, i.e. the legal estate in the land affected must be held by an *estate owner* whose function it is to give effect to the equitable interest. The very terminology, indeed, is changed. The correct expression now, for instance, is "entailed interest" not "estate tail", and "life interest" instead of "life estate".

Section 1 of the Law of Property Act 1925 runs as follows:

(1) The only estates in land which are capable of subsisting or of being conveyed or created at law are

6 P. 75, ante.
7 S. 1 (1), (2), (3).
8 Infra.
9 Chapter 14, p. 325, post.
10 Chapter 11, p. 245, post.
11 Chapter 12, p. 265, post.
12 Chapter 13, p. 275, post.

(*a*) An estate in fee simple absolute in possession;[13]

(*b*) A term of years absolute.[14]

(2) The only interests or charges in or over land which are capable of subsisting or of being conveyed or created at law are

(*a*) An easement, right, or privilege in or over land for an interest equivalent to an estate in fee simple absolute in possession or a term of years absolute;[15]

(*b*) A rentcharge in possession issuing out of or charged on land being either perpetual or for a term of years absolute;[16]

(*c*) A charge by way of legal mortgage;[17]

(*d*) Land tax,[18] tithe rentcharge,[19] and any other similar charge on land which is not created by an instrument;

(*e*) Rights of entry exercisable over or in respect of a legal term of years absolute, or annexed, for any purpose, to a legal rentcharge.

(3) All other estates, interests, and charges in or over land take effect as equitable interests.

It will be observed that in referring in the first sub-section to *estates* and in the second to *interests* the Act invented a new terminology that depends upon the difference between a right to the land itself and a right to some claim against the land of another person.

To be entitled to a legal as distinct from an equitable interest in the land itself it is necessary to hold an estate, and the only estate that qualifies for this purpose is either the fee simple absolute in possession or the term of years absolute according as the subject-matter is freehold or leasehold.

On the other hand, a claim against the land of another, if falling within the five items in sub-section (2) of section 1 of the Law of Property Act 1925 is termed an *interest* in that land, but to constitute a *legal* interest it must correspond in duration to one of the two legal estates. A person entitled in perpetuity or for 21 years to an easement, such as a right of way over Blackacre, owns a legal interest in Blackacre provided that the easement is created in the appropriate form. If he is only entitled to it for life, he is an equitable owner.

Thus, the ancient doctrine of estates under which the fee simple, the entail and the life interest were recognized as estates at common law, has been drastically abridged. There is only the one freehold estate at law—the fee simple absolute in possession. The doctrine, however, has only been "as it were, pushed back into equity"[20] in the sense that the interests that were formerly estates at law still subsist with equal vigour as equitable interests.

---

13 Chapter 8, p. 155, post.

14 Chapter 16, p. 357, post.

15 Chapter 17, p. 517, post.

16 Chapter 20, p. 645, post. The Rentcharges Act 1977 is phasing out the creation of certain kinds of rentcharge.

17 Chapter 21, p. 657, post.

18 Abolished by the Finance Act 1963, s. 73, Sch. 14, Pt. vi.

19 Extinguished by the Tithe Act 1936, s. 48, Sch. 9 and replaced by a sixty years' redemption annuity payable to the Crown. This is a legal interest within the meaning of "any other similar charge . . ." of para. (*d*). This was itself extinguished as from 2 October 1977 by FA 1977, s. 56.

20 Lawson, *Rational Strength of English Law*, p. 94.

(b) Legal estate as basis of conveyancing

This may be illustrated by two observations.

(i) Powers of appointment now equitable First, we have seen that it was a common practice before 1926 to limit land to A and B in fee simple to such uses as X might appoint, with the result that if X, who had no proprietary interest in the land, "appointed" to the use of Y and his heirs, A and B thereupon stood seised to the use of Y and he took a *legal* fee simple under the Statute of Uses.[1] This is no longer possible. The Statute of Uses has been repealed[2] and, though land may still be limited to A and B upon such trusts as X shall appoint, this merely empowers X to dispose of the equitable interest. With very few exceptions powers are now equitable.[3]

(ii) Title to legal estate alone investigated Secondly, if a legal estate that is held in trust for beneficiaries is offered for sale, the purchaser's sole concern in the normal case is to trace the title of the vendors to the legal estate. As we have seen,[4] he is entirely unaffected by the beneficial interests, for these are overreached, i.e. once the legal estate has been conveyed to a purchaser, they are no longer binding on the land but are transferred to the purchase money which has been paid to the trustees.[5]

(c) Settled land. Investigation of title. Overreaching of third party rights

(i) Conveyancing difficulties The policy of freeing the title to the legal estate from beneficial interests to which it may be subject, had begun in 1882 in the case of settled land. This was continued by the 1925 legislation. Furthermore the conveyancing machinery was greatly simplified. Before 1926 a settlement was created by a single deed which conferred legal estates and interests upon the successive beneficiaries, so that for instance the husband acquired a legal estate for life and the eldest son a legal estate tail.[6] When the tenant for life exercised, say, his statutory power of sale under the Settled Land Act 1882, his conveyance did, indeed, overreach these legal interests, but, as we have seen, the conveyancing difficulties were not inconsiderable.[7] These derived mainly from the fact that, since the fee simple was not vested in the tenant for life, his right to convey it rested solely upon the statutory powers of sale. The whole settlement required investigation, and before the purchaser was relieved from liability in respect of the beneficial limitations, it was incumbent upon him to make sure that the statutory conditions for the exercise of the power had been satisfied.

(ii) Settled Land Act 1925 These conveyancing difficulties, however, were

1 P. 69, ante.
2 LPA 1922, s. 207, Sch. 7.
3 LPA 1925, ss. 1 (7), 3. S. 205 (1) (xi) contains the following definitions: "Legal powers" include the powers vested in a chargee by way of legal mortgage or in an estate owner under which a legal estate can be transferred or created, and "equitable powers" mean all the powers in or over land under which equitable interests or powers only can be transferred or created.
4 Pp. 75, 76, ante.
5 For details, see pp. 814–5, 821–2, post.
6 These interests could also be equitable. After the re-introduction of the use in the form of the trust (pp. 52–4, ante) it was, of course, possible to create a strict settlement by the alternative method of a grant unto and to the use of trustees to hold the legal estate upon the requisite trusts, in which case the beneficiaries would be entitled to equitable interests.
7 Pp. 75–6, ante.

removed by the Settled Land Act 1925. Owing to the reduction in the number of legal estates, the limited and beneficial interests arising under a settlement are now necessarily equitable, and the legal fee simple out of which they have been carved must, in accordance with the statutory provisions, be vested in the first tenant for life and be transferred to each subsequent tenant for life as and when he becomes entitled to possession.[8]

(iii) Dual position of tenant for life Thus the tenant for life occupies a dual position. Although he is a mere tenant for life as regards beneficial enjoyment, he is the owner of the legal fee simple for conveyancing purposes. This means that within the scope of his statutory powers he can dispose of the legal estate, whether it be the fee simple absolute in possession or the term of years absolute, so as to pass to the purchaser a title free from the rights under the settlement; but it does not mean that he becomes entitled to the capital money arising from the transaction. It is, in fact, a condition of the purchaser's immunity that the money should be paid to the trustees.

(iv) Method of creating a settlement after 1925 In order to emphasize this separation of the legal estate from the beneficial and equitable interests and to facilitate conveyancing, a new method of creating a settlement, framed on the pattern of the trust for sale, was introduced by the Settled Land Act 1925. Every settlement *inter vivos* must now be made by two deeds. One (*the vesting deed*) vests the legal fee simple in the tenant for life, describes the property and names the trustees; the other (the *trust instrument*) declares the beneficial interests of the tenant for life and the other persons entitled under the settlement.[9]

(v) Overreaching of equitable interests The effect of a conveyance made by the tenant for life in his capacity as estate owner is to overreach the equitable interests of the beneficiaries, i.e. it clears them off the title to the legal fee simple and converts them into equivalent interests in the purchase money. Their fate is of no concern to the purchaser, provided that he pays the purchase money to the trustees, and not to the tenant for life. His sole object is to investigate the title to the *legal* estate. He must, therefore, trace that title down to the first vesting deed, i.e. he must require the vendor to show that the person who purported to vest the legal estate in the first tenant for life was in fact entitled to do so. He does not see, nor in general may he demand to see, the trust instrument. That instrument is the sole charter of the beneficiaries. The rights that it grants to the beneficiaries are still intact, still secure, but they are now transferred to the purchase money. The whole operation set in motion upon a conveyance by the tenant for life is an illustration of what is called the *curtain* principle. The vesting deed is, as it were, a curtain that veils the equitable interests.[10]

(d) Registrable third party rights

In the case, then, of a trust for sale and strict settlement, the beneficial interests are cleared altogether off the title to the legal estate and, since they

---

8 Pp. 179–82, 811–2, post.
9 SLA 1925, s. 4; pp. 179–82. In the case of a settlement made by a testator, the legal estate devolves upon his executors who hold it upon trust to convey it to the tenant for life. The will itself constitutes the trust instrument and the executors make a *vesting assent*, corresponding to the vesting deed, in favour of the tenant for life; p. 182, post.
10 For a detailed account of these matters, see pp. 811 et seq, post.

are transferred to the purchase money, no harm is done to their owners. Family rights and incumbrances in the nature of pecuniary claims do not impede a conveyance of the legal estate. There are, however, other equitable third party rights to which the doctrine of overreaching is necessarily inapplicable, since they are incapable of being attached to money. For instance, an estate contract or a restrictive covenant of which a purchaser has had notice must continue to affect the land after conveyance to him of the legal estate. In such cases the obvious method of simplifying the task of the purchaser and at the same time of protecting the equitable owner is to require rights of this nature to be publicly recorded if they are to remain binding against purchasers. This was the policy adopted by the legislature in 1925.

Legislation enabling rights against land to be registered has long been in force, but it has appeared in successive and somewhat slow stages. Thus life annuities charged upon land were made registrable as far back as 1777, and the system was extended to judgments in 1838, to pending land actions in 1839, to deeds of arrangement in 1887, and to what are called land charges in 1888. These several topics are the subject of full discussion later,[11] but what should be observed at once is that a great extension of the system of registration was made by the Land Charges Act 1925. Without going into details, it may be said that practically all equitable rights against land, except those which arise under a trust for sale or a settlement and are therefore overreachable, may be entered in one of the registers kept at the Land Charges Department of the Land Registry in Plymouth. Registration of a registrable right constitutes notice of it to the whole world; failure to register it carries the penalty that it is void against a purchaser[12]; and this is so even if the purchaser has actual notice of the unregistered right. Therefore in the case of a third party right that falls within the provisions of the Act, all now turns on registration; its owner can secure complete protection for himself by registration, while a purchaser need do no more than search at the Land Registry to discover whether the land is incumbered or not. An examination of section 2 (2) of the Land Charges Act 1972[13] will show that most of the charges which are registrable are equitable. The important exception is the puisne mortgage, that is to say, any legal mortgage not being a mortgage protected by a deposit of documents relating to the legal estate affected.[14] A puisne mortgage, although a legal interest, does not therefore bind a purchaser for value unless registered. It is made registrable, as will be seen later, in order to comply with the post-1925 scheme for the priority of mortgages.[15]

(4) SUMMARY OF CHANGES MADE BY LEGISLATION OF 1925

(a) Conveyance by estate owner

By way of summary, it may be said, then, that one of the principal objects of the 1925 legislation was to simplify and clear the title to the legal fee simple,

11 Pp. 756 et seq, post.
12 Some unregistered charges are void against a purchaser for value of any estate, legal or equitable; others are void only against a purchaser of a legal estate for money or money's worth: LCA 1972, s. 4 (5), (6); p. 764, post.
13 LCA 1925 has been replaced by LCA 1972 and Local Land Charges Act 1975.
14 Class C(i); p. 759, post.
15 P. 719, post. The Matrimonial Homes Act 1967 added a new Class F land charge which does not owe its origin to equity or to common law; p. 241, post.

which is the estate that the majority of purchasers wish to obtain. As a result of the legislation the general position is now as follows:

The only legal freehold estate in Blackacre is the fee simple absolute in possession. In all cases this will be vested in a definite person or body of persons called the *estate owner*. According to the circumstances the estate owner will be one of the following:

A beneficial owner entitled in his own right.
Trustees for sale.
The tenant for life or "statutory owners"[16] in the case of settled land.
Personal representatives.
A mortgagor.[17]
A bare trustee.[18]

A conveyance of the legal fee simple must be made by or in the name of the estate owner, not by anybody else. Thus the exercise of a power of appointment can no longer affect the legal estate,[19] and in the case of a settlement the tenant for life conveys the legal fee simple because the Settled Land Act 1925 requires that it shall be vested in him, not as formerly because he had a statutory power to convey what he had not got.

(b) Third party rights

The conveyance of a legal fee simple that is subject to equitable third party rights is considerably simplified:

(i)   Rights which arise under a settlement or a trust for sale continue to be overreached by the conveyance[20] and cleared off the title, for no injury is done to their owners by converting them into rights against the purchase money.

(ii) If the rights do not arise in that way (i.e. they came into existence before the creation of the settlement or the trust for sale) but are nevertheless convertible into rights against the money, the estate owner may clear them off the title by creating a settlement or a trust for sale for that particular purpose, called an *ad hoc* settlement or an *ad hoc* trust for sale.[1]

(iii) If the rights do not arise under a settlement or a trust for sale and are not convertible into money rights, such as an estate contract or a restrictive covenant, their continued enforcement depends in general on their registration as land charges.

---

16 These are the persons who take the legal fee simple in settled land when there is no person entitled to take it as tenant for life; p. 185, post.

17 In a mortgage of a legal fee simple, the mortgagor remains the estate owner of the legal fee simple, but nevertheless the mortgagee is entitled by virtue of his power of sale to convey it to a purchaser.

18 A bare or naked trustee is one who holds property for the absolute benefit of a beneficiary of full age, and who himself has no beneficial interest in the property and no duty except to transfer it to its owner: *Christie v Ovington* (1875) 1 Ch D 279; and, for an example in registered land, *Hodgson v Marks* [1971] Ch 892, [1971] 2 All ER 684. See H & M, pp. 72–73.

19 Save in a few exceptional cases; p. 93, n. 3, ante.

20 P. 94, ante; pp. 811–2, 824–5, post.

 1 Pp. 820–2, post.

(c) Effect on doctrine of bona fide purchaser for value of legal estate without notice

We have already seen the curtailment of the doctrine of the bona fide purchaser,[2] where overreaching operates in the case of beneficial interests under a settlement or trust for sale.[3] It has been further dramatically curtailed by the extension of the system of registration of land charges. In the case of registrable third party rights, their enforceability no longer depends on the state of the purchaser's mind; it is the state of the register which is crucial.

The doctrine, however, continues to apply to a residual category of equitable third party rights which are neither overreachable nor registrable. Here a purchaser is bound unless he is a bona fide purchaser of the legal estate for value without actual or constructive notice. This category is necessarily limited, because most equitable third party rights are in practice susceptible to overreaching or registration. Certain situations where the old rules concerning notice continue to apply were contemplated by the draftsmen of the 1925 legislation, for instance, a restrictive covenant entered into before 1926.[4] But in recent years the old rules have been applied in a number of situations which were presumably not foreseen.[5]

(d) Reconciliation of family and commercial needs

One aspect of the clear-cut distinction between the legal estate and the equitable interest deserves attention. Land is employed to satisfy at least two requirements, one affecting the family of its owner, the other affecting its commercial exploitation. It must be subject to rules that facilitate its employment as a continuing source of income for the present and future members of a family, but at the same time it must be under effective administration and above all be readily transferable by way of sale, lease, mortgage and similar transactions if good estate management so demands. These two requirements, at first sight contradictory, have been reconciled by English law. The estate owner, despite the existence of family trusts, is given full powers of management and disposal in respect of the land, but he holds them as trustee for such equitable beneficiaries as may exist. In this way the well-being of the land, the needs of the market and the prosperity of the family are harmonized.[6]

2 For the doctrine, see pp. 59 et seq, ante.
3 P. 94, ante.
4 P. 621, post.
5 *E.R. Ives Investment Ltd v High* [1967] 2 QB 379, [1967] 1 All ER 504; M & B p. 592 (licence by estoppel), p. 604, post; *Poster v Slough Estates Ltd* [1968] 1 WLR 1515, [1968] 3 All ER 257 (right of entry to remove a fixture on termination of lease), p. 531, n. 15, post; *Caunce v Caunce* [1969] 1 WLR 286, [1969] 1 All ER 722; M & B p. 273 (beneficial interest of wife who had contributed towards purchase price); *Kingsnorth Finance Co Ltd v Tizard* [1986] 1 WLR 783, [1986] 2 All ER 54, p. 63, n. 4, ante. *Shiloh Spinners Ltd v Harding* [1973] AC 691, especially at 720–721, [1973] 1 All ER 90 at 98–9, per Lord WILBERFORCE; M & B p. 36 (equitable right of re-entry on breach of covenant); *Midland Bank Ltd v Farmpride Hatcheries Ltd* (1980) 260 EG 493 (contractual licence); M & B p. 30; p. 63, ante.
6 Lawson, *Rational Strength of English Law*, pp. 91–2.

B. REGISTERED CONVEYANCING[7]

So far we have discussed the changes made by the 1925 legislation which were intended to simplify the law of real property within the framework of the system of unregistered conveyancing. The intention was that the unregistered system should be replaced by a simplified system of registered conveyancing. This has been gradually extended on a compulsory basis over the whole of England and Wales, a process which was completed in 1990.[8]

Registration of title was introduced into England as long ago as 1862.[9] At first it was voluntary; in 1897 provision was made to extend it to areas to be defined from time to time by Orders in Council;[10] and in 1990 it was finally extended to the whole of England and Wales.[11] The revised system is contained in the Land Registration Acts 1925 to 1986[12] which are supplemented by the Land Registration Rules 1925 as amended by subsequent rules.[13]

The object of the system is to replace the method of unregistered conveyancing by one whereby a registered title is guaranteed by the state. We have seen that the conveyancing of unregistered land depends upon the production by a vendor of a series of documents which recount previous transactions affecting the land and demonstrate to a purchaser the ability of

---

7 For detailed treatment, see pp. 784, et seq, post. The authoritative account is Ruoff and Roper (former Chief Land Registrars), *Law and Practice of Registered Conveyancing* (looseleaf edn). See also Ruoff, *Concise Land Registration Handbook* (1990); *Encyclopaedia of Forms and Precedents* (4th edn), vol. xvii. pp. 112–270 (R.B.Roper); Wolstenholme and Cherry, *Conveyancing Statutes* (13th edn), vol. 6; Barnsley, *Conveyancing Law and Practice* (3rd edn), chapters 2, 3, 4, 11, 15; Hayton, *Registered Land* (3rd edn); Wontner's *Guide to Land Registry Practice* (18th edn). The Land Registry issues Practice Notes in conjunction with the Law Society (2nd edn), and the Chief Land Registrar an Annual Report on H.M. Land Registry. The Law Commission is revising registered conveyancing. Its first report was published in 1983 (Law Com No. 125, HC 86) on Identity and Boundaries, Conversion of Title, the Treatment of Leases and the Minor Interests Index; its second report in 1985 on Inspection of the Register (Law Com No. 148, HC 551); its third report in 1987 on Overriding Interests, Rectification and Indemnity and Minor Interests (Law Com No. 158, HC 269) on which see [1987] Conv 334 (R. J. Smith). The recommendations on the last three topics of the 1983 Report were implemented in LRA 1986, pp. 512, 733, 787, post; and the 1985 Report was implemented in LRA 1988, p. 102, post. Its fourth and "for the time being final" report on Land Registration 1988 (Law Com No. 173, HC 680) presents a Land Registration Bill which incorporates the recommendations of the third report and "is a modern, and we hope, simpler version of the 1925 Act."
8 There were 14,439,253 separate titles on the register at 31 March 1993: Annual Report for 1992–3, p. 7. On computerisation of the system, see pp. 14–15. The number of titles connected to computerised format was 6.29 million at the end of March 1993. See AJA 1982, s. 66.
9 Land Registry Act 1862. For a history of land registration before 1926, see (1972) 36 Conv (NS) 390 (H. W. Wilkinson). See also *City of London Building Society v Flegg* [1988] AC 54 at 84, [1987] 3 All ER 435 at 448, per Lord OLIVER OF AYLMERTON.
10 Registered conveyancing must be distinguished from the system of registration of assurances practised in parts of Yorkshire which merely recorded conveyances and devises in a public register. These deeds registries are now closed: LPA 1969, ss. 16–22.
11 Registration of Title Order 1989.
12 I.e. LRA 1925, 1936, 1966 Land Registration and Land Charges Act 1971, Parts I and III, LRA 1986 and 1988.
13 See LRR 1956, 1964, 1967, 1976, 1978, 1986, 1987 and 1993; LR (Souvenir Land) R 1972; LR (Capital Transfer Tax) R 1975; LR (Companies and Insolvency) R 1986; LR (Powers of Attorney) R 1986; LR (Delivery of Applications) R 1986; LR (Matrimonial Homes) R 1990; LR (Open Register) R 1991; LR (Execution of Deeds) R 1990; LR (Charges) R 1990; LR (Charities) R 1993; LR (Fees) Order 1992; LR (Official Searches) R 1993; LR (Leasehold Reform) R 1993.

a vendor to convey what he has agreed to convey. "Title" to the interest to be conveyed is thus something deduced from evidence. It has to be proved afresh each time a disposition of land is made. The conveyancing of registered land is different in principle and in practice. Once the title to land is registered, its past history is irrelevant. The title thenceforth is guaranteed by the state, and a purchaser can do no other than rely on it. "Title" has now become something more than evidence; in a sense, it is itself the subject matter of the conveyance. Transfer of land becomes the substitution of one person's name for another's name in a registry. That transfer necessarily shifts the whole title registered in the former proprietor's name. The landowner receives from the registry a land certificate which reproduces the relevant entries on the register, but it is the register, not the land certificate, which establishes, and is, the source of title.

Registered conveyancing is not, however, a new system of land law. It is based on such familiar concepts as estates and interests, settlements, leases, mortgages, easements and covenants, and is an integral part of the 1925 Legislation. As we have seen, the only two legal estates which can exist at law are the fee simple absolute in possession and the term of years absolute,[14] and these are the only two legal estates which can be registered under separate titles.[15] Not all leases are so registrable, but the general effect of the legislation is that only leases with more than 21 years to run can be registered.[16] Other interests are dealt with in one of two ways:

(a) as overriding interests, in which case they bind a registered proprietor and his transferees whether or not they are entered on the register;[17]
(b) as minor interests, in which case they must be entered on the register of the land affected, if they are not to be overridden by a subsequent registered disposition of the land for value.[18]

(1) REGISTRATION AND ENTRY ON REGISTER

It is important to grasp the distinction between interests which may be *registered* and interests which may be *entered on the register*. The former are confined to the two legal estates,[19] the titles to which are substantively registered under their own separate title numbers. Minor interests, as the name implies, are interests lesser than registered interests and may be protected by the entry of a notice, caution, inhibition, or restriction[20] on the register of the title affected. The entry is made on the proprietorship or charges register[1] of that title, and operates by way of an incumbrance against it. It follows too that in the case of a strict settlement, the tenant for life, and,

14 P. 91, ante.
15 LRA 1925, s. 2 (1). For the suggestion that the Act creates a statutory estate, distinct from the fee simple or term of years at common law, see p. 161, post. Legal interests which may be registered in addition to those in corporeal land, are those in manors, mines and minerals, advowsons and rents: LRR 1925, r. 50. But legal easements may only be registered as appurtenant to the registered title of the dominant tenement: LRR 1925, r. 257; p. 580, post. In practice, rents means rent charges only. Undivided shares cannot be registered.
16 Ibid., s. 8, pp. 512, post.
17 P. 103, post.
18 P. 103, post.
19 Supra.
20 Pp. 801, et seq, post.
 1 P. 101, post.

in the case of a trust for sale, the trustees for sale, will be registered proprietors, and, as will be seen,[2] warning is given to a purchaser by the entry of a restriction on the registered title that the settlement or trust for sale exists, without however telling him what the individual beneficial interests are. Thus the doctrine of overreaching applies to the interests of the beneficiaries and the curtain principle is retained. "References to trusts shall, so far as is possible, be excluded from the register."[3] Registered conveyancing is thus not a new system of land law. It is, however, more than just a new system of conveyancing, and, as we shall see, has important effects on the substance of the land law.

The Land Registration Act 1925 lays down precise rules for dealings in the land, and attempts an enumeration of the powers of an owner under the Act.[4] The powers of disposition possessed by a registered proprietor are those expressly conferred on him by the Land Registration Act 1925, and he has no others.[5] This rule affects not only the land itself, but also the creation of other rights over it, such as easements and mortgages. But there remains a residual power[6] to negotiate and bring into existence equitable rights,[7] though these are minor interests and need protection through entry on the register. Obviously, then, a rule of fundamental importance is that the legal title can be affected only by observing the proper requirements.

In order to be effectual at law a disposition of registered land must be completed by registration. Thus a transfer for value of registered freehold or leasehold land must be completed by the Registrar entering on the register the transferee as the registered proprietor[8] and until he has done this the transferor is deemed to remain the proprietor.[9] As soon as he has done this, however, the legal estate will pass at once to the transferee.[10]

(2) TIMING OF REGISTRATION

Registration of a title need not be effected immediately the area in which it lies is made an area of compulsory registration. Title to freehold land must be registered on its first *sale* after the relevant date, while for registrable leaseholds the rule is that every *grant* of a leasehold for more than 21 years,

2 Pp. 202, 209, post.
3 LRA 1925, s. 74; cf s. 88 (1); *Abigail v Lapin* [1934] AC 491 at 500.
4 Ibid., ss. 18, 21, 25, 40, 101, 104, 106, 107, 109; LRR 1925, r. 74.
5 Ruoff and Roper, para. 8–04.
6 LRA 1925, ss. 101, 107. A contract of sale is an obvious example.
7 Leases for 21 years or less, although legal estates, cannot be registered substantively, and are usually overriding interests not requiring protection on the register; p. 513, post.
8 LRA 1925, ss. 19 (1), 22 (1). A prescribed form must be used: LRR 1925, rr. 98, 115. In practice the use of forms prescribed by r. 98 for freeholds is accepted by the Land Registry in the case of leasehold titles also. Registration is completed as of the day on which the application is delivered to the Registrar: LRR 1925, r. 83 (2), as substituted by LRR 1978, r. 8; LR (Delivery of Applications) R 1986: see letter from the Registrar, cited in (1976) 40 Conv (NS) 307; M & B p. 101.
9 Before registration, there may be a complete transfer in equity: *Mascall v Mascall* (1984) 50 P & CR 119 (intending donor executed transfer which he handed to donee together with land certificate: even though donee had not applied for registration, held to be complete gift in equity, since donor had done everything that he had to do to perfect gift: *Re Rose* [1952] Ch 499, [1952] 1 All ER 1217; M & B *Trusts and Trustees* 4th edn, pp 111–114). See Ruoff and Roper, para. 11–09; see also *E S Schwab & Co Ltd v McCarthy* (1975) 31 P & CR 196 at 212.
10 LRA 1925, ss. 20 (1), 23 (1) as amended by FA 1975, s. 52, Sch. 12, para 5, which set out in detail what appurtenances pass to the transferee, and also the matters subject to which his title subsists. See also LRR 1925, r. 251.

and every assignment on *sale* of a lease with more than 21 years still to run, must be registered.[11] If registration is not applied for within two months,[12] the legal estate will revest in the transferor, who then holds it upon trust for the transferee.[13]

Accordingly the system of registration of title will gradually supersede the system of conveyancing by title deeds; by 1992 there were already some 14 million titles on the register. The Chief Land Registrar has forecast that, with the existing triggers of sale and long lease, there should be 19 million titles on the register in 20 years' time; he has also suggested strategies for completing the register.[14]

(3) THE REGISTER

(a) **Tripartite**

The separate register for each individual title[15] is divided into three parts, a property register, a proprietorship register, and a charges register.[16] It was intended that the register should "mirror" the title, though, as we shall see, it does so in only a qualified manner. The register is kept on a card index system, and each of its three parts relating to any given title is filed on a separate card or part of a card. The register is a register of title, so that where there is more than one legal title subsisting in one piece of land (the obvious case is that of a registered reversion subject to a registered lease) there will be one register for each title. A copy of the various entries on the register and of the filed plan of the title, called a Land Certificate,[17] is given to the registered proprietor of the title, and can be retained by him or deposited in the registry. It is not the certificate but the register retained in the registry which is the title.

The property register describes and identifies the land,[18] and the interest in the land, which is the subject matter of the title, whether it be freehold or leasehold. The interest must, as we have said already, be a legal one. There

---

11 There were 313,706 first registrations during the year ended 31 March 1993. Annual Report 1992–3, p. 11. Compulsory registration does not extend to any area of land declared by the Registrar to be subject to a souvenir land scheme: Land Registration and Land Charges Act 1971, s. 4; LR (Souvenir Land) R 1972 (S.I. 1972 No. 985). See (1971) 35 Conv (NS) 390 at 397 (T. B. F. Ruoff and P. Meehan). On leaseholds, see LRA 1986, s. 2, p. 512, post.

12 This may be extended on application being made to the Registrar or to the Court of Appeal. See *Pinekerry Ltd v Kenneth Needs Contractors Ltd* (1992) 64 P & CR 245; [1993] CLJ 22 (A. J. Oakley).

13 LRA 1925, s. 123. The equitable interest of the transferee will be either a minor interest, or if he is in actual occupation of the land, an overriding interest.

Section 123 applies only to corporeal land, so that rentcharges are not thereby required to be registered. However, if land out of which a perpetual or terminable rentcharge is granted is itself registered, the title to the rentcharge must also be substantively registered, no matter how short the term of a terminable rentcharge. See Ruoff, *Rentcharges in Registered Conveyancing* (1961) chapters 1 and 2; p. 655, post.

14 Completing the Land Register in England & Wales: A Discussion and Consultation Paper (1992); [1993] Conv 101.

15 Registers of title are kept at nineteen District Registries: LR (District Registries) Order 1991 (S.I. 1991 No. 2634). The Headquarters of the Land Registry is at Lincoln's Inn Fields, London.

16 LRR 1925, r. 2.

17 For specimen Land Certificates, see M & B pp. 103–106. A new design for the cover was introduced in 1986.

18 See HM Land Registry: Practice Leaflet No. 16 on Boundaries in Land Registration, reproduced in [1990] Conv 401; Sara, *Boundaries and Easements*, ch. 4.

may also appear on this register mention of specific benefits capable of subsisting as legal interests, such as legal easements, and the effect will be to create a registered title of the same nature in them. There may also be a reference to other benefits, for instance, to the freedom of the land from specific overriding interests.[19]

The proprietorship register states the nature of the title, i.e. absolute, good leasehold, possessory or qualified, the name, address and description of the proprietor, and also any entries that affect his right of disposing of the land.[20] The charges register contains entries of incumbrances which burden the land, e.g. restrictive covenants and mortgages.

(b) Inspection of Register

Under the Land Registration Act 1988, the register was opened to inspection by the public.[1] It is also possible to discover whether or not a particular plot of land is registered by searching the Index Map and Parcels Index.[2]

(4) CLASSES OF TITLE

There are four different classes of title; absolute title, good leasehold title (for a lessee only), possessory title, and, finally, qualified title, where an application for one of the other titles cannot be substantiated.

An absolute title is the most frequent.[3] It cannot be registered until it has been approved by the Registrar,[4] who will carry out a full investigation of the title and who can compel the production of deeds and other evidence of title.[5] An applicant who has a title which professional opinion would regard as good under unregistered conveyancing may expect to be registered with an absolute title, for the Registrar seems "to occupy the position of a willing but prudent purchaser",[6] and is willing to overlook technical defects in a title if he is satisfied that there is no one who can impugn it. A title registered in this way is actually improved by registration. The technical defect is cured, for no one can subsequently raise it, save in the exceptional case of a rectification action.[7]

---

19 LRR 1925, r. 197; *Re Dances Way, West Town, Hayling Island* [1962] Ch 490, [1962] 2 All ER 42. The Land Registry is consulting as to whether the price paid for the land should appear on the register: (1994) 138 SJ 139.
20 P. 801, post.
 1 Substituting LRA 1925, ss. 112–113. LRA 1988 is based on the Second Report on Land Registration: Inspection of the Register (Law Com No. 148, HC 551) 1985. See (1990) 49 EG 44 (C. Coombe and H. Lewis); (1990) 41 LSG 19 (E. J. Pryer).
 2 LR (Open Register) R 1991 (S.I. 1991 No. 122); LRR 1993 (S.I. 1993 No. 3275); Land Registry Practice Direction reproduced in [1993] Conv 319. On searching the Index Map, see [1991] 6 LSG 24 (M. J. Russell).
 3 For the inferior titles, see p. 786, post. On first registration of freehold land, over 99 per cent of applications are registered with absolute title. The majority of the remainder relate to titles founded purely on adverse possession. See [1980] Conv, pp. 7–9, 96–8, 165–7.
 4 LRA 1925, s. 4.
 5 Ibid., s. 15. If the Registrar refuses to register a title as absolute, there is no appeal to the court: *Dennis v Malcolm* [1934] Ch 244; his action or inaction may be challengeable by an application for judicial review: RSC Ord 53; Ruoff and Roper, para. 5.02; *Quigly v Chief Land Registrar* [1993] 1 WLR 1435, [1993] 4 All ER 82.
 6 Hargreaves in *Stephens' Commentaries* (21st edn), vol. i, p. 624. See also Ruoff and Roper, para. 12.03 and (1963) 60 LS Gaz 345, and (1954) 18 Conv (NS) 130 (T. B. F. Ruoff). The registrar relies on the language of LRA 1925, s. 13, proviso (c); (1976) 40 Conv (NS) 122 (C. T. Emery). See *MEPC Ltd v Christian-Edwards* [1981] AC 205, [1979] 3 All ER 752.
 7 Infra; p. 787, post.

In the case of a leasehold,[8] an absolute title may be registered only if the Registrar approves not only the title to the leasehold itself, but also the titles to the freehold and to any intermediate leaseholds that may exist. If an absolute title to a leasehold is registered, it vests the leasehold in the first proprietor subject to the same rights, interests and incumbrances as in the case of a freehold registered with an absolute title, but subject to all implied and express covenants, obligations and liabilities incident to the registered land, including those arising under the lease.

(5) RECTIFICATION AND INDEMNITY

Once the title to the land has been registered, it vests in the registered proprietor, and is thenceforth guaranteed by the state. But, as in unregistered conveyancing, the title is still less than absolute. Section 82 of the Land Registration Act 1925 gives to the court and to the Registrar wide powers to rectify the register where there is any error or omission. Section 83[9] however provides for an indemnity for those who have suffered loss in certain cases by reason of such rectification or by refusal of rectification. So the system of registered conveyancing is to some extent an insurance system.[10]

(6) PROTECTION OF THIRD PARTY RIGHTS

We must now consider how third party rights are protected and how they affect a purchaser from the proprietor of registered land. We have seen that they are of two kinds, overriding interests and minor interests. The basic idea is simple enough. Some interests require protecon on the register; others do not. Overriding interests are those interests that bind a registered proprietor and his transferee, irrespective of entry on the register.[11] They override, or assume superiority over, the transferee's estate. They are mostly listed in section 70 (1) of the Land Registration Act 1925. The main examples are profits à prendre, legal easements, leases for not more than 21 years, local land charges, rights acquired or being acquired under the Limitation Act and in paragraph (g) of section 70 (1), the

rights of every person in actual occupation of the land or in receipt of the rents and profits thereof, save where enquiry is made of such person and the rights are not disclosed.[12]

Minor interests, on the other hand, are interests needing protection by entry on the register.[13] Some of them are incapable of binding a purchaser even if protected by entry, but nevertheless affect the method of disposing of

8 The provisions relating to leaseholds are contained in LRA 1925, ss. 8–12. Lease includes an underlease: LRA s. 3(x); p. 512, post.
9 As amended by Land Registration Act 1966 and Part I of the Land Registration and Land Charges Act 1971.
10 Pp. 787 et seq, post. The indemnity is payable by the Registrar out of moneys provided by Parliament. Land Registration and Land Charges Act 1971, s. 1. During 1992–93, 419 claims resulted in the payment of £5,093,848. This included a £3.65 million claim which arose from a fraud. Report of Chief Land Registrar for 1992–93, p. 19. Viewed against a fee revenue of about £200 million for the same year, the sums paid by way of indemnity "fade almost into insignificance".
11 LRA 1925, ss. 3 (xvi), 70; pp. 780 et seq, post.
12 For a fuller discussion of this most important category, see p. 791, post.
13 LRA 1925, ss. 3 (xv), 59 (6) (as amended by FA 1975, s. 52, Sch. 12, para. 5), 101. For the methods of protection, see pp. 801 et seq, post.

land. Thus, in the case of beneficial interests under a settlement or trust for sale that will be overreached on a sale of the land, a restriction will be entered on the proprietorship register indicating that the proprietor of the legal title is limited in his powers, but, if the terms of the restriction are complied with, a purchaser for value is not concerned with such beneficial interests. But other minor interests such as restrictive covenants, equitable easements, legal and equitable rentcharges, and estate contracts do bind purchasers for valuable consideration, if protected by entry on the register. Conversely, a purchaser will take free from them if they are not so protected by entry; and, as in unregistered conveyancing, this is so, even if he has actual notice of their existence.[14] A donee, however, will be bound by minor interests even if they are not protected by entry.

It is the former category of overriding interests which has attracted criticism.[15] Overriding interests, which do not appear on the register (they may do, in which case they cease to be overriding interests),[16] detract from the principle that the register should be a mirror of the vendor's title. Their existence will only be discovered by a purchaser if he resorts to the older methods of investigation, and this is particularly so where paragraph (*g*) applies. As Lord DENNING MR said in *Strand Securities Ltd v Caswell*:[17]

> Section 70 (1) (*g*) is an important provision. Fundamentally, its object is to protect a person in actual occupation of land from having his rights lost in the welter of registration. He can stay there and do nothing. Yet he will be protected. No one can buy the land over his head and thereby take away or diminish his rights. It is up to every purchaser before he buys to make inquiry on the premises. If he fails to do so, it is at his own risk. He must take subject to whatever rights the occupier may have. Such is the doctrine of *Hunt v Luck*,[18] for unregistered land. Section 70 (1) (*g*) carries the same doctrine forward into registered land . . .

But, as we shall see, paragraph (*g*) and the doctrine of *Hunt v Luck* are by no means identical.

C. COMPARISON OF UNREGISTERED AND REGISTERED SYSTEMS

We may now compare the position of a purchaser of the legal fee simple of Blackacre under the two systems of conveyancing. Under both systems he must satisfy himself on two separate matters: firstly, that the vendor is entitled to convey the fee simple, and, secondly, that there are no incumbrances in favour of third parties which will continue to bind the land after the conveyance.

As far as the first matter is concerned, the task of a purchaser is clearly simplified under the registered system. An investigation of the vendor's title deeds is replaced by a search of the register at the Land Registry. There is, however, no such clear cut difference in the matter of third party rights.

---

14 *Hodges v Jones* [1935] Ch 657 at 671, per LUXMOORE J; *De Lusignan v Johnson* (1973) 230 EG 499; LRA 1925, s. 59 (6). See, however, the much criticised decisions in *Peffer v Rigg* [1977] 1 WLR 285, [1978] 3 All ER 745; M & B p. 112; *Lyus v Prowsa Developments Ltd* [1982] 1 WLR 1044, [1982] 2 All ER 953; M & B p. 160; p. 801, n. 14, post.
15 See pp. 797–9, post.
16 LRA 1925, s. 3 (xvi). The relevant statutory protections then apply.
17 [1965] Ch 958 at 979–80, [1965] 1 All ER 820 at 826; see also RUSSELL LJ at 984, at 829.
18 [1902] 1 Ch 428. See p. 63, ante and p. 795, post.

Under the unregistered system since 1925, a purchaser must first search the Land Charges Register. He is bound by any registrable interests which have been registered at the time when he takes his conveyance from the vendor; if a registrable interest is not so registered, he takes free from it, even though he actually knows of its existence. Further, if the vendor is a tenant for life under a strict settlement or if the vendors are trustees for sale under a trust for sale, the purchaser takes free from the equitable interests of the beneficiaries under the doctrine of overreaching. Thirdly, under the unregistered system, a vendor is bound by certain rights which are neither registrable nor overreachable but which in the last resort can only be discovered by his own inquiries and inspection of Blackacre. These include: (*a*) legal third party rights, whether he knows about them or not, e.g. a legal estate, such as a lease, or a legal interest, such as a legal easement[19]; and (*b*) a residual category of equitable interests, unless he is a bona fide purchaser for value of the legal estate in Blackacre without actual or constructive notice, e.g. a pre-1926 restrictive covenant or a licence by estoppel.[20]

Under the registered system the position of a purchaser of Blackacre is different. On the one hand he is bound by minor interests which are entered on the register: if such an interest is not so entered, he takes free from it even though he actually knows of its existence. In this context an entry on the register has the same function that registration in the Land Charges Register has in unregistered conveyancing.[1] If, however, the vendor is a tenant for life or if the vendors are trustees for sale, the interests of the beneficiaries are also minor interests, but in these situations they will not bind a purchaser even when they have been protected by an entry on the register, because they will be overreached. On the other hand a purchaser is bound by overriding interests, even though he has no knowledge of them and even though they are not entered on the register. If they are entered, they cease to be overriding interests and take effect as minor interests. The statutory list in section 70 of the Land Registration Act 1925 is a collection of interests which it is held desirable to be binding on a purchaser but which, for some reason or another, do not fit into the pattern of the register. They are discoverable by, but only by, the purchaser's inspection of Blackacre and by inquiries which he must make without assistance from the register. As we have seen, they not only include legal rights which are familiar in unregistered conveyancing, e.g. legal easements and certain leases, but they also include the "rights of every person in actual occupation of the land or in receipt of the rents and profits thereof". It is this last category which may cause the kind of difficulty which was removed from unregistered conveyancing by the Land Charges Act 1925.

Thus in registered conveyancing there is no residual category of equitable interests to which the doctrine of the bona fide purchaser is applicable; that doctrine has been replaced by the provisions of the Land Registration Act 1925 for minor and overriding interests. Lord WILBERFORCE stated emphatically in *Williams and Glyn's Bank Ltd v Boland* that:

19 He is not bound by a puisne mortgage (any legal mortgage not being a mortgage protected by a deposit of documents relating to the legal estate affected) unless it is registered as a land charge; p. 95, ante, p. 720, post.
20 P. 97, n. 5, ante.
1 The provisions of the Land Charges Act 1972 are excluded from registered conveyancing; LRA 1925, s. 59; see also *Webb v Pollmount Ltd* [1966] Ch 584 at 599, [1966] 1 All ER 481 at 487, per UNGOED-THOMAS J.

the registered land system is designed to free the purchaser from the hazards of notice—real or constructive ... The only kind of notice recognised is by entry on the register;[2]

and PLOWMAN J, in *Parkash v Irani Finance Ltd*, found a plaintiff's reliance on the doctrine:

a little surprising, since one of the essential features of registration of title is to substitute a system of registration of rights for the doctrine of notice.[3]

The residual category of equitable interests, however, can exist under registered conveyancing, but any such interests which are not overriding interests must appear on the register if they are to bind a purchaser.[4]

Third party rights are treated differently under the two systems of conveyancing, and it is this different treatment that gives rise to differences in the substance of the land law; these differences we shall consider under the various topics in which they occur.[5]

2 [1981] AC 487 at 503, [1980] 2 All ER 408 at 412.
3 [1970] Ch 101 at 109, [1969] 1 All ER 930 at 933; *Hodgson v Marks* [1971] Ch 892, [1971] 2 All ER 684. But cf *Barclays Bank Ltd v Taylor* [1974] Ch 137, [1973] 1 All ER 752; M & B p. 809; p. 733, post; *Peffer v Rigg* [1977] 1 WLR 285, [1978] 3 All ER 745; M & B p. 112; *Lyus & Prowsa Developments Ltd* [1982] 1 WLR 1044 [1982] 2 All ER 953; M & B p. 160; p. 801, n. 14, post. See also CROSS J in *National Provincial Bank Ltd v Hastings Car Mart Ltd* [1964] Ch 9 at 16; *Miles v Bull (No 2)* [1969] 3 All ER 1585.
4 Pp. 606, 800 et seq, post.
5 See [1977] 41 Conv (NS) 405 (J. G. Riddall).

Chapter 6

Contract before conveyance[1]

SUMMARY

Section I Formation of contract 108
A. Open contract 108
B. Subject to contract 109
C. Lock-out agreement 110
D. Exchange of contracts 111

Section II Contracts made before 27 September 1989.
          Evidence of contract 111
A. Memorandum in writing 111
B. Act of part performance 117
C. Enforceability at law or in equity 121

Section III Contracts made after 26 September 1989.
          Requirement of writing 121

Section IV Effect of contract 124

Section V Option to purchase and right of pre-emption 127

Section VI Remedies of parties for breach of contract 129
A. Action for damages 129
B. Specific performance 133
C. Rescission 136
D. Rectification 138
E. Vendor and purchaser summons 139

A contract for the sale of land usually precedes the conveyance of the legal estate to the purchaser; and this is so whether the land is registered[2] or unregistered. Similarly, a contract for a lease may be made first, and then followed at a later date by a formal grant of the legal term of years absolute.[3] There are thus two distinct stages to be considered, the contract and the conveyance, and in this section we are concerned with the contract.

In 1990 the Council of the Law Society issued the National Conveyancing Protocol designed for use in domestic conveyancing of freehold and leasehold property. It sets out the steps to be followed by solicitors acting for the vendor

---

1 See generally Annand and Whish, *The Contract*; Barnsley, *Conveyancing Law and Practice* (3rd edn); *Emmet on Title* (19th edn); Farrand, *Contract and Conveyance* (4th edn). On the interpretation of contracts, see Lewison, *Interpretation of Contracts* (1989).
2 LRA 1925, s. 107 (1); Ruoff and Roper, *Registered Conveyancing*, para 15.04.
3 P. 374, post.

and purchaser, and its aim is to provide the purchaser's solicitor with as much information as possible about the property at the outset.[4]

SECTION I FORMATION OF CONTRACT

A contract for the sale or any other disposition of land is created in the same way as any other contract. There must be a final and complete agreement between the parties on its essential terms,[5] that is to say, the parties, the property, the consideration and, in the case of a lease, the commencement and the period of the tenancy.[6] If made before 27 September 1989, the contract is valid, even if oral, but, as we shall see, it will only be enforceable by action if it is evidenced by a signed memorandum in writing which complies with section 40 of the Law of Property Act 1925, or, failing that, if there is a sufficient act of part performance.

After 26 September 1989, this was superseded by section 2 of the Law of Property (Miscellaneous Provisions) Act 1989, under which there can be *no* contract unless it is in writing signed by or on behalf of both parties. The doctrine of part performance ceases to exist because there can be no oral contract to be partly performed.

A. OPEN CONTRACT

If a contract for the sale of land specifies merely the names of the parties, a description of the property and a statement of the price, it is called an *open contract*. When this form of contract is made, the parties are bound by certain obligations implied by the law. These implied obligations, as we shall see, impose a burdensome duty of proof of title upon the vendor, and in the majority of cases the vendor is anxious to produce the insertion in the written agreement of special stipulations, in order that his strict legal liability may be modified. The parties may incorporate into their contract such terms as they think fit, subject only to the rule that certain stipulations contrary to the policy of the law are void. Thus a stipulation that the conveyance shall be prepared at the expense of the purchaser by a solicitor appointed by the vendor is void.[7] In practice contracts for the sale of land are generally in standard form. The Law Society's Standard Conditions of Sale (Second Edition) 1992[8] contain standard forms of conditions and these are usually employed with such alterations as the parties may make to fit the particular

4 [1990] Conv 137 (H. W. Wilkinson). The Protocol (now in its third edition) is reproduced in *Emmet on Title*, Notes and Recommendations, pp. 93–119; Kenny, *Conveyancing Practice*, C.018–C030.
5 *Rossiter v Miller* (1878) 3 App Cas 1124 at 1151, per Lord BLACKBURN. See *Gibson v Manchester City Council* [1979] 1 WLR 294, [1979] 1 All ER 972; *Fletcher v Davies* (1980) 257 EG 1149 (flat in Inner Temple).
6 *Harvey v Pratt* [1965] 1 WLR 1025 at 1027, [1965] 2 All ER 786 at 788, per Lord DENNING MR; *James v Lock* (1977) 246 EG 395.
7 LPA 1925, s. 48 (1). See also s. 42.
8 Operative from 15 July 1992. They are reproduced in *Emmet on Title*, Practice Notes and Recommendations, p. 111. For explanatory notes by the Law Society, see (1992) 24 LSG 15. See also Aldridge, *Companion to the Standard Conditions of Sale* (1992); Silverman, *Standard Conditions of Sale* (4th edn); Wilkinson, *Standard Conditions of Sale of Land* (1980); [1990] Conv 179, [1992] Conv 316 (J. E. Adams).

transaction. Further, if the contract is made by correspondence, the Statutory Form of Conditions of Sale 1925 applies, except in so far as there is any modification or intention to the contrary expressed in the correspondence.[9]

DANCKWERTS LJ has referred to

the long-standing practice which has arisen among conveyancers of referring to the provisions in a contract for the sale of land as "conditions of sale", whether special or general (such as those provided by the common forms produced under the name of the National Conditions of Sale, or those produced by the Law Society). The word "condition" is traditional rather than appropriate, and these provisions are not so much concerned with the validity of the contract of sale as with the production of the title and the performance of the vendor's and purchaser's obligations leading up to completion by conveyance. Shortly, they are no more than the terms of the contract.[10]

B. SUBJECT TO CONTRACT

It is common practice in sales of land for the parties to agree a price "subject to contract".[11] The object of this procedure, "though it has drawbacks and is capable of being abused in certain circumstances, is based on a sound concept, namely, that the buyer should be free from binding commitment until he has had the opportunity of obtaining legal and other advice, arranging his finance and making the necessary inspections, searches and enquiries".[12] In 1975 the Law Commission recommended that there should be no change in this practice, even though one consequence is that the purchaser may be "gazumped" (i.e., the vendor may withdraw from the bargain or threaten to do so, in the expectation of receiving a higher price).[13]

The effect of such phrases as "subject to contract",[14] or "subject to a formal contract to be drawn up by our solicitors" is that there is no contract, unless there are some very exceptional circumstances necessitating a different construction.[15] Either party is free to repudiate the bargain until a formal contract has been made.

9 LPA 1925, s. 46; SR & O 1925 No. 779; *Stearn v Twitchell* [1985] 1 All ER 631 (contract arising out of acceptance by single letter of oral offer to buy or sell land held to be contract by correspondence). See (1974) 90 LQR 55 (A. M. Prichard).

10 *Property and Bloodstock Ltd v Emerton* [1968] Ch 94 at 118, [1967] 3 All ER 321 at 328.

11 See [1984] Conv 173, 251 (R. W. Clarke), comparing English and Irish Law. For its continued use in contracts after 26 September 1989, see p. 123 post.

12 Law Commission Report on "Subject to Contract" Agreements (Law Com No. 65, 1975), para 13. See *Cohen v Nessdale Ltd* [1981] 3 All ER 118 at 127–8; affd [1982] 2 All ER 97.

13 See the Law Commission Conveyancing Standing Committee's suggestion of a standard form of Pre-Contract Deposit Agreement, which would go some way towards deterring gazumping. It was called a paper-tiger: (1987) Times, 17 January, and has been abandoned: [1988] Conv. 79. See also the Committee's House Selling the Scottish Way for England and Wales (1987). Both are reproduced in *Emmet on Title* Practice Notes and Recommendations, pp. 10–15 and 37–49.

14 *Tiverton Estates Ltd v Wearwell Ltd* [1975] Ch 146, [1974] 1 All ER 209; *Munton v Greater London Council* [1976] 1 WLR 649, [1976] 2 All ER 815; *Sherbrooke v Dipple* (1980) 41 P & CR 173, [1981] Conv 165.

15 *Chillingworth v Esche* [1924] 1 Ch 97; *Alpenstow Ltd v Regalian Properties plc* [1985] 1 WLR 721, [1985] 2 All ER 545 (words "subject to contract" meaningless); *Westway Homes Ltd v Moores* [1991] 2 EGLR 193 (notice served by grantee of option to purchase headed "subject to contract" held to be surplusage and of no effect); *A-G of Hong Kong v Humphreys Estate (Queen's Gardens) Ltd* [1987] AC 114, [1987] 2 All ER 387 (estoppel "possible but unlikely" per Lord TEMPLEMAN at 127, at 395; M & B p. 71); *Salomon v Akiens* [1993] 1 EGLR 101; [1987] Conv 318.

Thus in *Winn v Bull*:[16]

a written agreement was entered into whereby the defendant agreed to take from the plaintiff a lease of a house for a certain time at a certain rent, "subject to the preparation and approval of a formal contract". No formal or other contract was ever entered into between the parties. It was held that there was no contract.

The parties may, however, be bound at once, although they intend to make a more formal contract later on. In *Branca v Cobarro*,[17] for example,

a written agreement to sell the lease and goodwill of a mushroom farm ended as follows: "This is a provisional agreement until a fully legalised agreement, drawn up by a solicitor and embodying all the conditions herewith stated, is signed". It was held by the Court of Appeal[18] that the parties, by using the word "provisional" had intended the document to be immediately binding and to remain so until superseded by a more formal document.

Finally we must notice that, where the parties have started their negotiations under a "subject to contract" formula, their later negotiations will continue to be qualified by it, unless and until they agree expressly or by necessary implication that the qualification should be expunged.[19]

C. LOCK-OUT AGREEMENT

As we have seen, a purchaser may be gazumped by a vendor (or a vendor by a purchaser) at any stage before completion. However he may avoid this hazard by entering into a lock-out agreement with the vendor, i.e. by making an agreement with him not to negotiate with any third party, provided that it is made for good consideration and a specified period of time. As Lord ACKNER said in *Walford v Miles*:[20]

See Wilkinson, *Standard Conditions of Sale of Land* (2nd edn), chapter 5 for a useful summary of standard conditional phrases; Barnsley, *Conveyancing Law and Practice*, pp. 129–135, (1975) 39 Conv (NS) 229–36, 311–13; *Emmet on Title* (19th edn), paras. 2.016–2.019. See for examples of valid phrases *Janmohamed v Hussam* (1976) 241 EG 609 ("subject to purchaser obtaining mortgage on terms satisfactory to himself within one month"); *Meehan v Jones* (1982) 56 ALJR 813; [1984] Conv 243; cf. *Lee-Parker v Izzet (No 2)* [1972] 1 WLR 775, [1972] 2 All ER 800; (1976) 40 Conv (NS) 37 (B. Coote); *Ee v Kakar* (1979) 40 P & CR 223 ("subject to survey"); (1981) 131 NLJ 771 (H. W. Wilkinson); *Duttons Brewery Ltd v Leeds City Council* (1981) 43 P & CR 160 ("at a price of £15,000 subject to a contract to be approved by me"); *Heron Garage Properties Ltd v Moss* [1974] 1 WLR 148, [1974] 1 All ER 421 ("conditional on purchaser obtaining detailed town planning consent"); cf. *Balbosa v Ayoub Ali* [1990] 1 WLR 914 ("subject to obtaining from the Town and Country Planning Department of all the necessary approvals for the transfer of the premises"); *Graham v Pitkin* [1992] 1 WLR 403, [1992] 2 All ER 235 ("subject to the purchaser obtaining a mortgage from [a building society] of $19,000 for 10 years"); [1992] Conv 318 (C. Harpum). See also *Provost Developments Ltd v Collingwood Towers Ltd* [1980] 2 NZLR 205 ("subject to a solicitor's approval"); [1981] Conv 90 (H. W. Wilkinson); Conv Prec pp. 8192–8195.

16 (1877) 7 Ch D 29.
17 [1947] KB 854, [1947] 2 All ER 101.
18 Reversing DENNING J, who construed "provisional" as equivalent to "tentative".
19 *Tevanan v Norman Brett (Builders) Ltd* (1972) 223 EG 1945 at 1947, per BRIGHTMAN J; *Sherbrooke v Dipple*, supra; *Cohen v Nessdale*, supra.
20 [1992] 2 AC 128 at 139, [1992] 1 All ER 453 at 461. In this case the agreement was void since it did not say for how long it was to last. Cf. *Pitt v PHH Asset Management Ltd* [1994] 1 WLR 327, [1993] 40 EG 149 (agreement whereby vendor agreed for valuable consideration not to negotiate with anyone else for 14 days held valid); [1993] CLJ 392 (C. MacMillan); [1994] Conv 58 (M. P. Thompson). A lock-out agreement does not have to satisfy the formalities required by LP (Miscellaneous Provisions) Act 1989, p. 123 post.

I stress that this is a negative agreement – B, by agreeing not to negotiate for a fixed period, locks himself out of such negotiations. He has in no legal sense locked himself into negotiations with A. What A has achieved is an exclusive opportunity, for a fixed period, to try to come to terms with B, an opportunity for which he has, unless he makes his agreement under seal, to give good consideration.

D. EXCHANGE OF CONTRACTS

Where a formal contract is drawn up, two copies are usually made, and each of the parties signs one of them. There is no binding contract until the copies have been physically exchanged.[1]

The Council of the Law Society has given advice on the various methods of exchange: Formulae A and B for exchange by telephone or telex, and Formula C for exchange in a chain of transactions.[2] The procedure may be adapted to an exchange by facsimile transmission (Fax).[3]

SECTION II   CONTRACTS MADE BEFORE 27 SEPTEMBER 1989. EVIDENCE OF CONTRACT

A. MEMORANDUM IN WRITING

Section 40 of the Law of Property Act 1925[4] provides that:

(1) No action may be brought upon any contract for the sale or other disposition of land or any interest in land, unless the agreement upon which such action is brought, or some memorandum or note thereof, is in writing and signed by the party to be charged or by some other person thereunto by him lawfully authorized.
(2) This section . . . does not affect the law relating to part performance.

It follows, therefore, that even when the parties are in complete accord upon all the terms of their agreement it will not be enforceable by either side in the absence of a sufficient memorandum or of an act of part performance as described later.[5]

---

1 *Trollope & Sons v Martyn Bros* [1934] 2 KB 436 at 455; *Eccles v Bryant and Pollock* [1948] Ch 93, [1947] 2 All ER 865; *Longman v Viscount Chelsea* (1989) 58 P & CR 189 at 190, per NOURSE LJ. If the exchange takes place by post the earliest date at which the contract is concluded is the date when the later of the two documents is posted; ibid,; *Harrison v Battye* [1975] 1 WLR 58, [1974] 3 All ER 830; cf *Smith v Mansi* [1963] 1 WLR 26, [1962] 3 All ER 857 (exchange unnecessary where there is only one document and the same solicitor acts for both vendor and purchaser); *Storer v Manchester City Council* [1974] 1 WLR 1403, [1974] 3 All ER 824; (1974) 38 Conv (NS) 385, 392; *Domb v Isoz* [1980] Ch 548, [1980] 1 All ER 942, (exchange by telephone); (1981) 78 LSG 961 (P. V. Baker and G. Woolf); *Brinkibon Ltd v Stahag GmbH* [1983] 2 AC 34, [1982] 1 All ER 293 (exchange by telex).
2 The Formulae are reproduced in *Emmet on Title*, Notes and Recommendations, pp. 8–9, 79–84A; Kenny, *Conveyancing Practice*, 4.082–4.097, C–010–041.
3 [1988] LS Gaz vol. 85.11; Kenny, F–005.
4 Replacing Statute of Frauds 1677, s. 4. For a detailed commentary, see Williams, *The Statute of Frauds, Section Four* (1932); Farrand, *Contract and Conveyance* (4th edn), pp. 321 et seq.; Barnsley, *Conveyancing Law and Practice*, pp. 105 et seq. For judicial criticism of the section, see *Wakeham v Mackenzie* [1968] 1 WLR 1175 at 1178, [1968] 2 All ER 783 at 785, per STAMP J; (1967) 31 Conv (NS) 182, 254 (H. W. Wilkinson) suggesting reform. See Law Commission Report on Formalities for Contracts of Sale etc. of Land 1987 (Law Com No. 164, HC 2). And for its relationship with part performance, see *Steadman v Steadman* [1974] QB 161 at 184, [1973] 3 All ER 977 at 995, per SCARMAN LJ.
5 P. 117 post.

(1) CONTRACTS WITHIN SECTION 40

The section applies to any contract for the sale or other disposition of land or any interest in land. This covers not only a contract for the sale of freehold land, but also includes a contract for the grant of a lease,[6] mortgage, easement or profit. It applies to a contract for the creation of a new interest in land as well as to a contract for the disposition of an existing interest; it also applies to a concluded unilateral contract to enter into a written contract for the sale of land.[7] Land is given a very wide definition in the Law of Property Act,[8] and has been held to include an interest in the proceeds of sale under a trust for sale of land.[9]

(2) CONTENTS OF MEMORANDUM

The contract itself need not be in writing. All that is required is that, before an action is brought, there should be a written memorandum containing not only the terms of the contract, but also an express or implied recognition that a contract was actually entered into. Thus, if an oral contract is followed by a writing which is expressed to be "subject to contract", there is no sufficient memorandum. As Lord DENNING MR said in *Tiverton Estates Ltd v Wearwell Ltd*:[10]

> I cannot myself see any difference between a writing which—(i) denies there was any contract; (ii) does not admit there was any contract; (iii) says that the parties are in negotiation; or (iv) says that there was an agreement "subject to contract", for that comes to the same thing. The reason why none of those writings satisfies the statute is because none of them contains any recognition or admission of the existence of a contract.

The memorandum may come into existence after the contract has been formed, and in *Barkworth v Young*[11] it was held that a memorandum made over fourteen years after the contract sufficed. It may even be made before the contract, where a written offer is accepted orally but unconditionally.[12]

The memorandum must contain not only the essential terms of the contract, that is to say, the names or adequate description of the parties, a

---

6 Cf LPA 1925, s. 54 (2) for the creation by parol of leases for a term not exceeding three years.
7 *Daulia Ltd v Four Millbank Nominees Ltd* [1978] Ch 231, [1978] 2 All ER 557. But it does not apply to compulsory purchase: *Munton v Greater London Council* [1976] 1 WLR 649, [1976] 2 All ER 815.
8 LPA 1925, s. 205 (1) (ix); p. 142, post.
9 *Cooper v Critchley* [1955] Ch 431, [1955] 1 All ER 520; M & B p. 294; *Steadman v Steadman* [1974] QB 161, [1973] 3 All ER 977, followed on this point without argument [1976] AC 536, [1974] 2 All ER 977; *Thompson's Trustee in Bankruptcy v Heaton* [1974] 1 WLR 605 at 610, [1974] 1 All ER 1239 at 1247.
10 [1975] Ch 146 at 160, [1974] 1 All ER 209 at 218. The Court of Appeal did not follow its own previous decision in *Law v Jones* [1974] Ch 112, [1973] 2 All ER 437 (holding that "subject to contract" was a suspensive condition capable of subsequent oral waiver); see the "explanatory observations" on *Law v Jones* by BUCKLEY LJ in *Daulia Ltd v Four Millbank Nominees Ltd*, supra, at 249, at 569; (1979) 95 LQR 7 (H. W. Wilkinson). See also *Griffiths v Young* [1970] Ch 675, [1970] 3 All ER 601; (1974) 38 Conv (NS) 127 (F. R. Crane); *Emmet on Title* (19th edn), para 2.017.
11 (1856) 4 Drew 1.
12 *Reuss v Picksley* (1866) LR 1 Exch 342; *Parker v Clark* [1960] 1 WLR 286, [1960] 1 All ER 93; *Tiverton Estates Ltd v Wearwell Ltd*, supra, at 166, at 222.

description of the property and the nature of the consideration, but also any other special terms deemed to be essential by the parties.[13]

There is this qualification, however, that:

> if a term is exclusively for the benefit of one party, that party may sometimes waive the benefit of it and sue on the contract for enforcement, even though the memorandum contains no evidence of that term.[14]

Further, if the oral term omitted from the memorandum is beneficial to the defendant, the plaintiff may submit to perform it and thus cure its omission from the memorandum.[15]

(3) CERTAINTY OF TERMS

The memorandum must either name the parties or describe them in such a manner that they can be identified without fair and reasonable dispute, and without resorting to parol evidence directly connected with the contract.

(a) Parties

If, for instance, the intending vendor is not named, but is referred to in the memorandum as the "proprietor" of the premises,[16] or as "executor"[17] or "trustee"[18] or "personal representative",[19] such description will suffice to satisfy the statute, since the identity of the person described can be easily ascertained; but if he were merely described as "the vendor",[20] or "landlord",[1] the memorandum would be useless, for the court would be driven to require parol evidence on the very point on which the statute requires written evidence.[2]

(b) Property

The same principle applies to the description of the property, which is the second point upon which the memorandum must furnish evidence. It is impossible to lay down beforehand what is a sufficient description of property, for, however detailed the expressions and even the plans may be, there is more often than not room for controversy,[3] but the general principle is—*id certum est quod certum reddi potest*,[4] and, provided that the

---

13 *Tiverton Estates Ltd v Wearwell Ltd*, supra, at 161, at 218; *Tweddell v Henderson* [1975] 1 WLR 1496, [1975] 2 All ER 1096.
14 *Hawkins v Price* [1947] Ch 645 at 659, [1947] 1 All ER 689 at 690, per EVERSHED J. The learned judge advisedly said "may *sometimes*", since it has been suggested (Fry, *Specific Performance* (6th edn), p. 243) that to be capable of waiver a term must be "of no great importance". If this vague test represents the law the result will surely be chaotic uncertainty. See also *Heron Garage Properties Ltd v Moss* [1974] 1 WLR 148, [1974] 1 All ER 421.
15 *Martin v Pycroft* (1852) 2 De GM & G 785; followed in *Scott v Bradley* [1971] Ch 850, [1971] 1 All ER 583, by PLOWMAN J in preference to *Burgess v Cox* [1951] Ch 383, [1950] 2 All ER 1212; (1951) 67 LQR 300 (R. E. M.); cf. *Topborough Ltd v Commodatos* [1993] EGCS 92.
16 *Rossiter v Miller* (1878) 3 App Cas 1124 at 1140.
17 *Hood v Lord Barrington* (1868) LR 6 Eq 218.
18 *Catling v King* (1877) 5 Ch D 660.
19 *Fay v Miller, Wilkins & Co* [1941] Ch 360, [1941] 2 All ER 18.
20 *Potter v Duffield* (1874) LR 18 Eq 4.
1 *Coombs v Wilkes* [1891] 3 Ch 77.
2 See *Sale v Lambert* (1874) LR 18 Eq 1; *Potter v Duffield* (1874) LR 18 Eq 4.
3 *Shardlow v Cotterell* (1881) 20 Ch D 90 at 93, per JESSEL MR.
4 *Plant v Bourne* [1897] 2 Ch 281 at 288.

memorandum furnishes something definite to go on, extrinsic evidence will be admitted to explain such descriptions as:

Mr Ogilvie's house,[5]

or

24 acres of land, freehold . . . at Totmonslow in the parish of Draycott, in the county of Stafford.[6]

Further, the whole of the property must be described in the memorandum, otherwise the entire contract will be unenforceable; thus an oral agreement for the sale of land and chattels together was held to be unenforceable where the only possible memorandum referred to the land.[7]

(c) Consideration

Thirdly, the memorandum must contain the consideration. This too must be stated with reasonable precision. Thus an option to purchase land "at a reasonable valuation" has been upheld as being sufficiently certain.[8]

(d) Contract for lease

Finally, in the case of a contract for a lease, the dates at which the tenancy is to begin and to end must appear in writing.

> It is settled beyond question that, in order for there to be a valid agreement for a lease, the essentials are not only for the parties to be determined, the property to be determined, the length of the term and the rent, but also the date of its commencement.[9]

The courts will not infer a stipulation that it is to commence within a reasonable time after the agreement.

(4) FORM OF MEMORANDUM

The memorandum need not be in any particular form, but may, for example, consist of a letter written by one of the parties to the other or to a third person, or of an affidavit or a will;[10] and it may also consist of a document that has been drawn up with the express intention of repudiating the parol agreement.[11] In fact any kind of signed document which contains all the essential terms that have been agreed between the parties will satisfy the statute.

(a) Signature

The signature must be that of "the party to be charged" or his agent, or, in other words, of the defendant in the action. If, therefore, in an agreement

---

5 *Ogilvie v Foljambe* (1817) 3 Mer 53.
6 *Plant v Bourne*, supra; *Auerbach v Nelson* [1919] 2 Ch 383.; *Harewood v Retese* [1990] 1 WLR 333.
7 *Ram Narayan s/o Shankar v Rishad Hussain Shah s/o Tasaduq Hussain Shah* [1979] 1 WLR 1349; *Hawkesworth v Turner* (1930) 46 TLR 389.
8 *Talbot v Talbot* [1968] Ch 1. See further p. 399, post.
9 *Harvey v Pratt* [1965] 1 WLR 1025 at 1027, [1965] 2 All ER 786 at 788, per Lord DENNING MR; *James v Lock* (1977) 246 EG 395.
10 *Re Holland* [1902] 2 Ch 360 at 383.
11 *Bailey v Sweeting* (1861) 9 CBNS 843; *Dewar v Mintoft* [1912] 2 KB 373.

between A and B the memorandum is signed by A only, it follows that B can enforce the contract, but that A cannot.[12] The signature need not be a subscription written at the foot of the agreement, but may appear anywhere, provided that it was written with the view of governing the whole instrument.[13] Indeed, the signature may consist merely of the defendant's initials[14] or of his printed name,[15] provided that the intention clearly is to authenticate the document.[16]

(b) Authority of agent to sign

An agent is "lawfully authorized" to sign the memorandum on behalf of his principal if his authority to do so has been conferred upon him in writing or orally, or if it is reasonably inferable from the attendant circumstances[17] and especially from his instructions. For instance:

> the mere appointment by an owner of an estate agent to dispose of a house confers no authority to make a contract; the agent is solely employed to find persons to negotiate with the owner; but, if the agent is definitely instructed to sell at a defined price, those instructions involve authority to make a binding contract and to sign an agreement.[18]

Where there is a sale by auction, the auctioneer becomes the agent of both parties upon the fall of the hammer. He derives his authority to act for the vendor from his instructions to sell, while his authority to sign on behalf of the purchaser is implied from the bid.[19] If, therefore, he signs a memorandum, either at the time of the sale or so soon afterwards that his signature can reasonably be regarded as part of the transaction of sale, the memorandum is binding upon both parties.[20]

(5) JOINDER OF DOCUMENTS

When the terms of the agreement are contained not in one, but in several documents, the difficult question often arises whether parol evidence is admissible to connect one document with another. Suppose, for instance, that:

> an intending lessee A has signed a document containing all the terms of the agreement and has paid a quarter's rent in advance. The other party, B, has not signed the written agreement, but has signed a receipt for the rent in the following terms:
>
> > "Received of A £30, being payment of one quarter's rent in respect of the house at Hammersmith."
>
> A cannot sue on the first document alone since it does not contain B's signature; nor on the receipt, because for one reason, though implicitly referring to a lease, it

---

12 *Laythoarp v Bryant* (1836) 2 Bing NC 735.
13 Cf *Johnson v Dodgson* (1837) 2 M & W 653; cf *Caton v Caton* (1867) LR 2 HL 127.
14 *Hill v Hill* [1947] Ch 231, [1947] 1 All ER 54.
15 Cf *Cohen v Roche* [1927] 1 KB 169; *Leeman v Stocks* [1951] Ch 941, [1951] 1 All ER 1043.
16 A further signature may be necessary if the memorandum is altered after the original signature. See *New Hart Builders Ltd v Brindley* [1975] Ch 342, [1975] 1 All ER 1007; (1975) 39 Conv (NS) 376 (C. T. Emery).
17 *Davies v Sweet* [1962] 2 QB 300 at 305, [1962] 1 All ER 92 at 94.
18 *Keen v Mear* [1920] 2 Ch 574 at 579, per ROMER J.
19 *Emmerson v Heelis* (1809) 2 Taunt 38.
20 *Bell v Balls* [1897] 1 Ch 663; *Chaney v Maclow* [1929] 1 Ch 461; *Phillips v Butler* [1945] Ch 358, [1945] 2 All ER 258.

does not state when it is to begin and end.[1] But if A is allowed to adduce parol evidence with a view to showing that the receipt is connected with and should be read with the memorandum, then taking the two together he will have a complete memorandum containing all that the statute requires.

In such a case, it has long been established that, if one document expressly refers to another, the latter can be put in evidence, but as the authorities now stand an implicit reference is also regarded as sufficient.[2]

The present law was stated by JENKINS LJ in *Timmins v Moreland Street Property Co Ltd*:[3]

> I think it is still indispensably necessary, in order to justify the reading of documents together for this purpose, that there should be a document signed by the party to be charged, which, while not containing in itself all the necessary ingredients of the required memorandum, does contain some reference, express or implied, to some other document or transaction. Where any such reference can be spelt out of a document so signed, then parol evidence may be given to identify the other document referred to, or, as the case may be, to explain the other transaction, and to identify any document relating to it. If by this process a document is brought to light which contains in writing all the terms of the bargain so far as not contained in the document signed by the party to be charged, then the two documents can be read together so as to constitute a sufficient memorandum for the purposes of section 40.

Suppose, for instance, that two parties to an agreement for a lease insert a carbon paper into a typewriter and type the following:

> I agree to take a lease of 50 High Street for five years at £100 a year from 25 December 1975, and to pay £25 by way of rent in advance.

"I", i.e. the tenant, signs the top paper; the landlord signs the carbon copy and also signs a receipt for £25. If, now, the tenant sues for specific performance he is met by a difficulty, for he cannot rely upon the carbon copy signed by the defendant, since it contains no description of "I." If, however, there is an implicit reference in the carbon copy to some document which describes "I", there is sufficient written evidence of the necessary terms. It is clear that the implicit reference exists in at least two forms, since the carbon copy indicates that there is (*a*) the original writing of which the carbon is a duplicate, and (*b*) a transaction connected with the payment of £25. This transaction may be represented by a document, e.g. a cheque signed by the plaintiff, and it is open to the plaintiff to show that it is so in fact.[4]

Under this rule the hypothetical agreement suggested above would be enforceable by the tenant against the landlord.

1 Cf. *Long v Millar* (1879) 4 CPD 450.
2 *Baumann v James* (1868) 3 Ch App 508; *Hill v Hill* [1947] Ch 231, [1947] 1 All ER 54.
3 [1958] Ch 110 at 130, [1957] 3 All ER 265 at 276; *Elias v George Sahely & Co (Barbados) Ltd* [1983] 1 AC 646, [1982] 3 All ER 801, where PC accepted this passage as a correct statement of the modern law.
4 This hypothetical case is based upon *Stokes v Whicher* [1920] 1 Ch 411, which was distinguished in *Timmins v Moreland Street Property Co Ltd* [1958] Ch 110, [1957] 3 All ER 265. See too *Fowler v Bratt* [1950] 2 KB 96, [1950] 1 All ER 662; *LD Turner Ltd v RS Hatton (Bradford) Ltd* [1952] 1 All ER 1286.

(6) EFFECT OF NON-COMPLIANCE

The effect of non-compliance with section 40 is not to invalidate the contract, but merely to prevent a party from bringing an action for damages or a claim for specific performance. The contract is valid, but unenforceable by action.[5] It may however be indirectly enforced. Thus if a purchaser defaults, the vendor may forfeit, or keep, a deposit, which has been paid under an oral contract.[6] Conversely, if a vendor defaults, the purchaser can recover his deposit by a claim in quasi-contract on a total failure of consideration.[7]

B. ACT OF PART PERFORMANCE

(1) BASIS OF PART PERFORMANCE[8]

It now remains to be noticed that even though there is no memorandum under the Law of Property Act 1925, yet, if there has been an oral contract followed by a sufficient act of part performance, the result in equity is in effect to exclude the operation of the statute. The attitude adopted by equity is that it would be fraudulent for a defendant to take advantage of the absence of a signed memorandum if he has stood by and allowed the plaintiff to alter his position for the worse by carrying out acts in performance of the contract.

If, for instance, B has orally agreed to let premises to A, and if A goes into actual possession of and improves the premises, it would be fraudulent, or at least inequitable, for B to refuse to implement his bargain on the ground that a sufficient memorandum was lacking.[9] Equity therefore grants a decree of specific performance of the contract against B. In doing this, however, it does not charge him on the contract itself, but holds him liable upon the equities arising from the changed position in which A finds himself.[10] A has prejudiced himself by acting on the assumption that B would carry out the bargain, and the fact that he has been allowed to do this gives him an undoubted equity against B. Upon proof of his act of part performance, therefore, he is allowed by equity to give parol evidence of an agreement that would otherwise require written evidence. If he satisfies the court in these two respects, he is entitled to a decree ordering the other party to execute a formal lease to include the terms which have been agreed upon.

(2) ELEMENTS OF PART PERFORMANCE

(a) Nature of the act

The crucial question is—what is an act of part performance? Although one of the parties may have done several things towards performing his side of the agreement, it does not at all follow that they will amount to part

---

5 *Leroux v Brown* (1852) 12 CB 801; *Maddison v Alderson* (1883) 8 App Cas 467 at 474, per Lord SELBORNE LC; *Delaney v TP Smith Ltd* [1946] KB 393, [1946] 2 All ER 23. If s. 40 is not pleaded by the defence, the court has discretion to allow pleadings to be amended: *Re Gonin* [1979] Ch 16, [1977] 2 All ER 720.
6 *Monnickendam v Leanse* (1923) 39 TLR 445.
7 *Pulbrook v Lawes* (1876) 1 QBD 284.
8 The doctrine is recognised and preserved by LPA 1925, ss. 40 (2), 55 (*d*).
9 *Caton v Caton* (1865) 1 Ch App 137 at 148, per Lord CRANWORTH.
10 *Maddison v Alderson* (1883) 8 App Cas 467 at 475, per Lord SELBORNE.

performance. The act must of itself on a balance of probability[11] establish the existence of the oral contract. It must be an act which is intelligible only on the assumption that some such contract as that alleged has been made, and if it is explicable on some other equally good ground, it does not satisfy the test. Further, there may be more than one act, and the acts when joined together "may throw light on each other; and there is no reason to exclude light".[12] The flexibility of this approach is enhanced when even "spoken words may themselves be part performance of a contract".[13]

(i) Possession A change of possession is, in the majority of cases, associated with the doctrine. Entry into possession is clearly sufficient. If, for instance, A is found to be in actual possession of land which has hitherto been owned and occupied by B, the only reasonable explanation of this change of possession is that the parties have entered into some contract, either of sale or lease, with regard to the land. Entry into possession, therefore, is an act of part performance, and if B resists a suit for specific performance by relying upon the absence of a written memorandum, A will be permitted to show by parol evidence what the actual contract was.[14]

On the other hand, remaining in possession, unless there are additional circumstances, is not sufficient. If A is the tenant in possession of lands under a lease which expires on 25 December, the mere fact that he is still in possession on 1 January is not sufficiently unequivocal to found a suit for specific performance of a parol agreement to grant him a new lease.

The possibility that the landlord has entered into a new contract relating to the land is certainly one explanation of A's continuance in possession, but it is not the only explanation. There are others equally good, as, for instance, that he refuses to go or that he has been given a few days' grace. But if, in addition to remaining in possession after the proper date, A begins to pay rent at a higher rate than under the old lease,[15] or if he spends money with the approval of the landlord on the improvement of the premises,[16] the requirement of part performance is satisfied, for what he has done is explicable only on the assumption that the landlord has agreed to grant a new lease. If the act relied upon by the plaintiff clearly refers to the type of contract that he seeks to prove, the fact that some ingenious mind might suggest a different explanation will not avail the defendant.[17]

Although possession generally forms the basis of a claim under the doctrine, this is not necessarily so. Thus in *Rawlinson v Ames*,[18]

> the defendant entered into an oral contract with the plaintiff to take a lease of a flat, part of the contract being that certain alterations should be made by the plaintiff. During the progress of the alterations the defendant frequently visited the flat and made suggestions as to the manner in which the work should be done. Her suggestions were carried out, and when, on the completion of the work, she repudiated the contract, she was adjudged liable in a suit for specific performance.

---

11 *Steadman v Steadman* [1976] AC 536 at 564–5, [1974] 2 All ER 977 at 1001, per Lord SIMON OF GLAISDALE and at 541–2, at 982, per Lord REID.
12 *Steadman v Steadman*, supra, at 564, at 1001, per Lord SIMON OF GLAISDALE.
13 Ibid.
14 *Morphett v Jones* (1818) 1 Swan 172; *Brough v Nettleton* [1921] 2 Ch 25; *Kingswood Estate Co Ltd v Anderson* [1963] 2 QB 169, [1962] 3 All ER 593.
15 *Miller and Aldworth v Sharp* [1899] 1 Ch 622.
16 *Nunn v Fabian* (1865) 1 Ch App 35.
17 Cf *Broughton v Snook* [1938] Ch 505, [1938] 1 All ER 411.
18 [1925] Ch 96; *Dickinson v Barrow* [1904] 2 Ch 339.

The submission of the plaintiff to interference by the defendant and the adoption of her suggestions were plainly referable to a contract relating to the premises.

A number of further questions arise from the decision of the House of Lords in *Steadman v Steadman*.[19] In that case:

a husband and wife, whose marriage had broken down, entered into an "oral package deal" by way of compromise. The wife would surrender to the husband her half interest in the matrimonial home for £1,500; the husband would pay £100 in respect of arrears of maintenance, and the maintenance order in favour of the wife would be discharged. This oral contract was made the subject of an order by the magistrates. The husband paid £100, and his solicitor prepared and sent a deed of transfer of the wife's interest to her for signature. The wife then refused to complete and relied upon the fact that the contract was oral and therefore unenforceable under section 40. The House of Lords held by a majority of four to one that both the payment of the £100 and the preparation and sending of the deed to transfer were sufficient acts of part performance, and, accordingly, ordered specific performance of the contract against the wife.

(ii) Referability to contract It will be seen that the acts performed by the husband did not of themselves prove the precise terms of the contract. It used to be said that the acts must be unequivocally referable to the contract. This strict rule was modified in *Kingswood Estate Co Ltd v Anderson*, and there was unanimous approval in *Steadman v Steadman* of UPJOHN LJ's statement[20] in that case:

The true rule is in my view stated in Fry on Specific Performance, 6th ed, p. 278, section 582: "The true principle, however, of the operation of acts of part performance seems only to require that the acts in question be such as must be referred to some contract, and may be referred to the alleged one; that they prove the existence of some contract, and are consistent with the contract alleged."

Accordingly, no act done in furtherance of an oral contract will satisfy the requirements of part performance unless it is one which demonstrates that *some* contract has been made. It need not refer to the precise terms of the contract upon which the plaintiff relies.[1]

(iii) Reference to land Even though it may not be necessary for the act of part performance to indicate the terms of the contract, it was argued in *Steadman v Steadman* that the act must at least be such as to show that there was a contract relating to land; and, in particular, the question arose whether if an oral contract contains several terms, but only one of which deals with an interest in land, it is sufficient that there has been part performance only of one or more of the *other* terms. Various opinions were expressed. Lord SALMON and Lord MORRIS OF BORTH-Y-GEST said that the act must indicate the term of the contract which concerns the disposition of an interest in

19 [1976] AC 536, [1974] 2 All ER 977; *Re Windle* [1975] 1 WLR 1628, [1975] 3 All ER 987.
20 [1963] 2 QB 169 at 189, [1962] 3 All ER 593 at 604; *Wakeham v Mackenzie* [1968] 1 WLR 1175, [1968] 2 All ER 783; *New Hart Builders Ltd v Brindley* [1975] Ch 342, [1975] 1 All ER 1007.
 1 In *Elsden v Pick* [1980] 1 WLR 898 at 905, [1980] 3 All ER 235 at 240, SHAW LJ said that the act relied on "must be in furtherance of the contract and not merely a recognition of its existence or of its contemplation" but need not amount to "the discharge of any primary obligation imposed by it".

land;[2] Lord REID and Viscount DILHORNE took the opposite view,[3] and Lord SIMON OF GLAISDALE found it unnecessary to determine the point because there were acts of part performance which specifically indicated the land in question.[4]

(iv) Payment of money Before *Steadman v Steadman* it was sometimes said that payment of money could never be a sufficient act of part performance.[5] This view, however, was decisively rejected by a majority of the House of Lords in that case.[6]

There may be many cases where the payment of money is an equivocal act. The *mere* payment of money without any admissible evidence of the surrounding circumstances need not imply a pre-existing oral contract; the payment is equally consistent with other hypotheses. But as *Steadman v Steadman* shows, such evidence may be admissible. Lord SALMON said:[7]

> The circumstances surrounding a payment may be such that the payment becomes evidence not only of the existence of the contract under which it was made but also of the nature of the contract . . . There is no rule of law which excludes evidence of the relevant circumstances surrounding the payment—save parol evidence of the contract on behalf of the person seeking to enforce the contract under which the payment is alleged to have been made . . . The wife's admission in open court plainly connected the payment of the £100 with the parol agreement relating to the disposition of an interest in land and showed that the payment was in part performance of that agreement. She has not repaid or ever offered to repay any part of the £100. This payment, in my opinion, bars the wife from relying on the statute and she is accordingly bound to perform her part of the agreement.

In summary, it is clear that the payment of money is not *per se* an act of part performance. But it would seem that, if it is paid in such circumstances that the payee is unwilling or unable to restore it (as, for instance, if he is insolvent), the mischief aimed at by the statute disappears, and the payment may be a sufficient act.

In *Re Windle*,[8] where there was an oral contract between husband and

---

2 *Steadman v Steadman* [1976] AC 536 at 567–70 and 547, [1974] 2 All ER 977 at 1003–6 and 986, respectively (Lord MORRIS OF BORTH-Y-GEST dissented). This view was followed by WALTON J in *Re Gonin* [1979] Ch 16 at 31, [1977] 2 All ER 720 at 731; [1979] Conv 402 (M. P. Thompson).

3 Ibid., at 541–2 and 554, at 982 and 992, respectively.

4 Ibid., at 562–3, at 999–1000.

5 *Thursby v Eccles* (1900) 49 WR 281; *Chapr’onière v Lambert* [1917] 2 Ch 356.

6 See (1974) 38 Conv (NS) 354 (F. R. Crane); 90 LQR 433 (H. W. R. Wade).

7 *Steadman v Steadman*, supra, at 570, 573, at 1006, 1008. See the two examples given at 570–1, at 1006–7; and Lord SIMON OF GLAISDALE at 565, at 1001–2.

8 [1975] 1 WLR 1628, [1975] 3 All ER 987. For other insufficient acts of part performance, see *New Hart Builders Ltd v Brindley* [1975] Ch 342, [1975] 1 All ER 1007 (submission by purchasers of application for planning permission); *Re Gonin* [1979] Ch 16, [1977] 2 All ER 720 (unmarried daughter's returning home after compassionate release from wartime service to look after ageing parents); *Daulia Ltd v Four Millbank Nominees Ltd* [1978] Ch 231, [1978] 2 All ER 557 (purchasers' tender of draft contract together with banker's draft for deposit); cf *Cohen v Nessdale* [1981] 3 All ER 118 (payment of one year's ground rent would have been sufficient act, if there had been final agreement); affd [1982] 2 All ER 97 (where the point was not considered). See *Take Harvest Ltd v Liu* [1993] AC 552, [1993] 2 All ER 459, where Sir Christopher SLADE said at 800: "The mere vacation by a tenant of the tenanted property cannot, by itself and without more, constitute an act of part performance because viewed in isolation it is equally consistent with the existence or non-existence of a contract to surrender the tenancy."

For sufficient acts of part performance, see *Liddell v Hopkinson* (1974) 233 EG 513 (vacation of matrimonial home by divorced wife so that husband could sell it, in return for wife for the transfer of property, GOFF J applied the principles of *Steadman v Steadman* and held that instructions to solicitors to prepare the transfer and the payment of their costs and disbursements were sufficient acts of part performance, but that the payment of mortgage arrears and instalments was not.

(b) Act by the plaintiff

Since the basis of the doctrine of part performance is that the plaintiff, having altered his position on the faith of the contract, acquires an equity against the defendant, it follows that the part performance must be by the plaintiff.

C. ENFORCEABILITY AT LAW OR IN EQUITY

It is important to observe that a person who is compelled to base his action on part performance is not in such a favourable position as one who can produce a memorandum satisfying all the requirements of the statute. If the plaintiff relies on a memorandum and proves his case, he is entitled as of right to an award of damages at common law: he may also be able to obtain a decree of specific performance in equity, but if for some reason, such as undue delay in seeking relief, he cannot obtain one, then he is limited to the recovery of damages only. On the other hand if he relies solely on part performance, he must show that the contract is one for which the court has jurisdiction to grant specific performance,[9] otherwise he is remediless, common law damages not being available. That is not to say that a plaintiff who relies on part performance will never recover damages. For Lord Cairns' Act 1858[10] gave to the Court of Chancery power to award damages either in addition to[11] or in substitution for specific performance. This includes a situation where no damages would be available at common law, as where the plaintiff relies on part performance, and is available even where a decree of specific performance would be refused on some discretionary ground. The damages are assessed in the same way as they would be at common law.[12]

SECTION III CONTRACTS MADE AFTER 26 SEPTEMBER 1989. REQUIREMENT OF WRITING

Section 2 of the Law of Property (Miscellaneous Provisions) Act 1989[13] provides as follows:

his offer of two-thirds of proceeds of sale if she would give up her right of occupation); *Sutton v Sutton* [1984] Ch 184, [1984] 1 All ER 168 (wife's consent to divorce on terms that matrimonial home be conveyed to her); *Dakin v Dakin* [1990] EGCS 45 (father's signing of draft conveyance as a result of son's deceit).

9 See *Lavery v Pursell* (1888) 39 Ch D 508 at 519; *Price v Strange* [1978] Ch 337, [1977] 3 All ER 371 (lack of mutuality does not deprive court of jurisdiction to grant specific performance).

10 Chancery Amendment Act 1858, s. 2; now Supreme Court Act 1981, s. 50. See (1975) 34 CLJ 224 (J. A. Jolowicz).

11 *Grant v Dawkins* [1973] 1 WLR 1406, [1973] 3 All ER 897.

12 *Johnson v Agnew* [1980] AC 367, [1979] 1 All ER 883; p. 133, post.

13 This was based on Law Commission Report on Formalities for Contracts of Sale etc. of Land 1987 (Law Com No. 164, HC 2); [1987] Conv 313; [1987] Conv 71. For the changes, see *Emmet on Title*, para. 2.037; Kenny, *Conveyancing Practice*, paras. 4.040–4.046; and generally (1989) 105 LQR 555 (R. E. Annand); [1989] Conv 431 (P. H. Pettit).

A contract for the sale or other disposition of an interest in land can only be made in writing and only by incorporating all the terms which the parties have expressly agreed in one document, or where contracts are exchanged, in both.

It follows, therefore, that, if the requirements as to writing are not complied with, there is *no* contract. This is a major change from the position under section 40 of the Law of Property Act 1925, where, as we have seen, non-compliance meant that the contract was merely unenforceable by action.

Although section 40 has been repealed, decisions on that section may still be relevant in interpreting section 2.

(1) CONTRACTS WITHIN SECTION 2

Section 2, like section 40, applies to any contract for the sale or other disposition of an interest in land. There are three exceptions:[14]

(a) a contract to grant a lease for a term not exceeding three years to which section 54 (2) of the Law of Property Act 1925 applies;[15]
(b) a contract made in the course of a public auction;
(c) a contract regulated under the Financial Services Act 1986.[16]

(2) INTERESTS IN LAND

Interests in land are widely defined as meaning:

any estate, interest or charge in or over land or in or over the proceeds of sale of land.

Accordingly, interests under a trust for sale are within section 2, thus following their inclusion under section 40 by judicial interpretation.[17]

(3) THE WRITING REQUIRED

The writing requirements are as follows:

(a)   The contract must incorporate all the terms which the parties have expressly agreed in one document or, where contracts are exchanged, in each.[17a]

This does not extend to terms implied by law, such as a term that where there is a sale with vacant possession, vacant possession must be given on completion.

(b)   The terms may be incorporated in a document either by being set out in it or by reference to some other document.

This provision differs from that for joinder of documents under section 40, where there could be joinder if there was an express or implied reference in a signed memorandum to some other document or transaction. The rule under section 2 is narrower in that it requires reference to some other document. It

14 S. 2(5). Nothing in the section affects the creation or operation of resulting, implied or constructive trusts: s. 2(5) (c).
15 P. 374, post. Such a contract was within s. 40.
16 Otherwise some forms of investment which include interests in land, such as unit trusts, would be within s. 2.
17 *Cooper v Critchley* [1955] Ch 431, [1955] 1 All ER 520; M & B p. 294, p. 236 post; *Steadman v Steadman* [1974] QB 161, [1973] 3 All ER 977.
17a *Milton Keynes Development Corpn v Cooper (Great Britain) Ltd* [1993] EGCS 142 (exchange of facsimiles held not to be contract or exchange of contracts).

is not clear whether that reference must be express or whether it can be implied.

(c) The document incorporating the terms, or where contracts are exchanged, one of the documents incorporating them (but not necessarily the same one) must be signed by or on behalf of each party to the contract.

Each party to the contract must sign. This is a marked change from the position under section 40, where, if there was only one signed memorandum, the contract could only be enforced by one party but not by the other. If a party does not himself sign the document, someone else may be authorised to sign on his behalf.

(d) If the court rectifies a document so that it comes within the scope of section 2 the contract shall come into being, or be deemed to have come into being, at such time as may be specified in the order.[17b]

(4) JUDICIAL INTERPRETATION OF SCOPE OF SECTION 2

Section 2 has so far been purposively interpreted by the courts, which have rejected technical arguments based upon it. As HOFFMANN J said:[18]

> The section was intended to prevent disputes over whether the parties had entered into a binding agreement or over what terms they had agreed.

The section has been held not to apply to:

(a) the exercise of an option to purchase land.[19] If the agreement under which the option is granted itself satisfies the requirements of the section, then the notice which exercises the option need not do so.

(b) a collateral contract. In *Record v Bell*:[20]

> before signed contracts were exchanged, the vendor offered to the purchaser a warranty as to the state of his title in order to induce him to exchange. This warranty was referred to in a side-letter which was attached to the contract, but which was only signed by the purchaser. It was held that the side-letter had not been incorporated into the main contract (there was no reference to it there), but that there was a collateral contract which fell outside section 2.

(c) an agreement which is supplemental to a contract, which has been duly carried out, and is therefore no longer executory.[1]

(5) CONTINUED USE OF "SUBJECT TO CONTRACT"

It would seem at first sight that the practice of heading pre-contract correspondence with the phrase "subject to contract" is no longer necessary, since no contract can come into existence until a document is signed by both parties. However, it is considered advisable to continue its use for two

---

17b *Wright v Robert Leonard (Developments) Ltd* [1994] EGCS 69 (contract rectified where parties failed to incorporate all terms as required by s. 2 (*a*)).
18 *Spiro v Glencrown Properties Ltd* [1991] Ch 537 at 541, [1991] 1 All ER 600 at 602; M & B p. 84.
19 Ibid., p. 127, post.
20 [1991] 1 WLR 853; (1991) 108 LQR 217 (R. J. Smith); [1991] CLJ 399 (C. Harpum); [1991] Conv 471 (M. Harwood); [1991] All ER Rev. 201 (P. J. Clarke). See also *Pitt v PHH Asset Management Ltd* [1994] 1 WLR 327, p. 110, ante (lock-out agreement).
 1 *Tootall Clothing Ltd v Guinea Properties and Management Ltd* [1992] 41 EG 117; 1993] Conv 89 (P. Luther); (1993) 109 LQR 191 (D. Wilde).

reasons. Firstly "it has a useful *aide memoire* effect in drawing a clear distinction in practice between the work preceding exchange of contracts and the work following exchange of contracts. It will serve as a useful reminder of the steps to be taken to exchange contracts. Secondly, there is the possibility that an exchange of letters (incorporating by reference the contractual terms) may amount to an exchange of contracts."[2]

(6) EFFECT OF ABOLITION OF PART PERFORMANCE

As we have seen, the doctrine of part performance supplemented the provisions of section 40 and enabled an oral contract to be enforceable in equity.[3] Under section 2 the doctrine is no longer available. However, other equitable doctrines, such as promissory or proprietary estoppel, may provide effective substitutes. In *Du Boulay v Raggett*[4] part performance was used as an alternative ground to reliance on the absence of writing being unconscionable.

SECTION IV EFFECT OF CONTRACT[5]

(1) VENDOR AS TRUSTEE FOR PURCHASER

If a contract for sale is capable of specific performance, an immediate equitable interest in the land passes to the purchaser. The legal estate remains in the vendor until the conveyance has been executed, but meanwhile equity regards the vendor as a trustee for the purchaser, and is prepared to decree specific performance at the instance of the latter.[6] In the words of JESSEL MR[7]

> The moment you have a valid contract for sale the vendor becomes in equity a trustee for the purchaser of the estate sold, and the beneficial ownership passes to the purchaser, the vendor having a right to the purchase money, a charge or lien on the estate for the security of that purchase money, and a right to retain possession of the estate until the purchase money is paid, in the absence of express contract as to the time of delivering possession.

Thus, for instance, pending completion the purchaser may dispose of his

2 Kenny, *Conveyancing Practice*, 4–044.
3 P. 117, ante.
4 (1988) 58 P & CR 138. See Law Commission Report on Formalities for Contracts for Sale etc. of Land 1987 (Law Com No. 164, HC 2), paras. 5.4–5.5; (1990) 10 LS 325 (L. Bently and P. Coughlan); (1990) 134 SJ 72 (P. Rank); *Kingswood v Estate Co Ltd v Anderson* [1963] 2 QB 169 at 179, [1963] 3 All ER 593 at 598, per WILMER LJ (promissory estoppel); *Lim Teng Huan v Ang Swee Chuan* [1992] 1 WLR 113 (agreement for transfer of land, although void for uncertainty, held to be evidence of parties' intentions and to give rise to proprietary estoppel); p. 597, post. See also *A-G of Hong Kong v Humphreys Estate (Queen's Gardens) Ltd.* [1987] AC 114, [1987] 2 All ER 387 at 395; M & B p. 71, per Lord TEMPLEMAN; *Saloman v Akiens* [1993] 1 EGLR 101.
5 See H & M, pp. 317–320; Farrand, *Contract and Conveyance* (4th edn), pp. 163–173; Barnsley, *Conveyancing Law and Practice* (3rd edn), pp. 228–232; Oakley, *Constructive Trusts* (2nd edn), chapter 6.
6 *Shaw v Foster* (1872) LR 5 HL 321 at 333, 338; *Howard v Miller* [1915] AC 318 at 326. There may be a decree, even though, between contract and completion, a compulsory purchase order has been made by a local authority: *Hillingdon Estates Co v Stonefield Estates Ltd* [1952] Ch 627, [1952] 1 All ER 85.
7 *Lysaght v Edwards* (1876) 2 Ch D 499 at 506; *Lake v Bayliss* [1974] 1 WLR 1073, [1974] 2 All ER 1114.

equitable interest by sale or otherwise; he becomes owner of the rents and profits which fall due after the time fixed for completion; and he can demand an occupation rent if the vendor remains in possession after that time.

On the other hand, as from the date of the contract, unless it otherwise provides, the purchaser must bear the risk of any loss or damage suffered by the property, as, for instance, from an accidental fire or from a fall in price; and from the date fixed for completion he must meet the cost of all necessary outgoings.

(a) Vendor's rights

Pending the completion of the sale, the vendor occupies a fiduciary position, and therefore he must manage and preserve the property with the same care as a trustee must show with regard to trust property. He must, for instance, relet the premises if an existing lease runs out, but before doing so he must consult the purchaser.[8] Nevertheless, the vendor is not an ordinary trustee, since he possesses certain rights of a valuable nature in the land, which he is entitled to protect on his own behalf. Thus:

(i) he has a right to remain in possession until the purchase money is paid, and to protect that possession, if necessary, by the maintenance of an action, though while in possession he is under a duty to maintain the property in a reasonable state of preservation and so far as may be in the state in which it was when the contract was made;[9]

(ii) he is entitled to take the rents and profits of the land[10] until the time fixed for completion; and

(iii) he possesses an equitable lien on the property for the amount of the purchase money. An equitable lien is in the nature of a charge on land and entitles the person in whom it resides to apply to the court for a sale of the property in satisfaction of his claim. Unlike a common law lien, it is not dependent on possession.[11]

Although the equitable ownership has passed to the purchaser, the vendor retains a substantial interest in the land, and for that reason is generally called a qualified trustee.[12] Lord CAIRNS, dealing with a case where a valid contract had been made for the sale of a London theatre, said:[13]

There cannot be the slightest doubt of the relation subsisting in the eye of a Court of Equity between the vendor and the purchaser. The vendor was a trustee of the property for the purchaser; the purchaser was the real beneficial owner in the eye of a Court of Equity of the property, subject only to this observation, that the vendor, whom I have called the trustee, was not a mere dormant trustee, he was a trustee having a personal and substantial interest in the property, a right to protect that interest, and an active right to assert that interest if anything should be done in derogation of it. The relation, therefore, of trustee and *cestui que trust* subsisted,

8 *Earl of Egmont v Smith* (1877) 6 Ch D 469; *Abdulla v Shah* [1959] AC 124.
9 *Clarke v Ramuz* [1891] 2 QB 456; *Phillips v Lamdin* [1949] 2 KB 33, [1949] 1 All ER 770; *Berkley v Poulett* (1976) 241 EG 911, 242 EG 39 (discussing the rights of a sub-purchaser); *Ware v Verderber* (1978) 247 EG 1081 (duty of vendor to take reasonable care of property).
10 Or dividends in the case of shares: *J. Sainsbury plc v O'Connor* [1991] STC 318.
11 White and Tudor, *Leading Cases in Equity* (9th edn), vol. ii. p. 857. See *Uziell-Hamilton v Keen* (1971) 22 P & CR 655.
12 *Rayner v Preston* (1881) 18 Ch D 1 at 6, per COTTON LJ.
13 *Shaw v Foster* (1872) LR 5 HL 321 at 338.

but subsisted subject to the paramount right of the vendor and trustee to protect his own interest as vendor of the property.

Thus, the trusteeship relates only to the property sold, which, failing express agreement, is confined to vacant possession of the land together with any physical accretions thereto. Therefore the vendor is entitled to retain compensation money payable in respect of the requisitioning of the property and falling due between the date of the contract and the date of the conveyance.[14]

(b) Insurance by purchaser

Likewise, if between these dates the premises are damaged by fire, the former rule was that the money paid by the insurance company in respect of the loss belonged to the vendor, not to the purchaser, for the policy of insurance was no part of the property sold.[15] This particular aspect of the principle, however, has been reversed by the Law of Property Act 1925, which provides[16] that where, after the date of any contract for sale or exchange of land, money becomes payable under any policy maintained by the vendor in respect of any damage to, or destruction of, property included in the contract, the money shall on completion of the contract be paid by the vendor to the purchaser. This obligation may be varied by the contract; it is subject to the liability of the purchaser to pay the premiums falling due after the date of the contract, and is also subject to any requisite consents of the insurers.[17]

(c) Standard Conditions of Sale

Under the Standard Conditions of Sale (1992), which are usually incorporated into the contract, a radical change has been made in the rules for the passing of risk. Condition 5 provides[18] that the vendor retains the risk until completion, that he is under no duty to the purchaser to insure the property, and that the provision for taking over the benefit of the vendor's insurance policy under section 47 is excluded. The purchaser has the right to rescind the contract if the physical state of the property has made it unusable for its purpose at the date of the contract, as a result of damage against which the vendor could not reasonably have insured or which it is not legally possible for him to make good.

In the light of this new condition, the Law Commission has recommended[19]

14 *Hamilton-Snowball's Conveyance* [1959] Ch 308, [1958] 2 All ER 319.
15 *Rayner v Preston*, supra. See also *Re Watford Corpn and Ware's Contract* [1943] Ch 82, [1943] 1 All ER 54.
16 LPA 1925, s. 47.
17 This would appear to put the purchaser in a doubtful position. If the house which is the subject of the sale is burnt down, the purchaser is nevertheless obliged to pay the purchase money, and if the insurance company refuses to give the requisite consent to the transfer of the insurance money, he will be unable to obtain payment of that money under the section. On the other hand, having regard to the nature of fire insurance, it seems clear that the vendor is not entitled both to the insurance money and to the purchase money. A purchaser is well advised to insure the property himself immediately after the contract and not to rely on this section. See [1984] Conv 43 (M. P. Thompson). On the insurer's potential liability both to the assured and to a third party, see *Lonsdale & Thompson Ltd v Black Arrow Group* [1993] Ch 361, [1993] 3 All ER 648; [1993] Conv 472 (M. Haley); [1993] CLJ 387 (A. J. Oakley).
18 P. 108, ante. For a critical analysis of Condition 5, see [1989] Conv 1 (H. W. Wilkinson); *Emmet on Title*, para. 1.082.
19 Report on Risk of Damage after Contract for Sale 1990 (Law Com No. 191, 323).

that it would be inappropriate to propose any legislative change at the present time.

(2) REGISTRATION OF CONTRACT

A binding contract for the sale of land is registrable as an estate contract under the Land Charges Act 1972.[20] If not registered it is void against later purchasers for money or money's worth of a legal estate in the land.[1] In the case of registered land, a notice or caution may be entered on the register; if no such entry is made, the contract will be overridden by a registered disposition made for valuable consideration. The purchaser may, however, have an overriding interest by virtue of his actual occupation of the land, in which case his rights will bind a subsequent purchaser whether he has notice or not.[2]

SECTION V OPTION TO PURCHASE AND RIGHT OF PRE-EMPTION

We must now consider two special cases, an option to purchase and a right of pre-emption (i.e., a right of first refusal).

An option to purchase[3] creates an immediate equitable interest in favour of the grantee as soon as it is granted. The grantee's right to call for a conveyance of the land is an equitable interest; as far as the grantor is concerned,

> his estate or interest is taken away from him without his consent, and the right to take it away being vested in another, the covenant giving the option must give that other an interest in the land.[4]

A question which has arisen is whether the contract to purchase is formed when the option is granted or when it is exercised. Section 2 of the Law of Property (Miscellaneous Provisions) Act 1989 provides that a contract for the sale of land must be made in writing which incorporates all the agreed terms and is signed by both parties.[5] In some contexts the grant of an option has been analysed as a conditional contract,[6] in which case section 2 would be satisfied as long as the grant of the option was in writing, incorporating all the terms and signed by both parties. Other authorities support the view

---

20 S. 2 (4) Class C (iv). The contract must be registered against the owner of the legal estate, s. 3 (1); *Barrett v Hilton Developments Ltd* [1975] Ch 237, [1974] 3 All ER 944.
1 Ibid., s. 4 (6); *Midland Bank Trust Co Ltd v Green* [1981] AC 513, [1981] 1 All ER 153; M & B p. 40; p. 766, post.
2 LRA 1925, s. 70 (1) (g), p. 791, post.
3 See generally Barnsley's, *Land Options* (2nd edn 1992); (1974) 38 Conv (NS) 8 (A. Prichard); [1984] CLJ 55 (S. Tromans).
4 *London and South Western Rly Co v Gomm* (1882) 20 Ch D 562 at 581, per JESSEL MR; *Griffith v Pelton* [1958] Ch 205 at 225; *Webb v Pollmount* [1966] Ch 584 at 597, [1966] 1 All ER 481 at 485; *Mountford v Scott* [1975] Ch 258, [1975] 1 All ER 198; *George Wimpey & Co Ltd v IRC* [1974] 1 WLR 975 at 980, [1974] 2 All ER 602 at 606; affd [1975] 1 WLR 995, [1975] 2 All ER 45; *Pritchard v Briggs* [1980] Ch 338 at 418, [1980] 1 All ER 294 at 328. For the application of the rule against perpetuities, see pp. 307, 317, post.
5 P. 121, ante.
6 *Helby v Matthews* [1895] AC 471 at 482 (Lord MACNAGHTEN); *Re Mulholland's Will Trusts* [1949] 1 All ER 460; *Griffith v Pelton* [1958] Ch 205, [1957] 3 All ER 75; *Armstrong & Holmes Ltd v Holmes* [1993] 1 WLR 1482.

that the grant of an option is an irrevocable offer, resulting in a contract only when accepted by the notice exercising the option.[7] If this is correct, section 2 would not be satisfied unless the grantor signed the notice of exercise, which he could not be compelled to do.

In *Spiro v Glencrown Properties Ltd*[8]

an option to purchase was granted by documents satisfying section 2 of the 1989 Act. The purchaser gave written notice to exercise it but failed to complete. When the vendor sued for damages for breach of contract, the purchaser claimed that there was no contract because the notice of exercise, which was not signed by the vendor, did not satisfy section 2. HOFFMANN J held that the grant of the option, and not its exercise, was a contract for the purposes of section 2.

Strictly speaking the grant of an option was neither a conditional contract nor an irrevocable offer, but created a relationship *sui generis*. The conditional contract was the more appropriate analogy in the context of section 2, as the purpose of an option would be destroyed if the purchaser had to obtain the vendor's signature to the notice of exercise, a result which had not been intended by the legislature. Thus the purchaser was liable to damages.

In *Pritchard v Briggs*, TEMPLEMAN LJ distinguished an option from a right of pre-emption as follows:[9]

Rights of option and rights of pre-emption share one feature in common: each prescribes circumstances in which the relationship between the owner of the property which is the subject of the right and the holder of the right will become the relationship of vendor and purchaser. In the case of an option, the evolution of the relationship of vendor and purchaser may depend on the fulfilment of certain specified conditions and will depend on the volition of the option holder. If the option applies to land, the grant of the option creates a contingent equitable interest . . . In the case of a right of pre-emption, the evolution of the relationship of vendor and purchaser depends on the grantor, of his own volition, choosing to fulfil certain specified conditions[10] and thus converting the pre-emption into an option. The grant of the right of pre-emption creates a *mere spes* which the grantor of the right may either frustrate by choosing not to fulfil the necessary conditions or may convert into an option and thus into an equitable interest by fulfilling the conditions.

The Court of Appeal held unanimously that, unlike an option, a right of pre-emption did not confer an equitable interest in the land on the holder of the right.[11] One difficulty was that many statutory provisions assumed that a right of pre-emption was a proprietary interest.[12] GOFF LJ held that these provisions were framed on a mistaken view of the law and were, therefore,

---

7 *Helby v Matthews*, supra, at 477 (Lord HERSCHELL) and 479–480 (Lord WATSON); *Beesly v Hallwood Estates Ltd* [1960] 1 WLR 549, [1960] 2 All ER 314; affd [1961] Ch 105, [1961] 1 All ER 90.

8 [1991] Ch 537, [1991] 1 All ER 600; [1991] Conv 140 (P. Smith); [1993] Conv 13 (P. Jenkins). If an option is registered, there is no need to register the ensuing contract when the option is exercised: *Armstrong & Holmes Ltd v Holmes*, supra.

9 Supra, at 418, at 438. See also *Brown v Gould* [1972] Ch 53 at 58, [1971] 2 All ER 1505 at 1509.

10 *Tuck v Baker* [1990] 32 EG 46 (pre-emption clause provided that there should be two months for acceptance of an offer of first refusal: the owner could change his mind about selling and withdraw the offer before acceptance within the two months).

11 See also *Manchester Ship Canal Co v Manchester Racecourse Co* [1901] 2 Ch 37; *Murray v Two Strokes Ltd* [1973] 1 WLR 823, [1973] 3 All ER 357, (1973) 89 LQR 462 (M. J. Albery); *First National Securities Ltd v Chiltern District Council* [1975] 1 WLR 1075, [1975] 2 All ER 766; cf *Birmingham Canal Co v Cartwright* (1879) 11 Ch D 421.

12 LCA 1972, s. 2 (4), where it is registrable as an estate contract: LPA 1925, ss. 2 (3), 186; PAA 1964, s. 9 (2).

of no effect.[13] Thus a right of pre-emption was not a proprietary interest capable of binding a successor in title, and could never be converted to such an interest, even if registered as an estate contract.[14] TEMPLEMAN and STEPHENSON LJJ, on the other hand, held that a right of pre-emption, while not initially an interest in land, was converted to an equitable interest as soon as the grantor fulfilled the condition on deciding to sell. If registered as an estate contract, either before or after fulfilment of the condition, the interest would be binding on the grantor's successors in title.[15] But neither view is free from difficulties, and the precise effect of a right of pre-emption remains uncertain.[16]

SECTION VI REMEDIES OF PARTIES FOR BREACH OF CONTRACT

The remedies which are available to either party in the event of a breach of a contract for sale are:[17]

A.   Action for damages,
B.   Specific performance,
C.   Rescission,
D.   Rectification,
E.   Vendor and purchaser summons.

A. ACTION FOR DAMAGES

In the event of a breach of any contract the general rule that governs the measure of damages is that the plaintiff is to be placed, so far as money can do it, in the same situation as if the contract had been performed.[18] This is however subject to the rule relating to remoteness of damage, which limits the defendant's liability to such losses as he ought reasonably to have contemplated as likely to occur, having regard to the knowledge, actual or constructive, possessed by him at the time of the contract.[19] The only duty cast upon a party in this respect is to foresee the loss that will occur in the

---

13 [1980] Ch 338 at 399, [1980] 1 All ER 294 at 313.
14 Ibid., at 396, at 311.
15 Ibid., at 418, 423, at 328, 332. In registered land, a right of pre-emption, if not registered as a minor interest, may be enforceable as an overriding interest under LRA 1925, s. 70 (1)(*g*): *Kling v Keston Properties Ltd* (1983) 49 P & CR 212; M & B, p. 88.
16 (1980) 96 LQR 488 (H. W. R. W.); [1980] Conv 433 (J. Martin).
17 See generally *Emmet on Title* (19th edn), chapter 8; Annand and Cain, *Remedies under the Contract* (1988). For liability in tort for negligent misstatement during pre-contract negotiations, see *Esso Petroleum Co Ltd v Mardon* [1976] QB 801, [1976] 2 All ER 5; *Howard Marine and Dredging Co Ltd v A. Ogden & Sons (Excavations) Ltd* [1978] QB 574, [1978] 2 All ER 1134 (liability in negligence and under Misrepresentation Act 1967, s. 2 (1)).
18 *Robinson v Harman* (1848) 1 Exch 850, 855 per PARKE B; *Surrey County Council v Bredero Homes Ltd* [1993] 1 WLR 1361; Treitel, *The Law of Contract* (8th edn), p. 836.
19 *Hadley v Baxendale* (1854) 9 Ex Ch 341; *Victoria Laundry (Windsor) Ltd v Newman Industries Ltd* [1949] 2 KB 528, [1949] 1 All ER 997; *Koufos v C Czarnikow Ltd, The Heron II* [1969] 1 AC 350, [1967] 3 All ER 686; Cheshire, Fifoot and Furmston, *Law of Contract* (12th edn), pp. 594 et seq.

usual course of things, unless he knows of exceptional circumstances by
which it may be increased. [20]

(1) DAMAGES RECOVERABLE BY VENDOR

In the case of a contract for the sale of land this general rule applies when it
is the vendor who brings the action. The loss caused to the vendor in the
usual course of things by the failure of the purchaser to complete is the
deprivation of the purchase price diminished by the value of the land that he
still holds, and he is therefore entitled to recover by way of damages the
difference, if any, between the value of the land which remains in his
possession and the price he would have got had the contract been completed. [1]
Thus, if he resells, he is entitled to recover both the difference in price and
the expenses attending the resale. [2]

(2) DAMAGES RECOVERABLE BY PURCHASER

(a) In contract

When it is the purchaser who sues for breach, the measure of damages
depends upon whether the contract was made

    (i) before 27 September 1989, or
    (ii) after 26 September 1989.

(i) Where the contract was made before 27 September 1989, the purchaser's
remedy depended upon a further distinction: whether the vendor's breach
was due merely to the vendor's inability to make a good title; or to his failure
to do all that he could to complete the conveyance.

Where the vendor was unable to complete the conveyance owing to a
defect in his title, the general rule—that damages are recoverable for loss of
bargain—was excluded by the rule in *Bain v Fothergill*, [3] under which the
purchaser was limited to the recovery of his deposit, if any, and of the
expenses incurred by him in investigating the title. [4] The justification for this
anomalous departure from the general rule was said to be the extreme
difficulty that attends the making of a good title to English land. [5] Thus if the
owner of leaseholds agreed to sell them without stating that his lessor's
licence was necessary, and if the licence was refused, the purchaser would
not be entitled to recover general damages. [6] But the anomaly was less

---

20 *Cottrill v Steyning and Littlehampton Building Society* [1966] 1 WLR 753, [1966] 2 All ER 295;
    dist. *Diamond v Campbell-Jones* [1961] Ch 22, [1960] 1 All ER 583.
1 *Laird v Pim* (1841) 7 M & W 474; *Harold Wood Brick Co Ltd v Ferris* [1935] 1 KB 613; affd
    [1935] 2 KB 198.
2 *Noble v Edwards* (1877) 5 Ch D 378; *Keck v Faber* (1915) 60 SJ 253.
3 (1874) LR 7 HL 158. For the abolition of the rule with effect from 27 September 1989, see
    infra.
4 *Flureau v Thornhill* (1776) 2 Wm Bl 1078; *Seven Seas Properties Ltd v Al-Essa* [1988] 1 WLR
    1272, [1989] 1 All ER 164; [1989] Conv 75 (H. W. Wilkinson); *Wards Construction (Medway)
    Ltd v Wajih* [1992] NPC 133.
5 *Bain v Fothergill* (1874) LR 7 HL 158; *Barnes v Cadogan Developments Ltd* [1930] 1 Ch 479 at
    488; *J W Café's Ltd v Brownlow Trust* [1950] 1 All ER 894; (1977) 41 Conv (NS) 341 (A.
    Sydenham); [1983] Conv 435 (C. Harpum); (1985) 82 LSG 2402; (1987) 137 NLJ 83 (M. P.
    Thompson); attacking the rule; (1978) 42 Conv (NS) 338 (C. T. Emery); (1986) 136 NLJ
    1205 (S. Farren) defending it.
6 *Bain v Fothergill*, supra.

compelling where the title to land is registered, and even before its abolition by the legislature, the courts had decided that the rule in *Bain v Fothergill* would not be extended.[7]

But a vendor who failed or refused to take the steps which were necessary to complete the title and which were within his power was liable in damages for loss of bargain.[8] In order to rely on the rule in *Bain v Fothergill*, the onus was on the vendor to show that he had used his best endeavours to fulfil his contractual obligations.[9] So if he had not acted honestly, or had refused or neglected to make a good title,[10] as for instance where a vendor of leaseholds induced his lessor to withhold the necessary licence,[11] or declined to carry out the contract, or failed to clear the land of a mortgage,[12] or was unwilling to persuade a co-owner to agree to the sale,[13] or had himself created the blot on his title,[14] or, where the contract was for vacant possession, he took no steps to determine a periodic tenancy under Part II of the Landlord and Tenant Act 1954,[15] or if his agreement to sell was unlawful,[16] he was liable to pay substantial damages. Fraud on the part of the vendor might also exclude the rule in *Bain v Fothergill*, and therefore give rise to damages for loss of bargain.[17]

(ii) Where, however, the contract was made after 26 September 1989, the measure of damages recoverable by the purchaser does not turn on whether or not the vendor's breach was due to his inability to make a good title. Since the abolition of the rule in *Bain v Fothergill*,[18] a purchaser is entitled in all cases to damages for loss of bargain. If the value of the property is greater than the purchase price, the plaintiff recovers the difference, though in this case he cannot recover his conveyancing costs.[19] If the value of the property

7 *Wroth v Tyler* [1974] Ch 30 at 52–6, [1973] 1 All ER 897 at 916–8; (spouse's right of occupation under Matrimonial Homes Act 1967, p. 241, post, held not to be a defect in title for the purpose of the rule, thus full damages recoverable against vendor unable to complete because after contract his wife entered a caution in respect of her rights under that Act). See (1973) 123 NLJ 393 (H. W. Wilkinson); *Sharneyford Supplies Ltd v Edge* [1987] Ch 305 at 318, [1987] 1 All ER 588 at 594, per BALCOMBE LJ. For the abolition of the rule, see n. 18, infra.
8 *Williams v Glenton* (1866) 1 Ch App 200 at 209; *Phillips v Lamdin* [1949] 2 KB 33, [1949] 1 All ER 770.
9 *Malhotra v Choudhury* [1980] Ch 52, [1979] 1 All ER 186; (1979) 38 CLJ 35 (D. J. Hayton).
10 *Wallington v Townsend* [1939] Ch 588, [1939] 2 All ER 225.
11 *Day v Singleton* [1899] 2 Ch 320.
12 *Thomas v Kensington* [1942] 2 KB 181; see also *Leominster Properties Ltd v Broadway Finance Ltd* (1981) 42 P & CR 372.
13 *Malhotra v Choudhury*, supra.
14 See *Ray v Druce* [1985] Ch 437, [1985] 2 All ER 482 (rule applied because blot created by earlier transaction of vendor), following *Goffin v Houlder* (1920) 90 LJ Ch 488; [1985] CLJ 348 (C. Harpum).
15 *Sharneyford Supplies Ltd v Edge*, supra; [1987] CLJ 212 (C. Harpum).
16 *Milner v Staffordshire Congregational Union (Incorporated)* [1956] Ch 275, [1956] 1 All ER 494.
17 See *McGregor on Damages* (15th edn) para. 727.
18 The rule was abolished by the Law of Property (Miscellaneous Provisions) Act 1989, ss. 3, 5(3); adopting the recommendations of the Law Commission Report on the Rule in *Bain v Fothergill* 1987 (Law Com No. 166, Cm 192). See *Newbury v Turngiant Ltd* (1991) 63 P & CR 458; *Grangeville Marketing Inc v Seven Seas Properties Ltd* [1990] EGCS 23.
19 *Re Daniel* [1917] 2 Ch 405. The loss for which compensation is recoverable is the difference between the purchase price and the value of the property if it had been conveyed in accordance with the contract. But if the property had in fact been so conveyed, the conveyancing costs would have fallen on the purchaser, and therefore he cannot recover both the difference and the costs; ibid., at 412, per SARGANT J.

is less than the purchase price, he is entitled to a return of the deposit with interest and also to damages in respect of the cost of investigating the title. [20]

(b) In tort

An alternative to suing for damages for breach of contract is to claim damages in tort. An action in deceit may lie if the vendor made a fraudulent misrepresentation,[21] and damages[1] may be recovered under the Misrepresentation Act 1967 for innocent misrepresentation, unless the vendor could prove that he had reasonable ground to believe and did believe up to the time the contract was made that the facts represented were true.[2] The measure of damages in tort does not however give recovery for loss of bargain; it puts the plaintiff in the position he would have been in had the tort not been committed.[3]

(3) DATE FOR ASSESSMENT OF DAMAGES

It was at one time thought that, while the general rule at common law requires damages to be assessed as at the date of the breach of contract, i.e. the date fixed for completion, a greater measure of damages, based on the value of the land at the date of the judgment, would be recoverable where the damages were awarded in substitution for specific performance under Lord Cairns' Act (Chancery Amendment Act 1858).[4] Lord Cairns' Act gave the Court of Chancery discretionary power to award damages either in addition to or in substitution for specific performance (in cases where the court had jurisdiction to award specific performance), the damages to be assessed in such manner as the court shall direct. Since the Judicature Act 1873, making the common law remedy of damages available in the Chancery Division, it is only necessary to invoke Lord Cairns' Act in a case where common law damages would not be available, for example where a contract is supported

---

20 *Wallington v Townsend*, supra; see also *Lloyd v Stanbury* [1971] 1 WLR 535, [1971] 2 All ER 267.
21 *Bain v Fothergill* (1874) LR 7 HL 158 at 207; *Derry v Peek* (1889) 14 App Cas 337.
1 Damages under s. 2 (1) Misrepresentation Act 1967 are assessed on the same basis as damages in the tort of deceit: *Royscot Trust Ltd v Rogerson* [1991] 2 QB 297, [1991] 3 All ER 294. See also *Sharneyford Supplies Ltd v Edge* [1986] Ch 128 at 149, [1985] 1 All ER 976 at 990–991; [1987] Ch 305 at 322, [1987] 1 All ER 588 at 598, per BALCOMBE LJ; [1987] Conv 423 (J. Cartwright); *Heinemann v Cooper* [1987] 2 EGLR 154; *Strover v Harrington* [1988] Ch 390, [1988] 1 All ER 769; *Cemp Properties (UK) Ltd v Dentsply Research and Development Corpn* [1991] 2 EGLR 197.
2 S. 2 (1). Damages in tort for negligent mis-statement are also a possibility: *Hedley Byrne & Co Ltd v Heller & Partners Ltd* [1964] AC 465, [1963] 2 All ER 595; *Cooper v Tamms* [1988] 1 EGLR 257. A plaintiff is however more likely to sue under the statute, where the burden of proof of honest and reasonable belief in the truth of the statement is thrown on the defendant. Under the Property Misdescriptions Act 1991, it is an offence to make false or misleading statements about property matters in the course of estate agency or property development business; Property Misdescriptions (Specified Matters) Order 1992 (S.I. 1992 No. 2834).
3 *McConnell v Wright* [1903] 1 Ch 546 at 554–555, per COLLINS MR; *Doyle v Olby (Ironmongers) Ltd* [1969] 2 QB 158, [1969] 2 All ER 119.
4 Now Supreme Court Act 1981, s. 50. *Wroth v Tyler* [1974] Ch 30, [1973] 1 All ER 897; *Grant v Dawkins* [1973] 1 WLR 1406, [1973] 3 All ER 897; (1975) 34 CLJ 224 (J. A. Jolowicz); [1981] Conv 286 (T. Ingman and J. Wakefield); (1981) 97 LQR 445 (S. M. Waddams). On the jurisdiction of the court to award damages before Lord Cairns' Act, see (1992) 108 LQR 652 (P. M. McDermott).

only by an act of part performance.[5] The position as to the time at which damages are to be assessed has now been clarified by the House of Lords in *Johnson v Agnew*.[6] Subject to the point that in some cases damages would be available under Lord Cairns' Act where none at all would be available at common law, the Act does not permit a departure from the common law rule on the quantum of damages. But there is no inflexible rule at common law that damages must be assessed as at the date of the breach of contract.[7] The principle is that the plaintiff should be put in the same position as if the contract had been duly performed. Where, after the breach, the innocent party has reasonably continued to try for completion, the damages, however awarded, should be assessed as at the date when the contract was lost.[8] This will normally be the date of the hearing, but an earlier date will be substituted if the plaintiff has delayed.[9]

Damages recoverable where completion is delayed, or where specific performance is ordered but enforcement subsequently proves impossible, are dealt with below.[10]

B. SPECIFIC PERFORMANCE

The most effective remedy available to either party is to sue for specific performance, i.e. to demand that the contract be completed according to its terms. One of the general principles established by equity is that this relief should be given only where damages do not afford an adequate remedy. But the subject matter of a contract for the sale of land[11] is of unique value, so that specific performance of the contract is available to a purchaser as a matter of course. Furthermore, even though a vendor could be adequately compensated by damages for the failure of a purchaser to complete, yet, in pursuance of the doctrine that remedies should be mutual, equity grants specific performance to a vendor as well as to a purchaser.[12]

An adequate discussion of specific performance is outside the scope of this book,[13] but it may be noticed that the remedy is discretionary, though the discretion is not exercised in an arbitrary or capricious manner, but according

---

5 Or perhaps where the case is based on proprietary estoppel, which gives rise to no action at law: *Crabb v Arun District Council (No 2)* (1977) 121 SJ 86. See also *Oakacre v Claire Cleaners (Holdings) Ltd* [1982] Ch 197, [1981] 3 All ER 667 (action for damages at law not accrued at date of writ).
6 [1980] AC 367, [1979] 1 All ER 883.
7 Ibid. See also *Wroth v Tyler*, supra, at 57, at 919; *Radford v De Froberville* [1977] 1 WLR 1262, [1978] 1 All ER 33; *Malhotra v Choudhury*, supra; *Techno Land Improvements Ltd v British Leyland (UK) Ltd* (1979) 252 EG 805; *Forster v Silvermere Golf and Equestrian Centre Ltd* (1981) 42 P & CR 255, (1979) 95 LQR 270 (D. Feldman and D. F. Libling); *Suleman v Shahsavari* [1988] 1 WLR 1181, [1989] 2 All ER 460.
8 In *Johnson v Agnew*, this was the date on which the vendor's mortgagees contracted to sell the property, thus preventing completion of the vendor's contract with the plaintiff.
9 *Radford v De Froberville*, supra; *Malhotra v Choudhury*, supra.
10 Pp. 132 et seq, post.
11 Specific performance may also be granted of a contractual licence to occupy land; *Verrall v Great Yarmouth Borough Council* [1981] QB 202, [1980] 1 All ER 839; M & B, p. 547; p. 589, post.
12 *Kenny v Wexham* (1822) 6 Madd 355 at 357, per LEACH V-C.
13 See generally H & M, chapter 23; *Snell's, Equity* (29th edn), pp. 585 et seq; Jones and Goodhart, *Specific Performance* (1986); White and Tudor, *Leading Cases in Equity* (9th edn), vol. ii, pp. 372 et seq.

to the rules that have been established by the judges. If the defendant can show any circumstances independent of the written contract which make it inequitable to decree specific performance, as for instance where the plaintiff has delayed, or in certain cases of mistake, misrepresentation and misdescription, or where the vendor or the purchaser has not acted fairly,[14] or where the completion of the contract would cause hardship to an innocent vendor or purchaser,[15] the court will not grant the remedy.

(1) SPECIFIC PERFORMANCE WHEN COMPLETION DELAYED

Where a contract for the sale of land is not completed upon the date fixed in the contract, specific performance may still be available, even at the instance of the delaying party.[16] *At law* time was always considered to be of the essence of the contract, and a party who failed to complete upon the agreed date was remediless. Thus, if the vendor failed to complete, the purchaser could repudiate the contract and recover the deposit and the costs of investigating the title. Equity, however, taking a different view that now prevails in all courts,[17] has always been prepared to decree specific performance notwithstanding failure to observe the exact date fixed for completion, *provided that this will not cause injustice to either party*.

But it must be emphasized that, even where time is not of the essence of a contract, failure to complete on the contractual date is a breach of contract, both at law and in equity. The contractual duty of the parties is not merely to complete on that date or within a reasonable time thereafter.[18] The fact that time is not of the essence merely means that the delaying party does not lose the right to specific performance, nor will he forfeit his deposit, provided that he is ready to complete within a reasonable time. If completion does not occur on the contractual date, the delaying party will be liable to pay damages, as, for example, where the innocent party incurs hotel or storage expenses as a result of the breach.

While the general position is that the party in breach of contract remains entitled to specific performance, that remedy will not be decreed if the parties have expressly stipulated that time shall be essential, or if there is something in the nature of the property or in the surrounding circumstances which renders it inequitable to treat the appointed date as non-essential.[19]

So, if the nature of the property is such as to make its conveyance at the agreed date imperative, e.g. when the contract is for the sale of licensed

---

14 See *Sang Lee Investment Co Ltd v Wing Kwai Investment Co Ltd* (1983) 127 SJ 410, per Lord BRIGHTMAN.

15 See *Patel v Ali* [1984] Ch 283, [1984] 1 All ER 978 (specific performance would inflict on vendor "a hardship amounting to injustice" per GOULDING J at 288, at 982); (1984) 100 LQR 337.

16 See generally Farrand, *Contract and Conveyance* (4th edn), pp. 208–210; Barnsley, *Conveyancing Law and Practice* (3rd edn), pp. 373–384. For the position where the plaintiff delays in enforcing the order for specific performance, see *Easton v Brown* [1981] 3 All ER 278.

17 LPA 1925, s. 41, re-enacting Judicature Act 1873, s. 25 (7). See generally (1980) 39 CLJ 58 (A. J. Oakley).

18 *Raineri v Miles* [1981] AC 1050, [1980] 2 All ER 145; *Oakacre v Claire Cleaners (Holdings) Ltd* [1982] Ch 197, [1981] 3 All ER 667. See also *Inns v D Miles Griffiths, Piercy & Co* (1980) 255 EG 623.

19 *Stickney v Keeble* [1915] AC 386 at 415–6, per LORD PARKER. See also *Rightside Properties Ltd v Gray* [1975] Ch 72, [1974] 2 All ER 1169; *Dean v Upton* [1990] EGCS 61.

premises,[20] or of a shop as a going concern, specific performance, even with compensation, will not be decreed; but if there is nothing special in the nature of the property or in the purposes for which it is required, the court will decree specific performance, subject to the condition that the defaulting party gives compensation for the delay. The principle in such a case is that specific performance will be awarded unless the plaintiff has delayed unreasonably. There is no statutory period of limitation barring claims to specific performance,[1] and no rule to lay down what is meant by unreasonable delay. It used to be thought that the plaintiff must normally seek specific performance well within one year,[2] but it now seems that this approach is too strict.[3] An exceptional case where delay will not be a bar is where the plaintiff has taken possession under the contract, so that the purpose of specific performance is merely to vest the legal estate in him.[4]

A new contract cannot be made at the will of one of the parties and therefore, where time is not initially essential, one party cannot make it so of his own volition.[5] Nevertheless, there must be some limit to delaying tactics, and it is established that after the date fixed for completion has passed one party may serve a notice on the other requiring completion within a specified time.[6] The notice will be valueless unless the time allowed is reasonable,[7] but if satisfactory in this respect it will bind both parties.[8]

(2) SPECIFIC PERFORMANCE WITH ABATEMENT

There are other circumstances where the court will decree specific performance in favour of the plaintiff subject to the condition that compensation is paid in respect of some term of the contract which has not been literally fulfilled. Such cases of specific performance with an abatement of the purchase price are primarily concerned with misdescription of the property.[9] Subject to any conditions of sale applying to the contract, the general rule is that if the misdescription is substantial, the vendor cannot obtain specific performance even subject to an abatement, while the purchaser may enforce the contract if he so chooses.[10] But if the

20 *Lock v Bell* [1931] 1 Ch 35.
1 Limitation Act 1980, s. 36 (1).
2 See Farrand, *Contract and Conveyance* (4th edn), p. 216.
3 *Lazard Bros & Co Ltd v Fairfield Properties Co (Mayfair) Ltd* (1977) 121 SJ 793; [1978] Conv 184.
4 *Williams v Greatrex* [1957] 1 WLR 31, [1956] 3 All ER 705 (delay of 10 years no bar in such a case).
5 *Green v Sevin* (1879) 13 Ch D 589 at 599.
6 *Finkielkraut v Monohan* [1949] 2 All ER 234; *Dimsdale Developments (South East) Ltd v De Haan* (1983) 47 P & CR 1; [1984] Conv. 34 (M. P. Thompson).
7 *Smith v Hamilton* [1951] Ch 174, [1950] 2 All ER 928; *Re Barr's Contract* [1956] 1 Ch 551, [1956] 2 All ER 853; *Ajit v Sammy* [1967] 1 AC 255.
8 *Finkielkraut v Monohan*, supra; *Quadrangle Development and Construction Co Ltd v Jenner* [1974] 1 WLR 68, [1974] 1 All ER 729; *Oakdown Ltd v Bernstein & Co* (1984) 49 P & CR 282; *Behzadi v Shaftesbury Hotels Ltd* [1992] Ch 1, [1991] 2 All ER 477; [1991] CLJ (C. Harpum); [1991] 107 LQR 534 (P. V. Baker).
9 See Farrand, *Contract and Conveyance* (4th edn) pp. 52–55; (1980) 40 CLJ 47 (C. Harpum).
10 *Flight v Booth* (1834) 1 Bing NC 370; *Rutherford v Acton-Adams* [1915] AC 866 at 870; *Rudd v Lascelles* [1900] 1 Ch 815. It is otherwise if the compensation cannot be assessed, or if the subject matter is entirely different from that contracted for; see p. 768, post.

misdescription is not substantial either party may obtain specific performance subject to compensation.[11]

(3) WHERE DEFENDANT FAILS TO COMPLY WITH DECREE OF SPECIFIC PERFORMANCE

Where the plaintiff obtains a decree of specific performance, but the defendant fails to comply with it, the plaintiff may apply either to enforce[12] or to dissolve the contract. The contract still exists after the grant of specific performance and does not merge into the decree; thus the plaintiff is not precluded in such a case from seeking damages at common law.[13] But any subsequent performance of the contract is regulated by the provisions of the order of specific performance and not by those of the contract.[14] If the order for specific performance is not complied with, the plaintiff, having elected to affirm the contract, cannot then unilaterally terminate it for breach. He must apply to the court either for further enforcement measures or for a dissolution of the order and termination of the contract;[15] in which case he may claim for damages.

C. RESCISSION[16]

(1) TERMINOLOGY

A distinction must be drawn between rescission ab initio and rescission in the sense of accepting the repudiation of the contract by the other party. Where rescission ab initio occurs, as, for example, in cases of fraud, mistake or lack of consent, the position is that the contract is treated as if it had never existed; thus the innocent party is entitled to an indemnity but cannot recover damages for breach of contract.[17] Where, however, the vendor fails to show a good title[18] or to deliver the actual land or interest described in the contract, or where the vendor or purchaser fails to complete after time has been made of the essence, it is commonly said that the innocent party may rescind. This is not rescission ab initio, but acceptance of a repudiation of the contract, discharging both parties from further performance. In such a case damages

---

11 *Jacobs v Revell* [1900] 2 Ch 858. This principle cannot be used so as to increase the price: *Re Lindsay and Forder's Contract* (1895) 72 LT 832.

12 See *Easton v Brown* [1981] 3 All ER 278, p. 134 n. 16, ante.

13 *Johnson v Agnew* [1980] AC 367, [1979] 1 All ER 883, confirming the views expressed in (1975) 91 LQR 337 (M. J. Albery) and (1977) 93 LQR 232 (F. Dawson); (enforcement impossible because after date of contract with purchaser, vendor's mortgagees contracted to sell the property).

14 *Singh v Nazeer* [1979] Ch 474, [1978] 3 All ER 817 (contractual completion notice served after decree of specific performance invalid); (1980) 96 LQR 403 (M. Hetherington).

15 *GKN Distributors Ltd v Tyne Tees Fabrication Ltd* (1985) 50 P & CR 403.

16 See generally H & M (14th edn), pp. 803–823; *Snell's Equity* (29th edn), pp. 616–623. For solicitors' liability in negligence for failing to advise purchaser of lease of his right to rescind, see *Peyman v Lanjani* [1985] Ch 457, [1984] 3 All ER 703.

17 For the position as to rescission for misrepresentation, see Cheshire Fifoot and Furmston, *Law of Contract* (12th edn), pp. 286–295; *Laurence v Lexcourt Holdings Ltd* [1978] 1 WLR 1128, [1978] 2 All ER 810; *Mustafa v Baptist Union Corporation* (1983) 266 EG 812.

18 A purchaser can rescind as soon as he discovers that the vendor has no title, i.e. before date fixed for completion: *Pips (Leisure Productions) Ltd v Walton* (1980) 43 P & CR 415 (contract to sell leasehold which was already forfeited); *Pinekerry Ltd v Needs (Kenneth) (Contractors) Ltd* (1992) 64 P & CR 245.

are recoverable at common law for breach of contract.[19] As discussed below, the terms of the contract may also confer a right to rescind in specified circumstances, and provide for the consequences. In the absence of any such terms, the innocent party may either accept the repudiation and proceed to claim damages (in which case he cannot later seek specific performance), or he may seek specific performance.[20] If an order for specific performance is made, but not complied with, he may apply to the court to enforce or to dissolve the order,[1] damages being recoverable in the latter case.[2]

(2) CONTRACTUAL RIGHT TO RESCIND

The right to rescind may also be conferred by the express terms of the contract.[3] There is commonly found in a contract of sale a condition that allows the vendor to rescind if the purchaser should insist on any requisition which the vendor is unable or unwilling to comply with.[4] But "a vendor, in seeking to rescind, must not act arbitrarily, or capriciously, or unreasonably. Much less can he act in bad faith ... Above all, perhaps, he must not be guilty of 'recklessness' in entering into his contract."[5] Thus, in *Baines v Tweddle*,[6] a vendor was unable to exercise a contractual right to rescind because he had failed to seek the concurrence of his mortgagees before contracting to sell free from the mortgage.

(3) FORFEITURE OF DEPOSIT

Where the purchaser defaults, the vendor is entitled, however, to retain any deposit that the purchaser may have paid. Thus in *Howe v Smith*,[7]

£500 was paid as deposit and part payment of the purchase money. The purchaser, who was in default in completing the contract, sued to recover the £500, but it was held that, since it was the intention of the parties that this sum should be deposited as a guarantee for the due performance of his obligations, it must be forfeited to the vendor.

19 *Johnson v Agnew* [1980] AC 367, [1979] 1 All ER 883, overruling *Henty v Schröder* (1879) 12 Ch D 666, and many other authorities. See *Tilcon Ltd v Land and Real Estate Investments Ltd* [1987] 1 WLR 46, [1987] 1 All ER 615.
20 If he proceeds for these remedies in the alternative, he must elect at the trial: *Meng Leong Development Pte Ltd v Jip Hong Trading Co Pte Ltd* [1985] 1 AC 511, [1985] 1 All ER 120.
 1 *Hillel v Christoforides* (1991) 63 P & CR 301 (where vendor has sought dissolution, purchaser cannot complete unless vendor has acted unconscionably).
 2 *Meng Leong Development Pte Ltd v Jip Hong Trading Co Pte Ltd*, supra; *GKN Distributors Ltd v Tyne Tees Fabrication Ltd* (1985) 50 P & CR 403.
 3 *Emmet on Title* (19th edn), paras 8.008–8.0010.
 4 See, e.g. Condition 4. 5. 2 of the Standard Conditions of Sale.
 5 *Selkirk v Romar Investments Ltd* [1963] 1 WLR 1415 at 1422, [1963] 3 All ER 994 at 999, per Lord RADCLIFFE.
 6 [1959] Ch 679, [1959] 2 All ER 724; *Re Des Reaux and Setchfield's Contract* [1926] Ch 178. See also, on misdescription, *Topfell Ltd v Galley Properties Ltd* [1979] 1 WLR 446, [1979] 2 All ER 388.
 7 (1884) 27 Ch D 89. On deposits generally, see Farrand, *Contract and Conveyance* (4th edn), pp. 203–208; Barnsley, *Conveyancing Law and Practice* (3rd edn), pp. 218–226; [1994] Conv 41, 100 (A. J. Oakley). For the position where an estate agent holds the pre-contract deposit of a prospective purchaser, see *Sorrell v Finch* [1977] AC 728, [1976] 2 All ER 371; *Ramsden v James Bennett* [1993] NPC 91 (£6,000 deposit for option to purchase villa in Spain); cf. *Ojelay v Neosale* [1987] 2 EGLR 167 and on stakeholders generally: *Sorrell v Finch*; *Tudor v Hamid* [1988] 1 EGLR 251; (1988) 138 NLJ 40 (H. W. Wilkinson); *Rockeagle Ltd v Alsop Wilkinson* [1992] Ch 47, [1991] 4 All ER 659.

Where a defaulting purchaser has not yet paid over the whole of the deposit, the whole or any unpaid part is recoverable by the vendor.[8] Similarly, where the vendor is in default, the purchaser may recover any deposit which he has paid. But whether the rule as to retention of the deposit applies or not is in each case a matter of construction, and if the terms show that the money has not been paid as a guarantee of performance, but solely by way of part payment, it is recoverable by the purchaser even though the contract is rescinded owing to his own default.[9]

A purchaser may be able to secure the return of his deposit under section 49(2) of the Law of Property Act 1925, which provides that:

> where the court refuses to grant specific performance of a contract, or in any action for the return of a deposit, the court may, if it thinks fit, order the repayment of any deposit.

In considering this provision BUCKLEY LJ has said that it was designed simply to do justice between vendor and purchaser:

> It confers on the judge a discretion, which is unqualified by any language of the subsection, to order or refuse repayment of the deposit, a discretion which must, of course, be exercised judicially and with regard to all relevant considerations, including the very important consideration of the terms of the contract into which the parties have chosen to enter . . . repayment must be ordered in any circumstances which make this the fairest course between the two parties.[10]

D. RECTIFICATION

If, as the result of a mistake common to both parties, the written evidence omits some material term and therefore does not express the true bargain

---

8 *Dewar v Mintoft* [1912] 2 KB 373 at 387–388; *Millichamp v Jones* [1982] 1 WLR 1422, [1983] 1 All ER 267 (where the authorities are fully reviewed by WARNER J); *Damon Cia Naviera SA v Hapag-Lloyd International SA* [1985] 1 WLR 435 (applied by CA in a case relating to ships); *John Willmott Homes Ltd v Read* (1985) 51 P & CR 90; cf. *Lowe v Hope* [1970] Ch 94, [1969] 3 All ER 605; Farrand, *Contract and Conveyance* (4th edn), p. 206.

9 *Mayson v Clouet* [1924] AC 980.

10 *Universal Corpn v Five Ways Properties Ltd* [1979] 1 All ER 552 at 555 (deposit of £88,500). Where the court orders the return of the deposit, the vendor is left to his remedy in damages. See also *James Macara Ltd v Barclay* [1944] 2 All ER 31 at 32; affd. on other grounds [1945] KB 148, [1944] 2 All ER 589; *Charles Hunt Ltd v Palmer* [1931] 2 Ch 287; *Finkielkraut v Monohan* [1949] 2 All ER 234; *Schindler v Pigault* (1975) 30 P & CR 328; *Faruqi v English Real Estates Ltd* [1979] 1 WLR 963 at 968; *Cole v Rose* [1978] 3 All ER 1121; *Maktoum v South Lodge Flats Ltd* (1980) Times, 22 April; 130 NLJ 668 (H. W. Wilkinson); *Dimsdale Developments (South East) Ltd v De Haan* (1983) 47 P & CR 1; *McGrath v Shah* (1987) 57 P & CR 452 (where no reference was made to LPA 1925, s. 49 (2)). See also Estate Agents Act 1979, ss. 12–17.

On the principles governing relief against forfeiture of deposit, see *Stockloser v Johnson* [1954] 1 QB 476, [1954] 1 All ER 630; *Linggi Plantations Ltd v Jagatheesan* [1972] 1 MLJ 89; *Windsor Securities Ltd v Loreldal Ltd and Lester* (1975) Times, 10 September; *Workers Trust & Merchant Bank Ltd v Dojap* [1993] AC 573, [1993] 2 All ER 370 (relief possible where deposit is a penalty and not a true deposit; deposit exceeding 10% held not to be a true "reasonable" deposit); [1989] Conv 377 (H. W. Wilkinson); [1993] CLJ 389 (C. Harpum); (1993) 109 LQR 524 (H. Beale); Goff and Jones, *The Law of Restitution* (4th edn), pp. 428–38. See generally *Snell's Equity* (29th edn), pp. 626–36; *Emmet on Title* (19th edn), paras. 8.026–8.029.

between the parties, the court has jurisdiction to rectify the contract.[11] In such a case it first rectifies the written contract by adding the oral omission or variation, and then decrees specific performance of the contract as rectified. At one and the same time it reforms and enforces the contract.[12] This remedy will be granted even where the mistake is embodied in the final deed of conveyance.[13]

Unilateral mistake may also give rise to a claim for rectification if the mistaken party can show that the other party was aware of the mistake, would benefit by it, and failed to draw it to the attention of the mistaken party.[14]

Whether the mistake was common or unilateral, the fact that it arose through the negligence of the plaintiff or his legal advisers is normally no bar to rectification.[15]

The mistake must be as to the effect of the document which it is sought to rectify; a mistaken belief as to its relation to another document is not sufficient.[16]

The benefit of the right to rectify in cases concerning land passes with the land,[17] but rectification will not be granted where a bona fide purchaser without notice has acquired an interest under the instrument.[18]

E. VENDOR AND PURCHASER SUMMONS

The Vendor and Purchaser Act 1874 introduced a new method whereby parties to a contract of sale, whose disagreement upon some matter prevents the completion of the contract, may apply in a summary way to a judge in chambers, and obtain such an order as may appear just. This summary proceeding is termed a vendor and purchaser summons, and is now governed by the Law of Property Act 1925.[19] Typical questions which lead to a summons are the sufficiency of the title shown by the vendor,[20] the sufficiency of an answer made to a requisition,[1] the construction of the contract, and the question whether a vendor is entitled to rescind.

The Act expressly excludes the possibility of raising any question that

11 *United States of America v Motor Trucks Ltd* [1924] AC 196; *Joscelyne v Nissen* [1970] 2 QB 86, [1970] 1 All ER 1213.
12 *United States of America v Motor Trucks Ltd*, supra, at 201, per Lord BIRKENHEAD.
13 *Craddock Bros Ltd v Hunt* [1923] 2 Ch 136. See also *Riverlate Properties Ltd v Paul* [1975] Ch 133, [1974] 2 All ER 656.
14 *A Roberts & Co Ltd v Leicestershire County Council* [1961] Ch 555, [1961] 2 All ER 545; *Thomas Bates & Son Ltd v Wyndham's (Lingerie) Ltd* [1981] 1 WLR 505, [1981] 1 All ER 1077; *Neptune Concrete Ltd v Kemp* [1988] 2 EGLR 87.
15 *Weeds v Blaney* (1977) 247 EG 211; *Central & Metropolitan Estates Ltd v Compusave* (1983) 266 EG 900; *Boots The Chemist Ltd v Street* (1983) 268 EG 817.
16 *London Regional Transport v Wimpey Group Services Ltd* [1986] 2 EGLR 41 (rent review).
17 *Boots The Chemist Ltd v Street*, supra; LPA 1925, s. 63.
18 *Garrard v Frankel* (1862) 30 Beav 445; *Smith v Jones* [1954] 1 WLR 1089, [1954] 2 All ER 823; *Taylor Barnard Ltd v Tozer* (1983) 269 EG 225; *Equity & Law Life Assurance Society Ltd v Coltness Group Ltd* (1983) 267 EG 949. In registered land, the right may be an overriding interest under LRA 1925, s. 70 (1)(g); *Blacklocks v JB Developments (Godalming) Ltd* [1982] Ch 183, [1981] 3 All ER 392, p. 793, n. 20, post.
19 LPA 1925, s. 49 (1).
20 See *MEPC Ltd v Christian-Edwards* [1981] AC 205, [1979] 3 All ER 752, illustrating that such proceedings are not necessarily expeditious or cheap.
1 See *Faruqi v English Real Estate Ltd* [1979] 1 WLR 963.

affects the existence or the validity of the contract in its inception, as for instance, the question whether there is a sufficient memorandum.

Not only may the court decide the question submitted to it, but it may also grant consequential relief, that is, may order such things to be done as are the natural consequence of the decision. For instance, it may order rescission in favour of a purchaser, together with the return of his deposit.

Chapter 7

The definition of land

SUMMARY

A. Distinction between corporeal and incorporeal hereditaments   141
B. Fixtures   143

As we are about to discuss the interests that may subsist in land, it is appropriate that we should first gain a clear idea of the meaning attributed by law to the word "land".

A. DISTINCTION BETWEEN CORPOREAL AND INCORPOREAL HEREDITAMENTS

Law is at one with the layman in agreeing that "land" includes the surface of the earth, together with all the sub-jacent and super-jacent things of a physical nature such as buildings, trees and minerals,[1] but it also gives the word a far wider meaning, and one which would not occur to those unversed in legal terminology. Using the word "hereditament" to signify a right that is heritable, i.e. capable of passing by way of descent to heirs, our legal ancestors reached the remarkable[2] conclusion that hereditaments are either corporeal or incorporeal. As Blackstone said:

> Hereditaments, then, to use the largest expression, are of two kinds, corporeal and incorporeal. Corporeal consist of such as affect the senses; such as may be seen and handled by the body; incorporeal are not the object of sensation, can neither be seen nor handled, are creatures of the mind and exist only in contemplation. Corporeal hereditaments consist of substantial and permanent objects.[3]

What this comes to is that the subject matter of estate ownership may consist either of corporeities or of incorporeities. There is nothing remarkable in this, for it is obvious that an incorporeity such as a right of way may, equally with a house or a piece of land, be held in fee simple or for life. What is remarkable, however, is a terminology which declares that an interest in a corporeity, i.e. a physical thing capable of carrying seisin, is itself a corporeal *interest*, but that an interest in an incorporeity is an incorporeal *interest*. This nomenclature will not bear a moment's examination, for no proprietary interest can be other than a mere *right* of ownership, and no matter what the nature of its subject matter may be, it must always be incorporeal.

> All property, of whatever kind, is an *incorporeal* right to the *corporeal* use and profit of some *corporeal* thing.[4]

1 As to waste products dumped on land, see *Rogers (Inspector of Taxes) v Longsdon* [1967] Ch 93, [1966] 2 All ER 49. See p. 156, post.
2 Co Litt 6a; *Lloyd v Jones* (1848) 6 CB 81 at 90.
3 *Commentaries*, vol. ii. p. 17.
4 (1857) 1 Jurid Soc, p. 542 (S. M. Leake).

It is difficult to answer the following criticism of Austin:

> With us *all* rights and obligations are not *incorporeal things*; but certain rights are styled *incorporeal hereditaments*, and are opposed by that name to *hereditaments corporeal*. That is to say, *rights* of a certain species . . . are absurdly opposed to the *things* (strictly so called) which are the *subjects* or *matter* of rights of another species. The word *hereditaments* is evidently taken in two senses in the two phrases which stand to denote the species of hereditaments. A corporeal hereditament is the thing itself which is the subject of the right; an incorporeal hereditament is not the subject of the right, but the right itself.[5]

The continued use to the present day of this unscientific terminology need not, however, disturb us. The two facts to bear in mind are: first, that whether an interest, such as a fee simple estate, exists in a corporeity or an incorporeity, it is an interest in *land*; secondly, that the number of incorporeities recognized by English law is considerable. Blackstone described no fewer than ten *incorporeal hereditaments* some of which are no longer of practical importance.[6] The most important now are easements,[7] profits[8] and rent charges.[9]

The following is the definition of *land* for the purposes of the Law of Property Act 1925:

> "Land" includes land of any tenure, and mines and minerals, whether or not held apart from the surface, buildings or parts of buildings (whether the division is horizontal, vertical or made in any other way) and other corporeal hereditaments; also a manor, an advowson, and a rent and other incorporeal hereditaments, and an easement, right, privilege, or benefit in, over, or derived from land; but not an undivided share in land . . .[10]

There is one class of corporeal things, namely *fixtures*, which are regarded as "land" and which are sufficiently important to merit a somewhat extensive treatment.

---

5 *Jurisprudence* (5th edn) vol. i. p. 362; but see Sweet's answer in Challis, *Law of Real Property* (3rd edn), pp. 48–58. LPA 1925, s. 1 (2), p. 92, ante, perpetuates the confusion in describing a right to, for instance, an easement as an interest in land, notwithstanding that in s. 205 (1) (ix) it includes an easement in the definition of "land". The truth is that an incorporeity, such as an easement, is neither an estate nor an interest, but something in which an estate or an interest can exist.

6 *Commentaries*, vol. ii. c. iii. The list is: advowsons, tithes, commons, ways, offices, dignities, franchises, corodies (a right to receive victuals for one's maintenance), annuities and rents. "Whether the benefit of a restrictive covenant can be described as an incorporeal hereditament is a very doubtful question": *Earl of Leicester v Wells-next-the-Sea UDC* [1973] Ch 110 at 119, [1972] 3 All ER 77 at 82, per PLOWMAN J. On franchises, see *Sevenoaks District Council v Pattullo & Vinson Ltd* [1984] Ch 211, [1984] 1 All ER 544 (right of market).

7 P. 519, post. "An easement is that familiar creature of English land law: an estate or interest carved out of a larger estate or interest, but nevertheless constituting a hereditament in its own right. It is a burden on the servient tenement, but also 'land' vested in the proprietor of the dominant tenement": *Willies-Williams v National Trust* (1993) 65 P & CR 359 at 361, per HOFFMANN LJ.

8 P. 562, post.

9 P. 645, post.

10 Section 205 (1) (ix); cf. the definitions in SLA 1925, s. 117 (1) (ix); TA 1925, s. 68 (6); LRA 1925, s. 3 (viii); LCA 1972, s. 17 (1). See also Interpretation Act 1978, s. 5, Sch. 1. As to whether land includes an interest under a trust for sale, see pp. 235 et seq, post.

B. FIXTURES

(1) DISTINCTION BETWEEN LAND AND CHATTELS

The primary meaning from a historical point of view of "fixtures" is chattels which are so affixed to land or to a building on land as to become in fact part thereof.[11] Such chattels lose the character of chattels and pass with the ownership of the land, for the maxim of the law is, *quicquid plantatur solo, solo cedit*.

This question whether a chattel has been so affixed to land as to become part of it is sometimes exceedingly difficult to answer. It is a question of law for the judge,[12] but the decision in one case is no sure guide in another, for everything turns upon the circumstances and mainly, though not decisively, upon two particular circumstances, namely, the *degree of annexation* and the *object of annexation*.[13] We will take these considerations separately.

(a) Degree of annexation

The general rule is that a chattel is not deemed to be a fixture unless it is actually fastened to or connected with the land or building. Mere juxtaposition or the laying of an article, however heavy, upon the land does not *prima facie* make it a fixture, even though it subsequently sinks into the ground. If a superstructure can be removed without losing its identity, it will not in general be regarded as a fixture. Examples are a Dutch barn, consisting of a roof resting upon wooden uprights, the uprights being made to lie upon brick columns let into the ground[14]; or a printing machine weighing several tons, standing on the floor and secured by its own weight;[15] or a white marble statue of a Greek athlete weighing half a ton and standing on a plinth.[16] The case is the same if the posts that support the roof of a corrugated iron building are not embedded in the concrete floor, but are held in position by iron strips fixed into the floor. The concrete foundation, which is of course a fixture, is regarded as a separate unit from the superstructure.[17] Again, a printing machine that stands by its own weight upon the floor is not a fixture, even though the driving apparatus is attached to the building at certain points.[18] On the other hand a chattel that is attached to land, however slightly, is prima facie to be deemed a fixture. Thus, a verandah connected with a house is a fixture,[19] as also are doors, windows, chimneypieces, ovens and other similar things.

11 Leake, *Uses and Profits of Land*, p. 103.
12 *Reynolds v Ashby* [1904] AC 466.
13 *Holland v Hodgson* (1872) LR 7 CP 328 at 334, per BLACKBURN J.
14 *Elwes v Maw* (1802) 3 East 38 at 55; *Wiltshear v Cottrell* (1853) 1 E & B 674; *HE Dibble Ltd v Moore* [1970] 2 QB 181, [1969] 3 All ER 1465 (greenhouses resting on own weight on concrete dollies held not to be fixtures); *Deen v Andrews* (1986) 52 P & CR 17; *Hynes v Vaughan* (1985) 50 P & CR 444 (chrysanthemum growing frame and sprinkler system held not to be fixtures).
15 *Hulme v Brigham* [1943] KB 152, [1943] 1 All ER 204.
16 *Berkley v Poulett* (1976) 241 EG 911, 242 EG 39; M & B p. 92; cf *Hamp v Bygrave* (1982) 266 EG 720 (stone and lead garden ornaments held to be fixtures); *Berkley v Poulett*, supra, was not cited; [1983] NZLJ 256 (H. W. Wilkinson).
17 *Webb v Bevis Ltd* [1940] 1 All ER 247; cf *Jordan v May* [1947] KB 427, [1947] 1 All ER 231 (electric lighting engine and dynamo bolted to a concrete bed. These were held to be fixtures, *aliter* the batteries). The degree of affixation is not necessarily the same in every type of case; see, e.g., *London County Council v Wilkins* [1955] 2 QB 653, [1955] 2 All ER 180; affd. [1957] AC 362, [1956] 3 All ER 38 (whether a wooden sectional hut is exempt from rateability).
18 *Hulme v Brigham*, supra.
19 *Buckland v Butterfield* (1820) 2 Brod & Bing 54.

Nevertheless the extent of annexation is not a decisive test. As BLACKBURN J said:

> Perhaps the true rule is, that articles not otherwise attached to the land than by their own weight are not to be considered as part of the land, unless the circumstances are such as to shew that they were intended to be part of the land, the onus of showing that they were so intended lying on those who assert that they have ceased to be chattels; and that, on the contrary, an article which is affixed to the land even slightly is to be considered as part of the land, unless the circumstances are such as to shew that it was intended all along to continue a chattel, the onus lying on those who contend that it is a chattel.[20]

It is for this reason that the second consideration mentioned above is material, namely:

(b) Object of annexation

The test here is to ascertain whether the chattel has been fixed for its more convenient use as a chattel, or for the more convenient use of the land or building.[1] BLACKBURN J gave the following example:

> Blocks of stone placed one on the top of another without any mortar or cement for the purpose of forming a dry stone wall would become part of the land, though the same stones, if deposited in a builder's yard and for convenience sake stacked on the top of each other in the form of a wall, would remain chattels.[2]

Again, a comparatively durable method of affixation will not render a chattel a fixture, if the method of annexation is necessary to its proper enjoyment as a chattel. Thus in the case of *Leigh v Taylor*:[3]

> A tenant for life, the owner of some valuable tapestry, laid strips of wood over the drawing-room paper and fixed them to the walls with two-inch nails. Canvas was stretched over these strips, and the tapestry was fastened by tacks to the strips. It was held that the tapestry had not become a fixture.

VAUGHAN WILLIAMS LJ said:

> In my judgment it is obvious that everything which was done here can be accounted for as being absolutely necessary for the enjoyment of the tapestry, and when one arrives at that conclusion there is an end of the case.[4]

The principle of this decision was adopted where a lessee had erected some oak and pine panelling and a chimney-piece[5]; and where a vendor had screwed pictures while still in their frames into the recesses in the panelling of a dining-room.[6]

On the other hand, chattels may be annexed to or placed on land in circumstances which show an obvious intention to benefit the use of the land, and if this is so they become fixtures. Examples are seats secured to the floor of a cinema hall,[7] and such objects as statues, stone seats and ornamental

---

20 *Holland v Hodgson* (1872) LR 7 CP 328 at 335; *Bradshaw v Davey* [1952] 1 All ER 350 (yacht mooring in the Hamble River held intended to be a chattel).
1 *Wake v Hall* (1883) 8 App Cas 195 at 204.
2 *Holland v Hodgson*, supra, at 335.
3 [1902] AC 157.
4 See the same case in CA sub nom. *Re De Falbe* [1901] 1 Ch 523 at 537.
5 *Spyer v Phillipson* [1931] 2 Ch 183.
6 *Berkley v Poulett*, supra.
7 *Vaudeville Electric Cinema Ltd v Muriset* [1923] 2 Ch 74. Cf *Lyon & Co v London City and Midland Bank* [1903] 2 KB 135.

vases, held in position merely by their own weight, which are part of the architectural design of a house and its grounds.[8]

(2) RIGHT TO REMOVE FIXTURES

Even if a chattel is affixed to the land so as to become part of the land, the person who affixed it or his successors in title may have a right to remove it. The question arises as between the following parties:[9]

(a) Landlord and tenant

In the course of time, the rule that an article becomes part of the land to which it has been affixed has been relaxed in favour of the tenant for years, and he is now allowed to remove three particular classes of articles notwithstanding that they are fixtures in the strict sense of the term:

(i) Trade fixtures First, it has long been the rule that during the term the tenant may remove fixtures that have been attached to the land for the purpose of carrying on his particular trade, since it is in the public interest that industry should be encouraged. Thus in *Poole's Case*[10] in 1703 it was held by Lord HOLT:

> that during the term the soap-boiler might well remove the vats he set up in relation to trade, and that he might do it by the common law (and not by virtue of any special custom), in favour of trade and to encourage industry. But after the term they become a gift in law to him in reversion, and are not removable.

Engines for working collieries,[11] salt pans,[12] coppers and pipes erected by a brewing tenant,[13] the fittings of a public house,[14] petrol pumps installed at a wayside garage[15] and floor coverings and light fittings[16] have been held to come within the description of trade fixtures.

(ii) Ornamental and domestic fixtures Secondly, it is now well established that during the term a tenant may remove such chattels as he has affixed to a house for the sake either of ornament or of convenience, but this relaxation of the strict rule is not supported by such strong reasons as apply in the case of trade fixtures and it will not be extended. Examples of objects which have been held removable on this ground are ornamental chimney-pieces, wainscot fixed to the wall by screws, fixed water-tubs, stoves and grates, ranges and ovens.[17]

But any fixture which partakes of the nature of a permanent improvement and which cannot be removed without substantial damage to the house, such

---

8 *D'Eyncourt v Gregory* (1866) LR 3 Eq 382; cf *Berkley v Poulett*, supra, where the statue was not an integral part of the design.
9 See too *Simmons v Midford* [1969] 2 Ch 415, [1969] 2 All ER 1269 (plaintiff's drainpipe under roadway held to be chattel with which neighbour claiming an easement of drainage could not interfere); cf. *Montague v Long* (1972) 24 P & CR 240.
10 (1703) 1 Salk 368.
11 *Lawton v Lawton* (1743) 3 Atk 13.
12 *Mansfield v Blackburne* (1840) 6 Bing NC 426.
13 *Lawton v Lawton*, supra.
14 *Elliott v Bishop* (1854) 10 Exch 496.
15 *Smith v City Petroleum Co* [1940] 1 All ER 260.
16 *Young v Dalgety plc* [1987] 1 EGLR 116.
17 See Woodfall, *Landlord and Tenant* (28th edn) vol. 1, paras. 1557–8.

as a conservatory connected by a door with one of the living rooms, does not come within the exception of an ornamental fixture.[18]

Trade, ornamental and domestic fixtures must be removed before the end of the tenancy, otherwise they become a gift in law to the reversioner,[19] but a further period of grace is allowed when the tenant continues in possession after the term under a reasonable supposition of consent on the part of the landlord.[20] Where the tenant surrenders his tenancy to his landlord, he loses the right to remove these fixtures if the surrender is express, in the absence of agreement to the contrary; but he does not lose the right if the surrender is implied by operation of law, as where the lease has expired by effluxion of time and is replaced by a new lease between the same parties.[1] If tenant's fixtures are removed, the premises must be made good to the extent of being left in a reasonable condition.[2]

(iii) Agricultural fixtures The third exception relates to agricultural fixtures. Formerly, a farmer was in an unfavourable position with regard to chattels that he had fixed to his holding, for it was held in *Elwes v Maw*[3] in 1802 that, though the sole purpose of their affixation was to further and improve his agricultural operations, yet they could not be regarded as trade fixtures. In that case, the tenant farmer had built at his own cost a beast-house, a carpenter's shed, a fuel-house, a wagon-house and a fold-yard, each of which he removed before the end of the lease, leaving the premises in the same state as when he first became tenant. He was held liable to pay damages to the landlord.

The only mitigation at common law of this rigour came in 1901, when it was decided that, though buildings put up by a farmer are not trade fixtures, yet glasshouses built by a market-gardener for the purposes of his trade do come within this description and may be removed before the end of the tenancy against the will of the landlord.[4]

This particular matter has, however, been put upon a more equitable footing by a succession of statutes and the position now is as follows:

Any engine, machinery, fencing *or other fixture* affixed to an agricultural holding by a tenant and any building erected by him thereon, for which he is not otherwise entitled to compensation, becomes his property and is removable by him during the tenancy or within two months after its termination. After the expiration of this period the property in fixtures is no longer vested in him.[5]

Within at least a month before the termination of the tenancy notice of removal must be given to the landlord, who thereupon acquires an option to purchase the fixture.[6] There is no right of removal until the tenant has paid all rent and satisfied his other obligations under the tenancy.

---

18 *Buckland v Butterfield* (1820) 2 Brod & Bing 54.
19 *Poole's Case* (1703) 1 Salk 368.
20 *Ex parte Brook* (1878) 10 Ch D 100 at 109; *Leschallas v Woolf* [1908] 1 Ch 641.
 1 *New Zealand Government Property Corpn v HM and S Ltd* [1982] QB 1145, [1982] 2 All ER 624; [1987] Conv 253 (G. Kodilinye).
 2 *Mancetter Developments Ltd v Garmanson Ltd* [1986] QB 121, [1986] 1 All ER 449 (holes left behind in landlord's brickwork).
 3 (1802) 3 East 38; *Smith's Leading Cases* (13th edn), vol. ii. p. 193.
 4 *Mears v Callender* [1901] 2 Ch 388.
 5 Agricultural Holdings Act 1986, ss. 10 (1), (2).
 6 Ibid., s. 10 (2). Under s. 10 (5) the tenant must make good any damage done when removing the fixture.

The result of these developments is that if a landlord disputes the right of his tenant to remove a certain chattel from the premises, there are two separate questions to be answered. First, has the chattel become a fixture by reason of its affixation to the land? If not, *cadit quaestio*. If, however, the answer is in the affirmative, the further question arises whether it is a landlord's or a tenant's fixture, and this of course depends upon whether the chattel falls within one of the three categories already described.[7]

(b) Mortgagor and mortgagee

Fixtures pass with the land to the mortgagee even though not mentioned in the deed,[8] as also do those which are added later by the mortgagor himself while in possession. Moreover, a mortgagor in possession is not entitled to remove "tenant's" fixtures, whether they have been annexed to the land before or after the mortgage transaction.[9] These rules apply whether the mortgage is legal or equitable, and whether it affects freehold or leasehold premises. Where, however, fixtures have been annexed to land by a *third party* under an agreement between him and the mortgagor which permits him to remove them in certain circumstances, his right of removal cannot in general be defeated by the mortgagee. The mortgagee, by allowing the mortgagor to remain in possession, implicitly authorizes him to make agreements usual and proper in his particular trade.[10]

(c) Vendor and purchaser

A conveyance of land, in the absence of express reservation, passes fixtures, but not chattels[11] to the purchaser without special mention,[12] and they cannot be removed by a vendor who remains in possession between the contract of sale and the completion of the transaction, even though they consist of articles which, as between landlord and tenant, would be "tenant's fixtures".[13] The fixtures are deemed to have been paid for by the price fixed for the land, and if the vendor desires to remove them or to receive an additional sum in respect of them a clause to that effect must be inserted in the contract.[14]

(d) Tenant for life and reversioner or remainderman

The general rule obtains that chattels annexed by a tenant for life so as to become part of the land belong to the owner of the fee simple. Nevertheless the personal representatives of a deceased tenant for life are entitled to

---

7 *Bain v Brand* (1876) 1 App Cas 762 at 767, per Lord CAIRNS.
8 *Vaudeville Electric Cinema Ltd v Muriset* [1923] 2 Ch 74; LPA 1925, ss. 62 (1), 205 (1) (ii).
9 *Longbottom v Berry* (1869) LR 5 QB 123.
10 *Gough v Wood & Co* [1894] 1 QB 713.
11 *Moffatt v Kazana* [1969] 2 QB 152, [1968] 3 All ER 271; *HE Dibble Ltd v Moore* [1970] 2 QB 181, [1969] 3 All ER 1465; *Deen v Andrews* (1986) 52 P & CR 17. See also *Berkley v Poulett* (1976) 241 EG 911, 242 EG 39 (sub-purchaser).
12 LPA 1925, s. 62 (1). The section is set out, p. 534, post.
13 *Gibson v Hammersmith Rly Co* (1863) 32 LJ Ch 337; *Phillips v Lamdin* [1949] 2 KB 33, [1949] 1 All ER 770.
14 On hire-purchase agreements and fixtures, see (1963) 27 Conv (NS) 30 (A. G. Guest and J. Lever); [1990] Conv 275 (G. McCormack).

remove "such fixtures as are removable by a tenant for years", i.e. objects affixed for purposes of trade, ornamentation or domestic use.[15]

(e) Executor of fee simple owner and devisee

If A, the tenant in fee simple of Blackacre, devises Blackacre to B, it might be argued that A's executors are entitled to remove, at any rate, "tenant's fixtures". The rule, however, is well established that all fixtures, no matter of what description, pass with the land to the devisee.[16]

15 *Lawton v Lawton* (1743) 3 Atk 13; p. 145, ante. There is some question whether the power of removal by the personal representative is not more restricted than in the case of a tenant for years.
16 *Re Whaley* [1908] 1 Ch 615; *Re Lord Chesterfield's Settled Estates* [1911] 1 Ch 237 (ornamental wood carvings by Grinling Gibbons).

Part II

Estates and interests in land

SUMMARY

Part II

Estates and interests in land

A. THE ESTATE IN FEE SIMPLE ABSOLUTE IN POSSESSION

SUMMARY

Introduction

After this brief introductory survey, the next task is to describe the estates and interests that may subsist in land. The general arrangement of the following account of this matter is based upon the distinction between family interests arising under a settlement or a trust for sale and what, for want of a better title, are called "commercial interests", i.e. interests such as leaseholds, mortgages and easements, that arise in the ordinary routine of business and for the most part are not inevitable parts of family endowment schemes. What deserves to be emphasized is that the propensity of land-owners to distribute portions of the fee simple among a succession of descendants or other relatives, a propensity that has been a feature of English social life for many centuries, though far less pronounced now in this age of increased taxation, has left an indelible mark upon the law of real property. To this sentiment is due the occurrence in conveyancing practice of entailed, life and future interests and of powers of appointment, interests that are never found except as cogs in the wheel of a settlement.

Before the proposed dichotomy of interests can be elaborated, however, it is necessary to describe the fee simple absolute in possession. This is the axis round which any account of landed interests must revolve, for it represents the subject matter out of which lesser proprietary rights, whether family or commercial, may be carved.

Chapter 8

The estate in fee simple absolute in possession

SUMMARY

SECTION I DEFINITION

(a) Fee simple

The first essential is to investigate the precise meaning of the statutory expression fee simple absolute in possession, which as we have seen is the only *freehold* interest capable of existing as a legal estate.[1] The word *fee* had by Littleton's day come to denote that the estate was inheritable, that is to say, that it would endure until the person entitled to it *for the time being*— whether the original donee or some subsequent alienee—died intestate and left no heir.[2] The word *simple* showed that the fee was one which was capable of passing to the heirs *general* and was not restricted to passing to a particular class of heirs.[3] This last fact therefore distinguishes a fee simple from another kind of fee which used to be called a fee tail and is now called an entailed interest, for this is a freehold that passes, on the intestacy of its owner, only to the particular class of lineal descendants specified in the instrument of creation.[4] Thus if a tenant in fee simple died intestate before 1926, his estate passed to his nearest heir, who according to the circumstances might be a descendant or an ascendant, a lineal or a collateral relative.[5]

An entailed interest, on the other hand (and this is still the law), was capable of passing only to lineal descendants, and these might, according to the terms of the instrument of gift, be either lineal descendants in general or a restricted class of descendants, such as male heirs or the issue of the tenant by a specified wife. The characteristic of general inheritability is still the attribute of a fee simple, but the significance of this is now modified, as will

1 LPA 1925, s. 1 (1) (*a*); pp. 91–2, ante.
2 Pollock and Maitland, *History of English Law* (2nd edn), vol. ii, p. 14.
3 Co Litt 1*a*, *b*, 18*a*, Blackstone, vol. ii. p. 105.
4 Pp. 249–52, post.
5 Pp. 871–5, post.

be explained later, by the abolition of the doctrine of heirship on intestacy except in the case of the entailed interest. The land itself no longer passes to the nearest heir but upon the death of the owner intestate is held by the administrators on trust for sale, for distribution among the nearest relatives according to a scheme introduced by the Administration of Estates Act 1925, as amended by subsequent legislation.[6] The relatives specified by the Act, however, comprise descendants and ascendants, both lineal and collateral, and it is therefore still true to say that a fee simple is an estate which is the subject of general inheritability.

(b) Absolute

It is not every fee simple that is a legal estate, for the Law of Property Act 1925 confines that attribute to a fee simple absolute in possession. Postponing for the moment the consideration of the last two words, we must inquire what is meant by the word "absolute". This is not defined in the Act, but it clearly excludes an estate that is defeasible either by the breach of a condition or by the possibility that it may pass to some new owner upon the happening of a specified event. Preston explained the purport of *absolute* in the following words:[7]

> The epithet *absolute* is used to distinguish an estate extended to any given time, without any condition to defeat, or collateral limitation to determine the estate in the mean time, from an estate subject to a condition or collateral limitation. The term absolute is of the same signification with the word pure, or *simple*, a word which expresses that the estate is not determinable by any event besides the event marked by the clause of limitation.

Thus a fee simple absolute is distinguished from a *determinable* fee simple, i.e. one which according to the express terms of its limitation may determine by some event before the completion of the full period for which it may possibly continue.[8]

If, for instance, premises are limited in fee simple to an incorporated golf club "so long as the premises are used for the purposes of the Club", the interest is a fee simple because it may possibly continue for ever, but it is not a fee simple absolute since it will cease and will return to the grantor or his successors if at some time in the future the premises are used for other purposes.

Again, the limitation of a fee simple may be accompanied by an executory limitation over which provides that if a certain event happens the estate shall pass from the grantee to another person. As, for instance, where there is a grant of Whiteacre,

> To A in fee simple, but if he becomes entitled to Blackacre, then to B in fee simple.

Here the fee simple given to A is not absolute, since it is liable to be divested from him on the occurrence of the specified event. There is one exception to this rule, for the Law of Property Act 1925 provides that a fee simple which is liable to be divested under the provisions of the Lands Clauses Acts or any

---

6 P. 875, post.
7 *Preston on Estates*, vol. i. pp. 125–6.
8 See p. 335, post.

similar statute is "for the purposes of the Act" a fee simple *absolute*.[9] The effect of this provision is that the interest may be a legal estate within section 1 (1) of the Law of Property Act 1925, and not an equitable interest giving rise to a settlement under the Settled Land Act. The conditions attached to the fee simple are not affected. Statutes of this type, which enable land to be acquired for certain public purposes, generally provide expressly that if the purpose fails or is not carried out the land shall revert to the original owner or shall vest in some other person. An express provision to this effect is not, however, essential to bring a statute within the exception. It is sufficient if the implication is that the grantee shall be divested of his interest upon the fulfilment or failure of the purpose for which the land was acquired.[10]

The Law of Property Act 1925 also provides that a fee simple vested in a corporation shall be regarded as absolute notwithstanding its liability to determine upon the dissolution of the corporate body.[11]

If a condition is annexed to the limitation of a fee simple providing that the grantor shall be entitled to re-enter and recover his interest if a certain event happens or does not happen, it is equally clear on general principles that the estate is not a fee simple absolute within the meaning of the description given by Preston.

Nevertheless the provision of the Law of Property Act 1925, which denied the character of a legal estate to an interest of this nature, caused considerable difficulty. In the North West of England and in the county of Avon (and especially in Manchester and Bristol), it has been a common practice for a purchaser of a fee simple, instead of paying the purchase money in a lump sum, to enter into a covenant to pay a perpetual annual rentcharge.[12] The payment of the rent is secured to the vendor and his successors by the reservation of either a right of entry or a right of re-entry. The former permits the vendor and his successors to enter the land at any time in the future if the annual payment falls into arrear and to hold the land *as a leasehold interest* until the arrears are paid.[13] The right of re-entry (which is more common in the case of a lease[14]) arises where the conveyance contains a condition that the purchaser and his successors will pay the rent and that the vendor shall

---

9 LPA 1925, s. 7 (1), as amended by Reverter of Sites Act 1987, which excludes from s. 7 (1) the School Sites Acts, the Literary and Scientific Institutions Act 1854 and the Places of Worship Sites Act 1873. The right of reverter in those cases is replaced by a trust for sale. Where, for example, a school site ceases to be used for purposes for which it was originally granted, the charitable trustees continue to hold the legal estate on trust for sale for the revertee: s. 1; *Marchant v Onslow* [1994] 13 EG 114. They may apply to the Charity Commissioners to have the interests of the revertee extinguished: s. 2. A revertee in some circumstances may be entitled to compensation: s. 2 (4). For the difficulties caused by the original s. 7 (1), see Law Commission Report on Rights of Reverter 1981 (Law Com No 111, Cmnd 8410). The Act departs in a significant number of respects from the Report's recommendations. See Current Law Statutes Annotated (J. Hill); [1987] Conv 408 (D. Evans).

10 *Tithe Redemption Commission v Runcorn UDC* [1954] Ch 383, [1954] 1 All ER 653 (highway vested in the local highway authority; Local Government Act 1929 held to be "a similar statute" within LPA 1925, s. 7 (1)).

11 S. 7(2). As to whether the lands of a corporation upon its dissolution reverted to the donor or escheated to the lord, see Co Litt 13b; Gray, *Rule against Perpetuities* (4th edn), ss. 44–52; Challis, *Law of Real Property* (3rd edn), pp. 35–6, 467–8; *Hastings Corpn v Letton* [1908] 1 KB 378; *Re Woking UDC* [1914] 1 Ch 300; *Re Sir Thomas Spencer Wells* [1933] Ch 29; (1933) 49 LQR 240; (1934) 50 LQR 33 (F. E. Farrer); (1935) 51 LQR 347 (M. W. Hughes), 361 (F. E. Farrer).

12 Pp. 647 et seq, post.

13 Litt s. 327; Co Litt 202*b*; ibid., note 93 by Hargrave and Butler.

14 Pp. 427, 434, post.

be entitled to re-enter if this condition is broken. In this case the person entitled to the rent may either re-enter upon the land or bring proceedings for its recovery, whereupon the interest of the purchaser is forfeited and the vendor *reacquires his old estate*.[15]

The fact that a fee simple liable to interruption in either of these ways was not a legal estate within the meaning of the Law of Property Act 1925 operated to the prejudice of a landowner, for not only did it seem to make the land subject to the Settled Land Act and thus to require the execution of a vesting deed, but it made it difficult to discover where the legal estate resided.[16]

In view of this inconvenience it was later enacted that:

> a fee simple subject to a legal or equitable right of entry or re-entry is for the purposes of this Act a fee simple absolute.[17]

The word "absolute" does not imply freedom from incumbrances. Thus a fee simple, though subject to a lien or a mortgage, whether legal or equitable, or to a mere charge, is none the less absolute.

(c) In possession

Finally, to have the character of a legal estate, a fee simple absolute must be *in possession*. "Possession" is not here confined to its popular meaning, for it includes receipt of rents and profits or the right to receive the same.[18] Therefore a tenant in fee simple who has leased the land to a tenant for years is the owner of a legal estate even though he is not in physical possession of the land. If, however, he is entitled to the fee simple only at some time in the future, as for instance in the case of a limitation:

> to A for life and then to B in fee simple,

A has an equitable life interest and B has an equitable fee simple. The land is settled land under the Settled Land Act 1925, unless the limitation takes effect under a trust for sale.[19]

SECTION II MODE OF CREATION

A. WORDS OF LIMITATION

We must first distinguish between "words of limitation" and "words of purchase". "Words of limitation" indicate the size of the interest given by some instrument; they limit or define it. On the other hand, "words of purchase" (*perquisitio*) point out, by name or description, the person who is to acquire (*perquirit*) an interest in land. A "purchaser" in this technical sense does not denote a person who buys land, but one to whom land is expressly transferred by *act of parties*, as for instance by conveyance on sale, by gift or by will. If land is given "to A and his heirs", A is a purchaser since he is

---

15 Litt s. 325.
16 (1926) 61 LJ News 49 (F. E. Farrer). See also M & B p. 7, n. 4.
17 LP(A)A 1926, Sch. The rentcharge, being perpetual, is a *legal* interest under LPA 1925, s. 1 (2) (*b*), p. 92, ante; and under s. 1 (2) (*e*), the right of entry, being "annexed to a legal rentcharge", is also a *legal* interest.
18 LPA 1925, ss. 205 (1) (xix), 95 (4); *District Bank Ltd v Webb* [1958] 1 WLR 148, [1958] 1 All ER 126; M & B, p. 8.
19 P. 176, post.

personally designated as the transferee, but the words "and his heirs" are words of limitation. They merely indicate the *quantum* of interest that A is to take, and give the heirs nothing by direct gift. The lands may, of course, descend to them as heirs if A dies intestate, but they will not be purchasers since the land comes to them by operation of law and not by act of parties.[20]

(1) NATURAL PERSONS

Whether a fee simple passes to a grantee or a devisee of land depends upon the words of limitation contained in the deed or will. In the case of deeds the law was in former times exceedingly strict upon this point. If certain expressions were adopted the effect was to create a fee simple; if others, a fee tail or life estate. Thus before 1882 the only way of creating a fee simple by a direct grant *inter vivos* was by a limitation to the grantee *and his heirs*. This expression has been common form since the birth of English law, and perhaps its original implication was that the tenant could not alienate his interest without first consulting the apparent heirs. In the thirteenth century, however, all restraints of that kind on alienation disappeared and it became settled that the expression did not confer rights of any sort upon the heir, but was used merely to show that the tenant had an estate that would endure at least as long as his heirs endured.[1]

If in a *deed* there was for instance a grant to:

A and his assignees;
A for ever;
A and his descendants;
A and his successors,[2]

then, however untechnical the expression might be, and however obvious the intention of the parties might be to convey the fee simple, the only effect was to pass a life estate to A. This strictness was mitigated and an alternative form of words was permitted by the Conveyancing Act 1881, which provided that in deeds executed after 31 December 1881, the fee simple should pass if the expression "in fee simple" was adopted.

In the case of land *devised by will* the law was more liberal in its definition of words of limitation than it was in the case of deeds. Thus in addition to the technical expression "and his heirs", any informal words which clearly showed that the testator intended to give the fee simple were allowed to have that effect,[3] but notwithstanding this more lenient attitude the fact remained that laxity in the use of words of limitation frequently defeated intention. The Wills Act 1837 therefore provided that:

20 See Fearne, *Contingent Remainders*, pp. 79–80; and *IRC v Gribble* [1913] 3 KB 212, where at 218 BUCKLEY LJ said: " 'Purchaser', as it seems to me, may mean any one of four things. First, it may bear what has been called the vulgar or commercial meaning; purchaser may mean a buyer for money. Secondly, it may also include a person who becomes a purchaser, for money's worth, which would include the case of an exchange. Thirdly, it may mean a purchaser for valuable consideration, which need not be money or money's worth, but may be, say, a covenant on the consideration of marriage. Fourthly it may bear that which in the language of real property lawyers is its technical meaning, namely a person who does not take by descent."
1 Pollock and Maitland, *History of English Law* (2nd edn), vol. ii. p. 13.
2 *Bankes v Salisbury Diocesan Council of Education Incorporated* [1960] Ch 631, [1960] 2 All ER 372.
3 *Jarman on Wills* (8th edn), p. 1802.

where any real estate shall be devised to any person without any words of limitation, such devise shall be construed to pass the fee simple, or other the whole estate or interest which the testator had power to dispose of by will in such real estate, unless a contrary intention shall appear by the will.[4]

The effect of this enactment was to reverse the former law.

Before 1837 the effect of using a non-technical expression was to pass only a life estate, unless an intention to pass the whole fee simple could be clearly deduced; but since 1837 the effect is to pass the entire interest which the testator happens to have in the lands, unless his intention clearly is to give some smaller interest. The burden of proving that a smaller interest passes lies on those who maintain that hypothesis.

The rule thus introduced for wills by the Act of 1837 was extended to deeds by the Law of Property Act 1925. It provides that:[5]

a conveyance of freehold land to any person without words of limitation, or any equivalent expression, shall pass to the grantee the fee simple or other the whole interest which the grantor had power to convey in such land, unless a contrary intention appears in the conveyance.

It will be noticed that the language of this section corresponds closely with that of the Wills Act 1837.

The position, then, at the present day, both for deeds and for wills, is that, if it is desired to confer a fee simple upon X, land may be limited "to X in fee simple" or "to X and his heirs"; but that, if any other expression is used, as for instance, "to X", or "to X for ever", the fee simple, if owned by the alienor, will pass unless the instrument clearly shows that there was no such intention.[6] In practice the words "to X in fee simple" are used, in order to avoid the possibility of a contrary intention appearing in the instrument.

A limitation before 1926, not *to A and his heirs*, but to A for life, remainder to his heirs

would have conferred a fee simple estate upon A under the rule known as the *Rule in Shelley's Case*. This rule, which is described below,[7] has, however, been abolished, and the effect of such a limitation now is to give a life interest to A and a fee simple estate to his heir.

(2) CORPORATIONS

Where it was desired to grant a fee simple to a corporation sole,[8] i.e. a body politic having perpetual succession and consisting of a single person, such as a bishop, a parson, the Crown or the Public Trustee, the old law was that the grant must be made to the person in question *and his successors*, otherwise it merely operated to confer an estate for life on the actual holder of the office.[9] This rule has, however, been altered,[10] and a conveyance of freehold land in which the word "successors" has been omitted passes to the corporation the fee simple or other the whole interest which the grantor has, unless a contrary intention appears in the conveyance.

---

4 S. 28.
5 LPA 1925, s. 60 (1).
6 See, for example, *Quarm v Quarm* [1892] 1 QB 184.
7 P. 256, post.
8 P. 934, post.
9 Co Litt 8*b*, 94*b*.
10 LPA 1925, s. 60 (2).

In the case of a corporation aggregate,[11] i.e. a collection of several persons united into one body under a special name and having perpetual existence, such as a limited liability company incorporated under the Companies Act 1985, it is sufficient to grant to the corporation under its corporate name.[12]

B. VOLUNTARY CONVEYANCES

If a feoffment were made before the Statute of Uses to a stranger in blood without the receipt of a money consideration (i.e. a voluntary conveyance), and *without declaring a use* in favour of the feoffee, the rule was that the land must be held by the feoffee to the use of the feoffor.[13] The equitable interest that thus returned by implication to the feoffor was called a resulting use. The effect of the enactment by the Statute of Uses that a *cestui que use* should have the legal estate was, of course, that the legal estate resulted to the feoffor.[14] In order to prevent this it became the practice in the case of such a conveyance to declare in the *habendum*[15] of the deed that the land was granted "unto and to the use of" the grantee. The repeal of the Statute of Uses by the legislation of 1925 would, in the absence of a further enactment, have restored the original rule, and it might have led practitioners to believe that the expression "to the use of" was still necessary in order to render a voluntary conveyance effective. It is, however, enacted that:

> in a voluntary conveyance a resulting trust for the grantor shall not be implied merely by reason that the property is not expressed to be conveyed for the use or benefit of the grantee.[16]

C. REGISTERED LAND

In registered land there are two points to notice about the fee simple absolute in possession. First, where the registered proprietor transfers it *inter vivos*, no words of limitation are required in the transfer.[17] Secondly, as we have seen, the legal estate will not pass to the transferee until the transfer is completed by registration.[18] For this reason it has been suggested[19] that the Land Registration Act 1925 really provides a new statutory title to land, one that is not the fee simple, but a new fee based on it. But the argument is really a verbal one as to how the consequences of registration affect the character of what is registered. Sections 5 and 69 (1) of the Act refer to a registered

---

11 P. 934, post.
12 Co Litt 94*b*.
13 Sanders, *Uses and Trusts*, (5th edn), vol. i. p. 60.
14 Ibid., p. 97; *Beckwith's Case* (1589) 2 Co Rep 56*b*.
15 P. 783, post.
16 LPA 1925, s. 60 (3).
17 P. 785, post; *AJ Dunning & Sons (Shopfitters) Ltd v Sykes & Son (Poole) Ltd* [1987] Ch 287 at 302, [1987] 1 All ER 700 at 708.
18 LRA 1925, s. 19 (1), 20 (1); p. 100, ante.
19 Ruoff and Roper, para. 2–15, referring to "a great deal of learned and hypothetical argument". See (1949) 12 MLR 139, 477 (A. D. Hargreaves); 205 (H. Potter); (1947) 11 Conv (NS) 184, 232 (R. C. Connell); (1972) 88 LQR 93 (D. Jackson); Farrand, *Contract and Conveyance* (2nd edn) pp. 178–80; Barnsley, *Conveyancing Law and Practice* (3rd edn), pp. 35–36.

proprietor as having a fee simple absolute in possession vested in him and it seems only a complication to depart from this terminology.[20]

SECTION III THE LEGAL POSITION OF A TENANT IN FEE SIMPLE

A. EXTENT OF OWNERSHIP

A tenant in fee simple has extensive property rights in the subject-matter of his interest. In accordance with the maxim:

cujus est solum, ejus est usque ad coelum et ad inferos[1]

the common law principle is that a tenant in fee simple is owner of everything in, on and above his land. As Lord WILBERFORCE said:[2]

At most the maxim is used as a statement, imprecise enough, of the extent of the rights, prima facie, of owners of land: BOWEN LJ was concerned with these rights when . . . he said "Prima facie the owner of the land has everything under the sky down to the centre of the earth".[3]

The rights are as extensive as common law and statute permit.[4]

(1) IN AND ON THE LAND

(a) Mines and minerals

At common law all mines and minerals that lie beneath the soil belong absolutely to the tenant in fee simple but by statute all interests in coal are vested in the British Coal Corporation[5] and petroleum existing in its natural condition in strata is vested in the Crown.[6] Further, the Crown is entitled to all gold and silver in gold and silver mines.[7]

(b) Chattels

In the absence of trustworthy evidence of ownership, there is a legal presumption that the fee simple owner, if in possession, is owner of chattels found on or under his land.[8]

---

20 See also ss. 18, 20.
 1 "A colourful phrase often upon the lips of lawyers since it was first coined by Accursius in Bologna in the 13th century": *Baron Bernstein of Leigh v Skyviews & General Ltd* [1978] QB 479 at 485, [1977] 2 All ER 902 at 905, per GRIFFITHS J.
 2 *Commissioner for Railways v Valuer-General* [1974] AC 328 at 351–2. The maxim was applied in *Grigsby v Melville* [1974] 1 WLR 80, [1973] 3 All ER 455 (cellar underneath drawing-room floor), *Graystone Property Developments Ltd v Margulies* (1983) 47 P & CR 472 (void space between false ceiling and underneath of floor of flat above).
 3 *Pountney v Clayton* (1883) 11 QBD 820 at 838.
 4 "It is quite plain that airspace is not something which even the most ingenious conveyancer of Lincoln's Inn has ever dealt with as an item of property unrelated to the ground over which it lies": *Rolfe v Wimpey Waste Management* [1988] STC 329 at 357, per HARMAN J.
 5 Coal Act 1938; Coal Industry Nationalisation Act 1946; Coal Industry Act 1987, s. 1 (2), Sch. 1, para 1.
 6 Petroleum (Production) Act 1934. See *Earl of Lonsdale v A-G* [1982] 1 WLR 887, [1982] 3 All ER 579 ("mines and minerals" in 1880 conveyance held not to include oil and natural gas).
 7 *The Case of Mines* (1567) 1 Plowd 310. Royal Mines Acts 1688, 1693.
 8 *South Staffordshire Water Co v Sharman* [1896] 2 QB 44; *Hannah v Peel* [1945] KB 509; *Hibbert v McKiernan* [1948] 2 KB 142; *Re Cohen* [1953] Ch 88, [1953] 1 All ER 378; *City of London Corpn v Appleyard* [1963] 1 WLR 982, [1963] 2 All ER 834; *Moffatt v Kazana* [1969] 2 QB 152, [1968] 3 All ER 271; *Parker v British Airways Board* [1982] QB 1004, [1982] 1 All ER 834 especially at 1017–1018, at 843 (gold bracelet found on floor in international executive

(c) Treasure trove

The proprietary rights of the tenant do not extend to treasure trove.

> Treasure trove is, where any gold or silver in coin, plate, or bullion is found concealed in a house, or in the earth, or other private place, the owner thereof being unknown, in which case the treasure belongs to the King or his grantee having the franchise of treasure trove; but if he that laid it be known or afterwards discovered, the owner and not the King is entitled to it; this prerogative right only applying in the absence of an owner to claim the property. If the owner, instead of hiding the treasure, casually lost it, or purposely parted with it,[9] in such a manner that it is evident he intended to abandon the property altogether, and did not purpose to resume it on another occasion, as if he threw it on the ground, or other public place, or in the sea, the first finder is entitled to the property as against every one but the owner, and the King's prerogative does not in this respect obtain. So that it is the hiding, and not the abandonment, of the property that entitles the King to it.[10]

Whether a coin or object is made of silver or gold is a question of fact. It must contain a substantial proportion of gold or silver. Thus, Roman coins of the third century AD with a silver content ranging from 0.2 to 18 per cent were held not to be treasure trove.[11]

(d) Sea-shore

An owner of land adjoining the sea is entitled to the sea-shore[12] down to a point which is reached by an ordinary high tide, but all the shore below that is vested in the Crown or its grantee.[13]

He is also entitled to land which is added by gradual and imperceptible accretion from the sea.[14]

lounge at Heathrow held to belong to finder); [1990] Conv 348 (D. C. Hoath); *Tamworth Industries v A–G* [1991] 3 NZLR 616; [1993] CLP Part I, p. 81 (P. Kohler). See Goodhart, *Essays in Jurisprudence and the Common Law*, pp. 75–90; Harris, *Oxford Essays in Jurisprudence* (ed. Guest), pp. 69–106.

9 *Quaere*, whether a possessor can divest himself of possession of a thing by its deliberate abandonment; Pollock and Wright, *Possession in the Common Law*, p. 124; *Haynes' Case* (1613) 12 Co Rep 113; *Arrow Shipping Co v Tyne Improvement Comrs* [1894] AC 508 at 532.

10 *Chitty on the Prerogative*, p. 152, cited *A–G v Moore* [1893] 1 Ch 676 at 683; *A–G v Trustees of British Museum* [1903] 2 Ch 598. On treasure generally, see Hill, *Treasure Trove in Law and Practice*.

11 *A–G of the Duchy of Lancaster v G E Overton (Farms) Ltd* [1982] Ch 277, [1982] 1 All ER 524; [1980] CLJ 281 (D. E. C. Yale); (1981) 44 MLR 178 (N. E. Palmer). See the Law Commission's *Treasure Trove: Law Reform Issues* (1987); Treasury's *Review of Ex Gratia Awards to Finders of Treasure Trove*, which decided that, in the absence of any criminal behaviour on the part of the finder, ex gratia payments equal to the full value of the find should continue to be made; if no museum wished to acquire the fund, it should be returned to the finder. See also the Earl of Perth's Private Members' Bill (1 March 1994), defining treasure as all objects of more than 200 years old, whether buried with intention of recovery, buried in a grave or simply lost. The law is to be reviewed by the Department of National Heritage.

12 See *Government of Penang v Beng Hong Oon* [1972] AC 425 at 435, 439, [1971] 3 All ER 1163 at 1170, 1173.

13 *Lowe v Govett* (1832) 3 B & Ad 863; *Blundell v Catterall* (1821) 5 B & Ald 268; *Alfred F Beckett Ltd v Lyons* [1967] Ch 449, [1967] 1 All ER 833. For the rights of the public over the sea-shore, see [1974] JPL 705 (A. Wharam).

14 *Gifford v Lord Yarborough* (1828) 5 Bing 163. See *Baxendale v Instow Parish Council* [1982] Ch 14 at 23, [1981] 2 All ER 620 at 627; Wisdom, *Law of Watercourses* (5th edn), chapter 2. The rule of accretion also applies to inland lakes: *Southern Centre of Theosophy Inc v State of South Australia* [1982] AC 706, [1982] 1 All ER 283 (accretion by fluvial action and river-blown sand); (1983) 99 LQR 412 (P. Jackson); [1986] Conv 255 (W. Howarth).

(e) Wild creatures

The owner's rights in respect of wild animals, such as game,[15] depend upon the circumstances. Such animals are not within the absolute ownership of any particular person. There are two exceptions, for wild animals which have been tamed belong to the person who has tamed them, and animals too young to escape belong to the occupier of the land on which they are until they gain their natural liberty.[16] In other cases the tenant in fee simple or, indeed, the occupier of the land, has not an absolute, but a qualified, right of ownership over the animals within the confines of his property in the sense that the exclusive right to catch and appropriate them belongs to him *ratione soli*.[17] Thus, game which is killed by a trespasser belongs to the occupier of the land on which it is killed. The only exception to this principle and one not altogether free from doubt is that if A starts game on the land of B, and hunts it on to the ground of C and kills it there, the ownership of the game belongs to A the hunter, though of course he is liable in trespass both to B and to C.[18]

(2) ABOVE THE LAND

Although the tenant does not acquire the ownership of anything that overhangs his land, such as a cornice, an illuminated advertisement, telephone wires or the bough of a tree, he can maintain an action of nuisance or of trespass against the person who allows it to be there,[19] unless it has been acquired by that person as an easement.[20] A tenant's rights in the airspace above as property do not, however, extend to an unlimited height, but are restricted to such height as is necessary for the ordinary use and enjoyment of his land. Thus, where an aircraft flew over land for the purpose of taking an aerial photograph of a house on it, an action for trespass failed.[1] And there was also a defence under the Civil Aviation Act 1982,[2] which provides that no action shall lie in respect of trespass or nuisance by reason

15 See *Inglewood Investment Co Ltd v Forestry Commission* [1988] 1 WLR 1278, [1988] 1 All ER 783 (game construed to mean feathered game and not deer).
16 *Case of Swans* (1592) 7 Co Rep 15b.
17 *Blades v Higgs* (1865) 11 HL Cas 621, per WESTBURY LC. The Crown has a prerogative right to swans, and royal fish, e.g. whales and sturgeon. Any such right to other wild creatures was abolished by the Wild Creatures and Forest Laws Act 1971, s. 1 (1) (*a*).
18 *Sutton v Moody* (1697) 1 Ld Raym 250, criticized by Lord CHELMSFORD in *Blades v Higgs* (1865) 11 HL Cas 621 at 639. It is a criminal offence under the Badgers Act 1973 (as amended by the Badgers Act 1991; Badgers (Further Protection) Act 1991) to kill badgers, and under the Wildlife and Countryside Act 1981 to kill wild animals listed in Sch. 5 (for example, swallowtail butterfly, common otter and red squirrel), and wild birds in Sch. 1 (for example, bee-eater, chough, fieldfare, hoopoe, kingfisher and barn owl). The Act was amended by the Wildlife and Countryside Act 1981 (Variation of Schedules) Order 1988 (S.I. 1988 No. 288); S.I. 1989 No. 906; and by the Wildlife and Countryside (Amendment) Act 1991. See also the Deer Act 1991.
19 *Wandsworth Board of Works v United Telephone Co* (1884) 13 QBD 904; *Lemmon v Webb* [1895] AC 1; *Gifford v Dent* [1926] WN 336; *Kelsen v Imperial Tobacco Co (of Great Britain and Ireland) Ltd* [1957] 2 QB 334, [1957] 2 All ER 343; *Woollerton and Wilson Ltd v Richard Costain Ltd* [1971] 1 WLR 411, [1970] 1 All ER 483; *Anchor Brewhouse Developments Ltd v Berkley House (Docklands Developments) Ltd* [1987] 2 EGLR 173 (tower cranes oversailing adjoining land held to be infringement of airspace and therefore trespass: injunction granted).
20 *Simpson v Weber* (1925) 41 TLR 302.
 1 *Baron Bernstein of Leigh v Skyviews and General Ltd* [1978] QB 479, [1977] 2 All ER 902. See McNair *Law of the Air* (3rd edn 1964), pp. 31 et seq.
 2 S. 76 (1).

only of the flight of an aircraft over any property at a height which is reasonable under the circumstances, provided that certain regulations are complied with.

(3) WATER[3]

A landowner has certain valuable rights over water that may run through or be situated on his land.

The right of abstraction at common law, however, has been substantially modified by statute. Under the Water Resources Act 1991 the National Rivers Authority runs a compulsory system of licensing for the abstraction of water.[4]

(a) Ponds and lakes

Water standing upon his land in a lake or pond is part of the land and belongs to him. If it stands partly upon his land and partly upon that of another, each is probably entitled to such part as lies opposite his own bank, but only up to a point half way between his and the opposite bank.[5]

(b) Percolating water

Water percolating underneath the land and not contained in a defined and contracted channel is a common supply in which nobody has any property, but at common law it becomes the absolute property of any occupier by whom it is appropriated.[6]

If an occupier abstracts percolating water, he becomes the owner of it and may take it regardless of the consequences, whether physical or pecuniary, to his neighbours.[7] Thus he will not be liable to his neighbours, though the effect may have been to dry up a spring or a well on their land.[8]

(c) Streams and rivers

The next type of case is where a river or stream runs in a *definite channel*, whether above or below the surface, though it must be noted that an underground stream does not come within this category until it is established that it follows a definite course.[9] Underground water, the course of which cannot be ascertained without excavation, ranks as percolating water. Two questions arise where a stream follows a definite course; first, the rights of the riparian owner or owners in the *bed*, secondly, their rights in the *water*.

---

3 See generally Wisdom, *Law of Watercourses* (5th edn); *Aspects of Water Law* (1981).
4 Ss. 24–72, replacing provisions under the Water Resources Act 1963, as amended.
5 See *Mackenzie v Bankes* (1878) 3 App Cas 1324.
6 *Ballard v Tomlinson* (1885) 29 Ch D 115 at 121, per BRETT MR.
7 *Stephens v Anglian Water Authority* [1987] 1 WLR 1381 at 1387, [1987] 3 All ER 379 at 384, per SLADE LJ; [1988] Conv 175 (M. Harwood).
8 *Acton v Blundell* (1843) 12 M & W 324; *Chasemore v Richards* (1859) 7 HL Cas 349; *Rugby Joint Water Board v Walters* [1967] Ch 397, [1966] 3 All ER 497; *Langbrook Properties Ltd v Surrey County Council* [1970] 1 WLR 161, [1969] 3 All ER 1424; *Thomas v Gulf Oil Refining Ltd* (1979) 123 SJ 787; *Brace v South Eastern Regional Housing Association Ltd* (1984) 270 EG 1286; *Home Brewery Co Ltd v William Davis & Co (Leicester) Ltd* [1987] QB 339, [1987] 1 All ER 637. See too *Bradford Corpn v Pickles* [1895] AC 587.
9 *Bleachers' Association Ltd v Chapel-en-le-Frith Rural Council* [1933] Ch 356.

(i) Rights in the bed

The bed of a *non-tidal* river belongs, when there is no evidence of acts of ownership to the contrary, to the owner of the land through which it flows, but when the lands of two owners are separated by a running stream, each owner is prima facie owner of the soil of the bed of the river *ad medium filum aquae*. The soil of the bed is not the common property of the two owners, but the share of each belongs to him separately, so that, if from any cause the stream becomes diverted, each owner may use his share of the bed in any way he chooses.[10] On the other hand, the bed of a *tidal* river, up to a point where the water flows and reflows regularly, belongs to the Crown unless it has been granted to a subject.[11]

(ii) Rights in the water

But the water as distinct from the bed of a river is not the subject of absolute ownership, and, though subject to certain rights exercisable by the owners of the lands through which it flows, it does not belong to them in the ordinary sense of the term. Such a riparian owner has at common law, as a natural incident of his ownership, certain riparian rights, which have been authoritatively described as follows:

> A riparian proprietor is entitled to have the water of the stream on the banks of which his property lies, flow down as it has been accustomed to flow down to his property, subject to the ordinary use of the flowing water by upper proprietors, and to such further use, if any, on their part in connection with their property as may be reasonable under the circumstances.[12]

The common law, as thus stated, may be elaborated into three propositions:[13]

1. A riparian owner may take and use the water for ordinary purposes connected with his riparian tenement (such as domestic purposes or the watering of his cattle),[14] even though the result may be to exhaust the water altogether.

2. A riparian owner may take the water for extraordinary purposes, provided, first that such user is connected with the riparian land, and secondly that he restores the water substantially undiminished in volume and unaltered in character. Common examples are where water is employed in the irrigation of the adjoining land or the working of a mill, for in such cases practically the same amount of water ultimately

---

10 *Bickett v Morris* (1866) LR 1 Sc & Div 47 (especially at 58).

11 *A-G v Lonsdale* (1868) LR 7 Eq 377 at 388.

12 *John Young & Co v Bankier Distillery Co* [1893] AC 691 at 698, per Lord MACNAGHTEN; *Provender Millers (Winchester) Ltd v Southampton County Council* [1940] Ch 131, [1939] 4 All ER 157; *Tate & Lyle Industries Ltd v Greater London Council* [1983] 2 AC 509, [1983] 1 All ER 1159; *Scott-Whitehead v National Coal Board* (1987) 53 P & CR 263; [1987] Conv 368 (S. Tromans); *Home Brewery Co Ltd v William Davis & Co (Leicester) Ltd* [1987] QB 339, [1987] 1 All ER 637; (1987) 137 NLJ 867 (H. W. Wilkinson). On water pollution, see *Cambridge Water Co v Eastern Counties Leather plc* [1994] 2 WLR 53 (civil liability); *Alphacell Ltd v Woodward* [1972] AC 824, [1972] 2 All ER 475; *National Rivers Authority v Sir Alfred McAlpine Homes East Ltd* (1994) Times, 3 February (criminal liability).

13 *Attwood v Llay Main Collieries* [1926] Ch 444 at 458.

14 But not spray irrigation: *Rugby Joint Water Board v Walters* [1967] Ch 397, [1966] 3 All ER 497.

returns to the stream.[15] Manufacture, in the present connection, is prima facie an extraordinary purpose, though the ultimate solution of this question depends upon local trading conditions, and on the use to which the water of rivers is put in the adjoining district.[16]

3. A riparian owner has no right whatever to take the water for purposes unconnected with the riparian tenement.[17] Thus it has been held that the mere possession of a mill on the bank of a stream does not entitle a waterworks company to collect the water in a reservoir for the benefit of a neighbouring town.[18]

(d) Abstraction under Water Resources Act 1991

The rights of taking water at common law have been curtailed by section 24 (1) of the Water Resources Act 1991[19] under which:

no person shall

(a) abstract water from any source of supply; or
(b) cause or permit any other person so to abstract any water,

except in pursuance of a licence under this Chapter granted by the [National Rivers] Authority and in accordance with the provisions of that licence.

The main exceptions to this are the abstraction of a quantity of water not exceeding:

(i) 5 cubic metres, provided that it does not form part of a continuous operation, or of a series of operations whereby in the aggregate more than 5 cubic metres are abstracted;[20]

(ii) 20 cubic metres in any 24 hours from underground water for the domestic purposes of the occupier's household and agricultural purposes other than spray irrigation.

In both these cases the water must be taken for use on a holding consisting of the riparian land and any other land held therewith.[1]

(e) Public rights in a river

The public have a common law right to navigation in a tidal river up to the point where the tide ebbs and flows,[2] but the non-tidal part of a river is analogous to a road running between two properties, and though the public may by dedication acquire the right of navigation thereon, it must be proved in case of dispute that this has been established by long enjoyment or by Act of Parliament.[3] Such a right of navigation if once established prevails over the ordinary rights of a riparian owner, and he cannot make any use of the bed of the river or of its water which will prejudice enjoyment by the public;

15 *Embrey v Owen* (1851) 6 Exch 353; cf *Rugby Joint Water Board v Walters,* supra.
16 *Ormerod v Todmorden Mill Co* (1883) 11 QBD 155 at 168, per Lord ESHER; see (1959) 22 MLR 35 (A. H. Hudson).
17 *McCartney v Londonderry and Lough Swilly Rly Co* [1904] AC 301; *Attwood v Llay Main Collieries,* supra.
18 *Swindon Waterworks Co v Wilts and Berks Canal Navigation Co* (1875) LR 7 HL 697.
19 Replacing the provisions of the Water Resources Act 1963 as amended.
20 *Cargill v Gotts* [1981] 1 WLR 441, [1981] 1 All ER 682 (series depends on taking, not quantity or frequency); (1981) 97 LQR 382 (P. Jackson).
1 Ss. 24, 27, 221.
2 *A–G v Tomline* (1880) 14 Ch D 58. See *Iveagh v Martin* [1961] 1 QB 232, [1960] 2 All ER 668; *Evans v Godber* [1974] 1 WLR 1317, [1974] 3 All ER 341.
3 *Orr-Ewing v Colquhoun* (1877) 2 App Cas 839.

he is not, for instance, entitled to erect a wharf or other building on the bed so as to obstruct to the smallest extent the passage of boats.[4]

(f) Fishing

As regards the person who possesses the right of fishing in a river, a distinction must again be drawn between tidal and non-tidal rivers, for while all members of the public are entitled to fish[5] in the former up to the point where the tide ebbs and flows,[6] the right in the case of a non-tidal river belongs to the owner of the bed of the stream, or to any person who has acquired a right from or against him. It is often thought that if a river is navigable the public have a right to fish in it, but this is not true in respect of that part of a river which lies above the flow of the tide, for the privilege of navigation no more confers a right to fish than the right to pass along a public highway entitles a member of the public to shoot upon it.[7] BOWEN LJ said:

> There is another most important matter to be recollected as regards such streams as the Thames, viz. that although the public have been in the habit, as long as we can recollect, and as long as our fathers can recollect, of fishing in the Thames, the public have no right to fish there—I mean they have no right as members of the public to fish there. That is certain law. Of course they may fish by the licence of the lord or the owner of a particular part of the bed of the river, or they may fish by the indulgence, or owing to the carelessness or good nature, of the person who is entitled to the soil, but right to fish themselves as the public they have none, and whenever the case is tried the jury ought to be told this by the judge in the most emphatic way, so as to prevent them from doing injustice under the idea that they are establishing a public right. There is no such right in law . . .[8]

The position is, then, that the owner of the bed of a river is presumptively entitled to the fishing, and if, for instance, the opposite banks are in different hands, each proprietor is owner of the fishing *usque ad medium filum aquae.*[9] But this fishing may become separated from the ownership of the bed and be vested as an incorporeal right in the hands of another person, and when this has been done it exists either as a several fishery or as a common of fishery. Both these rights are instances of what is called a *profit à prendre.* A several fishery is, as was said by Lord COLERIDGE:

---

4 *A–G v Terry* (1874) 9 Ch App 423. *Tate & Lyle Industries Ltd v Greater London Council* [1983] 2 AC 509, [1983] 1 All ER 1159 (construction of ferry terminals in River Thames caused silting at jetty of plaintiffs who succeeded in claim for special damage for public nuisance). Salvage is not recoverable on a non-tidal navigable river: *The Goring* [1988] 2 WLR 460, [1988] 1 All ER 641 (River Thames above Reading Bridge); [1987] CLJ 153 (D. E. C. Yale).

5 And to take worms as bait in exercise of their right to fish: *Anderson v Alnwick District Council* [1993] 1 WLR 1156.

6 It is an offence under the Salmon and Freshwater Fisheries Act 1975, s. 6 (1) to place a net in tidal and inland waters which obstructs the passage of salmon and migratory trout: *Champion v Maughan* [1984] 1 WLR 469, [1984] 1 All ER 680; *Gray v Blamey* [1991] 1 WLR 47, [1991] 1 All ER 1. See now Salmon Act 1986, s. 33 and generally, Robinson, *Law of Game, Salmon and Freshwater Fishing in Scotland* (1990).

7 *Smith v Andrews* [1891] 2 Ch 678 at 696. It is an offence to fish in such a river even though the fish are returned alive to the water: *Wells v Hardy* [1964] 2 QB 447, [1964] 1 All ER 953.

8 *Blount v Layard* [1891] 2 Ch 681n at 689.

9 *Hanbury v Jenkins* [1901] 2 Ch 401. If he is fishing for salmon by rod and line, he is entitled to stand on his own bank or to wade out to *medium filum*, and to fish as far across the river as he can reach by normal casting or spinning: *Fothringham v Kerr* (1984) 48 P & CR 173 (River Tay). See also *Welsh National Water Development Authority v Burgess* (1974) 28 P & CR 378 at 383 (salmon and trout-fishing in River Dovey).

a right to take fish *in alieno solo*, and to exclude the owner of the soil from the right of taking fish himself.[10]

A right to fish in the river of another in common with the owner, or in common with others to whom the same right has been granted, is called a "common of fishery", or "common of piscary".[11]

(4) FLYING FREEHOLDS

The *ad usque* maxim does not prevent a fee simple from existing in an upper storey of a building, separate and distinct from the rest. As Coke said:

A man may have an inheritance in an upper chamber though the lower buildings and soil be in another.[12]

This is known as a flying freehold. Land can thus be divided horizontally as well as vertically.

A fee simple may also be "a movable fee where 'the fee itself is a continuing estate, but it is an estate in land which from time to time changes its location'; as, for example, where it varies with changes of a boundary such as the foreshore".[13]

(5) LAW REFORM. COMMONHOLD. FREEHOLD FLATS

In 1987 a more sophisticated form of flying freeholds was recommended by the Aldridge Working Group on Freehold Flats and Freehold Ownership of Other Interdependent Buildings.[14] It proposes a new land ownership scheme for England and Wales, called Commonhold:

The purpose of the scheme is to regulate relations between owners of separate properties which lie in close proximity to each other and are interdependent. The scheme is suitable for, but not limited to, residential property. It gives people the chance to own flats freehold, without the present drawbacks, but the scheme can also apply to offices, commercial and industrial premises and other properties.

The Commonhold scheme is similar to Condominium legislation in Canada, the United States of America and, under the name of strata titles, in Australia and New Zealand.[15]

The "present drawbacks" which the new scheme is designed to overcome are, first, the difficulty which an owner of freehold property has in enforcing a positive covenant, for example, to repair or to pay service charges, against a purchaser from his original covenantor.[16] Hitherto this difficulty has been avoided by the owner of a block of flats granting *leases* of each separate unit

---

10 *Foster v Wright* (1878) 4 CPD 438 at 449. See *Loose v Castleton* (1978) 41 P & CR 19; *Lewis v Cavaciuti* [1993] NLJR 813 (extent of profit of piscary in River Usk).

11 Leake, *Uses and Profits of Land*, p. 176; p. 556, post.

12 Co Litt 48b; Lincoln's Inn Act 1860 which regulates flying freeholds in New Square, Lincoln's Inn. See the claim to a "subterranean flying freehold" of a cellar in *Grigsby v Melville* [1974] 1 WLR 80 at 83, [1973] 3 All ER 455 at 458.

13 *Baxendale v Instow Parish Council* [1982] Ch 14 at 20, [1981] 2 All ER 620 at 625, per MEGARRY V-C; *Welden v Bridgewater* (1592) Cro Eliz 421 (lot meadows, where two or more have a fee simple in a measured part of a meadow, but the precise part owned is determined by lots at specified times). See [1982] Conv 208 (R. E. Annand).

14 Cmnd 79. The Working Group was established in 1986 by the Chairman of the Law Commission as a result of the initiative of the Lord Chancellor: p.v.

15 Ibid., para 1.7. Similar legislation has been in force in Europe since the 1930s, and it has been introduced in many other parts of the world.

16 Pp. 611 et seq, post.

within it. In this case any positive covenant that relates to the property is enforceable against successive owners of the unit, in accordance with the rules for the running of leasehold covenants.[17] The system of leasehold flats, however, has brought a second drawback. Many leasehold schemes were evolved in the 1930s when leases were granted for 99 years. Today a lease with less than 40 years to run is an unattractive security for a mortgagee, and so the unit in many cases becomes unsaleable.

The general scope of Commonhold has been outlined by Mr Aldridge himself as follows:[18]

> Like other condominium systems, [Commonhold] would allow the freehold ownership of separate parts of a building. The problem of passing the benefit of positive obligations is overcome by legislation laying down the content of mutual obligations and easements, and making them bind the owners for the time being of each unit for the benefit of the rest of the development. Many see the standardisation of the mutual rights and obligations as a recommendation of the system.
>
> There would be an incorporated management association, the members of which are the owners of the freehold units. It is responsible for repairs and services and any common parts are vested in it. That structure is, of course, familiar here for leasehold flat schemes. When the commonhold is brought to an end, the owners would cease to have an exclusive interest in their respective units. They would then become equitable tenants in common of the whole property in pre-determined proportions. The legal estate would be vested in the association on trust for them. This avoids possible difficulties with the freehold ownership of blocks of air on a complete or partial destruction.
>
> The aim of the Working Group is to recommend a property ownership system which could be freely adopted by owners or developers for all types of property: existing or new, purpose-built in separate units or converted, of any type of construction, and put to any use, whether or not residential. With the progress of compulsory registration of title, it seems to us appropriate to base a new commonhold system wholly on registration. Commonholds would only be possible with a registered title. This should ensure that they are properly constituted, and will give easy access to the basic documentation.

The Aldridge Report produces a viable alternative to leasehold flat schemes.

In 1991 the Government announced its proposals for the introduction of commonhold.[19] The scheme will be for both residential and commercial property, and for both new and existing developments:

> Commonhold may be equally suited to a large Victorian house converted into flats, to a new purpose-built block of flats or to a parade of shops. Several detached houses, each having its own services but with a common recreational area or driveway, could also be a commonhold.[20]

A commonhold will be established by the registration of a declaration at the Land Registry. The consent of all tenants with tenancies of more than 21 years and of all business tenants must first be obtained. Where there are objections by up to 20% of shorter term tenants, the court will have power to override them. Once the land has become commonhold, no tenancy of more than 25 years can exist.

17 Pp. 444 et seq, post.
18 [1986] Conv 361.
19 Hansard, HL Deb 1601 Friday 12 July, 1991; Commonhold—A Consultation Paper 1990 (Cm 1345), which contains a draft Bill.
20 *Commonhold—The Way Ahead* (1992) Lord Chancellor's Department, p. 3.

B. RESTRICTIONS ON OWNERSHIP

In his account of the fee simple estate, written in 1885, Challis was able to give a comforting description of the extensive powers of enjoyment available to its owner:

> It confers, and since the beginning of legal history it always has conferred, the lawful right to exercise over, upon, and in respect, to the land, every act of ownership which can enter into the imagination, including the right to commit unlimited waste.[1]

Challis would, no doubt, have agreed with Samuel Johnson that a man cannot be allowed by society to be complete master of what he calls his own, and that he must submit to the restrictions placed by the law upon the exercise of his proprietary rights.[2] There is little doubt, however, that the restrictions now imposed by statute upon a landowner's right to enjoy what at common law is his own would have passed the understanding of both those writers. Even in Challis' time, of course, statutory interference with the freedom of a landowner was not unknown. He was obliged, for instance, to erect new buildings in conformity with local by-laws, and he might be compelled to demolish houses that were unfit for habitation. Later he became subject to legislation passed in the interests of the poorer sections of the community, such as the Housing Acts[3] and the Rent Acts,[4] which further increased his burdens and circumscribed his proprietary rights. Also from earlier times Parliament has frequently authorized the compulsory purchase or redistribution of land by private and public Acts, for purposes of inclosure or the provision of docks, canals, railways, utility undertakings and public works of all kinds.[5]

But the most vigorous attack upon the right of a man to do what he likes with his own has been made by the various Town and Country Planning Acts, which seek to prevent the evils that inevitably arise if no public control is placed upon the development of land. That building operations need to be controlled in the interests of the community is, of course, obvious. Land is scarce, the demand for houses increases with a rapidly rising population, the profit instinct is no weaker than formerly, and unless something is done to curb the activities of the speculative developer certain unfortunate results must inevitably ensue. Too often, uncontrolled development sacrifices agricultural land and places of natural beauty, defaces the countryside with unco-ordinated buildings sprawling along the main roads and causing embarrassment to the sanitary and educational authorities, and in general it is effected with little thought for the amenities of the neighbourhood or for the problems that it will raise in the future. Nevertheless, there is a need to preserve a just balance between the rights of landowners and the interests of the community.

Planning law and compensation rules together have produced a situation in which the market value of land, which includes development potential in addition to the value of the land in its existing use, is affected in a striking manner. The withholding of planning permission will deprive land of

---

1 *Law of Real Property* (3rd edn), p. 218.
2 In a letter to Boswell, 3 February, 1776.
3 Pp. 391–4, post.
4 Pp. 468 et seq, post.
5 See Blackstone, *Commentaries*, vol. i. p. 139; Dicey, *Law of the Constitution* (10th edn) p. 48.

development value which market demand would otherwise confer upon it. Compensation is payable for this loss of development value, but only rarely (except where land is compulsorily purchased).[6] There are great anomalies here, but little likelihood that they will be corrected other than by piecemeal changes without regard to fundamental principles.

To give an adequate account of these matters in the present chapter would upset the balance of the book and divert the attention of the reader from fundamental principles, but they are of such importance in the modern law that they are dealt with at a later stage in Part IV.[7]

6 Pp. 974, et seq, post.
7 P. 943, post.

Part II

Estates and interests in land

B. INTERESTS ARISING UNDER A STRICT SETTLEMENT OR TRUST FOR SALE

SUMMARY

Chapter 9

The strict settlement and the trust for sale

SUMMARY

The evolution of the strict settlement and the trust for sale has already been described in the historical introduction.[1]

The general idea of a settlement is to create, by either deed or will, out of real or personal property, a series of beneficial interests in favour of a succession of persons. The two methods by which land may be settled today are either by strict settlement under the Settled Land Act 1925, or by trust for sale under the Law of Property Act 1925.[2] They are mutually exclusive. Indeed it is expressly enacted that the statutory definition of a settlement contained in the Settled Land Act 1925 shall not apply to land held upon trust for sale.[3]

It is vital to distinguish the two methods of settlement. The chief practical importance of the distinction is that, upon the occasion of a conveyance, title to settled land must be made by the tenant for life, since the legal estate is vested in him, while title to land held upon trust for sale must be made by the trustees for sale. The result of a mistake in this regard is troublesome and expensive, for a purchaser who takes a conveyance from the trustees when the instrument is a settlement or from the tenant for life in the reverse case, does not thereby acquire the legal estate. We must also reiterate at the outset of the discussion that a purchaser, who takes a conveyance from the correct vendor, takes the land free from the interests of the beneficiaries under the settlement, provided that he pays the purchase money to at least two trustees

1 Pp. 67, et seq, ante.
2 See Harvey, *Settlements of Land*.
3 SLA 1925, s. 1 (7).

or to a trust corporation. The interests of the beneficiaries are transferred from the land to the purchase money and are overreached.[4]

Of these two methods of settling land we shall discuss first the strict settlement under the Settled Land Act 1925. In recent years however, mainly due to considerations of taxation, the strict settlement has become less widely used. In particular, the classic strict settlement, which was created on the occasion of a marriage so as to provide for all members of the family and thereby to keep the land as far as possible within the family,[5] is most unlikely to be created today. It is the trust for sale which is mainly used for family settlements, whether created *inter vivos* or by will; and furthermore its conveyancing machinery has been extended by the 1925 legislation to concurrent interests[6] and intestacy.[7]

SECTION I THE STRICT SETTLEMENT

A. THE DEFINITION OF A SETTLEMENT UNDER THE SETTLED LAND ACT 1925

The word *settlement* properly so called connotes succession. Its normal meaning is any instrument or series of instruments by which successive interests are carved out of realty or personalty and under which, in the case of land, there will usually be at any given time some person entitled in possession to a beneficial interest for life. But the Settled Land Act 1925 is not content to stop short at cases where there is a succession properly so called. Its further aim is to facilitate dealings wherever the disposition of the land is retarded or obstructed by some impediment affecting its title.

Infancy affords a simple illustration. If a favourable offer has been made for the purchase of land to which an infant is entitled in fee simple under a will, the rule that no person under 18 years of age[8] can execute a valid conveyance will cause the loss of a profitable bargain, unless some way out of the impasse can be contrived. But all difficulty disappears if the will is regarded as a "settlement" and if some person of full age is designated to exercise the statutory power of sale.

In a case of this nature there is, of course, no settlement and no tenant for life as usually understood, but any device which renders the statutory powers exercisable in respect of the infant's land is an undoubted advantage to all concerned. What the Act does, therefore, with the object of rendering an absolute title easily transferable despite the existence of what would normally be inhibitory factors, is to define "settlement" in broad terms so as to include a number of cases where there is no succession in the ordinary sense, and also, where necessary, to grant the statutory powers to a person who according to ordinary language is not a tenant for life. In fact, not only is the statutory definition of a "settlement" very wide, but wherever there is a settlement within the meaning of the Act and no tenant for life properly so called, and therefore no person normally competent to exercise the statutory powers, one of two things will occur, namely, either:

---

4 Pp. 75–7, ante. For a full discussion of overreaching, see pp. 813–5, 817–20, post.
5 Pp. 67–8 ante. For a detailed account see Cheshire, *Modern Real Property* (10th edn), pp. 126–31.
6 Pp. 213, et seq, post.
7 Pp. 875, et seq, post.
8 P. 921, post.

some person will be designated by the Act as entitled to exercise the powers; or the powers will be exercisable by trustees, who in this context are called "statutory powers".[9]

A settlement for the purposes of the Act exists in each of the following cases:[10]

(a) Succession

Where land stands limited in trust for any persons by way of succession.

This refers to the normal case where land is limited to a series of persons by way of succession, as for instance to A for life, remainder to B for life, remainder to C in fee simple.[11]

(b) Extended meaning of settlement

We now come to six cases where an extended meaning is given to the word "settlement".

(i) Entailed interest Where land stands limited in trust for any person in possession for an entailed interest whether or not capable of being barred or defeated.

(ii) Base or determinable fee[12] Where land stands limited in trust for any person in possession for a base or determinable fee or any corresponding interest in leasehold land.

Thus, under (i) and (ii), where the possessor is a tenant in tail or tenant of a base fee, the instrument of creation is a settlement, and the tenant holds the land under a settlement.

(iii) Limitation subject to gift over Where land stands limited in trust for any person in possession for an estate in fee simple or for a term of years absolute subject to an executory gift over on failure of issue or in any other event.

Thus, where a house is devised to A in fee simple subject to a condition that he resides and provides a home for X there, and if he breaks this condition, then devise over to B in fee simple, the will is a settlement and A is tenant for life within the meaning of the Act.[13]

---

9 P. 185, post.
10 SLA 1925, s. 1.
11 It need not be expressly limited. The trust may arise by operation of law, as, for instance, where there is a constructive trust under which the court gives protection to a licensee for the period of his life: *Bannister v Bannister* [1948] 2 All ER 133; M & B p. 557; *Binions v Evans* [1972] Ch 359, [1972] 2 All ER 70; M & B p. 555 (Lord DENNING MR dissented on this point at 366, at 74); p. 591, post; *Ungurian v Lesnoff* [1990] Ch 206; [1990] CLJ 25 (M. Oldham); [1990] Conv 223 (P. Sparkes); [1991] Conv 596 (J. Hill); *Costello v Costello* [1994] EGCS 40; cf *Ivory v Palmer* [1975] ICR 340, p. 604, n. 8, post. See Harvey, pp. 54, 82 et seq; *Emmet on Title* (19th edn), para 22.004; (1977) 93 LQR 561 (J. A. Hornby); Law Commission Report on Trusts of Land 1989 (Law Com No. 118), para. 4.2; p 211, post. On avoidance of an unintentional creation of a strict settlement in this situation, see *Griffiths v Williams* (1977) 248 EG 947, M & B p. 599, p. 604, post; [1978] Conv 250. For similar problems arising in connection with settlements on divorce, see *Morss v Morss* [1972] Fam 264, [1972] 1 All ER 1121; *Martin v Martin* [1978] Fam 12, [1977] 3 All ER 762; [1978] Conv 229 (P. Smith). See also *Allen v Allen* [1974] 1 WLR 1171, [1974] 3 All ER 385 (trust for sale).
12 Including a fee determinable by condition: SLA 1925, s. 117 (1) (iv).
13 *Re Richardson* [1904] 2 Ch 777.

(iv) Infant Where land stands limited in trust for any person in possession being an infant, for an estate in fee simple or for a term of years absolute.

A conveyance which purports to grant a fee simple absolute to an infant cannot take effect according to its terms, for an infant is incapable of holding a legal estate. Instead, the conveyance operates as an agreement by the grantor to execute a settlement by means of a vesting deed in favour of trustees (statutory owners),[14] and a trust instrument in favour of the infant.

(v) Springing interests Where land stands limited in trust for any person to take effect as a fee simple or term of years absolute on the happening of some event.

If, for instance, a fee simple estate is limited in trust for the two sons of X, who attain the age of eighteen years, the first son to reach that age becomes absolutely entitled to a half share, but also entitled to the fee simple in the entirety of the land contingent on the death of his brother during infancy.[15] This is one of the cases where, pending the occurrence of the contingency, the powers are exercisable by the statutory owners.[16]

(vi) Family charges Where land stands charged voluntarily,[17] or in consideration of marriage or by way of family arrangement[18] with the payment of any rentcharge for the life of any person, or any less period,[19] or of any sums for the portions, advancement, maintenance or otherwise for the benefit of any persons.[20]

If, for example, A charges his fee simple absolute with an annuity for his wife and capital sums for his children, the instrument which creates the charge is a "settlement", and, although the rentchargor, A, is not a tenant for life, yet by section 20 (1) (ix) of the Settled Land Act 1925 he is given the powers of a tenant for life. Strictly speaking, therefore, he should execute a vesting deed and appoint trustees. If he does so, he may sell the fee simple under the Act, and overreach the rentcharges so as to make them recoverable from the trustees to whom payment will have been made. If, however, the purchaser is willing to buy subject to the charges, A is permitted by the Law of Property (Amendment) Act 1926 to sell as absolute owner without the necessity of executing a vesting deed. Section 1 (1) of this Act provides as follows:

> Nothing in the Settled Land Act 1925 shall prevent a person on whom the powers of a tenant for life are conferred by section 20 (1) (ix) from conveying or creating a legal estate subject to a prior interest as if the land had not been settled land.

(c) Compound settlement

What emerges from the account given above is that a settlement may consist of a number of instruments. This will occur, for instance:

where lands, which in the first place have been settled on A for life with

---

14 SLA 1925, s. 27 (1); p. 185, post.
15 *Re Bird* [1927] 1 Ch 210.
16 SLA 1925, s. 23.
17 I.e. not for valuable consideration.
18 Presumably "family arrangement" in this context includes an arrangement made not voluntarily, but for valuable consideration; cf *Williams v Williams* (1867) 2 Ch App 294 at 301.
19 Chapter 20, p. 645, post.
20 SLA 1925, s. 1 (1) (v); *Re Austen* [1929] 2 Ch 155.

remainder in tail to his eldest son, are resettled on A for life, remainder (subject to the charges created by the original settlement) to the eldest son for life, with remainder over.

In this case the two settlements may be read as one, being together called a *compound settlement*,[1] and the Act provides that the word *settlement* shall be construed as referring to such compound settlement where it exists.[2]

B. THE MACHINERY OF A SETTLEMENT AFTER 1925

We have already seen that in order to emphasize the separation of the legal estate from the equitable interests of the beneficiaries and also to facilitate a conveyance of the former, the Settled Land Act 1925 introduced a new method for the creation of a settlement by enacting as follows:[3]

Every settlement of a legal estate in land *inter vivos* shall, save as in this Act otherwise provided, be effected by two deeds, namely, a vesting deed and a trust instrument and if effected in any other way shall not operate to transfer or create a legal estate.[4]

This method must now be examined in more detail.

(1) SETTLEMENT INTER VIVOS

(a) The vesting deed

The function of the vesting deed is to vest the legal fee simple in the person who for the time being is to have the actual enjoyment of the land, or, if he is an infant or otherwise legally incapable, then to vest it in some other person who is denominated a *statutory owner*.[5] The virtue of thus passing the legal fee simple to a person who is beneficially entitled to some lesser interest is that, should he later desire, in the interests of the beneficiaries generally, to dispose of the fee simple by way of sale, lease or otherwise under one of the powers conferred upon him by the Settled Land Act 1925, he can produce a document which not only shows that the legal estate is vested in him, but also certifies the facts essential to a valid exercise of the statutory power.

This vesting deed, then—called the *principal vesting deed*—conveys to the tenant for life or the statutory owner the whole legal estate which is held upon trust for persons by way of succession. It is a short document and must contain the following statements and particulars:[6]

(i) a description, either specific or general, of the settled land;
(ii) a statement that the settled land is vested in the person or persons to whom it is conveyed or in whom it is declared to be vested upon the trusts from time to time affecting the settled land;
(iii) the names of the trustees of the settlement;

1 *Re Ogle's Settled Estates* [1927] 1 Ch 229 at 232–33.
2 SLA 1925, s. 1 (1) (i), proviso.
3 P. 93, ante.
4 SLA 1925, s. 4 (1).
5 Ibid., ss. 23, 26, 117 (1) (xxvi).
6 Ibid., s. 5 (1).

(iv) a statement of any powers, over and above those conferred upon every tenant for life by the Act, which it is desired to give to the tenant for life under the settlement;

(v) the name of any person entitled to appoint new trustees of the settlement.

If after the execution of a principal vesting deed more land is acquired which is to become subject to the settlement, it is conveyed to the tenant for life by what is called a *subsidiary vesting deed*.[7]

The following is a precedent of a principal vesting deed:

This Vesting Deed made [&c.] between *John H* of [&c.] of the first part, *Jane W* of [&c.] of the second part, and *X* of [&c.], *Y* of [&c.] and *Z* of [&c.] (hereinafter called the trustees) of the third part.

Witnesseth and it is hereby declared as follows:—

1. In consideration of the intended marriage between *John H* and *Jane W* the said *John H* as Settlor hereby declares that

All that (*setting out the parcels by reference to a schedule or otherwise*) are vested in *John H* in fee simple (*or in the case of leaseholds refer to the terms*).

Upon the trusts declared concerning the same by a Trust Instrument bearing even date with but intended to be executed contemporaneously with these presents and made between the same parties and in the same order as these presents or upon such other trusts as the same ought to be held from time to time.

2. The trustees are the trustees of the settlement for all the purposes of the Settled Land Act, 1925.

3. The following additional or larger powers are conferred by the said trust instrument in relation to the settled land and by virtue of the Settled Land Act, 1925, operate and are exercisable as if conferred by that Act on a tenant for life. [*Here insert the additional powers.*]

4. The power of appointing a new trustee or new trustees of the settlement is vested in the said [*John H*] during his life.

In witness [&c.].[8]

(b) The trust instrument

At the same time a second deed, called the trust instrument, is executed which:

(i)   declares the trusts affecting the settled land;

(ii) appoints trustees of the settlement;

(iii) contains the power, if any, to appoint new trustees of the settlement;

(iv) sets out, either expressly or by reference, any powers intended to be conferred by the settlement in extension of those conferred by the Act;

(v) bears any ad valorem stamp duty which may be payable in respect of the settlement.[9]

Thus it is the trust investment which declares the trusts upon which the legal estate is to be held. If we look at the vesting deed alone, the tenant for life seems to be fully entitled to sell the fee simple. So he is. An intending purchaser need not look beyond the deed, but at the same time such a person is told in the vesting deed that the land is held upon trust and that there are trustees, and this knowledge throws upon him the obligation to pay the

7 SLA 1925, s. 10.
8 Ibid., Sch. 1 Form No. 2.
9 Ibid., s. 4 (3).

purchase money, not to the tenant for life, but to the trustees. If he does this, his obligations are at an end, and it is no concern of his what is done with the money. But what we need to look at for the moment is the trust instrument, since it records the equitable interests which it is the object of the settlement to confer upon the beneficiaries. The property comprised in the settlement, whether it remains in the form of land or is sold and converted into money, is actually enjoyed by the persons who are described in, and upon the conditions which are prescribed by, the trust instrument. We must not be misled by the vesting deed into thinking that the tenant for life, who is thereby declared to be the fee simple owner, can sell the whole estate and pocket the proceeds.

The following is a precedent of a trust instrument[10] which is the counterpart to that of the vesting deed set out above:[11]

This Trust Instrument is made [&c.] between *John H* of [&c.] (hereinafter called the Settlor) of the first part, *Jane W* of [&c.] of the second part, and *X* of [&c.], *Y* of [&c.], and *Z* of [&c.] (hereinafter called the trustees) of the third part.

Whereas by a deed (hereinafter called the Vesting Deed) bearing even date with but executed contemporaneously with these presents, and made between the same parties and in the same order as these presents, certain hereditaments situated at   in the county of   were vested in the Settlor Upon the trusts declared concerning the same by a trust instrument of even date therein referred to (meaning these presents).

Now in consideration of the intended marriage between the Settlor and *Jane W*, this Deed witnesseth as follows:

1. The Settlor hereby agrees that he will hold the hereditaments and property comprised in the Vesting Deed In trust for himself until the solemnisation of the said marriage and thereafter Upon the trusts following, that is to say:

2. Upon trust for the Settlor during his life without impeachment of waste with remainder Upon trust if *Jane W* survives him that she shall receive out of the premises during the residue of her life a yearly jointure rentcharge of [&c.] and subject thereto Upon trust for the trustees for a term of 800 years from the date of the death of the Settlor without impeachment of waste Upon the trusts hereinafter declared concerning the same. And subject to the said term and the trusts thereof Upon trust for the first and other sons of the said intended marriage successively according to seniority in tail male with remainder [&c.] *with an ultimate remainder in trust for the Settlor in fee simple.*

[*Here add the requisite trusts of the portions terms, and any other proper provisions including the appointment of the trustees to be trustees of the settlement for the purposes of the Settled Land Act, 1925, extension of Settled Land Act powers, and a power for the tenant for life for the time being of full age to appoint new trustees of the settlement.*]

In witness [&c.].

(2) SETTLEMENT BY WILL

The rule that an *inter vivos* settlement must be created by two contemporaneous deeds called the principal vesting deed and the trust instrument, applies differently to a settlement by will. In this case the legal estate devolves upon the personal representatives of the settlor, who hold it upon trust to convey it to the person entitled to the tenancy for life under the will.[12] This conveyance may be made by a *vesting assent*, i.e. by an assent in writing but not under

10 SLA 1925, Sch. 1 Form No. 3.
11 Supra.
12 SLA 1925, s. 6.

seal.[13] The position then is, that the vesting assent corresponds to the vesting deed that forms part of a settlement *inter vivos*, and the will itself is deemed to be the trust instrument.

(3) EFFECT OF MACHINERY

(a) Legal estate separated from equitable interests

As a result of this machinery, the legal estate conveyed to the tenant for life by the vesting deed is kept rigorously separate from the equitable interests of the beneficiaries which are created by and contained in the trust instrument. Throughout the duration of the settlement and however long that duration may be, the legal estate must and will be vested in a person or persons competent to deal with it as permitted by the Act. If no vesting deed has been executed, the tenant for life or statutory owner[14] can require the trustees of the settlement to repair the omission.[15] Normally, the legal estate will remain with the first tenant for life until his death, though in certain exceptional circumstances, as for example where his equitable life interest is forfeited under the terms of the settlement, it will pass to the trustees. On his death it will devolve on the trustees who will as soon as practicable convey it by a vesting assent to the person next entitled.[16]

(b) Evasion of Act prevented

The evasion of the statutory requirement of a vesting deed is prevented by section 13 of the Settled Land Act 1925.[17] This provides that where a tenant for life or statutory owner has become entitled to have a vesting deed or assent executed in his favour, then, until such an instrument has in fact been executed, no disposition of the land made *inter vivos* by any person shall operate to pass a legal estate, unless it is made in favour of a purchaser having no notice that the tenant for life or statutory owner has become so entitled. Such a purported disposition operates as a contract to convey the legal estate as soon as the vesting deed has been executed, and it is a contract that is registrable as a land charge.[18]

There is an exception, however, in favour of personal representatives, for they are allowed to sell settled land in the ordinary course of administration even though no vesting deed has been executed when their title accrues.[19]

(c) Where vesting deed not necessary

Moreover, there are three cases in which there is no necessity for a vesting deed:

(i) Where land ceases to be settled If, for instance, a tenant in tail in possession of settled land, free from any trusts or incumbrances, bars the entail before a vesting deed is executed in his favour, he thereby terminates the settlement, and can make title as a fee simple owner.[20]

---

13 SLA 1925, s. 8 (1).
14 P. 185, post.
15 SLA 1925, s. 9 (2).
16 P. 811, post.
17 SLA 1925, s. 13, as amended by LP(A)A 1926, Sch.
18 P. 759, post.
19 SLA 1925, s. 13.
20 *Re Alefounder's Will Trusts* [1927] 1 Ch. 360.

(ii) Where beneficiaries terminate settlement Beneficiaries, if of full age, may terminate the settlement and so avoid the necessity for a vesting deed. If, for instance, an owner devises his residence to his wife for life with remainder to his children in fee simple, the widow becomes tenant for life on his death and as such is entitled to a vesting deed. Instead, however, she may surrender her life interest to the remaindermen in fee, and then all the parties can create a trust for sale, with themselves as trustees, the income until sale and the ultimate proceeds to be held on trusts corresponding to those of the settlement.

(iii) Where land subject to family charges If the land has become settled merely because it has been voluntarily subjected to family charges,[1] the tenant for life, as we have seen, is allowed by the Law of Property (Amendment) Act 1926 to convey a legal estate subject to the charges without being required to procure the execution of a vesting deed.[2]

C. THE TENANT FOR LIFE

(1) DEFINITION OF TENANT FOR LIFE

A tenant for life is defined as follows in section 19 (1) of the Settled Land Act 1925:

> The person of full age who is for the time being beneficially entitled under a settlement to possession of settled land for his life is for the purposes of this Act the tenant for life of that land and the tenant for life under that settlement.[3]

He is deemed to be such, notwithstanding that the land or his estate therein is charged with the payment of incumbrances.[4] If two or more persons are jointly entitled to possession they together constitute the tenant for life.[5]

(a) Persons with powers of tenant for life

Obviously however there are several cases where land is settled in the sense that it is subject to a "settlement" within the statutory meaning of that word,[6] and yet where there is no tenant for life as defined in section 19. A tenant in tail in possession is a simple example of the situation.[7] The Act, therefore, takes care to ensure that wherever there is a "settlement" there shall always be some person with the powers of a tenant for life. In the first place section

---

1 SLA 1925, s. 20 (1) (ix).
2 P. 178, ante.
3 *Re Jefferys* [1939] Ch 205, [1938] 4 All ER 120 (an annuitant is not a tenant for life); *Re Carne's Settled Estates* [1899] 1 Ch 324 ("to occupy the land rent free so long as she might wish to do so" held to be a tenant for life); *Ayer v Benton* (1967) 204 EG 359; *Re Catling* [1931] 2 Ch 359 (wife as tenant at a nominal annual sum, the tenancy not to be determined so long as she made the property her principal place of residence; held not to be a tenant for life; and indeed there was no settlement); *Re Waleran Settled Estates* [1927] 1 Ch 522 (a term to a woman "for 99 years if she should so long live" held to be a tenant for life); *Re Ogle's Settled Estates* [1927] 1 Ch 229, p. 179, ante; *Re Cayley and Evans' Contract* [1930] 2 Ch 143; *Re Gallenga Will Trusts* [1938] 1 All ER 106.
4 SLA 1925, s. 19 (4).
5 Ibid., s. 19 (2).
6 Pp. 176–8, ante.
7 P. 177, ante.

20 provides that the following persons shall have the powers of a tenant for life and shall be included in the expression "tenant for life".[8]

(i) A tenant in tail, including both a tenant after possibility[9] and one who is by Act of Parliament restrained from barring his estate tail, but excluding a tenant in tail whose land has been bought with money provided by Parliament in consideration of public services.

(ii) A person entitled to land for an estate in fee simple or for a term of years absolute, subject to a gift over on failure of his issue or in any other event.[10]

(iii) A person entitled to a base[11] or a determinable fee[12] or a corresponding interest in leaseholds.

(iv) A tenant for years determinable on life, not holding merely under a lease at a rent.

We shall see that leases *at a rent* for a term of years determinable at the death of the tenant are now converted into terms for 90 years,[13] and that such a person cannot have the powers of a tenant for life,[14] but this conversion does not operate where such a term takes effect under a settlement. For instance, a devisee to whom lands are given for 30 years if he should so long live has the powers of a tenant for life.

(v) A tenant pur autre vie not holding merely under a lease at a rent.[15]

(vi) A tenant for his own or any other life, or for years determinable on life, whose interest is liable to cease in any event during that life, or is subject to a trust for accumulation of income.

For instance, a devise to A so long as he shall live on the estate for at least three months in each year, with a gift over to B upon failure to observe this condition, makes A tenant for life within section 20.[16]

(vii) A tenant by the curtesy.[17]

(viii) A person entitled to the *income* of land under a trust for payment thereof to him during his own or any other life,[18] or until sale of the land, or until some event (e.g. bankruptcy) terminates his interest. But if the land is subject to an immediate binding trust for sale, the person so entitled does not have the powers of a tenant for life.

(ix) A person beneficially entitled to land for an estate in fee simple or for a term of years absolute subject to any estates, interests, charges or powers of charging, subsisting or capable of being exercised under a settlement.

If, for instance, lands are settled on A for life with remainder in fee simple to

8 SLA 1925, s. 117 (1) (xxviii).
9 P. 251, post.
10 But a gift over on failure of issue becomes incapable of taking effect as soon as there is any issue who attains 18: LPA 1925, s. 134 (1), as amended by Family Law Reform Act 1969, s. 1 (3), Sch. 1.
11 Pp. 262–3, post.
12 Pp. 335 et seq, post.
13 LPA 1925, s. 149 (6), p. 361, post.
14 *Re Catling* [1931] 2 Ch 359.
15 *Re Johnson* [1914] 2 Ch 194.
16 *Re Paget* (1885) 30 Ch D 161.
17 P. 250, post.
18 *Re Llanover Settled Estates* [1926] Ch 626.

his eldest son B, with powers for A to charge the land with portions for his younger children, B, on the death of A, will hold the fee simple subject to any such charges that may have been created. He is tenant for life under the above clause and as such can deal with the estate, notwithstanding the charge to which it is subject.[19]

(b) Statutory owners

Comprehensive though this list is, it still fails to provide for the case of every settlement. For instance, a settlement within the meaning of the Settled Land Act 1925 exists if land is limited in trust for any person in fee simple contingently upon the happening of some event,[20] or when the person entitled in possession is entitled only to a *part* of the income from the trust[1] or where no person is entitled to any of its income at all as in the case of a discretionary strict settlement where the trustees are directed to pay the income to such members of a class of persons as they may think fit.[2] In none of these cases is the beneficiary a tenant for life or a person who has the powers of a tenant for life. The Act, therefore, provides that where such a situation arises the legal estate shall be vested in statutory owners—that is to say:

(a) any person of full age on whom they are conferred by the settlement; and

(b) in any other case the trustees of the settlement.[3]

Further, where the person who would otherwise be a tenant for life is an infant, the legal estate and statutory powers are vested during the minority of the infant in:

(a) a personal representative, if the settled land is vested in him and no vesting instrument has yet been executed; and

(b) in every other case, the trustees of the settlement.[4]

(2) POWERS OF TENANT FOR LIFE

In accordance with the policy that has prevailed since the Settled Land Act 1882, the person vested with the legal estate, normally the tenant for life in actual possession, is empowered by the Settled Land Act 1925 to manage and even to dispose of the fee simple, an aspect of his position that must now be developed in some detail. The general policy is that he shall have many of the powers of dealing with the land that are available to an estate owner entitled beneficially in his own right, but subject to this overriding proviso, that any gain accruing from the exercise of a power shall be held on trust for the equitable beneficiaries according to the limitations of the settlement. To this end the Act confers upon the tenant for life the right to exercise any of the following powers:

---

19 He also has the option under LP(A)A 1926, s. 1 (1), p. 178, ante, of conveying the legal estate to a purchaser subject to the charge, provided that the purchaser is agreeable.
20 *Re Bird* [1927] 1 Ch 210; p. 178, ante.
 1 *Re Frewen* [1926] Ch 580.
 2 *Re Gallenga Will Trusts* [1938] 1 All ER 106.
 3 SLA 1925, ss. 23, 117 (1) (xxvi).
 4 Ibid., s 26; pp. 922–5, post.

(a) Powers exercisable by tenant for life

(i) Powers to sell or exchange The tenant for life may sell the settled land, or any part thereof, or any easement, right or privilege of any kind over or in relation to the land.[5] Every sale must be made for the best consideration in money that can reasonably be obtained,[6] but instead of being made in return for a lump sum it may be made in consideration, wholly or partly, of a rent payable yearly or half-yearly and secured upon the land sold. Such a rent may be perpetual or terminable, and in the latter case—that is to say, when it will cease to be payable after a certain number of years—it must be treated partly as principal and partly as interest, and the part constituting principal must be dealt with as capital money. The interest accruing on the principal sum must be accumulated by way of compound interest and added each year to capital.[7] The rent must be the best that can reasonably be obtained, though for a period not exceeding five years from the sale it may be nominal.[8] The statutory remedies for the recovery of a rentcharge given by the Law of Property Act 1925[9] lie for recovery of the rent.[10]

It is also provided that where the land is sold to any company incorporated by special Act of Parliament or by any order having the force of an Act of Parliament, the purchase money may consist, either wholly or partially, of fully-paid securities of any description of the purchasing company.[11]

The tenant for life may make an exchange of the whole or part of the land, or of any easement, right, or privilege over it, for other land or for an easement, right, or privilege over other land, and he may pay or accept money in order to render the exchanges equal in value.[12]

When a sale or exchange is made, the tenant for life is permitted to except the mines and minerals, and in such a case to reserve for the settled land all proper rights and powers incidental to mining purposes.[13]

The powers of sale and exchange are exercisable with regard to any principal mansion-house which stands on the settled land, but in two cases mere notice to the trustees of the proposed transaction[14] does not suffice, and the tenant for life must first obtain either the consent of the trustees or an order of the court, namely:

(i) where the settlement existed before 1926, and does not expressly dispense with the necessity for such consent or order; and

(ii) where the settlement came into operation after 1925, but contains a provision that such consent or order is necessary.

The court must determine as a fact whether any particular house is a principal mansion-house,[15] but it is enacted that a house which is usually occupied as a farmhouse, or which, together with its pleasure-grounds and park and lands, does not exceed 25 acres in extent, is not a principal mansion-

---

5 SLA 1925, s. 38 (1).
6 Ibid., s. 39 (1); *Wheelwright v Walker (No 2)* (1883) 31 WR 912.
7 Ibid., s. 39 (2).
8 Ibid., s. 39 (3).
9 S. 121; p. 191, post.
10 LP(A)A 1926, Sch.
11 SLA 1925, s. 39 (5).
12 Ibid., ss. 38 (iii), 40.
13 Ibid., s. 50.
14 P. 191, post.
15 *Re Feversham Settled Estate* [1938] 2 All ER 210.

house within the meaning of the Act and can in all cases be disposed of without the consent of the trustees.[16]

(ii) Power to grant leases The tenant for life may lease the whole or part of the land or any easement, right, or privilege incidental thereto for any purpose whatever, whether involving waste or not, for any of the following maximum periods:

(a) 999 years for a building lease;
(b) 100 years for a mining lease;
(c) 999 years for a forestry lease;
(d) 50 years for any other kind of lease.[17]

When any of the above leases is made:

(i) the tenant for life must give one month's notice in writing to the trustees;[18]
(ii) he must procure the best rent reasonably obtainable;[19] and
(iii) the lease must be by deed[19] and must contain a covenant by the lessee for payment of the rent, and a condition allowing the tenant for life to re-enter if the rent is not paid within a specific time not exceeding 30 days.

The deed must be so framed that the lessee will take possession within twelve months, but if the land is already leased to a third person, then, provided that such existing lease has no more than seven years to run, it is lawful to grant what is called a reversionary lease to take effect in possession when the existing one determines.[20]

Without any notice to the trustees, a lease may be granted for a term not exceeding 21 years at the best rent that can reasonably be obtained without a fine, provided that the lessee is made impeachable for waste.[1] If the lease does not exceed three years, it may be made by writing without a deed, but the lessee must enter into a written agreement to pay the rent.[2]

As in the case of the power of sale, the tenant for life may lease the land and reserve the minerals,[3] and if he desires to lease the principal mansion-house, he must obtain the consent of the trustees in the cases which have been specified above.[4]

Special provisions are inserted in the Act with regard to building, mining and forestry leases:

(a) Building leases A building lease[5] must be made partly in consideration of the lessee or some other person erecting new or additional buildings or

16 SLA 1925, s. 65.
17 Ibid., s. 41. Law Reform Committee 23rd Report (The powers and duties of trustees) 1982 (Cmnd 8733), para 8.6 recommends that this period be increased to 99 years.
18 Ibid., s. 101.
19 Ibid., s. 42 (1) (ii); *Re Morgan's Lease* [1972] Ch 1, [1971] 2 All ER 235; (1971) 87 LQR 338 (D. W. Elliott). As to whether a tenant for life has power to insert a rent review clause in the lease, see [1979] Conv 258 (M. Dockray); Law Reform Committee 23rd Report, supra, para 8.4, recommends that this doubt be removed.
20 Ibid., s. 42 (1) (i).
1 For the meaning of waste, see p. 269, post.
2 SLA 1925, s. 42 (5).
3 Ibid., s. 50.
4 Ibid., s. 65, p. 186, ante.
5 P. 489, post.

improving or repairing buildings, and partly in consideration of the payment of rent. A peppercorn or nominal rent may be reserved for the first five years of the term.[6] A lease is valid although it does not specify a definite time within which the building or rebuilding shall begin.[7]

(*b*) *Mining leases* As regards minerals the rule at common law is that a tenant for life unimpeachable for waste[8] can *open* and work mines and retain the whole profits, though this right can no longer be exercised without the permission of the local planning authority, since it involves a material change in the user of land within the meaning of the Town and Country Planning Act 1990. A tenant for life impeachable for waste cannot *open* mines, but he can continue to work to his own profit those that have already been lawfully opened by a predecessor.[9] These rules have been varied by the Settled Land Act 1925. If the tenant for life is impeachable for waste in respect of minerals, three-quarters of the rent arising from a mining lease becomes capital; if unimpeachable, one-quarter becomes capital and the residue goes to him as income.[10] A tenant for life who is impeachable for waste under the settlement is not impeachable in respect of mines that have been lawfully opened by a predecessor, and therefore he is entitled to three-fourths of the rents.[11] These rules with regard to minerals have lost much of their importance since the passing of the Coal Industry Nationalisation Act 1946, but they are still material, for "minerals" include "all substances in, on or under the land, obtainable by underground or by surface working".[12]

(*c*) *Forestry lease* A forestry lease is defined by the Act as a "lease to the Forestry Commissioners for any purpose for which they are authorized to acquire land by the Forestry Act [1967]",[13] but this is now to be construed as a reference to the Minister of Agriculture, Fisheries and Food, in whom the former powers of the Commissioners to acquire land are now vested.[14] In a forestry lease the rent may be nominal for any period not exceeding the first ten years or may be made to vary according to the value of the timber cut in any one year, and any other provisions may be made for the sharing of the profits of the user of the land between the tenant for life and the Minister.[15]

(iii) **Power to raise money by the grant of a legal mortgage of the settled land** A capital sum of money may be raised by mortgage in order to meet some expense that is connected with the settled land or desirable in the interests of its prosperity. There are nine different purposes specified by the Act for which a tenant for life may raise money in this manner, but as five of these are connected with the conversion of copyhold into socage and perpetually renewable leases into long terms, it is only necessary to notice that a mortgage of the legal estate is permissible when the object is:[16]

---

6 SLA 1925, s. 44.
7 *Re Grosvenor Settled Estates* [1933] Ch 97.
8 For the meaning of waste, see p. 269, post.
9 *Re Hall* [1916] 2 Ch 488.
10 SLA 1925, s. 47. These provisions may be displaced by the settlement: s. 48.
11 *Re Chaytor* [1900] 2 Ch 804; *Re Fitzwalter* [1943] Ch 285, [1943] 2 All ER 328.
12 SLA 1925, s. 117 (1) (xv).
13 Ibid., s. 117 (1) (x); Forestry Act 1967, Sch. 6, para 5.
14 Forestry Act 1967, s. 50, Sch. 6, para. 5.
15 SLA 1925, s. 48.
16 Ibid., s. 71. See also Leasehold Reform Act 1967, s. 6 (5).

(a) The discharge of an incumbrance on the settled land.

If, for instance, different parts of the land are subject to three separate mortgages, the tenant for life may grant a new mortgage of the entire land to another mortgagee and use the money to pay off the three original debts.[17]

The incumbrance must be permanent, thus excluding any annual sum payable only during a life or for a term of years.[18]

(b) Payment for any improvement authorized by the Settled Land Act 1925 or by the settlement.

This is a valuable power that was introduced in 1925. A tenant for life may spend existing capital money on carrying out any of the improvements authorized by the Act.[19]

(c) Equality of exchange.
(d) Payment of the costs of any transaction effected under (a) to (c) above.

A legal mortgage by the tenant for life may take the form either of a charge by deed by way of legal mortgage or of a long lease,[20] and a tenant for life who grants a mortgage term for any of the above four purposes is not subject to those provisions of the Settled Land Act[1] which in a normal case restrict the length of lease that may be made.[2]

This must be distinguished from the case where the tenant for life borrows money for his own purposes by mortgaging his beneficial interest, as for instance his equitable life interest.[3]

(iv) Power to effect improvements The tenant for life is empowered to effect certain authorized improvements on the land and to have the cost defrayed out of capital.[4] Moreover, his right to this payment, unlike the practice prevailing before 1926, is no longer conditional on his submitting a scheme of operations to the trustees or to the court before the work is done.[5] The Act authorizes 34 specific improvements which are classified into three categories according to the permanence or impermanence of their results:[6]

Part I improvements comprise 25 different works that clearly increase the permanent capital value of the land, such as drainage, irrigation, bridges, defences against water, the provision of farmhouses and cottages for labourers and the rebuilding of the mansion house.

Part II improvements are those, the lasting value of which is more doubtful, such as the erection of houses for land agents, the repair of damage due to dry rot or boring for water.

Part III improvements are those whose value is transitory, as, for example, the installation of a heating or electric power apparatus for buildings, the wiring of a house for electricity or the purchase of moveable machinery for farming or other purposes.

17 *Re Clifford* [1902] 1 Ch 87.
18 SLA 1925, s. 71 (2).
19 Ibid., s. 83, infra.
20 Pp. 663, et seq, post.
 1 P. 187, ante.
 2 SLA 1925, s. 71 (3).
 3 P. 670, post.
 4 SLA 1925, s. 83.
 5 Ibid., s. 84 (1).
 6 Ibid., Sch. 3. For the significance of this classification, see p. 201, post.

(v) Power to accept leases of other land A new power was introduced by the Settled Land Act 1925 allowing the tenant for life to accept a lease of any other land[7] or of mines and minerals, or of any easement, right or privilege, "convenient to be held or worked with or annexed in enjoyment to the settled land", and there is no limit to the length of the term which he may so accept.[8]

(vi) Miscellaneous powers There are several miscellaneous powers which the tenant for life is entitled to exercise, and of these the following may be mentioned:

(*a*) *Power to contract* Power to contract to make any sale, exchange, mortgage, charge or other disposition authorised by the Act.[9] The transaction must be in conformity with the Act at the time of the performance of the contract. Thus in the case of a contract for a lease the lease must satisfy the requirement that the rent must be the best reasonably obtainable when the lease is granted.[10] Such contracts are enforceable by and against every successor in title of the tenant for life.[11]

(*b*) *Power to grant options* Power to grant, by writing, with or without consideration, an option to purchase or take a lease of settled land, or any easement, right, or privilege over it.[12] The price or rent must be the best reasonably obtainable and must be fixed when the option is granted.[13] The option must be made exercisable within an agreed number of years not exceeding ten.

(*c*) *Power to accept surrender of leases* Power to accept, with or without consideration, a surrender of any lease of settled land.[14]

(*d*) *Power to grant land for public purposes* Power, if the result will be for the general benefit of the settled land, to make grants or leases at a nominal price or rent for certain public and charitable purposes, e.g. the grant of land not exceeding one acre for a village institute or a public library.[15]

(*e*) *Power to provide land for working classes* Power to grant or lease a restricted amount of land at a nominal price or rent for the purpose of providing allotments or dwellings for the working classes.[16]

(*f*) *Power to sell timber* Power with the consent of the trustees or under an order of the court for a tenant for life who is impeachable for waste to sell timber that is ripe and fit for cutting, provided, however, that three-quarters of the net proceeds become capital money and one-quarter becomes income.[17]

7 This includes a power to accept an extended lease under Leasehold Reform Act 1967, s. 6 (2) (*a*); p. 493, post.
8 SLA 1925, s. 53.
9 Ibid., s. 90.
10 *Re Rycroft's Settlement* [1962] Ch 263, [1961] 3 All ER 581.
11 SLA 1925, s. 90 (2).
12 Ibid., s. 51.
13 *Re Morgan's Lease* [1972] Ch 1, [1971] 2 All ER 235; Law Reform Committee 23rd Report (The powers and duties of trustees) 1982 (Cmnd 8733) para 8.10 recommends that the tenant for life should be given the power to grant an option at a price to be fixed at the time of the exercise of the option.
14 SLA 1925, s. 52.
15 Ibid., s. 55.
16 Ibid., s. 57 (2).
17 Ibid., s. 66.

(*g*) *Power to sell heirlooms* Power under an order of the court to sell heirlooms, but in such a case the money arising from the sale becomes capital money, which in this case may be spent on the purchase of other heirlooms.[18]

(vii) Power to effect any transaction under order of court "Any transaction" within the powers of an absolute owner may be sanctioned by the court if this will be for the benefit of the settled land or the beneficiaries, even though it is a transaction not otherwise authorized by the Act or the settlement.[19] Thus approval was given to a scheme to raise money out of capital to enable the tenant for life to continue to reside in the mansion house;[20] and it has been held that the court has jurisdiction to authorise the tenant for life to vary the beneficial interest of an ascertained beneficiary of full age and capacity, even if that beneficiary did not consent.[21] Moreover the width of the definition of "transaction" enables the court to alter the beneficial interests under the settlement. This was commonly done for the purpose of saving estate duty on the death of beneficiaries, and the jurisdiction was largely superseded by that given to the court under the Variation of Trusts Act 1958.[1] Both jurisdictions still remain.

(b) Notice, consent or court order

As a general rule a tenant for life need not obtain the consent of the trustees to his exercise of a power, but if he intends to sell, exchange, mortgage or charge the land, to make a lease exceeding 21 years or to grant an option to purchase or to take a lease of the land, he must notify the trustees of his intention at least one month before he completes the transaction.[2] Except in the case of a proposed mortgage or charge, it is permissible, indeed usual, to give a general notice, i.e. one which states his intention to grant, for example, leases from time to time, without mentioning any specific lease already arranged.[3] There are, however, as we have seen, several cases in which something more than notice is required, and it may be helpful to restate these in summary form:

First, an order of the court must be obtained before the tenant for life may:

  (i)   grant more than the amount of land specified in the Act for providing allotments or dwellings for the working classes;[4]
  (ii) buy or sell heirlooms;[5]
  (iii) grant building or mining leases for terms longer than those specified in the Act.[6]

---

18 SLA 1925, s. 67.
19 Ibid., s. 64 (1). "Transaction" is defined in s. 64 (2) as amended by Settled Land and Trustee Acts (Court's General Powers) Act 1943, s. 2. *Re White-Popham Settled Estates* [1936] Ch 725, [1936] 2 All ER 1486; *Re Scarisbrick Re-Settlement Estates* [1944] Ch 229, [1944] 1 All ER 404; *Re Earl of Mount Edgcumbe* [1950] Ch 615, [1950] 2 All ER 242; *Re Simmons* [1956] Ch 125, [1955] 3 All ER 818; *Re Rycroft's Settlement* [1962] Ch 263, [1961] 3 All ER 581; M & B p. 233; *Raikes v Lygon* [1988] 1 WLR 281; [1988] 1 All ER 884.
20 *Re Scarisbrick Re-Settlement Estates*, supra.
21 *Hambro v Duke of Marlborough* (1994) Times, 25 March (Blenheim Parliamentary Estates).
 1 See generally H & M, chapter 21. Harris, *Variation of Trusts*, pp. 19–22.
 2 SLA 1925, s. 101 (1). Law Reform Committee 23rd Report, supra, para. 8.9, recommends that on receipt of the notice the trustees should require the tenant for life to submit to them a valuation, so that they may control the transaction more effectively.
 3 Ibid., s. 101 (2).   4 Ibid., s. 57 (2).
 5 Ibid., s. 67.   6 Ibid., s. 46.

Secondly, *either* an order of the court *or* the consent of the trustees must be obtained before the tenant for life may:

(i)   sell or lease the principal mansion-house in the cases specified above;[7]
(ii) sell the timber in the event of his being impeachable for waste.[8]

Thirdly, there are two cases in which the tenant for life must obtain the consent in writing of the trustees, namely, before he:

(i)   compromises or otherwise settles any claim or dispute relating to the settled land;[9]
(ii) releases, waives or modifies a right imposed on other land for the benefit of the settled land, as, for instance, an easement or a covenant.[10]

(3) POSITION OF TENANT FOR LIFE

(a) Additions to and reductions from powers

Such, then, are the powers conferred upon the tenant for life by the Act, but it must be remembered that there is nothing to prevent additional powers being given to him by the settlement, for it is expressly provided[11] that when a settlor authorizes the exercise of any powers additional to or larger than those enumerated above, they shall operate in exactly the same manner and with the same results as if they had been permitted by the Act. Thus a settlement may allow the tenant for life:

(i)   to grant a lease to take effect in possession not later than three years after its date;[12]
(ii)   to use as income the whole of the rent reserved on a mining lease;[13] or
(iii) to raise money on mortgage for the purchase of a dwelling house.[14]

In fact all the powers given by a settlement are expressly preserved, for it is provided that nothing in the Act shall take away, abridge or prejudicially affect any power under the settlement which is exercisable by the tenant for life or by the trustees with the consent of the tenant for life.[15] If, however, there is any conflict between the Act and the settlement, the Act prevails, and any power (not being a mere power of revocation or appointment[16]) conferred on the trustees becomes exercisable by the tenant for life as an additional power.[17]

Such a conflict occurs, for instance, if the settlement empowers the tenant for life to sell with the consent of a third person, for such a conditional power is inconsistent with the unfettered power of sale given by the Act.[18] Though

---

7 SLA 1925, s. 65; p. 186, ante.
8 Ibid., s. 66.
9 Ibid., s. 58 (1).
10 Ibid., s. 58 (2).
11 Ibid., s. 109.
12 *Encyclopaedia of Forms and Precedents* (4th edn), vol. 20. p. 700.
13 Ibid., p. 699.
14 Ibid., p. 702. For an example of such an express power, see *City of London Building Society v Flegg* [1988] AC 54, [1987] 3 All ER 435.
15 Ibid., s. 108 (1).
16 As, for example, where land is limited upon such trusts as T shall appoint, and subject thereto to A for life. Here, T's power to revoke the life interest and to appoint new interests remains exercisable by him: Wolstenholme and Cherry, vol. 3, p. 222.
17 SLA 1925, s. 108 (2).
18 *Re Jefferys* [1939] Ch 205; M & B p. 320; (1939) 55 LQR 22 (H.P.).

a settlor is allowed to confer upon the tenant for life the right to exercise powers additional to those permissible under the statute, it is enacted that any provisions inserted in the settlement with a view to cutting down the statutory powers shall be void. Section 106 of the Settled Land Act 1925 provides:

> If in a settlement, will, assurance, or other instrument . . . a provision is inserted:
> (a) purporting or attempting, by way of direction, declaration, or otherwise, to forbid a tenant for life or statutory owner to exercise any power under this Act, or his right to require the settled land to be vested in him; or
> (b) attempting, or tending, or intended, by a limitation, gift, or disposition over of settled land, or by a limitation, gift, or disposition of other real or any personal property, or by the imposition of any condition, or by forfeiture, or in any other manner whatever, to prohibit or prevent him from exercising, or to induce him to abstain from exercising, or to put him into a position inconsistent with his exercising, any power under this Act, or his right to require the settled land to be vested in him;
> that provision, as far as it purports, or attempts, or tends, or is intended to have or would or might have, the operation aforesaid, shall be deemed to be void.[19]

A condition that is sometimes inserted in settlements requiring the tenant for life to reside on the settled land will serve to illustrate the application of this section.

> Suppose that land is settled on X for life with a proviso that if he does not reside on the settled land for at least three months in each year he shall forfeit his interest.

Such a clause is void so far as it "tends" to hinder or obstruct the exercise by X of his statutory powers. This, of course, is its natural tendency, for if he sells or leases the estate he must necessarily infringe the condition as to residence. It is a deterrent of this nature that is within the mischief of the section, and the rule therefore is that, notwithstanding a disposition of the land under his statutory powers, his life interest in the income remains intact.[20] If, on the other hand, there is no question of the exercise of the powers, his failure to satisfy the condition operates as a forfeiture of his interest.[1] If it has never been his intention to exercise the powers, it cannot be said that the condition has in any way hampered his freedom of action.

Another example of the operation of the section is this:

> If the settlor vests a fund of money in the trustees, with authority to apply the income thereof upon the maintenance of the estate and to pay any surplus not required for that purpose to the tenant for life, X, the prospect of losing this income might tend to dissuade X from exercising his power of sale. As a general rule, therefore, if X sells the land he still remains entitled to the income for life.[2]

---

19 *Re Aberconway's Settlement Trusts* [1953] Ch 647, [1953] 2 All ER 350.
20 *Re Paget's Settled Estates* (1885) 30 Ch D 161; *Re Patten* [1929] 2 Ch 276 (an excellent example of the principle); *Re Orlebar* [1936] Ch 147.
1 *Re Acklom* [1929] 1 Ch 195; M & B p. 321; *Re Haynes* (1887) 37 Ch D 306; *Re Trenchard* [1902] 1 Ch 378.
2 *Re Ames* [1893] 2 Ch 479; M & B p. 320; *Re Herbert* [1946] 1 All ER 421; cf *Re Burden* [1948] Ch 160, [1948] 1 All ER 31; *Re Aberconway's Settlement Trusts*, supra; [1954] CLJ 60 (R. N. Gooderson).

(b) Non-assignability of powers

Again, as long as the land remains settled, the powers of a tenant for life are indestructible in the sense that they are not capable of assignment or release, but remain exercisable by him notwithstanding any assignment by operation of law or otherwise of his beneficial interest under the settlement.[3] Thus:

> If land stands settled on A for life, remainder to B for life with remainder over, and B sells his reversionary life interest for value to X, the statutory power to grant leases after the death of A is exercisable by B, for the design of the Act is to enable a tenant for life to exercise his powers whether he has disposed of his beneficial interest or not.[4]

In such a case as this the former rule was that B could not exercise his powers without the consent of his assignee for value, X, but the necessity for such consent has now been removed by the Act.[5] The rights of the assignee are, however, protected, for whatever interest he had in the property originally assigned to him he has a corresponding interest in any money, securities or land into which that property may have been converted as a result of the exercise of some power.[6] Moreover, notice of an intended transaction must be given to him.[7]

If, however, it is shown to the satisfaction of the court that a tenant for life has by reason of bankruptcy, assignment, incumbrance, or otherwise ceased to have a substantial interest in the settled land, and has unreasonably refused to exercise the statutory powers, an order may be made authorizing the trustees of the settlement to exercise the powers in his name.[8] The mere fact that he has grossly neglected the land and has allowed it to become derelict does not justify the making of an order. The court must be satisfied that there has been an unreasonable refusal to exercise the powers.[9]

Although any attempted assignment of the powers by the tenant for life is void, it is provided that if the life interest, with the intention of causing its extinction, is surrendered to the remainderman or reversioner next entitled under the settlement, the statutory powers shall cease to be available to the tenant for life and shall be exercisable as if he were dead.[10] For instance:

> if a tenant for life becomes bankrupt and the trustee sells his life interest to the tenant in tail in remainder,[11] or if a father surrenders his life interest to the tenant in tail in remainder, the statutory powers become exercisable by the tenant in tail.

---

3 SLA 1925, s. 104 (1).
4 *Re Barlow's Contract* [1903] 1 Ch 382; *Earl of Lonsdale v Lowther* [1900] 2 Ch 687.
5 SLA 1925, s. 104 (4).
6 Ibid., s. 104 (4) (*a*).
7 Ibid., s. 104 (4) (*c*).
8 Ibid., s. 24 (1). This section does not apply to a statutory owner: *Re Craven Settled Estates* [1926] Ch 985.
9 *Re Thornhill's Settlement* [1940] 4 All ER 83; affd [1941] Ch 24, [1940] 4 All ER 249; M & B p. 323.
10 SLA 1925, s. 105 (1). LP(A)A 1926, Sch. A remainderman or reversioner does not qualify if there is an intervening limitation which may take effect: *Re Maryon-Wilson's Instruments* [1971] Ch 789, [1969] 3 All ER 558.
11 *Re Shawdon Estates Settlement* [1930] 1 Ch 217; affd [1930] 2 Ch 1; M & B p. 323.

(c) Fiduciary nature of powers

(i) Tenant for life a trustee Finally, it must be observed that the tenant for life, though he is given an almost unfettered liberty to exercise the statutory powers, is at the same time constituted trustee for all interested parties. Section 107 (1) of the Settled Land Act 1925 provides that:

> A tenant for life or statutory owner shall, in exercising any power under this Act, have regard to the interests of all parties entitled under the settlement, and shall, in relation to the exercise thereof by him, be deemed to be in the position and to have the duties and liabilities of a trustee for those parties.[12]

Several judicial pronouncements have placed those duties on a high level. It has been said that the duty to "have regard to the interests of all parties" requires the tenant for life to consider all the interests in the widest sense, not merely pecuniary interests, but even the aspirations and sentiments of the family.[13] As Lord ESHER said:

> He must take all the circumstances of the family, and of each member of the family who may be affected by what he is about to do; he must consider them all carefully, and must consider them in the way that an honest outside trustee would consider them; then he must come to what, in his judgment, is the right thing to do under the circumstances—not the best thing, but the right thing to do.[14]

Nevertheless, having regard to the deliberate policy of the Act in conferring upon the tenant for life virtually the status of absolute owner, this super-imposed trusteeship is somewhat abnormal, for in the nature of things it must inevitably be "a highly interested trusteeship".[15] The mere imposition of a trust is insufficient to ensure that powers, so freely confided to the judgment of the tenant for life, will not be exercised from motives of selfishness and personal aggrandizement. A tenant for life, who, with the object of securing a larger income wherewith to meet his debts or to indulge expensive tastes, or in order to relieve himself from the cares of management, or because he is hostile to the remainderman, sells land that will obviously be of far greater value in a few years' time, owing perhaps to rapidly changing conditions in the neighbourhood, can scarcely be described as acting "as an upright independent and righteous man would act in dealing with the affairs of others",[16] and yet none of these facts alone is sufficient to render him liable, provided that he obtains the best price reasonably obtainable and otherwise observes the requirements of the Act.[17]

The Court may, however, intervene upon clear proof that the tenant for life has exercised a power with the sole object of conferring some benefit upon himself or upon some relative other than the remainderman, as, for

---

12 SLA 1925, s. 107 (1) re-enacting s. 53 of the 1882 Act; *Re Pelly's Will Trusts* [1957] Ch 1 at 18, [1956] 2 All ER 326 at 332.

13 *Re Marquis of Ailesbury's Settled Estates* [1892] 1 Ch 506, at 536, per LINDLEY LJ; and see BOWEN LJ passim. "He must act as an upright, independent and righteous man would act in dealing with the affairs of others," at 546, per FRY LJ.

14 *Re Earl of Radnor's Will Trusts* (1890) 45 Ch D 402 at 417.

15 *Re Stamford and Warrington* [1916] 1 Ch 404 at 420, per YOUNGER J.

16 See note 13, supra.

17 Cf the remarks of PEARSON J in *Wheelwright v Walker* (1883) 23 Ch D 752 at 761–2; M & B p. 325. See too *England v Public Trustee* (1967) 205 EG 651 where SELLERS LJ suggested that SLA 1925 should be amended to provide that notice of an intended sale by the tenant for life should be given to the other beneficiaries under the settlement.

example, where he accepts a bribe from a lessee,[18] where he makes an unsuitable investment,[19] or where a widow entitled for life *durante viduitate* makes a lease to her second intended husband in order to ensure her continued occupation of the premises.[20]

(ii) Acquisitions by tenant for life Subject to certain restrictions, a tenant for life may deal with the settled land for his own purposes. When a tenant for life exercises his statutory powers, he is normally dealing with persons who have no connection with the estate, but it may happen that in his private capacity and not as tenant for life he wishes to exercise one of the powers in favour of himself. The possibility of such a dealing between him and the settled estate was first allowed to a restricted extent by the Settled Land Act 1890, but his freedom in this respect has been extended by the Act of 1925, and it is now provided that any disposition of the settled land may be made to him, that capital money may be advanced on mortgage to him, and that land may be bought from or exchanged with him.[1]

Since a person can scarcely negotiate a transaction with himself, it is provided that in all such cases the trustees shall have all the powers of a tenant for life in reference to negotiating and completing the transaction, and the right to enforce any covenants entered into by the tenant for life.[2] Where the tenant for life is himself one of the trustees, he should be a conveying party as well as the person in whose favour the conveyance is made.[3]

D. THE TRUSTEES OF THE SETTLEMENT

(1) DEFINITION OF TRUSTEES

Section 30 (1) of the Settled Land Act 1925 gives a list of five different classes of persons competent to act as trustees of the settlement and arranges them in a binding order of priority as follows:[4]

(a) The persons who, under the settlement, are trustees with power to sell the settled land.

A power given to trustees to sell settled land is in fact abortive, since the Act provides that it shall be exercisable not by them, but by the tenant for life.[5] The only effect is to make the persons to whom it is given trustees *ex necessitate* of the settlement.

(b) The persons who are declared by the settlement to be trustees thereof for the purposes of the Settled Land Act.

These persons will normally constitute the trustees, for an express reservation of the power of sale contemplated by the first paragraph will rarely occur in practice.

---

18 *Chandler v Bradley* [1897] 1 Ch 315.
19 *Re Hunt's Settled Estates* [1906] 2 Ch 11.
20 *Middlemas v Stevens* [1901] 1 Ch 574; M & B p. 326.
　1 SLA 1925, s. 68 (1).
　2 Ibid., s. 68 (2).
　3 *Re Pennant's Will Trusts* [1970] Ch 75, [1969] 2 All ER 862.
　4 SLA 1925, s. 30 (1) (i)–(v).
　5 Ibid., s. 108 (2).

(c) The persons who, under the settlement, are trustees with power of sale of any *other* land comprised in the settlement which is subject to the same limitations as the land that is being dealt with.

(d) The persons who, under the settlement, are trustees with a *future* power of sale.

If, for example, a testator devises his land to his wife for life and after her death to X and Y upon trust to sell the fee simple, then, failing persons qualified under the first three paragraphs, X and Y will be the trustees of the settlement during the wife's life.

(e) The persons appointed by deed by the beneficiaries, provided that the beneficiaries are of full capacity and entitled to dispose of the whole equitable interest in the settled land.

Where a settlement is created by will, or has arisen by reason of an intestacy, and there are no trustees, the personal representatives of the deceased are trustees of the settlement until others are appointed; but if there is only one personal representative, not being a trust corporation, he must appoint an additional trustee to act with him.[6]

If at any time there are no trustees as defined above, or if for any reason it is expedient that new trustees should be appointed, the court may appoint fit persons to hold the office.[7]

(2) COMPOUND SETTLEMENT

(a) Definition

Where land is settled by a series of separate instruments, the instruments together form one settlement which is called a *compound settlement*.[8] The commonest example of this occurs in the case of a resettlement, which, as we have seen, involves three instruments, i.e. the original settlement, the disentailment and the resettlement.[9] The principle that the several instruments may be regarded as constituting one settlement becomes important when the tenant for life, in exercise of his statutory power of sale, desires to convey the fee simple to the purchaser free from the limitations of the various instruments.

(b) Conveyance by tenant for life

If, after a resettlement, a sale has been effected by the father as first tenant for life he can execute the conveyance in any one of three capacities:

(i) He may convey as tenant for life under the original settlement.

The merit of this is that his conveyance overreaches the limitations of both settlements, and if the purchase money is paid to the trustees of the original settlement the purchaser acquires a title free from the rights of the beneficiaries. The disadvantage is that the tenant for life, since he is acting under the original settlement, cannot avail himself of any additional powers which may have been reserved by the deed of resettlement.

6 SLA 1925, s. 30 (3).
7 Ibid., s. 34.
8 *Re Ogle's Settled Estates* [1927] 1 Ch 229 at 233–4, per ROMER J; M & B p. 306.
9 Pp. 67–9, ante.

(ii) He may convey as tenant for life under the resettlement.

The position here is reversed, for although he can exercise any additional powers, he cannot convey a title free from the rights of beneficiaries that have been created by the original settlement. Conveyancers sought before 1926 to overcome this difficulty by reciting in the re-settlement that the life interest resettled upon the father was "in restoration and by way of confirmation of" his life interest under the original settlement, but it was only on the eve of a statutory amendment of the law[10] that this device was held to be effective.[11] It had previously been held that "when once conveyancers have in fact transmuted the old body into a new body, they cannot claim to have retained the old body, whatever incantations they may use in the process".[12]

(iii) He may convey as tenant for life under the compound settlement.

This plan combines the advantages of the two preceding methods, since the tenant for life can exercise additional powers given by the resettlement and can overreach, within the statutory limits,[13] the limitations of both settlements. Under the old law, however, this method was often open to a fatal objection, for its efficacy depends upon the existence of compound trustees, and before the legislation of 1925, it frequently happened that there were no such trustees. If compound trustees had not been appointed in the original settlement it was impossible to rectify the omission in the resettlement, and unless all the beneficiaries were of full age (an improbable event), it was necessary to incur the expense of making an application to the court.

(c) Compound trustees

The difficulty that there may be no compound trustees has been avoided by the legislation of 1925 which is retrospective and is as follows:

(i) trustees under an instrument which is a settlement are trustees also of a settlement constituted by that instrument and any subsequent instruments, i.e. the original trustees are trustees of any compound settlement which later comes into being;[14]

(ii) trustees under a resettlement, where there are no trustees under the original settlement, are trustees of the compound settlement;[15]

(iii) where a resettlement states that a life interest limited to a tenant for life is *in restoration or confirmation* of his interest under the original settlement, he is entitled as of his former interest, and can exercise the statutory powers both under the original settlement and under the re-settlement.[16]

---

10 Infra.
11 *Parr v A-G* [1926] AC 239 (18 December 1925).
12 *A-G v Parr* [1924] 1 KB 916 at 931, per ATKIN LJ; *Re Constable's Settled Estates* [1919] 1 Ch 178.
13 Pp. 814–5, post.
14 SLA 1925, s. 31.
15 Ibid., as added by LP(A)A 1926, Sch.
16 Ibid., s. 22 (2); *Re Cradock's Settled Estates* [1926] Ch 944.

(3) PROTECTION OF TRUSTEES

It is not the policy of the legislature to subject the trustees of the settlement to a strict liability for the acts of the estate owner. Provisions are therefore inserted in the Settled Land Act 1925 designed to protect them in certain circumstances, and they now enjoy a greater measure of immunity than under the Act of 1882. Thus they are not liable for giving any consent or for not bringing any action which they might have brought, and, in the case of a purchase of land with capital money or in the case of a lease of the settled land by the tenant for life, they are not bound to investigate the propriety of the disposition.[17] Again, where the tenant for life directs capital money to be invested in any authorized security, the trustees are not liable for the acts of an agent employed by him or for failing to obtain a valuation of the proposed security;[18] neither are they liable for having delivered documents of title to the tenant for life, though they are responsible for securities representing capital money.[19] Each trustee is answerable only for what he actually receives, notwithstanding his signing any receipt for conformity, and he is not answerable for the acts and defaults of his co-trustees or for any loss not due to his own wilful default.[20] In short, the role of the trustees is to manage and protect the money that is paid to them.

E. CAPITAL MONEY

(1) DEFINITION OF CAPITAL MONEY

It is obvious that in several cases the exercise of a statutory power will result in the payment of money to the trustees; this is called *capital money*. Thus, for instance:

(i)   money which becomes due on the sale of the land or of heirlooms;[1]
(ii) fines paid by lessees in consideration of obtaining a tenancy;[2]
(iii) three-quarters or one-quarter (as the case may be) of a mining rent;[3]
(iv) three-quarters of the money arising from the sale of timber by a tenant for life who is impeachable for waste;[4]
(v)   consideration paid for an option to purchase or take a lease of the settled land;[5]
(vi) damages or compensation received by the tenant for life in respect of a breach of covenant by his lessee or grantee;[6] and
(vii) money raised by a mortgage of the land for the purposes authorized by the Act,[7]

are all examples of capital money.[8] The expression also covers money arising

17 SLA 1925, s. 97.
18 Ibid., s. 98 (1).
19 Ibid., s. 98 (3).
20 Ibid., s. 96. This is a rule applicable to trustees generally: TA 1925, s. 30 (1).
 1 Ibid., s. 67 (2).
 2 Ibid., s. 42 (4).
 3 Ibid., s. 47; p. 188, ante.
 4 Ibid., s. 66 (2).
 5 Ibid., s. 51 (5).
 6 Ibid., s. 80 (1).
 7 Ibid., s. 71; pp. 188-9, ante.
 8 And see SLA 1925, ss. 52, 54 (4), 55 (2), 56 (4), 57 (3), 58-61.

otherwise than under the Act which ought to be treated as capital,[9] as for example money paid under a fire insurance policy which the tenant for life was under an obligation to maintain.

(2) APPLICATION OF CAPITAL MONEY

As regards the manner in which capital money must be disposed of, the first point is that if raised for some particular purpose, it must be applied accordingly. Thus, money that has been borrowed on mortgage in order to carry out some specific improvement on the land must be so spent. If, however, the money has not been raised for some particular object, but is due, for instance, to the sale of the land, it must be applied in one or more of the modes set out in the Settled Land Act 1925.[10] In addition to any special mode permitted by the settlement itself there are 21 different modes indicated by the Act.[11] It would be inappropriate in a book of this nature to set out the whole list, but a few of the more important methods will be noted:

(a) Investment

The most usual destination of capital money is investment in what are called *trustee securities*—that is to say, investments in which the Trustee Investments Act 1961[12] authorizes trustees to invest trust funds. Money which is thus required to be invested is paid to the trustees or into court at the option of the tenant for life, and the investment is made according to his direction. It cannot afterwards be altered without his consent. The money, either before or after investment, represents the land from which it originated, and it is held in trust for the same persons for whom the land was held under the settlement and for the same interests, so that, for instance, the income arising from the investments is paid to the tenant for life in the same way as the annual profits of the land would have been paid prior to its sale.[13]

(b) Loan on mortgage

Provided that "proper advice" is taken, capital money may be lent on mortgage of "freehold property" in England and Wales or Northern Ireland and of "leasehold property in those countries" if the lease has at least 60 years to run;[14] further, a report of the value of the property must be obtained and not more than two-thirds of the value of any suitable property may be lent:[15] and when the settled land is sold in fee simple or for a term having at least 500 years to run, it is now enacted that a sum not exceeding two-thirds of the purchase money may be allowed to remain on mortgage of the land sold.[16]

9 SLA 1925, s. 81.
10 Ibid., s. 73.
11 See too Leasehold Reform Act 1967, s. 6 (5).
12 See generally H & M pp. 502, et seq; *Snell's Equity* (29th edn), pp. 215, et seq. Law Reform Committee 23rd Report (The powers and duties of trustees) 1982 (Cmnd 8733) paras. 9.1.II.6–10 recommend that the Trustee Investments Act be replaced by an up-to-date statute.
13 SLA 1925, s. 75. See *Re Cartwright* [1939] Ch 90.
14 Trustee Investments Act 1961, s. 1, Sch. I Part II, para 13. It appears that money should only be lent on a first legal mortgage; H & M, p. 513; *Snell's Equity*, p. 221.
15 TA 1925, s. 8.
16 SLA 1925, s. 10 (2).

(c) Purchase of land

Capital money may also be expended in the purchase of land or of mines or minerals convenient to be worked with the settled land, provided that the interest so bought is either the fee simple or a leasehold having at least 60 more years to run.[17] Again, it may be used to finance a person who has agreed to take a lease or grant for building purposes of the settled land, advances being made to him on the security of an equitable mortgage of his building agreement.[18]

(d) Improvements

Lastly capital money may be used in payment for any improvement authorized by the Settled Land Act 1925.

(i) Payment for improvement The procedure that governs payment varies according as the capital money is in the hands of the trustees or in court. In the former case the trustees, unless ordered by the court, must not pay for the improvement until they have obtained from a competent engineer or able practical surveyor, employed independently of the tenant for life, a certificate certifying that the improvement has been properly executed and declaring the amount that ought to be paid.[19] Where the capital money is in court, the court may, on a report or certificate of the Minister of Agriculture, Fisheries and Food, or of a competent engineer or able practical surveyor, approved by it, or on such other evidence as it may think sufficient, make what order it thinks fit for the application of the money in payment of the improvement.[20]

(ii) Repayment of cost In cases where the work done is not of lasting value it is economically sound that the tenant for life should ultimately restore the amount expended to capital by the creation of a sinking fund out of income, and it is with this object in view that the Act classifies the authorized improvements into the three categories that have already been mentioned.[1] The position is this:

Part I improvements The tenant for life cannot be required to set up a sinking fund.

Part II improvements Before meeting the cost out of capital, the trustees *may* if they think fit, and must if so directed by the court, require that the money shall be repaid to them out of the income of the settled land by not more than fifty half-yearly instalments.[2]

Part III improvements The trustees *must* require the whole cost to be paid out of income in the manner mentioned above.[3]

The court, when in possession of the capital money, is in the same position as the trustees with regard to requiring repayment of the money, except that it is not bound to require repayment in 25 years.

The effect of an order requiring repayment by instalments is that the

17 SLA 1925, s. 73 (1) (xi) and (xii).
18 Ibid., s. 73 (1) (xviii).
19 Ibid., s. 84 (2).
20 Ibid., s. 84 (3).
1 Ibid., Sch. 3; p. 189, ante. Law Reform Committee 23rd Report, supra, para 8.4 says that the provisions of this Sch. "undoubtedly require modernisation".
2 Ibid., s. 84 (2) (a).
3 Ibid., s. 84 (2) (b).

settled land becomes subject to a yearly rentcharge which takes effect as if it were limited by the settlement prior to the estate of the tenant for life.[4] If, however, the subject matter of the settlement is agricultural land used as such for the purposes of a trade or business,[5] capital money may be applied in the execution of any improvements specified in the Agricultural Holdings Act 1986,[6] without any provision being made for the replacement of the cost out of income.[7] How prejudicial this may be to remaindermen is evident from the inclusion in the specified improvements of the execution of running repairs other than those which the tenant is under an obligation to carry out.[8] This power to pay for improvements out of capital, however, is not available to trustees holding land under a trust for sale.[9]

F. REGISTERED LAND

The provisions of the Settled Land Act 1925 apply to registered land but take effect subject to the provisions of the Land Registration Act 1925.[10] The legal estate in the settled land is registered in the name of the tenant for life or statutory owner.[11] The beneficial interests under the settlement are included in the definition of minor interests[12] and "take effect as minor interests and not otherwise".[13] These interests are protected by restrictions entered on the proprietorship register[14] and are binding on the registered proprietor for his life but do not affect a disposition by his personal representative.[15]

   Thus, if X is the tenant for life and Y and Z are the trustees of a settlement, X will be the registered proprietor of the fee simple of the settled land and the register will contain a dual restriction, first preventing the registration of any disposition under which capital money arises unless the money is paid to Y and Z or into court[16] and then preventing the registration of any disposition not authorized by the Settled Land Act 1925. By this means, the beneficial interests of a strict settlement are protected without their details being brought onto the register. There is still a curtain, and a purchaser who complies with the restrictions will override the beneficial interests in the same way that he would overreach them in the case of unregistered land.

4 SLA 1925, s. 85.
5 Agricultural Holdings Act 1986, s. 1 (4).
6 Ibid., Sch. 7.
7 Ibid., s. 89 (1).
8 *Re Duke of Northumberland* [1951] Ch 202, [1950] 2 All ER 1181; *Re Sutherland Settlement Trusts* [1953] Ch 792, [1953] 2 All ER 27; *Re Lord Brougham and Vaux's Settled Estates* [1954] Ch 24, [1953] 2 All ER 655.
9 *Re Wynn* [1955] 1 WLR 940, [1955] 2 All ER 865; *Re Boston's Will Trusts* [1956] Ch 395, [1956] 1 All ER 593.
10 SLA 1925, s. 119 (3). See generally Ruoff and Roper, chapter 31. For settled land during a minority, see p. 927, post.
11 LRA 1925, s. 86 (1).
12 Ibid., s. 3 (xv) (b).
13 Ibid., s. 86 (2). See (1958) 22 Conv (NS) 14 at 23–4 (F. R. Crane) where it is suggested that, if no restrictions are entered, a beneficiary in possession of settled land cannot claim an overriding interest under LRA 1925, s. 70 (1) (g); p. 242, post. Law Commission Third Report on Land Registration 1987 (Law Com No. 158, HC 269) para 2.69 recommends that interests under settlements should be capable of being overriding interests.
14 LRR 1925, rr. 56–58, 104 and Forms 9–11. See Ruoff and Roper, paras. 31–01–31–06.
15 LRA 1925, s. 86 (3).
16 Or to at least two trustees or to a trust corporation.

SECTION II THE TRUST FOR SALE

An alternative method of settling land is to adopt the device of a trust for sale.

In general this arises where land is transferred by deed or will to trustees with an imperative direction that they are to effect a sale and to hold the proceeds thereof upon certain specified trusts. The manner of its formation has already been sufficiently described,[17] though it should be recalled that owing to the doctrine of conversion in equity, the land notionally becomes money, with the result that the interests of the beneficiaries are in the proceeds of sale and not in the land,[18] and are automatically overreached on a sale of the land by the trustees for sale.[19]

It is essential to define a trust for sale. As we have seen, the strict settlement and the trust for sale are mutually exclusive, and successive or limited interests in land create a settlement under the Settled Land Act 1925, unless the land is held upon trust for sale.[20]

A. THE DEFINITION OF A TRUST FOR SALE

The definition in section 205 (1) (xxix) of the Law of Property Act 1925 reads as follows:

"Trust for sale", in relation to land, means an immediate binding trust for sale, whether or not exercisable at the request or with the consent of any person, and with or without a power of discretion to postpone the sale.

We must now consider the meaning of the words "trust", "immediate", and "binding".

(1) TRUST

An instrument does not create a trust for sale unless it contains a direction imposing a duty upon the trustees to sell. A *trust* to sell must always be distinguished from a *power* to sell. A trust is obligatory upon the trustee, a power leaves it to his discretion whether he will sell or not. It has, indeed, been enacted that a disposition coming into operation after 1925 which directs that the trustees shall *either retain or sell* land shall constitute a trust for sale with power to postpone the sale,[1] but, apart from this statutory provision, whether an instrument creates a trust or confers a power is a question that can be answered only by construing its terms. What is in form a trust for sale may be nothing more than a discretionary power; what is in form a power may, when properly construed, be an imperative trust.[2] The distinction is of great importance in conveyancing, for if what is given to the trustees is a mere power of sale, it is exercisable not by them but by the tenant

17 Pp. 76–7, ante.
18 See *Irani Finance Ltd v Singh* [1971] Ch 59 at 80, [1970] 3 All ER 199 at 203, per Cross LJ; pp. 235, et seq, post.
19 P. 76, ante; p. 817, post.
20 SLA 1925, s. 1 (7); p. 175, ante.
1 LPA 1925, s. 25 (4).
2 *Re Newbould* (1913) 110 LT 6, per Swinfen Eady LJ: cf *Re White's Settlement* [1930] 1 Ch 179. For the distinction between a power and a trust, see H & M, pp. 61 et seq; M & B, *Trusts and Trustees* (4th edn), pp. 32 et seq; Maclean, *Trusts and Powers* (1989).

for life.[3] The trustees become trustees within the Settled Land Act 1925, the land is settled land within the meaning of that Act and is not subject to a trust for sale, and the proper person to make title is the tenant for life.[4]

(2) IMMEDIATE

The word "immediate" does not mean that the land must be sold at once, for power to postpone the sale is implied in every case, unless a contrary intention appears.[5] Its significance is to distinguish a trust for sale from a *future* trust for sale. A future trust is not immediately effective, and it is enacted that where it is imposed upon land, the trustees are to be trustees for the purposes of the Settled Land Act, not trustees for sale.[6] Thus, if land is devised to a wife for life and after her death upon trust for sale, the land *during her life* is settled land and is governed by the Settled Land Act.[7]

(3) BINDING

In its natural meaning "binding trust" is tautologous. A trust is different from a power because it is obligatory, not discretionary: the trustees are bound to sell the land ultimately, though the actual time of the sale is left to their discretion. A trust which imposes a duty upon the trustees as distinct from one which gives them a mere power may rightly be described as binding. Yet the word has been inserted in a statutory definition and the courts have searched for a secondary meaning. ROMER J suggested that, if it was not surplusage, the object of its insertion might be to emphasize the exclusion of a revocable trust for sale.[8] The cases in which the word has been discussed are concerned with the situation where settled land has been re-settled by way of trust for sale before the Settled Land Act settlement has been exhausted, and the judges have sought to find a solution in the word "binding" to the problem of whether the unexhausted settlement has precedence over the trust for sale or vice versa.

Thus in *Re Leigh's Settled Estates (No. 1)*:[9]

> X was tenant in tail of settled land which was subject to an equitable jointure rentcharge in favour of her mother. In 1923 X disentailed and conveyed the fee simple, still subject to the charge, to trustees upon trust for sale. The question arose whether in 1926 the land was settled land or whether it was held upon trust for sale.

It was clearly settled land[10] unless the conveyance made by X in 1923 was an "immediate binding trust for sale" within the meaning of the Law of Property Act 1925. TOMLIN J held that the land remained settled land and was not subject to a binding trust for sale, since in his opinion the word

3 SLA 1925, s. 108 (2).
4 Ibid., ss. 30 (1) (i), 108, 109; p. 196, ante. The position before 1926 involved a conflict of powers, since the tenant for life had a statutory, the trustees an express, power of sale. SLA 1882, s. 56 provided that in such a case the tenant for life should be unfettered in the exercise of the power, and that the trustees should not sell without his consent.
5 LPA 1925, s. 25 (1).
6 SLA 1925, s. 30 (1) (iv).
7 *Re Jackson's Settled Estate* [1902] 1 Ch 258; *Re Hanson* [1928] Ch 96; *Re Herklots' Will Trusts* [1964] 1 WLR 583, [1964] 2 All ER 66; M & B p. 224; *Re Nierop's Will Trusts* (23 April 1986, unreported), but discussed in *Williams on Wills* (6th edn), para. 1121.
8 *Re Parker's Settled Estates* [1928] Ch 247 at 261.
9 [1926] Ch 852; M & B p. 226.
10 SLA 1925, s. 1 (1) (v).

"binding" is not used to indicate that the trustees for sale are bound to sell sooner or later but refers to the interests that will be bound, i.e. overreached, when the trustees convey. To be "binding", the trust must enable the trustees to execute a conveyance which will bind the whole subject matter of the settlement, i.e. interests prior to the trust as well as those arising under its provisions. This test was not satisfied in the present case, for a conveyance in 1923 could not overreach the widow's prior equitable charge. To do this it would be necessary to obtain the additional powers of overreaching by creating an *ad hoc* trust for sale,[11] and this could only be done by replacing the trustees by a trust corporation or by having them approved by the court.[12]

This restricted view of the scope of the ordinary trust for sale has been implicitly[13] and expressly rejected.[14] In *Re Parker's Settled Estates*[15] ROMER J came to the conclusion that there can be a binding trust for sale notwithstanding that the trustees for sale are unable to overreach all charges having, under the settlement, priority to the trust for sale. He, however, then held that land cannot be described as held upon trust for sale so as to take it out of the Settled Land Act unless the *whole legal estate* is vested in the trustees. He was of the opinion that if there are prior *equitable* interests the trust for sale excludes the Settled Land Act, since the whole legal estate is in the trustees; but if there are prior *legal* estates or interests then the trust for sale is not sufficient to exclude that Act, since the *whole* legal estate is not in the trustees. In *Re Parker's Settled Estates* there was a prior legal term of years to secure portions and accordingly the land remained settled land.[16]

B. THE POWERS OF THE TRUSTEES FOR SALE

(1) POSTPONEMENT OF SALE

The powers of the trustees for sale are set out in the Law of Property Act 1925. Under section 25 a power to postpone a sale is implied in every trust for sale unless a contrary intention appears, and the trustees are not liable for an indefinite postponement in the absence of an express direction to the contrary.[17] A disregard of such an express direction, however, does not prejudice a purchaser of a legal estate, for it is enacted that he shall not be concerned with directions that relate to postponement.[18] The power to

11 LPA 1925, s. 2 (2); pp. 820 et seq, post.
12 After the trustees had been approved by the court TOMLIN J upheld the trust for sale: *Re Leigh's Settled Estates (No 2)* [1927] 2 Ch 13.
13 *Re Ryder and Steadman's Contract* [1927] 2 Ch 62 (land vested in X, Y and Z as tenants in common subject to an equitable jointure rentcharge in favour of A. CA held that after 1925 X, Y and Z held on a *statutory* trust for sale although they could not overreach A's prior equitable interest; p. 226, post).
14 *Re Parker's Settled Estates* [1928] Ch 247; M & B p. 226; see (1928) 65 LJ News 248, 272, 293 (J.M.L.).
15 Supra.
16 See too *Re Norton* [1929] 1 Ch 84; M & B p. 227; (1929) 67 LJ News 24 at 44 (J.M.L.). ROMER J held that there was no binding trust for sale since the trustees could not call for the legal estate from personal representatives due to a prior *equitable* charge: SLA 1925, s. 7 (5); *Re Beaumont's Settled Estates* [1937] 2 All ER 353; *Re Sharpe's Deed of Release* [1939] Ch 51, [1938] 3 All ER 449.
17 LPA 1925, s. 25 (1), (2); *Re Rooke* [1953] Ch 716, [1953] 2 All ER 110 (direction by testator to sell farm "as soon as possible after my death" held to be contrary intention); *Re Atkins' Will Trusts* [1974] 1 WLR 761, [1974] 2 All ER 1; M & B p. 364.
18 Ibid., s. 25 (2).

postpone must, like any other power given to trustees, be exercised unanimously by them;[19] if there is disagreement between the trustees for sale, the court may at its discretion direct them to carry out the sale.[20]

(2) MANAGEMENT AND SALE

The power of postponement may lead to the land remaining unsold for a considerable period, and it is essential that during the interval between the creation of the trust and the actual sale, the trustees should possess powers of disposition and management. These are given to them in abundance by the Law of Property Act 1925.

(a) Settled Land Act powers

Despite the fundamental distinction between a settlement and a trust for sale, it is provided by section 28 of the Law of Property Act 1925 that the trustees for sale, in relation to the land and the proceeds of sale, shall have all the powers both of a tenant for life and of trustees of a settlement under the Settled Land Act 1925.[1] Thus, for example, they may grant leases, raise money on mortgage for improvements and, so long as they retain some land, may invest the proceeds of sale in the purchase of other land.[2] It is further provided by the same section that they shall have the powers of management that are exercisable by trustees under section 102 of the Settled Land Act 1925 during the minority of a tenant for life of *settled* land.[3] Although, in the case of settled land these powers given by section 102 are exercisable only during the minority of the tenant for life, they may be exercised by trustees for sale whether there is a minority or not.[4]

(b) Delegation

In many cases the trustees for sale will not wish themselves to exercise the powers that have been given to them by section 28. Section 29 (1), therefore, provides that while the land remains unsold they may revocably and in writing delegate from time to time the *powers of leasing, of accepting surrenders of leases, and of management* to any person of full age (not merely being an annuitant), who is beneficially entitled in possession to the net rents and profits for his life or for any less period.[5] He must exercise the powers so delegated only in the names and on behalf of the trustees.[6] They are not liable for his acts or defaults. He alone is personally liable and in relation to the exercise of a power is deemed to be in the position of a trustee.[7] Thus,

19 *Re Roth* (1896) 74 LT 50; *Re Hilton* [1909] 2 Ch 548; *Re Mayo* [1943] Ch 302, [1943] 2 All ER 440; M & B p. 229; cf *Re 90 Thornhill Rd, Tolworth, Surrey* [1970] Ch 261, [1969] 3 All ER 685 (sale not ordered under SLA 1925, s. 93 when joint tenants for life disagreed as to the exercise of the power of sale). A power to act by a majority may be given in the trust deed, but it will be strictly construed: *Re Butlin's Settlement Trusts* (1974) 118 SJ 757; see also [1976] Ch 251 at 253, 259; [1976] 2 All ER 483 at 486.
20 LPA 1925, s. 30; pp. 208, 229, post.
 1 Ibid., s. 28 (1), as amended by LP(A)A 1926, s. 7. For the SLA powers, see pp. 185–92.
 2 *Re Wakeman* [1947] Ch 607, [1947] 2 All ER 74; *Re Wellsted's Will Trusts* [1949] Ch 296, [1949] 1 All ER 577; M & B p. 234.
 3 P. 926, post.
 4 *Re Gray* [1927] 1 Ch 242.
 5 LPA 1925, s. 29 (1); *Stratford v Syrett* [1958] 1 QB 107; *Napier v Light* (1974) 236 EG 273.
 6 Ibid., s. 29 (2).
 7 Ibid., s. 29 (3).

pending sale, the welfare of the land may be entrusted to the person most anxious to promote it. It must be noticed, however, that only those powers that are set out in section 29 may be delegated. The legal estate remains in the trustees for sale, and only they can convey the fee simple. That is the basis of their trust.

(c) Consents

The exercise of their powers by the trustees for sale, including that of sale itself, may be made subject to the consent of any persons.[8]

If the consent of not more than two persons is required, a purchaser[9] must ascertain that the requirement has been satisfied. If, however, the consent of more than two persons is required his obligation is satisfied if any two of the persons specified give their consent.[10] If the person whose consent is required is not sui juris or becomes subject to a disability, his consent, in favour of a purchaser, shall not be deemed to be required. But in the case of an infant the trustees should obtain the consent of his parent or guardian, and in the case of a mental patient that of the receiver.[11]

(d) Curtailment of powers

As we have seen, the powers of a tenant for life under the Settled Land Act 1925 cannot be cut down by any provisions inserted in the settlement.[12] There is no similar provision in the Law of Property Act 1925 for the curtailment of the powers of trustees for sale. Indeed their power of sale can be restricted by the imposition of a requirement of consent and the power to postpone sale may be excluded by a contrary intention. Apart from these cases, however, it would appear that the powers of trustees for sale, like those of a tenant for life, are irreducible.[13]

(e) Consultation

We must now consider how far the trustees for sale must observe the wishes of the beneficiaries. Under a statutory trust for sale[14] it is their duty, so far as practicable, to consult the persons of full age for the time being beneficially interested in possession in the rents and profits of the land until sale, and, so far as is consistent with the general interest of the trust, to give effect to the wishes of such persons, or, in the case of dispute, of the majority according to the value of their combined interests. A purchaser is not, however, concerned to see that this provision has been complied with.[15] It does not apply to express trusts for sale, unless a contrary intention appears in the

---

8 If they refuse to give it, any person interested may apply to the court for an order of sale: LPA 1925, s. 30; *Re Beale's Settlement Trusts* [1932] 2 Ch 15.
9 As defined by LPA 1925, s. 205 (1) (xxi).
10 Ibid., s. 26 (1).
11 Ibid., s. 26 (2) as amended by the Mental Health Act 1959, s. 149, Sch. 7.
12 SLA 1925, s. 106; p. 192, ante.
13 See *Re Davies' Will Trusts* [1932] 1 Ch 530 (life interest to nephew "so long as he shall reside upon and assist in the management of the farm" held not forfeitable by exercise of powers inconsistent with such condition. The decision related to statutory trusts for sale under LPA 1925, s 35, but the principle would appear to apply to express trusts for sale as well; [1978] Conv 229 (P. Smith)).
14 Infra.
15 LPA 1925, s. 26 (3), as substituted by LP(A)A 1926, Sch.; (1973) 117 SJ 518 (A. M. Prichard).

instrument creating the trust. Thus a settlor or testator may either give the trustees for sale complete freedom of discretion or compel them to consult the beneficiaries; but in the case of a statutory trust for sale there must be consultation.

(f) Application to court

Finally, if the trustees for sale refuse to sell or to exercise any of the powers conferred on them by sections 28 and 29 of the Law of Property Act 1925 or if any requisite consent cannot be obtained, any person interested may apply to the court under section 30 for an order directing the trustees to act accordingly, and the court may make such order as it thinks fit.[16] The court has the widest possible discretion under this section, and will take into account all the circumstances of the case.[17] In order to qualify as a person interested, the applicant must have some proprietary interest in the land.[18]

C. STATUTORY TRUSTS FOR SALE

A trust for sale may either be created expressly by act of parties or be imposed by statute. The following is a summary of the circumstances in which a statutory trust for sale is imposed by the 1925 legislation in pursuance of its policy to simplify conveyancing by separating the legal estate from the equitable interests:

    (i) Where an estate owner dies intestate.[19]

    (ii) Where property vested in trustees by way of security becomes discharged from the debtor's right of redemption.[20]

If, for example, trust money has been invested in a mortgage of a legal estate and the right of the mortgagor to redeem the land has been extinguished under the Limitation Act 1980[1] or by a foreclosure order,[2] the land, being thus subjected to a trust for sale, is regarded as converted into money and it will pass as such under a beneficiary's will.

In the following cases an express trust for sale is usually created, but, if not, a statutory trust arises automatically.

    (iii) Where land is devised or conveyed to two or more persons as tenants in common.[3]

---

16 See *Dennis v McDonald* [1981] 1 WLR 810 at 819, [1981] 2 All ER 632 at 640 per PURCHAS J; affd [1982] Fam 63, [1982] 1 All ER 590 (where an order for sale was refused, but one co-owner was ordered to pay an occupation rent to the other co-owner); *Bernard v Josephs* [1982] Ch 391 at 411, [1982] 3 All ER 162 at 175 per KERR LJ; p. 215, post; Law Commission Report on Trusts of Land 1989 (Law Com No. 181), paras. 12.6–12.13.
17 Pp. 229–31, post.
18 *Stevens v Hutchinson* [1953] Ch 299 at 305, [1953] 1 All ER 699 at 701 (a chargee); *Re Solomon* [1967] Ch 573, [1966] 3 All ER 255 (a trustee in bankruptcy); see also *First National Securities Ltd v Hegerty* [1985] QB 850, [1984] 3 All ER 641; *Harman v Glencross* [1986] Fam 81, [1986] 1 All ER 545 (judgment creditor under Charging Orders Act 1979, s. 3 (5)).
19 AEA 1925, s. 33 (1); pp. 835, 869, post.
20 LPA 1925, s. 31 (1).
 1 P. 684, post.
 2 P. 700, post.
 3 LPA 1925, s. 34 (2), (3); pp. 228–9, post.

   (iv) Where land is devised or conveyed beneficially to two or more persons as joint tenants.[4]

   (v) Where a legal estate is conveyed to an infant jointly with one or more persons of full age other than trustees or mortgagees.[5]

   (vi) Where the trustees of a *personalty* settlement or trustees for sale of land purchase land in virtue of a power contained in the settlement.[6] The effect of this, having regard to the doctrine of conversion, is that the land remains money in the eyes of equity and thus the original character of the settlement is preserved.

D. REGISTERED LAND

Where registered land is subject to a trust for sale, whether express or statutory,[7] the legal title to the land is registered in the names of the trustees for sale, not exceeding four in number.[8] As in the case of settled land, the interests of the beneficiaries are minor interests whether or not they are protected by restrictions entered on the proprietorship register. Where an express or statutory trust for sale appears on the title the Registrar will enter a restriction restraining a disposition, except by his order or that of the court, unless the proprietors are entitled for their own benefit, or can give valid receipts for the capital money, or unless one of them is a trust corporation.[9]

   A purchaser who complies with the restriction will override the beneficial interests in the same way that he would overreach them in the case of unregistered land.

SECTION III METHODS OF SETTLING LAND

We have seen that there are at present two methods open to a landowner who desires to provide for a succession of beneficiaries. He may create a settlement under the Settled Land Act 1925 or a trust for sale. Before, however, we discuss them as alternative methods of settling property, we must first notice that fiscal considerations dominate the advice to be given on the creation of any settlement. It is essential to preserve the family wealth by a method which attracts as little taxation as possible. In modern times various forms of taxation have all played their part in developing the law in this area: income tax, estate duty (replaced by capital transfer tax in 1974, in its turn replaced by inheritance tax in 1986), and capital gains tax (introduced in 1965). Details of these taxes are beyond the scope of this book and must be sought in specialist works.

---

4 LPA 1925, s. 36 (1); p. 229, post.
5 Ibid., s. 19 (2); p. 982, post.
6 Ibid., s. 32 (1). The statutory trust may be excluded by a contrary intention.
7 See further p. 242, post, and generally Ruoff and Roper, chapter 32.
8 LRA 1925, ss. 94, 95.
9 Ibid., s. 58 (3); LRR, r. 213, Form 62 (as amended by the Registrar); Ruoff and Roper, para. 32–08.

A. COMPARISON OF THE TWO METHODS

With the general warning that fiscal considerations are paramount, we may now discuss the strict settlement and trust for sale as methods of settling property.

Except in one respect, it is possible to reproduce by way of trust for sale the situation that obtains under a strict settlement. As we have seen, it was the deliberate policy of the 1925 legislation to extend the use of the trust for sale. Trustees for sale are given all the powers of a tenant for life and the trustees of a settlement under the Settled Land Act 1925;[10] they may revocably delegate the powers of leasing and management to any person of full age for the time being beneficially entitled to the net rents and profits of the land during his life;[11] and entailed interests may be created in personalty.[12] Thus, today, a settlement, the object of which is to keep the land or the capital money representing it in the family, may be achieved through a trust for sale. Paradoxically, it is easier to prevent the land from being sold if it is settled by way of trust for sale.[13] Not only may the trustees retain the land under their power to postpone sale indefinitely,[14] but they may be restrained from selling it unless they obtain the consent of certain persons,[15] and the settlor may choose as one of these the person beneficially entitled to the income for his life. The exception to the achievement of this similarity is that under the Settled Land Act 1925 the tenant for life is master in his own house;[16] he may exercise himself as of right all the powers given to him by that Act; and those powers are indefeasible.[17] Under a trust for sale, on the other hand, his counterpart can only exercise powers of leasing and management by way of revocable delegation from the trustees for sale; and the duty to sell cannot be delegated.[18]

Furthermore there are two ways in which the trust for sale is more flexible than the strict settlement. The strict settlement applies only to land, whereas the trust for sale may include all kinds of property, including land. Thus two separate trusts are required if a settlor desires to create a family trust of mixed property and insists on creating a strict settlement of the land. Secondly, a trust for sale is more convenient where the settlor desires to make provision for his children equally. They can be given concurrent interests in the land, and, as we shall see, this is one of the occasions on which a statutory trust for sale is imposed by the Law of Property Act 1925.[19]

Thus, if it were enacted that all settlements of land must be created by way of trust for sale, little of value would be lost. Any ambition to keep the land in the family could still be satisfied, in fact even more effectively than by employing a strict settlement. Admittedly the powers of management and the decision concerning sale would not be given as of right to the head of the family, who would have to rely on the revocable delegation of the powers by

10 LPA 1925, s. 28; p. 206, ante.
11 Ibid., s. 29; p. 206, ante.
12 Ibid., s. 130 (1); p. 258, post.
13 See in particular *Re Inns* [1947] Ch 576, [1947] 2 All ER 308; M & B p. 237.
14 LPA 1925, s. 25; p. 205, ante.
15 Ibid., s. 26; p. 207, ante.
16 (1944) 8 Conv (NS) 147 (H. Potter).
17 SLA 1925, s. 106; pp. 192–3, ante.
18 P. 206, ante.
19 P. 225, post.

the trustees for sale. On the other hand, this loss would be outweighed by the further simplification of conveyancing, if all settlements of land had to be created by way of trust for sale. For one thing, the occasional difficulty of deciding whether land is settled or held on trust for sale would no longer arise.[20] It would never be doubtful whether the trustees or the tenant for life were the appropriate parties to make title. It would always be made by the trustees. Furthermore under a trust for sale there is less complication and expense involved when the holder of the life interest dies. As we shall see, under the Settled Land Act the legal title to the settled land passes to the trustees of the settlement as special personal representatives, who must take out special letters of probate to the settled land and then by a vesting assent vest the legal title in the new tenant for life.[1] The cost of the special probate and the vesting instrument has to be borne by the trust. In the case of the trust for sale, however, on death the legal title remains in the trustees for sale, and if the powers of management have been delegated, the delegation automatically ceases. All the trustees for sale have to do is to make a new delegation to the next holder of the life interest.

Finally we must remember that under the present system of duality of settlement, the two forms are mutually exclusive.[2] In order to create a trust for sale, it is essential to use the appropriate technical language, such as "upon trust to sell"; failing that the settlement falls automatically under the Settled Land Act 1925. Thus, a testator who makes a home-made will, leaving his house to his widow for life and then to his children, unwittingly sets in motion the complicated machinery of the Act.[3] It would seem, indeed, that the task of the conveyancer would be facilitated and unnecessary expense avoided if the Settled Land Act were repealed and replaced by a short statute amplifying the provisions of the Law of Property Act with regard to trusts for sale.[4]

B. LAW REFORM

In 1989 the Law Commission published its Report on Trusts of Land.[5] It recommended that the present dual system of trusts for sale and strict

---

20 Pp. 203–5, ante. The problem may be solved by the purchaser taking a conveyance from both possible owners of the legal estate. See (1929) 67 LJ News 24 (J.M.L.).

1 P. 811, post.

2 SLA 1925, s. 1 (7); p. 175, ante.

3 If a testator, in a will made after 1982, leaves property to his spouse in terms which in themselves would give an *absolute* interest to the spouse, but also by the same will gives an interest in the same property to his issue, there is a rebuttable presumption that the gift to the spouse is absolute and the issue takes nothing: AJA 1982, s. 22: Law Reform Committee Report on the Interpretation of Wills 1973 (Cmnd 5301), paras. 60–62, 65 (9).

For the inadvertent settlement which arises when a person is given the right to reside in a property during his lifetime, see *Bannister v Bannister* [1948] 2 All ER 133; M & B p. 554; p. 177, n. 11, ante; p. 592, post. See also *Muir v Lloyds Bank plc* [1992] 28 LS Gaz R 32.

4 (1928) 166 LT 45; (1938) 85 LJ News 353 (J.M.L.); (1938) 54 LQR 576 (M. M. Lewis); (1944) 8 Conv (NS) 147 (H. Potter); (1957) CLP 152 (E. H. Scamell); (1961) 24 MLR 123 (G. A. Grove); (1962) CLP 104 (E. C. Ryder); Survey of the Land Law of Northern Ireland (1971) paras 88–100.

5 Law Com No. 181; (1989) 52 MLR 683 (A. Pottage); (1989) 3 Trust Law & Practice 66 (R. Sexton).

A draft Bill is being prepared: Law Commission Twenty-Seventh Annual Report 1992 (Law Com No. 210), para. 2.64.

settlements should be replaced by an entirely new system of trusts, applicable both to concurrent and to successive interests. The main recommendations are:

(1) *A New Trust of Land*   Trustees would hold the legal estate on trust with a *power* to sell and a *power* to retain the land, and, as at present, would be able to convey the legal estate free of equitable interests. (paras. 1.4.–1.7)

(2) *Concurrent Interests*   Land which previously would have become subject to an implied trust for sale should be held by trustees with a power to retain and a power to sell. The doctrine of conversion should be abolished in relation to all trusts, whatever the property and whenever created. It should still be possible for a duty to sell expressly to be imposed but a power to retain should be statutorily implied, contrary intention notwithstanding. (paras. 3.5–3.7)

(3) *Successive Interests*   It should no longer be possible to create Settled Land Act settlements and all successive interests should fall under the new system. (Existing settlements would not be affected.) (para. 4.3)

(4) *Minors*   Minority should remain a disability and an attempted conveyance of land to a minor should take effect as a declaration of trust, the land being held by the relevant trustee(s) under the new system.[6] (paras. 5.1–5.3)

(5) *Purchasers*   The new system should retain the overreaching mechanism, which would operate much as it currently does in relation to trusts for sale.[7] (paras. 6.1–6.2)

(6) *Bare Trusts*   These should come within the new system.[8] (para. 7.1)

(7) *Creation*   There should be no special formalities, the only requirement being that the trust be properly constituted within the terms of general trust law. The new system should apply to all trusts of land (whenever created and whether express, implied or constructive), with the exception of existing Settled Land Act settlements. There should be no new settled land and land newly acquired by an existing settlement, or which would continue to be settled land only by virtue of a new instrument, should be held under the new system. (paras. 8.1–8.3)

(8) *Powers of the Court*   Section 30 of the Law of Property Act 1925[9] should be amended (*a*) so as to enable any trustee or other interested person to apply to the court to intervene in any dispute relating to a trust of land; (*b*) to include guidelines for the exercise of the court's discretion.

In cases of insolvency, the provisions of section 336 of the Insolvency Act 1986[10] should be extended to cover all applications for sale in which a beneficiary has been adjudged bankrupt, but paragraphs (*b*), (*c*), and (*d*) of subsection (4) should apply only where the trust land is the home of the bankrupt or his spouse or former spouse.

In relation to successive interests, the relevant provisions of the Settled Land Act 1925 should be replaced by Section 30 of the Law of Property Act 1925 (as amended). (paras 12.6–12.13)

(9) *Entailed Interests*   An attempt to create an entailed interest in land should operate as a grant of a fee simple absolute (unless the grantor's interest is equitable only, in which case the attempt would take effect as a declaration of trust). It should no longer be possible to create entailed interests in any property.[11] (paras. 16.1)

6 P. 921, post.
7 Pp. 813, 817, post.
8 P. 818, post.
9 P. 229, post.
10 P. 231, post.
11 P. 245, post.

Chapter 10

Concurrent interests

SUMMARY

As we have already observed, the 1925 legislation used the statutory trust for sale to solve the conveyancing problems which arose from the holding of concurrent interests before 1926.[1] We must now examine this in some detail.

Several and concurrent ownership must first be distinguished. The owner of an interest in land may be entitled to possession either alone or in conjunction with other persons, and in both cases he may be entitled to take possession either now or at some time in the future. If he is entitled in his own right without having any other person joined with him in point of interest, he is said to hold in severalty; but where he and other persons have simultaneous interests in the land, they are said to hold concurrently, or in co-ownership, and to have concurrent interests. In other words, land may be the subject of several, that is, separate ownership, or of co-ownership.

SECTION I THE LAW BEFORE 1926

Such a fundamental change in the principles applicable to concurrent interests was effected by the legislation of 1925 that we need do little more than enumerate the various forms that such interests might take before 1926, and the methods by which they might be converted into several interests. At common law there are four possible forms of co-ownership, one of which,

---

1 Pp. 176, 208, ante. See generally Thompson, *Co-ownership* (1988).

tenancy by entireties, is now defunct;[2] while another, coparcenary, seldom arises.[3] The two found in practice are joint tenancy and tenancy in common.

A. JOINT TENANCY

(1) NATURE OF JOINT TENANCY

A joint tenancy arises whenever land is conveyed or devised to two or more persons without any words to show that they are to take distinct and separate shares, or, to use technical language, without words of severance.[4] If an estate is given, for instance, to:

A and B in fee simple,

without the addition of any restrictive, exclusive or explanatory words, the law feels bound to give effect to the whole of the grant, and this it can do only by creating an equal estate in them both.[5] From the point of view of their interest in the land they are united in every respect. But if the grant contains words of severance showing an intention that A and B are to take separate and distinct interests, as for instance where there is a grant to:

A and B equally,

the result is the creation not of a joint tenancy, but of a tenancy in common.

The two essential attributes of joint tenancy which must be kept in mind if the true meaning of the legislation of 1925 is to be grasped are the absolute unity which exists between joint tenants, and the right of survivorship.

(a) Unity between joint tenants

There is, to use the language of Blackstone,[6] a thorough and intimate union between joint tenants. Together they form one person. This unity is fourfold, consisting of unity of title, time, interest and possession. All the titles are derived from the same grant and become vested at the same time;[7] all the interests are identical in size; and there is unity of possession, since each tenant *totum tenet et nihil tenet*. Each holds the whole in the sense that in conjunction with his co-tenants he is entitled to present possession and enjoyment of the whole; yet he holds nothing in the sense that he is not entitled to the exclusive possession of any individual part of the whole.[8] Unity of possession is a feature of all forms of co-ownership. For this reason one co-owner cannot, as a general rule, maintain an action of trespass against the other or others, but can do so only if the act complained of amounts either

2 For a discussion, see 11th edn of this book, p. 338.
3 P. 222, post.
4 Litt s. 277; Blackstone, vol. ii. p. 179.
5 Blackstone, vol. ii. p. 180.
6 Ibid., p. 182.
7 In the case of a grant to uses, the fact that the interests vested at different times did not prevent the creation of a joint tenancy, e.g. under a grant to X and Y to the use of all the sons of A born within the lifetime of the settlor, sons born after the time of the grant became joint tenants with those alive at the time of its execution.
8 By Littleton's time the expression *totum tenet et nihil tenet* had become *per my et per tout*, which in Blackstone's view (vol. ii. p. 182) meant that each tenant was seised "by the half or moiety and by all". *My*, however, did not mean half, but was an early form of the French word *mie*.

to an actual ouster, or to a destruction of the subject matter of the tenancy;[9] nor can one co-owner in sole occupation be made to pay rent to another co-owner,[10] unless he has excluded or ousted him from possession.[11]

(b) Right of survivorship

The other characteristic that distinguishes a joint tenancy is the right of survivorship, or *jus accrescendi*, by which, if one joint tenant dies without having obtained a separate share in his lifetime, his interest is extinguished and accrues to the surviving tenants whose interests are correspondingly enlarged.[12] For example:

A and B may be joint tenants in fee simple, but the result of the death of B is that his interest totally disappears and A becomes owner in severalty of the land.

There are cases, however, where the right of survivorship does not benefit both tenants equally, for if there is (say) a grant to

A and B during the life of A

and A dies first, there is nothing that can accrue to B.[13]

(2) EQUITY PREFERS TENANCY IN COMMON TO JOINT TENANCY

From early times the right of survivorship caused a divergence of views between common law and equity. Common law favoured joint tenancies because they inevitably led to the vesting of the property in one person through the operation of the doctrine of survivorship, and thus facilitated the performance of those feudal dues that were incident to the tenure of land. But a tenancy in common never involved this right of survivorship, and equity, which was not over-careful of the rights of the lord, soon showed a marked inclination, in the interests of convenience and justice, to construe a joint tenancy as a tenancy in common.[14]

Equity aims at equality, a feature that is conspicuous for its absence if the survivor becomes the absolute owner of the land. This preference of equity for a tenancy in common has been shown in four cases:

(a) Where money is advanced on mortgage by two or more persons

Where two or more persons advance money, either in equal or in unequal shares, and take a mortgage of land from the borrower to themselves jointly,

9 Blackstone, vol. ii. p. 183; *Martyn v Knowllys* (1799) 8 Term Rep 145; *Murray v Hall* (1849) 7 CB 441; *Stedman v Smith* (1857) 8 E & B 1; *Wilkinson v Haygarth* (1847) 12 QB 837.
10 *M'Mahon v Burchell* (1846) 2 Ph 127; *Jones v Jones* [1977] 1 WLR 438, [1977] 2 All ER 231. See also *Chhokar v Chhokar* [1984] FLR 313. Rent received by one co-owner from a stranger will be shared with another co-owner.
11 *Dennis v McDonald* [1981] 1 WLR 810, [1981] 2 All ER 632 (ousted mistress); affd [1982] Fam 63, [1982] 1 All ER 590 (application under LPA 1925, s. 30); p. 229, post; *Bernard v Josephs* [1982] Ch 391, [1982] 3 All ER 162; cf *Stott v Radcliffe* (1982) 126 SJ 310; *Harvey v Harvey* [1982] Fam 83, [1982] 1 All ER 683 (application under Matrimonial Causes Act 1973, s. 25); [1982] Conv 305 (J. Martin). The rule of ouster has not always been applied in matrimonial cases where application was made under the Married Women's Property Act 1882, s. 17. See *Bedson v Bedson* [1965] 2 QB 666, [1965] 3 All ER 307 (rent of £1 a week ordered); *Leake v Bruzzi* [1974] 1 WLR 1528, [1974] 2 All ER 1196; *Suttill v Graham* [1977] 1 WLR 819, [1977] 3 All ER 819; [1978] Conv 161 (F. R. Crane); (1978) 97 Law Notes 78 (A. Treleaven).
12 Litt s. 280; Co Litt 181*a*; Blackstone, vol. ii. p. 183.
13 Co Litt 181*b*.
14 Burton, *Real Property*, para 165.

the rule *at law* is that they are joint tenants, so that the land and the right to the money belong absolutely to the survivor. The rule *in equity*, however, which prevails over the rule at law, is that they are tenants in common, and that the survivor is a trustee for the personal representatives of the deceased mortgagees.[15]

This equitable rule caused difficulty in those cases where trustees advanced trust money on mortgage. In practice a conveyance of land to trustees is always made to them as joint tenants, for the very nature of their office requires that the death of one shall not disturb the administration of the trust or deprive the survivor of power to execute conveyances and to give binding receipts for money. These advantages, however, will be lost if the trustees are to be regarded as tenants in common, for in that case each of them is entitled to a separate, though at present an unidentifiable, share of the land that passes on his death to his personal representatives. To avoid this inconvenience, it soon became the practice to insert a *joint account clause* in a mortgage to trustees. This declares that upon the death of one of the mortgagees the receipt of the survivor shall be a sufficient discharge for the money, and that the survivor shall be able to re-convey the land without the concurrence of the personal representatives of the deceased trustee.

The position has been made clearer by the Law of Property Act 1925,[16] which provides that where there is a mortgage for the payment of money and either the sum advanced is expressly stated to be advanced by more persons than one on a joint account, or a mortgage is *made to them jointly and not in shares*, the money lent shall, as *between the mortgagees and the mortgagor*, be deemed to belong to the mortgagees on a joint account, and the survivor shall be able to give a complete discharge for the money. Trustees always advance money on a joint account, and the fact that they are trustees is never disclosed in the mortgage.[17]

It will be noticed that the Act is not confined to loans of money made by trustees, but applies generally to all joint mortgages coming within the provisions of the section; and in a case where there is no question of trustees, it is important to remember that the joint account rule just stated applies only as between the mortgagor and the mortgagees, and not even between them if a contrary intention is shown in the deeds. As between the mortgagees themselves evidence is admissible to show that, despite the presence of a joint account clause, it was intended that the money should belong to them as tenants in common.[18]

(b)   Where joint purchasers of land provide purchase money in unequal shares

The invariable rule *at law* is that when purchasers take a conveyance to themselves in fee simple, they become joint tenants, and upon the death of one of them the whole estate passes to the survivor. Equity adopts the same attitude and does not treat the purchasers as being tenants in common, unless it can be inferred that they did not intend to take jointly.[19]

---

15 *Petty v Styward* (1631) 1 Eq Cas Abr 290; *Steeds v Steeds* (1889) 22 QBD 537; White and Tudor, *Leading Cases in Equity* (9th edn), vol. ii. pp. 882–5.
16 LPA 1925, s. 111, re-enacting Conveyancing Act 1881, s. 61.
17 *Encyclopaedia of Forms and Precedents* (4th edn), vol. 14. p. 201.
18 *Re Jackson* (1887) 34 Ch D 732.
19 *Lake v Gibson* (1729) 1 Eq Cas Abr 290, pl. 3; *Lake v Craddock* (1732) 3 PWms 158; White and Tudor, *Leading Cases in Equity* (9th edn), vol. ii. p. 881.

Thus, though this is not the only circumstance that will raise the inference, it is established that purchasers who contribute the money in unequal proportions are to be regarded as tenants in common of the land conveyed.[20]

(c) Where land is bought by partners

In the leading case of *Lake v Craddock*,[1] where five persons joined in buying some waterlogged land with a view to its improvement by drainage, the court laid down the general rule that persons who make a joint purchase for the purposes of a joint undertaking or partnership, either in trade or in any other dealing, are to be treated in equity as tenants in common. The right of survivorship is incompatible with a commercial undertaking—*jus accrescendi inter mercatores pro beneficio commercii locum non habet*.[2] Thus:

> If two partners take a grant or a lease of a farm and one dies, the survivor will be a trustee not only of the stock, but also of the land, for the personal representatives of the deceased partner.[3]

When once it is clear that property is partnership property, the rule in equity is that it is held by the partners as tenants in common, and it has been enacted by the Partnership Act 1890,[4] that all property brought into the business, or subsequently bought for the purposes of the business, or bought with money belonging to the business, is prima facie partnership property.

(d) Where joint purchasers of land hold it for their individual business purposes

In *Malayan Credit Ltd v Jack Chia-MPH Ltd*, where it was held that business tenants who had paid rent and service charges in agreed proportions were tenants in common, Lord BRIGHTMAN said:[5]

> Their Lordships do not accept that the cases in which joint tenants at law will be presumed to hold as tenants in common in equity are as rigidly circumscribed as the plaintiff asserts. Such are not necessarily limited to purchasers who contribute unequally, to co-mortgagees and to partners. There are other circumstances in which equity may infer that the beneficial interest is intended to be held by the grantees as tenants in common. In the opinion of their Lordships, one such case is where the grantees hold the premises for their several individual business purposes.

Despite these exceptional cases, the fundamental rule is that whenever land is granted or devised to two or more persons simply and without words of severance, the donees become joint tenants holding a single title, interest and possession, and when one dies his interest is extinguished and passes to the survivor or survivors.

(3) DETERMINATION OF JOINT TENANCY SEVERANCE

Since "each joint tenant stands, in all respects, in exactly the same position as each of the others",[6] it follows that anything which creates a distinction

---

20 *Robinson v Preston* (1858) 4 K & J 505; *Lake v Craddock*, supra; White and Tudor, vol. ii. p. 882.
1 Supra.
2 Co Litt 182a.
3 *Elliot v Brown* (1791) 3 Swan 489.
4 Ss. 20, 21.
5 [1986] AC 549 at 560, [1986] 1 All ER 711 at 715.
6 Challis, *Law of Real Property* (3rd edn), p. 367. See Law Commission Working Paper No. 94 Trusts of Land (1985), paras. 16.11–16.14.

between them severs the tenancy and converts it into a tenancy in common.[7]
Stated in more detail, its determination may be effected by:

(a) alienation by one joint tenant;
(b) acquisition by one tenant of a greater interest than that held by his co-tenants;
(c) partition;
(d) sale;
(e) mutual agreement;[8]
(f) any course of dealing sufficient to intimate that the interests of all were mutually treated as constituting a tenancy in common;[9] and
(g) where one joint tenant criminally kills another joint tenant.

These methods require some discussion.

(a) Alienation by a joint tenant

Although during the continuance of the tenancy one joint tenant holds nothing separately from his fellows, there is a general rule to the effect that *alienatio rei praefertur juri accrescendi*[10] and in accordance with this doctrine it has long been the law that one joint tenant can alienate his share to a stranger. The effect of such alienation, where by way of sale or mortgage,[11] is to convert the joint tenancy into a tenancy in common, since the alienee and the remaining tenant or tenants hold by virtue of different titles and not under that one common title which is essential to the existence of a joint tenancy.

If A and B are joint tenants in fee simple and A makes a grant in fee simple to X, the result is that B and X hold the lands as tenants in common, in equal undivided shares. If A, B and C are joint tenants in fee simple and A makes a grant to X in fee simple, X is tenant in common with B and C, though as between themselves the latter continue to hold as joint tenants.[12]

Severance may also be effected by involuntary alienation, as where a joint tenant is adjudicated bankrupt and his interest vests in his trustee in bankruptcy.[13]

---

7 Where the parties expressly create a beneficial joint tenancy, the shares of the tenants in common on severance are equal, even if they contributed unequally to the purchase price; where they do not, the beneficiaries may claim shares proportionate to their contributions: *Goodman v Gallant* [1986] Fam 106, [1986] 1 All ER 311; [1986] Conv 205 (S. Juss).
8 *Williams v Hensman* (1861) 1 John & H 546 at 557; *Burgess v Rawnsley* [1975] Ch 429, [1975] 3 All ER 142; M & B p. 268.
9 *Williams v Hensman*, supra, at 557, per PAGE WOOD V-C.
10 Co Litt 185a.
11 *Cedar Holdings Ltd v Green* [1981] Ch 129 at 138, [1979] 3 All ER 117 at 121, per BUCKLEY LJ; *First National Securities Ltd v Hegerty* [1985] QB 850, [1984] 3 All ER 641 (joint tenancy held to be severed where husband purported to mortgage jointly owned property by forging wife's signature); *Ahmed v Kendrick* (1988) 56 P & CR 120 (severance where husband sold jointly owned house by forging wife's signature on both contract and registered transfer); *Monarch Aluminium v Rickman* [1989] CLY 1526 (charging order nisi held to be severance); *Gore and Snell v Carpenter* (1990) 60 P & CR 456 (release of share to co-tenant held not to be severance).
12 Litt s. 292.
13 *Re Dennis* [1993] Ch 72, [1992] 3 All ER 436; *Re Gorman* [1990] 1 WLR 616, [1990] 1 All ER 717; *Re Pavlou* [1993] 1 WLR 1046, [1993] 3 All ER 955; *Re Gavin Palmer* (1994) Times, 30 March (insolvency administration order).

Owing to the doctrine of survivorship, no severance results from a disposition by will—*jus accrescendi praefertur ultimae voluntati.*[14]

(b) Acquisition of larger interest by a joint tenant

A joint tenancy is also severed if one of the joint tenants subsequently acquires an interest greater in quantum than that held by his co-tenants. This destruction of the unity of interest may result from the act of the parties or by operation of law. As an instance of the former:

If A and B are joint tenants for life and A purchases the fee simple in reversion, the joint tenancy is severed: A holding an undivided half in fee simple and B an undivided half for life. When B dies, the fee simple in the entirety of the land vests in A.[15]

Again, A may release his interest to B and so terminate the tenancy by vesting the whole ownership in B.[16]

A case in which a greater interest than that held by his co-tenants is cast upon a joint tenant by operation of law occurs where the reversion in fee descends to one of the joint tenants.[17]

If the joint tenants agree deliberately to put an end to the tenancy, the two methods open to them, in addition to a mutual agreement that henceforth they shall hold as tenants in common, are (c) partition and (d) sale.

(c) Partition

Partition is a method whereby the joint *possession* is disunited, and its effect is to make each former co-tenant a separate owner of a specific portion of the land, and thus to terminate the co-ownership for ever. Instead of holding an undivided share in the whole, each person will hold a divided share in severalty. If 50 acres are held by A and B as joint tenants in fee simple, the effect of the destruction of the unities of title or interest is, as we have seen, to create a tenancy in common; but the effect of partition is that each becomes absolute owner of 25 acres.

Before 1926, partition was either voluntary or compulsory. Compulsory partition was abolished in 1925.[18] Accordingly, co-owners may agree between themselves to divide the property into separate shares to be held in individual ownership. The actual amount or position of the land that is to be allotted to each party may be settled by the co-owners themselves, or by an arbitrator selected by them, or even by the drawing of lots.[19] The usual practice is first to enter into a preliminary agreement whereby the co-owners consent to the land being partitioned into allotments convenient to be held in separate

14 Blackstone, vol. ii. pp. 185–6.
15 Co Litt s. 182*b*; *Wiscot's Case* (1599) 2 Co Rep 60*b*.
16 *Re Schär* [1951] Ch 280, [1950] 2 All ER 1069.
17 Cruise, *Digest*, Tit. xviii. c. ii. s. 7. Contrary to the view of the majority of the Court of Appeal, it is submitted that the two methods of severance already discussed avail a husband or wife in respect of the matrimonial home: *Bedson v Bedson* [1965] 2 QB 666 at 688–91, [1965] 3 All ER 307 at 318–20, per RUSSELL LJ, dissenting, who said that the view was "without the slightest foundation in law or equity"; (1966) 82 LQR 29 (R.E.M.). The view of RUSSELL LJ has been preferred by PLOWMAN J in *Re Draper's Conveyance* [1969] 1 Ch 486 at 494, [1967] 3 All ER 853 at 858; M & B p. 265; and by LAWTON LJ in *Harris v Goddard* [1983] 1 WLR 1203 at 1208, [1983] 3 All ER 242 at 245.
18 I.e. by the repeal of the Partition Acts; LPA 1925, Sch. 7.
19 Litt ss. 55, 243–6.

ownership and as nearly as possible of equal values, provision being made for the payment of a sum of money to secure equality of partition where it is impossible to give each party land of equal value.[20] When the division has been settled, the last step is for the co-owners to execute that form of conveyance which is appropriate to the interest involved. A deed is necessary in the case of land, but joint tenants must execute a deed of release, while the proper form for tenants in common is a deed of grant.

(d) Sale

The normal and the simplest method of bringing a joint tenancy to an end is by sale. If all the joint tenants agree to sell, the joint title can be passed to the purchaser and the land will vest in him as single owner. Prior to 1926, if one joint tenant was obstructive, the others could compel a sale by the indirect method of bringing a partition action.

(e) Mutual agreement

The mutual agreement need not be specifically enforceable. The significance of the agreement is not that it binds the parties, but that it serves as an indication of a common intention to sever.[1]

(f) Course of dealing

A course of dealing need not amount to an agreement, express or implied, for severance. As Lord DENNING said:[2]

It is sufficient if there is a course of dealing in which one party makes clear to the other that he desires that their shares should no longer be held jointly but be held in common. I emphasise that it must be clear to the other party.

Thus, it was held that there was severance where one joint tenant negotiates with another for some rearrangement of interest, even though the negotiations break down.[3]

The onus of proving severance under this heading is on the party who desires to establish it.[4]

(g) By homicide

This occurs where one joint tenant criminally kills another joint tenant. No one may benefit in law from his own crime, so that there is necessarily a severance that prevents the killer from taking any beneficial interest by survivorship. In *Re K*, where a matrimonial home was owned jointly by the killer and his victim, it was held to have been rightly conceded that there was a severance of the joint tenancy, so that the beneficial interest (subject to

---

20 For a precedent, see *Encyclopaedia of Forms and Precedents* (4th edn), vol. 15. p. 856.
 1 *Burgess v Rawnsley* [1975] Ch 429 at 445, [1975] 3 All ER 142 at 152 per Sir John PENNYCUICK; M & B p. 268; *Hunter v Babbage* [1994] EGCS 8 (draft agreement).
 2 *Burgess v Rawnsley*, supra at 439, at 147.
 3 Ibid. See also *Re Draper's Conveyance* [1969] 1 Ch 486, [1967] 3 All ER 853; M & B p. 265; p. 234, post; *Greenfield v Greenfield* (1979) 38 P & CR 570 (conversion of house jointly owned by brothers into two self-contained maisonettes occupied separately held not to be severance); *Barton v Morris* [1985] 1 WLR 1257, [1985] 2 All ER 1032 (inclusion of jointly owned property as a partnership asset in the partnership accounts for tax purposes held not to be severance).
 4 *Re Denny* (1947) 177 LT 291; *McDowell v Hirschfield* [1992] 2 FLR 126.

relief under the Forfeiture Act 1982) vested in the deceased and the survivor as tenants in common. [5]

B. TENANCY IN COMMON

(1) CREATION OF TENANCY IN COMMON

A tenancy in common arises

(i) where land is limited to two or more persons with words of severance showing an intention, even in the slightest degree, [6] that the donees are to take separate shares, or

(ii) where equity reads what is at law a joint tenancy as a tenancy in common, [7] or

(iii) where one joint tenant disposes of his interest to a stranger, or acquires an interest greater than that of his co-tenants. [8]

The following expressions have at one time and another been construed as words of severance sufficient to create a tenancy in common:

equally to be divided;
to be divided;
in equal moieties;
equally;
amongst;
share and share alike.

So, also, if land is devised to A and B on condition that they pay in equal shares ten shillings a week to X during his life, this imposition of an equal burden on both donees shows that what would normally be a joint tenancy is to be a tenancy in common. [9]

The expression "jointly and severally", which is a contradiction in terms, has been solved by the court holding that the first word prevails in a deed (thus creating a joint tenancy), but the last in a will. [10] Similarly, the words in a deed "to hold in fee simple as beneficial joint tenants in common in equal shares" have been held to create a joint tenancy rather than a tenancy in common. [11]

(2) DIFFERENCES BETWEEN TENANCY IN COMMON AND JOINT TENANCY

There is a fundamental distinction between tenancy in common and joint tenancy.

---

5 *Re K* [1985] Ch 85, [1985] 1 All ER 403; affd [1986] Ch 180, [1985] 2 All ER 833. There was previously no English authority on the point. See *Schobelt v Barber* (1966) 60 DLR (2d) 519 and *Re Pechar* [1969] NZLR 574, where it was held that the law imposes a constructive trust of one undivided half share for the benefit of the next of kin of the deceased other than the killer. See p. 850, post.
6 *Robertson v Fraser* (1871) 6 Ch App 696 at 699; cf *Re Osoba* [1979] 1 WLR 247 at 260, [1979] 2 All ER 393 at 405.
7 Pp. 216–7, ante.
8 Pp. 218–9, ante.
9 *Re North* [1952] Ch 397, [1952] 1 All ER 609.
10 *Slingsby's Case* (1587) 5 Co Rep 18*b*.
11 *Joyce v Barker Bros (Builders) Ltd* (1980) 40 P & CR 512; cf *Martin v Martin* (1987) 54 P & CR 238, where similar words in a deed were held to create a tenancy in common. The second inconsistent clause constituted a severance of the joint tenancy and the creation of a tenancy in common; [1987] Conv 405 (J. E. Adams).

(a) Unity

In the first place, that intimate union which exists between joint tenants does not necessarily exist in a tenancy in common. In the latter case the one point in which the tenants are united is the right to possession.[12] They all occupy promiscuously, and if there are two tenants in common, A and B, A has an equal right with B to the possession of the whole land. But their union may stop at that point, for they may each hold different interests, as where one has a fee simple, the other a life interest; or where one is entitled to a two-thirds share, and the other to one third; and they may each hold under different titles, as for instance where one has bought and the other has succeeded to his share.[13] Each has a *share* in the ordinary meaning of that word. His share is undivided in the sense that its boundary is not yet demarcated, but nevertheless his right to a definite share exists.

(b) Survivorship

The second characteristic, and it is really the complement of the first, is that the *jus accrescendi* has no application to tenancies in common, so that, when one tenant dies, his share passes to his personal representatives, and not to the surviving tenant.[14] In the words of Challis:

> A tenancy in common, though it is an ownership only of an undivided share, is, for all practical purposes, a sole and several tenancy or ownership; and each tenant in common stands, towards his own undivided share, in the same relation that, if he were sole owner of the whole, he would bear towards the whole.[15]

Although the tenancy in common thus possesses certain advantages over a joint tenancy, it suffers from this disadvantage that, since the shares are distinct, it becomes necessary on a sale of the whole land to make a separate title to each separate share.

(3) DETERMINATION OF TENANCY IN COMMON

The three methods by which a tenancy in common is determined and converted into separate ownership are (a) partition, (b) sale, and (c) the acquisition by one tenant, whether by grant or by operation of law, of the shares vested in his co-tenants.

C. COPARCENARY

Coparcenary arose at common law wherever land descended to two or more persons who together constituted the heir. This occurred if a tenant in fee simple or a tenant in tail died intestate leaving only female heirs. In each case the females succeeded jointly to the estate and were called coparceners. Coparcenary also arose under the custom of gavelkind, according to which the land descended to all the sons equally, failing them to all the daughters equally, and failing them to all the brothers equally.[16] Gavelkind, however,

12 Co Litt 189*a*.
13 Blackstone, vol. ii. p. 191.
14 Ibid., p. 194.
15 *Law of Real Property* (3rd edn), p. 368.
16 P. 24, ante.

has been abolished; the rules regulating the disposition of a fee simple estate upon the intestacy of its owner have been altered by the Administration of Estates Act 1925;[17] and coparcenary can now arise only in the case of entailed interests.

If the owner of an entailed interest (other than an interest in tail male) dies without having either barred the entail or disposed of the interest by will, and if he leaves no male heirs who are entitled to succeed *per formam doni*, the interest passes to the female heirs of the appropriate class.[18] For instance:

Where the owner of an entailed interest general dies intestate leaving no sons, but three daughters, the interest descends to all the daughters jointly.[19] The daughters are called coparceners because, in the words of Littleton,

> by the writ, which is called *breve de participatione facienda*, the law will constrain them that partition shall be made among them.[20]

Coparceners constitute a single heir, and they occupy a position intermediate between joint tenants and tenants in common.[1] Like joint tenants they have unity of title, interest and possession; like tenants in common their estate is unaffected by the doctrine of survivorship, and if there are three coparceners and one dies, her share passes separately to her heirs or devisee, not to the survivors, though the unity of possession continues. It follows that unity of time is not necessary to constitute coparcenary, for if a man has two daughters to whom his estate descends and one dies leaving a son, such son and the surviving daughters will be coparceners.[2]

Coparcenary is converted into separate ownership (a) by partition, or (b) by the union in one coparcener of all the shares; and it is converted into a tenancy in common if one coparcener transfers her share to a stranger.[3]

The present position with regard to coparcenary is that interests held by coparceners are necessarily equitable, since for the most part they consist of entailed interests,[4] and these arise only under a settlement or a trust for sale. Therefore, it would seem that when a tenant in tail dies intestate, leaving female heirs, the legal fee simple vests in the trustees in the case of a settlement and is held by them on trust for sale and to give effect to the equitable rights of the coparceners.[5]

SECTION II THE LAW AFTER 1925

The object of the legislation of 1925 was to simplify conveyances of land, and where this simplicity could not otherwise be attained, to make radical

17 Pp. 875, et seq, post.
18 On entailed interests, see pp. 245 et seq, post.
19 Litt ss. 55, 241, 265; Blackstone, vol. ii. p. 187.
20 Litt s. 241. As distinct from the case of joint tenancy and tenancy in common, partition may be compelled at common law, since the co-tenancy arises, not by act of parties, but by operation of law.
1 Challis, *Law of Real Property* (3rd edn), p. 374.
2 Co Litt s. 164*a*.
3 Litt s. 309.
4 If a person who was a lunatic on 1 January 1926, and was therefore incapable of making a will, dies without recovering his testamentary capacity, his beneficial interest in land devolves according to the old canons of descent; AEA 1925, s. 51 (2). Coparcenary, therefore, may still arise under this provision in the case of a fee simple estate.
5 SLA 1925, s. 36 (1), (2).

alterations in the pre-1926 law. The law relating to concurrent interests was a subject that called for considerable alteration. If conveyancing is to be a simple matter, one primary essential is that the legal estate to be acquired by a purchaser should be vested in an easily ascertainable person and not distributed among a number of persons whose titles will each require to be investigated.

A. CONVEYANCING DIFFICULTIES BEFORE 1926

(1) JOINT TENANCY

Joint tenancy does not raise difficulties in this respect, for although several persons are interested in the land, yet there is but one title to be deduced, and if the purchaser is satisfied as to the validity of the deed or the will under which the tenancy stands limited, he is not concerned further with the tenants except to see that they are parties to the deed of sale.

(2) TENANCY IN COMMON

In tenancy in common, however, the case is different, for the existence of a number of persons interested in the land, each of whom, as we have seen, is entitled to a separate share, raises a serious hindrance to simplicity of transfer. An analogous difficulty occurs in the case of a settlement where the beneficial title is distributed among a number of persons *in succession*, but we have seen that this plurality of interests is not allowed to hinder conveyancing, since the tenant for life is treated as the fee simple owner for purposes of transmission, and the interests of the various beneficiaries are not allowed to affect a purchaser. The conveyancing problem raised by a number of successive interests is in fact comparatively simple, because the tenant for life is obviously marked out as the person to act as an intermediary for passing the legal estate.

But where land is held by tenants in common, there is no one person in whom the legal estate can appropriately be vested, for all the tenants have the equal right to present enjoyment, so that tenancy in common is a greater hindrance to simplicity of transfer than a settlement. The complication here is that the separate title of each tenant must be investigated.

Lastly, all this confusion is "worse confounded" by concurrent ownership in tenancy in common. Here is an example which recently came before me in my official capacity. A man by his will devised his freeholds to the use of his wife for life, and after her death to the use of his children in fee simple. He had ten children; one of them died during the widow's life, leaving a similar will, seven children, and a widow. This is quite a simple example; yet the result is that a house worth about £150 per annum is (the widow being dead) now vested (not merely in equity but at law) in seventeen persons in the following proportions:

Each of the nine living children of the testator or their assigns . . . . $\frac{7}{70}$

Each of the seven children of the deceased child, subject to
the prior life interest of their mother . . . . $\frac{1}{70}$

Moreover, several of the parties have mortgaged their shares, and in the result when the great expense of proving the title of each of the seventeen has been paid, a very small balance will remain for distribution. Thus, tenancy in common is (having regard to the Settled Land Acts) a far greater detriment to the proper management of land than settlements (which are popularly debited with this sin), and introduces infinitely greater difficulty with regard to its sale, as not only must the parties be unanimous, but the title of each of them has to be deduced.[6]

B. SCHEME OF 1925 LEGISLATION

(1) TENANCIES IN COMMON

In order to overcome such difficulties, the Law of Property Act 1925 revolutionized the law relating to tenancies in common.

The object was to enable land which is subject to such tenancies to be sold without casting upon the purchaser any obligation to consider the titles or the beneficial rights of the tenants.[7]

(a) Legal tenancies in common abolished

The first step in the attainment of this object is the enactment that:

> a legal estate is not capable of subsisting or of being created in an undivided share in land.[8]

What this particular enactment means is that there can never again be a *legal* tenancy in common, i.e. a tenancy in common of a legal estate.

(b) Legal estate held on trust for sale

It is then enacted that an undivided share in land shall not be created except behind a trust for sale.[9] This involves two consequences:

> First, the legal estate must be held by trustees holding as legal *joint* tenants upon trust for sale.
> Secondly, the subject matter of the tenancy in common is converted from land to money, for, as we have already seen, land directed to be sold is regarded by equity as having already been sold.[10]

(c) Legal joint tenancy cannot be severed

The corner stone of this new edifice is the vesting of the legal estate in joint tenants as trustees upon trust for sale, and since it is essential to the success of the scheme that this legal joint tenancy should remain invulnerable until

---

6 Sir Arthur Underhill in Fourth Report, 1919, p. 30.
7 See *City of London Building Society v Flegg* [1988] AC 54 at 77, [1987] 3 All ER 435 at 443, per Lord OLIVER OF AYLMERTON.
8 LPA 1925, s. 1 (6). The 1925 legislation refers to "undivided share" not to "tenancy in common".
9 SLA 1925, s. 36 (4).
10 P. 76, ante; pp. 235–8, post. The doctrine of conversion proved troublesome where a legal estate had been granted before 1926 to tenants in common in tail. The effect of the 1925 legislation was to make them equitable tenants in common of personalty, but as a result of this they became absolute owners, since before 1926 personalty could not be entailed and the new rule making this possible (p. 258, post), applied only to instruments executed after 1925. Hence the Law of Property (Entailed Interests) Act 1932, s. 1, overruling *Re Price* [1928] Ch 579, provides that in such a case the entail shall continue to exist in the personalty arising under the trust for sale.

terminated by sale, the old rules as to severance[11] have been abolished for *legal* joint tenancies. It is enacted that:

> no severance of a joint tenancy of a legal estate, so as to create a tenancy in common in land, shall be permissible.[12]

The basic effect of the scheme is that the legal estate is held by trustees for sale who hold it as legal joint tenants, but who are unable to sever; and, as in the case of all settlements by way of trust for sale, the beneficial interests exist in equity behind the trust for sale. On the sale of the legal estate by the trustees, a purchaser is not concerned with these equitable beneficial interests and takes free from them. They are overreached, provided that the purchase money is paid to at least two trustees or to a trust corporation; the beneficiaries then have corresponding rights in the purchase money.

(d) Trust for sale

If, therefore, it is desired to vest a fee simple absolute in possession or a term of years absolute in tenants in common, the correct method is to create an express trust for sale by conveying the legal estate to trustees upon trust for sale, i.e. upon trust to sell the land and to hold the rents and profits until sale and the ultimate proceeds of sale upon such trusts as the grantor may see fit to create.[13] He may provide, for instance, that the beneficiaries shall be entitled to the proceeds in unequal shares, in which case they become equitable tenants in common.

An alternative method is merely to convey the legal estate to trustees upon *the statutory trusts*, an expression which is defined by the Act to mean:

> upon trust to sell the land, with power to postpone the sale, and to hold the net rents and profits until sale and the ultimate proceeds of sale upon trust to give effect to the beneficial and equitable rights of the persons to whom the land was limited.[14]

(e) Effect of failure to create trust for sale

If the correct method of a conveyance upon trust for sale is not adopted, the Law of Property Act 1925 contains a number of provisions designed to ensure that, no matter what form the transaction may have taken, the effect shall be exactly the same as if the tenancy in common had been properly limited behind a trust for sale. There appear to be three normal cases, namely:

a direct conveyance of the legal estate to tenants in common;
a devise to tenants in common;
a contract to convey an undivided share.

(i) Conveyance With regard to a conveyance, section 34(2) of the Law of Property Act 1925 provides that:

> where [after 1925] land is expressed to be conveyed to any persons in undivided shares and those persons are of full age, the conveyance shall operate as if the land had been expressed to be conveyed to the grantees, or, if there are more than four grantors, then to the first four named in the conveyance, as joint tenants upon the statutory trusts.

11 Pp. 217–21, ante.
12 LPA 1925, s. 36 (2).
13 See *Encyclopaedia of Forms and Precedents* (4th edn), vol. 19. p. 1036.
14 LPA 1925, s. 35 (1).

Thus, if land is conveyed in fee simple to A, B, C, D and E in equal shares, A, B, C and D become joint tenants of the legal estate, while all five are entitled under the statutory trusts as equitable tenants in common to the proceeds of sale and the rents and profits until sale.

(ii) Devise A devise to two or more persons in undivided shares operates to vest the legal estate in the trustees (if any) of the will for the purposes of the Settled Land Act 1925, or, if there is none, in the personal representatives, but in either case the land is held on the statutory trusts and not as settled land.[15]

(iii) Contract to convey A contract to convey an undivided share in land is deemed to be fully performed by a conveyance of a corresponding share in the proceeds of sale arising under a trust for sale.[16]

(f) Settlement

As regards settlements, section 36(4) of the Settled Land Act 1925 provides that a tenancy in common shall not be capable of creation except under a trust instrument or under the above provisions of the Law of Property Act 1925, and shall then take effect under a trust for sale. Thus if it is desired to settle land on A and B for their lives in equal shares, with remainder to C in fee simple, the legal estate must be vested in the trustees upon trust for sale, and the disposition merely operates to give the beneficiaries a corresponding share of the net proceeds of sale and the rents and profits until sale.

If beneficiaries under an existing settlement become entitled in possession to the land, e.g. where in a

devise to X for life, remainder to X's children equally during their lives.

X dies leaving three children, the legal fee simple that was formerly held by X as tenant for life must be vested in the trustees of the settlement and held by them upon the statutory trusts.[17] The settlement within the meaning of the Settled Land Act 1925 comes to an end and is replaced by a trust for sale.

(g) Defect in scheme

The policy of the Law of Property Act 1925 is clearly to subject all forms of co-ownership to a trust for sale, except those which are within the Settled Land Act 1925. It seems doubtful, however, whether the language of these enactments covers all cases in which a tenancy in common may arise, as for example when two persons buy land and contribute the purchase price in unequal shares.[18] This was the position in *Bull v Bull*,[19] where:

15 LPA 1925, s. 34 (3). For an example, see *Re House* [1929] 2 Ch 166.
16 Ibid., s. 42 (6). Elaborate provisions are made in LPA 1925, Sch. 1, Part IV, for the conversion into equitable interests of tenancies in common that were in existence on 31 December 1925. These transitional provisions have given rise to a number of important decisions; see further *Gibson's Conveyancing* (20th edn), pp. 817–824.
17 SLA 1925, s. 36 (1), (2), (3).
18 P. 216, ante.
19 [1955] 1 QB 234, [1955] 1 All ER 253, followed in *Cook v Cook* [1962] P 181, [1962] 2 All ER 262; affd [1962] P 235, [1962] 2 All ER 811. See too *Re Buchanan-Wollaston's Conveyance* [1939] Ch 217; affd [1939] Ch 738, where a conveyance to purchasers as joint tenants (who contributed unequally) was treated as coming within LPA 1925, s. 36 (1); *Williams and Glyn's Bank Ltd v Boland* [1979] Ch 312 at 329, [1979] 2 All ER 697 at 703; affd [1981] AC 487, [1980] 2 All ER 408 (where a matrimonial home, to whose purchase both spouses contributed, was conveyed to one spouse only).

a mother and son bought a house as a dwelling place for themselves, the conveyance being made to the son only, who had provided the greater part of the purchase price. In an action in which the issue was the validity of a notice to quit served on the mother, the Court of Appeal, citing s. 36 (4) of the Settled Land Act 1925, held that the parties were tenants in common in equity, and that the legal estate vested in the son upon the statutory trusts for sale.

This decision, though expedient, is difficult to fit into the words of the legislation. There was nothing that could constitute a trust instrument within the meaning of the Settled Land Act 1925; and the land was not "expressed to be conveyed" to persons in undivided shares as required by the Law of Property Act 1925. It would seem, then, that the courts will readily impose a trust for sale if this will fulfil the intention of the parties.

(h) Advantages of scheme

Let us examine the effect of the statutory trust for sale that arises in these various cases from the point of view, first, of a purchaser of the land, secondly, of the beneficiaries.

(i) To purchaser The advantage to the purchaser is that he is no longer compelled to investigate the title of each tenant in common. He is concerned only with the legal estate held by the joint tenants upon trust for sale, since the rights of the persons beneficially entitled exist merely as equitable interests behind the trust for sale, and they are overreached upon a conveyance of the land by the trustees for sale, provided that the purchase money is paid to at least two trustees or to a trust corporation. It is a matter of indifference, therefore, that some of the tenants in common are infants, or that some of them are unwilling to acquiesce in the sale. Although it is true that in the case of a statutory, as distinct from an express, trust for sale the trustees are required, so far as practicable, to consult, and give effect to the wishes of the beneficiaries entitled in possession, or in the case of a dispute, of the majority in terms of value, yet it is expressly enacted that it shall be no concern of a purchaser to see that this requirement has been complied with.[20]

(ii) To tenants in common The advantage to the tenants in common is that, no matter how numerous they may be, a sale of the land effected is always possible without difficulty or undue expense. Neither are they prejudiced by the loss of their rights in the land itself, for they have corresponding rights in the money arising from the sale. Thus if A is entitled under the tenancy in common to a half share in the land, and B and C are entitled to a quarter share each, the duty of the trustees is to ensure that A, B and C receive the purchase money in the same proportions. They need not sell at once, nor indeed at any time, for they are statutorily empowered to postpone the same,[1] or, instead of selling, to partition the land among the persons beneficially entitled.[2] The tenants in common can still deal with their equitable interests as freely as they could formerly have dealt with their legal interests. If A, B and C are tenants in common and C sells his equitable interest to D, the legal joint tenancy remains vested in the trustees upon the statutory trusts for A, B and D.

20 LPA 1925, s. 26 (3); as amended by LP(A)A 1926, Sch.
 1 Ibid., s. 25.
 2 Ibid., s. 28 (3).

(2) JOINT TENANCIES

Certain consequential changes have also been effected in joint tenancies, and the law relating to this matter varies according as the land is, or is not, settled within the meaning of the Settled Land Act 1925.

(a) Settled land

The position with regard to settled land is what it was before 1926. If two or more persons are beneficially entitled for their lives under a settlement, as for example where land is devised to X and Y for their lives with remainder to Z in fee simple,[3] they together constitute the tenant for life within the meaning of the Settled Land Act and there is no question of any trust for sale.[4] They are invested with the legal estate, and it is their function to make title upon a sale or other disposition of the land.

(b) Joint tenants beneficially entitled

In the second case, however, where the land is not settled, but is *beneficially* limited for a legal estate to joint tenants, e.g.:

> where a father conveys Blackacre to his two sons in fee simple without words of severance,

it is enacted that the *legal* estate shall be held upon trust for sale in like manner as if the persons beneficially entitled were tenants in common.[5] This means, not that they become equitable tenants in common, but equitable joint tenants of the proceeds of sale and of the income until sale. Thus if land is granted to A, B and C jointly in fee simple, A, B and C become joint tenants of the legal estate upon trust for sale for themselves as equitable joint tenants. A legal and an equitable joint tenancy are automatically and inescapably brought into existence. A, B and C are trustees for sale of the legal estate[6] and can therefore make title with facility, but they are joint beneficiaries with regard to the equitable interests. They may postpone the sale of the land, indefinitely, but if the date at which it should be effected becomes a matter of dispute, any one of them may apply under section 30 of the Law of Property Act 1925 to the court which may make such order as it thinks fit. We have already seen that while it is the primary duty of the trustees for sale to sell, they have nevertheless a power to postpone sale.[7] Unless, therefore, A, B and C unanimously agree to exercise the power of postponement, the land must be sold.[8]

(c) Powers of court under section 30 of the Law of Property Act 1925

The powers of the court under section 30 are entirely discretionary. In exercising this discretion the court has regard to the underlying purpose of

---

3   See also *Re Gaul and Houlston's Contract* [1928] Ch 689; devise to X and Y in fee simple, subject to a charge, created voluntarily, of £1,000 in favour of Z. Thus, the land was settled by virtue of SLA 1925, s. 1 (1) (v); p. 178, n. 18, ante.
4   SLA 1925, s. 19 (2).
5   LPA 1925, s. 36 (1).
6   They must not exceed four in number: TA 1925, s. 34. See (1926) 42 LQR 478 at 480 (R. R. Formoy).
7   P. 205, ante.
8   *Re Mayo* [1943] Ch 302, [1943] 2 All ER 440; M & B p. 229.

the trust for sale and will not order a sale if some purpose of the trust remains to be discharged. Thus the court will refuse a sale on an application by A, if he has covenanted to sell only with the consents of B and C.[9] And likewise the court will refuse a sale where land has been acquired with some particular purpose in mind, as for instance, the joint occupation of a house and that purpose still subsists.[10]

> Thus, if the purpose was that the house should be the matrimonial home, then so long as that purpose is still alive, the court will not allow the husband or the wife arbitrarily to insist on a sale. But if the parties are divorced and in consequence the contemplated purpose is dead, then the trust for sale will take effect, subject always to the discretion of the court to postpone it.[11]

(i) Disputes between co-owners Litigation in recent years has been mainly concerned with the matrimonial or quasi-matrimonial home, where, on the breakdown of the relationship, A wants the house to be sold in order to realise his or her share of the proceeds of sale, and B wants it to be retained as accommodation for himself or herself and the children, if any. Where A and B have been married and their marriage has been ended under the Matrimonial Causes Act 1973,[12] application should be made to the Family Division under that Act, which gives to the court the widest jurisdiction to order a distribution of the spouses' property. Where A and B have not been married, the 1973 Act does not apply, and any application must be made under section 30.

In the matrimonial homes[13] cases the main question is whether the marriage still subsists in law[14] or in fact.[15] The court has regard to all the circumstances of the case, and, in particular, to the provision of a home for young and dependent children. Other factors to be taken into account include the conduct of the parties, their financial circumstances and the contribution which each has made to the acquisition of the property. Where children are concerned, however, there are conflicting approaches in the Court of Appeal. In *Re Evers' Trust*[16] the underlying purpose of the trust was to provide a *family* home, so that a sale would not be ordered while that purpose still existed; in *Re Holliday*[17] the purpose of the trust was to provide a *matrimonial* home and the interests of the children were only to be taken into account "so far as they affect the equities in the matter as between the two persons

  9 *Re Buchanan-Wollaston's Conveyance* [1939] Ch 738, [1939] 2 All ER 302; *Re Citro* [1991] Ch 142, [1990] 3 All ER 352; cf. *Abbey National plc v Moss* (1993) Times, 30 November. On s. 30, see also p. 208, ante.
 10 *Bull v Bull* [1955] 1 QB 234, [1955] 1 All ER 253; cf *Barclay v Barclay* [1970] 2 QB 677, [1970] 2 All ER 676.
 11 *Bedson v Bedson* [1965] 2 QB 666 at 678, [1965] 3 All ER 307 at 312, per Lord DENNING MR.
 12 As amended by Matrimonial and Family Proceedings Act 1984; *Williams v Williams* [1976] Ch 278 at 286; [1977] 1 All ER 28 at 31; (1977) 93 LQR 176 (M. W. Bryan); *Re Holliday* [1981] Ch 405 at 418, [1980] 3 All ER 385 at 393.
 13 See generally Cretney and Masson, *Principles of Family Law* (5th edn), pp. 257–262; M & B pp. 238–258.
 14 *Jones v Challenger* [1961] 1 QB 176, [1960] 1 All ER 785.
 15 *Rawlings v Rawlings* [1964] P 398, [1964] 2 All ER 804; *Re Solomon* [1967] Ch 573, [1966] 3 All ER 255; *Bernard v Josephs* [1982] Ch 391, [1982] 3 All ER 162 (co-habitees).
 16 [1980] 1 WLR 1327, [1980] 3 All ER 399; M & B p. 241.
 17 [1981] Ch 405, [1980] 3 All ER 385; M & B p. 245. The final judgment was delivered on the day after *Re Evers' Trust* was heard, and neither case refers to the other. See (1980) 77 LSG 288 (A. J. Oakley and D. Marks); [1981] Conv 79 (A. Sydenham); (1981) 97 LQR 200 (C. Hand); (1982) 98 LQR 519 (F. Webb); [1984] Conv 103 (M. P. Thompson).

entitled to the beneficial interests in the property". It has been suggested that the conflict is really a matter of language rather than substance.[18]

(ii) Bankruptcy Where the application is made under section 30 by the trustee in bankruptcy of A different considerations arise. The trustee is under a duty to realise A's assets, including his share of the matrimonial home, for the benefit of the creditors; whose rights are thus in conflict with the interests of B and B's children. The cases indicate that only in exceptional circumstances will the trustee in bankruptcy fail.[19]

The position is now governed by section 336 of the Insolvency Act 1986.[20] The application must be made to the court having bankruptcy jurisdiction, and that court is directed to make such order as it thinks just and reasonable having regard to:

(*a*) the interests of the bankrupt's creditors;
(*b*) the conduct of the spouse or former spouse, so far as contributing to the bankruptcy;
(*c*) the needs and financial resources of the spouse or former spouse;
(*d*) the needs of the children; and
(*e*) all the circumstances of the case other than the needs of the bankrupt.

These factors are similar to those taken into account by the court in bankruptcy cases before the Insolvency Act.[1]

Where, however, the application is made more than one year after the bankruptcy, the court must assume, unless the circumstances of the case are exceptional, that the interests of the creditors outweigh all other considerations.

The effect of the Act is probably to make no change in the outcome of an application, except that B's family will now have a statutory year's grace before the family home is sold.

Finally, section 336 is narrowly limited to cases where A and his spouse or former spouse are the trustees for sale; it therefore does not apply where A and B are unmarried or are co-owners, such as parent and child.[2]

(d) Determination of joint tenancy

This change in the law is unintelligible unless we remember that a *legal* joint tenancy can no longer be severed. It is essential to the success of the new rules for tenancies *in common* that the legal joint tenancy which must necessarily arise should continue undisturbed and should not be convertible

---

18 *Cousins v Dzosens* (1981) Times 12 December; M & B p. 249. See also *Chhokar v Chhokar* [1984] FLR 313; M & B pp. 145, 249, n. 10.
19 *Re Holliday* supra (husband bankrupt on own petition as tactical move to avoid transfer of property to divorced wife whom he had left with responsibility for children on her own; order for sale deferred until 1985); *Re Mott* [1987] CLY 212 ("It would be difficult to imagine a more extreme case of hardship than this one" per HOFFMANN J; M & B p. 256); *Re Gorman* [1990] 1 WLR 616, [1990] 1 All ER 717; M & B p. 256; (1991) 107 LQR 177 (S. M. Cretney).
20 The Act came into force on 15 December 1986. [1986] Conv 393 (J. G. Miller).
 1 *Re Solomon*, supra; *Re Turner* [1974] 1 WLR 1556, [1975] 1 All ER 5; *Re McCarthy* [1975] 1 WLR 807, [1975] 2 All ER 857; *Re Densham* [1975] 1 WLR 1519, [1975] 3 All ER 726; *Re Bailey* [1977] 1 WLR 278, [1977] 2 All ER 26; *Re Lowrie* [1981] 3 All ER 353; M & B p. 257; *Re Citro* [1991] Ch 142 at 159, [1990] 3 All ER 952 at 963; M & B p. 252; (1991) 107 LQR 177 (S. M. Cretney); [1991] CLJ 45 (J. C. Hall); [1991] Conv 302 (A. M. M. Lawson); (1992) 55 MLR 284 (D. Brown); cf. *Abbey National plc v Moss* (1993) Times, 30 November.
 2 Nor does it apply where A is a single trustee for sale holding on trust for himself and his spouse B. There is no reported case of an application against A's co-habitee.

into a tenancy in common by some transaction or event amounting to a severance, for otherwise the legal title would be split up into a number of separate titles and the old troubles incidental to a conveyance of the legal estate would return. Hence the new rule that a *legal* joint tenancy cannot be severed.[3] The object of the introduction of an equitable tenancy is to preserve to each tenant his right to sever his interest and thus to avoid the danger of his premature death and the consequent operation of the *jus accrescendi*.

We have already considered the methods by which a joint tenancy may be severed and converted into a tenancy in common,[4] but it is important to notice with some particularity the course open to a beneficial joint tenant who desires to prevent the survivorship of his equitable interest to the other tenants. If land has been conveyed to A and B as joint tenants, what is the effect upon A's beneficial interest if he predeceases B? The answer, of course, is that it survives absolutely to B to the detriment of A's successors. The further question then arises, what can A do in his lifetime to avoid this possible loss? In other words, how can the legal or the equitable joint tenancy, or both, be determined?

The solution is, either to determine the joint tenancy altogether, or, while retaining the legal joint tenancy, to sever it on its equitable side. Let us consider the two cases separately.

(i) Legal and equitable joint tenancy A joint tenancy is determined altogether by any one of the following methods.

1. *Sale of the legal estate* If A and B sell in their capacity as trustees for sale, their conveyance passes the legal fee simple to the purchaser freed from their rights as joint tenants. The purchaser is not concerned with these rights, since they exist behind the trust for sale and are merely equitable in nature.

A trust for sale cannot be exercised unless there are at least two trustees, but it is enacted by the Law of Property (Amendment) Act 1926 that a surviving joint tenant, who is solely and *beneficially* entitled to the land, may deal with the legal estate as if it were not held on a trust for sale.[5] Thus if land is devised in fee simple to a husband and wife jointly, the wife, on the death of her husband, can pass a good title to a purchaser of the legal estate without appointing another trustee in place of her husband.[6]

Such a conveyance, however, is not without its dangers, for a deceased tenant, without the knowledge of the survivor, may have severed his interest, a fact that will not appear on the vendor's abstract of title to the legal estate. It was formerly felt, therefore, that the only sure method of overreaching the equitable interest arising by virtue of the severance was for the survivor to reconstitute the trust for sale by appointing a new trustee. But this is no longer necessary. The Law of Property (Joint Tenants) Act 1964,[7] which is retrospective to 1 January 1926, provides that:

the survivor of two or more joint tenants shall, in favour of a purchaser of the legal

3 LPA 1925, s. 36 (2), p. 225, ante.
4 Pp. 217–21, ante.
5 Schedule amending LPA 1925, s. 36.
6 According to *Re Cook* [1948] Ch 212, [1948] 1 All ER 231 ; M & B p. 290, this would be the position apart from the Act of 1926, since, on the death of the husband the entire interest in the land, both legal and equitable, vests in the wife. The trust for sale ceases, since she is now owner and cannot be trustee for herself.
7 See Wolstenholme and Cherry, vol. 2, pp. 149–151 ; (1964) 28 Conv (NS) 329 ; (1966) 30 Conv (NS) 27 (P. Jackson).

estate, be deemed to be solely and beneficially interested if he conveys as beneficial owner[8] or the conveyance includes a statement that he is so interested.[9]

This provision, however, is not to apply if a memorandum of severance has been endorsed on or annexed to the conveyance by which the legal estate was vested in the joint tenants; or if a receiving order, or a petition for such an order, has been registered under the Land Charges Act 1972.[10]

2. *Partition* If all the joint tenants are of full age it is clear that as beneficial owners they may partition the land between themselves, whereupon the legal joint tenancy will be converted into separate ownership. Apart from this, however, the Law of Property Act 1925 provides, as we have seen, that where a legal estate is beneficially limited to persons as joint tenants it shall be held on trust for sale *in like manner as if the persons beneficially entitled were tenants in common.*[11] Then, another section provides that where the proceeds of sale have become absolutely vested in tenants in common of full age, the trustees may, with the consent of the persons (if any) of full age interested in possession in the profits of the land until sale:

(i) partition the land in whole or part, and
(ii) provide by way of mortgage or otherwise for the payment of any equality money.[12]

If the trustees or any of the beneficiaries refuse to agree to a partition, any person interested may apply to the court under section 30 of the Law of Property Act 1925.[13] The court may then make such order as it thinks fit, e.g. an order for sale.

3. *Release* Where land is held by A and B as joint tenants it is open to either of them to release his interest to the other, whereupon the alienee will become sole and several owner.[14] An agreement for such a release must satisfy the requirements for a contract for the sale or other disposition of land.[15]

(ii) Determination of equitable joint tenancy: severance It remains to be seen how it is possible to sever the equitable joint tenancy between A and B without disturbing the joint tenancy of the legal estate. This result is achieved if either of the tenants enters into any transaction which severs the tenancy and converts it into a tenancy in common, as for example where he alienates his share to a stranger; or if one of the tenants acquires an interest greater in quantum than that held by the other; or by mutual agreement; or by a course of dealing.[16]

The Law of Property Act 1925 added a new and very useful method of

---

8 As to the effect of conveying as beneficial owner, see p. 779, post.
9 S. 1 (1). The Act does not apply if the title to the land has been registered; ibid., s. 3.
10 LP (Joint Tenants) A 1964, s. 1 (1), proviso. Registration constitutes notice of the order or petition to the purchaser.
11 Section 36 (1); p. 229, ante.
12 LPA 1925, s. 28 (3). See *Re Gorringe and Brayton's Contract* [1934] Ch 614n; *Re Brooker* [1934] Ch 610.
13 Pp. 208, 229–31, ante.
14 LPA 1925, s. 36 (2).
15 Pp. 108, 111–124, ante; *Cooper v Critchley* [1955] Ch 431, [1955] 1 All ER 520; M & B p. 294.
16 Pp. 218–20, ante.

severance.[17] Section 36 (2) provides that if any tenant desires to sever the joint tenancy in equity, he may give to the other joint tenants a written notice[18] of such desire, whereupon he becomes entitled as tenant in common to his share of the profits of the land and of the purchase money after the land is sold.[19]

Suppose, for instance, that land is limited to A, B and C as joint tenants. We know that this creates both a legal and an equitable joint tenancy. If C dies without having dealt with his interest, A and B retain the legal estate as trustees for sale, and hold the equitable interest under the doctrine of survivorship, freed from the interest of C. But if in his lifetime C gives notice in writing of his desire to sever, his equitable joint tenancy becomes an equitable tenancy in common, and A and B hold the legal estate upon trust to sell and to divide the proceeds between themselves as equitable joint tenants and the personal representatives of C. The equitable tenancy in common will continue to exist until the sale is carried out, or the shares become vested in one person, or partition is effected.

C. PARTY-WALLS

We must finally examine the effect of the legislation of 1925 upon party-walls. According to FRY J the term "party-wall" may mean:[20]

(a) a wall of which two adjoining owners are tenants in common; or
(b) a wall divided vertically into two strips, one half of the thickness belonging to each of the neighbouring owners; or
(c) a wall belonging entirely to one owner, but subject to an easement in the other to have it maintained as a dividing wall; or
(d) a wall divided vertically into two equal strips, each strip being subject to a cross-easement in favour of the owner of the other.

It may be said that *most* of the party-walls in this country come within the first class, that is, are held by the adjoining owners as tenants in common, and in view of this it is clear that the effect of the statutory alterations relating to concurrent interests would have been absurd had special provisions for party-walls not been added. The effect would have been to render the majority of such walls subject to a trust for sale!

It is therefore enacted[1] that a wall which before 1926 would have been

---

17 Law Commission Working Paper No. 94 on Trusts of Land (1985) suggested that the only means of severance should be by notice in writing (para 6.12); and that it should be possible to sever by will (para 16.14).
18 *Re 88 Berkeley Road, London NW 9* [1971] Ch 648, [1971] 1 All ER 254 (notice properly served if sent by recorded delivery, even if not received by addressee: LPA 1925, s. 196 (4)).
19 *Re Draper's Conveyance* [1969] 1 Ch 486, [1967] 3 All ER 853; M & B p. 265 (issue of summons held to amount to notice in writing under s. 36 (2)); (1968) 84 LQR 462 (P.V.B.). Cf *Harris v Goddard* [1983] 1 WLR 1203, [1983] 3 All ER 242 (wife's prayer in a divorce petition for a property adjustment order to be made in respect of the former matrimonial home held not to be notice); [1984] Conv 148 (S. Coneys). Whether a unilateral act not amounting to notice under s. 36 (2) can effect severance is a matter of dispute: *Burgess v Rawnsley* [1975] Ch 429, [1975] 3 All ER 142; M & B p. 268; [1976] CLJ 20 (D. J. Hayton); (1977) 41 Conv (NS) 243 (S. M. Bandali).

As to whether beneficial joint tenancies should be abolished, see [1987] Conv 29, 225 (M. P. Thompson) in favour; 273 (A. M. Prichard) against.
20 *Watson v Gray* (1880) 14 Ch D 192 at 194–5. See generally Rudall, *Party Walls* (3rd edn).
1 LPA 1925, s. 38, Sch. I, part V; see also s. 187 (2).

held by tenants in common shall be regarded as severed vertically as between the respective owners, and that the owner of each part shall have such rights to support and user over the other part as he would have had *qua* tenant in common under the old law. In other words, most party-walls now fall within the last class enumerated by FRY J.[2]

SECTION III NATURE OF INTERESTS OF BENEFICIARIES UNDER A TRUST FOR SALE

As we have seen, the doctrine of conversion applies as soon as a trust for sale comes into operation.[3] As a result of this doctrine, the interests of the beneficiaries under the trust become automatically interests in the proceeds of the sale of land and not in the land itself. As CROSS LJ said:[4]

> The whole purpose of the trust for sale is to make sure, by shifting the equitable interests away from the land and into the proceeds of sale, that a purchaser of the land takes free from the equitable interests. To hold these to be equitable interests in the land itself would be to frustrate this purpose. Even to hold that they have equitable interests in the land for a limited period, namely, until the land is sold, would, we think, be inconsistent with the trust for sale being an "immediate" trust for sale working an immediate conversion, which is what the Law of Property Act 1925 envisages (see section 205 (1) (xxix)).[5]

A simple example of the effect of the doctrine is that, where a testator has left all his personal estate to P and all his real estate to R, an interest under a trust for sale passes to P and not to R.[6] The full logic of the doctrine of conversion has, however, not been applied by the courts. There are various situations where an interest under a trust for sale has been treated as if it were an interest in land. Thus, a beneficiary under a trust for sale can, with the consent of the other beneficiaries, if he and they are all adult and of sound mind, terminate the trust and call for a transfer of the land itself;[7] he is a "person interested" who may apply to the court for an order relating to the land under section 30 of the Law of Property Act 1925;[8] in the case of a statutory trust for sale, he has a right to be consulted by the trustees as to the

---

2 For statutory modification of these rules see e.g. London Building Acts (Amendment) Act 1939, Part VI; (1980) 256 EG 375 (K. A. Pollard). See also *London & Manchester Assurance Co Ltd v O & H Construction Ltd* [1989] 2 EGLR 185 (mandatory injunction granted for removal of building work where defendant failed to use proper procedure under the Act for demolition of party wall); *Lehmann v Herman* [1993] 1 EGLR 172.

3 P. 76, ante; (1971) 34 MLR 441 (S. M. Cretney); [1971] CLJ 44 (M. J. Prichard); [1978] Conv 194 (H. Forrest); [1981] Conv 108 (A. E. Boyle); [1986] Conv 415 (J. Warburton); H & M pp. 285–8; M & B pp. 292–302. See generally (1984) 100 LQR 86 (S. Anderson); Law Commission Report on Trusts of Land 1989 (No. 181), paras 3.4–3.7 recommends that the doctrine be abolished, p. 211, ante.

4 *Irani Finance Ltd v Singh* [1971] Ch 59 at 80, [1970] 3 All ER 199 at 203. For a critical analysis of the statutory provisions on overreaching and its relationship to the doctrine of conversion, see [1990] CLJ 277 (C. Harpum); M & B p. 287.

5 P. 203, ante. See *City of London Building Society v Flegg* [1988] AC 54 at 82, [1987] 3 All ER 435 at 447, where Lord OLIVER OF AYLMERTON quotes CROSS LJ verbatim as "a useful general analysis". The case is discussed p. 818, post.

6 *Re Kempthorne* [1930] 1 Ch 268; *Re Newman* [1930] 2 Ch 409; *Re Cook* [1948] Ch 212, [1948] 1 All ER 231; M & B p. 290.

7 *Saunders v Vautier* (1841) 4 Beav 115, p. 331, post.

8 P. 208, ante.

exercise of their powers over the land;[9] and, within the discretion of the court, he may be protected from eviction from the land by the holder of the legal estate.[10]

The nature of a beneficiary's interest has also arisen in the context of the interpretation of a statute. The question is whether a reference in a statute to "land" includes an interest under a trust for sale. Sometimes the statute deals expressly with the point; as in the Limitation Act 1980, where land includes "an interest in the proceeds of the sale of land held upon trust for sale".[11] Even though the Law of Property Act 1925 contains no such provision, it has been held that a contract for the sale of a beneficial interest under a trust for sale is a contract for the sale of "land or any interest in land" within section 40 and so requires a memorandum for its enforceability.[12] Similarly, under the Land Registration Act 1925, a beneficiary has been held to be a person interested in land within section 54 (1) and thereby entitled to lodge a caution to protect his interest as a minor interest;[13] and also to have "an interest

9 LPA 1925, s. 26 (3); p. 207, ante.
10 *Bull v Bull* [1955] 1 QB 234, [1955] 1 All ER 235 (order for possession refused); *Cook v Cook* [1962] P 235; [1962] 2 All ER 811; *Gurasz v Gurasz* [1970] P 11, [1969] 3 All ER 822; cf *Barclay v Barclay* [1970] 2 QB 677, [1970] 2 All ER 676 (order for possession granted); H & M pp. 272–274; M & B pp. 271, 293.
11 S. 38 (1).
12 *Cooper v Critchley* [1955] Ch 431, [1955] 1 All ER 520; M & B p. 294; (1955) 71 LQR 177 (R.E.M.); *Steadman v Steadman* [1974] QB 161 at 167, [1973] 3 All ER 977 at 982, p. 118, ante. Section 40 has been repealed in respect of contracts entered into after 26 September 1989: Law of Property (Miscellaneous Provisions) Act 1989, s. 2 (8), p. 121, ante. The replacement s. 2 (6) expressly includes "any interest in or over the proceeds of sale of land". Cf *Re Rayleigh Weir Stadium* [1954] 1 WLR 786, [1954] 2 All ER 283 (such a contract held not registrable under LCA 1925, where the definition of land expressly excludes an undivided share in land s. 17 (1)).
   In *Cedar Holdings Ltd v Green* [1981] Ch 129, [1979] 3 All ER 117, Mr and Mrs G were joint legal and beneficial owners of their matrimonial home. Mr G wished to raise money by a mortgage of the home. Mr G and a woman, who impersonated Mrs G, executed a legal charge in favour of CH Ltd. The question was whether this transaction charged Mr G's share of his beneficial interest in the home. CH Ltd argued that it did, since under LPA 1925, s. 63, "every conveyance is effectual to pass all the interest which the conveying parties respectively have in the property conveyed or expressed or intended so to be". CA rejected this argument because under the doctrine of conversion Mr G's interest was not "an interest in the property conveyed". On this point the CA decision was considered to have been wrongly decided in *Williams and Glyn's Bank Ltd v Boland* [1981] AC 487, [1980] 2 All ER 408, p. 793, post; *Ahmed v Kendrick* [1988] 2 FLR 22. See *Thames Guaranty Ltd v Campbell* [1985] QB 210, [1984] 2 All ER 585.
13 S. 3 (xv); *Elias v Mitchell* [1972] Ch 652, [1972] 2 All ER 153; M & B p. 295; cf. *Lynton International Ltd v Noble* (1991) 63 P & CR 453 (contractual right to share in proceeds of sale).
   See also Charging Orders Act 1979, s. 2 which provides that a charge may be imposed on a debtor's interest under any trust: *National Westminster Bank Ltd v Stockman* [1981] 1 WLR 67, [1981] 1 All ER 800. If the debtor or debtors together own the whole beneficial interest, then the order will be made against the legal estate (s. 2 (1) (b) (ii) and (iii)), and is thus registrable under the Land Charges Act 1972, s. 6; *Clark v Chief Land Registrar* [1993] Ch 294, [1993] 2 All ER 936, p. 757, ante. If it affects only part of the equitable interest, it is not registrable due to the doctrine of conversion: *Perry v Phoenix Assurance plc* [1988] 1 WLR 940, [1988] 3 All ER 60; M & B p. 298, not following *Harman v Glencross*, supra; [1988] All ER Rev 168 (P. J. Clarke); [1989] Conv 133 (N. S. Price); [1988] Cov 286 (J. E. Martin). It can only be protected by a notice to the trustees under LPA 1925, s. 137, p. 729, post; and, in registered land, by a caution: *Elias v Mitchell*, supra; *Howell v Montey* (1990) 61 P & CR 18; [1990] Conv 392 (P. Loughlan); *Clark v Chief Land Registrar*, supra.
   If a charging order is obtained, the judgment creditor may then apply to the court under LPA 1925, s. 30, p. 208, ante, for an order for sale of the property: *Midland Bank plc v Pike* [1988] 2 All ER 434, [1988] All ER Rev 234 (A. S. Zuckerman). For the reluctance of the

subsisting in reference to" registered land for the purpose of an overriding interest under section 70 (1) (g).[14] The latter point was decided by the House of Lords in *Williams and Glyn's Bank Ltd v Boland*.[15] In this case:

> a husband and wife each contributed to the purchase of a matrimonial home. The husband was registered under the Land Registration Act 1925 as the sole proprietor. By virtue of her contribution the wife had an equitable interest in the house; this created equitable beneficial co-ownership, and the husband held the legal title upon trust for sale for himself and his wife as equitable tenants in common.
>
> Later the husband, without the wife's consent, created a legal charge on the house in favour of the bank. On default being made in the mortgage payments, the bank brought an action for possession of the house.
>
> The question was whether the wife's interest was valid against the bank; it could only be so if it was an overriding interest due to her actual occupation of the house under section 70 (1) (g).[16]

The House of Lords held unanimously that the wife's interest was valid; her interest under the trust for sale was capable of existing as an overriding interest.[17] It was "an interest subsisting in reference to" registered land. Lord WILBERFORCE said that:

> to describe the interests of spouses in a house jointly bought to be lived in as a matrimonial home as merely an interest in proceeds of sale, or rents and profits until sale is just a little unreal.[18]

In the Court of Appeal ORMROD LJ had made the same point in more detail:[19]

> In converting such a relationship into a trust for sale the legislation of 1925 created, in effect, a legal fiction, at least in so far as the implied trusts are concerned. This may have been an inescapable consequence of the method adopted to achieve its primary objective, that is, the simplification of conveyancing. But to press this legal fiction to its logical conclusion and beyond the point which is necessary to achieve the primary objective is not justifiable, particularly when it involves the sacrifice of the interest of a class or classes of person. The consequence is that the interest of persons in the position of the wives ought not to be dismissed as a mere interest in

court to anticipate this application, see *First National Securities Ltd v Hegerty* [1985] QB 850, [1984] 3 All ER 641; cf *Harman v Glencross* [1985] Fam 49, [1984] 2 All ER 577 (competition between one co-owning spouse and judgment creditors of the other); affd [1986] Fam 81, [1986] 1 All ER 545, where BALCOMBE LJ sets out guidelines for the solution of this type of problem at 99, at 558; [1985] Conv 129 (P. F. Smith); (1985) 5 OJLS 132 (N. P. Gravells); *Austin-Fell v Austin-Fell* [1990] Fam 172, [1990] 2 All ER 455; *Lloyds Bank Plc v Byrne* (1993) 23 HLR 472. On charging orders generally, see Walker, *Charging Orders on Land* (1992).

14 P. 103, ante, p. 790, post.

15 [1981] AC 487, [1980] 2 All ER 408; p. 793, post.

16 A different conclusion was reached by STAMP J in *Caunce v Caunce* [1969] 1 WLR 286, [1969] 1 All ER 722; M & B p. 274 on identical facts in unregistered land. It was there held that the interest of the wife, being neither overreachable (p. 817, post) nor registrable, was not valid against the bank, which took free as a bona fide purchaser of the legal estate from the husband-mortgagor without actual or constructive notice. But, like RUSSELL LJ in *Hodgson v Marks* [1971] Ch 892 at 934–935, Lord SCARMAN in *Williams and Glyn's Bank Ltd v Boland*, supra at 511, at 418, was "by no means certain that *Caunce v Caunce* was rightly decided" and it was not followed in *Kingsnorth Finance Co Ltd v Tizard* [1986] 1 WLR 783, [1986] 2 All ER 54; p. 63, n. 4, ante.

17 Her interest could not be valid as a minor interest, since it had not been so protected on the register. Her only hope was in the safety-net provision of s. 70 (1) (g).

18 At 507, at 415.

19 [1979] Ch 312 at 336, [1979] 2 All ER 697 at 709; M & B p. 274.

the proceeds of sale except where it is essential to the working of the scheme to do so.

It follows that in construing this, and other legislation closely connected with it, it is permissible, and indeed necessary, to construe the relevant phraseology so as to do the least possible violence to the rights of holders of equitable interests in the property.

Enough has been said to show that the courts have in many circumstances rejected the logical consequences of the doctrine of conversion, and in so doing have equated law with reality. The doctrine is not necessary to enable a purchaser to overreach the beneficial interests under a trust for sale; since 1925 there has been statutory provision for this under the Law of Property Act 1925.[20] Perhaps the time has now come to reconsider the doctrine of conversion in its application to trusts for sale; and even to abolish it altogether.

SECTION IV THE MATRIMONIAL HOME

A. OWNERSHIP

The matrimonial home occupies a most important part in family property law,[1] and in many cases it is the only substantial asset of the family.[2] If a husband and wife wish to own a home jointly, they may do so by creating an express trust for sale, under which it is conveyed to trustees (who may be themselves), who become joint tenants of the legal estate upon trust for sale for themselves, as either equitable joint tenants or equitable tenants in common. The terms of the trust may declare not only the nature of the equitable beneficial interests, but also the quantum of the interest which each spouse is to own.[3] This is an application of the machinery invented by the 1925 legislation for concurrent interests. But in some cases it may not be so simple. The quantum may not be declared. Further, the legal estate in the property may be conveyed to *one* spouse only (usually the husband), but the beneficial interest is shared between husband and wife. The first question to decide in this type of case is whether, according to the strict principles of trust law,[4] each of the spouses has an interest in equity; if so, then the superstructure of the trust for sale is erected, and a statutory trust for sale

---

20 S. 2 (1) (ii), pp. 75–6, ante.
 1 See generally Bromley, *Family Law* (8th edn), pp. 585 et seq; Cretney and Masson, *Principles of Family Law* (5th edn) chapter 11; Law Commission Third Report on Family Property 1978 (Law Com No. 86), especially the critical review of the present law at pp. 62–69. This Report's proposal of automatic statutory co-ownership of the matrimonial home has not been implemented.
 2 The majority of married couples are owner occupiers. See Murphy and Clark, *The Family Home*, chapter 1.
 3 Fraud or mistake apart, this is conclusive: *Pettitt v Pettitt* [1970] AC 777 at 813, [1969] 2 All ER 385 at 405, per Lord UPJOHN; *Goodman v Gallant* [1986] Fam 106, [1986] 1 All ER 311; cf *City of London Building Society v Flegg* [1988] AC 54, [1987] 3 All ER 435. As to the effect of the Land Registry Transfer Form, see p. 242, post.
 4 *Gissing v Gissing* [1971] AC 886, [1970] 2 All ER 780. See generally H & M pp. 262–271; (1993) 109 LQR 263 (S. Gardner). Any special rules applying to married couples, such as Matrimonial Proceedings and Property Act 1970, s. 37, infra, apply also to property disputes between parties who have broken off their engagement to marry: Law Reform (Miscellaneous Provisions) Act 1970, s. 2 (1). See *Mossop v Mossop* [1989] Fam 77, [1988] 2 All ER 202.

comes into operation. Much of the case law concerns unmarried couples, in respect of whom similar principles apply.[5]

If husband and wife have made no express provision, there are two main situations in which a spouse may obtain a beneficial interest.

(a) Contribution

If, say, the wife contributes part of the purchase money, then, unless there is evidence of a contrary intention, there is a resulting trust in equity under which the husband, as purchaser, holds the property on trust for himself and his wife to the extent of their respective contributions.[6]

While direct contributions to the purchase price or mortgage instalments are clearly sufficient to acquire an interest, the position as to indirect contributions is less straightforward. Wifely services in looking after the home and children do not suffice;[7] but what if the wife contributes towards the family expenses, thereby enabling her husband to pay the mortgage instalments? Some decisions of the Court of Appeal under Lord DENNING MR favoured a liberal approach,[8] but this has now been rejected. Guidelines have been laid down by the House of Lords in *Lloyds Bank plc v Rosset*.[9] Where there is an express oral declaration or agreement (which does not satisfy the formality requirements of section 53 of the Law of Property Act 1925), a constructive trust will arise if the wife has relied on the agreement to her detriment. An excuse as to why the property has not been put in joint names may be treated as an expression of a common intention to share.[10] The requirement of detrimental reliance is shown by significant contributions in money or money's worth, which need not be direct,[11] but not by activities which any wife would do, such as decorating and supervising builders.[12]

In the absence of any express common intention, the House of Lords suggested that only direct contributions to the purchase price or mortgage instalments could suffice to confer an interest under a constructive trust. Direct contributions have, however, traditionally been regarded as giving

---

5 *Cooke v Head* [1972] 1 WLR 518, [1972] 2 All ER 38; *Eves v Eves* [1975] 1 WLR 1338, [1975] 3 All ER 768; *Bernard v Josephs* [1982] Ch 391, [1982] 3 All ER 162; *Gordon v Douce* [1983] 1 WLR 563, [1983] 2 All ER 228; *Burns v Burns* [1984] Ch 317, [1984] 1 All ER 244; *Grant v Edwards* [1986] Ch 638, [1986] 2 All ER 426; *Hammond v Mitchell* [1992] 2 All ER 109; [1992] All ER Rev 210 (P. J. Clarke).

6 See e.g. *Gissing v Gissing*, supra. The presumption of the resulting trust may also be rebutted by the presumption of advancement that a beneficial gift was intended. This presumption is applicable where the *husband* provides the purchase money, and is itself rebuttable. The presumption of advancement appears to be of little weight today: *Pettitt v Pettitt* [1970] AC 777, [1969] 2 All ER 385; *Falconer v Falconer* [1970] 1 WLR 1333, [1970] 3 All ER 449.

7 *Burns v Burns* [1984] Ch 317, [1984] 1 All ER 244.

8 *Hargrave v Newton* [1971] 1 WLR 1611, [1971] 3 All ER 866; *Hazell v Hazell* [1972] 1 WLR 301, [1972] 1 All ER 923; *Wachtel v Wachtel* [1973] Fam 72, [1973] 1 All ER 829.

9 [1991] 1 AC 107, [1990] 1 All ER 1111; (1990) 106 LQR 539 (J. Davies); [1990] Conv 314 (M. Thompson); [1991] CLJ 38 (M. Dixon); (1991) 54 MLR 126 (S. Gardner); *Ives v Blake* [1993] NPC 87. See also [1993] Conv 359 (J. Mee) on decisions in the Irish courts.

10 *Eves v Eves* [1975] 1 WLR 1338, [1975] 3 All ER 768; *Grant v Edwards* [1986] Ch 638, [1986] 2 All ER 426. The parties must communicate their common intention to each other; *Springette v Defoe* (1992) 65 P & CR 1; [1992] Conv 347 (H. Norman).

11 *Grant v Edwards*, supra; *Eves v Eves*, supra; *Hammond v Mitchell* [1991] 1 WLR 1127, [1992] 2 All ER 109 (unpaid assistance in business); [1992] Conv 218 (A. Lawson); (1993) 56 MLR 224 (P. O'Hagan).

12 *Lloyds Bank plc v Rosset*, supra.

rise to a resulting trust. The denial of any interest to a wife who has made substantial indirect contributions seems harsh, and not supported by authority.[13] It may be that the principles of proprietary estoppel will ultimately prevail as the solution to this problem.[14]

In the case of direct contributions, the size of the shares will be proportionate to the contributions. Where there is an express common intention to share, the size of the shares will be as agreed. If the parties have expressly agreed to share but have not directed their minds to the size of the shares, the court will determine what is a fair share in the circumstances.[15] Once the shares have been established, they must be valued at the date of realization of the property and not at the date of any earlier separation.[16]

(b) Improvements

Section 37 of the Matrimonial Proceedings and Property Act 1970 declares that a husband or wife who has made a substantial contribution in money or money's worth to the improvement of real or personal property in which either or both of them has a beneficial interest, will be treated as having a share or an enlarged share in that beneficial interest.[17] This is subject to any express or implied agreement to the contrary. The contributor is entitled to any share agreed, or in default as may seem in all the circumstances just.

Finally, it must be emphasized that a wife who is not a legal owner cannot claim any property interest in the matrimonial home during the marriage, unless she has made a contribution which entitles her to rely on the strict principles of trust law. However, if the marriage breaks down, and there is a decree of divorce, nullity of marriage or judicial separation, the court is given the widest discretionary powers.[18] under the Matrimonial Causes Act 1973[19] to order a distribution of the spouses' property, and disputes between spouses relating to property are best settled under that jurisdiction.[20] In particular, section 25 (2) (*f*) of the Act requires the court to have regard to:

> the contributions which each of the parties has made or is likely in the foreseeable future to make to the welfare of the family, including any contributions made by looking after the home or caring for the family.

First consideration must, however, be given to the welfare of any minor child of the family.[1]

13 See *Gissing v Gissing* [1971] AC 886, [1970] 2 All ER 780 (contributions must be "referable" to the costs of acquisition).
14 *Grant v Edwards*, supra; *Austin v Keele* (1987) 61 ALJR 605; *Lloyds Bank plc v Rosset*, supra; *Stokes v Anderson* [1991] 1 FLR 391. For proprietary estoppel, see pp. 595 et seq., post.
15 *Gissing v Gissing*, supra; *Stokes v Anderson*, supra.
16 *Turton v Turton* [1988] Ch 542, [1987] 2 All ER 641; [1987] Conv 378 (J. Warburton).
17 *Davis v Vale* [1971] 1 WLR 1022, [1971] 2 All ER 1021; *Kowalczuk v Kowalczuk* [1973] 1 WLR 930, [1973] 2 All ER 1042; *Griffiths v Griffiths* [1974] 1 WLR 1350, [1974] 1 All ER 932.
18 Including the power to order a sale of the matrimonial home where an order for financial relief is made on a decree of divorce, nullity or judicial separation. See s. 24A, added by Matrimonial Homes and Property Act 1981, s. 7. By s. 24A (6), a third party with a beneficial interest in the home may make representations before an order for sale is made. See [1981] Conv 404 (M. Hayes and G. Battersby).
19 Where this Act applies, it is inappropriate to make a separate award for improvements under s. 37: *Griffiths v Griffiths*, supra. For the relationship between the two jurisdictions generally, see (1974) 118 SJ 431 (S. M. Cretney).
20 *Williams v Williams* [1976] Ch 278 at 286, [1977] 1 All ER 28 at 31.
 1 Matrimonial Causes Act 1973, s. 25 (1), as substituted by the Matrimonial and Family Proceedings Act 1984, s. 3.

On the death of one spouse, the other becomes entitled to the matrimonial home by survivorship if they were beneficial joint tenants of it. In other cases the surviving spouse may acquire the home by will, under the intestacy laws[2] or by application under the Inheritance (Provision for Family and Dependants) Act 1975.[3]

B. OCCUPATION

Separate from any beneficial interest which a spouse may own is the right of occupation given by the Matrimonial Homes Act 1983.[4] This gives to one spouse, A, a right of occupation of a dwelling-house which the other spouse, B, is entitled to occupy:

> by virtue of a beneficial[5] estate or interest or contract or by virtue of any enactment[6] giving him or her the right to remain in occupation.[7]

More specifically, if in occupation, A has a right not to be evicted or excluded by B without the leave of the court; if not in occupation, A has a right with the leave of the court to enter and occupy the house.[8] The right is only available to A where A is "not so entitled", or has merely an equitable interest in the dwelling-house or in its proceeds of sale.[9] As we have seen, such an interest may arise from A's contribution to its acquisition or improvement. The court is given wide discretionary powers to make such order as it thinks just and reasonable.[10] The right is a charge on B's estate, and has priority, as if it were an equitable interest, from the date of B's acquisition of his estate, or of the marriage, or 1 January 1968,[11] whichever is the latest.[12] It ends on the death of B or on the termination of the marriage, unless the court makes an order to the contrary during the marriage.[13]

If B is adjudged bankrupt, A's charge binds the trustee in bankruptcy. A may apply for an order under the 1983 Act to the court having bankruptcy jurisdiction. The court shall make such order under the 1983 Act as it thinks

2 Intestates Estates Act 1952, Sch. 2; p. 876, post.
3 P. 827, post.
4 Replacing the Act of 1967. See generally the discussion of the Act by MEGARRY J in *Wroth v Tyler* [1974] Ch 30, [1973] 1 All ER 897; (1968) 32 Conv (NS) 85 (F. R. Crane); Bromley, *Family Law* (8th edn), pp. 612 et seq; Cretney and Masson, *Principles of Family Law* (5th edn), pp. 272 et seq; M & B pp. 275–281.
5 Including an interest under a trust. See further ss. 1 (8), 2 (2), (3).
6 E.g. Rent Act 1977; Housing Act 1988.
7 S. 1 (1). The Act does not apply to a dwelling-house that has at no time been a matrimonial home of the spouse in question: *Hall v King* [1987] 2 EGLR 121 (wife licensee of absent tenant husband).
8 S. 1 (1) (*a*), (*b*); *Watts v Waller* [1973] QB 153, [1972] 3 All ER 257 (spouse out of occupation can register before getting leave of court to re-enter); *Barnett v Hassett* [1981] 1 WLR 1385, [1982] 1 All ER 80 (spouse having no intention to occupy not permitted to register in attempt to freeze proceeds of intended sale).
9 S. 1 (11). Matrimonial Proceedings and Property Act 1970, s. 38, reversing *Gurasz v Gurasz* [1970] P 11, [1969] 3 All ER 822. Where the spouses are joint owners, s. 9 gives the court similar powers to prohibit, suspend or restrict the right of occupation of either party, or to require one spouse to permit the other to occupy. These powers were introduced by the Domestic Violence and Matrimonial Proceedings Act 1976, s. 4.
10 S. 1 (3). S. 1 (2) permits the exclusion of the spouse who is the legal owner.
11 The commencement date of the Matrimonial Homes Act 1967.
12 S. 2 (1).
13 S. 2 (4).

just and reasonable, having regard to various factors including the interests of B's creditors and the needs of A and any children. Where, however, the application is made more than one year after the vesting of B's estate in the trustee in bankruptcy, the court shall assume, save in exceptional circumstances, that the interests of B's creditors outweigh all other considerations.[14]

The statutory right of occupation is registrable as a Class F land charge.[15] In the case of registered land, it may be protected by the entry of a notice;[16] it is not an overriding interest, even if the spouse is in actual occupation.[17]

A may register the charge without notifying B of the registration, and thus cause difficulty where B later enters into a contract to sell the dwelling-house in ignorance of the registration. Further, A may register after B has contracted to sell and thus make it impossible for B to perform the contract, at the cost of substantial damages for its breach.[18]

SECTION V REGISTERED LAND

Where the trust for sale machinery of the Law of Property Act 1925 is used for the creation of concurrent interests, the restriction procedure operates, and there is no difficulty.[19] Where property is transferred to joint registered proprietors, the wording of the Land Registry transfer form should make it clear whether they are beneficially entitled. If the form states that the transferees are entitled for their own benefit and that the survivor can give a valid receipt for capital money, a beneficial joint tenancy is created.[20] But if the words "for their own benefit" are missing, the form is not regarded as an express declaration of a beneficial joint tenancy.[1] In such a case the beneficial interests must be established by other means.[2] Where the legal estate is vested in no fewer than two trustees for sale, payment to them will overreach the beneficial interests, whether or not the beneficiaries are in occupation.[3] But, as we have seen, a sole registered proprietor may nevertheless be a trustee, as where a husband and wife both contribute towards the purchase price of the matrimonial home, and the transfer is taken in the name of the

---

14 Insolvency Act 1986, s. 336, p. 231, ante.
15 LCA 1972, s. 2 (7). Such a registration entitles the spouse to be given notice of any proceedings by a mortgagee, and to be joined as a party to any action to enforce the mortgage: Matrimonial Homes Act 1983, s. 8 (3).
16 Matrimonial Homes Act 1983, s. 2 (8). Production of the land certificate is not necessary. The Law Commission has recommended that the Class F charge should be protected by notice if acknowledged by the proprietor, and by caution if not so acknowledged: Third Report on Land Registration, C. Minor Interests 1987 (Law Com No. 158, HC 269), para. 4.41.
17 Ibid.
18 *Watts v Waller* [1973] QB 153, [1972] 3 All ER 257; *Wroth v Tyler*, supra; (1974) 38 Conv (NS) 110, (1975) 39 Conv (NS) 78 (D. J. Hayton); (1974) CLP 76 (D. G. Barnsley).
19 P. 209, ante.
20 *Re Gorman* [1990] 1 WLR 616, [1990] 1 All ER 717 (whether or not the transferees have signed the form).
 1 *Harwood v Harwood* [1991] 2 FLR 274; *Huntingford v Hobbs* [1993] 1 FLR 736.
 2 P. 238, ante.
 3 *City of London Building Society v Flegg* [1988] AC 54, [1987] 3 All ER 435; p. 820, post.

husband who becomes the sole proprietor.[4] In this case, the husband should apply for a restriction to be entered on the register. If he does not, the wife may do so, if the land certificate is produced at the Registry or is already on deposit there, for instance, because there is a registered charge;[5] otherwise she may enter a caution.[6] Failing an entry on the register, a purchaser takes free from the interests of the beneficiaries under the trust, unless they are overriding under section 70 (1) (*g*) of the Land Registration Act 1925.[7] It has been held by the House of Lords that a beneficial interest under a trust for sale is an interest subsisting in reference to registered land for the purpose of paragraph (*g*), and is therefore capable of being an overriding interest if the owner of it is in actual occupation of the property.[8] Thus a wife in such a case may assert her interest in the home against a purchaser although not against a mortgagee who financed the original acquisition, as the legal owner's title was acquired subject to the mortgage.[9] A wife in occupation may be able to assert her interest against a later mortgagee by relying on section 70 (1) (*g*).[10] An interest under a settlement, however, is apparently excluded from paragraph (*g*) by the Act;[11] but to make a distinction between these two interests is surprising, and has been described as an anomalous and probably accidental result.[12]

As we have seen, a spouse's right of occupation under the Matrimonial Homes Act 1983[13] may be protected by the entry of a notice. This right of occupation is not an overriding interest.[14]

---

4   P. 237. See Ruoff and Roper, chapter 39, especially para. 39–04. Where there is a sole trustee the position in unregistered land is governed by the doctrine of notice. It is likely that a wife's occupation would give constructive notice: *Williams and Glyn's Bank Ltd v Boland*, supra; doubting *Caunce v Caunce* [1969] 1 WLR 286, [1969] 1 All ER 722; p. 237, n. 16, ante, p. 791, post; *Kingsnorth Trust Ltd v Tizard* [1986] 1 WLR 783; [1986] 2 All ER 54; p. 63, n. 4, ante.

5   P. 731, post.

6   *Elias v Mitchell* [1972] Ch 652, [1972] 2 All ER 153; (1973) 117 SJ 115, 136 (G. Miller); LRA 1925, s. 54 (1) proviso. See p. 103, post. The Law Commission recommends that production of the land certificate should not be necessary to support a restriction: Third Report on Land Registration, C. Minor Interests 1987 (Law Com No. 158, HC 269), para. 4.53, 4.54.

7   P. 103, ante.

8   *Williams and Glyn's Bank Ltd v Boland*, supra. This conclusion is now favoured by the Law Commission: Third Report on Land Registration, A. Overriding Interests 1987 (Law Com No. 158, HC 269), paras. 2.54–2.70; departing from earlier recommendations in 1978 (Law Com No. 86) and 1982 (Law Com No. 115).

9   *Abbey National Building Society v Cann* [1991] 1 AC 56, [1990] 1 All ER 1085.

10 Unless she knew about the proposed mortgage and did not reveal her interest to the mortgagee: *Paddington Building Society v Mendelsohn* (1985) 50 P & CR 244; *Bristol and West Building Society v Henning* [1985] 1 WLR 778, [1985] 2 All ER 606; *Equity and Law Home Loans Ltd v Prestidge* [1992] 1 WLR 137, [1992] 1 All ER 909 (remortgage); M & B p. 131, n. 6; [1992] CLJ 223 (M. Dixon); [1992] Conv 206 (M. P. Thompson); (1992) 108 LQR 371 (R. J. Smith).

11 LRA 1925, s. 86 (2); p. 202, n. 13, ante.

12 (1958) 22 Conv (NS) 14 at 24 (F. R. Crane). The Law Commission recommends that interests under settlements should be capable of being overriding interests: Third Report on Land Registration, A. Overriding Interests 1987 (Law Com No. 158, HC 269), para. 2.69.

13 S. 2 (8). Production of the land certificate is not required for the entry of such a notice; p. 242, n. 15, ante.

14 P. 242, ante.

Chapter 11

Entailed interests

SUMMARY

SECTION I HISTORY

A. CONDITIONAL FEE

The estate known to the common law as the conditional fee was the precursor of the estate tail. About the year 1200 it was becoming a common practice to limit lands to a man and a special or restricted class of his heirs, as for instance:

> to a man and "the heirs of his body"; or
> to a husband and wife and the heirs springing from their marriage; or
> to a woman and the heirs of her body—a form of gift that was called a *maritagium*.[1]

As the object of such a gift was to provide for a man's descendants, it was understood that if the donee or one of his issue to whom the land descended died without leaving any heirs of the class specified in the instrument of creation, the estate, being no longer required for the maintenance of the family, should revert to the donor, and should not, like a fee simple, pass to the general heirs of the donee.[2] The courts, however, animated probably by a desire to render land freely alienable and to this end to prevent it from being irrevocably ear-marked for a particular family, took an entirely different view of the matter, for they held that if a grant were made to A and

---

1 Holdsworth, *History of English Law*, vol. iii. pp. 74, 111; Plucknett, *Legislation of Edward I*, pp. 125–131.
2 If the gift took the form of what was called *liberum maritagium*, the rule was that after the land had descended three times there should no longer be any reverter to the donor and his heirs. Thus, the third heir became entitled in fee simple; Plucknett, pp. 126–9.

the heirs of his body, or to him and any similarly restricted class of heirs, A could make an out-and-out alienation of his estate, binding on his own heirs and on the donor, as soon as a child of the class indicated was born to him. They said that the effect of such a gift was to confer upon A a conditional fee, that is to say, an absolute fee simple, conditional however upon the birth of issue capable of inheriting the estate according to the terms of the original gift. When once the condition was satisfied, even though the child died the next minute, A was in as favourable a position as if the lands had originally been granted to him in fee simple, for at common law a condition once performed is utterly gone; but if the condition was not fulfilled by the birth of issue, then on A's death the estate reverted to the donor and his heirs.[3]

B. STATUTE DE DONIS 1285

This rule, which meant in effect that the donee could alienate the land and thus defeat both the right of his issue to succeed to the estate and the right of the donor to take the estate back if issue already born became extinct, was not popular. As early as 1258 there was an outcry against a doctrine that ran so contrary to the expressed intention of donors, and the result of this feeling was the passing in 1285 of the famous statute *De Donis Conditionalibus*.[4] This enacted that the intention of the donor according as it was manifestly expressed in the original gift, should thenceforth be observed, so that those to whom the land was given should have no power to alienate it, but that it should pass to their issue, or to the giver or his heirs if such issue failed, either by an absolute default of issue or, after the birth of issue, by its subsequent extinction.[5]

The result of this statute was the appearance of a new kind of fee or inheritable estate, called a fee tail, or in Latin *feodum talliatum*, and so called because the quantum of the estate was "cut down" in the sense that, unlike the case of the fee simple, the right to inherit was restricted to the class of heirs specially mentioned in the gift, and was not available to the heirs-general of the donee.[6]

The land could not be disposed of by the tenant in tail, it could not be seized in satisfaction of his debts after it had come into the hands of his successors, and it was not forfeitable for treason or felony—a fact which, in those disturbed times, was regarded by the Crown as a serious defect.[7]

Special remedies were given to the issue and to the donor for the recovery of the land in case the form of the original gift was not observed, and these were called respectively the *writ of formedon in the descender* and the *writ of formedon in the reverter*.[8]

There was thus set up an entailed interest in the true and proper sense of that term, that is to say, an interest in land that was bound to descend from one generation to another to the issue of the tenant, and which could not by any means whatsoever be removed from the family so long as any lineal heirs

3 Pollock and Maitland, *History of English Law* (2nd edn), vol. ii. pp. 16–19; Co Litt 19*a*; Challis, *Law of Real Property* (3rd edn), pp. 263–8.
4 Statute of Westminster II (1285), set out in full, Digby, *History of the Law of Real Property*, p. 226.
5 See Challis, *Law of Real Property* (3rd edn), p. 228.
6 Litt, s. 18; Challis, p. 60.
7 First Report of Real Property Commission, 1829, p. 22.
8 Holdsworth, *History of English Law*, vol. ii. p. 350.

of the class specified were in existence. It was an unbarrable entail, since neither the right of the issue to succeed, nor the right of the donor and his heirs to take on failure of issue, could be barred or taken away.[9] This state of affairs continued for some 200 years after the Statute *De Donis*, but the statute, instead of being a blessing calculated to ensure the stability of families, proved to be one of the most mischievous institutions in the realm. Blackstone has described some of its effects:[10]

> Children grew disobedient when they knew they could not be set aside; farmers were ousted of their leases made by tenants in tail; for, if such leases had been valid, then, under colour of long leases, the issue might have been virtually disinherited; creditors were defrauded of their debts, for if tenant in tail could have charged his estate with their payment, he might also have defeated his issue, by mortgaging it for as much as it was worth; innumerable latent entails were produced to deprive purchasers of the lands they had fairly bought, of suits in consequence of which our ancient books are full; and treasons were encouraged, as estates tail were not liable to forfeiture longer than for the tenant's life. So that they were justly branded as the source of new contentions and mischiefs unknown to the common law, and almost universally considered as the common grievance of the realm. But as the nobility were always fond of this statute, because it preserved their family estates from forfeiture, there was little hope of procuring repeal by the legislature.

C. METHODS OF BARRING FEE TAIL

Although the legislature did not step in to remedy a grievance that appears to have borne so heavily upon the community, the ingenuity of lawyers finally—and at least as early as 1472—contrived to discover means whereby estates tail could be barred and converted into estates in fee simple, free from the succession rights of heirs and from the rights of those persons who were entitled to take upon a failure or extinction of heirs. The actual methods invented are now a matter of history, and it must suffice here to state their names and their general effect.

(1) COMMON RECOVERY

The most usual method was *to suffer a common recovery*. In the earliest days of its history a common recovery was a collusive real action which a collaborator (called the *demandant*) brought against the tenant in tail for the recovery of the land entailed. The tenant in tail did not raise a substantial plea to the claim preferred against him, but stated, contrary to the truth, that he had obtained the land by conveyance from one X, who, at the time of the conveyance, had warranted for himself and his heirs that the title granted to the tenant in tail was a good one. X, who was an accomplice of the parties, admitted the warranty by disappearing from court. The court thereupon proceeded to deliver judgment, that on the one hand the demandant should recover the entailed lands for an estate in fee simple, and that on the other hand the tenant in tail should recover lands of equal value from X.

9 This apparently was not the intention of the draftsman of the statute. What was intended was that the land should be inalienable only until the third heir had entered, after which it could be alienated out of the family: Plucknett, *Legislation of Edward I*, pp. 131–5.
10 *Commentaries*, vol. ii. p. 116.

Now the effect of this collusive action was to defeat the rights both of the tenant's issue and of the persons entitled on failure of issue, because if lands of equal value had actually been recovered from X, which they never were, they would have replaced the original entailed estate and would have descended in the same manner. Ostensibly this was so, but none of the untrue allegations made in the course of the proceedings was traversable, and therefore all that the persons entitled after the death of the tenant acquired was a judgment enforceable against a man of straw. The court was not prepared to tolerate a plea that a judgment, solemnly pronounced, was in effect nugatory.[11]

After delivery of judgment the demandant would convey either the fee simple or its value to the former tenant in tail.

(2) FINE

The second method was to levy a fine. A fine, which from the earliest times had been regarded as the most sacred and efficacious form of conveyance known to the law,[12] was in substance a conveyance of land but in form an action.[13] It was an amicable composition or agreement of an action, made with the leave of the court, whereby the lands in question were acknowledged to belong to one of the parties, and it derived its name from the fact that it put an end (Lat. *finis*) to the action.[14] One of the purposes for which it was used was to bar an estate tail. The tenant in tail covenanted to sell the fee simple to a collaborator, and when he was sued by the latter in an action of covenant he decided to capitulate, and with the leave of the court a concord was drawn up acknowledging that the lands belonged to the plaintiff.

From one point of view the levying of a fine was not so effective as the suffering of a recovery, since it barred the rights only of the tenant's issue (thus setting up what is called a "base fee"), while a recovery barred not only the issue, but also everybody who became entitled to the estate on failure of issue. On the other hand, a fine, which was a personal action, enabled a tenant in tail who was not for the moment tenant in possession, e.g.:

where there was a grant to A for life and after his death to B in tail,

to bar his own issue without the necessity of obtaining the possessor's collaboration. In such circumstances, a common recovery was impossible unless the aid of the tenant for life, A, was obtained, because the proceedings reproduced the stages of a genuine action, and one of the fundamental rules of procedure was that a real action could be brought only against the person actually seised of the land.

(3) FINES AND RECOVERIES ACT 1833

Recoveries and fines, which even in their origin were collusive actions, gradually became wholly fictitious. Only formal matters were transacted in

---

11 For a full account see Blackstone, vol. ii. p. 357 et seq; Cruise, *Digest* Tit. xxxvi; Burton, *Real Property* (8th edn), paras. 682–697; Pollock, *The Land Laws*, pp. 80–9; Digby, *History of the Law of Real Property*, pp. 251–4; First Report of Real Property Commissioners, 1829, pp. 21–3; Holdsworth, *History of English Law*, vol. iii. pp. 118 et seq; Simpson, *A History of the Land Law* (2nd edn), pp. 126 et seq.

12 Holdsworth, *History of English Law*, vol. iii. p. 239.

13 Pollock and Maitland, *History of English Law* (2nd edn), vol. ii. p. 94.

14 Blackstone, vol. ii. p. 349; Challis, *Law of Real Property* (3rd edn), p. 304.

court. If a tenant in tail desired to bar his entail, all that he did was to instruct his solicitor to suffer a common recovery. But the solicitor, in carrying out the instructions, did not simply frame a deed expressing the tenant's intention, but was obliged to prepare a long and complicated document that recited all the stages and events of an action which was supposed, contrary to fact, to have been litigated. Moreover, the fees that would have been payable had the action been actually brought were still payable. The result was that to convert a fee tail into a fee simple was a tedious and expensive transaction, and one which, owing to the complicated and exceedingly difficult state of the law, required an expert for its completion, and even then often failed to produce a sound title. The Real Property Commissioners, in their Report issued in 1829, stated:

> there is no object, however complicated, that could not be effected by a simple instrument, expressing in clear and intelligible language the intentions of the parties.

The result of their recommendations was the passing of the Fines and Recoveries Act 1833, which abolished both recoveries and fines, and introduced a simple and straightforward method by which an estate tail might be barred.[15]

SECTION II CREATION OF ENTAILED INTERESTS

We have already seen that an entailed interest is one that is given to a person and after his death to a specified class of that person's heirs. The different classes of entailed interests depend upon the terms of the instrument of gift and vary according as the estate is descendible to the heirs of the donee by any spouse or by a particular spouse, and also according as the heirs are restricted as to sex or not.

A. CLASSES OF ENTAILED INTERESTS

(1) INTERESTS IN TAIL GENERAL

An interest in tail general is the widest type of entailed interest. Such an interest arises when land is limited to:

A and the heirs of his body begotten,

without any restriction either as to the wife upon whose body the heirs are to be begotten, or as to the sex of the heirs who are to take.[16] It matters not how many times A marries, for any child by any wife is eligible to succeed. If the entailed interest is not barred by the tenant during his lifetime nor disposed of by his will it still descends to his lineal descendants according to the old canons of descent which were formerly applicable to all inheritable fees,[17] but which were abolished by the Administration of Estates Act 1925, so far as regards the fee simple.

So where there is an interest in tail general limited to:

15 P. 259, post.
16 Litt, ss. 14, 15; Blackstone, vol. ii. p. 113.
17 LPA 1925, s. 130 (4). The canons are those that affected the descent of a fee simple before 1926 except those that relate to ancestors and collaterals; pp. 871–5, post.

A and the heirs of his body,

and A dies intestate having failed to bar the entail, his eldest son by his first wife will take first. If the eldest son has predeceased A leaving no children, the second son of A, or such son's representative if he is dead, will take, and so on through the sons in the order of their seniority. Failing sons or children of sons, the daughters of A will share equally as coparceners.[18]

(a) Curtesy

Before 1926 a husband was entitled in certain circumstances to a life interest in the whole of the land of which the wife died seised in fee simple or in tail. He became what was called a "tenant by the curtesy".[19] Curtesy has been abolished with regard to all interests except an entailed interest,[20] and therefore the subject can only now be of importance when a *female tenant in tail* dies intestate.

(b) Restriction as to sex

An interest in tail general may be restricted as to sex:

(i) In tail male general This arises where lands are limited to

A and the heirs *male* of his body begotten,

the factor in which this species of estate differs from an interest in tail general being that only male heirs are to succeed.[1] Sons by any wife are capable of inheriting, and so are any other male issue claiming continuously through male issue, but daughters and their issue, whether male or female, can never inherit.

(ii) In tail female general This is analogous to the last interest except that the only heirs entitled to take are females. Though this is a possible form of limitation, it never arises in practice.[2]

(2) INTERESTS IN TAIL SPECIAL

The characteristic of the remaining entailed interests is that by the words of the instrument of creation their descent is restricted to the heirs of the body of two specified persons, and not to the heirs of one, as in the cases described above. Such an estate may be limited either to one donee, e.g.:

to H and the heirs begotten by him on the body of W,

or to two donees, e.g.:

to H and W and the heirs of their two bodies begotten.[3]

In both cases it will be seen that it is not the heirs of H by any wife who

---

18 P. 222, ante.
19 Or more particularly, by the Curtesie of England: Co Litt 35.
20 AEA 1925, s. 45 (1) (*b*); LPA 1925, s. 130 (4). But curtesy in respect of a fee simple may still, though rarely, arise under AEA 1925, s. 51 (2). This provides that the old rules of descent shall apply to realty (excluding chattels real), to which a lunatic, living on 1 January 1926 and dying after that date without having recovered testamentary capacity, is entitled.
1 Litt s. 2; Blackstone, vol. ii. p. 114.
2 Co Litt 25*a*; Hargrave's note.
3 Litt s. 16; *Preston on Estates*, vol. ii. p. 413.

are capable of inheriting the interest, but only the children and their issue who can trace their descent from the particular wife W. If the limitation is to:

H and the heirs begotten by him on the body of his wife W,

H has an interest in tail special and the wife has nothing.[4] But the effect of a limitation to H and W and the heirs of their two bodies begotten varies according to the relative positions of H and W. If W is the wife of H or a person whom he may lawfully marry, the effect is to vest a joint interest in tail special in H and W;[5] but if H and W are persons who may not lawfully intermarry, by reason, for instance, of consanguinity, the limitation makes them joint tenants for life with separate inheritances.[6] That means that if H dies first and has issue, W becomes sole tenant for life, but that on the death of W the issue of H take one half and the issue of W the other half as tenants in common in tail.[7] The result will be the same if, though capable of intermarrying, H and W do not actually intermarry.

After what has been said it will be sufficient to give the appropriate words of limitation for granting the remaining species of entailed interests:

(a) In tail male special

Grant to:

A and his heirs male which he shall beget on the body of his wife X;

or to:

A and X and the heirs male of their two bodies begotten.[8]

(b) In tail female special

This arises from the same limitation as that just described, with the substitution of female for male.[9]

(3) INTERESTS IN TAIL AFTER POSSIBILITY OF ISSUE EXTINCT

An entailed interest special may by implication of law give rise to what is called an entailed interest after possibility of issue extinct. If lands are given to a man and his wife, or to the man or to the wife solely, in special tail, and one of them, or the designated spouse, dies before issue has been born, the survivor is termed a *tenant in tail after possibility*; and likewise if one dies leaving issue, but the other survives the issue.[10] In both these cases it will be seen that, owing to the premature death of one of the persons from whose body the appropriate heirs are to proceed, it is impossible that any person should become entitled to succeed to the interest in accordance with the terms of the original gift. The possibility of the right class of heirs coming into being no longer exists, and therefore the survivor is said to be a tenant after possibility. Such a person is virtually in the position of a tenant for life

4 Litt s. 29.
5 Co Litt 20*b*; 25*b*.
6 Litt 283; Preston, vol. ii. p. 417.
7 Co Litt 182*a*.
8 Litt 25.
9 For the whole of this section, see Challis, *Law of Real Property* (3rd edn), pp. 290–5.
10 Litt 32.

and he is not entitled to bar the entail.[11] He is given the statutory powers of a tenant for life by the Settled Land Act 1925.[12]

B. WORDS OF LIMITATION

We have now to consider what words of limitation must be used in order to create an entailed interest. Owing to the way in which the matter was dealt with by the Law of Property Act 1925, it is unfortunately necessary to discuss the rules which obtained under the previous law. The examples that have been given above of the various classes of entailed interests indicate the general nature of the proper words of limitation, and a short treatment of the subject will suffice here.

(1) WORDS OF LIMITATION BEFORE 1926

(a) Creation by deed

The first point is to ascertain the proper words of limitation necessary before 1926 for the creation of an entailed interest by *deed*.

(i) Word "heirs"

The requirement of common law here was that the word *heirs* must be used and not such analogous expressions as *seed, offspring, descendants, issue* and so on.[13] The effect of a grant, for example, to "A and his issue" was to confer upon A a mere life estate.

(ii) Words of procreation

The next requirement was that some expression denoting that the inheritance was to pass to the direct descendants of A should be used, and the surest phrase for this purpose was *of his body*. A grant to "A and the heirs of his body" always conferred an entailed interest on A, but common law, though insisting upon the use of the word *heirs*, was not so exacting with regard to this second requirement, and was satisfied with any words which expressly or by implication showed that the heirs were to issue from the body of A. Thus such expression as:

> of his flesh,
> from him proceeding, or
> which he shall beget of his wife,

were sufficient for the purpose.[14]

Before 1 January 1882, if the appropriate words of limitation as set out above were not adopted in a deed, the result was to confer a life estate upon the grantee, but the Conveyancing Act of 1881[15] provided that in deeds executed after that date it should be sufficient to use the words *in tail* instead

11 Fines and Recoveries Act 1833, s. 18; see p. 263, post.
12 SLA 1925, s. 20 (1) (i) *Hambro v The Duke of Marlborough* (1994) Times, 25 March; pp 185, 191, ante.
13 Co Litt 20*a*, *b*; Blackstone, vol. ii. p. 115.
14 Co Litt 20*b*.
15 S. 51.

of *heirs of the body*, and the words *in tail male* or *in tail female* instead of *heirs male* or *heirs female* of the body.[16]

(b) Creation by will

Greater latitude of terminology was, however, open to testators. It is more difficult to lay down hard and fast rules as to what words would, and what words would not, have created a certain interest when they were used in a testamentary as distinct from an *inter vivos* instrument, because the general principle of construction for wills is that the intention of the testator must be ascertained and given effect to, no matter what language he may have adopted. But at any rate it is clear that less formal language would create an entailed interest in a will than in a deed, and in fact any expressions that indicated an intention to give the devisee an estate of inheritance, descendible to his lineal as distinct from his collateral heirs, conferred an entailed interest upon him.[17]

Thus devises to:

A and his seed,[18]
A and his offspring,[19]
A and his family according to seniority,[20]
A and his issue,[1]
A and his posterity,[2]

have all, at one time or another, been held capable of passing an entailed interest when such a construction was consistent with the intention of the testator.

(c) Executory instruments

The same rule of construction was applied in the case of executory instruments *inter vivos*, that is, in instruments which do not finally express the limitations in technical language, but indicate their general nature and leave the settlor's intention to be carried out by apt phraseology. What are called "marriage articles" form the commonest example of an executory instrument. They constitute a contract by which an intending husband and wife specify in general the terms upon which they are willing to enter into a marriage settlement. Thus, if marriage articles provide for the limitation of an interest to the "issue" of the husband and wife, the presumed intention will be carried out in the formal settlement by the grant of an entailed interest to the first son of the marriage, with remainders in tail to the other children.[3]

(d) The rule in *Wild's Case*

A devise "to A and his children" requires particular attention because of the Rule in *Wild's Case*[4] laid down in 1599.[5] The rule was that where realty was

16 For criticism, see Challis, *Law of Real Property* (3rd edn), pp. 297–8.
17 *Jarman on Wills* (8th edn), p. 1825.
18 Co Litt 9*b*.
19 *Young v Davies* (1863) 2 Drew & Sm 167.
20 *Lucas v Goldsmid* (1861) 29 Beav 657.
 1 *Oxford University v Clifton* (1759) 1 Eden 473.
 2 *Wild's Case* (1599) 6 Co Rep 16*b*.
 3 *A-G v Bamfield* (1703) 2 Freem Ch 268.
 4 (1599) 6 Co 16*b*.
 5 See p. 256, n. 19, post.

devised to "A and his children", and A had no child *at the time of the devise*, the word children was prima facie construed as a word of limitation, with the result that A acquired an estate tail.

There was some justification for this. The testator clearly intended children to take in any event, but since they were not in existence they could take nothing except through A and he could transmit to them nothing unless he was given an estate of inheritance.[6]

The rule, however, was not inflexible and it was disregarded by the courts where it would operate to defeat the intention of the testator as gathered from other passages in the will.[7]

(2) WORDS OF LIMITATION AFTER 1925

(a) Formal words

We are now left with this question: what words are necessary and sufficient to create an entailed interest in the case of a deed or will that comes into operation after 1925? Section 130 (1) of the Law of Property Act 1925 enacts as follows:

> An interest in tail ... (in this Act referred to as "an entailed interest") may be created by way of trust in any property, real or personal, but only by the like expressions as those by which before [1926] a similar estate tail could have been created by deed (not being an executory instrument) in freehold land.

The result is that the law on the subject is more inflexible now than it was before 1926. The strict requirements of the common law applicable to deeds have been extended to wills. Thus, in both instruments the limitation must be to "A in tail", or to "A and the heirs of his body", except that in the last case any expressions will suffice that without expressly saying "of the body" indicate that the heirs are to issue from the body of A. The only exception to this rule is that a direction that personal property shall be enjoyed with land in which an entailed interest has already been created is sufficient to create a corresponding entailed interest in the personal property.[8]

On the other hand, informal expressions contained in the instrument which would not have been sufficient in a deed before 1926 to create an entailed interest, though they would have been sufficient in a will or executory instrument, no longer suffice to create an entailed interest.[9] If, for instance, a testator who dies after 1925 devises land to "A and his issue", an interest in tail does not pass to A.

(b) Informal words

The question that then arises is—what interest does pass to A when informal expressions such as "issue", "seed", "descendants" or "children" are contained in a conveyance or in a devise of land?[10] The Act purports to provide an answer in section 130 (2):

> Expressions contained in an instrument coming into operation after [1925], which, in a will, or executory instrument coming into operation before [1926], would have

---

6 *Radcliffe v Buckley* (1804) 10 Ves 195 at 202, per Sir WILLIAM GRANT MR.
7 *Byng v Byng* (1862) 10 HL Cas 171 at 178; *Grieve v Grieve* (1867) LR 4 Eq 180.
8 LPA 1925, s. 130 (3).
9 *Re Brownlie* [1938] 4 All ER 54.
10 See (1938) 6 CLJ 67 (S. J. Bailey); (1947) 9 CLJ 46 (R. E. Megarry); 185 (S. J. Bailey); 190 (J. H. C. Morris).

created an entailed interest in freehold land, but would not have been effectual for that purpose in a deed not being an executory instrument, shall ... operate in equity, in regard to property real or personal, to create absolute, fee simple or other interests corresponding to those which, if the property affected had been personal estate, would have been created therein by similar expressions before [1926].

The first point to notice is that this sub-section is not concerned with those formal expressions that would have been effectual in a deed before 1926 to create an estate tail in land. A gift of personalty to A and the heirs of his body or to A in tail formerly gave A the absolute ownership of the property,[11] but now, by virtue of section 130 (1),[12] it gives him an entailed interest. What we are concerned with here are informal expressions, and we are told that if they appear in a grant or a devise of land operating after 1925, the donee is to acquire in the land the interest that he would have acquired in personalty had the same expression been contained in a gift of personalty. The question then is, what interest passes under a gift of personalty, in the following typical cases:

To A and his issue;
To A for life and then to his issue;
To A and his descendants;
To A and his children.

Find this and we know what interest is taken if the same expressions are adopted in a grant or devise of land.

The primary difficulty is that, since the effect of such informal expressions has always varied according as they appear in deeds or in wills, it is not obvious whether the rules for deeds or for wills are to be adopted. Presumably the solution is that a devise containing informal expressions is to have the effect that has always been allowed to a bequest containing the like expressions, and that a grant *inter vivos* is to have the effect that has always been attributed to a corresponding gift by deed of personalty.

Let us examine only *bequests* of personalty, for it is unlikely in practice that any but formal expressions will be found in a conveyance *inter vivos* of land.[13] It must be realized at once, however, that no unqualified rule can be laid down with regard to the quantum of interest that passes under this or that expression, for since the object in each case is to ascertain and to implement the intention of the testator, what always has to be done is to construe the will as a whole. Strictly speaking, the only correct answer to make to the question, "What interest is taken under a gift of personalty to A and his issue?" is, "That interest which the testator intended to give". Certain canons of construction have, however, become established that cover most of the expressions found in practice.

(i) To A and his issue The primary canon of construction is that a gift of personalty *to A and his issue* shows an intention on the part of the testator that the issue alive when the will comes into operation shall take the property jointly with A.[14]

11 *Chatham v Tothill* (1771) 7 Bro PC 453; *Portman v Viscount Portman* [1922] 2 AC 473; Hawkins and Ryder, *Construction of Wills*, pp. 254–5.
12 P. 254, ante.
13 For the effect of gifts by deed containing informal expressions, see (1938) 6 CLJ p. 81.
14 *Re Hammond* [1924] 2 Ch 276.

Thus, if the gift be immediate, A and his issue (if any) living at the testator's death would take in joint tenancy; and if the gift be deferred, issue subsequently born before the period of distribution would be admitted along with them; and if no issue had come into existence before the period of distribution, A would take the whole.[15]

(ii) To A for life and then to his issue Again, if there is a bequest to A for life and after his death to his issue, A takes merely a life interest and the property is ultimately divided among the issue born during his life.[16]

Nevertheless this principle of construction which admits issue as beneficiaries in the instances given is displaced if it appears from the will as a whole that the testator meant to make A sole and absolute owner.

(iii) To A and his descendants The word "issue" has consistently been held to mean prima facie descendants of every degree,[17] and it therefore seems to follow that a gift of personalty *to A and his descendants* is construed, in the absence of a contrary intention, in the same way as a gift to A and his issue.[18] The descendants alive at the death of the testator take the absolute ownership jointly with A.

(iv) To A and his children A gift of personalty *to A and his children* is prima facie regarded as a gift to A and the children concurrently, so that A and his children alive at the testator's death take the property as joint tenants, or, if there are no children living at that time, A takes the whole absolutely.[19]

(3) RULE IN SHELLEY'S CASE

Finally, we must mention briefly the Rule in *Shelley's Case*,[20] which, though it has been abolished by the Law of Property Act 1925,[1] still applies to instruments coming into operation before 1926.[2]

(a) Statement of the rule

This rule, which was a rule of law applicable to deeds and to wills, ordained that if in the same instrument an estate of *freehold* was limited to A, with remainder, either immediately or after the limitation of an intervening estate, *to the heirs* or *to the heirs of the body* of A, the remainder, though importing an independent gift to the heirs as original takers, conferred the fee simple in the first case, and the fee tail in the second case, upon A, the ancestor.[3] Thus the effect of a grant:

to A for life, remainder to his heirs,

was to give A the fee simple; and the effect of a grant:

15 *Hawkins on Wills* (3rd edn), pp. 241–2; the words quoted are those of Hawkins himself.
16 *Knight v Ellis* (1789) 2 Bro CC 570; *Jarman on Wills* (6th edn), p. 1200.
17 Hawkins and Ryder, *Construction of Wills*, p. 148.
18 [1938] 6 CLJ p. 75.
19 Hawkins and Ryder, pp. 260–2. The rule in *Wild's Case* as stated above, p. 253 never applied to personalty.
20 See Challis, *Law of Real Property* (3rd edn), pp. 152 et seq; Cheshire, 11th edn of this book, pp. 198–202; [1981] Conv 128 (J. S. Coote).
 1 S. 131.
 2 *Re Routledge* [1942] Ch 457, [1942] 2 All ER 418 (testator died in 1874); *Re Williams* [1952] Ch 828, [1952] 2 All ER 502 (testator died in 1921).
 3 Hayes, *Introduction to Conveyancing*, vol. i. p. 542; *Preston on Estates*, vol. i. pp. 263–4.

to A for life, remainder to the heirs of his body,

was to give A an estate tail.

The interest which in terms was given to the heirs and which in most cases the donor, especially when he was a testator, meant the heirs to have, was in the eye of the law given to A. So A could dispose of the estate and thereby defeat his heir, who would take only if A died intestate still owning the estate.

Thus the operation of the rule was two-fold: it denied to a remainder the effect of a gift to the "heirs", and it attributed to the remainder the effect of a gift to A.[4] In fact, the legal effect of such a limitation was the direct opposite of what would naturally be expected, and it nearly always operated to defeat the intention of a testator.[5]

Another and more technical way of stating the rule is as follows:

> Where the ancestor by any gift or conveyance takes an estate of freehold, and in the same gift or conveyance an estate is limited, either mediately or immediately to his heirs, in fee or in tail, in such cases "the heirs" are words of limitation of the estate and not words of purchase.

We have already considered the distinction between words of limitation and words of purchase.[6] Thus, if land was given:

to A for life, remainder to the heirs of his body,

what the Rule in *Shelley's Case* declared was that the words "heirs of his body" were not words of purchase pointing out the heir as a person entitled to a definite interest in the land, but were words of limitation employed to mark out the extent of the interest given to A. Had the words "heirs of his body" been regarded as words of purchase, they would have indicated that the estate was given to the person who was found to be heir on the death of A. In other words, this person would have claimed the estate as having been given to him by the original conveyance. The result, in fact, was the same as if the grant had been:

to A and the heirs of his body,

but it is essential to notice that the Rule in *Shelley's Case* operated only where there were in terms two estates given, i.e. a freehold to the ancestor, A, and then a remainder to the heirs, e.g.:

to A for life and after his death to the heirs of his body.

It is true that a limitation *to A and his heirs* or *to A and the heirs of his body* gives A a fee simple in the first case and a fee tail in the second case, but these results do not ensue from *Shelley's Case*. The law had been so established at a far earlier date.[7]

(b) Abolition of the rule

The Rule in *Shelley's Case* was abolished by section 131 of the Law of Property Act 1925 for all instruments coming into operation after 1925. Accordingly, where there is a limitation to:

4 Hayes, *Introduction to Conveyancing*, vol. i. p. 534.
5 For the feudal reasons for this rule, see *Van Grutten v Foxwell* [1897] AC 658 at 668.
6 P. 158, ante.
7 If, for example, lands had been given "to W and her heirs for her and their use and benefit absolutely and for ever", the Rule in *Shelley's Case* would not have applied: *Re McElligott* [1944] Ch 216, [1944] 1 All ER 441; (1938) 54 LQR 70 (A. D. Hargreaves).

A for life and then to his heirs; or to
A for life and then to the heirs of his body,

the effect is to restrict A's interest to a life interest, and to appropriate a definite interest to the heir or to the heir of the body of A. The heir is ascertained in accordance with the canons of descent that obtained before 1926,[8] and he takes the interest by way of purchase. What interest he takes is perhaps a little doubtful, but presumably in all cases he takes the fee simple or otherwise the whole interest which the donor had power to convey, unless a contrary intention appears in the deed or will.[9]

The result, then, of the abolition of the Rule in *Shelley's Case* upon the expressions which are now essential to create an entailed interest, seems to be this:

(i)   A gift to A for life, remainder to the heirs of his body will no longer vest an entailed interest in A, despite the enactment that such an interest may be created by the like expressions as those by which before 1 January 1926 a similar estate tail could have been created by deed;[10]

(ii) A gift to A for life, remainder to the heirs of his body will be effectual to vest a definite interest in the *heir*, although such would not have been the result of a similar conveyance by deed under the old law.

SECTION III ENTAILED INTERESTS AFTER 1925

An entailed interest can no longer subsist as a legal estate. It is necessarily an equitable interest[11] and the only possible methods by which it can be created are (a) a settlement by deed or will, and (b) an agreement for a settlement in which the trusts upon which the land is to be held are sufficiently declared.[12]

A. ENTAILED INTERESTS MAY BE CREATED IN ANY FORM OF PROPERTY

(1) PERSONALTY

One of the radical changes introduced by the Law of Property Act 1925 is that any form of property, whether real or personal, may be limited in tail. At common law an estate tail could not be carved out of chattels or other personal property, but it appeared to the legislature that there was no reason why entailed interests should not be allowed in the case of such forms of property as stocks and shares and long leaseholds. Section 130 (1), therefore, provided that:

an interest in tail or in tail male or in tail female or in tail special (in this Act referred to as "an entailed interest") may be created by way of trust in any property,

8   Pp. 871–5, post.
9   LPA 1925, s. 60 (1); Wills Act 1837, s. 28; pp. 159–60, ante. The rule before the Wills Act 1837 was that a devise to the *heirs of the body* of a person conferred an estate tail (*Mandeville's Case* (1328) Co Litt 26b), and the question whether the fee simple could pass under s. 28 of the Wills Act does not seem to have arisen.
10 P. 254, ante.
11 LPA 1925, ss. 1, 130.
12 Ibid., s. 130 (6).

real or personal, but only by the like expressions as those by which before the commencement of this Act a similar estate tail could have been created by deed (not being an executory instrument) in freehold land, and with the like results, including the right to bar the entail either absolutely or so as to create an interest equivalent to a base fee, and accordingly all statutory provisions relating to estates tail in real property shall apply to entailed interests in personal property.[13]

One important effect of this subsection is that beneficial interests under a trust for sale, which, as we have seen, by the doctrine of conversion, are interests in personalty, may now be entailed.[14] Further an entail becomes subject to all rules, whether at common law or in equity, which governed and still govern estates tail in realty.[15]

(2) HEIRLOOMS

Before the Act it sometimes happened that when freeholds were limited by settlement to a series of legal tenants for life and in tail, it was desired to give the persons who for the time being were entitled to the land the enjoyment of certain family heirlooms such as valuable pictures and the like. As the heirlooms, being chattels, could not be carved into estates in the same way as the land, the only mode of carrying out the intention was to vest them in trustees upon trust that they should go along with the land so far as the rules of law and equity would permit.[16] In such a case law and equity permitted any legal tenant for life of the land for the time being to have an equitable life interest in the heirlooms, but required that the absolute ownership should vest in the first person to get an estate tail in the land. The Act now provides that when personal estate is directed to be held upon trusts corresponding with the trusts of land in which an entailed interest has been created, such direction shall create a corresponding entailed interest in the personal property.[17]

B. ENTAILED INTERESTS MAY BE BARRED

The Fines and Recoveries Act 1833, in a general enabling section, provides that every "actual tenant in tail", i.e. the tenant of an entailed interest that has not been barred,[18] whether entitled in possession, remainder, contingency[19] or otherwise shall have full power to dispose of the land for an estate in fee simple or for any lesser estate.[20] This right of the tenant to disentail and so enlarge his equitable interest into a legal fee simple is absolute, and it cannot be restricted by any device on the part of the grantor; so, for instance, a clause inserted in the instrument of creation providing that the interest shall not be barred, or that it shall pass from the owner upon

13 LPA 1925, s. 130 (1). A will is not within this section unless it takes effect after 1925: *Re Hope's Will Trust* [1929] 2 Ch 136.
14 P. 76, ante. See Law of Property (Entailed Interests) Act 1932, s. 1, p. 225, n. 10, ante.
15 *Re Crossley's Settlement Trusts* [1955] Ch 627, [1955] 2 All ER 801.
16 See *Re Morrison's Settlement* [1974] Ch 326, [1973] 3 All ER 1094.
17 LPA 1925, s. 130 (3).
18 Fines and Recoveries Act 1833, s. 1.
19 See, for example, *Re St. Albans' Will Trust* [1963] Ch 365, [1962] 2 All ER 402. Cf *Re Midleton's Will Trusts* [1969] 1 Ch 600, [1967] 2 All ER 402.
20 S. 15.

disentailment, is null and void.[1] The present mode of disentailment, however, falls to be considered under two heads according as the tenant is or is not entitled to actual possession.

(1) WHERE TENANT IN TAIL IS ENTITLED IN POSSESSION

A tenant in tail in possession and of full age may, without the concurrence of any other person, effectually bar the entailed interest and thereby enlarge it into a legal fee simple by adopting any form of conveyance which is sufficient to dispose of a fee simple estate in lands, provided, however, that in the case of an *inter vivos* disentailment the conveyance is effected by deed.[2] So the estate must be barred by a deed, called a disentailing assurance, and no disentailment can be effected by contract.[3]

The effect of a disentailing assurance which enlarges the entailed interest into a fee simple is to defeat entirely the rights both of the tenant's issue and of the persons whose estates are to take effect after the determination or in defeasance of the entailed interest. Suppose, for instance, that:

There is a grant of Blackacre to A in tail, remainder to B in tail, with a proviso that, if A becomes entitled to Whiteacre, his entailed interest in Blackacre shall cease and shall vest in C. If A, before he becomes entitled to Whiteacre, executes a disentailing deed of Blackacre for an estate in fee simple, the result is that he takes a fee simple estate which defeats:

first, his own issue;

secondly, B, who was entitled to take on the determination of the entailed interest; and

finally, C, whose estate was in defeasance of A's entailed interest.[4]

But, on the other hand, no disentailment can defeat interests that rank prior to the entailed interest.[5]

(2) WHERE TENANT IN TAIL IS NOT ENTITLED IN POSSESSION

Under the normal strict settlement, by which land is limited to A for life and then to his sons successively in tail, the eldest son upon birth becomes entitled to an entailed interest in remainder. During the lifetime of his father he is not entitled to possession. The only method under the law prior to the Fines and Recoveries Act by which a tenant placed in this situation could effect a complete disentailment was to suffer a common recovery. If he adopted this course, he obtained an absolute fee simple in remainder which defeated the rights both of his own issue and of the persons who were entitled to take on failure of issue. But the difficulty from his point of view was that a recovery could be suffered only if the collaboration of the tenant in actual possession of the land—that is, in the case of settled land, his father—were obtained. This was a beneficial rule of law, since it enabled the father to influence his son and gave him considerable power to check a disentailment that might be undesirable. The son, however, if he failed to obtain the collaboration of his

---

1 *Dawkins v Lord Penrhyn* (1878) 4 App Cas 51 at 64.
2 Fines and Recoveries Act 1833, ss. 15, 40. For the liability of a solicitor who failed to advise that a tenant in tail in possession should disentail, see *Otter v Church, Adams, Tatham & Co* [1953] Ch 280, [1953] 1 All ER 168.
3 Registration of the deed is no longer required: LPA 1925, s. 133.
4 See *Millbank v Vane* [1893] 3 Ch 79.
5 Fines and Recoveries Act 1833, ss. 15, 19.

father, was free to levy a fine, and though this did not, like a recovery, convert the entailed interest into an absolute fee simple, it did produce the effect of creating in its place what is called a base fee that was unassailable by the issue, but of no avail against the remainderman and reversioner if the issue became extinct. The base fee is described below.[6] When fines and recoveries were abolished in 1833, it seemed desirable to the legislature to retain in a different form this doctrine of the old law of recoveries, and thus to empower the father to check an ill-advised disentailment. To this end a new functionary called "the protector of the settlement" was instituted, in order to prevent a tenant in tail who was entitled only in remainder from effecting a complete disentailment.

The distinction between a tenant in tail *in possession* and a tenant in tail *in remainder*, therefore, is that the former can effect a complete bar without anyone's concurrence, while the latter can effect only a partial disentailment unless he obtains the consent of the protector.

The position at the present day is as follows.

(a) A tenant in tail in remainder can effect a complete bar by executing a disentailing deed with the consent of the protector

The protector of a settlement functions only where there is an entailed interest in remainder, preceded by one or more beneficial life interests. In this case, the Fines and Recoveries Act 1833 provides in effect that the protector shall be the owner of the prior life interest or of the first of several life interests, or who would have been the owner had he not disposed of his beneficial interest.[7] Until there has been a resettlement, there is usually only one life interest under a marriage settlement, namely that given to the husband:

Thus, if there is a limitation to H for life with remainder to his eldest son in tail, the father, H, is the protector, and the son will not be able to acquire a fee simple in remainder, valid against persons whose interests are to take effect after the determination or in defeasance of the entailed interest, unless the consent of his father is expressed in the disentailing assurance itself or in a separate deed executed on or before the day on which the assurance is executed.[8]

The effect of a resettlement, however, is that life interests stand limited first to the father, then to the son, with the result that the son succeeds to the protectorship on the death of his father.

If there is no resettlement, the office of protector ceases on the death of the father, and the son, as tenant in tail in possession, can dispose of the land as his fancy dictates.

---

6 Pp. 262–3, post.
7 Fines and Recoveries Act 1833, s. 22. The Act in s. 32, however, allowed a settlor to appoint any persons up to the number of three to act as protector in place of the person described in the text above. This power of nominating a special protector has been abolished as regards settlements made after 1925: LPA 1925, Sch. 7, repealing Fines and Recoveries Act 1833, s. 32. If there is no protector under s. 22, the court may be protector (s. 33), or the tenant in tail in remainder may disentail without consent: *Re Darnley's Will Trusts* [1970] 1 WLR 405, [1970] 1 All ER 319.
8 Ibid., ss. 34, 42.

(b) A tenant in tail in remainder can effect a partial bar by executing a disentailing deed without the consent of the protector

When lands are subject to a strict settlement, family dissension may cause the eldest son to bar his entailed interest in remainder against the wishes of his father. The father may be niggardly or the son contumacious, and in that unfortunate event the probability is that the son will effect the partial disentailment that is within his power and will then dispose of the resultant base fee upon the best terms obtainable. The Fines and Recoveries Act 1833[9] specifically enacts that a tenant in tail who is not for the moment entitled to actual possession of the land may execute a disentailing deed without the consent of the protector, but that the effect of such a disentailment shall be merely to set up a base fee—that is to say, a fee simple that will defeat the tenant's own issue, but will not defeat persons who are entitled to take estates in the land upon the determination of the entailed interest by failure of issue or otherwise. Suppose, for instance, that:

> Lands stand limited to A for life, remainder to A's eldest son in tail, remainder to A's second son in tail, and so on. If the eldest son of A disentails during his father's life and without his father's consent, he will acquire a fee simple which cannot be defeated by any of his own issue, but which nevertheless will go over to his brother's family if at any time in the future his own issue fails. In other words, the eldest son acquires a fee simple that will not fail, i.e. will not pass to somebody else, unless and until his descendants fail.

There may be other base fees than the one now under consideration,[10] but these are beside the present point, and as regards entailed interests section 1 of the Fines and Recoveries Act provides that:

> The expression "base fee" shall mean exclusively that estate in fee simple into which an estate tail is converted where the issue in tail are barred, but persons claiming estates by way of remainder or otherwise are not barred.

It is a less valuable fee simple than a fee simple absolute, since it will last only as long as there are in existence descendants who would have inherited the entailed interest had it never been barred; while a fee simple absolute continues as long as there exist any persons who are heirs, whether lineal or collateral, of the owner. In the example given above, if the eldest son of A, having barred the entail in his father's lifetime, conveys the interest so acquired to X and then dies without having issue, the base fee held by X ceases, and passes to the second son by way of remainder. On the other hand, had the interest conveyed to X been a fee simple absolute, the death of the eldest son without issue would have made no difference to the perpetual nature of X's interest.

A base fee, however, may be converted, or will automatically become enlarged, into a fee simple absolute in any one of the following ways.

(i) Union of base fee with remainder or reversion in fee Suppose there is a limitation to:

> A for life, remainder to B in tail, remainder to C in tail, remainder to B in fee simple.

9 S. 34.
10 Challis, *Law of Real Property* (3rd edn), pp. 325 et seq.

B creates a base fee in himself by executing a disentailing deed during the life of A and without his consent. The remainderman C dies in the lifetime of B without having issue. The position now is that both the base fee and the fee simple absolute in remainder are united in B without there being any intermediate estate between them, and whenever this occurs the Fines and Recoveries Act enacts that the base fee shall be enlarged into as great an estate as the tenant in tail could have created had he been in possession at the time of disentailment.[11] In plain language, it is enlarged into a fee simple absolute.

(ii) Fresh disentailing deed If a tenant in tail in remainder creates a base fee, he can convert it into a fee simple absolute by executing a fresh disentailing deed with the consent of the protector.[12] But if the protector no longer exists, as for instance where the tenant for life under a strict settlement dies, the tenant can enlarge the base fee, whether he has parted with it or not, by himself executing a fresh disentailing deed.[13]

(iii) Lapse of time A base fee becomes valid against remaindermen and reversioners if any person takes possession under the disentailing assurance, and if he or any other person remains in possession by virtue of that assurance[14] for twelve years from the time when the tenant in tail would have been entitled to possession and therefore free to effect a complete bar of his own accord.[15]

(iv) Devise The owner of a base fee *in possession* is now permitted to enlarge the base fee into a fee simple absolute by will.[16]

(c) Unbarrable entailed interests

Two classes of tenants in tail are unable to disentail their estates namely a tenant in tail after possibility[17] and a tenant in tail to whom or to whose ancestors an estate has been granted by Parliament as a reward for services rendered, if the statute by which the grant is made has expressly prohibited the right of disentailment. Examples are the Bolton, the Marlborough and the Wellington estates.[18]

C. ENTAILED INTERESTS MAY BE DISPOSED OF BY WILL

Prior to 1926 a tenant in tail could not devise his estate, and if he died without having disentailed, it passed by descent to the appropriate class of heirs. The Law of Property Act 1925, however, provides that in a will *executed* on or after 1 January 1926 a testator of full age may devise or bequeath all property of which he is tenant in tail *in possession* at the time of his death, and all

---

11 Fines and Recoveries Act 1833, s. 39.
12 Ibid., s. 35.
13 Ibid., s. 19; *Bankes v Small* (1887) 36 Ch D 716.
14 *Mills v Capel* (1875) LR 20 Eq 692.
15 Limitation Act 1980, s. 27. This section also applies to a disentailing assurance which, owing to some defect such as the lack of a deed, fails to bar the tenant's *issue*.
16 LPA 1925, s. 176 (1), (3); infra.
17 Fines and Recoveries Act 1833, s. 18; p. 251, ante.
18 Former examples were the Abergavenny, Shrewsbury and Arundel estates, but these have now been statutorily freed from restraints upon alienation. See also SLA 1925, s. 23 (2); *Hambro v The Duke of Marlborough* (1994) Times, 25 March.

money subject to be invested in the purchase of property, of which if it had been so invested he would have been tenant in tail in possession at his death.

The tenant has power to dispose of the estate:

> in like manner as if, after barring the entail, he had been tenant in fee simple or absolute owner thereof for an equitable interest at his death,[19]

and therefore the effect produced by the will is similar to that produced by a disentailing deed. But to guard against a disentailment by inadvertence, it is enacted that no will shall be sufficient to dispose of the estate unless it refers specifically either to the property entailed, or to the instrument creating the entail or to entailed property generally, and therefore a mere general devise or bequest is useless for the purpose.[20]

This power of disposition is also conferred by the Act[1] upon the owner of a base fee *in possession* provided that he is in a position to enlarge the base fee into a fee simple absolute. This position arises where a tenant in tail in remainder, having barred the entail without the consent of the tenant for life as protector, becomes entitled to possession upon the death of the tenant for life. In such a case, as we have already seen, the owner of the base fee may bar the entail and enlarge the base fee into a fee simple absolute in possession by executing a fresh disentailing assurance. The extension of this principle made by the Law of Property Act 1925 is that the owner may *devise* the base fee so as to pass a fee simple absolute to the devisee provided that the will refers specifically either to the base fee or to the instrument by which it was acquired. But he has no such testamentary power unless he is in possession of the base fee or of its rents and profits. It will thus be seen that the power to execute a fresh disentailing assurance given by the Fines and Recoveries Act is wider than the power of testamentary disposition given by the Law of Property Act, for the former can be exercised by the tenant in tail even after he has conveyed the base fee to a purchaser and has lost all right to possession of the land.[2]

D. LAW REFORM

In 1989 the Law Commission recommended[3] that it should no longer be possible to create entailed interests in any property. They are now an anachronism. As we have seen, they played an important part in the development of the old type of strict settlement. They are not, however, favoured today, when taxation is a predominant consideration in the creation of any settlement, and one which contains entailed interests given to a long list of beneficiaries makes no fiscal sense.

---

19 LPA 1925, s. 176 (1).
20 Ibid., s. 176 (1). The word *specifically* was interpreted in a liberal sense by Vaisey J in *Acheson v Russell* [1951] Ch 67, [1950] 2 All ER 572. For a criticism of the decision, see (1950) 66 LQR 449 (R.E.M.).
 1 LPA 1925, s. 176 (3).
 2 *Bankes v Small* (1887) 36 Ch D 716.
 3 Report on Trusts of Land (Law Com No. 181), para. 16.1; p. 211, ante.

Chapter 12

Life interests

SUMMARY

SECTION I THE GENERAL NATURE OF LIFE INTERESTS

A. HISTORY OF LIFE INTERESTS

The modern life interest differs fundamentally from that found in the days of feudalism. In those days, when lands were granted not in return for a rent nor by way of settlement, but on the condition that the tenant should render services of a military nature to the grantor, the tenant was given an interest merely for his life, because, although he was known to the lord and was presumably a man upon whose fidelity and courage reliance might be placed, yet the character of his eldest son was an unknown factor, and it would have been folly for a grantor to have tied his hands by pledging himself in advance to accept the son as a new tenant on his father's death. So in the twelfth century the life estate was the greatest interest that anyone could have in land, and it arose when a feudal grant was made by a lord to a tenant. At first the grantee of such a feud did not possess the free power of alienation, for to have permitted this would have prejudiced the lord's right to make the new tenant on the death of the old pay a fine (or relief, as it was called) for the privilege of obtaining the feud; and again, a tenant possessed of a free power of alienation might cause irreparable injury by granting the land to a personal enemy of the lord. But the restraints on alienation gradually disappeared, and it was recognized by the Statute *Quia Emptores* 1290[1] that a feudal tenant could grant his interest to whom he pleased.[2] By degrees it was also recognized that the feud was an inheritable interest that would descend to the heirs-general of the tenant, and which therefore would endure as long as there were any such heirs in existence. An estate greater than a life estate thus became known to the law, and an interest which could endure only for life, as distinguished from a fee simple which might endure for ever, was added to the list of possible estates. In the words of Hayes:

1 P. 14, ante.
2 For the growth of the power of alienation, see Holdsworth, *History of English Law*, vol. iii. pp. 73 et seq; Plucknett, *Concise History of the Common Law*, pp. 523 et seq; Simpson, *A History of the Land Law* (2nd edn), pp. 51–56.

Some time elapsed after the feudal relation began to be known in Europe, before the right of inheritable succession was fully conceded. In its primitive state the possession was held at pleasure, or for a short term only: afterwards, the tenure was for life, the lord resuming the land on the death of the tenant, and granting it out anew. But at length the son of the tenant was permitted to succeed: an indulgence which was followed by the extension of the grant, first to the tenant and his issue (i.e. in fee tail) and finally to him and his heirs (i.e. in fee simple, expressed in legal phraseology by the word fee, without more), the law marking out a course of descent, which, enlarging by degrees, embraced his relations, lineal and collateral, male and female.[3]

But though after the establishment of the fee simple it became possible and indeed common to create a life estate with peculiar incidents of its own, the object of this practice was materially different from that which underlies the life interest found in present-day conveyancing. The estate in those days was granted, generally by the rich ecclesiastical corporations, in return for an annual rent, and was the result of a purely business transaction analogous to the modern lease for a term of years. The tenant resembled the modern tenant farmer, except that he held for life instead of from year to year or for a fixed number of years, and although he was said to have a *lease*, the interest vested in him was a freehold interest and not a term of years. But in modern times the life interest is, as we have seen, created within the framework of a strict settlement or a trust for sale as an integral part of the beneficial interests thereunder.[4] This aspect of the nature of a life interest became more important in the nineteenth century, when the Settled Land Act 1882 gave to a tenant for life powers which extended beyond those that he had as the owner of a mere life interest.[5] The crucial question in a grant of land at the present day therefore is not whether a claimant may enjoy the land for his life, but whether he has the powers of a tenant for life under the Settled Land Act 1925.[6]

Another common example of a life interest today occurs where there is an intestacy, and the surviving spouse is given a life interest in half the residuary estate of the deceased under the Intestates' Estates Act 1952.[7]

B. CLASSES OF LIFE INTERESTS

A life interest is a freehold interest—generally called a *mere freehold* to distinguish it from fees simple and entails, which are estates of inheritance. After 1925 it can no longer exist as a legal estate, and is necessarily equitable.[8] It may be limited to endure for the life either of the tenant himself or of some other person, in which latter case it is called an interest *pur autre vie*.

(1) ESTATE FOR LIFE OF TENANT

An interest for the life of the tenant himself, though normally created expressly by a settlement, made either by deed or by will, may also arise by

---

3 *Introduction to Conveyancing*, vol. i. pp. 7–8.
4 P. 176, ante.
5 P. 73, ante.
6 See the problems which arise where the court seeks to protect a contractual licensee for the remainder of his or her life; p. 177, n. 11, ante; p. 604, post.
7 P. 876, post.
8 LPA 1925, s. 1 (3); p. 91, ante.

implication of law in the case of the tenant in tail after possibility,[9] or by operation of law where a husband becomes tenant by the curtesy in the entailed lands of his deceased wife.[10]

(2) ESTATE PUR AUTRE VIE

The interest *pur autre vie* is the lowest estate of freehold known to the law, and is not so great as an interest for the life of the tenant himself. It arises in two ways:

> The first is where there is an express limitation to A for the life of B. Such a limitation may be made, like an ordinary lease for years, in return for a rent, or as part of a settlement of land. A is called the tenant *pur autre vie*, and B the *cestui que vie*;[11]
> Secondly, if a person B, who is entitled to an estate for his own life assigns his interest to A, the effect is that A becomes the tenant pur autre vie.[12]

From the point of view of rights and liabilities a tenant pur autre vie is in the same position as an ordinary tenant for life.

Thus, at common law, he is entitled to the rents and profits of the land during the continuance of his interest and to cut timber within the limits of estovers, while on the negative side he is liable for waste to the same extent as if he were holding for his own life.[13] Unless holding merely under a lease at a rent, he may exercise any of the wide powers conferred by the Settled Land Act 1925.[14] No matter how the interest arises, he possesses an absolute power of alienation during his life,[15] and after his death his alienee is entitled to hold for the rest of the cestui que vie's life.[16] In the absence of such alienation the interest passes on the death of the tenant to his devisee,[17] or, if he has made no will, to the persons who are entitled to take his property under the rules that govern intestacy.[18] Prior to the legislation of 1925 there were certain peculiar rules which governed the devolution of an interest pur autre vie, but these have been abolished.[19]

9 P. 251, ante.
10 P. 250, ante.
11 Litt 56; Co Litt 41*b*.
12 Co Litt 41*b*. For example, the mortgage of an equitable life interest under a settlement; p. 670, post.
13 P. 269, post (waste); p. 271, post (estovers).
14 SLA 1925, s. 20 (1) (v); he is not so entitled if he is the assignee of a tenant for life holding under a settlement; p. 194, ante.
15 Co Litt 41*b*.
16 *Utty Dale's Case* (1590) Cro Eliz 182.
17 Wills Act 1837, s. 3.
18 AEA 1925, s. 46.
19 Ibid., s. 45 (1) (*a*); for the old law, see Challis, *Law of Real Property* (3rd edn), pp. 358 et seq. A tenant pur autre vie could not at common law devise his interest, and the question that arose was—what was to happen to the land if he died in the lifetime of the cestui que vie? This depended upon the form of the grant. If it were to *B during the life of A*, the land went on the death of B to the person who first took possession. This person was called the *general occupant* (Blackstone, vol. ii. p. 259). Neither the general occupant nor the land that he held was liable for the debts of B. If the grant were to *B and his heirs during the life of A*, the land went on the death of B to his heir, who took, not by descent, for title by descent can arise only in the case of an estate of inheritance, but as an occupant specially marked out and appointed by the original grant. He was called a *special occupant*, and again neither he nor the land was liable for the debts of B.
   The Statute of Frauds 1677, s. 3, made estates per autre vie devisable and liable for debts. This section was repealed and re-enacted by the Wills Act 1837, after which the position was

In view of the danger that a tenant pur autre vie may be tempted to conceal the death of the cestui que vie, the Cestui que Vie Act 1707 provides that a person entitled to the land upon the termination of the life interest may, after swearing an affidavit that he believes the cestui que vie to be dead, obtain an order from the High Court for the production of the cestui que vie. If the order is not compiled with, the cestui que vie is taken to be dead and the person next entitled to possession may enter upon the lands.

SECTION II THE RIGHTS AND OBLIGATIONS OF A TENANT FOR LIFE AT COMMON LAW

The rights and obligations at common law of a tenant for life entitled in possession may be summed up by saying that he may take the annual profits, but must not take or destroy anything that is a permanent part of the inheritance. He is entitled to fruits of all kinds, but must leave unimpaired the source of the fruits. He has certain positive rights, and one negative duty which is prescribed by the doctrine of *waste*. The object of these rules is to maintain a balance between the interests of the life tenant and those in reversion or remainder.

We have already seen the position of a tenant for life under the Settled Land Act 1925;[20] these old common law rules still apply to him today.[1]

A. EMBLEMENTS

There is little that need be said of his positive rights. The profits that arise from the land, whether they arise continuously, periodically or occasionally, belong to him. A particular hazard, however, that confronts him is that after he has sown crops his tenancy may end unexpectedly before they are ripe as, for instance, by the death of a *cestui que vie*. In this event, he is entitled to re-enter the land at harvest time and to reap what he has sown. This is known as the right to *emblements*.[2] It is enforceable, however, only in respect of crops such as corn, hemp, flax and potatoes, which bear an annual fruit.[3] One crop only can be taken,[4] and the right does not extend to seeds that do not produce a crop within a year of sowing, such as young fruit trees or the second crop of clover.[5]

The right can be exercised only if the estate comes to an end unexpectedly

as follows: (*a*) an estate pur autre vie was devisable; (*b*) if it was not devised and if there was no special occupant (i.e. if the grant was merely "to B during the life of A"), the estate passed to the personal representatives of B and was treated as personalty as regards its liability for the debts of B; (*c*) if it was not devised and if there was a special occupant (i.e. if the grant was "to B and his heirs during the life of A"), the estate went to the heirs and was treated as realty as regards liability for debts. General and special occupancy were abolished by AEA 1925, s. 45, and if B dies in the lifetime of A his interest in all cases passes to his personal representatives.

20 Pp. 185, et seq, ante.
 1 *Re Harker's Will Trusts* [1938] Ch 323, [1938] 1 All ER 145; but see (1938) 2 Conv (NS) 233 (H. Potter).
 2 Co Litt 55*b*. The right of the tenant for years to emblements has been replaced by a statutory right; p. 398, post.
 3 Co Litt 55*b*; Blackstone, vol. ii. p. 122.
 4 *Graves v Weld* (1833) 5 B & Ad 105.
 5 *Graves v Weld*, supra.

without any fault on the part of the tenant for life, and therefore, if it is forfeited in his lifetime owing to the breach of some condition, or if, being a determinable interest, it is brought to an end by the happening of the terminating event—as for instance by the re-marriage of a woman who is tenant *durante viduitate*—the crops belong to the reversioner.[6]

B. WASTE

The position of the tenant for life on the negative side is governed by the common law doctrine of waste as enlarged by statute and equity, a doctrine that also affects a tenant for years.[7]

(1) DEFINITION OF WASTE

Waste means in general such damage to houses or land as tends to the permanent and lasting loss of the person entitled to the inheritance, and it falls into two main classes:

(a) Voluntary waste

This is a wrong of commission consisting of a positive act of injury to the inheritance. It generally takes one of the following forms:

(i) Pulling down or altering houses[8] Thus if glass windows be broken or carried away, it is waste, although they may have been put in by the tenant himself, and so also in the case of benches, doors, furnaces and other things fixed to the land.

(ii) Opening pits or mines[9] It is waste to dig for gravel, lime, clay, stone and the like, unless for the reparation of buildings; also to open a new mine, but not to work one that is already open.

(iii) Changing the course of husbandry To convert wood, meadow or pasture into arable land, or to turn arable or woodland into meadow or pasture, is technically waste. The old writers state that such acts are waste, not only because they change the course of husbandry, but also because they destroy the owner's evidence of title, for if an estate which had been conveyed as pasture were found on the next conveyance to be arable, it might cause confusion.[10] This, of course, is no longer in itself a reason for regarding such an act of conversion as waste. In fact it is obvious that to change the system of husbandry must often have the effect of enhancing the value of land, as, for example, where a farm situated near a large town is tilled intensively as a market garden, and though such conversion is technically waste, the rule,

---

6 Co Litt 55*b*; *Oland's Case* (1602) 5 Co Rep 116*a*.
7 P. 397, post. For the history of "waste", see Holdsworth, *History of English Law*, vol. ii. pp. 248–9; vol. iii. pp. 121–3; vol. vii. pp. 275–81. See generally Woodfall, *Landlord and Tenant* (28th edn), paras 1.1513–1.1532.
8 Co Litt 53*a*; *Marsden v Edward Heyes Ltd* [1927] 2 KB 1; *Mancetter Developments Ltd v Garmanson Ltd* [1986] QB 1212, [1986] 1 All ER 449 (tenant, who failed to make good holes left behind in landlord's brickwork when removing trade fixtures, held liable in damages); p. 146, ante.
9 Co Litt 53*b*, 54*b*.
10 Blackstone, vol. ii. p. 282.

established since at least 1833,[11] is that it will entitle the owner of the inheritance to recover damages unless it causes an injury to the inheritance.[12] This kind of waste is known as *ameliorating waste*. In *Doherty v Allman*:[13]

> a tenant for 999 years of land and buildings was proceeding to convert some dilapidated store buildings into dwelling houses when the lessor filed a bill for an injunction.

The injunction was refused on the ground that acts which improve the inheritance cannot constitute actionable waste. A similar decision was reached where the tenant of an agricultural lease for 21 years converted part of the land into a market garden and erected glass-houses thereon for the cultivation of hot-house produce for the London market.[14]

(iv) Cutting timber   Timber trees are regarded as part of the inheritance and not part of the annual produce, and therefore it is waste to cut them, even though they are blown down by accident and have thus become what are called *windfalls*.[15] Sir George JESSEL MR defined "timber" as follows:[16]

> The question of what timber is depends, first on general law, that is, the law of England; and secondly, on the special custom of a locality. By the general rule of England, oak, ash and elm are timber, provided they are of the age of 20 years and upwards, provided also they are not so old as not to have a reasonable quantity of useable wood in them, sufficient . . . to make a good post. Timber, that is, the kind of tree which may be called timber, may be varied by local custom. There is what is called the custom of the country, that is, of a particular county or division of a county, and it varies in two ways. First of all, you may have trees called timber by the custom of the country—beech in some counties, hornbeam in others, and even whitethorn and blackthorn, and many other trees, are considered timber in peculiar localities—in addition to the ordinary timber trees.[17] Then again, in certain localities, arising probably from the nature of the soil, the trees of even 20 years old are not necessarily timber, but may go to 24 years, or even to a later period, I suppose, if necessary; and in other places the test of when a tree becomes timber is not its age but its girth.[18]

A tenant, whether for years or life, may cut and keep trees that do not fall within this definition of timber, such as larch, willows and chestnut, provided that they are ripe for felling and have not been planted for ornament, shelter or shade.[19] But only in three cases may he fell timber trees:

First, where the land is a timber estate, that is, where it is cultivated merely for the produce of saleable timber and where the timber is cut periodically.[20] In such a case it is obvious that to cut the trees does not injure the inheritance,

---

11 *Doe d Grubb v Earl Burlington* (1833) 5 B & Ad 507.
12 *Jones v Chappell* (1875) LR 20 Eq 539 at 541.
13 (1878) 3 App Cas 709; M & B p. 23.
14 *Meux v Cobley* [1892] 2 Ch 253. Although this case and that referred to in the previous note concerned a tenant for years, there would be even stronger reasons for adopting the same attitude towards a tenant for life.
15 *Garth v Cotton* (1753) 3 Atk 751.
16 *Honywood v Honywood* (1874) LR 18 Eq 306 at 309.
17 E.g. beech in Buckinghamshire: *Dashwood v Magniac* [1891] 3 Ch 306; M & B p. 21; birch in Yorkshire: *Countess of Cumberland's Case* (1610) Moore KB 812; willows in Hampshire: *Layfield v Cowper* (1694) 1 Wood 330.
18 If timber trees are blown down, they belong to the owner of the inheritance, but if they are dotards, i.e. decayed, they may be appropriated by the tenant: Co Litt 53a; *Herlakenden's Case* (1589) 4 Co Rep 62 at 63b; *Duke of Newcastle v Vane* (undated) 2 P Wms 241.
19 *Re Harker's Will Trusts* [1938] Ch 323, [1938] 1 All ER 145.
20 *Honywood v Honywood* (1874) LR 18 Eq 306 at 309.

because the total value of the timber on the estate remains, roughly speaking, the same throughout, though new trees take the place of old.[1]

Secondly, where there is a local custom to cut timber periodically according to the normal and ordinary course of husbandry practised in the neighbourhood.[2]

Thirdly, every tenant for life is entitled to cut timber or other trees for three specific purposes, namely for the fuelling or repair of a house (*housebote*), for making and repairing agricultural implements (*ploughbote*) and for repairing existing walls, fences and ditches (*haybote*). These are called *estovers*.[3] He will be liable for waste, however, if he exercises these rights in an unreasonable manner, as for instance if he fells growing trees for fuel when there is dead wood sufficient for the purpose.

(b) Permissive waste

Permissive waste arises from a mere act of omission, not of commission, and it is generally the result of allowing the buildings on an estate to fall into a state of decay.[4]

(2) EXTENT OF LIABILITY FOR WASTE

At common law, tenants for life or years whose tenancies arose by operation of law, such as the doweress or tenant by the curtesy, were liable for waste; but no liability arose in the case of tenancies, whether for life or years, created by act of parties, for the courts were disinclined to excuse the folly of the lessor in not imposing an express restraint upon the tenant.[5] This, however, was altered by the Statute of Marlborough[6] 1267, which provided as follows:

> Fermors, during their terms, shall not make waste, sale, nor exile of house, woods, nor of anything belonging to the tenements that they have to ferm, without special licence had by writing of covenant, making mention that they may do it.[7]

This reference to a "special licence" recognized, therefore, that a tenant for life might be expressly permitted to do acts that would normally constitute waste without incurring liability,[8] and from this point of view it led to the emergence of two classes of tenants for life, namely those impeachable for waste, and those unimpeachable for waste.

(a) Tenant impeachable

A tenant who is impeachable is liable for the commission of voluntary waste,[9] but is not liable for permissive waste[10] unless the settlor has imposed upon him an obligation to keep the property in repair.[11]

1 *Lloyd-Jones v Clark-Lloyd* [1919] 1 Ch 424 at 436.
2 *Dashwood v Magniac* [1891] 3 Ch 306; M & B p. 20; *Re Trevor-Batye's Settlement* [1912] 2 Ch 339.
3 Co Litt 41*b*.
4 Co Litt 53*a*, 54*b*.
5 *Countess of Shrewsbury's Case* (1600) 5 Co Rep 13*b*.
6 52 Hen 3, c. 23. Also called Marlbridge.
7 "Fermor" includes everybody holding for life or years.
8 *Woodhouse v Walker* (1880) 5 QBD 404 at 406–7; M & B p. 20.
9 Co Litt 53*a*.
10 *Re Cartwright* (1889) 41 Ch D 532; *Re Parry and Hopkins* [1900] 1 Ch 160; *Woodhouse v Walker*, supra.
11 *Woodhouse v Walker*, supra.

Where such an obligation is imposed, an action lies against the tenant or against his personal representative, on the general equitable principle that a person who accepts a benefit must take the benefit *cum onere*.[12]

Where, however, the property which is settled upon the tenant consists of leaseholds, he is bound to perform any covenants, such as a covenant to repair, contained in the lease under which the property is held. Thus, if a house which is held by a testator on a long lease is bequeathed to A for life, A must take the *onus* with the *commodum*, and instead of throwing the financial burden upon the testator's estate must meet the cost of performing the covenants out of his own pocket.[13]

(b) Tenant unimpeachable

If, as is nearly always the case under a settlement, a tenant for life is unimpeachable, he is not liable either for voluntary or for permissive waste, and at common law may fell timber or open new mines and deal with the produce as absolute owner.[14]

(c) Equitable waste

Equity, however, has consistently set its face against an abuse of this immunity and the rule has long been that any tenant who commits wanton or extravagant acts of destruction, will be restrained by injunction and ordered to rehabilitate the premises. As Lord CAMPBELL said:[15]

Equitable waste is that which a prudent man would not do in the management of his own property.

Examples of the application of this rule occur where the tenant dismantles a mansion or other house,[16] cuts saplings at unreasonable times,[17] or fells timber that has been planted for the ornament or shelter of the mansion-house and its grounds.[18] It is obviously difficult to decide whether timber is ornamental or not, but the question depends upon whether the person who carried out the planting intended the trees to be ornamental, and not upon the personal opinion of the court or anybody else.[19]

Wanton acts of destruction of the kinds specified are said to constitute equitable waste because prior to the Judicature Act 1873 they could be remedied only in a court of equity; but section 135 of the Law of Property Act 1925 now enacts that a tenant for life has no right to commit equitable waste unless an intention to confer such right appears in the instrument of creation.

A tenant pur autre vie is liable for waste to the same extent as a tenant for his own life,[20] but a tenant in tail after possibility of issue extinct incurs no liability by the commission of voluntary or of permissive waste.[1]

---

12 *Jay v Jay* [1924] 1 K B 826.
13 *Re Betty* [1899] 1 Ch 821; *Woodhouse v Walker*, supra.
14 *Lewis Bowles's Case* (1615) 11 Co Rep 79b; Tudor, *Leading Cases on Real Property* (4th edn), p. 153.
15 *Turner v Wright* (1860) 2 De GF & J 234 at 243; M & B p. 24.
16 *Vane v Lord Barnard* (1716) 2 Vern 738; M & B p. 24.
17 *Brydges v Stephens* (1821) 6 Madd 279.
18 *Downshire v Sandys* (1801) 6 Ves 107.
19 *Weld-Blundell v Wolseley* [1903] 2 Ch 664.
20 Co Litt 41b; *Seymor's Case* (1612) 10 Co Rep 95b, 98a.
 1 *Williams v Williams* (1810) 12 East 209.

Where an act of waste has been committed, the remainderman or reversioner may sue for an account in the Chancery Division, or bring an action in the Queen's Bench Division, either for conversion in respect of any things that may have been severed, or for money had and received as a result of their sale,[2] or for the recovery of damages; and he may sue in either Division for an injunction.

---

2 *Seagram v Knight* (1867) 2 Ch App 628 at 632. See generally Tudor, *Leading Cases on Real Property* (4th edn), p. 156.

Chapter 13

Future interests

SUMMARY

SECTION I FUTURE INTERESTS[1]

A. THE EFFECT OF THE LEGISLATION OF 1925

The law of future interests has the reputation of being unusually complex and difficult; Blackstone indeed said that "the doctrine of estates in expectancy contains some of the nicest and most abstruse learning of the English law".[2] Fortunately, the abstruse learning related mainly to various technical rules of the common law concerning *future legal estates*; and, as

---

1 For the history of this subject see Holdsworth, *History of English Law*, vol. vii. pp. 81 et seq; Simpson, *History of the Land Law* (2nd edn), pp. 208–241 and generally, see Gray, *The Rule against Perpetuities* (4th edn); Morris and Leach, *The Rule against Perpetuities* (2nd edn and Supplement); Maudsley, *The Modern Law of Perpetuities*.
2 Blackstone, vol. ii. p. 163.

explained above,[3] section 1 of the Law of Property Act 1925 restricted freehold legal estates[4] to the fee simple absolute in possession. There have therefore been no future legal estates for over 50 years.[5] After 1 January 1926, future interests can exist only in equity behind a trust; and a limitation which creates future interests in land will exist under either a settlement or a trust for sale. The only substantial restriction upon the creation or existence of future (equitable) interests in land since 1925 is the rule against perpetuities, which must be examined in some detail. At this stage, a short historical explanation will serve to show how great was the change made by the 1925 legislation, and to provide the background necessary to understand why the perpetuity rule developed in the way that it did.

B. THE DOCTRINE OF ESTATES

In accordance with the common law doctrine of estates, which developed from the feudal system, a subject of the King did not theoretically own the land; he held it as the feudal tenant of the King.[6] The tenant was said to own, not the land, but *an estate in* the land. The largest estate known to the law was the fee simple. The tenant, being entitled to a freehold estate in possession, was "seised" of the land.

The tenant could hold an estate less than the fee simple; typically, where he holds an estate for his life.[7] But the whole fee simple exists somewhere. The land may have been conveyed:

to A for life and after his death to B in fee simple,

in which case A is the owner of a life estate in possession, and B the owner of a fee simple estate in remainder; or, if the grantor only conveyed the land:

to A for life,

then the grantor would retain the fee simple; but in this case the land does not "stay away"[8] from the grantor on A's death, but "reverts" to the grantor; the grantor owns a reversion.[9]

C. REMAINDERS AT COMMON LAW

A remainder is a future interest. The term "future interest", however, is confusing. For a remainder was a present existing legal estate, capable of being bought and sold, capable of passing by succession on death, as any other item of real property. The only element of futurity in a vested remainder is that the owner is entitled only in the future to possession. For that reason, in the illustration given above, of a conveyance of land:

to A for life and after his death to B in fee simple,

---

3 P. 91, ante.
4 The only other legal estate is the term of years absolute.
5 Except for reversionary leases; p. 371, post.
6 One holding directly of the King is called the tenant in chief.
7 Or fee tail; chapter 11, p. 245, ante. Or estate *pur autre vie*, p. 267, ante.
8 *Remanere* meaning "to stay away" is the origin of the term remainder, in contrast to *reverti* meaning "to come back". See Pollock and Maitland, *History of English Law* (2nd edn), vol. ii. p. 21; (1890) 6 LQR 22 at 25 (F. W. Maitland).
9 See Co Litt 22*b*.

A owns a life estate in possession, B owns a fee simple in remainder. A is seised; A is responsible for the performance of feudal services to his feudal lord, and is entitled to the use of legal remedies which are based on seisin.[10] B will be entitled to seisin on A's death. Vested remainders were the first future interests recognized by the common law.

(1) VESTED AND CONTINGENT

Inevitably, the question arose of the rule which the common law should apply to a remainder where the remainder was dependent on a contingency. In the above illustration, the grantor might not wish to give the remainder to B unless B attained the age of 21. The grant would then be:

To A for life with remainder to B in fee simple if he attains the age of 21 years.

At first, the common law refused to recognize contingent remainders; later they were recognized, and held to be capable of alienation and of transmission on death. Thus, in the illustration, B, during his minority, has a contingent remainder; it becomes a vested remainder on B's attaining the age of 21. It is said that B's interest then "vests in interest". His estate will vest in possession on the death of A.

(2) DESTRUCTIBILITY OF CONTINGENT REMAINDERS

(a) **Failure to vest during continuance of prior estate**

A reader who has understood the crucial importance of *seisin* under the feudal system may well ask what happens if A dies before B attains the age of 21. If A dies before B attains the age of 21, B's estate will not vest until a future time; there would be an abeyance of seisin. An abeyance of seisin was not permitted by the common law;[11] and the rule was clear and uncompromising that, unless a contingent remainder vested (in interest) during the existence of the prior particular[12] estate, or at the same moment (*eo instanti*) as its termination, the contingent remainder was destroyed. This rule existed until the passing of the Contingent Remainders Act 1877.[13]

(b) **Merger; surrender; forfeiture by tortious feoffment**

These are all methods by which the tenant in possession, the owner of the prior particular estate, could, by conscious decision, destroy the contingent remainders which were dependent upon that particular estate. We have seen that a contingent remainder required a prior particular estate to support it; if the prior particular estate disappears, there is no such estate and the contingent remainder fails.

(i) **Merger; surrender** The principle of these two methods is similar. They both involve the unity of the prior particular estate with the remainder in fee. The simple case of merger is where the life tenant acquries, by conveyance or descent, the vested remainder in fee. The life estate merged with the

10 P. 25, ante.
11 *Preston on Estates*, vol. 1, pp. 17, 249.
12 So called because it is *particula*, or a small part, of the estate of inheritance.
13 The situation before the Statute of Uses was much relieved in the 17th century by the device of trustees to preserve contingent remainders; Holdsworth, *History of English Law*, vol. vii. pp. 111–115.

remainder and was no longer available to support the contingent remainder. Thus:

> To A for life, with remainder to such of A's children as shall attain the age of 21 for their lives with remainder to B in fee simple.

If A, having no adult children, should acquire B's remainder by conveyance; or if B should die and devise the remainder to A, A's life estate would merge with the fee simple, and the intervening contingent remainder would be destroyed.

But this doctrine of merger did not operate in all cases where the particular estate and the next vested estate in fee became united in the same person, for if it had, many settlements would have stultified themselves. To take a common illustration if there was a devise:

> to A for life, remainder in tail male to the successive sons of A, remainder to the heirs of A,

the devisee acquired, not only a life estate, but also by virtue of the Rule in *Shelley's Case*[14] the next vested estate in fee simple, so that, if the full consequences of merger were to ensue, the result, if A were childless, would be to destroy the contingent remainders in tail at the very moment at which they were created.

To obviate this, the law of merger was modified at an early date, and the rule was laid down that a merger which took place at the same instant as the creation of the particular estate should not be complete, but that the two estates thus temporarily united should reopen and let in the contingent remainders if they became vested during the lifetime of the particular tenant.[15]

(ii) Forfeiture by tortious feoffment The concept of the tortious feoffment has its origins in early land law, and is based on the duty of the tenant to protect the rights of the feudal lord. Any action inconsistent with this duty involved a forfeiture of the tenant's estate. A common way for this to occur was for a life tenant to purport to convey the fee to a third party; the life tenant's estate was forfeited.

In more modern times, a tortious conveyance is affected by suffering a recovery or levying a fine; these procedures were used for centuries, as we have seen, for the purpose of barring an entail.[16] They were used also when the tenant in possession decided to destroy the contingent remainders which were dependent upon his life estate. Thus, in the case of a simple limitation:

> To A for life with remainder to B in fee simple contingently on attaining the age of 21 years.

A could destroy B's contingent remainder in fee simple by suffering a recovery, and, with the co-operation of a friendly third party to whom the fee was conveyed, could obtain the fee simple for himself. This made a contingent remainder a peculiarly insecure form of estate. It may be added in passing that the rule of destructibility by tortious feoffment applied to contingent

---

14 P. 256, ante.
15 *Lewis Bowles's Case* (1615) 11 Co Rep 79*b*; Challis, *Law of Real Property* (3rd edn) p. 137.
16 P. 247, ante.

remainders only,[17] and not to vested remainders, nor to executory interests.[18] This distinction is crucial, and it played a large part in the need for the development of the modern rule against perpetuities.

(c) Abolition of destructibility of contingent remainders by merger, surrender or forfeiture. Real Property Act 1845

These methods of destructibility of contingent remainders were abolished in 1845 by the Real Property Act of that year.

(3) DISTINCTION BETWEEN VESTED AND CONTINGENT REMAINDERS

It thus became a matter of importance to determine whether a remainder was vested or contingent.[19] The distinction in general terms is obvious. A number of technicalities arose with which we are not concerned. For present purposes it is sufficient to say that a remainder is vested where:

    (a) the person (or persons) entitled to take are ascertained;

    (b) the interest is ready to take effect in possession forthwith, subject only to the prior interest.

Thus, we have seen that B's remainder is vested in a conveyance:[20]

    To A for life with remainder to B in fee simple.

It would be contingent if the remainderman were not ascertained, as where the remainder was:

    to A's eldest child living at his death; or
    to the survivor of B and C; or
    to B (an infant) if he attains the age of 21; or
    to B if he is called to the Bar,

or any other contingency. But the prospect of a life tenant in remainder surviving a life tenant in possession is not regarded as a contingency. Thus:

    to A for life with remainder to B for life with remainder to C in fee simple if he survives A.

A's death is not a contingency; it is a certainty, and B has a vested life estate in remainder. If B wishes to sell his remainder, its value will of course vary according to the statistical likelihood of his surviving A. C's remainder is contingent on his surviving A, because the limitation expressly so provides.

Viscount DILHORNE summed up the distinction between vested and contingent remainders as follows:[1]

In *Preston; Treatise on Estates*[2] an estate in possession is stated to be one which gives "a present right of present enjoyment". This was contrasted with an estate in remainder which it was said gave "a right of future enjoyment". In *Fearne on*

---

17 P. 279, post.
18 *Pells v Brown* (1620) Cro Jac 590.
19 On the distinction between vested and contingent, see Fearne, *Contingent Remainders*, pp. 65, 74, 89; Gray, s. 9 and chapter iii; Morris and Leach, chapter 2; *Theobald on Wills* (15th edn), chapter 43. In construing limitations, the court leans in favour of vested interests, sometimes in spite of language which at first sight appears to be contingent. See *Duffield v Duffield* (1829) 3 Bli NS 260 at 331, per BEST CJ.
20 P. 276, ante.
1 *Pearson v IRC* [1981] AC 753 at 772, [1980] 2 All ER 479 at 484.
2 (1820) p. 89.

Contingent Remainders,[3] it was said that an estate is vested when there is an immediate fixed right of present or future enjoyment; that an estate is vested in possession when there exists a right of present enjoyment; that an estate is vested in interest when there is a present fixed right of future enjoyment; and that an estate is contingent when a right of enjoyment is to accrue on an event which is dubious and uncertain.

(4) DEFINITION OF A REMAINDER

It will be seen that all the illustrations so far have been cases of gifts in remainder which are limited to take effect upon *the natural termination of a prior particular estate of freehold.*[4] This is the essential feature of a remainder. A remainder was the only future interest recognized by the early common law, though, as we shall see, other interests could be created behind a use,[5] and these were accepted as valid *legal estates* after execution by the Statute of Uses 1535, under the name of executory instruments. But, for the purposes of the present discussion, we are at common law, before 1535.

A remainder, then, is an interest which is limited to take effect in possession upon the natural termination of a prior particular estate. From this it follows that a future interest is not a remainder if it is designed so as to spring up in the future, as in a conveyance:

to A (an infant) for life if he attains the age of 21 years; or
at the date of the next election; or
1 year (or 1 day) from the date of this conveyance.

Such an interest, requiring an abeyance of seisin, could not exist at common law.

Nor could a limitation which purported to "shift" or transfer the estate from the tenant in possession to another on the happening of a future event. Thus, the common law did not recognize future interests in the following limitations:

to Mrs. A for life but if she remarries to X;
to A in fee simple, but if he should emigrate to the Colonies, to B in fee simple.

A further rule is commonly stated, which is self-evident. There can be no remainder after a fee simple. A remainder must be limited to take effect on the failure of a prior particular estate. The fee simple is the largest estate known to the law and is not a particular estate.

D. ESTATES IN EQUITY. SPRINGING AND SHIFTING USES

By and large, the Chancellor followed the law in the development of estates in equity. But where the common law, for technical reasons applicable only to the common law, frustrated the intention of the grantor, the Chancellor allowed new developments in equity.

A contingent remainder failed at common law if it failed to vest prior to or *eo instanti* with the termination of the prior particular estate. And it failed because an abeyance would otherwise be created in the seisin. The feudal system would not allow that. But, behind the use in equity, the problem

---

3 (10th edn. 1844) vol. 1. p. 2.
4 A life estate. But it could have been a fee tail or an estate *pur autre vie*.
5 Springing and shifting uses; infra.

disappeared, because the seisin was in the feoffees to uses. A gap in the beneficial interest behind the use created no problem in equity. Thus, contingent remainders in equity were valid whether they vested during the continuance of the prior estate, or at the moment of its termination, *or later*.

Further, the common law recognized only remainders as future interests. But no harm would be done in equity by allowing a grantor to create an equitable estate to "spring up" in the future, or to cause the equitable ownership to "shift" from the present equitable owner to another on the happening of a future event. The seisin was unaffected in either case, because the feoffees to uses remained seised throughout. Interests of this type were permitted in equity. Thus, the following gifts were valid in equity:

(i) to X, Y, Z to the use of B (an infant) when he attains the age of 21 years; or

when he is called to the Bar; or
one year from the date of this instrument.

(ii) to X, Y, Z to the use of Mrs B for life, but if she remarry to the use of C; or

to the use of B in fee simple but if he ceases to reside in the City of Oxford to the use of C and his heirs.

These interests are known as (i) springing uses and (ii) shifting uses. They played a crucial part in the history of future interests, as will be seen. For the passage of the Statute of Uses in 1535 executed the uses, turned them into legal estates and forced the common law courts into making a decision as to whether they were to be accepted as valid legal estates; and, secondly, the future interests in equity arose all over again, with the development of the trust in the place of the old use. The free acceptance of springing and shifting uses in equity gave to a settlor a power to create a perpetuity. But the problem was not faced until such interests had become legal executory interests after execution by the Statute. The problem of the possibility of creating executory interests in perpetuity was faced in the seventeenth century, and the basic rule applicable throughout the English-speaking world was laid down in the *Duke of Norfolk's Case* in 1681–1685.[6]

E. EXECUTORY INTERESTS

The situation before 1535 therefore was that the only legal future interests recognized by the common law were remainders, and contingent remainders were struck down if they failed to vest prior to or *eo instanti* with the prior particular estate of freehold.[7] But in equity the situation was more liberal. The Chancellor recognized remainders, and upheld them whether or not they had vested at the time of the termination of the prior particular estate. He also recognized springing and shifting uses.[8]

The Statute of Uses 1535 profoundly affected this scene. It had no effect, as such, on legal remainders, but it had the effect of "executing" the uses and

6 3 Ch Cas 1.
7 Future interests in chattels (including leaseholds) could not be remainders. Such interests if valid took effect as executory interests.
8 P. 281, post. It was said in the argument in *Hopkins v Hopkins* (1734) Cas temp Talb 45 at 51, that "springing uses are as old as uses themselves". For a case between 1417 and 1424 in which the aid of the Chancellor was supplicated, see (1896) 10 Selden Society, *Select Cases in Chancery*, 1364–1471, p. 114.

making legal estates out of the estates which had previously existed behind the use.[9] Thus a gift:

> to X, Y, Z to the use of A for life with remainder to the use of B (an infant) if he attains the age of 21,

was no longer an equitable contingent remainder, but a legal remainder. Similarly, springing and shifting interests behind a use became legal. The common law courts had to face the questions of determining whether to apply its own rules to the contingent remainder, and whether or not to recognize the springing and shifting interests at all. The common law could have decided that what had been valid in equity was valid now at law. They could have decided that these were now legal estates and would be treated in exactly the same way as similar grants at law, not preceded by a grant to uses. In fact, they compromised. They accepted as valid springing and shifting interests which were created by means of a grant to uses and the execution of the uses by the Statute of Uses. These became known as *executory interests*. It should be emphasized that such an interest would only be recognized by the common law in the case of a grant *inter vivos* if it were written in the form of a grant to uses (and the use executed by the Statute). But such interests, if *created by will*, were recognized as creating valid future legal estates even though not in the form of a grant to uses; these were *executory devises*.

Thus far the common law courts followed the rule in equity. But when they came to decide the fate of a grant of an equitable contingent remainder which was executed and made legal by the Statute, they could not bring themselves to depart from the old contingent remainder rule with which they were so familiar. It was held in *Purefoy v Rogers*[10] that any limitation which was in its nature a remainder was subject to the common law rules of destructibility.[11] As late as 1843, Lord St Leonards saw this rule as an article of faith:

> Now, if there be one rule of law more sacred than another, it is this, that no limitation shall be construed to be an executory or shifting use, which can by possibility take effect by way of remainder.[12]

And so the contingent remainder rule continued until it was abolished by the Contingent Remainders Act 1877.

F. MODERN TRUSTS. THE PROBLEM OF PERPETUITY

It has been seen that the use upon a use developed into, and allowed the creation of, modern trusts. Trusts, like uses before them, are free of the old technicalities which burden common law future interests. As explained above,[13] future interests can, since 1925, only exist in equity behind a trust. The old technicalities are mere history, and will be unlikely to affect any title which comes before a modern practitioner. But the history shows that the

---

9 It was held not to apply to active uses; nor to uses of leaseholds.
10 (1671) 2 Wms Saund 380; *Goodright v Cornish* (1694) 4 Mod Rep 255; *Brackenbury v Gibbons* (1876) 2 Ch D 417 at 419; *White v Summers* [1908] 2 Ch 256.
11 P. 277, ante.
12 *Cole v Sewell* (1843) 4 Dr & War 1 at 27.
13 P. 275, ante.

freedom permitted to uses before 1535 created a situation in which interests in equity could be projected into the future in perpetuity, and nothing was done to control them. After the Statute of Uses and the acceptance by the common law of executory interests, the same problem presented itself, this time in the form of future legal estates. The *Duke of Norfolk's Case*[14] decided that a projection into the future was valid provided that the interest must vest, if it vest at all, within the lifetime of a living person. Later developments[15] expanded the rule into one which said that the interest was void unless it must vest, if at all, within the period of a life or lives in being plus 21 years. This rule governed legal executory interests and equitable interests behind a trust.[16] Legal future interests have now disappeared; and the problem of future interests, apart from questions of construction and of tax liability, essentially resolve themselves into the question of the application of the perpetuity rule to equitable interests under trusts.

SECTION II DEVELOPMENT OF THE MODERN RULE AGAINST PERPETUITIES

A. PERPETUITY PROBLEMS THROUGHOUT HISTORY

The antagonism of the law to an unbarrable entail became apparent at an early date in its doctrine of the conditional fee.[17] The purpose of a grant to a man and a specified class of heirs of his body was that the land should serve the necessities of each generation and pass from heir to heir; but, as we have seen, the common law held that the grantee obtained a fee simple with an absolute power of alienation as soon as an heir of the prescribed class was born. Irritated by such a decisive defeat of their intention, the great landowners procured the passing of the Statute *De Donis* 1285, which enacted in effect that the intention of a donor was to prevail, and that an estate given to a man and the heirs of his body was perpetually to be reserved to the appropriate class of heir.[18] Thus for the moment the power to grant an inalienable interest in the shape of an unbarrable entail came within the powers of a grantor, but the right was soon lost, for at any rate by the fifteenth century the law had recognized recoveries as methods by which entails could be barred and converted into fees simple absolute by tenants in tail in possession.

When it had thus become impossible to ensure the maintenance of land in a family by the simple means of a grant to a man and the heirs of his body, settlors began to cast about for some device whereby they could attain their desire by a more indirect but equally effectual means. One plan was to insert in settlements a *clause of perpetuity*, that is, a condition to the effect that the interest of any tenant in tail who attempted to bar his entail should be

14 (1681–1685) 3 Ch Cas 1.
15 *Stephens v Stephens* (1736) Cas temp Talb 228; *Thellusson v Woodford* (1799) 4 Ves 227; affd (1805) 11 Ves 112; *Cadell v Palmer* (1833) 1 Cl & Fin 372; M & B p. 350: p. 285, post.
16 And contingent remainders: *Re Frost* (1889) 43 Ch D 246; *Re Ashforth* [1905] 1 Ch 535; *Whitby v Von Luedecke* [1906] 1 Ch 783; Maudsley, pp. 71–2.
17 P. 245, ante.
18 P. 246, ante.

forfeited. Such conditions were, however, held void in three cases decided between 1600 and 1613.[19]

For the next series of attempts contingent remainders were pressed into service. At first, probably about 1556,[20] it became usual to prolong the period during which the land should be inalienable by making a grant to a son for life with contingent remainders to his unborn children, instead of granting him an immediate estate tail. This form of settlement, however, did not fulfil even the limited purpose for which it was designed, since, owing to the common law rules relating to seisin, it was possible for the life tenant to deal with his estate in such a way as to cause the destruction of the contingent remainder to the children before their birth.[1] Such a premature destruction was, however, prevented at a later date by the appointment of trustees to preserve contingent remainders. Another attempt took the form of the limitation of a perpetual freehold, by which successive estates for life were granted to the unborn issue of a person *ad infinitum*. A settlor, A, would limit the land to his son for life, remainder to every person that should be his heir one after the other for the life of such heir; but it was held by the courts that all the contingent remainders after the life estate to the first unborn heir (i.e. A's son) were void.[2] This particular rule was generally, though incorrectly,[3] described as the rule against double possibilities, for it was said that the law would never countenance a possibility upon a possibility,[4] and in the limitation indicated one possibility was that A would not have a son, another that the son, if born, would himself not have a son. The rule enforced by the courts was not, however, based on any such narrow ground. It was really a particular application of the parent rule that the grant of an unbarrable entail is void, and it was reaffirmed in 1890 in the case of *Whitby v Mitchell*,[5] where the Court of Appeal decided once more that where lands were limited to a living person, and then to his unborn child, and then to the child of such an unborn child, the last remainder was absolutely void. A settlor could exercise control up to a point but not beyond. He could withhold the fee simple from the grasp of his son by granting him a mere life estate, and he could, by the grant of an estate tail to his son's heir, prevent the acquisition of a fee simple until his son's son attained 21; but nothing that he could do could prevent his son and grandson from collaborating to bar the entail when the grandson attained 21.

Still another device adopted by settlors was to carve a species of estate tail out of a term of years by the bequest of a long term to a person and his heirs one after the other *ad infinitum*. But such a limitation after the term to the first unborn heir was held void.[6]

Pausing here for a moment we see that the attempts which were constantly being made by settlors to keep their land within the family, although they varied in details, all had one object in common, namely, by a combination of estates tail and contingent remainders or executory bequests to set up

19 *Corbet's Case* (1600) 1 Co Rep 83*b*; *Mildmay's Case* (1605) 6 Co Rep 40*a*; *Mary Portington's Case* (1613) 10 Co Rep 35*b*.
20 (1855) 1 Jurid Soc 47 (Joshua Williams); cited Scrutton, *Land in Fetters*, pp. 116–17.
1 P. 277, ante.
2 Fearne, *Contingent Remainders*, p. 502.
3 Challis, *Law of Real Property* (3rd edn), pp. 116–18; *Jarman on Wills* (8th edn), p. 293; Holdsworth, *Historical Introduction to Land Law*, p. 222, n. 6.
4 Co Litt 184*a*.
5 (1890) 44 Ch D 85.
6 *Sanders v Cornish* (1631) Cro Car 230; *Jarman on Wills*, p. 291.

unbarrable entails, and it was this particular species of inalienable estate that was regarded by the lawyers of the seventeenth century as a perpetuity. As Lord NOTTINGHAM said:

> A perpetuity is the settlement of an estate or interest in tail, with such remainders expectant upon it as are in no sort in the power of the tenant in tail in possession to dock by any recovery or assignment.[7]

Thus at an early date contingent remainders ceased to endanger the free alienability of land, for they failed altogether unless they had vested when the particular tenant died; they were easily destructible; and, if they were nothing more than unbarrable entails in disguise, they were void on the ground that they virtually created an inalienable interest.

B. EMERGENCE OF THE MODERN RULE AGAINST PERPETUITIES

The modern rule began to emerge about 1660,[8] and it was finally completed by the House of Lords in *Cadell v Palmer* in 1833.[9] The main stages in its development may be shortly stated.[10] In *The Duke of Norfolk's Case*, 1681–85,[11] there was a:

> grant of a term of 200 years to trustees upon trust for the grantor's second son Henry and the heirs male of his body, but if his eldest son Thomas died without issue male *in Henry's lifetime*, then in trust for Charles, his third son.

Lord NOTTINGHAM held that the last limitation was good, since the shifting to Charles must take place, if it ever took place at all, upon the dropping of a life in being, namely that of Thomas. Thus the case did not fix the maximum period during which vesting might be suspended, but decided that an interest that must vest if ever within lives in being was valid. *Stephens v Stephens*,[12] in 1736, held that an executory devise to the unborn child of a living person upon attaining 21 was good, and thereby in effect extended the maximum period to lives in being plus a further 21 years. In *Thellusson v Woodford*,[13] in 1805, Lord ELDON was of opinion that the persons whose lives were chosen need have no connection with the settled property, but might be strangers chosen at random. This opinion was endorsed by *Cadell v Palmer*,[14] which also decided that a term of 21 years without any reference to minorities might be added to existing lives.

In 1925 the rule in *Whitby v Mitchell* was abolished by section 161 of the Law of Property Act:

> (1) The rule of law prohibiting the limitation, after a life interest to an unborn person, of an interest in land to the unborn child or other issue of an unborn person is hereby abolished, but without prejudice to any other rule relating to perpetuities.

---

7 *Duke of Norfolk's Case* (1681–1685) 3 Ch Cas 1.
8 *Snowe v Cuttler* (1664) 1 Lev 135; *Wood v Saunders* (1669) 1 Ch Cas 131; Holdsworth, *History of English Law*, vol. vii. pp. 222 et seq.
9 (1833) 1 Cl & Fin 372; M & B p. 350.
10 Pollock, *Land Laws*, Appendix Note G; Gray, ss. 123 et seq.; Holdsworth, *Historical Introduction to Land Law*, p. 224; Morris and Leach, pp. 8–11.
11 (1681–85) 3 Ch Cas 1.
12 (1736) Cas temp Talb 228.
13 (1799) 4 Ves 227; (1805) 11 Ves 112.
14 (1833) 1 Cl & Fin 372.

(2) This section only applies to limitations or trusts created by an instrument coming into operation after the commencement of this Act.[15]

Thus the rule against perpetuities, fortified by the rules against accumulations,[16] is now the sole determinant of whether an interest is too remote. It applies both to realty and personalty out of which future contingent interests have been carved.

SECTION III THE MODERN RULE AGAINST PERPETUITIES[17]

A. INTRODUCTORY NOTE

The rule has been summarized by *Gray on Perpetuities* as follows:

> No interest is good, unless it must vest, if at all, not later than 21 years after some life in being at the creation of the interest.[18]

Four comments should be made upon this statement at the outset.

(i) This is not a statutory provision. It is a distinguished author's formulation of the basic operation of the rule. There are, as will be seen, several areas of operation where special factors have to be taken into consideration.

(ii) The requirement of the rule is that the interest must vest in *interest*, if at all, within the perpetuity period. The time at which it vests in possession is immaterial. The distinction between interests which are contingent, vested in interest or vested in possession has been explained above.[19]

(iii) How is it to be determined when the interest must vest, if at all, and within 21 years of which lives? These two basic questions on the working of the rule are not legal questions; nor are they asked because Gray's statement of the rule is obscure. The key to understanding the operation of the rule is to appreciate that what is sought is a *relationship* between the vesting and persons living. When does the interest vest? Examine the language of the instrument to find out. Is that vesting certain to occur within 21 years of the death of some living person, if it occurs at all? Examine the *relationship* between the vesting and living persons. The relationship will be either logical or biological. Thus, in a gift:

to the first child of A to attain the age of 21,

A's first child must attain that age, if at all, within 21 years of A's death. For A cannot procreate children after his death.[20] A's is the measuring life. But if the gift were:

15 A limitation to the unborn issue of an unborn taker is void under the modern rule, unless it is expressly confined within due limits, as in *Re Nash* [1910] 1 Ch 1. As to the meaning of "coming into operation after" the Act, see *Re Leigh's Marriage Settlement* [1952] 2 All ER 57.

16 P. 327, post.

17 See the accounts of this difficult subject in Morris and Leach, *The Rule against Perpetuities* (2nd edn, 1962), with supplement (1964) on PAA 1964; Maudsley, *The Modern Law of Perpetuities* (1979); *Theobald on Wills* (15th edn) chapter 44. See also (1964) 80 LQR 486 (J. H. C. Morris and H. W. R. Wade); (1981) 97 LQR 593 (R. L. Deech). This account owes much to Maudsley and M & B, chapter 7. In 1993 the Law Commission published a Consultation Paper on the Rules against Perpetuities and Excessive Accumulations (Law Com No. 133), pp. 327, 333, post.

18 S. 201.

19 Pp. 276, 279, ante.

20 A period of gestation is allowed, if in fact gestation takes place.

to the first child of A to marry,

the gift would be void. There is no living person within 21 years of whose death A's child is certain to marry, if at all. Of course a living child of A must marry, if at all, within that *child's* lifetime. That is logical (and obvious). But logically also, the first child of A to marry may be a future born child of A, if A has no married child and is alive at the date of the gift. A focus on the logical and biological *relationship* between the vesting and living people is the simplest way to understand the rule. Many millions of persons are "lives" in the sense that they are alive, but only those persons, within 21 years of whose death the interest must vest, if at all, are the measuring lives, and it is only possible to discover who they are after an examination of the *relationship* between the time of vesting and the living persons. A gift:

to the first great-great-grandchild of A to go for a walk with X

is valid. It must vest, if at all, in X's lifetime. Application of the rule has led to a number of innocent-looking limitations being held void because of the theoretical possibility of the happening of the practically impossible, such as an old lady of 70 having further children.[1] To an ordinary person such freakish possibilities would be incomprehensible. The special situations have to be learned and recognized from the cases.

(iv) Largely for the reasons given in the previous paragraph, there were strong movements for reform. We will see that the Perpetuities and Accumulations Act 1964[2] effected major reforms, providing, not only for detailed reforms in particular situations, but by introducing the principle of "wait and see". Rather than hold an interest void because it is not certain to vest, if at all, within the period, why not wait and see whether or not it does vest within the period, and hold it valid if it does, and void if it does not? That is a very attractive solution, and has been used in many jurisdictions in Australia, Canada, Northern Ireland, New Zealand, and the United States of America.[3] Manitoba has gone further in abolishing the rule and in its place widening the court's jurisdiction to vary trusts.[4] The 1964 Act creates a number of difficulties in the application of the principle.

1 *Jee v Audley* (1787) 1 Cox Eq Cas 324; M & B p. 357; *Re Dawson* (1888) 39 Ch D 155; M & B p. 372; *Ward v Van der Loeff* [1924] AC 653; M & B p. 358.
2 Which came into operation on 16 July 1964, and gave substantial effect to the recommendations of the Law Reform Committee Fourth Report (1956) Cmnd 18; p. 311, post.
3 In the United States, the rule against perpetuities was considered by the Commissioners on Uniform State Laws, who favoured retention of the common law (with amendments, including the introduction of wait and see) and its codification in statutory form. This led to the Uniform Statutory Rule Against Perpetuities being approved by the National Conference of Commissioners in 1986. Up to July 1991 it had been implemented in 16 states.
4 Perpetuities and Accumulations Act 1983 (SM 1982–1983, c 43); Manitoba Law Reform Commission Report on the Rules against Accumulations and Perpetuities (1982 No. 49); see (1984) 4 OJLS 454 (R. Deech) for a detailed review and criticism of this legislation; M & B pp. 347, 401; (1983) Manitoba LJ 245 (A. I. McClean) "Abolition is a great step into the unknown. The Manitoba Law Reform Commission and the Manitoba Legislator are not to be numbered amongst the law's timorous souls"; (1984) 62 Can Bar Rev 618 (J. M. Glenn), criticizing the legislation. Abolition has also been recommended by the Law Reform Committee of South Australia (73rd Report, *Relating to the Reform of the Law of Perpetuities* (1984)) and the Law Reform Commission of Saskatchewan (*Proposals Relating to the Rules Against Perpetuities and Accumulations* (1987)). See p. 333, n. 5, post.

B. THE RULE APPLICABLE TO INSTRUMENTS TAKING EFFECT BEFORE 16 JULY 1964

(1) APPLICABILITY OF THE COMMON LAW RULE

It is still necessary to understand the working of the common law rule: firstly, because the 1964 Act only applies to instruments taking effect after 15 July 1964, and questions of perpetuity have a habit of turning up many years after the instrument comes into effect; secondly, because the 1964 Act provides[5] that the "wait and see" principle is applicable to instruments which fail to comply with the common law rule.[6] The common law rule, therefore, applies to all dispositions; if the limitation complies with that rule, it is valid, but, if it fails to comply with the rule it may be saved by the application of the principle of "wait and see".

(2) STATEMENT OF THE RULE

The inquiry, then, in cases governed by the common law rule is to determine whether the interest in question is certain to vest in interest, if it vests at all, within a life in being plus 21 years, plus a period of gestation if gestation in fact takes place. For the purposes of the rule, conception is treated as equivalent to birth.[7] Thus a child, whether a beneficiary or not, who is *en ventre sa mère*[8] at the time when the instrument of gift takes effect may constitute a life in being,[9] and a child *en ventre sa mère* at the end of the perpetuity period may qualify as a beneficiary under the limitation.[10]

The test for certainty of vesting is made as of the date when the instrument comes into effect, i.e. if the instrument is a deed, when the deed is executed; if it is a will, when the testator dies. Or, to put the rule another way, an interest is void if it might by any possibility vest outside the period of a life in being plus 21 years. A number of points arising out of the rule will now be examined.

(a) Vesting

The rule is concerned with the time of vesting in interest. The rules for such vesting are explained above.[11] The rule is in no way concerned with the time at which an interest may vest *in possession*. It is necessary to examine the language of the instrument to determine the time at which the interest will vest. Further, the rule is not concerned with the duration of interests, the time for which they may continue. Thus:

> to A for life and after his death to the first of A's children to attain the age of 21 in fee simple. A is alive and has infant children.

5 S. 3.
6 For a criticism, see p. 313, post.
7 *Re Stern* [1962] Ch 732 at 737, [1961] 3 All ER 1129 at 1132.
8 "In simple English, it is an unborn child inside the mother's womb": *Royal College of Nursing of the United Kingdom v Department of Health and Social Security* [1981] AC 800 at 802, [1981] 1 All ER 545, at 554 per Lord DENNING MR. For the effect on the rule against perpetuities of delayed posthumous births by means of sperm banks or other devices, see (1979) 53 ALJ 311 (C. Sappideen). See also Human Fertilisation and Embryology Act 1990; Human Fertilisation (Disclosure of Information) Act 1992; Law Commission Report on The Rules against Perpetuities and Excessive Accumulations 1993 (Law Com No. 133), paras. 2.20, n. 30; 2.21, n. 45; 5.79.
9 *Long v Blackall* (1797) 7 Term Rep 100; *Re Wilmer's Trusts* [1903] 2 Ch 411.
10 Gray, s. 220; Challis, *Law of Real Property* (3rd edn), p. 182.
11 P. 279, ante; Gray, s. 323.

This interest will vest in *interest* when the first of A's children attains the age of 21. That interest will vest in *possession* when A dies. The fact that the interest of A's child, being a fee simple, may last forever is immaterial. That interest is alienable, and the freedom of disposition of the property is not restricted in any way.[12]

It is sometimes said also that the rule does not apply to vested gifts. This is a truism. The requirement of the rule is that the interest must vest, if at all, within the period. If the interest is vested, no question arises. The rule is concerned with interests which are contingent, not vested.

(b) Requirement of certainty. Remorseless construction

The rule requires that the interest must be absolutely certain to vest, if at all, within the perpetuity period. This does *not* mean that the interest must be certain to vest; for we are dealing with contingent interests, and there is no such thing as a contingency which is certain to occur. It is sometimes easier to look at the alternative formulation of the rule, and say that the interest is void if by any possibility it *might vest outside the period*.

The requirement of certainty of vesting, if at all, within the period means what it says. If there is any possible way, however freakish and unlikely, in which the interest might vest outside the period, the interest is void. And possibilities which are known to be not only freakish and unlikely, but also those which are physically impossible, such as that a woman over 70 may have a baby,[13] have been allowed to render gifts void. Further, the lawyers of olden days were so concerned at the possibility of the appearance of a perpetuity, that it became established that the language of the limitation must be remorselessly construed; the fact that the settlor or testator obviously did not intend the interest to fail to comply with the perpetuity rule is ignored. Lord SELBORNE LC said in 1880:[14]

> You do not import the law of remoteness into the construction of the instrument, by which you investigate the expressed intention of the testator. You take his words, and endeavour to arrive at their meaning, exactly in the same manner as if there had been no such law, and as if the whole intention expressed by the words could lawfully take effect.

and Gray:

> Its object is to defeat intention. Therefore every provision in a will or settlement is to be construed as if the rule did not exist, and then to the provision so construed the rule is to be remorselessly applied.[15]

The rule is applied in relation to the facts existing at the time when the instrument comes into effect. Invalidity is unaffected by the fact that, as the facts *subsequently* work out, the interest does in fact vest within the period. There is no wait and see at common law. That principle will be discussed in connection with the 1964 Act.[16]

Much of the difficulty in applying the rule stems from the fact that interests have been held void by reason of the possibility of an occurrence which would not normally be foreseen. These points will be demonstrated by a

12 P. 279, ante.
13 *Jee v Audley*, supra; *Re Dawson*, supra; *Ward v Van der Loeff*, supra.
14 *Pearks v Moseley* (1880) 5 App Cas 714 at 719.
15 S. 629.
16 P. 313, post.

number of illustrations below. It is thought better to take the illustrations together, because more than one important point is demonstrated in each case.

(c) The perpetuity period. Measuring lives

The perpetuity period at common law was that of a life or lives in being plus 21 years. To be valid the interest must be certain to vest, if at all, within the period. The requirement of vesting has been explained. Once the time of vesting is ascertained, the problem is to determine whether that vesting event must occur, if at all, within the period of a life or lives in being plus 21 years. This is what was meant by saying, above, that it is necessary to understand the *relationship* between the lives and the vesting. Which lives? Anybody: so long as that (living) person's relationship with the vesting is such as to enable it to be known with certainty that the vesting must occur, if at all, within 21 years of the dropping of that life. As has been said:[17]

> What one is really looking for at common law is some life in existence at the commencement of the period which shows, in the light of the circumstances existing at that date, that the interest must vest in time. In other words, one is looking for a life that will show the gift to be valid and one rejects all others as irrelevant. . . . The search, at common law, is for a life in being at the commencement of the period which is (i) certain and identifiable and (ii) so related to the vesting contingency that the gift must vest if at all within twenty-one years of its termination. A life that does not satisfy these requirements can be of no assistance in determining the validity of the gift at common law and is therefore rejected as irrelevant (or simply not considered at all).

Some simple illustrations will explain.

(i) When no lives have been expressly selected

1. *To the first child of A to attain the age of 21 years*   This is valid, because it is absolutely certain that A's first child will attain the age of 21 years, if he/she ever does, within 21 years of the death of A. We will see that the rule assumed that it was possible for a man or woman to have a child at any age, however advanced, but A cannot procreate children after his death. A's is the measuring life. Of course, if A were dead, his living children are certain to attain the age of 21, if they ever do, within their own lifetimes. Theirs would then be the measuring lives.

2. *To the first child of A to marry*   A is alive and has unmarried children. This is void.[18] It is not certain that A's first child to marry will do so within 21 years of the death of any person now living. The first child to marry *may* do so within 21 years of the death of A, or Mrs A, or A's parents or A's neighbours, but he/she may not. Of course, each of A's children living at the date of the gift must marry, if at all, within their own lifetimes, but the first child to marry may be future born, and may marry more than 21 years after the death of A, Mrs A, the children alive at the date of the gift, A's parents or A's neighbours. The gift is void. There is no measuring life. Of course, if A were dead at the date of the gift, the gift would be valid. Any child of A is

---

17 (1965) 81 LQR 106 at 107 (D. E. Allan); Maudsley, pp. 94–95; M & B p. 366. See also (1981) 97 LQR 593 (R. L. Deech); p. 318, n. 9, post.
18 Similarly, a gift to the first child of A to attain the age of 22 years was void prior to 1926; the gift was saved by LPA 1925, s. 163; p. 293, post.

certain to marry, if at all, during that child's lifetime. The children's would be the measuring lives.

3. *To the first of A's great-great-grandchildren to go for a walk with X* This is valid. It must occur, if at all, in X's lifetime. X's is the measuring life. The fact that X is unlikely to live that long is not relevant. The interest must vest, if it ever does, within X's lifetime. The gift is likely to fail, not for perpetuity, but because it will probably never vest.

4. *To the first grandchild of A to attain the age of 21* A is alive, has two children and four infant grandchildren. This is void. It is not certain that the first grandchild of A to attain the age of 21 will do so within 21 years of the death of any person now living. It is possible that A, regardless of age or sex, will have a third child. All the family, except the newborn child, then die. Suppose that newborn child has a child 30 years later, and that child attains the age of 21 years, 51 years after the death of persons living at the date of the gift. The gift is void; there are no measuring lives.

The result would be different if A were dead at the date of the gift. All of A's grandchildren would necessarily be children of the children of A, alive at the date of the gift, and *their* children must attain the age of 21, if at all, within 21 years of the death of those living children of A. A's living children are the measuring lives. Similarly if A, by his will, makes a gift to "the first of my grandchildren to attain the age of 21"; A, being a testator, is necessarily dead.

Again, the gift would be valid if it had been a gift to such of A's grandchildren as shall attain the age of 21, being children of a child of A alive at the date of the gift.

Now let us go back to the first paragraph of this illustration, and assume that A is an old lady of 80. It is obvious that the settlor or testator intended the gift to be in favour of the then living children of A. The settlor would not even consider the possibility of the old lady bearing another child. But the rule requires that possibility to be taken into consideration. And the courts were not even willing to construe the limitation to accord with what would have been the obvious intention of the settlor if he had been asked.[19]

As the number of contingencies is unlimited, so could this list of illustrations be endless. What they are intended to show is that it is necessary in every case to determine *the relationship between the vesting and the lives*, in order to discover whether that relationship is such as to enable us to say that the interest must vest, if at all, within 21 years of the death of some life.

(ii) Expressly selected lives Thus far, the settlor has taken no steps to select the lives to be used for the purpose. He may select the lives, and he may choose whomsoever he wishes, but it must be substantially practicable to ascertain the date of the death of the survivor. If, however, the number of the selected lives is so great as to render it impossible to ascertain the death of the survivor, as for instance where a testator defined the period as:

> twenty-one years from the death of the last survivor of all persons who shall be *living at my death*,

the gift, though not infringing the rule against perpetuities, is void for

---

19 P. 295, post.

uncertainty.[20] The selected lives need have no connection with the beneficial interests. Young and healthy babies would be a good selection if it is decided to extend the period as long as possible. It became the general practice in the nineteenth century to select:

the lineal descendants of Queen Victoria living at my death.

There were many of them, and they were in the public eye and easily traceable. But, the fact that as a result of World War I descendants of Queen Victoria would be scattered as refugees throughout the world could not have been foreseen.

These problems were discussed in *Re Villar*:[1]

The testator died on 6 September 1926, having made his will in 1921, and confirmed it in a codicil in 1926. He provided that his estate was to be held upon certain family trusts for the duration of "the period of restriction" after the expiration of which the estate was to be finally distributed. The "period of restriction" was defined as "the period ending at the expiration of 20 years from the day of the death of the last survivor of all the lineal descendants of Her late Majesty Queen Victoria who shall be living at the time of my death".

Since there were about 120 descendants scattered among at least ten countries in Europe alone, it was obvious that the difficulty of proving the fact and date of death of each descendant might be almost insuperable. Nevertheless, the trust was held to be valid.

Assuming that the measuring lives selected by the settlor or testator comply with the rule requiring ascertainability, the application of the rule to cases where lives are expressly selected is exactly the same as that in which no mention is made of measuring lives. The question is still the same; is it certain that the interest must vest, if at all, within 21 years of the death of some person or persons now living?

It will be noticed that the limitation in *Re Villar* was that the estate was to be finally distributed at the end of "the period of restriction". The final vesting would necessarily take place 20 years from the death of the survivor of persons living at the death of the testator, which must necessarily be within the period. But if the testator makes a gift

to such of my lineal descendants as shall be living 20 years from the death of the survivor of my friends X, Y and Z,

then, unless the court construes the language of the gift as intending to restrict the vesting to those descendants who vest within 20 years from the death of the survivor, the gift is void. All lineal descendants could claim at any time in the future. Measuring lives are nominated. But there is no *relationship* between the lives and the vesting.

(iii) Human lives The lives must be those of human beings, and not "of animals or trees in California".[2]

---

20 *Re Moore* [1901] 1 Ch 936. And not even valid for 21 years; see *Muir v IRC* [1966] 1 WLR 1269 at 1282, [1966] 3 All ER 38 at 44.
1 [1928] Ch 471, affd [1929] 1 Ch 243; M & B p. 354; *Re Leverhulme (No. 2)* [1943] 2 All ER 274, where MORTON J added a warning against "using the formula in the case of a testator who dies in the year 1943 or at any later date". See, however, *Re Warren's Will Trusts* (1961) 105 SJ 511, where a testatrix died in 1944 and CROSS J upheld the will.
2 *Re Kelly* [1932] IR 255, per MEREDITH J; M & B p. 356.

(iv) No lives specified If no lives are specified, an absolute period of 21 years, and no longer, is allowed.[3] In *Re Hooper*,[4] a gift:

for the upkeep of certain monuments so far as the trustees legally can do so,

was upheld for a period of 21 years.

(3) OPERATION OF THE RULE. REMORSELESS APPLICATION

A number of cases will now be examined as illustrations of the perpetuity rule at work. In each case, the language of the instrument should be examined in order to see when the interest is limited to vest, and then the *relationship* between the time of vesting and the lives of living people should be examined to see if the vesting is certain to occur, if at all, within 21 years of the death of some person now living.

(a) Standard illustrations of void gifts

Limitations were held void where a gift was to vest:

when a candidate for the priesthood "comes forward from St. Saviour's Church, St. Albans;"[5]

or,

when a house ceases to be maintained as a dwelling place;[6]

or,

where an advowson was devised to the first or other son of A that should be bred a clergyman and be in Holy Orders;[7]

or,

where there was a gift by will of an annuity of £100 to be provided to the Central London Rangers on the appointment of the next lieutenant-colonel.[8]

In each of these cases it will be seen that the time of vesting is in no way related to the lives of living people. The vesting may occur on the day after the instrument came into force. But it may not. All living people may be dead before the interest vests. This is unlikely, but we are concerned with what *might* happen, not with what is likely to happen, and we do not wait at common law to see what does happen.

(b) Vesting postponed to a date later than 21 years

The most common cause of invalidity in the older cases was the selection of an age of vesting greater than the age of 21. The child of A is certain to attain

---

3 *Palmer v Holford* (1828) 4 Russ 403.
4 [1932] 1 Ch 38.
5 *Re Mander* [1950] Ch 547, [1950] 2 All ER 191.
6 *Kennedy v Kennedy* [1914] AC 215.
7 *Proctor v Bishop of Bath and Wells* (1794) 2 Hy Bl 358.
8 *Lord Stratheden and Campbell* [1894] 3 Ch 265. Other illustrations are: *Edwards v Edwards* [1909] AC 275 (when the coal under certain land is exhausted); *Re Wood* [1894] 3 Ch 381 (when a gravel pit is worked out); *Re Engels* [1943] 1 All ER 506 (after termination of the present war with Germany); *Re Fry* [1945] Ch 348 at 352, [1945] 2 All ER 205 at 206 (when an unborn person, ascertainable within the perpetuity period, takes the testator's surname); *Re Jones* [1950] 2 All ER 239 ("upon the realization of my foreign estate"); *Re Flavel's Will Trusts* [1969] 1 WLR 444, [1969] 2 All ER 232 (fund to provide superannuation benefits for present and past employees of a company).

the age of 21 within 21 years of A's death. But the child of A is not certain to attain the age of 22 (or more commonly 25) within 21 years of the death of any living person. In order to avoid the necessity of holding such gifts void, section 163 of the Law of Property Act 1925 provided that:

> Where in a will, settlement or other instrument the absolute vesting either of capital or income of property, or the ascertainment of a beneficiary or class of beneficiaries, is made to depend on the attainment by the beneficiary of members of the class of an age exceeding twenty-one years, and thereby the gift to that beneficiary or class or any member thereof, or any gift over, remainder, executory limitation, or trust arising on the total or partial failure of the original gift, is, or but for this section would be, rendered void for remoteness, the will, settlement, or other instrument shall take effect for the purposes of such gift, gift over, remainder, executory limitation, or trust as if the absolute vesting or ascertainment aforesaid had been made to depend on the beneficiary or member of the class attaining the age of twenty-one years, and that age shall be substituted for the age stated in the will, settlement, or other instrument.

It will be seen that the age was only to be reduced to 21 years where the gift would thereby be validated. Section 163 was repealed by the Perpetuities and Accumulations Act 1964[9] in respect of dispositions to which the Act applies.

(c) Leach's caricature cases

The trouble with the perpetuity rule was that, because of its remorseless application, it rendered void a number of perfectly reasonable dispositions, in cases in which the settlor's or testator's intention could have been achieved if the draftsman had been competent.[10] Professor Barton Leach listed and named a number of such situations.[11]

(i) **The magic gravel pits** This situation may arise when a testator assumes that his estate will be administered by his personal representatives within a reasonably short time, and then his will is drafted in such a way that a contingent interest may, beyond all reasonable expectation, vest outside the perpetuity period. Thus, in *Re Wood*:[12]

> a testator, who was a gravel contractor, directed his trustees "to carry on my said business of a gravel contractor until my gravel pits are worked out" and then to sell them and to divide the proceeds among his issue "then living". At the date of the will it was clear that the testator knew that the gravel pits would soon be worked out, and they were in fact worked out within six years of his death.

It was held that the gift was void because there was a possibility that the gravel pits might not have been worked out within the perpetuity period of 21 years. As has been said, "like the widow's cruse, the gravel pits might have replenished themselves for ever—or at least for more than 21 years".[13]

---

9 P. 322, post.
10 (1952) 68 LQR 35 at 36 (W. Barton Leach); Maudsley, pp. 37–8.
11 (1938) 51 HLR 1329; (1952) 65 HLR 721; (1952) 68 LQR 35 at 44.
12 [1894] 2 Ch 310, affd. [1894] 3 Ch 381; M & B p. 364. See also *Re Lord Stratheden and Campbell* [1894] 3 Ch 265; p. 293, ante (a perpetual lieutenant-colonel); *Re Atkins' Will Trusts* [1974] 1 WLR 761, [1974] 2 All ER 1; M & B p. 364 (contingency was that of a bank complying with its duty to sell land within the period. Held to be valid as there was no reason to assume that the bank would commit a breach of trust).
13 Morris and Leach, p. 74.

(ii) The unborn widow(er) Gifts to children may fail because of the possibility that a mother (or father) who is now married may lose her husband (or wife) by death or divorce, and then may marry again, his second wife being someone who is now unborn. Thus, in *Re Frost*[14] there was a gift to:

Emma, a spinster, for life, and after her death to any husband she may marry for his life, and then to each of their children as shall be living at the death of the survivor of Emma and such husband.

The gift to the children was void. It was contingent on the children surviving Emma and her husband. Emma was unmarried at the date of the gift, and might marry a husband who was unborn at that date. If he then survived Emma by more than 21 years, the interests of the children would not vest within 21 years of Emma's death. The result would have been the same even if Emma had been married at the date of the gift.

Re Frost must be contrasted with *Re Garnham*,[15] where there was a gift:

to Thomas, a bachelor, for life, then to any woman he may marry for life, and then to the children of Thomas at 21.

The gift was held to be valid. The interests of the children vested in *interest* on the death of Thomas, and not, as in *Re Frost*, on the death of the *survivor* of Emma and her husband.

(iii) The fertile octogenarian The common law recognized no upper (or lower) limit of age at which a living person was supposedly capable of reproduction; and this led to the necessity to hold void a number of dispositions in which there was no physical possibility of the interest vesting outside the period, and no thought or expectation that there might be a problem. The leading case is *Ward v Van der Loeff*:[16]

By his will the testator devised his residuary estate upon trust for his widow for life and then, in the events which happened, upon trust for the children of his brothers and sisters.

By a codicil he declared that his widow's life interest should be terminable on her remarriage, unless such remarriage should be with a natural born British subject; and that, on her death or remarriage, the trustees should hold the residuary estate upon trust for such of the children of his brothers and sisters as should attain the age of 21 (or, being daughters, attain that age or marry). The widow married a Dutchman.

At the date of the testator's death, his parents were both alive, aged 66. Two brothers and two sisters were alive, each of whom was over 30 and had infant children, one of whom was born after the remarriage of the widow.

The House of Lords held that the gift in the codicil was void, because a future born niece or nephew might have attained the age of 21 outside the period. The living nieces and nephews would attain that age, if at all, in their own lifetimes. And future born children of the testator's brothers and sisters living at the time would also attain that age, if at all, within 21 years of the death of their parents (the living brothers and sisters of the testator). But if the testator's parents were still alive, they might have another child, a new brother or sister to the testator. Everyone else might die, and then that child might have a child which might attain the age of 21 more than 21 years after

14 (1889) 43 Ch D 246; M & B p. 362.
15 [1916] 2 Ch 413; M & B p. 363.
16 [1924] AC 653; M & B p. 358.

the death of any person living at the date of the testator's death. The rule relating to class gifts, as will be seen, is that the gift to the class is valid only if its exact composition must be known within the period. The result was that the gift in the codicil failed.[17]

For all its complications, this case reduces itself to an illustration of the simple proposition, discussed above, that a gift to the grandchildren of living persons is void.[18] It illustrates dramatically the application of the rule of remorseless construction. What would the testator have said if he had been asked the question: By "children of my brothers and sisters", do you mean the children of your *living* brothers and sisters,[19] or do you wish to include the children of a future brother or sister to which your 66 year old mother might give birth after your death? It will be seen that the Perpetuities and Accumulations Act 1964 has enacted the permissible periods of reproduction for males and females.[20]

(iv) The precocious toddler Logically, the presumption of fertility attributed to the old should equally affect the young. Whether it must be presumed that no person can be too young to beget children was canvassed in *Re Gaite's Will Trusts*[1] but was not determined. On the facts of that case, the argument in favour of such a presumption rested upon the possibility that within the short space of five years after the settlor's death a child might be born to his widow, already 65 years old, and might then marry and have issue. The judge evaded the question of physical impossibility by holding that such a hypothetical marriage, contracted by a person under 16 years of age contrary to the Age of Marriage Act 1929,[2] was a legal impossibility. And the court will not take into account an event which presupposes a contravention of statute or a breach of trust.[3]

(4) GIFTS TO A CLASS

(a) General

(i) Meaning of gift to a class As Lord SELBORNE said in *Pearks v Moseley*:

> A gift is said to be to a class of persons when it is to all those who shall come within a certain category or description defined by a general or collective formula, and who, if they take at all, are to take one divisible subject in certain proportionate shares.[4]

There is a gift to a class if the limitation is:

to all the children of A who shall attain 21.

17 But the story had a happier ending. The House of Lords further held that (i) the codicil did not revoke the gift in the will, by applying the doctrine of dependent relative revocation (p. 862, post) and (ii) the gift in the will itself was valid. That was saved by the inter-relation of the class closing rules and the perpetuity rule, as a result of which the child who was born after the remarriage of the widow was excluded. See p. 298, post; Maudsley, pp. 54–6.
18 One of the grandparents in fact died before the litigation. But that of course made no difference.
19 In which case the gift would have been valid. In the Court of Appeal ATKIN LJ would have upheld the codicil on the ground that this was the testator's obvious intention: *Re Burnyeat* [1923] 2 Ch 52 at 70. See p. 856, post.
20 P. 312, post.
 1 [1949] 1 All ER 459; M & B p. 353.
 2 Now the Marriage Act 1949, s. 2.
 3 *Re Atkins' Will Trusts* [1974] 1 WLR 761, [1974] 2 All ER 1; M & B p. 364.
 4 (1880) 5 App Cas 714 at 723.

On the other hand, a gift of:

£2,000 to each of the daughters of B,

is not a class gift.[5]

(ii) Vesting of interest of member of class We have seen that,[6] for the purpose of determining whether an individual member of a class has a vested interest, each member of the class obtains a vested interest on satisfying the necessary qualifications. Thus in a gift:

to A for life and after his death to such of his children as shall attain 25,

each child of A obtains a vested interest on reaching that age. The significance of this vesting is that the child's interest is then indefeasible. If his interest vests and he then dies before A, the child's estate will claim. If however he dies at the age of 24, it will have no claim. The interest of a child of A who attains 25 is said to be vested "subject to open"; that is to say, subject to open and admit future born children of A:

Thus if A has three children and all have attained 25, they all have vested interests. But if A then has three more children, the interest of the three eldest will be reduced from one third each to one sixth; and will increase again if any of the younger children dies under the age of 25.

(iii) Requirement that interest of each member vest within period However, for the purpose of determining the validity of a gift on the ground of remoteness, the rule is that the gift to a class is only valid if the interest of every possible member of the class must vest, if at all, within the perpetuity period. If the interest of even one potential member could possibly vest outside the period, the *whole* gift fails. Those whose interests have already vested take nothing.[7] "The vice of remoteness affects the class as a whole, if it may affect an unascertained number of its members."[8] In other words, a class gift cannot be partially good, partially bad.

Suppose, for instance, that a testator leaves his residuary estate:

to such of the children of A who shall marry.

If A survives the testator, the whole gift is void. Even if, when the testator dies, A already has children who therefore marry, if at all, within their own lifetimes, there is no certainty that all his children who marry will do so within the perpetuity period. For A may have a future born child who marries more than 21 years after the death of lives in being. The whole gift, however, would be valid if it were expressed to be to the *living* children of A who marry; or if, when the testator dies, A were dead and therefore unable to have further children.[9]

---

5 *Wilkinson v Duncan* (1861) 30 Beav 111; M & B p. 382.
6 P. 217, ante.
7 *Leake v Robinson* (1817) 2 Mer 363.
8 *Pearks v Moseley* (1880) 5 App Cas 714 at 723, per Lord SELBORNE.
9 The gift would also be saved if one of the children of A were married when the testator dies. This would have the effect of bringing into operation the class-closing rules, and of artificially closing the class at the date of the gift, to include only those children of A who were alive at that time. They must marry, if at all, within their own lifetimes. For these rules and the interrelation between them and the rule against perpetuities, see infra.

(b) Class closing rules[10]

(i) Rule in *Andrews v Partington* Rules of construction, sometimes known as the rule in *Andrews v Partington*,[11] have developed, which have the effect of determining which members of a class can take. They have the effect of artificially closing the class, and of excluding members who would otherwise have taken. They are rules of construction only, and defer to a contrary intention; and the courts in recent years, it seems, are more ready than previously to find that intention.[12]

A class is artificially closed under these rules in order to allow the trustees to make a distribution[13] when one member of the class attains a vested interest and is entitled to be paid. Let us consider the position of trustees where there is a gift "to such of the children of A who shall attain 21"; and when A's eldest child, X, becomes 21, there is a brother, Y, aged 11 and a sister, Z, aged 1. X asks the trustees for payment; what are they to pay to him? If A is still alive, there is danger in paying to X a one-third share, because future born children of A would reduce X's entitlement. So the class closing rules, for the convenience of the administration of the trust, say that the trustees may calculate X's share by providing for only those children of A who have been born. His future born children are excluded. Y and Z can claim their shares when they attain 21. This is very convenient for the trustees and for X, Y and Z; but inconvenient for any future born children of A.

The key to understanding when the class closes is to appreciate that it closes when the time for distribution arises; when, that is, the first claimant becomes entitled to be paid. Thus, in an immediate gift to a class, such as "to the children of A", that class closes to include those alive at the date of the gift. If vesting is postponed, for example, "to such of the children of A who shall attain 21", the class closes when the first child of A becomes 21. If it is an interest in remainder, for example, "to X for life, remainder to the children of A who shall attain 21", the class closes when X has died and when the first child of A has attained 21, whichever event happens last, because that is the time at which the first member of the class becomes entitled to be paid. There is an exception to these rules where there is an immediate gift and no existing claimant. Thus if there is a gift to the children of A and A has no children, the class remains open to include all A's children.[14]

(ii) Inter-relation between class-closing and perpetuity rules We have seen that the purpose of the class-closing rules is to simplify the administration of a trust by enabling the trustees to make payment to beneficiaries as soon as

10 For a full discussion of these rules see (1954) 70 LQR 61 (J. H. C. Morris); (1958) CLJ 39 (S. J. Bailey); Morris and Leach, pp. 109–125; Maudsley, pp. 17–25; *Theobald on Wills* (15th edn), chapter 32; p. 858, post.

11 (1791) 3 Bro CC 401.

12 *Re Bleckly* [1951] Ch 740, [1951] 1 All ER 1064; *Re Cockle's Will Trusts* [1967] Ch 690, [1967] 1 All ER 391; *Re Kebty-Fletcher's Will Trusts* [1969] 1 Ch 339, [1969] 3 All ER 1076; *Re Harker's Will Trusts* [1969] 1 WLR 1124, [1969] 3 All ER 1; *Re Henderson's Trusts* [1969] 1 WLR 651, [1969] 3 All ER 769; (1970) 34 Conv (NS) 393 (J. G. Riddall); *Re Edmondson's Will Trusts* [1972] 1 WLR 183, [1972] 1 All ER 444; *Re Deeley's Settlement* [1974] Ch 454; [1973] 3 All ER 1127; *Re Chapman's Settlement Trusts* [1977] 1 WLR 1163, [1978] 1 All ER 1122; [1978] Conv 73 (F. R. Crane); *Re Clifford's Settlement Trusts* [1981] Ch 63, [1980] 1 All ER 1013; *Re Tom's Settlement* [1987] 1 WLR 1021, [1987] 1 All ER 1081; *Re Drummond* [1988] 1 WLR 234, [1988] 1 All ER 449; [1988] Conv 427 (P. Luxton).

13 The rules apply to all forms of property, and to settlements as well as to wills.

14 *Weld v Bradbury* (1715) 2 Vern 705; *Re Ransome* [1957] Ch 348 at 359, [1957] 1 All ER 690 at 695, per UPJOHN J.

they have become entitled. Essentially the rules have nothing to do with the rule against perpetuities. But it will be appreciated that there may be situations in which the rules interact, as for instance where there is a gift to a class in which the interests of some of the members must vest within the perpetuity period, but there is a possibility that those of others may vest outside it, with the result that the whole gift is void under the rule against perpetuities. But if, as it were by a fluke, the class-closing rules exclude all the members whose interests would invalidate the gift, then it will be valid. Thus if there is a gift before 1926 "to the children of A who shall attain 25", that is void. But, if at the date of the gift there is a child of A who is already 25, the class-closing rules operate to include only those children of A who are alive at the date of the gift; and they will clearly attain 25, if at all, within their own lifetimes. The gift is therefore valid.[15] Further, to return to our earlier example[16] of a gift "to such of the children of A who shall marry": we saw that this is void, if A is alive at the date of the gift. If, however, one of the children of A is then married, the gift is valid.[17]

(5) POWERS OF APPOINTMENT

We now deal with a number of situations in which it is necessary to apply special rules. Gray's formulation of the rule is no longer adequate. The first of these situations concerns powers of appointment.

Before stating the law on this, however, we must first explain the nature of powers of appointment.

(a) Definition and terminology

A power of appointment gives to the donee of the power the right to effect dispositions of property which he does not own, and in which he may have no interest at all.[18] Thus, property may be given by a testator on trust:

> To my widow for life and after her death to such of our children and in such shares as she shall in her absolute discretion appoint.

Or the power of appointment may be given to the trustees; or to one who holds no legal or equitable interest in the property, as where the testator gives property:

> To my widow for life and after her death to such of my nieces and nephews as my brother, X, in his absolute discretion shall appoint.

As regards terminology, when A gives X the right to exercise a power of appointment, A is called the *donor*; X the *donee* or *appointor*; the person in whose favour the appointment is made is termed the *appointee*; and when the donee exercises the power he is said to make an appointment.

---

15 *Picken v Matthews* (1878) 10 Ch D 264.
16 P. 298, ante.
17 See [1988] Conv 339 (P. Sparkes and R. Snape), arguing that the rules should be applied during the "wait and see" period.
18 Powers of appointment were unknown at common law, but originated with uses in equity. See Co Litt 237a; Sugden, *Gilbert on Uses*, p. xxxix, 158 n.; Hayes, *Introduction to Conveyancing*, vol. 1. p. 70. On powers generally, see *Farwell on Powers* (3rd edn); H & M, chapter 6; Maclean, *Trusts and Powers* (1989).

(b) General and special powers

Powers of appointment may be either general, or special.

If the appointor is authorized to appoint in favour of anybody in the world, including himself, without being required to obtain the consent of another person, he is said to have a *general power*, but if he may appoint only to the members of a restricted class, as for instance, "amongst the children of A", he has a *special power*, and the persons whom he may select to take the property are called the *objects* of the power.

(c) Powers and the rule against perpetuities

A power of appointment may infringe the rule against perpetuities in two respects, for either its *creation* or its *exercise* may be too remote.

To give a person a general power is in effect to give him the absolute fee, for it entitles him to vest the whole fee in any person in the world, including himself, and therefore it does not tend to the creation of remote interests:

> He has an absolute disposing power over the estate, and may bring it into the market whenever his necessities or wishes may lead him to do so . . . The donee may sell the estate the next moment.[19]

On the other hand, the grant of a special power has an immediate tendency to be a perpetuity, for, since the objects in whose favour it is exercisable are restricted, it imposes from the moment of its creation a fetter upon the free disposability of the land.[20] It is important to notice, however, that a general power exercisable jointly by two or more persons or by one person with the consent of another is a special power for the purposes of the rule against perpetuities, the view taken by the law being that a power which cannot be exercised without the concurrence of two minds is not equivalent to property.[1]

(i) General powers

1. *Validity of creation* A general power to appoint by deed, or either by deed or by will, is void unless it will become effectively exercisable, if at all, within the perpetuity period. At the date when the instrument of creation takes effect, it must be possible to say that within that period the donee will be ascertainable, the event upon which the power is to arise will have occurred and any condition precedent to the right of exercise will have been satisfied.

On this basis, each of the following powers is void:

A power given to the survivor of two living persons and their children.[2]
A power to arise upon the general failure of the issue of a marriage.[3]

---

19 Sugden, *Powers* (8th edn), pp. 395–6, cited Morris and Leach, p. 148.
20 Co Litt 272*a*, Butler's note.
 1 *Re Churston Settled Estates* [1954] Ch 334, [1954] 1 All ER 725; *Re Earl of Coventry's Indentures* [1974] Ch 77, [1973] 3 All ER 1. This is an example of a power which is intermediate or hybrid in the sense that it conforms neither to special nor general powers. For an account, see Morris and Leach, *The Rule against Perpetuities* (2nd edn) pp. 136–8; Fourth Report of Law Reform Committee 1956 (Cmnd 18), paras 44–6. See *Re Lawrence's Will Trusts* [1972] Ch 418, [1971] 3 All ER 433 where that category is discussed by MEGARRY J.
 2 *Re Hargreaves* (1889) 43 Ch D 401.
 3 *Bristow v Boothby* (1826) 2 Sim & St 465. Prima facie, "issue" includes descendants of every degree. See *Theobald on Wills* (15th edn), pp. 415–418.

A power given to an unborn person upon his marriage.[4]

If a general power to appoint by deed, or either by deed or by will, is exercisable within the perpetuity period, it is not rendered objectionable by the fact that it may possibly be exercised after the period has expired, as may well happen, for instance, if it is given to the unborn child of a living person. By virtue of the power, such a donee ascertained within due limits acquires an unrestricted right of alienation, and as in the case of any absolute owner he is free to decide when he will exercise that right.[5]

On the other hand, a general testamentary power, i.e. one that is exercisable only by will, though it will vest in the donee, if at all, within the perpetuity period, is void if it may be exercised beyond that period. The reason is that the property is tied up during the lifetime of the donee in the sense that he possesses no right of alienation until his death. Therefore, such a power is void if, as in the case of one given to the unborn child of a living person, it may be exercisable at too remote a time.[6]

2. *Validity of appointment* The donee of a general power, since he can appoint to anybody in the world, including himself, has complete and absolute freedom of disposition, and therefore for the purpose of testing the validity of his appointments the perpetuity period is reckoned from the exercise of the power, not from its creation.

This rule applies whether the general power is exercisable *inter vivos*, or whether it is a general testamentary power, exercisable only by will. It is arguable that the validity of an appointment made under a general testamentary power should be subject to the restrictions imposed on special powers, discussed below, on the ground that the disposition of the property is restricted during the lifetime of the donee. This, indeed, is the rule in all the American States except for Rhode Island. However, the donee has complete power of disposition on death, and the restriction imposed during the donee's lifetime is not thought to be a substantial breach of perpetuity policy. This view is confirmed, as we shall see, by the Act of 1964.

(ii) Special powers

1. *Validity of creation* As regards the validity of its creation, a special power is subject to the following rule:

> A special power which, according to the true construction of the instrument creating it, is capable of being exercised beyond lives in being and 21 years afterwards is, by reason of the rule against perpetuities, absolutely void.[7]

As in the case of a general power, a special power is too remote in its creation if the donee may not be ascertained or if the condition precedent to its exercise may not have occurred within lives in being and 21 years afterwards. But in the case of a special power there is the further requirement that the objects must be ascertainable within the same period. The difference in this respect between the two classes of powers may be illustrated by a power, to be exercised by deed, given to an unborn person.

A special power to this effect, as, for instance, one conferred by settlement

---

4 *Morgan v Gronow* (1873) LR 16 Eq 1 (in the case of the original appointment).
5 *Re Fane* [1913] 1 Ch 404 at 413.
6 *Wollaston v King* (1869) LR 8 Eq 165; *Morgan v Gronow*, supra.
7 *Re De Sommery* [1912] 2 Ch 622 at 630, per PARKER J; M & B p. 379.

upon the eldest son of X, a bachelor, to appoint to his children, is void *ab initio*.[8] At the time of the settlement, it can no doubt be said that the appointor will be ascertained, if at all, within 21 years from the death of the life in being, X; but it cannot be said that the children in whose favour alone the appointment may be made will be ascertainable, if at all, within the same period. In other words, the occasion upon which the power is to become operative may be too remote.[9]

On the other hand, as we have seen, a general power to the same effect exercisable by deed is valid. The donee, being ascertainable within the perpetuity period; has complete control over the property and, once ascertained, is in the same position as if he were already its absolute owner.[10]

Provided that a special power is so limited that it cannot be *exercised* beyond the perpetuity period, it is immaterial that under its terms an appointment may possibly be made that will be too remote, as in the case, for instance, of a devise:

to X for life, remainder to such of his issue as he shall by will appoint.[11]

At the date of such a devise, it is impossible to say whether the perpetuity rule will be transgressed or not, but this uncertainty does not invalidate the power. The appointments will fail only if in fact they are too remote.[12] The question is not what may be done, but what in fact is done. In other words this is an exceptional case at common law where it is necessary to wait and see what happens.

2. *Validity of appointment* Presuming now, that the power itself is valid in the sense that it is exercisable only within the perpetuity period, it remains to consider the test that governs the validity of appointments in fact made. It differs radically from that applicable to a general power.

In the case of a special power, the disposition of the property remains controlled by the donor; the donee has power only to appoint to a limited class. As Lord ROMER said:

It is as though the settlor had left a blank in the settlement which [the donee] fills up for him if and when the power of appointment is exercised.[13]

The rule therefore is that, for the purposes of the perpetuity rule, the appointment which is in fact made must be "read back" into the instrument which created the power; and the perpetuity period is reckoned from the time when the instrument came into operation.

Thus, in *Whitby v Von Luedecke*:[14]

A settlement made in 1844, upon the marriage of H and W, limited land to W for

8 *Wollaston v King* (1869) LR 8 Eq 165.
9 Gray, ss. 475, 477.
10 *Bray v Bree* (1834) 2 Cl & Fin 453.
11 *Slark v Dakyns* (1874) 10 Ch App 35; *Re Vaux* [1939] Ch 465 at 472, [1938] 4 All ER 297 at 302.
12 *Re Fane* [1913] 1 Ch 404 at 413–4.
13 *Muir (or Williams) v Muir* [1943] AC 468 at 483.
14 [1906] 1 Ch 783; *Re Legh's Settlement Trusts* [1938] Ch 39, [1937] 3 All ER 823. W, however, might have achieved her object by making the interest in the entire income vested instead of contingent. An appointment of one-half to X for life with remainder to Y for life, and of one-half to Y for life with remainder to X for life, would have been valid. The rule against perpetuities is, indeed, of a highly technical nature; see (1952) 68 LQR, pp. 47–9 (W. B. Leach). See also *Re Brown and Sibly's Contract* (1876) 3 Ch D 156; M & B p. 380.

life and after her death to such of her children as she should appoint. The terms of her appointment were that the income of the land should be divided equally between her two daughters, X and Y, during their respective lives, but that upon the death of one it should pass in its entirety to the survivor.

It was held that the gift to the survivor was void. It was a contingent gift, and the event upon which it was to vest—the death of one of the daughters—would not necessarily occur within 21 years from the deaths of H and W who constituted the sole lives in being when the special power was created in 1844.

The rule, that the appointment ultimately made must be regarded as having been made in the original instrument of creation, merely ensures that the donee of the power shall not grant interests that the donor himself could not have granted. It is permitted, however, to read and construe the appointments in the light of the circumstances existing at the time when they are intended to take effect, not at the time when the power was created.[15]

Thus in *Re Paul*,[16] a disposition was saved by the application of the rule:

A testator died in 1895, leaving a share in his residuary estate to his daughter, Mrs. A, for life and after her death as she should appoint among her children. She made an appointment in 1919 to her son on attaining the age of 25 years. The son was then 18. The appointment was read back into the will as an appointment by Mrs. A to her son at an age which he must attain, if at all, within 21 years of Mrs. A's death. It was therefore valid.

(6) EFFECT OF INFRINGEMENT ON SUBSEQUENT INTERESTS[17]

Where one of a series of limitations is void for perpetuity, the question arises as to the effect of that void limitation upon the other limitations which are not in themselves void. The obvious solution would seem to be to ignore the void limitation, and to let the valid limitations take effect as if the void limitation never existed. But the matter is not so simple.[18]

(a) Where subsequent limitation is subject to a void contingency

Where the subsequent limitation is itself subject to a void contingency, whether the same as or different from that of the earlier void limitation, the subsequent limitation is of course void. Thus a limitation:

to A for life with remainder to such of his grandchildren as shall marry, but if no grandchildren of A shall marry, then to the children of B (who is alive) absolutely.

The gift to the children of B is void. Those who qualify may include future born children of B; and the takers will not be ascertained until it is known whether any of A's grandchildren marry, and that may not be known until a time outside the perpetuity period.

15 Gray, s. 523; *Wilkinson v Duncan* (1861) 30 Beav 111; M & B p. 382; *Von Brockdorff v Malcolm* (1885) 30 Ch D 172; *Re Thompson* [1906] 2 Ch 199; *Re Paul* [1921] 2 Ch 1; M & B p. 381.
16 Supra.
17 See (1950) 10 CLJ 392 (J. H. C. Morris); (1950) 14 Conv (NS) 148 (A. K. R. Kiralfy).
18 Many questions of this type are settled in the United States by the application of the doctrine of "infectious invalidity". Under this doctrine, the invalidity of an important part of a limitation may cause the whole limitation to be held void. The justification is that, if the testator's plan is so changed by the invalidity of one part, then he may well prefer to rely on the intestacy provisions instead.

If the gift over had been to the living (or named) children of B for their lives, the gift over would be valid; for the gift over in those circumstances must vest, if at all, within the lifetime of those living children of B. The contrary was, however, held in *Re Hewett's Settlement*:[19]

> In a marriage settlement, life interests were given to the husband and wife, and after their deaths the property was to be divided between such of their children as should attain the age of 25, and "if there should be no child of the marriage who should attain twenty-five" then on trust for the testator's three sisters, Helga, Hilda and Hulda.

The gift to the sisters was held to be void. Such a result could only be reached by failing to appreciate that the gift must vest in the sisters, if at all, during their own lifetimes. They were therefore the lives in being in relation to the gift to themselves; and the fact that that intermediate gift was void should have been treated as irrelevant.

(b) Intention that subsequent limitation should take effect only after termination of prior void limitation

In *Re Abbott*,[20] STIRLING J said, in a famous dictum:

> It is settled that any limitation depending or expectant upon a prior limitation which is void for remoteness is invalid. The reason appears to be that the persons entitled under the subsequent limitation are not intended to take unless and until the prior limitation is exhausted; and as the prior limitation which is void for remoteness can never come into operation, much less be exhausted, it is impossible to give effect to the intentions of the settlor in favour of the beneficiaries under the subsequent limitation.

There is little to be said in support of this proposition. But some cases can only be supported on this ground. In *Re Backhouse*:[1]

> A picture was bequeathed for a series of life interests, some of which were void for perpetuity, with an ultimate gift to the testator's right heirs. This last gift was in favour of persons who would be ascertained at the testator's death, and would therefore vest at that time. Even so, it was held void on the ground that it was subsequent to the prior void limitations.

The modern and better view is that the subsequent limitation, valid in itself, should be accelerated so as to take effect in the place of the earlier void limitation.

(c) Later limitation not dependent

Where an interest is created which will not take effect in possession until a future date, but must vest in interest within the perpetuity period, and its possessory enjoyment is not dependent on the exhaustion of the precedent interests, it will be unaffected by remoteness in any of the antecedent interests.[2] This is illustrated by *Re Coleman*:[3]

---

19 [1915] 1 Ch 810; *Re Thatcher's Trusts* (1859) 26 Beav 365 at 369; *Re Hubbard's Will Trusts* [1963] Ch 275, [1962] 2 All ER 917; M & B p. 383; *Re Buckton's Settlement Trusts* [1964] Ch 497, [1964] 2 All ER 487.
20 [1893] 1 Ch 54 at 57.
 1 [1921] 2 Ch 51.
 2 *Re Hubbard's Will Trusts*, supra, at 285–7, at 921–3. *Re Backhouse*, supra, however, is inconsistent with this proposition.
 3 [1936] Ch 528; followed in *Re Allan* [1958] 1 WLR 220, [1958] 1 All ER 401.

A testator left his residuary estate on discretionary trusts to H for life; after H's death upon similar discretionary trusts for any widow who might survive him; and after the death of such widow upon trust (not discretionary) for the children of H at 21 in equal shares.

By virtue of the discretionary trusts, the trustees were empowered to make payments of income to H or his widow. But this trust in the widow's case was void, for H might marry a woman born after the testator's death, and if so the discretion of the trustees, which was a condition precedent to her right to an interest, might be exercisable beyond the perpetuity period. Nevertheless, it was held that the limitation to the children was valid. The interests of the children would necessarily vest, if at all, within 21 years of H's death. Their interests were not dependent on the validity of the discretionary power to pay income to the widow.

(d) Divestment on occurrence of void condition

Where a testator or settlor gives property to A either immediately or at some future date which is not too remote, but so frames his trusts that the interest of A may be displaced by the exercise of some power or discretion, the interest of A will be unaffected by any invalidity of that power or discretion on the ground of remoteness.[4]

In one case, for instance, a testator allocated a fund to be used at the discretion of trustees upon the maintenance of a mansion-house so long as any person entitled to the house under a strict settlement should be under 21 years of age, "and subject thereto" upon trust for A absolutely. The discretionary trust for the maintenance of the house was admittedly too remote, but it was held that the trust in favour of A was an independent limitation and was valid.[5]

The destination of the property affected by a remote limitation differs according as the disposition is made by deed or by will. In the former case it results to the settlor. In the case of a will, it goes to the residuary legatee or devisee, but to the persons entitled as on an intestacy of the testator if there is no residuary gift or if the residue itself is the subject matter of the limitation. If the void limitation is effected by the exercise of a special power of appointment, the property concerned passes to the persons entitled in default of appointment.

(7) ALTERNATIVE LIMITATIONS

Where a settlor makes the vesting of a future gift dependent upon two alternative events, one of which is too remote and the other not, the gift is allowed to take effect if the event which is not too remote is the one that actually happens.[6] This doctrine provides an exception to the rule that possible, not actual, events are alone considered, for the court waits to see

---

4 *Re Hubbard's Will Trusts*, supra at 287, at 923, per BUCKLEY J.
5 *Re Canning's Will Trusts* [1936] Ch 309; see also *Re Abbott* [1893] 1 Ch 54. The difficulties arising from this doctrine of dependency no longer affect instruments taking effect after 15 July 1964; PAA 1964, s. 6; p. 325, post.
6 *Longhead v Phelps* (1770) 2 Wm Bl 704; *Leake v Robinson* (1817) 2 Mer 363; *Re Curryer's Will Trusts* [1938] Ch 952, [1938] 3 All ER 574; Gray, chapter ix.

which of the two events in fact occurs.[7] Thus in the early case of *Longhead v Phelps*[8] a marriage settlement declared that certain trusts should arise:

> if H should die without issue male *or* if such issue male should die without issue.

The latter contingency was obviously too remote, for whether H's male issue died without themselves leaving issue might not necessarily be known within 21 years of the death of any person living at the date of the testator's death, but in fact he died without male issue and it was held that the trusts were valid. In a more recent case[9] a testator created a trust to take effect:

> upon the decease of my last surviving child *or* the death of the last surviving widow or widower of my children as the case may be whichever shall last happen.

Here again the last contingency was too remote, since one or more of the children might marry a person born after the testator's death, but it was held that the trust would be valid if the first contingency in fact happened, i.e. if all the widows and widowers were dead when the last surviving child died.

The courts, however, have consistently held that this indulgence will not be shown to the valid gift unless the settlor has himself expressly and distinctly designated the two alternative contingencies.[10] If vesting is in terms made dependent upon a single event which in fact includes two contingencies, one too remote the other not too remote, the future gift is void, although the contingency which actually happens is the one that satisfies the perpetuity rule. The court will not split the expression used by the settlor, i.e. will not separate and state in an alternative form the two events that the expression in fact includes. By way of illustration we may refer once more to *Proctor v Bishop of Bath and Wells*.[11] In that case the fee simple was devised:

> to the first or other son of A that should be bred a clergyman, and be in Holy Orders, but in case he should have no such son, then to B in fee simple.

It is clear on analysis that the event upon which the gift to B was dependent included two contingencies, namely:

(a) failure of A to leave sons;
(b) failure of any son to take Holy Orders.

A gift to B to take effect if A left no sons would obviously be valid, but though A did in fact die childless, it was held that B was not entitled to the fee simple. If the description of the event had been alternative, instead of single, in point of expression, all would have been well; i.e. if the testator had expressly stated that the fee simple was to vest in B:

> if A had no son *or* if he had no son who should take Holy Orders,

B's claim would have been upheld, since it was the first contingency that in fact happened. What the court refused to do was to redraft in an alternative form the single expression appearing in the will. In cases of this kind the court does not concentrate upon implementing the testator's intention, for a man who says that an estate is to go over to B if none of A's sons becomes a

7 Morris and Leach, pp. 181–4.
8 (1770) 2 Wm Bl 704.
9 *Re Curryer's Will Trusts*, supra.
10 *Re Bence* [1891] 3 Ch 242; *Miles v Harford* (1879) 12 Ch D 691 at 702, per JESSEL MR.
11 (1794) 2 Hy Bl 358; p. 293 ante.

clergyman obviously means it to go over if A never has a son. Whether the intention will prevail is purely a question of words:

> You are bound to take the expression as you find it, and if, giving the proper interpretation to that expression, the event may transgress the limit, then the gift over is void.[12]

(8) EXCEPTIONS TO THE RULE AGAINST PERPETUITIES

(a) Limitations after entailed interests

A tenant in tail can bar his own and all subsequent interests. The rule, therefore, is that no limitation after an entailed interest is void for remoteness, provided that the subsequent limitation must vest, if at all, at or before the end of the perpetuity period. There is in fact no perpetuity.[13]

(b) Contracts and options[14]

"It is settled beyond argument that an agreement merely personal, not creating any interest in land, is not within the rule against perpetuities."[15] Therefore, it is not void simply because the obligation it creates may last for an indefinite time.[16] For instance, in *Walsh v Secretary of State for India*:[17]

> the East India Company entered into a covenant in 1770 whereby they promised to pay a certain sum of money if, at any time after 1794, they should cease to have a military force in their pay and service in the East Indies. It might have been centuries before such a state of things occurred, and in point of fact it was nearly a century, but nevertheless the court upheld the validity of the obligation.

It is equally well settled at common law that even a contract which creates an interest in land remains binding upon the parties themselves, notwithstanding that it may be enforceable beyond the perpetuity period. So long as privity of contract exists, there is no room for the rule against perpetuities. Thus in *Hutton v Watling*:[18]

> A written agreement by which X sold his business to Y stipulated that Y should have the option, exercisable at any time in the future, to purchase the premises in which the business was carried on.

An action by Y for specific performance brought seven years later was met by the plea that the stipulation was void for remoteness. The plea failed. In such a case, Y is entitled not only to recover damages from X,[19] but also to a decree of specific performance if the land is still retained by X, for "specific performance is merely an equitable mode of enforcing a personal obligation with which the rule against perpetuities has nothing to do".[20]

But once the promisee seeks to enforce the promise against a third person,

12 *Miles v Harford* (1879) 12 Ch D 691 at 703, per JESSEL MR.
13 *Nicholls v Sheffield* (1787) 2 Bro CC 215; *Heasman v Pearse* (1871) 7 Ch App 275.
14 See (1954) 18 Conv (NS) 576 (J. H. C. Morris and W. B. Leach).
15 *South Eastern Rly Co v Associated Portland Cement Manufacturers (1900) Ltd* [1910] 1 Ch 12 at 33, per FARWELL J.
16 *Witham v Vane* (1883); Challis, *Law of Real Property* (3rd edn), p. 440.
17 (1863) 10 HL Cas 367.
18 [1948] Ch 26, [1947] 2 All ER 641; affd on other grounds [1948] Ch 398, [1948] 1 All ER 803.
19 *Worthing Corpn v Heather* [1906] 2 Ch 532.
20 *Hutton v Watling* [1948] Ch 26 at 36, [1947] 2 All ER 641 at 645, per JENKINS J. This rule has been reversed in the case of instruments taking effect after 15 July 1964; p. 325, post.

the position is changed. We now pass from the law of contract to the law of property, with the result that such an option as that in *Hutton v Watling* or an option given to a lessee to purchase the reversion, since it creates an executory interest in land, cannot be enforced against third persons who later acquire the promisor's land unless it is confined within the perpetuity period.[1] Thus where a railway company sold land to one Powell subject to a right of repurchase if at any time thereafter the land was required for the railway, it was held that the right was unenforceable against the appellant, to whom Powell's heir had sold the land.[2]

JESSEL MR said:

> If then the rule as to remoteness applies to a covenant of this nature, this covenant clearly is bad as extending beyond the period allowed by the rule. Whether the rule applies or not depends upon this as it appears to me—does or does not the covenant give an interest in the land? If it is a bare or mere personal contract it is of course not obnoxious to the rule, but in that case it is impossible to see how the present appellant can be bound. He did not enter into the contract, but is only a purchaser from Powell who did. If it is a mere personal contract it cannot be enforced against the assignee. Therefore the company must admit that it somehow binds the land. But if it binds the land it creates an equitable interest in the land. The right to call for a conveyance of the land is an equitable interest or equitable estate.

Thus, an option to call for a lease of land exemplifies this principle and is void if it is exercisable beyond the perpetuity period, but it has long been recognized that an option given to a tenant to *renew* his existing lease is entirely unaffected by the rule against perpetuities.[3]

(c) Certain easements and mortgages

A further illustration of the principles laid down by JESSEL MR is that the grant of an easement to arise *in futuro* may be void on the ground of remoteness, as for example where it entitles the grantee to use the drains and sewers "now passing *or hereafter to pass*" under a private road.[4]

The rule against perpetuities has no application to mortgages, and therefore a postponement of the right of redemption for longer than the perpetuity period is not void for remoteness,[5] though it may be void on other grounds.[6]

(d) Certain rights of entry

The rule affects certain rights of entry, but not others.

(i) Forfeiture of lease The right usually reserved to a lessor to enter upon the land and to terminate the lease if the tenant commits a breach of covenant[7] is not subject to the rule.[8]

1 *Woodall v Clifton* [1905] 2 Ch 257; M & B p. 386; *London and South Western Rly Co v Gomm* (1882) 20 Ch D 562; M & B p. 387; *Griffith v Pelton* [1958] Ch 205, [1957] 3 All ER 75.
2 *London and South Western Rly Co v Gomm*, supra.
3 *Woodall v Clifton*, supra, at 265, 268; *Weg Motors Ltd v Hales* [1961] Ch 176, [1960] 3 All ER 762; affd [1962] Ch 49, [1961] 3 All ER 181.
4 *Dunn v Blackdown Properties Ltd* [1961] Ch 433, [1961] 2 All ER 62; (1961) 25 Conv (NS) 415 (G. Battersby); *Newham v Lawson* (1971) 22 P & CR 852.
5 *Knightsbridge Estates Trust Ltd v Byrne* [1939] Ch 441 at 463, [1938] 4 All ER 618 at 631; affd. [1940] AC 613, [1940] 2 All ER 401.
6 Pp. 674–6, post.
7 Pp. 427, 434, post.
8 *Re Tyrrell's Estate* [1907] 1 IR 292 at 298, per WALKER LC.

(ii) Enforcement of rentcharge There are three situations to consider in relation to the enforcement of a rentcharge.

First, the owner of a rentcharge, i.e. a person, other than a reversioner, entitled to the payment of an annual sum of money out of land,[9] is empowered by the Law of Property Act 1925,[10] in the event of non-payment to enter upon the land and to recover the money due either by levying distress or by leasing the land to a trustee until all arrears have been paid. The Act puts this right of entry, together with its attendant remedies, outside the rule against perpetuities.[11]

If the instrument creating the charge expressly empowers the creditor to enter the land and to determine the fee simple estate of the debtor for non-payment of rent, or to enter and enforce some covenant other than that to pay the sum due, it is doubtful whether such a power is excluded from the perpetuity rule by virtue of the Act.[12]

Secondly, a rentcharge is sometimes created merely by way of indemnity against another rentcharge.[13] If, for instance, an estate which as a whole is subject to a rentcharge is being sold off in lots, it is a common practice to throw the burden of the charge entirely upon one lot. In practice the purchaser of that lot then gives the purchasers of the other lots an indemnity rentcharge issuing out of his land, so that if they as purchasers of parts of the whole land are compelled by the rent-owner to pay the charge, they will have a right to reimburse themselves out of the lot on which it has been thrown.

The former doubt whether the law of remoteness applied to such cases was dispelled by the Law of Property Act 1925, which provides that rentcharges created only by way of indemnity against other rentcharges and powers to distrain or to take possession of land affected by such rentcharges, shall be excluded from the operation of the rule against perpetuities.[14]

Thirdly, if a fee simple is sold in return for a perpetual annual rentcharge, the right of entry or re-entry that accrues to the vendor in the event of non-payment,[15] although exercisable for an unlimited period, does not withdraw the land from commerce and therefore is unaffected by the rule against perpetuities.[16]

(iii) Condition broken A right of entry for condition broken attached to a fee simple is void if it is exercisable beyond the perpetuity period.[17]

(e) Accumulative trust of income for the purpose of paying debts

The rule does not apply to a trust directing that income shall be accumulated with a view to the payment of the settlor's debts, or for the discharge of incumbrances charged upon the land, for such a trust, though capable of enduring for an indefinite time, may be determined at any moment either by the beneficiaries paying the debts and freeing the land, or by the creditors

9 P. 651, post.
10 S. 121.
11 S. 121 (6).
12 See Morris and Leach, p. 218. The doubt has been removed by PAA 1964, s. 11, which, however, is not retrospective; see p. 326, post.
13 P. 653, post.
14 LPA 1925, s. 162 (1) (*a*).
15 P. 157, ante; p. 647, post.
16 Compare the remarks of Lord BROUGHAM in *Keppell v Bailey* (1834) 2 My & K 517 at 528–9.
17 *Re Hollis' Hospital Trustees and Hague's Contract* [1899] 2 Ch 540; LPA 1925, s. 4 (3); p. 341, post.

enforcing their claims by the seizure of the land.[18] Neither does the rule apply to a trust under which money is to be accumulated for the reduction of the National Debt.[19]

(f) Pension and superannuation funds

If there were no specific exemption for pension and superannuation funds, they would become void after the end of the perpetuity period, because interests in the fund might vest at too remote a time.[20] Under the common law rule, the trust fund would have been wholly void unless expressly limited to the perpetuity period. In order to avoid this problem, the Social Security Act 1973 makes express provision for all qualifying occupational pension schemes to be exempt from the rule.[1]

(g) Administrative powers of trustees

The former rule was that administrative powers given to trustees, such as a power to sell or lease land, or to receive remuneration for their services, were void if they were capable of being exercised at too remote a time, notwithstanding that they were attached to a trust which itself was not too remote. This may be illustrated by *Re Allott*:[2]

> A testator left his mines to trustees upon trust to pay annuities to his daughters out of the profits. He directed that if a daughter married, and was survived by her husband, such survivor should be entitled for his life to her annuity.
> After the testator's death, a deed of family arrangement was entered into which incorporated the trusts of the will and which inter alia gave the trustees powers to grant leases not exceeding 99 years.

The life interest given to any surviving husband was valid despite the fact that he might be a person not born at the date of the execution of the deed. His life interest would necessarily arise, if it ever arose at all, immediately on the death of his wife. Nevertheless, the power of leasing was void, since it might be exercised, and so create a fresh interest, more than 21 years after the dropping of the lives in being if the husband lived so long.

The effect of administrative powers is not to tie up the property, but to facilitate its management, and therefore the Law Reform Committee recommended that they should be excluded from the perpetuity rule provided that the trusts to which they are ancillary are valid and subsisting. This recommendation has been accepted by the Perpetuities and Accumulations Act 1964, in the only section that is retrospective. It provides that:

> The rule against perpetuities shall not operate to invalidate a power conferred on trustees or other persons to sell, lease, exchange or otherwise dispose of property for full consideration, or to do any other act in the administration (as opposed to the distribution) of any property, and shall not prevent the payment to trustees or other persons of reasonable remuneration for their services.[3]

18 *Tewart v Lawson* (1874) LR 18 Eq 490; *Lord Southampton v Marquis of Hertford* (1813) 2 Ves & B 54.
19 Superannuation and Other Trust Funds (Validation) Act 1927, s. 9.
20 *Re Flavel's Will Trusts* [1969] 1 WLR 444, [1969] 2 All ER 232; p. 294, n. 12, ante.
 1 S. 69; Personal and Occupational Pension Schemes (Perpetuities) Regs 1990 (S.I. 1990 No. 1143).
 2 [1924] 2 Ch 498.
 3 S. 8 (1). If a power has been created before the commencement of the Act, i.e. 16 July, 1964, this section is applicable, provided that the exercise is effected after that date: s. 8 (2).

It should be noticed that it is only *administrative* powers that are exempt from the rule against perpetuities. The rule applies to beneficial powers such as powers of appointment,[4] powers of distribution under a discretionary trust and powers of maintenance and advancement.[5]

(h) Certain limitations to charities

An interest given to a charity, like any other gift, is void unless it will vest within the perpetuity period.[6] On the other hand, a limitation transferring property from one charity to another upon a certain contingency is valid, although the contingency may not occur until some indefinite time in the future. Provided that the interest of the first charity will begin within the perpetuity period, it is immaterial that the second charity may not take until a remote date. Thus in one case, where:

> a testator bequeathed £42,000 to the London Missionary Society with a gift over to the Blue Coat School if the Society failed to keep his family vault in repair,

it was held that the gift over was valid.[7] Had the gift over been, not to another charity, but to private persons, it would have been void.[8]

A gift to a charity is not void as a perpetuity merely because it creates an interest that may remain subject to the charitable trust for an indefinite period.[9]

C. THE RULE APPLICABLE TO INSTRUMENTS TAKING EFFECT AFTER 15 JULY 1964[10]

The Perpetuities and Accumulations Act 1964 came into operation on 16 July 1964.[11] It can be regarded as achieving two things: first, it provided a number of specific solutions to specific problems created by the common law rule,[12] and secondly, it altered the whole basis of operation of the perpetuity rule, by introducing the principle of "wait and see". "Wait and see" is applicable, in the place of the common law rule requiring certainty of vesting, to dispositions which fail to comply with the common law rule. The draftsman expected the question of the validity of a disposition to be determined by the application first of the common law rule; if valid, all is well; if void, the disposition may be saved by the application of "wait and see". It will be

---

4 P. 299, ante.
5 *Pilkington v IRC* [1964] AC 612, [1962] 3 All ER 622; *Re Hastings-Bass* [1975] Ch 25, [1974] 2 All ER 193 (statutory power of advancement under TA 1925, s. 32).
6 *Chamberlayne v Brockett* (1872) 8 Ch App 206; *Re Lord Stratheden and Campbell* [1894] 3 Ch 265; *Re Mander* [1950] Ch 547, [1950] 2 All ER 191.
7 *Re Tyler* [1891] 3 Ch 252; following *Christ's Hospital v Grainger* (1849) 1 Mac & G 460. For a criticism of this decision see Gray, s. 603.
8 *Re Talbot* [1933] Ch 895; *Re Bland-Sutton's Will Trusts* [1951] Ch 485, [1951] 1 All ER 494; revsd in part [1952] AC 631, [1952] 1 All ER 984.
9 *Chamberlayne v Brockett* (1872) 8 Ch App 206 at 211; *Goodman v Saltash Corpn* (1882) 7 App Cas 633 at 650, 651; *Re Bowen* [1893] 2 Ch 491 at 494.
10 See generally Morris and Leach, Supplement; (1964) 80 LQR 486 (J. H. C. Morris and H. W. R. Wade); Wolstenholme and Cherry, vol. 2. pp. 135 et seq.; Maudsley, chapters 4, 5 and 6.
11 The Act applies where there is a disposition contained in an instrument. On disposition, see *Re Thomas Meadows & Co Ltd* [1971] Ch 278, [1971] 1 All ER 239; and on instrument, see *Re Holt's Settlement* [1969] 1 Ch 100, [1968] 1 All ER 470 (court order approving an arrangement under the Variation of Trusts Act 1958 constitutes an instrument).
12 Ss. 1, 2, 5, 6 and 7.

seen, when section 3 is discussed, that this method has caused a number of unnecessary difficulties. It would have been preferable to abolish the common law rule, and to replace it by "wait and see". The sections of the Act will be examined in order.

(1) SECTION 1. THE PERPETUITY PERIOD

As an alternative to the common law period during which it is permissible to suspend the vesting of interests, section 1 allows the settlor to specify a fixed period of years not exceeding 80.[13] This provision was intended to provide a more attractive option than the royal lives clause[14] in cases where, as is usual with discretionary trusts, the settlor or testator intended to lay down the period of duration of a trust; and it has had that effect.

It must be emphasized that this alternative period must be expressly specified in the instrument. And, in order to be valid under the common law rule, the vesting of interests under the trust must be related to the period selected. Thus, it is a valid specification of the alternative period of years if the settlor or testator provides for a "trust period" of 80 years (or smaller period) during which the trustee can exercise various discretionary powers, with a provision that the trust assets vest in identifiable beneficiaries at the conclusion of the period. The vesting is then related to the alternative perpetuity period. But a disposition would be void under the common law rule if the gift was not related to the alternative period. There is no "wait and see" period of 80 years. Thus, either of the two following dispositions would be void under the rule:

> to such of the issue of X as may be living at the expiration of 80 years after X's death. The period was not specified.
> to the lineal issue of X. I specify the period of 80 years as the perpetuity period applicable to this disposition. The period was specified, but the vesting was not related to the period.

In each case, the gift being void, the "wait and see" provisions of section 3 will apply. Those beneficiaries whose interests in fact vest within 21 years of the dropping of the survivor of the *statutory* measuring lives will take.

The donor of a special power may provide that the perpetuity period applicable to the limitations shall be a fixed number of years not exceeding 80. Such period will, of course, begin to run from the effective creation of the power, and it cannot be extended by the donee when he makes an appointment.[15]

(2) PRESUMPTIONS AS TO FERTILITY

The rule at common law that a person of whatever age must be regarded as capable of having children[16] has been abolished in the case of instruments taking effect after 15 July 1964.

Under the Act it is to be presumed in any proceedings that a male can

---

13 PAA 1964, s. 1 (1); *Re Green's Will Trusts* [1985] 3 All ER 455; M & B p. 352 (period specified as "from the date of my death to the 1st day of January 2020" held valid as being "unambiguously identified" or "made clear" as a period of 43$\frac{11}{12}$ years from the testator's death on 1 February 1976 to 1 January 2020). This provision does not apply to certain options to acquire an interest in land; s. 9 (2), p. 317, post.
14 P. 292, ante.
15 PAA 1964, s. 1 (2).
16 Pp. 295–6, ante.

beget a child at, but not under, the age of 14 years; and that a female can have a child at, but not over, the age of 55 years.[17] In the case of a living person, however, evidence may be given to rebut these presumptions, by showing that he or she will not be able to have a child at the time in question.[18]

The Act extends these presumptions to the possibility that a person will at any time have a child by adoption, legitimation or other means.[19] If a person is adopted or legitimated, the question arises whether or not he will take as a "child" of an adopting or legitimating parent under a gift to that person's "children". The rule prior to the coming into force of the Children Act 1975 was that an adopted or legitimated child took under such a disposition if he had been adopted or legitimated *before* the instrument came into effect.[20] Under the Children Act 1975, which applies to instruments coming into effect after 1 January 1976, such a person can take whether the adoption or legitimation was before or after the date of the instrument.[1]

A further question arises in relation to the presumption in section 2 of the Perpetuities and Accumulations Act 1964 to the effect that a woman over the age of 55 is incapable of giving birth to a child. A woman over that age might, of course, adopt or legitimate a child.[2] For the purpose of the perpetuity rule, however, the presumption remains.[3] If property has been distributed on the basis of the presumption, and a woman does give birth to, or adopt, or legitimate, a child inconsistently with it, the High Court is empowered to make such order "so far as may be just", for placing the beneficiaries in the position they would have held had the presumption not been applied.[4]

(3) UNCERTAINTY AS TO REMOTENESS. SECTION 3. WAIT AND SEE

It has been seen that a disposition is void under the common law rule unless it is certain to vest, if at all, within 21 years of the death of some person living at the date when the instrument comes into effect. The disposition is void even though it is 99 per cent certain that it will vest, if at all, within the period. And the void disposition is not helped by the fact that it *does in fact vest* within the period. We saw that a gift to the first child of A to marry is void under the common law rule. It is immaterial that, at the date of the gift, three of A's children are engaged to be married, and do in fact marry on the following Saturday.

Factors like these brought the rule into disrepute. The Law Reform Committee[5] examined the problem and accepted the very convincing argument that, instead of basing the decision on the certainty of vesting as seen from the date when the instrument came into effect, it would be very

17 PAA 1964, s. 2 (1) (*a*).
18 Ibid., s. 2 (1) (*b*).
19 See also the effect of the Family Law Reform Act 1969, s. 15 and the Family Law Reform Act 1987, s. 1 (1), p. 859, post.
20 Adoption Act 1958, s. 16; Legitimacy Act 1926, s. 3.
1 Adoption Act 1976, s. 39. On legitimation, see Legitimacy Act 1976, s. 5, Schs. 1 and 2.
2 Or even give birth to a child.
3 PAA 1964, s. 2 (4). As it does also in relation to an adoption after the date of the instrument: Adoption Act 1976, s. 42 (5) and n. 1, supra.
4 Ibid., s. 2 (2).
5 Fourth Report, 1956 (Cmnd 18).

much better to wait and see whether it did in fact vest within the period. If it did vest within the period, it was valid. If it did not, it was void.

This solution is deceptively simple. Two important principles have to be observed if "wait and see" is to be made to work. The first principle is that, if "wait and see" is enacted, that is, if validity is to be determined by waiting to see whether the disposition vests within the period of a life in being plus 21 years—it is essential to specify which lives are to be used to measure the period of a life in being plus 21 years. Otherwise, it is not known how long to wait and see.[6]

The Act introduces a comprehensive list of lives to be used to measure the period of waiting and seeing. The list will be examined in detail below.[7]

The second principle is that, once "wait and see" is enacted, the common law rule becomes irrelevant, and should be abolished. The common law rule becomes irrelevant, because it is no longer relevant to know whether or not a disposition complies with the common law rule. If an interest *must* vest, if at all, within the period, then it *will* vest, if at all, within the period. To say that it *must* vest, if at all, says nothing; the trustees still have to wait until the interest vests before paying out the money to the beneficiaries. Compare two dispositions:

(a) to the first child of A to attain the age of 21. A is alive and has a child aged 16.
(b) to the first great-grandchild of A to attain the age of 21. A is alive and has a great-grandchild aged 16.

The first disposition is valid under the common law rule. The trustees wait for 5 years to see if the child attains the age of 21, and then pay out the money.

The second disposition is void under the common law rule. So, under the Act, the trustees wait and see whether the first great-grandchild attains the age of 21 within the period.

There is no difference between these cases in the era of "wait and see", and they should both be solved on the principle of "wait and see".

If the Act had *replaced* the common law rule by "wait and see", the whole of the learning on the common law rule would have disappeared. It is impossible, however, to ignore it, because the list of measuring lives in section 3 fails to include *all* the lives which could be used to determine validity at common law. There are situations in which the disposition may be valid at common law, using the common law lives, but not so if the measuring lives listed in section 3 are used. Illustrations are cases where the settlor or testator has selected his own lives; these are omitted from the list in section 3. There are other cases of which the following may be taken as an example:

to the first of A's lineal descendants to go for a walk with X.

This would be valid at common law. But X is not included in the statutory list. If the walk takes place more than 21 years after the death of the survivor

---

6 It seems that the Law Reform Committee did not consider this question, nor did many jurisdictions which have selected wait and see; (1965) 81 LQR 106 (D. E. Allan); Maudsley, Appendix D. But the draftsman came to the rescue. In 1987 the American Uniform Act of Perpetuities adopted a period of 90 years as the wait and see period, in preference to a life in being and 21 years: (1987) 21 Real Property, Probate & Trust Journal 569; [1987] CLJ 234 (L. W. Waggoner).

7 S. 3 (5); p. 317, post.

of the persons in the statutory list, it will be void under the "wait and see" provision but valid under the common law.

There seems to be no point in preserving all the old learning on the common law rule to deal with situations of this type. But that is what happened. It is necessary therefore to understand both the common law and the "wait and see" principle. Simple alterations to the Act would make this unnecessary.[8]

Section 3 provides that,[9] where an interest would be void under the common law rule on the ground that it might vest outside the common law perpetuity period, the disposition shall be treated as not subject to the rule, until it becomes established that the vesting can only occur *outside* the period. Subsection (4) provides that where the section applies, the perpetuity period shall be measured by the lives of the persons listed in subsection (5), plus 21 years.[10] In other words, if the disposition is void under the common law rule, using either the common law lives plus 21 years or, if so specified, the specified period not exceeding 80 years, the interest will be treated as valid (unless it becomes clear that the interest will *not* vest within the period) during a period measured by the *statutory* lives plus 21 years. In short, if the disposition is void under the common law rule, there is "wait and see" for a period measured by the statutory lives plus 21 years.

As a result of the Act, there are no less than three perpetuity periods and two basic doctrines.[11] This reinforces the argument made above that the common law rule should have been abolished and replaced by "wait and see". There would then have been one period, one doctrine, and one set of lives.[12] Illustrations of the working of the principle of "wait and see" will be delayed until the statutory lives have been examined.

(a) Each part of limitation a separate disposition

In the application of the "wait and see" principle, each distinct part of a limitation is treated by the Act as a separate disposition. For instance:

A testator devises land to A for life, remainder to his widow for life, remainder to such of the children of A as are alive at the death of the widow; but if there be no such children, then to the first son of X to marry.

In such a case, the gift to the children of A and the gift to the first son of X to marry are distinct dispositions subject to different waiting periods.

(b) Special power of appointment

The "wait and see" principle applies equally to the validity of appointments made by the exercise of a special power:

Suppose that a testator, who dies in 1965, devises land to A, a bachelor, for life, remainder to such of his issue as he shall by will appoint. A appoints in favour of his infant daughter, X *on her marriage*. A dies in 1975.

8 Maudsley, Appendix E.
9 Apart from ss. 4 and 5.
10 See ss. 1 (80 year period), p. 312, ante; 9 (2) (21 year period in connection with options to purchase).
11 I.e., certainty of vesting and "wait and see".
12 Or two, if the 80 year period were applicable for "wait and see".

At common law the appointment is too remote.[13] Under the Act, it is valid provided that the daughter marries within 21 years after A's death.

(c) Intermediate income

One problem raised by these provisions is the destination of the intermediate income during the waiting period.[14] The general rule, subject to certain exceptions, is that, although the vesting contingency may ultimately never be satisfied, a contingent gift carries the income arising from the corpus, except so far as such income has been otherwise disposed of by the donor.[15] Suppose, for example, that a testator bequeaths the residue of his estate to his grandchild, X, upon her marriage and that she is an infant and unmarried at the time of the testator's death. In these circumstances, the income is accumulated during her infancy and the trustees may use it for her maintenance and education,[16] and may make advances to her out of capital,[17] but at her majority the income becomes and remains payable to her even though she may never marry.[18]

The rights of the beneficiaries in such a case, however, are subject to the perpetuity rule, the effect of which varies according as the disposition falls to be determined by the common law or by the Act of 1964:

> Suppose, for instance, that a will bequeaths the residue of the estate to the daughters of X when they marry, and that X is childless at the time of the testator's death.

At common law the bequest is void *ab initio*. It is impossible to say at the time when the will takes effect that, if any daughters born to X marry, they will do so within 21 years from her death.

But under the statutory "wait and see" provisions the gift is not void *ab initio*. It is void only if at the end of 21 years from the death of the last of the statutory lives none of X's daughters, if any, has married. The destination of the income of the corpus during this waiting period therefore presents a problem. If a daughter is born to X, is she to receive the benefit of the income although the bequest may ultimately become void for remoteness? The recommendation of the Law Reform Committee that such should be the rule[19] was accepted by the Act of 1964, which provides that when it becomes established that the vesting of a gift must occur, if at all, after the end of the perpetuity period, "the validity of anything previously done in relation to the interest disposed of by way of advancement, application of intermediate income or otherwise" shall not be affected.[20]

(d) General powers of appointment

A general power of appointment that may possibly be exercised beyond the perpetuity period, and which is therefore void at common law,[1] is to be

---

13 Compare the example, discussed, p. 302, ante.
14 See Morris and Leach, pp. 93–5.
15 See e.g. LPA 1925, s. 175 (2).
16 Trustee Act 1925, s. 31 (1) (i); 31 (2). For dispositions taking effect after 1969 the age of majority has been reduced to 18: Family Law Reform Act 1969, s. 1. Schs. 1, 3, para. 5.
17 Ibid., s. 32.
18 Ibid., s. 31 (1) (ii).
19 Para 22 (1956 Cmnd 18).
20 PAA 1964, s. 3 (1).
 1 P. 301, ante.

treated as valid until it is established that it will not in fact be exercised at too remote a time.[2] If, for instance, it is exercisable only by will and is given to the unborn child of X, it will be valid if the donee is born and dies within 21 years after X's death; if it is exercisable by deed, or either by deed or by will, but only on the marriage of the unborn child, it will be valid if the marriage occurs within the same period.

(e) Any power, option or other right

In a more comprehensive section, the Act deals separately with the remote exercise of "any power, option or other right". It provides that a power, option or other right is no longer to be rendered void merely because it may possibly be exercised at too remote a time. It will be void only if it is not in fact fully exercised within the perpetuity period:[3]

> For instance, a special power granted by a deed of settlement to the eldest son of X, a bachelor, is void *ab initio* at common law;[4] but under the Act it is not void unless exercised beyond the perpetuity period calculated from the date of the settlement.

On the other hand, if the exercise of a special power satisfies the test of remoteness prescribed by this subsection, the question whether the appointed interests are too remote is governed, as we have seen, by an earlier subsection.[5]

The reference in this enactment to an "option" means, inter alia, that a right conferred by contract upon one person to purchase the land of another at some unspecified time in the future is no longer void *ab initio*,[6] but void only if it is not in fact exercised within the perpetuity period.

But, except where the option is one that entitles a tenant to purchase his landlord's reversion, which is exercisable throughout the continuance of the lease however long this may be,[7] the only period applicable to an option to acquire for valuable consideration any interest in land is 21 years.[8]

(4) DURATION OF THE WAITING PERIOD. THE STATUTORY LIVES

(a) General

Before examining the statutory list of measuring lives, three important preliminary points need to be made. First, as explained above, there is the obvious point that it is impossible to wait and see for lives in being plus 21 years unless it is known whose lives are to be used for the period of waiting and seeing. Those lives need to be known exactly and precisely; otherwise difficult questions will be asked when the period comes to an end. And, for the convenience of the trustees administering the fund, it is more important to have the lives specified at the time when the intrument comes into operation. Otherwise, they will have to add new "lives" as the years go by.

2 PAA 1964, s. 3 (2).
3 Ibid., s. 3 (3). It will be noticed that a general power is caught by this subsection as well as by subsection (2).
4 Pp. 301–3, ante.
5 PAA 1964, s. 3 (1); see the example given, p. 315, ante.
6 As under the common law, *London and South Western Rly Co v Gomm* (1882) 20 Ch D 562; p. 307, ante; *Dunn v Blackdown Properties Ltd* [1961] Ch 433, [1961] 2 All ER 62; p. 308, ante.
7 PAA 1964, s. 9 (1); p. 326, post.
8 Ibid., s. 9 (2).

The second point is that the common law lives will not do. The common law lives, as has been seen, are those within 21 years of whose death the interest must vest, if it vest at all. They are, in other words, the lives which validate the gift. There are no other common law lives additional to the validating lives.[9] The "wait and see" system cannot work if only the common law validating lives are used; one could only wait and see where the disposition was already valid. As Professor Allan said: "There would never be any occasion for waiting and seeing at all."[10]

Thirdly, it is necessary to consider who the measuring lives ought to be for "wait and see". The common law lives are irrelevant, and have nothing to do with the choice. The basic question under "wait and see" is to ask: if that person does in fact live to a date within 21 years of the actual time of vesting, would it be sensible policy that that person should be used as a life which validates the gift?

For example, a settlor creates a trust under which interests are given to such of the grandchildren of A as shall marry. A is alive and has infant children. The gift is void at common law. If a grandchild of A should marry within 21 years of the death of A, or of Mrs A, or of any of the living children of A, or of the settlor, *should* each or any of those lives be used for the purpose of validating the gift? The statutory lives have been selected on that basis. In such a case they would indeed be A, Mrs A, A's living children and the settlor.

(b) Statutory lives

(i) Definition The statutory lives are defined in section 3 (5) as follows:

(a) The person by whom the disposition is made, if made by deed, even though he himself takes no interest in the property.[11]

(b) Any of the following persons in whose favour the disposition is made, namely:

(i) In the case of a class gift, any member or potential member of the class.[12]

---

9 P. 290, ante. A different view is expressed in many of the books, and, in most detail, in (1964) 80 LQR 496 (J. H. C. Morris and H. W. R. Wade). It is there suggested that the common law lives are persons whose lives may or may not validate the interest. It is necessary to ascertain who the lives are, and the test is said to be whether there is a causal relationship between the lives and the vesting. Some lives which are causally connected will validate the interest, but others may not. It is further suggested that this principle is the one that should have been used for the measuring lives applicable to "wait and see".

The problem is to determine who those lives are. Causal connection is too uncertain. The standard example which is usually taken is that of a gift to the grandchildren of A who is still alive. The article in 80 LQR seems to suggest that the grandparent is a measuring life because he is causally connected, and so are his living children. It is suggested however that the living grandchildren themselves are inappropriate. It is difficult to see how the grandparent is causally connected with the vesting, because the vesting might occur at any time quite independently of the life or death of the grandparent. On the other hand, the living grandchildren would appear to be measuring lives because it is the continuance of their lives which causes the vesting to occur.

For a detailed discussion of this controversy, see Maudsley pp. 87–109; (1981) 97 LQR 593 (R. L. Deech); (1986) 102 LQR 250 (J. Dukeminier).

10 (1965) 81 LQR 109.

11 PAA 1964, s. 3 (5) (a).

12 Ibid., s. 3 (5) (b) (i).

A person is a member of the class if he has satisfied all the conditions that entitle him to an interest; he is a potential member if he has satisfied only some of the conditions but may in time satisfy the remainder.[13] If, for instance, there is a gift by will to such of the daughters of X as may marry and if at the time of the testator's death X has an unmarried daughter, she constitutes a life. She has satisfied the condition relating to birth and there is a possibility that she may later marry.

(ii) In the case of an individual disposition to a person subject to certain conditions, any person as to whom some of the conditions are satisfied and the remainder may in time be satisfied.[14]

This would be the position, for instance, if in the last illustration the gift had been to the first granddaughter of X to marry, and if at the time of the testator's death a granddaughter had been born but was not yet married.

(iii) The above two provisions apply equally to special powers of appointment.[15]

If, for instance, the power is conferred by will and is exercisable in favour of any of the issue of X, descendants of X alive at the testator's death constitute statutory lives.

(iv) The person on whom any power, option or other right is conferred.[16]

Trustees who possess a special power of appointment, for instance, fall within this category.

(c) In certain circumstances, the parents and grandparents of the designated beneficiaries also constitute persons whose lives are relevant in the present context. The Act provides in section 3 (5) that:

> The persons capable of ranking as "statutory lives" shall include a person having a child or grandchild who would be a life in being under the rules (*b*) (i) to (iv) given above; and also a person any of whose children or grandchildren, if subsequently born, would by virtue of descent be a life in being under the same rules.[17]

It must be remembered that a person has two parents and four grandparents. The "in-laws" are included by this provision.

Suppose, for instance, that a bequest is made to such of X's daughters as may marry, and that at the testator's death a daughter has been born to X but has not yet married. In these circumstances, as we have seen in dealing with rule (*b*) (i),[18] the daughter ranks as a statutory life. So also is X, and so are Mrs X, X's parents, and the parents of Mrs X. Under the instant rule, therefore, X is equally qualified in that respect, and so also are such of X's parents and grandparents who are alive at the testator's death.[19]

Again, suppose that there is a bequest to the first granddaughter of X to marry, and that at the testator's death X has one unmarried son. In these circumstances, X, X's wife and X's unmarried son are lives in being under

13 PAA 1964, s. 15 (3).
14 Ibid., s. 3 (5) (*b*) (ii).
15 Ibid., s. 3 (5) (*b*) (iii) and (iv).
16 Ibid., s. 3 (5) (*b*) (v). For a view that this relates only to the *validity* of the power, and not to appointments made under the power, see Maudsley, pp. 133–7.
17 Ibid., s. 3 (5) (*c*).
18 Supra.
19 See [1969] CLJ 284 (M. J. Prichard).

the instant rule, because, if a daughter is subsequently born to X's son, she would qualify under rule (*b*) (ii). If X's son were married after the testator's death, his wife and her parents would also qualify.

(*d*) Any person on the failure or determination of whose prior interest the disposition is limited to take effect constitutes a life in being.[20]

A simple illustration of this is that under a limitation to A for life, remainder to the first grandchild of X to marry, A ranks as a life in being. It would seem, however, that he will not qualify as such under a limitation to A for life, remainder to B for life, remainder to the first grandchild of X to marry, for it is on the determination of B's interest that the gift to the grandchild is to take effect.[1] Nor, it seems, would X be a statutory life in a gift:

> to the first son of X that should be bred a clergyman and be in Holy Orders, but in case X should have no such son, then to B in fee simple,[2]

because the gift over is to take effect on the failure of the interest of the son, and not that of X. These omissions appear to be unintended, and to be an oversight on the part of the draftsman.

(ii) In being and ascertainable Subsection (4) (*a*) limits the statutory lives to those individuals in subsection (5) who are:

> in being and ascertainable to the commencement of the perpetuity period.

The object of this provision is that the trustees are able to make their list of statutory lives when the instrument comes into operation, and will not be required to add new ones. "In being" includes children *en ventre sa mère*.[3]

(iii) Impracticability of ascertainment Following the common law rule relating to expressly selected lives,[4] the statutory list limits the lives in subsection (4) (*a*) by providing that the:

> lives of any description of persons falling within paragraph (*b*) or (*c*) of subsection (5) shall be disregarded if the number of persons of that description is such as to render it impracticable to ascertain the date of death of the survivor.[5]

It has been assumed that this is an attempt to enact the common law rule relating to the selection of express lives.[6] Clearly, some provision of this nature is required. The problem is likely to arise in cases, which are common in modern practice, where a successful business executive sets up a trust in favour of his family, and employees and their dependants.[7] It would not be possible to ascertain each beneficiary, and the restriction in subsection (4) (*a*) will come into operation. The difficulty is to know which person shall be "disregarded". It is tempting to assume that the "dependants" would be disregarded, or the "employees", but the subsection refers to the "lives of any description of persons falling within paragraph (*b*) or (*c*)" of subsection

---

20 PAA 1964, s. 3 (5) (*d*); *Re Thomas Meadows & Co Ltd* [1971] Ch 278, [1971] 1 All ER 239.
1 See (1964) 80 LQR, p. 505 (J. H. C. Morris and H. W. R. Wade).
2 *Proctor v Bishop of Bath and Wells* (1794) 2 Hy & Bl 358.
3 PAA 1964, s. 15 (2).
4 P. 291, ante.
5 I.e., rules (*b*) and (*c*); pp. 318–9, ante.
6 (1964) 80 LQR 486, p. 502.
7 *McPhail v Doulton* [1971] AC 424, [1970] 2 All ER 228; M & B, *Trusts and Trustees* (4th edn), p. 65.

(5). If the categories of subsection (5) determine who shall be disregarded, the beneficiaries are all in the same category and should all be disregarded. Perhaps the statute intends their parents and grandparents to be disregarded; for that is a separate description in the Act. No doubt the courts will determine the matter in a way which makes the Act workable. It should be noted also that the subsection on its terms applies only when it is the "number of persons" that renders impracticable the ascertainment of the date of death of the survivor. This appears to be a wrong emphasis. Very large numbers can be traced in modern times through births and deaths registers. But there are many other reasons why the ascertainment of the date of death of the survivor may be impossible to determine; as in the case of the ascertainment of the grandparents of an immigrant from a third world country where no such records are kept. Again, the Act will presumably be construed in a pragmatic manner, with no undue emphasis on the word "number".

(iv) No statutory lives If there are no statutory lives and no specified period, a period in gross of 21 years is allowed.[8]

(5) SPECIAL PROVISIONS DESIGNED TO SAVE REMOTE INTERESTS

The Act of 1964 contains three additional provisions designed to cure the vice of remoteness, but it is essential to bear in mind that these are not to be invoked until it has become clear that the limitations in question will not be saved by the "wait and see" rule.[9] The provisions are as follows:

(a) Provisions concerning death of surviving spouse

This deals with the case of the possibly unborn spouse. Suppose for instance that the limitations contained in a will are:

to X, a bachelor, for life, remainder to his future wife for life, remainder to such of his children as are living at the death of the survivor of X and such wife.

As we have seen, the limitation to the children is void at common law.[10] It is possible that X may marry a woman not yet born, and therefore it cannot be affirmed at the time of the testator's death that the vesting contingency will necessarily occur within the perpetuity period.

If X marries a woman who is alive at the date of the will, the gift to the children will not be saved by the "wait and see" rule unless she dies not later than 21 years after X's death. The wife cannot qualify as a "statutory life", though possibly and most probably she is alive at the date of the testator's death, for under the Act of 1964 lives in being for the purposes of the "wait and see" rule must be ascertainable at the commencement of the perpetuity period.[11]

It is therefore provided by the Act of 1964 that a disposition such as that given above, which fails for remoteness, shall be treated for all purposes as if it had been limited to take effect immediately before the end of the perpetuity period, if to do so will save it from being void for remoteness.[12]

---

8 PAA 1964, s. 3 (4) (*b*).
9 Because s. 3, which introduces the "wait and see" rule is expressed to operate "apart" from ss. 4 and 5 which contain these three additional provisions.
10 P. 295, ante.
11 PAA 1964, s. 3 (4) (*a*); p. 320, ante.
12 Ibid., s. 5.

If, then, in the case of the above example, X marries, and his wife dies within 21 years of his death, the limitation to the children is saved under the "wait and see" rule. If she survives beyond that time, the "wait and see" rule is impotent, but the limitation is none the less saved, since by virtue of the above enactment it vests at the end of 21 years from X's death in the children then living and will take effect in possession on the death of the wife.

(b) Age reduction provisions

An interest whose vesting is postponed until the attainment by the beneficiary of an age exceeding 21 years is void *ab initio* at common law, but as we have already seen it was provided by section 163 of the Law of Property Act 1925 that in such a case the age of 21 years should be substituted for that specified by the donor.[13]

Such a disposition contained in an instrument taking effect after 15 July 1964 may well be saved by the "wait and see" provisions of the Act of 1964:

Suppose, for instance, that a gift is made by will to the first son of X, a bachelor, to attain the age of 30 years; and that X is survived by a son aged 10.

If the son satisfies the prescribed contingency, he will have done so within 21 years from the death of X, the life in being.

On the other hand, the "wait and see" rule may be ineffective. If, for instance, in the example just given the eldest son is only 5 years of age at X's death, the vesting contingency cannot be satisfied within the perpetuity period, though if section 163 were applicable the gift to him would be saved by the reduction of the vesting age from 30 to 21 years.

It was felt, however, that instead of mechanically reducing the age to 21 years in every case, it would be preferable to conform more closely with the donor's wishes and to reduce it only to whatever age would suffice to prevent the limitation from being too remote. The Act of 1964, therefore, repeals section 163 of the Law of Property Act 1925[14] though not retrospectively,[15] and replaces it by the following provision:

Where a disposition is limited by reference to the attainment by any person or persons of a specified age exceeding twenty-one years, and it is apparent at the time the disposition is made or becomes apparent at a subsequent time

(*a*) that the disposition would, apart from this section, be void for remoteness, but

(*b*) that it would not be so void if the specified age had been twenty-one years,

the disposition shall be treated for all purposes as if, instead of being limited by reference to the age in fact specified, it had been limited by reference to the age nearest to that age which would, if specified instead, have prevented the disposition from being so void.[16]

Suppose that in a will there is a gift to the first son of X, a bachelor, to attain the age of 30 and that, at the death of the last of the statutory lives,[17] his son is only 4 years old. In these circumstances it has become apparent

---

13 P. 293, ante.

14 PAA 1964, s. 4 (6), (7) as added by Children Act 1975, s. 108, Sch. 3, para 43. See (1965) 81 LQR 346 (J. D. Davies) which had argued that the repeal of s. 163 by s. 4 (6) was defective; (1976) 120 SJ 498 (F. A. R. Bennion).

15 Ibid., s. 15 (5).

16 Ibid., s. 4 (1).

17 X and X's parents.

that the "wait and see" rule cannot save the ultimate limitation. The son cannot attain the prescribed age within the perpetuity period. Hence the above section operates, and the qualifying age is reduced from 30 to 25 years.

If the disposition is in favour of two or more persons, as for example to the children of X at 30 years of age, and if at X's death his son is 4 and his daughter 5 years old, the reduction of the specified age to 25, necessary to save the son's interest, affects the daughter also.[18]

If the disposition specifies different ages for distinct classes of beneficiaries, as for instance 30 for sons and 25 for daughters, the classes are segregated for the purpose of estimating the extent of the reduction. The reduction must be such as is necessary in each separate class.[19]

(c) Class exclusion provisions

We have already seen that at common law a class gift cannot be partly good, partly bad. If some members of the class may possibly fail to satisfy the vesting contingency within the perpetuity period, the whole gift fails even in respect of those members whose interests are already vested.[20]

The Act however abolishes this rule and in its place provides that the disposition shall take effect in favour of those members who acquire vested interests within the perpetuity period to the exclusion of those who fail to qualify within that time. This policy applies to two distinct cases.

First, it applies where the only cause of failure at common law is that some members of the class may not be ascertainable within the perpetuity period.

In such a case, the Act provides that, unless their interests are saved by virtue of the "wait and see" provision, those members shall be excluded from the class.[1]

> Suppose, for instance, that a disposition is made by will to X, a bachelor, for life, remainder to such of his children as may marry. Suppose further that X dies leaving a married son and an unmarried daughter.

If the daughter marries within 21 years after the death of the last of the statutory lives, her interest is saved by the "wait and see" provisions; if she is still a spinster at the expiry of that time, she is excluded from the class. In the latter event, the gift, which would have been wholly void at common law, takes effect in favour of the son.

The second case is where neither the "wait and see" principle nor the age reduction provisions will save the gift, as may occur if the attainment by the members of the class of an age exceeding 21 is part of the vesting contingency. The following is an example of such a case:

> A bequest to X, a bachelor, for life, remainder to such of his children as marry and attain the age of 25 years.
> X dies leaving a married daughter aged 19 and a son aged 3.

The inability of the son to reach the prescribed age within the perpetuity period which ends 21 years from the death of the last of the statutory lives,

---

18 The reason is that there is only one "disposition", not several "dispositions" to cover all members of the class; (1964) 80 LQR p. 509 (J. H. C. Morris and H. W. R. Wade). See [1969] CLJ 284 at 286–91 (M. J. Prichard).

19 PAA 1964, s. 4 (2).

20 Pp. 296–7, ante.

1 PAA 1964, s. 4 (4).

may no doubt be rectified under the age reduction provisions.[2] But the marriage contingency remains, for whether this is satisfied may not be established until too remote a time. If in fact he marries within 21 years after the death of the last of the statutory lives, the "wait and see" rule will operate to validate the whole gift. If not, then the daughter becomes the sole beneficiary, for the effect of the Act of 1964 is to exclude the son from the class of designated beneficiaries.[3]

(6) GENERAL AND SPECIAL POWERS OF APPOINTMENT

We have already discussed the importance of the distinction between general and special powers of appointment in the context of the doctrine of remoteness.[4] We have also seen that it is sometimes difficult to determine whether a so-called "hybrid" power is to be classed as general or special.[5] This difficulty is removed by the Act of 1964 which defines what powers shall be treated as special powers for the purposes of the rule against perpetuities, but only for those purposes. By virtue of this enactment a power is to be treated as a special power, unless:

(a) in the instrument creating the power it is expressed to be exercisable by one person only, and

(b) it could, at all times during its currency when that person is of full age and capacity, be exercised by him so as immediately to transfer to himself the whole of the interest governed by the power without the consent of any other person or compliance with any other condition, not being a formal condition relating to the mode of exercise of the power.[6]

The result is that the only general power is one under which "there is a sole donee who is at all times free without the concurrence of any other person to appoint to himself".[7]

Thus, for instance, a power is to be regarded as a special power if it is exercisable by the donee jointly with other persons or only with the consent of other persons; or exercisable in favour of any persons alive at the donee's death; or exercisable in favour of any person except the donee. On the other hand, a power to appoint to any person in the world except X should be classified as general.[8]

But the general testamentary power, i.e. one unrestricted in respect of objects but exercisable only by will,[9] is treated as exceptional by the Act. Under the existing case law, such a power is regarded as special so far as the validity of its creation is concerned;[10] but as general when the question is whether an appointment is too remote.[11] The perpetuity period runs from the date of the instrument of creation in the former case, in the latter from the date of the appointment. To classify such a power as general in respect of the appointments is illogical for, unlike the case where exercise by deed is permissible, the donee is in no sense the virtual owner of the property. Any

---

2 P. 322, ante.
3 PAA 1964, s. 4 (3).
4 Pp. 299 et seq, ante.
5 P. 300, n. 1, ante.
6 PAA 1964, s. 7.
7 Fourth Report of Law Reform Committee (1956 Cmnd 18), para 47.
8 Morris and Leach, p. 137.
9 P. 301, ante.
10 *Wollaston v King* (1869) LR 8 Eq 165; *Morgan v Gronow* (1873) LR 16 Eq 1; p. 301, ante.
11 *Rous v Jackson* (1885) 29 Ch D 521.

transfer of the ownership to himself is necessarily ineffective until after his death. Nevertheless, it was felt to be unwise to revise a rule that had obtained for some 70 years, and one upon which conveyancing precedents in constant use had been based. Therefore, the distinction between the validity of the power itself and the validity of appointments is retained by the Act.[12]

The expression "power of appointment" includes any discretionary power to transfer a beneficial interest in property without the furnishing of consideration.[13] It ranks as a special power.

(7) EXTENDED SCOPE OF THE RULE

(a) Possibilities of reverter

The scope of the rule against perpetuities is enlarged in two respects by the Act of 1964. It is extended to possibilities of reverter and analogous possibilities, a matter that is dealt with in a later chapter;[14] and its effect upon certain contracts for the purchase of land is expanded.

(b) Contract for purchase of land

We have seen that at common law a contract for the purchase of land, since it creates an equitable interest in favour of the promisee, is not enforceable by or against third parties if it is too remote; but that it remains enforceable without any limit of time between the parties themselves, since the rule against perpetuities is not concerned with personal obligations.[15]

The second limb of the common law rule, however, is now abolished. The Act provides in effect that:

> where a disposition, made inter vivos and creating proprietary rights capable of transfer, would be void for remoteness as between persons other than the original parties, it shall be void as between the person by whom it was made and the person in whose favour it was made or any successor of his.[16]

(8) EFFECT OF AN INFRINGEMENT OF THE RULE UPON SUBSEQUENT INTERESTS

The Law Reform Committee, after castigating the doctrine of dependency, recommended that:

> no limitation which itself complies with the rule should be invalidated solely by reason of being preceded by one or more invalid limitations, whether or not it expressly or by implication takes effect after or subject to, or is dependent upon, any such invalid limitations.[17]

The Act of 1964 deals with this recommendation in the following terms:

> A disposition shall not be treated as void for remoteness by reason only that the interest disposed of is ulterior to and dependent upon an interest under a disposition which is so void, and the vesting of an interest shall not be prevented from being

12 PAA 1964, s. 7, proviso.
13 Ibid., s. 15 (2).
14 Pp. 341–2, post.
15 Pp. 307–8, ante.
16 S. 10. See (1964) 80 LQR pp. 524–5 (J. H. C. Morris and H. W. R. Wade).
17 Para 33 (1956 Cmnd 18).

accelerated on the failure of a prior interest by reason only that the failure arises because of remoteness.[18]

Thus each limitation in a chain of limitations must be considered separately according to its own intrinsic validity and without regard to the remoteness of its predecessors. An interest which is already vested or which will necessarily vest, if at all, within the perpetuity period takes effect according to its individual terms.

It will be noticed that the concluding words of the enactment do not direct that the ulterior interest *shall* be accelerated, i.e. allowed to take effect immediately upon the failure for remoteness of the prior interest, but that such failure *shall not prevent* acceleration. The reason for this negative approach is that there may be other obstacles to acceleration. If, for example, the interest that fails is followed by a contingent interest, which in turn is followed by a vested interest, the latter is not accelerated until it is established whether or not the contingent interest will take effect.[19]

(9) EXCEPTIONS TO THE RULE

The exceptions to the rule recognized by the common law have been affected in three respects.

(a) Administrative powers

First, as we have already seen, the administrative powers of trustees are excluded from the rule even in respect of instruments taking effect before 16 July 1964.[20]

(b) Option to purchase leasehold reversion

Secondly, an option to acquire for valuable consideration the freehold interest expectant upon a lease, is wholly exempted from the rule regardless of the length of the lease, provided that it is exercisable only by the lessee or his successors in title, and provided that it is not exercisable later than one year after the end of the lease.[1]

(c) Remedies for recovery of rentcharge

Thirdly, the former doubt as to the ambit of section 121 of the Law of Property Act 1925[2] has been removed. It is provided by the 1964 Act that the perpetuity rule shall not apply to any powers or remedies for recovering or compelling the payment of an annual sum to which that section relates, or otherwise becoming exercisable or enforceable on the breach of any condition or other requirement relating to that sum.[3]

18 S. 6.
19 *Re Townsend's Estate* (1886) 34 Ch D 357.
20 PAA 1964, s. 8 (1); pp. 310–1, ante.
 1 Ibid., s. 9 (1).
 2 P. 309, ante.
 3 PAA 1964, s. 11 (1).

D. LAW REFORM

In 1993 the Law Commission published a Consultation Paper on the Rules against Perpetuities and Excessive Accumulations,[4] which criticises the rule on various grounds: complexity, uncertainty, inconsistency, interference with commercial transactions, harshness, lack of adaptability and expense (Part IV). Against that background it sets out four options:

Option I   Do nothing, which it rejects as not being realistic given the strength of the criticisms of the rule. (paras. 5.8–5.10.)

Option II   Abolish the rule without replacing it, for which it adduces the cogent arguments that:

> its existence is inconsistent with principles of freedom of disposition and testation; it is unnecessary in modern society since there is little desire on the part of property owners to tie up property for unacceptably long periods; the policy functions of the rule in so far as they are necessary would be performed adequately by other existing rules of law, such as tax legislation and powers to vary trusts; the effectiveness of the rule is in many cases limited since it can be successfully avoided; and abolition may be justified by the simplification of the law which it would bring about. (paras. 5.11–5.48.)

Option III   Replace the rule with a new rule. Two possibilities are considered:

(a) the introduction of a general rule limiting the duration of trusts, for example, for one hundred years from the date when the trust comes into existence;

(b) the conferral on the courts of a wide discretion to vary trusts.

This option is rejected because it might create more practical difficulties and objections than it would solve. (paras. 5.49–5.56.)

Option IV   Reform the rule, by:

(a) removing the need to apply the common law before "wait and see";

(b) making a fixed period of years the only perpetuity period;

(c) introducing a cy-près power for the court to reform dispositions;

(d) making provision for advancements in reproductive technology;

(e) introducing new exceptions to the rule for pension schemes, future easements, options and contracts, rights of pre-emption, contingent dispositions to charity, and, more comprehensively, all commercial dispositions. (paras. 5.57–5.91.)

Overall the Law Commission recommends that, whether abolition or reform is preferred, the legislation should be retrospective, subject to the restriction that it should not cause any person to be deprived of an interest which has already vested. (paras. 5.3–5.7.)

SECTION IV THE RULES AGAINST ACCUMULATIONS OF INCOME[5]

At common law, the rule against perpetuities governs not only the right to suspend the vesting of an estate, but also the right to direct the accumulation

---

4 Law Com No. 133.
5 See Morris and Leach, pp. 266–306; *Theobald on Wills* (15th edn), pp. 631–638; Maudsley, chapter 7; Simes, *Public Policy and the Dead Hand*, chapter iv.

of income arising from an estate. Therefore, before the law was altered by statute in 1800 it was held that a direction for the accumulation of income for a period which did not exceed the perpetuity period was valid.[6] This was decided in the famous case of *Thellusson v Woodford*,[7] where the facts were these:

> At the end of the eighteenth century a certain Peter Thellusson, a man of great wealth, took advantage of the rule and made a will the object of which was to accumulate an enormous fortune for the benefit of certain future and unascertained members of his family. He directed that the income arising from his land should be accumulated at compound interest during the lives of all his sons, grandsons and great-grandsons living at his death or born in due time afterwards, and that, on the death of the survivor, the capital sum so produced should be divided amongst the male representatives of his son's families. At the time of the controversy engendered by this will it was calculated that the accumulation would endure for about 80 years, and produce an amount of approximately 100 million pounds.[8] It was held that these trusts for accumulation were valid, but a statute generally called the Thellusson Act,[9] was subsequently passed in order to prevent further examples of what has been called posthumous avarice.

An explanation of the statutory permitted periods will follow. But it may first be useful to put the whole question of accumulations of income in perspective. It has been customary for nearly two hundred years to concentrate upon the criticisms of Mr Thellusson's testamentary plan; and this has brought accumulations of income into disrepute with suggestions that accumulations are evil in themselves. The truth is that they are in some areas encouraged. Thus, accumulation of income is permitted during the infancy of a beneficiary, and, since 1925, trustees holding property on trust for an infant for any interest, whether vested or contingent, have power, under section 31 of the Trustee Act 1925, provided that the gift carries the intermediate income,[10] to apply the income for the maintenance and education of the beneficiary, and they are required to accumulate the surplus. Again, it is common to provide for the accumulation of the income of a discretionary trust. The trustees would be under a duty to distribute the income to some member or members of the class of beneficiaries, unless power is given to them to accumulate the income.

A social problem could arise if many testators made provision for large accumulations for the period of perpetuity, as did Mr Thellusson. In fairness to him, however, it should be pointed out that he made ample provision for his widow and children, and that he refrained from giving more to the children for the very good reason that he wanted them to have to work for their living.[11] Furthermore, on the failure of the provisions in favour of those

---

6 Fearne, *Contingent Remainders*, p. 537, note.

7 (1798) 4 Ves 227; affd (1805) 11 Ves 112; M & B p. 391.

8 Challis, *Law of Real Property* (3rd edn), p. 201; Holdsworth, *History of English Law*, vol. vii, pp. 228 et seq.; Morris and Leach, p. 267 n. 5; (1970) NILQ 131 (G. W. Keeton). "On the death of the last surviving grandson in 1856, the estate was divided (not without more litigation) between the two male representatives of two of Peter Thellusson's sons who had left issue. But owing to mismanagement and costs of litigation, the estate realised a comparatively small amount": Holdsworth, at p. 230.

9 Accumulations Act 1800.

10 H & M p. 563, p. 337, post.

11 "The Provision which I have made for my said three sons, and the very great success they have met with, will be sufficient to procure them comfort, and it is my earnest wish and desire, that they will avoid ostentation, vanity and pompous show; as that will be the best fortune they can possess."

remote successors, he provided an alternative gift to the Crown to the use of the Sinking Fund.

A. STATUTORY PERIODS

The Thellusson Act has been re-enacted and amended by the Law of Property Act 1925,[12] as well as by the Perpetuities and Accumulations Act 1964,[13] and the position now is that a person[14] who desires the income of his property to be accumulated is restricted to choose *one* only[15] of the following periods for the duration of the accumulation:

(1) the life of the grantor or settlor;
(2) a term of 21 years from the death of the grantor, settlor or testator;
(3) the minority[16] or respective minorities of any person or persons living or *en ventre sa mère* at the death of the grantor, settlor or testator;
(4) the minority or respective minorities only of any person or persons who, under the limitations of the instrument directing the accumulations, would for the time being, if of full age, be entitled to the income directed to be accumulated;[17]
(5) a term of 21 years from the date of the making of the disposition;
(6) the minority or respective minorities of any person or persons in being at that date.[18]

The last two periods were added by the Act of 1964 with the object of giving a wider choice to persons who make an *inter vivos* settlement. They apply only to instruments taking effect after 15 July 1964.

B. SELECTION OF PERIODS

The difference between the third and fourth periods is that while the third period is for the minority of a person living at the death of the settlor or testator, the fourth includes the minority of any person who may *afterwards* become entitled to an interest in the land.[19] Thus by the choice of the fourth period an accumulation may lawfully be directed for the minorities of persons who are not alive at a testator's death. This is illustrated by the case of *Re Cattell*,[20] where:

12 Ss. 164–6. The Act affects not only an express direction to accumulate income, but also a power of accumulation: *Re Robb* [1953] Ch 459, [1953] 1 All ER 920; see also PAA 1964, s. 13 (2). The same point was decided in Scotland under Trusts (Scotland) Act 1961, s. 5; *Baird v Lord Advocate* [1979] AC 666, [1979] 2 All ER 28.
13 See Law Reform Committee, Fourth Report, Section C (1956 Cmnd 18).
14 A corporate settlor is not a person within the section: *Re Dodwell & Co Ltd's Trust Deed* [1979] Ch 301, [1978] 3 All ER 738.
15 *Jagger v Jagger* (1883) 25 Ch D 729.
16 In the case of dispositions taking effect after 1969, minority ends at the age of 18: Family Law Reform Act 1969, s. 1. There are transitional provisions so that the change from 21 to 18 shall not invalidate any direction for accumulation in a settlement or other disposition made by a deed, will or other instrument which was made before 1970: ibid., s. 1 (4), Sch. 3, para 7.
17 LPA 1925, s. 164 (1) (a), (b), (c), (d).
18 PAA 1964, s. 13 (1).
19 Fearne, *Contingent Remainders*, p. 537, Butler's note citing Preston.
20 [1914] 1 Ch 177; M & B p. 394.

a testator vested property in trustees upon trust for the children of his sons and daughters. He directed that the income of the property should be accumulated during the minorities of any of the children. The testator died in 1880. Gladys was born to one of his sons in 1885 and Frederick to another of his sons in 1912. It was argued that it was inadmissible to accumulate the income during these minorities, since the infants were not alive at the testator's death.

The Court of Appeal held that accumulation during both minorities was warranted by the statute. Lord PARKER said:

> In my opinion the fourth alternative period covers not only children who are born or *en ventre sa mère* at the death of the settlor, but children who are subsequently born, and I think that the fact that the fourth alternative comes immediately after, and in contrast with, the third alternative, which refers only to born children, and children *en ventre sa mère*, at the time of the death of the settlor, points strongly to this conclusion.[1]

This interpretation necessarily admits of accumulations during successive minorities, and is open to the objection that income may be withdrawn from use for a very considerable time; but, as Challis points out,[2] this latitude of choice is set off by the fact that the minorities chosen must be those of persons who are prospectively entitled to the income.

A settlor sometimes directs an accumulation of income to be made, not for the purpose of dividing the capital among children, but for the purchase of land. It is provided by section 106 of the Law of Property Act 1925,[3] that an accumulation for this particular purpose may be made to endure only for the fourth statutory period.

C. EFFECT OF EXCESSIVE ACCUMULATION

Where an excessive accumulation has been directed, the effect differs according as the direction violates the general perpetuity period or one of the six statutory periods. A direction for accumulation which transgresses the rule against perpetuities, by designating a period longer than a life or lives in being and 21 years afterwards, is void *in toto* and no income can be accumulated;[4] but a direction which, while it exceeds the statutory periods yet keeps within the general perpetuity period, is good *pro tanto*, and is void only in so far as it exceeds the appropriate statutory period.[5] The excess alone is void.[6] So if accumulation is ordered for the life of a person other than the settlor (which is not one of the statutory periods), it will be good for 21 years.[7]

1 [1914] 1 Ch 177 at 188.
2 *Law of Real Property* (3rd edn), p. 202.
3 Re-enacting Accumulations Act 1892.
4 *Curtis v Lukin* (1842) 5 Beav 147. It seems unfortunate that PAA 1964 left the test of compliance with the perpetuity rule to be governed still by the common law rule. A provision for "wait and see" to be applied in this situation would have been welcomed.
5 What is the appropriate period raises a difficult question of construction that must be determined according to the language of the instrument and the facts of the case: *Re Watt's Will Trusts* [1936] 2 All ER 1555 at 1562, a test described by UPJOHN J as "artificial and difficult": *Re Ransome* [1957] Ch 348 at 361, [1957] 1 All ER 690 at 696; M & B p. 399.
6 For the destination of the excessive accumulation, see e.g. *Green v Gascoyne* (1864) 4 De G J & Sm 565; M & B p. 398; *Theobald on Wills* (15th edn), p. 637.
7 *Longden v Simson* (1806) 12 Ves 295; *Griffiths v Vere* (1803) 9 Ves 127. See also *Re Ransome*, supra.

If the person entitled to property under a trust is an infant, there is a statutory power given to the trustees to maintain the infant out of the income, and to accumulate any surplus income during the remainder of the minority.[8] Where, in accordance with the directions of a settlor, income has been accumulated for one of the statutory periods, and at the termination of that period the beneficiary is an infant, so that a further accumulation may be necessary, it is enacted that the two accumulations shall not be counted together and so held to amount to an infringement of the Act.[9]

D. RULE IN *SAUNDERS v VAUTIER*

In the case of instruments taking effect after 15 July 1964, the presumption that no woman over 55 years of age can have a child, introduced by the Act of 1964,[10] applies to the right of beneficiaries to put an end to accumulations.[11] That right is defined in *Saunders v Vautier*[12] and later cases and is as follows: Where there is a gift of capital and income to a beneficiary absolutely, but subject to a trust that the income is to be accumulated beyond the time of his majority, he may, on reaching it, stop the accumulation and insist that the capital and accumulated income be paid to him forthwith. Once the property belongs to him absolutely, his free enjoyment of it cannot be fettered. This right, however, will not avail existing beneficiaries if it is possible that further beneficiaries may come into existence, and before 16 July 1964 the possibility that a woman over 55 years of age might have children sufficed to exclude the rule in *Saunders v Vautier*.[13]

E. EXCEPTIONS TO RULE AGAINST ACCUMULATIONS

Section 164 of the Law of Property Act 1925 sets out certain exceptions to the rule against accumulations.[14] If a settlor directs income to be accumulated for any of the following purposes, the direction will be valid although it may exceed the statutory periods.

(a) Payment of debts

Provisions for the payment of the debts of any person need not be confined within one of the six periods.[15]

(b) Raising of portions

Provisions for raising portions for any children or remoter issue of the grantor, settlor or testator, or for any children or remoter issue of a person

---

8 Trustee Act, 1925, s. 31; p. 927, post.
9 LPA 1925, s. 165; *Re Maber* [1928] Ch 88.
10 P. 312, ante.
11 PAA 1964, s. 14.
12 (1841) 4 Beav 115; *Wharton v Masterman* (1895) AC 186; Morris and Leach, pp. 289–95; Fourth Report of Law Reform Committee (1956 Cmnd 18) para 14.
13 *Re Deloitte* [1926] Ch 56.
14 Re-enacting Accumulations Act 1800, s. 2.
15 LPA 1925, s. 164 (2) (i).

taking any interest under the settlement, or for a person to whom any interest is thereby limited,[16] are excepted from the Act.[17]

The reason appears to be that unless such accumulations were permissible, it would be necessary for large owners to sell part of their estates in order to make provision for their younger children; but at the same time it must be recognized that this particular exception admits of a latitude that may be productive, in a great degree, of all the inconveniences that were felt or apprehended under the rules of the common law, because, by a will artfully prepared, every purpose aimed at by Mr Thellusson may be accomplished.[18]

But on the whole the courts have construed this enactment (which repeats the corresponding section of the Thellusson Act) in such a way as to render a flagrant evasion of the spirit of the statute impossible. Thus, an accumulation for the purpose of creating a fund out of which it would be possible to pay portions is not within the exception.[19] Again, an accumulation of the whole of a testator's property with a view to swelling a portions fund has been held void.[20]

As Lord CRANWORTH said, in *Edwards v Tuck*:[1]

> a direction to accumulate all a person's property to be handed over to some child or children when they attain twenty-one can never be said to be a direction for raising portions for the child or children; it is not raising a portion at all, it is giving everything. "Portion" ordinarily means a part or a share, and although I do not know that a gift of a whole might not, in some circumstances, come under the term of a gift of a portion, yet I do not think it comes within the meaning of a portion in this clause of the Act which points to the raising of something out of something else for the benefit of some children or class of children ... If every direction for accumulation for a child was a portion, the intention of the Legislature, which was to prevent accumulations, such accumulations being most frequently directed for the benefit of children, would be entirely defeated.

(c) Timber or wood

The Act does not apply to any provision respecting the accumulation of the produce of timber or wood.[2]

The probable explanation of this exception is that timber is not usually regarded as annual income, but merely as a resource for some particular occasion, so that a direction concerning its accumulation, provided that it conforms to the rule against perpetuities,[3] does not in effect withdraw income from the owner of the estate.[4]

---

16 I.e., the interest need not be carved out of the precise property, the income of which is to be accumulated.
17 LPA 1925, s. 164 (2) (ii).
18 Fearne, *Contingent Remainders*, p. 541, note by Preston.
19 *Re Bourne's Settlement Trusts* [1946] 1 All ER 411.
20 *Wildes v Davies* (1853) 1 Sm & G 475.
 1 (1853) 3 De GM & G 40 at 58.
 2 LPA 1925, s. 164 (2) (iii).
 3 *Ferrand v Wilson* (1845) 4 Hare 344.
 4 Fearne, *Contingent Remainders*, p. 537, Butler's note.

F. LAW REFORM

In its Consultation Paper in 1993[5] on The Rules against Perpetuities and Excessive Accumulations, the Law Commission adopts a similar approach to both rules. It criticises the existing rule against Excessive Accumulations on grounds of complexity, uncertainty, inconsistency in its effect on dispositions, frustrating the reasonable wishes of settlors, applying to charitable trusts, and not fitting well with other statutory provisions, for example, section 71 of the Inheritance Tax Act 1984 (paras. 4.20–4.36). Similarly, it sets out three options:

Option I   Do nothing (para. 6.3).
Option II   Abolish the rule (paras. 6.4–6.21).[6]
Option III Reform the rule, in particular by:

   (a) changing the accumulation periods;
   (b) codifying all the relevant law in one statute;
   (c) adding new exceptions to the rule, for example, the exclusion of commercial transactions;
   (d) extending "wait and see" to directions to accumulate (paras. 6.22–6.34).

The Law Commission rejects Option 1, and sets out cogent arguments in favour of abolition.

Again, whether abolition or reform is accepted, the legislation should be retrospective, provided that it does not deprive any person of a vested interest in property.

5 Law Com No. 133.
6 Western Australia (Law Reform (Property, Perpetuities and Succession) Act (WA) 1962, s. 17), New Zealand (Perpetuities Act (NZ) 1964, s. 21), Victoria (Perpetuities and Accumulations Act (V) 1968, s. 19), Alberta Perpetuities Act (SA) 1972, c. 121, s. 24 (see now RSA 1980, c. P-4, s. 24), and British Columbia Perpetuities Act, (SBC) 1975, c. 53, s. 24 (1) (see now Perpetuity Act (RSBC) 1979, c. 321, s. 24 (1)) have repealed the rule but have retained a rule against perpetuities. Manitoba has abolished both rules simultaneously (The Perpetuities and Accumulations Act (SM) 1982–83, c. 43, p. 282, ante). The Law Reform Commission of Saskatchewan (Proposals Relating to the Rules Against Perpetuities and Accumulations (1987)) has made a similar proposal which has not yet been implemented.

Chapter 14

Determinable interests

A. DEFINITION AND TERMINOLOGY

A determinable interest is one that may come to an end before the completion of the maximum period designated by the grantor. For instance, the first clause in a deed of strict settlement, made by a man in view of his approaching marriage, provides that the settlor shall hold the land in trust for himself in fee simple *until the solemnization of the intended marriage*.[1] In such a case the maximum interest taken by the settlor is a fee simple, but it is a modified, not an absolute fee, since it will not run its full course if the terminating event—the marriage—supervenes:

> A *direct* limitation marks the duration of estate by the life of a person; by the continuance of heirs; by a space of precise and measured time; making the death of the person in the first example; the continuance of heirs in the second example; and the length of the given space in the third example, the boundary of the estate or the period of duration.
> A *collateral* [i.e. determinable] limitation, at the same time that it gives an interest which may have continuance for one of the times, in a direct limitation, may, on some event which it describes, put an end to the right of enjoyment *during the continuance of that time*.[2]

Much confusion of terminology is apparent among the writers on this subject. Thus Preston, in the above quotation, speaks of *collateral* limitations; Littleton describes the terminating event as a *condition in law*, while most of the other early writers adopt the expression *conditional limitations*. The words *collateral* and *conditional*, however, besides being obscure, are used in many different senses, and the modern practice is to describe this particular species of modified interest as a determinable interest, and the limitation by which it is created as a determinable limitation.[3]

---

1 See the precedent of a trust instrument, p. 180, ante.
2 *Preston on Estates*, vol. i. p. 42, cited Challis, *Law of Real Property* (3rd edn), pp. 252–3.
3 Challis, pp. 253–4.

B. DETERMINABLE FEE SIMPLE

The older writers deal fully with determinable fees simple, and the classic example is that given by Blackstone, who states that the effect of a grant to A and his heirs, *tenants of the manor of Dale*, is to give A and his heirs a fee simple which will be defeated as soon as they cease to be tenants of that manor.

In such a case there resides in the grantor and his heirs what is called a *possibility of reverter*,[4] since there is a possibility that the terminating event will occur and so cause the estate to revert.[5]

Another example of a determinable fee is afforded by *Re Leach*,[6] where freeholds were devised:

> upon trust to pay the rents to Robert until he should assign, charge or otherwise dispose of the same, or become bankrupt.

It was held that Robert took an equitable fee simple which would determine if one of the specified events occurred in his lifetime, but which would become absolute if he died without their having occurred.

Determinable fees, however, disappeared from practical conveyancing (and gave way to shifting future estates operating under the Statute of Uses) when it was once decided that the fee simple in the case of a determinable limitation could not be made to pass to a stranger on the occurrence of the terminating event. The common law has never allowed a fee to be limited after a fee simple. As was said by Lord CAIRNS in *The Buckhurst Peerage Case*:[7]

> There is no instance in the books that we are aware of in which a fee simple, or a fee tail qualified in the way that I have mentioned, as by the addition of the words "lords of the manor of Dale", is followed by a remainder to other persons upon the first takers ceasing to be lords of the manor.

Thus at the present day, if it is desired to make a fee simple pass from the grantee to some other person when a given event does or does not happen, the limitation will take the form of the grant of an equitable future interest.

(a) Settled land

The uncertain duration of a determinable fee does not impede its effective disposition, for the instrument by which it is limited constitutes a settlement for the purposes of the Settled Land Act 1925.[8] The person entitled to possession is a tenant for life within the meaning of the same Act, and as such he may convey the land by way of sale, mortgage or lease under his statutory powers.[9]

(b) Rule against perpetuities

The matter aroused considerable controversy, but, in one case it was decided that the possibility of reverter arising on the grant of a determinable fee

---

4 Blackstone, vol. ii. p. 109.
5 Co Litt 18*a*.
6 [1912] 2 Ch 422.
7 (1876) 2 App Cas 1 at 23.
8 S. 1 (1) (ii) (*c*); p. 177, ante.
9 Pp. 183 et seq., ante.

simple was subject to the rule against perpetuities.[10] This view has now been adopted by the Perpetuities and Accumulations Act 1964.[11] Thus, if the terminating event in fact occurs within the perpetuity period (i.e. 21 years, unless the instrument of creation refers to lives in being or specifies a fixed period of years not exceeding 80), the reverter will take effect by virtue of the "wait and see" provisions of the Act. Otherwise, it will be void and the determinable fee will become absolute.[12]

(c) Resulting trust

An interest analogous to a possibility of reverter arises where a testator gives *personalty* to trustees upon trust to pay the income to a corporation or other body until some event occurs that may not occur within the perpetuity period. In such a case, the occurrence of the event raises a resulting trust in favour of the person entitled to the undisposed residue of the testator's estate. Formerly, a resulting trust of this nature was exempt from the rule against perpetuities,[13] but it has been subjected to the rule by the Act of 1964.[14]

C. DETERMINABLE LIFE INTEREST

There may be a limitation of a determinable *life* interest:

> If a man grant an estate to a woman *dum sola fuit*, or *durante viduitate*, or *quamdiu se bene gesserit*, or to a man and a woman during the coverture, or so long as such a grantee dwell in such a house, ... or for any like incertaine time, which time, as Bracton saith, is *tempus indeterminatum*: in all these cases if it be of lands or tenements, the lessee hath in judgment of law an estate for life determinable.[15]

The *protective trust* is a common example of a determinable life interest. Its basis is a life interest subject to an executory gift over upon the happening of a certain event such as bankruptcy or attempted alienation. The gift over may be in favour of other members of the family, but today it is more commonly in favour of trustees to hold upon discretionary trusts for a class which includes the tenant for life and members of his family; and the latter is the basis of the protective trust adopted by section 33 of the Trustee Act 1925. It is now common practice, in drafting settlements, to give a protected life interest to a beneficiary, especially if the beneficiary is an infant, or if there is some doubt as to the beneficiary's financial stability. The protected life interest is followed by discretionary trusts stating how the trustees may deal with the income of the property if the interest of the beneficiary is determined. These trusts were formerly set out in detail, but this is no longer necessary, for section 33 enacts that a mere declaration directing income to be held on *protective trusts* shall confer certain discretionary powers upon the

10 *Hopper v Liverpool Corpn* (1943) 88 Sol Jo 213 (limitation of a house in fee simple so long as it shall be used as a news room and coffee room). On the subject generally, see Morris and Leach, *Rule against Perpetuities* (2nd edn), pp. 209–18.
11 S. 12 (1) (*a*).
12 Law Reform Committee Fourth Report, 1956 (Cmnd 18) para 39.
13 *Re Randall* (1888) 38 Ch D 213; *Re Blunt's Trust* [1904] 2 Ch 767; *Re Chardon* [1928] Ch 464; *Re Chambers' Will Trusts* [1950] Ch 267.
14 S. 12 (1) (*b*).
15 Co Litt 42*a*.

trustees.[16] The statutory effect of using the expression is that the interest of the beneficiary automatically determines if he attempts to alienate or charge it or if he becomes bankrupt,[17] and the trustees at their discretion may apply the income during the rest of his life for the maintenance or support, or otherwise for the benefit, of any one or more of the following persons:

> The husband, the wife and the issue of the marriage, or, if there is no wife or issue, the persons who, if the husband were dead, would be entitled to the settled property or its income.

In cases of a determinable life interest the grantee takes an interest that may endure for life, or may determine sooner by the occurrence of the terminating event. It differs from a determinable fee in that it may be followed by a gift over to a third party which may validly take effect when the event occurs.[18]

A tenant for life whose estate is liable to cease on some event during that life has the powers of a tenant for life under the Settled Land Act 1925.[19]

D. DETERMINABLE TERM OF YEARS

Lastly, a *term of years* may be made determinable upon the happening of some uncertain event before the period of the term has expired.

As Lord TEMPLEMAN said in *Prudential Assurance Co Ltd v London Residuary Body*:[20]

> A lease can be made for five years subject to the tenant's right to determine if the war ends before the expiry of five years. A lease can be made from year to year subject to a fetter on the right of the landlord to determine the lease before the expiry of five years unless the war ends. Both leases are valid because they create a determinable certain term of five years.

---

16 See generally H & M, pp. 192 et seq; *Snell's Equity* (29th edn), pp. 274 et seq; (1957) 21 Conv (NS) 110; 323 (L. A. Sheridan).

17 If, by virtue of a power contained in the settlement, the husband makes an advancement to an infant beneficiary, this is a disposition that will cause his life interest to be forfeited: *Re Shaw's Settlement* [1951] Ch 833, [1951] 1 All ER 656.

18 Blackstone, vol. ii. p. 155.

19 SLA 1925, s. 20 (1) (vi); p. 184, ante.

20 [1992] 2 AC 386 at 395, [1992] 3 All ER 504 at 510; p. 372, post.

Chapter 15

Interests upon condition subsequent

SUMMARY

SECTION I GENERAL NATURE AND EFFECT

A. DEFINITION

An interest upon condition subsequent arises where a qualification is annexed to a conveyance, whereby it is provided that, in case a particular event does or does not happen, or in case the grantor or the grantee does or omits to do a particular act, the interest shall be defeated.[1] Examples of such interests taken from the Law Reports are:

grant to trustees in fee simple on condition that, if the land granted shall ever be used for other than hospital purposes, it shall revert to the heirs of the grantor;[2]

devise in fee simple to the council of a school on condition that the council shall publish annually a statement of payments and receipts;[3]

devise of land to J "on condition that he never sells out of the family";[4]

devise to A for life provided that he makes the mansion-house his usual common place of abode and residence;[5]

devise to A for life on condition that he assumes the name and arms of the testator within 12 months.[6]

In all cases of this type there vests in the grantor, his heirs and assignees a

---

1 Litt s. 325; Cruise, *Digest*, Tit. xiii. c. 1. This must be distinguished from a condition *precedent* where the qualification provides that the interest will not *commence* until the occurrence of some event, e.g., a grant to A if he becomes a barrister; p. 279, ante.
2 *Re Hollis' Hospital Trustees and Hague's Contract* [1899] 2 Ch 540.
3 *Re Da Costa* [1912] 1 Ch 337.
4 *Re Macleay* (1875) LR 20 Eq 186.
5 *Wynne v Fletcher* (1857) 24 Beav 430.
6 *Re Evans's Contract* [1920] 2 Ch 469.

right of re-entry, the exercise of which determines the estate of the grantee. In principle, therefore, a fee simple subject to a condition subsequent should be classified as an equitable interest, not as a legal estate, for since it may be defeated by a re-entry before its full course is run it can scarcely be described as "absolute". Nevertheless, for reasons already explained,[7] it has been given the status of a legal estate by the Law of Property (Amendment) Act 1926,[8] in words that are wide enough to include any right of re-entry. They state that:

> a fee simple subject to a legal or equitable right of entry or re-entry is for the purposes of [the Law of Property Act 1925] a fee simple absolute.

B. DISTINCTION BETWEEN INTEREST UPON CONDITION AND DETERMINABLE INTEREST

There is a fundamental and somewhat subtle distinction[9] between limitations upon condition and determinable limitations. Some writers contend that the distinction is a mere matter of words. On this basis the effect of such expressions as *until, so long as, whilst, during,* is to create a determinable interest; while such phrases as *on condition that, provided that, if, but if it happen that,*[10] will raise an interest upon condition.

But the distinction goes deeper than this. We must differentiate between a limitation properly so called, and a condition.

A limitation is a form of words which creates an estate and denotes its extent by designating the event upon which it is to commence and the time for which it is to endure.[11] It marks the utmost time for which the estate can continue. It appears in two forms. A direct limitation marks the time by denoting the size of the estate in familiar terms, e.g. by using such expressions as "for life" or "in fee simple"; a determinable limitation gives an interest for one of the times possible in a direct limitation, but also denotes some event that may determine the estate during the continuance of that time. In the simple example of a grant to A and his heirs, tenants of the manor of Dale, the terminating event is incorporated in, and forms an essential part of, the whole limitation, and if the estate expires because the tenancy of Dale is no longer in A's family, it is none the less considered to have lasted for the period originally fixed by the limitation. So in general the province of a limitation is to fix the period for the commencement and the duration of an estate, and to mark its determinable qualities.[12]

A condition, on the other hand, specifies some event which, if it takes place during the time for which an estate has already been limited to continue, will defeat that estate:

---

7 P. 178, ante.

8 LPA 1925, s. 7 (1) as amended by LP(A)A 1926, Sch.; M & B p. 7, n. 4.

9 It has been referred to as "extremely artificial" by PENNYCUICK V-C in *Re Sharp's Settlement Trusts* [1973] Ch 331 at 340, [1972] 3 All ER 151 at 156; M & B p. 25; and as "little short of disgraceful to our jurisprudence" by PORTER MR in *Re King's Trusts* (1892) 29 LR IR 401 at 410.

10 See *Sanders on Uses*, vol. i. p. 156; *Sheppard's Touchstone*, 122; Bacon Abr Condition (A); Challis, *Law of Real Property* (3rd edn), p. 283.

11 *Sheppard's Touchstone*, 117; Blackstone, vol. ii. p. 155; *Preston on Estates*, vol. i. p. 40.

12 Fearne, *Contingent Remainders*, p. 11, Butler's note.

And here is condition, because there is not a new estate limited over but the estate to which it is annexed is destroyed.[13]

In short, if the terminating event is an integral and necessary part of the formula from which the size of the interest is to be ascertained, the result is the creation of a determinable interest; but if the terminating event is external to the limitation, if it is a divided clause from the grant, the interest granted is an interest upon condition.[14]

C. EFFECT OF DISTINCTION

Outwardly a condition resembles a determinable limitation, for the difference between a grant:

to a woman for life, but if she remarries then her life interest shall cease,

and a grant:

to a woman during widowhood,

is not apparent at first sight. The natural inference is that the legal effect must be the same in each case. Nevertheless, certain practical distinctions between the two limitations existed at common law and to a diminished degree still exist.[15] The present position appears to be as follows.

(i) Determination A determinable interest comes to an end automatically upon the occurrence of the terminating event, as for example upon the remarriage of a woman to whom an estate has been granted during her widowhood. This is inevitable, for according to the limitation itself, i.e. according to the words fixing the space of time for which the widow's right of enjoyment is to continue, her interest ceases with her remarriage and nothing remains to be done to defeat her right. There can, indeed, be no question of defeating what has already come to an end.[16]

The effect of a condition operating by way of re-entry, on the other hand, is to defeat an interest *before* it has reached the end of the period for which it has been limited. The interest becomes voidable upon the breach of the condition. It does not become void unless and until the grantor, his heir or assignee re-enters upon the land.[17]

(ii) Rule against perpetuities The rule against perpetuities applies both to conditions subsequent and to a possibility of reverter arising on the grant of a determinable fee.

The position as regards common law conditions was established long before the rule came into existence, and the old authorities never doubted that a right of entry was enforceable at any distance of time by the grantor or

---

13 *Serjeant Rudhall's Case* (1586) Sav 76, cited *Re Hollis' Hospital Trustees and Hague's Contract* [1899] 2 Ch 540 at 549.

14 Fearne, p. 11, note (*h*); vol. ii. s. 36 (Smith, *An Original View of Executory Interests*); Challis, *Law of Real Property* (3rd edn), p. 260.

15 "Although in some respects a condition and a limitation may have the same effect, yet in English law there is a great distinction between them": *Re Moore* (1888) 39 Ch D 116 at 129, per COTTON LJ.

16 *Preston on Estates*, vol. i. p. 47; Challis, p. 219; *Re Evans's Contract* [1920] 2 Ch 469 at 472.

17 Co Litt 218*a*. At common law, the seisin transferred by livery cannot be divested without its actual resumption by re-entry: Co Litt 214*b*.

his heirs.[18] But, after several dicta in favour of subjecting conditions to the rule,[19] the point was finally decided to that effect[20] and was later confirmed by the Law of Property Act 1925.[1]

As we have already seen, a possibility of reverter appertaining to a determinable fee simple has been subjected to the rule by the Perpetuities and Accumulations Act 1964.[2]

(iii) Assignability At common law, a right of entry affecting a fee simple was neither devisable nor alienable *inter vivos*, and availed only the grantor and his heirs.[3] This, however, is no longer the position. The Wills Act 1837 allows a testator to devise "all rights for condition broken and other rights of entry",[4] and the Law of Property Act 1925 deals with their assignment *inter vivos* by providing that:

> All rights and interests in land may be disposed of, including—a right of entry into or upon land whether immediate or future, and whether vested or contingent.[5]

Whether a possibility of reverter is on the same footing in both these respects is not so clear. It has, indeed, been held that it may be disposed of by a testator since it is covered by the words of the Wills Act cited above.[6] But its assignment *inter vivos* presents some difficulty. In the view of the common law, what was left in the grantor of a determinable interest was not an estate but a possibility that he might acquire an estate at a future time. Such a *bare possibility*, as it was called, was not assignable at common law,[7] but it seems a reasonable assumption that it now falls within the wide language quoted above from the Law of Property Act 1925.

(iv) Void conditions As will be seen in the next section, a condition attached to any limitation of property may prove to be void for a variety of reasons. A condition subsequent that is thus invalidated is totally cancelled, and the limitation takes effect as if it had not been imposed;[8] but a determinable interest fails altogether if the possibility of reverter is invalidated, for to treat it as absolute would be to alter its quantum as fixed by the limitation.[9]

(v) Interest followed by remainder At common law, a remainder might be limited to take effect after a determinable life estate, but not after a life estate

---

18 Challis, *Law of Real Property* (3rd edn), pp. 187 et seq.
19 *Re Macleay* (1875) LR 20 Eq 186; *London and South Western Rly Co v Gomm* (1882) 20 Ch D 562 at 582; *Dunn v Flood* (1883) 25 Ch D 629.
20 *Re Hollis' Hospital Trustees and Hague's Contract* [1899] 2 Ch 540; *Re Da Costa* [1912] 1 Ch 337. A contrary view was expressed by PALLES CB in *A-G v Cummins* [1906] 1 IR 406, and his view has prevailed in Northern Ireland: *Walsh v Wightman* [1927] NI 1.
1 S. 4 (3).
2 S. 12 (1) (*a*); p. 325, ante.
3 Fearne, *Contingent Remainders*, Butler's note, p. 381.
4 S. 3.
5 LPA 1925, s. 4 (2) (*b*).
6 *Pemberton v Barnes* [1899] 1 Ch 544, where it was held that the possibility of reverter arising upon the grant of a determinable fee in copyholds was within the Act.
7 As to the three different meanings of the word *possibility*, see Challis, *Law of Real Property* (3rd edn), p. 76, note.
8 *Re Wilkinson* [1926] Ch 842 at 846; *Re Croxon* [1904] 1 Ch 252. If the illegal condition is *precedent*, the gift fails entirely.
9 *Re Moore* (1888) 39 Ch D 116. If, however, a possibility of reverter or a condition subsequent is void under the rule against perpetuities, the interest of the grantee becomes absolute: PAA 1964, s. 12.

that was defeasible by a condition subsequent. If, for instance, there were a feoffment:

> to A during widowhood and then to B for life,

the remainder to B was valid, since by force of the limitation itself it took effect upon the natural determination of the particular estate. But had the limitation been:

> to A, a widow, for life on condition that if she remarried then to B for life,

B's remainder would have come into conflict with three rules of ancient origin: a remainder was not allowed to cut short a particular estate;[10] none but the grantor and his heirs could exercise a right of re-entry; and in any event, the effect of re-entry was to defeat all the estates that depended upon the original livery of seisin.[11]

The matter has long been of only historical interest, for a settlor, minded to impose such a condition upon a widow's interest, could at an early date frame his limitation as a shifting use, and can now effect the same result by way of a future trust.

SECTION II VOID CONDITIONS

There are three types of conditions subsequent that are void when annexed to the grant of an estate or interest.

A. CONDITIONS REPUGNANT TO THE INTEREST GRANTED[12]

A condition that is repugnant to the interest to which it is annexed is absolutely void.[13] For instance, a condition attached to the grant of a fee simple that the grantee shall always let the land at a definite rent, or cultivate it in a certain manner or be deprived of all power of sale, is void on the ground of its incompatibility with that complete freedom of enjoyment, disposition and management that the law attributes to the ownership of such an estate.[14] It is not permissible to grant an interest and then to provide that the incidents attached to it by law shall be excluded. The most important examples of repugnant conditions that arise in practice are those designed to prohibit alienation or to exclude the operation of the bankruptcy laws.

(1) CONDITIONS AGAINST ALIENATION

(a) Total restraints

In accordance with the cardinal principle that the power of alienation is necessarily and inseparably incidental to ownership, it has been held in a long line of decisions that if an *absolute* interest is given to a donee—whether it be a fee simple, a fee tail, a life interest or any other interest, and whether

---

10 P. 280, ante.
11 Fearne, *Contingent Remainders*, pp. 261–2, 381, note; *Preston on Estates*, vol. i. pp. 50 et seq.
12 For a trenchant criticism of this doctrine, see (1943) 59 LQR 343 (G. L. Williams).
13 *Re Dugdale* (1888) 38 Ch D 176; *Bradley v Peixoto* (1797) 3 Ves 324.
14 *Jarman on Wills* (8th edn), p. 1477.

it be in possession or *in futuro*—any restriction which *substantially* takes that power away is void as being repugnant to the very conception of ownership.[15] Therefore, a condition[16] that the donee:

> shall not alienate at all;[17] or
> shall not alienate during a particular time, such as the life of a certain person,[18] or during his own life;[19] or
> shall alienate only to one particular person,[20] or to a small and diminishing class of persons, such as to one of his three brothers;[1]
> or shall not adopt some particular mode of assurance such as a mortgage,[2] or shall not bar an entail,[3]

is void.

(b) Partial restraints

A restraint that is partial, however, and which therefore does not substantially deprive the owner in fee of his power of alienation, is valid. Thus it has been held that a condition is valid which restrains the owner from alienating to a specified person,[4] or to anyone except a particular class of persons, provided, however, that the class is not too restricted.[5] But when does a restraint cease to be total? In the case of *Re Macleay*,[6] where there was a devise:

> to my brother J on the condition that he never sells out of the family,

the condition was held by JESSEL MR to be valid, though some doubt has been thrown on the correctness of this decision by a later case.[7]

The difficulty, indeed, is to ascertain the principle upon which such restraints have been permitted, for they would seem to be just as repugnant to ownership as a total restraint. Perhaps the truth is that the courts, losing sight of the fundamental doctrine of repugnancy, have, unintentionally and unwittingly, allowed the necessities of public policy to engraft certain exceptions on the main rule.[8]

---

15 Cf the position of a tenant for life under SLA 1925 the exercise of whose powers cannot be prohibited or limited, s. 106; p. 192, ante. But restraints even of a general nature may be valid in the case of a determinable interest: *Re Dugdale*, supra; *Re Leach* [1912] 2 Ch 422; p. 336, ante; and this is the basis of the protected life interest under TA 1925, s. 33; p. 337, ante.

16 But a *covenant* against alienation is not repugnant: *Caldy Manor Estate Ltd v Farrell* [1974] 1 WLR 1303, [1974] 3 All ER 753.

17 Litt s. 360; Co Litt 206*b*, 223*a*; *Re Dugdale*, supra.

18 *Re Rosher* (1884) 26 Ch D 801.

19 *Corbett v Corbett* (1888) 14 PD 7.

20 *Muschamp v Bluet* (1617) J Bridg 132; *Re Cockerill* [1929] 2 Ch 131.

1 *Re Brown* [1954] Ch 39, [1953] 2 All ER 1342; M & B p. 9.

2 *Ware v Cann* (1830) 10 B & C 433.

3 *Mildmay's Case* (1605) 6 Co Rep 40*a*; *Mary Portington's Case* (1613) 10 Co Rep 35*a*; *Dawkins v Lord Penrhyn* (1878) 4 App Cas 51.

4 Co Litt 223*a*.

5 *Doe d Gill v Pearson* (1805) 6 East 173 ("except to four sisters or their children"). But racial discrimination in the disposal of property is made unlawful by the Race Relations Act 1976, s. 21. See also Sex Discrimination Act 1975, s. 30.

6 (1875) LR 20 Eq 186.

7 *Re Rosher*, supra. But the restriction was placed only on a sale, and it was to endure only for the life of J. See too *Re Brown*, supra; (1954) 70 LQR 15 (R.E.M.).

8 *Re Rosher* (1884) 26 Ch D 801 at 813.

(2) CONDITIONS EXCLUDING OPERATION OF BANKRUPTCY LAWS

Just as the donee of property cannot be deprived of the normal rights of ownership, so also is it impossible to render his interest immune from involuntary alienation for insolvency or bankruptcy.[9] It is not permissible, for instance, to annex to the grant of a life interest a condition that it shall not be liable to seizure for debt. Thus in *Graves v Dolphin*:[10]

> a testator directed his trustees to pay £500 a year to his son for life, and declared that it should not on any account be subject or liable to the debts, engagements, charges or incumbrances of his son, but that it should always be payable to him and to no other person. The son became bankrupt, and it was held that the annuity became the property of his creditors.

But, as we have seen in discussing the protective trust,[11] there is no objection to the grant by one person to another of an interest which is to determine upon the bankruptcy of the grantee. Lord ELDON, adverting to the distinction between a determinable limitation and a limitation upon condition, made this clear over 180 years ago:

> A disposition to a man until he shall become bankrupt, and after his bankruptcy over, is quite different from an attempt to give to him for his life, with a proviso that he shall not sell or alien it. *If that condition is so expressed as to amount to a limitation*, reducing the interest short of a life interest, neither the man nor his assignees can have it beyond the period limited.[12]

The distinction at first sight seems fine and far from obvious, but in fact it is fundamental. In one case the only interest passing under the limitation is an interest *until* the donee becomes bankrupt; in the other, an absolute interest is first limited for life, and then an attempt is made to remove one of the incidents, namely liability for debts, to which all absolute interests are subject.

Thus, if husband and wife both bring property into a marriage settlement, the wife's property may be limited to the husband until he becomes bankrupt and then over to the trustees. But the husband cannot settle his own property upon himself in the same manner, for this would be a fraud on the bankruptcy laws.[13] On the other hand, it has long been recognized that a settlor may protect himself against other forms of alienation, voluntary and involuntary. Thus a man may settle his own property upon himself until he attempts to assign, charge or incumber it, or until he does something that makes it liable to be taken in execution by a particular creditor, and if so over to another person. The limitation over, once it has taken effect, is not avoided by the subsequent bankruptcy of the settlor.[14]

---

9 *Re Machu* (1882) 21 Ch D 838; *Re Dugdale* (1888) 38 Ch D 176.
10 (1826) 1 Sim 66.
11 P. 337, ante.
12 *Brandon v Robinson* (1811) 18 Ves 429 at 432, 433–434. See TA 1925, s. 33, as to these protected life interests; pp. 337–8, ante.
13 *Mackintosh v Pogose* [1895] 1 Ch 505 at 511; *Re Brewer's Settlement* [1896] 2 Ch 503; *Re Burroughs-Fowler* [1916] 2 Ch 251. This principle is retained by TA 1925, s. 33 (3).
14 *Brooke v Pearson* (1859) 27 Beav 181; *Re Detmold* (1889) 40 Ch D 585.

B. CONDITIONS CONTRARY TO PUBLIC POLICY

Any condition which has a tendency to conflict with the general interest of the community, even though it will not necessarily do so, is void.[15]

The following categories include the types of condition which most frequently occur.

(1) CONDITIONS IN RESTRAINT OF MARRIAGE

The law as to the validity of conditions in restraint of marriage differs according as the gift is of real or of personal property.

(a) Personalty

The rules governing personalty have come to us from the Roman Law through the ecclesiastical courts and the Court of Chancery. They are marked by numerous and fine distinctions, and in the words of a learned judge are "proverbially difficult";[16] but it is sufficient for our purposes to say that a condition in total restraint of marriage is void, while one in partial restraint is good, provided that it is reasonable from the point of view of public policy.[17]

For instance, a condition that a person shall not marry a named person,[18] a Papist,[19] a Scotchman,[20] or a domestic servant[1] is valid, but a condition that he shall not marry at all is void. But a partial restraint is not upheld unless there is a bequest over to another person in default of compliance with the condition. In the absence of such a bequest, the condition is treated as ineffectual on the ground that it has merely been imposed *in terrorem*, i.e. as an idle threat calculated to secure compliance by the donee.[2] A condition, however, is valid which restrains a *second* marriage, either of a man or of a woman.[3] Similarly, a condition requiring consent to marriage is not invalid.[4]

(b) Realty

The rules relating to real estate, on the other hand, are both few and simple. While a condition in general restraint of marriage if attached to a gift of personalty is void *per se*, in the case of realty it is not void *per se*, but only if there is an intention to promote celibacy. Thus in *Jones v Jones*:[5]

> a man after devising land to three women during their lifetime added:
> "provided the said Mary . . . shall remain in her present state of single woman, otherwise . . . if she shall bind herself in wedlock, she is liable to lose her share of

---

15 *Egerton v Earl Brownlow* (1853) 4 HL Cas 1; *Re Wallace* [1920] 2 Ch 274.
16 *Re Hewett* [1918] 1 Ch 458 at 463, per YOUNGER J.
17 *Re Lanyon* [1927] 2 Ch 264. A determinable gift, however, is valid: *Re Lovell* [1920] 1 Ch 122.
18 *Re Bathe* [1925] Ch 377.
19 *Duggan v Kelly* (1848) 10 I Eq R 473.
20 *Perrin v Lyon* (1807) 9 East 170.
 1 *Jenner v Turner* (1880) 16 Ch D 188. Quaere, however, whether this example and those given in the preceding two notes would not nowadays be treated as void for uncertainty; see, pp. 349–51, post.
 2 *Re Whiting's Settlement* [1905] 1 Ch 96; *Re Hewett*, supra. *Leong v Chye* [1955] AC 648, [1955] 2 All ER 903.
 3 *Allen v Jackson* (1875) 1 Ch D 399.
 4 *Re Whiting's Settlement*, supra.
 5 (1876) 1 QBD 279.

the said property immediately, and her share to be possessed and enjoyed by the other mentioned parties, share and share alike."

It was held that the condition was valid since its object was not to prevent her from marrying but to provide for her whilst unmarried.[6]

The *in terrorem* doctrine does not apply to realty,[7] and it may be said that a condition in partial restraint of marriage attached to real estate is always good,[8] and that one in total restraint *may* be good. However, a general restraint cannot be imposed upon a tenant in tail, since it is incompatible with and repugnant to an interest that is expressly made descendible to the heirs born of the marriage of the donee.[9]

(2) CONDITIONS ENCOURAGING SEPARATION AND DIVORCE

Similarly conditions designed to encourage the separation or divorce of a married couple are invalid as being contrary to public policy;[10] but where the parties are already separated, a limitation to a woman with a condition that the interest shall cease if she and her husband live together again, is valid as constituting a maintenance of the wife while she is unprovided for, unless there is evidence showing that the donor's object is to induce her not to return to her husband.[11]

(3) CONDITIONS AFFECTING PARENTAL DUTIES

A condition designed to separate a parent from his child, even where the parents are divorced, is contrary to public policy:[12] likewise a condition designed to interfere with the performance of parental duties.[13] But the operation of this principle was restricted by the House of Lords in *Blathwayt v Lord Cawley*,[14] where a condition which divested property if a child became a Roman Catholic was argued to be void on the ground that it would hamper parental duties in religious instructions. This argument was rejected by Lord WILBERFORCE:

> To say that any condition which in any way might affect or influence the way in which a child is brought up, or in which parental duties are exercised, seems to me to state far too wide a rule.

6 As to the admissibility of any evidence of the donor's intention, see *Re Johnson's Will Trusts* [1967] Ch 387, [1967] 1 All ER 553.
7 *Jenner v Turner* (1880) 16 Ch D 188 at 196, per BACON V-C.
8 *Re Bathe* [1925] Ch 377.
9 *Earl of Arundel's Case* (1575) 3 Dyer 342b.
10 *Re Moore* (1888) 39 Ch D 116; distinguished *Re Thompson* [1939] 1 All ER 681. *Re Caborne* [1943] Ch 224, [1943] 2 All ER 7; *Re Johnson's Will Trusts* [1967] Ch 387, [1967] 1 All ER 152; *Re Hepplewhite Will Trusts* (1977) Times, 21 January.
11 See *Re Lovell* [1920] 1 Ch 122.
12 *Re Sandbrook* [1912] 2 Ch 471 (condition held void which divested property if the donees "should live with or be or continue under the custody, guardianship or control of their father"). See also *Re Piper* [1946] 2 All ER 503.
13 *Re Borwick* [1933] Ch 657 (condition held void which divested a gift if the infant donee during minority became a Roman Catholic, for this tended to influence the parent in the discharge of his duty of religious instruction). But see now *Blathwayt v Lord Cawley* [1976] AC 397, [1975] 3 All ER 625.
14 Supra.

(4) CONDITIONS RESTRICTING FREEDOM OF RELIGION

Conditions restricting the beneficiaries' freedom of religion have frequently been encountered. Sometimes they have failed on the ground of uncertainty,[15] but they have never been held to be contrary to public policy.[16] In *Blathwayt v Lord Cawley*[17] the House of Lords held that a condition in a will under which a beneficiary would forfeit his interest if he should "be or become a Roman Catholic" was not invalid. Although conceptions of public policy move with the times, it is not against public policy for an adherent of one religion to distinguish in disposing of his property. To invalidate such conditions would go far beyond the mere avoidance of discrimination on religious grounds:

> To do so would bring about a substantial reduction of another freedom, firmly rooted in our law, namely that of testamentary disposition. Discrimination is not the same thing as choice: it operates over a larger and less personal area, and neither by express provision nor by implication has private selection yet become a matter of public policy.[18]

(5) CONDITIONS AFFECTING RACE

The Race Relations Act 1976 has no application to conditions imposed by settlors and testators. There is little authority on the point, which has mainly arisen in connection with charitable trusts, but it appears that it is not contrary to public policy for a settlor to discriminate on these grounds.[19]

(6) OTHER CONDITIONS

We have seen that any condition having a tendency to conflict with the general interest of the community is void. Thus in *Egerton v Earl Brownlow*:[20]

> Lands were devised to Lord Alford for 99 years if he should so long live, and then to the heirs male of his body, with a proviso that if Lord Alford should not in his lifetime acquire the dignity of Duke or Marquis of Bridgewater, the estates should pass from his heirs male immediately on his decease.

After great conflict of opinion the condition was held invalid by the House of Lords as being contrary to public policy. But there were special considerations applicable to that case. For instance, since the rank to be obtained was among the highest in the peerage, and one that conferred legislative rights and imposed legislative duties upon the holder, there was a danger that efforts to obtain the qualifying position would be pushed so far as to come into conflict with the general interests of the community. These special considerations were recognized in a later case, where a limitation that property should go to a certain person provided that he acquired the title of baronet was held to be capable of taking effect upon the fulfilment of the

---

15 *Clayton v Ramsden* [1943] AC 320, [1943] 1 All ER 16, p. 350, post. The Race Relations Act 1976 does not apply to religion as such, although the position of the Jewish religion is unclear. See Race Relations Board First Annual Report. A condition relating to Jewish parentage was considered racial in *Clayton v Ramsden*.
16 Even in the case of charitable trusts. See *Re Lysaght* [1966] Ch 191, [1965] 2 All ER 888, where discrimination against Jews and Roman Catholics was merely "undesirable".
17 [1976] AC 397, [1975] 3 All ER 625.
18 Ibid., at 426 and 636, per Lord WILBERFORCE.
19 Underhill and Hayton, *Law of Trusts and Trustees* (14th edn), pp. 166–7.
20 (1853) 4 HL Cas 1.

condition.[1] Unlike a peerage, no legislative powers and duties would be involved, thus the public interest could not be affected. But conditions forbidding entry into the naval or military services could affect the public interest, and have been accordingly held void.[2]

Difficulty has been encountered in the past with "name and arms clauses", whereby settlors attempt to ensure that the beneficiary adopts the settlor's name and coat of arms. In addition to problems of certainty,[3] such clauses were at one time held to be contrary to public policy on the ground that, in the case of a married woman beneficiary, the taking of another name might lead to dissension between husband and wife. But it was held by the Court of Appeal in *Re Neeld*,[4] overruling many previous decisions, that such clauses are not contrary to public policy.

C. UNCERTAIN CONDITIONS

A condition subsequent, designed to defeat a vested estate, is void if it is uncertain either in expression or in operation. It must be possible, not only to affirm with precision exactly what the words imposing the condition mean, but also to ascertain with certainty the circumstances that will cause a forfeiture.[5] In a well-known passage Lord CRANWORTH stated the position as follows:

> I consider that, from the earliest times, one of the cardinal rules on the subject has been this: that where a vested estate is to be defeated by a condition on a contingency that is to happen afterwards, that condition must be such that the court can see from the beginning, precisely and distinctly, upon the happening of what event it was that the preceding vested estate was to determine.[6]

Several cases have been concerned with conditions designed to secure the observance by a donee of a particular religion, as for example by requiring him "to be a member of" or "to conform to"[7] the Church of England, or not

---

1 *Re Wallace* [1920] 2 Ch 274 (baronetcy is "a barren title", per WARRINGTON LJ at 289). The condition here was precedent, but a condition, if contrary to public policy, is invalid whether precedent or subsequent. The *effect* of invalidity, however, is different; p. 351, post.

2 *Re Beard* [1908] 1 Ch 383.

3 P. 350, post.

4 [1962] Ch 643, [1962] 2 All ER 335.

5 *Re Sandbrook* [1912] 2 Ch 471 at 477, per PARKER J; *Re Murray* [1955] Ch 69 at 77–8, [1954] 3 All ER 129 at 132–3, per Lord EVERSHED MR. A less strict test applies in the case of a condition precedent, where even conceptual uncertainty may not defeat it: *Re Allen* [1953] Ch 810; [1953] 2 All ER 898. Lord DENNING MR in *Re Tuck's Settlement Trusts* [1978] Ch 49 at 60, [1978] 1 All ER 1047 at 1052, described this distinction as a "deplorable dichotomy", serving only to defeat the settlor's intention; M & B, *Trusts and Trustees* (4th edn), p. 629. But the distinction was acknowledged by the House of Lords in *Blathwayt v Lord Cawley* [1976] AC 397 at 425, [1975] 3 All ER 625 at 635. An example is *Re Barlow's Will Trusts* [1979] 1 WLR 278, [1979] 1 All ER 296; M & B, *Trusts and Trustees* (4th edn), p. 82 (option to purchase a painting at a low price from the testatrix's estate on satisfying the description "any members of my family and any friends of mine" upheld as a valid condition precedent). See Underhill, pp. 59–61; [1980] Conv 263 (L. McKay).

6 *Clavering v Ellison* (1859) 7 HL Cas 707 at 725.

7 *Re Tegg* [1936] 2 All ER 878.

to marry any person "not of Jewish parentage and of the Jewish faith".[8] Such phrases are shrouded in uncertainty and are generally held to be ineffective. Of those, for instance, who profess membership of the Church of England, many are devout observers of its practice and doctrines, but the conduct of countless others affords little evidence of any religious conviction. Faith varies infinitely in degree, and, even if it were possible to do so, a donor does not normally specify the exact degree that will satisfy his anxiety.[9] Again, whether a person "conforms to" a particular religion defies any certain answer.[10] Does, for instance, conformity to the Church of England necessitate attendance at religious services? If so, how regular must the attendance be? On the other hand, a condition for the forfeiture of an interest if the donee should "become a convert to the Roman Catholic religion" has been upheld, for such a conversion requires the performance of certain definite acts.[11] The court can, therefore, say with certainty what has to be done and whether it has in fact been done.

Many other examples might be given of uncertain conditions. For instance, provisions that an interest should be forfeited if the donee(s) have "in any way associated, corresponded or visited with any of my present wife's nephews or nieces",[12] or "social or other relationship with" a named person,[13] have been held void, since it is impossible to say with reasonable certainty which of the many connections included in the words "association" or "relationship" offend the prohibition.

Again, a condition that property shall be enjoyed by a beneficiary "only so long as she shall continue to reside in Canada" is too vague to be enforced, for there are many forms and degrees of residence and it is impossible to say precisely which of them fall under the ban.[14] But the law does not exact too high a standard of certainty. The condition need not be clear beyond peradventure. So in one case a requirement of "taking up permanent residence in England" was held to be sufficiently certain, since the word "permanent" postulates an intention to live in a place for life as opposed to living there temporarily or for a fixed period.[15]

In several cases decided between 1945 and 1960, courts of first instance, in disregard of what had been conveyancing practice for at least a century,

---

8 *Clayton v Ramsden* [1943] AC 320, [1943] 1 All ER 16; *Re Moss's Trusts* [1945] 1 All ER 207; *Re Tarnpolsk* [1958] 1 WLR 1157, [1958] 3 All ER 479; *Re Krawitz's Will Trusts* [1959] 1 WLR 1192, [1959] 3 All ER 793. Cf *Blathwayt v Lord Cawley* [1976] AC 397, [1975] 3 All ER 625; *Re Tuck's Settlement Trusts*, supra (marriage to an "approved wife" of Jewish blood and faith not uncertain as condition precedent); *Re Tepper's Will Trusts* [1987] Ch 358, [1987] 1 All ER 970 (gift by a devout and practising Jewish testator to children provided that "they shall not marry outside the Jewish faith": SCOTT J was reluctant to find the condition subsequent void for uncertainty and adjourned the case for further evidence of the Jewish faith as practised by the testator and his family; [1987] All ER Rev 260 (C. H. Sherrin)).
9 *Re Donn* [1944] Ch 8.
10 *Re Tegg*, supra.
11 *Re Evans* [1940] Ch 629; *Blathwayt v Lord Cawley*, supra.
12 *Jeffreys v Jeffreys* (1901) 84 LT 417.
13 *Re Jones* [1953] Ch 125, [1951] 1 All ER 357.
14 *Sifton v Sifton* [1938] AC 656, [1938] 3 All ER 425. See also *Re Brace* [1954] 1 WLR 955, [1954] 2 All ER 354, when a condition requiring the donee "to provide a home for" X was held to be so vague as to be unintelligible.
15 *Re Gape's Will Trusts* [1952] Ch 743, [1952] 2 All ER 579. Compare *Bromley v Tryon* [1952] AC 265, [1951] 2 All ER 1058, when it was held that a condition for forfeiture if a beneficiary became entitled to specified settled land "or the bulk thereof" was not void for uncertainty, since "bulk" meant anything over half.

showed a surprising tendency to stigmatize as void for uncertainty clauses in a will or settlement providing for the forfeiture of an interest given to X upon his failure to assume the surname and arms of Y. It has been held more than once, for instance, that to decree forfeiture, if X "disuses" the surname Y, does not show with sufficient precision what degree of disuser he must avoid.[16]

The Court of Appeal, however, has now overruled these decisions on the ground that they imposed an unreasonably rigorous test of certainty:[17]

> Each of us has a surname, and it seems to me altogether fanciful to suggest that there is any real ambiguity in a requirement that I should adopt and use a surname in place of that which I at present have: for the requirement does no more nor less than postulate that I should thereafter use the new surname, just as I at present use my existing name. Equally, as it seems to me, there is no real ambiguity in a divesting provision expressed to take effect if I should at any time "disuse" or "discontinue to use" the surname which I have adopted.[18]

D. EFFECT OF VOID CONDITIONS

If realty is conveyed to a person on a condition which is void, then, in the case of a condition precedent, the conveyance is void, and the interest does not arise;[19] but where a gift is subject to several conditions, some of which are valid and others void, the valid conditions are severable from the others, which alone are to be disregarded.[20] In the case of a condition subsequent the condition alone is void, and the donee takes an absolute interest in the property free from the restrictive clause.[1]

---

16 *Re Bouverie* [1952] Ch 400 at 404, [1952] 1 All ER 408 at 410, per VAISEY J.
17 *Re Neeld* [1962] Ch 643, [1962] 2 All ER 335. We have seen that the Court of Appeal also held that a name and arms clause is not contrary to public policy; p. 349, ante. See too *Re Neeld (No 3)* [1969] 1 WLR 988, [1969] 2 All ER 1025.
18 Ibid., at 667, at 346, per Lord EVERSHED. See also at 679, at 354, per UPJOHN LJ, ibid, at 682, at 355, per DIPLOCK LJ, as to disuser.
19 A bequest of *personalty* subject to an illegal condition precedent is void if the condition is *malum in se*, i.e. wrong in itself, but if the condition is only *malum prohibitum*, i.e. indifferent in itself but made unlawful by statute, the bequest takes effect unfettered by the condition: *Re Elliott* [1952] Ch 217, [1952] 1 All ER 145; *Re Piper* [1946] 2 All ER 503. See (1955) 19 Conv (NS) 176 (V. T. H. Delany).
20 *Re Hepplewhite's Will Trusts* (1977) Times, 21 January.
1 Co Litt 206a; *Re Croxon* [1904] 1 Ch 252; *Re Turton* [1926] Ch 96 (impossible condition). This is also the case with personalty. But in the case of a determinable interest, we have seen that the whole interest fails if the determining event is unlawful: *Re Moore* (1888) 39 Ch D 116; p. 341, ante.

Part II

Estates and interests in land

C. COMMERCIAL INTERESTS

I INTERESTS CONFERRING A RIGHT TO THE LAND
   ITSELF

II INTERESTS CONFERRING A RIGHT ENFORCEABLE
    AGAINST THE LAND OF ANOTHER

SUMMARY

Part II

Estates and interests in land

Chapter 16

Leasehold interests[1]

SUMMARY

1 See generally Aldridge, *Leasehold Law*; Foa, *Law of Landlord and Tenant* (8th edn); Hill and Redman, *Law of Landlord and Tenant* (18th edn); Woodfall, *Landlord and Tenant* (28th edn); Evans and Smith, *Law of Landlord and Tenant* (4th edn); Partington, *Landlord and Tenant* (2nd edn); Yates and Hawkins, *Landlord and Tenant Law* (2nd edn). The Law Commission has published ten reports on the law of landlord and tenant: (*a*) The Obligations of Landlords and Tenants 1975 (Law Com No. 67, HC 377); (*b*) Covenants Restricting Dispositions, Alterations and Change of User 1985 (Law Com No. 141, HC 278); (1985) 135 NLJ 991, 1015 (P. F. Smith); (*c*) Forfeiture of Tenancies 1985 (Law Com No. 142, HC 279); (*d*) Landlord and Tenant: Reform of the Law 1987 (Law Com No. 162, Cm 145) which reviews the law and identifies areas which require reform; (*e*) Leasehold Conveyancing 1987 (Law Com No. 161, HC 360); (*f*) Privity of Contract and Estate 1988 (Law Com No. 174, HC 8); (*g*) Compensation for Tenants' Improvements 1989 (Law Com No. 178, HC 291); (*h*) Distress for Rent 1991 (Law Com No. 194, HC 138); (*i*) Business Tenancies: A Periodic Review of the LTA 1925 Part II 1992 (Law Com No. 208, HC 224); (*j*) Termination of Tenancies Bill 1994 (Law Com No. 221, HC 135).

The Law Commission has also published two further Working Papers: (*a*) Implied Covenants for Title 1988 (No. 107); (*b*) Part II of the Landlord and Tenant Act 1954 (1988 No. 111); and one Consultation Paper: Responsibility for State and Condition of Property 1992 (No. 123).

In its Fourth Programme of Law Reform, the Law Commission recommends that an examination be made of Repairing Obligations, Civil Liability of Vendors and Lessors for Defective Premises, Waste and Distress for Rent; and of the Basic Law of Landlord and Tenant with a view to its modernisation and simplification and the codification of such parts as may appear appropriate (Law Com No. 185, pp. 4, 11, 12).

Several cases on leases are reported only in the Property and Compensation Reports and the Estates Gazette (issued weekly) and thence in Estates Gazette Digest (published annually until 1984) and thereafter in the Estates Gazette Law Reports.

We have already seen how the leasehold interest developed during the Middle Ages. It was then established as personalty and classified as a chattel real; for a leasehold interest, though personalty, is land. It remains personalty today, but we have seen how realty and personalty were assimilated before and by the 1925 legislation.

We begin this chapter with an examination of the general principles of leasehold law. Superimposed on this general law is a large body of statutory material dealing with specialized topics; there are, in fact, at least eight distinct statutory codes. Although they are in many respects radically different from each other, their general policy is to limit the rent which a landlord can obtain, and to restrict his right to recover possession of the premises at the end of the lease. An outline of these codes is given in Section IX below.

SECTION I MEANING OF TERM OF YEARS ABSOLUTE

A. GENERAL NATURE

A leasehold is capable of subsisting as a legal estate,[2] but it must be created in the manner required by the law[3] and satisfy the definition of a "term of years absolute" contained in the Law of Property Act 1925.[4] Otherwise it is

2 LPA 1925, s. 1 (1).
3 Pp. 374 et seq, post.
4 LPA 1925, s. 205 (1) (xxvii).

an equitable interest.[5] A term of years absolute means a term that is to last for a certain fixed period, even though it may be liable to come to an end before the expiration of that period by the service of a notice to quit; the re-entry of the landlord;[6] operation of law;[7] or a provision for cesser on redemption, as in the case of a mortgage term.[8] It includes a term for less than a year,[9] or for one year, or for a year or years and a fraction of a year, and also the tenancy from year to year that is common in the case of agricultural leases.

The Act provides that:[10]

A legal estate may subsist concurrently with or subject to any other legal estate in the same land in like manner as it could have done before the commencement of this Act,

and it therefore follows, for instance, that A, who owns the legal fee simple in Blackacre, may grant a legal lease to B, who then grants a legal sub-lease to C. In such a case three legal estates exist at once in the same land.

A term of years absolute is a legal estate notwithstanding that it does not entitle the tenant to enter into immediate possession, but is limited to begin at a future date. Such a lease is called a reversionary lease.[11]

B. PERPETUALLY RENEWABLE LEASES

There is no limit of time for which a lease may be made to endure; periods of 99 or 999 years are common, and longer periods are possible, but leases cannot exist for unspecified or for indeterminate periods, such as leases in perpetuity or until war breaks out.[12] The nearest approach to a perpetual lease before 1926 was one which was perpetually renewable, that is one in which the lessor covenanted that he would from time to time grant a new lease on the determination of the one then existing, if the lessee should so desire and should pay a fine for the privilege.

Perpetually renewable leases were inconvenient[13] and were modified by the Law of Property Act 1922. Those which existed on 1 January 1926 were converted into leases for 2,000 years calculated from the date at which the existing term began; and any perpetually renewable sub-lease granted by the tenant out of his interest was converted into a term of 2,000 years less one day.[14] Any fine that was due on renewal became payable as additional rent.[15]

If a contract is made after 1925 which, when properly construed, provides for the grant of a lease with a covenant for perpetual renewal, it operates as

5 LPA 1925, s. 1 (1) (*b*). For this important aspect of leases under *Walsh v Lonsdale*, see pp. 375 et seq., post.
6 Pp. 427, 434, post.
7 For example, where the purposes for which a portions term has been created are satisfied, the term merges in the reversion and ceases accordingly: LPA 1925, s. 5 (1), (2).
8 P. 663, post.
9 See *Re Land and Premises at Liss, Hants* [1971] Ch 986 at 991, [1971] 3 All ER 380 at 382, per GOULDING J; *EWP Ltd v Moore* [1992] QB 460, [1992] 1 All ER 880.
10 LPA 1925, s. 1 (5).
11 P. 371, post.
12 *Sevenoaks, Maidstone and Tunbridge Rly Co v London, Chatham and Dover Rly Co* (1879) 11 Ch D 625 at 635.
13 See remarks by JESSEL MR in *Re Smith's Charity* (1882) 20 Ch D 516.
14 LPA 1922, s. 145, Sch 15, para 1.
15 Ibid., para 12. For the meaning of a fine, see p. 361, n. 6, post.

a contract to grant a lease for 2,000 years, but the lessor is not entitled to convert into additional rent any fine that may have been reserved.[16] Thus a lessor may find to his discomfiture that a lease, though not expressly made renewable, is converted, by reason of the language used, into a term that will endure for 2,000 years unless the tenant chooses to determine it sooner. This will be the case, for instance, if a lease for three years certain contains a covenant that:

the lessor will on request of the tenant grant him a tenancy at the same rent containing the like provisions as are herein contained including the present covenant for renewal.[17]

Such a clause contains the seeds of its own reproduction[18] in the sense that a lease granted for a second period of three years would also contain a covenant for renewal, and so on *ad infinitum*.

On the other hand, it was held in *Marjorie Burnett Ltd v Barclay*[19] that a perpetual lease was not created where a seven year lease contained a covenant by the landlord to grant to the tenant at his request:

a new lease of the premises hereby demised for a further term of seven years, to commence from and after the expiration of the term hereby granted at a rent to be agreed between the parties....
And such lease shall also contain a like covenant for renewal for a further term of seven years on the expiration of the term thereby granted.

NOURSE J, having remarked that the courts lean against perpetual renewals, said that the second paragraph of the covenant was not part of the covenant for renewal, and the notion of a 2,000 year term was completely inimical to a lease containing provision for rent review every seven years.[20]

The result, then, of the legislation is that there may be a valid contract for renewal, but not for perpetual renewal. In order to keep permissible renewals within reasonable bounds, however, it is enacted that an agreement to renew for a longer period than 60 years from the end of the lease in question shall be void.[1]

A term for 2,000 years that arises as a result of this legislation is in general subject to the covenants, conditions and provisions of the original lease, but the following special incidents have been attached to it by statute:

(*a*) The lessee or his successor in title may terminate the lease by giving at least ten days' written notice before any date at which, but for its conversion, it would have expired if no renewal had taken place.[2]

(*b*) The lessee is bound to register with the lessor every assignment or devolution of term within six months of its taking place.[3]

---

16 LPA 1922, Sch 15, para 5.
17 *Parkus v Greenwood* [1950] Ch 644, [1950] 1 All ER 436; *Northchurch Estates Ltd v Daniels* [1947] Ch 117, [1946] 2 All ER 524; *Caerphilly Concrete Products Ltd v Owen* [1972] 1 WLR 372 at 376, [1972] 1 All ER 248 at 252; M & B p. 417, where SACHS LJ refers to "an area of the law in which the courts have manoeuvred themselves into an unhappy position". Cf *Centaploy Ltd v Matlodge Ltd* [1974] Ch 1, [1973] 2 All ER 720; M & B p. 467.
18 An expression used by counsel in the court below [1950] Ch 33 at 34.
19 (1980) 258 EG 642; (1981) 131 NLJ 683 (H. W. Wilkinson); M & B p. 419.
20 At 644.
 1 LPA 1922, Sch. 15, para 7 (2).
 2 Ibid., Sch. 15, para 10 (1) (i).
 3 Ibid., 10 (1) (ii).

(*c*) A lessee, who assigns the term to another, ceases after the assignment to be liable on the covenants contained in the lease.[4] This applies even to the original lessee, and is therefore an exception to the general rule that despite an assignment he remains liable on his contractual obligations.[5]

C. LEASES FOR LIVES OR UNTIL MARRIAGE

Certain other leases have also been modified by the Law of Property Act 1925.

A lease *at a rent, or in consideration of a fine*,[6] made:

(i)   for life or lives, e.g. to T for life or during the lives of A and B; or
(ii) for any term of years determinable with a life or lives, e.g. to T for 9 years or to T for 99 years, if X shall so long live; or
(iii) for any term of years determinable on the marriage of the lessee, e.g. to T for 20 years until T marries,

now takes effect as a lease for 90 years.[7] This lease may be terminated upon the death or the marriage, as the case may be, of the original tenant, for after these events have occurred a month's notice in writing to terminate the tenancy upon one of the usual quarter days may be given by either side.[8]

The policy of the Act is not altogether clear. In the case of a lease for life, 90 years is chosen as a term long enough to exceed the specified life, but it is difficult to see why *all* terms determinable with life or lives should be converted into 90 years irrespective of the term actually granted:

'Why should a term of 3 years "if X shall so long live" automatically become a term of 90 years determinable by notice after X's death? It is possible (although one hardly dares whisper such a suggestion about the great conveyancers who drafted the statute) that it was simply a mistake.'[9]

SECTION II THE ESSENTIALS OF A TERM OF YEARS

For a term of years to arise and for the relation of landlord and tenant to be created, one person, called the landlord or lessor, must confer upon another, called the tenant or lessee, the right to the exclusive possession of certain land for a period that is definite or capable of definition. The lessor retains an interest which is called a reversion.

---

4 LPA 1922, Sch. 15, para 11 (1).
5 Pp. 453 et seq, post.
6 A fine is usually the single payment of a lump sum made by the tenant, and is additional to the rent. By statute the word includes "a premium or foregift and any payment, consideration or benefit in the nature of a fine, premium or foregift": LPA 1925, s. 205 (1) (xxiii). *Skipton Building Society v Clayton* (1993) 66 P & CR 223. The rent or fine excludes beneficial tenancies for life under a settlement; these are equitable interests and subject to SLA 1925: *Binions v Evans* [1972] Ch 359 at 366, [1972] 2 All ER 70 at 74; *Ivory v Palmer* [1975] ICR 340; p. 604, n. 8, post.
7 LPA 1925, s. 149 (6).
8 Ibid.
9 *Bass Holdings Ltd v Lewis* (1986) unreported, per HOFFMANN J; affd [1986] 2 EGLR 40.

A. THE RIGHT TO EXCLUSIVE POSSESSION MUST BE GIVEN

A necessary feature of a lease is that the lessee shall be given the right to exclude all other persons from the land, including the lessor.[10] This does not mean, however, that whenever a person is let into exclusive possession he necessarily becomes a lessee. It may well be that he obtains only a personal privilege in the shape of a licence which may be revoked according to the express or implied terms of the contract.[11] It is of particular importance to determine whether a transaction creates a lease or a licence, since a lease is enforceable against third parties as a legal estate or an equitable interest,[12] whereas a contractual licence is not, unless the circumstances give rise to a constructive trust[13] or proprietary estoppel.[14] The plethora of cases in recent years has arisen from the applicability of the Rent Act 1977,[15] which conferred substantial security of tenure and other rights on a tenant but not on a licensee.[16]

In deciding whether a transaction creates a lease or a licence,[17] the test has now come full circle. In the nineteenth century the crucial issue was whether the occupier had exclusive possession of the land or not;[18] if he was in exclusive possession, other than as a freeholder or copyholder, he was a tenant; if not, he was a licensee.[19] During the last forty years the emphasis shifted from the rigid test of exclusive possession to the flexible test of the intention of the parties to be inferred from all the circumstances. In 1985 the House of Lords in *Street v Mountford*[20] considered the distinction for the first time and decisively rejected the flexible test. In that case

---

10 *London and North Western Rly Co v Buckmaster* (1874) LR 10 QB 70 at 76.
11 Pp. 589 et seq, post.
12 P. 381, post.
13 *Ashburn Anstalt v Arnold* [1989] Ch 1, [1988] 2 All ER 147; M & B pp. 550, 557.
14 P. 595, post.
15 Now phased out; p. 468, post.
16 Section IX, pp. 468 et seq, post. The distinction is also relevant in the application of the Landlord and Tenant Act 1954 (business tenancies); the duty of care owed to an occupier in respect of his chattels by a licensor but not by a landlord: *Appah v Parncliffe Investments Ltd* [1964] 1 WLR 1064, [1964] 1 All ER 838; the warranty of suitability of premises for their intended purpose implied into a licence: *Wettern Electric Ltd v Welsh Development Agency* [1983] QB 796, [1983] 2 All ER 629; (1983) 80 LSG 2195 (H. W. Wilkinson); there is no such warranty in respect of a lease, apart from express guarantee by the landlord; p. 390, n. 10, post; and the length of notice required for the termination of a licence: *Smith v Northside Developments Ltd* [1987] 2 EGLR 151, p. 466, n. 2, post. A difference was removed by *National Carriers Ltd v Panalpina Ltd* [1981] AC 675, [1981] 1 All ER 161, p. 462, post, where HL held that the doctrine of frustration is applicable to a lease; for licences, see *Krell v Henry* [1903] 2 KB 740.
17 Megarry, *Rent Acts* (10th edn), pp. 53–64; Evans and Smith, *Law of Landlord and Tenant* (4th edn), ch. 3; Martin, *Residential Security* (1989), pp. 6–24.
18 The giving of a right of exclusive possession should be distinguished from the giving of an exclusive or sole right to use the premises for a particular purpose which has never been held to create a tenancy: *Hill v Tupper* (1863) 2 H & C 121; *Wilson v Tavener* [1901] 1 Ch 578; *Clore v Theatrical Properties Ltd and Westby & Co Ltd* [1936] 3 All ER 483.
19 In *Lynes v Snaith* [1899] 1 QB 486, LAWRENCE J said: "As to the first question, I think it is clear [the defendant] was a tenant at will and not a licensee; for the admissions state that she was in exclusive possession, a fact which is wholly inconsistent with her having been a mere licensee"; *Allan v Liverpool Overseers* (1874) LR 9 QB 180; *Glenwood Lumber Co Ltd v Phillips* [1904] AC 405. Cf *Taylor v Caldwell* (1863) 3 B & S 826.
20 [1985] AC 809, [1985] 2 All ER 289; M & B, p. 433; [1985] All ER Rev 190 (P. J. Clarke); [1985] Conv 328 (R. Street); [1985] CLJ 351 (S. Tromans); 48 MLR 712 (S. Anderson); (1986) 130 SJ 3, 27 (P. M. Rank); [1986] Conv 39 (D. N. Clarke); [1986] Conv 344 (S. Bridge).

there was a licence agreement under which it was conceded that Mrs Mountford was given exclusive possession of furnished rooms for £37 a week. She had signed a statement at the end of the agreement that she understood and accepted that it "does not and is not intended to give me a tenancy protected under the Rent Acts". As SLADE LJ said in the Court of Appeal, "It was a plain expression of the intentions of both parties that what she was being given was a licence rather than a tenancy. There is no plea by her of misrepresentation, undue influence or *non est factum* and no claim to rectification."[1]

The House of Lords reversed the Court of Appeal and held that the agreement was a tenancy. Lord TEMPLEMAN said:

Where the only circumstances are that residential accommodation is offered and accepted with exclusive possession for a term at rent, the result is a tenancy . . . The courts will, save in exceptional circumstances, only be concerned to inquire whether as a result of an agreement relating to residential accommodation the occupier is a lodger or a tenant.[2]

If these three hallmarks of exclusive possession, for a fixed or periodic term and at a rent are present,[3] then there will be a tenancy[4] unless there are exceptional circumstances which reduce it to a licence:

The manufacture of a five-pronged implement for manual digging results in a fork even if the manufacturer, unfamiliar with the English language, insists that he intended to make and has made a spade.[5]

The intentions of the parties as to the nature of the agreement are irrelevant; the only intention which is relevant is the intention to grant exclusive possession.

1 (1984) 271 EG 1261 at 1262.
2 [1985] AC 809 at 827, [1985] 2 All ER 289 at 300.
3 Rent is not essential for a lease; LPA 1925, s. 205 (1) (xxvii); *Ashburn Anstalt v Arnold* [1989] Ch 1, [1988] 2 All ER 147; M & B p. 550, p. 365, n. 14, post (occupier let into possession for business purposes under rent-free arrangement pending re-development; only outgoings payable during occupation; held to be a tenant); *Skipton Building Society v Clayton* (1993) 66 P & CR 223; [1983] Conv 478 (L. Crabb).
    For a residential tenancy to be protected under the Rent Act 1977, the rent must be not less than two-thirds of the rateable value or, if not in money, quantifiable: *Barnes v Barratt* [1970] 2 QB 657, [1970] 2 All ER 483; *Bostock v Bryant* (1990) 61 P & CR 23 (Uncle Joe who owned a house and lived in one room paid general and water rates in respect of the whole house, and the respondents, who lived in the rest of the house, the gas and electricity likewise for the whole; CA held that, assuming the respondents were tenants, the rent was not quantifiable).
    Where no rent is payable, a licence may be the more likely construction: *Barnes v Barratt*, supra.
4 A simple example of the rule is *Caplan v Mardon* [1986] CLY 1873 (held in the county court that three students were joint tenants in spite of a signed agreement that nothing in it should create a tenancy).
5 [1985] AC 809 at 819; [1985] 2 All ER 289 at 294. See *Antoniades v Villiers* [1990] 1 AC 417 at 444, [1988] 3 All ER 309 at 315, where BINGHAM LJ said: "The House of Lords [in *Street v Mountford*] has not, I think, held that assertions in a document that it is a licence should be ignored. It has held that the true legal nature of a transaction is not to be altered by the description the parties choose to give it. A cat does not become a dog because the parties have agreed to call it a dog. But in deciding whether an animal is a cat or a dog the parties' agreement that it is a dog may not be entirely irrelevant."

(1) THE RIGHT TO EXCLUSIVE POSSESSION

(a) Tenant or lodger

Sometimes it may be difficult to discover whether, on the true construction of an agreement, exclusive possession is conferred. As JESSEL MR said:[6]

> I think it wiser and safer to say that the question whether a man is a lodger, or whether he is an occupying tenant, must depend on the circumstances of each case.

It is clear that the reservation by the landlord of the right to enter and view the state of the premises and to repair and maintain them does not derogate from the exclusive possession of the tenant. It merely serves to emphasise the fact that the occupant is entitled to exclusive possession and is a tenant.[7] It is also clear that the occupier of residential accommodation at a term for a rent is a lodger, if the landlord provides attendance or services which require the landlord or his servants to exercise unrestricted access to and use of the premises.[8] But such provision, or the lack of it, is not by itself decisive. Lord TEMPLEMAN did not say in *Street v Mountford* that the occupier was a lodger if, and only if, such attendance or services were provided.[9] And in *Brooker Settled Estates Ltd v Ayers*[10] the Court of Appeal reversed the county court judge who had held that there was a tenancy where:

> a written agreement purported to license an individual occupier of one room in a three room flat to occupy the whole flat, repeatedly asserting that nobody had exclusive possession of anything and reserving to the licensor the right to put another person into that room. "There is no evidence that Brooker & Co provided any attendance or services to Miss Ayers. By that definition, she must have had the exclusive use of the room. She was not a lodger, *ergo* she was a tenant."

In reversing the judgment, the Court of Appeal pointed out that in *Street v Mountford* the right to exclusive possession had been conceded, and ordered a new trial as to the nature of the possession given when the agreement was made and as to the credibility and honesty of the licensor as a witness.

Useful guidance was given in *Crancour Ltd v Da Silvaesa*,[11] where PURCHAS LJ considered the signals for which the court should look in order to decide whether the occupier is a tenant or a lodger. He identified the criteria which the court should ignore or, alternatively, should not be treated as decisive; namely:

(*a*) the description of the agreement chosen by the parties, for example, "lease" or "licence";

(*b*) the actual subjective intention of the parties, even if they are *ad idem*;[12]

(*c*) the effects of the Rent Acts are irrelevant to the construction of the document;

---

6 *Bradley v Baylis* (1881) 8 QBD 195 at 218.

7 *Street v Mountford*, supra at 818, at 293.

8 At 818, at 293. See also *Royal Philanthropic Society v County* [1985] 2 EGLR 109. On the equivocal significance of the retention of keys by the landlord, see *Aslan v Murphy* [1990] 1 WLR 766, [1989] 3 All ER 130; M & B p. 458.

9 *Crancour Ltd v Da Silvaesa* [1986] 1 EGLR 80 at 85, per RALPH GIBSON LJ.

10 [1987] 1 EGLR 50.

11 [1986] 1 EGLR 80 at 88. These criteria mainly summarise points raised by Lord TEMPLEMAN in *Street v Mountford*. See (1987) 50 MLR 226 (A. J. Waite). See also Lord DONALDSON OF LYMINGTON in *Aslan v Murphy* [1990] 1 WLR 766, [1989] 3 All ER 130; M & B p. 458.

12 Unless they do not intend to enter into the agreement at all: *Isaac v Hotel de Paris Ltd* [1960] 1 WLR 239, [1960] 1 All ER 348, cited in *Street v Mountford* at 823, at 297.

(*d*) the exercise or failure to exercise rights provided by the agreement by one, other or both parties to the agreement is not of decisive importance;

(*e*) the court should not draw up a "shopping list" of clauses;

(*f*) the court should not award marks for drafting.

(b) Business tenant or licensee

The decision in *Street v Mountford*, which related to residential accommodation, has been applied to business tenancies not only where the three indicia of exclusive possession and payment of rent for a term are present,[13] but even where the indicium of rent is lacking.[14] The Court of Appeal, however, held in *Dresden Estates Ltd v Collinson*[15] that "an unusual provision" in a licence agreement which reserved to the licensor of an industrial unit the right to relocate the licensee to an adjoining unit effectively deprived the licensee of the right to exclusive permission. GLIDEWELL LJ said[16] that the test in relation to residential premises as to whether the occupier is a tenant or a lodger:

> is of course of itself not applicable to business tenancies because there is no such person as a lodger in relation to business premises. For myself, I think that the indicia, which may make it more apparent in the case of a residential tenant or a residential occupier that he is indeed a tenant, may be less applicable or be less likely to have that effect in the case of some business tenancies.

The decision of the Court of Appeal in *IDC Group Ltd v Clark*,[17] holding that an agreement for the occupation of business premises, which was made by a deed which was *professionally* drawn and described as a licence, was a licence and not an easement, may be significant in the construction of an agreement for business, but not for residential accommodation.

13 *London and Associated Investment plc v Calow* [1986] 2 EGLR 80, M & B p. 446; [1987] Conv 137 (S. Bridge); *Dellneed Ltd v Chin* (1987) 53 P & CR 172 (Mai Toi agreement); [1987] Conv 298 (S. Bridge); cf *Smith v Northside Development Ltd* [1987] 2 EGLR 151 (*oral* agreement where occupier said that he "would take unit 17 on my own" held not to be grant of exclusive possession). See also *Bracey v Read* [1962] 3 All ER 472 at 475, per CROSS J; *University of Reading v Johnson-Houghton* (1985) 276 EG 1353 (grant of right to "gallops for racehorses at Blewbury in Berkshire" held to be a lease on the balance of probabilities . . . despite its title ("licence") and much of its language), per LEONARD J at 1356; [1986] Conv 275 (C. P. Rodgers); *Wigan Borough Council v Green & Son (Wigan) Ltd* [1985] 2 EGLR 242 ("permission to use exclusively" stalls in covered market for "a very substantial butcher's shop" held to be tenancy).

14 *Ashburn Anstalt v Arnold* [1989] Ch 1, [1988] 2 All ER 147; M & B p. 550; p. 363, n. 3 ante: "We are unable to read Lord TEMPLEMAN's speech in *Street v Mountford* as laying down a principle of 'no rent, no lease'", per FOX LJ at 9.

15 [1987] 1 EGLR 45; M & B p. 445; (1987) Conv 220 (P. E. Smith); (1987) 50 MLR 655 (S. Bridge).

16 At 47. See also *London and Associated Investment plc v Calow* supra at 84, where Judge BAKER QC said: "There might be special cases of some sort of trading properties, areas in shops and so forth, or stalls in markets, and there might be difficulties with agricultural properties, where licences are frequent."; *McCarthy v Bence* [1990] 1 EGLR 1 (joint venture in form of sharing milk arrangement held to be licence for purposes of s. 2 (2) (*b*) of the Agricultural Holdings Act 1986; agreement would not involve "exclusive occupation", and area of land and fields available for licensee's cows might be altered from time to time by the licensor, who also enjoyed access for several purposes such as the exercise of sporting rights, felling dead elm trees, hedging and ditching and "walking with his dog, taking his thistle spud in the thistle season to pull out thistles or doing any other minor tidying up that caught his eye" [1991] Conv 58 (C. Rodgers), 207 (M. Slater)).

17 [1992] 65 P & CR 179 p. 529, post.

(2) SHAM OR GENUINE. MULTIPLE OCCUPATION

Before 1985 some landlords had drafted occupation agreements in terms designed to ensure that the premises were occupied under a licence and not under a lease. Their object was to avoid the application of the Rent Acts. Thus in *Somma v Hazelhurst*:[18]

> Mr H and Miss S each entered into separate but identical agreements with the owner of a dwelling-house to occupy a double bed-sitting room. Each agreement repeatedly proclaimed itself to be a licence and stated that the licensor was not willing to grant exclusive possession of any part of the rooms, and that the use of the rooms was to be "in common with the licensor and such other licensees as the licensor may permit to use the said rooms". Each occupant was severally liable for his or her rent.

The Court of Appeal held that each agreement was a licence, CUMMING-BRUCE LJ saying:[19]

> We can see no reason why an ordinary landlord . . . should not be able to grant a licence to occupy an ordinary house. If that is what both he and the licensee intend and if they can frame any written agreement in such a way as to demonstrate that it is not really an agreement for a lease masquerading as a licence, we can see no reason in law or justice why they should be prevented from achieving that object. Nor can we see why their common intentions should be categorised as bogus or unreal or as sham merely on the ground that the court disapproves of the bargain.

In *Street v Mountford* the House of Lords strongly disapproved of this case saying that both agreements were a sham:[20]

> Although the Rent Acts must not be allowed to alter or influence the construction of an agreement, the court should be astute to detect and frustrate sham devices and artificial transactions whose only object is to disguise the grant of a tenancy and to evade the Rent Acts.[1]

18 [1978] 1 WLR 1014, [1978] 2 All ER 1011. Followed in *Aldrington Garages Ltd v Fielder* (1978) 247 EG 557; *Sturolson & Co v Weniz* (1984) 272 EG 326. Cf *O'Malley v Seymour* (1978) 250 EG 1083; *Walsh v Griffiths-Jones* [1978] 2 All ER 1002, where the agreements were held to be sham. For a detailed review, see (1980) 130 NLJ 939, 959 (A. Waite).
19 At 1024, at 1121. HL Appellate Committee (Lords WILBERFORCE, SALMON and FRASER OF TULLYBELTON) refused leave to appeal: [1978] 2 All ER 1011 at 1025.
20 See *Snook v London and West Riding Investments Ltd* [1967] 1 All ER 518 at 528, where DIPLOCK LJ defines "this popular and perjorative word": "If it has any meaning in law, it means acts done or documents executed by the parties to the 'sham' which are intended by them to give to third parties or to the court the appearance of creating between the parties legal rights and obligations different from the actual legal rights and obligations (if any) which the parties intend to create."
1 At 825, at 299. Cf the similar approach in the House of Lords to tax avoidance schemes which involve "a pre-ordained series of transactions (whether or not they include the achievement of a legitimate commercial end) into which there are inserted steps which have no commercial purpose apart from the avoidance of a liability to tax which in the absence of those particular steps would have been payable": *IRC v Burmah Oil Co Ltd* [1982] STC 30 at 32, per Lord DIPLOCK. See also *WT Ramsay v IRC* [1982] AC 300, [1981] 1 All ER 865; *Furniss v Dawson* [1984] AC 474, [1984] 1 All ER 530. These cases made very severe inroads on the ambit within which the earlier doctrine of *IRC v Duke of Westminster* [1936] AC 1 at 19 had been applied. See M & B, *Trusts and Trustees* (4th edn, 1990), pp. 525–528. See also *Gisborne v Burton* [1989] QB 390, [1988] 3 All ER 760, where CA invoked the tax doctrine to strike down a scheme to deny a sub-tenant the protection of the Agricultural Holdings Act 1948, s. 24 (1); cf *Hilton v Plustitle Ltd* [1989] 1 WLR 149, [1988] 3 All ER 1051 (company let scheme held not to be a sham because the company tenant, rather than the occupier, performed all the obligations under the tenancy); *Kaye v Massbetter Ltd* (1990) 62 P & CR 558 (letting to limited company tenant with a view to excluding the Rent Acts held to be

In *AG Securities v Vaughan* and *Antoniades v Villiers*[2] (which were heard simultaneously) the House of Lords went further and overruled *Somma v Hazelhurst*. Both cases concerned separate flat-sharing agreements, both were described as "licences", and both denied exclusive possession (in terms drafted before *Street v Mountford*). In both cases the House of Lords reversed the Court of Appeal, holding that in the first there was a licence, and in the second a joint tenancy.

In *AG Securities v Vaughan*:

> Four young men signed separate agreements on different dates with different amounts of payment. The documents were described as licences, denied exclusive possession of any part and required the occupier to share with not more than three other persons. When there was a change, there was a pecking order for the best rooms.

The House of Lords held that the four occupiers were individual licensees, and not joint tenants. The differences of date and payment made it impossible for the four unities (of possession, interest, time and title) of a joint tenancy to exist.[3]

As Lord BRIDGE OF HARWICH said:[4]

> The arrangement seems to have been a sensible and realistic one to provide accommodation for a shifting population of individuals who were genuinely prepared to share the flat with others introduced from time to time who would, at least initially, be strangers to them. There was no artificiality in the contracts concluded to give effect to this arrangement.

In *Antoniades v Villiers*:

> There were two separate agreements based on the *Somma v Hazelhurst* precedent. They were entered into by a man and a woman who wished to live together in a small flat in undisturbed quasi-connubial bliss.[4a] They chose a double rather than single beds. They were to use the flat in common with the owner or other licensees permitted by him.

Unlike *AG Securities v Vaughan*, "the two agreements were interdependent, not independent of one another. Both would have signed or neither. The two

genuine); [1992] Conv 58 (P. Luther); *Estavest Investments Ltd v Commercial Express Travel Ltd* [1988] 2 EGLR 91: [1991] 11 OJLS 136 (S. Bright). See also the 1986 Blundell Memorial Lecture, summarised at (1986) 83 LSG 3736 (K. Lewison); (1987) 84 LSG 403 (P. Freedman).
2 [1990] 1 AC 417, [1988] 3 All ER 1058; M & B p. 448; [1989] 1 CLJ 19 (C. Harpum); (1989) 105 LQR 165 (P. V. Baker); (1989) Conv 128 (P. F. Smith); (1989) 52 MLR 408 (J. Hill); [1988] All ER Rev 171 (P. J. Clarke); (1992) 142 NLJ 575 (S. Bright) (arguing that the co-occupants may be tenants in common).
3 On the four unities, see pp. 214–5, post; cf *Mikeover Ltd v Brady* [1989] 3 All ER 618; M & B p. 455 (where each of two occupants was liable for his own share of the payments, CA held that there was no unity of interest and therefore each had a licence). See, however, Lord TEMPLEMAN in *Antoniades v Villiers* at 461, at 106 ("a tenancy remains a tenancy even though the landlord may choose to require each of two joint tenants to agree expressly to pay one-half of the rent").
  AG Securities v Vaughan was followed in *Stribling v Wickham* [1989] 2 EGLR 35; M & B p. 454; [1989] Conv 192 (J. E. Martin) (three friends signed identical agreements; on change of occupation the new occupant signed an agreement ending on expiry of agreements of the remaining occupiers; on that date all then in occupation signed new arrangements with common expiry date; CA held each occupier to have a separate licence).
4 At 454, at 1061.
4a *Street v Mountford* [1985] AC 809 at 825, [1985] 2 All ER 289 at 299, per Lord TEMPLEMAN.

agreements must therefore be read together".[5] The sharing term was "contrary to the provisions of the Rent Acts and, in addition was in the circumstances, a pretence intended only to get round the Rent Acts."

Lord TEMPLEMAN went on to set out the matters to be taken into consideration when construing one or more documents in order to decide whether a tenancy has been created.[6]

> The court must consider the surrounding circumstances including any relationship between the prospective occupiers, the course of negotiations and the nature and extent of the accommodation and the intended and actual mode of occupation of the accommodation.

(3) EXCEPTIONAL CIRCUMSTANCES

Where the occupier has the right to exclusive possession, there are certain exceptional circumstances where he may nevertheless only be a licensee. In *Street v Mountford* Lord TEMPLEMAN identified as exceptional[7] those cases where:

(a) the occupancy is within one of a number of special categories, i.e. under a contract for the sale of land, or pursuant to a contract of employment or referable to the holding of an office.[8] The Court of Appeal has interpreted the first exception narrowly, in holding that a *potential* purchaser of a dwelling-house who entered into exclusive

---

5 At 460, at 1066, per Lord TEMPLEMAN. Followed in *Aslan v Murphy* [1990] 1 WLR 766, [1989] 3 All ER 130; M & B p. 458; [1989] All ER Rev 172 (P. J. Clarke); *Nicolaou v Pitt* [1989] 1 EGLR 84 ("after a certain amount of humming and hawing the owner said he did contemplate introducing a stranger into the flat. I do not believe him." CA held that there was a tenancy, even though the flat had a spare bedroom and had been previously occupied by three persons).

6 At 458, at 1064.

7 [1985] AC 809 at 826, [1985] 2 All ER 289 at 300. The categories are "illustrative and not exhaustive"; *Dellneed Ltd v Chin* (1986) 53 P & CR 172 at 187, per MILLETT J. See *Royal Philanthropic Society v County* [1985] 2 EGLR 109, where CA rejected a number of submitted exceptional circumstances; [1986] Conv 215 (P. F. Smith); *Whitbread West Pennines Ltd v Reedy* [1988] ICR 807.

Another possible exception is homeless persons: *Westminster City Council v Clarke* [1992] 2 AC 288, [1992] 1 All ER 695, [1992] Conv 112 (J. E. Martin), 285 (D. S. Cowan); [1992] All ER Rev 225 (P. J. Clarke) (grant of "licence to occupy" to occupant of single room in men's hostel run by appellant council, in pursuance of its duty to house the homeless under Housing Act 1985, s. 65 (2), held to be a licensee and not a secure tenant; "a very special case which depends on the peculiar nature of the hostel maintained by the council, the use of the hostel by the council, the totality, immediacy, and objectives of the powers exercisable by the council and the immediate restrictions imposed on Mr. Clarke. The decision in this case will not allow a landlord, private or public, to free himself from the Rent Acts or from the restrictions of a secure tenancy merely by adopting or adapting the language of the licence to occupy": per Lord TEMPLEMAN at 238, at 703). See also Housing Act 1985, s. 79 (3), Sch 1, para 4 and Housing Act 1988, s. 1 (6), which exclude most tenancies granted in such circumstances from statutory protection.

8 *Mayhew v Suttle* (1854) 4 E & B 347; *Smith v Seghill Overseers* (1875) LR 10 QB 422 distinguish a service occupant who is a licensee from a service tenant who is not. The latter is a person to whom a dwelling-house is let in consequence of his employment, but who is not required to live there for the better performance of his duties: *Torbett v Faulkner* [1952] 2 TLR 659. See *Royal Philanthropic Society v County*, supra; *Norris v Checksfield* [1991] 1 WLR 1241, [1991] 4 All ER 327 (semi-skilled mechanic held to be service licensee, even though he was never in a position to perform the duties required of him); *Burgoyne v Griffiths* [1991] 1 EGLR 14 (farm cottage); *South Glamorgan County Council v Griffiths* [1992] 2 EGLR 232; *Greenwich London Borough Council v Hughes* [1993] EGCS 166 (employer providing facility, but not imposing obligation).

possession for a term at a rent under an arrangement with the ultimate intention of negotiating for its sale was a tenant;[9]

(b) the owner has no power to grant a tenancy;[10]

(c) the circumstances show that there is no intention to create legal relationships as, for example, "where there has been something in the circumstances, such as a family arrangement, an act of friendship or generosity, or such like, to negative any intention to create a tenancy".[11] It would appear that the test of intention is relevant in deciding whether there is an intention to create a legal relationship, but irrelevant in deciding which legal relationship is created.

(4) EXAMPLES OF LICENCES

Licences rather than leases have been created where an employer allowed his retiring servant to remain in his cottage rent free for the rest of his life;[12] where a father, wishing to provide a home for his son and daughter-in-law, allowed them to occupy a house that he had bought in return for their promise to pay the instalments still due to a building society;[13] where a landlord allowed the daughter of his deceased employee to remain in her father's cottage rather than evict her immediately;[14] where a woman bought a house and allowed her brother to occupy it, rent free;[15] where a man aged 85

9 *Bretherton v Paton* [1986] 1 EGLR 172. See also *Essex Plan Ltd v Broadminster Ltd* (1988) 56 P & CR 353 (licence where occupier continued in possession after expiry of option; no exclusive possession) [1989] Conv 55 (J. E. Martin); cf. *Heslop v Burns* [1974] 1 WLR 1241, [1974] 3 All ER 406; M & B p. 463, p. 383, post, where SCARMAN LJ held that occupation prior to a contract of sale was a paradigm case of a tenancy at will; *Vandersteen v Agius* (1992) 65 P & CR 266 (occupation pursuant to sale of goodwill of osteopathy practice not an exception). On purchasers in possession generally, see [1987] Conv 278 (P. Sparkes).

10 *Street v Mountford* [1985] AC 809 at 821, [1985] 2 All ER 289; *Camden London Borough Council v Shortlife Community Housing Ltd* (1992) 90 LGR 358 (which contains a critique on the exceptions by MILLETT J); [1993] Conv 157 (D. S. Cowan).

11 *Facchini v Bryson* [1952] 1 TLR 1386 at 1389–1390, per DENNING LJ, cited *Street v Mountford* at 821, at 296. See *Booker v Palmer* [1942] 2 All ER 674; *Marcroft Wagons Ltd v Smith* [1951] 2 KB 496, [1951] 2 All ER 271; *Heslop v Burns* supra; *Sharp v McArthur* (1987) unreported, where owner of flat, with empty "For Sale" notice board prominently displayed, let defendant into possession as a favour pending sale. Held by CA to be a licence, even though defendant had exclusive possession and was given a rent book for the purpose of enabling him to obtain payment from the D.H.S.S. for outgoings for accommodation; *Carr Gomm Society v Hawkins* [1990] CLY 2811 (self-employed gardener held to be licensee of registered charity which had 60 homes in London and a continuing need to move people if necessary); *Westminster City Council v Basson* [1991] 1 EGLR 277 (girl friend who remained in exclusive possession of flat after her boy friend's tenancy had been terminated held to be licensee, even though she had received rent rebates from the council, which had made it clear that no tenancy was intended); [1992] Conv 113 (J. E. Martin); *Colchester Borough Council v Smith* [1991] Ch 448 at 485–486, [1991] 1 All ER 29 at 53–54 (no intention to create legal relations where occupant's implied offer to pay reasonable rent was rejected, and where there was insistence on his occupation at his own risk and on his giving up possession at short notice if land required for other purposes). Cf *Nunn v Dalrymple* (1989) 59 P & CR 231; *Ward v Warnke* (1990) 22 HLR 496 (in both cases a *family* arrangement in which exclusive possession of a cottage in return for regular payments was held to be a tenancy). See also *Abbeyfield (Harpenden) Society v Woods* [1968] 1 WLR 374, [1968] 1 All ER 352n; *Barnes v Barratt* [1970] 2 QB 657, [1970] 2 All ER 483 (house-sharing arrangement without rent or fixed term held to be licence).

12 *Foster v Robinson* [1951] 1 KB 149; *Binions v Evans* [1972] Ch 359, [1972] 2 All ER 70; M & B p. 555 (widow of deceased employee).

13 *Errington v Errington and Woods* [1952] 1 KB 290, [1952] 1 All ER 154.

14 *Marcroft Wagons Ltd v Smith* [1951] 2 KB 496.

15 *Cobb v Lane* [1952] 1 All ER 1199. See also *Heslop v Burns* [1974] 1 WLR 1241, [1974] 3 All ER 406.

occupied a room in an old people's home;[16] where a lodger occupied a room in a self-contained residential hotel for men;[17] where "under an informal family arrangement" a mother bought a house and allowed her son and his second wife to live there on payment of £7 a week;[18] and where a gardener-handyman occupied a cottage rent and rates free.[19]

(5) SUMMARY

The effect of *Street v Mountford* and the subsequent cases is to prevent a landlord from driving a coach and horses through the Rent Acts.[20] Its rejection of the relevance of the *intention* of the parties is of paramount importance; and the consequent rigidity of the test for distinguishing between a lease and a licence may have led to the overprotection of the tenant at the expense of the landlord, especially where it is a business tenancy.

The crux of the matter is that an owner of residential property is reluctant to grant a lease to a tenant which will have the consequences of rent control and of security of tenure after the end of the contractual term. A status of irremovability is particularly unattractive to an owner. The Housing Act of 1980 introduced the protected shorthold tenancy as a method of letting residential premises without security of tenure after the contractual term ended. The Housing Act[1] of 1988 phased out the Rent Act 1977 and extended the concept of the shorthold tenancy. Tenancies created before 15 January 1989 were not affected. The object is to provide an incentive to landlords to let premises and to ease the housing shortage in the private rented sector. The new tenancies (assured tenancies and assured shorthold tenancies) preserve the basic principle of security of tenure, but the grounds of possession are strengthened and the tenant enjoys only minimal rights of succession and rent control.

There is now less incentive for the landlord of residential property to create a lease instead of a licence. There will, however, be many cases of licences created before *Street v Mountford* which will have to be interpreted in the light of that decision.

B. THE PERIOD MUST BE DEFINITE

(1) COMMENCEMENT OF PERIOD

Though a lease may be limited to endure for any specified number of years, however many, it cannot be limited in perpetuity.[2] It may even be for a

---

16 *Abbeyfield (Harpenden) Society Ltd v Woods*, supra.
17 *Marchant v Charters* [1977] 1 WLR 1181, [1977] 3 All ER 918. The decision was approved, but not its reasoning, in *Street v Mountford* at 824, at 298.
18 *Hardwick v Johnson* [1978] 1 WLR 683, [1978] 2 All ER 935; M & B, p. 546; cf. *Tanner v Tanner* [1975] 1 WLR 1346, [1975] 3 All ER 776; M & B p. 538.
19 *Scrimgeour v Waller* (1980) 257 EG 61; *De Rothschild v Wing RDC* [1967] 1 WLR 470, [1967] 1 All ER 597.
20 At 819, at 294. In *Brooker Settled Estates Ltd v Ayers* [1987] 1 EGLR 50, O'CONNOR LJ said at 51: "Lord TEMPLEMAN reviewed the authorities dealing with this tortured question, and sought to introduce some order into the law for the better administration of the law and guidance of the learned judges, particularly in the county courts, who have to deal with this problem."
1 P. 469, post.
2 *Sevenoaks, Maidstone and Tunbridge Rly Co v London, Chatham and Dover Rly Co* (1879) 11 Ch D 625 at 635–6. The effect of an instrument purporting to create a perpetual lease at a

discontinuous period, for example, a single letting for three successive bank holidays. In the context of time-sharing of holiday homes, it was held that the lease of a cottage for 1 week in each year for 80 consecutive years was a lease for a discontinuous period of 80 years.[3]

The term must be for a definite period in the sense that it must have a certain beginning[4] and a certain ending. This does not necessarily mean that the parties must immediately fix the exact date of commencement, for it is open to them to agree that the lease shall *begin* upon the occurrence of an uncertain event, as for example, upon the declaration of war by Great Britain[5]; or:

upon possession of the premises becoming vacant.[6]

Such an agreement, though at first conditional, becomes absolute and enforceable as soon as the event occurs.[7]

(2) REVERSIONARY LEASES

A term expressed to begin from a past date[8] or, as is more usual, from the date of the lease is called a lease *in possession*. It is also possible to create a *reversionary* lease, by which the term is limited to commence at some future date. Formerly such a term might be granted so as to commence at any time in the future, as, for instance, where a lease was made in 1917 to commence in 1946,[9] but a restriction was imposed upon this right by the Law of Property Act 1925, which provides that:

A term, at a rent or granted in consideration of a fine, limited after the commencement of this Act to take effect more than 21 years from the date of the instrument purporting to create it, shall be void, and any contract made after such commencement to create such a term shall likewise be void.[10]

The first limb of this enactment nullifies the creation of a reversionary lease limited to take effect more than 21 years from the date of the lease, e.g. a lease executed in 1994 for a term of ten years to run from 2021. The second limb nullifies a contract to create *such a term*, i.e. a term that will commence more than 21 years from the date of the lease by which it will eventually be

---

rent may perhaps be either to create a yearly tenancy or to pass the fee simple to the lessee subject to the payment of an annual rentcharge in perpetuity: *Doe d Roberton v Gardiner* (1852) 12 CB 319 at 333.
3 And not for "a term certain exceeding 21 years" within VATA 1983, s. 1, Sch. 2, para 4. VAT was therefore chargeable: *Cottage Holiday Associates Ltd v Customs and Excise Comrs* [1983] QB 735. See Timeshare Act 1992; [1992] Conv 30; [1983] Conv 248 (H. W. Wilkinson).
4 *Harvey v Pratt* [1965] 1 WLR 1025, [1965] 2 All ER 786 (contract for lease void for failing to specify date of commencement).
5 *Swift v Macbean* [1942] 1 KB 375, [1942] 1 All ER 126.
6 *Brilliant v Michaels* [1945] 1 All ER 121. In this case, however, it was held that no final agreement had been made.
7 Ibid., at 126, citing Fry, *Specific Performance* (6th edn), p. 458.
8 *James v Lock* (1977) 246 EG 395. Such a lease cannot retrospectively vest an estate in the lessee. A grant of a term of 7 years from this day a year ago merely creates a term of 6 years from today. See *Bradshaw v Pawley* [1980] 1 WLR 10 at 14, [1979] 3 All ER 273 at 276.
9 *Mann, Crossman and Paulin Ltd v Registrar of the Land Registry* [1918] 1 Ch 202.
10 S. 149 (3). This restriction does not affect terms, such as portions terms, taking effect in equity under a settlement.

created. For example, a contract, which is made in 1994 to grant a lease for ten years in 1996, the term to run from 2021 is void.[11]

Thus, the Act relates the period of 21 years to the date of the lease, not to the date of the contract. Therefore a contract in a lease for 35 years giving the tenant an option to renew it for a further period of 35 years by making a written request to this effect 12 months before the expiration of the current term, is not void, since the contractual option, if exercised, will result in a term to begin upon the execution of the second lease. It is immaterial that it will be more than 21 years before the contractual right is exercised.[12]

(3) ENDING OF PERIOD

The date upon which a lease is to terminate is generally expressed specifically, but in accordance with the maxim—*id certum est quod certum reddi potest*—it is sufficient if made to depend upon some uncertain event, provided that the event occurs before the lease takes effect; as for example where lands are let to A for so many years as B shall fix.

On the other hand a lease is void if the date of its termination remains uncertain after it has taken effect. It was accordingly held in *Lace v Chantler*,[13] for instance, that an agreement to let a house for the duration of the war did not create a valid tenancy.[14]

This principle, which has been judicially accepted for 500 years, was reaffirmed by the House of Lords in *Prudential Assurance Co Ltd v London Residuary Body*[15] in which:

> the London County Council granted a lease of a strip of land fronting a road on terms that "the tenancy shall continue until the land is required by the council for the purposes of widening the road".

The lease was held to be void for uncertainty, since it was not possible to say at the outset what the maximum duration of the lease would be.

(4) INTERESSE TERMINI ABOLISHED

There was a troublesome doctrine of the common law which established, in the case of a lease not operating under the Statute of Uses, that the lessee acquired no estate in the land until he actually entered into possession. Until

---

11 *Re Strand and Savoy Properties Ltd* [1960] Ch 582, [1960] 2 All ER 327; M & B p. 414; *Weg Motors Ltd v Hales* [1961] Ch 176, [1960] 3 All ER 762; affd [1962] Ch 49, [1961] 3 All ER 181; M & B p. 415; see (1960) 76 LQR, pp. 352–4 (R.E.M.).

12 *Re Strand and Savoy Properties Ltd*, supra.

13 [1944] KB 368, [1944] 1 All ER 305; M & B p. 412.

14 A conveyancing device by which the difficulty may be surmounted is to grant a lease for a fixed period determinable upon the happening of the uncertain event, e.g. to A for 99 years terminable on the cessation of hostilities; *Prudential Assurance Co Ltd v London Residuary Body* [1992] 2 AC 386 at 389, [1992] 3 All ER 504 at 506, per Lord TEMPLEMAN. In *Great Northern Rly Co v Arnold* (1916) 33 TLR 114, ROWLATT J managed even to construe a lease similar to that in *Lace v Chantler* as a lease for 999 years terminable on the cessation of the 1914 War. The effect of *Lace v Chantler* was to defeat so many leases made before and during the war of 1939 that it was found necessary to save them by a temporary measure, the Validation of War-time Leases Act 1944.

15 Supra; (1993) 109 LQR 93 (P. Sparkes); [1993] Conv 461 (P. F. Smith); (1994) 57 MLR 117 (D. Wilde); [1993] CLJ 26 (S. Bridge); [1992] 13 LS 38 (S. Bright); [1992] All ER Rev 223 (P. J. Clarke); [1993] CLP Part I 69 (P. Kohler). For the subsequent holding that the purported lease was valid as a periodic tenancy on the terms of the agreement in so far as they were consistent with a yearly tenancy, see p. 384, post.

that time he was said to have a mere right to take possession, and this right was called an *interesse termini*. This requisite of entry to perfect a lease was, however, abolished by the Law of Property Act 1925, and all terms of years absolute, created before or after the commencement of the Act, take effect from the date fixed for the commencement of the term without actual entry.[16]

SECTION III CREATION OF TERMS OF YEARS

A term of years may be brought into existence either at law by a lease or in equity by a contract for a lease.

A lease is a conveyance, and if made in the form required by law, it passes a *legal* term of years to the tenant and creates the legal relationship of landlord and tenant—either at once in the case of an immediate letting or at the agreed future date in the case of a reversionary lease. The tenant thereby acquires a proprietary interest in the land, which, being legal, is enforceable against all the world.[17]

A contract for a lease, on the other hand, does not operate as a conveyance at law, but is a contract that binds the parties, the one to grant a lease and the other to accept it.[18]

Such a contract does not create the relationship of landlord and tenant *at law*. But, as we shall see, the position of the parties *in equity* is different. An *equitable* term of years may pass to the person who holds under a contract for a lease.[19] If that contract is capable of being enforced by specific performance, then he will hold under the same terms in equity as if a lease had actually been granted to him. The relationship of landlord and tenant will thus be created *in equity*, and as between the parties the rights and duties of that relationship will be the same as if the lease had been granted.[20] But, in this case, the tenant has only an equitable interest in the land, which, according to general principle, is enforceable against all the world *except* a bona fide purchaser for value of the legal estate without notice.[1]

A lease which is framed in formal and technical language will state that:

The landlord hereby demises unto the tenant all that messuage or dwelling-house, etc.

but the mere fact that an instrument is drafted as a contract does not preclude it from taking effect as an actual demise. Whether the contract operates as a lease or as a contract depends upon the intention of the parties, which must be collected from all the circumstances.[2]

We will now deal separately with these two modes of creation, beginning with the contract for a lease.

---

16 LPA 1925, s. 149 (1), (2).
17 P. 56, ante.
18 *Borman v Griffith* [1930] 1 Ch 493.
19 Cited by Lord SIMON OF GLAISDALE in *National Carriers Ltd v Panalpina (Northern) Ltd* [1981] AC 675 at 784, [1981] 1 All ER 161 at 178. See pp. 379 et seq, post.
20 *Walsh v Lonsdale* (1882) 21 Ch D 9; M & B p. 79, p. 378, post.
 1 For further detail, and for the effect of registration under LCA 1972, see pp. 377 et seq, post.
 2 See Woodfall, *Landlord and Tenant* (28th edn), paras 1–0455–8.

A. CONTRACT FOR A LEASE

We have already discussed the requirements for a valid and enforceable contract for the sale or other disposition of land.[3] For a contract for a lease to be valid, there must be a final agreement on the terms of the lease,[4] that is to say, on the parties, the property, the consideration or rent, the duration of the lease and any other special terms. The contract must also comply with the formalities required for a contract for the sale or other disposition of land.[5]

As we have seen, it is usual for a contract for the sale of land to precede the conveyance of the legal estate to the purchaser.[6] However, this is the exception rather than the rule in the case of a lease.[7] Where there is a building lease, a contract is often made first, and then a lease is subsequently granted when the building is complete. But in most cases, the transaction is effected either by a contract for a lease, or by a lease, but rarely by a combination of both.[8]

B. LEASES

(1) FORMALITIES

(a) Leases not exceeding three years

At common law a parol lease was sufficient to create the relation of landlord and tenant in the case of corporeal hereditaments, and there was no necessity to employ either a deed or a writing. This is still the law with regard to leases *not exceeding three years*, for the Law of Property Act 1925,[9] re-enacting in effect the Statute of Frauds 1677, provides that:

> the creation by parol of leases taking effect in possession for a term not exceeding three years (whether or not the lessee is given power to extend the term) at the best rent which can be reasonably obtained without taking a fine,

shall be valid.

Thus a mere oral lease suffices to create a *legal* term of years, provided that it is to take effect in possession, that it reserves the best rent reasonably obtainable, and that it is not to last for longer than three years. A lease exceeds three years within the meaning of the Act only if it is for a definite term longer than that period. It is immaterial in such a case that it contains a provision allowing its earlier determination by notice.[10] On the other hand, a periodic tenancy for an indefinite period, such as one from year to year or week to week, may be validly created by a parol lease, for, though it may endure for much longer than three years, it may equally well be determined at an earlier date.

---

3 Pp. 107 et seq, ante.
4 See e.g. *Fletcher v Davies* (1980) 257 EG 1149 (flat in Inner Temple).
5 Pp. 111, 121, ante.
6 P. 107, ante.
7 See *Hollington Bros Ltd v Rhodes* [1951] 2 TLR 691 at 694.
8 *Emmet on Title* (19th edn), para 26.001.
9 S. 54(2).
10 *Kushner v Law Society* [1952] 1 KB 264, [1952] 1 All ER 404.

Although a lease not exceeding three years may be created orally, it cannot be assigned at law without a deed.[11]

(b) Leases exceeding three years

A lease, however, which exceeds three years will not pass a legal estate immediately and directly to the tenant unless it is made by deed. The history of this requirement is as follows. Section 1 of the Statute of Frauds 1677 enacted that:

> All leases ... or terms of years ... made or created ... by parol, and not put in writing, and signed by the parties so making or creating the same, or their agents thereunto lawfully authorized by writing, shall have the force and effect of leases or estates *at will* only.

The second section excepted leases not exceeding three years at a rent of two-thirds at least of the full improved value of the land.

The next enactment was the Real Property Act 1845[12] which required a further formality by providing that:

> A lease, required by law to be in writing, of any tenements or hereditaments ... made after the first day of October, 1845, shall be void at law unless also made by deed.

Thus it was only in the case of leases exceeding three years that a deed became necessary, since it was these alone that had previously been "required by law to be in writing". A lease exceeding three years and not executed as a deed had and still has a greater effect than is indicated by the language of the two statutes cited but since 1845 it has never sufficed to pass to the tenant an immediate legal interest equivalent to that which the parties intended to create. The Statutes of 1677 and 1845 have been in effect re-enacted by the Law of Property Act 1925 in the two following sections:

> 54.—(1) All interests in land created by parol and not put in writing and signed by the persons so creating the same, or by their agents thereunto lawfully authorized in writing, have, notwithstanding any consideration having been given for the same, the force and effect of interests at will only.
>
> (2) Nothing in the foregoing provisions ... shall affect the creation by parol of leases taking effect in possession for a term not exceeding three years ... at the best rent which can be reasonably obtained without taking a fine.
>
> 52.—(1) All conveyances of land or of any interest therein are void for the purpose of conveying or creating a legal estate unless made by deed.
>
> (2) This section does not apply to—
>
> (*d*) leases or tenancies or other assurances not required by law to be made in writing.

We must now attempt to define the exact effect of a lease exceeding three years which fails to satisfy the statutory requirements.

(2) EFFECT OF LEASES EXCEEDING THREE YEARS WHICH ARE NOT MADE IN ACCORDANCE WITH THE REQUIRED FORMALITIES

The scope of the following inquiry is to ascertain, first what was the legal effect between 1677 and 1845 of a lease not put into writing as required by

---

11 *Crago v Julian* [1992] 1 WLR 372, [1992] 1 All ER 744; [1992] Conv 375 (P. Sparkes). For assignment of a lease, see p. 453, post. On informal short term leases, see [1992] Conv 252, 337 (P. Sparkes).

12 S. 3.

the Statute of Frauds; secondly, what has been the effect since 1845 of a lease not made by deed as required by the Real Property Act of that year. Inasmuch as both these Statutes have been re-enacted by the Law of Property Act 1925, the result of this inquiry will be a statement of the present law on the subject.

(a) Effect at common law

The Statute of Frauds said that a lease which was not put in writing should create a mere tenancy at will, and this was the view taken by the common law when a tenant did nothing more than enter into possession of the premises under a parol lease. But common law went further and presumed that a tenant who had not merely gone into possession, but had also paid rent on a yearly basis, became tenant from year to year, and that he held this yearly tenancy subject to such of the terms and conditions of the unwritten lease as were consistent with a yearly tenancy.[13]

The provision of the Real Property Act 1845 that an unsealed lease should be *void at law* was construed in the same manner. The document was void as a lease in the sense that it did not create the agreed term of years, but if the intended tenant entered into possession and paid rent at a yearly rate, he was presumed to be a yearly tenant.[14]

Moreover the above represents the legal position at the present day *if we confine our attention to the common law*. A conveyance of land, and this includes a lease,[15] is void under the Law of Property Act 1925 for the purpose of creating a legal estate unless made by deed (except of course in the case of a lease not exceeding three years), but nevertheless, if the tenant enters into possession and pays a yearly rent, he will become a yearly tenant. Again, by the same Act a term exceeding three years which is not put in writing is to have the force and effect of an interest at will only, but, given the same two facts of possession and payment of rent, it also will be converted into a legal yearly tenancy. It is expressly provided that the requirements of the Act with regard to formalities shall not "affect the right to acquire an interest in land by virtue of taking possession".[16]

(b) Effect in equity

Equity, however, took a very different view of the effect of a lease for more than three years which was not put in writing as required by the Statute of Frauds, or which, after 1845, was not made by deed. While admitting that the statutes rendered such a lease incapable of passing the term agreed upon by the parties, courts of equity held that the abortive lease must be regarded as *a contract for a lease*, provided, of course, that the constituents of an enforceable contract, as described above,[17] were present. In other words, an *oral* lease followed by an act of part performance, and a *written* lease signed by the party to be charged and constituting a sufficient memorandum of the

13 *Doe d Rigge v Bell* (1793) 5 Term Rep 471; *Mann v Lovejoy* (1826) Ry & M 355; *Clayton v Blakey* (1798) 8 Term Rep 3; *Richardson v Gifford* (1834) 1 Ad & El 52; *Hamerton v Stead* 1824) 3 B & C 478 at 483, per LITTLEDALE J. See p. 387, post.
14 *Martin v Smith* (1874) LR 9 Exch 50; *Rhyl UDC v Rhyl Amusements Ltd* [1959] 1 WLR 465, [1959] 1 All ER 257, where the lease was void for lack of compliance with the Public Health Act 1875, s. 177.
15 S. 205 (1) (ii).
16 S. 55 (c).
17 P. 374, ante.

terms of the bargain, were both allowed to have the same effect as a contract for a lease. It becomes necessary, therefore, to ascertain what the effect has always been in equity of such a contract.

A contract for a lease is a contract to which the equitable remedy of specific performance is peculiarly appropriate. If a party can prove to the satisfaction of the court that such a contract has been entered into, he can bring a suit for specific performance requiring the other party to execute a deed in the manner required by statute so as to create that legal term which the parties intended to create. One effect, therefore, of such a specifically performable contract is that the prospective tenant immediately acquires an equitable interest in the land in the sense that he has an equitable right to a legal estate.[18]

As was said in a case prior to 1845:[19]

The defendant was let into possession under an agreement, which gave the parties a right to go to equity to compel the execution of it by making out a formal lease.

The same view was upheld even when the Real Property Act 1845 had enacted that a lease exceeding three years made otherwise than by deed should be void at law. As Lord CHELMSFORD said in *Parker v Taswell*:[20]

The legislature appears to have been very cautious and guarded in language, for it uses the expression "shall be void at law". If the legislature had intended to deprive such a document of all efficacy, it would have said that the instrument should "be avoided to all intents and purposes". There are no such words in the Act. I think it would be too strong to say that because it is void at law as a lease, it cannot be used as an agreement enforceable in Equity, the intention of the parties having been that there should be a lease, and the aid of Equity being only invoked to carry that intention into effect.

(3) DOCTRINE OF *WALSH V LONSDALE*

(a) The doctrine

The effect of this divergence between the views of common law and equity was that, prior to the passing of the Judicature Act 1873, an unsealed lease and a contract for a lease resulted in the creation of two entirely different interests, according as the common law or the equitable doctrine was invoked. At common law the tenant acquired the interest of a tenant from year to year if he paid rent and entered into possession: in equity he was entitled to call for the execution of a legal lease and to have inserted therein all the provisions of the void lease or of the contract.

The Judicature Act, however, materially affected the position. It provides in effect that, whenever an action is brought in any court, the plaintiff may set up equitable claims and the defendant may raise equitable defences, and that:

[Where] there is any conflict or variance between the rules of equity and the rules of the common law with reference to the same matter, the rules of equity shall prevail.[1]

The particular point of variance which existed in the case of an unsealed

18 *Palmer v Carey* [1926] AC 703 at 706.
19 *Doe d Thompson v Amey* (1840) 12 Ad & El 476 at 479, per Lord DENMAN CJ.
20 (1858) 2 De G & J 559 at 570.
1 Supreme Court of Judicature Act 1873, s. 25 (11); now Supreme Court Act 1981, s. 49 (1).

lease fell to be considered in the leading case of *Walsh v Lonsdale*,[2] decided in 1882. In that case:

> the plaintiff agreed in writing to take a lease of a mill for seven years, and part of the agreement was that a deed should be executed containing inter alia a provision that *on any given day* the lessor might require the tenant to pay one year's rent in advance. No deed was executed, and the plaintiff, who was let into possession, paid rent quarterly, but not in advance, for a year and a half. The landlord then demanded a year's rent in advance and upon refusal distrained for the amount. The plaintiff brought an action to recover damages for illegal distress, for specific performance of the contract for a lease and for an interim injunction to restrain the distress.
>
> The main ground upon which he rested his claim was that, as he had been let into possession and had paid rent under a contract which did not operate as a lease, he was in the position of a tenant from year to year and held the mill upon such of the agreed terms as were consistent with a yearly tenancy. The condition making a year's rent always payable in advance was obviously inconsistent with a yearly tenancy which could be determined by half a year's notice, and for this reason it was argued that the distress was illegal.

This argument did not prevail. It was decided that a tenant who holds under a contract for a lease of which specific performance will be decreed occupies the same position *vis à vis the landlord*, as regards both rights and liabilities, as he would occupy if a formal lease under seal had been executed.

If a lease by deed had been executed in this case on the lines of the contract, the defendant would have been entitled to distrain for rent not paid in advance, and the mere fact that the formal lease had not been actually made was not to prejudice his rights. Sir George JESSEL MR put the matter thus:

> There is an agreement for a lease under which possession has been given. Now since the Judicature Act the possession is held under the agreement. There are not two estates as there were formerly—one estate at common law by reason of the payment of the rent from year to year, and an estate in equity under the agreement.There is only one court, and the equity rules prevail in it. The tenant holds under an agreement for a lease. He holds, therefore, under the same terms in equity as if a lease had been granted, it being a case in which both parties admit that relief is capable of being given by specific performance. That being so, he cannot complain of the exercise by the landlord of the same rights as the landlord would have had if a lease had been granted. On the other hand, he is protected in the same way as if a lease had been granted; he cannot be turned out by six month's notice as a tenant from year to year. He has a right to say: "I have a lease in equity and you can only re-enter if I have committed such a breach of covenant as would, if a lease had been granted, have entitled you to re-enter according to the terms of a proper proviso for re-entry". That being so, it appears to me that being a lessee in equity he cannot complain of the exercise of the right of distress merely because the actual parchment has not been signed and sealed.

Such, then, is the doctrine of *Walsh v Lonsdale*. It is one example of the principle that equity regards as already done what the parties to a transaction have agreed to do—a principle that is by no means confined to a contract for a lease, for it applies to any contract to convey or create a legal estate of which equity will order specific performance, as for instance, a contract for

2 (1882) 21 Ch D 9; M & B p. 79; (1988) OJLS 350 (P. Sparkes).

the sale of land,[3] or for the grant of a mortgage,[4] an easement[5] or a profit à prendre.[6]

(b) Application of doctrine

In the context of landlord and tenant, *Walsh v Lonsdale* has been followed,[7] qualified[8] and explained[9] in later cases. It has also been applied "once removed",[10] as where V entered into a contract to sell the fee simple of land to P, who then agreed to grant a lease of the land to T. T was treated as a lessee in equity by virtue of a double application of the doctrine. T could not become a lessee at common law until a legal lease had been properly granted. As Lord DENNING said:[11]

> It is quite plain that, if the lease to T was defective in point of law, nevertheless it was good in equity, and for this simple reason. There were two agreements of which specific performance would be granted. One was the agreement by V to convey to P. The other was the agreement by P to grant a lease to T. In respect of each of these agreements, equity looks upon that as done which ought to be done. It follows that, by combining the two agreements, the tenant, T, hold upon the same terms as if a lease had actually been granted by V to T. This is, of course, an extension of the doctrine of *Walsh v Lonsdale* where there was only one agreement. But I see no reason why the doctrine should not be extended to a case like the present, where there were two agreements, each of which was such that specific performance would be granted.

The doctrine is now the governing rule whenever it is necessary to ascertain the effect of a lease or contract for a lease which is not made by deed as required by the Law of Property Act 1925. Section 52(1)[12] of the Act provides that all conveyances of land:

> are void for the purpose of conveying or creating a legal estate unless made by deed,

but, if a tenant has an enforceable right to call for a deed, he is, as far as his rights and liabilities in relation to the landlord are concerned, in practically the same position as if he actually had a deed.

(4) A CONTRACT FOR A LEASE IS NOT EQUAL TO A LEASE

It must not, however, be concluded that a contract for a lease is as effective in all respects and against all persons as a lease. This is not so.[13] What Sir

---

3 P. 124, ante.
4 P. 669, post.
5 P. 532, post.
6 P. 570, post.
7 *Lowther v Heaver* (1889) 41 Ch D 248; *Coatsworth v Johnson* (1885) 55 LJQB 220; M & B p. 82; *Tottenham Hotspur Football and Athletic Co Ltd v Princegrove Publishers Ltd* [1974] 1 WLR 113, [1974] 1 All ER 17; (1974) 90 LQR 149 (M. Albery); *Re A Company (No 00792 of 1992), ex p Tredegar Enterprises Ltd* [1992] 29 EG 122.
8 *Cornish v Brook Green Laundry Ltd* [1959] 1 QB 394, [1959] 1 All ER 373, where it was held that it cannot be invoked if the contract to grant a term of years is subject to a condition precedent performable by the proposed tenant and not yet performed; *Shelley v United Artists Corpn Ltd* [1990] 1 EGLR 103.
9 *Manchester Brewery Co v Coombs* [1901] 2 Ch 608; M & B p. 522; *Gray v Spyer* [1922] 2 Ch 22.
10 *Industrial Properties (Barton Hill) Ltd v Associated Electrical Industries Ltd* [1977] QB 580, [1977] 2 All ER 293; M & B p. 80.
11 Ibid., at 598, at 303. Letters have been substituted for the names of the parties.
12 P. 375, ante.
13 *Manchester Brewery Co v Coombs* [1901] 2 Ch 608 at 617.

George JESSEL MR meant in *Walsh v Lonsdale* was that if, in litigation between the parties, the circumstances would justify a decree for the execution of a sealed lease, then both in the Queen's Bench Division and in the Chancery Division, the case must be treated as if such a lease had been granted. There are at least three facts which illustrate the limitations of the doctrine, and the advantages of a lease as compared with a contract for a lease.

(a) Specific performance

First, the doctrine stands excluded if the contract is one of which equity will not grant specific performance.[14] This is still a discretionary remedy and will not be granted in all cases, as for instance where a lessee who seeks the aid of the court will be unable to perform the covenants in the lease owing to his insolvent state, or where he has already committed a breach of covenant that would have formed part of the lease. Thus, in *Coatsworth v Johnson*:[15]

> The plaintiff entered into possession under an agreement that the defendant would grant him a lease for twenty-one years. Before any rent was due or had been paid, the defendant gave him notice to quit and evicted him on the ground that he had done that which amounted to a breach of a covenant contained in the agreement and intended to be inserted in the lease.

The plaintiff sued in trespass, but failed. At common law, having paid no rent, he was a mere tenant at will and as such could be evicted at the pleasure of the defendant; in equity he was precluded from obtaining a decree of specific performance, since he had broken a covenant into which he had entered.

STAMP J, in explaining that the doctrine only applies where the tenant is entitled to specific performance, said in *Warmington v Miller*:[16]

> The equitable interests which the intended lessee has under an agreement for a lease do not exist in vacuo, but arise because the intended lessee has an equitable right to specific performance of the agreement. In such a situation that which is agreed to be and ought to be done is treated as having been done and carrying with it in equity the attendant rights.

Further, specific performance will not be granted if the court has no jurisdiction to grant it. Thus a county court has such jurisdiction only where the value of the property claimed by the plaintiff does not exceed £30,000.[17]

(b) Conveyance

Secondly, the statutory definition of "conveyance"[18] includes a lease but not a contract for a lease. Thus, a tenant under a contract cannot claim those privileges which are granted by section 62 of the Law of Property Act 1925[19] to one who takes a "conveyance" of land.[20]

14 For criticism of this requirement, see (1987) 7 OJLS 60 (S. Gardner).
15 (1886) 55 LJQB 220; M & B p. 82.
16 [1973] QB 877 at 887, [1973] 2 All ER 372 at 377.
17 County Courts Act 1984, s. 23 (*d*); County Courts Jurisdiction Order 1981, S.I. 1981 No. 1123; *Foster v Reeves* [1892] 2 QB 255; cf *Cornish v Brook Green Laundry Ltd* [1959] 1 QB 394, [1959] 1 All ER 373; *Kingswood Estate Co Ltd v Anderson* [1963] 2 QB 169, [1962] 3 All ER 593; *Rushton v Smith* [1976] QB 480, [1975] 2 All ER 905.
18 LPA 1925, s. 205 (1) (ii).
19 P. 534, post.
20 *Borman v Griffith* [1930] 1 Ch 493; M & B p. 478.

(c) Third parties

Thirdly, the doctrine does not in all cases affect the rights of third parties.[1] For instance, privity of estate exists between a landlord and an assignee from a tenant holding *under a lease*, so as to make the covenants enforceable by and against the assignee,[2] but no such privity exists in the case of an assignee from a person "whose only title to call himself a lessee depends on his right to specific performance of the agreement".[3] But a more important fact is that, since a specifically enforceable contract confers an equitable right upon the lessee, it will not on general principles be enforceable against a bona fide purchaser for value of a legal estate without notice in the land to which the contract relates. To quote the words of MAITLAND:

> An agreement for a lease is not equal to a lease. An equitable right is not equal to a legal right; between the contracting parties an agreement for a lease may be as good as a lease; just so between the contracting parties an agreement for the sale of land may serve as well as a completed sale and conveyance. But introduce the third party and then you will see the difference. I take a lease; my lessor then sells the land to X; notice or no notice my lease is good against X. I take a mere agreement for a lease, and the person who has agreed to grant the lease then sells and conveys to Y, who has no notice of my merely equitable right. Y is not bound to grant me a lease.[4]

It must be observed, however, that a contract for a lease is now an estate contract within the meaning of the Law of Property Act 1925,[5] and that therefore it will only be enforceable against third parties who acquire the land from the lessor, if it has been registered as a land charge at the Land Registry.[6] Registration constitutes notice to the whole world, lack of registration renders the contract void against a later purchaser of the legal estate for money or money's worth, even though in actual fact he may have known of its existence.[7] Thus:

> if A takes such a contract from B and then B wrongfully sells and conveys the land to an unsuspecting purchaser, Y, the estate contract of A *if registered* will prevail against Y, but *if not registered* will be defeated by the conveyance, even though Y, far from being unsuspecting, actually knew that it had been made.

1 *Manchester Brewery Co v Coombs* [1901] 2 Ch 608; M & B p. 522; *Purchase v Lichfield Brewery Co* [1915] 1 KB 184; M & B p. 525.
2 P. 444 et seq, post.
3 *Purchase v Lichfield Brewery Co*, supra, at 188, per LUSH J; M & B pp. 520–521. See H & M, pp. 712–713; (1978) 37 CLJ 98 (R. J. Smith).
4 Maitland, *Equity*, p. 158. But if, when Y buys, I am in possession of the land, Y will have constructive notice of my equitable right: *Hunt v Luck* [1902] 1 Ch 428 at 432, 433; M & B p. 48; p. 63, ante.
5 S. 2 (3) (iv).
6 LCA 1972, ss. 2 (4), Class C (iv); 4 (6); p. 759, post. For the position in registered land, see pp. 513–4, post.
7 LPA 1925, s. 199 (1); *Sharp v Coates* [1948] 1 All ER 136; on appeal, [1949] 1 KB 285, [1948] 2 All ER 871. See *Midland Bank Trust Co Ltd v Green* [1981] AC 513, [1981] 1 All ER 153; M & B p. 40; *Hollington Bros Ltd v Rhodes* [1951] 2 TLR 691, [1951] 2 All ER 578n; M & B p. 48; p. 765, post; *Markfaith Investment Ltd v Chiap Hua Flashlights Ltd* [1991] 2 AC 43 ("indistinguishable from the decision of HARMAN J in *Hollington Bros Ltd v Rhodes*", per Lord TEMPLEMAN). See also *Lyus v Prowsa Developments Ltd* [1982] 1 WLR 1044, [1982] 2 All ER 953, p. 801, post, where a sale expressly subject to an estate contract gave rise to a constructive trust; *Ashburn Anstalt v Arnold* [1989] Ch 1, [1988] 2 All ER 147 p. 594, post, per Fox LJ, at 25, at 164.

If, however, in the case given A goes into possession of the land before the sale to Y and pays rent on a yearly basis, he acquires a yearly tenancy which will be binding upon Y.[8] The failure of A to register does not affect the *legal* estate that arises in him at common law under the rules already discussed. If this is so, Y can, of course, determine the tenancy by half a year's notice.[9]

(5) SUMMARY

We have now reviewed the methods whereby the relation of landlord and tenant may be constituted, and it may be helpful in conclusion to summarize the present state of the law:

(*a*) A lease not exceeding three years, whether by parol, in writing or by deed, confers a legal term of years upon the tenant.

(*b*) A lease by deed exceeding three years has the same effect.

(*c*) A written lease exceeding three years confers an equitable term upon the tenant by virtue of the doctrine of *Walsh v Lonsdale*, provided that the formalities for a contract for the sale or other disposition of land have been complied with.[9a] Where they have been, there will be no occasion, owing to the superior efficacy of the *Walsh v Lonsdale* doctrine, to rely upon the common law rule that possession plus payment of a yearly rent may give rise to a yearly tenancy. The contract should, however, be registered as a land charge.

(*d*) A contract for a lease of any period confers an equitable term upon the tenant by virtue of the doctrine of *Walsh v Lonsdale*. If, however, the term does not exceed three years, the contract is exempt from formalities. Any such contract is registrable as a land charge.[10]

SECTION IV TENANCIES AT WILL, AT SUFFERANCE, FROM YEAR TO YEAR AND BY ESTOPPEL

This section deals with various types of tenancy, apart from a lease for a fixed period of time.

A. TENANCY AT WILL

A tenancy at will exists when A occupies the land of B as tenant with B's consent, on the understanding that either A or B may terminate the tenancy when he likes. Littleton says:

> Tenant at will is where lands or tenements are let by one man to another, to have and to hold to him at the will of the lessor, by force of which lease the lessee is in possession. In this case the lessee is called tenant at will, because he hath no certain or sure estate, for the lessor may put him out at what time it pleaseth him.[11]

But such a tenancy equally arises when possession is held at the will of the lessee, and indeed it is important to notice that, even though a lease is made determinable at the will of the lessor only, it is also by implication

8 See e.g. *Bell Street Investments Ltd v Wood* (1970) 216 EG 585.
9 P. 464, post.
9a Pp. 111, 121, ante.
10 P. 759, post.
11 Litt, s. 68.

determinable at the will of the lessee. In other words, every tenancy at will must be at the will of both parties.[12] In the words of Lord SIMONDS:

> A tenancy at will, though called a tenancy, is unlike any other tenancy except a tenancy at sufferance, to which it is next-of-kin. It has been properly described as a personal relation between the landlord and his tenant: it is determined by the death of either of them or by one of a variety of acts, even by an involuntary alienation, which would not affect the subsistence of any other tenancy.[13]

A tenancy at will may be created either expressly[14] or by implication, as, for example, where a tenant, with the consent of his landlord, holds over after the expiry of the lease; or where he goes into possession under a contract for a lease or under a void lease;[15] or where a purchaser goes into possession prior to completion, or a prospective tenant goes into possession during negotiations for a lease.[16] These situations apart, the courts have restricted the scope of implied tenancies at will. They are now disinclined to infer such a tenancy from an exclusive possession of premises for an indefinite period.[17] As SCARMAN LJ said in 1974:[18]

> It may be that the tenancy at will can now serve only one legal purpose, and that is to protect the interests of an occupier during a period of transition. If one looks to the classic cases in which tenancies at will continue to be inferred, ... one sees that in each there is a transitional period during which negotiations are being conducted touching the estate or interest in the land that has to be protected, and the tenancy at will is an apt legal mechanism to protect the occupier during such a period of transition: he is there and can keep out trespassers: he is there with the consent of the landlord and can keep out the landlord as long as that consent is maintained.

Despite the termination of his tenancy, a tenant at will has always been allowed a right to emblements, i.e. a right to re-enter the land at harvest and recover the crops that he has sown. This situation, in which the land reverted to the lessor but the right to enjoyment remained in effect with the tenant, seemed unsatisfactory to the common law courts and if the circumstances warranted it they were disposed to treat a tenancy at will as having been converted into one from year to year.[19]

B. TENANCY AT SUFFERANCE

Lord COKE said:

> Tenant at sufferance is he that at first comes in by lawful demise and after his estate ended continueth in possession and wrongfully holdeth over.[20]

12 Co Litt 55*a*; *Fernie v Scott* (1871) LR 7 CP 202.
13 *Wheeler v Mercer* [1957] AC 416 at 427, [1956] 3 All ER 631 at 634.
14 E.g. *Manfield & Sons Ltd v Botchin* [1970] 2 QB 612, [1970] 3 All ER 143; *Hagee (London) Ltd v AB Erikson and Lawson* [1976] QB 209, [1975] 3 All ER 234. A tenancy at will avoids the provisions of Landlord and Tenant Act 1954, Part II; p. 503, post.
15 P. 376, ante.
16 *British Railways Board v Bodywright Ltd* (1971) 220 EG 651. See also *City of Westminster Assurance Co Ltd v Ainis* (1975) 29 P & CR 469; p. 267, ante.
17 As in *Lynes v Snaith* [1899] 1 QB 486.
18 *Heslop v Burns* [1974] 1 WLR 1241 at 1253, [1974] 3 All ER 406 at 416.
19 Smith's *Leading Cases* (13th edn), notes to *Clayton v Blakey* (1798) 8 Term Rep 3, vol. ii, 120, p. 385, post.
20 Co Litt 57*b*.

A man, for example, becomes a tenant at sufferance if having an estate *pur autre vie*,[1] he continues to hold after the death of the *cestui que vie*; or if being tenant for a fixed term, he "holds over", i.e. remains in possession without the consent of the landlord, after the term has come to an end.

Such a person differs from a tenant at will because his holding over after the determination of the term is a wrongful act, and he differs from a disseisor in that his original entry upon the land was lawful.[2]

A tenant at sufferance, unless he is a tenant of premises within the Rent Acts, is in a precarious position. He may be ejected at any moment and has no right to emblements, while he becomes liable to statutory penalties if he remains in occupation after he should have departed. In the view of the common law tenants at sufferance came under no liability to pay rent, since it was the folly of the owners that suffered them to continue in possession after their estate had ended,[3] but the Landlord and Tenant Act 1730[4] enacts that any tenant (or any other person getting possession under or by collusion with him) who shall wilfully hold over after the determination of the term, and after demand made and written notice given for delivery up of possession, shall pay double the yearly value of the lands for the time the premises are detained. A tenant is not deemed to hold over "wilfully" unless he is well aware that he has no right to retain possession.[5]

Similarly, by the Distress for Rent Act 1737, a tenant holding under a periodic tenancy who gives notice to quit and who does not give up possession in accordance with his notice is liable to pay double the rent for the time he remains in possession after the notice expires.[6] Such a person is not a tenant at sufferance, but his tenancy is statutorily prolonged at double rent.

On the other hand, a tenant at sufferance, since he is in possession, may maintain trespass against a third party or recover in ejectment against a mere wrongdoer,[7] and if he remains in possession for twelve years without paying rent, he defeats the right of the landlord and of those claiming under the landlord to recover the land.[8]

C. TENANCY FROM YEAR TO YEAR

(1) NATURE

A tenancy from year to year differs from a tenancy for a fixed number of years, in that, unless terminated by a proper notice to quit, it may last indefinitely; and from a tenancy at will, in that the death of either party or the alienation of his interest by either party does not effect its determination. It is practically the universal form of letting in the case of agricultural lands.[9]

The rule in *Lace v Chantler*[10] that requires certainty of duration in the case of a lease for a fixed term applies also to a tenancy from year to year (or to

---

1 P. 267, ante.
2 Co Litt 57*b*, and Butler's note to 270*b*.
3 Cruise, *Digest,* Tit. ix., c. ii. s. 5.
4 S. 1.
5 *French v Elliott* [1960] 1 WLR 40, [1959] 3 All ER 866.
6 S. 18.
7 *Asher v Whitlock* (1865) LR 1 QB 1; M & B p. 203.
8 *Re Jolly* [1900] 2 Ch 616.
9 It is greater than a tenancy for one year: *Bernays v Prosser* [1963] 2 QB 592, [1963] 2 All ER 321. See p. 509, post.
10 [1944] KB 368, [1944] 1 All ER 305; M & B p. 412; p. 372, ante.

any other periodic tenancy). The term, although originally indeterminate, is determinable by either party.[11] As Lord TEMPLEMAN explained:[12]

> A tenancy from year to year is saved from being uncertain because each party has power by notice to determine at the end of the year. The term continues until determined as if both parties made a new agreement at the end of each year for a new term for the ensuing year. A power for nobody to determine or for one party only to be able to determine is inconsistent with the concept of a term from year to year.

(2) CREATION

A tenancy from year to year may arise from express agreement, or by operation of law.

(a) Express

Where the tenancy is created by express agreement, the phrase best adopted for carrying out the intention of the parties is "from year to year", since this enables the tenancy to be determined at the end of the first or any subsequent year.[13] But it sometimes happens that the parties by inadvertence use expressions which have the effect of creating a tenancy for at least two years, as for example:

> for one year and so on from year to year,

in which case the tenancy can be determined only by notice in the second or any later year.[14]

(b) Implied

A tenancy from year to year will arise by operation or presumption of law whenever a person is in occupation of land with the permission of the owner, not as a licensee nor for an agreed period, and rent measured by reference to a year is paid and accepted. The two important cases where this occurs are where either a tenant at will or a tenant at sufferance pays a yearly rent.

(i) Where a tenant at will pays a yearly rent It has been the law from an early date that the payment and acceptance of rent is presumptive evidence of an intention by the parties to establish a yearly tenancy, provided that the rent is contractually assessed on a yearly basis.[15] CHAMBRE J said:

> If he accepts yearly rent, or rent measured by any aliquot part of a year, the courts have said that is evidence of a taking for a year.[16]

The assessment of rent on a yearly basis is evidence of an intention to create a yearly tenancy, even though payment may fall due at more frequent intervals such as every quarter or month. If the rent is fixed by reference to some period less than a year it creates a shorter tenancy.[17] Where, for

---

11 Partington, *Landlord and Tenant* (2nd edn), p. 45.
12 *Prudential Assurance Co Ltd v London Residuary Body* [1992] 2 AC 386 at 394, [1992] 3 All ER 504 at 510; p. 372, ante.
13 *Doe d Clarke v Smaridge* (1845) 7 QB 957.
14 *Re Searle* [1912] 1 Ch 610; *Cannon Brewery v Nash* (1898) 77 LT 648.
15 *Clayton v Blakey* (1798) 8 Term Rep 3.
16 *Richardson v Langridge* (1811) 4 Taunt 128 at 132.
17 *Ladies' Hosiery and Underwear Ltd v Parker* [1930] 1 Ch 304.

example, a lease for one year reserves a rent of £3 weekly, the tenant holds under a weekly tenancy if he remains in possession after the end of the year.[18]

But the presumption in favour of a yearly tenancy raised by the payment and acceptance of rent may be rebutted by contrary evidence, as for instance by proof that, unknown to the lessor, the payments have been made by a squatter who disseised the original occupier,[19] or where the tenant has a right to remain in possession as a statutory tenant of a residential letting within the Rent Act.[20] As Lord DENNING said:[1]

> If the acceptance of rent can be explained on some other footing than a contractual tenancy, as, for instance, by reason of an existing or possible statutory right to remain, then a new tenancy should not be inferred.

In *Javad v Aqil*,[2] where a prospective tenant was let into possession of premises during negotiations, NICHOLLS LJ thought that it would be artificial to impose a periodic tenancy on the parties, and said:[3]

> They cannot sensibly be taken to have agreed that he shall have a periodic tenancy, with all the consequences flowing from that, at a time when they are still not agreed about the terms on which the prospective tenant shall have possession under the proposed lease, and when he has been permitted to go into possession or remain in possession merely as an interim measure in the expectation that all will be regulated and regularised in due course when terms are agreed and a formal lease granted.

In essence, the court must look at all the circumstances of the case and determine what is a fair inference to be drawn.[4]

(ii) Where a tenant at sufferance pays a yearly rent This is the second case in which a tenancy from year to year may arise by presumption of law. In brief, this conversion takes place if the landlord waives the tort of the tenant.[5]

A. L. SMITH LJ explained this in *Dougal v McCarthy*:[6]

> If the landlord consents to such holding over by the tenant, and the tenant consents to remain in possession as tenant, then the implication of law is, unless there is evidence to rebut it, that the tenant holds over as tenant from year to year on the terms of the old tenancy so far as they are not inconsistent with a tenancy from year to year.

The best evidence of this consent is the payment and acceptance of rent on a yearly basis. But other indications suffice. Thus in *Dougal v McCarthy*:

---

18 *Ladies' Hosiery and Underwear Ltd v Parker*, [1930] 1 Ch 304 at 327–9; *Adler v Blackman* [1953] 1 QB 146, [1952] 2 All ER 945; M & B p. 464.
19 *Tickner v Buzzacott* [1965] Ch 426, [1965] 1 All ER 131. In this case, the original occupier was not a tenant at will but was holding under a lease for an unexpired period of 75 years. See too *Manfield & Sons Ltd v Botchin* [1970] 2 QB 612, [1970] 3 All ER 143.
20 *Marcroft Wagons Ltd v Smith* [1951] 2 KB 496, [1951] 2 All ER 271. The same applies to renewable business tenancies: *Lewis v MTC (Cars) Ltd* [1975] 1 WLR 457, [1975] 1 All ER 874, and to long leases under the Leasehold Reform Act 1967: *Baron v Phillips* (1978) 38 P & CR 91.
1 Ibid., at 506, at 277.
2 [1991] 1 WLR 1007, [1991] 1 All ER 243; M & B, p. 465; [1991] CLJ 232 (S. Bridge); (1990) 140 NLJ 1538 (H. W. Wilkinson). The possibility of a licence was not raised: pp. 368–9, ante.
3 At 1012, at 248; *Brent London Borough Council v O'Bryan* [1993] EGLR 59.
4 *Longrigg, Burrough and Trounson v Smith* (1979) 251 EG 847, per Lord SCARMAN; *Cardiothoracic Institute v Shrewdcrest Ltd* [1986] 1 WLR 368, [1986] 3 All ER 633.
5 *Right d Flower v Darby and Bristow* (1786) 1 Term Rep 159.
6 [1893] 1 QB 736; *Lowther v Clifford* [1926] 1 KB 185; affd [1927] 1 KB 130.

Premises were let at an annual rent of £140 for one year ending 1 February. The tenants remained in possession after 1 February and on 25 February they received a demand from the landlord for £35, being one quarter's rent due in advance. The tenants did not answer this demand, but wrote on 26 March intimating their intention to discontinue the tenancy.

It was held that under the circumstances the parties must be taken to have consented to a tenancy from year to year on the terms of the original lease.

A. L. SMITH LJ said:

> In the present case there is a direct statement by the landlord to the tenants that he consents to their holding over, because on 25 February, three weeks after the expiration of the tenancy, he writes asking for a quarter's rent as on a fresh tenancy. For a whole month the tenants do nothing, but hold over with notice that the landlord is demanding rent from them as tenants on the terms of the agreement which expired on 1 February. Speaking for myself, I should say that the proper inference from that was that the tenants consented to hold over on the terms of the old agreement.

If, however, the contractual tenant who holds over occupies premises that are within the Rent Acts, the landlord has no alternative but to accept the rent, for the tenant becomes a "statutory tenant" and not a tenant holding under a new contractual agreement.[7]

(3) TERMS OF TENANCY FROM YEAR TO YEAR

It will have been observed that where a yearly tenancy arises by implication of law there is often some instrument of agreement under which the premises were formerly held, or under which it was intended that they should be held. For instance, there is the old lease when a tenant holds over with the consent of the landlord and, as in *Walsh v Lonsdale*,[8] there is the void lease or the contract for a lease where the formalities for the creation of the relationship of landlord and tenant at common law are wanting. The problem that arises in these cases is whether the covenants and the terms of the instruments in question continue to bind the parties after they have changed their former position and the tenant holds the land subject to all the terms of the old or the void lease or the contract, as the case may be, where they are not inconsistent with the general nature of a yearly tenancy.

Examples of terms which in this way will be read into an implied yearly tenancy are agreements to pay rent,[9] to keep a house in repair,[10] to keep the premises open as a shop and to promote its trade as far as possible.[11]

On the other hand, covenants by the tenant to build,[12] or to paint every three years,[13] and a covenant by the lessor giving the tenant an option to purchase the freehold at a certain price[14] are incompatible with a yearly tenancy and will not be enforced.

---

7 *Morrison v Jacobs* [1945] KB 577, [1945] 2 All ER 430; p. 468, post.
8 P. 377, ante.
9 *Lee v Smith* (1854) 9 Exch 662.
10 *Cole v Kelly* [1920] 2 KB 106; *Felnex Central Properties Ltd v Montague Burton Properties Ltd* (1981) 260 EG 705.
11 *Sanders v Karnell* (1858) 1 F & F 356.
12 *Bowes v Croll* (1856) 6 E & B 255 at 264.
13 *Pinero v Judson* (1829) 6 Bing 206.
14 *Bradbury v Grimble* [1920] 2 Ch 548.

D. TENANCY BY ESTOPPEL[15]

(1) THE DOCTRINE

The doctrine of estoppel may be applied to create a tenancy. If a person purports to grant a lease of land in which he has no estate, he is estopped from repudiating the tenancy and the tenant is estopped from denying its existence. There thus arises what is called a *tenancy by estoppel* which, as between the parties estopped, possesses the attributes of a true tenancy:

> It is true that a title by estoppel is only good against the person estopped and imports from its very existence the idea of no real title at all, yet as against the person estopped it has all the elements of a real title.[16]

Thus, the covenants contained in the lease are enforceable by the lessor against the tenant, and the successors in title to either party are themselves equally estopped.[17] The estoppel does not, however, bind strangers to it; for example, the lessor cannot exercise his right to distrain goods, which are not owned by the tenant, for rent in arrear.[18]

The estoppel operates from the time when the landlord puts the tenant into possession, and continues to operate after the tenant has given up possession, unless he has been evicted by someone claiming by title paramount.[19] Thus the covenants contained in the lease are enforceable by the landlord in respect of breaches which occurred before the tenant surrendered his lease.[20] The tenant, however, can show that the landlord no longer has a title; if for example, the landlord assigns his reversion to A and then sues the tenant for rent, the tenant can deny the landlord's title and claim that the rent is now due to A. Similarly, if the landlord's title is a lease which has expired, the tenant can withhold the rent even though no third party is claiming it.[1]

The doctrine applies to all types of tenancy.

(2) FEEDING THE ESTOPPEL

A tenancy by estoppel, however, may be transformed into an effective tenancy. The rule is that if the lessor later acquires the legal estate in the land, the effect is to "feed the estoppel" and to clothe the tenant also with a legal estate. The lessee then acquires a legal tenancy and ceases to rely on the estoppel. The tenancy commenced by estoppel, but for all purposes it has

---

15 For a full discussion, see Spencer Bower and Turner, *Estoppel by Representation* (3rd edn) pp. 191–211; (1964) 80 LQR 370 (A. M. Prichard). For the origin of the word, see Co Litt s. 667; *McIlkenny v Chief Constable of the West Midlands* [1980] QB 283 at 317, [1980] 2 All ER 227 at 235 (estoupail meaning "a bung or cork by which you stopped something from coming out", per Lord DENNING MR).

16 *Bank of England v Cutler* [1908] 2 KB 208 at 234, per FARWELL LJ.

17 *Cuthbertson v Irving* (1859) 4 H & N 742. If the lessor has any legal estate in the land, though one less in extent than that which he purports to lease, there is no estoppel. The tenant acquires the interest, whatever it may be, that the lessor holds: *Hill v Saunders* (1825) 4 B & C 529. There may be an estoppel if the lessor has an equitable interest: *Universal Permanent Building Society v Cooke* [1952] Ch 95 at 102, [1951] 2 All ER 893 at 896.

18 *Tadman v Henman* [1893] 2 QB 168. For distress, see p. 423, post.

19 Or the equivalent, e.g. where the tenant, without going out of possession, acknowledges the title of a third person by attorning tenant to him.

20 *Industrial Properties (Barton Hill) Ltd v Associated Electrical Industries Ltd* [1977] QB 580, [1977] 2 All ER 293; M & B p. 469, where CA did not follow its own previous decision in *Harrison v Wells* [1967] 1 QB 263, [1966] 3 All ER 524, on the ground that it was decided per incuriam; (1977) 40 MLR 718 (P. Jackson); [1978] Conv 137 (J. Martin).

1 *National Westminster Bank Ltd v Hart* [1983] QB 773, [1983] 2 All ER 177; M & B p. 470; [1984] Conv 64 (J. W. Price). But if the plaintiff is an assignee of the reversion from the landlord the tenant must prove a valid title paramount.

now become an estate or interest.[2] Formerly this gave rise to difficulties where the landlord purchased land on mortgage. For instance:

P agrees to purchase a house from V and is let into possession before completion. Though at present entitled only to an equitable interest, he purports to lease the premises to T, whereupon a tenancy by estoppel arises between these two parties. The conveyance of the legal estate to P is completed some weeks later and this is followed immediately by a mortgage of the premises to M who has agreed to advance the purchase money and who pays it direct to V.

It had been held[3] that there was a *scintilla temporis* between the conveyance to P (which fed the estoppel and gave T a legal tenancy) and the mortgage to M, with the result that the legal tenancy acquired by T preceded and took priority over M's mortgage.

In *Abbey National Building Society v Cann,*[4] the House of Lords has now reversed this approach and held that the transactions are "not only precisely simultaneous but indissolubly bound together", with the result that M takes free from T's tenancy.

SECTION V RIGHTS AND LIABILITIES OF LANDLORD AND TENANT

In the majority of cases the rights and the liabilities of a landlord and a tenant are fixed by the express covenants that, having been settled by the parties, are incorporated in the lease or the contract under which the premises are held. But a contract may be silent on several matters of importance, or there may be no agreement at all, and therefore it is necessary to consider, first, what the position of the parties is where there are no express covenants, and then to notice shortly the usual covenants common to all ordinary leases.[5]

A. POSITION WHERE THERE ARE NO EXPRESS COVENANTS OR CONDITIONS

(1) IMPLIED OBLIGATIONS OF THE LANDLORD

(a) Quiet enjoyment

A covenant that the lessee shall have quiet enjoyment[6] of the premises is implied in every lease that does not expressly deal with the matter.[7] The

---

2 *Webb v Austin* (1844) 7 Man & G 701 at 724, per TINDAL CJ, citing Preston, *Treatise on Abstracts*; M & B p. 468.
3 *Church of England Building Society v Piskor* [1954] Ch 553, [1954] 2 All ER 85.
4 [1991] 1 AC 56, [1990] 1 All ER 1085; M & B p. 472; preferring *Coventry Permanent Economic Building Society v Jones* [1951] 1 All ER 901; *Security Trust Co v Royal Bank of Canada* [1976] AC 503, [1976] 1 All ER 381. See also *Walthamstow Building Society v Davies* (1989) 60 P & CR 99 (where mortgagee took a second charge to replace a first charge, held no scintilla temporis between discharge of first and creation of second charge during which unauthorised tenancy granted by mortgagor became binding on mortgagee).
5 The Unfair Contract Terms Act 1977 does not apply to a covenant in a lease "in so far as it relates to the creation or transfer of an interest in land": Sch 1, para 1 (b); *Electricity Supply Nominees Ltd v IAF Group Ltd* [1993] 1 WLR 1059, [1993] 3 All ER 372 (anti-set off clause excluded); Conv Bulletin 1993/6, p. 9 (P. H. Kenny).
6 See (1976) 40 Conv (NS) 427; (1977) 40 MLR 651; [1978] Conv 419 (M. J. Russell); Arden and Partington, *Quiet Enjoyment* (3rd edn).
7 *Markham v Paget* [1908] 1 Ch 697. In early days there was no such implication unless the word demise had been used in the lease; ibid. See *Gordon v Selico Co Ltd* [1986] 1 EGLR 71 at 77, where SLADE LJ held that no covenants were to be implied "where it was intended by all parties to provide a comprehensive code in regard to repair and maintenance".

meaning of this is that the lessee shall be put into possession[8] and that he shall be entitled to recover damages[9] if his enjoyment is substantially disturbed by the acts, either of the lessor or of somebody claiming under the lessor.[10] "It is a covenant for freedom from disturbance by adverse claimants to the property."[1] Instances are, where the lessor, having reserved the right to work minerals under the land, so works them as to cause the land to subside;[2] or where, in a lease of shooting rights, he erects buildings so as substantially to reduce the area over which the rights are exercisable,[3] or where, with a view to getting rid of the tenant, he removes the doors and windows of the demised premises,[4] or subjects him to persistent and prolonged intimidation,[5] or inflicts physical discomfort on him by cutting off his gas and electricity,[6] or where he erects scaffolding which obstructs access to the premises.[7] There is no liability under the covenant, however, if the act of disturbance is committed by a person claiming not under the lessor, but under a title paramount to his;[8] nor is there liability if a landlord enters into possession as a result of a court order on the ground of forfeiture of the lease, which is subsequently reversed on appeal.[9]

(b) Fitness for habitation

In general, there is no implied undertaking by the landlord that the premises are or will be fit for habitation; and no covenant is implied that he will do any repairs whatever.[10] There are, however, five exceptions to this rule.

(i) Furnished houses Upon the letting of a furnished house, there is an implied warranty, in the nature of a condition, that the premises shall be reasonably fit for habitation at the date fixed for the commencement of the

---

8 *Miller v Emcer Products Ltd* [1956] Ch 304, [1956] 1 All ER 237.
9 For criminal offences in this connection, see p. 486, post.
10 *Jones v Lavington* [1903] 1 KB 253; *Sanderson v Berwick-upon-Tweed Corpn* (1884) 13 QBD 547 at 551; *Matania v National Provincial Bank Ltd* [1936] 2 All ER 633; *Sampson v Hodson-Pressinger* [1981] 3 All ER 710 at 714; *Guppys (Bridport) Ltd v Brookling* (1983) 269 EG 846 (exemplary damages); *Mira v Aylmer Square Investments Ltd* [1990] 1 EGLR 45 (damages for loss of revenue from sublettings).
1 *Hudson v Cripps* [1896] 1 Ch 265 at 268 per NORTH J.
2 *Markham v Paget*, supra.
3 *Peech v Best* [1931] 1 KB 1 (a case, however, of an express covenant).
4 *Lavender v Betts* [1942] 2 All ER 72.
5 *Kenny v Preen* [1963] 1 QB 499, [1962] 3 All ER 814; *Branchett v Beaney* [1992] 3 All ER 910, where CA reviewed the authorities and held that damages are not recoverable for mental distress; doubting *Sampson v Floyd* [1989] 2 EGLR 49 (constructive eviction where tenant was frightened for himself and for his wife; damages awarded for loss of lease, conveyancing costs and distress).
6 *Perera v Vandiyar* [1953] 1 WLR 672, [1953] 1 All ER 1109.
7 *Owen v Gadd* [1956] 2 QB 99, [1956] 2 All ER 28, a case of an express covenant, but equally applicable to an implied covenant: *Queensway Marketing Ltd v Associated Restaurants Ltd* (1984) 271 EG 1106.
8 *Jones v Lavington*, supra. See also *Celsteel Ltd v Alton House Holdings Ltd (No 2)* [1987] 1 WLR 291, [1987] 2 All ER 240 (lessor not liable on covenant for what predecessor in title had done).
9 *Hillgate House Ltd v Expert Clothing Service & Sales Ltd* [1987] 1 EGLR 65.
10 In *Wettern Electric Ltd v Welsh Development Agency* [1983] QB 796, [1983] 2 All ER 629 a term was implied into a contractual *licence* of business premises that they were of sound construction and would be reasonably fit for the purposes required by the licensee; (1983) 80 LSG 2195 (H. W. Wilkinson); cf *Morris-Thomas v Petticoat Lane Rentals* (1986) 53 P & CR 238.

tenancy.[11] Thus, if the house is infested with bugs,[12] if its drainage is defective,[13] or if it has been lately occupied by a person suffering from tuberculosis,[14] the tenant is entitled to repudiate the tenancy and to recover damages. But provided that the house is fit for habitation at the beginning of the tenancy, the fact that it later becomes uninhabitable imposes no liability upon the landlord.[15]

This implied condition does not extend to unfurnished premises.[16]

(ii) Premises in multiple occupation A landlord who retains control of the means of access to demised premises in a high-rise block of flats, such as lifts and staircases and other common facilities, such as rubbish chutes or lighting, is under an implied duty to keep them in repair. The implied duty is not absolute, but only a duty to take reasonable care to maintain them in a state of reasonable repair and usability.[17]

(iii) Houses let at low rent The Landlord and Tenant Act 1985[18] provides for the protection of persons taking houses at a low rental. Where a contract is made on or after 6 July 1957 for letting for human habitation a house or part of a house at a rent not exceeding £80 a year in Greater London and £52 elsewhere, there shall be implied a condition by the landlord, notwithstanding any stipulation to the contrary, that the house is fit for human habitation at the commencement of the tenancy, and an undertaking that he will keep it so throughout the tenancy.[19] There is no such stipulation, however, if the letting is for at least three years upon the terms that the tenant will put the house into a condition reasonably fit for human habitation, and if the lease is not determinable by either party before the expiration of three years.[20]

Whether the statutory condition has been broken is a question of fact and one not always easy to determine, but the Act provides that a house shall be deemed to be unfit for human habitation if and only if it is unreasonably defective in respect of one or more of the following matters—repair, stability, freedom from damp, internal arrangement, natural lighting, ventilation, water supply, drainage and sanitary conveniences, facilities for preparation and cooking of food and for the disposal of waste water.[1]

11 *Collins v Hopkins* [1923] 2 KB 617.
12 *Smith v Marrable* (1843) 11 M & W 5.
13 *Wilson v Finch-Hatton* (1877) 2 Ex D 336.
14 *Collins v Hopkins*, supra.
15 *Sarson v Roberts* [1895] 2 QB 395.
16 *Hart v Windsor* (1844) 12 M & W 68; *Robbins v Jones* (1863) 15 CBNS 221; *Cruse v Mount* [1933] Ch 278; *Cavalier v Pope* [1906] AC 428; *Bottomley v Bannister* [1932] 1 KB 458; *Otto v Bolton and Norris* [1936] 2 KB 46, [1936] 1 All ER 960.
17 *Liverpool City Council v Irwin* [1977] AC 239, [1976] 2 All ER 39, p. 527, post. It was held on the facts that there was no breach of the duty; cf *Duke of Westminster v Guild* [1985] QB 688, [1984] 3 All ER 144 (no repairing covenant implied on part of landlord in respect of drains running under retained land).
18 Ss. 8–10, replacing Housing Act 1957, ss. 4, 6 and 7. See Arden and Partington, *Housing Law* (1983), paras 15.28–15.31, and commentary on LTA 1985 in *Current Law Statutes Annotated* by A. Arden and S. McGrath.
19 LTA 1985, s. 8. In the case of a contract made before 6 July 1957 and after 31 July 1923, the equivalent figures are £40 for London and £26 elsewhere. In view of inflation, the section must now have remarkably little application: *Quick v Taff Ely Borough Council* [1986] QB 809 at 817, [1985] 3 All ER 321 at 324, per DILLON LJ.
20 Ibid., s. 8 (5).
1 Ibid., s. 10. As to the test of unfitness in the case of disrepair, see *Summers v Salford Corpn* [1943] AC 283 at 293, [1943] 1 All ER 68 at 70, per Lord ATKIN; and generally M.H.L.G. circular 69/67.

In the event of a breach of the implied condition, the tenant may repudiate the tenancy and recover damages for breach of the undertaking,[2] providing that the landlord had notice of the existence of the defect and failed to remedy it.[3] The landlord's obligation is restricted to cases where the house is capable of being made fit at reasonable expense for human habitation.[4]

(iv) Houses let for short term The Landlord and Tenant Act 1985[5] imposes further obligations on the landlord, where he has let a dwelling-house after 24 October 1961 for a term of less than seven years.[6] In the case of such a lease or an agreement for a lease,[7] he is subjected to an implied covenant:

> (*a*) to keep in repair the structure and exterior[8] of the dwelling-house[9] (including drains, gutters and external pipes); and
> (*b*) to keep in repair and proper working order[10] the installations in the dwelling-house—
>
>> (i) for the supply of water,[11] gas and electricity, and for sanitation (including basins, sinks, baths and sanitary conveniences); and
>> (ii) for space heating or heating water.[12]

This implied covenant was extended by the Housing Act 1988 to include any part of the building in which the lessor has an estate or interest, if the

2 *Walker v Hobbs & Co* (1889) 23 QBD 458.
3 *Morgan v Liverpool Corpn* [1927] 2 KB 131; *McCarrick v Liverpool Corpn* [1947] AC 219, [1946] 2 All ER 646.
4 *Buswell v Goodwin* [1971] 1 WLR 92 at 96–7, [1971] 1 All ER 418 at 421–2; *Hillbank Properties Ltd v Hackney London Borough Council* [1978] QB 998, [1978] 3 All ER 343; [1979] Conv 414 (D. Morgan); *FFF Estates Ltd v Hackney London Borough Council* [1981] 1 All ER 32; *Phillips v Newham London Borough Council* (1981) 43 P & CR 54; *Kenny v Kingston upon Thames Royal London Borough Council* [1985] 1 EGLR 26; *R v Ealing London Borough* (1982) 265 EG 691.
5 Ss. 11–16, replacing Housing Act 1961, ss. 32–33. See the commentary in *Current Law Statutes Annotated* (1985). S. 11 does not bind the Crown: s. 15 (5). See *Department of Transport v Egoroff* [1986] 1 EGLR 89.
6 A lease is treated as one for less than seven years if, though made for that period or longer, it is determinable at the lessor's option within seven years: LTA 1985, s. 13 (2) (*c*). See *Parker v O'Connor* [1974] 1 WLR 1160, [1974] 3 All ER 257; *Brikom Investments Ltd v Seaford* [1981] 1 WLR 863, [1981] 2 All ER 783.
7 *Brikom Investments Ltd v Seaford*, supra; [1981] Conv 396.
8 *Brown v Liverpool Corpn* [1969] 3 All ER 1345 (outside steps and path held to be essential part of access and therefore included): cf *Hopwood v Cannock Chase District Council* [1975] 1 WLR 373, [1975] 1 All ER 796 (backyard path not giving access excluded); *King v South Northamptonshire District Council* [1992] 1 EGLR 53. See also *Campden Hill Towers v Gardner* [1977] QB 823, [1977] 1 All ER 739 (exterior of flat not exterior of whole building). The decision was reversed by Housing Act 1988, s. 116. See also *Douglas-Scott v Scorgie* [1984] 1 WLR 716, [1984] 1 All ER 1086 (roof over a top-floor flat); *Irvine v Moran* [1991] 1 EGLR 261, where structure was defined as consisting of those elements of the overall dwelling-house which gave it its essential appearance, stability and shape; *Staves v Leeds County Council* (1990) 23 HLR 107 (plaster part of structure).
9 As to the meaning of a dwelling-house, see *Okereke v Brent London Borough Council* [1967] 1 QB 42, [1966] 1 All ER 150.
10 But not to put in a new efficient system: *Liverpool City Council v Irwin* [1977] AC 239 at 269–70, [1976] 2 All ER 39 at 56–7 (water closet cistern which flooded due to bad design held not to be in proper working order); nor to lag water pipes: *Wycombe Area Health Authority v Barnett* (1982) 47 P & CR 394; nor to install a damp-course: *Wainwright v Leeds City Council* (1984) 270 EG 1289.
11 *Sheldon v West Bromwich Corpn* (1973) 117 Sol Jo 486.
12 For a miscellany of "severe defects" leading to repudiation of lease, see *Hussein v Mehlman* [1992] 2 EGLR 87, p. 464, post.

disrepair is such as to affect the lessee's enjoyment of the dwelling-house, or of any common parts, which the lessee is entitled to use.[13]

The duty to repair means that the tenant must show physical damage to that part of the premises which has to be made good; it is not enough to show that it is defective or inherently inefficient for living in or ineffective in providing the condition of ordinary habitation.[14]

The statutory obligations do not require the landlord to reinstate the premises if they are damaged by fire or by tempest, flood or other inevitable accident; or to effect repairs necessitated by the tenant's failure to use the premises in a tenant-like manner.[15] In determining the standard of repair, regard must be had to the age, character and prospective life of the dwelling-house and to the locality.[16] The landlord is liable for any consequential expenditure to which the tenant is put, such as redecoration or alternative accommodation during the repairs.[17] But he is only liable for defects of which notice[18] is given, and only then if after a reasonable time, he fails to remedy the defect.[19]

The parties cannot contract out of the Act,[20] but with their consent the county court may exclude or modify the repairing obligations of the landlord if it is considered reasonable to do so.[1] It is further enacted that any covenant to repair by the tenant shall be of no effect in so far as it relates to the matters covered in the landlord's statutory obligations.[2]

Local authorities have wide powers under the Housing Act 1985 of requiring the person who has control of a dwelling-house or of a house in multiple occupation[3] to make it fit for human habitation,[4] or to carry out repairs where, even though the house is not unfit:

---

13 LTA 1985, s. 11 (1A), as added by Housing Act 1988, s. 116.

14 *Quick v Taff Ely Borough Council* [1986] QB 809, [1985] All ER 34 (living conditions appalling due to condensation, but no damage to walls or windows of house); *McNerny v Lambeth London Borough Council* [1989] 1 EGLR 81.

15 Landlord and Tenant Act 1985, s. 11 (2).

16 Ibid., s. 11 (3); *London Borough of Newham v Patel* [1979] JPL 303; *McLean v Liverpool City Council* [1987] 2 EGLR 56; *Trustees of the Dame Margaret Hungerford Charity v Beazeley* [1993] 29 EG 100; [1994] Conv 145 (J. Morgan).

17 *McGreal v Wake* (1984) 269 EG 1254; *Bradley v Chorley Borough Council* [1985] 2 EGLR 49.

18 *O'Brien v Robinson* [1973] AC 912, [1973] 1 All ER 583; *McGreal v Wake*, supra; *Al Hassani v Merrigan* [1988] 1 EGLR 93. The notice may be from a person other than the tenant: *Dinefwr Borough Council v Jones* [1987] 2 EGLR 58; and may be by way of a valuation report sent to the landlord: *Hall v Howard* [1988] 2 EGLR 75.

19 *Porter v Jones* [1942] 2 All ER 570 (landlord who failed for eight months from notice to remedy disrepair held liable in damages); *Morris v Liverpool City Council* [1988] 1 EGLR 47 (delay of one week for emergency repairs held unreasonable).

20 LTA 1985, s. 12 (1).

1 Ibid., s. 12 (2). For the extension of the obligations by express provision in the lease or by any subsequent variation of its terms, see *Palmer v Sandwell Metropolitan Borough* [1987] 2 EGLR 79.

2 Ibid., s. 11 (4).

3 *Pollway Nominees Ltd v Croydon London Borough Council* [1987] AC 79, [1986] 2 All ER 849; *R v Lambeth London Borough Council, ex p Clayhope Properties Ltd* [1988] QB 563, [1987] 3 All ER 545.

4 Part VI (Repair Notices), replacing Housing Act 1957, ss. 9 (as amended by Housing Act 1980 s. 149), 10, 16, 39; *White v Barnet London Borough Council* [1990] 2 QB 328. See also Part VII (Improvement Notices); Part IX (Slum Clearance: Demolition or closing of unfit premises beyond repair at reasonable cost); *Cole v Swansea City Council* [1989] 1 EGLR 52; Part XI (Houses in multiple occupation); (for amendments to these Parts, see Local Government and Housing Act 1989, Sch 9, Part I); Environmental Protection Act 1990, Part III, replacing Public Health Act 1936, s. 93; *Birmingham District Council v McMahon* (1987)

substantial repairs are necessary to bring it up to a reasonable standard, having regard to its age, character and locality.[5]

A tenant may prefer to invoke action by the local authority rather than to enforce his rights directly under the covenant.

(v) Duty of care for safety A landlord may owe a duty of care in tort for negligence in respect of defective premises. Under the common law rule in *Cavalier v Pope*[6] a landlord of unfurnished premises does not owe a duty of care to his tenant in respect of the state of the premises at the time when they are let. In *Rimmer v Liverpool City Council*,[7] however, the Court of Appeal held that a landlord who is also a builder owner, i.e. who designs or builds premises, does owe a duty of care qua designer or qua builder, to his tenant or other person who may reasonably be expected to be affected by the design or construction of the premises.

(vi) Correlative obligation on landlord A repairing covenant may be implied against a landlord where a tenant's express covenant as to internal repairs would eventually become impossible to perform in the absence of a correlative obligation on the landlord as to outside repairs. The imposition of such an obligation on the landlord is necessary in order to give business efficacy to the lease.[8]

The landlord's immunity under *Cavalier v Pope* has been eroded by the Defective Premises Act 1972. The Act applies to all types of tenancy, and any agreement to contract out of it is void.[9]

---

19 HLR 452; [1988] Conv 377 (D. C. Health); Building Act 1984, s. 76; London Building Acts (Amendment) Act 1939, as extended outside London by Building Act 1984, s. 77, and, generally, Evans and Smith, *Law of Landlord and Tenant* (4th edn), pp. 199–202.

5 Housing Act 1985, s. 190 (1) as amended by Housing Act 1988, Sch. 15, paras. 1 and 2; and Local Government and Housing Act 1989, Sch. 9, Part I.

6 [1906] AC 428; *McNerny v Lambeth London Borough Council* [1989] 1 EGLR 81; [1989] Conv 216 (P. F. Smith).

7 [1985] QB 1, [1984] 1 All ER 930 (tenant injured by defective glass panel). The Defective Premises Act 1972 infra did not apply; at 7, at 933; *Targett v Torfaen Borough Council* [1992] 3 All ER 27 (where CA held that *Rimmer* was not overruled by *Murphy v Brentwood District Council* [1991] 1 AC 398, [1990] 2 All ER 908). See also *Dutton v Bognor Regis UDC* [1972] 1 QB 373, [1972] 1 All ER 462; *Anns v Merton London Borough Council* [1978] AC 728, [1977] 2 All ER 492; *Batty v Metropolitan Property Realisations Ltd* [1978] QB 554, [1978] 2 All ER 445; *Eames London Estates Ltd v North Hertfordshire District Council* (1980) 259 EG 491; (1978) 94 LQR 60, 331 (I. N. Duncan-Wallace); [1979] Conv 97 (N. P. Gravells); *Balcomb v Wards Construction Ltd* (1981) 259 EG 765; *Lyons v FW Booth Ltd* (1981) 262 EG 981; *Bluett v Woodspring District Council* (1983) 266 EG 220; *Dennis v Charnwood Borough Council* [1983] QB 409, [1982] 3 All ER 486; *Junior Books Ltd v Veitchi Co Ltd* [1983] 1 AC 520, [1983] 2 All ER 201; *Governors of the Peabody Donation Fund v Sir Lindsay Parkinson & Co Ltd* [1985] AC 210, [1984] 3 All ER 529; *Hambro Life Assurance plc v White Young & Partners* [1985] 2 EGLR 165; *Investors in Industry Commercial Properties Ltd v South Bedfordshire District Council* [1986] QB 1034, [1986] 1 All ER 787, especially SLADE LJ at 1062, at 805; *Percival v Walsall Metropolitan Borough Council* [1986] 2 EGLR 136; *Curran v Northern Ireland Co-ownership Housing Association Ltd* [1987] AC 718, [1987] 2 All ER 13; *D & F Estates Ltd v Church Comrs for England* [1989] AC 177, [1988] 2 All ER 992; *Norwich City Council v Harvey* [1989] 1 WLR 828, [1989] 1 All ER 1180; *Murphy v Brentwood District Council*, supra; (1990) 107 LQR 228 (I. N. Duncan-Wallace); *Richardson v West Lindsey District Council* [1990] 1 WLR 522, [1990] 1 All ER 296; *Targett v Torfaen District Council*, supra; *Department of the Environment v Thomas Bates & Son Ltd* [1991] 1 AC 499, [1990] 2 All ER 943.

8 *Barrett v Lounova (1982) Ltd* [1990] 1 QB 348, [1989] 1 All ER 351; cf. *Demetriov v Poolaction Ltd* [1991] 1 EGLR 100.

1. *Duty to build dwellings properly*

Under section 1 any person who takes on work[10] for or in connection with the provision of a dwelling, whether by the erection, conversion or enlargement of a building, is under a duty to see that the work is done in a workmanlike or professional manner, with proper materials and so that as regards that work the dwelling will be fit for habitation when completed. The tenant[11] may recover damages for any damage or injury that arises within six years of the dwelling being completed.[12] The remedy lies not only against the landlord, if he has the duty, but also against third parties, including the builder and architect.[13]

The statutory duty under this section does not apply to dwellings built in accordance with an "approved scheme" of purchaser protection.[14] Most houses built within recent years are covered by the Housebuilders' Agreement backed by the National House-Building Council.[15] This provides, in effect, a guarantee against defects which arise from non-compliance with the Council's standard specification.[16] The Council guarantees the liability of the house-builder within certain financial limits.[17]

2. *Duty of care for safety*

Under section 4 of the Act,[18] a landlord owes to all persons,[19] who might reasonably be expected to be affected by defects in the state of the premises, a duty to take reasonable care to see that they are reasonably safe from personal injury or from damage to their property. Such a duty arises when the landlord is under an obligation to the tenant for the maintenance or

9 S. 6. The Act is based on the Law Commission Report on Civil Liability of Vendors and Lessors for Defective Premises 1970 (Law Com No. 40); *D & F Estates Ltd v Church Comrs for England*, supra, at 793, at 996. See Holyoak and Allen, *Civil Liability for Defective Premises*, as supplemented by (1984) 134 NLJ 347, 369, 411, 425; Speaight and Stone, *Law of Defective Premises* (1982).
10 *Alexander v Mercouris* [1979] 1 WLR 1270, [1979] 3 All ER 305; (1980) 255 EG 241 (H. W. Wilkinson).
11 Or a contractual licensee: s. 6 (1).
12 Defective Premises Act 1972, s. 1 (5).
13 See also Health and Safety at Work etc. Act 1974, s. 71; *Westminster City Council v Select Management Ltd* [1985] 1 WLR 576, [1985] 1 All ER 897; and for the liability at common law for defective design by a sub-contractor: *Independent Broadcasting Authority v EMI Electronics and BICC Construction Ltd* (1980) 14 BLR 1 (collapse of 1,250 ft television mast).
14 Defective Premises Act 1972, s. 2.
15 The two millionth house protected under the scheme was opened by HM The Queen in February 1981.
16 Clause 4 of the Agreement contains a warranty similar to the duty imposed by s. 1 of the Act, except that "efficient" is substituted for "professional".
17 House-Building Standards (Approved Scheme etc) Order 1979 (S.I. 1979 No. 381). On the operation of this scheme, see (1964) 28 Conv (NS) 385 (G. Dworkin), and on its revision in 1979, (1980) 130 NLJ 171, 195, 219 (J. E. Adams); Tapping and Rolfe, *Guarantees for New Homes: A Guide to the NHBC Scheme* (2nd edn 1981); *Keating on Building Contracts* (5th edn 1991), pp. 362–5. The scheme was relaunched in 1988 under the name Buildmark with further revision; (1989) 35 LSG 4 Oct 17, 11 Oct 19 (P. Palmer); Kenny, *Conveyancing Practice* F-004. For an alternative scheme, see Foundation 15, which began in 1989; (1988) 132 SJ 1644.
18 Replacing Occupiers' Liability Act 1957, s. 4.
19 Including a tenant: *Smith v Bradford Metropolitan Council* (1982) 44 P & CR 171; *McNerny v Lambeth London Borough Council* [1989] 1 EGLR 81.

repair of the premises, or when he has an express or implied right[20] to enter the premises[1] to maintain and repair them. This duty, however, is owed only if the landlord knows or ought to have known of the defect, and if the defect arises from his failure to carry out his obligation or right to maintain or repair.

(c) Non-derogation from grant[2]

The only other covenant to which a landlord becomes implicitly subject is one that he shall not derogate from his grant. He must not frustrate the use of the land for the purposes for which it was let;[3] or, as BOWEN LJ put it, "a grantor having given a thing with one hand is not to take away the means of enjoying it with the other".[4] WOOD V-C in one case said:

> If a landowner conveys one of two closes to another, he cannot afterwards do anything to derogate from his grant; and if the conveyance is made for the express purpose of having buildings erected upon the land so granted, a contract is implied on the part of the grantor to do nothing to prevent the land from being used for the purpose for which to the knowledge of the grantor the conveyance is made.[5]

In the case of leases this general principle of law becomes particularly applicable when the landlord makes an inconsiderate use of land adjacent to the tenant's holding. Thus where lands were leased to a tenant for the purpose of carrying on the business of a timber merchant, and the landlord proceeded to erect buildings on adjoining land in such a way as to interrupt the free flow of air to the tenant's drying sheds, it was held that damages were recoverable against the landlord's assigns for breach of the implied covenant.[6] Again, where a flat is leased in a building, the whole of which is clearly intended to be used solely by residential tenants, the landlord commits a breach of the

---

20 *McAuley v Bristol City Council* [1992] QB 134, [1992] 1 All ER 749; [1992] Conv 346 (J. Martin).
1 Including a back concrete patio: ibid.
2 For a comprehensive discussion, see (1964) 80 LQR 244 (D. W. Elliott); criticized in part, (1965) 81 LQR 28 (M. A. Peel); Gale, pp. 100–105.
3 *Browne v Flower* [1911] 1 Ch 219 at 225–7, where illustrations are given by PARKER J.
4 *Birmingham, Dudley and District Banking Co v Ross* (1888) 38 Ch D 295 at 313; *Johnston & Sons Ltd v Holland* [1988] 1 EGLR 264 at 267–268, per NICHOLLS LJ: "The expression 'derogation from grant' conjures up images of parchment and sealing wax, of copperplate handwriting and fusty title deeds. But the principle is not based on some ancient technicality of real property ... it is a principle which merely embodies in a legal maxim a rule of common honesty".
5 *North Eastern Rly Co v Elliott* (1860) 1 John & H 145 at 153.
6 *Aldin v Latimer Clark Muirhead & Co* [1894] 2 Ch 437; *Harmer v Jumbil (Nigeria) Tin Areas Ltd* [1921] 1 Ch 200. See also *Lyme Valley Squash Club Ltd v Newcastle under Lyme Borough Council* [1985] 2 All ER 405 (easement of light). The principle is also applicable if the tenant is prevented from entering the lessor's land in order to execute essential repairs to the demised premises: *Ward v Kirkland* [1967] Ch 194 at 226–227, [1966] 1 All ER 609 at 617.
  The Access to Neighbouring Land Act 1992 enables a person to obtain an order of the County Court for access to neighbouring land, in order to carry out works which are reasonably necessary for the preservation of his own land. The Act is based on the Law Commission Report on Rights of Access to Neighbouring Land 1985 (Law Com No. 151, Cmnd 9692). The Act had a chequered history: [1992] 26 EG 136 (J. Adams). It came into force on 31 January 1993. An access order is registrable as a writ or order under LCA 1925, s. 6 (1) (*d*), and is regarded as a pending land action under s. 5 (1). If the land is registered, the order is registrable by way of notice under LRA 1925, s. 49 (1) (*j*), and cannot be an overriding interest: Access to Neighbouring Land Act 1992, s. 5.

covenant if he subsequently lets the greater part of the premises for business purposes.[7]

The covenant is enforceable against the landlord and his successors not only by the original tenant but also by those claiming under him.[8]

(2) IMPLIED OBLIGATIONS AND RIGHTS OF THE TENANT

(a) Obligations

(i) General A tenant, including one from year to year,[9] is subject to an implied obligation to keep and to deliver up the premises in a tenant-like manner and to keep the fences in a state of repair.[10]

(ii) Liability for waste Further, tenants are subject to the doctrine of waste,[11] though in varying degrees.

A tenant for a fixed number of years is liable for voluntary and also for permissive waste,[12] though perhaps a doubt still lingers with regard to the latter question.[13].

A tenant from *year to year* is liable for voluntary waste, but otherwise his only obligation, it would seem, is to use the premises in a "tenant-like" manner.[14]. This expression is obscure if not unintelligible, and all that it means apparently is that the tenant must do such work as is necessary for his own reasonable enjoyment of the premises. DENNING LJ gave some illustrations in *Warren v Keen*:[15]

> The tenant must take proper care of the place. He must, if he is going away for the winter, turn off the water and empty the boiler.[16] He must clean the chimneys, when necessary, and also the windows. He must mend the electric light when it fuses. He must unstop the sink when it is blocked by his waste. In short, he must do the little jobs about the place which a reasonable tenant would do. In addition, he must, of course, not damage the house, wilfully or negligently; and he must see that his family and guests do not damage it: and if they do, he must repair it. But apart from such things, if the house falls into disrepair through fair wear and tear or lapse of time, or for any reason not caused by him, then the tenant is not liable to repair it.

There is however some authority for the view that he must keep the premises wind and water tight in the sense that, although he is not bound to do

---

7 *Newman v Real Estate Debenture Corpn Ltd* [1940] 1 All ER 131; distinguished in *Kelly v Battershell* [1949] 2 All ER 830.
8 *Molton Buildings Ltd v City of Westminster London Borough Council* (1975) 30 P & CR 182 at 186, per Lord DENNING MR.
9 *Marsden v Edward Heyes Ltd* [1927] 2 KB 1.
10 *Cheetham v Hampson* (1791) 4 Term Rep 318; *Goodman v Rollinson* (1951) 95 SJ 188. For the tenant of an agricultural holding, see *Wedd v Porter* [1916] 2 KB 91.
11 Pp. 269–73, ante.
12 *Yellowly v Gower* (1855) 11 Exch 274; *Mancetter Developments Ltd v Garmanson Ltd* [1986] QB 1212, [1986] 1 All ER 449.
13 See cases collected in Hill and Redman, *Law of Landlord and Tenant* para. A1032.
14 *Warren v Keen* [1954] 1 QB 15, [1953] 2 All ER 1118; (1954) 70 LQR 9 (R.E.M.); [1954] CLJ 71 (H. W. R. Wade).
15 Supra, at 20, at 1121. The expression is an extension to tenants generally of the rule that the agricultural tenant must farm the land in a "husbandlike" manner. In this context, "husbandlike" has a definite meaning. The tenant must observe the custom of the country, i.e. the local usages of husbandry.
16 Not, however, for two nights, even when the temperature fell to below 6 or 7 degrees below freezing. The test is reasonable foresight of frozen pipes in a cold climate: *Wycombe Health Authority v Barnett* (1982) 264 EG 619.

anything of a substantial nature, he must carry out such repairs as are necessary to prevent the property from lapsing into a state of decay.[17] But the existence of this obligation was doubted by the Court of Appeal in *Warren v Keen*.

A tenant *at will* is not liable for either kind of waste, though the effect of the commission by him of any act of voluntary waste is to terminate his tenancy and to render him liable to an action of trespass.[18] A tenant *at sufferance* is liable for voluntary waste, but probably not for permissive waste.[19].

(b) Rights

(i) **Estovers** A tenant for years, notwithstanding the doctrine of waste, is entitled to take estovers from the land, that is to say, wood, even though it be timber,[20] for the purpose of carrying out certain repairs. Estovers fall into three classes, namely: house-bote (wood to be used either as fuel or for building purposes); plough-bote (wood for making and repairing agricultural implements); and hay-bote (wood for repairing hedges).[1]

This right is limited by immediate necessity: a tenant cannot cut and store wood with a view to future requirements.

(ii) **Emblements** A tenant for years is entitled at common law to emblements.[2] It is obvious that a tenant for a fixed term of years cannot be entitled to this right, because he knows when his tenancy will end, and it his own fault if he sows crops which will not come to maturity until after that date. But there may be cases where a tenancy comes to an end unexpectedly, as for instance upon the sudden determination of a tenancy at will or upon the determination of the estate out of which the term has been created, in which the common law right to emblements exists. The right is obviously inconvenient to both parties, and in one type of case, i.e. where the lessor's estate ended prematurely, it was modified by the Landlord and Tenant Act 1851. This provided that a tenant for years at a rack rent (i.e. a rent which represents the full annual value of the land[3]) whose lease expired owing to the failure of his lessor's estate, should in lieu of emblements be entitled to remain in occupation until the end of the current year of tenancy.

In the case of agricultural tenancies, however, the Agricultural Holdings Act 1986[4] provides that a tenant at a rack rent, whose term ceases by the death, or the cesser of the estate, of a landlord entitled only for life or for any other uncertain interest, shall continue to hold and occupy the holding until the occupation is determined by a twelve-month's notice to quit, expiring at the end of a year of the tenancy.

(iii) **Right to remove certain fixtures** The extent of this right of removal has already been discussed.[5]

---

17 *Ferguson v* — (1797) 2 Esp 590; *Wedd v Porter*, supra, at 100.
18 *Countess of Shrewsbury's Case* (1600) 5 Co Rep 13*b*.
19 *Burchell v Hornsby* (1808) 1 Camp 360.
20 For the definition of "timber", see pp. 270–1, ante.
1 Co Litt 41*b*.; cf p. 567, post.
2 See p. 268, ante.
3 *Re Sawyer and Withall* [1919] 2 Ch 333.
4 S. 21(1).
5 Pp. 145–8, ante.

B. POSITION WHERE THERE ARE EXPRESS COVENANTS AND CONDITIONS

In the majority of cases the rights and the liabilities of a lessor and a lessee are regulated by express covenants inserted in the lease, but, as the number of matters that may be the subject of agreement is infinite, and as the agreed terms will naturally vary widely in different cases, it is obvious that in a treatise of this limited scope we cannot do more than notice shortly the more important covenants that find a place in a normal lease.

Generally speaking, and where no exceptional circumstances exist, a lessee will enter into covenants with regard to the payment of rent, rates and taxes, and the maintenance, repair and insurance of the premises; while the lessor will undertake to keep the lessee in quiet enjoyment, and may perhaps take upon himself part of the burden of repairs. The following covenants require special mention.

(1) COVENANT BY TENANT TO PAY RENT

(a) Rent service

The rent payable by a tenant for years is properly called a rent service,[6] and though it generally consists of the payment of money, it may equally well take the form of the delivery of personal chattels,[7] as corn, or the performance of personal services;[8] and there may even be no rent at all.[9]

(b) Certainty of rent

The rent must be certain, but this does not mean that it must be certain at the date of the lease. Rent is sufficiently certain if it can be calculated with certainty at the time when payment comes to be made. Thus a condition in a council tenant's rent book, providing that the rent was "liable to be increased or decreased on notice being given" was held to be valid.[10] So also was an option to purchase a farm "at a reasonable valuation",[11] and an option to renew a lease "at a rent to be fixed at a price to be determined having regard to the market valuation of the premises at the time of exercising the option".[12]

---

6 P. 421, post.
7 Co Litt. 142*a*.
8 *Duke of Marlborough v Osborn* (1864) 5 B & S 67.
9 LPA 1925, s. 205 (1) (xxvii); *Ashburn Anstalt v Arnold* [1989] Ch 1, [1988] 2 All ER 147; M & B, p. 550.
10 *Greater London Council v Connolly* [1970] 2 QB 100, [1970] 1 All ER 870.
11 *Talbot v Talbot* [1968] Ch 1, [1967] 2 All ER 920.
12 *Brown v Gould* [1972] Ch 53, [1971] 2 All ER 1505; M & B p. 421; *Smith v Morgan* [1971] 1 WLR 803, [1971] 2 All ER 1500 (right of pre-emption "at a figure to be agreed upon" held to be valid); cf *King's Motors (Oxford) Ltd v Lax* [1970] 1 WLR 426, [1969] 3 All ER 665 (option for lease "at such rental as may be agreed upon between the parties" held to be void for uncertainty); *Courtney and Fairbairn Ltd v Tolaini Bros (Hotels) Ltd* [1975] 1 WLR 297, [1975] 1 All ER 716 (building agreement to "negotiate fair and reasonable contract sums" held to be void for uncertainty); *Bushwall Properties Ltd v Vortex Properties Ltd* [1976] 1 WLR 591, [1976] 2 All ER 283 (contract for sale of 51½ acres of land for £50,000 payable in three unequal instalments held unenforceable because of provision that on each payment "a proportionate part of the land shall be released"); *ARC Ltd v Schofield* [1990] 2 EGLR 52 (option to renew lease at a rent "to be agreed between the landlord and tenant, being a fair and reasonable market rent at that time" held valid); *Corson v Rhuddlan Borough Council* [1990] 1 EGLR 255; M & B p. 424 (option to renew lease of golf course for further 21 years "at a rental to be agreed" [but not to exceed £1,150 per annum] held valid with implication

The parties may also provide machinery for the application of the formula, e.g. by directing that the rent shall be fixed by a third party;[13] but, if that machinery proves to be ineffective, the court may substitute its own. In *Sudbrook Trading Estate Ltd v Eggleton*:[14]

> a lease gave to the lessees an option to purchase the reversion "at such a price not being less than £12,000 as may be agreed upon by two valuers one to be nominated by the lessor and the other by the lessees or in default of such agreement by an umpire appointed by the said valuers". The lessor refused to appoint a valuer.

In granting specific performance of the option at "a fair and reasonable price", the House of Lords held that, if the ineffective machinery is merely subsidiary and inessential, the court will provide its own, but it will not do so if the machinery constitutes an essential term of the contract. As Lord FRASER OF TULLYBELTON said:[15]

> Where an agreement is made to sell at a price to be fixed by a valuer who is named, or who, by reason of holding some office such as auditor of a company whose shares are to be valued, will have special knowledge relevant to the question of value, the prescribed mode may well be regarded as essential. Where, as here, the machinery consists of valuers and an umpire, none of whom is named or identified, it is in my opinion unrealistic to regard it as an essential term. If it breaks down there is no reason why the court should not substitute other machinery to carry out the main purpose of ascertaining the price in order that the agreement may be carried out.

(c) Date of payment

The covenant should state precisely the dates at which rent is payable, but if no mention is made of the matter, payment is due at the end of each period by reference to which the rent has been assessed. Thus in the case of a yearly

of term that rent was to be a fair rent with an upper limit of £1,150): [1990] Conv 290 (J .E. Martin); *Miller v Lakefield Estates Ltd* [1989] 1 EGLR 212 (option to purchase "at a price to be agreed", but if no sale took place within six months of notice given to exercise option, then property should be sold at public auction, held valid); *King's Motors (Oxford) Ltd v Lax* was doubted in *Corson v Rhuddlan Borough Council*; and *Smith v Morgan* was doubted in *Miller v Lakefield Estates Ltd*; *Walford v Miles* [1992] 2 AC 128, [1992] 1 All ER 453, p. 110, ante (agreement to continue to negotiate "in good faith" held void for uncertainty). For the validity of an index-linked rent, see *Blumenthal v Gallery Five Ltd* (1971) 220 EG 31 (index of retail prices); *Cumshaw Ltd v Bowen* [1987] 1 EGLR 30; (1987) 132 NLJ 288 (H. W. Wilkinson).

13 E.g. *Lloyds Bank Ltd v Marcan* [1973] 1 WLR 1387, [1973] 3 All ER 754 (rent to be fixed by person chosen by President of the Royal Institution of Chartered Surveyors).

14 [1983] 1 AC 444, [1982] 2 All ER 1; M & B p. 425; [1983] Conv 76 (K. Hodkinson). Followed in *Re Malpass* [1985] Ch 42, [1984] 2 All ER 313 (testamentary option to purchase farm "at the agricultural value thereof determined for agricultural purposes . . . as agreed with the District Valuer"; the valuer declined to act). See also *Campbell v Edwards* [1976] 1 WLR 403, [1976] 1 All ER 785 (valuation fixed by an agreed valuer held binding); *Trustees of National Deposit Friendly Society v Beatties of London Ltd* [1985] 2 EGLR 59, where GOULDING J held valid an option agreement for a new lease in favour of tenants who had carried on a business of selling model railways for 75 years "the rent payable . . . to be the greater of £33,000 per annum exclusive or such rent as may be agreed as from the architect's certificate of completion". In rejecting claims that it was void for uncertainty in regard to the date of the commencement of the term, the amount of rent and the covenants and conditions, he said at 61: "There has been such performance on the tenant's side as to justify the court in a much more liberal approach to the validity of the document than in the case of a purely executory option where nothing but perhaps a nominal consideration has been given on either side."; *R & A Millett (Shops) Ltd v Leon Allen International Fashions Ltd* [1989] 1 EGLR 138 (sublease rent to be 78/85ths of fair market rent as fixed in manner provided by head lease).

15 At 483, at 10.

rent nothing need be paid until the end of each year of the term.[16] If a day for payment is fixed, it becomes due on the first moment of that day and is held to be in arrear if it is not paid by midnight.[17]

(d) Rent review clauses

Many leases today contain a rent review clause,[18] the object of which is to enable the rent to be raised at regular intervals to what is then the fair market value of the property let. The clause may provide for a revision to be made every seven years, and, not infrequently, every four or even three years. In some leases of commercial premises granted for longer terms, there may be a provision to allow the landlord to reduce the interval between rent reviews after, for example, the first 35 years; this "review of reviews" operates in the same way as a rent review.[19] The clause usually lays down the administrative procedure or machinery by which the fair market rent is to be ascertained. Wide varieties of formulae are used.[20] In practice many clauses have not been well drawn,[1] and, in particular, there has been considerable litigation on the question of whether time is of the essence in construing clauses which specify time limits for the operation of the rent review procedure. In *United Scientific Holdings Ltd v Burnley Borough Council*[2] the House of Lords held that there was a presumption that time was not of the essence of the contract. Accordingly a landlord who fails to serve a notice on the tenant by a specified date may still serve a notice late and implement the rent review. Unreasonable delay, and even delay which causes hardship to the tenant, will not disentitle him from exercising his contractual right to claim a rent review which will be retrospective to the relevant date. The right continues to exist unless and until it is abrogated by mutual agreement, breach of contract, frustration or

---

16 *Coomber v Howard* (1845) 1 CB 440; *Collett v Curling* (1847) 10 QB 785.
17 *Dibble v Bowater* (1853) 2 E & B 564.
18 See generally Aldridge, *Leasehold Law*, paras. 4.038–48; Bernstein and Reynolds, *Handbook of Rent Review* (2nd edn); Clarke and Adams, *Rent Reviews and Variable Rents* (3rd edn); *Emmet on Title*, paras. 26.031–26.051; Barnsley, *Land Options* (2nd edn), chapter 10; Rent Review Journal (which began in 1981), superseded in 1992 by Rent Review and Lease Renewal Journal.
19 Aldridge, para. 4.039.
20 For precedents, see Aldridge, p. 011–020; Conv. Prec. vol. i, para. 2108–9; 5–57. And for revised model forms by the Joint Working Party of the Law Society and the Royal Institution of Chartered Surveyors (2nd edn, 1986), see Conv Precedents 5.61–561B.
 1 *United Scientific Holdings Ltd v Burnley Borough Council* [1976] Ch 128 at 146, [1976] 2 All ER 220 at 231, per ROSKILL LJ. See *London Regional Transport v Wimpey Group Services Ltd* [1986] 2 EGLR 41 at 42 where HOFFMANN J said: "Rent formulae can often be expressed more simply and unambiguously in algebraic form and this case shows that a very modest degree of numeracy can save a great deal of money", and *Freehold & Leasehold Properties Ltd v Friends Provident Life Office* (1984) 271 EG 451, where OLIVER LJ referred to the "somewhat Delphic pronouncement" of the definition of rent for the D. H. Lawrence House, Nottingham: "It may be doubted whether the distinguished author after whom the premises were named would have approved of the obscurity of language with which the parties have chosen to veil their intentions". See (1992) 12 LS 349 (G. D. Goldberg and P. F. Smith).
   On professional negligence in connection with a rent review clause in a commercial lease, see *County Personnel (Employment) Agency Ltd v Alan R Pulver & Co* [1987] 1 WLR 916, [1987] 1 All ER 289.
 2 [1978] AC 904, [1977] 2 All ER 62; [1979] Conv 10 (P. F. Smith); *Dean and Chapter of Chichester Cathedral v Lennards Ltd* (1977) 35 P & CR 309; cf *Commission for the New Towns v R Levy & Co Ltd* [1990] 2 EGLR 121.

failure of consideration, or by an estoppel by words or conduct.[3] The tenant, however, can serve a counter-notice making time of the essence.[4]

There is also a presumption that time is of the essence of an agreement which has granted an option to acquire an interest in property, and of a landlord's or tenant's break clause in a lease.[5]

The presumption may be rebutted either expressly,[6] or impliedly by other provisions in the lease or by inference from surrounding circumstances; as where the tenant has an option to determine the lease which is linked to the rent review.[7] Where time is of the essence, the court will not intervene to impose a rent review, if notice is served out of time.[8]

The doctrine of time not being of the essence is one of substance and not

3 *Amherst v James Walker (Goldsmith & Silversmith) Ltd (No 2)* [1983] Ch 305, [1983] 2 All ER 1067, per OLIVER LJ at 316, at 1074; per LAWTON LJ at 320, at 1077.

4 *Factory Holdings Group Ltd v Leboff International Ltd* [1987] 1 EGLR 135.

5 *Chiltern Court (Baker Street) Residents Ltd v Wallabrook Property Co Ltd* [1989] 2 EGLR 207.

6 On the construction and effect of an express provision, (*a*) where time has been held to be of the essence, see *Drebbond Ltd v Horsham District Council* (1978) 37 P & CR 237 (reference to arbitration within three months of original notice "but not otherwise"); *Weller v Akehurst* [1981] 3 All ER 411; *Pips (Leisure Productions) Ltd v Walton* (1980) 43 P & CR 415 ("would use their best endeavours"); *Lewis v Barnett* (1981) 264 EG 1079 (notice to review "shall be void and of no effect"); *Trustees of Henry Smith's Charities v AWADA Trading and Promotion Services Ltd* (1982) 47 P & CR 607 ("shall be deemed to be a market rent"); *Greenhaven Securities Ltd v Compton* (1985) 275 EG 628 (rent to be "a sum equal to the rent payable immediately before the review date"); *Mammoth Greetings Cards Ltd v Agra Ltd* [1990] 2 EGLR 124 (rent "shall be conclusively fixed"; "This evinces the concept of finality", per MUMMERY J at 125); *Norwich Union Life Insurance v Sketchley* [1986] 2 EGLR 126 ("but not otherwise"); *Chelsea Building Society v RSA Millett (Shops) Ltd* [1994] 09 EG 182 ("it shall be a condition precedent": "clearest possible intention"); (*b*) where time has been held not to be of the essence, see *Amherst v James Walker* (1980) 254 EG 123 (two time-limit steps out of three stated to be "of the essence"; held third step to be not of the essence); *Laing Investment Co Ltd v GA Dunn & Co* (1981) 262 EG 879; *Touche Ross & Co v Secretary of State for the Evironment* (1982) 46 P & CR 187 (reference to surveyor "as soon as practicable but in any event not later than three months"); *Thorn EMI Pension Fund Trust v Quinton Hazell plc* (1983) 269 EG 414; *Mecca Leisure Ltd v Renown Investments (Holdings) Ltd* (1984) 271 EG 989 ("shall be deemed to have agreed to pay the increased rent specified in the Rent Notice"); *Taylor Woodrow Property Co Ltd v Lonrho Textiles Ltd* (1985) 52 P & CR 28; *Phipps-Faire Ltd v Malbern Construction Ltd* [1987] 1 EGLR 129; *Power Securities (Manchester) v Prudential Assurance Co* [1987] 1 EGLR 121 (rent to be agreed between landlord and tenant within six months after end of second term; *Panavia Air Cargo Ltd v Southend-on-Sea Borough Council* [1988] 01 EG 60 (if review not completed until twelve months of relevant period, rent payable during the period would be current rent increased by 25%); *Kings (Estate Agents) Ltd v Anderson* [1992] 1 EGLR 121 (determination of rent (time to be of the essence) "three months prior to commencement of second or third rent period", failure to mention fourth period); *North Hertfordshire District Council v Hitchin Industrial Estate Ltd* [1992] 2 EGLR 121 (service of landlord's notice "shall be a condition precedent"); *Richurst Ltd v Pimenta* [1993] 1 WLR 159, [1993] 2 All ER 559 (acknowledgment of receipt of late service of notice held not to be agreement to extend time); [1993] Conv 382 (M. Haley); *Prudential Services v Capital Land Holdings* [1993] 15 EG 147 (effective counter-notice).

7 *United Scientific Holdings Service Ltd v Burnley Borough Council* [1978] AC 904 at 929, [1977] 2 All ER 62 at 71, per Lord DIPLOCK; *Al Saloom v Shirley James Travel Service Ltd* (1981) 42 P & CR 181; *Rahman v Kenshire* (1980) 259 EG 1074; *Coventry City Council v J Hepworth & Son Ltd* (1982) 265 EG 608; *Legal and General Assurance (Pension Management) Ltd v Cheshire County Council* (1983) 269 EG 40; *William Hill (Southern) Ltd v Govier* (1983) 269 EG 1168; *Edwin Woodhouse Trustee Co Ltd v Sheffield Brick Co plc* (1983) 270 EG 548; *McLeod Russel (Property Holding) Ltd v Emerson* (1985) 51 P & CR 176; *Metrolands Investments Ltd v JH Dewhurst Ltd* [1986] 3 All ER 659; *Stephenson & Son v Orca Properties Ltd* [1989] 2 EGLR 129.

8 *Weller v Akehurst* [1981] 3 All ER 411.

of form. The fact that the time limit is to be found partly in a definition and partly in a substantive clause of the lease makes no difference.[9]

A rent review clause usually contains a formula for the assessment of the revised rent. In this context, where rent has been paid and accepted up to the review date, the courts have been astute not to hold a formula void for uncertainty; they are more concerned with the amount of rent payable for the remainder of the term, and with the construction of the formula in such a way as to render the clause effective. Thus in *Beer v Bowden*[10] the court held that "such rent as shall thereupon be agreed" should be construed to mean "such fair rent as shall thereupon be agreed", and this formed the basis for the valuation of the revised rent.[11]

(e) Recovery of rent

The landlord's remedies for the recovery of rent will be considered later.[12]

(2) COVENANT TO REPAIR[13]

Various expressions are used to describe the extent of the obligation imposed by a covenant to repair the premises. The following are typical examples:

good tenantable repair;
good and tenantable order and repair;
well and substantially repair;
perfect repair.

By the use of appropriate language, the parties can, of course, settle the standard of repair as high or as low as they choose, but it is generally admitted that such epithets as "good", "perfect" or "substantial" do not increase the burden connoted by the simple word "repair".[14] By way of caution, it should be noticed that, if the premises are in a state of disrepair at the beginning of the lease, a covenant by the tenant to "keep" them in repair obliges him to

---

9 *Pembroke St Georges Ltd v Cromwell Developments Ltd* [1991] 2 EGLR 129.
10 [1981] 1 WLR 522, [1981] 1 All ER 1070; M & B p. 427; *Corson v Rhuddlan Borough Council* [1990] 1 EGLR 255 at 257.
11 *Thomas Bates & Son Ltd v Wyndham's (Lingerie) Ltd* [1981] 1 WLR 505, [1981] 1 All ER 1077; M & B p. 428; *Beer v Bowden*, supra; *Lear v Blizzard* [1983] 3 All ER 662; M & B p. 429, n. 7.
　For rent reviews where improvements have been made to the premises, see *Ponsford v HMS Aerosols Ltd* [1979] AC 63, [1978] 2 All ER 837, approving *Cuff v J & F Stone Property Co Ltd* [1979] AC 87, [1978] 2 All ER 833; *Hambros Bank Executors and Trustee Co Ltd v Superdrug Stores Ltd* [1985] 1 EGLR 99; *Lear v Blizzard* supra; *Pleasurama Properties Ltd v Leisure Investments (West End) Ltd* (1985) 273 EG 67 (conversion of shop premises into a dolphinarium); *Brett v Brett Essex Golf Club Ltd* (1986) 52 P & CR 330; *Panther Shop Investments Ltd v Keith Pople Ltd* [1987] 1 EGLR 131; *Ravenseft Properties Ltd v Park* [1988] 2 EGLR 164; *Ipswich Town Football Club Co Ltd v Ipswich Borough Council* [1988] 2 EGLR 146; *Laura Investment Co Ltd v Havering London Borough Council* [1992] 1 EGLR 155 (where HOFFMANN J reviews the authorities); *ibid (No. 2)* [1993] 88 EG 120; *Historic House Hotels v Cadogan* [1993] 30 EG 94 (improvements to be disregarded in spite of provision that premises so altered were to be comprised in lease at outset).
12 Pp. 423 et seq, post.
13 See generally West's *Law of Dilapidations* (9th edn 1988); Williams, *Handbook of Dilapidations* (1992). Whether the matter has been dealt with by covenant or not, the lessor is under a statutory obligation to repair a dwelling-house that has been let for less than seven years; p. 392, ante.
14 *Anstruther-Gough-Calthorpe v McOscar* [1924] 1 KB 716 at 722–3; but see at 731–2.

put them into the required state at his own expense.[15] A state of disrepair means a deterioration in the condition of the premises from a former better condition.[16]

In *Brew Brothers Ltd v Snax (Ross) Ltd*,[17] SACHS LJ set out the approach to be adopted in construing a covenant to repair:

> It seems to me that the correct approach is to look at the particular building, to look at the state which it is in at the date of the lease, to look at the precise terms of the lease, and then come to a conclusion as to whether, on a fair interpretation of those terms in relation to that state, the requisite work can fairly be termed repair. However large the covenant it must not be looked at in vacuo.[18]

(a) Extent of obligation

The extent of the obligation assumed by a covenantor who has agreed to repair the premises is that, after making due allowance for the locality, character and age of the premises at the time of the lease, he must keep them in the condition in which they would be kept by a reasonably minded owner.[19]

(i) **Locality** The locality is a material consideration, for the state of repair suitable for a house, say, in Grosvenor Square, differs from that which is appropriate to a house in Spitalfields.

(ii) **Character of premises** The character of the premises is also material. Thus the standard of repairs will vary according as the premises are the mansion-house or a labourer's cottage on the estate. The essential fact to notice, however, is that it is the character of the premises at the beginning, not at the end, of the lease that is material in this context. Thus in one case:

> a new house, situated in what was then a fashionable part of London was let in 1825 to a good class of tenant on a 95 year lease. In course of time the character of the neighbourhood deteriorated to such an extent that the only persons willing to occupy the house expected nothing more than that the rain should be kept out.

The covenantor, therefore, argued that the standard of repair required of him was to be measured by the needs and expectations of prospective tenants in 1920. The argument failed. The obligation of a covenantor is neither increased nor diminished in extent by a change in the character of the neighbourhood.[20]

(iii) **Age of premises** The age of a house is also material, though only in the sense that the covenantor's obligation is not to bring it up to date, but to keep

---

15 *Payne v Haine* (1847) 16 M & W 541; *Proudfoot v Hart* (1890) 25 QBD 42; *Credit Suisse v Beegas Nominees Ltd* [1994] 11 EG 151, 12 EG 189.
16 *Post Office v Aquarius Properties Ltd* [1987] 1 All ER 1055, per RALPH GIBSON LJ; *Plough Investments Ltd v Eclipse Radio and Television Services Ltd* [1989] 1 EGLR 244.
17 [1970] 1 QB 612 at 640, [1970] 1 All ER 587 at 602; *Smedley v Chumley and Hawke Ltd* (1982) 44 P & CR 50 at 54; *McDougall v Easington District Council* [1989] 1 EGLR 93.
18 "I have found most assistance in the judgment of SACHS LJ . . . It contains a timely warning against attempting to impose the crudities of judicial exegesis upon the subtle and often intuitive discriminations of ordinary speech": *Post Office v Aquarius Properties Ltd* [1985] 2 EGLR 105 at 107, per HOFFMANN J.
19 *Proudfoot v Hart* (1890) 25 QBD 42; *Lurcott v Wakely and Wheeler* [1911] 1 KB 905; *Anstruther-Gough-Calthorpe v McOscar* [1924] 1 KB 716; *Lloyd's Bank Ltd v Lake* [1961] 1 WLR 884, [1961] 2 All ER 30; *Firstcross Ltd v Teasdale* (1982) 47 P & CR 228; *Credit Suisse v Beggas Nominees Ltd* [1994] 11 EG 151, 12 EG 189.
20 *Anstruther-Gough-Calthorpe v McOscar*, supra.

it in a reasonably good condition for a building of that age. He cannot escape liability by the allegation that to keep so old a building in the covenanted condition requires renewal, not mere repairs. Repair always involves renewal. The covenant must be fulfilled, even though this necessitates the replacement of part after part until the whole is renewed.[1] The correct antithesis is between renewal and reconstruction. The former is required, the latter not. Whether the work necessary for the maintenance of a building is renewal or reconstruction is a question of degree, the test being whether the replacement affects a subordinate part or substantially the whole of the building.[2] Thus the tenant of an old house is not bound to replace defective foundations by foundations of an entirely different character;[3] but he must demolish and replace a dangerous wall if it is but a subsidiary part of the whole building.[4]

An inherent defect of design in the premises may be within the ambit of a covenant to repair, but the covenantor is not liable to remedy a design fault, unless that fault has caused or contributed to a proved state of disrepair:[5] As FOSTER J said:[6]

> the true test is that it is always a question of degree whether that which the tenant is being asked to do can properly be described as repair, or whether on the contrary it would involve giving back to the landlord a wholly different thing from that which he demised.

(b) Exception of fair wear and tear

It is usual to qualify the covenant to repair by a clause to the effect that the covenantor shall not be liable for "fair wear and tear", or, what signifies the same thing, for "reasonable wear and tear". The effect of these words is to exempt the covenantor from liability for damage that is due to the ordinary operation of natural causes, always presuming that he has used the premises

---

1 *Lurcott v Wakely and Wheeler*, supra, at 916–17, per FLETCHER-MOULTON LJ.
2 Ibid.; *Sotheby v Grundy* [1947] 2 All ER 761.
3 *Lister v Lane and Nesham* [1893] 2 QB 212; *Sotheby v Grundy*, supra; *Pembery v Lamdin* [1940] 2 All ER 434 (landlord's covenant); *Brew Bros Ltd v Snax (Ross) Ltd* [1970] 1 QB 612, [1970] 1 All ER 587 (tenant's covenant).
4 *Lurcott v Wakely and Wheeler*, supra; cf *Smedley v Chumley & Hawke Ltd* (1982) 44 P & CR 50 (underpinning of foundations of *recently* constructed restaurant in motel complex held to be work of repair). Cf *Halliard Property Co Ltd v Nicholas Clarke Investments Ltd* (1983) 269 EG 1257 (no duty to rebuild jerry-built structure); *Post Office v Aquarius Properties Ltd* [1985] 2 EGLR 105 (remedial scheme for failure of "kicker joint" more than repair); affirmed on other grounds [1987] 1 All ER 1055; *Elmcroft Developments Ltd v Tankersley-Sawyer* (1984) 270 EG 140 (defective damp course below ground level to be repaired by silicone injection); cf *Yanover v Romford Finance & Development Co Ltd* (1983) unreported but noted at (1984) 272 EG 250 (D. W. Williams); *Elite Investments Ltd v T I Bainbridge Silencers Ltd* [1986] 2 EGLR 43 (replacement of roof held to be repair) where the authorities are reviewed; [1987] Conv 140 (P. F. Smith); *New England Properties plc v Portsmouth News Shops Ltd* [1993] 1 EGLR 84.
5 *Ravenseft Properties Ltd v Davstone (Holdings) Ltd* [1980] QB 12, [1979] 1 All ER 929; [1979] Conv 429 (P. F. Smith); *Quick v Taff-Ely Borough Council* [1986] QB 809, [1985] 3 All ER 321; *Post Office v Aquarius Properties Ltd*, supra; [1987] Conv 224 (P. F. Smith); *Stent v Monmouth District Council* [1987] 1 EGLR 59; *Murray v Birmingham County Council* [1987] 2 EGLR 53; *Staves v Leeds City Council* [1992] 2 EGLR 36 (condensation affecting plasterwork).
6 *Ravenseft Properties Ltd v Davstone (Holdings) Ltd*, supra, at 21, at 937. For more detailed formulations of the test, see *McDougall v Easington District Council* [1989] 1 EGLR 93 at 95–96, per MUSTILL LJ; [1990] Conv 735 (P. F. Smith); *Holding and Management Ltd v Property Holding & Investment Trust plc* [1990] 1 EGLR 65 at 68, per NICHOLLS LJ.

in a reasonable manner.[7] As TINDAL CJ put it in a case where a tenant had invoked such a clause:

> What the natural operation of time flowing on effects, and all that the elements bring about in diminishing value, constitute a loss which, so far as it results from time and nature, falls upon the landlord.[8]

But where the defect, though initially due to natural causes, will obviously cause further and lasting damage unless rectified, the clause will not continue to avail a covenantor who stands idly by and allows the ravages of time and nature to take their course. TALBOT J made this clear in a passage later adopted by the House of Lords:

> The tenant is bound to do such repairs as may be required to prevent the consequences flowing originally from wear and tear from producing others which wear and tear would not directly produce. For example, if a tile falls off the roof, the tenant is not liable for the immediate consequences; but, if he does nothing and in the result more and more water gets in, the roof and walls decay and ultimately the top floor, or the whole house, becomes uninhabitable, he cannot say that it is due to reasonable wear and tear. . . . On the other hand, take the gradual wearing away of a stone floor or staircase by ordinary use. This may in time produce a considerable wear and tear, and the tenant is not liable in respect of it.[9]

(c) Covenant not to make improvements without consent

A covenant against the making of improvements without consent is statutorily subject to a proviso that consent shall not unreasonably be withheld, though the landlord is entitled to demand the payment of a reasonable sum for any damage or loss of value that may be caused to the premises or to neighbouring premises belonging to him.[10] The word "improvements" refers to improvements from the point of view of the tenant, and the statute applies even though what he proposes to do, e.g. the demolition of part of the main structure of a building, will temporarily diminish the value of the premises.[11] In such a case no injury is, in theory, suffered by the landlord, since he is permitted by the statute to demand an undertaking from the tenant that the premises will be reinstated.[12]

---

7 *Haskell v Marlow* [1928] 2 KB 45 at 59.
8 *Gutteridge v Munyard* (1834) 1 Mood & R 334 at 336. The words quoted do not appear in the report 7 C & P 129.
9 *Haskell v Marlow*, supra, at 59. This decision was overruled by the Court of Appeal in *Taylor v Webb* [1937] 2 KB 283, [1937] 1 All ER 590, but the principles laid down in this second case, after being stigmatized as inconsistent with earlier authorities by a later Court of Appeal in *Brown v Davies* [1958] 1 QB 117, [1957] 3 All ER 401, were finally overruled by the House of Lords in *Regis Property Co Ltd v Dudley* [1959] AC 370, [1958] 3 All ER 491, and the authority of *Haskell v Marlow* restored.
10 Landlord and Tenant Act 1927, s. 19 (2). The tenant may apply to the High Court or the County Court for a declaration that the landlord has unreasonably withheld his consent: Landlord and Tenant Act 1954, s. 53 (1) (*b*) as amended by County Courts Act 1984, s. 148 (1), Sch. 2, para 23.
11 *Lambert v Woolworth & Co* [1938] Ch 883, [1938] 2 All ER 664.
12 In 1989 the Law Commission published a Report: Compensation for Tenants' Improvements (No. 178), which recommends that (a) the statutory scheme in Part I of the Landlord and Tenant Act 1927 for compensating tenants of business properties for improvements which they have made should be abolished; and (b) there should not be a statutory compensation scheme for residential tenants who improve their premises.

(d) Landlord's right of entry

If the landlord is to perform his covenant to repair, he must have a right of entry to the premises. This may be expressly authorised by the terms of the lease or by statute; and if the landlord is liable to repair the premises he has an implied right to enter for a reasonable time to carry out the work.[13] Otherwise he has no right to enter during the currency of the lease,[14] because, as we have seen, the tenant has the right to exclusive possession.[15]

(e) Remedies for breach of covenant to repair

(i) Remedies of landlord

1. Injunction and specific performance Apart from forfeiture, the usual remedy for breach of a covenant to repair is damages. Injunction and specific performance are inappropriate where the covenant is broken by the tenant, because damages are an adequate remedy for the landlord. The landlord may himself do the work, if the lease authorises him to enter to do repairs.[16]

2. Damages The measure of damages *at common law* for breach of a contract to repair varies according as the breach occurs during the tenancy or at the end of the tenancy. In the first case the measure is the amount by which the value of the reversion has diminished; but in the second case, where the premises are delivered up in disrepair, it is the amount that it will cost to carry out the repairs required by the covenant.[17] If, for instance, a tenant converts into flats a house which he has covenanted to keep suitable for single occupation, the first rule applies and the measure of damages is not necessarily the full cost of reinstatement, but the sum that represents the loss which the lessor has sustained.[18] It was found that the second rule might inflict unnecessary hardship upon an outgoing tenant, since it enabled a landlord to recover substantial damages even though the performance of the covenant would have been entirely useless, as, for instance, where the premises were to be demolished, or where the want of repair would not diminish by one penny the rent obtainable on a re-letting. It is, therefore, provided by the Landlord and Tenant Act 1927[19] that whether the breach is of a covenant to repair during the currency of a lease or to leave premises in repair at the termination of a lease:

> the damages shall in no case exceed the amount (if any) by which the value of the reversion (whether immediate or not) in the premises is diminished, owing to the breach of the covenant or agreement.

The diminution in the value of the reversion is the amount that it will cost within the terms of the covenant to make the house reasonably fit for the class of tenant likely to take it. The fact that the landlord has been able to relet it, though spending less than that amount on repairs, is an irrelevant

---

13 *Saner v Bilton* (1878) 7 Ch D 815; *Mint v Good* [1951] 1 KB 517, [1950] 2 All ER 1159.
14 *Stocker v Planet Building Society* (1879) 27 WR 877.
15 P. 362, ante.
16 *Regional Properties Ltd v City of London Real Property Co Ltd* (1979) 257 EG 64; *Stocker v Planet Building Society* (1879) 27 WR 877, per JAMES LJ.
17 *Joyner v Weeks* [1891] 2 QB 31.
18 *Duke of Westminster v Swinton* [1948] 1 KB 524, [1948] 1 All ER 428. See also *James v Hutton and J Cook & Sons Ltd* [1950] 1 KB 9, [1949] 2 All ER 243.
19 S. 18 (1); *Haviland v Long* [1952] 2 QB 80, [1952] 1 All ER 463; *Mather v Barclays Bank plc* [1987] 2 EGLR 254; (1988) 104 LQR 372 (D. N. Clarke).

consideration.[20] In other words the primary test of the measure of damages still seems to be the cost of doing the covenanted repairs. There are many cases where the sale of the property unrepaired will fetch as high a price as its sale in a state of good repair, so that in one sense the value of the reversion as a whole is undiminished, as, for example, where the tenancy relates only to a few rooms in a large building and they cannot be made fit for occupation unless the covenanted repairs are done. In such a case it is now recognized that the cost of the necessary repairs prima facie represents the diminution in value of the reversion.[1]

In one particular case the landlord is denied any right to damages. The Act provides that no damages shall be recoverable for breach of the covenant:

> if it is shown that the premises, in whatever state of repair they might be, would at or shortly after the termination of the tenancy have been or be pulled down, or such structural alterations made therein as would render valueless the repairs covered by the covenant or agreement.[2]

Thus the Act requires the tenant to prove that the landlord had decided to demolish the premises and that this decision still held at the end of the lease. If this be shown, it is immaterial that the decision is later changed and the premises not demolished.[3] Damages are irrecoverable.[4] The onus, therefore, that lies upon the tenant is to show that the demolition or structural alteration of the premises was firmly intended, not merely contemplated, by the landlord and also that the achievement of the plan was reasonably possible.[5] Damages will, however, be recoverable, if the premises are demolished as a result of the tenant's breach of his covenant to repair.[6]

(ii) Remedies of tenant The landlord is not liable on his covenant to repair until he has notice of the need to repair. This is usually given to him by the tenant, but notice from any source is probably sufficient.[7]

The remedies of the tenant are:

1. Injunction and specific performance
Where it is the landlord who breaks the covenant, damages may be an inadequate remedy for the tenant; and, in the case of dwellings, the Landlord and Tenant Act 1985 gives the court discretion to order specific performance

---

20 *Jaquin v Holland* [1960] 1 WLR 258, [1960] 1 All ER 402; *Hanson v Newman* [1934] Ch 298. Cf *Family Management v Gray* (1979) 253 EG 369; [1980] Conv 244; *Crown Estate Comrs v Town Investments Ltd* [1992] 1 EGLR 61.

1 *Jones v Herxheimer* [1950] 2 KB 106, [1950] 1 All ER 323; *Smiley v Townshend* [1950] 2 KB 311 at 322–3, [1950] 1 All ER 530 at 534; *Drummond v S and U Stores Ltd* (1980) 258 EG 1293 (where the landlord was awarded the bulk of the cost of repairs, including Value Added Tax, and a sum representing three months' loss of rent); *Culworth Estates Ltd v Society of Licensed Victuallers* [1991] 2 EGLR 54 (damage to reversion greater than cost of carrying out necessary repairs).

2 Landlord and Tenant Act 1927, s. 18(1).

3 *Keats v Graham* [1960] 1 WLR 30, [1959] 3 All ER 919.

4 *Salisbury v Gilmore* [1942] 2 KB 38, [1942] 1 All ER 457.

5 *Cunliffe v Goodman* [1950] 2 KB 237, [1950] 1 All ER 720.

6 *Hibernian Property Co Ltd v Liverpool Corpn* [1973] 1 WLR 751, [1973] 2 All ER 1117.

7 *Torrens v Walker* [1906] 2 Ch 166; *McCarrick v Liverpool Corpn* [1947] AC 219, [1946] 2 All ER 646; *O'Brien v Robertson* [1973] AC 912, [1973] 1 All ER 583. See also *Sheldon v West Bromwich Corpn* (1973) 117 SJ 486 (landlord liable for damage of which he ought to have recognised warning signs on inspection); *Dinefwr Borough Council v Jones* [1987] 2 EGLR 58 ("actual notice from some responsible source"). For the landlord's liability to all persons likely to be affected by his failure to repair under Defective Premises Act 1972, s. 4, see p. 395, ante.

of the covenant whether or not the breach relates to part of the premises let to the tenant.[8] Further, where a landlord has failed to carry out repairs within his express or implied covenant, the tenant, after giving due notice, may carry out the repairs himself and deduct the proper costs of repair from future payments of rent.[9] The right of set-off may be excluded by clear words in the lease.[10]

2. Damages

The tenant has a wide range of remedies in damages. He may recover the cost of repairs and redecoration, the cost of reasonable alternative accommodation and of storage of furniture, and general damages for inconvenience and discomfort. If the premises, to the knowledge of the landlord, had been purchased for re-sale or sub-letting or if the tenant was forced to sell because of the breach of covenant, then he can recover the loss in market value or of rental value as the case may be.[11]

3. Appointment of a receiver[12]

Where the landlord is in breach of his covenant to repair and neglects the property, the court may appoint a receiver to collect the rent and to carry out repairs, "if it is just and convenient to do so".

4. Appointment of a manager: leasehold flats

The Landlord and Tenant Act 1987[13] makes special provision for tenants of residential premises consisting of "the whole or part of a building containing two or more flats". Parts II and III of the Act apply where the court is

---

8 Ss. 17, 32 (1). *Jeune v Queens Cross Properties Ltd* [1974] Ch 97, [1973] 3 All ER 97 (specific performance granted before the Act); *Francis v Cowcliffe Ltd* (1976) 33 P & CR 368; *Parker v Camden London Borough Council* [1986] Ch 162, [1985] 2 All ER 141; *Posner v Scott-Lewis* [1987] Ch 25, [1986] 3 All ER 513 (covenant to employ resident porter). See (1975) 119 SJ 362, (1976) 120 SJ 428 (H. E. Markson).

9 *Lee-Parker v Izzet* [1971] 1 WLR 1688, [1971] 3 All ER 1099; (1976) 40 Conv (NS) 190 (P. M. Rank). See *Asco Developments Ltd v Gordon* (1978) 248 EG 683 at 683, where MEGARRY V-C said that this right of deduction was equally applicable to arrears of rent. See also *British Anzani (Felixstowe) Ltd v International Marine Management (UK) Ltd* [1980] QB 137, [1979] 2 All ER 1063; *Melville v Grapelodge Developments Ltd* (1978) 39 P & CR 179; (1980) 131 NLJ 330 (P. F. Smith); [1981] Conv 199 (A. Waite).

10 *Connaught Restaurants Ltd v Indoor Leisure Ltd* [1994] 1 WLR 501 (payment of rent "without any deduction" ambiguous and insufficient to exclude right of set-off). Such a clause is not subject to the test of reasonableness under the Unfair Contract Terms Act 1977, p. 389, n. 15, ante.

11 *Calabar Properties Ltd v Stitcher* [1984] 1 WLR 287, [1983] 3 All ER 759; *McGreal v Wake* (1984) 269 EG 1254; *Bradley v Chorley Borough Council* [1985] 2 EGLR 49; (1984) 134 NLJ 379 (H. W. Wilkinson); *Chiodi's Personal Representatives v De Marney* [1988] 2 EGLR 64.

　See Secure Tenancies (Right to Repair Scheme) Regulations 1985 (S.I. 1985 No. 1493), which entitles a secure tenant (p. 487, post) to carry out his landlord's repairs ("other than a repair to the structure or exterior of a flat"), the cost of which may then be recouped from the landlord; cf *Lee-Parker v Izzet*, supra; (1986) 83 LSG 1376 (P. M. Rank).

12 Supreme Court Act 1981, s. 37(1); *Hart v Emelkirk Ltd* [1983] 1 WLR 1289, [1983] 3 All ER 15; *Daiches v Bluelake Investments Ltd* [1985] 2 EGLR 67; cf *Parker v Camden London Borough Council* [1986] Ch 162, [1985] 2 All ER 141; *Evans v Clayhope Properties Ltd* [1988] 1 WLR 358, [1988] 1 All ER 444; [1988] Conv 363 (C. P. Rodgers); *Blawdziewicz v Diadon Establishment* [1988] 2 EGLR 52 (balance of convenience).

13 As amended by Housing Act 1988, Sch 13. The Act implements the main recommendations of the Nugee Committee of Inquiry on the Management of Privately Owned Blocks of Flats (1985). This valuable report contains statistics about private sector flats in England and Wales in chapter 3, and discusses the problems of owning a flat in chapter 6. See (1988) 51 MLR 97 (M. E. Percival).

satisfied that the landlord is in breach of any obligations under the tenancy that relate to the management of the premises, including their repair, maintenance and insurance.[14] The court must also be satisfied that the circumstances by which he is in breach of any such obligation are likely to continue, and that it is just and convenient to make the order in all the circumstances of the case. The court then has power under Part II to appoint a manager to carry out:[15]

(a) such functions in connection with the management of the premises, or
(b) such functions of a receiver,
or both, as the court thinks fit.

Part III of the Act makes provision for a person to be nominated by the tenants to acquire their landlord's interest in the premises without his consent. In order to qualify under this Part, the tenants must be tenants of residential premises under a *long* lease[16] (i.e. a lease granted for a term exceeding 21 years). On the application by not less than two-thirds[17] of the qualified tenants, the court may make an acquisition order if the landlord is in breach, and, is likely to continue to be in breach, of his obligations, or if the appointment of a manager has been in force for at least three years, and, in either case, the court considers it appropriate to make the order in the circumstances. Under the order the nominated person is entitled to acquire the landlord's interest on such terms as may be determined by agreement between the parties, or, in default of agreement, by a rent assessment committee.[18]

(iii) Apportionment of liability There are circumstances in which liability may be apportioned between landlord and tenant, for example, where a tenant was in breach of his covenant to repair, but had a claim against the landlord in tort for nuisance and negligence in respect of neglect which contributed to the damage, liability was apportioned 90 per cent to the landlord and 10 per cent to the tenant.[19]

(3) COVENANT BY TENANT TO INSURE AGAINST FIRE

By the Fires Prevention (Metropolis) Act 1774[20] no action may be brought against any person in whose house a fire shall *accidentally* begin, though it is

---

14 On service charges, see *Freedman and Shapiro, Service Charges, Law and Practice* (1986); Sherriff, *Service Charges in Leases; A Practical Guide* (1989).
15 Landlord and Tenant Act 1987, s. 24 (1). If a tenant applies for an order under s. 24, he may not apply for the appointment of a receiver under Supreme Court Act 1981, s. 37 (1), supra: s. 21 (6). See *Howard v Midrome Ltd* [1991] 1 EGLR 58 (manager of a company owned by the tenants).
16 Tenancies under the Landlord and Tenant Act 1954 Part II are excluded: ss. 21 (7), 26 (1). A lease includes a sub-lease, and an agreement for a lease or for a sub-lease: s. 59 (1).
17 Landlord and Tenant Act 1987, s. 25, as amended by Leasehold Reform, Housing and Urban Development Act 1993, s. 85.
18 See also Part IV, as amended by Leasehold Reform, Housing and Urban Development Act 1993, s. 86, under which the court may vary the terms of any long lease of a flat if they fail to make satisfactory provision for repair or maintenance, insurance, provision or maintenance of services, recovery of expenditure or computation of a service charge payable under the lease.
19 *Tennant Radiant Heat Ltd v Warrington Development Corpn* [1988] 1 EGLR 41.
20 S. 86. The Act applies to the whole of England. As to its interpretation, see *Goldman v Hargrave* [1967] 1 AC 645, [1966] 2 All ER 989; *Mason v Levy Auto Parts of England Ltd* [1967] 2 QB 530, [1967] 2 All ER 62; *Reynolds v Phoenix Assurance Co Ltd* (1978) 247 EG 995.

expressly enacted that this provision shall not defeat an agreement made between landlord and tenant. The result is that, when the property has been burnt, a landlord can maintain an action against his tenant in two cases:

first, where the tenant has covenanted to repair, for his contractual liability is not excluded by the happening of an inevitable accident against which he might have expressly protected himself; [1] and

secondly, where the fire has begun or been allowed to spread by reason of the negligence of the tenant or of those for whom he is responsible. [2]

But, in addition, it is usual for a tenant to covenant that he will insure the demised buildings to their full value and will keep them insured during the term. It has been held in such a case that the omission to keep the premises insured for any period, no matter how short, and even though no fire breaks out during the period, constitutes a breach of the covenant. [3]

A covenant to insure is usually coupled with a covenant to apply any insurance moneys received in the reinstatement of the premises, [4] and this is effective unless it is impossible to rebuild. There is an implied duty to lay out the insurance moneys within a reasonable time. [5]

If the landlord himself takes out a policy without having agreed to do so, he is not liable to expend the insurance money on the reinstatement of the premises in the event of their destruction, unless the cost of the premiums is reflected in the rent. [6] Reinstatement of the premises may be impossible, for example, because of restrictions on building or compulsory acquisition of the site. In that case the insurance proceeds belong to the party who paid the premium. [7]

(f) Law reform

In 1975 the Law Commission reported on a wide range of obligations undertaken by parties to leases, including the covenant to repair. [8] In 1992 it published a Consultation Paper on Responsibility for State and Condition of Property, covering some of the same ground as the earlier Report, although it ranged more widely. [9]

Under Reform Options (Part V), the Consultation Paper sets out three approaches to reform:

1. No change (paras. 5.2–5.4)

The first option is to make no changes. The scope of the contractual property maintenance bargain between the parties to leases, however the obligation has been allocated, has remained unaltered for many years, although litigation has served to clarify aspects of it and to demonstrate how it applies to particular

1 *Redmond v Dainton* [1920] 2 KB 256.
2 *Musgrove v Pandelis* [1919] 2 KB 43.
3 *Penniall v Harborne* (1848) 11 QB 368; *Naumann v Ford* [1985] 2 EGLR 70.
4 *Lonsdale & Thompson Ltd v Black Arrow Group plc* [1993] Ch 361, [1993] 3 All ER 648.
5 *Farimani v Gates* (1984) 271 EG 887.
6 *Mumford Hotels Ltd v Wheler* [1964] Ch 117, [1963] 3 All ER 250. Cf *Re King* [1963] Ch 459, [1963] 1 All ER 781; M & B p. 517; *Mark Rowlands Ltd v Berni Inns Ltd* [1985] QB 211, [1986] 3 All ER 473; (1986) 83 LSG 1046 (H. W. Wilkinson).
7 *Re King*, supra; cf *Beacon Carpets Ltd v Kirby* [1985] QB 755, [1984] 2 All ER 726.
8 Report on Obligations of Landlord and Tenant (Law Com. No. 67).
9 No. 123. Part II contains a valuable summary of the present law; (1992) 27 EG 128 (S. Murdock).

circumstances. At least those who enter into a lease with professional advice and have the implications explained to them, should be reasonably clear about the scope and limitations of the duties undertaken . . . (para 5.2).

Some may be of the view that the matters of concern to which we have referred occasion real difficulty only rarely and that a complex reform is not justified. As Sir John Megaw said, after referring to difficulties arising from the distinction between repairs and remedial work which are not repairs: It may be, however, that in practice—in real life as distinct from legal theory—the cases where such difficulties would arise would be rare, since the carrying out of such works will usually be very much in the interest of both landlord and tenant; and an attempt to cover by legislation such rare cases where the parties have failed to agree might lead to more problems than it would solve.[10]

2. A new approach (paras. 5.5–5.35)

An alternative approach to the present rules could place emphasis on the purpose for which the property was let. . . . A duty to maintain premises in a state suitable for a particular use has been adopted elsewhere: it is common in civil law countries, and it is spreading into common law jurisdictions in the United States. It cannot therefore be dismissed as unworkable, but it would be a considerable change in this country. The traditional imposition of repairing obligations treats the need to maintain the condition of the property as independent from the purpose for which the property is to be used. The standard of repair is not dictated by what is needed for that use, and indeed the premises may be unusable even though the repairing duty has been discharged. The attraction of a duty linked to the use is that it treats the grant of the lease as an integrated transaction, recognising that the physical state of the property can determine whether the tenant is able to obtain the intended benefit. Such a use-based approach would clearly be a radical change for English law, and it therefore requires detailed examination.

3. Individual reforms (paras. 5.36–5.64)

As an alternative to a comprehensive approach, a number of individual reforms are suggested. They include:

(i) Meaning of repair

The definition of repair could be adjusted in a number of ways:

- (a) Some improvements might be included. Would it be satisfactory to extend the repairing duty to include improvements which enable a building to perform its intended function? Should an obligation to repair a whole building include the obligation to repair improvements? (paras. 5.38–5.46.)
- (b) In relation to defects in the property existing at the date of the lease, a tenant's repairing liability might not extend to any known to the landlord, or possibly any which ought to have been known to him, unless the tenant was notified. (paras. 5.49–5.51.)
- (c) The standard of repair could be judged at the date it was being considered, rather than as at the date of the lease, or perhaps no date is relevant. (para. 5.52.)
- (d) The statutory obligation in relation to fitness for human habitation could be amended to dispense with the rent limits and to apply the new statutory definition of fitness. Possible alternative limits on the application of the duty are: to apply it only to lettings for less than seven years or only to those for up to twenty-one years. (paras. 5.53–5.55.)

10 *McDougall v Easington District Council* [1989] 1 EGLR 93 at 96.

(e) Repairing obligations could extend to neighbouring property on which the demised premises are dependent, if the party responsible for repair had a right of entry. A landlord's duty could extend to property over which the tenant had an easement, where the landlord was entitled to do the work. (paras. 5.56–5.57.)

(ii) Waste

The doctrine of waste could cease to apply between landlord and tenant, but a new rule should be introduced. This would be either that lease provisions would continue for so long as the former tenant remained in possession, or, in those circumstances, that only the former tenant's obligations would continue. (paras. 5.58–5.59)

(iii) Enforcement

The objective of enforcement should be to place an emphasis on ensuring that necessary work is done. The following possibilities arise:

(a) Specific performance should be the primary method of enforcing property maintenance duties. The statutory provisions facilitating this in the case of residential property should extend to all types of property; (para. 5.61)
(b) Damages for breach of a duty to maintain property awarded while the lease continues should be of the amount required to pay for the work when damages are awarded. The court should be able to impose a condition that the money be spent on the work; (para. 5.62)
(c) Legislation in this field should bind the Crown. (paras. 5.63–5.64)

(4) COVENANT BY TENANT NOT TO ASSIGN OR UNDERLET OR PART WITH POSSESSION[11]

Unless there is a special agreement to the contrary, a tenant is free to grant his interest to a third party either by assignment or by underlease,[12] but as it is undesirable from the landlord's point of view that the premises should fall into the hands of an irresponsible person, it is usual to provide for the matter by express covenant. In this case, even though the assignment or underlease is made in breach of the covenant, it is nevertheless valid, but the breach may give rise to forfeiture or to a claim for damages.[13]

(a) Construction of covenant

The courts, however, have always construed this covenant with great strictness and have insisted that the restraint imposed upon the tenant shall not go beyond the letter of the express agreement.[14] Thus, a covenant *not to assign or underlet* is not broken by an equitable mortgage accompanied by deposit of title deeds,[15] nor by a deed of arrangement whereby the tenant constitutes himself trustee for his creditors,[16] nor by permitting another

---

11 Crabb, *Leases, Covenants and Consents* (1991).
12 *Keeves v Dean* [1924] 1 KB 685 at 691; *Leith Properties Ltd v Byrne* [1983] QB 433.
13 *Old Grovebury Manor Farm Ltd v W Seymour Plant Sales and Hire Ltd (No 2)* [1979] 1 WLR 1397, [1979] 3 All ER 504; *Governors of the Peabody Donation Fund v Higgins* [1983] 1 WLR 1091, [1983] 3 All ER 122.
14 *Church v Brown* (1808) 15 Ves 258 at 265, per Lord ELDON; *Grove v Portal* [1902] 1 Ch 727 at 731.
15 *Doe d Pitt v Hogg* (1824) 4 Dow & Ry KB 226; p. 669, post.
16 *Gentle v Faulkner* [1900] 2 QB 267.

person to have the use of the premises without giving him legal possession,[17] nor in general by any transfer which is involuntary, as, for instance, one which results from the bankruptcy of the tenant.[18] A provision that "this lease shall be non-assignable" does not embrace a sub-lease of the premises.[19] An agreement *not to sublet* is not broken by a sub-lease of part of the premises;[20] but a covenant *not to assign or underlet any part of the premises* is broken if the tenant assigns or underlets the whole of the premises.[1] A covenant *not to part with the possession of the premises or any part thereof* is not broken by the grant of a licence to place an advertisement hoarding on the wall of the demised premises, since the tenant is not thereby deprived of legal possession;[2] but a covenant *"not to underlet or part with possession of the premises"* is broken if the tenant assigns his lease, since this involves a parting with possession.[3] It would seem that the letting of lodgings is no breach of a covenant *not to underlease the premises*.[4]

(b) Effect of breach of covenant

The result of a tenant's breach depends upon the nature of the covenant by which he has bound himself. A covenant is either absolute or qualified.

(i) Absolute covenant An absolute covenant is one which imposes an unconditional prohibition upon the tenant, there being no provision for its relaxation at the will of the lessor. In this case any assignment contrary to the terms of the covenant renders the tenant liable, notwithstanding that it is in no way prejudicial to the lessor's interest.

(ii) Qualified covenant

1. Unreasonable withholding of consent by lessor A qualified covenant, which is far more common in practice, is one which merely prohibits an assignment without the consent of the lessor. It has long been usual to qualify this type of covenant even further by a provision that the lessor's consent shall not be unreasonably withheld, and the Landlord and Tenant Act 1927 makes this qualification inevitable by providing that:

> In all leases whether made before or after the commencement of this Act containing a covenant condition or agreement against assigning, underletting, charging or parting with the possession of demised premises or any part thereof without licence or consent, such covenant condition or agreement shall, notwithstanding any

---

17 *Chaplin v Smith* [1926] 1 KB 198.
18 *Re Riggs* [1901] 2 KB 16; *Marsh v Gilbert* (1980) 256 EG 715 (vesting in new trustee by order of court). As to whether a bequest of a leasehold interest breaks a covenant not to assign, see (1963) 27 Conv (NS) 159 (D. G. Barnsley).
19 *Sweet and Maxwell Ltd v Universal News Services Ltd* [1964] 2 QB 699, [1964] 3 All ER 30.
20 *Cook v Shoesmith* [1951] 1 KB 752; *Esdaile v Lewis* [1956] 1 WLR 709, [1956] 2 All ER 357.
 1 *Field v Barkworth* [1986] 1 WLR 137, [1986] 1 All ER 362, approved in *Troop v Gibson* [1986] 1 EGLR 1 (landlord estopped from enforcing covenant); (1985) 129 SJ 781, 867.
 2 *Stening v Abrahams* [1931] 1 Ch 470; *Lam Kee Ying Sdn Bhd v Lam Shes Tong* [1975] AC 247, [1974] 3 All ER 137.
 3 *Marks v Warren* [1979] 1 All ER 29.
 4 *Doe d Pitt v Laming* (1814) 4 Camp 73 at 77, doubted in *Greenslade v Tapscott* (1834) 1 Cr M & R 55; *Victoria Dwellings Association Ltd v Roberts* [1947] LJNCCR 177; *Phillips v Woolf* [1953] CLY 1966; *Re Smith's Lease* [1951] 1 All ER 346.

express provision to the contrary, be deemed to be subject to a proviso to the effect that such licence or consent is not to be unreasonably withheld.[5]

Thus, the Act requires that the grounds for the refusal of consent shall in fact be reasonable, and therefore its operation cannot be curtailed by a provision in the lease that certain specified grounds shall not be deemed unreasonable.[6] But, if the lease contains a covenant that, before the tenant assigns or underlets , he must first offer to surrender his lease to the landlord, the landlord may demand surrender and so obtain the value of a premium obtainable on an assignment.[7]

It is enacted by the Law of Property Act 1925 that the lessor may not require the payment of a fine in return for his consent, unless express provision for such a payment is contained in the lease.[8]

The tenant must apply for consent to assign, even if it could not reasonably be refused; the landlord must be given a reasonable opportunity to consider whether to give his consent or not.[9] If the tenant assigns the premises without asking for consent, he is in breach of covenant, and liable to pay damages, and also at common law to the forfeiture of his interest.[10] He may, however, apply to the court for relief against such forfeiture.[11] If, on the other hand, the tenant asks for consent and the landlord refuses consent unreasonably, the tenant may proceed with the assignment without consent.[12]

2. Landlord and Tenant Act 1988 This "curious little Act"[13] imposes statutory duties on a landlord in relation to applications for consent to an assignment, underletting, charging or parting with possession. It applies to applications served after 28 September 1988, and only affects qualified covenants.[14] Its object is to prevent undue delay by the landlord in dealing with a consent

5 S. 19 (1) (*a*); this section does not apply to an absolute covenant: per ROMER LJ in *FW Woolworth & Co Ltd v Lambert* [1937] Ch 37 at 58, 59; and MEGAW LJ in *Bocardo SA v S and M Hotels Ltd* [1980] 1 WLR 17 at 22, [1979] 3 All ER 737 at 741, but see DANCKWERTS LJ in *Property and Bloodstock Ltd v Emerton* [1968] Ch 94 at 119–20, [1967] 3 All ER 321 at 330; *Vaux Group plc v Lilley* [1991] 1 EGLR 60 at 63, per KNOX J. Nor does it apply to the lease of an agricultural holding: s. 19 (4).
6 *Re Smith's Lease* [1951] 1 All ER 346.
7 *Bocardo SA v S and M Hotels Ltd*, supra; *Adler v Upper Grosvenor Street Investment Ltd* [1957] 1 WLR 227, [1957] 1 All ER 229; (1957) 73 LQR 157 (R.E.M.); *Creer v P and O Lines of Australia Pty Ltd* (1971) 45 ALJR 697; (1972) 88 LQR 317. This surrender proviso was doubted by CA in *Greene v Church Comrs for England* [1974] Ch 467, [1974] 3 All ER 609. It is registrable as an estate contract: LCA 1972, s. 2 (4); *Greene v Church Comrs for England*, supra. For the position of business tenancies under Landlord and Tenant Act 1954, Part II, see *Allnatt London Properties Ltd v Newton* [1981] 2 All ER 290; [1980] Conv 418 (C. G. Blake); (1983) 127 SJ 855 (C. Coombe).
8 S. 144; *Gardner & Co Ltd v Cone* [1928] Ch 955; *Comber v Fleet Electrics Ltd* [1955] 2 All ER 161. An increase in rent as a condition to giving consent is in the nature of a fine: *Jenkins v Price* [1907] 2 Ch 229.
9 *Wilson v Fynn* [1948] 2 All ER 40.
10 *Barrow v Isaacs & Son* [1891] 1 QB 417.
11 *Lambert v FW Woolworth & Co Ltd (No 2)* [1938] Ch 883 at 893.
12 The tenant may apply to the High Court or to the County Court for a declaration that the landlord has unreasonably withheld his consent: Landlord and Tenant Act 1954, s. 53 (1) (*a*), as amended by County Courts Act 1984, s. 148 (1), Sch. 2, para. 23.
13 *Venetian Glass Gallery Ltd v Next Properties Ltd* [1989] 2 EGLR 42 at 46, per HARMAN J. The Act is based on Law Commission Report: Leasehold Conveyancing 1987 (Law Com. No. 161, HC 360); [1989] Conv 1. See also the earlier Report on Covenants Restricting Dispositions, Alterations and Change of User 1985 (Law Com. No. 141, HC 278), paras. 8.50–8.131: (1985) 135 NLJ 491, 1015 (P. F. Smith); [1986] Conv 240 (A. J. Waite).
14 S. 1 (1). It does not apply to a secure tenancy under the Housing Act 1985: s. 5 (3).

application by the tenant, especially where the landlord decides to refuse consent.[15]

Where the landlord receives written application for consent from the tenant, he owes a duty to the tenant within a reasonable time:[16]

(a) to give consent, except in a case where it is reasonable not to give consent,

(b) to serve on the tenant written notice of his decision whether or not to give consent specifying in addition:

　　(i) if the consent is given subject to conditions, the conditions,
　　(ii) if the consent is withheld, the reasons for withholding it.

The landlord is also under a duty to forward the application to any other person whose consent to the transaction is needed, for example, to a superior landlord or to a mortgagee. In this case the superior landlord owes a similar duty.[17]

Where any duty imposed by the Act is broken, an action lies for the tort of breach of statutory duty.[18]

The burden of proof, which at common law was placed on the tenant to prove that consent cannot be unreasonably refused, is reversed by the Act in regard to all the duties, i.e. as to reasonable time, reasonable conditions and reasonable refusal.[19] The Act contains no definition of reasonableness in any of its connotations.[20] These matters will still depend on the application of common law principles.[1]

3. Test of reasonableness The crucial question is—What does the law regard as a reasonable refusal? This was answered in *Houlder Bros & Co Ltd v Gibbs*,[2] where TOMLIN J at first instance said:

It is by reference to the personality of the lessee or the nature of the user or occupation of the premises that the court has to judge the reasonableness of the lessor's refusal.

And where SARGANT LJ in the Court of Appeal said:

I was very much impressed by counsel's argument that in a case of this kind the landlord's reason must be something affecting the subject matter of the contract which forms the relationship between the landlord and the tenant, and that it must not be something wholly extraneous and completely dissociated from the subject matter of the contract.[3]

In that case it was held that:

it was unreasonable for a landlord, who had let Blackacre to X and Whiteacre to Y,

15 See *29 Equities Ltd v Bank Leumi (UK) Ltd* [1986] 1 WLR 1490 at 1494, [1987] 1 All ER 108 at 111, per DILLON LJ.
16 S. 1 (3).
17 Ss. 2, 3.
18 S. 4.
19 S. 1 (6). The Act has not changed the rule that it is not necessary for the landlord to prove that his conclusions were justified if he can show that they were reasonably reached in the circumstances: *Air India v Balabel* [1993] 2 EGLR 66; *Beale v Worth* [1993] EGCS 135.
20 In the 1985 Report the Law Commission had recommended a 28-day period: para. 8.125. On the obscure s. 1 (5), see (1989) 133 SJ 1277 (T. Aldridge).
 1 *Midland Bank plc v Chart Enterprises Inc* [1990] 2 EGLR 59 (gap of two and a half months between application and notice of decision held unreasonable).
 2 [1925] Ch 198 at 209. See generally [1988] Conv 45 (G. Kodilinye).
 3 [1925] Ch 575 at 587; *Bromley Park Garden Estates Ltd v Moss* [1982] 1 WLR 1019, [1982] 2 All ER 890 (where the object of the refusal was to promote good estate management); *Anglia Building Society v Sheffield County Council* (1982) 266 EG 311.

to forbid an assignment of Blackacre by X to Y, on the ground that Y might terminate his tenancy of Whiteacre.

Although this approach has been criticized by the House of Lords on the ground that it involved adding glosses to the plain words of the covenant,[4] it has been generally followed by the Court of Appeal.[5] The question of reasonableness is essentially a question of fact depending on all the circumstances of the case;[6] and there is now more emphasis on this approach.[7] As Lord DENNING MR said:[8]

> Seeing that the circumstances are infinitely various, it is impossible to formulate strict rules as to how a landlord should exercise his power of refusal. The utmost that the Courts can do is to give guidance to those who have to consider the problem. As one decision follows another, people will get to know the likely result in any given set of circumstances. But no one decision will be a binding precedent as a strict rule of law. The reasons given by the judges are to be treated as propositions of good sense—in relation to the particular case—rather than propositions of law applicable to all cases.

In considering whether the landlord's refusal of consent is reasonable, there is a divergence of authority as to whether it is permissible to have regard to the consequences to the tenant if consent is withheld. In *International Drilling Fluids Ltd v Louisville Investments (Uxbridge) Ltd*, BALCOMBE LJ reconciled this divergence by saying that:[9]

> while a landlord need usually only consider his own relevant interests, there may be cases where there is such a disproportion between the benefit to the landlord and the detriment to the tenant if the landlord withholds his consent to an assignment that it is unreasonable for the landlord to refuse consent.

In that case it was held that, where a user clause permitted only one specified type of use ("for any purpose other than as offices"), it was unreasonable to refuse consent to an assignment on the grounds of use (being within the only specified type of use) where the result would be that the property was left vacant and where the landlord was fully secured for payment of the rent.

4. Examples of reasonable refusal It has been held that a landlord has a valid reason for withholding his consent:

4 *Viscount Tredegar v Harwood* [1929] AC 72 at 78, 81.
5 *Lee v K Carter Ltd* [1949] 1 KB 85 at 96, [1948] 2 All ER 690; *Swanson v Forton* [1949] Ch 143 at 149, [1949] 1 All ER 135 at 138; *Pimms Ltd v Tallow Chandlers in the City of London* [1964] 2 QB 547, [1964] 2 All ER 145; *Bickel v Duke of Westminster* [1977] QB 517, [1976] 3 All ER 801, per ORR and WALLER LJJ; contra Lord DENNING MR, who considered that no such rule bound the Court of Appeal; *Bromley Park Garden Estates Ltd v Moss*, supra; *International Drilling Fluids Ltd v Louisville Investments (Uxbridge) Ltd* [1986] Ch 513, [1986] 1 All ER 321, where BALCOMBE LJ gives seven propositions of law deduced from the authorities at 519, at 325.
6 *Brann v Westminster Anglo-Continental Investment Co Ltd* (1975) 240 EG 927 at 931; *Bickel v Duke of Westminster*, supra, at 524, at 804, per LORD DENNING MR; *West Layton Ltd v Ford* [1979] QB 593 at 605, 606, [1979] 2 All ER 657, at 663, 664, per ROSKILL and LAWTON LJJ.
7 See e.g. *Leeward Securities Ltd v Lilyheath Properties Ltd* (1983) 271 EG 279 at 282, per OLIVER LJ; *International Drilling Fluids Ltd v Louisville Investments (Uxbridge) Ltd*, supra, at 521, at 326, where it is the seventh proposition to which all the others are subject.
8 *Bickel v Duke of Westminster*, supra at 524, at 804.
9 [1986] Ch 513 at 521, [1986] 1 All ER 321 at 326; *Leeward Securities Ltd v Lilyheath Properties Ltd*, supra, at 283, per OLIVER LJ. Cf *Ponderosa International Development Inc v Pengap Securities (Bristol) Ltd* [1986] 1 EGLR 66 ("nothing like as grave a detriment as was in question in *International Drilling*"); *FW Woolworth plc v Charlwood Alliance Properties Ltd* [1987] 1 EGLR 53; [1987] Conv 381 (L. Crabb).

if the assignee's references[10] or financial standing[11] are unsatisfactory; or
if he considers that other property belonging to him will be injured by the
use that the assignee intends to make of the demised premises;[12] or
if, where the lease is of a tied public-house, he fears that the value of the
trade will depreciate because the assignee is a foreigner who does not
intend to reside on the premises;[13] or
if the effect of the assignment will be to nullify a collateral agreement made
at the time of the lease;[14] or
if the assignment will enable the assignee to acquire a statutory tenancy
protected by the Rent Acts,[15] or in due course to acquire the freehold
under the Leasehold Reform Act 1967;[16] or
if the rent reserved in a proposed sub-lease is well below that obtainable in
the open market, but the sub-lessee agrees to pay a large sum by way of
premium;[17] or
if the assignment will embarrass the future development of the property of
which the demised premises form part;[18] or
if, where there are breaches of a covenant to repair, he is not really sure
that the assignee will remedy them;[19] or
if the effect of the assignment will be to reduce the rent by 50 per cent.[20]

5. *Giving of reasons by landlord* The landlord is not bound to give any reasons
for withholding his consent.[1] But if he does not give a reason, the court may
be more inclined to infer that the refusal of consent was unreasonable.[2]

If the landlord gives reasons at the time of his refusal of consent, is he then
limited to those reasons, or may he also put forward further reasons at the

10 *Shanly v Ward*, (1913) 29 TLR 714; *Rossi v Hestdrive Ltd* [1985] 1 EGLR 50. See also *Shires v Brock* (1977) 247 EG 127 (fictitious transaction by tenant in favour of nominee with first class references, the object being to give difficult landlord "a bit of a fright"); *City Hotels Group Ltd v Total Property Investments Ltd* [1985] 1 EGLR 253 (extent of enquiries for information of tenant's capabilities); *Warren v Marketing Exchange for Africa Ltd* [1988] 2 EGLR 247 ("references of a particularly qualified and non-enthusiastic character").
11 *Ponderosa International Development Inc v Pengap Securities (Bristol) Ltd*, supra; *British Bakeries (Midlands) Ltd v Michael Testler & Co Ltd* [1986] 1 EGLR 64.
12 *Governors of Bridewell Hospital v Fawkner and Rogers* (1892) 8 TLR 637.
13 *Mills v Cannon Brewery Co Ltd* [1920] 2 Ch 38; cf *Parker v Boggon* [1947] KB 346, [1947] 1 All ER 46; *Rayburn v Wolff* (1985) 50 P & CR 463 (absentee American attorney resident in Washington).
14 *Wilson v Fynn* [1948] 2 All ER 40.
15 *Lee v K Carter Ltd*, supra; *Swanson v Forton*, supra; *Dollar v Winston* [1950] Ch 236, [1949] 2 All ER 1088, n.; cf. *Thomas Bookman Ltd v Nathan* [1955] 1 WLR 815, [1955] 2 All ER 821; *Re Cooper's Lease* (1968) 19 P & CR 541; *Brann v Westminster Anglo Continental Investment Co Ltd*, supra; *West Layton Ltd v Ford*, supra; cf. *Deverall v Wyndham* [1989] 1 EGLR 57 (unreasonable).
16 *Norfolk Capital Group Ltd v Kitway Ltd* [1977] QB 506; *Bickel v Duke of Westminster*, supra. See also *Welch v Birrane* (1974) 29 P & CR 102; *Leeward Securities Ltd v Lilyheath Properties Ltd*, supra. For the Leasehold Reform Act 1967, see pp. 490 et seq, post.
17 *Re Town Investments Ltd Underlease* [1954] Ch 301, [1954] 1 All ER 585.
18 *Pimms Ltd v Tallow Chandlers in the City of London*, supra.
19 *Orlando Investments Ltd v Grosvenor Estates Belgravia* [1989] 2 EGLR 74; [1989] Conv 371 (P. F. Smith); cf. *Farr v Ginnings* (1928) 44 TLR 249.
20 *Oil Property Investment Ltd v Olympia & York Canary Wharf Ltd* [1993] EGCS 129.
 1 *Young v Ashley Gardens Properties* [1903] 2 Ch 112 at 115; *Parker v Boggan* [1947] KB 346, [1947] 1 All ER 461. See Housing Act 1985, ss. 94 (6), 98 (4), 99 (2), which reverse the rule in the case of secure tenancies (p. 487, post).
 2 *Frederick Berry Ltd v Royal Bank of Scotland* [1949] 1 KB 619 at 623, [1949] 1 All ER 706 at 708.

time of the hearing? In *Bromley Park Garden Estates Ltd v Moss*[3] SLADE LJ thought that there was much to be said for the view that he should not be allowed to do so, but on the assumption that he were so allowed,[4] he added a proviso that the landlord could only rely on those reasons which actually influenced his mind when he refused his consent.[5]

6. Test objective or subjective No decisive answer has yet been given to the fundamental question whether the test of reasonableness is objective and not subjective, as some affirm,[6] but others deny.[7] Must the court merely inquire whether the landlord's refusal of consent is in fact unreasonable? Or, must it also consider what influenced his mind in reaching his decision? This difference of opinion is not purely academic, for if the state of his mind is relevant, certain difficult problems will inevitably arise.

For instance, if the landlord has justified his refusal on some unsupportable ground he will presumably be unable at the date of the trial to rely upon an alternative and better ground. Again, a refusal will apparently be ineffectual if, though justifiable in the circumstances, it is justified on inadmissible grounds, as for instance where the proposed assignee is in fact an undischarged bankrupt, but the landlord's only declared objection is to his religion.

It is submitted that the question must be approached objectively, and that, as it has been aptly put, the landlord's "mental processes or uttered words" are irrelevant.

In short, what must be tested for unreasonableness is the withholding and not the landlord, the act and not the man.[8]

7. Racial discrimination The Race Relations Act 1976 provides that it is unlawful to discriminate on racial grounds by withholding consent.[9] This provision does not apply if the person withholding consent, or a near relative of his, resides and intends to continue to reside on the premises, there is shared accommodation, and the premises are small premises.[10]

(iii) Building leases It is also provided by the Landlord and Tenant Act 1927 that in the case of a lease for more than 40 years made in consideration of the erection or the substantial improvement, alteration or addition of buildings, the tenant may, notwithstanding a prohibition of assignment without the lessor's consent, assign the premises without such consent, provided that the assignment is made more than seven years before the end of the term, and provided that within six months after its completion it is notified in writing to the lessor.[11]

---

3 [1982] 1 WLR 1019 at 1034, [1982] 2 All ER 890 at 902; *CIN Properties Ltd v Gill* [1993] 37 EG 152 (landlord so allowed; Landlord and Tenant Act 1988, s. 1 (3) (*a*), p. 415, ante).
4 *Parker v Boggon*, supra; *Sonnenthal v Newton* (1965) 109 SJ 333; *Welch v Birrane* (1974) 29 P & CR 102.
5 *Rossi v Hestdrive Ltd* [1985] 1 EGLR 50.
6 *Re Smith's Lease* [1951] 1 All ER 346 at 349, per ROXBURGH J.
7 *Lovelock v Margo* [1963] 2 QB 786 at 789, [1963] 2 All ER 13 at 15, per Lord DENNING MR.
8 (1963) 79 LQR 479 at 482 (R.E.M.). See *Deverall v Wyndham* [1989] 1 EGLR 57; (1989) 139 NLJ 413 (H. W. Wilkinson).
9 S. 24. For the meaning of racial discrimination, see ss. 1, 2 and 3. See also Sex Discrimination Act 1975, s. 31.
10 S. 24 (2). For the definition of small premises, see s. 22 (2).
11 S. 19 (1) (*b*). This section does not apply if the lessor is a Government department, a local or public authority, or a statutory or public utility company; *Vaux Group plc v Lilley* [1991] 1 EGLR 60.

(iv) Rule in Dumpor's Case The rule at common law as laid down in *Dumpor's Case*[12] is that a condition is an entire and indivisible thing and therefore incapable of enforcement if once the person entitled to enforce it has allowed it to be disregarded. The effect of this doctrine was that, if a lease from A to B contained a covenant or condition against assigning without licence, and A permitted B to assign to C, A's right to stop further assignments was utterly gone. When once consent had been given to an assignment, the term became freely assignable. Again, and as a result of the same doctrine, if a lease was made to several lessees, upon condition that neither they nor any one of them should assign without a licence, a licence given to one of the lessees destroyed the condition with regard to the others. Again, if a tenant was allowed to assign part of the land leased, the condition ceased to apply to the whole of the land. This absurd doctrine was, however, abrogated by statute[13] in 1859 so far as conditions contained in leases were concerned, and the present position is regulated by the Law of Property Act 1925.[14] This provides that:

> where a licence is granted to a lessee to do any act, the licence, unless otherwise expressed, extends only
>
> (a) to the permission actually given; or
> (b) to the specific breach of any provision or covenant referred to; or
> (c) to any other matter thereby specifically authorised to be done;
>
> and the licence does not prevent any proceeding for any subsequent breach unless otherwise specified in the licence.

Moreover, it is enacted that where a lease contains a covenant or condition against assigning or doing any other act without licence, and a licence is granted to one or more of several lessees, or is granted in respect of part only of the property, it shall not operate to extinguish the lessor's remedy in case the covenant is broken either by the other lessees or with regard to the rest of the property.[15]

The result is that the rule in *Dumpor's Case* no longer applies to leases.

(5) THE USUAL COVENANTS

Although there are many other covenants which may figure in a lease, those that are normally found have been mentioned. It should be noticed that, where the lease is preceded by a contract for a lease,[16] there is an implied term of the contract that it shall include the *usual covenants*. It was generally considered, on the authority of *Hampshire v Wickens*,[17] that the only covenants by a tenant which could be described as "usual" were:

> to pay rent;
> to pay tenant's rates and taxes;
> to keep and deliver up the premises in repair;
> to allow the lessor to enter and view the state of repair;

---

12 (1603) 4 Co Rep 119b; *Smith's Leading Cases* (13th edn), vol. i. p. 35; Holdsworth, *History of English Law*, vol. vii. p. 282. In *GMS Syndicate v Gary Elliott Ltd* [1982] Ch 1, [1981] 1 All ER 619, NOURSE J relied on *Dumpor's Case* as establishing that a landlord can in certain circumstances forfeit a lease in part only; p. 440, post.
13 LP(A)A 1859, s. 1.
14 S. 143 (1).
15 LPA 1925, s. 143 (3).
16 P. 374, ante.
17 (1878) 7 Ch D 555 at 561, per JESSEL MR; *Charalambous v Ktori* [1972] 1 WLR 951, [1972] 3 All ER 701.

and that the covenant for quiet enjoyment was the only usual covenant binding the lessor.

It has now been decided, however, that the list is neither fixed nor closed. The question whether particular covenants are usual is a question of fact dependent upon the circumstances of each case, which can be resolved only after considering the evidence of conveyancers, the books of precedents, the practice in the particular district and the character of the property.[18]

SECTION VI REMEDIES OF THE LANDLORD FOR THE ENFORCEMENT OF THE COVENANTS

From the point of view of remedies, the covenant to pay rent must be distinguished from all other covenants entered into by the tenant. These two classes will now be treated separately.

A. COVENANT TO PAY RENT

(1) MEANING OF RENT

A rent is either a rentservice or a rentcharge.

(a) Rentservice

Rentservice consists of an annual return, made by the tenant in labour, money or provisions, in retribution for the land that passes,[19] and this is the rent which is due whenever a tenant holds his lands of a reversioner.[20] A reversion is an estate that arises by operation of law whenever the owner of an estate carves a smaller estate, called a *particular estate*, out of it in favour of another. The residue of the estate continues in him that made the particular estate.[1]

Thus, where lands are leased at a rent for a term of years, the lessor is the *reversioner* and the rent payable by the tenant is called a *rentservice*.

Since rentservice is that rent which is due from a tenant who holds of a reversioner, it follows that rent which is reserved on the grant of an estate in fee simple cannot be a rentservice, for since *Quia Emptores* 1290 such a grantee no longer holds of the grantor, but is substituted for him.[2] There is no reversion, no residue left in the grantor.

The origin of the term rentservice lies far back in legal history. Originally the services due from a tenant took many forms, but in course of time they were commuted into fixed money payments called rents service, since they represented the services that formerly issued out of the land. If the tenant failed to perform the services or to pay the rent into which they had been commuted, the lord enjoyed of common right, i.e. independently of statute or agreement, the remedy of distress, a feudal institution of very ancient

---

18 *Flexman v Corbett* [1930] 1 Ch 672. For usual covenants where there was a contract for a lease of garage workshops in Chelsea in 1971, see *Chester v Buckingham Travel Ltd* [1981] 1 WLR 96, [1981] 1 All ER 386; (1981) 97 LQR 385 (G. Woodman).

19 *Gilbert on Rents*, p. 9. For the history of the subject, see *Holdsworth, History of English Law*, vol. vii. pp. 262 et seq.

20 Litt, s. 213.

1 Co Litt 22*b*.

2 P. 14, ante.

origin, which entitled him to seize cattle and other chattels found upon the land. This remedy existed of common right only where the distrainor had an interest in the shape of a reversion in the land upon which the chattels lay, for otherwise it could scarcely be said with justice that there was anything he was entitled to seize.[3]

Today rent is regarded as a contractual sum to which a landlord becomes entitled for the use of his land, and, therefore, "the time and manner of the payment is to be ascertained according to the true construction of the contract, and not by reference to out-dated relics of medieval law".[4] As Lord DIPLOCK said:[5]

> The mediaeval concept of rent as a service rendered by the tenant to the landlord has been displaced by the modern concept of a payment ... for the use of his land. The mediaeval concept has, however, left as its only surviving relic the ancient remedy of distress.

(b) Rentcharge

From a rentservice must be distinguished a rentcharge. This differs from rentservice in that its owner has no tenurial interest in the land out of which it is payable, and having no such interest, is not entitled as of common right to the remedy of distress. It is, then, any rent *expressly* made payable out of land, other than rent payable by a tenant to a reversioner. For instance, if A sells land to B in fee simple, he may agree to accept an annual sum of money from B in perpetuity instead of a lump sum down, and it is expressly agreed that the fee simple estate shall be charged in favour of A with a power of distress should the rent fall into arrears, the rent (whatever name may be given to it by local usage, such as quit rent, ground rent, chief rent, etc.) is a rentcharge.

> It is called a rentcharge because the land for payment thereof is charged with a distresse.[6]

(c) Rentseck

Formerly, if a rent was made payable out of a fee simple and for some reason an express power of distress was not reserved, the rent was called a *rentseck* or dry rent—*dry* because it did not confer the power to distrain.[7]

---

3 Litt, s. 213; Gilbert, p. 9; Co Litt 78*b*, 142*b*; Bacon Abr tit Rent (A) 1.
4 *CH Bailey Ltd v Memorial Enterprises Ltd* [1974] 1 WLR 728 at 732, [1974] 1 All ER 1003 at 1007, per Lord DENNING MR, approved in *United Scientific Holdings Ltd v Burnley Borough Council* [1978] AC 904 at 956, [1977] 2 All ER 62 at 93, per Lord SALMON; *T and E Homes Ltd v Robinson* [1979] 1 WLR 452, [1979] 2 All ER 522; *Bradshaw v Pawley* [1980] 1 WLR 10, [1979] 3 All ER 273 (rent payable under contract from a date prior to execution of lease). See also *Property Holding Co Ltd v Clark* [1948] 1 KB 630 at 648, [1948] 1 All ER 165 at 173, per EVERSHED LJ; [1991] Conv 270 (R. G. Lee).
   For further emphasis on the contractual nature of a lease, see *National Carriers Ltd v Panalpina (Northern) Ltd* [1981] AC 675, [1981] 1 All ER 161, p. 462, post (frustration); *Hammersmith and Fulham London Borough Council v Monk* [1992] 1 AC 478, [1992] 1 All ER 1; p. 467 (notice to quit by one of two joint landlords); *Hussein v Mehlman* [1992] 2 EGLR 87; p. 464, post (repudiation).
5 *United Scientific Holdings Ltd v Burnley Borough Council*, supra, at 935, at 76.
6 Co Litt 144*a*. See also *Jenkin R Lewis Ltd v Kerman* [1971] Ch 477 at 484, [1970] 1 All ER 833 at 838. On rentcharges, see chapter 20, post.
7 Litt, s. 218.

Thus, at common law the three kinds of rent are rentservice, rentcharge and rentseck. But rentsseck have long ceased to exist, for the inability of their owners to distrain was removed by the Landlord and Tenant Act 1730,[8] which enacted that the owners of rentsseck, rents of assize and chief rents should have the same remedy by distress as was available to the owner of a rentservice.

LINDLEY LJ said:

> Bearing in mind what was done by the Act of Geo. II, which by section 5 gave a power of distress for all rents, there is now no magic in the word rentcharge. Whether you speak of a rentcharge or only of a rent, if it is a rent and not merely a sum covenanted to be paid, seems to me to be utterly immaterial, because under the Act of Geo. II you have a power of distress in respect of it.[9]

The same remedy is given by the Law of Property Act 1925.[10] For the purpose of this Act, "rent"

> includes a rentservice or a rentcharge, or other rent, toll, duty, royalty, or annual or periodical payment, in money or money's worth, reserved or issuing out of or charged upon land, but does not include mortgage interest.[11]

This is not the place to elaborate the subject of rentcharges.[12] The historical difference between them and rentservice has been demonstrated, and we may now proceed to set out the remedies that are available to a landlord for the recovery of the rentservice due to him.

(2) DISTRESS

The right of distress which has existed in England since the Conquest was originally allowed for the enforcement of a great number of services that in feudal days might be incidental to tenure, such as rentservice, suit-service, heriot-service, aids, reliefs and so on, but most of these are now obsolete, and practically the only purpose for which common law distress is exercisable is the recovery of rent in arrear.[13] It is not dependent on an express right of re-entry, and the landlord is entitled to exercise it unless he contracts not to do so.[14]

The value of the remedy to a landlord is that he can seize and sell the chattels found on the land and thus procure the rent without the necessity of taking legal proceedings. It is a self-help remedy[15] which operates outside the machinery of the courts except in the case of tenancies subject to the Rent Acts. In 1969 the Payne Committee recommended the abolition of "the highly complex technical and archaic law" of distress for rent.[16] This was

8 S. 5.
9 *Re Lord Gerard and Beecham's Contract* [1894] 3 Ch 295 at 313.
10 S. 121.
11 S. 205 (1) (xxiii).
12 See chapter 20, p. 645, post.
13 The common law right to recover compensation by way of distress for damage caused by trespassing livestock was replaced by a statutory provision for detention and sale: Animals Act 1971, s. 7.
14 *T and E Homes Ltd v Robinson* [1979] 1 WLR 452 at 453, [1979] 2 All ER 522 at 527, per TEMPLEMAN LJ.
15 At common law he could only retain the goods: a power of sale was given by the Distress for Rent Act 1689, s. 1.
16 Report of the Committee on the Enforcement of Judgment Debts (1969), Cmnd 3909, paras 912–932; see also Law Com. Interim Report on Distress for Rent (1966); Law Com. Report on Rentcharges 1975 (Law Com. No. 68), para 94.

also the view of the Law Commission in 1991, which, however, recommended[17] that distress should not be abolished until improvements to the court system make the other remedies available to landlords effective alternatives to distress.

It is essential that the reversion should be vested in the distrainor at the time when the rent falls due and also when the distress is levied.

Thus if L has assigned the reversion to X at a time when rent is due, L cannot distrain, since he no longer holds the reversion; and X is under the same disability, since he was not the reversioner at the critical moment.

(a) Time and place

Distress cannot be made until the rent is in arrear, which does not occur until the day after it is due,[18] nor can it be levied between sunset and sunrise.[19]

As a general rule the right of seizure is confined to chattels upon the actual land out of which the rent issues, but it may be extended by agreement to other premises, and by the Distress for Rent Act 1737 goods which have been fraudulently and secretly removed by a tenant after the rent became due, in order to avoid distress, may be seized by the landlord within 30 days wherever found.

A distrainor must enter the demised premises[20] and in so doing may commit what in anyone else would be a trespass,[1] as for example by entry through an unlocked door;[2] but he may neither break open a door, whether of a dwelling-house or of an outhouse,[3] nor effect an entrance through a closed but unfastened window.[4]

(b) Distrainable goods

The general rule of the common law is that all personal chattels found upon the premises out of which the rent issues, whether they belong to the tenant or to a stranger, can be distrained, but this extensive power is cut down in two ways.

(i) Privileged goods It is outside the scope of this work to deal with this question in detail, and the reader is referred to the notes given in Smith's *Leading Cases* to *Simpson v Hartopp*.[5] It will suffice here to say that the following articles are absolutely privileged in the sense that they can never be seized:

> machinery belonging to a third person which is on an agricultural holding under a contract of hire;[6]

---

17 Report on Distress for Rent (Law Com. No. 194, HC 138). See [1985] Conv 451 (A. Hill-Smith) and (1985) Law Notes 21 (M. Maddock), arguing that distress is speedier and more comprehensive than an action for the arrears of rent.
18 *Duppa v Mayo* (1669) 1 Wms Saund 275; *Re Aspinall* [1961] Ch 526, [1961] 2 All ER 751.
19 *Tutton v Darke* (1860) 29 LJ Ex 271.
20 *Evans v South Ribble Borough Council* [1992] QB 757, [1992] 2 All ER 695; [1993] Conv 77 (J. E. M. Sulek) (posting draft walking possession agreement and distress notice through letter-box in sealed envelope insufficient).
1 *Long v Clarke* [1894] 1 QB 119 at 122.
2 *Southam v Smout* [1964] 1 QB 308, [1963] 3 All ER 104.
3 *American Concentrated Must Corpn v Hendry* (1893) 62 LJQB 388.
4 *Nash v Lucas* (1867) LR 2 QB 590.
5 (1744) Willes 512; *Smith's Leading Cases* (13th edn), vol. i. p. 137.
6 Agricultural Holdings Act 1986, s. 18.

livestock belonging to a third person which is on an agricultural holding solely for breeding purposes;[7]
animals *ferae naturae*;
things delivered to a person in the way of his trade, such as cloth given to a tailor to be made into a suit;
things in actual use, such as a horse drawing a cart;
things in the custody of the law, such as property already taken in execution;
clothes and bedding belonging to the tenant and his family up to a total value of £100;[8]
tools and implements of the tenant's trade up to a total value of £150, if not in actual use.[9]

The following things are conditionally privileged, that is to say, they can be seized only if there is not a sufficiency of other distrainable goods to be found upon the premises:

beasts of the plough;
sheep and instruments of husbandry;
the instruments of a man's trade or profession, such as the text-books of a solicitor;
the livestock of a third person found on the land of an agricultural tenant as a result of a contract of agistment.[10]

(ii) Goods belonging to third parties BLACKBURN J said:

The general rule at common law was that whatever was found upon the demised premises, whether belonging to a stranger or not, might be seized by the landlord and held as a distress till the rent was paid or the service performed. This state of things produced no harm, because at common law the landlord not being able to sell the distress he generally gave up the goods as soon as he found they were not the tenant's, as his continuing to hold them would not induce the tenant to pay. But in the reign of William and Mary a very harsh and unjust law was passed by which the right was given to the landlord to sell any goods seized, and to apply the proceeds to the payment of the rent unless the tenant or the owner of the goods first paid it; and this held out a great temptation to a landlord to seize the goods of a stranger although he knew they were not the tenant's.[11]

This has gradually been put on a more equitable footing, and at the present day the Law of Distress Amendment Act 1908,[12] except in the case of certain specified goods,[13] provides a means by which a lodger or under-tenant or indeed any person not being a tenant of the premises and not having any beneficial interest in the tenancy, may avoid the seizure of his belongings. Suppose for instance that:

7 Agricultural Holdings Act 1986, s. 18.
8 Protection from Execution (Prescribed Value) Order 1980 (S.I. 1980 No. 26), art. 2 (*a*).
9 Ibid., art. 2 (*b*).
10 Agricultural Holdings Act 1986, s. 18. If distrained because of an insufficiency of other goods the landlord cannot thereby recover more than the amount due and unpaid under the contract of agistment.
11 *Lyons v Elliott* (1876) 1 QBD 210 at 213.
12 S. 1.
13 I.e. goods belonging to the husband or wife of the tenant; goods comprised in a bill of sale, hire-purchase agreement or settlement made by the tenant; and goods of which the tenant is the reputed owner: *Perdana Properties Bhd v United Orient Leasing Co Sdn Bhd* [1981] 1 WLR 1496, [1982] 1 All ER 193.

L has leased premises to T, and that X is the lodger or the under-tenant of T. If in such a case L levies a distress on any goods belonging to X for arrears of rent due from T, X may serve L with a notice declaring that:

> T has no right of property in the goods;
> the goods are not goods excepted from the Act;
> so much rent is due from X to T;
> future instalments will become due on stated days;
> he will pay such rent to L.

With this notice, which is of no effect unless it contains the requisite written declarations,[14] X must also send an inventory of his goods. If L distrains on the goods of X after receipt of this notice and inventory, he is guilty of an illegal distress, and X may apply to a justice of the peace or to a magistrate for the restoration of his goods. The protection afforded by the Act applies only to a tenant whose rent equals the full annual value of the premises.

(c) Levying of distress

A landlord may distrain in person, or by employing a certificated bailiff, who has been authorized to levy distress (either in the one particular case or in general cases) by a certificate in writing under the hand of a county court judge.[15]

Such a bailiff should be provided by the landlord with a distress warrant authorizing him to make the levy. The first step is to seize and impound the goods. At common law the impounding had to take place off the premises but now it is lawful to secure the goods in some part of the premises themselves.[16]

The usual practice is to leave a man in possession, but this is not essential, for goods are deemed to be impounded if what is called "walking possession" is taken of them, i.e. if they are left on the premises but periodically inspected by the bailiff.[17] Anyone who interferes with goods after they have been impounded is liable in treble damages for pound breach.[18] As soon as the seizure is complete, the landlord is bound to give the tenant[19] notice of the distress and of the place, if any, to which the goods have been removed,[20] and he is not at liberty to sell them until five days have elapsed since the service of the notice. Thus a tenant is allowed five days within which to pay what is due, but he is entitled to an extension of this period to 15 days if he makes a request in writing to this effect to the landlord and gives security for any additional expense that the delay may involve.[1] The sale is generally though not necessarily by auction, and it usually takes place on the premises

---

14 *Druce & Co Ltd v Beaumont Property Trust Ltd* [1935] 2 KB 257. It may be signed by an agent: *Lawrence Chemical Co Ltd v Rubinstein* [1982] 1 WLR 284, [1982] 1 All ER 653. See *Rhodes v Allied Dunbar Pension Services Ltd* [1987] 1 WLR 1703.
15 Law of Distress Amendment Act 1888, s. 7; Distress for Rent Rules 1988 (S.I. 1988 No. 2050), rr. 3–5. See also *Rhodes v Allied Dunbar Pension Services Ltd* [1989] 1 WLR 800, [1989] 1 All ER 1161.
16 Distress for Rent Act 1737, s. 10.
17 *Lavell v O'Leary* [1933] 2 KB 200.
18 Distress for Rent Act 1689, s. 3 (1).
19 Ibid., s. 1; Distress for Rent Rules 1988 (S.I. 1988 No. 2050), r. 12 Appx. 2 Form 7.
20 Distress for Rent Act 1737, s. 9.
 1 Law of Distress Amendment Act 1888, s. 6.

unless the tenant has requested in writing that the goods shall be removed to a public auction-room. If it does not produce sufficient proceeds, no second sale is as a general rule permissible.[2]

Only six years' arrears of rent may be recovered by the remedy of distress, whether or not the lease is by deed.[3] When the demised premises consist of an agricultural holding only one year's arrears are recoverable by this method.[4]

(d) Amount recoverable

The tenant may set off any sums due to him from the landlord against a claim to levy distress. Otherwise a landlord would be able to recover more by distress than he could in an action for the debt.[4a]

(3) ACTION FOR ARREARS OF RENT

(a) Arrears recoverable

Whether a lease is made by deed or not, only six years' arrears of rent are recoverable by action.[5] Thus a landlord must bring his action within six years after the rent has become due or has been acknowledged in writing to be due, or after some payment has been made by the tenant.[6] A payment of part of the rent does not entitle the landlord to sue for the remainder more than six years after it became due.[7]

But while the relation of landlord and tenant continues under a lease for a fixed term of years, the right of the landlord to recover rent is not *totally* barred by non-payment no matter how long the rent is in arrear.[8] Suppose, for instance, that:

A holds lands of B for 99 years at £100 a year, and that A has not paid rent for 25 years. B's right to recover rent is not extinguished, but is limited to the recovery of the last six years' arrears.

The only case in which the right of a landlord is extinguished altogether occurs where for a period of 12 years the rent has been paid to a third person who wrongfully claims to be entitled to the reversion.[9]

(b) Inter-relation of remedies

The rule is that a landlord cannot pursue the two remedies of action and distress at one and the same time. If he has levied a distress, he cannot bring an action for recovery until he has sold the distrained articles and found the purchase money insufficient to satisfy his demand.[10] If he has sued to judgment first, then, even though the judgment remains unsatisfied, he loses his remedy of distress altogether for that particular rent.[11]

2 *Rawlence and Squarey v Spicer* [1935] 1 KB 412.
3 Limitation Act 1980, s. 19.
4 Agricultural Holdings Act 1986, s. 16.
4a *Eller v Grovecrest Investments Ltd* [1994] EGCS 28.
5 Limitation Act 1980, s. 19.
6 Limitation Act 1980, s. 29 (5).
7 Ibid., s. 29 (6).
8 *Grant v Ellis* (1841) 9 M & W 113; *Archbold v Scully* (1861) 9 HL Cas 360.
9 *Lehain v Philpott* (1875) LR 10 Exch 242; pp. 901–3, post.
10 *Archbold v Scully*, supra.
11 *Chancellor v Webster* (1893) 9 TLR 568.

(4) FORFEITURE

(a) Right to forfeit

(i) Distinction between covenant and conditions The breach of a covenant by
a tenant does not entitle the lessor to resume possession by a re-entry upon
the premises, unless the right to do so is expressly reserved in the lease. On
the other hand, an undertaking by the tenant which is framed not as a mere
covenant, but as a condition, carries with it at common law a right of re-
entry if the condition is broken. Whether a stipulation amounts to a covenant
or a condition is sometimes a question of considerable nicety, but it depends
entirely upon the intention of the parties. A condition is a clause which shows
a clear intention on the part of the landlord, not merely that the tenant shall
be personally liable if he fails in his contractual duties, but that the lease shall
determine in the event of such a failure. The tenancy is to remain conditional
upon the fulfilment by the tenant of his obligations. In an early case,
BAYLEY J said:

> In a lease for years no precise form of words is necessary to make a condition. It is
> sufficient if it appears that the words used were intended to have the effect of
> creating a condition. They must be the words of the landlord, because he is to
> impose the condition.[12]

In this case it was "stipulated and conditioned" in the lease that the tenant
should not assign or underlet the premises, otherwise than to his wife or
children, and it was held that these words were sufficient to create a condition.
Mere words of agreement, however, as for example when the tenant "agrees
that he will not assign the premises without the consent of the landlord",
create nothing more than a covenant.[13]

(ii) Express proviso for re-entry and forfeiture of lease It is, however, the
usual practice for a lease to contain, in clear and unmistakable language, an
express clause which reserves to the lessor the right of re-entry if one or more
of the covenants are broken, and which provides that upon re-entry the lease
shall be forfeited.[14] The virtue of this is that the lessor, if he finds himself
saddled with an impecunious tenant who is a persistent defaulter in the
payment of rent, may regain possession instead of being driven to constant
litigation.

The following is a precedent of a proviso for forfeiture:

> Provided always that if any part of the said rent shall be in arrears for 21 days,
> whether lawfully demanded or not, the lessor or his assigns may re-enter upon the
> said premises, and immediately thereupon the said term shall absolutely determine.

(b) Effect of breach

In such a case the effect of allowing the rent to fall into arrears for more than
21 days is to render the tenant's interest liable to forfeiture, and not ipso facto
to cause a forfeiture. However clearly the proviso may state that the lease

---

12 *Doe d Henniker v Watt* (1828) 8 B & C 308 at 315.
13 *Crawley v Price* (1875) LR 10 QB 302.
14 See *Richard Clarke & Co Ltd v Widnall* (1976) 33 P & CR 339, where a clause in a lease under
   which the landlord was entitled to serve a notice to terminate in the event of a breach of
   covenant to pay rent was construed as a proviso for re-entry. Cf *Clays Lane Housing Co-
   operative Ltd v Patrick* (1984) 49 P & CR 72 (for a clause to be a forfeiture clause it must bring
   the lease to an end earlier than the actual termination date).

shall be void on breach of condition, it has been held in a long series of decisions that its only effect is to render the lease voidable.[15] It is at the option of the landlord whether the tenancy shall be determined or not, and it is only if he does some unequivocal act which shows his intention to end it that the lease will be avoided.[16] Thus an actual entry by the landlord[17] or the grant of a lease to a new tenant works a forfeiture,[18] but the usual practice at the present day is to sue for the recovery of possession instead of making a re-entry;[19] for, as WILLES J said:

> The bringing of an action of ejectment is equivalent to the ancient entry. It is an act unequivocal in the sense that it asserts the right of possession upon every ground that may turn out to be available to the party claiming to re-enter.[20]

It is the service of the writ for possession, and not its issue which is equivalent to re-entry.[1] But the forfeiture does not become final until the landlord has obtained judgment for possession. Until then, for example, the covenants in a lease remain potentially good, since the forfeiture may not be established; or relief against forfeiture may be granted to the tenant, in which case the lease is re-established as from the beginning.[2] But where an application for relief is pending the position appears to be one-sided. As STEPHENSON LJ said:[3]

> A landlord who has unequivocally elected to determine a lease by serving a writ and forfeiting it cannot himself rely on any covenants of the lease in any shape or form, or any covenants in it, but the tenant who has not elected to determine the lease can do so.

The landlord may forfeit a lease in respect of part only of the premises where that part is physically separate and capable of being distinctly let.[4]

(c) Waiver of right to forfeit

The question whether the landlord has by some unequivocal act elected to treat the lease as forfeited is an important one from the point of view of

---

15 *Davenport v R* (1877) 3 App Cas 115 at 128.
16 *Toleman v Portbury* (1871) LR 6 QB 245 at 250; *Eaton Square Properties Ltd v Beveridge* [1993] EGCS 91 ("there can hardly be a more unequivocal act than changing the locks").
17 See *Hone v Daejan Properties Ltd* (1976) 239 EG 427, where re-entry by a landlord who had taken an assignment of his tenant's mortgage did not effect a forfeiture. He was "wearing two hats" (of landlord and mortgagee in possession) and that was equivocal.
18 But not an agreement with a sub-lessee that he remain in occupation as tenant of a term of an *existing* sub-lease: *Ashton v Sobelman* [1987] 1 WLR 177, [1987] 1 All ER 755.
19 In the case of tenancies of residential premises a re-entry other than pursuant to a court order for possession is prohibited. See p. 486, post.
20 *Grimwood v Moss* (1872) LR 7 CP 360 at 364.
1 *Canas Property Co Ltd v KL Television Services Ltd* [1970] 2 QB 433, [1970] 2 All ER 795; *Richards v De Freitas* (1975) 29 P & CR 1; *Ashton v Sobelman* [1987] 1 WLR 177, [1987] 1 All ER 755; *Hammersmith and Fulham London Borough Council v Top Shop Centres Ltd* [1990] Ch 237, [1989] 2 All ER 655; *Capital and City Holdings Ltd v Dean Warburg Ltd* (1988) 58 P & CR 346.
2 *Driscoll v Church Comrs for England* [1957] 1 QB 330 at 339, [1956] 3 All ER 802 at 806, per DENNING LJ. For the effect of relief against forfeiture, see p. 431, post.
3 *Peninsular Maritime Ltd v Padseal Ltd* (1981) 259 EG 860 at 866. See also *Meadows v Clerical Medical and General Life Assurance Society* [1981] Ch 70, [1980] 1 All ER 454; *Associated Deliveries Ltd v Harrison* (1984) 50 P & CR 91; *Official Custodian for Charities v Mackey (No. 2)* [1985] 1 WLR 1308, [1985] 2 All ER 1016; *Hillgate House Ltd v Expert Clothing Service & Sales Ltd* [1987] 1 EGLR 65.
4 *GMS Syndicate Ltd v Gary Elliott Ltd* [1982] Ch 1, [1981] 1 All ER 619, p. 440, post.

waiver. Common law dislikes conditions of forfeiture, and it will always treat such a condition as waived and therefore unenforceable if, after the act of forfeiture has been committed, the landlord clearly shows that he regards the tenancy as still existing. The two essentials for waiver are that:

1. the landlord must be aware of the commission of an act of forfeiture by the tenant, and
2. he must do "some unequivocal act recognizing the continued existence of the lease."[5]

Thus a merely passive attitude on his part has no effect,[6] nor does his failure to take action because he thinks that he will not be able to prove a suspected breach of covenant;[7] but on the other hand (and this applies to all conditions of forfeiture, whether in respect of the non-payment of rent or of the non-performance of other covenants), a waiver will be implied if a landlord, with knowledge of the breach.[8]

1. demands or sues for rent,[9] or accepts payment of it notwithstanding that his acceptance is stated to be "without prejudice",[10] or a clerk of his agents accepts it by mistake;[11] or
2. distrains for rent whether due before or after the breach,[12] or
3. grants a new lease to the defaulting tenant.[13]

It is a question of fact whether money has been tendered and accepted as rent,[14] and its acceptance as such is in law conclusive against the landlord. Intention is irrelevant.

As Lord DENNING MR said:

> It does not matter that the landlords did not intend to waive. The very fact that they accepted the rent with the knowledge constitutes the waiver.[15]

---

5 *Matthews v Smallwood* [1910] 1 Ch 777 at 786, per PARKER J; M & B p. 500; *Dendy v Nicholl* (1858) 4 CBNS 376.
6 *Perry v Davis* (1858) 3 CBNS 769.
7 *Chrisdell Ltd v Johnson* [1987] 2 EGLR 123.
8 *Metropolitan Properties Co Ltd v Cordery* (1979) 39 P & CR 10 (landlords' acceptance of rent for flat with knowledge, through their porters, of facts which pointed to breach of covenant held to be waiver). Cf *Trustees of Henry Smith's Charity v Willson* [1983] QB 316, [1983] 1 All ER 73 (uncommunicated rent demand); *Official Custodian for Charities v Parway Estates Developments Ltd* [1985] Ch 151, [1984] 3 All ER 679 (publication in London Gazette of compulsory liquidation held not to be imputed knowledge so as to constitute waiver).
9 *Dendy v Nicholl*, supra; dist. *Clarke v Grant* [1950] 1 KB 104, [1949] 1 All ER 768.
10 *Segal Securities Ltd v Thoseby* [1963] 1 QB 887, [1963] 1 All ER 500.
11 *Central Estates (Belgravia) Ltd v Woolgar (No. 2)* [1972] 1 WLR 1048, [1972] 3 All ER 610. See also *Expert Clothing Service & Sales Ltd v Hillgate House Ltd* [1986] Ch 340, [1985] 2 All ER 998 (proffering of negotiating document held not to be waiver where no acceptance of rent or demand for rent involved): *Church Comrs for England v Nodjoumi* (1985) 51 P & CR 155 (service of s. 146 notice held not to be waiver of right to forfeit lease on grounds other than those set out in notice); *Re National Jazz Centre Ltd* [1988] 2 EGLR 57 (mere entry into negotiations held not to be waiver).
12 *Doe d David v Williams* (1835) 7 C & P 322.
13 *Ward v Day* (1864) 5 B & S 359.
14 *John Lewis Properties plc v Viscount Chelsea* [1993] 34 EG 116 ("arguments very finely balanced").
15 *Windmill Investments (London) Ltd v Milano Restaurant Ltd* [1962] 2 QB 373, [1962] 2 All ER 680; see also *Bader Properties Ltd v Linley Property Investments Ltd* (1967) 19 P & CR 620 at 638–41; *Central Estates (Belgravia) Ltd v Woolgar (No. 2)*, supra; *David Blackstone Ltd v Burnetts (West End) Ltd* [1973] 1 WLR 1487, [1973] 3 All ER 782; *Welch v Birrane* (1974) 29 P & CR 102; (1988) 138 NLJ 95 (H. W. Wilkinson); *Van Haarlam v Kasner* [1992] 2 EGLR

The waiver of a covenant or of a condition does not operate as a general waiver, but extends only to the particular breach in question.[16] An important distinction should be noticed between continuing and non-continuing breaches of covenant, for acceptance of rent or the levy of distress after the breach of a continuing covenant, e.g. to keep in repair the premises,[17] waives the forfeiture only up to the date of distress or payment of rent. The proviso for re-entry may be enforced if the breach subsequently continues.[18]

But when once a landlord unequivocally and finally elects to treat a lease as void, as, for instance, where he serves a writ for recovery of the land, no subsequent receipt of rent or other act will amount to waiver so as to deprive him of his right to enforce the clause of re-entry.[19]

(d) Formal demand for rent

In the precedent which is set out above it will be noticed that the landlord reserves a power of re-entry for non-payment of rent *whether lawfully demanded or not*. The object of inserting these words is to avoid the strictness of the common law which requires the landlord, failing a contrary agreement, to make a formal demand upon the premises themselves for the exact amount of rent due, and to make it between the hours of sunrise and sunset so as to afford the tenant an opportunity of counting out the money while light remains.[20] This common law rule has, however, been partly abrogated by a statute which enacts that, even though the formal demand has not been dispensed with in the lease, yet, if one-half year's rent is in arrear and there are not sufficient distrainable goods upon the premises and a power of re-entry has been reserved, the landlord can recover the premises by action at the end of the period fixed in the proviso for re-entry without making any formal demand of rent.[1] The restricted nature of this statutory modification makes it desirable, in the interests of a sure and speedy remedy, to obviate by express words the necessity for a formal demand.

(e) Relief against forfeiture

One of the aims of the old Court of Chancery was to prevent the enforcement of a legal right from producing hardship, and therefore, since the sole object of a right of re-entry was to give a landlord security for the rent, it was always prepared to relieve the tenant against the forfeiture, provided that he paid all that was due by way of arrears of rent, together with costs and interest. In this way, the landlord obtained all that the right of re-entry was intended to secure to him, and it would be inequitable for him to take advantage of the forfeiture.[2]

Originally a tenant might petition for and obtain this relief at any time

59; [1993] Conv 288 (J. Martin); *Iperion Investments Corpn v Broadwalk House Residents Ltd* [1992] 2 EGLR 235.
16 LPA 1925, s. 148.
17 *Penton v Barnett* [1898] 1 QB 276; *Cooper v Henderson* (1982) 263 EG 592 (covenant as to user); *City and Westminster Properties (1934) Ltd v Mudd* [1959] Ch 129, [1959] 2 All ER 733; M & B 502; cf *Farimani v Gates* (1984) 271 EG 887.
18 *Doe d Hemmings v Durnford* (1832) 2 Cr & J 667; *Doe d Baker v Jones* (1850) 5 Exch 498.
19 *Civil Service Co-operative Society Ltd v McGrigor's Trustee* [1923] 2 Ch 347; *Evans v Enever* [1920] 2 KB 315.
20 Notes to *Duppa v Mayo* (1669) 1 Wms Saund 282 at 287.
1 Common Law Procedure Act 1852, s. 210.
2 *Howard v Fanshawe* [1895] 2 Ch 581; and authorities there cited.

after he had been ejected under the power of re-entry, but his right has been restricted by statute. The present position depends upon sections 210–212 of the Common Law Procedure Act 1852 and upon section 38 of the Supreme Court Act 1981.[3] The result of these Acts is as follows.

If the lessor sues for possession and the tenant at any time before the trial pays or tenders to the lessor or pays into court the rent and arrears and costs, all further proceedings are stayed and he regains possession under the old lease.[4] It has now been held, however, that there is no case for such a stay of proceedings unless six months' rent is in arrear.[5]

If the tenant does not, or cannot, take this opportunity and judgment is given against him, he may, nevertheless, apply for relief within six months after execution of the judgment.[6] If he applies within this period, the court is empowered to relieve him from the forfeiture subject to such terms and conditions as to payment of rent, costs and otherwise, as could formerly have been imposed by the old Court of Chancery. The effect of a grant of relief is that he holds the land according to the terms of the original lease without the necessity of a new lease.[7]

The grant of relief within this extended time of six months, however, is a matter of discretion, the general principle being that, so far as rent is concerned, the landlord can claim nothing more than to be restored to the position that he would have occupied had the forfeiture not been incurred. The position has been stated in the following authoritative passage:

> The function of the court in exercising this equitable jurisdiction is to grant relief when all that is due for rent and costs has been paid up, and (in general) to disregard any other causes of complaint that the landlord may have against the tenant. The question is whether, provided all is paid up, the landlord will not have been fully compensated; and the view taken by the court is that if he gets the whole of his rent and costs, then he has got all that he is entitled to so far as rent is concerned, and extraneous matters of breach of covenant, and so forth, are, generally speaking, irrelevant.[8]

Even so, however, exceptional circumstances may justify the refusal of relief, such as the inordinate conduct of the tenant himself or the fact that the landlord has altered his position in the belief that the forfeiture is effective. Thus, for instance, relief was refused to a tenant who did not apply until just before the six months had elapsed, by which time the landlord, after incurring expenditure upon the maintenance of the property, had "made an arrangement" to let another party into possession.[9]

If relief is granted upon conditions to be performed within a limited time,

---

3 Replacing Landlord and Tenant Act 1730, ss. 2, 4, and Supreme Court of Judicature (Consolidation) Act 1925, s. 46 respectively. A useful summary of the law is given by Sir Nicolas BROWNE-WILKINSON V-C in *Billson v Residential Apartments Ltd* [1992] 1 AC 494 at 510, [1991] 3 All ER 265 at 276.
4 Common Law Procedure Act 1852, s. 212. For a "trial" to come within the meaning of this section, it must be an effective trial binding on all the necessary parties: *Gill v Lewis* [1956] 2 QB 1, [1956] 1 All ER 844, where judgment was signed against only one of two joint tenants.
5 *Standard Pattern Co Ltd v Ivey* [1962] Ch 432, [1962] 1 All ER 452 criticized (1962) 78 LQR pp. 168–171 (R.E.M.).
6 Common Law Procedure Act 1852, ss. 210–212.
7 Supreme Court Act 1981, s. 38 (2).
8 *Gill v Lewis* [1956] 2 QB 1 at 13, [1956] 1 All ER 844 at 853, per JENKINS LJ. See also *Belgravia Insurance Co Ltd v Meah* [1964] 1 QB 436, [1963] 3 All ER 828.
9 *Stanhope v Haworth* (1886) 3 TLR 34.

the court has jurisdiction to extend the time if it is just and equitable to do so.[10]

Relief may be granted to the tenant where the landlord, instead of bringing an action for recovery of the land, enters into peaceable possession. In such a case the tenant cannot claim relief under the Act which only applies where the landlord sues for possession. He may, however, rely on the ancient inherent equitable jurisdiction of the court, and, provided that he acts with reasonable promptness, may obtain relief even if he brings his action more than six months after the landlord resumes possession.[11]

(f) Relief to under-lessees

Where a lease is forfeited, any under-leases created out of it automatically come to an end. But an under-lessee has the same right of applying to the court for relief against forfeiture of the head lease as the tenant has under the head lease.[12] The Law of Property Act 1925,[13] provides that where a head lessor proceeds by action or otherwise to enforce a forfeiture, the court may, on the application of an under-lessee, make an order vesting the whole or any part of the property in the under-lessee "for the whole term of the lease or any less term" upon such conditions as it thinks fit,[14] "but in no case shall any such under-lessee be entitled to require a lease to be granted to him for any longer term than he had under his original sub-lease".[15]

There is an important difference between relief granted to an under-lessee and relief granted to a tenant. In the case of the under-lessee a new term is created in him; the lease which has been forfeited is not revived and continued. Accordingly the rent from any under-lease is payable to the landlord between the forfeiture of the old lease and the creation of the new one.[16]

Relief is available to the mortgagee of a leasehold interest holding under a sub-demise or under a charge by way of legal mortgage,[17] and also to an

---

10 *Chandless-Chandless v Nicholson* [1942] 2 KB 321, [1942] 2 All ER 315.
11 *Howard v Fanshawe* [1895] 2 Ch 581; *Lovelock v Margo* [1963] 2 QB 786, [1963] 2 All ER 13; *Thatcher v CH Pearce & Sons (Contractors) Ltd* [1968] 1 WLR 748 (four days over six months); *Ladup Ltd v Williams & Glyn's Bank plc* [1985] 1 WLR 851, [1985] 2 All ER 577. See [1969] JPL pp. 251–252. See also *Billson v Residential Apartments Ltd* [1992] 1 AC 494 at 516, [1991] 3 All ER 256 at 276, where CA held that there was no similar inherent jurisdiction in the case of relief for breach of covenant other than the covenant to pay rent; p. 441, post.
 For the jurisdiction of the County Court to grant relief, see the County Courts Act 1984, s. 138, as amended by AJA 1985, s. 55; *United Dominions Trust Ltd v Shellpoint Trustees Ltd* [1993] 4 All ER 310 (containing a detailed examination of the sections).
12 Common Law Procedure Act 1852, s. 210; *Doe d Wyatt v Byron* (1845) 1 CB 623. See generally [1986] Conv 187 (S. Tromans).
13 S. 146 (4). This is the only part of s. 146 which applies to forfeiture for non-payment of rent.
14 See *Chatham Empire Theatre (1955) Ltd v Ultrans Ltd* [1961] 1 WLR 817, [1961] 2 All ER 381 (relief granted on payment of proportionate share of rent by applicant sub-lessees).
15 *Factors (Sundries) Ltd v Miller* [1952] 2 All ER 630; *Cadogan v Dimovic* [1984] 1 WLR 609, [1984] 2 All ER 168.
16 *Official Custodian for Charities v Mackey* [1985] Ch 168, [1984] 3 All ER 689; [1985] Conv 50 (J. Martin).
17 *Belgravia Insurance Co Ltd v Meah* [1964] 1 QB 436, [1963] 3 All ER 828; *Hammersmith & Fulham London Borough Council v Top Shop Centres Ltd* [1990] Ch 237, [1989] 2 All ER 655; [1989] All ER Rev 194. As to these forms of mortgage, see p. 665, post.

equitable chargee.[18] It is not available to a squatter who has dispossessed a lessee.[19]

B. COVENANTS OTHER THAN THE COVENANT TO PAY RENT

(1) DAMAGES OR INJUNCTION

If the tenant fails to observe any of the covenants contained in the lease, it is open to the lessor either to sue for damages for breach or to obtain an injunction to restrain the breach.[20]

(2) FORFEITURE

As a further safeguard to the landlord it is the common practice, just as in the case of the covenant to pay rent, to ensure the observance of all other covenants by inserting an express proviso for re-entry and forfeiture in the event of their breach. The following is a typical clause in a lease:

> If there shall be any breach or non-observance of any of the covenants by the tenant hereinbefore contained, then and in any such case the lessor may, at any time thereafter, into and upon the demised premises, or any part thereof, in the name the whole, re-enter, and the same have again, repossess and enjoy as in his former estate.[1]

In two respects, what has already been said above about forfeiture for non-payment of rent applies equally to these other covenants, namely, the effect of a breach is to render the lease voidable, not void; and the right of avoidance is lost by any act on the part of the lessor which amounts to a waiver of the condition.[2] But until the legislature intervened, the jurisdiction of the court to relieve the tenant varied according as the forfeiture was due to non-payment of rent or to the breach of a covenant relating to some other matter. The question soon arose whether equity would protect a tenant against the loss of his interest under such a clause if, having incurred a forfeiture by breaking one of the covenants, he was prepared to put the matter right by paying all costs and compensation. To cite the words of KAY LJ:

> At first there seems to have been some hesitation whether this relief [grantable in the case of non-payment of rent] might not be extended to other cases of forfeiture for breach of covenants such as to repair, to insure, and the like, where compensation could be made; but it was soon recognized that there would be great difficulty in

---

18 *Ladup Ltd v Williams & Glyn's Bank plc* [1985] 1 WLR 851, [1985] 2 All ER 577 (under the court's inherent jurisdiction, p. 433, ante).
19 *Tickner v Buzzacott* [1965] Ch 426, [1965] 1 All ER 131.
20 *Coward v Gregory* (1866) LR 2 CP 153.
 1 In this case forfeiture is provided for by the act of the parties, but it also occurs by operation of law if the tenant asserts a title in himself adverse to the landlord (e.g. by a written declaration that he, not the landlord, is entitled to the freehold), or if he lets a stranger into possession with the intention of enabling him to set up such an adverse title. But in all cases, it is a question of fact whether the tenant's act shows an intention to deny the landlord's title: *Wisbech St Mary Parish Council v Lilley* [1956] 1 WLR 121, [1956] 1 All ER 301; *Warner v Sampson* [1959] 1 QB 297, [1959] 1 All ER 120; *W G Clark (Properties) Ltd v Dupre Properties Ltd* [1992] Ch 297, [1992] 1 All ER 596; [1993] Conv 299 (J. Martin). See generally, Hill and Redman, *Law of Landlord and Tenant* (18th edn), para A 2181.
 2 Pp. 429–31, ante.

estimating the proper amount of compensation; and since the decision of Lord Eldon in *Hill v Barclay*[3] it has always been held that equity would not relieve, merely on the ground that it could give compensation, upon breach of any covenant in a lease except the covenant for payment of rent. But of course this left unaffected the undoubted jurisdiction to relieve in case of breach occasioned by fraud, accident, surprise, or mistake.[4]

This denial of relief was maintained even though the breach, instead of causing loss to the landlord, operated to his advantage by restoring to him, at a much earlier date than he had a right to expect, premises upon which the tenant, in the expectation of continued tenure, might have already expended large sums of money. The strongest example of this was where a tenant failed to re-insure for a short time after the previous year's policy had run out. If in such a case no fire had occurred in the uninsured period the landlord had obviously lost nothing, and yet it was held in several cases that such a breach was sufficient to produce a forfeiture against which no relief could be given.[5] This particular case of forfeiture (by failure to insure) received legislative attention in 1859,[6] when relief was made possible on certain conditions, but it still remained true that the merely technical and innocuous breach of any other covenant inevitably led to the loss of his interest by the tenant if the landlord chose to take advantage of a proviso for re-entry.

The law, however, was fundamentally changed in two respects by the Conveyancing Act of 1881,[7] which first required certain conditions to be satisfied before forfeiture could be enforced, and then gave to the tenant the right to petition for relief.

These provisions were re-enacted by section 146 of the Law of Property Act 1925 and amended by three further Acts in 1927, 1938 and 1954.[8] The law now stands as follows.

(a) The statutory restriction on the landlord's right to enforce a forfeiture

(i) The notice Section 146 of the Law of Property Act 1925 provides as follows:

A right of re-entry or forfeiture under any proviso or stipulation in a lease for a breach of any covenant or condition in the lease shall not be enforceable, by action or otherwise, unless and until the lessor serves on the lessee a notice

   (*a*) specifying the particular breach complained of; and
   (*b*) if the breach is capable of remedy, requiring the lessee to remedy the breach; and
   (*c*) in any case, requiring the lessee to make compensation in money for the breach;

and the lessee fails, within a reasonable time thereafter, to remedy the breach, if it is capable of remedy, and to make reasonable compensation in money, to the satisfaction of the lessor, for the breach.

---

3 (1810) 16 Ves 402.
4 *Barrow v Isaacs & Son* [1891] 1 QB 417 at 425; *Shiloh Spinners Ltd v Harding* [1973] AC 691 at 722 et seq, [1973] 1 All ER 90 at 100 et seq, per Lord WILBERFORCE.
5 See e.g. *Doe d Muston v Gladwin* (1845) 6 QB 953.
6 LP(A) A 1859, ss. 4–9; later repealed by the Conveyancing Act 1881.
7 S. 14.
8 Landlord and Tenant Act 1927; Leasehold Property (Repairs) Act 1938; Landlord and Tenant Act 1954.

A period of three months is normally regarded as a "reasonable time", but in special circumstances it may be much less.[9] This statutory rule is designed to afford the tenant an opportunity of considering the matter before an action is brought against him and of making up his mind whether he can admit the breach and whether he ought to offer compensation.[10]

The section has effect notwithstanding any stipulation to the contrary.[11] The parties cannot even contract out of its requirements indirectly. Thus, where a tenant agreed to lodge a deed of surrender executed in escrow with the president of the local law society, who had authority to deliver it to the landlord if the tenant committed a breach of covenant, it was held that the deed was void as being a device to circumvent the section.[12] As PLOWMAN J said:[13]

> A forfeiture in the guise of a surrender . . . remains a forfeiture for the purposes of section 146.

(ii) Method of service The notice may be served in accordance with the general provisions of section 196 of the Law of Property Act 1925 governing all notices under the Act. It can be sent to "the lessee"[14] or to "the persons interested", and may be left at the tenant's address[15] or sent there by registered letter or recorded delivery.[16] The notice may also be served by affixing it to or leaving it for the tenant at the demised premises.[17]

In the case of a covenant to repair, it is enacted by the Landlord and Tenant Act 1927,[18] that a right of re-entry shall not be enforceable unless the lessor proves that service of the notice was known either:

(a) to the lessee; or
(b) to an under-lessee holding under an under-lease which reserved a nominal reversion only to the lessee; or
(c) to the person who last paid the rent,

and that a reasonable interval had elapsed since the time when the fact of

---

9 *Civil Service Co-operative Society Ltd v McGrigor's Trustee* [1923] 2 Ch 347; *Scala House and District Property Co Ltd v Forbes* [1974] QB 575, [1973] 3 All ER 308; M & B p. 490 (fourteen days held to be sufficient where breach of covenant against assigning or sub-letting held to be incapable of remedy); *Cardigan Properties Ltd v Consolidated Property Investments Ltd* [1991] 1 EGLR 64 (ten days to comply with insurance covenant held to be insufficient); [1991] Conv 223 (J. E. Martin); *Bhojwani v Kingsley Investment Trust Ltd* [1992] 2 EGLR 70; [1993] Conv 296 (J. E. Martin).
10 *Horsey Estate Ltd v Steiger* [1899] 2 QB 79 at 91.
11 LPA 1925, s. 146 (12).
12 *Plymouth Corpn v Harvey* [1971] 1 WLR 549, [1971] 1 All ER 623; M & B p. 497.
13 At 554, at 627.
14 Lessee includes an under-lessee and the persons deriving title under the lessee: LPA 1925, s. 146 (5) (*b*). Where a lessee assigns his lease in breach of covenant, the assignment is effective and the notice must be served on the assignee and not on the original lessee: *Old Grovebury Manor Farm Ltd v W Seymour Plant Sales and Hire Ltd (No 2)* [1979] 1 WLR 1397, [1979] 3 All ER 504; *Governors of the Peabody Donation Fund v Higgins* [1983] 1 WLR 1091, [1983] 3 All ER 122; *Fuller v Judy Properties Ltd* [1992] 1 EGLR 75; [1992] Conv 343 (J. E. Martin); *Greenwich London Borough Council v Discreet Selling Estates Ltd* [1990] 2 EGLR 65; [1991] Conv 222 (J. E. Martin) (a landlord, who had served notice for breach of covenant to repair and then waived breach by acceptance of rent, need not serve a fresh notice).
15 Even though the lessee is in prison and unlikely to receive it: *Van Haarlam v Kasner* [1992] 2 EGLR 59.
16 Recorded Delivery Service Act 1962, s. 1; [1990] Conv 147 (J. E. Adams).
17 *Trustees of Henry Smith's Charity v Kyriakou* [1989] 2 EGLR 110.
18 S. 18 (2).

service was *known to* such person. In this case, the sending of the notice by registered letter or recorded delivery to a person is only to be regarded prima facie as good service.[19]

(iii) Contents of notice It is now established that the statutory notice need not contain a demand for compensation if the lessor does not desire to be indemnified.[20] We must now see whether the statutory notice will be ineffective if it omits to require a breach to be remedied.

If a positive covenant has been broken, e.g. a covenant to repair, that is clearly capable of remedy and accordingly the notice must require it to be remedied. In *Expert Clothing Service and Sales Ltd v Hillgate House Ltd*[1] the Court of Appeal held that, where a tenant had committed a once-and-for-all breach of a covenant to reconstruct premises by a certain date, the breach was capable of remedy even after that date. SLADE J said:[2]

> The breach of a positive covenant (whether it be a continuing breach or a once-and-for-all breach) will ordinarily be capable of remedy. The concept of capability of remedy for the purpose of section 146 must surely be directed to the question whether the harm that has been done to the landlord by the relevant breach is for practical purposes capable of being retrieved. In the ordinary case, the breach of a promise to do something by a certain date can for practical purposes be remedied by the thing being done, even out of time.

There may, however, be rare cases where the breach of a positive covenant is incapable of remedy, for example, where there is a breach of a covenant to insure at a time when the premises have already been burnt down.

Where, however, the covenant which has been broken is a negative one, there is some difficulty. If, for instance, the tenant has agreed not to permit the premises to be used for illegal or immoral purposes and he is convicted of using them for habitual prostitution, it may be that the landlord is already branded locally as the owner of a brothel. If so, the tenant may discontinue his immoral use of the premises, his only mode of redemption, but mere cesser will not wipe out the past and remove the stigma on the landlord's reputation. In this sense the breach is not capable of remedy. If, therefore, the landlord can show that he has suffered lasting damage of this nature, his statutory notice need not require the breach to be remedied.[3] But the position is different where the action for forfeiture is brought against the original tenant in respect of immoral user permitted not by him, but by his sub-tenant or assignee. In these circumstances, it is the duty of the original tenant to take immediate steps to stop the wrongful user and also to enforce the forfeiture against the wrongdoer. It is only if he fails to do so within a

19 If a tenant is making a claim under the Leasehold Reform Act 1967 (p. 490 post), no proceedings to enforce any right of re-entry or forfeiture may be brought during the currency of the claim without the leave of the court, which shall not be granted unless it is satisfied that the claim was not made in good faith, i.e. to avoid forfeiture: ss. 22, 34, Sch. 3, para 4 (1); *Central Estates (Belgravia) Ltd v Woolgar* [1972] 1 QB 48, [1971] 3 All ER 647.
20 *Lock v Pearce* [1893] 2 Ch 271; *Governors of Rugby School v Tannahill* [1935] 1 KB 87; M & B p. 488.
1 [1986] Ch 340, [1985] 2 All ER 998; M & B p. 494.
2 At 355, at 1008.
3 *Governors of Rugby School v Tannahill*, supra; *Egerton v Esplanade Hotels London Ltd* [1947] 2 All ER 88; *Hoffman v Fineberg* [1949] Ch 245, [1948] 1 All ER 592; *Ali v Booth* (1966) 110 SJ 708; *D R Evans & Co Ltd v Chandler* (1969) 211 EG 1381; *Dunraven Securities Ltd v Holloway* (1982) 264 EG 709; *British Petroleum Pension Trust Ltd v Behrendt* (1985) 52 P & CR 117; *Van Haarlam v Kasner* [1992] 2 EGLR 59 (paraphernalia for spying found in flat).

reasonable time after learning the facts that the breach will be regarded as incapable of remedy.[4]

In *Scala House and District Property Co Ltd v Forbes*[5] the Court of Appeal held that a covenant not to assign or sublet is a once-and-for-all breach which cannot be remedied, even by obtaining a surrender from the tenant of the sub-lease. In reaching that decision RUSSELL LJ reviewed the cases of *user* of premises in breach of covenant and said:[6]

> We have a number of cases . . . in which the decision that the breach is not capable of remedy has gone upon the "stigma" point, without considering whether a short answer might be—if the user had ceased before the section 146 notice—that it was *ex hypothesi* incapable of remedy, leaving the lessee only with the ability to seek relief from forfeiture and the writ unchallengeable as such.

Hitherto, as we have seen, the test applicable to such breaches has been whether or not the stigma attaching to the premises can be removed by cesser of the immoral or illegal user. It might be preferable to adopt the approach of RUSSELL LJ and to revert to the "attractive and easy" view[7] that *all* negative covenants are incapable of remedy. Recovery of possession by the landlord would then depend solely on whether the court would grant to the tenant relief from forfeiture under section 146 (2).

As regards the details which must be brought to the knowledge of the tenant, the rule has been laid down that the notice must be sufficiently precise to direct his attention to the particular things of which the landlord complains, so that he may understand with reasonable certainty what he is required to do and may be in a position to put matters right before the action is brought.[8] If, for instance:

> the tenant holds six houses from the landlord and he is merely notified that he has broken his covenant to repair, the notice will be bad as not indicating which of the houses are involved.

(iv) Exceptional case of covenant to repair Where a landlord sues for damages or to enforce a forfeiture in respect of a covenant to keep or put the premises in repair,[9] he is subject to a further statutory restriction under the Leasehold Property (Repairs) Act 1938.[10] This Act applies to premises, other than an

---

4   *Glass v Kencakes Ltd* [1966] 1 QB 611, [1964] 3 All ER 807. These difficulties will be avoided if the statutory notice requires the tenant to remedy the breach *if it is capable of remedy*. The landlord can then claim in his action (1) that the breach is incapable of remedy, or (2) if it is capable of remedy that it has not been remedied: at 629–30, at 818–9.

5   [1974] QB 575, [1973] 3 All ER 308; M & B p. 490, (1973) 89 LQR 460 (P.V.B.); (1973) 37 Conv (NS) 455 (D. Macintyre); *Billson v Residential Apartments Ltd* [1992] 1 AC 494, [1991] 3 All ER 265 (where Sir Nicolas BROWNE-WILKINSON V-C doubted whether breach of covenant not to make alterations without prior consent of landlord was irremediable).

6   At 588, at 314. For criticism of some of the reasoning in this decision, see *Expert Clothing Service and Sales Ltd v Hillgate House Ltd* [1986] Ch 340 at 364, [1985] 2 All ER 998 at 1015; M & B p. 493 n. 3, per O'CONNOR LJ.

7   *Hoffman v Fineberg* [1949] Ch 245 at 254, [1948] 1 KB 592 at 596, per HARMAN J, referring to the ratio of MACKINNON J in *Governors of Rugby School v Tannahill* at first instance [1934] 1 KB 695 at 700–1. While affirming his decision, CA rejected his view that all breaches of negative covenant are irremediable: [1935] 1 KB 87 at 90, 92.

8   *Fletcher v Nokes* [1897] 1 Ch 271 at 274; approved *Fox v Jolly* [1916] 1 AC 1; *John Lewis Properties plc v Viscount Chelsea* [1993] 34 EG 116.

9   An obligation to cleanse is not an obligation to repair: *Starrokate Ltd v Burry* (1982) 265 EG 871.

10 S. 1 (1); as amended by the Landlord and Tenant Act 1954, s. 51 (1).

agricultural holding, which have been let for a period of not less than seven years, of which at least three years remain unexpired. The landlord must serve on the tenant a notice under section 146 of the Law of Property Act 1925 not less than one month before the commencement of the action, and inform him in that notice of his right to serve a counter-notice.[11] The tenant may within 28 days of receiving the notice serve a counter-notice on the landlord claiming the benefit of the Act.

The effect of a counter-notice is that no proceedings whatsoever may be taken by the landlord for the enforcement of any right of re-entry or forfeiture, or for the recovery of damages, in respect of a breach of the repairing covenant, unless he first obtains the leave of the court. But as soon as the lease has less than three years to run, there is no longer any need to apply for this leave.[12] The circumstances in which leave is to be given are specifically enumerated by the statute.[13] At this stage of the proceedings the landlord need only show a prima facie case of a breach by the tenant.[14]

The Act applies where the landlord is claiming forfeiture or damages, but not where he is claiming for a contract debt. A claim for expenses incurred in the preparation and the service of a section 146 notice is a claim for a contract debt and therefore no leave to enforce it under the Act is required.[15] There are conflicting decisions at first instance as to whether this extends to a case where the lease contains a covenant that the landlord can enter and carry out repairs at the tenant's expense, if the tenant fails to do them, and that the tenant will reimburse his proper expenditure. The better view is that an action for the recovery of the cost of repair is an action for debt and therefore no leave of the court is required under the Act.[16]

(b) Suspension of covenant

There may exist lawful excuses for the non-performance of a covenant in a lease. If so, the lease is not forfeitable; the covenant is merely suspended, but

11 Leasehold Property (Repairs) Act 1938, s. 1 (4) *Middlegate Properties Ltd v Messimeris* [1973] 1 WLR 168, [1973] 1 All ER 645; *BL Holdings Ltd v Marcolt Investments Ltd* (1978) 249 EG 849. See *Swallow Securities Ltd v Brand* (1983) 45 P & CR 328 (where a landlord failed in his attempt to circumvent the requirement of serving a notice).
12 *Baker v Sims* [1959] 1 QB 114, [1958] 3 All ER 326.
13 Leasehold Property (Repairs) Act 1938, s. 1 (5); (*a*) where substantial damage has been caused, or will be caused if breach not remedied; (*b*) where an immediate remedy is required for giving effect to any enactment, by-law or order of a local authority respecting the safety, repair, maintenance or sanitary condition of the house; (*c*) where the tenant does not occupy the whole of the house and the breach is injurious to the other occupant; (*d*) where the cost of repair is relatively small as compared with the much greater expense that a postponement will involve; or (*e*) where it is "just and equitable" that leave should be given. It is sufficient to give the court jurisdiction if the landlord proves any one of these five grounds: *Phillips v Price* [1959] Ch 181, [1958] 3 All ER 386. And he must prove it on the balance of probabilities; *Associated British Ports v C H Bailey plc* [1990] 2 AC 703, [1990] 1 All ER 929; [1990] CLJ 401 (S. Bridge); [1990] Conv 305 (P. F. Smith).
14 *Sidnell v Wilson* [1966] 2 QB 67, [1966] 1 All ER 681; *Land Securities plc v Receiver for Metropolitan Police District* [1983] 1 WLR 439, [1983] 2 All ER 254 (Scotland Yard).
15 *Bader Properties Ltd v Linley Property Investments Ltd* (1967) 19 P & CR 620; *Middlegate Properties Ltd v Gidlow-Jackson* (1977) 34 P & CR 4.
16 *Hamilton v Martell Securities Ltd* [1984] Ch 266, [1984] 1 All ER 665, not following *Swallow Securities Ltd v Brand* (1983) 45 P & CR 328, and preferred in *Colchester Estates (Cardiff) v Carlton Industries plc* [1986] Ch 80, [1984] 2 All ER 601, but only because it was decided later; *Elite Investments Ltd v T I Bainbridge Silencers Ltd* [1986] 2 EGLR 43. See also *SEDAC Investments Ltd v Tanner* [1982] 1 WLR 1342, [1982] 3 All ER 646; (1984) 134 NLJ 791 (H. W. Wilkinson); [1986] Conv 85 (P. F. Smith).

the lease remains valid. Lord RUSSELL OF KILLOWEN recognised obiter that there may be excuses for the non-performance of a building covenant short of full frustration:[17]

> It may well be that circumstances may arise during the currency of the term which render it difficult, or even impossible, for one party or the other to carry out some of its obligations as landlord or tenant, circumstances which might afford a defence to a claim for damages for their breach, but the lease would remain.

This dictum was applied in *John Lewis Properties plc v Viscount Chelsea*[18] where a tenant was unable to perform a covenant to demolish and rebuild property owing to his inability to obtain planning permission, which had become necessary on its subsequent listing as a Grade II building.

(c) The statutory right of the tenant to claim relief

(i) Power of court to grant or refuse relief After requiring the above preliminaries from a lessor before he can enforce a forfeiture the Act of 1925 then provides that, when the lessor is proceeding by action[19] or entry to recover the premises, the lessee may apply to the court for relief,[20] and the court may, after reviewing the circumstances of the case and the conduct of the parties, refuse such relief, or grant it upon such terms as to costs, expenses, damages, compensation, penalty, etc., as seem fit.[1] This application must be made by all the tenants if the premises are held by joint lessees.[2] Where the court grants relief, the effect is as if the lease had never been forfeited.[3] If the relief is granted upon terms to be performed by the tenant in the future, the order for relief falls to the ground if they are not performed; but, until the time comes for performance, the tenant who remains on the premises is there not as a tenant under the lease, but as a tenant at will or on sufferance.[4] The court has jurisdiction to extend the time.[5]

Further, where the tenant has under-let the premises, if the court grants relief to the tenant, the effect is to revive the under-lease in its entirety. In a case, however, where part of the demised premises had been under-let by the tenant, and where those premises were physically separated and the breach of covenant was committed by the under-lessee on his part of the property only, it was held that relief could be granted to the tenant without reviving the under-lease.[6]

---

17 *Cricklewood Property and Investment Trust Ltd v Leighton's Investment Trust Ltd* [1945] AC 221 at 233–234, [1945] 1 All ER 252 at 258; so too Lord GODDARD at 244, at 264.

18 [1993] 34 EG 116 (25 Cadogan Gardens "once described as the most wonderful house in the world"). Frustration was not pleaded; p. 462, post.

19 Such an action is a pending land action under LCA 1972, s. 17 (1) and is registrable under s. 5; and, in the case of registered land, is required to be protected by a caution under LRA 1925, s. 59 (1), (5); *Selim Ltd v Bickenhall Engineering Ltd* [1981] 1 WLR 1318, [1981] 3 All ER 210.

20 He may apply as soon as the s. 146 notice has been served: *Pakwood Transport Ltd v 15 Beauchamp Place Ltd* (1977) 36 P & CR 112.

1 LPA 1925, s. 146 (2).

2 *T M Fairclough & Sons v Berliner* [1931] 1 Ch 60.

3 *Dendy v Evans* [1910] 1 KB 263; *Meadows v Clerical Medical and General Life Assurance Society* [1981] Ch 70, [1980] 1 All ER 454.

4 *City of Westminster Assurance Co Ltd v Ainis* (1975) 29 P & CR 469.

5 *Chandless-Chandless v Nicholson* [1942] 2 KB 321, [1942] 2 All ER 315; *Starside Properties Ltd v Mustapha* [1974] 1 WLR 816, [1974] 2 All ER 567.

6 *GMS Syndicate Ltd v Gary Elliott Ltd* [1982] Ch 1, [1981] 1 All ER 619, relying on *Dumpor's Case* (1603) 4 Co Rep 119*b*, p. 419, ante. For an under-lessee's independent right to claim relief, see infra.

Attempts have been made to specify the principles upon which this relief should be granted or withheld,[7] but the House of Lords has held that though such statements are useful and may reflect the judicial view for normal cases, yet the discretion given by the statute is so wide that it is better not to lay down rigid rules for its exercise.[8] Although the court will rarely exercise its discretion in favour of a lessee who knowingly suffers premises to be used for immoral purposes, it may nevertheless do so where there are special mitigating circumstances.[9]

(ii) Time of application After the statutory notice under section 146 has been served, the tenant may apply for relief under subsection (2). He may do so not only where the landlord proceeds by action, but also where he peaceably re-enters without a court order. The latter was decided by the House of Lords in *Billson v Residential Apartments Ltd*,[10] as a result of a purposive interpretation of the opening words of the section:

> Where a lessor is proceeding, by action or otherwise, to enforce such a right of re-entry or forfeiture.

Before *Billson*, these words had been construed to mean that the tenant could only apply for relief during the time when *the lessor is proceeding*, and that, once the lessor had recovered possession, it would be too late. The House of Lords has now held that the effect of the subsection is that the tenant may apply for relief if the landlord *proceeds or has proceeded* to forfeit by action or otherwise. Accordingly, the tenant may apply where the landlord has peaceably re-entered without first obtaining a court order.[11]

Where the landlord proceeds by action, the tenant must apply before the landlord has entered into possession pursuant to a final judgment; but where the landlord forfeits by peaceable re-entry, there is no time limit. In deciding whether to grant relief, the court will take into account all the circumstances, including delay on the part of the tenant.[12]

(iii) Under-lessees The jurisdiction of the court to relieve an under-lessee, or a person deriving title under him,[13] against a forfeiture due to the under-lessor's failure to pay rent[14] is equally exercisable where the failure relates to

---

7 E.g. *Rose v Hyman* [1911] 2 KB 234.

8 *Hyman v Rose* [1912] AC 623 at 631, per Lord ELDON LC; *Southern Depot Co Ltd v British Railways Board* [1990] 2 EGLR 39; *Darlington Borough Council v Denmark Chemists Ltd* [1993] 1 EGLR 62.

9 *Borthwick-Norton v Romney Warwick Estates Ltd* [1950] 1 All ER 798; *Borthwick-Norton v Dougherty* [1950] WN 481; *Central Estates (Belgravia) Ltd v Woolgar (No 2)* [1972] 1 WLR 1048, [1972] 3 All ER 610; *Burfort Financial Investments v Chotard* (1976) 239 EG 891; *British Petroleum Pension Trust Ltd v Behrendt* (1985) 52 P & CR 117; *Ropemaker Properties Ltd v Noonhaven Ltd* [1989] 2 EGLR 50; (1989) 139 NLJ 1747 (H. W. Wilkinson). See also *Earl Bathurst v Fine* [1974] 1 WLR 905, [1974] 2 All ER 1160 (relief refused to unsatisfactory tenant, where personal qualifications were important); *Southern Depot Co Ltd v British Railways Board* [1990] 2 EGLR 39 (relief granted despite wilful breaches involving "a thoroughly deceptive course of conduct" towards the landlord).

10 [1992] 1 AC 494, [1992] 1 All ER 141; M & B p. 503; [1992] CLJ 216 (S. Bridge); [1992] Conv 273 (P. F. Smith); (1992) 02 EG 154 (P. Dollar and C. Peet).

11 An application for relief was subsequently refused: [1993] EGCS 150.

12 At 539–540, at 149, per Lord TEMPLEMAN; at 543–544, at 152, per Lord OLIVER OF AYLMERTON.

13 *Re Good's Lease* [1954] 1 WLR 309, [1954] 1 All ER 275; as for example, a mortgagee by way of sub-demise: *Grand Junction Co Ltd v Bates* [1954] 2 QB 160, [1954] 2 All ER 385.

14 Pp. 433, ante.

some other covenant.[15] This is so, even though the nature of the breach, e.g. the bankruptcy of a publican, precludes the under-lessor from applying for relief.[16] It is a jurisdiction that should be sparingly exercised.[17]

(iv) Inherent equitable jurisdiction The Court of Appeal in *Billson*[18] first decided that there was no statutory jurisdiction to grant relief against forfeiture and then held by a majority that it had no inherent equitable jurisdiction either. The section was an exhaustive provision. As Sir Nicolas BROWNE-WILKINSON V-C said:[19]

> If Parliament intended the court to be able to grant relief even when the landlord is *not* proceeding to enforce his rights but has enforced them, what was the reason for including in section 146 (2) and (4) the limitation that the powers of relief could be exercised only when the landlord is proceeding?

The House of Lords did not refer to this equitable jurisdiction, since it had reversed the Court of Appeal and held that it had statutory jurisdiction to grant relief.

(v) Decorative repairs A special rule was introduced by the Law of Property Act 1925 for covenants relating to the internal decorative repair of a house.[20] It is provided that where a statutory notice has been served by the landlord indicating a breach of such a covenant, the court, after reviewing all the circumstances and in particular the length of the term, may wholly or partially relieve the tenant from liabilities for such repairs. But this power to set a covenant aside is not exercisable when a tenant, having expressly agreed to put the property in a decorative state of repair, has never performed the covenant, nor is it to apply to anything which is necessary for keeping the property in a sanitary condition or in a state which makes it fit for human habitation.

(d) Exceptions to the statutory requirements

The particular subsections of the Act already considered are general in nature and would, without more, apply to every covenant contained in a lease, but there are three covenants for the breach of which a lessor need not serve the statutory notice as a preliminary to enforcing the forfeiture, and in respect of which relief is not grantable. The covenants so excepted are the following.

(i) Covenant to pay rent[1]

(ii) Covenant for inspection in mining lease If a mining tenant, under obligation to pay royalties according to the quantity of minerals got, breaks the covenant by which he has agreed to give access to his books, accounts, weighing machines or other things, or to the mine itself, forfeiture may be enforced without service of the statutory notice and no relief is grantable.[2]

15 LPA 1925, s. 146 (4).
16 LP(A)A 1929, s. 1.
17 *Creery v Summersell and Flowerdew & Co Ltd* [1949] Ch 751; *Hill v Griffin* [1987] 1 EGLR 81.
18 [1992] 1 AC 494, [1991] 3 All ER 265, supra.
19 Ibid., at 517, at 282. The equitable jurisdiction is available in cases of non-payment of rent, see p. 433, ante. RSC (Amendment No. 2) 1986 (S.I. 1986 No. 1187) rr. 2 and 3 require a landlord to notify any person entitled to relief against forfeiture of whom he is aware.
20 S. 147.
1 LPA 1925, s. 146 (11); pp. 427, et seq, ante.
2 Ibid., s. 146 (8) (ii).

(iii) Condition of forfeiture on the bankruptcy of tenant or where lease is taken in execution It is common to provide in a lease that the premises shall be forfeited to the lessor if the tenant becomes bankrupt[3] or if his interest is taken in execution. There are certain classes of property in which it is vital to the landlord that he should recover his property in either of these events, and where the lease relates to such property the Act provides that the statutory provisions shall be excluded. The following are the leases concerned:[4]

(*a*) agricultural or pastoral land,
(*b*) mines or minerals,
(*c*) a house used or intended to be used as a public house or beer shop,
(*d*) a house let as a dwelling-house, with the use of any furniture, books, works of art, or other chattels not being in the nature of fixtures,
(*e*) any property with respect to which the personal qualifications of the tenant are of importance[5] for the preservation of the value or character of the property, or on the ground of neighbourhood to the lessor,[6] or to any person holding under him.

In such a lease, then, the lessor can proceed to enforce a forfeiture as soon as the bankruptcy occurs, and the tenant has no claim to relief.

If the demised land is not within one of the classes enumerated above, the extent to which the statutory provisions concerning notice and relief apply depends upon whether the lessee's interest is sold, or is not sold, for the benefit of his creditors within one year from the bankruptcy or taking in execution. The two rules on the matter, which are designed to enable the trustee in bankruptcy to decide whether he will disclaim the lease or use it for the benefit of the creditors, are as follows:[7]

(*a*) If the interest is sold within the year, the statutory provisions apply without any limit of time. This means, in the case of bankruptcy, that if the trustee in bankruptcy is able to sell the tenant's interest under the lease within the year for the benefit of the creditors, then, despite proceedings for forfeiture, he can apply for relief even after the year has elapsed, and the court may grant the application and confirm the title of the purchaser.[8]

(*b*) If the interest is not sold within the year, the statutory provisions apply only during that year, i.e., although the landlord cannot take steps to regain possession during that period without serving the statutory notice and without the risk of defeat by a successful application for relief, yet, after the year has elapsed, his right to recover the premises is absolute. No notice need be served; no relief can be granted.[8]

In practice, however, leases do not usually contain a proviso for forfeiture on the bankruptcy of the tenant, except in the five cases enumerated above, since it is troublesome for the landlord to be deprived of his rent until a

---

3 But not if his surety does: *Halliard Property Co Ltd v Jack Segal Ltd* [1978] 1 WLR 377, [1978] 1 All ER 1219.
4 LPA 1925, s. 146 (9).
5 *Earl Bathurst v Fine* [1974] 1 WLR 905, [1974] 2 All ER 1160.
6 *Hockley Engineering Co Ltd v V & P Midlands Ltd* [1993] 1 EGLR 76.
7 LPA 1925, s. 146 (10). Any wider equitable jurisdiction is ousted by ss. 10: *Official Custodian for Charities v Parway Estates Developments Ltd* [1985] Ch 151, [1984] 3 All ER 679; *Billson v Residential Apartments Ltd* [1991] 1 AC 494, [1991] 3 All ER 265, p. 442, ante.
8 *Civil Service Co-operative Society v McGrigor's Trustee* [1923] 2 Ch 347 at 355; *Horsey Estate Ltd v Steiger* [1899] 2 QB 79; *Gee v Harwood* [1933] Ch 712; affd [1934] AC 272.

decision has been reached by the trustee, and if he accepts rent falling due after the date of bankruptcy the forfeiture is thereby waived.[9]

(e) Law Commission Report on Forfeiture of Tenancies, 1985

The Law Commission Report[10] recommends radical changes in the law of forfeiture. "It is complex and confused; its many features fit together awkwardly; and it contains a number of uncertainties, anomalies and injustices." (para. 3.2.)

The Report recommends that the present law of forfeiture, both statutory and non-statutory, be swept away, and with it, the doctrine of re-entry. They are to be replaced by a scheme under which there is to be no distinction between termination for non-payment of rent and termination for other reasons, and under which the tenancy is to continue in force until the date on which the court orders that it should terminate. "The landlord's right to terminate is merged with the tenant's right to resist termination so as to produce one single rule that the court has a primary discretion as to whether the tenancy should terminate or not." The court is to have power to make a *termination order* which can be applied for only on the occasion of a *termination order event*, i.e. (*a*) breach of covenant by the tenant, or (*b*) disguised breach of covenant, that is, broadly, a breach by the tenant of an obligation imposed on him otherwise than by covenant, or (*c*) insolvency of the tenant. The order may be either *absolute* (to terminate the tenancy unconditionally on a date specified) or *remedial* (to terminate the tenancy on a date specified unless the tenant takes remedial action by that time). In both cases the court may grant or refuse to grant the order according to a discretion exercisable within guidelines. (paras. 3.25–3.71.)

Finally a tenant is given a new right to terminate a tenancy in cases of fault on the part of the landlord. The right is analogous to the landlord's right to terminate, and the tenant exercising this right is given a right to claim damages from the landlord for the loss of his tenancy. (paras. 3.72–3.93.) The new scheme applies to existing tenancies as well as to those created in the future. (para. 3.29.)

In 1994 the Law Commission published a further Report,[10a] which is in effect a republication of the 1985 Report, together with minor amendments and a draft Termination of Tenancies Bill. The recommendation for a Tenants Termination Order has been shelved.[10b]

SECTION VII COVENANTS WHICH RUN WITH THE LAND AND WITH THE REVERSION[11]

A covenant in a lease is prima facie a contract binding only on the lessor and the lessee—the actual contracting parties. But it was early seen that to enforce this doctrine of privity of contract was highly undesirable in the case

---

9 *Doe d Gatehouse v Rees* (1838) 4 Bing NC 384.
10 Law Com No. 142 (HC 279); [1986] Conv 165 (P. F. Smith); [1987] LSG 1042 (J. Cherryman).
10a Termination of Tenancies Bill (Law Com No. 221, HC 135). Appendix C contains an updated summary of the present law of forfeiture and its defects.
10b Paras. 1.7 and 1.13.
11 Holdsworth, *History of English Law*, vol. vii. pp. 287–92.

of leases, since both parties had transmissible interests the value of which depended largely upon the obligations that each had assumed. Thus the mediaeval land law, although it never lost sight of the general principle that a stranger to a contract cannot sue or be sued upon it, did recognize that covenants contained in a lease might have a wider operation than ordinary contracts. As Holdsworth remarked:

> they were regarded in a sense as being annexed to an estate in the land, so that they could be enforced by anyone who took that estate in the land.[12]

The scope, then, of our present inquiry is to ascertain in what circumstances persons other than the original lessor and lessee can sue or be sued upon the covenants. Two events may occur—an assignment of the term by the tenant or an assignment of the reversion by the lessor.[13] In each case the two questions that arise are whether the benefit and burden of the covenants pass to the assignee. In short, do the covenants run with the land and with the reversion? Four cases, therefore, fall to be considered:

1. The lessee assigns his interest to A. Can A enforce the covenants inserted in the lease in favour of the lessee? Does the benefit of these covenants run with the land?
2. The lessee assigns his interest to A. Can A be sued on the covenants inserted in the lease in favour of the lessor? Does the burden of the covenants entered into by the lessee run with the land?
3. The lessor assigns his interest, i.e. the reversion, to Z. Can Z enforce the covenants inserted in the lease in favour of the lessor? Does the benefit of the covenants run with the reversion?
4. The lessor assigns his reversion to Z. Can Z be sued upon the covenants inserted in the lease in favour of the lessee? Does the burden of the lessor's covenants run with the reversion?

In this section we are concerned only with the rules laid down by common law and by statute. It must be realized, however, that these rules may in certain limited circumstances be modified by the doctrine of *Tulk v Moxhay*,[14] under which a restrictive covenant between landlord and tenant is sometimes enforceable by and against third parties in cases where this would be impossible either at common law or under the statutes that we shall presently consider.

A. COVENANTS TOUCHING AND CONCERNING THE LAND

It will simplify our task if, before dealing separately with the four divisions of the subject given above, we describe what is meant by covenants that *touch and concern the land demised*, for it is only these, as distinct from those merely affecting the person, that are capable of running either with the reversion or with the land.

From the present point of view all covenants fall into one or other of two classes, being either personal to the contracting parties, or such as touch and concern the land.

12 Holdsworth, *History of English Law*, vol. iii. p. 158.
13 For the meaning of assignment, see pp. 456, post.
14 Pp. 614 et seq, post.

The time-honoured expression "touching and concerning the land" was replaced in the Law of Property Act 1925 by the phrase *having reference to the subject-matter of the lease*.[15] This affords a clue to the meaning of what is at first sight a little vague. If the covenant has direct reference to the land, if it lays down something which is to be done or is not to be done upon the land, or, and perhaps this is the clearest way of describing the test, *if it affects the landlord in his normal capacity as landlord or the tenant in his normal capacity as tenant*, it may be said to touch and concern the land.
Lord RUSSELL CJ said:

> The true principle is that no covenant or condition which affects merely the person, and which does not affect the nature, quality, or value of the thing demised or the mode of using or enjoying the thing demised, runs with the land,[16]

and BAYLEY J at an earlier date asserted the same principle:

> In order to bind the assignee, the covenant must either affect the land itself during the term, such as those which regard the mode of occupation, or it must be such as per se, and not merely from collateral circumstances, affects the value of the land at the end of the term.[17]

If a simple test is desired for ascertaining into which category a covenant falls, it is suggested that the proper inquiry should be whether the covenant affects either the landlord *qua* landlord or the tenant *qua* tenant. A covenant may very well have reference to the land, but, unless it is reasonably incidental to the relation of landlord and tenant, it cannot be said to touch and concern the land so as to be capable of running therewith or with the reversion.[18] Tested by this principle the following covenants have been held to touch and concern the land.

(1) EXAMPLES OF COVENANTS TOUCHING AND CONCERNING THE LAND

Covenants by the tenant:

to pay rent or taxes;[19]
to repair or leave in repair;[20]
to spend a stated yearly sum on repairs, or in default to pay to the landlord the difference between this sum and the amount actually expended;[1]
to lay dung on the land annually;[2]

15 Ss. 141, 142.
16 *Horsey Estate Ltd v Steiger* [1899] 2 QB 79 at 89.
17 *Mayor of Congleton v Pattison* (1808) 10 East 130 at 138; cited Behan, *Covenants Affecting Land*, p. 52.
18 Cited with approval in *Hua Chiao Commercial Bank Ltd v Chiaphua Industries Ltd* [1987] AC 99 at 107, [1987] 1 All ER 1110 at 1112, per Lord OLIVER OF AYLMERTON; and in *Breams Property Investment Co Ltd v Stroulger* [1948] 2 KB 1 at 7, [1948] 1 All ER 758 at 759, per SCOTT LJ. See also formulations of the test by Sir Nicolas BROWNE-WILKINSON V-C in *Kumar v Dunning* [1989] QB 193 at 204, [1987] 2 All ER 801 at 810; and by Lord OLIVER OF AYLMERTON in *P & A Swift Investments v Combined English Stores Group plc* [1989] AC 632 at 642, [1988] 2 All ER 885 at 890; M & B pp. 512–513. And generally [1989] 47 LSG 24, 48 LSG 22 (J. Adams and H. Williamson).
19 *Parker v Webb* (1693) 3 Salk 5. Cf a premium payable by instalments: *Hill v Booth* [1930] 1 KB 381. A covenant by a surety guaranteeing the tenant's rent also touches and concerns the land: *Kumar v Dunning*, supra.
20 *Martyn v Clue* (1852) 18 QB 661.
 1 *Moss' Empires Ltd v Olympia (Liverpool) Ltd* [1939] AC 544, [1939] 3 All ER 460.
 2 *Sale v Kitchingham* (1713) 10 Mod Rep 158.

to renew tenant's fixtures;[3]
to reside on a farm during the term;[4]
to insure the premises against fire;[5]
by a publican tenant to buy all beer from the lessor;[6]
not to assign or under-let without the landlord's consent;[7]
not to allow a third party, X, to be concerned in the conduct of the business carried on at the demised premises.[8]

Covenants by the landlord:

to renew the lease;[9]
to supply the demised house with good water;[10]
not to build on adjoining land so as to depreciate the amenity of the demised land;[11]
to erect a new building in place of an old one;[12]
to keep a housekeeper to act as servant of the lessee;[13]
not to serve a notice to quit for three years, unless he requires the premises for his own occupation.[14]

Covenant by a third party:

to guarantee the tenant's performance of his obligations.[15]

(2) EXAMPLES OF PERSONAL COVENANTS

On the other hand personal, or collateral, covenants do not touch and concern the land, since they have no direct reference to the subject-matter of the lease. The word *collateral*, admittedly ambiguous, in this context, indicates a covenant relating to a matter not normally relevant to the relationship of landlord and tenant. For instance, a covenant by either party to pay a sum of money to the other is merely collateral,[16] unless it is inextricably bound up with other covenants that touch and concern the land.[17]

Thus a covenant by a lessee, in furtherance of his express undertaking to repair, to

3 *Williams v Earle* (1868) LR 3 QB 739.
4 *Tatem v Chaplin* (1793) 2 Hy Bl 133.
5 *Vernon v Smith* (1821) 5 B & Ald 1.
6 *Clegg v Hands* (1890) 44 Ch D 503.
7 *Goldstein v Sanders* [1915] 1 Ch 549.
8 *Lewin v American and Colonial Distributors Ltd* [1945] Ch 225 at 236, [1945] 2 All ER 271, n.
9 *Muller v Trafford* [1901] 1 Ch 54; *Weg Motors Ltd v Hales* [1961] Ch 176, [1960] 3 All ER 762; affd. [1962] Ch 49, [1961] 3 All ER 181.
10 *Jourdain v Wilson* (1821) 4 B & Ald 266.
11 *Ricketts v Enfield Churchwardens* [1909] 1 Ch 544.
12 *Easterby v Sampson* (1830) 6 Bing 644.
13 *Barnes v City of London Real Property Co* [1918] 2 Ch 18.
14 *Breams Property Investment Co Ltd v Stroulger* [1948] 2 KB 1, [1948] 1 All ER 758.
15 *Kumar v Dunning* [1989] QB 193, [1987] 2 All ER 801; [1988] CLJ 180 (C. Harpum); approved *P & A Swift Investments v Combined English Stores Group plc* [1989] AC 632, [1988] 2 All ER 885, where Lord TEMPLEMAN said at 637, at 887: "A surety for a tenant is a quasi tenant who volunteers to be a substitute or twelfth man for the tenant's team and is subject to the same rules and regulations as the player he replaces. A covenant which runs with the reversion against the tenant runs with the reversion against the surety".
   See also *Coronation Street Industrial Properties Ltd v Ingall Industries plc* [1989] 1 WLR 304, [1989] 1 All ER 979 (covenant by surety of tenant to accept new lease replacing lease granted to tenant, where that lease was disclaimed by liquidator on tenant's insolvency, held to touch and concern).
16 *Re Hunter's Lease* [1942] Ch 124, [1942] 1 All ER 27.
17 *Moss' Empires Ltd v Olympia (Liverpool) Ltd,* supra; *Boyer v Warbey* [1953] 1 QB 234, [1952] 2 All ER 976.

expend £500 yearly upon repairs, or to pay the lessor the difference between this amount and what is actually expended, is not a bare obligation personal to the contracting parties. It touches and concerns the land, since it is part and parcel of the repairing covenant.[18]

In *Thomas v Hayward*:[19]

where the lessor of a public house had covenanted that he would not open another beer or spirit house within half a mile of the demised premises, the question arose whether this covenant could be enforced by an assignee of the lessee.

It was held that it could not, because it was collateral in the sense that it did not oblige the lessor to do or to refrain from doing anything on the demised premises. On the other hand a covenant by the tenant of a public house to conduct the business in such a manner as to afford no ground for the suspension of the licence, was held to touch and concern the land, since it concerned the manner in which the covenantor was to use the premises as tenant.[20]

A covenant that entitles the tenant to purchase the fee simple at a given price at any time during the term, affects the parties *qua* vendor and purchaser, not *qua* landlord and tenant. It is collateral to the lease and as such it cannot run as a matter of course with the land or with the reversion as being one that touches and concerns the land.[1] Nevertheless, if it does not infringe the rule against perpetuities,[2] its effect is to confer upon the tenant an equitable interest in the land[3] which, like any other piece of property, is freely assignable unless the terms of its grant show that it is personal to him. Therefore, the option will pass on an assignment of the demised land and will be enforceable by an assignee of the tenant against the landlord; and if registered as an estate contract[4] it will be enforceable against an assignee of the reversion.[5]

It has also been held that a covenant by the tenant to pay to the landlord a substantial security deposit on the terms that it would be repayable at the end of the lease if there was no breach of the tenant's covenants did not touch and concern the land.[6] The obligation was entered into with the landlord *qua* payee rather than *qua* landlord.[7]

B. RUNNING OF COVENANTS AT COMMON LAW AND BY STATUTE

We can now take up the four cases that have been indicated above and determine in what circumstances the covenant will run in each case. The

---

18 *Moss' Empires Ltd v Olympia (Liverpool) Ltd*, supra.
19 (1869) LR 4 Exch 311.
20 *Fleetwood v Hull* (1889) 23 QBD 35.
 1 A right of pre-emption over adjoining land is also collateral: *Collison v Lettson* (1815) 6 Taunt 224; *Charles Frodsham & Co Ltd v Morris* (1972) 229 EG 961.
 2 P. 325, ante.
 3 *London and South Western Rly Co v Gomm* (1882) 20 Ch D 562; pp. 127, 325, ante.
 4 P. 759, post.
 5 *Griffith v Pelton* [1958] Ch 205, [1957] 3 All ER 75, explaining *Woodall v Clifton* [1905] 2 Ch 257; *Re Button's Lease* [1964] Ch 263, [1963] 3 All ER 708. See generally (1958) 74 LQR 242 (W. J. Mowbray).
 6 *Hua Chiao Commercial Bank Ltd v Chiaphua Industries Ltd* [1987] AC 99, [1987] 1 All ER 1110; M & B p. 513.
 7 At 107, at 1112, per Lord OLIVER OF AYLMERTON.

rules depend partly upon the common law as finally enunciated in *Spencer's Case*, 1583,[8] and partly upon statutes. The statutes that formerly regulated the matter were the Grantees of Reversions Act, passed in 1540[9] after the dissolution of the monasteries, and the Conveyancing Act 1881,[10] but these were both repealed and replaced by the Law of Property Act 1925.[11]

(1) BENEFIT OF COVENANT RUNS WITH LAND

The lessee assigns his interest to A. Can A enforce the covenants which were inserted in the lease in favour of the lessee? The rule even at common law is that the benefit of the covenants runs with the land, enabling an assignee (A) from the lessee to sue the lessor on any covenants which touch and concern the land demised and which enure for the benefit of the lessee, such as a covenant by the lessor to supply the demised premises with pure water. The authority for this rule is *Spencer's Case*, in the fourth resolution of which the court, dealing with a covenant for quiet enjoyment, said:

> for the lessee and his assignee hath the yearly profits of the land, which shall grow by his labour and industry for an annual rent; and therefore it is reasonable when he hath applied his labour and employed his cost upon the land, and be evicted (whereby he loses all), that he shall take such benefit of the demise and grant, as the first lessee might . . . .

(2) BURDEN OF COVENANT RUNS WITH LAND

The lessee assigns his interest to A. Can A be sued upon the covenants which were inserted in the lease in favour of the lessor? The common law answers this also in the affirmative, provided that the covenant touches and concerns the land, for it was said in *Spencer's Case* that:

> When the covenant extends to a thing *in esse*, parcel of the demise, the thing to be done by force of the covenant is *quodammodo* annexed and appurtenant to the thing demised, and shall go with the land and shall bind the assignee, although he be not bound by express words.

It is true that the judgment then proceeded to draw a distinction between a covenant which referred to something already in existence (such as to repair an existing wall), and one which related to a thing not in existence at the time of the lease (such as a covenant to build a new wall), and laid down that though the former would bind assignees in all cases, yet the latter would not do so unless the original lessee had covenanted for himself *and his assigns*. This distinction rested upon no solid basis, but, though adversely criticized,[12] it remained law until 1926. It was abolished by the Law of Property Act 1925, which provides that:[13]

> A covenant relating to any land of a covenantor or capable of being bound by him, shall, unless a contrary intention is expressed,[14] be deemed to be made by the

---

8 (1583) 5 Co Rep 16; M & B p. 514.
9 32 Hen 8, c. 34, s. 1.
10 Ss. 10, 11.
11 Ss. 141, 142.
12 *Minshull v Oakes* (1858) 2 H & N 793. See Behan, *Covenants Affecting Land*, pp. 75 et seq.
13 S. 79 (1).
14 I.e. unless an indication to the contrary is found in the instrument, and this may be expressed or implied: *Re Royal Victoria Pavilion, Ramsgate* [1961] Ch 581, [1961] 3 All ER 83, per PENNYCUICK J at 589, at 87; M & B p. 840.

covenantor on behalf of himself his successors in title and the persons deriving title under him or them, and, subject as aforesaid, shall have effect as if such successors and other persons were expressed.

This subsection extends to a covenant to do some act relating to the land, notwithstanding that the subject-matter may not be in existence when the covenant is made.

This section, however, applies only to covenants made on or after 1 January 1926. In the case of a lease executed before 1926, the burden of a covenant relating to something not in existence will not run with the land unless it was expressly imposed upon the lessee *and his assigns*.

(3) BENEFIT OF COVENANT RUNS WITH REVERSION

The lessor assigns his interest, i.e. the reversion, to Z. Can Z enforce the covenants which were inserted in the lease in favour of the lessor? The rule at common law is that the grantee of a reversion can sue upon an implied covenant, that is, one which automatically results from the relationship of landlord and tenant (such as a covenant to pay rent), but he cannot sue upon express covenants contained in the lease.[15] The difficulty is said to be that in the case of a reversion there is no corporeal thing to which the covenant can be regarded as annexed, such as there is where the land is assigned.[16]

A mitigation of this strict rule of the common law became urgent when the monasteries were dissolved by Henry VIII in 1539, because, if the law had not been altered, it would have precluded the grantees of the monastic lands from enforcing against existing lessees the express covenants in leases granted by the monasteries before their dissolution. Hence the Grantees of Reversions Act 1540, which, though designed merely to accommodate grantees of monastic lands, soon came to be regarded as having universal application and as laying down the law for assignees of reversions in general. This statute, which remained the only law on the subject until the Conveyancing Act 1881, enacted that assignees of reversions should have the same right of enforcing forfeitures, and the same right of suing for a breach of any covenant, as the original lessors.[17]

Both these statutes have been repealed, and the right of an assignee of a reversion to enforce the covenants now rests upon the Law of Property Act 1925,[18] which, in a section that applies to all leases whether made before or after the Act provides that:

(1) Rent reserved by a lease, and the benefit of every covenant or provision therein contained, having reference to the subject-matter thereof,[19] and on the lessee's part to be observed or performed, and every condition of re-entry and other condition therein contained, shall be annexed and incident to and shall go with the reversionary estate in the land, or in any part thereof, immediately expectant on the term granted by the lease, notwithstanding severance of that reversionary estate, and without prejudice to any liability affecting a covenantor or his estate.[20]

(2) Any such rent, covenant or provision shall be capable of being recovered, received, enforced and taken advantage of, by the person from time to time entitled, subject

15 *Platt on Covenants*, p. 531; *Wedd v Porter* [1916] 2 KB 91 at 100–101.
16 E.g. *Smith's Leading Cases* (13th edn), vol. i. pp. 61–2.
17 S. 10.
18 S. 141.
19 I.e., touching and concerning the land demised.
20 *London and County (A and D) Ltd v Wilfred Sportsman Ltd* [1971] Ch 764, [1970] 2 All ER 600; M & B p. 519.

to the term, to the income of the whole or any part, as the case may require, of the land leased.

(3) Where that person becomes entitled by conveyance or otherwise, such rent, covenant or provision may be recovered, received, enforced or taken advantage of by him notwithstanding that he becomes so entitled after the condition of re-entry or forfeiture has become enforceable, but this subsection does not render enforceable any condition of re-entry or other condition waived or released before such person becomes entitled as aforesaid.

(a) Form of lease

One result of this enactment, which provides, in repetition of the Conveyancing Act 1881, that "rent reserved by a lease,[1] and the benefit of every covenant or provision therein contained" shall pass with the reversion, is to abolish the old construction that was put upon the Grantees of Reversions Act 1540, viz. that the assignee of a reversion could not sue upon the covenants unless the original lease was under seal. The rule now is that the assignee can sue if the lease is in writing or if the tenancy is the result of a written agreement for a lease,[2] even though in the latter case the agreement is signed by the landlord only.[3] The same is the case if a parol lease is made for a period not exceeding three years, or if an agreement for a lease complies with the formality requirements for the sale or other disposition of an interest in land.[4]

(b) Breach of covenant committed before assignment

The Court of Appeal has held that, under this section of the Act, the assignee of the reversion is the only person entitled to sue the tenant for any breach of covenant, whether of a continuous nature or not and even though committed before the date of the assignment:[5]

> The expression "go with" must be intended to add something to the concept involved in the expression "annexed and incident to" and in my view connotes the transfer of the right to enforce the covenant from the assignor to the assignee with the consequent cessation of the right of the assignor to enforce the covenant against the tenant.[6]

(4) BURDEN OF COVENANT RUNS WITH REVERSION

The lessor assigns his reversion to Z. Can Z be sued upon the covenants which were inserted in the lease in favour of the lessee? There was no right of action against Z at common law, but a right was given by the Grantees of Reversions Act 1540 which enacted that a lessee and his assigns should have

1 "Lease" includes "an under-lease or other tenancy": s. 154.
2 *Rickett v Green* [1910] 1 KB 253; M & B p. 524; *Boyer v Warbey* [1953] 1 QB 234, [1953] 1 All ER 269; M & B p. 524; [1978] 37 CLJ 98 (R. J. Smith).
3 *Rye v Purcell* [1926] 1 KB 446.
4 *Boyer v Warbey* [1953] 1 QB 234, [1953] 1 All ER 269; M & B p. 525; Law of Property (Miscellaneous Provisions) Act 1989, s. 2, p. 121 ante.
5 *Re King* [1963] Ch 459, [1963] 1 All ER 781; M & B p. 517 (covenant to repair and reinstate); *London and County (A and D) Ltd v Wilfred Sportsman Ltd* [1971] Ch 764, [1970] 2 All ER 600, M & B p. 519 (covenant to pay rent); *Arlesford Trading Co Ltd v Servansingh* [1971] 1 WLR 1080, [1971] 3 All ER 1130; *Electricity Supply Nominees Ltd v Thorn EMI Retail Ltd* [1991] 2 EGLR 46.
6 Ibid., at 497, at 798, per DIPLOCK LJ.

the same remedy against the assignees of the lessor as the original lessee would have had against the lessor. This enactment was attended by certain difficulties, which are no longer of interest, since they were removed by the Conveyancing Act 1881,[7] in a section now replaced by section 142 (1) of the Law of Property Act 1925, and applicable to all leases whenever made:[8]

> The obligation under a condition or of a covenant entered into by a lessor with reference to the subject-matter of the lease shall, if and as far as the lessor has power to bind the reversionary estate immediately expectant on the term granted by the lease, be annexed and incident to and shall go with that reversionary estate, or the several parts thereof, notwithstanding severance of that reversionary estate, and may be taken advantage of and enforced by the person in whom the term is from time to time vested by conveyance, devolution in law, or otherwise; and, if and as far as the lessor has power to bind the person from time to time entitled to that reversionary estate, the obligation aforesaid may be taken advantage of and enforced against any person so entitled.

The word "covenant" as used in this section is not confined to its strict meaning of a contract under seal, but includes any promise touching and concerning the land[9] that is contained in a tenancy agreement made otherwise than by deed.[10]

(a) Breach of covenant committed before assignment

Section 142 differs in one respect from its counterpart, section 141. It does not contain subsections corresponding to subsections (2) and (3) of section 141. As a result of the omission, it has been held that, although a tenant can sue the assignee of the reversion for breach of a repairing covenant which occurred before the assignment, because the property is still in disrepair, he cannot sue him for consequential damages flowing from the breach.[11]

(b) Severance of reversion

One particular difficulty which arose under the Grantees of Reversions Act was that, owing to its indivisible nature,[12] a condition could not be enforced by an assignee of *part* of the reversion. If the reversion was severed, the condition could not be apportioned. The statutory rule now, however, is that, where such a severance has taken place, every condition contained in the lease is apportioned and remains annexed to the severed parts of the reversion.[13] The tenancy itself, however, is not severed, with the result that there is still a single tenancy, even though the reversion has been severed.[14] If the owner of a severed part of the reversion determines the tenancy by a notice to quit,[15] the lessee is permitted within one month to determine the

7 S. 11.
8 S. 142 (1).
9 *Davis v Town Properties etc* [1903] 1 Ch 797.
10 *Weg Motors Ltd v Hales* [1962] Ch 49, [1961] 3 All ER 181.
11 *Duncliffe v Caerfelin Properties Ltd* [1989] 2 EGLR 38; [1990] Conv 127 (J. E. Martin). For another difference between the sections, see *City and Metropolitan Properties Ltd v Greycroft Ltd* [1987] 1 WLR 1085, [1987] 3 All ER 839, p. 454, post.
12 P. 419, ante.
13 LPA 1925, s. 140 (1); replacing LP(A)A 1859, s. 3, and Conveyancing Act 1881, s. 12.
14 LPA 1925, s. 140 (2). The severance must be genuine, and not, e.g., where the landlord conveys part of the reversion to bare trustees for himself: *Persey v Bazley* (1984) 47 P & CR 37.
15 See, e.g., *Smith v Kinsey* [1936] 3 All ER 73.

whole tenancy by serving notice on the owner in whom the rest of the reversion is vested.[16]

C. ESSENTIALS OF ENFORCEABILITY

Before we conclude the subject of covenants that run with the land or the reversion, there are two general observations of considerable importance to be made.

(1) PRIVITY OF CONTRACT OR ESTATE

First, there can be no question of the enforcement of covenants between two parties unless there exists between them either privity of estate or privity of contract. *Privity of contract* denotes that relationship which exists between the lessor and the lessee—and between them only—by virtue of the covenants contained in the lease. This relationship is created by the contract itself and continues to subsist between the lessor and lessee despite an assignment of their respective interests. *Privity of estate* describes the relationship between two parties who respectively hold the same estates as those created by the lease. This is the position where one holds the original reversion and the other the original term, or rather, the whole of what is now left of the original term. Thus there is privity of estate between the lessor and an assignee from the lessee of the residue of the term; also between the lessee and an assignee of the reversion; also between an assignee of the reversion and an assignee of the residue of the term. In the absence of assignment, therefore, there is privity both of contract and of estate between the lessor and lessee.[17]

(a) Original lessee always liable to original lessor

There are certain important rules that flow from this general principle. Thus:

> It is perfectly settled by a multitude of decisions that, notwithstanding an assignment of his lease, the lessee continues liable on the personal privity of the contract to the payment of the rent and the performance of the covenants during the whole term; although the lessor concur in the assignment, or, by acceptance of rent or otherwise, recognize the assignee as his tenant.[18]

This continuing liability of the original lessee for all breaches of covenant throughout the duration of the lease, even after he has assigned it, is a hazard to the lessee.[19] Recent cases have highlighted this, and in one of them:[20]

---

16 *Jelley v Buckman* [1974] QB 488, [1973] 3 All ER 853; *Nevil Long & Co (Boards) Ltd v Firmenich & Co* (1984) 47 P & CR 59.

17 *Bickford v Parson* (1848) 5 CB 920 at 929. See also *Platt on Leases*, vol. ii. p. 351: "Privity of estate is the result of tenure; it subsists by virtue of the relation of landlord and tenant, and follows alike the devolution of the reversion, and of the term".

18 *Platt on Leases*, vol. ii. pp. 352–3; *Warnford Investments Ltd v Duckworth* [1979] Ch 127 at 137, [1978] 2 All ER 517 at 525. Distinguish, however, the liability of a lessee who acquires a statutory term of 2000 years under the provisions for converting perpetually renewable leases; pp. 359, ante.

19 The original tenant is released if the landlord unconditionally releases the assignee by accord and satisfaction: *Deanplan Ltd v Mahmoud* [1993] Ch 151, [1992] 3 All ER 945; (1993) 143 NLJ 28 (H. W. Wilkinson); *City of London Corpn v Fell* [1993] 3 WLR 1164 (where lease, assigned by original lessee, had run its term and had been extended under Landlord and Tenant Act 1954, original lessee's obligations held to cease on completion of term); [1994]

a warehouse was let for 21 years at a rent of £17,000 a year, subject to a rent review at the end of 14 years. The original lessee assigned the lease and in the following year the landlord and the assignee agreed a revised rent of £40,000 a year. When the assignee failed to pay the rent for two quarters, the lessee was held liable to pay the £20,000 then outstanding.

As HARMAN J said:[1]

Each assignee is the owner of the whole estate and can deal with it so as to alter it or its terms. The estate as so altered then binds the original tenant, because the assignee has been put into the shoes of the original tenant and can do all such acts as the original tenant could have done.

Although the point does not often arise, the landlord is in the same position as the lessee. He remains personally liable on his covenants in the lease even after he has assigned his reversion.[2] Likewise he remains liable to the tenant, even after the tenant has assigned his lease.[3]

(b) Assignee liable and entitled only in respect of matters occurring while he holds the land

Again, as the liability of an assignee of the tenant is based upon the privity[4] of estate between him and the lessor or the latter's assignee, it follows that the tenant's assignee cannot be liable for a breach of covenant committed before he took the estate under the assignment,[5] and cannot sue the lessor for breaches committed prior to that time. Lastly, and consistently with the same principle, an assignee ceases to be liable for breaches occurring after he has assigned his interest to a third party, for such a re-assignment obviously destroys the privity of estate which previously existed.[6] He is liable, however, even for these subsequent breaches, if he expressly covenants with the landlord at the time of taking the assignment that he will perform the terms of the lease.[7] Moreover, in any event, he remains liable after re-assignment for any breaches which occurred while the tenancy was vested in him.[8]

CLJ 28 (S. Bridge); cf. *Herbert Duncan Ltd v Cluttons* [1993] QB 589, [1993] 2 All ER 449; [1993] Conv 164 (P. F. Smith). See also *Norwich Union Life Insurance Society v Low Profile Fashions Ltd* [1992] 1 EGLR 86; [1992] CLJ 425 (S. Bridge) (no duty of care on landlord to ensure solvency of assignee when consenting to assignment, and no equitable principle which obliges landlord to sue assigns and his surety before original tenant).

20 *Centrovincial Estates plc v Bulk Storage Ltd* (1983) 46 P & CR 393; [1984] Conv 443 (P. McLoughlin). The other cases are *Allied London Investments Ltd v Hambro Life Assurance Ltd* [1985] 1 EGLR 45; *Selous Street Properties Ltd v Oranel Fabrics Ltd* (1984) 270 EG 643; *Thames Manufacturing Co Ltd v Perrotts (Nichol & Peyton) Ltd* (1984) 50 P & CR 1; *Gus Property Management Ltd v Texas Homecare Ltd* [1993] 27 EG 130.

For the continuing liability of a surety for the original lessee, see *P & A Swift Investments v Combined English Stores Group plc* [1989] AC 632, [1988] 2 All ER 885; *Becton Dickinson UK Ltd v Zwebner* [1989] QB 208; *Johnsey Estates Ltd v Webb* [1990] 1 EGLR 80. And for his liability to an assignee of the lessee, see *Cerium Investments Ltd v Evans* [1991] 1 EGLR 80.

1 At 396.
2 *Stuart v Joy* [1904] 1 KB 362.
3 *City and Metropolitan Properties Ltd v Greycroft Properties Ltd* [1987] 1 WLR 1085, [1987] 3 All ER 839 (tenant who assigned lease at reduced value because of landlord's breach of covenant to repair held able to recover damages from landlord after assignment); [1987] Conv 374 (P. F. Smith).
4 *Purchase v Lichfield Brewery Ltd* [1915] 1 KB 184; M & B p. 525.
5 *Grescot v Green* (1700) 1 Salk 199.
6 *Paul v Nurse* (1828) 8 B & C 486.
7 *J Lyons & Co Ltd v Knowles* [1943] 1 KB 366, [1943] 1 All ER 477.
8 *Harley v King* (1835) 2 Cr M & R 18; cf *Richmond v Savill* [1926] 2 KB 530.

(c) Implied indemnity by assignee

It will thus be seen that, where one of the lessee's covenants has been broken after an assignment of the term, the lessor has the option of suing either the original lessee on the privity of contract or the particular assignee who had the estate when the breach occurred, but although this joint liability undoubtedly exists, the rule is that the assignee in possession is the principal debtor, while the lessee occupies the position of a surety.[9] Nevertheless the continuing liability of the original lessee is an obvious menace to him, and it became the invariable practice for every assignee expressly to covenant to indemnify his assignor against future breaches of the provisions contained in the lease. This is no longer necessary, for it is now enacted that every assignment for valuable consideration[10] shall be deemed to include a covenant by the assignee that he will pay all rent falling due in the future and will perform all the covenants, agreements and conditions binding upon the original lessee. This implied covenant of indemnity binds all persons, such as later assignees, deriving title under the assignee.[11] To take an example:

L leases land to T. Later successive assignments of the land are made first to U, then to V, and finally to W. If L sues T for the breach committed by W of some condition contained in the lease, the implied covenant of indemnity entitles T to make U a party to the action. Similarly U can join V, and V can join W as a party. In this way judgment can be given against the person who has actually committed the breach.[12]

(d) Law reform

In 1988 the Law Commission recommended in its Report on Privity of Contract and Estate[13] that tenants should automatically be released from their liabilities when they dispose of their interests, unless the landlord's consent to a transfer was needed and he could prove that it was reasonable that they should guarantee their immediate successor's liability. Likewise tenants should be protected when the freehold changes hands between landlords.

In 1993 the Government announced that it would implement these recommendations, with two modifications.[14] The scope of the reform should be limited to future but not to existing leases, and to commercial but not residential leases; and notice of claims for arrears of rent or service charges should be served within nine months after the money becomes due.

---

9 *Humble v Langston* (1841) 7 M & W 517 at 530, per PARKE B.

10 On valuable consideration, see *Johnsey Estates Ltd v Lewis & Manley (Engineering) Ltd* [1987] 2 EGLR 69.

11 LPA 1925, s. 77 (1) (*c*); Sch. 2, Part IX; and in registered land, LRA 1925, s. 24 (whether or not there is valuable consideration). It may be excluded by an express term of the contract: *Re Healing Research Trustee Co Ltd* [1992] 2 All ER 481.

12 As to the nature of this covenant, see *Butler Estates Co v Bean* [1942] 1 KB 1, [1941] 2 All ER 793. See also *Re Mirror Group Holdings Ltd* [1992] EGCS 126 (original lessee cannot compel his assignee to enforce the benefit of its own indemnity covenant against an ultimate assignee if the latter has re-assigned the lease).

13 Law Com. No. 174; [1989] Conv 145; (1991) 11 LS 47 (R. Thornton); [1992] Conv 393 (H. W. Wilkinson).

14 See also Landlord and Tenant Law Amendment Act (Ireland) 1860, s. 16; [1993] Conv 151 (J. McRobert).

(2) ASSIGNMENT

(a) Whole interest must be transferred

The second observation is that the rules laid down above with regard to the running of covenants apply only where there has been an assignment in the true and proper sense of that term, for it is only then that privity of estate exists between the reversioner and the person who is in occupation of the land. The term "assignee" is very comprehensive: it applies to all persons who take the estate either by act of party[15] or by act of law, such as the executors of a lessee or assignee, and persons taking the premises by way of execution for debt, but in the eyes of the law no person occupies the position of assignee of the land unless he takes the *identical term* which the lessee had, and also takes the *whole of that term.*[16]

Thus if the lessee, on making what purports to be an assignment of his term, reserves to himself a reversion, no matter how trifling it may be—as where he assigns the remainder of his lease less one day—the transaction amounts to an under-lease and not to an assignment. In such a case it is obvious that there is neither privity of contract nor privity of estate between the superior landlord and the under-lessee, and therefore neither of them can sue or be sued *at law* upon the covenants of the lease,[17] though as we shall see later the under-lessee may be liable under the equitable doctrine of *Tulk v Moxhay* on purely negative covenants.[18] But there is no magic in words. If a man has acquired an interest in the tenancy and a question arises with regard to his position, the first point that falls to be considered is whether he has taken the whole of the tenant's interest. Thus where the tenant executes a deed couched in the form of an under-lease, which purports to sub-let the property for the whole of the remainder of his term or for a longer period, the transaction amounts to an assignment.[19]

(b) Identical interest must be transferred

The other point, as we have observed, is that if there is to be an assignment, the alienee must take the identical interest which the alienor possessed. If, for instance, a tenant deposits his lease with X by way of mortgage, X obtains a mere equitable right to the land and not the legal term to which the tenant was entitled. Therefore, whether he goes into possession or not, he can neither sue nor be sued on the covenants.[20] A similar result again ensues where a person obtains a title under the Limitation Act against the lessee, as was decided in *Tichborne v Weir.*[1] The facts of this case were as follows:

> In 1802 D leased land to B for 89 years.
> In 1836 G seized the land and remained in possession of it until 1876, paying D the rent which had been fixed by the lease of 1802.
> In 1876 G by deed assigned all his interest to the defendant, who remained in

---

15 *Old Grovebury Manor Farm Ltd v W Seymour Plant Sales and Hire Ltd (No 2)* [1979] 1 WLR 1397, [1979] 3 All ER 504; p. 436, n. 14, ante.

16 *Platt on Leases*, vol. ii. pp. 419–20.

17 *South of England Dairies Co v Baker* [1906] 2 Ch 631; M & B p. 520.

18 P. 619, post.

19 *Beardman v Wilson* (1868) LR 4 CP 57; *Hallen v Spaeth* [1923] AC 684; *Milmo v Carreras* [1946] KB 306, [1946] 1 All ER 288; M & B p. 520.

20 *Cox v Bishop* (1857) 8 De GM & G 815; M & B p. 524. He may, however, be liable under the doctrine of *Tulk v Moxhay*, pp. 614 et seq, post.

 1 (1892) 67 LT 735; M & B pp. 208, 838, followed in *Taylor v Twinberrow* [1930] 2 KB 16.

possession until 1891, paying the same rent to the plaintiff, who had succeeded to D.

The original lease between D and B contained a covenant by B to keep the premises in repair, and the plaintiff now sued the defendant for breach of that covenant. The right of the original covenantor B to his tenancy of the land had been extinguished by lapse of time when the defendant came to the land in 1876, but the question that arose was whether the defendant was an assignee of B through G. It was clear, if the identical lease which was vested in B had passed to G and from him to the defendant, that the latter would be liable as assignee on the repairing covenant, and it was strenuously argued that the effect of the Real Property Limitation Act 1833, which was the statute then in force, was to transfer the term from B to G.

But it was held that the only effect of the statute was to extinguish B's right of recovering the land and not to convey what he had to G. It therefore followed that the defendant was not liable on the repairing covenant, because, not possessing the very estate to which it was attached, he was not an assignee.

But the limits of the decision must be noted. It was said by a learned Irish judge:[2]

> It appears to me to decide only this, that the Statute of Limitations operates by way of extinguishment, and not by way of assignment of the estate, which is barred; and that a person who becomes entitled to a leasehold interest by adverse possession for the prescribed period is not liable to be sued *in covenant as assignee* of the lease, unless he has estopped himself from denying that he is assignee.

So, in the first place, the decision will not apply where the occupier of the lands has estopped himself from denying that he holds on all the terms of the original lease,[3] but although this point was pressed in *Tichborne v Weir*, it was held that the terms under which the defendant paid rent did not warrant the conclusion that he stood for all purposes in the shoes of the original tenant B.[4] But where a lease contains a proviso that the rent shall be reduced by a half if all the covenants are duly observed, and an adverse possessor avails himself of the privilege, he is estopped from denying that he is subject to the burden of the lease.[5]

Secondly, the case only goes to show that an adverse possessor cannot be sued in covenant as assignee, and when we come to deal with equitable doctrines, we shall see that he is liable on such negative covenants as create an equitable burden on the estate he takes.[6]

SECTION VIII DETERMINATION OF TENANCIES

A. TENANCIES FOR A FIXED PERIOD

A tenancy for a fixed period may be terminated by forfeiture, surrender, merger, enlargement, effluxion of time, frustration, or, where an agreement to that effect has been made, by a notice to quit given by either party.

(1) FORFEITURE

There is no need to add to the account already given of forfeiture.[7]

2 FITZGIBBON LJ in *O'Connor v Foley* [1906] 1 IR 20 at 26.
3 As for instance in *Rodenhurst Estates Ltd v Barnes Ltd* [1936] 2 All ER 3.
4 For another instance, see *Official Trustee of Charity Lands v Ferriman Trust Ltd* [1937] 3 All ER 85.
5 *Ashe v Hogan* [1920] 1 IR 159.
6 *Re Nisbet and Potts' Contract* [1905] 1 Ch 391; M & B pp. 208, 838; pp. 620–1, post.
7 Pp. 428–34, 434–44, ante.

(2) SURRENDER

Surrender occurs where the tenant yields up his estate to the lessor. In the case of a joint tenancy, a surrender is not effective unless made by all the tenants.[8]

(a) Express surrender

The express surrender of a lease not exceeding three years may be effected by a written instrument,[9] but in terms for longer periods it must be made by deed.[10] If an express surrender is not made by deed, but complies with the formalities required for a contract for the sale or other disposition of land[10a] and is made for value (for example, where the landlord releases the tenant's arrears of rent), it is effective in equity as a contract to surrender the lease.[11]

(b) Surrender by operation of law

If, however, the intention of the parties as inferred from their conduct is that the lease should be yielded up, surrender results by operation of law without the necessity either of a writing or a deed.[12] This doctrine rests upon the principle of estoppel.[13] It operates where the owner of a particular estate, such as a tenant for years, is a party to some transaction that would not be valid if his estate continued to exist. If, for example, the lessor grants to him a new lease which is to begin during the currency of the existing lease, the latter is implicitly surrendered and the tenant is estopped from disputing the validity of the new lease.[14] Before there can be such an implied surrender, there must be something in the nature of an agreement, and that agreement must amount to more than a mere variation of the terms of an existing tenancy.[15] In particular, an agreed increase in rent does not necessarily amount to an implied surrender.[16]

Other examples of implied surrender occur, if:

possession is delivered by the tenant to the lessor and accepted by the latter;[17]

---

8 *Leek and Moorlands Building Society v Clark* [1952] 2 QB 788, [1952] 2 All ER 492. For the effect of surrender by a tenant on his sub-tenant's estate, see *Bromley Park Garden Estates Ltd v George* [1991] 2 EGLR 95, p. 916, post.

9 LPA 1925, ss. 53 (1) (*a*), 54 (2); *Crago v Julian* [1992] 1 WLR 372, [1992] 1 All ER 744, p. 375, ante.

10 Ibid., s. 52; *Greenwich London Borough Council v McGrady* (1982) 46 P & CR 223 at 224.

10a P. 108, ante.

11 *Tarjomani v Panther Securities Ltd* (1982) 46 P & CR 32. It is not an actual surrender as required by Landlord and Tenant Act 1954, s. 24 (2).

12 LPA 1925, s. 52 (2) (*c*).

13 For its operation in the creation of a tenancy, see p. 388, ante.

14 *Lyon v Reed* (1844) 13 M & W 285; *Fenner v Blake* [1900] 1 QB 426; *Knight v Williams* [1901] 1 Ch 256. To produce a surrender, the new lease must be effective, not, for example, one which is beyond the powers of the lessor: *Barclays Bank Ltd v Stasek* [1957] Ch 28, [1956] 3 All ER 439.

15 *Smirk v Lyndale Developments Ltd* [1975] Ch 317 at 339, [1975] 1 All ER 690 at 694, per LAWTON LJ; *Bush Transport Ltd v Nelson* [1987] 1 EGLR 71 (oral agreement).

16 *Jenkin R Lewis & Son Ltd v Kerman* [1971] Ch 477, [1970] 3 All ER 414; *Take Harvest Ltd v Liv* [1993] AC 552, [1993] 2 All ER 459.

17 *Dodd v Acklom* (1843) 6 Man & G 672. See *Chamberlaine v Scally* [1992] EGCS 90 (no unequivocal conduct which was inconsistent with continuance of existing tenancy; tenant's belongings and two cats still on premises, which she visited to attend to them); cf. *Brent London Borough v Sharma* [1993] 1 EGLR 59.

the tenant is permitted to remain in occupation of the premises as a licensee paying no rent;[18]

the lessor grants a new lease to a third party, or accepts a third party as the new tenant, with the assent of the existing tenant;[19]

the tenant has been absent from the premises for a substantial period and owes a substantial amount of rent.[20]

(3) MERGER

The term of years and the reversion are concurrent interests that cannot be held by one and the same person at the same time. If, therefore, they become united in one person in the same right, as for example where the lessor conveys the fee simple to the tenant, the term is at common law immediately destroyed. It is said to be "merged", i.e. sunk or drowned in the greater estate.[1] It will be explained later, however, that in equity the union of a smaller and a greater estate in one person does not always result in merger.[2]

(4) ENLARGEMENT

A tenant may by deed enlarge his lease into a fee simple under the Law of Property Act 1925.[3]

Before the enlargement can be effected, however, the following conditions must exist:

(i)   The term must originally have been created for not less than 300 years, and at the time of the proposed enlargement there must be at least 200 more years to run.

(ii) There must be no trust or right of redemption[4] still existing in favour of the reversioner.

(iii) The term must not be one which is liable to be determined by re-entry for condition broken.

(iv) There must be no rent of any money value.[5]

A fee simple, so acquired by enlargement, is subject to all the same covenants, provisions and obligations as the lease would have been subject to if it had not been so enlarged.[6]

As we shall see, this statutory power provides a possible, but as yet untried, method of making the burden of positive covenants run with freehold land.[7]

(5) EFFLUXION OF TIME

In principle there is no need for a notice to quit in the case of a lease for a definite term, since the tenancy terminates automatically upon the expiration of the agreed period. The scope of this rule, however, has been drastically

---

18 *Foster v Robinson* [1951] 1 KB 149, [1950] 2 All ER 342; *Scrimgeour v Waller* (1980) 257 EG 61; *Tarjomani v Panther Securities Ltd* (1982) 46 P & CR 32.
19 *Wallis v Hands* [1893] 2 Ch 75; *Metcalfe v Boyce* [1927] 1 KB 758.
20 *Preston Borough Council v Fairclough* (1982) 8 HLR 70 (test not satisfied).
 1 Blackstone, vol. ii. p. 177.
 2 P. 916, post.
 3 S. 153. See (1958) 22 Conv (NS) 101 (T. P. D. Taylor).
 4 I.e., under a mortgage. See p. 672, post.
 5 *Re Chapman and Hobbs* (1885) 29 Ch D 1007; *Re Smith and Stott* (1883) 29 Ch D 1009.
 6 LPA 1925, s. 153 (8); p. 613, post.
 7 P. 613, post.

restricted by legislation, for there are several cases in which there is no automatic cessation of a tenancy upon the expiration of the period for which it was granted. These cases are the following:

Private Residential Lettings.[8]
Public Sector Housing.[9]
Long Tenancies.[10]
Business Tenancies.[11]
Agricultural Holdings.[12]

In the result there are comparatively few cases in which effluxion of time has its normal effect.

(6) NOTICE TO QUIT

(a) When necessary

A notice to quit is necessary in the case of yearly and other periodic tenancies, and also in the case of a lease for a fixed period if a stipulation to that effect is made. There is special protection in the case of a dwelling-house. The Protection from Eviction Act 1977[13] provides that no notice shall be valid unless it is given not less than four weeks before the date on which it is to expire; the notice must be in writing and contain such information as may be prescribed by the Secretary of State.[14] The common law rule applies in this context and the provision is satisfied by a notice given on one day to expire that day four weeks hence.[15]

(b) Essentials of validity

Since the notice is a unilateral act performed in the exercise of a contractual right, it must conform strictly to the terms of the contract.[16] The onus of proving its validity lies upon the person by whom it is given.[17] Three matters in particular upon which its validity depends may be observed.

(i) **Must indicate correct day** First, it is void unless it either names the correct date for the termination of the tenancy[18] or uses a formula from which the correct date is ascertainable with certainty. A familiar example of the latter is when the notice requires the yearly tenant to quit the premises:

---

8   P. 468, post.
9   P. 487, post.
10 P. 489, post.
11 P. 502, post.
12 P. 509, post.
13 S. 5 (1) (b). This section only applies where the true relation between the parties is that of landlord and tenant: *Alliance Building Society v Pinwill* [1958] Ch 788, [1958] 2 All ER 408; *Crane v Morris* [1965] 1 WLR 1104, [1965] 3 All ER 77; *Peckham Mutual Building Society v Rigiste* (1980) 42 P & CR 186. Four weeks is also the minimum notice for a residential contract in respect of a caravan: Caravan Sites Act 1968, s. 2.
14 Ibid., s. 5 (1) (a). See Notices to Quit (Prescribed Information) Regulations 1988 (S.I. 1988 No. 2201).
15 *Schnabel v Allard* [1966] 3 All ER 816.
16 *Dagger v Shepherd* [1946] KB 215 at 220, [1946] 1 All ER 133 at 135; *Hankey v Clavering* [1942] 2 KB 326 at 330, [1942] 2 All ER 311 at 314.
17 *Lemon v Lardeur* [1946] KB 613, [1946] 2 All ER 329.
18 *Hankey v Clavering*, supra.

at the expiration of the year of your tenancy, which shall expire next after the end of one half-year from the service of this notice.[19]

Where, however, the date in the notice is one which no reasonable tenant could possibly have supposed was the date correctly intended by the landlord, the notice will be valid. Thus, where by a clerical error a notice served in 1974 referred to a 1973 date instead of a 1975 date, GOULDING J held the notice valid and said:[20]

I would put the test generally applicable as being this: "Is the notice quite clear to a reasonable tenant reading it? Is it plain that he cannot be misled by it?"

A gloss was put on this test in *Land v Sykes*,[1] where SCOTT LJ held that it was:

subject perhaps to the qualifications that the reasonable tenant reading the notice is to be taken to have had the knowledge of the surrounding facts and circumstances which the actual landlord and tenant enjoyed.

(ii) Must be unconditional Secondly, a notice to quit must be unconditional. It must be expressed in such decisive and unequivocal terms, that the person to whom it is directed can entertain no reasonable doubt as to its intended effect. In particular, although no precise form is required, "there must be plain unambiguous words claiming to determine the existing tenancy at a certain time".[2] Thus a notice given by a tenant would be ineffective if it expressed his intention to quit the premises on 25 March, unless he was unable to obtain alternative accommodation.

Where, however, the naming of a certain day for the termination of the tenancy is followed by an intimation that the lease shall continue if the other party assents to certain terms, as for example to an increase[3] or diminution[4] of rent, the courts are inclined to treat the document as a valid notice accompanied by an offer of a new tenancy capable of acceptance or refusal by the other party. In *Dagger v Shepherd*,[5] for instance, the question arose whether a notice, given on 21 December, directing the tenant to quit the premises:

on or before the 25th March next,

was valid and effective. It was objected by the tenant that the notice was void for uncertainty, since he was left in doubt as to its intended effect. In his submission the document contained nothing more than a statement that the tenancy was to end on some unspecified date between 21 December and 25 March. The court, however, rejected this submission. It construed the

19 *Addis v Burrows* [1948] 1 KB 444, [1948] 1 All ER 177. See (1974) 38 Conv (NS) 312.
20 *Carradine Properties Ltd v Aslam* [1976] 1 WLR 442, [1976] 1 All ER 573, approved and followed by CA in *Germax Securities Ltd v Spiegal* (1978) 37 P & CR 204 (where the clerical error was not in the operative part of the notice, and was clear from association of the notice with a covering letter from the landlord); (1977) 40 MLR 490 (P. F. Smith). See also *Safeway Food Stores v Morris* (1980) 254 EG 1091 (notice, which failed to identify subsidiary part of property necessarily enjoyed with main part of it, held to apply to whole); *Crawford v Elliott* [1991] 1 EGLR 13; *Divall v Harrison* [1992] 2 EGLR 64 (notice which failed to identify correct landlord held invalid).
1 [1992] 1 EGLR 1 at 3 (9 ft by 200 ft strip not material in context of 290 acre farm).
2 *Gardner v Ingram* (1889) 61 LT 729 at 730, per Lord COLERIDGE.
3 *Ahearn v Bellman* (1879) 4 Ex D 201; but Lord ESHER vigorously dissented.
4 *Bury v Thompson* [1895] 1 QB 696.
5 [1946] KB 215, [1946] 1 All ER 133.

document as an irrevocable notice to quit on 25 March in any event, but
followed by an offer to accept the termination of the tenancy at an earlier
date at which the tenant might elect to give up possession. Similarly, a notice
to quit "by" a certain day is valid.[6] And, where the landlord has a right to
determine a lease by giving to the tenant "not less than three months' notice",
a notice to vacate the premises "within a period of three months from the
date of the service of the notice" is valid. As NOURSE LJ said:[7]

> I see no difference between the meanings of "within" and "during" . . . If someone
> is required to vacate premises within or during a specified period, he will comply
> with the requirement by walking out of the door either before, or on, the stroke of
> midnight on the last day of that period.

(iii) Must relate to whole of premises A notice to quit given by a lessor must
relate to the whole of the premises. It is void if it directs the tenant to
surrender possession of part only of what he holds, unless this is permitted
by the lease itself or by statute.[8] Such a statutory power is vested in the lessor
of an agricultural holding if he requires part of the land for certain purposes,
such as the erection of cottages or the provision of allotments, specified by
the Agricultural Holdings Act 1986.[9] If, however, he takes advantage of this
power, the tenant may treat the notice as a notice to quit the entire holding.[10]

(7) FRUSTRATION

In *National Carriers Ltd v Panalpina (Northern) Ltd*,[11] the House of Lords,
by a majority of four to one, held that the doctrine of frustration is applicable
to leases. In so doing, it reconsidered its former opinions in *Cricklewood
Property and Investment Trust Ltd v Leighton's Investment Trust Ltd*,[12] in
which Viscount SIMON LC and Lord WRIGHT were of opinion that the
doctrine could apply; the second Lord RUSSELL OF KILLOWEN and Lord
GODDARD that it never could, and Lord PORTER reserved his opinion. The
effect of the decision is unlikely to produce any dramatic change, and as Lord
HAILSHAM OF ST MARYLEBONE LC said:[13]

> It is the difference immortalised in *H.M.S. Pinafore* between "never" and "hardly
> ever", since both Viscount Simon and Lord Wright conceded that, though they
> thought the doctrine applicable in principle to leases, the cases in which it could
> properly be applied must be extremely rare.

As a result of this decision,[14] it is no longer necessary to draw the
anomalous distinctions between:[15]

6 *Eastaugh v Macpherson* [1954] 1 WLR 1307, [1954] 3 All ER 214.
7 *Manorlike Ltd v Le Vitas Travel Agency & Consultancy Services Ltd* [1986] 1 All ER 573.
8 *Re Bebington's Tenancy* [1921] 1 Ch 559. The actual decision is now out of date owing to LPA
    1925, s. 140 (1), (2); p. 452, *ante*.
9 S. 31.
10 S. 32.
11 [1981] AC 675, [1981] 1 All ER 161; (1981) 131 NLJ 189 (H. W. Wilkinson). For the doctrine
    generally, see Cheshire, Fifoot and Furmston, *Law of Contract* (12th edn), chapter 20.
12 [1945] AC 221, [1945] 1 All ER 252.
13 At 688, at 166.
14 The third Lord RUSSELL OF KILLOWEN, with filial piety, dissented; and followed the views of
    the second Lord RUSSELL and Lord GODDARD in the *Cricklewood case*. For him also "the
    second answer of the *Pinafore's* captain on the subject of mal de mer is to be preferred to his
    first." He was prepared to accept the doctrine where the lease is merely incidental to an
    overall commercial adventure, or where the subject-matter has totally disappeared. The

(i) a lease and a licence. Hitherto the doctrine has been applicable to a licence, as in *Krell v Henry*[16] and the other Coronation cases, where an agreement to let a room for the purpose of viewing the coronation procession of Edward VII was frustrated when the procession was cancelled owing to the illness of the king;

(ii) a lease and a contract for a lease. In *Rom Securities Ltd v Rogers (Holdings) Ltd*[17] GOFF J had assumed, without deciding, that the doctrine was applicable to a contract for a lease;

(iii) the charter of a ship by demise[18] and a demise of land, e.g. a short lease of an oil storage tank and a demise charter for the same term of an oil tanker to serve such a storage tank, and a supervening event then frustrating the demise charter and equally affecting the use of the storage tank.

In the *National Carriers* case the House of Lords held unanimously that a ten year lease of a warehouse was not in fact frustrated when it was made unusable for twenty months by the closing of an access street to it. Previous cases are also examples of a lease not being frustrated.

In the *Cricklewood* case itself, a building lease for 99 years from May 1936 was not frustrated by war-time legislation prohibiting building. It has also been held that a tenant must continue to pay his rent notwithstanding that the premises are utterly destroyed by fire,[1] or by a hostile bomb,[2] or are requisitioned by the Crown acting under statutory powers or under the prerogative,[3] even though the Crown itself is the lessor.[4]

Similarly, a covenant to repair imposes an absolute obligation for the non-performance of which the covenantor remains liable, notwithstanding that owing to some extraneous cause beyond his control, such as the refusal of the authorities to grant him a building licence[5] or the requisitioning of the premises,[6] he is unable to execute the necessary work.[7]

---

majority view has an anomaly of its own: the doctrine would apply to a lease but not to the sale of land, whether for a freehold or leasehold interest. It would seem, however, to apply to a contract for the sale of land; see Lord SIMON OF GLAISDALE at 705, at 179, and Lord ROSKILL at 714, at 185. See also *Universal Corpn v Five Ways Properties Ltd* [1979] 1 All ER 552, where the Court of Appeal assumed that the doctrine so applied.

For the effect of the unforeseen event of "mountainous inflation and the pound dropping to cavernous depths" on the construction of the terms of a covenant in a lease, see *Staffordshire Area Health Authority v South Staffordshire Waterworks Co* [1978] 1 WLR 1387, [1978] 3 All ER 769; *Pole Properties Ltd v Feinberg* (1981) 43 P & CR 121.

15 See Lord SIMON OF GLAISDALE at 701, at 176.
16 [1903] 2 KB 740.
17 (1967) 205 EG 427.
18 See *Blane Steamships Ltd v Minister of Transport* [1951] 2 KB 965; LR (Frustrated Contracts) Act 1943, s. 2 (5) (*a*).
 1 *Matthey v Curling* [1922] 2 AC 180.
 2 See *Redmond v Dainton* [1920] 2 KB 256; *Denman v Brise* [1949] 1 KB 22, [1948] 2 All ER 141.
 3 *Whitehall Court v Ettlinger* [1920] 1 KB 680. But see the Landlord and Tenant (Requisitioned Land) Act 1942, which allows a tenant to disclaim a lease if the land is requisitioned by the Crown.
 4 *Crown Land Comrs v Page* [1960] 2 QB 274, [1960] 2 All ER 726.
 5 *Eyre v Johnson* [1946] KB 481, [1946] 1 All ER 719.
 6 *Smiley v Townshend* [1950] 2 KB 311, [1950] 1 All ER 530. But the Landlord and Tenant (Requisitioned Land) Act 1944 relieves the tenant of liability for damages to the land during the period of requisition.
 7 See *John Lewis Properties plc v Viscount Chelsea* [1993] 34 EG 116 (excuse for non-performance short of full frustration).

(8) REPUDIATION

A similar development is taking place as far as the repudiation of a lease is concerned. In spite of the Court of Appeal suggestion in *Total Oil Great Britain Ltd v Thompson Garages (Biggin Hill) Ltd*[8] that a repudiatory breach of a lease is not possible, it has recently been held in the county court that it is. Not only can there now be frustration of a lease, but also there is a line of nineteenth century cases in which it has been "treated as axiomatic that a contract of letting could be terminated by the innocent party without notice if the other party failed to fulfil a fundamental term of the contract".[9]

In *Hussein v Mehlman*:

> there was a miscellany of serious breaches of the implied covenant to repair (one of them "vitiated the central purpose of the contract of letting")[10] by the landlord who persistently attempted to evade compliance with his covenant.

It was held that the tenant had accepted the repudiation by vacating the premises and returning the keys, and so was entitled to damages.

B. YEARLY AND OTHER PERIODIC TENANCIES

(1) TENANCIES FROM YEAR TO YEAR

(a) Half a year's notice necessary

A tenancy from year to year does not expire at the end of the first or any subsequent year, but continues until it is determined by a notice served by either the landlord or the tenant.[11] It has been the rule since the reign of Henry VIII that not less than half a year's notice is necessary, unless a different agreement has been made by the parties.

It is well established what is meant by "half a year". If the tenancy began on one of the usual quarter days,[12] it means the interval between a quarter day and the next quarter day but one, notwithstanding that, measured by days, such a period may not amount to half a year.[13] Thus in a Lady Day tenancy notice to quit will be good if given on or before Michaelmas Day, though the actual period is five days short of 182. If the tenancy began at some day falling between two quarter days, then the length of notice must be 182 days at least.[14]

---

8 [1972] 1 QB 318 at 324. There can be repudiation of a contract for a lease: *Sweet & Maxwell Ltd v Universal News Services Ltd* [1964] 2 QB 699, [1964] 3 All ER 30. For Australian authority in favour of repudiation, see [1985] Conv 262 (J. W. Carter); [1986] Conv 262 (J. W. Carter and J. Hill).

9 *Hussein v Mehlman* [1992] 2 EGLR 87 at 89, per Mr Stephen Sedley QC; [1993] CLJ 212 (C. Harpum).

10 At 90.

11 See *Youngmin v Heath* [1974] 1 WLR 135, [1974] 1 All ER 461 (personal representative of deceased weekly tenant liable for rent until notice to quit given).

12 Lady Day (25 March); Midsummer Day (24 June); Michaelmas (29 September); Christmas (25 December).

13 *Right d Flower v Darby* (1786) 1 Term Rep 159.

14 1 Wms Saunders 276 C; *Sidebotham v Holland* [1895] 1 QB 378 at 384.

(b) Exceptions

There are two exceptions to the rule requiring half a year's notice.

(i) Contrary agreement First, where the parties have made a different arrangement:

> I know of nothing which prevents parties, in entering into an agreement for a tenancy from year to year, from stipulating that it should be determinable by a notice to quit shorter than the usual six months' notice; or that the notices to quit to be given by the landlord and the tenant respectively should be of unequal length; or that the tenancy should be determinable by the one party only by notice to quit and by the other party either by notice to quit or in some other way.[15]

Any such agreement must not be repugnant to the nature of a yearly tenancy. Thus a term under which neither of the parties may determine, or under which only one of them may determine, is inconsistent with the concept of a yearly tenancy,[16] and will be struck out, thereby enabling a landlord to terminate on giving the appropriate notice.

(ii) Agricultural holding Secondly, it is provided by statute in the case of an agricultural holding, that, notwithstanding any express stipulation to the contrary, a notice to quit shall be invalid if it purports to terminate the tenancy before the expiration of twelve months from the end of the current year of the tenancy.[17]

(c) Notice to expire at end of current year

A yearly tenancy is terminable only at the end of the current year, and therefore a notice, given for example by the landlord, must require the tenant to quit the holding on that date—no earlier, no later. Literally interpreted, the end of the current year is midnight of the day prior to the anniversary of the day on which the tenancy began.

> For instance, if a yearly tenancy began on 29 September,[18] its current period ends each year on 28 September. In strictness, therefore, a notice given, say, by the landlord, must direct the tenant to quit on 28 September and it must reach the tenant at least half a year before that day. A notice, for instance, that is not served upon him till after 25 March, and which directs him to quit on the next ensuing 28 September is bad, and he will be entitled to remain until 28 September in the following year.

---

15 *Allison v Scargall* [1920] 3 KB 443 at 449, per SALTER J.
16 *Prudential Assurance Co Ltd v London Residuary Body* [1992] 2 AC 386 at 394, [1992] 3 All ER 504 at 510, p. 372, ante (reversing *Re Midland Rly Co's Agreement* [1971] Ch 725, [1971] 1 All ER 1007); *Doe d Warner v Browne* (1807) 8 East 165; *Cheshire Lines Committee v Lewis & Co* (1880) 50 LJQB 121.
17 Agricultural Holdings Act 1986, s. 25 (1); p. 510, post.
18 There is a presumption that a tenancy from a named date commences on the first moment of the day following: *Ladyman v Wirral Estates Ltd* [1968] 2 All ER 197. The presumption was rebutted in *Whelton Sinclair v Hyland* [1992] 2 EGLR 158 (application of presumption would have left premises undemised for one day, where parties were mistaken as to correct date of renewed lease under Landlord and Tenant Act 1954).

The courts, however, after some hesitation, have extended the strict meaning of the expression "end of the current year" to include the anniversary of the day on which the tenancy began. "A notice to quit at the first moment of the anniversary," said LINDLEY LJ, "ought to be just as good as a notice to quit on the last moment of the day before."[19] A notice, therefore, given not later than Lady Day, will be good if it purports to terminate a Michaelmas tenancy on 29 September.[20]

(2) OTHER PERIODIC TENANCIES

Similar rules apply in the case of other periodic tenancies. Subject to the statutory rule in the case of a dwelling-house,[1] the length of the notice must be not less than the length of the tenancy, e.g. at least seven days' notice is necessary to terminate a weekly tenancy, and the notice must purport to terminate the tenancy at the end of the current period,[2] i.e. either on the anniversary of the date of its commencement[3] or on the preceding day. In computing the period of seven days or the other appropriate period, the day of expiry but not the day of service is included. Thus, a tenancy that began on a Saturday may be terminated by a notice to quit given on a Saturday, notwithstanding that this does not give the tenant seven clear days' notice. In *Lemon v Lardeur*:[4]

> A tenant who held on a four-weekly tenancy was given "a month's notice as from 1 August, 1945, to vacate" the premises. No evidence was given of the date on which the tenancy began.

The notice was invalid, for, since it had not been shown that 1 August was the first day of one of the four-weekly periods, it was impossible to ascertain whether the month's notice would expire at the end of the current period.

These rules may be varied by the parties. Subject to the statutory rule that four weeks' notice is necessary to terminate a lease of a dwelling-house, the length of the notice and the date at which it may be given are matters upon which the parties may make what arrangement they like.[5]

A notice to quit given by one of two joint landlords[6] or by one of two joint

---

19 *Sidebotham v Holland* [1895] 1 QB 378 at 383.
20 *Sidebotham v Holland*, supra; *Crate v Miller* [1947] KB 946, [1947] 2 All ER 45 (dealing with the analogous case of a weekly tenancy). Where notice is given in months, the period of notice ends on the day of the month which bears the same number as that on which the notice was given. February, having only 28 and 29 days, is an exception: *Dodds v Walker* [1981] 1 WLR 1027, [1981] 2 All ER 609; *EJ Riley Investments Ltd v Eurostyle Holdings Ltd* [1985] 1 WLR 1139, [1985] 3 All ER 181.
1 Protection from Eviction Act 1977, s. 5 (1); p. 460, ante; p. 486, post.
2 *Lemon v Lardeur* [1946] KB 613, [1946] 2 All ER 329; *Queen's Club Garden Estates Ltd v Bignell* [1924] 1 KB 117; *Bathavon RDC v Carlisle* [1958] 1 QB 461, [1958] 1 All ER 801. The payment period of a week is not necessarily the appropriate test in the case of a licence: in that case, the test is: what is the reasonable period in all the circumstances of the case? *Smith v Northside Developments Ltd* (1987) 283 EG 1211.
3 *Crate v Miller*, supra.
4 [1946] KB 613, [1946] 2 All ER 329.
5 *Land Settlement Association Ltd v Carr* [1944] KB 657, [1944] 2 All ER 126. As regards the actual decision in this case, see Agricultural Holdings Act 1986, s. 2 (1). See also *Harler v Calder* [1989] 1 EGLR 88.
6 *Doe d Aslin v Summersett* (1830) 1 B & Ad 135; *Parsons v Parsons* [1983] 1 WLR 1390 (two of four joint tenants); criticised in [1983] Conv 194 (F. Webb). For a similar rule in licences, see *Annen v Rattee* (1985) 273 EG 503; [1985] Conv 218 (J. Martin).

tenants is effective to determine a periodic tenancy, even though the other joint owner does not concur.[7]

In *Hammersmith and Fulham London Borough Council v Monk*[8] the House of Lords held that this was so, in spite of the law that a single joint tenant cannot exercise a break clause in a lease,[9] surrender the term, make a disclaimer, exercise an option to renew the lease or apply for relief against forfeiture. As Lord BRIDGE OF HARWICH said:[10]

> All these positive acts which joint tenants must concur in performing are said to afford analogies with the service of notice to determine a periodic tenancy, which is likewise a positive act. But this is to confuse the form with the substance. The action of giving notice to determine a periodic tenancy is in form positive; but both on authority and on the principle so aptly summed up in the pithy Scottish phrase "tacit relocation" the substance of the matter is that it is by his omission to give notice of termination that each party signifies the necessary positive assent to the extension of the term for a further period.

C. TENANCIES AT WILL

A tenancy at will may be expressly terminated at any time by either party. The strict rules that govern a notice to quit do not, however, apply in this case, for, as has been said by TINDAL CJ:

> Anything which amounts to a demand of possession, although not expressed in precise and formal language, is sufficient to indicate the determination of the landlord's will.[11]

Thus a declaration, that the landlord will take steps to recover possession unless the tenant complies with certain conditions, determines the tenancy if the conditions are not accepted.[12]

The tenancy is also implicitly determined if the lessor does acts inconsistent with its continuance, as for instance if he alienates the reversion or removes material, such as stones, from the land.[13]

Implicit determination also occurs if the tenant does acts incompatible with his limited rights, as for instance if he commits waste or assigns the land to a stranger.[14]

The death of either party also determines the tenancy.

A premature determination is not allowed to prejudice the rights of either party. If the tenant quits before the day on which his rent is due, he does not escape liability;[15] while if he has sown crops he has a right at common law

---

7 For one joint tenant to give notice without the consent of others might be a breach of trust: *Parsons v Parsons*, supra; *Harris v Black* (1983) 46 P & CR 366; *Featherstone v Staples* [1986] 1 WLR 861 at 875, [1986] 2 All ER 461 at 472.
8 [1992] 1 AC 478, [1992] 1 All ER 1; [1992] Conv 279 (S. Goulding); CLJ 218 (L. Tee); 108 LQR 375 (J. Dewar).
9 *Hounslow London Borough Council v Pilling* [1993] 1 WLR 1242.
10 At 490, at 9.
11 *Doe d Price v Price* (1832) 9 Bing 356 at 358.
12 *Doe d Price v Price*, supra; *Fox v Hunter-Paterson* [1948] 2 All ER 813.
13 *Doe d Bennett v Turner* (1840) 7 M & W 226.
14 *Pinhorn v Souster* (1853) 8 Exch 763 at 772.
15 Cruise, *Digest*, Tit. ix., c. 1, s. 13.

to re-enter and reap them if the lessor determines the tenancy before they are ripe.[16]

SECTION IX SECURITY OF TENURE AND CONTROL OF RENT

Land in overcrowded England is a scarce commodity which all need but many cannot afford to own. The forces of supply and demand, if left unchecked, would give landlords a bargaining superiority over their tenants which twentieth-century ideas of social justice have been unwilling to accept. In consequence, ever since the First World War, legislation has been used to redress the balance in favour of the tenant.[17] Restrictions have been imposed upon the amount of rent recoverable and the landlord's common law right to recover possession. With changes in government the tide of protection has ebbed and flowed. The highwater-mark of tenants' rights in the private sector was the Labour Rent Act 1974. At the time of writing the tide is very much on the ebb. The Conservative Housing Act 1980 reduced the tenant's protection, and further significant reduction was achieved by the Housing Act 1988. But the need for protection of some kind is today generally accepted and it is highly unlikely that landlord and tenant will ever be restored to their nineteenth-century freedom of contract.

Statutory protection was at first afforded only to tenants who held periodic tenancies or short leases of unfurnished residential premises;[18] but protection has been extended to most residential lettings by private landlords who do not themselves reside in the same house,[19] while different systems of control have been devised for public sector housing,[1] long leaseholders,[2] business tenants,[3] and agricultural holdings.[4] The result of somewhat haphazard historical development is that there are today many distinct statutory codes of protection, in various respects radically different from each other. The detailed provisions of this legislation are extremely complex and the subject matter of a number of specialised works. What follows is no more than a brief outline of how the various codes operate.

A. PRIVATE RESIDENTIAL LETTINGS[5]

Statutory control of residential lettings dates back to 1915, but almost all the provisions now in force will be found in the Rent Act 1977 and the Housing Act 1985. A tenancy falling within the Rent Act 1977 is known as a "protected tenancy".

Tenants under protected tenancies are given security of tenure by the

---

16 Co Litt 55*b*; see p. 398, ante.
17 See *Johnson v Moreton* [1980] AC 37 at 65, [1978] 3 All ER 37 at 53, per Lord SIMON OF GLAISDALE.
18 Increase of Rent and Mortgage Interest (War Restrictions) Act 1915.
19 Rent Act 1977; Housing Act 1988.
 1 Part IV of the Housing Act 1985, p. 487, post.
 2 Part I of the Landlord and Tenant Act 1954; Leasehold Reform Act 1967; p. 489, post; Leasehold Reform, Housing and Urban Development Act 1993.
 3 Part II of the Landlord and Tenant Act 1954; p. 501, post.
 4 Agricultural Holdings Act 1986; p. 509, post.
 5 For detailed discussion, see *Megarry on The Rent Acts* (11th edn); Martin, *Residential Security*; Rodgers, *Housing, The New Law*.

mechanism of the "statutory tenancy"—a status of irremovability which attaches to a tenant remaining in occupation after his protected tenancy has come to an end and which cannot be terminated by the landlord except by an order of the court made upon limited and specified grounds. For the purposes of rent regulation, both protected and statutory tenancies are termed "regulated tenancies" and are subject to machinery for determining a "fair rent" which is the maximum that the tenant can be required to pay. The "fair rent" is lower than a market rent because market rents are determined by supply and demand, whereas in assessing a "fair rent" it must be assumed that the demand for similar dwellings in the locality is not substantially greater than the supply.[6]

The philosophy behind the Housing Act 1988 is that the reduction of security and rent control will increase the supply of rented accommodation by encouraging owners to let. The effect of the 1988 Act is to phase out the regulated tenancy (and also the "restricted contract", an inferior form of protection under the Rent Act 1977 applying primarily to tenants of resident landlords). The operation of the Rent Act 1977 is much reduced in that, subject to narrow exceptions,[7] no new protected tenancies may be granted after 15 January 1989, the date upon which the 1988 Act came into operation. Tenancies created before that date continue to enjoy the protection of the Rent Act 1977, but the 1988 Act hastens their termination by diminishing the succession rights which previously existed on the death of a protected or statutory tenant.

The key concepts of the Housing Act 1988 are the "assured tenancy" and its variant the "assured shorthold tenancy". The basic principle of security of tenure remains, but the grounds for possession are strengthened and there are only very limited rights of succession and rent control. In order to dissuade landlords from evicting Rent Act tenants unlawfully in order to get the benefit of the new Housing Act regime, the 1988 Act strengthened the Protection from Eviction Act 1977 by extending criminal and civil liability for unlawful eviction and harassment.

The account which follows deals only with assured and assured shorthold tenancies under the Housing Act 1988. Much of the Rent Act case law, however, remains relevant, as many provisions of the 1988 Act are modelled on those of the 1977 Act, in particular in relation to the conditions for protected status, the exceptions to protection and the grounds for possession.

It is not yet clear whether the 1988 Act has achieved its objective of increasing the pool of private rented accommodation. The increased availability of such accommodation at present is primarily attributable to the difficulty of selling in a depressed property market.

(1) THE ASSURED TENANCY

(a) **Definition**

By section 1 of the Housing Act 1988, a tenancy under which a dwelling-house is let as a separate dwelling is an assured tenancy if and so long as:

   (a) the tenant or each of joint tenants is an individual; and

---

6 Rent Act 1977, s. 70 (2).
7 Housing Act 1988, s 34.

(b) the tenant or at least one of joint tenants occupies the dwelling-house
     as his only or principal home; and
(c) the tenancy is not one which cannot be an assured tenancy by virtue of
     the exclusions in Schedule 1[8] or by virtue of section 1 (6).[9]

Further, the tenancy cannot be assured unless it was entered into on or
after the commencement of the 1988 Act on 15 January 1989.[10]
Each part of the definition will now be examined.

(i) Dwelling-house . . . let as a separate dwelling

Every word of this phrase has been the subject of judicial interpretation and
the last five words are among the most litigated on the statute book.

(a) Dwelling-house A "dwelling-house", which may be a house or part of a
house, includes a flat and even an hotel,[11] but the premises must be
structurally suitable for occupation as a residence and must have some degree
of permanence. Caravans are therefore not normally within the definition
and their occupants are protected, if at all, by different legislation.[12]

(b) Let The use of the word "let" connotes the relationship of landlord and
tenant. Contractual licensees, such as lodgers and other persons not having
exclusive possession, are therefore not within the Act.[13] Since the decision
of the House of Lords in *Street v Mountford*[14] it is clear that exclusive
possession for a fixed or periodic term gives rise to a strong presumption of a
tenancy, rebuttable only by special circumstances. These special circumstances include cases where there was no intent to create legal relations
(sometimes called the "generosity factor"[15] cases) or where the occupation is
attributable to another legal relationship, such as a contract for sale.[16] Where
the court is satisfied that the arrangement amounts to a tenancy, it will pay
no regard to the fact that the parties have chosen to label their relationship a
licence,[17] and will be astute to detect sham devices.[18] If two or more persons
share occupation, they will be joint tenants if they have exclusive possession;
otherwise they will be licensees.[19]

The most common examples of residential licensees are lodgers, who lack
exclusive possession because the owner provides attendance or services
which require him to exercise unrestricted access to the premises,[20] and the
"service occupant", i.e. the employee who is required by his contract of

8 P. 473, post.
9 This excludes tenancies granted to homeless persons by private landlords by arrangement
   with the local authority.
10 Housing Act 1988, Sch. 1, para 1.
11 *Luganda v Service Hotels Ltd* [1969] 2 Ch 209, [1969] 2 All ER 692.
12 The Caravan Sites Act 1968 and the Mobile Homes Act 1983; *R v Rent Officer of Nottingham
    Registration Area, ex p Allen* (1985) 52 P & CR 41.
13 See *Brooker Settled Estates Ltd v Ayers* [1987] 1 EGLR 50.
14 [1985] AC 809, [1985] 2 All ER 289; p. 362, ante.
15 *Marcroft Wagons Ltd v Smith* [1951] 2 KB 496, [1951] 2 All ER 271; *Heslop v Burns* [1974] 1
    WLR 1241, [1974] 3 All ER 406. Similarly, if there is no legal power to grant a tenancy:
    Camden London Borough Council v Shortlife Community Housing Centre (1992) 25 HLR 330.
16 See, however, *Bretherton v Paton* [1986] 1 EGLR 172.
17 *Facchini v Bryson* [1952] 1 TLR 1386.
18 *Crancour Ltd v Da Silvaesa* [1986] 1 EGLR 80.
19 *AG Securities v Vaughan*; *Antoniades v Villiers* [1990] 1 AC 417, [1988] 2 All ER 1058;
    Mikeover Ltd v Brady [1989] 3 All ER 618.
20 See *Street v Mountford*, supra.

employment to occupy a particular dwelling for the better performance of his duties.[1] Caretakers occupying flats in blocks or office buildings usually come within this category. Agricultural workers in tied cottages also do so, but they are now subject to a separate code under the Rent (Agriculture) Act 1976. But a service occupant must be distinguished from a "service tenant", i.e. a person to whom a dwelling-house is let in consequence of his employment, but who is not required to live there for the better performance of his duties.[2] Service tenants are within the Housing Act 1988, although the Act contains a special provision to enable the employer to recover possession from a tenant who has left his service.[3]

(c) As The requirement that the house must be let *as* a separate dwelling means that one has regard to the purpose for which it was let, which will not necessarily be the same as the purpose for which it is actually being used. If a lease contains a covenant confining the use of the premises to business purposes, the tenancy will not be protected merely because the tenant in fact uses them as a dwelling.[4] If there is no specific user covenant in the lease, the question will turn upon the use contemplated by the parties at the time of the letting,[5] and if they had no particular use in mind, it will depend upon the nature of the premises and their *de facto* use at the time when the question arises for decision.

(d) A The house (or part of a house) must be let as a single dwelling. A house let to one person as a number of separate dwellings in multiple occupation is not protected.[6] Similarly, in *St. Catherine's College v Dorling*,[7] the owner of a house in Oxford let it to the college for the purpose of enabling it to grant sub-tenancies or licences of rooms to undergraduates. The Court of Appeal held that a letting for the purpose of allowing a number of people the exclusive use of particular rooms was not a letting of the house as a single dwelling.

(e) Separate The requirement that the premises must be let as a separate dwelling would, if unqualified, exclude all cases where the tenant shares some living accommodation, either with another tenant or with his landlord.[8] This was in fact the position before 1949, by which time the courts had evolved a great deal of learning on what constituted sharing and what amounted to "living accommodation". Now, however, the tenant who shares with another tenant nevertheless has an assured tenancy,[9] while a tenant who shares with his landlord is normally excluded by the resident landlord exception.[10]

(f) Dwelling The word "dwelling" has its ordinary meaning of premises used for normal domestic purposes such as cooking, feeding and sleeping, of

1 *Norris v Checksfield* [1991] 1 WLR 1241, [1991] 4 All ER 327.
2 *Royal Philanthropic Society v County* [1985] 2 EGLR 109.
3 Housing Act 1988, Sch. 2, Ground 16.
4 *Wolfe v Hogan* [1949] 2 KB 194, [1949] 1 All ER 570.
5 Ibid.
6 *Horford Investments Ltd v Lambert* [1976] Ch 39, [1974] 1 All ER 131.
7 [1980] 1 WLR 66, [1979] 3 All ER 250.
8 *Neale v Del Soto* [1945] KB 144, [1945] 1 All ER 191; *Goodrich v Paisner* [1957] AC 65, [1956] 2 All ER 176.
9 Housing Act 1988, s. 3.
10 Ibid., Sch. 1, para. 10. See p. 473, post.

which sleeping seems to be the most important.[11] If premises are let partly as a dwelling and partly for business purposes (as in the common case of a shop with living accommodation above) the tenancy will be subject only to the code governing business tenancies[12] and not come within the Housing Act 1988 at all.[13]

(ii) The tenant is an individual

This part of the definition makes it clear that a corporate tenant cannot have an assured tenancy. It has long been established that a "company let" cannot attract security of tenure under the Rent Act 1977 because that Act, although not expressly requiring the tenant to be an "individual", imposes a residence requirement[14] which corporate tenants cannot satisfy.[15] The courts have been reluctant to regard company lettings as shams even where the mechanism has clearly been adopted solely as a device to avoid statutory protection,[16] although it remains possible that a letting to a company could be construed as a letting to the individual who occupies.[17]

(iii) Occupation as only or principal home

The purpose of the Housing Act 1988 and its predecessors is to protect a tenant in the occupation of his home, not to confer rights on those who do not occupy, because they have sublet or for some other reason. The occupation requirement of the 1988 Act may be best understood by first considering the authorities under the Rent Act 1977, which remain to a great extent relevant. The rule under section 2 of the 1977 Act is that the tenant must occupy the dwelling-house as his residence. Clearly he need not be there all the time, so long as he preserves a sufficient intention to return and leaves some visible indication of continued occupation. In other words, he must establish the necessary *animus possidendi* and *corpus possessionis*.[18] The presence of the tenant's furniture and effects, his wife[19] or other member of his family are the usual ways in which the latter requirement is satisfied while the tenant is away on business, at sea or in prison.[20] A tenant who has sublet part of the premises continues to satisfy the requirement so long as he resides in the other part.

The "only or principal home" requirement of the assured tenancy is stricter. Although a tenant who has two homes is not excluded, he can only have an assured tenancy in relation to his principal home. This is a question

---

11 *Wright v Howell* (1947) 92 SJ 26; *Palmer v McNamara* [1991] 1 EGLR 121; *Westminster City Council v Clarke* [1992] 2 AC 288, [1992] 1 All ER 695.
12 See p. 502, post.
13 Housing Act 1988, Sch. 1, para. 4. Unless the business element is "de minimis": *Lewis v Weldcrest Ltd* [1978] 1 WLR 1107, [1978] 3 All ER 1226.
14 Rent Act 1977, s. 2.
15 *Hiller v United Dairies (London) Ltd* [1934] 1 KB 57; *Firstcross Ltd v East-West (Export/ Import) Ltd* (1980) 41 P & CR 145.
16 *Hilton v Plustitle Ltd* [1989] 1 WLR 149, [1988] 3 All ER 1051; *Kaye v Massbetter Ltd* (1990) 62 P & CR 558.
17 See *Gisborne v Burton* [1989] QB 390, [1988] 3 All ER 760 (tax doctrine of "artificial transaction" applicable in landlord and tenant context).
18 *Brown v Brash* [1948] 2 KB 247, [1948] 1 All ER 922; *Skinner v Geary* [1931] 2 KB 546. This is a question of fact and degree.
19 Occupation by the tenant's spouse satisfies the requirement even if the tenant does not intend to return: Matrimonial Homes Act 1983, s. 1 (6).
20 *Brown v Brash*, supra.

of fact. The requirement is the same as that which applies to public sector secure tenants under the Housing Act 1985. Decisions concerning secure tenancies may thus afford guidance.[1] In the case of joint tenancies, only one need occupy as his only or principal home.[2] Hence assured status is not lost if the tenants are a married couple who separate. As in the case of the Rent Act 1977, occupation by the tenant's spouse (where there is no joint tenancy) will satisfy the requirement.[3]

(b) The exceptions

The Act contains a fairly long list of exceptions.[4] Only the more important ones will be considered here.

(i) Houses let by an exempted body Tenancies granted by certain specified bodies, which include local authorities, the Commission for New Towns, and housing action trusts are not assured.[5] They are instead subject to the code of protection for public sector housing now found in the Housing Act 1985.[6] Similar exemption from the Housing Act 1988 (and from the public sector code) has been conferred upon educational institutions and similar bodies who let premises to students,[7] and upon Crown lettings.[8] Housing associations are not, however, exempted.

(ii) Lettings by resident landlords A tenancy is not assured if the dwelling forms part of a building[9] (other than a purpose-built block of flats) in which the landlord was also residing when the tenancy began and in which he has since continued to reside.[10]

This exception was introduced by the Rent Act 1974 and is hedged about with qualifications of great complexity which can only be explained (though not excused) by its legislative history. Until 1974 the law took no account of whether or not the landlord resided on the premises. Instead, there was a general exception for furnished lettings. The furnished tenancy exception was socially controversial because it was comparatively easy and inexpensive for a landlord to provide enough furniture to prevent the tenant from acquiring security of tenure.[11] This was hard on the many persons (including a substantial proportion of recent immigrants and "single-parent families") who had to take furnished accommodation because they could not find or afford any other. On the other hand, there is a need for a pool of short-term

---

1 See *Peabody Donation Fund Governors v Grant* (1982) 264 EG 925; *Crawley Borough Council v Sawyer* (1987) 20 HLR 98. See also, on the Leasehold Reform Act 1967, *Dymond v Arundel-Timms* [1991] 1 EGLR 109.
2 Housing Act 1988, s. 1.
3 Matrimonial Homes Act 1983, s. 1 (6), as amended by Housing Act 1988, Sch. 17, para. 33. This does not apply where the occupier is the tenant's cohabitee: *Colin Smith Music Ltd v Ridge* [1975] 1 WLR 463, [1975] 1 All ER 290; or former spouse *Metropolitan Properties Co Ltd v Cronan* (1982) 44 P & CR 1. The court may order the transfer of the tenancy on divorce; see p. 475, post.
4 See Housing Act 1988, Sch. 1.
5 Ibid., para. 12.
6 See p. 487, post.
7 Housing Act 1988, Sch. 1, para. 8; Housing Act 1985, Sch. 1, para. 10.
8 Ibid., para. 11 (no exemption for Crown Estate Commissioners or Duchies of Lancaster or Cornwall).
9 See *Bardrick v Haycock* (1976) 31 P & CR 420; *Griffiths v English* (1982) 261 EG 257.
10 Housing Act 1988, Sch. 1, para. 10.
11 See *Woodward v Docherty* [1974] 1 WLR 966, [1974] 2 All ER 844.

accommodation which would dry up if all tenants were given full protection. The Rent Act 1974 compromised by abolishing the furnished lettings exception and trying to preserve the pool of short-term accommodation by introducing the new exception for resident landlords.

The present Act deals in two ways with the amount of residence which a landlord must put in to keep his tenant within the exception. In the first place, it provides that the landlord, or at least one of joint landlords, must occupy as his only or principal home.[12] Secondly, the Act specifies periods of non-residence which may be overlooked, such as up to six months for a purchaser landlord to move in and up to two years after a landlord has died and while the premises are vested in his estate.[13]

Finally, where the landlord is not only resident but also shares accommodation with the tenant, the tenancy is excluded from the requirements of the Protection from Eviction Act 1977 relating to notices to quit and recovery of possession by court order.[14]

(iii) Holiday lettings These are outside the Housing Act 1988[15] or any other system of control.[16] The lack of statutory definition of "holiday" has facilitated attempts to avoid the Act. In the leading case of *Buchmann v May*[17] there was a three month letting in Norbury to an Australian with a temporary visitor's permit, who had already occupied under a series of short lettings. The document, signed by her, stated that the letting was "solely for the purpose of the tenant's holiday in the London area". The Court of Appeal held that where the tenancy is stated to be for a holiday, the onus is on the tenant to establish that the document is a sham or the result of mistake or misrepresentation, but added that the court would be astute to detect a sham if evasion was suspected. On the facts, the tenant failed.

(iv) Tenancies at a low rent Tenancies under which no rent is payable[18] or, if entered into on or after 1 April, 1990 (when domestic rating was abolished), at a rent not exceeding £1,000 a year in Greater London or £250 elsewhere[19] are excluded. Tenancies entered into before that date are excluded if the current rent is less than two thirds of the rateable value on 31 March 1990.[20] The effect of these provisions is to exclude tenants under leases, usually for long terms such as 99 years, which have been granted at a low or "ground" rent in return for payment of a substantial premium. Such tenants are, from an economic point of view, owner-occupiers, and the machinery of the 1988 Act is not appropriate for them. As we shall see, they have substantial protection under other statutory codes.[1]

(v) Tenancies at a high rent Tenancies granted on or after 1 April 1990 cannot be assured if the current rent exceeds £25,000 a year.[2] At this level

12 Housing Act 1988, Sch. 1, para. 10 (1) (*b*). See p. 472, ante.
13 Ibid., paras. 17, 20.
14 Protection from Eviction Act 1977, s. 3A, p. 486, post.
15 Housing Act 1988, Sch. 1, para. 9.
16 Protection from Eviction Act 1977, s. 3A, p. 486, post.
17 [1978] 2 All ER 993.
18 Housing Act 1988, Sch. 1, para. 3.
19 Ibid., para. 3A, inserted by References to Rating (Housing) Regulations 1990 (S.I. 1990 No. 434).
20 Ibid., para. 3B.
 1 See p. 489, post.
 2 Housing Act 1988, Sch. 1, para. 2, as substituted by References to Rating (Housing) Regulations 1990 (S.I. 1990 No. 434).

there is no hardship in allowing a free market. Tenancies granted prior to that date, before the abolition of domestic rating, are excluded if the property (or such part as is subject to the tenancy) had a rateable value on 31 March 1990 exceeding £1,500 in Greater London or £750 elsewhere.[3]

(c) Implied terms of the assured tenancy

The most important implied term relates to assignment and subletting. In the case of an assured periodic tenancy, there is an implied term that the tenant shall not assign, sublet or part with possession (in whole or in part) without the landlord's consent.[4] Section 19 of the Landlord and Tenant Act 1927,[5] implying that the landlord's consent shall not be unreasonably withheld, is excluded.

No such term is implied in the case of a periodic tenancy (which is not a statutory periodic tenancy[6]) if there is an express term either prohibiting or permitting assignment and so forth (absolutely or conditionally).[7] In the case of an express conditional prohibition, section 19 of the 1927 Act will apply.

Nor is such a term implied in the case of a fixed-term assured tenancy, where the general law on assignment and subletting (including section 19 of the 1927 Act) applies. It should be noted that the court has power to order the transfer of an assured tenancy on divorce.[8]

In the case of all assured tenancies there is an implied term that the tenant shall afford the landlord access for doing repairs which the landlord is entitled to execute.[9]

The jurisdiction of the rent assessment committee to vary the terms of a statutory periodic tenancy is dealt with below.[10]

(2) THE ASSURED SHORTHOLD TENANCY

An assured shorthold tenancy is one which is within the definition of an assured tenancy, as discussed above, and which satisfies three further conditions.[11]

(a) it is a fixed-term tenancy granted for a term certain of not less than six months; and

(b) the landlord has no power to determine[12] the tenancy at any time earlier than six months from the beginning of the tenancy; and

(c) a notice in prescribed form[13] was served by the prospective landlord on the prospective tenant before the assured tenancy was entered into, stating that the tenancy was to be a shorthold tenancy.

3 Housing Act 1988, Sch. 1, para. 2A.
4 Ibid., s. 15
5 See p. 414, ante.
6 See p. 478, post.
7 Housing Act 1988, s. 15 (3) (*a*). Nor is such a term implied where a premium is payable on the grant or renewal of the tenancy: s. 15 (3) (*b*).
8 Matrimonial Homes Act 1983, Sch. 1, as amended.
9 Housing Act 1988, s. 16.
10 See p. 479, post.
11 Housing Act 1988, s. 20 (1).
12 The existence of a right of re-entry is not treated as a power to determine the tenancy; ibid., s. 45 (4). Forfeiture is not a means of determining assured tenancies; see p. 478, post.
13 See Assured Tenancies and Agricultural Occupancies (Forms) Regulations 1988 (S.I. 1988 No. 2203), Form 7, as amended by S.I. 1990 No. 1532; *Panayi v Roberts* [1993] 28 EG 125. The court has no power to dispense with this requirement.

As an anti-avoidance measure, a shorthold tenancy cannot be granted to a person who, immediately before the grant, had an assured tenancy which was not shorthold.[14] In exceptional cases, an assured shorthold tenancy may exist even though the three conditions set out above are not all satisfied,[15] although normally failure to satisfy the three conditions will result in the creation of an assured tenancy, so long as section 1 of the 1988 Act is satisfied.

The attraction of the assured shorthold tenancy to landlords is that they may recover possession more easily than in the case of an assured tenancy because of the availability of a special mandatory ground of possession applicable only to assured shorthold tenancies. This ground, which is available in addition to the grounds which apply to assured tenancies generally, is explained below.[16] The other distinction between assured tenancies and assured shorthold tenancies is that a greater degree of rent control applies to assured shortholds.[17]

(3) CONTROL OF RENT

Rent control under the "fair rent" system of the Rent Act 1977[18] took the form of keeping the rent below market levels. In order to encourage letting, the philosophy of the Housing Act 1988 is to impose a form of rent control which seeks merely to prevent excessive rents and does not prohibit the recovery of a market rent. Unlike the Rent Act 1977, the payment of a premium on the grant or assignment of an assured tenancy is not prohibited.

(a) Fixed-term assured tenancy

The rent control scheme of the 1988 Act does not apply to such a tenancy during the period of the fixed term. The rent under such a tenancy is that which the parties have agreed. It may be increased if there is a rent review clause (or by agreement).

(b) Periodic assured tenancy and statutory periodic assured tenancy

As will be explained below,[19] the scheme of the Housing Act 1988 is that a periodic assured tenancy continues until a ground for possession becomes available, and cannot be terminated by a landlord's notice to quit. The security mechanism for a fixed-term assured tenancy is that, on expiry of the fixed term, a statutory periodic assured tenancy arises, which continues until a ground for possession becomes available and cannot be ended by a landlord's notice to quit. In both of these cases section 13 of the 1988 Act provides a means of increasing the rent.

The landlord may serve on the tenant a notice in prescribed form proposing a new rent to take effect at the beginning of a new period of the tenancy specified in the notice.[20] Except in the case of a statutory periodic tenancy, the increase cannot take effect within a year of the commencement of the tenancy. If the rent has already been increased under this procedure, no

14 Housing Act 1988, s. 20 (3).
15 Ibid., s. 20 (4) (where prior assured shorthold); s. 34 (2) (where prior shorthold tenancy under Rent Act 1977); s. 39 (7) (succession on death of shorthold tenant under Rent Act 1977).
16 Ibid., s. 21, p. 482, post.
17 See p. 477, post.
18 P. 469, ante.
19 P. 478, post.
20 Housing Act 1988, s. 13 (2).

further increase can take effect within a year of the date on which the previous increase took effect. Subject to these two rules, the Act provides that the increased rent cannot take effect within certain minimum periods from the date of service of the notice, such as six months in the case of a yearly tenancy.[1]

The rent specified in the landlord's notice will take effect unless the tenant refers the notice to a rent assessment committee before the beginning of the new period specified in the notice.[2] Alternatively, the rent may be varied by agreement without following these procedures.[3]

If the tenant refers the landlord's notice to a rent assessment committee, the committee will determine the rent which the dwelling "might reasonably be expected to be let in the open market by a willing landlord under an assured tenancy".[4] In assessing the market rent, certain matters must be disregarded, such as any increase in value attributable to relevant improvements by the tenant or any decrease in value attributable to a breach of covenant by the tenant, such as a failure to repair.[5] The rent determined by the committee takes effect from the beginning of the new period specified in the landlord's notice (unless the parties agree otherwise), although a later date may be substituted if it appears that the earlier date would cause undue hardship to the tenant.[6]

(c) Assured shorthold tenancy

The procedures described above can apply to assured shorthold tenancies. Such tenancies are normally fixed-term,[7] and accordingly outside these provisions. If, however, the landlord does not recover possession on expiry, the tenancy will become a statutory periodic tenancy, in which case the provisions discussed in (b) above will apply.

The 1988 Act provides a further procedure which is applicable only to assured shorthold tenancies, and which enables the tenant to refer the rent initially agreed to a rent assessment committee.[8] This differs from the procedure already discussed, which merely facilitates a review of the rent after it has operated for a certain period. A shorthold tenant may apply by notice in prescribed form for a determination by the committee, which will then determine the rent which "the landlord might reasonably be expected to obtain under the assured shorthold tenancy".[9] This procedure may be invoked only once, and is not available if the fixed term has expired and a statutory periodic tenancy has arisen.[10]

The committee is not to make a determination unless it considers that there is a sufficient number of similar dwellings in the locality let on assured tenancies (whether or not shorthold), and that the agreed rent is significantly higher than the rent which the landlord might reasonably be expected to be

1 Housing Act 1988, s. 13 (3).
2 Ibid., s. 13 (4).
3 Ibid., s. 13 (5).
4 Ibid., s. 14 (1).
5 Ibid., s. 14 (2). The default must be that of the present tenant: *N & D (London) Ltd v Gadsdon* [1992] 1 EGLR 112.
6 Ibid., s. 14 (7).
7 See p. 475, ante.
8 Housing Act 1988, s. 22.
9 Ibid., s. 22 (1).
10 Ibid., s. 22 (2).

able to obtain.[11] The committee has no power to increase the rent. The effect of these limitations is that the tenant will not succeed if there are insufficient comparables nor if the rent is insufficiently excessive. His lack of security of tenure may in any event make him reluctant to apply.

If the committee does determine the rent, it takes effect from such date as it directs, not being earlier than the date of the application.[12]

Finally, information as to rents which have been the subject of applications to rent assessment committees is publicly available, to assist in the establishment of comparables.[13]

(4) SECURITY OF TENURE

An assured tenancy may be terminated only in the manner laid down by the Housing Act 1988. As in the case of the Rent Act 1977, it is clear from the mandatory wording of the Act that the parties cannot contract out of security of tenure. If, however, the tenancy has ceased to be assured, as where the tenant no longer occupies as his only or principal home, the landlord may terminate it by any methods which are available under the general law.

(a) Periodic assured tenancy

In the case of a periodic tenancy, section 5 of the 1988 Act provides that service of a notice to quit by the landlord shall be of no effect.[14] Such a tenancy may be terminated by a tenant's notice to quit[15] or by a court order based on a ground for possession, as explained below.

(b) Fixed-term assured tenancy

Such a tenancy may be terminated by "surrender or other action on the part of the tenant".[16] The "other action" would include the operation of a break clause (a provision permitting premature termination of a fixed term) by the tenant. The landlord cannot terminate the tenancy except by a court order based on a ground for possession or, "in the case of a fixed-term tenancy which contains a power for the landlord to determine the tenancy in certain circumstances, by the exercise of that power".[17] It is further provided that, unless the tenancy is terminated by the tenant or by a court order, the tenant is entitled to remain after termination of the fixed term as a statutory periodic tenant.[18] This will occur, for example, where the fixed term ends by expiry or is determined by the exercise of a break clause by the landlord. The provisions relating to forfeiture are obscurely drafted, but the position appears to be as follows. The reference in section 5 to ending the tenancy by the exercise of a landlord's power to determine it does not include forfeiture,[19] which is not, therefore, an available method of terminating an assured

11 Housing Act 1988, s. 22 (3).
12 Ibid., s. 22 (4). Any excess is irrecoverable from the tenant. The landlord cannot serve a notice of increase under s. 13 within a year of this date.
13 Ibid., s. 42.
14 See *Love v Herrity* [1991] 2 EGLR 44.
15 Notice by one of joint tenants will suffice; *Hammersmith and Fulham London Borough Council v Monk* [1992] 1 AC 478, [1992] 1 All ER 1.
16 Housing Act 1988, s. 5 (2).
17 Ibid., s. 5 (1).
18 Ibid., s. 5 (2).
19 Ibid., s. 45 (4).

tenancy. A notice under section 146 of the Law of Property Act 1925[20] would be ineffective, and the concept of relief from forfeiture does not apply. A landlord who would have had grounds for forfeiture may, however, be able to invoke a statutory ground for possession. Only certain grounds are available during the currency of a fixed term,[1] and the terms of the tenancy must provide for termination on the ground in question (whether by forfeiture, notice or otherwise).[2] It is not clear whether the forfeiture clause or other terminating provision in the tenancy must refer specifically to the grounds for possession. In the absence of amending legislation to clarify the position, the safest course would be to make specific reference.

Where a statutory periodic tenancy arises on termination of the fixed term, it can be ended only by the tenant or by a court order based on a ground for possession, as described in (a) above. The periods of this tenancy are the same as those for which rent was last payable under the fixed term. The other terms (including rent) are the same as those of the fixed term immediately before it ended.[3] The implied terms relating to assignment and subletting and the procedure for increasing the rent have already been discussed.[4] Either party may seek a variation in the terms of the tenancy (other than rent) by serving a notice proposing different terms on the other party. If the other party does not accept the new terms he may refer the notice to a rent assessment committee, which will determine whether those terms or some other terms might reasonably be expected in an assured periodic tenancy of the dwelling-house in question.[5]

(c) The grounds for possession

The court may make an order for possession, which determines the assured tenancy, only if the judge is satisfied of the existence of one of the grounds for possession specified in the Act.[6] In some cases the establishment of a statutory ground for possession concludes the matter. An order for possession is then mandatory.[7] In other cases, the judge may not make such an order unless he considers it reasonable to do so.[8] The requirement gives the judge a wide discretion, enabling him to consider all relevant circumstances at the date of the hearing. There are 16 grounds for possession, 8 mandatory and 8 discretionary. In addition, there is the special mandatory ground which applies only to assured shorthold tenancies.[9] The position as to termination during the currency of a fixed-term assured tenancy has already been discussed.[10] Where a fixed-term tenancy has come to an end, the possession

---

20 See p. 435, ante.
1 The available grounds are Grounds 2, 8 and 10 to 15, which are explained at pp. 480–484, post.
2 Housing Act 1988, s. 7 (6). See (1989) 139 NLJ 326 (C. Rodgers).
3 Ibid., s. 5 (3).
4 See s. 15 (assignment etc.), p. 475, ante, and s. 13 (rent), p. 476, ante.
5 Housing Act 1988, s. 6.
6 As to consent orders, see *R v Bloomsbury & Marylebone County Court ex p Blackburne*, [1985] 2 EGLR 157; *R v Worthing Borough Council, ex p Bruce* (1991) 24 HLR 261.
7 Housing Act 1988, Sch. 2, Part I.
8 Ibid., Sch. 2, Part II.
9 Housing Act 1988, s. 21, post.
10 Supra.

order operates to terminate also any statutory periodic tenancy which has arisen.[11] In certain cases an accelerated procedure is available.[11a]

In order to invoke a ground for possession, the landlord must serve a notice[12] in prescribed form under section 8 of the 1988 Act, specifying the ground or grounds relied on.[13] He must then begin proceedings within the time limits laid down by section 8, which vary according to the ground in question.

(i) Mandatory grounds

The following grounds are those upon which the court must order possession.

(a) Ground 1: Landlord occupied or intends to occupy This ground applies either where the landlord (or at least one of joint landlords) occupied the dwelling as his only or principal home at some time before the beginning of the tenancy or, without any such condition, the landlord (or at least one of joint landlords) requires the dwelling as his or his spouse's only or principal home. In the latter case the landlord must not have acquired the reversion for money or money's worth. In the former case there is no requirement that the landlord intends to occupy. In both cases the ground is available only if the landlord gave written notice no later than the beginning of the tenancy that possession might be recovered on this ground, although the court may dispense with this requirement if of the opinion that it is just and equitable to do so.

Compensation is payable where the landlord recovers possession but it later appears that he obtained the order by misrepresentation or concealment of material facts.[14]

(b) Ground 2: Mortgagee's power of sale Where the landlord mortgaged the property before granting the tenancy, this ground is available where the mortgagee requires possession in order to exercise the power of sale. Written notice[15] must have been given before the beginning of the tenancy, unless the court dispenses with the requirement, as in the case of Ground 1.

Where the mortgage was granted after the tenancy, the mortgagee's power of sale can be exercised only subject to the tenancy,[16] and so this ground is not available. A tenancy granted after the mortgage will be binding on the mortgagee only if the mortgagor's leasing power under section 99 of the Law of Property Act 1925[17] has not been excluded, or if he has consented to the grant or accepted the tenant. It is in these cases that Ground 2 is relevant. Where the tenancy is not binding on the mortgagee, the latter may recover possession under the general law without regard to the Housing Act 1988,[18] although the landlord could not do so. If the subject of the mortgage is the

---

11 Housing Act 1988, s. 7 (7).

11a County Court (Amendment No. 3) Rules 1993 (S.I. 1993 No. 2175) (Grounds 1, 3, 4, 5 and expiry of assured shortholds).

12 The court may dispense with this requirement (except in the case of Ground 8) if it considers it just and equitable to do so: ibid., s. 8 (1) (*b*).

13 The statutory grounds need not be set out verbatim in the notice but the substance must be fully set out; *Mountain v Hastings* [1993] 29 EG 96 (Ground 8).

14 Housing Act 1988, s. 12.

15 It appears that the notice in question must have been a notice under Ground 1.

16 See p. 696, post.

17 See p. 687, post.

18 See, on the Rent Act 1977, *Britannia Building Society v Earl* [1990] 1 WLR 422, [1990] 2 All ER 469.

assured tenancy itself, the mortgagee's right to possession is not affected by the Housing Act 1988.[19]

(c) Ground 3: Out of season lettings This ground applies to a fixed-term tenancy not exceeding eight months where the dwelling has been occupied for a holiday within the twelve month period before the beginning of the tenancy. The landlord must have given written notice to the tenant no later than the beginning of the tenancy that possession might be recovered on this ground. The effect of this ground is that landlords may let holiday accommodation out of season and be able to recover possession when the property is again required for holiday lettings, which, as has been seen, cannot be assured tenancies.[20]

(d) Ground 4: Vacation lettings of student accommodation This is based on the same principle as Ground 3. Student lettings themselves cannot be assured.[1] If the landlord wishes to utilise the accommodation in the vacation, possession may be recovered on this ground when the property is again required for student lettings. The vacation letting must be for a fixed term not exceeding twelve months, the dwelling must have been subject to an excluded student letting during the twelve-month period before the beginning of the tenancy, and written notice must have been given to the tenant no later than the beginning of the tenancy that possession might be recovered on this ground.

(e) Ground 5: Occupation by minister of religion This ground applies to a dwelling which is held for the purposes of being available as a residence for a minister of religion, where the court is satisfied that the dwelling is now required for that purpose. Notice must have been given to the tenant no later than the beginning of the tenancy that possession might be recovered on this ground.

(f) Ground 6: Intention to demolish or reconstruct A landlord who intends to demolish or reconstruct the whole or a substantial part of the dwelling or to do substantial works may invoke this ground, which is based on one of the business tenancy grounds in the Landlord and Tenant Act 1954.[2] The landlord will not succeed if the work could reasonably be done without the tenant giving up possession. The tenant may, for example, be willing to take an assured tenancy of a reduced part of the dwelling or to give the landlord access and facilities, where the nature of the work is such that either course would be practicable.

This ground is available only to the original landlord or a successor who acquired the reversion other than for money or money's worth. In other words, he must not have purchased the property subject to the tenancy.

Where Ground 6 is established, the landlord must pay reasonable removal expenses to the tenant.[3] Compensation is also payable in cases of misrepresentation or concealment, as mentioned in relation to Ground 1, above.

(g) Ground 7: Death of periodic tenant Where a periodic assured tenant dies

19 S. 7 (1).
20 See p. 474, ante.
1 See p. 473, ante.
2 S. 30 (1) (*f*), p. 506, post.
3 Housing Act 1988, s. 11.

without leaving a spouse who is qualified to succeed to the assured tenancy,[4] it devolves under his will or intestacy and becomes subject to termination by Ground 7. The landlord must begin proceedings not later than twelve months after the death or after the date on which the court considers that the landlord became aware of it. If the landlord does not act in time, the tenancy will continue until some other ground for possession becomes available, provided the beneficiary satisfies the conditions required for an assured tenancy. If he does not, the tenancy may be terminated by a notice to quit, without recourse to Ground 7.

Ground 7 does not apply to a fixed-term assured tenancy. On the death of the tenant such a tenancy will pass under his will or intestacy and will continue assured if the beneficiary satisfies the conditions required for an assured tenancy. A statutory periodic tenancy will then arise at the end of the fixed term, which will be subject to Ground 7 on the tenant's death. If the beneficiary does not satisfy the conditions required for an assured tenancy, the tenancy will terminate on expiry of the fixed term.

(h) Ground 8: Three months' rent unpaid There are three grounds for possession relating to rent, one mandatory and two discretionary.[5] Ground 8 applies where the arrears exist both at the date of service of the notice of proceedings under section 8[6] and at the date of the hearing. The amount of arrears necessary to establish the ground varies according to how frequently the rent is payable under the tenancy, but broadly at least three months' rent must be unpaid. The rent must be "lawfully due", which will not be the case, for example, so far as it exceeds any figure determined by a rent assessment committee.[7]

As the ground is mandatory, the court has no power to suspend or postpone the order subject to conditions as to payment.[8] If, however, the tenant pays the arrears before the hearing, Ground 8 will no longer apply. The discretionary grounds applicable to rent may still apply, and so the landlord should include these in his section 8 notice.

(i) Assured shorthold tenancy Section 21 provides a further mandatory ground which is confined to assured shorthold tenancies. Where the tenancy has ended and no further tenancy is in existence other than a statutory periodic tenancy, the court must make a possession order if the landlord has given the tenant not less than two months' notice stating that he requires possession.[9] The court cannot stay or suspend the order.[10] The notice may be given on or before the day on which the fixed term ends, although obviously the order cannot take effect before the fixed term has ended.

Where the tenancy has already become a statutory periodic tenancy before the notice is served, the date specified in the landlord's notice cannot be earlier than the earliest date upon which the tenancy could have been ended[11] by notice to quit.

4 See p. 485, post.
5 Grounds 10 and 11, post.
6 P. 480, ante. See *Mountain v Hastings* [1993] 29 EG 96.
7 Housing Act 1988, ss. 14, 22; see p. 477, ante. Other examples would include non-compliance with Landlord and Tenant Act 1987, ss. 47, 48 (duty to provide information to tenant).
8 Ibid., s. 9.
9 A notice of proceedings under s. 8 is not required; *Panayi v Roberts* [1993] 28 EG 125.
10 Housing Act 1988, s. 9. An accelerated possession procedure is available; see p. 479, ante.
11 But for s. 5 (1), which prohibits termination by a landlord's notice to quit.

(ii) Discretionary grounds

The grounds discussed below are those upon which the court may make an order for possession if it considers it reasonable to do so.[12] In the case of these discretionary grounds the court may adjourn the proceedings or stay or suspend execution of the order or postpone the date of possession for such period as it thinks just.[13] In such a case the court will impose conditions as to the payment of any rent arrears or such other conditions as it thinks fit. Where the tenant complies with the conditions, the possession order may be discharged.

(a) Ground 9: Alternative accommodation The court can make an order for possession if it is satisfied that "suitable alternative accommodation" is available for the tenant or will be available for him when the order takes effect. Alternative accommodation is suitable if (as will normally be the case) the tenant will have an assured tenancy or equivalent security of tenure,[14] and if the premises are reasonably suitable to the means of the tenant and the needs of his family as regards proximity to place of work, extent and character.[15] Although the alternative accommodation must be suitable for the tenant and his family, it need not be as pleasant and commodious as the existing premises.[16] The test is suitability to the means and needs of the tenant and not comparison with what the tenant has got.[17] Indeed, landlords would seldom in practice offer alternative accommodation if it had to be in all respects equivalent to the existing premises. Furthermore, the rent may be higher than that of the existing premises. If the tenant has the means to pay, the accommodation will nevertheless be suitable.[18] It should however be observed that although comparisons with the existing premises and rent are not admissible on the question of suitability, they are nevertheless matters which the judge may take into account in deciding whether or not it is reasonable to make an order for possession.[19]

An ingenious piece of judicial interpretation has made the "alternative accommodation" provision a means of regaining possession of parts of the premises which the tenant has sub-let. We have seen that as long as the tenant himself resides somewhere on the premises as his only or principal home, he may sub-let the rest and retain his assured tenancy of the whole.[20] An assured tenant may thus be able to make more out of sub-lettings of parts than he pays his landlord for the whole premises. But the landlord may be able to put an end to this situation by offering the tenant as "alternative

12 Housing Act 1988, s. 7 (4).
13 Housing Act 1988, s. 9. As to the mandatory grounds, see Housing Act 1980, s. 89 (14 days or up to 6 weeks if exceptional hardship).
14 Ibid., Sch. 2, Part III, para. 2. A tenancy subject to Grounds 1–5 or an assured shorthold will not suffice.
15 Ibid., para. 3. See *Siddiqui v Rashid* [1980] 1 WLR 1018, [1980] 3 All ER 184, in which a room in a house in Luton (where the tenant worked) was held to be a suitable alternative to a room in Islington, where the tenant had cultural, social and religious connections. The Rent Act cases discussed in this section remain authoritative, as Ground 9 is closely modelled on the equivalent Rent Act provisions.
16 See *Hill v Rochard* [1983] 1 WLR 478, [1983] 2 All ER 21 (proximity to sport, entertainment and recreation not relevant).
17 *Warren v Austen* [1947] 2 All ER 185.
18 *Cresswell v Hodgson* [1951] 2 KB 92, [1951] 1 All ER 710.
19 *Warren v Austen*, supra; *Redspring Ltd v Francis* [1973] 1 WLR 134, [1973] 1 All ER 640 (relevance of environmental factors).
20 For terms as to subletting, see p. 475, ante.

accommodation" a tenancy of the part of the premises which he is actually occupying, and on this ground seeking an order for possession of the whole.[1] As the tenant is voluntarily confining himself to the part in question, it is difficult for him to say that it is not suitable to his needs. The end result is that the tenant obtains a new tenancy of his part, while the landlord takes over his sub-tenants.

Finally, a landlord who recovers possession under Ground 9 must pay reasonable removal expenses to the tenant.[2]

(b) Ground 10: Some rent unpaid This ground applies where some rent lawfully due was unpaid at the date on which the possession proceedings were begun and was in arrears at the date of service of the notice under section 8.[3] Unlike mandatory Ground 8, the rent need not be unpaid at the date of the hearing, and may be less than three months in arrears. The possibility of suspension or postponement of the order has been dealt with.[4] It is most unlikely that an immediate possession order will result from an isolated breach.

(c) Ground 11: Persistent delay in paying rent Persistent delay in paying rent which is lawfully due is a ground for possession even if there are no arrears on the date on which possession proceedings are begun. Again, the court may suspend or postpone the execution of the order, subject to conditions.[5]

(d) Ground 12: Other breaches Breach of any obligation of the tenancy other than non-payment of rent affords a ground for possession. Where the breach is not serious or can be remedied, the order is likely to be refused or suspended, as is also the case with the following three grounds.

(e) Ground 13: Condition of the dwelling-house This ground applies where the dwelling (or common parts) has deteriorated owing to the act, neglect or default of the tenant or other person residing in the tenant's dwelling. If the guilty party is the tenant's lodger or sub-tenant, the ground applies only if the tenant has not taken reasonable steps to remove him.

(f) Ground 14: Nuisance or annoyance or conviction for using the dwelling for illegal or immoral purposes It is a ground for possession if the tenant or any person residing in the dwelling has been guilty of conduct falling within this description, though the degree of control which the tenant could have exercised over the person in question would no doubt be taken into account in deciding whether it was reasonable to make an order. In the case of illegal or immoral user, the conviction must relate to the premises.[6]

(g) Ground 15: Condition of furniture Deterioration in the condition of furniture provided under the tenancy owing to ill-treatment by the tenant or any other person residing in the dwelling is a ground for possession. Where the person responsible is the tenant's lodger or sub-tenant, the ground applies only if the tenant has not taken reasonable steps to remove him.

(h) Ground 16: Tenant ceasing to be in landlord's employment This ground for

1 *Mykolyshyn v Noah* [1970] 1 WLR 1271, [1971] 1 All ER 49; cf *Yoland Ltd v Reddington* (1982) 263 EG 157.
2 Housing Act 1988, s. 11.
3 See p. 480, ante.
4 See p. 483, ante.
5 Housing Act 1988, s. 9. Ground 11 is modelled on the business tenancy ground in s. 30 (1) (*b*) of the Landlord and Tenant Act 1954.
6 *Abrahams v Wilson* [1971] 2 QB 88, [1971] 2 All ER 1114 (possession of drugs).

possession lies only against a "service tenant", i.e. a person to whom the premises were let in consequence of his employment.[7] The court may make an order for possession if the tenant has ceased to be in the landlord's employment, whether or not the premises are needed for another employee.

(d) Succession to an assured tenancy

Section 17 of the 1988 Act creates succession rights to an assured periodic tenancy (including a statutory periodic tenancy). It provides that on the death of a sole[8] tenant under such a tenancy, the tenancy vests in the tenant's spouse, provided the spouse was occupying as his or her only or principal home immediately before the death. "Spouse" is defined as including a person living with the tenant as his or her wife or husband.[9] No minimum period of cohabitation is specified. A similar provision relating to public sector secure tenancies has been held not to apply to homosexual couples.[10] In the unlikely event of more than one claimant, only one can be the successor. Failing agreement, the county court will decide the matter.[11] Where succession rights are established, the tenancy will not devolve under the tenant's will or intestacy.[12] It appears that these provisions apply also to a shorthold tenancy, provided that it has continued beyond the fixed term and thereby becomes a statutory periodic tenancy.

Succession can occur only once, because section 17 applies only where the deceased tenant was not himself a successor.[13] On the death of the successor a mandatory ground for possession becomes available.[14]

These succession rights do not apply on the death of a tenant holding under a fixed-term assured tenancy.[15] If the beneficiary who acquires the tenancy on the death satisfies the assured tenancy requirements, the tenancy will continue to be assured.[16] If the beneficiary does not qualify as an assured tenant (for example because he does not occupy as his only or principal home), the tenancy will terminate under the general law at the end of the term.

Where there is no person who qualifies to be a successor on the death of an assured periodic tenant, the tenancy will devolve as part of the deceased tenant's estate, but a mandatory ground for possession is available.[17]

7 See p. 471, ante.
8 On the death of a joint tenant, the other joint tenant will take by survivorship, and no further succession will be possible: Housing Act 1988, s. 17 (2), post.
9 Housing Act 1988, s. 17 (4).
10 *Harrogate Borough Council v Simpson* [1986] 2 FLR 91, p. 489, post. See also *Westminster City Council v Peart* (1991) 24 HLR 389.
11 Housing Act 1988, s. 17 (5).
12 Ibid., s. 17 (1).
13 Ibid., s. 17 (1) (c). "Successor" has an extended meaning, including, for example, the survivor of joint tenants or a person who inherited a fixed-term assured tenancy by will or intestacy: s. 17 (2), (3).
14 Ground 7, p. 481, ante.
15 Nor does Ground 7 apply.
16 If a statutory periodic tenancy subsequently arises, there can be no succession rights under s. 17 on the tenant's death (see s. 17 (2)), and Ground 7 will be available.
17 Ground 7, p. 481, ante. The tenancy ceases to be assured if the person entitled to it does not occupy, in which case it may be terminated by notice to quit.

(e) Subtenants

The Housing Act 1988 applies between tenant and subtenant in the same way as between landlord and tenant. The question to be considered here is whether the subtenant has any security of tenure against the head landlord when the tenancy terminates. In addition to any rights he may have at common law,[18] he will retain security if he falls within section 18 of the 1988 Act. This section protects only lawful subtenants (whose presence does not constitute a breach of a covenant against subletting) and who qualify as assured tenants against their immediate landlord. Its effect is that, on termination of the superior tenancy (in any way), the sub-tenant becomes assured tenant of the superior landlord.[19] There is no requirement that the mesne landlord should have had an assured tenancy, and it seems unlikely that this could have been the case. If the mesne landlord was not also occupying as his only or principal home, he would not have satisfied the residence requirement of an assured tenancy,[20] whereas if he was occupying part as his only or principal home, the sub-tenancy would not have been assured because of the resident landlord exception.[1]

(f) Unlawful eviction and harassment

Where a tenancy or licence of a dwelling comes to an end by expiry or notice to quit, eviction without a court order is prohibited if the occupier is still residing.[2] This rule is subject to certain exceptions, for example where the tenant or licensee shares accommodation with the owner or occupies for a holiday.[3] Rights of forfeiture of residential tenancies may not be enforced without court proceedings where any person is lawfully residing.[4] It is a criminal offence for any person unlawfully to deprive the residential occupier of his occupation of the premises or any part thereof.[5] The separate offence of harassment consists in doing certain specified acts with the intention of causing a residential occupier to give up the occupation of all or part of the premises or to refrain from exercising any of his rights, such as a right to the use of shared accommodation.[6] The specified acts are acts likely to interfere with the peace or comfort of the occupier or members of his household or the persistent withdrawing or withholding of services reasonably required for the occupation of the premises as a residence. The Housing Act 1988 introduced a further offence of harassment which does not require a specific intent and will thus be easier to prove.[7] The acts constituting the offence are as in the original offence, but it suffices that the landlord (or his agent) knows or has reasonable cause to believe that the occupier will give up occupation or refrain from exercising his rights. Prosecutions for these offences can be

18 P. 433, ante.
19 Unless the landlord's interest is such that the tenancy cannot be assured, for example where the superior landlord is the Crown: Housing Act 1988, s. 18 (2).
20 See p. 472, ante.
 1 See p. 473, ante.
 2 Protection from Eviction Act 1977, s. 3, as amended by Housing Act 1988, s. 30.
 3 Ibid., s. 3A, introduced by Housing Act 1988, s. 31. See also Criminal Law Act 1977, s. 6.
 4 Ibid., s. 2.
 5 Ibid., s. 1 (2).
 6 Ibid., s. 1 (3), as amended by Housing Act 1988, s. 29 (1). See *R v Burke* [1991] 1 AC 135, [1990] 3 All ER 385.
 7 Housing Act 1988, s. 29 (2), inserting s. 1 (3A) into the Act of 1977.

brought by the victim, the police or the local authority, although in practice the police refer complaints to the local authority.

Section 27 of the Housing Act 1988 confers a new civil action for damages for unlawful eviction or harassment causing the occupier to give up occupation. The measure of damages is the difference in value between the landlord's interest in the building subject to the occupier's rights and not so subject.[8] Where section 27 is not satisfied, general law remedies in contract or tort are likely to be available to the occupier for the acts of harassment.

B. PUBLIC SECTOR HOUSING

Until the Housing Act 1980 the residential tenants of landlords in the public sector (by far the most numerous category of tenants) were altogether excluded from statutory protection. They may now enjoy a "secure tenancy", which is modelled upon the Rent Act protected tenancy with certain variations and modern improvements. The provisions are now found in the Housing Act 1985.[9]

(1) DEFINITION OF A SECURE TENANCY

A secure tenancy is a tenancy:

(i) under which a dwelling-house is let as a separate dwelling;[10]

(ii) in respect of which the interest of the landlord belongs to one or other of a list of "public sector" bodies such as local authorities, new town corporations, and housing action trusts;[11]

(iii) in respect of which the tenant is an individual who occupies the house as his only or principal home or, where the tenancy is a joint tenancy, each of the joint tenants is an individual and at least one of them occupies the house as his only or principal home;[12]

(iv) which does not fall within any of the exceptions listed in the Housing Act 1985.

The first of these conditions reproduces part of the definition of a protected or assured tenancy in the private sector. The second mirrors (with certain exceptions) the list of tenancies excluded from the definition of a protected or assured tenancy on account of the identity of the landlord.[13] The third is the same as the conditions as to occupation which apply to assured tenancies.[14] The list of exceptions has some common ground with the exceptions for protected tenancies (long tenancies,[15] student lettings,[16]

---

8 Housing Act 1988, s. 28. See *Tagro v Cafane* [1991] 1 WLR 378, [1991] 2 All ER 235 (£31,000); *Jones v Miah* [1992] 2 EGLR 50 (£8,000); *Haniff v Robinson* [1993] QB 419, [1993] 1 All ER 185 (£26,000). For county court decisions on the measure of damages, see the monthly issues of *Legal Action*.

9 Part IV. See also Part V and Leasehold Reform, Housing and Urban Development Act 1993, Part II (the right to buy). See generally Hughes, *Public Sector Housing Law* (2nd edn).

10 Housing Act 1985, s. 79. Certain licences are included: s. 79 (3), (4).

11 Ibid., s. 80, as amended by Housing Act 1988, s. 83.

12 Ibid., s. 81.

13 Rent Act 1977, ss. 14–16; Housing Act 1988, Sch. 1, para. 12.

14 See p. 469, ante.

15 Housing Act 1985, Sch. 1, para. 1.

16 Ibid., para. 10.

business tenancies[17] and agricultural holdings[18]) but also includes important arrangements which exist only in the public sector, such as the provision of accommodation for homeless persons under Part III of the Housing Act 1985,[19] lettings of "short-life" premises acquired for development,[20] the provision of temporary accommodation for persons who have come to the area to seek employment[1] and lettings to local authority or other public sector employees.[2]

(2) NO CONTROL OF RENTS

There is no control of the rents which may be charged in the public sector in any way analogous to the machinery provided by rent officers and rent assessment committees in the private sector.

(3) SECURITY OF TENURE

The mechanism for giving security of tenure in the public sector resembles that which applies to assured tenancies in the private sector.[3] The scheme of the Act is that the landlord cannot recover possession without obtaining a court order based on one of the grounds for possession.[4] Thus a periodic tenancy cannot be terminated by notice to quit[5] unless a ground for possession is available. Where the tenancy is for a fixed term, a periodic tenancy automatically arises on its expiry, which cannot be terminated without a ground for possession.[6] A similar principle applies to the forfeiture of a fixed-term tenancy: on termination by forfeiture a periodic tenancy arises, which again cannot be terminated without a ground for possession.[7] There is a list of cases in which orders for possession may be made, and the order has the effect of terminating the tenancy on the date when the tenant is ordered to give up possession.

Several of the grounds upon which orders for possession may be made are the same or similar to the grounds upon which the court may make such an order in the private sector. Non-payment of rent or breach of covenant,[8] nuisance or annoyance to neighbours,[9] neglect of the premises,[10] furniture[11] or common parts are examples. These "default" grounds are discretionary. But there are other grounds special to public sector dwellings, e.g. that the dwelling has features designed to make it suitable for occupation by a

---

17 Ibid., para. 11.
18 Ibid., para. 8.
19 Housing Act 1988, Sch. 1, para. 4. Homeless persons are not excluded in all cases. See *Westminster City Council v Clarke* [1992] 2 AC 288, [1992] 1 All ER 695.
20 Ibid., para. 3.
 1 Ibid., para. 5.
 2 Ibid., para. 2.
 3 See p. 478, ante.
 4 Housing Act 1985, s. 82 (1). It is otherwise if the tenancy is not secure: *Sevenoaks DC v Emmott* (1979) 39 P & CR 404.
 5 Except by the tenant: *Hammersmith and Fulham London Borough Council v Monk* [1992] 1 AC 478, [1992] 1 All ER 1.
 6 Housing Act 1985, s. 86.
 7 Ibid., s. 82 (3). The ground for forfeiture will not necessarily constitute a ground for possession.
 8 Ibid., Sch. 2, Part 1, Ground 1.
 9 Ibid., Ground 2.
10 Ibid., Ground 3.
11 Ibid., Ground 4.

physically disabled person and such a person no longer resides in the dwelling house.[12] In such a case suitable alternative accommodation must be available for the tenant.[13]

(4) SUCCESSION

As in the case of the private sector, the Housing Act confers certain rights of succession to the secure tenancy. As with an assured tenancy, succession can occur once only.[14] The successor must have occupied the dwelling-house as his only or principal home[15] at the time of the tenant's death, and must either be the tenant's spouse or another member of his family. In the latter case he must have resided with the tenant for the period of twelve months ending with the tenant's death,[16] although not necessarily in the same dwelling.[17] If there is more than one claimant, the landlord selects the successor in default of agreement.[18] The Housing Act contains a definition of "family",[19] which includes persons who live together as husband and wife.[20]

C. LONG TENANCIES

A long tenancy for the purposes of the landlord and tenant codes means primarily a tenancy granted for a term exceeding 21 years.[1] In 1967 it was estimated that about a million and a quarter houses in England and Wales were let on long tenancies. Most of them originate in the Victorian and Edwardian practice of developing land for residential purposes by means of "building leases". This usually involved an agreement between a landowner and a speculative builder. The builder would enter upon the land and put up houses. When the houses were completed, the landowner would let them to the builder on long leases. Ninety-nine years was a common period.[2] The leases would reserve a rent representing the value of the site as building land but ignoring the value of the houses, which the builder had erected at his own expense. It was therefore called a "ground rent". The landowner would thus obtain an immediate enhanced return on his land and the somewhat distant prospect of the reversion in the houses when the leases came to an end. The builder would make his profit by selling the leases to individual purchasers for capital sums. Or sometimes the landowner would grant the leases directly to individual purchasers nominated by the builder, in return for payment of a capital sum to the builder and the reservation of a ground rent for himself. In all these cases the main object of the builder was to take his profit and disappear from the scene, but more recently some developers

12 Ibid., Part III, Ground 13. See *Freeman v Wansbeck DC* [1984] 2 All ER 746.
13 See *Enfield LBC v French* (1984) 49 P & CR 223; *Wandsworth LBC v Fadayomi* [1987] 1 WLR 1473, [1987] 3 All ER 474 (wife's position).
14 Housing Act 1985, s. 87.
15 See *Peabody Donation Fund Governors v Grant* (1982) 264 EG 925.
16 Housing Act 1985, s. 87.
17 *Waltham Forest London Borough Council v Thomas* [1992] 2 AC 198, [1992] 3 All ER 244.
18 Housing Act 1985, s. 89 (2).
19 Ibid., s. 113.
20 This does not include a lesbian relationship; *Harrogate Borough Council v Simpson* [1986] 2 FLR 91. See also *Westminster City Council v Peart* (1991) 24 HLR 389.
 1 Landlord and Tenant Act 1954, s. 2 (4); Leasehold Reform Act 1967, s. 3 (1).
 2 Because leases for 100 years and over attracted a higher rate of stamp duty.

of residential estates have chosen to grant long leases rather than sell freeholds in order to retain control over the management of the estate. Positive covenants are easier to enforce against tenants than against freeholders and the expiry of all leases simultaneously would allow the landlords to undertake a comprehensive redevelopment.

Long tenancies seldom fall within the Rent Act 1977 or the Housing Act 1988. This is not because the Acts exclude long tenancies as such but because they are usually within the exception for tenancies granted at a low rent.[3] Such tenancies are, however, by no means lacking in statutory protection. The Leasehold Reform Act 1967 allows a duly qualified long leaseholder of a house to acquire the freehold or an extended long tenancy upon terms which the Act describes as "fair"[4] but which can be highly advantageous to the tenant. The existence of these rights has reduced the importance of the second code, contained in Part I of the Landlord and Tenant Act 1954, which merely allows the tenant to remain in possession at a regulated rent after the expiration of his lease. Now long leaseholders of flats may collectively purchase the freehold of their block or may individually extend their leases under the Leasehold Reform, Housing and Urban Development Act 1993.[5] The following is a brief account of these statutes.

(1) THE LEASEHOLD REFORM ACT 1967

The Act confers upon a duly qualified tenant the right to acquire the freehold (commonly called "enfranchisement" of the tenancy) or an extended long lease of his house and premises. Contracting out is not permitted.[6] The discussion of the Act can conveniently be divided into four parts. First, the conditions which must be satisfied by the tenant; secondly, the procedure by which he must exercise his rights; thirdly, the nature of the interests he may acquire and finally the terms upon which he may do so.

(a) The qualifying conditions

The qualifying conditions concern the terms of the tenancy, the character and value of the premises and the way in which they have been occupied.

(i) Long tenancy at a low rent A tenant must hold under a tenancy granted originally for a term of years certain exceeding 21 years[7] and at a rent which is less than two-thirds of the rateable value of the premises.[8] He need not of course be the original tenant. It is possible to buy a long lease which has only a short time left to run and then (subject only to the residence requirements discussed below) claim the benefits of the Act. A tenant who had bought the

---

3 Rent Act 1977, s. 5; Housing Act 1988, Sch. 1, para. 3 (1).
4 Leasehold Reform Act 1967, s. 1 (1).
5 Such tenants were given a right of pre-emption over the landlord's interest in certain circumstances by the Landlord and Tenant Act 1987, Parts I and III.
6 Leasehold Reform Act 1967, s. 23. See *Rennie v Proma Ltd* [1990] 1 EGLR 119.
7 Ibid., s. 3 (1); *Roberts v Church Comrs for England* [1972] 1 QB 278, [1971] 3 All ER 703.
8 Ibid., s. 4; *Duke of Westminster v Johnston* [1986] AC 839, [1986] 3 All ER 613. For tenancies created after the abolition of domestic rating on 1 April 1990 the rent must not exceed £1,000 in Greater London or £250 elsewhere: Local Government and Housing Act 1989, s. 149 and References to Rating (Housing) Regulations 1990 (S.I. 1990 No. 434). The "low rent" rule has been modified by the Leasehold Reform, Housing and Urban Development Act 1993, which introduces an alternative rule which may be satisfied if the rent during the first year of the tenancy did not exceed specified limits; Leasehold Reform Act 1967, ss. 1A (2), 4A.

short residue of a long lease in the years immediately before the passing of the Act found that Parliament had given him a substantial windfall gain.

(ii) House, not flat The Act applies to houses in the ordinary sense of that word ("any building designed or adapted for living in and reasonably so called"[9]) but not to flats or maisonettes. Where a building is horizontally divided into flats or maisonettes, the building itself can be a "house", but the units cannot. For the avoidance of conveyancing difficulties, it is further provided that the Act does not apply to a house "of which a material part lies above or below a part of the structure not comprised in the house".[10] "House" has been widely interpreted, and, according to a majority of the House of Lords, even includes a purpose-built shop with a flat above in a parade, where the shop constituted 75% of the total area of the property.[11] Flats and maisonettes were excluded because their conversion into freeholds would present problems over the enforceability of positive covenants.[12] Proposals for the reform of the law on positive covenants, which would[13] resolve the difficulties, remain unimplemented. It is difficult to see, however, why long leaseholders of flats were not given the right to an extended lease, as is the case with secure tenancies of flats in the public sector.[14] The Government's White Paper which preceded the Act also said rather mysteriously that "different considerations of equity" applied to flats,[15] although it is not easy to guess what these could be. The sale of flats on long leases has become a widespread practice in recent years, being considered a more profitable proposition than letting them on short regulated or assured tenancies. Long leaseholders of flats could be assisted by the reform of the law on positive covenants, or, more radically, by the introduction of a system of "common-hold" tenure under which the ownership of freehold flats would be facilitated.[16] Pending these reforms, the rights of long leaseholders of flats have been increased by the Leasehold Reform, Housing and Urban Development Act 1993. Qualifying leaseholders may acquire a new extended lease or may collectively acquire the freehold of the block. This is discussed below.[17]

(iii) Rateable value Formerly the Act did not apply if the rateable value of the house exceeded certain limits or, after the abolition of domestic rating, if the premium paid for the lease exceeded a specified figure.[18] Tenants of houses previously so excluded have now been given the right to acquire the freehold by the Leasehold Reform, Housing and Urban Development Act

---

9 Ibid., s. 2 (1).
10 Leasehold Reform Act 1967, s. 2 (2); see *Parsons v Trustees of Henry Smith's Charity* [1974] 1 WLR 435, [1974] 1 All ER 1162; *Cresswell v Duke of Westminster* [1985] 2 EGLR 151.
11 *Tandon v Trustees of Spurgeon's Homes* [1982] AC 755, [1982] 1 All ER 1086.
12 "Flying freeholds . . . give rise to peculiarly difficult conveyancing problems": *Gaidowski v Gonville and Caius College, Cambridge* [1975] 1 WLR 1066 at 1069, [1975] 2 All ER 952 at 955, per ORMROD LJ.
13 See the Wilberforce Report on Positive Covenants, p. 614, post; Law Commission Report on Positive and Restrictive Covenants 1984 (Law Com. No. 127), pp. 640–2, post.
14 Housing Act 1985, Part V.
15 *Leasehold Reform in England and Wales* (1966) Cmnd 2916, para 8. For the Government's view on the consideration of equity applicable to houses, see p. 495, post.
16 See the Lord Chancellor's Commonhold Discussion Paper 1990 (Cmnd 1345); p. 169, ante.
17 See p. 498, post.
18 Leasehold Reform Act 1967, s. 1 (1) (*a*), as amended.

1993.[19] As will be explained below, the price to be paid by such tenants is assessed in a manner more favourable to the landlord.

(iv) Occupation as a residence The tenant may exercise his rights only when he has been occupying the house or some part of it in right of his tenancy as his only or main residence for the last three years or for three out of the last ten years.[20] A tenant who has more than one residence may claim only in respect of his "main" residence.[1] Thus a person with a freehold principal residence in London and a long lease of a country cottage, or a principal residence abroad and a long leasehold pied-à-terre in London, cannot claim the benefits of the Act at all. Whether the tenant can satisfy the requirement of residence may involve difficult questions of fact and degree.[2]

It is sufficient if the tenant resides in only part of the house comprised in his tenancy.[3] Thus, although the tenant of a flat cannot qualify under the Act,[4] a tenant of the whole house who has converted it into flats and resides in one, underletting the rest, can claim the freehold of the house. It is also no objection that part of the house is used for business purposes, either by the tenant or his sub-tenant or licensee.[5] A tenant of a shop with living accommodation above can therefore qualify if he lives on the premises, whether he uses the shop himself or underlets it to someone else.[6]

It is ordinarily necessary that the statutory period of residence should coincide with the existence of a long tenancy at a low rent.[7] Thus a tenant who has been occupying a house for five years under a short tenancy at a full rent and then buys a long lease at a low rent cannot claim the freehold at once on the ground that he has already been in residence for more than three years. But there is an exception in favour of a tenant who has succeeded to a qualifying tenancy by reason of the death of a member of his family.[8] Such a tenant may include any period during which he was residing with his predecessor in the house.

The object of the residence provisions was to confine the benefits of the Act to persons who were genuinely occupying the property as their homes and to exclude speculators who might buy up leases simply to make a profit by acquiring the freeholds. But the benefit of a tenant's notice claiming the freehold or an extended lease is assignable together with the tenancy[9] and there is nothing to stop a speculator from buying the lease and the benefit of the notice from an outgoing tenant who was residentially qualified and served his notice before completion.

---

19 S. 63, introducing s. 1A (1) of the 1967 Act.
20 Leasehold Reform Act 1967, s. 1 (1) (*b*), as amended by Housing Act 1980.
 1 Compare the capital gains tax exemption provisions in Taxation of Chargeable Gains Act 1992, s. 222.
 2 See *Poland v Earl Cadogan* [1980] 3 All ER 544; *Dymond v Arundel-Timms* [1991] 1 EGLR 109.
 3 Leasehold Reform Act 1967, s. 1 (2). See *Harris v Swick Securities Ltd* [1969] 1 WLR 1604, [1969] 3 All ER 1131.
 4 Ibid., s. 2 (2); see supra.
 5 Ibid., s. 1 (2).
 6 *Lake v Bennett* [1970] 1 QB 663, [1970] 1 All ER 457; *Tandon v Trustees of Spurgeon's Homes* [1982] AC 755, [1982] 1 All ER 1086.
 7 Leasehold Reform Act 1967, s. 1 (1) (*b*).
 8 Ibid., s. 7. "Family" is narrowly defined.
 9 Ibid., s. 5 (2).

(b) Enfranchisement procedure

A tenant exercises his rights under the Act by serving upon his landlord a notice in the prescribed statutory form, stating that he desires to acquire the freehold or an extended lease.[10] In particular the notice must make it clear whether he wants the one or the other. A notice claiming the freehold or an extended lease in the alternative is invalid.[11] The effect of service of the notice is to create a contract between landlord and tenant, registrable as an estate contract[12] under which the one is bound to grant and the other to take the freehold or an extended lease, as the case may be, on the terms laid down by the Act.[13] The landlord can oppose enfranchisement or extension if the house is reasonably required for occupation as the only or main residence of the landlord or an adult member of his family.[14]

(c) Freehold or extended lease

(i) Freehold A tenant who claims the freehold is entitled to have it conveyed to him free of incumbrances.[15] Any intermediate leasehold interests will be merged in the freehold and there are provisions for dividing up the purchase money between the freeholder and intermediate leaseholders according to the value of their respective interests.[16]

The effect of enfranchisement is of course ordinarily to extinguish the covenants between landlord and tenant in the lease and thereby to deprive the landlord of all rights which he may have had under the lease to control the use, appearance or state of repair of the house. The Act did however provide for exceptional cases in which the former landlord was allowed to retain limited "powers of management".[17] This exception was intended to apply to substantial residential estates which were held from one landlord where the Secretary of State for the Environment certified that it was in the general interest "in order to maintain adequate standards of appearance and amenity and regulate development in the area" that the landlord should retain some control. Applications for the Minister's certificate had to be made before 1 January 1970.[18] If the certificate was granted, the landlord could apply to the High Court for approval of a scheme giving him the appropriate powers.

(ii) Extended lease A tenant who claims an extended lease is entitled to the grant of a new tenancy, in substitution for the existing tenancy, for a term

---

10 For the position where there is a claim to forfeiture, see Sch. 3, para. 4 (1); *Central Estates (Belgravia) Ltd v Woolgar* [1972] 1 QB 48, [1971] 3 All ER 647.
11 *Byrnlea Property Investments Ltd v Ramsay* [1969] 2 QB 253, [1969] 2 All ER 311. The prescribed form has since been amended.
12 Leasehold Reform Act 1967, s. 5 (5).
13 Ibid., ss. 8 (1), 14 (1).
14 Ibid., s. 18. Compensation is payable.
15 Ibid., s. 8 (1).
16 Ibid., Sch. 1.
17 Ibid., s. 19.
18 For houses which became enfranchisable only by virtue of the increases in rateable value limits effected by Housing Act 1974, s. 118, the date was 31 July 1976. For houses brought within the 1967 Act by the Leasehold Reform, Housing and Urban Development Act 1993, the landlord's application must be made within two years of the coming into force of the 1993 Act.

expiring 50 years after the term date of the existing tenancy[19] and on terms as to rent which will be considered in the next paragraph.

Compared with the freehold, the extended tenancy is a weak and unattractive thing and it is seldom in practice requested.[20] After the expiry of the original term it carries no further rights, either to claim the freehold or even another extension.[1] A tenant under an extended tenancy does not even have the ordinary long leaseholder's right to security of tenure after the expiry of his term.[2] Furthermore, the landlord may at any time from twelve months before the commencement of the last 50 years of the term apply to the court for an order terminating the tenancy (on payment of compensation) if he can show that he intends to demolish or reconstruct the whole or a substantial part of the house and premises.[3]

(d) Terms of acquisition

(i) Extended tenancy The rent for the new substituted tenancy is the old rent for the remainder of the old term and then, for the 50 year extension, a "modern ground rent" representing the letting value of the site without including anything for the value of the buildings on the site, calculated at the date when the extension commences, with a review after 25 years.[4]

(ii) Freehold The Act now contains three different methods of calculating the price which the tenant must pay for the freehold. The first, contained in the original Act, now applies to houses of a rateable value on 31 March 1990 of less than £500 (£1,000 in Greater London). The second, introduced by the Housing Act 1974, applies to houses of which the rateable value exceeds those figures but does not exceed £750 (£1,500 in Greater London).[5] The third applies to high value houses brought within the 1967 Act by the Leasehold Reform, Housing and Urban Development Act 1993. Under the original scheme, the price of the freehold is the price which it would fetch if sold in the open market by a willing seller subject to the lease, on the assumption that the lease had already been extended by 50 years in accordance with the Act,[6] but without regard to any enhanced bid which might be expected from the tenant himself or a member of his family.[7] In practice, therefore, the price will be the capitalised value of the rent payable under the lease as extended together with the value (if any) of the reversion. In the case of a lease which still has a very long time to run, the calculation is comparatively easy because the reversion has no value. No one will give anything simply for the right to possession of a property in 90 years' time.

---

19 Leasehold Reform Act 1967, s. 14 (1). This option is not available to tenants given enfranchisement rights by the Leasehold Reform, Housing and Urban Development Act 1993.

20 However, it is more valuable than the rights under the 1954 Act (post) because the rent is lower and the tenant acquires a saleable asset.

1 Leasehold Reform Act 1967, s. 16 (1) (*a*) and (*b*).

2 Parts I and II of the Landlord and Tenant Act 1954 are excluded by s. 16 (1) (*c*).

3 Leasehold Reform Act 1967, s. 17.

4 Ibid., s. 15 (2).

5 See p. 495, post. For houses built after the abolition of domestic rating, see post.

6 Leasehold Reform Act 1967, s. 9 (1). See also Leasehold Reform Act 1979, protecting a tenant against artificial inflation of the price he has to pay; the Act negatives the effect of the device considered by HL in *Jones v Wrotham Park Settled Estates* [1980] AC 74, [1979] 1 All ER 286.

7 Housing Act 1969, s. 82.

The value is therefore simply a capitalisation of the rent. Thus the freehold reversion upon a lease of a house at a ground rent of £20 a year with 70 years unexpired is likely to be worth today about eight years' purchase or £160. On the other hand, as the term date approaches, the reversion begins to acquire some value. However, because of the deemed extension, there will always be at least 50 years to run. If the reversion does have any value, this must be added to the value of the right to receive the rent for the rest of the term. If the parties cannot agree on the value, it must be determined by the Leasehold Valuation Tribunal.[8]

The terms upon which the freehold can be acquired are perhaps the most controversial feature of the Leasehold Reform Act 1967. The effective disregard of the value of the reversion to the building means that the terms can be highly advantageous to the tenant whose lease has a short period left unexpired. This method of calculation was intended to give effect to the Government's declaration in the White Paper that "the price of enfranchisement must be calculated in accordance with the principle that in equity the bricks and mortar belong to the qualified leaseholder and the land to the landlord".[9] The word "equity" is clearly used in the sense of social justice and not in any sense which would have been recognised by Lord ELDON. Even so, it is not easy to understand. It is presumably intended to reflect the situation on the grant of a building lease, when the landlord reserves a rent which reflects the value of the land alone and the builder is able to dispose at a profit of the building he has erected.[10] At this stage, however, the reversion is so remote that the question of whether it should in equity be a reversion in the land alone or the land and building is entirely academic; in either case it will have no value. But the position is very different when the lease is approaching its end, as was the case with many Victorian building leases at the time when the Act was passed. At this point the reversion has a value which is enhanced by the fact that it includes the house as well as the land and a person who bought the reversion would have paid a price which reflected this enhanced value. A purchaser of the residue of the term will have paid a price which was correspondingly lower in order to allow for the fact that he was buying a wasting asset. The "equity" of the Act deprives the landlord of part of the value of his reversion and gives the tenant a windfall gain. It can be justified only on the general ground that it is desirable to enrich tenants at the expense of their landlords.[11]

It was no doubt for these reasons that a different method of calculating the price was applied to the more expensive houses which were brought within the scope of the Act by the Housing Act 1974. In the case of houses having a rateable value on 31 March 1990 of between £500 and £750 (the figures are £1,000 and £1,500 in Greater London) the price is calculated upon a set of assumptions which result in the tenant paying more or less the market value of the reversion, including the reversion to the building as well as the site.[12]

8 Leasehold Reform Act 1967, s. 21 (1), as amended by Housing Act 1980.
9 *Leasehold Reform in England and Wales* 1966 (Cmnd 2916) para. 4.
10 See p. 489, ante.
11 A claim that the Act contravened the European Convention on Human Rights was rejected in *James v United Kingdom* (1986) 8 EHRR 123; M & B p. 409.
12 Leasehold Reform Act 1967, s. 9 (1A). This method applies also to leases of houses built after the abolition of domestic rating if the premium paid for the lease exceeds a limit based on a mathematical formula. Otherwise the original method applies: Local Government and Housing Act 1989, s. 149 and References to Rating (Housing) Regulations 1990 (S.I. 1990 No. 434).

Instead of assuming a 50 year extension, as in the case of low rateable value properties, it is assumed that the tenant has the right to remain at the end of his contractual term under Part I of the Landlord and Tenant Act 1954. Unlike the low rateable value properties, the fact that the tenant himself might make an enhanced bid is not to be disregarded. The price, therefore, includes the value of the rent for the residue of the contractual term, the value of the "fair rent" for the dwelling-house (not just the site) during continuation under the 1954 Act, the value of the reversion to the site and building subject to these rights, and an addition to reflect the higher bid a sitting tenant would make.

It became apparent that a tenant of a high rateable value property could achieve a substantial reduction in the price by first extending the lease for 50 years under the 1967 Act prior to enfranchising.[13] This effectively gave the tenant the benefit of the formula applicable to low rateable value properties, and thereby diminished the value of the reversion. This is now prohibited by the Housing and Planning Act 1986, whereby it is assumed, for the purpose of calculating the price, that the tenant has no right to an extension, and that, where the lease has been extended, that it will end on the original term date.[14]

In the case of high value houses brought within the 1967 Act by the Leasehold Reform, Housing and Urban Development Act 1993, the price of the freehold is calculated on a basis similar to the second method described above, but with certain modifications which operate in the landlord's favour.[15] For example, there is no assumption that the tenant is entitled to remain in possession at the end of the tenancy under Part I of the Landlord and Tenant Act 1954. This, accordingly, increases the value of the freehold. Further, compensation is payable to the landlord if the enfranchisement causes the value of his other property to diminish.[16]

(2) PART I OF THE LANDLORD AND TENANT ACT 1954[17]

Part I of the Landlord and Tenant Act 1954 gives security of tenure to long leaseholders who, at common law, would be obliged to give up possession on the ground that their leases had terminated by effluxion of time. In effect, it allows them to remain in possession as Rent Act statutory tenants. It is not possible to contract out of Part I of the 1954 Act.[18] Nowadays, however, long leaseholders of houses will usually also be entitled to the more attractive privileges of the Leasehold Reform Act 1967, while long leaseholders of flats have been given enhanced rights by the Leasehold Reform, Housing and Urban Development Act 1993.

(a) The qualifying tenancy

The Act protects the tenant if he holds under a long tenancy at a low rent[19] and if he satisfies what the Act calls the "qualifying condition".[20] This

---

13 *Mosley v Hickman* (1986) 52 P & CR 248.
14 S. 23, amending s. 9 of the 1967 Act, but not retrospectively.
15 S. 9 (1C) of the 1967 Act, introduced by s. 66 of the 1993 Act.
16 S. 9A, introduced by s. 66 of the 1993 Act.
17 See Woodfall, *Landlord and Tenant* (28th edn) paras. 3181–3210.
18 Landlord and Tenant Act 1954, s. 17; *Re Hennessey's Agreement* [1975] Ch 252, [1975] 1 All ER 60.
19 As defined in Rent Act 1977, s. 5 (rent less than two-thirds of the rateable value on a specified

requires him to show that, if his tenancy had not been at a low rent, he would have been entitled to retain possession of all or part of the premises under the Rent Act 1977. Thus the premises must have been let as a separate dwelling,[1] they must fall within the appropriate limits of rateable value,[2] the tenant must have been occupying them wholly or in part as his residence,[3] and so forth. The crucial moment when the qualifying condition must be satisfied is on what the Act calls "the term date",[4] i.e. the date on which the tenancy would expire at common law. Thus in *Herbert v Byrne*[5] the tenant bought the last five months' residue of the 99 year lease which was due to expire at Christmas 1962. In November 1962 he moved in a few pieces of his furniture and when Christmas came he was "pigging it" in a part of the house while his family lived elsewhere. The whole exercise was admittedly performed solely in order to obtain the protection of the Act, but the Court of Appeal held that he satisfied the qualifying condition on the relevant date and had therefore succeeded.

(b) Security of tenure

At common law the landlord would be entitled to possession on the term date. But the Act provides that he shall be entitled to possession only if he can show the existence of certain specified discretionary grounds.[6] These grounds are similar to those upon which a court may make an order for possession under the Rent Act[7] but with one important addition, namely, that for the purposes of redevelopment after the termination of the tenancy the landlord proposes to demolish or reconstruct the whole or a substantial part of the relevant premises.[8] This ground is available only where the landlord is a public body.[9] If the landlord is unable to prove the existence of any of the statutory grounds, the tenant is entitled to retain possession as a Rent Act tenant,[10] paying a fair rent determined by the rent officer in the normal way.[11] Possession may thereafter be recovered under the Rent Act grounds for possession.

The machinery by which the Act provides security of tenure is rather different from that applicable to ordinary short protected tenancies. The Act artificially prolongs the existence of the long tenancy until it has been

---

day). For tenancies granted on or after 1 April 1990, the rent must not exceed £1,000 a year in Greater London or £250 elsewhere: Local Government and Housing Act 1989, s. 149 and References to Rating (Housing) Regulations 1990 (S.I. 1990 No. 434).

20 Landlord and Tenant Act 1954, s. 2 (1).

1 See p. 470, ante; *Regalian Securities Ltd v Ramsden* [1981] 1 WLR 611, [1981] 2 All ER 65; *Grosvenor Estates Belgravia v Cochran* [1991] 2 EGLR 83.

2 Defined in Rent Act 1977, s. 4. For tenancies granted on or after 1 April, 1990, this rule is replaced by a requirement that the premium paid for the tenancy did not exceed a limit based on a mathematical formula: Local Government and Housing Act 1989, s. 149 and S.I. 1990 No. 434.

3 This is less strict than the test under the Housing Act 1988, because there is no requirement that it be the tenant's only or principal home. See p. 472, ante.

4 Landlord and Tenant Act 1954, s. 2 (6).

5 [1964] 1 WLR 519, [1964] 1 All ER 882.

6 Landlord and Tenant Act 1954, s. 12.

7 For example, breach of covenant, nuisance or annoyance, or requirement for occupation by landlord or family.

8 Landlord and Tenant Act 1954, s. 12 (1) (*a*). Compensation is not payable.

9 Leasehold Reform Act 1967, s. 38.

10 Landlord and Tenant Act 1954, ss. 6 (1) (*a*), 22 (1).

11 Leasehold Reform Act 1967, Sch. 5, para. 4.

determined in accordance with a complicated procedure of notices, counter-notices and (if necessary) applications to the county court. If the landlord wishes to retake possession, he must serve the appropriate notice on the tenant at least six months but less than twelve months in advance, stating the ground upon which he claims that he is entitled to possession.[12] If the tenant replies with a counter-notice electing to remain in possession, or simply stays there and continues to fulfil the "qualifying condition",[13] the landlord must apply to the court for an order for possession.[14] If he is successful, the tenancy will of course come to an end. If he is unsuccessful, or if he did not want to retake possession in the first place, he may terminate the long tenancy by a notice proposing a Rent Act statutory tenancy.[15] Such a notice must specify the date upon which the long tenancy is to come to an end. Except in the case of a notice served after an unsuccessful application for possession (when the minimum period is three months)[16] the notice must also be given at least six months but less than one year in advance.[17] The notice must also propose the terms of the new statutory tenancy (apart from the rent) and in particular the obligations of the parties concerning repairs.[18] If these are not agreed, they must be settled by an application to the court.[19] The rent will continue (in the absence of agreement between the parties) at the old rate[20] until a fair rent for the statutory tenancy has been determined by the rent officer.[1]

(c) New assured tenancy regime

The policy of the Housing Act 1988 was to phase out Rent Act tenancies and to introduce the assured tenancy. The Act of 1988 did not, however, amend the 1954 Act. That was done by the Local Government and Housing Act 1989,[2] which applies to long tenancies entered into on or after 1 April 1990. Where the long tenancy was created before that date but still exists on 15 January 1999, it becomes subject to the new régime on termination. The new rules will apply to long tenancies which would be assured tenancies under the Housing Act 1988 but for the low rent.[3]

The main difference between the old régime and the new is that a landlord who cannot establish a ground for possession[4] must propose an assured monthly tenancy instead of a Rent Act statutory tenancy in order to terminate a long tenancy after its term date. Thus a market rent will be payable instead of the lower "fair rent" under the Rent Act 1977. If the parties cannot agree

---

12 Landlord and Tenant Act 1954, s. 4 (2), (3) (*b*).
13 Landlord and Tenant Act 1954, s. 13 (1). For the meaning of "qualifying condition", see p. 496, ante.
14 Ibid., s. 13 (1).
15 Ibid., s. 4 (3) (*a*).
16 Ibid., s. 14 (3).
17 Ibid., s. 4 (2).
18 Ibid., s. 7 (3). Remedies for disrepair are restricted by s. 16.
19 Ibid., s. 7 (1); *Etablissement Commercial Kamira v Schiazzano* [1985] QB 93, [1984] 2 All ER 465.
20 Leasehold Reform Act 1967, Sch. 5, para. 3 (1).
 1 Ibid., para. 4.
 2 S. 186 and Sch. 10.
 3 The property must be "let as a separate dwelling" at the time when the question arises: Local Government and Housing Act 1989, Sch. 10, para. 1 (7).
 4 For the applicable grounds, see Sch. 10, para. 5.

on the rent under the assured tenancy, the matter may be referred to the rent assessment committee, which will determine the market rent.[5]

(3) THE LEASEHOLD REFORM, HOUSING AND URBAN DEVELOPMENT ACT 1993

Long leases of flats have been a source of dissatisfaction to tenants for two reasons. First, they are wasting assets which in time become unsaleable. Secondly, the tenants have insufficient control over the level of service charges and the standard of maintenance. We have seen that flat-dwellers have no rights of enfranchisement under the Leasehold Reform Act 1967.

The Leasehold Reform, Housing and Urban Development Act 1993 seeks to improve the position of long leaseholders of flats by giving them a collective right to acquire the landlord's interest in the building. It should be appreciated that this Act does not enable a leaseholder to acquire the freehold of his *flat*, as a system of commonhold tenure would do. Also, such a leaseholder is given an individual right to an extended lease of his flat. Contracting out of either of these rights is prohibited.[6]

(a) Conditions for enfranchisement

The right to collective enfranchisement is conferred on "qualifying tenants",[7] namely lessees of flats[8] who hold under long leases (granted for a term exceeding 21 years[9]) at low rents.[10] As explained below, a proportion of the qualifying tenants must also satisfy the residence condition, requiring occupation of the flat as the tenant's only or principal home for the last twelve months or for periods amounting to three years in the last ten years.[11]

The premises must be a self-contained building or a self-contained part of a building containing at least two flats held by qualifying tenants and such tenants must hold at least two-thirds of the total number of flats in the premises.[12] The right to enfranchisement is excluded if there is a resident landlord and the premises contain no more than four units,[13] or if more than 10% of the internal floor area (disregarding common parts) is non-residential.[14] Thus the Act does not apply to a building consisting of a row of flats above shops.

(b) Procedure

The statutory procedure requires the tenants to serve a notice on the landlord, who must respond by counter-notice.[15] In outline, the tenants' notice must

---

5 Ibid., para. 11. The Committee also has jurisdiction to settle other terms of the assured tenancy. An interim rent may be fixed during the statutory continuation of the long tenancy; ibid., para. 6.
6 Leasehold Reform, Housing and Urban Development Act 1993, s. 93.
7 Ibid., s. 5. Business leases are excluded. Long leaseholders were given limited rights to acquire the landlord's interest by the Landlord and Tenant Act 1987.
8 Defined in s. 101 of the 1993 Act.
9 Ibid., s. 7.
10 Ibid., s. 8. The requirement of low rent relates to the first year of the lease. For leases granted on or after 1 April, 1990 the limits are £1,000 per annum in Greater London or £250 elsewhere. In other cases the limit is based on the letting value or the rateable value.
11 Ibid., s. 6. Occupation by a company or artificial person does not suffice.
12 Ibid., s. 3.
13 Ibid., s. 4 (4). "Resident landlord" is defined in s. 10, and "unit" in s. 38.
14 Ibid., s. 4 (1).
15 Ibid., ss. 13, 21. By s. 28, the tenants' notice may be withdrawn before a binding contract is made.

provide the landlord with information such as the names of the qualifying tenants and must propose a purchase price. The landlord's counter-notice must state whether he accepts the right to enfranchise and whether the price is acceptable. If the right is denied, the matter will be resolved by the court.[16] If the landlord accepts the right but rejects the proposed price, his counter-notice must include a counter-offer.

An important restriction on the right to collective enfranchisement is that the tenants' notice cannot be served unless at least two-thirds of the total number of qualifying tenants participate. Secondly, the tenants serving the notice must be the lessees of at least half the number of flats in the premises. Thirdly, at least half of the tenants serving the notice must satisfy the residence condition described above.[17] Other qualifying tenants may later elect to participate if the tenants who served the notice agree.

The landlord may defeat the claim by applying to court and establishing an intention to redevelop the whole or a substantial part of the premises. This course is open to him only if at least two-thirds of all the long leases of flats in the premises are due to end within five years from the date of the tenants' notice.[18]

Enfranchisement proceedings are conducted by the "nominee purchaser", who will take a conveyance of the freehold on behalf of the participating tenants.[19] This will normally be a company formed to act for the purpose, in which the tenants hold the shares. The nominee purchaser must grant a lease back to the former landlord of any flats subject to secure tenancies. This lease will be for 999 years at a peppercorn rent. The former landlord may also require such a lease of non-residential units or flats having no qualifying tenant.[20]

It will be appreciated that, after enfranchisement, the tenants (via the "nominee purchaser") will be responsible for the management of the premises.

Where it is necessary for the maintenance of standards of appearance and amenity of an estate, the former landlord may be permitted to retain limited control over an enfranchised building by means of a management scheme along the lines of section 19 of the Leasehold Reform Act 1967.[1]

(c) The price[2]

The tenants must pay the market value of the landlord's interest, which includes the capitalised value of the rents for the residue of the leases and the value of the reversion on expiry of the leases, allowing for the tenants' rights to remain in possession under the Landlord and Tenant Act 1954, Part I, but disregarding the right to enfranchise or to extend the lease. If the landlord does not take a lease of any non-qualifying parts, the value of the reversion to these parts must be included. In addition, the tenants must pay at least

---

16 Ibid., s. 22.
17 Leasehold Reform, Housing and Urban Development Act 1993, s. 13 (2).
18 Ibid., s. 23.
19 Ibid., s. 15.
20 Ibid., Sch. 9. Likewise a flat occupied by a resident landlord (i.e. where the right to enfranchise is not excluded because the premises contain more than four units: s. 4).
 1 Ibid., s. 69. The landlord must apply to a leasehold valuation tribunal for approval within two years of the coming into force of s. 70.
 2 Ibid., Sch. 6. Only an outline can be given here. Failing agreement, the price will be determined by a leasehold valuation tribunal; s. 24.

half of the "marriage value"[3] of the landlord's and tenants' interests. This means that the landlord can share in the increased value accruing to the tenants as a result of their ability to acquire new long leases from the nominee purchaser without paying a premium. The price must also include any compensation payable to the landlord on account of loss or damage to his other property as a result of the enfranchisement.

(d) Extended lease

The 1993 Act also confers on long leaseholders individual rights to a new extended lease of their flats, on payment of a premium. In order to qualify, the existing lease must be a long lease (granted for a term exceeding 21 years),[4] at a low rent,[5] and the tenant (or at least one of joint tenants) must have occupied the flat as his only or principal home for the three years prior to giving notice of his claim, or for periods amounting to three years during the ten years before that date.[6] The statutory procedure requires a tenant's notice and a landlord's counter-notice.[7] The tenant's rights may be assigned along with the lease of the flat, but cannot be exercised during the currency of any claim to acquire the freehold of the block.[8] Where the original lease is due to end within five years from the date of the tenant's notice, the landlord may defeat the right to a new lease by applying to court and establishing his intention to redevelop the premises in which the flat is contained.[9]

A qualifying tenant is entitled, on payment of premium, to a new lease at a peppercorn rent for a term expiring 90 years after the term date of his existing lease.[10] This lease, which replaces the existing lease, is otherwise on the same terms as the original lease, but excluding any express renewal right or option to purchase.[11] The tenant is not entitled to any security of tenure (for example under the Landlord and Tenant Act 1954) at the end of the new lease, but the new lease may itself be renewed under the statutory procedure.[12]

The premium which the tenant must pay for the new lease is the aggregate of (a) the diminution in the value of the landlord's interest in the flat (on the assumption that the tenant had no enfranchisement or extension rights), (b) the landlord's share (at least 50%) of the "marriage value", and (c) any compensation payable to the landlord on account of loss or damage to his other property as a result of the grant of the new lease.[13]

The landlord may subsequently terminate the new lease if he satisfies the court of his intention to redevelop the premises in which the flat is contained.[14] In such a case he must pay compensation to the tenant based on the open market value of the new lease.[15]

It is likely in practice that this right to a new lease will be more attractive

3 Ibid., Sch. 6, para. 4. For drafting problems, see [1993] 43 EG 104 (M. Daiches).
4 Leasehold Reform, Housing and Urban Development Act 1993, s. 7.
5 Ibid., s. 8. The definition was given at p. 499, ante.
6 Ibid., s. 39. Occupation by a company or other artificial person does not suffice.
7 Ibid., ss. 42, 45.
8 Ibid., s. 54.
9 Ibid., s. 47.
10 Ibid., s. 56.
11 Ibid., s. 57.
12 Ibid., s. 59.
13 Ibid., Sch. 13. Only an outline is given here. "Marriage value" is defined in para. 4.
14 Ibid., s. 61. The application may be during the twelve months ending with the original term date or during the period of five years ending with the term date of the new lease.
15 Ibid., Sch. 14.

to tenants than the collective right to acquire the freehold of the block, not least because the conditions are easier to satisfy.

D. BUSINESS TENANCIES[16]

Protection is necessary for business tenants principally because a tenant with an established business is in a vulnerable position. If he has built up a goodwill attaching to the premises, such as that of a successful shopkeeper, he may suffer a severe loss of custom if he is required to remove elsewhere at the end of his tenancy. Furthermore, he will often have adapted the premises at his own cost to the needs of his particular business, so that removal would involve him in considerable further outlay. A landlord may therefore be able to extract a higher rent from his sitting tenant than he would obtain by letting the premises to a new tenant in the open market. Parliament has thought it unfair that the landlord should be able to force the tenant to pay this additional rent merely to preserve goodwill and improvements[17] created by his own effort and expense. It has therefore made provision for a system of security of tenure and rent control which is now contained in Part II of the Landlord and Tenant Act 1954, as amended by Part I of the Law of Property Act 1969.[18]

(1) THE QUALIFYING TENANCY

A tenancy qualifies for the protection of Part II of the Landlord and Tenant Act 1954 if the property comprised in the tenancy "is or includes" premises which are occupied by the tenant "and are so occupied for the purposes of a business carried on by him or for those and other purposes".[19] There are some features of this definition which require closer examination.

(a) "is or includes premises . . . occupied by the tenant . . ."

A tenant will enjoy the protection of the Act if he occupies[20] any part of the property comprised in his lease for the purposes of his business, although his protection will ordinarily extend only to what the Act defines as his "holding". This means the part of the property occupied by the tenant himself (whether for business or other purposes) or by a person employed in his business.[1] Thus the tenant of a shop with a flat above who carries on business in the shop and lives in the flat, or sub-lets it to an assistant or manager working in the shop will enjoy protection in respect of the whole premises. If he has sub-let the flat to someone who does not work in the shop, the tenancy will be within the Act but his "holding" will be the shop alone.[2] If he has sub-let the

---

16 See Woodfall, *Landlord and Tenant*, chapter 22.
17 As to compensation for improvements, see Landlord and Tenant Act 1954, Part I.
18 The Law Commission has proposed improvements to the working of the Act by amending certain details while leaving the fundamentals undisturbed: Landlord and Tenant: Business Tenancies 1992 (Law Com. No. 208); [1993] Conv 334 (M. Haley).
19 Landlord and Tenant Act 1954, s. 23 (1).
20 For the meaning of "occupy", see *Linden v Secretary of State for Social Services* [1986] 1 WLR 164, [1986] 1 All ER 691.
 1 Landlord and Tenant Act 1954, s. 23 (3).
 2 *Narcissi v Wolfe* [1960] Ch 10, [1959] 3 All ER 71.

whole premises, his tenancy will not be protected at all, although that of the sub-tenant probably will be.

(b) "occupied for the purposes of a business"

"Business" is very widely defined, to include a "trade, profession or employment" and, rather curiously, "*any* activity carried on by a body of persons, whether corporate or unincorporate". Thus the tenancy of a members' tennis club has been held within the Act, because playing tennis is undoubtedly an activity and it was carried on by a body of persons.[3] For an individual, on the other hand, activity is not enough. It must be a "trade, profession or employment". Accordingly a tenant who ran a free Sunday school in a disused shop was held to be outside the definition.[4]

Under the Housing Act 1988, where the key phrase is "let as a separate dwelling", attention is concentrated on the purpose for which the premises were let rather than the purpose for which they are actually being used.[5] The business code, on the other hand, is more concerned with actual user at the time when the question has to be decided.[6] Prima facie, the fact that the tenant is carrying on business upon the premises is enough. But in some cases the fact that the business user is in breach of covenant will exclude the application of the Act.[7] And there is nothing in the Act to restrict the landlord's common law right to forfeit the tenancy for breach of covenant.[8]

(c) "or for those and other purposes"

The tenant need use only a part of the premises for the purposes of his business, or he may use the same part for business purposes some of the time and other purposes at other times. If the premises are used partly for business and partly for residential purposes, residential security is excluded and only the Landlord and Tenant Act 1954 applies.[9] But the business user must be significant "and not merely ancillary to the residential user" such as maintaining a study where one can work in the evenings or at weekends.[10]

(2) EXCLUSIONS

Expressly excluded from the protection of the Act are short fixed-term lettings not exceeding six months,[11] tenancies excluded by agreement which the court has authorised on a joint application,[12] and certain other tenancies

---

3 *Addiscombe Garden Estates Ltd v Crabbe* [1958] 1 QB 513, [1957] 3 All ER 563.
4 *Abernethie v A M and J Kleiman* [1970] 1 QB 10, [1969] 2 All ER 790; see also *Lewis v Weldcrest Ltd* [1978] 1 WLR 1107, [1978] 3 All ER 1226 (taking lodgers).
5 See p. 471, ante.
6 The critical dates are the contractual term date (because unless the premises are then being used for business purposes the term will not be artificially prolonged) and the date when a notice to determine the tenancy is served: *Cheryl Investments Ltd v Saldanha* [1978] 1 WLR 1329 at 1337, [1979] 1 All ER 5 at 12, per GEOFFREY LANE LJ.
7 Landlord and Tenant Act 1954, s. 23 (4); see *Bell v Alfred Franks and Bartlett Co Ltd* [1980] 1 WLR 340, [1980] 1 All ER 356.
8 Ibid., s. 24 (2).
9 Housing Act 1988, Sch. 1, para. 4.
10 *Cheryl Investments Ltd v Saldanha*, supra.
11 Landlord and Tenant Act 1954, s. 43 (3).
12 Ibid., s. 38 (4), p. 509, post.

such as agricultural holdings and mining leases.[13] Although not expressly excluded, the Act does not apply to tenancies at will, even if expressly created,[14] nor to licences. With respect to the latter, the effect of the decision in *Street v Mountford*[15] must be considered.[16]

(3) SECURITY OF TENURE AND RENT

The Act gives a business tenant security of tenure by providing, first, that his tenancy (whether periodic or for a term certain) cannot be terminated except by the notice procedure laid down by the Act, and secondly, that upon the termination of his tenancy the tenant shall be entitled as of right to the grant of a new tenancy unless the landlord can establish one of a list of specified grounds of opposition.

(a) Termination procedure

A business tenancy can be terminated only in accordance with the system of notices, counter-notices and applications to court provided by the Act.[17] Until this procedure has run its course, the tenancy continues, whatever its term might be. At common law, if a tenant for a term certain at an annual rent holds over after the end of the term and rent continues to be paid at the old rate, the normal inference is that he is holding over as a tenant from year to year.[18] But a business tenant who stays after the term date is not holding over. There can be no inference of a tenancy from year to year because the old tenancy has not yet come to an end.

(i) Termination by landlord The landlord may terminate the tenancy by a notice in a prescribed form, specifying the date of termination.[19] This must be at least six months but not more than twelve months after service of the notice and not earlier than the date on which the tenancy would have terminated, or could have been terminated, at common law.[20] A landlord's notice to terminate is commonly known as a "section 25 notice".

The notice must state whether or not the landlord would oppose the grant of a new tenancy, and if he intends to do so, the statutory grounds upon which he will rely.[1]

A tenant who has been served with a section 25 notice must within two months serve a counter-notice stating whether or not he is willing to give up possession of the premises.[2] If he does not serve such a notice (or states that he is willing to give up possession) the tenancy will end upon the date specified in the notice. Having served the necessary counter-notice, a tenant who wishes to preserve his right to a new tenancy must apply to the court not

13 Ibid., s. 43 (1). Tenancies of public houses are no longer excluded: Landlord and Tenant (Licensed Premises) Act 1990.
14 *Manfield & Sons Ltd v Botchin* [1970] 2 QB 612, [1970] 3 All ER 143.
15 [1985] AC 809, [1985] 2 All ER 289, p. 362, ante.
16 See *University of Reading v Johnson-Houghton* [1985] 2 EGLR 113; *London & Associated Investment Trust plc v Calow* (1986) 53 P & CR 340; *Dellneed Ltd v Chin* (1986) 53 P & CR 172; *Dresden Estates Ltd v Collinson* [1987] 1 EGLR 45; p. 365, ante.
17 Landlord and Tenant Act 1954, s. 24 (1).
18 See p. 385, ante.
19 Landlord and Tenant Act 1954, s. 25 (1).
20 Ibid., s. 25 (2).
 1 Ibid., s. 25 (6).
 2 Ibid., s. 29 (2). Law Commission Report on Business Tenancies 1992 (Law Com No. 208, HC 224), para. 2.39 recommends the abolition of this requirement.

less than two months nor more than four months after the date of service of the section 25 notice.[3] If he does not, the tenancy will expire on the date specified in the notice. Most applications are adjourned while the parties negotiate the new terms, and only in a minority of cases are these settled by the court. The negotiation of the terms of a new tenancy usually takes some time, but a tenant who has been served with a section 25 notice and allows the four months to pass in negotiation without protecting himself by an application to court will find that he has lost all his rights. Once an application for a new tenancy has been made, the old tenancy continues until three months after the proceedings have been "finally disposed of".[4]

(ii) Termination by tenant A tenant who simply wants to go out of possession can terminate his tenancy in any way open to him at common law.[5] Furthermore, a tenant who holds under a tenancy for a term of years certain exceeding one year, or a term of years certain and thereafter from year to year, can serve a notice requesting the grant of a new tenancy.[6] This notice is the counterpart of the landlord's section 25 notice. Like the section 25 notice, it must specify the date on which the current tenancy is to terminate, and it is subject to the same time limits.[7] A landlord who wishes to oppose the grant of a new tenancy must serve a counter-notice stating his grounds of opposition within two months of the tenant's notice,[8] but whether he does so or not, the tenant will lose his right to a new tenancy unless he follows up his notice by an application to the court not less than two months nor more than four months after the date of his notice.[9]

(iii) Who is the "landlord"? The scheme of the Act contemplates an exchange of notices followed by negotiations for a new tenancy and, if necessary, the adjudication of the court, between landlord and tenant. "Tenant", however, includes a sub-tenant;[10] the immediate landlord of the tenant carrying on the business may himself hold only a leasehold interest. But there is little point in the grant of a new tenancy by a "landlord" whose own interest in the premises is shortly about to expire. The Act deals with this problem by disregarding altogether a landlord who has himself only a short remaining leasehold interest. For the purposes of the Act, the "landlord" must be the owner of the fee simple or a leasehold interest which will not come to an end within fourteen months by effluxion of time or in respect of which a notice to terminate has been served under the Act.[11] If the immediate landlord does not fulfil these conditions, the competent landlord for the purposes of the Act will be the next superior landlord who does.

---

3 Ibid., s. 29 (3). Cf. *Kammins Ballrooms Co Ltd v Zenith Investments (Torquay) Ltd* [1971] AC 850, [1970] 2 All ER 871 (waiver of time limits possible), see also *Dodds v Walker* [1981] 1 WLR 1027, [1981] 2 All ER 609. Law Commission Report, supra, paras. 2.58–2.59 propose relaxation of the time limits. For assessment of damages for failure by solicitors to apply within prescribed time for a new tenancy, see *Ricci v Masons* [1993] 37 EG 154 (£111,410).
4 Landlord and Tenant Act 1954, s. 64.
5 Ibid., s. 24 (2).
6 Ibid., s. 26 (1).
7 Ibid., s. 26 (2).
8 Ibid., s. 26 (6).
9 Ibid., s. 29 (3).
10 Ibid., s. 69 (1).
11 Ibid., s. 44 (1).

(b) The grounds of opposition

The Act specifies seven grounds upon which a landlord may oppose the grant of a new tenancy.[12] These may be briefly summarised as follows: (a) the tenant's failure to repair, (b) persistent delay in paying rent, (c) other misbehaviour by the tenant, (d) alternative accommodation available, (e) that the tenant is, in relation to the landlord, a sub-tenant of part of the property originally let and that the landlord could realise a better rent by reletting the property as a whole, (f) the landlord's intention to demolish or reconstruct the premises, and (g) the landlord's intention to occupy the premises himself, either for the purposes of his business or as a residence. The last two grounds are in practice the most frequently relied upon and the only ones upon which any further comment will be made.

(i) Intention to demolish or reconstruct The burden is upon the landlord to establish the necessary intention at the time of the hearing.[13] "Intention" involves more than thinking that demolition or reconstruction would be desirable. The landlord must be able to show that he means business. As Lord ASQUITH said in a famous passage:[14]

> An "intention" . . . connotes a state of affairs which the party "intending" . . . does more than merely contemplate: it connotes a state of affairs which, on the contrary, he decides, so far as in him lies, to bring about, and which, in point of possibility, he has a reasonable prospect of being able to bring about, by his own act of volition . . . The term "intention" [is] unsatisfied if the person professing it has too many hurdles to overcome, or too little control of events . . . [The scheme must have] moved out of the zone of contemplation—out of the sphere of the tentative, the provisional and the exploratory—into the valley of decision.

The landlord may therefore have to satisfy the court that his scheme of redevelopment is commercially viable, that he has the means to carry it through and the necessary planning permissions and other consents, or a reasonable prospect of obtaining them.

The landlord must also show that he could not reasonably carry out his work of demolition or reconstruction without obtaining possession of the holding.[15] "Possession" in this context means legal possession, not merely physical occupation of the premises. Thus a landlord who has reserved a wide right to enter and do works upon the premises may be entitled to go into occupation for a lengthy period without ousting his tenant from legal possession.[16] Such a right will prevent him from opposing the grant of a new tenancy in similar terms. Even if the lease does not include such rights of entry, the tenant may be able to preserve his right to a new lease by offering to include them. The Act provides that the landlord cannot oppose the grant of a new tenancy on this ground, if the tenant agrees to the inclusion of terms giving the landlord reasonable access and other facilities and the work could then be carried out without obtaining possession and without interfering "to a substantial extent or for a substantial time" with the use of the holding for

---

12 Ibid., s. 30 (1) (*a*) to (*g*).
13 *Betty's Cafés Ltd v Phillips Furnishing Stores Ltd* [1959] AC 20, [1958] 1 All ER 607.
14 *Cunliffe v Goodman* [1950] 2 KB 237 at 253–254, [1950] 1 All ER 720 at 724.
15 Landlord and Tenant Act 1954, s. 30 (1) (*f*).
16 *Health v Drown* [1973] AC 498, [1972] 2 All ER 561.

the purposes of the tenant's business.[17] Similarly, the tenant may be entitled to claim a new tenancy of "an economically separable part"[18] of the holding, if possession of the rest and (if necessary) access and facilities over the part retained would be reasonably sufficient to enable the landlord to carry out his work.[19]

(ii) Intention to use for own business or residence Again the burden is upon the landlord to establish the necessary intention at the time of the hearing.[20] The Act provides, however, that the landlord cannot rely upon this ground if his own interest has been purchased or created less than five years before "the termination of the current tenancy".[1] The purpose of this provision, as in the case of the parallel provision in the Housing Act 1988,[2] is to prevent persons wanting premises with vacant possession from buying them over the heads of sitting tenants and then opposing their normal security of tenure on the ground that they are required for the landlord's own use.

(c) Compensation

A tenant who is unable to obtain a new tenancy because the landlord can establish one of the grounds of opposition listed above as (e), (f) or (g) is entitled to be paid compensation for disturbance.[3] If his business has been carried on at the premises (whether by himself or a predecessor) for more than fourteen years, the compensation will be twice the rateable value of the premises. Otherwise it will be the rateable value.[4] A tenant need not go to court and lose merely in order to claim his compensation. If the landlord states in his section 25 notice, or his counter-notice opposing the tenant's request for a new tenancy, that he intends to rely on grounds (e), (f) or (g), the tenant will be entitled to his compensation if he makes no application to court, or makes one and later withdraws it.[5]

(d) Terms of the new tenancy

If the parties cannot agree on the terms of the new tenancy, they must be fixed by the court. The court has a discretion in fixing the length of the term but it must not exceed fourteen years.[6] Other terms (apart from rent) must be fixed by having regard to the terms of the current tenancy and to "all relevant circumstances".[7] This means in practice that the court will follow the terms

---

17 Landlord and Tenant Act 1954, s. 31A (1) (*a*). See *Cerex Jewels Ltd v Peachey Property Corp plc* (1986) 52 P & CR 127; *Romulus Trading Co Ltd v Trustees of Henry Smith's Charity* (1989) 60 P & CR 62.
18 Defined in Landlord and Tenant Act 1954, s. 31A (2).
19 Landlord and Tenant Act 1954, s. 31A (1) (*b*). On the other hand, if the landlord wants to use the whole holding for the purposes of the work, the tenant cannot argue that the landlord could do as well or better by using only a part. See *Decca Navigator Co Ltd v Greater London Council* [1974] 1 WLR 748, [1974] 1 All ER 1178.
20 See *Westminster City Council v British Waterways Board* [1985] AC 676, [1984] 3 All ER 737.
1 Landlord and Tenant Act 1954, s. 30 (2).
2 Housing Act 1988, Sch. 2, Ground 1. See also Ground 6.
3 Landlord and Tenant Act 1954, s. 37 (1).
4 Ibid., s. 37 (2) and (3); Local Government and Housing Act 1989, Sch. 7; Landlord and Tenant Act 1954 (Appropriate Multiplier) Order 1990 (S.I. 1990 No. 363).
5 Until the Act was amended by LPA 1969 the tenant had to go to court.
6 Landlord and Tenant Act 1954, s. 33. Law Commission Report on Business Tenancies 1992 (Law Com No. 208, HC 224), para. 2.79, recommends a maximum of 15 years.
7 Ibid., s. 35.

of the current tenancy unless there is a good reason for not doing so. In *O'May v City of London Real Property Co Ltd*[8] the current tenancy made the landlord responsible for repair and services, the tenant paying a fixed service charge. The House of Lords refused to alter the tenancy to make the tenant liable for repairs and the full cost of services, paying a correspondingly lower rent, because the effect would be to transfer the risk of indeterminate financial burdens to the tenant.

(e) Rent

The rent under the new tenancy is that which the premises could command if let in the open market, but disregarding any effect on the rent of the fact that the tenant or his predecessors in title have been in occupation, or any goodwill attaching to the holding on account of the tenant's business, or any improvements made during the current tenancy or in certain cases in previous tenancies within the past 21 years.[9] When the court has to determine the rent, it will usually do so after hearing the evidence of expert surveyors, giving their opinions of the letting value of the premises supported by evidence of lettings of comparable properties in the same area. It may be questioned whether the court's function could not be better performed by a body which was itself expert in these matters, such as the Lands Tribunal.

Until 1970, the tenant continued to be liable only for the rent under the old tenancy until it was duly terminated in accordance with the Act and the new tenancy had begun. In the absence of contrary agreement, as we have seen, the old tenancy could not terminate until three months after the proceedings for the grant of the new tenancy had been finally disposed of.[10] In times of inflation, when the difference between the old rent and the new might be very considerable, it was therefore greatly in the tenant's interest to prolong the proceedings (and his tenancy) as much as possible. Time might be gained by taking fine points on the validity of the section 25 notice and similar procedural matters, while even an unsuccessful appeal to the House of Lords might be financed out of the difference in rents. This situation led to an amendment which allowed the landlord to apply to the court to fix an interim rent, payable from the date of termination specified in the section 25 notice or the tenant's request for a new tenancy or the date of the application to fix the interim rent, whichever is the later.[11] In a rising market, the interim rent will commonly be more than the current rent but less than the rent which would be payable under any statutory renewal of the tenancy. This is for two reasons. First, it is fixed upon the assumption that a new tenancy from year to year is being granted, the rent for such a tenancy normally being less than that of a tenancy for a fixed term. Secondly, the court must "have regard" to the rent payable under the existing tenancy in determining the interim rent.[12] This usually has the effect of reducing the interim rent below a market rent in order to provide a "cushion" for the tenant against the shock of a steep

---

8 [1983] 2 AC 726, [1982] 1 All ER 660. See also *Cairnplace Ltd v CBL (Property Investment) Co Ltd* [1984] 1 WLR 696, [1984] 1 All ER 315 (guarantor term imposed).
9 Landlord and Tenant Act 1954, s. 34.
10 Ibid., s. 64. See p. 504, ante.
11 Landlord and Tenant Act 1954, s. 24A. See *Stream Properties Ltd v Davis* [1972] 1 WLR 645, [1972] 2 All ER 746.
12 Ibid., s. 24A (3).

increase if a market rent were to be imposed.[13] In a falling market the interim rent could be lower than the old rent. For this reason the Law Commission recommends that the tenant should be able to make the application.[14]

(f) Contracting out

Until 1970 the parties could not by agreement exclude the provisions of the Act.[15] Although landlords could avoid the Act by granting terms not exceeding six months or licences,[16] it was found that this prohibition discouraged landlords from letting premises which they intended eventually to use themselves or redevelop. Whatever the terms of the letting, the protected tenant will be entitled to at least six months' notice to terminate[17] and can usually prolong his tenancy for several months more by an unsuccessful application for a new tenancy.[18] When it finally expires, he may delay the landlord still further by compelling him to commence proceedings for possession. Many landlords therefore preferred to leave their building temporarily empty. The Act now allows the parties to agree to exclude the Act if their agreement is approved by the court, which will have to be satisfied that the tenant understands his position and has not been oppressed or overborne.[19]

E. AGRICULTURAL HOLDINGS[20]

Tenant farmers need security of tenure to encourage them to spend money on improving the land and buying stock and other capital equipment. Some statutory protection was introduced soon after the First World War,[1] but this was greatly strengthened and improved during and after the Second World War as part of the general effort made to increase home food production at the time. The code now in force is contained in the Agricultural Holdings Act 1986.

(1) THE AGRICULTURAL HOLDING

The key concept in the Agricultural Holdings Act 1986 is the "agricultural holding". This is defined as "the aggregate of the land (whether agricultural land or not) comprised in a contract of tenancy which is a contract for an agricultural tenancy",[2] but excluding service tenancies granted during the continuance of some office or employment. A contract for an agricultural tenancy is one where, having regard to the terms of the tenancy, the actual

13 See *English Exporters (London) Ltd v Eldonwall Ltd* [1973] Ch 415, [1973] 1 All ER 726; *Charles Follett Ltd v Cabtell Investments Co Ltd* [1987] 2 EGLR 88.
14 Law Commission Report on Business Tenancies 1992 (Law Com No. 208, HC 224), para 2.63.
15 Landlord and Tenant Act 1954, s. 38 (1); *Allnatt London Properties Ltd v Newton* [1984] 1 All ER 423 (effect of s. 38 (1) on "offer to surrender" clause), p. 415, ante.
16 P. 503, ante.
17 See p. 504, ante.
18 See p. 508, ante.
19 Landlord and Tenant Act 1954, s. 38 (4). Law Com. No. 208 (1992), para. 2.19, recommends removing the requirement of court approval.
20 See Muir Watt, *Agricultural Holdings* (13th edn).
 1 Agricultural Holdings Act 1923.
 2 Agricultural Holdings Act 1986, s. 1 (1).

or contemplated use of the land at the date of the contract or subsequently and any other relevant circumstances, substantially the whole of the land is let for use as agricultural land.[3] "Agriculture" is very widely defined[4] and there is no minimum size for an agricultural holding. "Agricultural land" means land which is not merely used for agriculture but is "so used for the purposes of a trade or business."[5] Provided the use is agricultural, the business need not be,[6] but non-commercial agricultural use does not qualify.

(2) SECURITY OF TENURE

(a) The deemed yearly tenancy

The Act confers security of tenure by limiting the circumstances in which a landlord can validly serve a notice to quit. Prima facie this machinery can operate only on periodic tenancies, because only in such cases is a notice to quit necessary to terminate the tenancy. But the Act deals with this problem in sweeping fashion by providing that tenancies for an interest less than a tenancy from year to year shall take effect as if they were yearly tenancies,[7] while a tenancy for a term certain of two years or upwards shall (unless a notice to quit has been served) thereafter continue as a yearly tenancy.[8] Licences to occupy the land for any period also take effect as tenancies from year to year.[9] Thus most agricultural tenancies, whatever their express terms, are deemed to be or become yearly tenancies.

It will be noticed, however, that there is a curious gap in these provisions. A tenancy for a term certain which is more than a year but less than two years does not appear to be converted into a yearly tenancy. It will therefore expire by effluxion of time and the security of tenure machinery cannot apply to it.[10] Furthermore, the Act contains an express exception in the case of a letting or licence "in contemplation of the use of the land only for grazing or mowing (or both) during some specified period of the year".[11] The owner of a country house who has some surplus fields can therefore let them to a neighbouring farmer for grazing for up to 364 days at a time[12] without committing himself to the security of tenure provisions of the Act. Finally, the security provisions do not protect subtenants against the head landlord.[13]

---

3 Ibid., s. 1 (2). S. 1 (3) deals with change of user.
4 Ibid., s. 96 (1).
5 Ibid., s. 1 (4). See *Brown v Teirnan* [1993] 1 EGLR 11.
6 *Rutherford v Maurer* [1962] 1 QB 16, [1961] 2 All ER 775 (grazing horses of a riding school).
7 Agricultural Holdings Act 1986, s. 2 (1).
8 Ibid., s. 3 (1). Subject to an exception in s. 5, it is not possible to contract out of this provision.
9 Ibid., s. 2 (2); *Bahamas International Trust Co Ltd v Threadgold* [1974] 1 WLR 1514, [1974] 3 All ER 881 (exclusive occupation necessary). See also *McCarthy v Bence* [1990] 1 EGLR 1, discussing the effect of this subsection on *Street v Mountford* [1985] AC 809, [1985] 2 All ER 289, p. 364, ante.
10 *Gladstone v Bower* [1960] 2 QB 384, [1960] 3 All ER 353; *Keen v Holland* [1984] 1 WLR 251, [1984] 1 All ER 75. Nor is it protected as a business tenancy: *EWP Ltd v Moore* [1992] QB 460, [1992] 1 All ER 880.
11 Agricultural Holdings Act 1986, s. 2 (3).
12 *Reid v Dawson* [1955] 1 QB 214, [1954] 3 All ER 498; *Scene Estate Ltd v Amos* [1957] 2 QB 205, [1957] 2 All ER 325; *Stone v Whitcombe* (1980) 40 P & CR 296; *Watts v Yeend* [1987] 1 WLR 323, [1987] 1 All ER 744.
13 See, however, *Gisborne v Burton* [1989] QB 390, [1988] 3 All ER 760 (subtenant treated as tenant under "artificial transaction" doctrine).

(b) The notice to quit

At common law a yearly tenancy may be terminated by at least six months' notice expiring on the anniversary of the tenancy.[14] For an agricultural holding the notice period is extended to one year.[15] The common law requirement that the notice must terminate on the anniversary is retained. It may therefore be up to two years before a notice to quit can expire.

(c) Validity of notice to quit

A notice to quit an agricultural holding can operate effectively in only two kinds of circumstances. The first is when the landlord at the time of service can rely upon one of eight specified grounds.[16] The second is when the local Agricultural Land Tribunal consents to the operation of the notice after it has been served.[17] This consent also may be given only upon certain specified grounds, for example, that greater hardship would be caused by withholding than by giving consent. Compensation is payable except in default cases.

The grounds upon which a notice may be served and operate without further consent may be summarised briefly as follows: (a) the tenant of a smallholding has attained the age of 65, (b) land required for non-agricultural use,[18] (c) bad husbandry by the tenant, (d) failure to pay rent or to remedy remediable breach after statutory demand, (e) irremediable breach of covenant by the tenant, (f) bankruptcy, (g) death of the tenant or sole surviving tenant within three months before the giving of the notice, (h) amalgamation of the land pursuant to Minister's certificate.

Ground (g) is in practice the most important because it is the only one which (unless the tenant is a limited company) must become available to the landlord sooner or later. Its significance was reduced when the Agriculture (Miscellaneous Provisions) Act 1976 gave certain members of the deceased tenant's family a right to succeed to the tenancy. These succession rights, however, have now been largely confined to tenancies granted before 12 July 1984.[19]

(d) Notice procedure

A tenant who has been served with a notice to quit and wishes to invoke the security of tenure provisions of the Act must serve a counter-notice.[20] If the notice does not purport to have been given on one of the permitted grounds, he must simply claim the protection of the relevant section whereby the Tribunal's consent is required.[1] If the notice relies on certain of the permitted grounds, the tenant's notice must claim an arbitration on whether the

---

14 See p. 465, ante.
15 Agricultural Holdings Act 1986, s. 25 (1). Contracting out is not permitted; cf. *Elsden v Pick* [1980] 1 WLR 898, [1980] 3 All ER 235 (waiver).
16 Agricultural Holdings Act 1986, Sch. 3.
17 Ibid., ss. 26, 27.
18 This ground has been amended by the Agricultural Holdings (Amendment) Act 1990.
19 Agricultural Holdings Act 1986, s. 34, re-enacting Agricultural Holdings Act 1984, s. 2. Where succession rights are available, they apply also on the tenant's retirement.
20 It is not possible to deprive the tenant by contract of his right to serve a counter-notice: *Johnson v Moreton* [1980] AC 37, [1978] 3 All ER 37. See also *Featherstone v Staples* [1986] 1 WLR 861, [1986] 2 All ER 461.
 1 Agricultural Holdings Act 1986, s. 26 (1). See *Crawford v Elliott* [1991] 1 EGLR 13.

appropriate ground existed.[2] There are stringent time limits for these notices and the tenant may lose all protection if they are not correctly served.[3] It is perhaps questionable whether such a complicated procedure is suitable for farmers.[4]

(3) RENT

The rent for an agricultural holding is, in the absence of agreement, fixed by an arbitrator appointed under the Act.[5] The landlord is entitled to the rent at which the holding might reasonably be expected to be let by a prudent and willing landlord to a prudent and willing tenant, taking into account the current level of rents for comparable lettings (as to which any scarcity element must be disregarded). Certain matters must be disregarded, including the fact that the tenant is in occupation, any improvements he has made and any deterioration for which he is responsible.[6] The rent may be reviewed (by agreement or arbitration) at intervals of not less than three years.[7]

SECTION X REGISTERED LAND[8]

As we have seen, a term of years absolute is one of the two legal estates which can be registered as a separate title on the property register.[9] Not every lease is so registrable, but if it is, then the legal estate will not finally pass to the lessee until registration is completed in accordance with the provisions of the Land Registration Act 1925.

The Land Registration Act 1986 simplified the requirements for the registration of leases.[10]

(a) Provisions for registration

All leases,[11] which are granted after 1986 for more than 21 years out of registered land are substantively registrable; and so are all assignments of unregistered leases in compulsory areas, which have more than 21 years to run.[12]

---

2 Ibid., s. 2 (2) and Sch. 4. But a notice containing statements which the landlord knows to be false is of no effect: *Rous v Mitchell* [1991] 1 WLR 469, [1991] 1 All ER 676.
3 As in *Magdalen College Oxford v Heritage* [1974] 1 WLR 441, [1974] 1 All ER 1065.
4 The position has been somewhat mitigated by the requirement that a notice based on failure to pay rent (or other breach) must now be in prescribed form, informing the tenant of his right to seek arbitration: Agricultural Holdings Act 1986, Sch. 3, para. 10.
5 Agricultural Holdings Act 1986, s. 12.
6 Agricultural Holdings Act 1986, Sch. 2, paras. 1–3.
7 Ibid., para. 4. See *Mann v Gardner* (1990) 61 P & CR 1.
8 See generally Ruoff and Roper, chapter 21; Barnsley, *Conveyancing Law and Practice* (3rd edn), pp. 425–431; *Registered Land Practice Notes* (2nd edn), pp. 21–24; M & B pp. 526–531.
9 P. 99, ante.
10 The Act was based on the Law Commission Report on Land Registration 1983 (Law Com. No. 125, HC 86).
11 For the classes of leasehold title which may be registered, see p. 102, ante; p. 786, post.
12 LRA 1986, s. 2 substituted periods of "more than 21 years" for those of "not less than 40 years" in LRA 1925, s. 123 (1), p. 99, ante, thereby eliminating the anomaly that, in areas of compulsory registration where leases were granted for more than 21 years but less than 40 years, or were assigned having more than 21 years but less than 40 years to run at the date of assignment, registration was compulsory, if the superior title was registered, but only optional if the superior title was not registered.

These include assignments by consent of inalienable leases, i.e. those which contain an absolute prohibition or restriction against all dealings therewith inter vivos.[13]

(b) Effect of registration and non-registration

(i) Registration It is important to notice the effect of the substantive registration of a registrable lease. It is only on registration that the lessee finally acquires a legal estate: furthermore, as part of the machinery of registration, notice of the lease is automatically entered by the Registrar against the lessor's registered title, if the land certificate is lodged in the registry.[15]

(ii) Non-registration We must now consider the effect of the failure on the part of the lessee to register his lease. There are two different situations. If, on the one hand, it is registrable because his lessor's title is itself registered, then until registration is completed "the transferor shall be deemed to remain proprietor of the registered estate".[16] If, on the other hand, the transaction is one which calls for first registration of title, then, if registration is not applied for within two months, the transaction is "void so far as regards the grant ... of the legal estate".[17] In the latter case the lessee acquires the legal estate at the time of the grant, but if he fails to register it within the time limit, it reverts to the lessor. "The effect of not registering the title to a lease when granted would at best seem to be that the lessee holds the demised premises, not as legal owner of the term, but as a person who has entered into a binding agreement for a lease."[18]

(c) Leases for 21 years or less. Contracts for lease

It follows from the registration provisions that a lease granted for a term of 21 years or less (and a lease which has 21 years or less unexpired[19]) cannot be substantively registered. Nor can a contract for a lease: this is, as we have seen, an equitable interest and is therefore incapable of registration as a legal estate.[20] But this does not mean that such transactions afford no protection to a lessee or to a holder under a contract for a lease.

Under section 70 (1) (*k*) of the Land Registration Act 1925:[1]

Leases granted for a term not exceeding twenty-one years,

are overriding interests, and here the lessee is protected against a transferee from the lessor without the need for any entry on the register. A contract for

13 Ibid., s. 3. Previously these were not registrable. Mortgage terms "where there is a subsisting right of redemption" are not registrable: LRA 1925, ss. 8 (1) (*a*), 19 (2) (*b*), 22 (2) (*b*). They are best protected by registration of a charge under s. 26.
15 LRR 1925, r. 46. For an account of the procedure, see *Strand Securities Ltd v Caswell* [1965] Ch 958 at 976–979, [1965] 1 All ER 820–5, per LORD DENNING MR; M & B p. 531; [1981] Conv 395.
16 LRA 1925, ss. 18 (5), 19 (1), 19 (2), 21 (5), 22 (1), 22 (2).
17 Ibid., s. 123 (1) as amended by LRA 1986, s. 2 (1).
18 Ruoff and Roper, para. 1–10. For the effect in equity, see p. 100, ante.
19 LRA 1925, ss. 8 (1) (*a*), 19 (2) (*a*), 22 (2) (*a*).
20 P. 98, ante.
1 As substituted by LRA 1986, s. 4 (1). Previously gratuitous leases and leases granted for a premium were excluded. Such existing leases are transitionally overriding interests: s. 4 (4). See Law Commission Third Report on Land Registration: A. Overriding Interests 1987 (Law Com. No. 158), paras. 2.38–2.53, p. 799, post.

a lease, however, cannot be protected as an overriding interest under this paragraph.[2]

If there is no overriding interest under paragraph (*k*), i.e. if the lease is over 21 years and registration is not yet completed, or if the transaction is a contract for a lease, then the right is a minor interest and should be protected by the entry of a notice or, if a notice cannot be entered, of a caution on the lessor's registered title.

The question now arises as to how far such a lessee or a holder under a contract for a lease is protected if he fails to enter a notice or a caution on the register. It is here that there is a striking difference between the two systems of conveyancing. In the unregistered system, failure to register a contract for a lease as a land charge under the Land Charges Act 1972 renders it void as against a purchaser of the legal estate for money or money's worth, even if the purchaser has actual notice of the agreement.[3] But in registered land the position is both similar and different. On the one hand the failure to protect a contract as a minor interest by an entry on the lessor's registered title has similar consequences; it will be overridden if the lessor makes a registered disposition for valuable consideration.[4] On the other hand the contract may be saved by section 70 (1) (*g*) of the Land Registration Act 1925, under which:

> the rights of every person in actual occupation of the land or in receipt of the rents and profits thereof, save where inquiry is made of such person and the rights are not disclosed

are overriding interests.[5] Similarly if a lessee is let into occupation before formal transfer and there is no entry on the register of his interest, the mere fact of the occupation turns his minor interest into an overriding one.[6] It would seem that a lessee in occupation (irrespective of the length of his lease) can always rely on just his occupation for protection. A lessor in receipt of rent, or in occupation through a servant or agent is also protected under paragraph (*g*) but a tenant who allows another to occupy his property rent free is not.[7]

(d) Determination

The Registrar is required to notify on the register the determination, whether whole or partial, of a lease. It must be proved to his satisfaction that it has so determined.[8] The general principles which govern the determination of leases apply equally to registered as to unregistered land. A lease which is determined by effluxion of time will only be cancelled on the register, if the Registrar is satisfied that it has not been statutorily extended, e.g. under the Landlord and Tenant Act 1954.[9]

2 *City Permanent Building Society v Miller* [1952] Ch 840, [1952] 2 All ER 621; M & B p. 529, p. 796, post. A lease granted to a secure tenant exercising his right to buy under Housing Act 1985, s. 118 is also excluded from para (*k*): LRA 1986, s. 2 (4); p. 796, post. It must always be substantively registered regardless of its length: s. 154 (1).
3 P. 381, ante.
4 P. 800, post.
5 P. 103, ante; p. 790, post.
6 *Woolwich Equitable Building Society v Marshall* [1952] Ch 1, [1951] 2 All ER 769; *Mornington Permanent Building Society v Kenway* [1953] Ch 382, [1953] 1 All ER 951.
7 *Strand Securities Ltd v Caswell* [1965] Ch 958, [1965] 1 All ER 820; p. 794, post; M & B p. 141.
8 LRA 1925, s. 46. On determination by surrender, see *Spectrum Investment Co v Holmes* [1981] 1 WLR 221, [1981] 1 All ER 6; M & B p. 210; p. 914, post.
9 See ss. 1–3, 23, 24.

Part II

Estates and interests in land

C. COMMERCIAL INTERESTS

Estate and interests in

COMMON LAW DISTINCT

Chapter 17

Easements and profits

SUMMARY

SECTION I RIGHTS *IN ALIENO SOLO* GENERALLY

A. INCORPOREAL INTERESTS

In this chapter our concern is with rights *in alieno solo*, i.e. with the case where X possesses some right that is enforceable against the land of another. If the owner of Blackacre is entitled to an easement, such as a right of way, over Whiteacre, he is said, in the curious language of English law, to have an incorporeal interest. Perhaps it is more intelligible to describe him as holding an interest in an incorporeity.[1]

1 Pp. 141–2, ante.

Like corporeal estates and interests, incorporeal interests may exist at law and in equity. A legal interest must be created by deed,[2] and can exist only for the same periods as those for which a legal estate can exist. Thus a legal easement may exist in fee simple or for a term of years absolute. An easement for any other period, e.g. for life, or an easement created otherwise than by deed, can only exist in equity.[3]

As we have seen, the *jura in re aliena* which are known to English law cover a very wide field and include such diverse subjects as rentcharges,[4] advowsons, tithes and so on,[5] but our present concern is solely with what Roman lawyers called "praedial servitudes". Though servitude is a word that is occasionally adopted by the judges,[6] it is not admitted as a term of art in English law, and yet it is a suitable expression to denote the particular legal interests which form the subject of this chapter.

A praedial servitude in Roman law meant a right *in rem*, annexed to a definite piece of land, the *praedium dominans*, which entitled the owner of that land to do something or to prevent the doing of something on another piece of land, the *praedium serviens*.[7] This is a sufficiently accurate description of easements and profits which represent the praedial servitudes of English law.

B. EASEMENTS

An easement is a privilege without a profit,[8] that is to say, it is a right attached to one particular piece of land which allows the owner of that land (the dominant owner) either to use the land of another person (the servient owner) in a particular manner, as by walking over or depositing rubbish on it, or to restrict its user by that other person to a particular extent, but which does not allow him to take any part of its natural produce or its soil.[9]

Thus an easement may be either positive or negative.[10] It is positive if it consists of a right to do something upon the land of another, as, for example, to walk or to place erections such as signboards thereon.

A negative easement, on the other hand, does not permit the execution of an act, but imposes a restriction upon the use which another person may make of his land. For instance, the easement of light signifies that the servient owner must not build so as unreasonably to obstruct the flow of light, and again an easement of support implies that the servient owner must not interfere with his own land or building so as to disturb his neighbour's.

An easement confers upon its owner no proprietary or possessory right in the land affected. It merely imposes a particular restriction upon the proprietary rights of the owner of the servient land. A right which entitles one person to the unrestricted use of the land of another may be an effective right to ownership or possession, but it cannot be an easement.[11]

---

2 Pp. 530, post.
3 Pp. 530, post.
4 Chapter 20, p. 645, post.
5 P. 142, n. 6, ante.
6 E.g. *Dalton v Angus* (1881) 6 App Cas 740 at 796, per Lord SELBORNE.
7 Moyle, *Institutes of Justinian* (5th edn), p. 214.
8 *Hewlins v Shippam* (1826) 5 B & C 221; Termes de la Ley, *sub voce* "Easement".
9 *Manning v Wasdale* (1836) 5 Ad & El 758.
10 *Dalton v Angus* (1881) 6 App Cas 740 at 821.
11 See p. 527, post.

C. PROFITS À PRENDRE

A profit à prendre is a right to enter another's land and to take something off that land,[12] and it is this participation in the produce of the soil or in the soil itself that principally distinguishes a profit from an easement. A right is a profit only if the thing to be taken is something that is capable of ownership. Thus the rights to pasture cattle on another's land, or to take sand or fish from another's river, or to take turf, stones or pheasants from another's estate are all examples of profits, for such things are capable of ownership; but a right to collect and carry away water from a spring on another person's land, or to water cattle in another's stream is an easement, since water is no part of the soil like sand, nor the produce of soil like grass, and unless stored in a tank or other receptacle is not capable of private ownership.[13]

SECTION II EASEMENTS[14]

A. NATURE OF EASEMENTS

A question that not infrequently arises is whether some right exercisable over the land of another is an easement or a right of an inferior nature, and it is a question of crucial importance. An owner may grant a number of different rights over his land to X, but it will make a world of difference to the position of X whether they are easements or not. A legal easement is a *jus in rem*, not a mere *jus in personam*; it permanently binds the land over which it is exercisable and permanently avails the land for the advantage of which it exists.[15] If X acquires an easement either in fee simple or for a term of years absolute, he becomes the owner of an actual legal interest in the land[16] and can enforce it against anybody who comes to the land whether by way of purchase, lease, gift or as a squatter, and whether with or without notice of the easement.

Thus at common law the benefit of an easement passes with a transfer of the land to which it is annexed without being specially mentioned,[17] and it is expressly provided that a conveyance of land shall be deemed to include and shall operate to convey all easements which are attached to the land conveyed.[18]

On the other hand, if X is given some right over the land of Y which may bear some similarity to an easement but which nevertheless the law does not regard as an easement, X acquires a mere personal right. Its infringement may give him a remedy in damages against Y, and if negative in nature it may be enforceable in equity against a person who acquires Y's land with notice of its existence,[19] but it is not a real right enforceable irrespective of

---

12 *Duke of Sutherland v Heathcote* [1892] 1 Ch 475 at 484.
13 Co Litt 4*a*; Blackstone, vol. ii. 18; *Mason v Hill* (1833) 5 B & Ad 1; *Race v Ward* (1855) 4 E & B 702; *Lowe v J W Ashmore Ltd* [1971] Ch 545 at 557, [1971] 1 All ER 1057 at 1068.
14 See generally Gale, *Law of Easements* (15th edn); Jackson, *Law of Easements and Profits*; Sara, *Boundaries and Easements* (1991).
15 *Leech v Schweder* (1874) 9 Ch App 463 at 474; LPA 1925, s. 187 (1).
16 P. 530, post.
17 Co Litt 121*b*.
18 LPA 1925, s. 62 (1), re-enacting Conveyancing Act 1881, s. 6 (1); pp. 534, post.
19 See the doctrine of *Tulk v Moxhay*, p. 614, et seq, post.

notice against all subsequent owners of that land. Nor can a right be given the status of an easement at the free will of the parties who create it, for the rule is that no right over land will be regarded as an easement unless it possesses certain attributes which the law has determined.

This being so, the first task must be to discover what those attributes and characteristics are.

(1) CHARACTERISTICS OF EASEMENTS

If an interest is to be an easement it must possess the four following characteristics.[20]

(a) There must be a dominant and a servient tenement[1]

The very nature of an easement, as being a right *in alieno solo*, requires that there shall be a tenement over which it is exercisable, the *servient tenement*, but in addition to this the law requires that there shall be another tenement, the *dominant tenement*, for the benefit of which the easement exists. To adopt legal phraseology an easement must be appurtenant or attached to land.

> If X, the owner of Blackacre, has acquired a right of way over the adjoining tenement Whiteacre, he is entitled to an easement of way not because he is X, but because he is the fee simple owner of Blackacre. The easement exists because Blackacre exists.[2]

It follows from this that there cannot be an easement *in gross*,[3] an easement that is independent of the ownership of land by the person who claims the right. Of course a person who does not own a yard of property may be granted a privilege to pass over Whiteacre, but though this may give him a personal right it certainly does not entitle him to an easement. It amounts to a licence confined in its effect to the actual parties.[4]

(b) An easement must accommodate the dominant tenement

It is a fundamental principle that an easement must not only be appurtenant to a dominant tenement, but must also be connected with the normal enjoyment of that tenement.[5] There must be a direct *nexus* between the enjoyment of the right and the user of the dominant tenement.[6] This requirement has been stated in various ways:

> An easement must be connected with the enjoyment of the dominant tenement and must be for its benefit.[7]

20 *Re Ellenborough Park* [1956] Ch 131, [1955] 3 All ER 667; M & B p. 621; (1964) 28 Conv (NS) 450 (M.A. Peel).
1 Holdsworth, *History of English Law*, vol. vii. pp. 324 et seq.
2 *Rangeley v Midland Rly Co* (1868) 3 Ch App 306 at 311; *Ackroyd v Smith* (1850) 10 CB 164 at 188; *Hawkins v Rutter* [1892] 1 QB 668.
3 *Ackroyd v Smith*, supra; *Weekly v Wildman* (1698) 1 Ld Raym 405, per TREBY CJ; *London & Blenheim Estates Ltd v Ladbroke Retail Parks Ltd* [1994] 1 WLR 31, [1993] 4 All ER 157 (right intended as easement and attached to servient tenement before dominant tenement identified held not to be an easement); *Voice v Bell* [1993] EGCS 128. In the USA both easements and profits may be *in gross*. See American Law Institute *Restatement of the Law of Property* (1944), Vol. 5. paras. 454, 489–96; and generally (1980) 96 LQR 557 (M. F. Sturley), criticising the rule; (1982) 98 LQR at p. 305 (S. Gardner).
4 Pp. 585, et seq, post.
5 *Ackroyd v Smith* (1850) 11 CB 19.
6 *Re Ellenborough Park* [1956] Ch 131 at 174, [1955] 3 All ER 667 at 680.
7 *Gale on Easements* (12th edn), p. 20; *Clapman v Edwards* [1938] 2 All ER 507.

It must have some natural connection with the estate, as being for its benefit.[8]
The incident sought to be annexed, so that the assignee of the land may take advantage of it, must be beneficial to the land in respect of the ownership.[9]

To take a simple example, a right of way in order to rank as an easement need not lead right up to the dominant tenement, but it must at least have some natural connection with it.[10] You cannot, remarked BYLES J, have a right of way over land in Kent appurtenant to an estate in Northumberland,[11] for a right of way in Kent cannot possibly be advantageous to Northumberland land.[12] We may expand the statement of the principle thus: a right enjoyed by one over the land of another does not possess the status of an easement unless it accommodates and serves the dominant tenement, and is reasonably necessary for the better enjoyment of that tenement, for if it has no necessary connection therewith, although it confers an advantage upon the owner and renders his ownership of the land more valuable, it is not an easement at all, but a mere contractual right personal to and only enforceable between the two contracting parties.[13]

Whether the necessary *nexus* exists depends greatly upon the nature of the dominant tenement and the nature of the right alleged. If, for example, the dominant tenement is a residential house and if there is annexed to it by express grant a right to use an adjoining garden for purposes of relaxation and pleasure, this is a clear case where the right is sufficiently connected with the normal enjoyment of the house to rank as an easement.[14] The fact that the right enhances the value of the dominant tenement is a relevant, but not a decisive, consideration.[15] The principle is perhaps best illustrated by *Hill v Tupper*,[16] where the facts were as follows:

> A canal company leased land adjoining the canal to Hill and gave him the "sole and exclusive right" to let out pleasure boats on the canal. Tupper, an innkeeper, disregarded this privilege by himself letting out boats for fishing purposes. Hill thereupon brought an action in his own name against Tupper, his alleged cause of action being a disturbance of his easement to put boats on the canal.

It was held that the right conferred upon Hill by the contract with the company was not an easement but a mere licence personal to himself, since it was acquired in order to exploit an independent business enterprise, not to accommodate the riparian land as such.[17] The right was not beneficial to the land as land; rather, the land was required for the exploitation of the right.

The principle applies equally to profits appurtenant, and may be illustrated by the remark of COKE that the right of cutting turfs for fuel cannot be

---

8 *Bailey v Stephens* (1862) 12 CBNS 91 at 115, per BYLES J.
9 Ibid.
10 *Todrick v Western National Omnibus Co* [1934] Ch 561; *Birmingham, Dudley and District Banking Co v Ross* (1888) 38 Ch D 295 at 314; *Pugh v Savage* [1970] 2 QB 373, [1970] 2 All ER 353 (intervening land between dominant and servient tenements).
11 *Bailey v Stephens* (1862) 12 CBNS 91.
12 *Todrick v Western National Omnibus Co* [1934] Ch 561 at 580, per ROMER LJ.
13 Cited with approval in *Re Ellenborough Park*, supra at 170, at 677.
14 *Re Ellenborough Park*, supra; M & B p. 621.
15 Ibid., at 173, at 679.
16 (1863) 2 H & C 121; M & B p. 619.
17 *Re Ellenborough Park*, supra, at 175, at 681. Contrast the Pennsylvanian case of *Miller v Lutheran Conference and Camp Association* 331 Pa 241 (1938); Aigler, Smith and Tefft, *Cases on Property* (1960), vol. ii. p. 212, where a somewhat similar right was treated as an easement *in gross* capable of assignment.

claimed as appurtenant to land, but only to a house, because the use of fuel has no connection with land as such. In the leading case of *Bailey v Stephens*:[18]

> A, who was seised in fee of a piece of land called Bloody Field, claimed the right to enter an adjoining close for the purpose of cutting down, carrying away and converting to his own use the trees and wood growing thereon. It was held that, as the wood was not employed for the beneficial enjoyment of Bloody Field, it was not connected therewith and so was not a valid profit.

(c) Dominant and servient owners must be different persons

If one person owns two adjoining properties which, physically speaking, are separate properties, any rights that he may have been in the habit of exercising over one or other of them, as, for example, by passing over one to reach the highway, are not easements (though they are often called "quasi-easements"), because they derive from his ownership not of the quasi-dominant land, but of the quasi-servient land itself.[19] FRY LJ in one case said:

> Of course, strictly speaking, the owner of two tenements can have no easement over one of them in respect of the other. When the owner of Whiteacre and Blackacre passes over the former to Blackacre, he is not exercising a right of way in respect of Blackacre; he is merely making use of his own land to get from one part to another.[20]

Thus, if X is the owner of two separate tenements and he lets one of them to a tenant, the latter cannot acquire by prescription an easement over the other, for his occupation is in the eyes of the law the occupation of his landlord, a person who cannot acquire an easement against himself.[1] As will be seen later, however, the right to light is exceptional in this respect.[2]

If the principle were otherwise and if rights exercised by a man over one of two properties both owned by him were to be treated as easements, they would necessarily remain vested in him after a sale of the quasi-servient tenement. They would also pass without express mention to a purchaser of the quasi-dominant tenement. But these consequences do not ensue. To quote an ancient instance:

> J.S. had a close, and a wood adjoining to it, and time out of mind a way had been used over the close to the wood to carry and re-carry. He granted the close to one, and the wood to another. The question was, if the grantee of the wood shall have the way? And it was adjudged he should not, for the grantor by the grant of the close had excluded himself of the way, because it was not saved to him; and he himself could not use it, no more can his grantee.[3]

The moral to be drawn from this rule is that, when a large estate is split up and sold to different purchasers, any quasi-easements which were enjoyed by

---

18 (1862) 12 CBNS 91.
19 *Bolton v Bolton* (1879) 11 Ch D 968.
20 *Roe v Siddons* (1888) 22 QBD 224 at 236; and see *Metropolitan Rly Co v Fowler* [1892] 1 QB 165; *Derry v Sanders* [1919] 1 KB 223.
 1 *Warburton v Parke* (1857) 2 H & N 64; *Gayford v Moffatt* (1868) 4 Ch App 133. A tenant may, however, grant an easement, for a period not exceeding that of his lease, in favour of another tenant of the same landlord; p. 546, post.
 2 Pp. 556, 562, post.
 3 *Dell v Babthorpe* (1593) Cro Eliz 300.

the former owner should be expressly reserved to the purchaser of the quasi-dominant tenement.[4]

(d) A right over land cannot amount to an easement unless it is capable of forming the subject-matter of a grant

As we shall see, apart from statute, every easement must originate in a grant, either express, implied or presumed. It follows from this that no right can have the status of an easement unless it is the possible subject-matter of a grant.[5] This characteristic has three aspects.

(i) Certainty of description The nature and extent of the right must be capable of reasonably exact description. If it is so vague or so indeterminate as to defy precise definition, it cannot rank as an easement. This requirement, which is common to all forms of grant, is especially important in the present context, for a right over the land of another is allowed to ripen into an easement if it has been enjoyed for a long time without any interruption by the servient owner, but this necessarily implies that there should be something definite capable of interruption.[6]

A right to the flow of light to a particular window satisfies the test of certainty, for not only does the light pass over the servient tenement along a defined channel, but it can be interrupted by an obstruction placed across its line of approach.[7] Again, it has been held that a *jus spatiandi*, i.e. a right to wander at large over the servient tenement, is sufficiently determinate to constitute an easement if it is limited by express grant to a particular house or group of houses and is exercisable over an adjoining garden.[8] So also the right to a flow of air can subsist as an easement if it is claimed in respect of some definite channel, such as a ventilator in a building,[9] but not if what is claimed is that the current of air flowing indiscriminately over the entire servient tenement shall not be interrupted.[10]

In *Harris v De Pinna*,[11] where a claim to the general flow of air was made, BOWEN LJ said:

> It would be just like amenity of prospect,[12] a subject-matter which is incapable of definition. So the passage of undefined air gives rise to no rights and can give rise to no rights for the best of all reasons, the reason of common sense, because you cannot acquire any rights against others by a user which they cannot interrupt.

4 *Wheeldon v Burrows* (1879) 12 Ch D 31 at 49; pp. 540–3, post.
5 *Potter v North* (1669) 1 Wms Saund 347, *arguendo*; *Goodman v Saltash Corpn* (1882) 7 App Cas 633 at 654; *Dalton v Angus* (1881) 6 App Cas 740 at 795; *Chastey v Ackland* (1895) 11 TLR 460; *Harris v De Pinna* (1886) 33 Ch D 238 at 262; *Bryant v Lefever* (1879) 4 CPD 172 at 178, per BRAMWELL LJ.
6 *Webb v Bird* (1862) 13 CBNS 841 at 843.
7 *Harris v De Pinna* (1886) 33 Ch D 238 at 259.
8 *Re Ellenborough Park* [1956] Ch 131, [1955] 3 All ER 667; M & B p. 621.
9 *Cable v Bryant* [1908] 1 Ch 259; M & B p. 621.
10 *Webb v Bird*, supra; *Bryant v Lefever* (1879) 4 CPD 172; M & B p. 620.
11 (1886) 33 Ch D 238 at 262. This may, however, be enforceable under the doctrine of non-derogation from grant. See *Aldin v Latimer Clark, Muirhead & Co* [1894] 2 Ch 437; p 396, ante; *Lyme Valley Squash Club Ltd v Newcastle under Lyme Borough Council* [1985] 2 All ER 405 (easement of light); p. 537, n. 19, post.
12 *Bland v Moseley* (1587) cited in 9 Co Rep 58a. But a right to a prospect or view over neighbouring land may be framed as a restrictive covenant enforceable under the doctrine of *Tulk v Moxhay*; p. 614, post. See *Wakeham v Wood* (1981) 43 P & CR 40; *Gilbert v Spoor* [1983] Ch 27, [1982] 2 All ER 576; p. 638, n. 10, post.

(ii) Capable grantee A claimant to an easement must be a person capable of receiving a grant, that is, he must be a definite person or a definite body such as a corporation. Thus a claim put forward by a vague fluctuating body of persons, such as the inhabitants of a village, will not be sustainable as an easement.[13]

(iii) Capable grantor Again, the same principle demands that the servient owner should have been lawfully entitled to grant the right claimed to be an easement. Thus a claim[14] against a company incorporated by statute will fail upon proof that the grant was *ultra vires*.[15]

(2) EXAMPLES OF EASEMENTS

(a) List of easements not closed

Such, then, are the essential characteristics of easements, and it is important that they should be borne in mind, for otherwise certain judicial statements that new kinds of rights *in rem* cannot be created at will may be misunderstood. Thus Lord BROUGHAM said:[16]

> There are certain known incidents to property and its enjoyment, among others, certain burdens wherewith it may be affected, or rights which may be created and enjoyed over it by parties other than the owner. . . . But it must not therefore be supposed that incidents of a novel kind can be devised and attached to property at the fancy or caprice of any owner; . . . great detriment would arise and much confusion of rights, if parties were allowed to invent new modes of holding and enjoying real property, and to impress upon their land and tenements a peculiar character, which should follow them into all hands, however remote.

This means not that an easement of a kind never heard of before cannot be created, but that a new species of incorporeal hereditament or a new species of burden cannot be brought into being and given the status and legal effect of an easement. In other words, if a right exhibits the four characteristics described above, it is an easement that will run with the dominant and against the servient tenement, even though its object may be to fulfil a purpose for which it has not hitherto been used; but if it lacks one or more of those characteristics, it may, indeed, be enforceable between the parties who create it, but it cannot, like an easement, be enforceable by or against third parties.[17] One of the main purposes of law is to keep pace with the requirements of society and to adapt itself to new modes of life and new business methods, a fact that was present in the mind of Lord ST LEONARDS when he said:

> The category of servitudes and easements must alter and expand with the changes that take place in the circumstances of mankind.[18]

Thus in a case where an easement was claimed to place stores and casks upon land reclaimed from the sea, the Privy Council said:

> The law must adapt itself to the conditions of modern society and trade, and there

---

13 But a local customary right may be established; pp. 529, 575 et seq, post.
14 *Paine & Co Ltd v St. Neots Gas and Coke Co* [1939] 3 All ER 812.
15 *Mulliner v Midland Rly Co* (1879) 11 Ch D 611.
16 *Keppell v Bailey* (1834) 2 My & K 517 at 535. See also *Hill v Tupper* (1863) 2 H & C 121 at 127–8, per POLLOCK CB.
17 *Re Ellenborough Park* [1956] Ch 131 at 140–1, [1955] 2 All ER 38 at 42–3.
18 *Dyce v Hay* (1852) 1 Macq 305.

is nothing in the purposes for which the easement is claimed inconsistent in principle with a right of easement as such.[19]

(b) Examples

The following list of easements, which begins with the most important kinds and which, of course, is not exhaustive, will afford some idea of how great their variety is:

(i) **Way** Rights of way, whether for general or special purposes, and whether exercisable in all modes or limited to a carriage way, bridle way, foot way or a way for cattle.

(ii) **Light** A right that the light flowing over adjoining land to a window shall not be reasonably obstructed.[20]

(iii) **Water** Rights in connection with water, such as a right to the uninterrupted passage of water over adjoining land,[1] or a right to enter upon adjoining land to divert the course of a stream for irrigation purposes, or a right to pollute a river or to discharge water onto the land of another.[2]

(iv) **Support** A right to the support of buildings by adjoining land or buildings. Though a landowner has a natural right to have his *land* supported by adjoining land, yet a right to have *buildings* supported can be claimed only if it has actually been acquired as an easement.[3]

(v) **Fencing** A right to have a fence maintained by an adjoining owner.

This has been recognised by the Court of Appeal as "a right in the nature of an easement". As Lord DENNING said in *Crow v Wood*:[4]

> It is not an easement strictly so called because it involves the servient owner in the expenditure of money. It was described by Gale as a "spurious kind of easement".[5] But it has been treated in practice by the courts as being an easement . . .[6]
>
> It seems to me that it is now sufficiently established—or at any rate, if not established hitherto, we should now declare—that a right to have your neighbour keep up the fences is a right in the nature of an easement which is capable of being granted by law so as to run with the land and to be binding on successors. It is a right which lies in grant.[7]

19 *A-G of Southern Nigeria v John Holt & Co* [1915] AC 599 at 617; *Simpson v Godmanchester Corpn* [1896] 1 Ch 214 at 219; *Dowty Boulton Paul Ltd v Wolverhampton Corpn (No 2)* [1976] Ch 13 at 23, [1973] 2 All ER 491 at 495 ("A tendency in the past to freeze the categories of easements has been overtaken by the defrosting operation in *Re Ellenborough Park*", per RUSSELL LJ).
20 See generally *Colls v Home and Colonial Stores Ltd* [1904] AC 179; M & B p. 692; pp. 554–6, post.
1 *Rance v Elvin* (1985) 50 P & CR 9; *Coopind (UK) Ltd v Walton Commercial Group Ltd* [1989] 1 EGLR 241 ("right to receive supply of water gas electricity and heat").
2 A landowner may have certain natural rights in respect of water; p. 165, ante; p. 529, post.
3 The leading case is *Dalton v Angus & Co* (1881) 6 App Cas 740. See also London Buildings Acts (Amendment) Act 1939, s. 50.
4 [1971] 1 QB 77 at 84, [1970] 3 All ER 425 at 428; M & B p. 631. See (1971) 87 LQR 13 (P. V. Baker).
5 Gale, *Law of Easements* (11th edn), p. 432. See too *Lawrence v Jenkins* (1873) LR 8 QB 274 at 279, per ARCHIBALD J. Cf *Hilton v Ankesson* (1872) 27 LT 519.
6 See *Jones v Price* [1965] 2 QB 618 at 633, [1965] 2 All ER 625 at 630, per WILMER LJ; and at 639, at 634, per DIPLOCK LJ; *Egerton v Harding* [1975] QB 62, [1974] 3 All ER 689.
7 It may also be acquired (1) as an easement by prescription: *Lawrence v Jenkins* (1873) LR 8 QB 274: *Jones v Price* [1965] 2 QB 618, [1965] 2 All ER 625; (2) by custom: *Egerton v Harding*, supra.

(vi) Miscellaneous easements Such are the only easements commonly found in practice, but we may add examples of some variations and extensions of these interests:[8]

- (i) Right to hang clothes on a line passing over neighbouring soil.[9]
- (ii) Right to run telephone lines over neighbouring land.[10]
- (iii) Right to use a close for the purpose of mixing muck and preparing manure thereon for the use of an adjoining farm.[11]
- (iv) Right to fix a signboard to the walls of another's house.[12]
- (v) Right of a landowner to use a particular seat in a parish church.[13]
- (vi) Right to nail trees to a wall.[14]
- (vii) Right to lay stones upon adjoining land to prevent sand from being washed away by the sea.[15]
- (viii) Right to store casks and trade produce on a neighbour's land.[16]
- (ix) Right to use a lavatory situated on the servient tenement.[17]
- (x) Right to use a letter-box.[18]
- (xi) Right to use an airfield.[19]
- (xii) Right to park a car anywhere on the forecourt of a block of flats.[20]

(c) New easements

New easements may arise, but no right which fails to exhibit the four characteristics described above can exist as an easement. Whether or not a new right, complying with the accepted requirements of an easement, will be judicially recognised or not is very difficult to forecast.

There are, however, three situations in which such recognition is unlikely to be granted.

(i) Expenditure by servient owner First, where the owner of the servient tenement would be under a duty to spend money.[1] There is only one right in

---

8 For further examples, see *Gale on Easements* (15th edn), pp. 36–38.
9 *Drewell v Towler* (1832) 3 B & Ad 735.
10 *Lancashire and Cheshire Telephone Exchange Co v Manchester Overseers* (1884) 14 QBD 267.
11 *Pye v Mumford* (1848) 11 QB 666.
12 *Moody v Steggles* (1879) 12 Ch D 261; *William Hill (Southern) Ltd v Cabras* [1987] 1 EGLR 37.
13 *Mainwaring v Giles* (1822) 5 B & Ald 356; *Brumfitt v Roberts* (1870) LR 5 CP 224; *Re St. Mary's Banbury* [1986] Fam 24, [1986] 2 All ER 611; affd [1987] Fam 136, [1987] 1 All ER 247.
14 *Hawkins v Wallis* (1763) 2 Wils 173.
15 *Philpot v Bath* (1905) 21 TLR 634.
16 *A-G of Southern Nigeria v John Holt & Co (Liverpool) Ltd* [1915] AC 599; *Smith v Gates* (1952) 160 EG 512 (right to keep chicken coops on a common).
17 *Miller v Emcer Products Ltd* [1956] Ch 304, [1956] 1 All ER 237; M & B p. 629.
18 *Goldberg v Edwards* [1950] Ch 247; M & B p. 646.
19 *Dowty Boulton Paul Ltd v Wolverhampton Corpn (No 2)* [1976] Ch 13, [1973] 2 All ER 491.
20 *Newman v Jones* (22 March 1982, unreported); M & B p. 631; *London and Blenheim Estates Ltd v Ladbroke Retail Parks Ltd* [1992] 1 WLR 1278 at 1288; [1993] 1 All ER 307 at 317; *Handel v St. Stephen's Close Ltd* [1994] 05 EG 159.
1 *Regis Property Co Ltd v Redman* [1956] 2 QB 612, [1956] 2 All ER 335 (covenant to supply hot water and central heating, involving the performance of services, not an easement); *Rance v Elvin* (1983) 49 P & CR 65 (right to metered water supply paid for by servient owner held not to be an easement, even though dominant owner agreed to reimburse water charges); (1985) 50 P & CR 9 (CA held that the right was to the uninterrupted passage of water, and not to its supply; it was therefore an easement, and the servient owner was liable in quasi-contract to reimburse); [1985] CLJ 458 (A. J. Waite); *Coopind (UK) Ltd v Walton Commercial Group Ltd* [1989] 1 EGLR 241 (right to receive a supply of gas under service roads retained by lessors held to extend to right to lay new gas main).

this category, that of fencing, where the servient owner is under a duty to take positive steps to maintain the fence, including the expenditure of money. As we have seen, its exceptional nature is recognized by the Court of Appeal.[2] There may also be cases where the parties have expressly or impliedly agreed that the servient owner shall bear the burden; as where:

a local authority, which owned a high-rise block of flats, let them to tenants. Easements of access over the common parts of the building retained by the local authority (the servient owner) were implied in favour of the tenants. The local authority was held liable, as on an implied contract, to maintain those parts.[3]

(ii) Negativity Secondly, where the easements is negative, in the sense that it gives the owner of the dominant tenement a right to stop his neighbour doing something on his (the neighbour's) own land. This has long been recognized in the cases of the easements of light and support. But in *Phipps v Pears*,[4] where the premises had been exposed to damp and frost owing to the demolition of an adjacent house, the Court of Appeal held that there was no easement of protection against the weather. Lord DENNING said:[5]

A right to protection from the weather ... is entirely negative. Seeing that it is a negative easement, it must be looked at with caution. Because the law has been very chary of creating any new negative easements. ... If such an easement were to be permitted, it would unduly restrict your neighbour in his own enjoyment of his own land.

It is, however, possible for such rights to be framed as covenants which may be enforceable under the doctrine of *Tulk v Moxhay*.[6]

(iii) Exclusive or joint user Finally, it must be remembered that no right will be recognized as an easement which is in effect a claim to exclusive or joint

2 *Jones v Price* [1965] 2 QB 618; *Crow v Wood* [1971] 1 QB 77, [1970] 3 All ER 425; M & B p. 631.
3 *Liverpool City Council v Irwin* [1977] AC 239, [1976] 2 All ER 39; *King v South Northamptonshire District Council* [1992] 1 EGLR 53; [1992] Conv 347 (J. E. Martin); *Duke of Westminster v Guild* [1985] QB 688, [1984] 3 All ER 144 (tenant qua dominant owner of right of drainage held to be liable for repairs). See also *Stokes v Mixconcrete (Holdings) Ltd* (1978) 38 P & CR 488; *Holden v White* [1982] QB 679, [1982] 2 All ER 328 (servient owner owed no duty of care at common law to milkman injured by disintegrating manhole cover on private footpath giving access to terraced house, nor under Occupiers' Liability Act 1957. See now Occupiers' Liability Act 1984, in effect reversing the decision).
4 [1965] 1 QB 76, [1964] 2 All ER 35; M & B p. 629 criticised in (1964) 80 LQR 318 (R.E.M.); (1964) 27 MLR 614; (1965) 28 MLR 264 (H. W. Wilkinson), and supported (1964) 27 MLR 768 (J. F. Garner). Followed in *Marchant v Capital and Counties Property Co Ltd* (1982) 263 EG 661; (1983) 267 EG 843 (award under London Building Acts (Amendment) Act 1939). Under Public Health Act 1961, s. 29 (5), a local authority may serve a notice on anyone demolishing a building, requiring him to weatherproof any surface of adjacent buildings exposed by the demolition. In *Regional Properties Ltd v City of London Real Property Co Ltd* (1979) 257 EG 64 at 70, it was suggested that a right to protection against the weather by a *roof* might be an easement, thereby limiting *Phipps v Pears* to an easement of protection against the weather in the vertical plane. For liability for weatherproofing of party walls where there is a right of support, see *Bradburn v Lindsay* [1983] 2 All ER 408 (servient owner held liable in negligence for infestation of dominant tenement by dry rot, and in nuisance for loss of support to, and consequent exposure of, the side of the dominant tenant to rot and decay); [1984] Conv 54 (P. Jackson); [1987] Conv 47 (A. J. Waite). See also *Brace v South East Regional Housing Association Ltd* (1984) 270 EG 1286 (interference with right of support); *Tollemache & Cobbold Breweries Ltd v Reynolds* (1983) 268 EG 52 (fire damage); (1984) 269 EG 200 (C. M. Brand and D. W. Williams).
5 At 83, at 37.
6 P. 614, post.

user of the servient tenement. Thus in *Copeland v Greenhalf*,[7] it was held that a wheelwright had no easement to store and repair an unlimited number of vehicles on a strip of his neighbour's land. In the words of UPJOHN J:[8]

> I think that the right claimed goes wholly outside any normal idea of an easement, that is, the right of the owner or the occupier of a dominant tenement over a servient tenement. This claim really amounts to a claim to a joint user of the land by the defendant. Practically, the defendant is claiming the whole beneficial user of the strip of land on the south-east side of the track there; he can leave as many or as few lorries there as he likes for as long as he likes; he may enter on it by himself, his servants and agents to do repair work thereon. In my judgment, that is not a claim which can be established as an easement. It is virtually a claim to possession of the servient tenement, if necessary to the exclusion of the owner; or, at any rate, to a joint user, and no authority has been cited to me which could justify the conclusion that a right of this wide and undefined nature can be the proper subject-matter of an easement. It seems to me that to succeed, this claim must amount to a successful claim of possession by reason of long adverse possession.[9]

The question is really one of degree. As ROMER LJ said in *Miller v Emcer Products Ltd*,[10] where a right to use a lavatory situated on the servient tenement was held to be an easement:

> It is true that during the times when the dominant owner exercised the right the owner of the servient tenement would be excluded, but this in greater or less degree is a common feature of many easements (for example, rights of way) and does not amount to such an ouster of the servient owner's rights as was held by UPJOHN J to be incompatible with a legal easement in *Copeland v Greenhalf*.

The problem has recently arisen in connection with the right to park cars. In *Newman v Jones*[11] it was held that a right for a landowner to park a car anywhere in a defined area nearby was capable of existing as an easement; and the mere risk of there being not enough space for all to park simultaneously was not a reason for denying that any rights at all exist. Nor may it be an objection that charges are made by the servient owner, whether for the parking itself or for the general upkeep of the park. As Judge Paul Baker QC said in *London & Blenheim Estates Ltd v Ladbroke Retail Parks Ltd*:[12]

> The essential question is one of degree. If the right granted in relation to the area over which it is to be exercisable is such that it would leave the servient owner without any reasonable use of his land, whether for parking or anything else, it could not be an easement though it might be some larger or different grant.[13]

---

7 [1952] Ch 488, [1952] 1 All ER 809; M & B p. 626; *Ward v Kirkland* [1967] Ch 194, [1966] 1 All ER 609; cf *Wright v Macadam* [1949] 2 KB 744, [1949] 2 All ER 565; M & B p. 643 (right to store domestic coal in shed held to be an easement). This case was not cited in *Copeland v Greenhalf*. See also *Grigsby v Melville* [1972] 1 WLR 1355, [1973] 1 All ER 385; affd [1974] 1 WLR 80, [1973] 3 All ER 455; M & B p. 628 (claim to exclusive right of storage in cellar under drawing-room floor); *Thomas W Ward v Alexander Bruce (Grays) Ltd* [1959] 2 Lloyds Rep 472 (right to ground ships on silt in defendant's dock in course of plaintiff's business as shipbrokers held not to be an easement: "it involves an almost complete exclusion of the alleged servient owner" per HARMAN LJ at 477).
8 [1952] Ch 488 at 498, [1952] 1 All ER 809 at 812.
9 Chapter 26, p. 887, post. See (1968) Conv (NS) 270 (M. J. Goodman).
10 [1956] Ch 304 at 316, [1956] 1 All ER 237 at 240; p. 629; (1956) 72 LQR 172 (R.E.M.).
11 (22 March 1982, unreported); M & B p. 631; *Handel v St Stephens Close Ltd* [1994] 05 EG 159.
12 [1992] 1 WLR 1278 at 1288; [1993] 1 All ER 307 at 317; affd [1994] 1 WLR 31, [1993] 4 All ER 157.
13 For example, a lease, for which exclusive possession would be necessary; p. 364, ante.

B. EASEMENTS DISTINGUISHED FROM OTHER RIGHTS

Having seen something of the nature of easements, we will conclude this part of the subject by adverting to other rights of a somewhat similar nature from which they must be distinguished.[14]

(1) LICENCES

A licence is created in favour of B if, without being given any legal estate or interest, he is permitted by A to enter A's land for an agreed purpose. It is an authority that justifies what would otherwise be a trespass.

We shall discuss in chapter 18 the categories of licence and the different rules which are applicable to each of them.[15] Here it is sufficient to mention that an easement is narrower than a licence.

Thus an easement must be created by a deed of grant, whether actual, implied or presumed; whereas a licence may be created informally; further, an easement is not a personal right, but is of necessity annexed to a dominant tenement; and, once established, there can never be any question of its unilateral revocation by the servient owner.

The distinction was illustrated in *IDC Group Ltd v Clark*,[16] where an agreement, which was made by deed and described as a licence, provided for a fire escape route through a party wall between two adjoining properties; the parties to the deed were expressed to include their respective successors and assigns. The Court of Appeal held that the deed, being professionally drawn and described as a licence, created personal and not property rights, and was therefore a licence.

(2) LOCAL CUSTOMARY RIGHTS

Indefinite and fluctuating classes of persons, such as the inhabitants of a village, may be entitled to exercise over another's land rights which, if the matter rested between the servient owner and a definite dominant owner, would properly be termed easements. Illustrations from the cases are:

(a) where the inhabitants of a village pass across another's land on their way to church,[17] or
(b) where the fishing inhabitants dry their nets on certain property.[18]

Such rights are not easements, for an easement lies in grant, and a vague and fluctuating body of persons such as fishing inhabitants is not a legal person, and is therefore incapable of taking under a grant. If, therefore, they are to be established, some other title than grant must be shown, and this, as we shall see later, is what the law calls *custom*.[19]

(3) NATURAL RIGHTS

This is an expression often used to describe a right that is one of the ordinary and inseparable incidents of ownership, though its exercise requires an

14 For the difference between an easement and a profit, see pp. 562–4, post.
15 P. 585, post. For the difference between a licence and a lease, see pp. 362–70, ante.
16 [1992] 1 EGLR 187; p. 365, ante.
17 *Brocklebank v Thompson* [1903] 2 Ch 344.
18 *Mercer v Denne* [1904] 2 Ch 538.
19 Pp. 575–80, post.

adjacent owner to forbear from doing something on his own land that otherwise he would be free to do. The epithet "natural" serves to distinguish such rights from easements, which do not automatically accompany ownership but must be acquired by grant, either actual, implied or presumed.[20] Thus *ex jure naturae*, an owner has a right to so much support from his neighbour's land as will support his own land, unincumbered by buildings, at its natural level;[1] and a riparian owner is entitled to demand that other riparian owners shall not divert the natural course of the stream.[2] Such natural rights differ from easements in at least two respects—their existence does not depend upon some form of grant, and they cannot be extinguished by unity of seisin.[3]

(4) PUBLIC RIGHTS

Public rights are rights which anyone may exercise as a member of the public. Main examples are the right to pass along a public highway,[4] or to fish in the sea or to navigate over the foreshore.[5] These rights exist by virtue of the general law and do not require a dominant tenement.

C. LEGAL AND EQUITABLE EASEMENTS

An easement is capable of subsisting as a legal interest. It will be legal if (i) it complies with the Law of Property Act 1925 and is held for "an interest equivalent to an estate in fee simple absolute in possession or a term of years absolute",[6] and (ii) is created either by statute, deed or prescription.[7] If it does not satisfy both requirements, then it may be an equitable easement: e.g. if it is for the life of the grantee (even if it is created by deed), or if it is created for value informally,[8] as for instance by a contract to grant an easement.

This distinction is important in relation to the enforceability of the easement against third parties. In accordance with general principle, a legal easement is enforceable against all the world, an equitable easement against all the world except the bona fide purchaser for value of the legal estate without notice. An equitable easement is registrable as a Class D (iii) land charge under the Land Charges Act 1972,[9] and if it is not so registered, is void against a purchaser of the legal estate for money or money's worth.

It is therefore important to define an equitable easement. The Law of Property Act 1925 refers to:

> Any easement, liberty, or privilege over or affecting land and being merely an equitable interest (in this Act referred to as an "equitable easement").[10]

20 *Backhouse v Bonomi* (1861) 9 HL Cas 503.
1 Ibid; *Midland Bank plc v Bardgrove Property Services Ltd* [1991] 2 EGLR 283.
2 Pp. 163 et seq, ante.
3 For extinguishment of easements, see p. 558, post.
4 The law is consolidated in Highways Act 1980 as amended by Local Government (Miscellaneous Provisions) Act 1982, s. 20, Sch. 5, and Highways (Amendment) Act 1986.
5 P. 167, ante.
6 S. 1 (2) (*a*).
7 Pp. 531 et seq, post.
8 P. 532, post.
9 Ss. 2 (5), 4 (6).
10 S. 2 (5) (iii); the definition in LCA 1972 s. 2 (5) substitutes the word "right" for "liberty".

In spite of some earlier views to the contrary,[11] it is now settled that this definition is to be construed narrowly.[12] It may be limited to such proprietary interests in land as would before 1926 have been recognized as capable of being conveyed or created at law, but which since 1925 only take effect as equitable interests, as for instance, an easement granted for the life of the grantee.[13] It thus excludes such informal equitable rights as an equitable right of re-entry,[14] or any rights arising in equity by reason of an estoppel licence or the doctrine of mutual benefit and burden.[15] The effect of this in unregistered conveyancing is that there are certain informal third party rights which do not require registration; they cannot therefore be void for want of registration as land charges, and their enforceability against third parties depends solely on the doctrine of notice.[16]

D. ACQUISITION OF EASEMENTS

The basic principle is that every easement must have had its origin in grant.[17]

All the methods of acquisition except one are traceable to a grant which has been or which might have been made, and the one exception, namely statute, is not of frequent occurrence. It may facilitate exposition to set the subject out in tabular form.

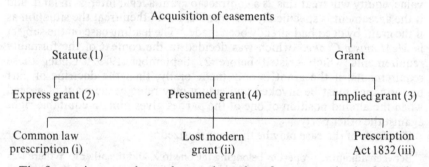

The figures in parentheses denote the order of treatment in the following pages.

(1) ACQUISITION BY STATUTE

An example of statutory creation is an Inclosure Act. This is a statute that discharges land from rights of common to which it has hitherto been subject

---

11 See (1935) 15 Bell Yard 18 (G. Cross).
12 *Shiloh Spinners Ltd v Harding* [1973] AC 691, [1973] 1 All ER 90; M & B p. 36; p. 96, ante.
13 *E R Ives Investment Ltd v High* [1967] 2 QB 379 at 395, [1967] 1 All ER 504 at 508, per Lord DENNING; M & B p. 592; (1937) 53 LQR 259 (C. V. Davidge); (1948) 12 Conv (NS) 202 (J. F. Garner).
14 *Shiloh Spinners Ltd v Harding*, supra.
15 *E R Ives Investment Ltd v High*, supra, followed in *Poster v Slough Estates Ltd* [1969] 1 Ch 495, [1968] 3 All ER 257 (right of entry to remove fixtures at end of lease). See also *Lewisham Borough Council v Maloney* [1948] 1 KB 50, [1947] 2 All ER 36 (requisitioning authority's right to possession); (1969) 33 Conv (NS) 135 (P. Jackson).
16 See p. 96, ante.
17 *Angus & Co v Dalton* (1877) 3 QBD 85 at 102, per COCKBURN CJ.

and distributes it in plots among a number of absolute owners.[18] As part of the scheme of distribution easements of ways over adjoining plots are frequently reserved to the respective owners.[19] Modern examples of easements created by statute are to be found in local Acts of Parliament. Statutory rights similar to easements are also created by general Acts and are sometimes called statutory easements.[20]

(2) ACQUISITION BY EXPRESS GRANT

(a) Creation

(i) At common law An easement is an incorporeal hereditament and therefore, in accordance with the historic rule of the common law, it must be granted by deed, for:

the deed of incorporeate inheritances doth equal the livery of corporeate.[1]

(ii) In equity At common law, a grant of an easement, made orally or by writing not executed as a deed, creates only a licence.[2] But this may create an equitable easement where equity acts on the principle that what ought to be done must be regarded as actually done—a view which has given us the doctrine of *Walsh v Lonsdale*.[3] If the grant satisfies the formalities required for a contract for the sale or other disposition of an interest in land and is for value, equity will treat this as a contract to grant a legal interest in land, and if the agreement is specifically enforceable, it will then treat the situation as if the grant by deed had already been made.[4] The leading case on the subject is *McManus v Cooke*,[5] which was decided in the context of the formality requirements which existed before 27 September 1989.[6] Under those requirements, if the grant is only made orally, then the doctrine of part performance must be invoked and equity may remedy the want of a deed when the altered position of one of the parties gives him an equitable right against the other party.[7]

The facts of the case may be thus summarized:

Between adjoining properties belonging the one to X and the other to Y there was a high party wall of unnecessary width. It was orally agreed between X and Y that in order to give more space to each owner the wall should be pulled down by X and replaced by one which was lower and thinner, the work to be at their joint expense. It was also agreed orally that each of the parties should erect a lean-to skylight, and that both of these should rest on the new wall and incline upwards and outwards to the respective houses. X duly carried out his part of the work, but Y, instead of building a lean-to skylight on his side, built one so shaped that part of it showed

18 P. 573, post. See also Access to Neighbouring Land Act 1992, p. 396, ante.
19 For example, *Adeane v Mortlock* (1839) 5 Bing NC 236.
20 Jackson, chapter 12; (1956) 20 Conv (NS) 208 (J. F. Garner). The Conveyancing Standing Committee of the Law Commission considered a scheme for the implication by statute of standard-form easements into transfers of plots of land on new residential developments: Second Annual Report 1986–87 (Law Com No. 169), para 2.12.
1 Co Litt 9a, b; LPA 1925, s. 52 (1).
2 *Wood v Leadbitter* (1845) 13 M & W 838; M & B p. 535; *Fentiman v Smith* (1803) 4 East 107, pp. 586–7, post.
3 Pp. 376 et seq, ante.
4 *May v Belleville* [1905] 2 Ch 605.
5 (1887) 35 Ch D 681; M & B p. 83; pp. 117 et seq, ante.
6 P. 111, ante.
7 *Dann v Spurrier* (1803) 7 Ves 231 at 235; *Duke of Devonshire v Eglin* (1851) 14 Beav 530.

above the wall and in consequence obstructed the access of light to X's skylight. X sued for an injunction to restrain Y from maintaining an erection which infringed the agreement.

KAY J decided in favour of the plaintiff X on the ground that the effect of the oral agreement was to give each party an easement of light over the other's land, and that despite the want of a deed this easement was enforceable by the party who had gone to expense in carrying out his side of the agreement, thereby giving to Y all the advantages to which he was entitled under the contract.

(iii) Identification of dominant tenement If the dominant tenement has not been clearly described by the parties, the court will identify it by construing the instrument that created the easement, and for this purpose extrinsic evidence of all material facts and surrounding circumstances in which the instrument was executed is admissible.[8]

(b) Express reservation

If the owner of two adjoining properties desired, upon the sale of one of them, to retain an easement over that one, he could do so at common law either by way of *exception* from the grant or by way of *reservation*.[9] The only things that could be excepted were specific parts of the land, such as timber and minerals; and the word "reservation" was only appropriate where services, such as the payment of rent, were to be rendered for the tenure of land.[10] It was formerly necessary, therefore, either that the conveyance of the land should be executed by the *grantee* (whereupon the easement would arise by way of re-grant from him),[11] or that the conveyance should be made to him to the *use* that the vendor should enjoy the easement and subject thereto *to the use* of the purchaser in fee simple.[12]

With the repeal of the Statute of Uses the latter method is now impossible, and the former is unnecessary, for section 65 (1) the Law of Property Act 1925 provides that:

a reservation of a legal estate shall operate at law without any execution of the conveyance by the grantee of the legal estate out of which the reservation is made, or any regrant by him.

Such a reservation, however, still operates by way of re-grant. Thus, where an easement is reserved by a vendor of land, the terms of the reservation in cases of doubt are to be construed against the purchaser and not against the vendor.[13]

It is also provided by section 65 (2) that:

a conveyance of a legal estate expressed to be made subject to another legal estate

8 *Johnstone v Holdway* [1963] 1 QB 601, [1963] 1 All ER 432; M & B p. 683; *Shannon Ltd v Venner Ltd* [1965] Ch 682, [1965] 1 All ER 590; *Land Reclamation Co Ltd v Basildon District Council* [1979] 1 WLR 106 at 110, [1978] 2 All ER 1162 at 1165. Cf the judgment of UPJOHN J in *Newton Abbot Co-operative Society Ltd v Williamson and Treadgold Ltd* [1952] Ch 286, [1952] 1 All ER 279; M & B p. 864; p. 628, post.
9 *Durham and Sunderland Rly Co v Walker* (1842) 2 QB 940.
10 Leake, *Uses and Profits of Land*, p. 265.
11 *Wickham v Hawker* (1840) 7 M & W 63.
12 Conveyancing Act 1881, s. 62 (1).
13 *Johnstone v Holdway* [1963] 1 QB 601, [1963] 1 All ER 432; *St Edmundsbury and Ipswich Diocesan Board of Finance v Clarke (No 2)* [1975] 1 WLR 468, [1975] 1 All ER 772; M & B p. 634.

not in existence immediately before the date of the conveyance shall operate as a reservation unless a contrary intention appears.[14]

(c) Section 62 of the Law of Property Act 1925

(i) The section It is of the greatest practical importance to observe that, owing to section 62 of the Law of Property Act 1925, a grant of land may have a far-reaching, and sometimes an unexpected, effect upon the creation of easements. This section provides that unless a contrary intention is expressed in the conveyance:

> A conveyance of land shall be deemed to include and shall by virtue of this Act operate to convey, with the land, all buildings, erections, fixtures, commons, hedges, ditches, fences, ways, waters, watercourses, liberties, privileges, easements, rights, and advantages whatsoever, appertaining or reputed to appertain to the land or any part thereof, or, at the time of conveyance, demised, occupied, or enjoyed with, or reputed or known as part or parcel of or appurtenant to the land or any part thereof.[15]

The object of this section is to ensure that a grantee, without inserting numerous descriptive terms, usually called *general words*, in the conveyance, shall automatically acquire the benefit not only of easements and other rights appurtenant to the land in the strict sense, but also of quasi-easements and other privileges which have hitherto been enjoyed in respect of the land. It is obvious that easements already appurtenant to the land conveyed continue in favour of the grantee, but the statutory words are so sweeping and comprehensive that the conveyance, unless expressly limited in its operation, may have an effect far wider than the grantor intends. The effect indeed may be catastrophic in the sense that privileges which have hitherto been enjoyed by the permission of the grantor in respect of the land conveyed, a permission which could at any moment have been revoked, may acquire the status of permanent easements as a result of the conveyance.

Suppose, for example, that A, the owner of two adjoining closes, Blackacre and Whiteacre, leases Blackacre to X, and as a friendly act allows X to use a path over Whiteacre as a short cut to the main road and also to store his coal in a shed on Whiteacre. Later A either sells or conveys the fee simple of Blackacre to X or renews X's lease of Blackacre.

In this case at the time of the conveyance there is a "privilege . . . enjoyed with the land" conveyed. The statute therefore comes into operation, and the effect of the conveyance, unless it expresses a contrary intention, is that a right of way over Whiteacre and a right to use the shed become appurtenant to Blackacre.[16]

Again, if B, the owner of a mansion and park, allows Y, the tenant of the lodge at one of the gates, to use the main drive as a means of access to the neighbouring village, and later sells and conveys the fee simple of the lodge to him, a similar result follows. Y acquires an easement of way over the drive.[17]

14 *Wiles v Banks* (1983) 50 P & CR 80 (conveyance "subject to a right of way").
15 S. 62 (1), re-enacting Conveyancing Act 1881, s. 6 (1).
16 *International Tea Stores Co v Hobbs* [1903] 2 Ch 165; *Wright v Macadam* [1949] 2 KB 744, [1949] 2 All ER 565; M & B p. 643.
17 *International Tea Stores Co v Hobbs*, supra, at 172; *Goldberg v Edwards* [1950] Ch 247; M & B p. 646.

The permissive nature of the privilege enjoyed prior to the conveyance is quite irrelevant in these cases. The question is not whether the grantee had an enforceable right to enjoy the privilege, but, whether it was in fact enjoyed by him qua occupant of the land prior to the conveyance.[18]

(ii) Limits of the section In spite of the wide wording of section 62, there are strict limits to its operation:

(a) Conveyance

The section does not operate unless there has been a "conveyance" of land, a word which statutorily includes:

> a mortgage, charge, lease, assent, vesting declaration, vesting instrument, disclaimer, release and every other assurance of property or of an interest therein by any instrument, except a will.[19]

This definition does not comprise an oral lease.[20] Nor does it comprise a contract for a lease or for the sale of land, since an assurance is "something which operates as a transfer of property"[1] and a mere contract has no such operation, notwithstanding that under the doctrine of *Walsh v Lonsdale*[2] it is for many purposes as effective as a lease.[3]

The right must not only be enjoyed prior to the conveyance, it must also be enjoyed with the land[4] at the time of the conveyance. As MEGARRY V-C said in *Penn v Wilkins*:[5]

> Section 62 was apt for conveying existing rights, but it did not resurrect mere memories of past rights.

And likewise the section is not concerned with future rights.[6]

A right which is enjoyed with only part of the land conveyed may nevertheless benefit the whole. Thus in *Graham v Philcox*[7] the purchaser of the freehold of a converted coach house was also the tenant of a first floor flat in it which had the benefit of a right of way. The Court of Appeal held that, under section 62, the benefit of the right of way enured to the whole of the building. In effect the section operated to enlarge the extent of an existing easement.

---

18 *Wright v Macadam*, supra at 750–1; *Phipps v Pears* [1965] 1 QB 76, [1964] 2 All ER 35; M & B p. 648. For a critical attitude to this effect of s. 62 (1), see *Wright v Macadam*, supra, at 755, at 573, per TUCKER LJ; *Green v Ashco Horticulturist Ltd* [1966] 1 WLR 889 at 896, [1966] 2 All ER 232 at 239, per CROSS J.
19 LPA 1925, s. 205 (1) (ii).
20 *Rye v Rye* [1962] AC 496, [1962] 1 All ER 146; M & B p. 474.
1 *Re Ray* [1896] 1 Ch 468 at 476.
2 P. 376, ante.
3 *Borman v Griffith* [1930] 1 Ch 493; M & B p. 478.
4 Enjoyment is not synonymous with user: *Re Yateley Common, Hampshire* [1977] 1 WLR 840 at 850, [1977] 1 All ER 505 at 515. See *MRA Engineering Ltd v Trimster Co Ltd* (1987) 56 P & CR 1 (rights of access granted to an existing tenant held not to pass under s. 62 on sale of freehold after surrender of the lease); *Re St Clement's, Leigh-on-Sea* [1988] 1 WLR 720.
5 (1974) 236 EG 203.
6 *Nickerson v Barraclough* [1981] Ch 426, [1981] 2 All ER 369.
7 [1984] QB 747, [1984] 2 All ER 643; M & B p. 689, following *Wright v Macadam* [1949] 2 KB 744, [1949] 2 All ER 565; [1985] Conv 60 (P. Todd); [1985] CLJ 15 (S. Tromans).

(b)   Nature of right

No right will be conveyed by virtue of the Act, however, unless it is a right known to the law.[8]

As Lord DENNING MR said in *Phipps v Pears*:[9]

> A fine view, or an expanse open to the winds, may be an "advantage" to a house, but it would not pass under section 62. Whereas a right to use a coal shed or to go along a passage would pass under section 62. The reason being that these last are rights known to the law, whereas the others are not. A right to protection from the weather is not a right known to the law. It does not therefore pass under section 62.

And it must not be a right which the grantor at the time of the grant had no power to grant;[10] nor one which is merely a matter of personal contract;[11] nor one the enjoyment of which could only be expected to be temporary.[12] Further, the section only operates to pass rights which are part and parcel of the land conveyed. A conveyance of land is deemed to include all "buildings, erections and fixtures", and it has been held that a greenhouse resting on its own weight on concrete dollies was neither a fixture nor an erection within the section.[13]

(c)   Diversity of ownership or occupation

The section will not operate unless, as in the examples given above, there has been some diversity of ownership or occupation of the two closes prior to the conveyance.[14] If, for instance, the grantor, the common owner and occupier of Blackacre and Whiteacre, has been in the habit of passing over Blackacre in order to reach the highway, his conveyance of Whiteacre does not entitle the grantee to invoke the statute and to establish a right of way over Blackacre. What the grantor was accustomed to do was attributable to his general rights as the occupying owner of both closes, not to a privilege deriving from his occupation of Whiteacre, as distinct from his occupation of Blackacre.[15] In approving what has come to be called the rule in *Long v Gowlett*, Lord WILBERFORCE said in *Sovmots Investments Ltd v Secretary of State for the Environment*:[16]

> When land is under one ownership one cannot speak in any intelligible sense of rights, or privileges, or easements being exercised over one part for the benefit of another. Whatever the owner does, he does as owner and until a separation occurs,

8   *International Tea Stores Co v Hobbs*, supra at 172; *Goldberg v Edwards*, supra; *Ward v Kirkland* [1967] Ch 194, [1966] 1 All ER 609; *Green v Ashco Horticulturist Ltd*, supra; *Phipps v Pears*, supra; *Crow v Wood* [1971] 1 QB 77, [1970] 3 All ER 425; M & B, p. 631.
9   Supra at 84, at 38; M & B p. 648.
10   *Quicke v Chapman* [1903] 1 Ch 659.
11   *Regis Property Co Ltd v Redman* [1956] 2 QB 612, [1956] 2 All ER 335.
12   *Wright v Macadam* [1949] 2 KB 744 at 751, [1949] 2 All ER 565 at 571, per JENKINS LJ, citing COTTON LJ in *Birmingham and Dudley District Banking Co v Ross* (1888) 38 Ch D 295 at 307; *Green v Ashco Horticulturist Ltd*, supra at 897, at 239.
13   *H.E. Dibble Ltd v Moore* [1970] 2 QB 181, [1969] 3 All ER 465.
14   *Sovmots Investments Ltd v Secretary of State for the Environment* [1979] AC 144 at 169, 176, [1977] 2 All ER 385 at 391, 397; M & B p. 651, approving *Long v Gowlett* [1923] 2 Ch 177; M & B p. 537. See *Ward v Kirkland*, supra, at 227–231, at 617–20; *Wright v Macadam*, supra, at 748, at 569; *Squarey v Harris-Smith* (1981) 42 P & CR 118 at 129, per OLIVER LJ. For criticism of the rule, see Jackson, pp. 100–103; (1966) 30 Conv (NS) 342–348; [1978] Conv 449 (P. Smith); and in favour [1979] Conv 113 (C. Harpum).
15   *Long v Gowlett*, supra, at 200–1. The right to light, however, stands on a different footing: ibid., at 202–3, citing *Broomfield v Williams* [1897] 1 Ch 602.
16   [1979] AC 144 at 169, [1979] 2 All ER 385 at 391.

of ownership, or at least of occupation, the condition for the existence of rights, etc., does not exist.

In order to substantiate his claim, the grantee would have to bring himself within the doctrine of an implied grant under the rule in *Wheeldon v Burrows*.[17]

Enough has now been said to show that a grantor, who retains property adjoining that granted, or a landlord about to renew a lease, should be extremely vigilant to ensure that any advantages or privileges hitherto enjoyed in respect of the land are either revoked or expressly excepted from the conveyance, unless he wishes them to continue.[18]

If an intention is shown in the preliminary contract of sale that a certain privilege shall not pass to the purchaser, the vendor is entitled to insert a clause in the deed of conveyance restrictive of the operation of the statute.[19] Moreover, in such a case he is entitled to have the conveyance rectified if, owing to the common mistake of the parties, it does not include a restrictive clause of this nature.[20]

(3) ACQUISITION BY IMPLIED GRANT[1]

An owner, as we have seen, cannot have an easement over his own land.[2] Where, however, he has been accustomed to use one part in a particular manner, as for example by crossing a field to reach the highway, his practice is conveniently described as the exercise of a *quasi-easement*. If he later severs his ownership by granting part only of the land to another, such a quasi-easement is capable of ripening by implication into an easement properly so called in favour either of the land granted or the land retained.

The principle of this mode of creation is that although there has been no express mention of an easement in the grant of the land, yet it may very well be that the common intention of the parties cannot be carried out unless some particular easement is deemed to arise by implication. For the purposes of the doctrine, however, a lease and a devise are on the same footing as a grant.

The premises for the application of the doctrine are, first, that A, the owner of two separate tenements, has been in the habit of enjoying certain quasi-easements over one of them; and secondly, that the common ownership of A has been severed. Thus, if A sells the quasi-servient tenement, certain easements may be implied in his favour over the part sold (*implied reservation*); if he sells the quasi-dominant tenement, certain easements may be implied against him and in favour of the purchaser (*implied grant*); while the question of implication may also arise when he disposes of both the tenements to different persons. We will now consider these three cases separately.

17 P. 538, post.
18 See Standard Conditions of Sale, Condition 3.4.2.; Wilkinson, *Standard Conditions of Sale of Land* (5th edn), pp. 29–33.
19 *Squarey v Harris-Smith* (1981) 42 P & CR 118 (where a standard condition that the purchaser should not acquire any rights which would restrict the free use of the vendor's other land for building was held to negative the operation of s. 62); cf. *Lyme Valley Squash Club Ltd v Newcastle under Lyme Borough Council* [1985] 2 All ER 405, in which *Squarey v Harris-Smith* was not cited, and the opposite conclusion reached; [1985] Conv 243. See also *William Hill (Southern) Ltd v Cabras Ltd* [1987] 1 EGLR 37; *Pretoria Warehousing Co Ltd v Shelton* [1993] EGCS 120.
20 *Clark v Barnes* [1929] 2 Ch 368.
1 See generally Farrand, *Contract and Conveyance* (2nd edn), pp. 337–92.
2 P. 522, ante.

(a) Implied reservation. Common owner sells quasi-servient tenement

The law is disinclined to imply easements in favour of a grantor. The reason is not far to seek. In the case of a grant of land the law is guided by two principles: the words of a deed must be construed as far as possible in favour of the grantee;[3] and the grantor cannot derogate from his own absolute grant by claiming rights over the thing granted.[4] If the grantor intends to retain a right over the land, it is his duty to reserve it expressly in the grant.[5] As a general rule there will be no implication in his favour.[6]

(i) Easements of necessity There are, no doubt, exceptions to this rule, the most obvious of which is the way of necessity. This arises where land which is entirely surrounded by other land is segregated by the common owner, and either retained by him or conveyed to another person. In such a case a way is implied either in favour of the grantor or against him:

> Where a man, having a close surrounded with his own land, grants the close to another in fee, for life or for years, the grantee shall have a way to the close over the grantor's land as incident to the grant; for without it he cannot derive any benefit from the grant.[7]

This rule applies where the landlocked close is devised,[8] and also where part of the surrounding land is owned by third persons.[9]

The same doctrine also applies where the grantor disposes of the surrounding land and keeps that which is enclosed.[10]

The extent of the implied right is strictly limited and depends upon the mode of enjoyment of the surrounded land prevailing at the time of the grant. The way may be used for any purpose which is essential to maintain that mode of enjoyment: it may not be used for other purposes. Thus:

> Where at the time of the grant the surrounded close was used only for agricultural purposes, it was held that the grantor was not entitled to carry over it timber and other materials.[11]

(ii) Easements of common intention Easements will also be implied in favour of the grantor as may be necessary to give effect to the common intention of grantor and grantee as for example where mutual easements of support are implied on the conveyance of one of two adjacent buildings supported by each other.[12] There may be other cases where such easements will be implied

---

3 *Neill v Duke of Devonshire* [1882] 8 App Cas 135 at 149, per Lord SELBORNE.
4 *Suffield v Brown* (1864) 4 De GJ & Sm 185, per Lord WESTBURY. See generally (1964) 80 LQR 244 (D. W. Elliott). The rule may be varied by contract, see, e.g., the draft forms of standard contracts of sales of land published by the Lord Chancellor under the Law of Property Act 1925, s. 46, which provide that a vendor who sells a house reserving adjoining land shall retain the right to build on such land. This right may, of course, operate to the prejudice of the house sold.
5 *Wheeldon v Burrows* (1879) 12 Ch D 31 at 49, per THESIGER LJ.
6 *Wheeldon v Burrows*, supra; *Aldridge v Wright* [1929] 2 KB 117; *Liddiard v Waldron* [1934] 1 KB 435; *Re Webb's Lease* [1951] Ch 808, [1951] 2 All ER 131; M & B p. 656.
7 *Promfret v Ricroft* (1669) 1 Wms Saund 321; *Union Lighterage Co v London Graving Dock Co* [1902] 2 Ch 557 at 573; *Pinnington v Galland* (1853) 9 Exch 1.
8 *Pearson v Spencer* (1861) 1 B & S 571.
9 *Barry v Hasseldine* [1952] Ch 835, [1952] 2 All ER 317; M & B p. 641.
10 *Pomfret v Ricroft*, supra; *London Corpn v Riggs* (1880) 13 Ch D 798; M & B p. 654.
11 *London Corpn v Riggs*, supra; *Serff v Acton Local Board* (1886) 31 Ch D 679.
12 *Richards v Rose* (1853) 9 Exch 218; *Shubrook v Tufnell* (1882) 46 LT 886.

in favour of a grantor without express reservation,[13] but the scales are heavily weighted against him. The necessary inference from the circumstances must be that he was intended to retain the precise easement that he claims.[14]

(b) Implied grant. Common owner sells quasi-dominant tenement

The law is much more inclined to imply easements in favour of the grantee than in favour of the grantor.

(i) Easements of necessity As we have seen, easements of necessity may be impliedly reserved in favour of a grantor over the quasi-servient tenement which he has granted. Consistently with the principle that a grantor may not derogate from his grant, the law more readily implies easements in favour of the grantee of the quasi-dominant tenement; *a fortiori* an easement of necessity will be implied in his favour.[15]

In *Nickerson v Barraclough*,[16] the Court of Appeal rejected an argument that, if the implied grant of a way of necessity has been negated by an express contrary provision, such a grant may nevertheless be implied under a rule of public policy that "no transaction should, without good reason, be treated as effectual to deprive land of a suitable means of access".[17] BRIGHTMAN LJ said:[18]

> The doctrine of way of necessity is not founded upon public policy at all but upon an implication from the circumstances ... There would seem to be no particular reason to father the doctrine ... upon public policy when implication is such an obvious and convenient candidate for paternity.

The Court of Appeal held that a way of necessity could only exist in association with a grant of land, and depended on the intention of the parties and the implication from the circumstances that, unless some way was implied, the land would be inaccessible. Public policy could not help the court to ascertain that intention;[19] it could only require the court to frustrate that intention where a contract was against public policy.

(ii) Easements of common intention Similarly the law more readily implies easements of common intention in favour of the grantee. As Lord PARKER OF WADDINGTON said:[20]

> The law will readily imply the grant or reservation of easements as may be necessary to give effect to the common intention of the parties to a grant of real property, with

---

13 *Re Webb's Lease* [1951] Ch 808 at 816–7, 823, [1951] 2 All ER 131 at 136–7, 141; M & B p. 656.
14 Ibid., at 828, at 144.
15 See *Liverpool City Council v Irwin* [1977] AC 239, [1976] 2 All ER 39; p. 527, ante; cf. *Manjang v Drammeh* (1990) 61 P & CR 194 (PC held no easement of necessity where available access by water across the River Gambia "albeit perhaps less convenient than access across *terra firma*"); *MRA Engineering Ltd v Trimster Co Ltd* (1987) 56 P & CR 1 (no easement of necessity because access on foot was "merely difficult and inconvenient"; land was not inaccessible or useless without right of way claimed).
16 [1981] Ch 426, [1981] 2 All ER 369 reversing MEGARRY V-C [1980] Ch 325, [1979] 3 All ER 312; (1982) 98 LQR 11 (P. Jackson). For a comparative study of legal solutions on access to landlocked land, see (1982) 10 Syd LR 39 (A. J. Bradbrook).
17 [1980] Ch 325 at 334, [1979] 3 All ER 312 at 323, per MEGARRY V-C.
18 [1981] Ch 426 at 440, [1981] 2 All ER 369 at 379.
19 EVELEIGH LJ at 383 thought that in a rare case public policy might help.
20 *Pwllbach Colliery Co Ltd v Woodman* [1915] AC 634 at 646; cf. *Stafford v Lee* (1992) 65 P & CR 172.

reference to the manner or purposes in and for which the land granted . . . is to be used. But it is essential for this purpose that the parties should intend that the subject of the grant . . . should be used in some definite and particular manner. It is not enough that the subject of the grant should be intended to be used in a manner which may or may not involve this definite and particular use.

In *Wong v Beaumont Property Trust Ltd*:[1]

three cellars in Exeter were let by B's predecessor in title to W's predecessor in title for the purpose of being used as a Chinese restaurant. By certain statutory regulations no premises could be used for this purpose unless they were provided with a ventilation system. In the circumstances, it was impossible to install this without affixing a duct to the outside walls of B's superjacent building.

The Court of Appeal granted a declaration that W was entitled to an easement of necessity,[2] and was entitled to construct and maintain the duct.

(iii) Easements within the Rule in *Wheeldon v Burrows*[3] The rule has been laid down in an obiter dictum by THESIGER LJ in *Wheeldon v Burrows*, which has been accepted as a correct statement of the law, that:

on the grant by the owner of a tenement of part of that tenement as it is then used and enjoyed, there will pass to the grantee all those continuous and apparent easements (by which, of course, I mean quasi-easements), or, in other words, all those easements which are necessary to the reasonable enjoyment of the property granted,[4] and which have been and are at the time of the grant used by the owner of the entirety for the benefit of the part granted.

This rule is also a rule of intention, based on the proposition that a man may not derogate from his grant. As Lord WILBERFORCE said:[5]

He cannot grant or agree to grant land and at the same time deny to the grantee what is at the time of the grant obviously necessary for its reasonable enjoyment.

Thus, for instance, it has been law since 1663 that if a man grants a house in which there are windows, he cannot build on his own adjoining land so as to obstruct the light.[6] It also follows that the rule cannot apply in the case of a compulsory purchase of land; that would mean substituting for the intention of a reasonable voluntary grantor the unilateral, opposed, intention of the acquirer.[7]

It will be noticed that, unlike section 62 of the Law of Property Act 1925, the rule in *Wheeldon v Burrows* is limited to continuous and apparent

---

1 [1965] 1 QB 173, [1964] 2 All ER 119; M & B p. 640; *Stafford v Lee* (1992) 65 P & CR 172.
2 The court classified this as an easement of necessity, but this must be *per incuriam*. "An easement is surely not an 'easement of necessity' merely because it is necessary to give effect to the intention" (1964) 80 LQR 322 (R.E.M.). But the two headings may overlap: see *Nickerson v Barraclough* [1980] Ch 325 at 332, [1979] 3 All ER 312 at 320.
3 *Wheeldon v Burrows* (1879) 12 Ch D 31 at 49; M & B p. 638. The case itself is a decision on implied reservation.
4 At 58 THESIGER LJ appears to treat these as two alternative requirements, and not, as here, synonymous. See *Ward v Kirkland* [1967] Ch 194 at 224, [1966] 1 All ER 609 at 615, per UNGOED-THOMAS J; M & B p. 639; *Squarey v Harris-Smith* (1981) 42 P & CR 118 at 124, per OLIVER LJ (where it was held that a right of way was necessary to the reasonable enjoyment of land "having regard to the purpose for which, in the contemplation of both parties, it was sold", but any implied right was excluded by a condition of sale incorporated into the contract); (1967) 83 LQR 240 (A. W. B. Simpson).
5 *Sovmots Investments Ltd v Secretary of State for the Environment* [1979] AC 144 at 168, [1977] 2 All ER 385 at 391; (1977) 41 Conv NS 415 (C. Harpum).
6 *Palmer v Fletcher* (1663) 1 Lev 122; *Phillips v Low* [1892] 1 Ch 47.
7 *Sovmots Investments Ltd v Secretary of State for the Environment*, supra.

easements. Strictly speaking a continuous easement is one, such as the right to light, the constant enjoyment of which does not, as in the case of a right of way, require the active intervention of the dominant owner. The word "continuous", however, is not in this context to be taken in its strict sense but rather in the sence of permanence. The two words "continuous" and "apparent" must be read together and understood as pointing to an easement which is accompanied by some obvious and permanent mark on the land itself, or at least by some mark which will be disclosed by a careful inspection of the premises.[8] Instances are:

(i) watercourses consisting of some actual construction such as pipes;[9]
(ii) a made road;[10]
(iii) light flowing through windows;[11]
(iv) drains which can be discovered with ordinary care.[12]

A right of way is not necessarily such a quasi-easement as will pass under the rule in *Wheeldon v Burrows*. To do so it must be apparent. There is no difficulty where there is a definite made road over the quasi-servient tenement to and for the apparent use of the quasi-dominant tenement. Such will clearly pass upon a severance of the common tenement.[13] But the existence of a formed road is not essential, and if there are other indicia which show that the road was being used at the time of the grant for the benefit of the quasi-dominant tenement and that it is necessary for the reasonable enjoyment of that tenement,[14] it will pass to a purchaser of the latter.[15] Thus:

A man built four cottages on his own land and left a strip between the rear of the cottages and the boundary of his land in order to afford a back means of access to the main highway. It was held that the quasi-easement of way was sufficiently continuous and apparent to pass under the present doctrine, for at the time of the grant the strip, though not formed into a made road, was worn and marked with rough tracks, so that no one seeing it could doubt that it was used as a way to the cottages.[16]

This doctrine of *Wheeldon v Burrows* has been shorn of much of its importance by section 62 of the Law of Property Act 1925,[17] but it still remains available in those cases where section 62 is inapplicable, either because there has been no diversity of occupation prior to a conveyance,[18]

---

8 *Pyer v Carter* (1857) 1 H & N 916 at 922, adopting *Gale on Easements*; *Ward v Kirkland* [1967] Ch 194, [1966] 1 All ER 609 (right to enter neighbour's land to repair and maintain a wall held to be not continuous and apparent; it was, however, held to be an easement created under LPA 1925, s. 62; p. 534, ante).
9 *Watts v Kelson* (1870) 6 Ch App 166; *Schwann v Cotton* [1916] 2 Ch 120; affd [1916] 2 Ch 459.
10 *Brown v Alabaster* (1887) 37 Ch D 490.
11 *Allen v Taylor* (1880) 16 Ch D 355.
12 *Pyer v Carter*, supra.
13 *Brown v Alabaster*, supra; *Davies v Sear* (1869) LR 7 Eq 427.
14 "Necessary" must not be confused with "necessity" (see "way of necessity", p. 538, ante). A way of necessity is one without which the property cannot be used at all, but "necessary" in the present connection indicates that the way conduces to the reasonable enjoyment of the property.
15 *Hansford v Jago* [1921] 1 Ch 322; *Borman v Griffith* [1930] 1 Ch 493 at 499. This paragraph was cited with approval in *Ward v Kirkland* [1965] Ch 194 at 225, [1966] 1 All ER 609 at 616.
16 *Hansford v Jago*, supra.
17 Pp. 534–7, ante.
18 P. 536, ante.

or because there has been no "conveyance" as defined by the Act.[19] Thus in *Borman v Griffith*:[20]

> X, who owned a large park containing two houses, The Gardens and The Hall, agreed in writing to lease the former to the plaintiff for seven years. A drive ran from the public road to The Hall, passing en route close to The Gardens. There was no separate drive for The Gardens, but at the time of the agreement X was constructing, and he later completed, an unmetalled way which ran from the back door of the house to the public road. The agreement reserved no right of way to the plaintiff, but he constantly used The Hall drive in preference to the unmetalled way. Later, the defendant took a lease from X of The Hall and the rest of the park, and began to obstruct the plaintiff in his use of the drive. In the ensuing action the plaintiff claimed to be entitled to a right of way over the drive.

The question, therefore, was whether the plaintiff had acquired the quasi-easement which the common owner of the whole land had exercised over the drive when passing from The Gardens to the public road. There was clearly no easement of necessity, since the unmetalled way provided a means of approach to the outside world. It was equally clear that section 62 was inapplicable to a contract for a lease. Nevertheless it was held that an easement of way had arisen by implication in favour of the plaintiff according to the doctrine of *Wheeldon v Burrows*. Thus, under that doctrine a grantee acquires only those easements to which he has an implied contractual right; but under section 62 of the Law of Property Act 1925, the conveyance may vest in him an easement to which he has no contractual right whatsoever.[1]

(c)   Contemporaneous sales to different persons

Where, instead of a sale of part of the land and a retention by the common owner of the other part, there have been simultaneous sales effected of separate but *contemporaneous* conveyances to different persons, all those continuous and apparent quasi-easements which were in use at the time of the sales pass by implication with the respective parts.[2] In other words, when the sales are by the same vendor and take place at one and the same time, the rights of the parties are exactly the same as if the common owner had sold the dominant part and kept the rest of the land.

Thus in *Schwann v Cotton*:[3]

> where a testator devised Blackacre to X and Whiteacre to Y, it was held that a right to the free passage of water which flowed through an underground pipe running across Blackacre to Whiteacre passed by implication to the devisee of Whiteacre.

If the sales are not simultaneous, the later purchaser is in the same position as his vendor. So if the vendor first sells the quasi-servient tenement, he will not, in the absence of an express reservation, be entitled to easements over the part sold, except a way of necessity where one exists, nor will a subsequent purchaser from him be in any better position;[4] but if the vendor first sells the

---

19 P. 535, ante. S. 62, however, is wider, in that the right need not be "continuous and apparent", nor "necessary to the reasonable enjoyment of the property granted".

20 [1930] 1 Ch 493; M & B p. 478; *Horn v Hiscock* (1972) 223 EG 1437.

1 (1952) 15 MLR pp. 265–6 (A. D. Hargreaves).

2 *Allen v Taylor* (1880) 16 Ch D 355; *Swansborough v Coventry* (1832) 9 Bing 305; *Barnes v Loach* (1879) 4 QBD 494; *Schwann v Cotton* [1916] 2 Ch 120, affd 459; *Hansford v Jago* [1921] 1 Ch 322.

3 Supra.

4 *Murchie v Black* (1865) 19 CBNS 190.

quasi-dominant tenement, the purchaser thereof can enforce quasi-easements against a subsequent purchaser of the quasi-servient tenement to the same extent as he could have done against the vendor.

(4) ACQUISITION BY PRESUMED GRANT OR PRESCRIPTION

Proof of the existence of an easement may be, and usually is, based upon a mere presumption that at some time in the past it has been granted by deed. There are three possible methods by which a claimant may avail himself of this presumption, for he may plead prescription:

  (i) at common law; or
 (ii) under the doctrine of lost modern grant; or
(iii) under the Prescription Act 1832.

Each method is based upon identical reasoning. The established principle no doubt is that an easement must be created by deed of grant, since incorporeal hereditaments lie in grant.[5] On the other hand, it is obviously undesirable that a man should be deprived of an easement long and continuously enjoyed merely because its formal creation by deed is incapable of proof. Therefore, in accordance with the maxim—*omnia praesumuntur rite et sollemniter esse acta*—the law is prepared to infer from this long enjoyment that all those acts were done that were necessary to create a valid title.[6] In this way, a claim, founded upon actual enjoyment without interruption by the servient owner, is referred to a lawful origin.

(a) Nature of user

Long enjoyment, however, is not in itself sufficient to raise the presumption of a grant. It must be of a particular nature, and this is so whether an easement is claimed by prescription at common law, or under the doctrine of lost modern grant or under the Prescription Act 1832. As we shall see, the user must be as of right and continuous, and only a grant in fee simple will be presumed.

All forms of prescription ultimately depend on the acquiescence of the servient owner. Why should long user confer a right protected by the courts? The answer is, that if the servient owner has allowed somebody to exercise an easement over his land for a considerable period and if he has omitted to prevent such exercise when he might very well have done so, it is only reasonable to conclude that the privilege has been rightfully enjoyed, for otherwise some attempt to interfere with it would long ago have been made by any owner who possessed even a modicum of common sense. FRY J said in *Dalton v Angus*:[7]

> In my opinion, the whole law of prescription and the whole law which governs the presumption or inference of a grant or covenant rest upon acquiescence. The courts and the judges have had recourse to various expedients for quieting the possession of persons in the exercise of rights which have not been resisted by the persons against whom they are exercised; but in all cases it appears to me that acquiescence

---

5 P. 523, ante.

6 *Philipps v Halliday* [1891] AC 228 at 231; *Foster v Warblington Urban Council* [1906] 1 KB 648 at 679.

7 (1881) 6 App Cas 740 at 773. Lord PENZANCE (at 803) was "in entire accord with" FRY J, and Lord BLACKBURN (at 823) described it as "a very able opinion". THESIGER LJ had used very similar language to that of FRY J in *Sturges v Bridgman* (1879) 11 Ch D 852 at 863.

and nothing else is the principle upon which these expedients rest. It becomes then of the highest importance to consider of what ingredients acquiescence consists. . . . I cannot imagine any case of acquiescence in which there is not shewn to be in the servient owner:

(1) a knowledge of the acts done;
(2) a power in him to stop the acts or to sue in respect of them; and
(3) an abstinence on his part from the exercise of such power.

(i) User as of right   This stress upon the element of acquiescence gives the clue to the kind of user required for a prescriptive title. In technical language, it must be *user as of right*,[8] or, to use the expression taken by Coke from Bracton,[9] *longus usus nec per vim, nec clam, nec precario*. The servient owner cannot be said to have acquiesced in an easement that has been enjoyed *vi, clam* or *precario* (by force, by secrecy or by permission).

Thus, if the dominant owner has used coercion, or if his user is contentious in the sense that the servient owner continually and unmistakably protests against it, there is clearly no acquiescence, and the user, being *vi*, will not avail the claimant.[10] Again, there is no acquiescence if the user has been *clam*, i.e. by stealth, for a man cannot assent to something of which he is ignorant, and the law allows no prescriptive right to be acquired where there has been any concealment or where the enjoyment has not been open.[11] It must always be found that the servient owner had actual or constructive knowledge of the enjoyment upon which the claimant relies.[12] Lastly, where the user has been *precario*, that is, where it is enjoyed by the permission of the servient owner and the permission is one which he may withdraw at any moment, it cannot be said that he has acquiesced in the existence of the easement as a matter of right. To ask permission is to acknowledge that no right exists. In this case an explanation of the user is forthcoming, and an irrevocable right to the perpetual enjoyment of the easement is not consistent with the explanation. What a plaintiff must show is that he claims the privilege not as a thing permitted to him from time to time by the servient owner, but as a thing that he has a right to do.[13]

For instance:

A woman relied upon sixty years' user of a cartway from her stables through the yard of an adjoining inn, but on it appearing that she had paid 15*s.* each year for

---

8 *Gardner v Hodgson's Kingston Brewery Co Ltd* [1903] AC 229; M & B p. 661; *Tickle v Brown* (1836) 4 Ad & El 369; *Healey v Hawkins* [1968] 1 WLR 1967, [1968] 3 All ER 836; M & B p. 664.
9 Co Litt 113*b*.
10 *Eaton v Swansea Waterworks Co* (1851) 17 QB 267; *Dalton v Angus* (1881) 6 App Cas 740 at 786; *Hollins v Verney* (1884) 13 QBD 304 at 307.
11 *Union Lighterage Co v London Graving Dock Co* [1902] 2 Ch 557; M & B p. 674, in which a dock-owner's claim to an easement of support by means of invisible rods sunk under the adjoining land was disallowed; *Dalton v Angus*, supra, at 827; *Wilson's Brewery v West Yorkshire Metropolitan County Council* (1977) 34 P & CR 224; *Liverpool Corpn v Coghill* [1918] 1 Ch 307 (injurious substances discharged into the public sewer at night for more than 20 years); *Scott-Whitehead v National Coal Board* (1987) 53 P & CR 263.
12 *Lloyds Bank Ltd v Dalton Ltd* [1942] Ch 466, [1942] 2 All ER 352; *Davies v Du Paver* [1953] 1 QB 184, [1952] 2 All ER 991; M & B p. 664; Cf *Dance v Triplow* [1992] 1 EGLR 190 (where "the plaintiffs failed to prove both their unwillingness to tolerate the interruption and some word or act making that clear to the defendant", per GLIDEWELL LJ); [1992] Conv 197 (J. Martin).
13 *Patel v W H Smith (Eziot) Ltd* [1987] 1 WLR 853.

this privilege, it was held by the House of Lords that the user, being *precario*, was not *as of right*.[14]

Thus a common method of preventing user from developing into a right is to exact a small periodical payment, and although in such a case there is in one sense a right to enjoy what has been paid for, yet it does not amount to a right to a permanent easement, but at the most to a right to damages for breach of contract.[15]

Finally, an easement cannot be acquired by conduct which is prohibited by a public statute. The user cannot be *as of wrong*.[16]

(ii) User must be continuous In addition to being *as of right*, user must also be continuous, though the continuity varies according to the nature of the right in question. For instance, a right of way from the nature of the case admits only of occasional enjoyment, and therefore if it is used as and when occasion demands, the requirement of continuity is satisfied.[17] But so far as a discontinuous easement, such as a right of way, is concerned, it is impossible to define what in every case constitutes sufficient continuity of user. Every case must depend upon the exact nature of the right claimed, and all that can be said is that the user must be such as to disclose to the servient owner the fact that a continuous right to enjoyment is being asserted and that therefore it ought to be resisted if it is not to ripen into a permanent right.[18] The user must assert a right, and not be merely dependent for its continuance upon the tolerance and neighbourly good nature of the servient owner.[19]

The right which is claimed on the ground of its continuous and uninterrupted exercise for a period of time need not have been exercised by the same person throughout the whole period: it is sufficient that it has been exercised by the successive owners of the estate in the dominant tenement to which the easement is appurtenant. Nor need it continue to be exercised in precisely the same manner; thus, where the dominant and servient owners agreed upon a variation of the route of a right of way for their own convenience, it was held that the user of the substituted route was substantially an exercise of the old right.[20]

14 *Gardner v Hodgson's Kingston Brewery Co Ltd* [1903] AC 229; M & B p. 661; *Diment v N H Foot Ltd* [1974] 1 WLR 1427, [1974] 2 All ER 785 (agent's knowledge); *Patel v W H Smith (Eziot) Ltd* [1987] 1 WLR 853, [1987] 2 All ER 569.
15 *Gardner v Hodgson's Kingston Brewery Co Ltd* [1903] AC 229, at 231. For the effect of mistake on user as of right, see *Bridle v Ruby* [1989] QB 169, [1988] 3 All ER 64, where CA held that a right of way was acquired under the doctrine of lost modern grant even though there was a mistaken view of both parties as to existing rights. See too *Thomas W Ward v Alexander Bruce (Grays) Ltd* [1959] 2 Lloyd's Rep 472, where HARMAN LJ also reviewed *Earl de la Warr v Miles* (1881) 17 Ch D 535 and *Chamber Collery Co v Hopwood* (1886) 32 Ch D 549; *Hamilton v Joyce* [1984] 3 NSWLR 279; [1986] Conv 356 (A. H. Hudson).
16 *Hanning v Top Deck Travel Group Ltd* [1993] Times, 6 May (LPA 1925, s. 163).
17 *Dare v Heathcote* (1856) 25 LJ Ex 245.
18 *Hollins v Verney* (1884) 13 QBD 304 at 315. In that case a right of way was claimed for the purpose of removing wood cut upon adjoining land, but the evidence showed that the right had been exercised only on three occasions at intervals of twelve years. The Court of Appeal held that there had not been sufficient continuity of enjoyment.
19 *Ironside, Crabb and Crabb v Cook, Cook and Barefoot* (1978) 41 P & CR 326 (user of verge, although sufficiently continuous, held not to be easement of way); *Mills v Silver* [1991] Ch 271, [1991] 1 All ER 449; M & B p. 662 (tolerance is "fundamentally inconsistent with the whole notion of acquisition of rights by prescription", per DILLON LJ, at 279, at 455).
20 *Davis v Whitby* [1974] Ch 186, [1974] 1 All ER 806; M & B p. 676; *Payne v Shedden* (1834) 1 Mood & R 382.

(iii) User in fee simple Since the basis of a prescriptive claim is immemorial user, an easement can be prescribed for only in respect of a fee simple estate. The rule is absolute that an easement claimed either by prescription at common law, or under the doctrine of a lost grant or under the Prescription Act 1832 must be claimed in favour of the fee simple estate in the dominant tenement.[1] An easement may be granted expressly for a lesser interest than a fee simple, but it cannot arise by virtue of a presumed grant. A tenant for years, no matter what the length of his lease may be, cannot for instance acquire a right of way over the adjoining land of his lessor.[2] He may, however, acquire by prescription an easement against the land of a stranger, though if he does so it enures for the benefit of the fee simple and does not cease with the cessation of his leasehold interest.[3] Furthermore, if the servient tenement is occupied by a tenant for years[4] or a tenant for life[5] at the beginning of the period of user, there can be no claim for an easement by prescription. But if the user begins against a fee simple owner, then the fact that the servient tenement is subsequently let or settled will not prevent this claim.[6]

Owing, however, to the wording of the Prescription Act 1832, the right to light is an exception to these rules.[7]

(b) Methods of prescription

We must now discuss the three methods of prescription.

(i) Prescription at common law[8] At common law a man may assert a prescriptive title to an easement founded upon long enjoyment. This, however, immediately raises the question—how long must his enjoyment have lasted before a grant in his favour will be presumed? The conclusion reached by the courts was that he must have enjoyed his right from *time immemorial*, that is to say, "from time whereof the memory of men runneth not to the contrary".[9]

It is obvious that this designation of what is generally termed *legal memory* is vague and unsatisfactory, and so the courts soon solved the difficulty in a rough and ready fashion by fixing some date at which the memory of man was supposed to begin. They did not choose a date at random, but took as their guide the statutes that from time to time restricted the period within which actions for the recovery of land had to be brought. At first those statutes, instead of fixing a given number of years, adopted the singular expedient of making the period of limitation run from particular dates or events as, for example, from the last return of King John into England. The

---

1 *Bright v Walker* (1834) 1 Cr M & R 211 at 221 (prescription at common law); *Wheaton v Maple & Co* [1893] 3 Ch 48; *Kilgour v Gaddes* [1904] 1 KB 457 at 466; M & B p. 665 (Prescription Act 1832); *Simmons v Dobson* [1991] 1 WLR 720, [1991] 4 All ER 25; M & B p. 666 (lost modern grant); criticised [1992] Conv 107 (P. Sparkes); [1992] CLJ 222 (C. Harpum), following (1958) 74 LQR 82 (V. T. H. Delany).
2 *Gayford v Moffatt* (1868) 4 Ch App 133; *Kilgour v Gaddes*, supra.
3 *Wheaton v Maple & Co*, supra, at 63; *Pugh v Savage* [1970] 2 QB 373, [1970] 2 All ER 353.
4 *Daniel v North* (1809) 11 East 372.
5 *Roberts v James* (1903) 89 LT 282.
6 *Palk v Shinner* (1852) 18 QB 568; *Pugh v Savage*, supra.
7 P. 554, post.
8 For the history of prescription, see Holdsworth, *History of English Law*, vol. vii. pp. 343 et seq.
9 Co Litt 170.

last statute which adopted this plan was the Statute of Westminster in 1275, which fixed the first year of the reign of Richard I, i.e. 1189, as the period of limitation for the recovery of land by a writ of right. These statutes were, of course, not concerned with prescription, but the courts, from time to time, adopted the various statutory dates as the time at which *legal memory* was to be taken as beginning. Thus after the Statute of Westminster, a prescriptive claim to an easement had to be based on an enjoyment carried back to 1189. Unfortunately, this policy of keeping in line with successive statutes of limitation was not maintained, for when the legislature set up a different principle in 1623[10] by enacting that actions for the recovery of land must be brought within a fixed number of years (20 years for the action of ejectment), the courts omitted to restrict *legal memory* to the same period.[11] So, absurd though it is, 1189 is at the present day still considered to be the time from which a claimant who is prescribing at common law must prove enjoyment of the easement. The result has been the adoption of what COCKBURN CJ described as a "somewhat startling rule",[12] for, in order to lighten the burden of a claimant, the courts are willing to presume that enjoyment has lasted from 1189 if proof is given of an actual enjoyment from as far back as living witnesses can speak.[13] A lifetime's enjoyment or even a shorter period raises the presumption that the enjoyment has stretched back to the reign of Richard I.[14]

This principle that the court will be satisfied with something like a lifetime's enjoyment affords some alleviation to claimants who, in strict theory of law, should stretch their enjoyment back to 1189, but in the majority of cases it is ineffectual because of another difficulty that confronts a claim based on prescription. If it can be shown that there was a time subsequent to 1189 when for some reason or other the easement could not possibly have existed, it is obvious that user enjoyed even for several centuries will be of no avail, since despite its length it must have started after the removal of the impossibility, and that was after 1189.[15] This almost precludes prescription at common law in the case of easements appurtenant to buildings, such as a right to light, for proof that the building did not exist in the time of Richard I must inevitably defeat the claim.[16]

(ii) Prescription under lost modern grant The "lost modern grant" represents the second stage in the history of acquisition by presumed grant. If easements which were fortified by long enjoyment, but for the grant of which no deed could be produced, were to receive the protection they deserved, it was soon seen that something must be done to turn the flank of the rule that a prescriptive claim at common law failed if it was shown that the easement must have come into existence at some time later than 1189. Stimulated by a

10 Following 32 Henry VIII, c. 2.
11 See the judgment of COCKBURN CJ in *Bryant v Foot* (1867) LR 2 QB 161 at 180–1; M & B p. 659.
12 *Bryant v Foot*, supra, at 181.
13 First Report of Real Property Commissioners (1829), p. 51.
14 *Bailey v Appelyard* (1838) 8 Ad & El 161 at 166. See *Darling v Clue* (1864) 4 F & F 329 at 334, per WILLES J: "At common law twenty years uninterrupted user as of right will be prima facie evidence of the right liable to be rebutted." See also *Bealey v Shaw* (1805) 6 East 208 at 215, per Lord ELLENBOROUGH.
15 *Hulbert v Dale* [1909] 2 Ch 570 at 577.
16 *Bury v Pope* (1588) Cro Eliz 118; *Norfolk v Arbuthnot* (1880) 5 CPD 390; First Report of Real Property Commissioners, p. 51.

determination to support ancient user at all costs, judicial astuteness in course of time evolved the very questionable theory[17] of the lost modern grant. After actual enjoyment of an easement has been shown for a reasonable length of time, the court presumes that an actual grant was made at the time when enjoyment began, but that the deed has been lost. The justification for this attitude is that if a claimant, despite his inability to prove enjoyment back to 1189 or to produce a deed of grant, has clearly exercised the easement for (say) the last 60 years, it is possible that at some time an actual grant was made to him or his predecessor, and that it was subsequently lost. Therefore, since long enjoyment must be upheld, the only course open to the court is to leave it to the jury to presume that the grant was in fact made.

The virtue of this theory is that it avoids the disaster which overtakes common law prescription when it is shown that the easement could not have existed (say) in 1750, for it does not matter what the state of affairs was then if you rely on a grant made some years later.

COCKBURN CJ said:[18]

> Juries were first told that from user, during living memory or even during twenty years, they might presume a lost grant or deed, [and here the courts did act by analogy to the Limitation Act 1623];[19] next they were recommended to make such presumption; and lastly, as the final consummation of judicial legislation, it was held that a jury should be told, not only that they might, but also that they were bound to presume the existence of such a lost grant, although neither judge nor jury, nor anyone else, had the shadow of a belief that any such instrument had ever really existed.

So the lost grant fiction rested and still rests upon the basis of long user, and though in theory the user is merely presumptive evidence, in practice and effect it is decisive. At the present day it is the last expedient of a claimant who finds himself unable to rely upon prescription at common law or upon the provisions of the Prescription Act 1832.[20]

The general rule is that 20 years' enjoyment is enough to raise the presumption,[1] and a period of 21 years, eight and a half months has been held to suffice.[2]

The same kind of user must be shown as in the case of prescription at common law, so that if it is *vi, clam* or *precario* the doctrine will not be invoked by the court.[3] Again, in accordance with general principles, it must be clear that there was some person or body of persons to whom the grant might have been made;[4] that there was a fee simple owner capable of

---

17 *Bryant v Foot* (1867) LR 2 QB 161 at 181, per COCKBURN CJ.
18 Ibid.; M & B p. 660.
19 *Bright v Walker* (1834) 1 Cr M & R 211 at 217, per PARKER B.
20 *Hulley v Silversprings Bleaching and Dyeing Co Ltd* [1922] 2 Ch 268; see e.g. *Hulbert v Dale* [1909] 2 Ch 570; M & B p. 668; *Healey v Hawkins* [1968] 1 WLR 1967, [1968] 3 All ER 836; *Ward (Helston) Ltd v Kerrier District Council* (1981) 42 P & CR 412 (easement); *Tehidy Minerals Ltd v Norman* [1971] 2 QB 528, [1971] 2 All ER 475; M & B p. 669 (profit à prendre); *Mills v Silver* [1991] Ch 271, [1991] 1 All ER 449; M & B p. 662; *Simmons v Dobson* [1991] 1 WLR 720, [1991] 4 All ER 25; M & B p. 666.
1 *Bryant v Foot* (1867) LR 2 QB 161 at 181, per COCKBURN CJ.
2 *Tehidy Minerals Ltd v Norman*, supra.
3 *Hanna v Pollock* [1900] 2 IR 664 at 671; *Partridge v Scott* (1838) 3 M & W 220; *Oakley v Boston* [1976] QB 270, [1975] 3 All ER 405.
4 *Tilbury v Silva* (1890) 45 Ch D 98 at 122.

executing the grant;[5] and that the right claimed was one which might have been the subject matter of a grant.[6]

In *Tehidy Minerals Ltd v Norman*,[7] the Court of Appeal, after reviewing the difference of judicial opinion in *Angus v Dalton*,[8] decided that the presumption of a lost modern grant cannot be rebutted by evidence that no such grant was in fact made. If for instance a claim to an easement of support in respect of a house were made, it might be a simple matter to prove that no grant had ever been executed, but it would not be a good reason for refusing to apply the doctrine. The doctrine is plainly a fiction; it is a means to an end, and the end is that some technical ground may be found for upholding a right that has been openly enjoyed.

A lost grant, however, will not be presumed if, during the period of user, there was no person capable of making the grant,[9] or if such a grant would have been in contravention of a statute.[10]

As BUCKLEY LJ said:[11]

> In our judgment *Angus v Dalton* decides that, where there has been upwards of 20 years' uninterrupted enjoyment of an easement, such enjoyment having the necessary qualities to fulfil the requirements of prescription, then unless, for some reason such as incapacity on the part of the person or persons who might at some time before the commencement of the 20-year period have made a grant, the existence of such a grant is impossible, the law will adopt a legal fiction that such a grant was made, in spite of any direct evidence that no such grant was in fact made.
>
> If this legal fiction is not to be displaced by direct evidence that no grant was made, it would be strange if it could be displaced by circumstantial evidence leading to the same conclusion, and in our judgment it must follow that circumstantial evidence tending to negative the existence of a grant (other than evidence establishing impossibility) should not be permitted to displace the fiction.

(iii) Prescription under the Prescription Act 1832 The two chief objects of the Prescription Act were to shorten the time of legal memory, and to make it impossible in actions brought under the Act for a claim to be defeated by proof that at some point of time later than 1189 the easement could not have existed. For these purposes the Act separates the right to light from all other easements, and deals with each class in a different manner.

(a) Easements other than light

1. *20 and 40 year periods* Section 2 enacts in effect that:

> where an easement has been actually enjoyed without interruption for twenty years, it shall not be defeated by proof that it commenced later than 1189, but it may be defeated in any other way possible at common law.

Thus a claimant who relies on the Act is untroubled by the doctrine of

5 *Daniel v North* (1809) 11 East 372; *Oakley v Boston*, supra.
6 *Bryant v Lefever* [1879] 4 CPD 172.
7 [1971] 2 QB 528, [1971] 2 All ER 475; M & B p. 669.
8 (1877) 3 QBD 85; on appeal (1878) 4 QBD 162; affd sub nom *Dalton v Angus & Co* (1881) 6 App Cas 740. The views are summarized in *Tehidy Minerals Ltd v Norman*, supra, at 547, at 487.
9 *Oakley v Boston* [1976] QB 270, [1975] 3 All ER 405 (incumbent of glebe land held to be capable grantor with consent of Ecclesiastical Commissioners).
10 *Neaverson v Peterborough RDC* [1902] 1 Ch 557.
11 *Tehidy Minerals Ltd v Norman*, supra, at 552, at 491.

legal memory, but he may still be met by the defences admissible in a case
where common law prescription is pleaded, as for instance that the right is
not the possible subject matter of a grant;[12] or that the user is not as of right,
i.e. it has been *vi, clam* or *precario*. The same section goes on to enact that an
easement which has been enjoyed without interruption for 40 years shall be
deemed absolute and indefeasible unless it appears that it was enjoyed by
some consent or agreement expressly given by deed or writing.

The advantage derived from enjoyment for the longer of these periods will
be explained below.[13]

2. *Next before some suit or action*   The two periods specified do not mean *any*
period of 20 or 40 years, but the period *next before some suit or action* wherein
the claim is brought into question.[14] Thus, the plaintiff must prove
uninterrupted enjoyment for the period which immediately precedes and
which terminates in an action.[15] For instance:

> suppose that a claimant proves that he and his predecessors in title have
> enjoyed a right of way over adjoining lands for more than a hundred years,
> except for a short period of 18 months 12 years ago, when he happened to
> be seised in fee simple of both tenements. Although this is a case where
> the court will still presume a lost modern grant,[16] a claim under the Act
> will fail, because during part of the *last* 20 years he has enjoyed the
> privilege not as the owner of an easement over the land of another, but as
> the owner of the servient tenement.[17]

3. *Without interruption*   It is essential that the enjoyment for the period of 20
or 40 years should be uninterrupted, but the Act provides that nothing is to
be deemed a statutory interruption unless it has been submitted to or
acquiesced in by the dominant owner for one year after he had notice of the
interruption and of the person responsible therefor.[18]

"Interruption" means some overt act, such as the obstruction of a right of
way, which shows that the easement is disputed.[19] Thus:

> if A has regularly passed over a track on B's land for 25 years and is then
> sued in trespass by B, his user of the way for the 20 years next preceding
> the action will entitle him to judgment. If, however, before his right has
> been contested, he submits to or acquiesces in an interruption that
> continues for one year, his previous enjoyment for 25 years becomes
> unavailing to him and he must start it afresh in order to satisfy the statute.

The crucial question, therefore, is—what amounts to submission or
acquiescence? This is a question of fact dependent upon the circumstances,
but the test that should be applied seems a little obscure.

---

12 *Staffordshire Canal Co v Birmingham Canal Co* (1866) LR 1 HL 254 at 278.
13 Pp. 551, post.
14 Prescription Act 1832, s. 4.
15 *Jones v Price* (1836) 3 Bing NC 52; *Parker v Mitchell* (1840) 11 Ad & El 788; *Hyman v Van
    den Bergh* [1907] 2 Ch 516; affd [1908] 1 Ch 167; M & B p. 674; *Newnham v Willison* (1987)
    56 P & CR 8 (interruption lasting more than one year before action brought); [1989] Conv
    357 (J. E. Martin).
16 Cf *Hulbert v Dale* [1909] 2 Ch 570; M & B p. 668.
17 *Bright v Walker* (1834) 1 Cr M & R 211 at 219.
18 S. 4.
19 *Carr v Foster* (1842) 3 QB 581, per PARKE B.

Suppose, in the case above, that B erects a fence across the track over which A has been passing for 25 years and that A, though he protests violently and threatens legal proceedings, lets thirteen months elapse without forcing the issue by a positive act of resistance.[20]

Does his protest suffice to negative his submission to or acquiescence in the interruption? It has been held that he need not go so far as to remove the obstruction or to take legal proceedings. It is said to be enough that he communicate to the servient owner, with sufficient force and clarity, his opposition to the interruption.[1] This vague test is scarcely satisfactory. Strictly speaking, no doubt, submission or acquiescence is a state of mind, but if a dissident state of mind, unfortified by some positive act of resistance, is to nullify an aggressive act of interruption, what certainty will remain in the title to the servient tenement? A single protest will remain effective after the year has elapsed and the statutory rule that interruption for a year shall defeat a claimant will be deprived of its intended force. The weight of judicial opinion, however, is disinclined to regard inactivity by the dominant owner for longer than a year after the interruption and after his protest as necessarily fatal to his claim.[2]

An interruption that occurs after the enjoyment of an easement has persisted for 19 years and a fraction of a year will not avail the servient owner, provided that the dominant owner sues to vindicate his right within a year afterwards.[3] The interruption is not yet an interruption within the meaning of the statute. Nevertheless, the acquisition of an easement requires enjoyment for the full period of 20 years immediately preceding an action, and therefore if the servient owner brings an action before the period has elapsed he will be entitled to a declaration that no easement exists, notwithstanding the deficiency of the interruption.[4]

4. *User as of right* The nature of the enjoyment necessary for the statutory periods must be similar to that required at common law, that is to say, it must be *as of right*.[5] This is so even where user has been shown for the full period of 40 years. The Act does not mean that easements enjoyed for 40 years otherwise than by written permission are in all circumstances indefeasible, but only if their enjoyment has been open and notorious. Lord MACNAGHTEN gave a warning against reading too much into the Act:

> The Act was passed, as its preamble declares, for the purpose of getting rid of the inconvenience and injustice arising from the meaning which the law of England attached to the expressions "time immemorial" and "time whereof the memory of man runneth not to the contrary". The law as it stood put an intolerable strain on the consciences of judges and jurymen. The Act was an Act "for shortening the time of prescription in certain cases". And really it did nothing more.[6]

This enables us to appreciate the significance of enjoyment for the longer

20 Cf *Davies v Du Paver* [1953] 1 QB 184, [1952] 2 All ER 991; M & B p. 664.
 1 *Bennison v Cartwright* (1864) 5 B & S 1; *Glover v Coleman* (1874) LR 10 CP 108.
 2 *Davies v Du Paver*, supra (where, however, that view was not shared by SINGLETON LJ); *Ward v Kirkland* [1967] Ch 194, [1966] 1 All ER 609.
 3 *Flight v Thomas* (1841) 8 Cl & Fin 231.
 4 *Reilly v Orange* [1955] 2 QB 112, [1955] 2 All ER 369; M & B p. 675.
 5 *Tickle v Brown* (1836) 4 Ad & El 369 at 382; *Bright v Walker* (1834) 1 Cr M & R 211; *Lyell v Hothfield* [1914] 3 KB 911.
 6 *Gardner v Hodgson's Kingston Brewery Co Ltd* [1903] AC 229 at 236; M & B p. 672.

period of 40 years. A hasty reading of section 2 might induce the belief that a right enjoyed for 40 years is indefeasible unless it can be proved that it was enjoyed by virtue of a written grant. But this is not so. In the case of enjoyment for the *shorter* period the claim cannot be met by the objection that enjoyment originated subsequently to 1189, but it can be met and defeated by any one of the common law defences, namely:

(a) that the right claimed lacks one or more of the characteristics essential to an easement;[7] or

(b) that the right in question, though enjoyed for 20 years, is prohibited by law, as for example, because a grant would have been *ultra vires* the grantor[8] or the grantee;[9] or

(c) that the user was not *as of right*,[10] i.e. that it was forcible, or secret, or enjoyed by permission *whether written or oral*.[11]

Next, a claim to an easement based upon 40 years' enjoyment can likewise be defeated upon the first two grounds, and also by proof that the user was forcible or secret or enjoyed by *written* permission. What is not sufficient to nullify a user lasting for this longer period is the oral permission of the servient owner. On general principles user that is precarious in any sense cannot originate an easement, but the statute, by enacting that user for 40 years is not to be considered precarious unless enjoyed by written permission, has, in the case of this longer period, given a special and restricted meaning to "precarious" if the claim is based on statutory prescription.[12] The difference, then, between the two periods is that an oral consent may defeat enjoyment for 20 years, but not enjoyment for 40 years.

The circumstances when this may do so have been elucidated by the courts. It is clear that permission of any sort, whether written or oral, is fatal to a claim based upon prescription at common law, however long the enjoyment may have lasted. The case of a claim based on the statutory periods, however, depends upon whether the permission is given during or at the beginning of the period of user. If permission is given from time to time *during* the 20 or 40 years, the user becomes *precario* and this is fatal to the claim.[13] On the other hand, if the permission is given at the *beginning* of the period of user and extends over the whole period[14] (i.e. a permission given more than 20 or 40 years ago and not since renewed), then, if it is written, it is fatal to a claim based upon either of the statutory periods, and, if oral, it is only fatal to a claim based upon the 20 year period.

As GOFF J said in *Healey v Hawkins*:[15]

---

7 *Mouncey v Ismay* (1865) 3 H & C 486.
8 *Rochdale Canal Co v Radcliffe* (1852) 18 QB 287 at 315; *Staffordshire Canal Co v Birmingham Canal Co* (1866) LR 1 HL 254 at 278.
9 *National Manure Co v Donald* (1859) 4 H & N 8.
10 Pp. 544–9, ante.
11 *Burrows v Lang* [1901] 2 Ch 502.
12 *Gardner v Hodgson's Kingston Brewery Co Ltd* [1901] 2 Ch 198 at 214; for the facts see p. 544, ante. The annual payment of 15s had been orally fixed some 60 years before the action. That was held, however, to be no evidence that an oral agreement granting the easement had in fact been made.
13 *Gardner v Hodgson's Kingston Brewery Co Ltd* [1903] AC 229; M & B pp. 661, 672.
14 Whether it does so depends on the circumstances: *Gaved v Martyn* (1865) 19 CBNS 732; *Healey v Hawkins* [1968] 1 WLR 1967, [1968] 3 All ER 836; M & B p. 664. See (1968) 32 Conv (NS) 40 (P. S. Langan).
15 At 1973, at 841.

In principle it seems to me that once permission has been given, the user must remain permissive and not be capable of ripening into a right save where the permission is oral and the user has continued for 40 . . . years, unless and until, having been given for a limited period only, it expires or, being general, it is revoked, or there is a change in circumstances from which revocation may fairly be implied. . . .

Of course, when the user has continued for 40 . . . years a prior parol consent affords no answer, because it is excluded by the express terms of section 2 of the Prescription Act, but, even so, permission given during the period will defeat the claimant because it negatives user as of right. That is, in my judgment, the explanation of the distinction drawn by the House of Lords in *Gardner v Hodgson's Kingston Brewery* between antecedent and current parol consents.

Oral permission given within the period will also negative user *as of right*, where the user continues on a common understanding that the user is and continues to be permissive.[16]

5. *Disabilities* Another difference between the two statutory periods is that certain disabilities of the servient owner, which obstruct a claim based on 20 years' user, do not affect a claimant who has enjoyed an easement for 40 years.

The Act provides that a right, even though enjoyed for the statutory periods, shall not ripen into a legal easement if the servient owner has been under certain disabilities. The time during which such person may have been an infant, idiot, *non compos mentis* or tenant for life, or during which an action has been pending and diligently prosecuted, is excluded by section 7 from the period of 20 years, though it begins to run again *at the point where it was interrupted* as soon as the disability is removed. Suppose, for instance, that

the claimant began to exercise the right in 1960, when the servient owner was the fee simple owner. In 1965 the latter became tenant for life under a settlement, but on his death in 1977 his successor came to the estate as tenant in fee simple. The claimant has exercised the right continuously from 1960 until 1994, when the action is brought. Five of these 34 years preceded the disability of a tenancy for life and 17 came afterwards. The 12 years during which the disability lasted must of course be excluded, but the question is whether the claimant may add the periods of 5 and 17 years together and allege enjoyment for the statutory period; or whether he will be defeated by his inability to show enjoyment for the last 20 years.

He will not be defeated, for the rule is that a claimant must show 20 years' enjoyment either:

(i) wholly before the disability if it still exists at the time of the action, or
(ii) partly before or partly after, if the disability be ended.[17]

Except for that of a tenancy for life, these disabilities do not affect a claim based on a 40 years' enjoyment;[18] this is to say, an uninterrupted user as of right for so long will confer an absolute title, no matter what the position of the servient owner may have been. Section 8, however, provides that where the servient tenement has been held during the whole or any part of the 40 years for a term of life or for a term of years exceeding three years, the period

16 *Jones v Price* (1992) 64 P & CR 404.
17 Cf. *Clayton v Corby* (1842) 2 QB 813.
18 S. 7.

during which such term lasted shall be excluded in the computation, provided that the claim is resisted by the reversioner within three years of the determination of the term.[19]

A curious feature of these rules is that the deduction of the time during which the servient tenement has been held by a tenant for a term exceeding three years only affects the computation of the longer period of 40 years. Thus an easement of way may be acquired by 20 years' user, though for the greater part of that time the servient tenement has been in the hands of a tenant.[20]

None of the disabilities applies to the easement of light.

(b) Easement of light

As the Act treats this particular easement quite differently from all others, it is necessary to cite the section dealing with it in full:[1]

> When the access and use of light to and for any dwelling house, workshop or other building[2] shall have been actually enjoyed therewith for the full period of 20 years without interruption, the right thereto shall be deemed absolute and indefeasible, any local usage or custom to the contrary notwithstanding, unless it shall appear that the same was enjoyed by some consent or agreement expressly made or given for that purpose by deed or writing.

1. *User need not be as of right* We have seen that where a claim to an easement is made under the Act, it must clearly appear that the enjoyment has been *as of right*, and the reason is that the statutory words *claiming right thereto* have been construed as equivalent to the common law expression *as of right*. Since these words, however, are omitted from the section dealing with light, it follows that in the case of this particular easement a fresh mode of creation has been statutorily introduced.[3] All that the claimant need show, if he claims not at common law but under the Act, is actual user and absence of written agreement,[4] but the user must have continued for the period of 20 years next before the action in which the claim is brought into question. In other words, the right is not absolute and indefeasible after 20 years' user, but remains merely inchoate until it has been established in legal

---

19 The section is in words restricted to ways and watercourses, but there is reason to believe that the word "convenient" has crept into the section instead of "easement"; see *Wright v Williams* (1836) Tyr & Gr 375 at 380; *Laird v Briggs* (1880) 50 LJ Ch 260 at 261, per FRY J.
20 *Palk v Shinner* (1852) 18 QB 568.
 1 S. 3. Ellis, *Rights to Light* (1992); *Colls v Home and Colonial Stores Ltd* [1904] AC 179; M & B p. 692 (where an injunction was refused); cf. *Pugh v Howells* (1984) 48 P & CR 298 (where a mandatory injunction was granted); *Blue Town Investments Ltd v Higgs and Hill plc* [1990] 1 WLR 696, [1990] 2 All ER 897; *Marine and General Mutual Life Assurance Society v St James' Real Estate Co Ltd* [1991] 38 EG 230 (measure of damages); *Voyce v Voyce* (1991) 62 P & CR 290 (right of light enforceable against equitable owner); *Deakins v Hookings* [1994] 14 EG 133.
 2 *Clifford v Holt* [1899] 1 Ch 698 (church); *Hyman v Van den Bergh* [1908] 1 Ch 167 (cowshed); *Allen v Greenwood* [1980] Ch 119, [1978] 1 All ER 819; M & B p. 694 (greenhouse), where it was held that a right to a specially high degree of light may be acquired by prescription. GOFF LJ left open the question whether a right to light would include the properties of the sun in relation to solar heating. See [1979] Conv. 298 (F. R. Crane); [1984] Conv. 408 (A. H. Hudson); Conv. Precedents 19–32. See also *Carr-Saunders v Dick McNeil Associates Ltd* [1986] 1 WLR 922, [1986] 2 All ER 888 (dominant owner's right under s. 3 is for access of light to the building as a whole and not to any particular room).
 3 *Scott v Pape* (1886) 31 Ch D 554 at 571, per BOWEN LJ.
 4 *Truscott v Merchant Taylors' Co* (1856) 11 Exch 855; *Frewen v Phillips* (1861) 11 CBNS 449; *Colls v Home and Colonial Stores Ltd* [1904] AC 179 at 205; *Kilgour v Gaddes* [1904] 1 KB 457.

proceedings.[5] To defeat a claim to light, based upon user for the statutory period, the servient owner must produce an express agreement by deed or writing which shows that the user has been permissive during the last 20 years.[6] Thus, for instance, user of light for 20 years is not dismissed as precarious, merely because it has been enjoyed under an oral permission extending over the whole period.[7] Even the payment of rent by the dominant owner under an oral agreement will not prevent the acquisition of the easement,[8] unless some receipt or acknowledgment has been given which can be construed as a written agreement.

2. *Interruption* A right to light cannot, of course, be acquired if its enjoyment has been effectively interrupted within the meaning of the Prescription Act, i.e. if there has been some adverse act by the servient owner which has lasted for at least one year.[9] In this type of easement, the adverse act must in the nature of things take the form of some physical structure, such as a hoarding, so sited as to obstruct the flow of light to the dominant tenement. An alternative to this cumbrous and unsightly method, however, was introduced by the Rights of Light Act 1959,[10] which enables the access of light to be notionally obstructed by the registration of a notice as a local land charge.

A notice in the prescribed form must be submitted to the local authority by the servient owner,[11] and it must state that its registration is intended to represent the obstruction to the access of light that would be caused by an opaque structure of certain specified dimensions, whether of unlimited height or not, erected upon the servient tenement.[12] The notice must also be accompanied by a certificate from the Lands Tribunal certifying either that adequate notice of the proposed registration has been given to all persons likely to be affected, or that the case is one of exceptional urgency and that therefore registration for a limited time is essential.[13] The notice, if not cancelled, expires one year after registration or, where accompanied by a certificate of exceptional urgency, at the end of the period specified in the certificate.[14]

For the purpose of determining whether a right to light has been acquired either at common law or under the Prescription Act, the access of light to the dominant tenement is to be treated as obstructed by a registered notice to the same extent and with the like consequences as if the structure specified in

5 *Hyman v Van Den Bergh* [1907] 2 Ch 516; affd [1908] 1 Ch 167; M & B p. 674. The reason is that the third section, cited above, must be read in connection with the fourth section which requires the period to be *next before* some action.

6 *Foster v Lyons* [1927] 1 Ch 219; *Willoughby v Eckstein* [1937] Ch 167, [1937] 1 All ER 257.

7 *Mallam v Rose* [1915] 2 Ch 222.

8 *Plasterers' Co v Parish Clerks' Co* (1851) 6 Exch 630.

9 P. 550, ante.

10 As amended by Local Land Charges Act 1975, s. 17, Sch. I. The Act embodies the recommendations of the Harman Committee on Rights of Light, 1958 (Cmnd 473); (1959) CLJ 182 (H. W. R. Wade). See *Hawker v Tomalin* (1969) 20 P & CR 550 at 551, per HARMAN J.

11 I.e., the owner of a legal fee simple or of a term of years absolute of which at least seven years remain unexpired, or the mortgagee in possession of such a fee or term: Rights of Light Act 1959, s. 7 (1).

12 Rights of Light Act 1959, s. 2 (1), (2); Lands Tribunal Rules 1975 Part VI (S.I. 1975 No. 299); Local Land Charges Rules 1977, r. 10. (S.I. 1977 No. 985). See p. 767, post.

13 Ibid., s. 2 (3). 938 definitive and 211 temporary certificates were issued between 1959 and 1980. See (1978) 122 SJ 515, 534; (1981) 259 EG 123 (W. A. Greene).

14 Ibid., s. 3 (2).

the application for registration has in fact been erected;[15] and any right of action that the dominant owner would have had in that event is available by reason of the notice.[16] In order to obviate the difficulties that may arise where the right is interrupted after it has been enjoyed for nineteen years and a fraction,[17] the Act provides in effect that the enjoyment by the dominant owner of the flow of light shall be notionally prolonged for one year if he sues for cancellation of the notice.[18]

3. *Not limited to prescription in respect of fee simple* Owing to the wording of the Prescription Act 1832 the right to light is an exception to the rule that an easement can be prescribed for only in respect of a fee simple.[19] It is peculiar in two respects:

First, the fee simple estate of a landlord is bound by an easement of light acquired over the land while in the occupation of a tenant.[20] Suppose, for instance, that:

A, the fee simple owner of Blackacre, leases it to a tenant for 25 years. During the tenancy, X, the owner of an adjoining house, builds a window overlooking Blackacre and enjoys access of light to it for 20 years. A right to light is thereby acquired that is enforceable against A, his tenant and all successors in title of Blackacre.

Secondly, if two tenements are held by different lessees under a common landlord, and one lessee enjoys the use of light over the other tenement for the necessary period, he and his successors acquire an indefeasible right to the light not only against the other tenant, but also against the common landlord and all succeeding owners of the servient tenement.[1]

(c) Common law not displaced by Prescription Act 1832

The Act is only supplementary to the common law—it provides an additional method of claiming easements, but leaves the other two methods untouched. If, for instance, the claimant is unable to show enjoyment for the statutory period of the last 20 years, as will happen if there has been unity of possession for part of that period, he may either prescribe at common law or invoke the doctrine of a lost grant.[2] Normally, he will rely on the Act. Failing this, he will base his case on prescription at common law; and, failing that, he will plead a lost modern grant, but only if driven to it, for, as Lord LINDLEY said:

that doctrine only applies where the enjoyment cannot be otherwise reasonably accounted for.[3]

Although a plaintiff can succeed only on one ground, it may be advisable

15 Rights of Light Act 1959, s. 2 (1).
16 Ibid., s. 3 (3).
17 P. 551, ante.
18 Rights of Light Act 1959, s. 1 (1), (2).
19 P. 546, ante.
20 *Simper v Foley* (1862) 2 John & H 555.
 1 *Morgan v Fear* [1907] AC 425; M & B p. 696; *Willoughby v Eckstein* [1937] Ch 167 at 170.
 2 See *Hulbert v Dale* [1909] 2 Ch 570, argument of counsel at 573.
 3 *Gardner v Hodgson's Kingston Brewery Co Ltd* [1903] AC 229 at 240.

to plead alternative claims by statute, common law prescription and lost modern grant.[4]

E. EXTENT OF EASEMENTS

In ascertaining the nature and extent of an easement, the principles to be applied vary with the method of its creation.

As WILLES J said in *Williams v James*:[5]

> The distinction between a grant and prescription is obvious. In the case of proving a right by prescription the user of the right is the only evidence. In the case of a grant the language of the instrument can be referred to, and it is of course for the court to construe that language; and in the absence of any clear indication of the intention of the parties, the maxim that a grant must be construed most strongly against the grantor must be applied.

(a) Express grant

It follows that, if the easement is created by express grant, the question is one of construing the terms of the grant, and, in cases of difficulty, the physical circumstances of the *locus in quo* must be considered. Thus, in determining whether the grant or reservation of "a right of way" is a right exercisable on foot only or with vehicles and, if so, what kind of vehicles, the condition of the way itself and the nature of the dominant tenement may be taken into account.[6] Furthermore, an unrestricted right of way is not confined to the use of the dominant tenement contemplated by the parties at the time of the grant. Thus, where an unrestricted right of way was granted as appurtenant to a house, and the house was subsequently converted into an hotel, its owner became entitled to a right of way for the general purposes of the hotel.[7] But a grant of an

---

4 See Bullen and Leake and Jacob, *Precedents of Pleadings* (12th edn), p. 1049. The three alternative claims were pleaded together in *Bailey v Stephens* (1862) 12 CBNS 91; *Norfolk v Arbuthnot* (1880) 5 CPD 390; *Wheaton v Maple* [1893] 3 Ch 48; *Roberts v James* (1903) 89 LT 282. See too *Pugh v Savage* [1970] 2 QB 373, [1970] 2 All ER 353.

5 (1867) LR 2 CP 577 at 581.

6 *Cannon v Villars* (1878) 8 Ch D 415 at 420; *St Edmundsbury and Ipswich Diocesan Board of Finance v Clark (No 2)* [1975] 1 WLR 468, [1975] 1 All ER 772; M & B p. 682; *United Land Co v Great Eastern Rly Co* (1875) 10 Ch App 586; *Robinson v Bailey* [1948] 2 All ER 791 (right of way to building plot held to include business user); *Jalnarne Ltd v Ridewood* (1989) 61 P & CR 143 (right of way held to permit its use by juggernaut lorries and customers in vans and cars for access to dominant tenements subsequently used for motorcar dealing, frozen food business and snooker club with bar); *Soames-Forsythe Properties Ltd v Tesco Stores Ltd* [1991] EGCS 22 ("full and free right of way on foot only" from supermarket to car park held to include right for customers to use supermarket trolleys on it); [1992] Conv 199 (J. Martin); *London and Suburban Land and Building Co (Holdings) Ltd v Carey* (1991) 62 P & CR 480 (express grant of a right of way to commercial premises did not imply a right to unload from the access way onto the dominant tenement).

7 *White v Grand Hotel Eastbourne Ltd* [1913] 1 Ch 113; *Kain v Norfolk* [1949] Ch 163, [1949] 1 All ER 176; *Bulstrode v Lambert* [1953] 1 WLR 1064, [1953] 2 All ER 728; *Keefe v Amor* [1965] 1 QB 334, [1964] 2 All ER 517; M & B p. 679; *McIlraith v Grady* [1968] 1 QB 468, [1967] 3 All ER 625; *Bracewell v Appleby* [1975] Ch 408, [1975] 1 All ER 993 (right to pass over close A to reach close B held to be not usable as access to close C lying beyond close B), following *Harris v Flower* (1904) 74 LJ Ch 127; *Nickerson v Barraclough* [1980] Ch 325 at 336, [1979] 3 All ER 312 at 324 (such a right held to be usable as access where close B is itself used as access to close C at time of grant); *Scott v Martin* [1987] 1 WLR 841, [1987] 2 All ER 813 (plan used to explain "private road"); *Hamble Parish Council v Haggard* [1992] 1 WLR 122 ("I have to put myself into the shoes of the notional judge visiting the site with the conveyance in one hand and gazing about him to identify on the ground those features which would enable him to ascertain the extent of the dominant land", per MILLETT J at 130).

unrestricted right of way does not authorise excessive use which would be an unreasonable interference with the rights of others entitled to use it. [8]

(b) Implied grant

If the easement is created by implied grant, we have already seen that where it is implied in favour of the grantor, an easement of necessity is strictly limited to the circumstances of the necessity prevailing at the time of the grant. [9] In the case of an easement implied in favour of the grantee, the grantee must establish that the parties intended that the subject of the grant should be used in some definite and particular manner; the law will then imply the grant of such easements as may be necessary to give effect to it. [10]

(c) Prescription

The extent of a prescriptive easement is comensurate with its user. Once the purposes for which it has been used during the period of its acquisition have been determined by evidence, its use for purposes radically different in character is not permissible. In other words, the burden upon the servient tenement must not be increased by reason of a radical change in the character of the dominant tenement. [11] For example, a right of way that has been used to carry agricultural produce to a farm cannot lawfully be used to meet the requirements of a factory into which the farm is later converted. [12] But if the character or nature of the user remains constant, there is no objection to an increase in its intensity. [13] A right of way appurtenant to a golf club, for instance, is not misused merely because the membership of the club has greatly increased. [14]

F. EXTINGUISHMENT OF EASEMENTS

An easement may be extinguished by statute or by release or as the result of unity of seisin. There is no statutory procedure for their discharge or modification as there is in the case of restrictive covenants. [15]

---

8 *Jelbert v Davis* [1968] 1 WLR 589, [1968] 1 All ER 1182; M & B p. 682; (1968) 112 SJ 172 (S. M. Cretney) (right to be used "in common with all other persons having the like right"); *Rosling v Pinnegar* (1986) 54 P & CR 124; cf. *National Trust v White* [1987] 1 WLR 907; *White v Richards* [1993] RTR 318 (track not intended to carry juggernauts).
9 P. 538, ante.
10 *Milner's Safe Co Ltd v Great Northern and City Rly Co* [1907] 1 Ch 208; *Stafford v Lee* (1992) 65 P & CR 172.
11 *Wimbledon and Putney Common Conservators v Dixon* (1875) 1 Ch D 362; *Ward (Helston) Ltd v Kerrier District Council* (1981) 42 P & CR 412.
12 *Williams v James* (1867) LR 2 CP 577 at 582, per WILLES J.
13 *British Railways Board v Glass* [1965] Ch 587, [1964] 3 All ER 418; M & B p. 684 (Lord DENNING MR dissenting); (1965) 87 LQR 17 (R.E.M.); *Woodhouse & Co Ltd v Kirkland (Derby) Ltd* [1970] 1 WLR 1185, [1970] 2 All ER 560 (considerable increase in number of customers using right of way held to be "mere increase in user and not a user of a different kind or for a different purpose"); *Giles v County Building Constructors (Hertford) Ltd* (1971) 22 P & CR 978 (erection of seven modern dwelling units in place of two houses held to be "evolution rather than mutation"); *Cargill v Gotts* [1981] 1 WLR 441, [1981] 1 All ER 682 (drawing of extra water from neighbour's millpond for agricultural purposes held to be mere increase in user), p. 165, ante.
14 Ibid., at 568, at 432, per DAVIES LJ.
15 P. 634, post.

(1) STATUTE

Easements may be extinguished by statute. Important examples are to be found in the Town and Country Planning Act 1990, under which acquiring authorities are enabled to extinguish:

> all private rights of way and rights of laying down, erecting, continuing or maintaining any apparatus on, under or over the land.

Further, local authorities may build or carry out work on land acquired for planning purposes, even though it involves interference with "any easement, liberty, privilege, right or advantage annexed to land and adversely affecting other land, including any natural right of support".[16]

(2) RELEASE

An extinguishment may be effected by a release, either express or implied.

(a) Express release

The dominant owner is free to execute a deed of release relieving the servient tenement from the burden of any easement to which it is subject. At common law a deed is necessary,[17] but if the servient owner, in reliance on an agreement to release, has prejudiced his position to such an extent that it would be inequitable and oppressive to treat the easement as still in being, equity will disregard the absence of formalities and will hold the dominant owner to his bargain.[18] If, for instance, a person who is entitled to an easement of light orally agrees to an alteration in the servient tenement which must necessarily obstruct the flow of light to the window, he cannot, after expense has been incurred in making the alteration, bring an action in respect of the resulting obstruction.

(b) Implied release
(i) Abandonment

A more important and at the same time more difficult point is whether in any given case there has been an implied release or abandonment of the easement by the dominant owner.

The onus of proving abandonment lies fairly and squarely on the person who alleges it, and the onus is a very heavy one.[19] As BUCKLEY LJ said in *Tehidy Minerals Ltd v Norman*:[20]

> Abandonment of an easement or of a profit à prendre can only, we think, be treated as having taken place where the person entitled to it has demonstrated a fixed intention never at any time thereafter to assert the right himself or to attempt to transmit it to anyone else.

---

16 TCPA 1990, ss. 236, 237. See also Housing Act 1985, s. 295 (1)–(3); New Towns Act 1981, s. 19; Local Government, Planning and Land Act 1980, s. 144, Sch 6; Railways Act 1993, s. 34.
17 Co Litt, 264b.
18 *Davies v Marshall* (1861) 10 CBNS 697; *Waterlow v Bacon* (1866) LR 2 Eq 514.
19 *James v Stevenson* [1893] AC 162.
20 [1971] 2 QB 528 at 553, [1971] 2 All ER 475 at 492; M & B p. 698.

The general principle is that whether he intended to abandon his right depends upon the proper inference to be drawn from the circumstances.[1]

No one circumstance necessarily implies an abandonment, and thus, it has been laid down again and again that mere non-user is not decisive of the question.[2] If the non-user is explicable only on the assumption that the dominant owner intended to give up his right, it will amount to an abandonment, but not if there are other circumstances which go to show that he regarded the right as still alive. In other words, a cessation may show either an abandonment or a mere abeyance of an easement according to the particular circumstances of each case.

The principle was re-stated by POLLOCK MR in *Swan v Sinclair*:

Non-user is not by itself conclusive evidence that a private right of easement is abandoned. The non-user must be considered with, and may be explained by, the surrounding circumstances. If those circumstances clearly indicate an intention of not resuming the user then a presumption of a release of the easement will, in general, be implied and the easement will be lost.[3]

Thus in the leading case of *Moore v Rawson*:[4]

a plaintiff, who had some ancient windows, pulled down the wall in which they were situated and rebuilt it as a stable with no windows. Some fourteen years later the defendant erected on his adjoining land a building which would have obstructed the flow of light to the windows had they still been there. After another three years the plaintiff made a window in the stable in the exact spot where one of the old windows had been, and then proceeded to bring an action against the defendant for obstruction of light.

It was held that he could not succeed, because, in erecting a building entirely different from the old one, he had shown an intention to abandon the enjoyment of his former right.

However, as was stated by HOLROYD J:

If he had done some act to shew that he intended to build another in its place, then the new house, when built, would in effect have been a continuation of the old house, and the rights attached to the old house would have continued. If a man has a right of common attached to his mill, or a right of turbary attached to his house, if he pulls down the mill or the house, the right of common or of turbary will prima facie cease. If he shows an intention to build another mill or another house, his right continues.

The same principle can be seen at work in the case of rights of way. So:

where the exercise of a right of way had been discontinued for many years because the dominant owner had a more convenient route over his own land, it was held that the non-user was adequately explained and did not constitute an abandonment.[5]

But any non-user of a right of way caused by something which is adverse to the enjoyment of the right will be regarded as an abandonment. Thus in *Swan v Sinclair*:[6]

---

1 *Cook v Bath Corpn* (1868) LR 4 Eq 177.
2 *R v Chorley* (1848) 12 QB 515; *Ward v Ward* (1852) 7 Exch 838; *Crossley & Sons Ltd v Lightowler* (1867) 2 Ch App 478; *Re Yateley Common, Hampshire* [1977] 1 WLR 840 at 845, [1977] 1 All ER 505 at 510; *Gotobed v Pridmore* (1970) 115 SJ 78; *Benn v Hardinge* (1992) 66 P & CR 246 (no abandonment in spite of 175 years' non-user).
3 *Swan v Sinclair* [1924] 1 Ch 254 at 266; affd [1925] AC 227.
4 (1824) 3 B & C 332; M & B p. 699.
5 *Ward v Ward* (1852) 7 Exch 838.
6 [1924] 1 Ch 254; affd [1925] AC 227.

Certain houses were put up for sale in lots in 1871, one of the conditions being that a strip of land running at the back of the houses should be formed into a roadway, and that the purchaser of each lot should have a right of way along the road when made. At the time when the action was brought in 1923 the road had not been constructed, fences lay across its proposed site between each pair of lots, and in 1883 the then owner of lot 1 nearest the exit of the proposed road had levelled up the site, and by so doing had caused a sheer drop of 6 feet to occur between that lot and lot 2. The plaintiff was now desirous of building a garage on lot 2, and the question arose whether he was still entitled to a right of way over the strip of land at the back of lot 1.

The majority of the court dismissed his claim on the ground that, though as a rule mere non-user is insufficient to extinguish a right of way, yet in this case the continued existence of the dividing fences and the raising of the level of lot 1 were circumstances adverse to a right of enjoyment, sufficient to show an intention on the part of the various owners to abandon the project.

(ii) Alterations to dominant tenement

Alterations to the dominant tenement which make the enjoyment of an easement impossible or unnecessary may show an intention to abandon the right. For example, where a right of water is appurtenant to a mill, and the mill is demolished, without any intention of replacing it, the easement is impliedly released.[7] Furthermore, the easement may be extinguished where the dominant tenement is so altered as to throw a substantially increased burden on the servient tenement to the detriment of its owner.[8]

(iii) Frustration

In *Huckvale v Aegean Hotels Ltd*, the Court of Appeal considered a novel claim that an easement can be extinguished by its ceasing to accommodate the dominant tenement. In granting an interlocutory injunction, SLADE LJ said:[9]

> In the absence of evidence of proof of abandonment, the court should be slow to hold that an easement has been extinguished by frustration, unless the evidence shows clearly that because of a change of circumstances since the date of the original grant there is no practical possibility of its ever again benefiting the dominant tenement in the manner contemplated by that grant.

(3) UNITY OF SEISIN

Easements are also extinguished by unity of seisin, that is to say, if the fees simple of both the dominant and the servient tenements become united in the same owner, all easements properly so called come to an end, for the owner can do what he likes with his own land, and any right that formerly ranked as an easement because it was exercisable over another's land is now merely one of the ordinary incidents of his ownership.[10] An easement which

---

7 *Liggins v Inge* (1831) 7 Bing 682 at p 693; *Ecclesiastical Comrs for England v Kino* (1880) 14 Ch D 213; *Scott v Pape* (1886) 31 Ch D 554.

8 *Ankerson v Connelly* [1906] 2 Ch 544; affd [1907] 1 Ch 678 (easement of light); *Ray v Fairway Motors (Barnstaple) Ltd* (1968) 20 P & CR 261 (easement of support); *Lloyds Bank Ltd v Dalton* [1942] Ch 466 at 471–2, [1942] 2 All ER 352 at 357, per BENNETT J; cf *Graham v Philcox* [1984] QB 747, [1984] 2 All ER 643; M & B p. 689; p. 535, ante; *Gale on Easements* (15th edn), pp. 355 et seq.

9 (1989) 58 P & CR 163 at 173; [1990] Conv 292 (K. Kodilinye).

10 Co Litt 313a; *Lord Dynevor v Tennant* (1888) 13 App Cas 279.

has been destroyed by this union of title in one hand may, however, be re-created under the doctrine of *Wheeldon v Burrows* if the property is again severed into its original parts.[11] A complete extinguishment occurs when both the tenements become united in one person for an estate in fee simple, but if he acquires only a particular estate in one of them, as for instance a life interest or a term of years, the easement is merely suspended and will revive again if upon the determination of his particular estate the tenements are once more in different hands.[12]

Unity of seisin without unity of possession does not extinguish an easement of light, as, for example, where the owner of the servient tenement acquires the fee simple in the dominant tenement while the latter is in the possession of a tenant for years.[13] It is doubtful, however, whether this is true in the case of easements other than light.[14]

SECTION III PROFITS À PRENDRE

A. GENERAL NATURE OF PROFITS À PRENDRE

(1) DIFFERENCES BETWEEN PROFITS AND EASEMENTS

Profits à prendre differ from easements in the fact that they import the taking of some thing which is capable of ownership from the servient tenement. Such things are numerous and diverse, as for instance, the soil itself, the grass growing on or the minerals lying below the soil, animals such as fish and fowl,[15] sand from the seashore, ice from a canal, heather, turf, acorns and so on.

But in addition to this fundamental distinction there are the following important differences between profits and easements.

(a) Existence in gross

Unlike an easement,[16] a profit may be granted in gross to be held independently of the ownership of land.[17] From early times it was held that an express grant by deed to a man, his heirs and assigns of a perpetual right to a profit was a valid grant,[18] and as the possibility of a grant is the basis of all the methods whereby profits as well as easements may be acquired, it was later held that a profit in gross might be prescribed for at common law.[19] Such profits in gross are not common, but once established they may be sold or leased to a third party,[20] and they will pass under a will or intestacy.

---

11 (1879) 12 Ch D 31; p. 540, ante. But not under LPA 1925, s. 62, since there would be no diversity of occupation; p. 536, ante.
12 *Thomas v Thomas* (1835) 2 Cr M & R 34.
13 *Lord Richardson v Graham* [1908] 1 KB 39; M & B p. 700.
14 In *Buckby v Coles* (1814) 5 Taunt 311, MACDONALD CB was of opinion that a right of way was not extinguished by mere unity of seisin (at 315), but the Court of Common Pleas expressed a "decided opinion" to the opposite effect (at 315–6) and counsel abandoned the argument.
15 *Peech v Best* [1931] 1 KB 1 at 9.
16 P. 520, ante.
17 *Lord Chesterfield v Harris* [1908] 2 Ch 397 at 421, per BUCKLEY LJ.
18 1495 YB 11 Hen, fol. 8a, cited by PARKE B in *Wickham v Hawker* (1840) 7 M & W 63 at 79.
19 *Welcome v Upton* (1840) 6 M & W 536; *Johnson v Barnes* (1872) LR 7 CP 592; 8 CP 527; *Shuttleworth v Le Fleming* (1865) 19 CBNS 687; *Goodman v Saltash Corpn* (1882) 7 App Cas 633 at 658.
20 *Goodman v Saltash Corpn*, supra.

(b) Longer periods under Prescription Act 1832

Profits as well as easements may be prescribed for under the Prescription Act 1832, but the statutory periods of enjoyment are fixed at 30 and 60 years respectively instead of 20 and 40.[1]

(c) Remedies

In as much as a profit imports the privilege of carrying away something from the servient tenement, the dominant owner enjoys such possessory rights as will enable him to maintain trespass or nuisance at common law for an infringement of his right, but the owner of an easement is restricted to the remedies of abatement or an action of nuisance.[2]

(d) Quasi-profits

A right in the nature of an easement can be acquired by an indefinite and fluctuating class of persons such as the inhabitants of a village, while a profit à prendre cannot be directly claimed by such persons, for otherwise the result would be to exhaust the servient tenement,[3] though in exceptional cases it can be indirectly acquired, as we shall see later.[4]

(e) Profit may be appendant

A profit may be *appendant* to land, that is annexed to the land by operation of law, but an easement may not. If before the passing of the Statute *Quia Emptores* in 1290 the lord of a manor granted *arable* land to be held of him by a freehold tenant, the common law automatically appended to the grant a right in the tenant to pasture upon the waste lands of the manor such cattle as were necessary to plough and manure the arable land.[5]

This right of pasture was held to be appendant, and necessarily appendant, to a grant of arable land within a manor, for the grantee obviously could not till the arable land without beasts of plough, and he would have no means of sustaining the animals unless he could pasture them on the manorial waste.[6] This right, therefore, arose from common right upon the grant of arable land within a manor and it must be distinguished from profits or easements appurtenant to land, which are opposed to common right and must be deliberately acquired by an actual or presumed grant.[7] Profits appendant are still possible, but they must have come into existence before 1290,[8] for the effect of *Quia Emptores* is that all sales by the lord of a manor since that date take the land out of the manor altogether, so that the grantee does not hold of the manor in the waste of which he claims a right.

---

1 Prescription Act 1832, s. 1.
2 *Fitzgerald v Firbank* [1897] 2 Ch 96; *Peech v Best*, supra; *Nicholls v Ely Beet Sugar Factory Ltd* [1936] 1 Ch 343.
3 P. 575, post.
4 Pp. 575–7, post.
5 Co Litt 122*a*; Blackstone, vol. ii. p. 33; *Earl of Dunraven v Llewellyn* (1850) 15 QB 791 at 810; Holdsworth, *History of English Law*, vol. iii. pp. 147 et seq; Hall, *Law of Profits à Prendre and Rights of Common*, p. 224.
6 Blackstone, vol. ii. p . 33.
7 *Tyrringham's Case* (1584) 4 Co Rep 36*b*; *Warrick v Queen's College, Oxford* (1871) 6 Ch App 716.
8 See *Davies v Davies* [1975] QB 172, [1974] 3 All ER 817.

(2) SIMILARITIES BETWEEN PROFITS AND EASEMENTS

Apart from the differences indicated, the nature of a profit is in general similar to that of an easement. Thus, for instance, it is necessary that a profit which is *appurtenant* to land should be connected with the dominant tenement in the sense of increasing its beneficial enjoyment.[9] The law does not recognize an unlimited profit appurtenant, as for instance a right to cut turf[10] or to catch salmon for sale,[11] or to dig clay wherever it is required for making bricks.[12] A profit appurtenant must be limited, and the limit is arrived at by estimating the needs of the dominant tenement.[13]

Further, a profit, like an easement, is capable of subsisting as a legal interest; it may also be equitable[14] and, if so, is registrable as a Class D (iii) land charge under the Land Charges Act 1972.[15]

B. CLASSES OF PROFITS À PRENDRE

(1) SEVERAL PROFITS AND PROFITS IN COMMON

Profits fall into two classes, namely those enjoyed by their owner to the exclusion of everybody else, and those enjoyed by him in common with other persons including the owner of the servient tenement.

The first are called "several" profits à prendre, and the latter profits à prendre in "common", or rights of common, or more often simply *commons*:

> A right of common may be said to exist where two or more take, in common with each other, from the soil of a third person a part of the natural profits thence produced.[16]

Thus, while every common is a profit à prendre, it does not follow that all profits à prendre are commons.

Profits à prendre are rights which have existed from a very early date in the history of this country, and which in their origin[17] were exercised by numbers of persons in common with each other. Moreover, that is the form in which they are most frequently found nowadays. It may of course happen that a man possesses the right to take something off the land of another without affecting the right of the owner to take similar things for his own use; or he may be entitled to the exclusive right of taking something, as often occurs in the case of pasturage rights over the Sussex Downs; but the type of profit that a practising lawyer will most likely to have to consider is a right of common properly so called.

---

9 *Clayton v Corby* (1843) 5 QB 415 at 419; *Bailey v Stephens* (1862) 12 CBNS 91; cf. pp. 520–2, ante.
10 *Valentine v Penny* (1605) Noy 145.
11 *Lord Chesterfield v Harris* [1908] 2 Ch 397; affd [1911] AC 623.
12 *Clayton v Corby*, supra.
13 See pp. 565–6, post, in reference to common of pasture.
14 *Mason v Clarke* [1955] AC 778, [1955] 1 All ER 914; M & B p. 81, p. 570, post; see *Lowe v J W Ashmore Ltd* [1971] Ch 545, esp. at 557–8, [1971] 1 All ER 1057 at 1068.
15 S. 2 (5). Pp. 530–1, ante, which apply *mutatis mutandis* to profits.
16 *Woolrych on Commons* (2nd edn), p. 13.
17 For the history of profits, see the 11th edn of this book, pp. 547–8.

(2) RIGHTS OF COMMON

(a) Classification

Rights of common are classified into:

   (i) rights appendant,
  (ii) rights appurtenant,
 (iii) rights in gross, and
  (iv) rights *pur cause de vicinage*. A common *pur cause de vicinage*, which is the only one we have not explained, is restricted to the right of pasturage, and arises where adjacent commons are open and unfenced and there is a custom for the cattle to inter-common, that is, for the cattle rightfully put upon the common of one manor to stray and feed upon the common of the adjoining manor without being treated as trespassers.[18]

Rights of common may also be classified according to their subject matter into four kinds, namely, common of pasture, of piscary, of turbary and of estovers.[19]

(i) Common of pasture This, the most usual common, arises when the owner of cattle is, in common with others, entitled to put his cattle to feed on the land of another.[20] In the case of a common *appendant* the right is limited to "commonable cattle", that is, horses and oxen to plough the land and cows and sheep to manure it.[1] A common *appurtenant* is not limited in this way, but depends upon the extent of the enjoyment proved or upon the terms of the grant if there is one, and so a right may well be established to pasture such animals as hogs, goats and geese.[2] Common in gross may also be enjoyed in respect of any animal. Commons of pasture appendant and appurtenant are also restricted in another manner, as we have already had occasion to notice, for there is no right to pasture an unlimited number of commonable cattle.[3] The rule at common law is that the right is exercisable only in respect of cattle *levant et couchant* on the land, i.e. the number that the dominant tenement is çapable of supporting through the winter.[4] Again a right of pasturage in gross cannot be prescribed for unless it is restricted in the same manner.[5]

This doctrine of *levancy et couchancy* was, however, abolished by the Commons Registration Act 1965,[6] which requires all rights of grazing to be registered, but limits registration to a defined number of animals.[7] In the case of a common in gross there is no objection in principle to the existence of pasture without stint, or, in other words, to a right to put an unlimited

18 Co Litt 122*a*; *Tyrringham's Case* (1584) 4 Co Rep 366. See *Newman v Bennett* [1981] QB 726, [1980] 3 All ER 449 (three straying cows in the New Forest).
19 Blackstone, vol. ii. p. 32; Co Litt 122*a*.
20 *Tyrringham's Case* (1584) 4 Co Rep 36*b*, 37.
 1 Ibid. This pasture may be claimed for certain animals only, e.g. sheep (when it is called "sheep walk"): *Robinson v Duleep Singh* (1878) 11 Ch D 798; or swine (called common of "pannage"); *Chilton v Corpn of London* (1878) 7 Ch D 562.
 2 *Bennett v Reeve* (1740) Willes 227; *Tyrringham's Case,* supra.
 3 *Anderson v Bostock* [1976] Ch 312, [1976] 1 All ER 560.
 4 *Robertson v Hartopp* (1889) 43 Ch D 484 at 517; Holdsworth, *History of English Law*, vol. vii. p. 320 and authorities there cited; *Re Ilkley and Burley Moors* (1983) 47 P & CR 324.
 5 *Mellor v Spateman* (1669) 1 Saund 339.
 6 P. 567, post.
 7 S. 15.

number of cattle on the servient tenement, because, as it is not appurtenant to anything, there is no dominant tenement with reference to the needs of which the content of the right must be proportioned. Thus, as was said by BUCKLEY LJ:[8]

> it may well be that there can exist in law a right in gross to enter and take without limitation—without stint—the profits or proceeds of another's land commercially for the purposes of sale.

Such an unstinted right might no doubt be granted expressly by deed, but, though there is no objection to it in principle, the case of *Mellor v Spateman*[9] clearly decided that it could not be prescribed for:

> And the court did not dislike any part of the plea, but only it was not said in the plea "*levant et couchant* within the town". And KELYNGE CJ said positively that there cannot be any common in gross without number.[10]

The old expression *common sans nombre* which is met with in earlier cases is not inconsistent with this principle, for it merely meant that the right was for beasts *levant et couchant*, the point being in such a case that the number was not positively fixed at a definite figure.

(ii) Common of piscary A stranger may acquire a right to catch fish in inland waters, such as lakes, ponds and non-navigable rivers, belonging to private owners. This right takes two forms:

(i) A "several fishery" or a "free fishery", which is not a right of common, but is a right to take fish *in alieno solo* and to exclude the owner of the water from the right to take fish himself;[11]

(ii) A "common of fishery" which is a liberty of fishing in another man's water in common with other persons.[12]

"Common of piscary being given for the sustenance of the tenant's family"[13] must, if appurtenant to a house, be limited to the needs of that house, and the fish cannot be caught for sale.[14] It should be noted that though the fishery in arms of the sea and in tidal rivers is open to all subjects of the realm,[15] yet a prescriptive right to a several fishery or a common of fishery therein may be established.[16] The presumption, however, is in favour of the public.

(iii) Common of turbary Common of turbary is the right of cutting turf or peat in another man's land to be expended as fuel in the house of the commoner.[17] For the last 400 years this right has always been treated as a common appurtenant, with the qualification that it must be appurtenant to an ancient house or to a new house erected in continuance of the ancient

8 *Lord Chesterfield v Harris* [1908] 2 Ch 397 at 421.
9 (1669) 1 Wms Saund 339.
10 At 346.
11 *Foster v Wright* (1878) 4 CPD 438 at 449. See *Loose v Castleton* (1978) 41 P & CR 19; *Lovett v Fairclough* (1990) 61 P & CR 385 (claim to profit in gross of piscary over Jeffrey's Pool in the River Tweed failed).
12 Blackstone, vol. ii. p. 34; *Seymour v Courtenay* (1771) 5 Burr 2814, per MANSFIELD CJ.
13 Ibid., p. 35.
14 *Lord Chesterfield v Harris* [1908] 2 Ch 397.
15 *Fitzwalter's Case* (1674) 1 Mod Rep 105; *Carter v Murcot* (1768) 4 Burr 2162 at 2164.
16 *Carter v Murcot*, supra.
17 Blackstone, vol. ii. p. 34.

one.[18] It cannot be appurtenant to land,[19] for, as we have seen, a thing which is appurtenant must agree in nature and quality with the thing to which it is attached, and the idea of using fuel on land apart from a house is absurd.

(iv) Common of estovers Blackstone has said:

> Common of estovers or estouviers; that is, necessaries (from *estoffer*, to furnish), is a liberty of taking necessary wood, for the use or furniture of a house or farm, from off another's estate. The Saxon word, *bote*, is used by us as synonymous to the French *estovers*; and therefore house-bote is sufficient allowance of wood to repair or to burn in the house (which latter is sometimes called fire-bote); plough-bote and cart-bote are wood to be employed in making and repairing instruments of husbandry; and hay-bote, or hedge-bote, is wood for repairing hays, hedges or fences.[20]

This right, which very closely resembles common of turbary, is generally appurtenant to a house,[1] though of course it may be attached to land for the purpose of repairing fences. When it is appurtenant to a house, the wood taken must be expended on that house, and cannot be used for the reparation of new buildings which may have been erected, or as fuel in new fireplaces which have been built in the original house.[2] But when the old dominant house is demolished and replaced by another one, the right continues to exist according to its original extent:

> If an ancient cottage which had common be fallen down, and another cottage be erected in the place where the old cottage stood; this is no new cottage, but it may claim common as an ancient cottage by prescription.[3]

A right similar to the common of estovers and also called estovers is given at common law to a tenant for life or years enabling him to cut timber which would otherwise be waste.[4] The only difference between the common law right and that which we have just considered is that the former arises in the tenant by virtue of the possession of the land rented and is exercisable over that land, while the latter is a profit to be taken out of somebody else's land.

(b) Registration

The Commons Registration Act 1965[5] requires the registration with county

---

18 *A-G v Reynolds* [1911] 2 KB 888; *Warrick v Queen's College, Oxford* (1871) 6 Ch App 716 at 730.
19 *Tyrringham's Case* (1584) 4 Co Rep 36*b*.
20 Blackstone, vol. ii. p. 35.
1 *A-G v Reynolds* [1911] 2 KB 888.
2 *Luttrel's Case* (1601) 4 Co Rep 86*a*.
3 *Bryers v Lake*, cited Hall, *Law of Profits à Prendre and Rights of Common*, p. 322.
4 P. 398, ante.
5 See generally Gadsden, *The Law of Commons* (1988); Oswald, *Common Land* (1989); Harris and Ryan, *Outline of the Law relating to Common Land and Public Access to the Countryside* (1967); Clayden, *Our Common Land* (1985); [1977] JPL 352 (R. Vane); Report of Royal Commission on Common Land, 1955–1958 (Cmnd 462); (1972) 122 NLJ 1127 (V. Chapman); M & B p. 62. Decisions of the Commons Commissioners are reported in Campbell, *Decisions of the Commons Commissioners* (1972), in Current Law and in the Annual Reports of Commons, Open Spaces and Footpaths Preservation Society. See (1973) 117 SJ 537; (1974) 118 SJ 424 (I. Campbell). See Commons Registration (General) Regulations 1966 (S.I. 1966 No. 1471), as amended by S.I. 1968 No. 658; S.I. 1980 No. 1195; S.I. 1982 Nos. 209, 210; S.I. 1989 No. 2167. There will be further legislation about the management and improvement of registered common land as well as about its user by the public. In 1978 the Department of the Environment issued a consultative document and in 1986 the Countryside Commission

councils of common land in England and Wales[6] of persons claiming to be or found to be its owners, and of claims to rights of common over such land before August 1970.[7] The Act also applies to town or village greens,[8] and to waste land of a manor not subject to rights of common.[9]

The expression "rights of common" includes:[10]

cattlegates or beastgates[11] and rights of sole or several vesture[12] or herbage or of sole or several pasture, but does not include rights held for a term of years or from year to year.

Registration under the Act may be final or provisional. It is final if no objection was lodged before August 1972;[13] and final registration is conclusive evidence of the matters registered at the date of registration.[14] If there is any such objection, the registration is provisional, and only becomes final if it is confirmed after a hearing before a Commons Commissioner.[15]

published the Report of the Commons Land Forum. This contains recommendations for the amendment of the Act, which Lord DENNING MR said "is ill-drafted and has given rise to many difficulties": *Corpus Christi College Oxford v Gloucestershire County Council* [1983] QB 360 at 370, [1982] 3 All ER 995 at 1002. See Appendices C and D for a detailed and critical summary of the present law and practice; [1985] Conv 24 (A. Samuels) which contains a bibliography; (1987) 151 LG Rev 24; (1990) 29 LSG 17 (P. Reeves).

6 There are some 1½ million acres of common land.
7 Commons Registration Act 1965, ss. 1–4 as amended by LGA 1972, s. 272 (1), Sch. 30, and LGA 1985, s. 16, Sch. 8, para 10 (6). The Act does not apply to the New Forest, Epping Forest or to any land exempted by an order of the Secretary of State: s. 11; S.I. 1965 No. 2001.
8 Ibid., s. 22 (1); *Re The Rye, High Wycombe, Bucks* [1977] 1 WLR 1316, [1977] 3 All ER 521; *New Windsor Corpn v Mellor* [1975] Ch 380, [1975] 3 All ER 44; *Re White Land Pond, Four Dales and Clay Pitts, Thorne and Stainforth, South Yorkshire (No 1)* [1984] CLY 287; cf. *Re River Don and its Banks* [1984] CLY 284; *Re Foreshore, East Bank of River Ouse, Nabum, Selby District, North Yorkshire* [1989] CLY 276; [1992] Conv 434 (A. Samuels); M & B p. 64.
9 Ibid., s. 22 (1) (*b*); *Re Britford Common* [1977] 1 WLR 39, [1977] 1 All ER 532; *Re Yateley Common, Hampshire* [1977] 1 WLR 840, [1977] 1 All ER 505; *Re Chewton Common* [1977] 1 WLR 1242, [1977] 3 All ER 509; *Baxendale v Instow Parish Council* [1982] Ch 14, [1981] 2 All ER 620; *Hampshire County Council v Milburn* [1991] 1 AC 325, [1990] 2 All ER 257 (waste land of a manor held by HL to mean "waste land now or formerly of a manor" or "waste land of manorial origin").
10 Commons Registration Act 1965, s. 22 (1).
11 Cattlegate or beastgate, sometimes called *stinted pasture*, is a right to pasture a fixed number of beasts on the land of another, generally for a part of the year only. See e.g. *Rigg v Earl of Lonsdale* (1857) 1 H & N 923; *Brackenbank Lodge Ltd v Peart* (1993) Times, 4 June.
12 The right of sole vesture, *vestura terrae*, is not merely to graze cattle, but to take away the product of the land, such as grass, corn, underwood, turf, peat, and so forth.
13 S.I. 1968 No. 989, as amended by S.I. 1970 No. 384; *Smith v East Sussex County Council* (1977) 76 LGR 332.
14 Commons Registration Act 1965, s. 10; *New Windsor Corpn v Mellor*, supra, at 392, at 51, per Lord DENNING MR; *Cooke v Amey Gravel Co Ltd* [1972] 1 WLR 1310, [1972] 3 All ER 579 (provisional registration is itself no evidence of the existence of the right registered); *Corpus Christi College Oxford v Gloucestershire County Council* [1983] QB 360, [1982] 3 All ER 995 (registration conclusive even where entry on register was wrong); *R v Mid-Sussex District Council* [1993] EGCS 183.
15 Ibid., ss. 4–7; S.I. 1971 No. 1727; S.I. 1972 No. 437, as amended by S.I. 1993 No. 1771; S.I. 1973 No. 815. The onus of establishing the validity of the registration is on the person making the registration: *Re Sutton Common, Wimborne* [1982] 1 WLR 647, [1982] 2 All ER 376; *Re West Anstey Common* [1985] Ch 329, [1985] 1 All ER 618; *Re Newton Fell* [1988] CLY 285. When deciding whether to confirm a provisional registration, the Commissioner should consider not only the situation as it was at the date of registration, but also events occurring since that date; *Re Merthyr Mawr Common* [1989] 1 WLR 1014, [1989] 3 All ER 451.

There is a right of appeal from his decision by a person aggrieved to the High Court on a point of law.[16]

After July 1970, no land capable of being registered under the Act is to be deemed to be common land unless it is so registered, and no rights of common shall be exercisable over any such land unless they are either registered under the Act or have been previously registered under the Land Registration Act 1925.[17] Thus not only are unregistered rights existing before that date extinguished, but there can be no future acquisition of rights over registered commons.[18] New commons may, however, arise, for example, by grant or by prescription, and be registered.[19] In this case the land does not cease to be common land nor do the rights of common cease to be exercisable, if not registered.

The Common Land (Rectification of Registers) Act 1989 provides that land may be removed from the register, if it can be shown that at all times since 5 August 1945 (i.e. 20 years before the passing of the Commons Registration Act 1965) the land has included or has been ancillary to a dwelling-house.[20]

C. ACQUISITION OF PROFITS À PRENDRE

It will not be necessary to consider this topic at any length for the methods by which easements may be acquired are applicable, with very few exceptions, to the acquisition of profits à prendre, whether rights of common or not. At the outset we can dismiss profits appendant because they have been impossible of acquisition since *Quia Emptores* in 1290, and a claimant will be required to prove that he holds arable land which was granted by the lord of a manor to a freehold tenant before that date.[1]

The four possible methods of acquiring easements are set out on page 531. We will take each one of these and show to what extent it applies to profits:

16 Commons Registration Act 1965, s. 18. See *Wilkes v Gee* [1973] 1 WLR 742, [1973] 2 All ER 1214; *R v Chief Commons Comr* (1977) 37 P & CR 67; *Re Tillmire Common, Heslington* [1982] 2 All ER 615.

17 Ibid., s. 1 (2); S.I. 1970 No. 383. Applications for registration had to be made before 3 January 1970. For registration where land becomes common land or a town or village green after 2 January 1970, see Commons Registration (New Land) Regulations 1969 (S.I. 1969 No. 1843); *Central Electricity Generating Board v Clwyd County Council* [1976] 1 WLR 151, [1976] 1 All ER 251 (right of common not registered by closing date held to be extinguished); *Re Turnworth Down, Dorset* [1978] Ch 251, [1977] 2 All ER 105. For the liability of a solicitor who failed to search the register, see *G and K Ladenbau (UK) Ltd v Crawley and De Reya* [1978] 1 WLR 266, [1978] 1 All ER 682.

18 Ibid., s. 13 (*b*); S.I. 1969 No. 1843, r. 3 (2).

19 S.I. 1969 No. 1843, r. 3 (1), and n. 5 on p. 11.

20 Applications must have been made before 21 July 1992: Common Land (Rectification of Registers) Regulations 1990 (S.I. 1990 No. 311); Guidance Note (Chief Commons Commissioners) 30 September 1990 (set out in [1990] Conv 463; [1989] Conv 384 (A. Samuels)); *Re 1–4 White Row Cottages, Bewerley* [1991] Ch 441, [1991] 4 All ER 50 (dwellinghouse held to include an unoccupied house or one which had become derelict and unfit for human habitation); *Cresstock Investments Ltd v Commons Comrs* [1992] 1 WLR 1088, [1993] 1 All ER 213 (uncultivated woodland ancillary to dwelling house); cf. *Re Land at Freshfields* (1993) 66 P & CR 9 (pasture land not ancillary); *Storey v Commons Comr* (1993) 66 P & CR 206 (derelict orchard ancillary to Settrington House), even though enjoyed by more than one house before present ownership).

1 *Viner's Abridgment*—Common C. p. 1; *Comyns' Digest*, Tit. Covenant B.

(a) Statute

Profits may be acquired by statute, as when Inclosure Acts confer new rights upon manorial lords by way of compensation for the interest lost by them in the soil itself.

(b) Express grant

Profits, whether appurtenant or in gross, may be created by an express grant, which at common law must be made by deed.[2] The want of a deed, however, is not necessarily fatal to the grantee, for if he can prove a specifically enforceable contract for the grant of the profit, he may invoke the familiar doctrine of equity that the grantor must be regarded as having already done what he ought to have done.

Thus in an early case:[3]

> The defendant signed a written memorandum by which he agreed in return for valuable consideration that the plaintiff should have the exclusive right of sporting over and killing the game on the defendant's lands, but some years later he revoked the agreement.

At the instance of the plaintiff, WOOD V-C decreed specific performance by ordering the execution of a formal deed and meanwhile granting an injunction forbidding the defendant to interfere with the enjoyment of the right.

Section 62 of the Law of Property Act 1925, which, as we have already seen, provides that a conveyance of land shall operate to pass rights and advantages appertaining to the land at the time of the conveyance,[4] applies not only to easements but also to profits, such as a right of depasturing sheep on an adjoining mountain.[5]

(c) Implied grant

The next method whereby easements may be acquired is that of an implied grant under the doctrine of *Wheeldon v Burrows*, but since this is confined to interests of a continuous and apparent nature, it can have no application to profits, which can scarcely possess either of these characteristics.

(d) Presumed grant or prescription

(i) Prescription at common law Profits can be acquired by prescription at common law, and when this method of claim is adopted it must conform to all those general principles which obtain in the case of easements, so that:

---

2 Co Litt 9 *a, b*; *Wood v Leadbitter* (1845) 13 M & W 838 at 842–3; *Mason v Clarke* [1954] 1 QB 460, [1954] 1 All ER 189.
3 *Earl Frogley v Lovelace* (1859) John 333; *Mason v Clarke* [1955] AC 778, [1955] 1 All ER 914 (part performance); M & B p. 81.
4 P. 534, ante.
5 *White v Williams* [1922] 1 KB 727; *White v Taylor (No 2)* [1969] 1 Ch 160, [1968] 1 All ER 1015; *Anderson v Bostock* [1976] Ch 312, [1976] 1 All ER 560 (exclusive right of grazing without limit held to be unknown to the law), p. 535, ante; *Re Yateley Common, Hampshire* [1977] 1 WLR 840 at 850, [1977] 1 All ER 505 at 514; *Re Broxhead Common, Whitehill, Hampshire* (1977) 33 P & CR 451.

    (i) the possibility of a grant must be shown;

   (ii) use is required to be *as of right*; and

  (iii) the claim is liable to be defeated by proof of its origin since 1189.

There is this difference, however, between easements and profits, that although a man can only prescribe in a *que estate* for an easement, he may prescribe in himself and his ancestors for a profit.[6] Examples of this personal prescription are rare,[7] since profits in gross themselves are rare, and such cases as are to be found in the Law Reports refer to *several* profits and not to rights of common.[8] Where a man does prescribe in the person, he must adduce evidence to show that either he and his ancestors, or some other person and *his* ancestors from whom the plaintiff acquired the title to the profit, have enjoyed the right from time immemorial.[9]

(ii) Lost modern grant Profits à prendre may be claimed by virtue of a lost modern grant, but instances are rarely found. If a claim is so made, it must conform to the rules and surmount the objections that apply where an easement is founded on a lost grant.[10] Even though the Prescription Act 1832 requires 30 years' user in respect of a claim to a profit, only 20 years' user is necessary to support a presumption of a lost grant.[11]

(iii) Prescription Act 1832 The Prescription Act 1832 treats profits differently from easements in that it requires longer periods of enjoyment. The periods fixed for profits are 30 years and 60 years instead of 20 and 40. But, for the purposes of the Commons Registration Act 1965,[12] the time during which the servient tenement has been requisitioned, or a right of grazing has been prevented by reason of animal health, must be ignored in computing the period of 30 or 60 years or in determining whether there has been an interruption within the meaning of the Prescription Act.[13] Further, any objection to the registration of a right of common under the Commons Registration Act is deemed to be a suit or action within section 4 of the Prescription Act.[14] Otherwise the provisions of the Act of 1832 are exactly the same for both interests.

    The Act of 1832 applies only to profits appurtenant, not to those in gross, for it requires the claimant to allege in his pleading that the right has been enjoyed "by the occupiers of the tenement in respect whereof the same is claimed. . . ."[15] As Montague Smith J said in the leading case:

> The whole principle of this pleading assumes a dominant tenement and an enjoyment of the right by the occupiers of it. The proof must of course follow and support the pleading. It is obvious that rights claimed in gross cannot be so pleaded or proved.[16]

----

6 Co Litt 122*a*. *Que estate* is Norman French for "whose estate"; land in which an interest, in the nature of an easement or profit à prendre, has been acquired by prescription.

7 *Shuttleworth v Le Fleming* (1865) 19 CBNS 687, per Montague Smith J.

8 *Welcome v Upton* (1840) 6 M & W 536; *Shuttleworth v Le Fleming*, supra; *Johnson v Barnes* (1873) LR 8 CP 527.

9 *Welcome v Upton* (1839) 5 M & W 398; *Lovett v Fairclough* (1990) 61 P & CR 385.

10 *Neaverson v Peterborough RDC* [1902] 1 Ch 557; *Mills v New Forest Commission* (1856) 18 CB 60; *Loose v Castleton* (1978) 41 P & CR 19 (several fishery).

11 *Tehidy Minerals Ltd v Norman* [1971] 2 QB 528, [1971] 2 All ER 475.

12 P. 567, ante.

13 Commons Registration Act 1965, s. 16.

14 Ibid., s. 16 (2).

15 Prescription Act 1832, s. 5.

16 *Shuttleworth v Le Fleming* (1865) 19 CBNS 687 at 711.

D. EXTINGUISHMENT OF PROFITS À PRENDRE

Several profits and profits in common may be extinguished by any of the following methods:

(a) Unity of seisin

If the owner of the profit or common also becomes owner of the land over which the right is exercisable, the right is extinguished, provided that his estates in the right and in the land are similar both in quantum and in quality.[17] Thus a profit appurtenant is extinguished if one person becomes seised in fee both of the dominant and of the servient tenement, but if the owner of the profit takes a lease of the servient tenement, the result of this unity of possession, as distinguishd from unity of seisin in the former case, is that the profit is only suspended and will revive again upon the expiration of the lease.[18]

(b) Release

A release of a profit in favour of the servient owner extinguishes the right in the sense that it ceases to exist as a right *in alieno solo*, since a man cannot have a profit or common in his own land.

(c) Alteration of dominant tenement

Although it has been said that:

common is obtained by long sufferance and also it may be lost by long negligence,[19]

it is not true that mere non-user of a profit will by itself produce an extinguishment of the right,[20] but if the character of the dominant tenement is so altered as to make any further appurtenancy impossible, a presumption is raised in favour of extinguishment. If, for instance, land to which a common of pasture was appurtenant entirely loses its agricultural character by conversion into a building estate, the common is destroyed, but if the conversion is not irrevocable, as where arable land is turned into an orchard, the profit is merely suspended and is capable of being resumed on the restoration of the land to its original state.[1]

(d) Approvement and inclosure of commons

Rights of common may be partially extinguished by the process known as approvement or wholly extinguishd by inclosure.

(i) Approvement

At common law it appears that the lord of a manor was entitled to *approve* the manorial waste upon which the freehold tenants had the right of pasturing their cattle, by appropriating part thereof to himself and holding it in separate ownership.[2] This practice was justified by the lords on the ground that the multiplicity of commoners rendered the manor unprofitable, but as it not unnaturally caused dissension it was ultimately regulated by two statutes—the Statute of Merton 1235, chapter 4, and the

---

17 *Tyrringham's Case* (1584) 4 Co Rep 36*b*; *White v Taylor (No 2)* [1969] 1 Ch 150, [1967] 3 All ER 349; *Re Yateley Common, Hampshire* [1977] 1 WLR 840, [1977] 1 All ER 505; Hall, *Law of Profits à Prendre and Rights of Common*, p. 335.

18 Co Litt 313*a*, 114*b*.

19 *Gateward's Case* (1607) 3 Leon 202.

20 *Seaman v Vawdrey* (1810) 16 Ves 390; *Re Yateley Common, Hampshire*, supra.

 1 *Carr v Lambert* (1866) LR 1 Exch 168; *Tyrringham's Case* (1584) 4 Co Rep 36*b*.

 2 See authorities collected in Hall, *Law of Profits à Prendre and Rights of Common*, pp. 345 et seq.; *Re Broxhead Common, Whitehill, Hampshire* (1977) 33 P & CR 451.

Statute of Westminster the Second 1285, chapter 46.[3] These expressly permitted the lord of a manor to appropriate or approve the manorial waste, subject to the condition that he left sufficient pasturage for the commoners, determined according to the aggregate number of animals which they were entitled to turn out, and not according to the number which they had for a fixed number of years been in the habit of turning out.[4]

The Commons Act 1876 requires a person seeking to approve a common to publish his intention in the local press on three successive occasions,[5] and the Law of Commons (Amendment) Act 1893 further provides that an approvement of any part of a common purporting to be made under the Commons Acts of 1236 and 1285 shall not be valid unless it is made with the consent of the Board of Agriculture and Fisheries (now the Secretary of State for the Environment).

(ii) Inclosure The other method of deliberate extinguishment is inclosure under the various Inclosure Acts. Inclosure differs in three respects from approvement:

   (i) it applies to all kinds of commonable rights, such as common of turbary and estovers, and is not restricted to pasture;
  (ii) it involves the discharge of the whole of the lands from the rights of common; and finally
 (iii) it does not depend upon the discretion of any one man, but requires for its validity the sanction of an Act of Parliament.

Inclosure is the process whereby a commoner, in place of the rights over the manorial waste which he formerly enjoyed, is granted a definite piece of land to be held in fee simple. It is now virtually a dead letter, but in the comparatively short period of a hundred years, from about 1760 to 1860, it led to the almost entire disappearance of those rights of common which from the earliest days had been such a striking feature of English landholding. To understand this sudden and rapid extinction of ancient rights, it is necessary to realize that even as late as the eighteenth century the greater part of the cultivated land of England was still farmed under the medieval village community system. That system[6] had outlived its *raison d'être* and had become by the eighteenth century nothing but a hindrance to proper cultivation.

At first inclosures were carried out by private Acts of Parliament by which allotments of land to be held in separate ownership and discharged from commonage were awarded to the lord and the commoners. The expense of these private Acts was very great, and in 1801 the procedure was simplified by the passing of the Inclosure (Consolidation) Act, which set out a number of general provisions capable of being incorporated into private Acts.[7]

The Inclosure Act 1845 established a central body in the shape of the Inclosures Commissioners for England and Wales, whose duties are now

---

3 The Statute Law Revision Act 1948 renamed these two chapters as the Commons Act 1236, and the Commons Act 1285. The former was repealed *in toto* by the Statute Law Revision Act 1953.
4 *Robertson v Hartopp* (1889) 43 Ch D 484.
5 S. 31.
6 See Holdsworth, *History of English Law*, vol. ii. pp. 56 et seq, and the 11th edn of this book, pp. 547–8.
7 See e.g. *Fisons Horticulture Ltd v Bunting* (1976) 240 EG 625.

carried out by the Secretary of State for the Environment, and required the consent of Parliament for inclosures.[8]

The result of this Act, was that between 1845 and 1875, 590,000 acres were inclosed and divided among 25,930 persons. But during the last decade of this period it became practically impossible to obtain parliamentary sanction for inclosure awards, since, under the influence of the Commons Preservation Society, the nation became convinced that one of the most urgent national needs was the provision of open spaces. The new policy was not to parcel out common lands among private owners, but to throw them open to the public and provide for their management and regulation by public bodies. Effect was given to this by the Commons Act 1876, which, after reciting that:

> inclosure in severalty as opposed to regulation of commons should not be hereinafter made unless it can be proved to the satisfaction of the said Commissioners and of Parliament that such inclosure will be of benefit to the neighbourhood as well as to private interests,

contained provisions designed to protect the public and to give local authorities an opportunity of acquiring land for the public. Thus the Secretary of State for the Environment when making a provisional award for submission to Parliament must now insert provisions, where applicable, for securing free access to any particular prospect, the preservation of objects of historical interest, the reservation of the right of playing games where a recreation ground has not been set out, and so on.[9]

The procedure for an inclosure is governed by the Act of 1876, and the stages are as follows:

(a) An application supported by persons representing at least one-third of the value of the lands must first be made to the Secretary of State for the Environment.

(b) The application must explain why inclosure is preferable to the regulation of the land as a public common.

(c) If the Secretary of State is of opinion that a *prima facie* case has been made out he orders a local inquiry to be made by one of his officers.

(d) The officer inspects the locality, holds a public meeting at which he hears the views of all persons who wish to be heard and makes a report to the Secretary of State.

(e) The Secretary of State, if he is satisfied that the matter ought to go further, prepares a draft provisional order which is ultimately submitted to Parliament.

---

8 Or the Secretary of State for Wales: S.I. 1967 No. 156; S.I. 1970 No. 1681.
9 S. 7. For the regulation and management of commons, see also Metropolitan Commons Act 1866; Metropolitan Commons Amendment Act 1869; Commons Act 1899; Commons (Schemes) Regs 1982 (S.I. 1982 No. 209). For the rights of the public of access for air and exercise to commons and waste lands, see LPA 1925, ss. 193, 194; *Mienes v Stone* (1985) CO/ 1217/84 noted [1985] Conv 415 (J. R. Montgomery). See also National Parks and Access to the Countryside Act 1949, ss. 59–83; Countryside Act 1968, ss. 6, 9; *R v Doncaster Metropolitan Borough Council* (1986) Times, 11 October (Doncaster Common "best known as the site of the St. Leger" held to be an open space within LGA 1972, s. 123 (2A)); [1988] Conv 369 (J. Hill).

So then at the present day inclosures are still possible, but owing to the very strong case which must be made out by the petitioners, and also to the important part played by local authorities, who are afforded facilities for making a portion of the land common to the public, it is unlikely that they will be continued.

(e) Commons Registration Act 1965

As we have seen, rights of common are no longer exercisable over land in England and Wales which is common land or a town or village green, unless they have been registered under the Commons Registration Act 1965 or the Land Registration Act 1925.[10]

SECTION IV RIGHTS IN THE NATURE OF EASEMENTS AND PROFITS À PRENDRE ACQUIRED BY FLUCTUATING AND UNDEFINED CLASSES OF PERSONS

There is no doubt that indefinite and fluctuating classes of persons, such as the inhabitants of a village, may acquire rights, analogous in nature to easements, over the land of another.[11] For example, they have succeeded in establishing rights to enter another's close and take water from a spring,[12] to dry their fishing nets on the land of a private person,[13] to hold horse races[14] or a fair[15] on such land, and to pass to church[16] or market over a man's private property.

A. RIGHTS IN NATURE OF EASEMENTS

Such rights are not easements capable of acquisition by prescription, for all forms of prescription presuppose the possibility of a grant, and no grant can be made to an indefinite body of persons. Nevertheless, the law, in its anxiety to protect the long sustained enjoyment of a privilege, has surmounted the technical difficulty incident to prescription by allowing rights of this nature to be established by *custom*. Hence the name *customary* rights. Custom is an unwritten rule of law which has applied from time immemorial in a particular locality and which displaces the common law in so far as that particular locality is concerned.[17] To quote the words of TINDAL CJ:[18]

> A custom which has existed from time immemorial without interruption within a certain place, and which is certain and reasonable in itself, obtains the force of a law, and is, in effect, the common law within that place to which it extends, though contrary to the general law of the realm.

10 S. 1 (2); p. 567, ante.
11 *Gateward's Case* (1607) 6 Co Rep 59*b*; *Race v Ward* (1855) 4 E & B 702.
12 *Weekly v Wildman* (1698) 1 Ld Raym 405; *Race v Ward*, supra.
13 *Mercer v Denne* [1905] 2 Ch 538.
14 *Mounsey v Ismay* (1865) 3 H & C 486.
15 *Tyson v Smith* (1838) 9 Ad & El 406.
16 *Brocklebank v Thompson* [1903] 2 Ch 344.
17 See *Termes de la Ley, sub voce* "Custom"; *Tanistry Case* (1608) Dav Ir 28; Litt s. 169; *Hammerton v Honey* (1876) 24 WR 603.
18 *Lockwood v Wood* (1844) 6 QB 50 at 64.

(a) Requisites for custom

It has been said[19] that a custom must be

(1) certain,[20]
(2) not unreasonable,[1]
(3) commencing from time immemorial,
(4) continued without interruption, and
(5) applicable to a particular district.

The two outstanding requirements are existence from time immemorial[2] and restriction to a definite locality.[3]

Strictly speaking the first of these requirements means that the custom must have existed since 1189, but although the nature of the right precludes the court from presuming a lost modern grant if enjoyment cannot be proved for so long, yet the practice is to presume that the right originated at the proper time if it is obviously of respectable antiquity.[4] It is generally enough to show continuous enjoyment going as far back as living testimony can go.

To quote TINDAL CJ again:

> As to the proof of the custom, you cannot, indeed, reasonably expect to have it proved before you that such a custom did in fact exist before time of legal memory, that is, before the first year of the reign of Richard I; for if you did, it would in effect destroy the validity of almost all customs; but you are to require proof, as far back as living memory goes, of a continuous, peaceable, and uninterrupted user of the custom.[5]

Although the presumption in favour of enjoyment from time immemorial will readily be raised, it can undoubtedly be rebutted by positive evidence showing that it actually began at some later date.[6] The courts, however, are slow to rebut the presumption. In *Mercer v Denne*:

> it was proved by witnesses that for as long as they could remember—a matter of 70 years—the fishing inhabitants of Walmer had used part of the defendant's beach for the purpose of drying their nets. The defendant, having proved that in 1844 a considerable portion of this part of the beach was under water, argued that the custom of using that particular portion must be disallowed as obviously having arisen since 1189.

In rejecting this plea FARWELL J said:[7]

> A defendant may no doubt defeat a custom by shewing that it could not have existed in the time of Richard I, but he must demonstrate its impossibility, and the onus is on him to do so if the existence of the custom has been proved for a long period; this was done, for instance, in *Simpson v Wells*,[8] where the claim of a

---

19 *Mercer v Denne* [1905] 2 Ch 538; *New Windsor Corpn v Mellor* [1975] Ch 380, [1975] 3 All ER 44 (right to indulge in lawful sports and pastimes).
20 I.e., the persons entitled to the right must be certain and not, e.g., "poor householders": *Selby v Robinson* (1788) 2 Term Rep 758.
1 E.g. a custom to do something which would exhaust the subject matter is void, as for inhabitants of a parish to fish in a river: *Bland v Lipscombe* (1854) 4 E & B 713n.
2 Blackstone, vol. i. p. 76; *Chapman v Smith* (1754) 2 Ves Sen 506.
3 *R v Rollett* (1875) LR 10 QB 469 at 480.
4 *Mercer v Denne*, supra, at 556; *Wolstanton Ltd and A-G of Duchy of Lancaster v Newcastle-under-Lyme Borough Council* [1940] AC 860 at 876, [1940] 3 All ER 101 at 109.
5 *Bastard v Smith* (1838) 2 Mood & R 129 at 136.
6 *Hammerton v Honey* (1876) 24 WR 603 at 604, per JESSEL MR.
7 [1904] 2 Ch 534 at 555.
8 (1872) LR 7 QB 214.

custom to set up stalls at the Statute Sessions for the hiring of servants was defeated by shewing that such sessions were introduced by the Statutes of Labourers, the first of which was in the reign of Edward III. But no such impossibility is shewn in the present case. If the beach was of its present extent in 1795, why am I bound to infer that it cannot have been the same in 1189 from the mere fact that between 1795 and 1844 the extent diminished and has since again increased? The mere non-user during the period that the sea flowed over the spot is immaterial, for it was no interruption of the right but only of the possession, and an "interruption of the possession only for ten or twenty years will not destroy the custom".[9]

A customary right, once acquired, cannot be lost by mere non-user or by waiver.[10]

(b) Custom and prescription

Enough has been said to show that custom bears a close and striking resemblance to prescription. Both methods depend on continuous and uninterrupted enjoyment which has lasted for the time whereof the memory of man runneth not to the contrary, and both are liable to be defeated in the same manner. COKE CJ emphasized the resemblance in quaint language:

> Prescription and custom are brothers, and ought to have the same age, and reason ought to be the father, and congruence the mother, and use the nurse, and time out of memory to fortify them both.[11]

But for all that there is an important difference between the two methods, for while prescription always connects the right with a definite person, custom connects it with some particular locality. Prescription is personal, custom is local. A right is always prescribed for in the name of a certain person and his ancestors, or of those whose estate he owns, or in the name of corporations and their predecessors.[12] But a right claimed by custom is not alleged to be vested in any definite person or body of persons, but is claimed on the ground that it is vested in the shifting class of persons connected from time to time with the definite locality to which the right is attached.[13] In custom you first prove the attachment of the right to a locality and then prove your connection with that locality; while in prescription you show the existence of the right in some person from whom your title is derived, or else you prove yourself to be the owner of a tenement to which the right is attached.

The importance of the distinction lies in the fact that persons who are quite unable to establish their claim to an easement by means of prescription, because prescription presupposes a grant to some definite person, may very well succeed under the cover of custom. A customary right is part of the general law applicable to a particular locality; and persons resident there, whether capable grantees or not, are entitled to enjoy the benefit of the law which runs throughout the locality.

---

9 Blackstone, vol. 1. p. 77; Co Litt 114*b*.
10 *Wyld v Silver* [1963] Ch 243, [1962] 3 All ER 309; *New Windsor Corpn v Mellor* [1975] Ch 380, [1975] 3 All ER 44.
11 *Rowles v Mason* (1612) 2 Brownl 192 at 198.
12 4 Co Rep 32*a*, per Sir Edward COKE.
13 Co Litt 113*b*; Blackstone, vol. ii. p. 263; *Foiston v Crachroode* (1587) 4 Co Rep 31*a*; *Gateward's Case* (1607) 6 Co Rep 59*b*.

B. RIGHTS IN NATURE OF PROFITS À PRENDRE

So far our account has been restricted to the capacity of a fluctuating and ever-changing class of persons to establish a claim to quasi-easements, and it remains to be considered whether such persons can sustain a claim to *profits à prendre*. It has been the law at least since 1607[14] that indefinite persons cannot acquire a profit by custom.[15] JAMES LJ, in one case, said:

> Of course it is settled and clear law that you cannot have any right to a profit *à prendre in alieno solo* in a shifting body like the inhabitants of a town or residents of a particular district.[16]

Were the rule otherwise the result would be to exhaust and destroy the subject matter of the custom. Thus claims by inhabitants or classes of persons equally indefinite have been disallowed where the customs alleged were to enjoy common of pasture,[17] to collect dead wood for fuel,[18] to carry away sand that has drifted from the sea shore,[19] or to take minerals from the soil.[20]

But in all cases where ancient claims are in question we have to reckon with the tendency of the courts to presume everything reasonably possible in order to uphold a right of which there has been long enjoyment, and it is in furtherance of this general principle that two methods have been evolved whereby fluctuating classes can in certain circumstances maintain a claim even to profits *in alieno solo*. These may be termed (1) the "presumed Crown grant" method and (2) the "presumed charitable trust" method.

(1) PRESUMED CROWN GRANT

To take the Crown grant first, we start with this, that although a private person cannot make a grant to indefinite classes of persons, yet the Crown may do so. Lord ROMILLY said:[1]

> The distinction between a grant by a private individual and a grant by the Crown is this, that as the Crown has the power to create corporations, so, if it is necessary for the purpose of establishing the validity of the grant, the grantees will be treated as a corporation *quoad* the grant, which is not the case with a grant by a private individual, because a private individual has no power of creating a corporation.

The Crown by virtue of this power may make a grant to the inhabitants of a town, with the result that they become by implication a corporation for the purposes of the grant and, as such, capable of enjoying a profit in the land of another. So in *Willingale v Maitland*:

> where an actual Crown grant had been made in the time of Elizabeth to the inhabitants of a parish allowing a certain section of the parishioners to lop the branches of trees growing in the waste of a manor, it was held on demurrer that the grant was legal.[2]

---

14 *Gateward's Case*, supra.
15 Ibid.; *Race v Ward* (1855) 4 E & B 702; *Chilton v London Corpn* (1878) 7 Ch D 735; *Constable v Nicholson* (1863) 14 CBNS 230.
16 *Sewers Comrs of the City of London v Glasse* (1872) 7 Ch App 456 at 465.
17 *Grinstead v Marlowe* (1792) 4 Term Rep 717.
18 *Selby v Robinson* (1788) 2 Term Rep 758.
19 *Blewett v Tregonning* (1835) 3 Ad & El 554.
20 *A-G v Mathias* (1858) 4 K & J 579.
 1 *Willingale v Maitland* (1866) LR 3 Eq 103 at 109.
 2 Ibid.

Cases where an actual grant can be found must be rare, and the real question is whether the court will presume a grant so as to incorporate the inhabitants and thus render them eligible to take profits. All that can be said is that such a presumption will be raised only where the circumstances that have accompanied the enjoyment go to show that the claimants have always regarded themselves as a corporation and have acted as such.

Such a grant was presumed in the *Faversham Fishery Case*;[3] but in *Lord Rivers v Adams*,[4] where it appeared that the enjoyment of an alleged right of inhabitants to carry away wood from a manorial waste was inconsistent with the fact that the tenants of the manor had openly asserted and exercised control over the wood, the court refused to raise the presumption.

KELLY CB in this case said:

> If the inhabitants had held meetings in reference to this right, or appointed any officer to look to the right, or done any act collectively of that description, the case would be different. We should then have the inhabitants acting in a corporate capacity in reference to this right, and from their doing so, and from their existence *de facto* as a corporation, we might according to the ordinary rule find a legal origin by a grant from the Crown.[5]

(2) PRESUMED CHARITABLE TRUST

The second method, whereby uncertain bodies may establish a claim to profits, namely, that of a presumed charitable trust, is very similar to the one just described. It depends upon the decision of the House of Lords in *Goodman v Saltash Corpn*,[6] where the principle was in effect established that, where it appears that a definite body capable of taking by grant, such as the corporation of a borough, has enjoyed a profit *in alieno solo* for a great number of years, and where it also appears that an indefinite body has shared in this enjoyment, then the court presumes a lost grant in favour of the corporation, but declares that the corporation must hold the profit in trust for the indefinite body.

In *Goodman v Saltash Corpn*:

> Two facts were clearly proved: first, that the Corporation of Saltash had from time immemorial exercised the right of dredging for oysters in the river Tamar; secondly, that the free inhabitants of ancient tenements in the borough had each year from Candlemas (22 February) to Easter Eve exercised a similar right for the previous 200 years. An action was brought by the corporation against two free inhabitants of ancient tenements for trespass committed in the Tamar and for converting to their own use quantities of oysters.

After holding that the free inhabitants could not be presumed to be separately incorporated, the House addressed itself to the task of discovering a legal origin for the right which undoubtedly had been enjoyed for a very considerable time. The majority of the House (Lord BLACKBURN dissenting) held that the fishery must have originally been granted to the corporation

3 *Re Free Fishermen of Faversham* (1887) 36 Ch D 329; see especially at 343, per BOWEN LJ.
4 (1878) 3 Ex D 361.
5 *Lord Rivers v Adams* (1878) 3 Ex D 361 at 366–7. This is a most instructive case on the whole subject of claims to profits by fluctuating bodies.
6 (1882) 7 App Cas 633; *Peggs v Lamb* [1994] 2 WLR 1 (charitable trust for freemen and widows of freemen of the ancient borough of Huntingdon).

subject to a condition that the free inhabitants were to be allowed to fish for a certain period each year. Lord CAIRNS said:

> It appears to me that there is no difficulty at all in supposing such a grant, a grant to the corporation before the time of legal memory of a several fishery, a grant by the Crown, with a condition in that grant in some terms which are not before us, but which we can easily imagine—a condition that the free inhabitants of ancient tenements in the borough should enjoy this right, which as a matter of fact the case tells us they have enjoyed from time immemorial. . . . Such a condition would create that which in the very wide language of our courts is called a charitable, that is to say a public, trust or interest, for the benefit of the free inhabitants of ancient tenements.[7]

But for this principle to apply, it must be established that the enjoyment of the profit was regarded by the indefinite body of persons as a right to which they were entitled without anybody's permission, not as a privilege of little significance that was tolerated by the indulgence or good nature of the servient owner.[8]

In conclusion, then, we may say that before a fluctuating class can sustain a claim to a profit, they must show either that a grant was probably made in such a way as to incorporate them, or that there is some definite corporation which is capable of taking a grant and of holding the right granted in trust for them.

SECTION V   REGISTERED LAND[9]

A.   CREATION

An easement, right or privilege may be created over registered land in the same way as it can over unregistered land.

(i) Express grant When the right is created by express grant, it may appear on either the property register of the title to the dominant tenement, or on the charges register of that to the servient tenement, or on both. Provision is made for the entry of a right on the property register, if it is appurtenant to land and is capable of subsisting as a legal estate.[10] The noting of a profit in gross, as opposed to a profit appurtenant, is thus excluded. As far as the charges register is concerned, the Registrar has a mandatory duty to enter a note thereon of any easement, right or privilege which has been created by an instrument[11] and which adversely affects the servient land at the time of first registration.[12] Thereafter, he has a discretion to enter a notice of an adverse easement upon proof of its existence.[13]

Furthermore, even if the easement is not referred to on the property register, it will nevertheless be enjoyed by each registered proprietor of the dominant tenement. This stems from the rule that section 62 of the Law of

---

7 At 650.
8 *Alfred F Beckett Ltd v Lyons* [1967] Ch 449, [1967] 1 All ER 833.
9 Registered Land Practice Notes (2nd edn 1986), pp. 36–38.
10 LRR 1925, rr. 3 (2) (c), 252–257. See *Re Evans' Contract* [1970] 1 WLR 583, [1970] 1 All ER 1236.
11 This does not include a statute, unless the statute creates a settlement: LRA 1925, s. 3 (vii).
12 LRA 1925, s. 70 (2); *Re Dances Way, West Town, Hayling Island* [1962] Ch 490 at 508, [1962] 2 All ER 42 at 52; M & B p. 705.
13 Ibid., s. 70 (3); LRR 1925, r. 41 (1). The difficulties in determining from available evidence the nature and extent of easements is considerable. See generally *Re Dances Way*, supra.

Property Act 1925, under which general words may be implied in a conveyance, applies equally to a transfer of registered land.[14]

In this context it is important to reiterate the rule that in order to perfect the title of any easement or profit at law, the disposition creating it must itself be completed by registration.[15] Until this has been done, the grantor remains the proprietor. The consequence is that the transaction takes effect in equity, and a type of equitable easement, peculiar to registered conveyancing, is thereby created.

(ii) Implied grant In the case of an easement created by implied grant,[16] it would appear that the rule in *Wheeldon v Burrows*[17] applies also to registered land, although there is no specific reference to it in the Land Registration Act or the Rules. It is clear, however, that an easement or profit may be created by implied grant under section 62 of the Law of Property Act 1925.[18] Here too no legal right can be created until the grantee is registered as proprietor.

(iii) Prescription Rule 250 (1) of the Land Registration Rules 1925 provides:[19]

> easements, rights and privileges adversely affecting registered land may be acquired in equity by prescription in the same manner and to the same extent as if the land were not registered.

An easement or profit acquired by prescription will take effect at law if it is capable of subsisting as a legal interest, and in equity, in any other case. If it takes effect at law, it becomes an overriding interest,[1] and, if the Registrar thinks fit, he may enter a notice of it on the charges register of the servient tenement, and on the property register of the dominant tenement.[2]

B. RUNNING OF BURDEN

As far as the running of the burden of an easement or profit is concerned, a purchaser of the servient tenement, in accordance with the general principles of registered conveyancing, takes subject to any rights which appear on the register. He also takes subject to any overriding interests, and, in this context, section 70 (1) (*a*) of the Land Registration Act 1925 provides that the following are such:

> Rights of common,[3] drainage rights, customary rights (until extinguished), public rights, profits à prendre, rights of sheepwalk, rights of way, watercourses, rights of

---

14 LRR 1925, r. 251. See also LRA 1925, ss. 5–7, 9–12, 19 (3), 20 (1), 22 (3), 23 (1), 72.
15 LRA 1925, ss. 19 (2), 22 (2).
16 See Ruoff and Roper, para. 6–07; Farrand, *Contract and Conveyance* (2nd edn), pp. 390–2.
17 (1879) 12 Ch D 31, p. 540, ante.
18 P. 534, ante.
19 See also LRA 1925, s. 75 (5).
1 LRA 1925, s. 70 (1) (*a*); infra.
2 Ibid., s. 7 (3); LRR 1925, r. 250 (2). Ruoff and Roper, para. 6–07, 29–10. In most cases, as easements in course of prescription are inchoate until court action, the note in the property register will merely state that the easement is claimed and not that it actually subsists.
3 No rights of common can be registered under LRA 1925 over land which is capable of registration under the Commons Registration Act 1965, s. 1 (1). See also s. 12; p. 567, ante.

water, and other easements not being equitable easements required to be protected
by notice on the register.

This paragraph is ill-drafted. It mixes public and private rights, and specifies
some easements (e.g. rights of way) and not others (e.g. rights of support or
light). The general intention of the paragraph seems to be to include
everything in the nature of easements and profits. Its jumbled nature is
probably due to its history.[4]

The paragraph was examined in *Celsteel Ltd v Alton House Holdings Ltd*,[5]
where it was held that a right of way to a garage, which had been created in
a written contract for a lease and was therefore an equitable easement, came
within rule 258 of the Land Registration Rules 1925:

> Rights, privleges and appurtenances appertaining or reputed to appertain to land
> or demised, occupied or enjoyed therewith or reputed or known as part or parcel of
> or appurtenant thereto, which adversely affect registered land.[6]

The right, which was not protected by an entry on the register, had been
openly exercised and enjoyed as appurtenant to the garage, and was therefore
binding as an overriding interest on a subsequent registered proprietor.

This rule, however, may have a more limited effect. Its wording suggests
that its purpose was to "ensure that where, as the result of the registration of
a person as proprietor of land, the benefit of rights vests in him under section
62 of the Law of Property Act 1925,[7] the burden of those rights, if affecting
other registered land, should in any event be overriding interests. Thus if A
sells part of his registered freehold property to B, the registration of B as
proprietor of the part may vest[8] in B the benefit of some unspecified 'right'
previously enjoyed over the land retained by A. The register of A's title after
the sale will contain no reference to this right, and were it not for the fact
that rule 258 makes the right an overriding interest burdening A's land, a
purchaser from A would take free from it.".[9]

In *Celsteel*, SCOTT J also rejected counsel's argument that, as nothing in the
Land Registration Act 1925 *required* easements to be protected on the
register, it followed that all equitable easements were overriding interests.
He preferred to interpret "required to be protected" as "needed to be
protected", with the result that only those easements which did not need to
be protected on the register came within paragraph (*a*): "the most obvious
example would be equitable easements which qualified for protection under
paragraph (*g*) as part of the rights of a person in actual occupation".[10]

The result of this case then is that an equitable easement is an overriding
interest if the owner of it exercises it at the time that the servient land is
transferred or if he is in actual occupation of the servient land; otherwise the

4 See Law Commission Working Paper: Land Registration No. 37 (1971), para. 35; Ruoff and
   Roper, para. 6–06; Barnsley, *Conveyancing Law and Practice* (3rd edn), pp. 48–49; Farrand
   (2nd edn), pp. 188–190.
5 [1985] 1 WLR 204, [1985] 2 All ER 562; M & B p. 702; [1986] Conv 31 (M. P. Thompson).
6 R. 258 was incorporated into the Act by LRA 1925, s. 144 (2). It was held that this was not
   ultra vires, in spite of its being in wider terms than the Act.
7 P. 534, ante.
8 Under LRR 1925, r. 251, p. 580, ante.
9 Law Commission Working Paper on Land Registration (Second Paper) 1971 (No. 37), para.
   48.
10 At 220, at 575.

easement will be overridden by a transfer for value, unless it is protected on the register.[11]

In 1987 the Law Commission recommended that equitable easements should no longer be overriding interests.[12]

SECTION VI LAW REFORM COMMITTEE REPORT ON ACQUISITION OF EASEMENTS AND PROFITS BY PRESCRIPTION[13]

In *Tehidy Minerals Ltd v Norman* BUCKLEY LJ said:[14]

> The co-existence of three separate methods of prescribing is, in our view, anomalous and undesirable, for it results in much unnecessary complication and confusion. We hope that it may be possible for the Legislature to effect a long-overdue simplification in this branch of the law.

In 1966 the Law Reform Committee recommended the abolition of the prescriptive acquisition of easements and of profits à prendre;[15] in the former case by a majority of eight to six, in the latter unanimously. The Committee, however, also considered the ways in which prescriptive acquisition—if it should be retained for easements—should operate, and was unanimous on the new system to be adopted.

The main recommendations, in brief outline, are:

(1) All existing methods of acquisition of easements and profits by prescription should be abolished. This recommendation includes the abolition of prescription at common law and under the doctrine of a lost modern grant, and the repeal of the Prescription Act 1832.[16]

(2) The following method should be adopted, if it were decided to substitute a new system for easements only:[17]

(*a*) The prescriptive period should be a period in gross of 12 years (i.e., it need not be "next before action brought").[18]

(*b*) There should be no "disabilities".[19]

(*c*) An easement should be capable of being acquired against the owner of a limited interest in the servient land so as to subsist as long as that

11 LRA 1925, ss. 49 (1) (*f*), 54 (1).
12 Third Report on Land Registration A. Overriding Interests (Law Com No. 158, HC 269), para. 2.33. See [1987] Conv 328 (A. M. Prichard).
13 Fourteenth Report (1966) Cmnd. 3100. See Jackson, chapter 15; (1967) 30 MLR 189 (H. W. Wilkinson); M & B pp. 705–707.
  In 1971 the Law Commission Working Paper on Rights Appurtenant to Land (No. 36) suggested that "easements and covenants should be assimilated along lines hitherto regarded as appropriate to easements" (para. 9) and, in relation to prescription, "as at present advised we are inclined to agree in principle with the majority, but only on the basis that some alternative to prescription can be found. In the meantime it will be assumed that prescription will continue" (para. 99). It should be reformed along the lines recommended by the Law Reform Committee (Proposition 10). For further criticism of the Prescription Act 1832, see Holdsworth, *Historical Introduction to the Land Law*, pp. 284–6; *History of English Law*, vol. vii. pp. 350–62; Simpson, *A History of the Land Law* (2nd edn), pp. 266–269; Underhill, *Century of Law Reform*, p. 308.
14 [1971] QB 528 at 543, [1971] 2 All ER 475 at 484.
15 Paras. 32, 98.
16 Paras. 40, 98, 99 (1)–(3).
17 Para. 99 (6).
18 Paras. 41–43. Prescription Act 1832, s. 4.
19 Para. 44. Prescription Act 1832, ss. 7, 8.

servient owner's interest subsists.[20] Prescription by the owner of a limited interest in the dominant land should continue, as at present, in favour of the freeholder.[1] A tenant should be able to prescribe against his landlord and vice versa.[2]

(*d*) Enjoyment:

    (i) by force should not count in favour of the dominant owner;[3]

    (ii) must have been actually known to the servient owner or ought reasonably to have been known to him;[4]

    (iii) must be of such a kind and frequency as would only be justified by the existence of an easement;[5]

    (iv) by consent or agreement, whether written or oral, should not count. If so enjoyed for one year or more, the consent, like an interruption, would prevent earlier enjoyment being added to later enjoyment for the purpose of making up the required total of 12 years. A consent which is indefinite in duration should operate for one year.[6]

(*e*) Notional interruption, on the lines of the Rights of Light Act 1959, should be extended to easements generally; this should be by registration against the dominant land in the local land charges register after notice given. Interruption, notional or actual, should endure for 12 months in order to be effective.[7]

(*f*) An easement, acquired by prescription, should be lost by 12 years' continuous non-user.[8]

(3) The Committee was unanimous about provisions to facilitate, subject to compensation where appropriate, the acquisition of easements of support for buildings by land or for buildings by buildings.[9]

(4) Shelter of building by an adjoining building should be treated in the same way as support.[10]

(5) The Lands Tribunal should be empowered to discharge easements or substitute more convenient ones, subject to payment of compensation where appropriate.[11]

---

20 Paras. 47–49.
1 Para. 50.
2 Para. 51.
3 Para. 57.
4 Para. 58.
5 Para. 59.
6 Paras. 61–63.
7 As at present. Prescription Act 1832, s. 4. Paras 64–69, 75.
8 Para. 81.
9 Paras. 89–95, 99 (8)–(11).
10 Paras. 96, 99 (12); *Phipps v Pears* [1965] 1 QB 76, [1964] 2 All ER 35; M & B p. 629, p. 527, ante.
11 Paras. 97, 99 (13).

Chapter 18

Licences[1]

As we have seen, a licence is essentially a permission to enter upon the land of another for an agreed purpose.[2] The permission justifies what would otherwise have been a trespass.[3] The main issue through the years has been firstly, whether the licensee is entitled to protection against eviction by the licensor, and, if so, whether that protection is effective also against third party transferees from the licensor, not being bona fide purchasers of a legal estate for value without notice. In both these issues, the availability of equitable remedies after the passing of the Judicature Act 1875 played an important part, and developments in recent years have revolutionized the position of the licensee. These come from the recognition, as relevant and applicable in this field, of the doctrine of proprietary estoppel, under which a licensee may be entitled, not only to protection from eviction, but also to a transfer of the interest or estate in the land which the licensor, by his acts or statements, had led the licensee to expect to receive.[4] Further, licensees have been protected by finding that a constructive trust arises in their favour, and this jurisdiction to find a constructive trust has been widened and developed in recent cases.[5]

The facts in the cases will show the wide variety of circumstances in which questions of the protection of licensees can arise. They range from a visit to the grandstand at Doncaster race-course in 1845 to the provision of a house

---

1 See generally M & B, chapter 9; Dawson and Pearce, *Licences Relating to the Occupation or Use of Land*; (1954) 70 LQR 326 (Lord EVERSHED).
2 P. 529, ante.
3 *Thomas v Sorrell* (1673) Vaugh 330 at 351, per VAUGHAN CJ.
4 Pp. 595, et seq, post.
5 Pp. 592, et seq, post.

for a mistress in more modern times. The courts have been astute to adapt the law of licences to solve problems arising from the occupation of a quasi-matrimonial home.

SECTION I THE LICENSEE AT COMMON LAW

Licences at common law may be divided into three categories:

(1) BARE OR GRATUITOUS LICENCE

A bare or gratuitous licence is a mere permission for the licensee to enter upon the licensor's land, as for instance when permission is given to play cricket on a field. As we shall see, this permission may be withdrawn at any time by the licensor.

(2) LICENCE COUPLED WITH A GRANT OR INTEREST

A licence coupled with a grant or interest, on the other hand, may be irrevocable. It is said to be *coupled with a grant or interest* when the licensee, having been granted a definite proprietary interest in the land or in chattels lying on the land, is given permission to enter in order that he may enjoy or exploit the interest. Such a licence, as distinct from a *bare* licence, is of this nature if given to a man who is entitled to chattels,[6] or to growing timber[7] or to game on the land.[8] There are here two separate matters—the grant and the licence.

> But a licence to hunt in a man's park and to carry away the deer killed to his own use; to cut down a tree in a man's ground and to carry it away the next day after to his own use, are licences as to the acts of hunting and cutting down the tree; but as to the carrying away of the deer killed and the tree cut they are grants.[9]

Such a licence is not effective at common law unless the grant is formally valid. Thus a grant merely by writing of a right to shoot and carry away game, coupled with a licence to enter the land, is ineffective, since a deed is necessary at common law for the grant of a *profit à prendre*.[10] But the rule in equity, which now prevails and which is illustrated in another context by *Walsh v Lonsdale*,[11] is that a contract to grant an interest is treated as if the formalities required by law had been observed. Thus a contract to grant a right of shooting over land is specifically enforceable and as between the parties is as effective as an actual grant by way of deed;[12] to be enforceable against third parties, it must be registered as a land charge under the Land Charges Act 1972.[13] Equity may grant an injunction to the licensee to present the licensor from revoking the licence so long as the term of the grant of the ancillary interest continues.

6 *Wood v Manley* (1839) 11 Ad & El 34.
7 *James Jones & Sons Ltd v Earl of Tankerville* [1909] 2 Ch 440.
8 *Frogley v Earl of Lovelace* (1859) John 333. See also *Vaughan v Hampson* (1875) 33 LT 15 (right of solicitor to attend a creditors' meeting), described as a "curiosity" in *Hounslow London Borough Council v Twickenham Garden Developments Ltd* [1971] Ch 233 at 254, [1970] 3 All ER 326 at 343.
9 *Thomas v Sorrell* (1673) Vaugh 330 at 551, per VAUGHAN CJ.
10 *Wood v Leadbitter* (1845) 13 M & W 838; M & B p. 535.
11 Pp. 376, ante.
12 *Hurst v Picture Theatres Ltd* [1915] 1 KB 1; M & B p. 535; *Frogley v Earl of Lovelace*, supra.
13 P. 759, post.

(3) CONTRACTUAL LICENCE

A contractual licence is a licence supported by consideration, as for instance where the licensee buys a ticket for a race meeting or a theatre,[14] or where he is contractually entitled to the exclusive privilege of supplying refreshment in a theatre.[15]

In considering the effect of these licences as between licensor and licensee, common law drew a distinction between a mere licence, whether gratuitous or contractual, and a licence coupled with a grant.[16] We have seen that a licence coupled with a grant may be irrevocable. On the other hand a mere licence may, at common law, be revoked at any moment, and it was held[17] that this was so even where the licensee had entered by contract, and the revocation of the licence by the licensor was in breach of contract. The licensee became a trespasser, and liable to be evicted. He had to be satisfied with a financial remedy for breach of contract.[18]

SECTION II THE INTERVENTION OF EQUITY. REMEDIES

The tide turned with the availability of equitable remedies after 1875. In *Hurst v Picture Theatres Ltd*:[19]

> the plaintiff purchased a ticket[20] to attend the cinema. The proprietors, erroneously thinking that Hurst had not paid for the ticket, evicted him, using no more force than was reasonably necessary. Hurst successfully sued for damages for assault.

The matter was authoritatively settled by the House of Lords in *Winter Garden Theatre (London) Ltd v Millennium Productions Ltd*.[1] This case finally established that the rights of the parties to a contractual licence must be determined upon the proper construction of the contract. Their Lordships favoured the argument that, if on its construction a contractual licence is irrevocable, then, even though it is not coupled with a grant, its revocation in breach of the contract should be prevented where possible[2] by the grant of

---

14 *Wood v Leadbitter*, supra; *Hurst v Picture Theatres Ltd*, supra.

15 *Frank Warr & Co Ltd v LCC* [1904] 1 KB 713.

16 For a doctrine of long standing, but little relied on, that a licence is irrevocable if it has been acted on, see *Webb v Paternoster* (1619) Palm 71; *Hounslow London Borough Council v Twickenham Garden Developments Ltd* [1971] Ch 233 at 255, [1970] 3 All ER 326 at 344; (1965) 29 Conv (NS) 19 (M. C. Cullity).

17 *Wood v Leadbitter*, supra; *Thompson v Park* [1944] KB 408, [1944] 2 All ER 477.

18 *Kerrison v Smith* [1897] 2 QB 445; *Tanner v Tanner* [1975] 1 WLR 1346, [1975] 3 All ER 776, p. 588, post.

19 Supra. See also *Cowell v Rosehill Racecourse Co Ltd* (1937) 56 CLR 605; M & B p. 536.

20 For 6d.

 1 [1948] AC 173, [1947] 2 All ER 331; M & B p. 540; for a critique of this case, see *Hounslow London Borough Council v Twickenham Garden Developments Ltd*, supra at 245 et seq, at 335 et seq; (1971) 87 LQR 309; *Mayfield Holdings Ltd v Moana Reef Ltd* [1973] 1 NZLR 309.

 2 *Thompson v Park* [1944] KB 408, [1944] 2 All ER 477 (where an injunction was refused to a licensee who "had been guilty at least of riot, affray, wilful damage, forcible entry and, perhaps, conspiracy", per GODDARD LJ at 409); *Brynowen Estates Ltd v Bourne* (1981) 131 NLJ 1212; cf. *Williams v Staite* [1979] Ch 291, [1978] 2 All ER 928 (effect of misbehaviour by estoppel licensee); *J Willis & Sons v Willis* [1986] 1 EGLR 62, p. 602, post. See also *Ivory v Palmer* [1975] ICR 340 (licensee, whose occupation of premises was dependent on his employment, not protected when dismissed in breach of contract).

an injunction.[3] In other words, equity does what it can by means of a decree of injunction to preserve the sanctity of a bargain[4] and by that remedy it is prepared to restrain a revocation that would derogate from the right of occupation conferred by the contract. If the contract does not expressly state the time for which the licence is to last, a promise by the licensor must be implied that he will not revoke the permission in a manner contrary to the intention of the parties.[5] The exact scope of the implied promise, if any, must be ascertained in each case, for it will, of course, vary with the circumstances. For instance a spectator who buys a ticket for a theatre is a licensee with a right to occupy his seat until the spectacle is over;[6] a licence of the "front of the house rights" at a theatre cannot be revoked until a reasonable time has been afforded to the licensee for his withdrawal.[7] In those cases such as *Hurst v Picture Theatres Ltd*, where there is no time or opportunity to obtain an injunction, the court will presumably give judgment on the basis of what the rights of the parties would have been, had the grant of this remedy been practicable.

The injunction will last for the period of the contract or for such other period as the court thinks appropriate. The situation is simpler where, as in the *Winter Garden* case, there is an express contract. But the courts have, in some recent cases, including family or "mistress" situations, found the existence of a contractual licence where the evidence of the contract was of the flimsiest. Indeed, in *Tanner v Tanner,*[8] where the mistress had vacated the premises in obedience to an order of the lower court, and an injunction would have been sterile, Lord DENNING went so far as to say that the court should "imply a contract by him . . . or if need be impose the equivalent of a contract by him".[9] Similarly, in *Hardwick v Johnson*[10] and *Chandler v Kerley*[11] contractual licences were found, though, in the former, Lord DENNING would have preferred to find a licence by estoppel. In *Chandler v Kerley*:

Mr and Mrs K jointly purchased a house intending it to be their matrimonial home,

---

3 The House of Lords construed the licence as being revocable by the licensor, and so their views were obiter. The Court of Appeal, however, had construed it as irrevocable and had protected the licensee by granting an injunction against the licensor: [1946] 1 All ER 678 at 684, per Lord GREENE MR; M & B p. 541. For a full discussion of contractual licences, see MEGARRY J in *Hounslow London Borough Council v Twickenham Garden Developments Ltd* supra, where this approach was followed.
4 *Winter Garden Theatre (London) Ltd v Millennium Productions Ltd*, supra, at 202, at 343 per Lord UTHWATT.
5 *Errington v Errington and Woods* [1952] 1 KB 290 [1952] 1 All ER 149; M & B p. 551.
6 *Hurst v Picture Theatres Ltd* [1915] 1 KB 1.
7 *Winter Garden Theatre (London) Ltd v Millennium Productions Ltd*, supra.
8 [1975] 1 WLR 1346, [1975] 3 All ER 776; M & B p. 538; cf *Horrocks v Forray* [1976] 1 WLR 230, [1976] 1 All ER 737, where no contract was implied in similar circumstances (described in (1976) 40 Conv (NS) 362 (M. Richards) as "*Tanner v Tanner* in a middle class setting"); *Coombes v Smith* [1986] 1 WLR 808, p. 600, n. 18, post (no contract implied that man would provide mistress with house for rest of her life).
9 At 1350, at 780.
10 [1978] 1 WLR 683, [1978] 2 All ER 935; M & B p. 546 (where mother purchased house for son and his bride, who were to pay her £7 a week; on breakdown of marriage son left bride now pregnant for another woman. Mother sued for possession. Daughter-in-law held entitled to protection as contractual licensee for indefinite period on payment of £7 a week).
11 [1978] 1 WLR 693, [1978] 2 All ER 942; M & B p. 542. See also *Roach v Johannes* [1976] CLY 1549 (licence of "paying guest" terminable on giving reasonable notice, which in the circumstances was not less than 21 days); *Piquet v Tyler* [1978] CLY 119 (irrevocable licence for life of defendants, who had, by arrangement with plaintiff, surrendered protected tenancy to look after plaintiff's aged mother).

the mortgage payments being made by Mr K. On the breakdown of the marriage, Mr K left, never to return, and Mrs K remained with their two children. She became the mistress of C, who moved into the house with her. Mr K then ceased to pay the mortgage instalments, and Mrs K and he tried without success to sell the house for £14,300. Finally C purchased it from them for £10,000, out of which the mortgagee was repaid and the balance divided between Mr and Mrs K. Six weeks later C terminated the relationship with Mrs K and claimed possession of the house. Mrs K claimed that she was a licensee for life or for so long as the children remained in her custody. The Court of Appeal held that she was a contractual licensee for a period terminable on twelve months' notice.

It is possible even for the contractual licensee to obtain specific performance of the contractual licence. In *Verrall v Great Yarmouth Borough Council*:[12]

The Conservative council granted a licence to the National Front to hold its annual conference at the Wellington Pier Pavilion for £6,000. After the local government elections, the new Labour council purported to revoke the licence.

In granting specific performance of the contractual licence, Lord DENNING MR said:[13]

Since the *Winter Garden* case, it is clear that once a man has entered under his contract of licence, he cannot be turned out. An injunction can be obtained against the licensor to prevent his being turned out. On principle it is the same if it happens before he enters. If he has a contractual right to enter, and the licensor refuses to let him come in, then he can come to the court and in a proper case get an order for specific performance to allow him to come in.

SECTION III CONTRACTUAL LICENCES AND THIRD PARTIES

Once the courts gave protection to a contractual licensee, the next question inevitably arose—whether that protection was good against a third party, not being a bona fide purchaser of a legal estate for value without notice. On the one hand, protection of a licensee may be of little value if the licensor can defeat him by transfer to a third party. On the other hand, protection of the licensee against third parties goes a long way towards the recognition of a licence as an interest in land.

A bare licence is revocable by the licensor at any time, but the licensee cannot be treated as a trespasser until a reasonable time after notice that the licence has been or will be withdrawn.[14] It clearly, therefore, does not bind his successors in title. If, however, the licence is coupled with a grant or interest, it is irrevocable by the licensor. If the interest granted is legal, it binds any successor in title; if it is equitable, as for instance where there is a

---

12 [1981] QB 202, [1980] 1 All ER 839; M & B p. 547. For the reasons given by the court for exercising its discretion to grant specific performance in the interests of freedom of speech, see at 216–18, at 844–5.

13 At 216, at 844.

14 *Minister of Health v Bellotti* [1944] KB 298, [1944] 1 All ER 238; *Greater London Council v Jenkins* [1975] 1 WLR 155 at 158, [1975] 1 All ER 354, at 357, per Lord DIPLOCK; *Canadian Pacific Rly Co v R* [1931] AC 414; *Australian Blue Metal Ltd v Hughes* [1963] AC 74, [1962] 3 All ER 335; *Wallshire Ltd v Advertising Sites Ltd* [1988] 2 EGLR 167; *Express Newspapers plc v Silverstone Circuits Ltd* (1989) Times, 20 June (right to place advertisements on bridge at Woodcote Corner). For the abandonment of a licence, see *Bone v Bone* [1992] EGCS 81 (no formalities are necessary: "it is enough that the parties have so conducted themselves that it ought to be inferred that they have mutually agreed to bring the contract to an end").

contract to grant in writing, which is not executed as a deed, the interest, and with it the licence, binds all successors in title except a bona fide purchaser of the legal estate without notice from the licensor. Such a contract, however, is registrable under section 2(4) of the Land Charges Act 1972, and, if not registered, will be void against a purchaser of a legal estate in the land for money or money's worth.[15]

The main controversy has been in relation to contractual licences and third parties. On principle, a contract between A and B is not capable of imposing a burden on C.[16] Nor is it an answer to say that, on the principle of *Tulk v Moxhay*,[17] the fact that A has a right to an injunction against B to restrain revocation, gives him also a right to an injunction against C, not being a bona fide purchaser of a legal estate for value without notice. That, indeed, was the early view of *Tulk v Moxhay*, but was found to be impracticable in the real property cases,[18] and was never applied in cases relating to chattels.[19] The injunction is available against a third party only in cases where policy considerations justify it. And, while there may be compelling cases in the field of contractual licences, a rule that every contractual licence is binding on third parties, not being bona fide purchasers of a legal estate for value without notice, would cause serious difficulties.

Authority is to the same effect. In *King v David Allen & Sons, Billposting Ltd*:[20]

> the licensor gave to the licensee an exclusive permission to affix advertisements to the walls of a cinema. Later the licensor granted a lease of the cinema to a cinema company, but the lease contained no reference to the licence. When the company refused to allow the advertisements to be affixed to the building, the licensee brought an action against the licensor for breach of contract. The liability of the licensor depended on whether the lease to the company had deprived the licensee of his contractual right to affix advertisements. The House of Lords held that it had, and therefore the action for damages succeeded.

There are, however, two cases which are quoted as authority for the proposition that contractual licences are binding on third parties, in one case a volunteer devisee,[1] and in the other a purchaser who took the premises "expressly subject" to the contract.[2]

---

15 LCA 1972, s. 4 (6), p. 764, post.
16 *Tweddle v Atkinson* (1861) 1 B & S 393; *Dunlop Pneumatic Tyre Co Ltd v Selfridge & Co Ltd* [1915] AC 847; *Beswick v Beswick* [1968] AC 58, [1967] 2 All ER 1197; *Woodar Investment Development Ltd v Wimpey Construction (UK) Ltd* [1980] 1 WLR 277, [1980] 1 All ER 571; Cheshire, Fifoot and Furmston, *Law of Contract* (12th edn, 1991), chapter 14; Treitel, *Law of Contract* (8th edn, 1991), chapter 15. See Law Commission Consultation Paper No. 121: Privity of Contract: Contracts for the Benefit of Third Parties (1991).
17 (1848) 2 Ph 774; chapter 19, p. 609, post.
18 *Formby v Barker* [1903] 2 Ch 539; *LCC v Allen* [1914] 3 KB 642, p. 617, post.
19 *De Mattos v Gibson* (1859) 4 De G & J 276; *Lord Strathcona SS Co Ltd v Dominion Coal Co Ltd* [1926] AC 108; *Port Line Ltd v Ben Line Steamers Ltd* [1958] 2 QB 146, [1958] 1 All ER 787; *Law Debenture Trust Corpn plc v Ural Caspian Oil Corpn Ltd* [1993] 1 WLR 138, [1993] 2 All ER 355. See, however, *Swiss Bank Corpn v Lloyds Bank Ltd* [1979] Ch 548 at 569–575, [1979] 2 All ER 853 at 869–874; revsd on different grounds [1982] AC 584, [1981] 2 All ER 449; (1982) 98 LQR 279 (S. Gardner).
20 [1916] 2 AC 54; M & B p. 549. See also *Clore v Theatrical Properties Ltd and Westby & Co Ltd* [1936] 3 All ER 483.
 1 *Errington v Errington and Woods* [1952] 1 KB 290, [1952] 1 All ER 149; M & B p. 551.
 2 *Binions v Evans* [1972] Ch 359, [1972] 2 All ER 70; M & B p. 555.

In *Errington v Errington and Woods*:

A father bought a house for £750. He paid £250 in cash and borrowed £500 from a building society, the loan being secured by a mortgage of the house and repayable by instalments of fifteen shillings a week. He allowed his son and daughter-in-law to go into possession and told them that if they paid all the instalments he would convey the legal estate to them. They paid the instalments as they became due, but the payments were not all completed when the father died nine years later having devised the house to his widow. The son then left his wife, but the latter remained in occupation of the house and continued to pay the instalments.

An action brought by the widow for possession against the daughter-in-law was dismissed. The Court of Appeal held that the son and daughter-in-law were neither tenants at will nor weekly tenants, but licensees entitled to occupy the house as long as they paid the instalments. This licence was binding upon the licensor's devisee.

Substantially, the reasoning adopted by the court was that, since the son and daughter-in-law were entitled in equity to restrain the revocation of the licence contrary to the terms of the implied contract, they acquired in effect an equitable interest, or at least an equity[3] in the land that was capable of binding third parties, as in the case of a restrictive covenant.[4]

The reasoning must be considered afresh in the light of *National Provincial Bank Ltd v Ainsworth*,[5] in which Lord UPJOHN and Lord WILBERFORCE in the House of Lords and RUSSELL LJ in the Court of Appeal showed their reluctance to regard the contractual licensee as possessing more than a personal right. RUSSELL LJ, in particular, resisted the view that this personal right is converted into some form of equitable interest binding on third parties merely because the licensor may be restrained from revoking his permission.[6]

In *Binions v Evans*[7] a contractual licence was enforced against a purchaser who took a conveyance of land expressly subject to a licence, having in consequence paid a reduced price:

Mrs Evans was the widow of an employee of the Tredegar Estate. In 1968 the Estate entered into a written agreement with her under which she was permitted to reside in a cottage on the Estate for the remainder of her life free of rent and rates. She agreed to keep the cottage in a proper manner. In 1970 the Estate sold and conveyed it to the plantiffs expressly subject to the agreement. The plaintiffs paid a reduced price because of this. Six months later they claimed possession of the cottage.

The Court of Appeal unanimously held that Mrs Evans was protected, but differed in their reasons. MEGAW and STEPHENSON LJJ held that the

3 P. 60, ante.
4 This reasoning was defended by G. C. Cheshire in (1953) 16 MLR 1; but rejected in (1952) 68 LQR 337 (H. W. R. Wade). For an attack on the decision from a different angle, see (1953) 69 LQR 466 (A. D. Hargreaves). See also *Re Solomon* [1967] Ch 573 at 582–6, [1966] 3 All ER 255 at 259–61, per GOFF J. The decision may be sustainable on the principle of estoppel by acquiescence; pp. 595 et seq, post.
5 [1965] AC 1175, [1965] 2 All ER 472, rejecting the so-called "deserted wife's equity", p. 603, post. The decision gave rise to the Matrimonial Homes Act 1967, now Matrimonial Homes Act 1983, p. 241, ante.
6 [1964] Ch 665 at 698.
7 [1972] Ch 359, [1972] 2 All ER 70; M & B p. 555; (1972) 88 LQR 336 (P. V. B.); (1972) 36 Conv (NS) 266 (J. Martin), 277 (D. J. Hayton); (1973) CLJ 123 (R. J. Smith); (1973) 117 SJ 23 (B. W. Harvey); (1977) 93 LQR 561 (J. A. Hornby).

agreement conferred a life interest and that Mrs Evans was a tenant for life under the Settled Land Act 1925.[8] Lord DENNING, however, held that the plaintiffs were bound by Mrs Evans's contractual licence, saying, firstly, that the plaintiffs, having purchased *expressly subject* to the rights of Mrs Evans, could not ignore them; and, secondly, on the wider ground that the contractual licence created a constructive trust which bound the plaintiffs to permit her to reside in the cottage during her life or as long as she wished. It is submitted that the former view is preferable. It is difficult to see how the wider view is consistent with earlier authority on contractual licences, and the expressions of opinion in the House of Lords in *National Provincial Bank Ltd v Ainsworth*.

Clearly these cases provide no support for the view that contractual licences generally are binding on third parties.[9] Moreover in *Ashburn Anstalt v Arnold*[10] the Court of Appeal has recently held, obiter, that, where land was conveyed to a purchaser expressly "subject to" a contractual licence, the licence was not a property interest and therefore not enforceable against the third party. In rejecting the wide implications of *Errington v Errington and Woods* and *Binions v Evans*, FOX LJ emphasised that there was no other case in which a contractual licence had been held to bind a third party in the absence of a finding that the third party took the land as a constructive trustee:

> The far-reaching statement of principle in *Errington* was not supported by authority, not necessary for the decision of the case and *per incuriam* in the sense that it was made without reference to authorities which, if they would not have compelled, would surely have persuaded the court to adopt a different ratio. Of course, the law must be free to develop. But as a response to problems which had arisen, the *Errington* rule (without more) was neither practically necessary nor theoretically convincing. By contrast, the finding on appropriate facts of a constructive trust may well be regarded as a beneficial adaptation of old rules to new situations.[11]

SECTION IV CONSTRUCTIVE TRUST

We have seen that gratuitous licences and contractual licences do not of themselves constitute interests in land, and so do not bind third parties. The analysis of a person's occupation of land as constituting a gratuitous or contractual licence does not however preclude the finding that some other interest has also been created which is an interest in land and which is therefore capable of binding a third party. In particular, the courts will

---

8 Following *Bannister v Bannister* [1948] 2 All ER 133, infra. This is not without difficulty, p 604, n. 8, post. MEGAW LJ also suggested at 371, at 78, that the plaintiffs would be guilty of the tort of interference with existing contractual rights if they were to evict the defendant; (1977) 41 Conv (NS) 318 (R. J. Smith).

9 Nor does *Midland Bank Ltd v Farmpride Hatcheries Ltd* (1980) 260 EG 493, where the issue was not raised; p. 63, n. 9, ante.

10 [1989] Ch 1, [1988] 2 All ER 147; M & B p. 550. The case was decided against the purchaser on the ground that the agreement created a tenancy which was binding on him; p. 363, ante. See also *Patel v Patel* (1983) unreported, where SLADE LJ said: "A mere licence to occupy land, albeit of a contractual nature, as opposed to a lease, does not confer any interest on the licensee in the land".

11 At 22, at 164.

consider whether the person is in occupation of the land pursuant to a constructive trust or an estoppel licence.[12]

A few cases have been decided on the basis of a constructive trust. Such a trust arises by operation of law when the court is of the opinion that it is in the interests of justice or for the prevention of unjust enrichment that such a trust should be found.[13]

The first, *Bannister v Bannister*,[14] could more appropriately have been treated as a licence by estoppel;[15] but licences by estoppel had not generally been recognized in 1948. In that case:

> the defendant, who owned two cottages, sold them in 1943 to her brother-in-law, the plaintiff, for £250 (which was £150 below market price). They made an oral agreement under which the brother-in-law would let her stay in one of the cottages "as long as you like, rent free". In 1945 the defendant gave up possession of the cottage except for one room. In 1947 the plaintiff claimed possession of the room on the ground that she was a tenant at will.

The defendant was unable to rely on an express trust, because that was required to be in writing.[16] The Court of Appeal, however, held that it would be a fraud to disregard the oral trust and that she was entitled under a constructive trust to a life interest determinable upon her ceasing to reside in the cottage.

Re Sharpe[17] could likewise have been treated as a licence by estoppel. In that case:

> an elderly aunt lent money to her nephew to purchase and improve a house on the understanding that she would live there and be looked after by the nephew and his wife for the rest of her life. The aunt moved in, and the nephew went bankrupt. His trustee in bankruptcy then entered into a contract to sell the house with vacant possession to a purchaser, and sought to recover possession of the house from the aunt.

In holding that the aunt was entitled under a constructive trust as against the trustee to remain in the house until she was repaid[18] the sums she advanced, BROWNE-WILKINSON J said:

> In my judgment, whether it be called a contractual licence or an equitable licence or an interest under a constructive trust, the aunt would be entitled as against the

---

12 In *Ashburn Anstalt v Arnold*, supra, for example, the Court of Appeal held that the contractual licence did not create an interest in land; they went on however to consider whether the facts also gave rise to a constructive trust, which would have created such an interest. They found that, on the facts, there was no constructive trust.

13 See generally Oakley, *Constructive Trusts* (2nd edn), chapter 11, H & M pp. 326–330, M & B, *Trusts and Trustees*, chapter 7; *Snell's Equity* (29th edn), pp. 192–197; Underhill and Hayton, *Law of Trusts and Trustees* (14th edn), chapter 7, especially pp. 325–31.

14 [1948] 2 All ER 133; M & B p. 554; *Hussey v Palmer* [1972] 1 WLR 1286, [1972] 3 All ER 744.

15 P. 595, post.

16 LPA 1925, s. 53(1); p. 773, post.

17 [1980] 1 WLR 219, [1980] 1 All ER 198; M & B p. 608; [1980] Conv 207 (J. Martin); 96 LQR 336 (G. Woodman). In *Bristol and West Building Society v Henning* [1985] 1 WLR 778, [1985] 2 All ER 606; p. 597, n. 3, post, BROWNE-WILKINSON LJ said at 783, at 610, that "nothing in this judgment should be taken as expressing any view on the question . . . whether the decision in *Re Sharpe* was correct."

18 The purchaser was not a party to the action, and it was left open whether he was also bound.

nephew to stay in the house ... The introduction of a constructive trust is an essential ingredient if the plaintiff has any right at all.[19]

In *Hussey v Palmer*[20] and *Binions v Evans*[1] (where the constructive trust was relied on as a second ground) the constructive trust was described as an available remedy in the widest terms. Such a remedy is both too wide and too severe. "The dicta are ... certainly fine sounding, but one needs more guidance as to when such trusts will be implied."[2]

In *Ashburn Anstalt v Arnold*[3] the Court of Appeal took the view that the mere fact that land is expressed to be conveyed "subject to" a contract does not necessarily imply that the grantee is to be under an obligation, not otherwise existing, to give effect to the provisions of the contract:

> The Court will not impose a constructive trust unless it is satisfied that the conscience of the estate owner is affected ... The words "subject to" will, of course, impose notice. But notice is not enough to impose on somebody an obligation to give effect to a contract into which he did not enter.[4]

Binions v Evans was regarded as a legitimate application of the doctrine of constructive trusts, since the facts that the Tredegar Estate provided the purchasers with a copy of the agreement with Mrs Evans, and that the purchasers paid a reduced purchase price, indicated that the intention of the Estate and the purchasers was that the purchasers should give effect to Mrs Evans's agreement. If they had failed to do so, the Estate would have been liable in damages to Mrs Evans.[5]

The remedy of the constructive trust is also too severe. For it creates, in this situation, undocumented proprietary interests in land, and they can cause difficulties for the conveyancing system. If the constructive trust creates an equitable fee simple, it will be one which is not registrable, though it may

---

19 See *Re Basham* [1986] 1 WLR 1498 at 1504, [1987] 1 All ER 405 at 410; M & B p. 612, where Edward NUGEE QC, in holding that a claim for proprietary estoppel succeeded, treated it "as giving rise to a species of constructive trust"; [1981] Conv 211 (J. Martin); [1987] CLJ 215 (D. Hayton). See also Sir Christopher SLADE's Child & Co Oxford Lecture 1984 on *The Informal Creation of Interests in Land* at p. 12.

20 [1972] 1 WLR 1286, [1973] 3 All ER 744 (elderly widow, invited to live with daughter and son-in-law, paid cost of extra bedroom built onto house for her accommodation; held entitled to recover money when she left). See also *DHN Food Distributors Ltd v Tower Hamlets London Borough Council* [1976] 1 WLR 852, [1976] 3 All ER 462 (irrevocable contractual licence which gave rise to constructive trust, under which DHN had "a sufficient interest in the land to qualify them for disturbance" upon compulsory purchase by local authority); (1977) 93 LQR 170 (D. Sugarman and F. Webb); (1977) 41 Conv (NS) 73; *Sparkes v Smart* [1990] 2 EGLR 245 (collusive transaction between purchaser of freehold farm and ageing tenant, purchaser's father-in-law, with object of destroying youngest son's tenancy; CA held obiter constructive trust in favour of the son).

1 Supra.

2 [1973] CLJ p. 142 (R. J. Smith).

3 [1989] Ch 1, [1988] 2 All ER 147; M & B, p. 550. The Appeal Committee dismissed a petition for leave to appeal [1989] Ch 32; [1988] CLJ 353 (A. J. Oakley); 104 LQR 175 (P. Sparkes); 51 MLR 226 (J. Hill); Conv 201 (M. P. Thompson); All ER Rev 176 (P. J. Clarke).

4 At 25, per FOX LJ. See also *IDC Group Ltd v Clark* [1992] 1 EGLR 187, where Sir Nicolas BROWNE-WILKINSON V-C said at 189: "The Court of Appeal put what I hope is the *quietus* to the heresy that a mere licence creates an interest in land. They also put the *quietus* to the heresy that parties to a contractual licence necessarily become constructive trustees". A purchaser may, however, make a bargain with the vendor that he undertakes *de novo* to honour existing contractual obligations: ibid., at p. 190, approving the analysis of DILLON J in *Lyus v Prowsa Developments Ltd* [1982] 1 WLR 1044, [1982] 2 All ER 953.

5 In *Ashburn Anstalt v Arnold* the purchaser had not paid a reduced price, nor would the licensor have been liable in damages to the licensee.

be overreachable;[6] and if it creates an interest for life, it may bring the provisions of the Settled Land Act 1925 into operation. The problem will be discussed in more detail below,[7] where it will be seen that a similar problem arises on the application of the doctrine of proprietary estoppel.

SECTION V LICENCES BY ESTOPPEL[8]

A. THE DOCTRINE

The development of the doctrine of estoppel in the context of licences over the past 30 years has been remarkable. The general principle is that an estoppel arises where one party (A) makes a representation or promise to another party (B), intending B to act in reliance on the representation or promise, and B does so act to his detriment. A is estopped from acting inconsistently with his representation or promise. If A is the licensor and B the licensee, there is a compelling case for the intervention of equity to protect the licensee. Estoppel by representation is ancient. Early authority can be found for promissory estoppel,[9] but it was not generally recognized until the *High Trees* case in 1947.[10]

There is also an equitable doctrine of "encouragement and acquiescence" which has recently been treated as a type of estoppel and is now called proprietary estoppel. The early cases deal almost exclusively with situations in which a landlord encouraged the occupier of his land to believe that the latter held under a lease.[11] The principle was explained in a well-known and generally accepted dictum in a dissenting speech of Lord KINGSDOWN:[12]

> If a man, under a verbal agreement with a landlord for a certain interest in land, or, what amounts to the same thing, under an expectation, created or encouraged by the landlord, that he shall have a certain interest, takes possession of such land, with the consent of the landlord, and upon the faith of such promise or expectation, with the knowledge of the landlord, and without objection by him, lays out money upon the land, a court of equity will compel the landlord to give effect to such promise or expectation.

In *Willmott v Barber*[13] FRY J set out the requirements in more detail:

> It has been said that the acquiescence which will deprive a man of his legal rights must amount to fraud, and in my view that is an abbreviated statement of a very

---

6 See *Hodgson v Marks* [1971] Ch 892, [1971] 2 All ER 684.
7 P. 602, post.
8 Finn, *Essays in Equity* (1985), pp. 59–94; Spencer Bower and Turner, *Estoppel by Representation* (3rd edn) passim, and especially chapter 12; Dawson and Pearce, pp.29–36, 97–9, 144–5, 161–3; Snell, pp. 568–579; [1981] Conv 347 (P. N. Todd); [1983] CLJ 257 (M. P. Thompson); (1986) 49 MLR 741 (J. Dewar); (1984) 100 LQR 376 (S. Moriarty); Sir Christopher SLADE, *The Informal Creation of Interests in Land* (1984) Child & Co Oxford Lecture; [1988] Conv 346 (P. T. Evans); [1991] Conv 36 (G. Battersby).
  On the relationship between contractual and estoppel licences, see the controversy between [1981] Conv 212; [1983] Conv 285 (A. Briggs) and [1983] Conv 50, 471 (M. P. Thompson).
9 *Hughes v Metropolitan Rly Co* (1877) 2 App Cas 439.
10 *Central London Property Trust Ltd v High Trees House Ltd* [1947] KB 130, [1956] 1 All ER 256 n; *Combe v Combe* [1951] 2 KB 215, [1951] 1 All ER 767; *A-G of Hong Kong v Humphreys Estate (Queen's Gardens) Ltd* [1987] AC 114 at 121, [1987] 2 All ER 387 at 390.
11 *Huning v Ferrers* (1710) Gilb Ch 85; *Stiles v Cowper* (1748) 3 Atk 692; *East India Co v Vincent* (1740) 2 Atk 83; *Jackson v Cator* (1800) 5 Ves 688.
12 *Ramsden v Dyson* (1866) LR 1 HL 129 at 170.
13 (1880) 15 Ch D 96 at 105–6.

true proposition. A man is not to be deprived of his legal rights unless he has acted in such a way as would make it fraudulent for him to set up those rights.

What, then, are the elements or requisites necessary to constitute fraud of that description? In the first place the plaintiff must have made a mistake as to his legal rights. Secondly, the plaintiff must have expended some money or must have done some act (not necessarily upon the defendant's land) on the faith of his mistaken belief. Thirdly, the defendant, the possessor of the legal right, must know of the existence of his own right which is inconsistent with the right claimed by the plaintiff. If he does not know of it he is in the same position as the plaintiff, and the doctrine of acquiescence is founded upon conduct with a knowledge of your legal rights. Fourthly, the defendant, the possessor of the legal right, must know of the plaintiff's mistaken belief of his rights. If he does not, there is nothing which calls upon him to assert his own rights. Lastly, the defendant, the possessor of the legal right, must have encouraged the plaintiff in his expenditure of money or in the other acts which he has done, either directly or by abstaining from asserting his legal right. Where all these elements exist, there is fraud of such a nature as will entitle the Court to restrain the possessor of the legal right from exercising it, but, in my judgment, nothing short of this will do.

These five probanda, as they have been called, have been listed and applied in some cases[14] and ignored in others. The courts have indicated that they prefer a much broader approach based on the defendant's unconscionable behaviour. In *Taylors Fashions Ltd v Liverpool Victoria Trustees Co Ltd*,[15] OLIVER J held that, contrary to the requirements of FRY J, proprietary estoppel is not restricted to cases where the defendant knows his rights, and that it is not possible to formulate strict and rigid rules:

The more recent cases indicate that the application of the *Ramsden v Dyson* principle—whether you call it proprietary estoppel, estoppel by acquiescence or estoppel by encouragement is really immaterial—requires a very much broader approach which is directed rather at ascertaining whether, in particular individual circumstances, it would be unconscionable for a party to be permitted to deny that which, knowingly, or unknowingly, he has allowed or encouraged another to assume to his detriment than to inquiring whether the circumstances can be fitted within the confines of some preconceived formula serving as a universal yardstick for every form of unconscionable behaviour.[16]

14 *E and L Berg Homes Ltd v Grey* (1979) 253 EG 473 (where the plaintiff failed because he was unable to satisfy the first and fifth requirements); *Crabb v Arun District Council* [1976] Ch 179, [1975] 3 All ER 865; M & B p. 585. See also the approval of the probanda in *Kammins Ballrooms Co Ltd v Zenith Investments (Torquay) Ltd* [1971] AC 850 at 884, [1970] 2 All ER 871 at 895, per Lord DIPLOCK, and their application in detail by Jonathan PARKER QC in *Coombes v Smith* [1986] 1 WLR 808. See also *Gloucestershire County Council v Farrow* [1983] 2 All ER 1031.
15 *Taylors Fashions Ltd v Liverpool Victoria Trustees Co Ltd* [1982] QB 133n, [1982] 1 All ER 897; M & B p. 563. OLIVER J approved at 151, at 915, the broad test (applied by CA in *Shaw v Applegate* [1977] 1 WLR 970, [1978] 1 All ER 123) of "whether in the circumstances the conduct is unconscionable without the necessity of forcing those circumstances into a Procrustean bed constructed from some unalterable criteria". The statement in the text was approved by OLIVER LJ in *Habib Bank Ltd v Habib Bank AG Zurich* [1981] 1 WLR 1265 at 1285, [1981] 2 All ER 650 at 666; (1981) 97 LQR 513. See also SCARMAN LJ in *Crabb v Arun DC* [1976] Ch 179 at 194, [1975] 3 All ER 865 at 876; M & B p. 585; MEGARRY V-C in *Appleby v Cowley* (1982) Times, 14 April; M & B p. 604; ROBERT GOFF LJ in *Amalgamated Investment and Property Co Ltd v Texas Commerce International Bank Ltd* [1982] QB 84 at 103, [1981] 1 All ER 923 at 935; affd [1982] QB 84, [1981] 3 All ER 577; (1982) 79 LSG 662 (P. Matthews); *Esso Petroleum Co Ltd v Anthony Gibbs Financial Services Ltd* (1981) 262 EG 661 at 667–668: *Pacol Ltd v Trade Lines Ltd and R/I Sif IV* [1982] 1 Lloyd's Rep 456; *Waltons Stores (Interstate) Ltd v Maher* (1988) 164 CLR 387; (1988) 104 LQR 362 (A. Duthie).
16 At 151, at 915.

The effect of this approach is that the court now regards the five probanda no longer as rigid criteria to be satisfied, but as being "guidelines which will probably prove to be the necessary and essential guidelines, to assist the court to decide the question whether it is unconscionable for the plaintiffs to assert their legal rights by taking advantage of the defendant".[17] OLIVER J suggested that the five probanda might be necessary where the defendant had done no positive act, and merely "stands by without protest".[18]

Unconscionability was the basis of the decision of the Privy Council in *Lim Teng Huan v Ang Swee Chuan*,[19] where:

A built a house on land which he jointly owned with L. A and L entered into a contract, under which L acknowledged that he had no title to the house and agreed to exchange his half share in the land for unspecified land which he expected to obtain from the Government of Brunei. The contract was void for uncertainty. L claimed that he was the sole beneficial owner of A's share.

In rejecting L's claim, the Privy Council held that L was estopped from denying A's title to the whole of the land, and that he was entitled to compensation representing a half-share in the present value of the land without the house; on payment L should convey his half-share in the land to A. Lord BROWNE-WILKINSON said:[20]

The decision in *Taylors Fashions* showed that, in order to found a proprietary estoppel, it is not essential that the representor should have been guilty of unconscionable conduct in permitting the representee to assume that he could act as he did: it is enough if, in all the circumstances, it is unconscionable for the representor to go back on the assumption which he permitted the representee to make.

Two important limitations on the doctrine have been emphasised by the Court of Appeal. Firstly, in *Western Fish Product Ltd v Penwith District Council*, where MEGAW LJ said:[1]

We know of no case, and none has been cited to us, in which the principle set out in *Ramsden v Dyson* ... has been applied otherwise than to rights and interests created in and over land. It may extend to other forms of property[2] ... In our judgment there is no good reason for extending the principle further.

And, secondly, in *Brinnand v Ewens*,[3] where NOURSE LJ said:

The acting [to the detriment] must have taken place in the belief either that the

---

17 *Swallow Securities Ltd v Isenberg* [1985] 1 EGLR 132 at 134, per CUMMING-BRUCE LJ.
18 *Taylors Fashions Ltd v Liverpool Victoria Trustees Co Ltd*, supra, at 146, at 911.
19 [1992] 1 WLR 113; [1993] Conv 173 (S.K. 600).
20 At 117.
 1 [1981] 2 All ER 204 at 218 (no estoppel where owner spent money on his own land in the expectation encouraged by a local authority that he would acquire a planning permission).
 2 *Re Foster* [1938] 3 All ER 610 (life insurance policy); *Moorgate Mercantile Co Ltd v Twitchings* [1976] QB 225 at 242, [1975] 3 All ER 314 at 323, per Lord DENNING MR.
 3 [1987] 2 EGLR 67 (expenditure incurred on work "done to make the home more comfortable"). See also *Bristol and West Building Society v Henning* [1985] 1 WLR 778, [1985] 2 All ER 606, where, in a case concerning the priority between the beneficial interest of a spouse and the rights of a mortgagee, BROWNE-WILKINSON LJ said at 782, at 609, that "in the absence of express agreement, an intention or assumption [that a party other than the legal owner should have a beneficial interest in the property] must be proved in order to found the lesser interest of an irrevocable licence conferring a property interest: see *Re Sharpe* [1980] 1 WLR 219, [1980] 1 All ER 198, p. 593, ante." See also *Paddington Building Society v Mendelsohn* (1985) 50 P & CR 244; (1985) CLJ 354 (M. Welstead); *Grant v Edwards* [1986] Ch 638 at 657, [1986] 2 All ER 426 at 439.

claimant owned a sufficient interest in the property to justify the expenditure or that he would obtain such an interest.[4]

The doctrine has been held to apply in a wide range of situations.[5] Many of its recent applications, under the name of "proprietary estoppel", have been in licence cases, where it has proved to be particularly useful because it is capable of producing a positive remedy, as opposed to the negative protection by injunction provided by estoppel by representation and promissory estoppel. It provides not only a shield, but a sword.

B. ILLUSTRATIONS. REMEDIES

Once it is established that an estoppel is working in favour of a licensee, the court will decide which of the available remedies is most appropriate. As has been said many times in the case:

> The court must look at the circumstances in each case to decide in what way the equity can be satisfied.[6]

(1) INJUNCTION TO RESTRAIN

Before the doctrine of proprietary estoppel was introduced into the licence cases, negative protection was the only remedy available. In *Inwards v Baker*:[7]

> B's son wished to build a bungalow on land which he had hoped to purchase, but the project was beyond his means. B then said to his son "Why not put the bungalow on my land and make the bungalow a little bigger?" The son did so, building it mainly through his own labour and expense. He lived there continuously until B died in 1951, and then from B's death until the proceedings began in 1963. B had left the land elsewhere in a will dated 1922 to trustees on trust for sale in favour of

---

4 Adapted from *Snell's Equity*, p. 575.
5 *East India Co v Vincent* (1740) 2 Atk 83; *Dann v Spurrier* (1802) 7 Ves 231; *Duke of Devonshire v Eglin* (1851) 14 Beav 530; *Duke of Beaufort v Patrick* (1853) 17 Beav 60; *Unity Joint Stock Mutual Banking Association v King* (1858) 25 Beav 72; *Ramsden v Dyson*, supra; *Willmott v Barber*, supra; *Plimmer v Wellington Corpn* (1884) 9 App Cas 699; M & B p. 583; *Foster v Robinson* [1951] 1 KB 149, [1950] 2 All ER 342; *Vaughan v Vaughan* [1953] 1 QB 762, [1953] 1 All ER 209; *Hopgood v Brown* [1955] 1 WLR 213, [1955] 1 All ER 550; M & B p. 580; *Armstrong v Sheppard and Short* [1959] 2 QB 384, [1959] 2 All ER 651; *Inwards v Baker* [1965] 2 QB 29, [1965] 1 All ER 446; M & B p. 578; *Ward v Kirkland* [1967] Ch 194, [1966] 1 All ER 609; *E R Ives Investment Ltd v High* [1967] 2 QB 279, [1967] 1 All ER 504; M & B p. 592; *Siew Soon Wah v Yong Tong Hong* [1973] AC 836; *Dodsworth v Dodsworth* (1973) 228 EG 1115; M & B p. 598; *Holiday Inns Inc v Broadhead* (1974) 232 EG 951; *Crabb v Arun District Council* [1976] Ch 179, [1975] 3 All ER 865; M & B p. 585; *Jones v Jones* [1977] 1 WLR 438, [1977] 2 All ER 231; M & B p. 581; *Griffiths v Williams* (1977) 248 EG 947; M & B p. 599; *Williams v Staite* [1979] Ch 291, [1978] 2 All ER 928; *E and L Berg Homes Ltd v Grey* (1979) 253 EG 473; *Pascoe v Turner* [1979] 1 WLR 431, [1979] 2 All ER 945; M & B p. 594; *Greasley v Cooke* [1980] 1 WLR 1306, [1980] 3 All ER 710; M & B p. 574; *Taylors Fashions Ltd v Liverpool Victoria Trustees Co Ltd*, supra; *Salvation Army Trustee Co Ltd v West Yorkshire Metropolitan County Council* (1980) 41 P & CR 179; *Appleby v Cowley*, supra; *Re Basham* [1986] 1 WLR 1498, [1987] 1 All ER 405; M & B p. 612; *Burrows v Sharp* (1991) 23 HLR 82; [1992] Conv 54 (J. E. Martin); *Baker v Baker* (1993) 25 HLR 408. See the review of the authorities by Lord TEMPLEMAN in *A-G of Hong Kong v Humphreys Estate (Queen's Gardens) Ltd* [1987] AC 114, [1987] 2 All ER 387 (where PC refused to apply the doctrine). See Snell, *Equity*, pp. 577–578; M & B p. 576.
6 *Plimmer v Wellington Corpn* (1884) 9 App Cas 699 at 713.
7 [1965] 2 QB 29, [1965] 1 All ER 446; M & B p. 578; (1965) 81 LQR 183 (R. H. Maudsley).

others. When the trustees sought possession, the Court of Appeal held that the son "can remain there as long as he desires to use it as his home".[8]

The remedy has been held to be available against third parties, whether volunteers, as in *Inwards v Baker*, or a purchaser with constructive notice, as in *Hopgood v Brown*.[9] *Inwards v Baker* should be contrasted with *Dillwyn v Llewelyn*,[10] where, however, the father had signed an unexecuted and gratuitous memorandum of conveyance in favour of his son, and the son had spent no less than £14,000 in building himself a home, with his father's knowledge and approval. The House of Lords ordered a conveyance of the land without payment. No mention was made in the House of Lords of estoppel or of the equitable doctrine of encouragement and acquiescence, but some writers have claimed that this is an illustration of the doctrine of proprietary estoppel.[11] It might be thought, in either of the cases, that a better solution would have been to give the son the option of taking a conveyance of the land on payment of site value or of receiving compensation for the value of his expenditure on the land.

(2) PROPRIETARY ESTOPPEL

Lord KINGSDOWN's principle was applied in *Plimmer v Wellington Corpn*,[12] where the plaintiff had expended money on the development of a jetty in New Zealand at the encouragement of the Government, and the question was whether he was entitled to compensation on the ground that, within the terms of the compensation statute, he had "any estate or interest" in the jetty. He received compensation.

The doctrine of proprietary estoppel received the approval of the Court of Appeal in *Crabb v Arun District Council*.[13] SCARMAN LJ, who did not think that "the distinction between promissory and proprietary estoppel" was helpful, said:[14]

> If the plaintiff has any right, it is an equity arising out of the conduct and relationship of the parties. In such a case I think it is now well settled law that the court, having analysed and assessed the conduct and relationship of the parties, has to answer three questions. First, is there an equity established? Secondly, what is the extent of the equity, if one is established? And, thirdly, what is the relief appropriate to satisfy the equity?

In *Crabb v Arun District Council*:

> C owned a two acre plot of land which had access in the northern part (at point A) onto a lane owned by the defendants and thence along a right of way over that lane to the highway. In 1967 C decided to sell the northern and southern parts of the plot separately. Since he had no means of access from the southern part to the highway (except over the northern part), he made an oral agreement with the defendants under which they would give to him a further point of access (point B) together with a further right of way along the lane. No formal grant of the right of access or easement was made. As a result of the agreement, the defendants erected

8 At 37, at 449, per Lord DENNING MR.
9 [1955] 1 WLR 213, [1955] 1 All ER 550; M & B p. 580; [1981] Conv 347 (P. N. Todd).
10 (1862) 4 De GF & J 517.
11 Dawson and Pearce, p. 34.
12 (1884) 9 App Cas 699; M & B p. 583.
13 [1976] Ch 179, [1975] 3 All ER 865; M & B p. 585; (1976) 40 Conv (NS) 156 (F. R. Crane); (1976) 92 LQR 174 (P. S. Atiyah); 342 (P. J. Millett).
14 At 193, at 875.

a fence between their land and C's land, and gates at the two access points. C, relying on this agreement, sold the northern part with the point A access to X, without reserving a right of way over it in favour of the retained southern part. In 1969 the defendants removed the gate at point B, and fenced the gap, thus making C's southern plot land-locked; further, they asked C to pay "close on £4,000 in order to provide him with that which their representative had undertaken to provide".

The Court of Appeal held that the defendants were estopped from denying C's right of access at point B and the right of way therefrom to the highway, and, in view of the sterilisation of his land for a considerable period, the rights would be granted without any payment by him to the defendants.[15]

It will be seen from the illustrations so far that the emphasis has shifted from the paradigm case, where the licensee has spent money on the land of the licensor, to one where he has suffered detriment arising from some activity or inactivity on his part. In *Crabb v Arun District Council* the detriment to the licensee was that, in reliance on the agreement with the licensor that he would have an access to and a right of way over the licensor's lane, he refrained from expressly reserving an easement of way over the northern plot when he sold and conveyed it to X. Furthermore the doctrine is not limited to acts done in reliance on a belief relating to an existing right, but is extended to acts done in reliance on a belief that future rights will be granted; as, for example, where a step-daughter acted to her detriment in reliance on her belief that she would ultimately benefit by receiving the deceased's property under his will.[16] The doctrine has also been widened in *Greasley v Cooke*[17] in connection with the burden of proof; in that case the Court of Appeal held that, once there is proof that a representation has been made by the licensor, the onus is on him to prove that the licensee did not rely on it. It spite of this rule, however, the basic requirement of detriment remains unimpaired. As DUNN LJ said in that case:[18]

> There is no doubt that for proprietary estoppel to arise the person claiming must have incurred expenditure or otherwise have prejudiced himself or acted to his detriment.

Other cases have examined the facts and circumstances in great detail

15 See *Crabb v Arun District Council (No. 2)* (1977) 121 SJ 86 where C was refused an enquiry as to damages. See also *Salvation Army Trustee Co Ltd v West Yorkshire Metropolitan County Council* (1980) 41 P & CR 179 (where proprietary estoppel was extended to the *disposal* of an interest in land where the disposal was closely linked by an arrangement that also involved the acquisition of an interest in land); discussed in *A-G of Hong Kong v Humphreys Estate (Queen's Gardens) Ltd* [1987] AC 114 at 126, 127, [1987] 2 All ER 387 at 394.
16 *Re Basham* [1986] 1 WLR 1498, [1987] 1 All ER 405; M & B p. 612; [1987] Conv 211 (J. E. Martin); [1987] CLJ 215 (D. J. Hayton); [1987] All ER Rev 156 (P. J. Clarke), 260 (C. H. Sherrin); (1988) 8 LS 92 (M. Davey); cf. *Layton v Martin* [1986] 2 FLR 227 (offer of "financial security" too vague).
17 [1980] 1 WLR 1306, [1980] 3 All ER 710.
18 At 1313, at 715. See *Dann v Spurrier* (1802) 7 Ves 231 at 235–236, per Lord ELDON LC, cited in *Taylors Fashions Ltd v Liverpool Victoria Trustees Co Ltd* [1982] QB 133 at 156, [1981] 1 All ER 897 at 919; *Christian v Christian* (1981) 131 NLJ 43; *Watkins v Emslie* (1982) 261 EG 1192; *Watts v Story* [1983] CA Transcript 319; M & B p. 575, where DUNN LJ explains the observations of Lord DENNING MR in *Greasley v Cooke*; *Coombes v Smith* [1986] 1 WLR 808 (no detriment where wife left husband and went to live with lover and their child); [1986] CLJ 394 (D. J. Hayton); *Hammersmith and Fulham London Borough Council v Top Shop Centres Ltd* [1990] Ch 237, [1989] 2 All ER 655 (failure to negotiate for grant of new lease or to apply for relief against forfeiture held to be detriment; reliance presumed); *Wayling v Jones* [1993] EGCS 153.

with a view to finding a solution especially adjusted to the circumstances. For example in *Dodsworth v Dodsworth*:[19]

the plaintiff lived alone in a bungalow. Her younger brother and his wife, the two defendants, returned to England from Australia and were looking for a home. The plaintiff persuaded them to join her in her bungalow. They did so, and spent some £700 on improvements to the bungalow, in the expectation, encouraged and induced by the plaintiff, that the defendants and the survivor of them would be able to remain in the bungalow as their home for as long as they wished to do so. Nine months later, the plaintiff repented of her invitation and started proceedings for possession; she died before the hearing in the Court of Appeal.

The Court of Appeal held that the equity would best be satisfied by securing the occupation of the defendants until the expenditure had been reimbursed.

It might be thought that the solution in *Pascoe v Turner*[20] was too extreme.

In 1963 P, a businessman, and T, a widow with an invalidity pension and a small amount of capital, lived together in his house. In 1965 P purchased another house, into which they moved and lived as man and wife. In 1973 P started an affair with another woman. T remained in the house and was told by P that the house and everything in it was hers. In reliance on this statement, T spent, to P's knowledge, her own money on repairs and improvements, and also on furniture. P moved out in 1973 when the relationship ended, and in 1976 he gave T two months' notice to determine the licence.

The Court of Appeal held that there was a gift of the contents, since T was in possession of them as a bailee when P declared the gift. As far as the house was concerned, there was no valid declaration of trust,[1] but an estoppel arose in her favour. The court rejected a solution that would give T a licence to occupy the house for her lifetime, and ordered that the fee simple be conveyed to her.

Only in this way could the defendant be "assured of security of tenure, quiet enjoyment, and freedom of action in respect of repairs and improvements without interference from the plaintiff."[2] Instead of granting a life interest to T, as a result of which she might have become tenant for life under the Settled Land Act 1925,[3] and leaving her to her remedies in tort against P, if necessary, the Court awarded T the fee simple of a house worth £16,000 at the time of the judgment for an outlay of less than £1,000.[4]

19 (1973) 228 EG 1115; M & B p. 598. See *Baker v Baker* (1993) 25 HLR 408 (order not to be oppressive to licensor).
20 [1979] 1 WLR 431, [1979] 2 All ER 945; M & B p. 594; [1979] Conv 379 (F. R. Crane); (1979) 42 MLR 574 (B Sufrin). Cf. *Dillwyn v Llewelyn* (1862) 4 De GF & J 517, p. 599, ante; *Voyce v Voyce* (1991) 62 P & CR 290 (donee of farm and cottage from licensee ordered to convey fee simple to licensee).
 1 It was not in writing as required by LPA 1925, s. 53 (1), p 773, post.
 2 At 438, at 951.
 3 For the powers of a tenant for life, see p. 185, ante. See also p. 604, post.
 4 See also *Re Basham* [1986] 1 WLR 1498, [1987] 1 All ER 405; M & B p. 612, where a step-daughter was held to be entitled to the whole of the deceased's estate, including his house. For the other extreme, see *Appleby v Cowley* (1982) Times, 14 April; M & B p. 604, where MEGARRY V-C envisaged the possibility of *no* remedy being granted.

C. TERMINATION OF LICENCE

A licence is revocable when it is not binding on the licensor or his successors in title in accordance with the rules stated in this chapter. A question has arisen whether an irrevocable licence can be made revocable by the serious misconduct of the licensee. In *Williams v Staite*,[5] where the estoppel licensee announced that the successor in title of the licensor was in for "bloody trouble" and blocked the entrance to the house which he had purchased, the Court of Appeal held that the licence did not thereby become revocable. As GOFF LJ said:

> Excessive user or bad behaviour towards the legal owner cannot bring the equity to an end or forfeit it. It may give rise to an action for damages for trespass or nuisance or to injunctions to restrain such behaviour, but I see no ground on which the equity, once established, can be forfeited.[6]

Lord DENNING MR thought that, in an extreme case, the licence might be revocable.

The effect of serious misconduct may, however, prevent an estoppel licence from arising in the first place, for example, where a forged document is used to bolster the claim. This is a simple application of the equitable maxim that "he who comes to equity must come with clean hands".[7]

D. TRANSFER OF BENEFIT OF LICENCE

There is no English authority on the transfer of the benefit of an estoppel licence. In New South Wales, however, the Supreme Court held in *Hamilton v Geraghty*[8] that the benefit of an estoppel based on passive acquiescence was assignable and in fact had been assigned. The estoppel was not a personal right to sue which could not be assigned, but an interest in the land itself.[9]

Whether a licence is transferable depends on the circumstances and in particular on its construction. In *Inwards v Baker*,[10] where the son's licence was to remain in the bungalow as long as he desired to use it as his home, the right was clearly personal and not transferable. In *E R Ives Investment Ltd v High*,[11] however, the benefit of High's licence would run with the land.

SECTION VI SUMMARY

Sufficient has been said to demonstrate the dramatic development of the law of licences in the past 40 years or so. *Hurst v Picture Theatres Ltd*[12] was then

---

5　[1979] Ch 291, [1978] 2 All ER 928.
6　At 300, at 934. Cf. a contractual licence where misconduct may be a breach of an implied term in it, and so prevent the licensee from relying on equitable relief against revocation: *Brynowen Estates Ltd v Bourne* (1981) 131 NLJ 1212 (driving car at speed along roads of caravan park with sounding of horn at night; and swearing at and making obscene gestures at visitors to it); p. 587, n. 12, ante.
7　*J. Willis & Son v Willis* [1986] 1 EGLR 62.
8　(1901) 1 SRNSW Eq 81; *Lands Comr v Hussein* [1968] EA 585; (1969) ASCL 354 (E. H. Burn).
9　At 89, per OWEN J.
10　[1965] 2 QB 29, [1965] 1 All ER 446, M & B p. 578; p. 598, ante.
11　[1967] 2 QB 379, [1967] 1 All ER 504, M & B p. 592; p. 604, post.
12　[1915] 1 KB 1; p. 587, ante.

the only glimmer of hope for the contractual licensee. And the phrase "licence by estoppel" had no meaning. Now, as has been seen, a right of way,[13] a life interest,[14] and a fee simple[15] have been awarded to licensees, even though they were volunteers and had no documentary title to such estate or interest. But this progress has produced a number of problems.

It will be remembered that in the 1950s there grew up the concept of the deserted wife's licence. A husband who deserted his wife could not turn her out of the home, even though he owned it. And this protection was extended through a series of cases[16] to protect the deserted wife against third parties to whom the home might be transferred, not being bona fide purchasers of a legal estate for value without notice. This situation created conveyancing complications, and the doctrine was disapproved by the House of Lords in *National Provincial Bank Ltd v Ainsworth* in 1965,[17] on the ground that the wife held no proprietary interest recognized by the law. The deserted wife was thus left unprotected against third parties. The criticism which followed led to the registration of a deserted wife's "right of occupation" under the Matrimonial Homes Act 1967.[18]

The new problem presented in *National Provincial Bank Ltd v Ainsworth* is a very real one in the context of the conveyancing system. One basic principle of the 1925 legislation was to provide for the documentation of all dealings with the legal estate and for equities and equitable interests to be either overreachable or registrable. The principle is all the more obvious with registered land, when the intention is to record everything except overriding interests. From a conveyancer's point of view, these are good principles, but the system, apart from licences, has not remained intact in the case of unregistered land;[19] nor, because of the literal construction of section 70 (1) (g) of the Land Registration Act 1925, in the case of registered land.[20] The biggest inroad into these principles of conveyancing is found in the modern development of licences. Even where negative protection only is

---

13 *Crabb v Arun District Council* [1976] Ch 179, [1975] 3 All ER 865; p. 599, ante; *E R Ives Investment Ltd v High* [1967] 2 QB 379, [1967] 1 All ER 504; p. 604, post.

14 *Inwards v Baker* [1965] 2 QB 29, [1965] 1 All ER 446; p. 598, ante. See *Griffiths v Williams* (1977) 248 EG 947, 604, post.

15 *Pascoe v Turner* [1979] 1 WLR 431, [1979] 2 All ER 945; p. 601, ante.

16 *Bendall v McWhirter* [1952] 2 QB 466, [1952] 1 All ER 1307; *Ferris v Weaven* [1952] 2 All ER 233; *Street v Denham* [1954] 1 WLR 624, [1954] 1 All ER 532; *Lee v Lee* [1952] 2 QB 489, [1952] 1 All ER 1299; *Jess B Woodcock & Sons Ltd v Hobbs* [1955] 1 WLR 152, [1955] 1 All ER 445; *Westminster Bank Ltd v Lee* [1956] Ch 7, [1955] 2 All ER 883; *Miles v Bull* [1969] 1 QB 258, [1968] 3 All ER 632.

17 [1965] AC 1175, [1965] 2 All ER 472; M & B pp. 121, 614. See also *Hall v King* [1987] 2 EGLR 121 where Sir John DONALDSON MR said at 212: "A wife's right to occupy the matrimonial home is of a very special nature, depending upon her status as a wife and not upon any leave or licence of her husband ... This accords with common sense and experience. Whoever heard of a husband expressly saying to his wife 'Do come and stay with me in the matrimonial home, dear'".

18 Now Matrimonial Homes Act 1983; p. 241, ante.

19 *E R Ives Investment Ltd v High* [1967] 2 QB 379, [1967] 1 All ER 504; M & B p. 592 (licence by estoppel), infra; *Poster v Slough Estates Ltd* [1969] 1 Ch 495, [1968] 3 All ER 257 (right of entry to remove a fixture on termination of lease); *Caunce v Caunce* [1969] 1 WLR 286, [1969] 1 All ER 722; M & B p. 274; *Kingsnorth Finance Ltd v Tizard* [1986] 1 WLR 783, [1986] 2 All ER 54; p. 63, ante (beneficial interest of wife who had contributed towards purchase price); *Shiloh Spinners Ltd v Harding* [1973] AC 691, [1973] 1 All ER 90; M & B p. 36 (equitable right of entry on breach of covenant); p. 97, ante.

20 *Hodgson v Marks* [1971] Ch 892, [1971] 2 All ER 684; *Williams and Glyn's Bank Ltd v Boland* [1981] AC 487, [1980] 2 All ER 408; M & B p. 122; p. 792, post.

given,[1] a purchaser is faced with the interest of the licensee as a blot on his title. The licensee may be in possession, and the purchaser may thus have what would be considered to be constructive notice under the pre-1926 cases.[2] But these rules are now taken over by provisions for registration, and licences have been held not to be registrable under the Land Charges Act 1925. Indeed, it would be a disaster for the licensee if they were; for many of the licence situations arise in connection with personal family affairs, without legal advice, and as a matter of practice would hardly ever be registered; and, further, if they were registrable and not registered, they would be void even against a purchaser who actually knew of the licence. The point was decided in *E R Ives Investment Ltd v High*,[3] where:

> the defendant, High, built a house on his own land. His neighbour then erected a block of flats whose foundations encroached on High's land. They agreed orally that the foundations should remain and that High should have a right of way across the neighbour's yard. High, relying on this agreement, built a garage on his own land so sited that it could only be approached across the yard. The neighbour sold the block of flats to a purchaser, who resold it to the plaintiffs, expressly subject to High's right of way. The right of way was not a legal interest since it had not been formally created; nor had it been registered as an equitable easement under the Land Charges Act 1925.[4] The Court of Appeal held that High had a right by estoppel, which, not being registrable as a land charge, was binding on the plaintiffs who had purchased the legal estate of the licensor with actual notice.[5]

The difficulties are even greater where the licensee receives an award of an undocumented proprietary interest or estate. Once the case has been determined, the proper documentation can be prepared, but the licensee's protection cannot depend upon the trial of the action. The protection is given in equity, and not by the court's decision. Where the court's decision is to award a life interest, the question is whether the licensee will become a tenant for life under the Settled Land Act 1925. The point was first noticed by Scott LJ in *Bannister v Bannister*,[6] a case decided on the theory of constructive trust. The point was overlooked in many of the licence cases.[7] The view has been expressed that the Settled Land Act 1925 would not apply.[8] Russell LJ, on the other hand, noted in *Dodsworth v Dodsworth*,[9] that the award of a life interest:

> will lead, by virtue of the provisions of the Settled Land Act, to a greater and more extensive interest than was ever contemplated by the plaintiff and the defendants,

and in *Griffiths v Williams*,[10] the Court of Appeal went out of its way to provide for the protection of Mrs Williams, without deciding that she had a life interest, and thus avoiding the risk of the application of the Settled Land

---

1 *Inwards v Baker*, supra.
2 *Hunt v Luck* [1901] 1 Ch 45; p. 63, ante.
3 Supra; (1967) 31 Conv (NS) 332 (F. R. Crane).
4 S. 2 (5) Class D (iii); p. 760, post.
5 The CA also relied on the doctrine of *Halsall v Brizell* [1957] Ch 169, [1957] 1 All ER 371, that he who takes the benefit must accept the burden; p. 612, post.
6 [1948] 2 All ER 133; M & B p. 592; p. 593, ante.
7 Cf *Inwards v Baker*, supra.
8 *Binions v Evans* [1972] Ch 359 at 366, [1972] 2 All ER 70 at 74, per Lord Denning MR (unintended settlement), p. 177, ante. See also *Ivory v Palmer* [1975] ICR 340 at 347, where Cairns LJ said "*Binions v Evans* stretched to the very limit the application of the Settled Land Act". See (1977) 93 LQR 561 (J. A. Hornby).
9 (1973) 228 EG 1115; M & B p. 598.
10 (1977) 248 EG 947; M & B p. 599.

Act 1925. Instead of giving her a life interest, the Court obtained the same effect by making a consent order, granting to her a long lease of the house determinable on her death at a nominal rent of less than two-thirds of its rateable value (thereby keeping the house outside the protection of the Rent Act), the lease containing an absolute covenant against assignment.[11]

A similar problem arises where a fee simple is awarded, as in *Pascoe v Turner*.[12] The licensor holds the legal estate, and the licensee has an equitable fee simple. There is no provision, in such a situation, for registration or overreaching; though, in registered land, the licensee would be held to have an overriding interest.[13] With unregistered land, the old principle of notice presumably applies; and its application must be particularly difficult where, as in *Pascoe v Turner*, the licensee had not the slightest idea that she was entitled to a fee simple.

This raises the question whether a licence should now be regarded as an interest in land. This is a difficult discussion, made impossible by the lack of agreement as to what an "interest in land" means in the context. It is clear that the early analysis of a licence did not treat it as an interest in land. Although licensees in the nineteenth century found little protection in the decisions, the courts took the view that a licence granted under seal was irrevocable; from which one might conclude that if a licence was granted under seal, it must be the subject matter of a grant, and that makes it look like an interest in land. That theory, however, was largely exploded once it was decided that there could be no easement in gross; for that, at best, is what a licence granted under seal could claim to be.[14] From the 1940s, the doctrine has been accepted that a contractual licensee or licensee by estoppel may be protected by injunction. Whether such injunction will lie also against a third party is a matter of controversy in the case of a contractual licensee, the leading cases of *Errington v Errington and Woods*[15] and *Binions v Evans*[16] being special cases and capable of having been decided on other grounds. Licences by estoppel have always been held to be binding on third parties, not being bona fide purchasers for value of a legal estate without notice.

But such interests would not qualify as interests in land if the test was whether the interest could be bought and sold. Now, however, that positive remedies are awarded, by way of constructive trust, or by the application of the doctrine of proprietary estoppel, it is clear that the licensee may have an interest which is both binding on third parties and capable of being bought and sold. In such circumstances, the conclusions cannot be avoided that, in view of recent developments, some licences are indeed interests in land. The law on this point is still in the process of development,[17] but it seems that a

11 See also *J. T. Douglas Development Ltd v Quinn* [1991] 2 EGLR 257.
12 [1979] 1 WLR 431, [1979] 2 All ER 945; M & B p. 594.
13 LRA 1925, s. 70 (1) (g), p. 791, post.
14 See *Cowell v Rosehill Racecourse Co Ltd* (1937) 56 CLR 605 at 616; M & B p. 536, per LATHAM CJ: "the right to see a spectacle cannot, in the ordinary sense of legal language, be regarded as a proprietary interest. Fifty thousand people who pay to see a football match do not obtain fifty thousand interests in the football ground".
15 [1952] 1 KB 290, [1952] 1 All ER 149, M & B p. 551; p. 589, ante.
16 [1972] Ch 359, [1972] 2 All ER 70; M & B p. 555. See, however, *Ashburn Anstalt v Arnold* [1989] Ch 1, [1988] 2 All ER 147; M & B p. 550; p. 592, ante.
17 See (1967) 31 Conv (NS) 341 (F. R. Crane); (1969) ASCL 354 (E. H. Burn). See also *Pennine Raceway Ltd v Kirklees Metropolitan Council* [1983] QB 382, [1982] 3 All ER 628, where a licensee of land was held entitled to compensation under TCPA 1971, s. 164 as a person "interested in land" on withdrawal of planning permission: [1982] All ER Rev 173 (P. J. Clarke).

new right *in alieno solo* has emerged in this century as did one in the previous century under the doctrine of *Tulk v Moxhay*.[18]

SECTION VII   REGISTERED LAND

There are three kinds of licence to be considered:

(1) LICENCE COUPLED WITH GRANT OR INTEREST

Where a licence coupled with a grant or interest is in essence a profit à prendre, it may be protected as a minor interest by the entry of a notice or caution on the licensor's registered title, but, in any event, it is an interest subsisting in reference to registered land under section 70 (1) of the Land Registration Act 1925 and enforceable against third parties as an overriding interest under paragraph (*a*).[19] And this is so whether the profit is legal or equitable.

(2) CONTRACTUAL LICENCE

If a contractual licence is not an interest in land, then it will not be enforceable against third parties, and, as in the case of a bare licence, no question of registration arises. But, if it is an interest in land,[20] then the contractual licensee must protect it by the entry of a notice or caution, or rely on its being an overriding interest by virtue of actual occupation under paragraph (*g*) of section 70 (1).[1]

(3) LICENCE BY ESTOPPEL

As we have seen, a licence by estoppel in unregistered land is not registrable as a land charge under the Land Charges Act 1972, and its enforceability against third parties depends on the doctrine of notice.[2] In registered land, however, such a licence must be protected by the entry of a notice or caution on the register,[3] unless it is an overriding interest under paragraph (*g*) of section 70 (1). In *Inwards v Baker*,[4] for example, where a son expended money in building a bungalow on his father's unregistered land, under the expectation created by his father that he could remain there, the Court of Appeal held that the son's right to remain in the bungalow for life or as long as he wished was enforceable against a purchaser with notice. It would seem that, if the title to the land were registered, the son's right would be protected,

18 Chapter 19, p. 614, post.
19 P. 581, ante.
20 See *Errington v Errington and Woods* [1952] 1 KB 290, [1952] 1 All ER 149; M & B p. 551; p. 590, ante; *Binions v Evans* [1972] Ch 359, [1972] 2 All ER 70; M & B p. 555; p. 591, ante; *Ashburn Anstalt v Arnold* [1989] Ch 1, [1988] 2 All ER 147; M & B p. 550; p. 592, ante.
 1 P. 791, post.
 2 *E. R. Ives Investments Ltd v High* [1967] 2 QB 379, [1967] 1 All ER 504; M & B p. 592; p. 604, ante.
 3 LRA 1925, ss. 49 (1) (*f*), 54 (1): Ruoff and Roper, para. 35–33.
 4 [1965] 2 QB 29, [1965] 1 All ER 446; M & B p. 578; p. 598, ante.

by virtue of his actual occupation as an overriding interest under section 70 (1) (*g*) of the Land Registration Act 1925. On the other hand, such protection would not be accorded to the estoppel licensee in *E R Ives Investment Ltd v High*,[5] where the garage was sited on his own land. Nor might the intermittent user of his right over the licensor's land amount to actual occupation.[6]

5 Supra. See also *Crabb v Arun District Council* [1976] Ch 179, [1975] 3 All ER 865; M & B p. 585; p. 599, ante, where the licensee was also not in actual occupation.
6 *Epps v Esso Petroleum Co Ltd* [1973] 1 WLR 1071, [1973] 2 All ER 465; M & B p. 168. See also *Lee-Parker v Izzet (No. 2)* [1972] 1 WLR 775, [1972] 2 All ER 800.

Chapter 19

Restrictive covenants

It sometimes happens that a landowner desires to impose a positive or a
negative duty upon the owner of neighbouring land with the object of
preserving the saleable value or the residential amenities of his own property.
X, the owner of Whiteacre, for instance, who sells part of his garden
(Blackacre) to Y, may wish to control the manner in which Y uses the land.
Accordingly X may require Y to covenant that he will not build shops on
Blackacre (a negative or a restrictive covenant) or that he will erect and
maintain a fence between it and X's retained land (a positive covenant), for
the benefit of X and his successors in title. Such a covenant remains binding
qua contract between X and Y personally, but does its benefit run with
Whiteacre and its burden with Blackacre in the sense that it is enforceable
by the successors in title of the former against the successors in title of the
latter?

If the privilege granted by the covenant constitutes a legal easement, there
is no difficulty. It permanently binds the servient tenement Blackacre and
permanently enures for the benefit of the dominant tenement Whiteacre. If
the covenant is contained in a lease, again there is no difficulty, for it will
normally run both with the land and with the reversion. [1] Otherwise there is
the fundamental objection that a stranger to a contract can neither enforce
nor be bound by its terms. [2]

---

1 Pp. 610, et seq, ante.
2 See Cheshire, Fifoot and Furmston, *Law of Contract* (12th edn), chapter 14.

We must now consider the extent to which in this context the doctrine of privity of contract has been relaxed, first by the common law, secondly by equity.

SECTION I THE EXTENT TO WHICH COVENANTS MADE ON THE OCCASION OF A SALE IN FEE SIMPLE RUN AT COMMON LAW[3]

A. BENEFIT MAY RUN AT COMMON LAW

The rule at law for several centuries has been that the *benefit* of covenants, whether positive or negative, which are made with a covenantee, having an interest in the land to which they relate, passes to his successors in title.[4] Thus in *Sharp v Waterhouse*[5] it was admitted that:

> a covenant by the owner of a mill that he "his heirs executors and administrators" would supply pure water to the adjacent land of X, ran with that land and could be put in suit by X's devisee.

The covenantor is liable to the successors in title of the covenantee merely because of the covenant that he has made, not because of his relationship to any servient tenement.[6] He is liable even though he himself owns no land.[7]

Four things, however, are essential to bring this rule into operation at common law:

(i)   The covenant must touch and concern the land of the covenantee.[8] In general, the test for this requirement is the same as that for covenants in leases.[9]

(ii) There must be an intention that the benefit should run with the land owned by the covenantee at the date of the covenant.[10]

(iii) The covenantee, at the time of making the covenant, must have the legal estate in the land which is to be benefited.[11]

(iv) An assignee who seeks to enforce the covenant must have the same legal estate in the land as the original covenantee, for the covenant is incident to that estate.[12]

Thus, at common law a covenant taken by an owner in fee simple does not avail his lessee. This rule, however, has been abrogated for covenants made after 1925 by section 78 of the Law of Property Act 1925, which provides that:

> A covenant relating to any land of the covenantee shall be deemed to be made with

---

3 See (1954) 18 Conv (NS) 546 (E. H. Scammell).

4 *The Prior's Case* (1368) YB 42 Ed III, Pl. 14, fol. 3A; Co Litt 385*a*; *Shayler v Woolf* [1946] Ch 320, [1946] 2 All ER 54 (express assignment by covenantee of the benefit of the covenant); *Smith and Snipes Hall Farm Ltd v River Douglas Catchment Board* [1949] 2 KB 500, [1949] 2 All ER 179; 1 *Smith's Leading Cases* (13th edn), pp. 51, 65, 73; M & B, p. 842.

5 (1857) 7 E & B 816.

6 *Smith and Snipes Hall Farm Ltd v River Douglas Catchment Board*, supra.

7 Ibid.

8 *Rogers v Hosegood* [1900] 2 Ch 388 at 395.

9 Pp. 444–8, ante.

10 *Rogers v Hosegood* [1900] 2 Ch 388 at 396; *Shayler v Woolf* [1946] Ch 320, [1940] 2 All ER 54; *Smith and Snipes Hall Farm Ltd v River Douglas Catchment Board*, supra, at 506, at 183.

11 *Webb v Russell* (1789) 3 Term Rep 393.

12 *Smith and Snipes Hall Farm Ltd v River Douglas Catchment Board*, supra, at 516, at 189.

the covenantee and his successors in title and the persons deriving title under him or them, and shall have effect as if such successors and other persons were expressed.[13]

In the present context, of course, this provision will avail a successor in title, such as a lessee, only where the covenant is one that touches and concerns the land that he holds.

The benefit of a covenant may also be transferred by assignment as a chose in action under section 136 of the Law of Property Act 1925. To be effective in law, the assignment must be in writing, and express notice in writing given to the covenantor.[14]

B. BURDEN DOES NOT RUN AT COMMON LAW

In *Austerberry v Corporation of Oldham*[15] the view was expressed by two Lords Justices that the burden of a positive covenant made between a vendor and a purchaser does not run with the fee simple at common law.

This view was reaffirmed by the House of Lords in *Rhone v Stephens*,[16] where:

> Walford House and Walford Cottage were in common ownership until 1960 when Walford Cottage was sold. The vendor covenanted to keep the common roof which covered part of Walford Cottage in wind and water tight condition. Both properties were sold after 1960. The question arose whether the covenant was enforceable against the owners of Walford House.

In holding that the covenant was not enforceable, Lord TEMPLEMAN said:[16a]

> In the *Austerberry* case the owners of a site of a road covenanted that they and their successors in title would make the road and keep it in repair. The road was sold to the defendants and it was held that the repair covenant could not be enforced against them.
>
> For over a hundred years it has been clear and accepted law that equity will enforce negative covenants against freehold land but has no power to enforce positive covenants against successors in title of the land. To enforce a positive covenant would be to enforce a personal obligation against a person who has not covenanted. To enforce negative covenants is only to treat the land as subject to a restriction.[17]

The House of Lords held further that *Austerberry v Corporation of Oldham* had not been "reversed remarkably but unremarked" by section 79 of the

---

13 *Smith and Snipes Hall Farm Ltd v River Douglas Catchment Board*, supra (where one of the plaintiffs was a yearly tenant); *Williams v Unit Construction Co Ltd* (1955) 19 Conv (NS) 262 (where the plaintiff was a weekly tenant). This wide interpretation of the section was followed in *Federated Homes Ltd v Mill Lodge Properties Ltd* [1980] 1 WLR 594, [1980] 1 All ER 371, M & B p. 851, p. 623, post, where CA was considering the running of the benefit in equity. For a criticism of the CA decision in *Smith and Snipes Hall Farm Ltd v River Douglas Catchment Board*, see 18 Conv (NS) at 553–6. It would seem that the section was intended to abrogate (ii) and not (iv) and thus to be a "word-saving" section only. See also Wolstenholme and Cherry, vol. 1. pp. 162–3; (1972B) 31 CLJ, pp. 171–5 (H. W. R. Wade).
14 See Cheshire, Fifoot and Furmston, *Law of Contract* (12th edn), pp. 505 et seq. See also LPA 1925, s. 56, p. 632, post.
15 (1885) 29 Ch D 750; M & B p. 826; *E. and G. C. Ltd v Bate* (1935) 79 LJ News 203.
16 [1994] 2 WLR 429.
16a At 434.
17 Pp. 614 et seq, post

Law of Property Act 1925 where a covenant was made after 1925. The section provides that:

> A covenant relating to any land of a covenantor or capable of being bound by him, shall, unless a contrary intention is expressed, be deemed to be made by the covenantor on behalf of himself his successors in title and the persons deriving title under him or them, and, subject as aforesaid, shall have effect as if such successors and other persons were expressed.

This is a welcome and restrictive interpretation of section,[18] which is at variance with the wide construction of the corresponding section 78 on the running of the benefit of a covenant.[19]

(1) DEVICES TO CIRCUMVENT RULE

There are, however, "a number of current techniques and devices by which lawyers attempt to surmount or circumvent the difficulties of enforcing positive covenants."[20]

(a) Lease instead of sale

The land may be leased instead of sold, and the positive covenants enforced under the doctrine of privity of estate.[21]

(b) Chains of indemnity covenants

As we have seen, an original covenantor remains liable even after he has parted with the land, and so he may protect himself by taking a covenant of indemnity from his purchaser. Each successive purchaser may give a similar covenant to his vendor with the result that a chain of indemnity covenants is created. In theory the original covenantee should be able to secure the indirect enforcement of the positive covenant by the current owner of the land by suing the original covenantor. "But in practice this device sooner or later becomes ineffective, either in consequence of the death or disappearance of the original covenantor, or because a break occurs in the chain of indemnities."

(c) The doctrine of *Halsall v Brizell*[22]

"In some cases a positive covenant can be enforced in practice by the operation of the maxim *'qui sentit commodum sentire debet et onus'*. This

---

18 For its construction as a word-saving section, see *Tophams Ltd v Earl of Sefton* [1967] 1 AC 50 at 73, 81, [1966] 1 All ER 1039, at 1048, 1053, per Lords UPJOHN and WILBERFORCE respectively; *Federated Homes Ltd v Mill Lodge Properties Ltd*, supra, per BRIGHTMAN LJ; M & B, pp. 851, 861. See *Emmet on Title* (19th edn) para 17.007; and the laconic "No" given as an answer by Sir Benjamin Cherry in his *Lectures on the New Property Acts* (1926), p. 131, to the question "Is the case of *Austerberry v Corporation of Oldham* overruled by s. 79 of the *Law of Property Act?*".

19 See n. 13, supra.

20 Report of the Committee on Positive Covenants Affecting Land (1965), Cmnd 2719, para. 8, whence the quotations in this paragraph are taken. See also Law Commission Report on Positive and Restrictive Covenants 1984 (Law Com No. 127, HC 201), paras. 3.19–3.42; Farrand (2nd edn), pp. 422–427; George and George, *The Sale of Flats* (5th edn), pp. 76–89; (1973) 37 Conv (NS) 194 (A. M. Prichard); Conv Prec, 5–22, 19–11; McAuslan, *Land, Law and Planning*, pp. 292–302

21 Pp. 444 et seq, ante.

22 [1957] Ch 169, [1957] 1 All ER 371; *E R Ives Investment Ltd v High* [1967] 2 QB 379, [1967] 1

obliges a person who wishes to take advantage of a service or facility (e.g. a road or drains) to comply with any corresponding obligation to contribute to the cost of providing or maintaining it. The maxim cannot, however, be invoked where the burdened owner does not enjoy any service or facility to which his obligations attach or has no sufficient interest in the continuance of these benefits."[23]

(d) Enlargement of long leases into freeholds

This is an "untried and artificial" device, whereby a long lease is enlarged under section 153 of the Law of Property Act 1925, and the freehold is then subject "to all the same covenants . . . as the term would have been subject to if it had not been so enlarged".[1]

(e) Estate rentcharge

An estate rentcharge may be created to secure the payment of money or contribution to the maintenance of property.[2] The Rentcharges Act 1977 makes special provision for this type of rentcharge.[3]

(f) Right of re-entry

A right of re-entry may be reserved, exercisable on events which amount to the breach of a positive covenant. This right of re-entry runs with the land, but is subject to the rule against perpetuities.[4]

(g) Restriction under Land Registration Act, section 58

"Where the title to plots on a newly developed estate is going to be registered and the developer is interested in the continuing observance of the covenants, he can insert a covenant in the original conveyances that the plot shall not be sold without his consent. He can then enter a restriction in the register[5] to ensure compliance with the covenant and can refuse to give his consent to any sale under which the purchaser does not assume the appropriate positive obligations."

All ER 504; M & B p. 592; *Four Oaks Estate Ltd v Hadley* (1986) Times, 2 July (no benefit to which burden could be attached); *Law Debenture Trust Corpn plc v Ural Caspian Oil Corpn Ltd* [1993] 1 WLR 138; *Rhone v Stephens*, [1994] 2 WLR 429, [1994] 2 All ER 65 (doctrine not invoked where benefit "technical or minimal"). For a detailed discussion of the doctrine, see *Tito v Waddell (No. 2)* [1977] Ch 106, 289–311, [1977] 3 All ER 129 at 293–8, where MEGARRY V-C held at 303, at 292 that it covered not merely successors in title but also "anybody whose connection with the transaction creating the benefit and burden is sufficient to show that he has some claim to the benefit whether or not he has a valid title to it." See also (1977) 41 Conv (NS) 432–435 (F. R. Crane); [1985] Conv 12 (F. P. Aughterson); *Emmet on Title* (19th edn) para. 17.020.

23 *Rhone v Stephens* [1994] 2 WLR 429 at 437, where Lord TEMPLEMAN said: "The condition must be relevant to the exercise of the right. The obligation to repair the roof was an independent provision".

1 P. 459, ante. See also Leasehold Reform Act 1967, s. 8(3), p. 490, ante.

2 *Morland v Cook* (1868) LR 6 Eq 252; *Austerberry v Oldham Corpn* (1885) 29 Ch D 750–782.

3 S. 2 (3) (c), (4), (5). See p. 647, post.

4 *Shiloh Spinners Ltd v Harding* [1973] AC 691, [1973] 1 All ER 90. The possibility of relief against forfeiture reduces its effectiveness as a device. See (1950) 14 Conv (NS) 350 at 354–7 (S. M. Tolson).

5 LRA 1925, s. 58, p. 803, post.

(2) LAW REFORM

In spite of these methods of circumvention, the burden of a covenant, whether positive or negative, does not run with the servient land upon which it is imposed. As we are about to see, this rule has been radically relaxed by equity in the case of a negative covenant which merely restricts an owner from making certain defined uses of his land, but it still governs a positive covenant, such as one to maintain a fence for the benefit of a neighbouring owner or to contribute towards the cost of constructing and maintaining a private road. That such a covenant should be unenforceable against the successors in title of the covenantor is in many cases unreasonable, as, for instance, where the purchaser of a freehold flat has entered into positive covenants that are essential to the comfort of his neighbours in the same building. "This rule, whose discovery has shocked more than one eminent judge unversed in the subtleties of property law"[6] was considered in 1965 by the Wilberforce Committee which recommended that, subject to certain conditions, the burden of positive covenants should run, and again in 1984 by the Law Commission on the wider topic of both Positive and Restrictive Covenants.[7] In 1991 the Government announced that it would introduce commonhold[8] and implement with modifications the 1984 Report.

SECTION II   THE EXTENT TO WHICH RESTRICTIVE COVENANTS, WHETHER MADE BETWEEN LESSOR AND LESSEE, OR BETWEEN THE VENDOR AND THE PURCHASER OF A FEE SIMPLE, RUN WITH THE LAND IN EQUITY

A. GENERAL NATURE OF THE EQUITABLE DOCTRINE

In the historic case of *Tulk v Moxhay*,[9] the common law rule, that the burden of a covenant does not run with the land of the covenantor except in the case of a lease, was radically modified by equity so far as negative covenants are concerned. The general effect of the doctrine established by this case is that, subject to certain conditions to be discussed at length later, a covenant *negative in substance* entered into by the owner of Blackacre with the neighbouring owner of Whiteacre, imposes an equitable burden upon Blackacre that is enforceable to the same extent as any other equitable

---

6 *Rhone v Stephens* [1994] 2 WLR 429, [1994] 2 All ER 65, per NOURSE LJ.
7 Report of the Committee on Positive Covenants Affecting Land 1965 (Cmnd 2719); Law Commission Report on Restrictive Covenants 1967 (Law Com No. 11); Law Commission Report on Positive and Restrictive Covenants 1984 (Law Com No. 127, HC 201); p. 640, post; (1972B) 31 CLJ 157 (H. W. R. Wade). See *Rhone v Stephens* [1994] 2 WLR 429, where Lord TEMPLEMAN said at 436: "Parliamentary legislation to deal with the decision in the *Austerberry* case would require careful consideration of the consequences. Moreover, experience with leasehold tenure where positive covenants are enforceable by virtue of privity of estate, has demonstrated that social injustice can be caused by logic. Parliament was obliged to intervene to prevent tenants losing their homes and being saddled with the costs of restoring to their original glory buildings which had languished through wars and economic depression for exactly 99 years."
8 P. 169 , ante.
9 (1848) 2 Ph 774; M & B p. 833; [1981] Conv 55 (C. D. Bell); (1982) 98 LQR 279 (S. Gardner); [1983] Conv 29 (R. Griffith); 327 (C. D. Bell). On restrictive covenants generally, see Preston and Newsom, *Restrictive Covenants Affecting Freehold Land* (8th edn); Elphinstone, *Covenants Affecting Land*; Farrand (2nd edn), pp. 404–429; Maitland, *Equity,* pp. 162–178; (1971) 87 LQR 539 (D. J. Hayton). For a historical account, see Simpson, *A History of the Land Law* (2nd edn), pp. 116–118, 140–141, 256–260.

interest, such as a contract for a lease. The right to obtain an injunction[10] against a breach of the negative undertaking will pass to the subsequent owners of Whiteacre, and the duty to observe it will pass to all persons who take the burdened Blackacre, except a bona fide purchaser for value of the legal estate therein without notice, actual or constructive, of the covenant. The facts of *Tulk v Moxhay* were as follows:

> In 1808 the plaintiff, being then the owner in fee of the vacant piece of ground in the middle of Leicester Square, London, sold the ground to one Elms in fee, Elms covenanting for himself, his heirs and assigns that he and they would:
>
> > keep and maintain the said piece of ground and Square Garden, and the iron railing round the same in its then form, and in sufficient and proper repair as a Square Garden and Pleasure Ground, in an open state, uncovered with any buildings in neat and ornamental order.
>
> The piece of ground passed by divers conveyances into the hands of the defendant Moxhay, who, although he had made no similar covenant with his immediate vendor, admitted that he took the land with notice of the original covenant. The defendant then openly proposed to erect buildings upon the square, but the plaintiff, who still remained the owner of several adjacent houses, succeeded in obtaining an injunction to stop the breach of covenant.[11]

This doctrine has been the subject of development, in the course of which the nature of the right and obligation arising from a restrictive covenant has undergone a radical change.[12] The earlier decisions, culminating in *Luker v Dennis* in 1877,[13] proceeded solely upon the fact of notice,[14] since this was the element that Lord COTTENHAM stressed in *Tulk v Moxhay* in the following words:

> It is said that, the covenant being one which does not run with the land, this court cannot enforce it, but the question is, not whether the covenant runs with the land, but whether a party shall be permitted to use the land in a manner inconsistent with the contract entered into by his vendor, and with notice of which he purchased.[15]

To rest the enforcement of a contract against a third party on this basis is not without its dangers.

First, if the emphasis is laid upon whether the conscience of the third party acquiring the land of the covenantor is affected, instead of upon whether the land itself is affected, there will be certain persons, such as a squatter obtaining a title by 12 years' adverse possession,[20] who will enjoy an immunity that they do not deserve.

Secondly, if notice alone justifies the issue of an injunction, the remedy can scarcely be withheld in principle even though the contract is collateral, in the sense that its purpose is not to protect the covenantee's land against an

---

10 The court has power to grant damages in lieu of an injunction under Supreme Court Act 1981, s. 50 (formerly Chancery Amendment Act 1858, s. 2). See *Sefton v Tophams Ltd* [1965] Ch 1140, [1965] 3 All ER 1; *Baxter v Four Oaks Properties Ltd* [1965] Ch 816, [1965] 1 All ER 906; *Surrey County Council v Bredero Homes Ltd* [1992] 3 All ER 302; [1992] Conv 457 (N.S. Price). Preston and Newsom, paras. 8–11 to 8–19.
11 For the continued enforceability of the covenant, see *R v Westminster City Council and London Electricity Board* (1989) 59 P & CR 51, where SIMON BROWN J describes Leicester Square as "one of London's ornaments".
12 See especially Behan, *Covenants Affecting Land*, pp. 27 et seq.
13 (1877) 7 Ch D 227.
14 *LCC v Allen* [1914] 3 KB 642 at 658–9, 664–6.
15 (1848) 2 Ph 774 at 777.
20 P. 620, post.

undesirable use of the covenantor's land but to confer some personal privilege upon the covenantee.

Since the end of the nineteenth century the judicial approach to the matter has altered. The courts, choosing as the appropriate analogy either the negative easement, such as the right to light, or the tenant's covenant that is annexed to the land by virtue of *Spencer's Case*,[1] have required a restrictive covenant to possess what may be called a real, as distinct from a personal, flavour, before it becomes available to and enforceable against third parties. It must, as VAUGHAN WILLIAMS LJ said, "arise from the relation of two estates one to the other",[2] or, to use more familiar language, it must touch and concern the dominant tenement of the covenantee and must be intended to protect that land against certain uses of the servient tenement. But once it satisfies this requirement it creates an equitable right that will run with the dominant tenement and a corresponding equitable obligation binding on the servient tenement. Being an equitable burden, it affects every person in the world who comes to the servient tenement, except one who bona fide acquires the legal estate for value therein without notice, actual or constructive, of the covenant. The position cannot be better described than in the words of COLLINS LJ:

> When the benefit has been once clearly annexed to one piece of land, it passes by assignment of that land, and may be said to run with it . . . without proof of special bargain or representation on the assignment. In such a case it runs, not because the conscience of either party is affected, but because the purchaser has bought something which inhered in or was annexed to the land bought. That is the reason why, in dealing with the burden, the purchaser's conscience is not affected by notice of covenants which were part of the original bargain on the first sale, but were merely personal and collateral, while it is affected by notice of those which touch and concern the land. The covenant must be one that is capable of running with the land before the question of the purchaser's conscience and the equity affecting it can come into discussion.[3]

As the law now stands, certain essentials must be satisfied before the burden of a covenant can be laid upon an assignee of the servient tenement or before its benefit can be exploited by an assignee of the dominant tenement. These will now be stated.

B. CONDITIONS PRECEDENT TO THE ENFORCEMENT OF A RESTRICTIVE COVENANT IN EQUITY

(1) THE RUNNING OF THE BURDEN WITH THE LAND OF THE COVENANTOR

The burden of a restrictive covenant will bind an assignee of the servient tenement if the following essentials are satisfied.

(a) The conditions precedent

(i) The covenant must be negative in nature It is essential that the covenant should be negative in substance, not a positive one requiring the expenditure

---

1 P. 449; ante; *London and South Western Rly Co v Gomm* (1882) 20 Ch D 562 at 583; M & B p. 837; *Rhone v Stephens* [1994] 2 WLR 429, [1994] 2 All ER 65.
2 *Formby v Barker* [1903] 2 Ch 539 at 553. No such relation existed, for instance, in *Tophams Ltd v Earl of Sefton* [1967] 1 AC 50, [1966] 1 All ER 1039.
3 *Rogers v Hosegood* [1900] 2 Ch 388 at 407.

of money for its performance.[4] This condition is satisfied if the owner of the land undertakes to use the premises for private residence only, or to keep certain windows obscured, or not to build, not to open a public house, not to carry on a business, and so on. But in every case it is the substance and not the form of the contract that must be regarded, for if an undertaking, though couched in affirmative terms, clearly implies a negative, it will be caught by the doctrine of *Tulk v Moxhay*. Indeed, in that case itself, the covenant was not in terms restrictive, but its provision that the piece of ground was to be used only as an ornamental garden implied a prohibition against building.[5] Again, a covenant to give the first refusal of land is regarded as negative in substance, since in effect it is a promise not to sell without giving the covenantee an option to buy.[6]

(ii) The covenantee must at the time of the creation of the covenant and afterwards own land for the protection of which the covenant is made A restrictive covenant taken from the purchaser of a freehold estate is a mere covenant in gross personal to the contracting parties, unless it imposes an equitable burden upon the covenantor's land for the protection of land owned by the covenantee. Equity, acting on the analogy of a negative easement, will not regard a restrictive covenant as other than personal, unless there is the relation of dominancy and serviency between the respective properties.

It follows, therefore, that, if the covenantee retains no adjacent land or owns no land capable of being protected by the covenant, the covenant cannot be enforced against a person other than the covenantor, even if he has notice of it.[7]

Thus in *London County Council v Allen*:[8]

A, a builder, in return for permission to lay out a new street on his land, entered into a covenant with LCC not to build upon a plot of land which lay across the end of the proposed street. The plot was eventually conveyed to Mrs. A, who built on it and mortgaged it to B. The Court of Appeal held that the restrictive covenant was not binding on Mrs. A and B, even if they had had notice of it.

4 *Haywood v Brunswick Permanent Benefit Building Society* (1881) 8 QBD 403. Positive and negative obligations may be set in a single covenant. "There cannot be any doctrine of contagious proximity whereby the presence of the positive inhibits the enforcement of the neighbouring negative": *Shepherd Homes Ltd v Sandham* (No 2) [1971] 1 WLR 1062, [1971] 2 All ER 1267, per MEGARRY J.
5 *Clegg v Hands* (1890) 44 Ch D 503 at 519; *Bridges v Harrow London Borough* (1981) 260 EG 284 at 288 (covenant to retain trees in hedgerow held to be probably negative in substance); *Bedwell Park Quarry Company v Hertfordshire County Council* [1993] JPL 349 ("It is hard to think of an obligation which was more positive in substance as well as in form").
6 *Manchester Ship Canal Co v Manchester Racecourse Co* [1901] 2 Ch 37.
7 But a lessor's interest in the reversion suffices to make a covenant touching and concerning the land enforceable against a sub-lessee: *Hall v Ewin* (1887) 37 Ch D 74; *Regent Oil Co Ltd v J A Gregory (Hatch End) Ltd* [1966] Ch 402 at 432–3, [1965] 3 All ER 673 at 680. For statutory exceptions to the rule, see National Trust Act 1937, s. 8; *Gee v The National Trust* [1966] 1 WLR 170 at 174, [1966] 1 All ER 954 at 957; Green Belt (London and Home Counties) Act 1938, s. 22; Water Act 1945, s. 15; National Parks and Access to Countryside Act 1949, s. 16 (4); Forestry Act 1967, s. 5 (2); Endowments and Glebe Measure 1976, s. 22; Ancient Monuments and Archaeological Areas Act 1979, s. 17 (5); Wildlife and Countryside Act 1981, s. 39 (3); Local Government (Miscellaneous Provisions) Act 1982, s. 33; Housing Act 1985, s. 609; Town and Country Planning Act 1990, s. 106; and a number of local authorities have power under local Acts. See also *Governors of the Peabody Donation Fund v London Residuary Body* (1987) 55 P & CR 355 (Artisans and Labourers Dwellings Improvement Act 1875, s. 9; "a valuable site in Covent Garden").
8 [1914] 3 KB 642; M & B p. 834; *Formby v Barker* [1903] 2 Ch 539; M & B p. 836.

BUCKLEY LJ in the course of his judgment said:[9]

> In the present case we are asked to extend the doctrine of *Tulk v Moxhay* so as to affirm that a restrictive covenant can be enforced against a derivative owner taking with notice by a person who never has had or who does not retain any land to be protected by the restrictive covenant in question. In my opinion the doctrine does not extend to that case. The doctrine is that a covenant not running with the land, but being a negative covenant entered into by an owner of land with an adjoining owner, binds the land in equity and is enforceable against a derivative owner taking with notice. The doctrine ceases to be applicable when the person seeking to enforce the covenant against the derivative owner has no land to be protected by the negative covenant. The fact of notice is in that case irrelevant.[10]

Again, once a covenantee has assigned the whole of the dominant land, he cannot enforce the covenant against the servient owner. His one remedy is to sue the covenantor personally on the contract, but even so he is entitled only to nominal damages, not to an injunction. The principle of *London County Council v Allen*[11] is that the equitable doctrine ought to be applied with the sole object of protecting the enjoyment of the land which the covenant was intended to protect. If it were possible for a covenantee to enforce a covenant, despite the fact that he never retained any land at all or that he later disposed of the land which he had retained, the result would be to place an unwarranted and useless burden upon subsequent purchasers from the covenantor.[12]

(iii) The covenant must touch and concern the dominant land The covenant must be capable of benefiting the dominant land in the sense that it must be one which touches and concerns that land.[13] To satisfy this condition in the case where a freehold estate is conveyed:

> the covenant must either affect the land as regards mode of occupation, or it must be such as *per se*, and not merely from collateral circumstances, affects the value of the land.[14]

Whether the covenant benefits the dominant land is a question of fact to be determined on expert evidence presented to the court.[15] The onus is on the defendant to show that it does not do so, either originally or at the date of the action.[16] This means that, if there were possible opinions either way, the defendant will still fail unless he can show that the opinion that the covenant benefits the land could not reasonably be held.[17]

(iv) It must be the common intention of the parties that the burden of the covenant shall run with the land of the covenantor This intention may appear

9 At 654.

10 See, however, n. 7, supra, as to the modern statutory power of local authorities to enforce restrictive covenants otherwise than for the protection of land.

11 [1914] 3 KB 642; *Formby v Barker*, supra; *Kelly v Barrett* [1924] 2 Ch 379.

12 *Chambers v Randall* [1923] 1 Ch 149 at 157; *Re Union of London and Smith's Bank Ltd's Conveyance, Miles v Easter* [1933] Ch 611 at 632.

13 *Rogers v Hosegood* [1900] 2 Ch 388 at 395; *Kelly v Barrett* [1924] 2 Ch 379 at 395; *Marquess of Zetland v Driver* [1939] Ch 1 at 8, [1938] 2 All ER 158 at 161.

14 *Rogers v Hosegood*, supra, at 395, per FARWELL J, adopting BAYLEY J in *Congleton Corpn v Pattison* (1808) 10 East 130.

15 *Marten v Flight Refuelling Ltd* [1962] Ch 115 at 137; *Earl of Leicester v Wells-next-the-Sea UDC* [1973] Ch 110, [1972] 3 All ER 77; *Wrotham Park Estate Co Ltd v Parkside Homes Ltd* [1974] 1 WLR 798, [1974] 2 All ER 321.

16 *Wrotham Park Estate Co Ltd v Parkside Homes Ltd*, supra.

17 [1974] JPL at 133 (G. H. Newsom).

from the wording of the covenant itself, as, for instance, where the covenant is made by the covenantor for himself, his heirs and assigns. Covenants which are made after 1925 and relate to any land of the covenantor, or are capable of being bound by him,[18] are deemed by section 79 of the Law of Property Act 1925 to be made by the covenantor on behalf of himself, his successors in title and the persons deriving title under him or them, unless a contrary intention is expressed.[19]

(b) Persons against whom burden runs

We must now examine more closely the effect of a covenant which satisfies the four conditions set out above, and in particular consider those persons against whom the covenant is enforceable.

The doctrine of *Tulk v Moxhay* stands on quite a different footing from the rules which regulate the running of covenants at law, and being of a far more elastic nature it affects a more extensive class of persons and embraces a more extensive class of covenants. The essence of the matter is that when once the above conditions are satisfied a restrictive covenant becomes an equitable interest, and as such is enforceable on general principles against all persons who acquire the burdened land, with the one exception of the bona fide purchaser for valuable consideration of the legal estate therein without notice of the covenant. Moreover, the occupier of the burdened land is liable irrespectively of the character of his occupation. This is in sharp contrast with the common law and statutory rules that govern covenants contained in a lease. Under these rules, as we have seen,[20] the burden of a covenant, whether positive or negative, that touches and concerns the land passes to an assignee of the tenant, and it is immaterial that the landlord retains no dominant land.[1] But no one is an assignee for this purpose unless there is privity of estate between him and the reversioner. Thus, though the burden is traditionally said to run with the land, what in fact it runs with is the estate created by the lease. Under the developed doctrine of *Tulk v Moxhay*, on the other hand, it runs with the servient land as such, and there is no question of privity of estate. A restrictive covenant is enforceable against the successors in title of the original covenantor, including a mere occupier of the land.[2]

The effect of this distinction between running with the land and running with the estate may be illustrated by a reference to three classes of persons who are all caught by the doctrine of *Tulk v Moxhay*, but none of whom is liable at common law under the rules derived from *Spencer's Case*.

(i) Under-lessees A restrictive covenant imposed upon a lessee binds an under-lessee, despite the absence of privity of estate between him and the lessor.[3]

(ii) Mere occupiers A person who is merely occupying land without having

---

18 *Lynnthorpe Enterprises Ltd v Sidney Smith (Chelsea) Ltd* [1990] 1 EGLR 148 (land need not belong to covenantor at time of covenant); M & B p. 840.

19 *Re Royal Victoria Pavilion (Ramsgate)* [1961] Ch 581, [1961] 3 All ER 83; M & B p. 840; *Tophams Ltd v Earl of Sefton* [1967] 1 AC 50 at 81, [1966] 1 All ER 1039 at 1053; M & B p. 839; p. 615, n. 10, ante; *Rhone v Stephens* [1994] 2 WLR 429, [1994] 2 All ER 65.

20 P. 455, ante.

1 *Regent Oil Co Ltd v J. A. Gregory (Hatch End) Ltd* [1966] Ch 402, [1965] 3 All ER 673.

2 LPA 1925, s. 79 (2).

3 *Clements v Welles* (1865) LR 1 Eq 200; *Hall v Ewin* (1887) 37 Ch D 74; *John v Holmes* [1900] 1 Ch 188.

any definite estate or interest therein is bound by restrictive covenants. Thus in *Mander v Falcke*:[4]

a lessee who had covenanted not to use the demised premises for purposes which would cause annoyance or inconvenience to adjoining property owned by the lessor granted an under-lease of the premises. The reversion was ultimately assigned to the plaintiff and the under-lease became vested in X. Apparently X did not occupy the premises himself, but allowed his father to have possession, and the evidence clearly showed that the latter, while purporting to keep an oyster bar, was in fact using the place as a brothel to the great scandal of the neighbourhood.

In seeking an injunction to restrain a breach of the covenant it was argued that such relief could not be granted against the father, as he had no interest whatever, either legal or equitable, in the land. This argument failed, and an injunction was granted against the father, LINDLEY LJ saying:

I treat him simply as an occupier managing the business. He may be neither an assignee nor purchaser, but he is in occupation, and that is enough to affect him, he having notice of the covenants in the lease.[5]

(iii) Disseisors A person who acquires a title to land by lapse of time under the Limitation Act 1980 is bound by any restrictive covenants which are annexed to the land. We have seen that a covenant entered into between landlord and tenant does not at law bind a person who by long-continued possession of the premises acquires a superior right to the tenant, because the effect of the Limitation Act is merely to extinguish the right of the tenant and not to transfer his identical interest to the adverse possessor.[6] There is no privity of estate between the disseisor and the lessor. This lack of privity, however, will not free a disseisor of the servient land from a restrictive covenant unless he can prove that he is a bona fide purchaser for value of the legal estate without notice. The case of *Re Nisbet and Potts' Contract*[7] affords an illustration:

Lands were sold in 1867 by A to W, a covenant being entered into by the latter that he would not build on the purchased property within 30 feet of a certain road. This covenant was for the benefit of other property owned by A. In 1872 W re-sold the land to X with a similar covenant. Somewhere about 1878 Y wrongfully seized the land and remained in occupation for over 12 years, after which he automatically acquired what is called a possessory title, and became entitled to keep the land as against X. In 1890 Y's son, who had succeeded his father, sold the land to Z, who agreed that instead of requiring the title to be proved for the last 40 years[8] he would be content with proof that Y had been in possession since before 1878. Later still the land was sold to Nisbet, and he agreed in 1903 to sell it to Potts. The question was whether Potts, if he took a conveyance of the land, would be subject to the restrictive covenant imposed by the original deed of 1867.

It was argued that the covenant no longer bound assignees of the servient land, for Y, who had seized the land in 1878, acquired a title quite independent of any prior holder's title, and that, even if it made any difference, which was denied, neither Z nor Nisbet had notice of the covenant and therefore could not be bound thereby. But it was held that the equitable

4 [1891] 2 Ch 554.
5 At 557
6 *Tichborne v Weir* (1892) 67 LT 735; M & B p. 838; p. 456, ante.
7 [1905] 1 Ch 391, affd [1906] 1 Ch 386; M & B p. 839.
8 P. 62, ante.

interest created by the covenant remained enforceable against Z and Nisbet, unless they could satisfy the court that they had acquired the legal estate for valuable consideration without notice.

They certainly had acquired the legal estate for value without actual notice, but nevertheless they were affected by constructive notice, for if they had insisted, as they might have done, upon proof of a good root of title at least 40 years old, they would have been led back through the squatter Y to the original covenantor W. If they chose to accept less than they might have done, they were bound to take the consequences.

Further, it was clear that the lapse of time and the changes of title that had occurred since 1867 did not bar the remedy of the person in whom the benefit of the covenant was now vested. Time under the Limitation Act does not begin to run against a person until his right of action accrues. In the instant case no right or action would accrue until the covenant was broken, and there had been no question of this until 1903.

(c) Registration of restrictive covenants

A final word is now required as to the binding effect of restrictive covenants. Since 1925 restrictive covenants have been divided into two classes.

(i) Covenants created before 1926 The rule, which governs covenants created before 1 January 1926, is that laid down above, viz. that they bind all persons who acquire the burdened land, with the exception of a bona fide purchaser for value of the legal estate therein without notice, actual or constructive, of the covenants. Such a purchaser can, however, pass a title free from the restriction to a purchaser from him, even though the latter has actual notice of the covenant.[9]

(ii) Covenants created after 1925 Covenants created after 1925, except those made between lessor and lessee,[10] are void against a purchaser (including a mortgagee and lessee) of the *legal estate* in the burdened land *for money or money's worth*, unless they are registered as land charges in the appropriate register.[11] If not registered they are void against the purchaser for value of the legal estate even though he had express notice of them. Thus non-registration does not avail an assignee of a mere equitable interest in the burdened land, or an assignee of the legal estate who does not give money or money's worth. The reason why a restrictive covenant between a lessor and lessee cannot be registered, is that it is a simple and normal step for an assignee to inspect the lease which contains the terms of the tenancy.

(2) THE RUNNING OF THE BENEFIT WITH THE LAND OF THE COVENANTEE

Suppose that on the sale of Whiteacre to X a restrictive covenant has been taken from him for the protection of Blackacre still retained by the vendor, A; and suppose further that A has subsequently sold Blackacre, the dominant land, to B. Can B enforce the covenant against X or against Y who is an

---

9 *Wilkes v Spooner* [1911] 2 KB 473; M & B p. 28.
10 *Dartstone Ltd v Cleveland Petroleum Co Ltd* [1969] 1 WLR 1807, [1969] 3 All ER 668; [1956] 20 Conv (NS) 370 (R. G. Rowley).
11 LCA 1972, ss. 2 (5) Class D (ii), 4 (6); s. 17 (1), p. 764, post. Positive and negative covenants entered into with a local authority, a Minister of the Crown or Government Department (otherwise than as between landlord and tenant) are registrable as local land charges: LLCA 1975, ss. 1, 2, p. 767, ante.

assignee of X's land? The answer is that enforcement is not automatic merely because the dominant land has come into the hands of B. B must go further. He must prove, not only that he has acquired the land, but also that he has acquired the benefit of the covenant itself.[12]

We have already seen that the benefit of a covenant runs at common law subject to certain conditions.[13] If B can satisfy these, there is no need for him to rely on the rules evolved by equity for the running of the benefit. There are however circumstances in which the common law rules are inapplicable, and it is then that B must prove that he has satisfied the conditions which equity imposes.

The situations in which B must do this are:

(*a*) where B is, or A the original covenantee, was, a mere equitable owner of Blackacre;[14]

(*b*) where B does not have the same legal estate in Blackacre as A had, this would only apply to covenants made before 1926;[15]

(*c*) where Whiteacre has been conveyed to Y and enforcement against Y depends upon the equitable doctrine of *Tulk v Moxhay;*[16]

(*d*) where B relies upon an express assignment of the benefit of the covenant from A, and the assignment does not comply with section 136 of the Law of Property Act 1925;[17]

(*e*) where part only of Whiteacre has been conveyed to B, for "at law, the benefit could not be assigned in pieces. It would have to be assigned as a whole or not at all";[18]

(*f*) where B relies upon his land being part of a scheme of development.[19]

In these situations there are only three ways[20] in which B can show that he has acquired the benefit of the covenant itself, namely by proving:

(*a*) that the benefit of the covenant has been effectively annexed to the dominant land, and that he had acquired the whole of that land, or the part of it to which the covenant was annexed; or,

(*b*) that the benefit of the covenant was separately and expressly assigned to him at the time of the sale; or,

(*c*) that both the dominant and servient lands are subject to a scheme of development.

Let us take these methods separately.

---

12 [1938] CLJ 339 (S. J. Bailey); [1971] 82 LQR 539 (D. J. Hayton); (1982) 2 Legal Studies 53 (D. J. Hurst); (1982) 98 LQR 279 (S. Gardner).

13 P. 610, ante.

14 *Fairclough v Marshall* (1878) 4 Ex D 37; *Rogers v Hosegood* [1900] 2 Ch 388 (a mortgagor before 1926); M & B p. 848.

15 LPA 1925, s. 78 (1); p. 610, ante.

16 *Renals v Cowlishaw* (1878) 9 Ch D 125; M & B p. 777; *Re Union of London and Smith's Bank Ltd's Conveyance, Miles v Easter* [1933] Ch 611 at 630 per ROMER LJ; M & B p. 863; *Marten v Flight Refuelling Ltd* [1962] Ch 115, [1961] 2 All ER 696; M & B p. 868.

17 Pp. 627 et seq, post.

18 *Re Union of London and Smith's Bank Ltd's Conveyance,* supra, at 630, per ROMER LJ; *Federated Homes Ltd v Mill Lodge Properties Ltd* [1980] 1 WLR 594, [1980] 1 All ER 371; M & B p. 851.

19 Pp. 630 et seq, post.

20 *Re Pinewood Estate, Farnborough* [1958] Ch 280, [1957] 2 All ER 517; M & B p. 846.

(a) Annexation of covenant to dominant land

(i) **Intention to annex** Whether or not the benefit of a restrictive covenant runs with the dominant land by virtue of its express annexation to that land depends on the intention of the parties to be inferred from the language which they used in the deed creating the covenant. This intention to annex is commonly inferred when the covenant is made:

"with so and so, owners or owner for the time being of whatever the land may be". Another method is to state by means of an appropriate declaration that the covenant is taken "for the benefit of" whatever the lands may be.[1]

Thus in *Rogers v Hosegood*[2] the following covenant was held to be annexed to the land:

with intent that the covenants might so far as possible bind the premises thereby conveyed and every part thereof and might enure to the benefit of the vendors ... their heirs and assigns and others claiming under them to all or any of their lands adjoining or near to the said premises.

(ii) **Dominant land must be ascertainable** Furthermore, the exact land to which the parties intend to annex the benefit of the covenant must be ascertainable. Whether this is so depends primarily upon the construction of the deed of conveyance. A competent draftsman will describe the land in precise terms, as for instance by declaring that the covenant is taken for the benefit of "the property known as Blackacre"; or for the "land marked red on the plan drawn on these presents". If the description is more vague, as for instance "the land adjoining" the servient land, extrinsic evidence is admissible to identify the particular land that the parties had in mind.[3]

In summary, the land must be clearly,[4] or easily,[5] identified in the conveyance creating the covenant. As we shall see, this is a stricter rule of identification than that which applies in the case of express assignment.[6]

(iii) **Law of Property Act, section 78** However, the problem of determining whether the language of a conveyance is sufficient to show an intention to annex the covenant has disappeared in respect of a covenant entered into after 1925 since the decision of the Court of Appeal in *Federated Homes Ltd v Mill Lodge Properties Ltd*.[7] In that case:

A owned land for development which was subject to restrictions on the overall number of houses to be built on it. A sold three parts of the land (blue, red and green) to separate purchasers. The blue land was sold to M who covenanted with A that:

"in carrying out the development the Purchaser shall not build at a greater density than a total of 300 dwellings so as not to reduce the number of units which the Vendor might eventually erect on the retained land." The conveyance contained

1 *Drake v Gray* [1936] Ch 451 at 456, [1936] 1 All ER 363 at 377, per GREENE LJ.
2 [1900] 2 Ch 388; M & B p. 848. Cf. *Renals v Cowlishaw* (1878) 9 Ch D 125; M & B p. 850 (covenant with the vendors "their heirs, executors, administrators and assigns" held insufficient to annex, since no dominant land was specified). See also *J. Sainsbury plc v Enfield London Borough Council* [1989] 1 WLR 590, [1989] 2 All ER 817; M & B p. 850.
3 See Preston and Newsom, *Restrictive Covenants*, para 2.19.
4 *Newton Abbot Co-operative Society Ltd v Williamson and Treadgold Ltd* [1952] Ch 286 at 289, [1952] 1 All ER 279, at 283, per UPJOHN J.
5 *Marquess of Zetland v Driver* [1939] Ch 1 at 8, [1938] 2 All ER 158 at 161, per FARWELL J.
6 P. 628, post.
7 [1980] 1 WLR 594, [1980] 1 All ER 371; M & B, p. 851.

a reference to the retained lands as "any adjoining or adjacent property retained" by A.

It will be seen that the terms of the covenant were not such as, from its express language, to annex the benefit of it to A's land under the rule in *Rogers v Hosegood*.

A then sold the red and green lands to other purchasers, and eventually F became owner of both of them. In the case of the green land, there was a complete chain of assignments of the benefit of the covenant through the various purchasers to A, but not in the case of the red land.

F sought an injunction to restrain M from breaking the restrictive covenant.

In granting the injunction the Court of Appeal held that F was entitled to the benefit of the covenant in respect of the green land, by reason of the chain of assignments.[8] This was sufficient to entitle F to relief, but the Court then went on to consider whether F also had the benefit of the covenant in his capacity as owner of the red land. It was held that F had that benefit under section 78 (1) of the Law of Property Act 1925.[9] The actual wording of the covenant was "sufficient to intimate that the covenant was one relating to the land of the covenantee",[10] and, therefore, the benefit was annexed to the land without the need to use appropriate language from which an intention to annex might be inferred. As BRIGHTMAN LJ said:[11]

> If the condition precedent of section 78 is satisfied—that is to say, there exists a covenant which touches and concerns the land of the covenantee—that covenant runs with the land for the benefit of his successors in title, persons deriving title under him or them and other owners and occupiers.

This decision simplifies the rules as to the passing of the benefit of a restrictive covenant, but it has been criticized on the ground that a narrow construction of the section is preferable, i.e. that it is merely a statutory shorthand for reducing the length of legal documents.[12] On this view the section would only operate when annexation had already been established according to the general rule. There are strong arguments in favour of the narrow view. The Law of Property Act 1925 is a consolidation statute and "if the words are capable of more than one construction then the Court will give effect to the construction which does not change the law".[13] Further, if a far-reaching and substantial alteration to the law had been intended by Parliament, one would expect it to be expressed in unambiguous terms,[14]

8　P. 629, post.

9　P. 610, ante. The Court of Appeal found support for this wide construction in *Smith and Snipes Hall Farm Ltd v River Douglas Catchment Board* [1949] 2 KB 500, [1949] 2 All ER 179; M & B p. 769; p. 610, ante; *Williams v Unit Construction Co Ltd* (1955) 19 Conv NS 262; M & B p. 845. John Mills QC had decided in favour of F at first instance, but under LPA 1925, s. 62; p. 534, ante; p. 625, n. 19, post.

10　See *Bridges v Harrow London Borough Council* (1981) 260 EG 284; [1982] Conv 313 (F. Webb).

11　At 605, at 379.

12　[1980] JPL 371; [1981] 97 LQR 32; [1981] JPL 295; (1982) 98 LQR 202 (G. H. Newsom); (1980) 43 MLR 445 (D. J. Hayton); 130 NLJ 531 (T. Bailey); [1985] Conv 177 (P. N. Todd). And there is no suggestion of a wide construction in Sir Benjamin Cherry's book (Wolstenholme and Cherry's *Conveyancing Statutes*, 11th edn, 1925). See also *J. Sainsbury plc v Enfield London Borough Council* [1989] 1 WLR 590, [1989] 2 All ER 817 (benefit of covenant made in 1894 not annexed by Conveyancing Act 1881, s. 58 (1), the forerunner of LPA 1925, s. 78(1)).

13　*Beswick v Beswick* [1968] AC 58 at 87 and 105, [1967] 2 All ER 1197 at 1121 and 1223, per Lord GUEST and Lord UPJOHN respectively. In that case the rule was used to restrict the scope of LPA 1925, s. 56; p. 632, post.

14　*Beswick v Beswick*, supra at 93, at 1215, per Lord PEARCE.

and a formula was ready to hand to do this; the repetition of the wording in the two immediately preceding sections would have given the effect of the wider construction without any ambiguity.[15] The Court of Appeal's view is also at variance with the narrow interpretation by the House of Lords of the similar but not identical section 79 in respect of the running of the burden of a covenant.[16].

The decision in *Federated Homes Ltd v Mill Lodge Properties Ltd* was further considered in *Roake v Chadha*,[17] where a covenant contained the words

> so as to bind ... the land hereby transferred into whosoever hands the same may come ... but so that this covenant shall not enure for the benefit of any owner or subsequent purchaser of any part of the estate unless the benefit of this covenant shall be expressly assigned.

It was held that the annexation of the benefit under section 78 was not automatic, notwithstanding that section 78, unlike its counterpart, section 79, does not contain the words "unless a contrary intention is expressed". Even where a covenant is deemed to be made with successors in title as section 78 requires, "one still has to construe the covenant as a whole to see whether the benefit of the covenant is annexed".[18]

(iv) Annexation to whole of covenantee's land Even if the language of the covenant indicates an intention to annex the benefit of the covenant to the whole of the land of the covenantee, such annexation will not be effected unless substantially the whole of the land is capable of benefiting. Thus in *Re Ballard's Conveyance*[19]

> the benefit of a covenant which imposed a restriction on 18 acres was annexed by the conveyance to "the Childwickbury Estate". The area of this estate was about 1700 acres, far the largest part of which could not possibly be directly affected by a breach of the covenant.

Although it would seem that an injury to a part of any unity is inevitably an injury to the whole, CLAUSON J held that the covenant was not enforceable by assignees of the whole of the dominant land. Moreover, he refused to

---

15 LPA 1925, ss. 76 (6) (covenants for title), 77 (5) (implied covenants in conveyances subject to rents); p. 781, post. The two sub-sections have identical wording: "The benefit of a covenant implied as aforesaid shall be annexed to, and shall go with, the estate of interest of the implied covenantee, and shall be capable of being enforced by every person in whom that estate or interest is, for the whole or any part thereof, from time to time vested." See also ss. 141 (1), 142 (1); p. 450, ante.
16 *Rhone v Stephens* [1994] 2 WLR 429, [1994] 2 All ER 65; p. 613, ante.
17 [1984] 1 WLR 40, [1983] 3 All ER 503; M & B p. 855; [1983] All ER Rev 331 (P. J. Clarke); [1984] Conv 68 (P. N. Todd).
18 Per Judge Paul Baker QC at 46, at 508. He also held that the benefit of the covenant did not pass under LPA 1925, s. 62; p. 534, ante. It was not a right "appertaining or reputed to appertain" to land. He also thought that the rights in s. 62 might be confined to legal rights, thereby excluding the benefit of a restrictive covenant, which is an equitable right. See also *Kumar v Dunning* [1989] QB 193, [1987] 2 All ER 801, where BROWNE-WILKINSON V-C said at 198, at 805: "A right under covenant cannot appertain to the land unless the benefit is in some way annexed to the land. If the benefit of a covenant passes under s. 62 even if not annexed to the land, the whole modern law of restrictive covenants would have been established on an erroneous basis".
19 [1937] Ch 473, [1937] 2 All ER 691.

sever the covenant and thus to regard it as annexed to the part of the land that was in fact touched and concerned. The decision seems to amount to this: that if a covenantee over-estimates to a moderate degree the area of the dominant land capable of deriving advantage from a restrictive covenant, his attempt to preserve the amenities of the neighbourhood and to maintain the selling value of what he retains will fail.[1] Why the well-known doctrine of severance should be excluded from this type of contract is difficult to appreciate.[2]

On the other hand, a covenant which is annexed to the whole *or any part or parts* of the dominant land is enforceable by a successor in title to any part of that land which is in fact benefited by the covenant. In *Marquess of Zetland v Driver*,[3] for instance:

> The covenant was expressed to be for the benefit and protection of "such part or parts of the [dominant land] (a) as shall for the time being remain unsold or (b) as shall be sold by the vendor or his successors in title with the express benefit of this covenant." Certain parts of the unsold land were contiguous to the land of the covenantor, but other parts were more than a mile distant. The covenant, therefore, did not benefit the whole of the dominant land.

It was held that the person who succeeded to the dominant land could enforce the covenant against a purchaser of the servient land. The Court of Appeal, without expressing approbation of *Re Ballard's Conveyance*, distinguished it on the ground that:

> in that case the covenant was expressed to run with the whole estate, whereas in the present case . . . the covenant is expressed to be for the benefit of the whole or any part or parts of the unsold settled property.[4]

Extrinsic evidence is admissible to show whether a covenant is capable of operating to the advantage of the dominant land;[5] and, as we have seen, the onus is on the defendant to show that it does not do so, either originally, or at the date of the action.[6]

(v) Annexation to part of covenantee's land The benefit of a restrictive covenant, once it has been annexed to the dominant land, runs automatically with that land and is enforceable by the successors in title of the covenantee, even though they do not learn of its existence until after execution of the conveyance.[7] If a successor in title acquires the whole of the land, the benefit passes to him without question; but if he acquires only part he must show that the benefit was annexed to that particular part alone or to each portion of the whole.

For instance, A, the owner of a large property, sells part of it to Y and

1 (1941) 57 LQR pp. 210–11 (G. R. Y. Radcliffe).
2 See Elphinstone, *Covenants Affecting Land*, p. 60, n. 10.
3 [1939] Ch 1, [1938] 2 All ER 158.
4 Ibid., at 10, at 163.
5 *Marten v Flight Refuelling Ltd* [1962] Ch 115, [1961] 2 All ER 696; M & B, p. 868; *Earl of Leicester v Wells-next-the-Sea UDC* [1973] Ch 110, [1972] 3 All ER 77 (expert evidence admitted to show that a covenant restricting 19 acres afforded "great benefit and much needed protection to the Holkham Estate as a whole" i.e. to 32,000 acres). In *Re Ballard's Conveyance*, supra, no evidence was offered to show benefit to the dominant land as a whole.
6 *Wrotham Park Estate Co Ltd v Parkside Homes Ltd* [1974] 1 WLR 798, [1974] 2 All ER 321; p. 618, ante; *Cryer v Scott Bros (Sunbury) Ltd* (1986) 55 P & CR 183; [1988] Conv 172 (J. E. Adams).
7 *Rogers v Hosegood* [1900] 2 Ch 388; M & B p. 848.

takes a covenant that no public house shall be opened on it. This covenant is annexed to A's land. Later A sells part of the dominant land to B. If B seeks to enforce the covenant by virtue of its annexation to A's land, he must prove that its benefit was annexed to each and every part of those lands or to the very part bought by him.

Whether or not there has been effective annexation to each and every part of the land is once again a question of construction of the language of the covenant. Thus in *Re Selwyn's Conveyance*[8] it was held that:

a covenant "to enure for the protection of the adjoining or neighbouring land part of, or lately part of, the Selwyn Estate"

was annexed to each part of the dominant land.

Furthermore, even if the covenant has been annexed only to the whole of the dominant land, a purchaser of part of it will be able to enforce the covenant if the benefit of the covenant has been expressly assigned to him.[9]

Finally, we must notice that this problem of construction will disappear if the approach of the Court of Appeal in *Federated Homes Ltd v Mill Lodge Properties Ltd*[10] is subsequently adopted. In that case the court found it difficult to understand how a covenant, which is annexed to the land as a whole, is not also annexed to the individual parts of that land. It favoured a rule that the benefit of such a covenant annexed to the whole is prima facie annexed to every part thereof, unless a contrary intention clearly appears.

(b) Express assignment of covenant

Failure to establish the annexation described above is not necessarily fatal to an assignee of the covenantee's land, for he will succeed in an action for an infringement of the restriction if he shows that he is not only an assignee of the land, but also the express assignee of the *covenant* itself.[11]

Such an express assignment will be necessary in fewer instances in the future, as a result of the decision in *Federated Homes Ltd v Mill Lodge Properties Ltd*,[12] in which, as we have seen, annexation was held to be effected under section 78 of the Law of Property Act 1925 without the need for appropriate language in the deed creating the covenant. Instances may, however, still arise, as for example, where there is express provision to the

---

8 [1967] Ch 674, [1967] 1 All ER 339. Cf *Russell v Archdale* [1964] Ch 38, [1962] 2 All ER 305; M & B, p. 860; *Re Jeff's Transfer (No. 2)* [1966] 1 WLR 841, [1966] 1 All ER 937; *Stilwell v Blackman* [1968] Ch 508, [1967] 3 All ER 514. See *Griffiths v Band* (1974) 29 P & CR 243 ("this somewhat muddy corner of legal history", per GOULDING J at 246); Law Commission Report on Restrictive Covenants 1967 (Law Com No. 11), p. 15 which recommends that the benefit of a land obligation should be annexed to each and every part unless a contrary intention is expressed. See too a valuable article in (1968) 84 LQR 22 (P. V. Baker).

9 *Russell v Archdale*, supra (against the original covenantor who was still owner of the servient land); *Stilwell v Blackman*, supra (against a successor in title of the original covenantor).

10 [1980] 1 WLR 594 at 606, 607, [1980] 1 All ER 371 at 380, 382; M & B p. 851. This would involve re-consideration of the decisions in n. 8, supra.

11 *Reid v Bickerstaff* [1909] 2 Ch 305 at 320; *Re Union of London and Smith's Bank Ltd's Conveyance, Miles v Easter* [1933] Ch 611.

12 [1980] 1 WLR 594, [1980] 1 All ER 371; M & B p. 851; p. 623, ante.

effect that express assignment of the covenant shall be required, [13] or where there is no identification in the conveyance of the land to be benefited. [14]

As we have already seen, the benefit of a covenant may be transferred at law by assignment as a chose in action under section 136 of the Law of Property Act 1925. [15] "Where the defendant is liable at law (as the original covenantor or his personal representative) there is no difficulty peculiar to the case of covenants affecting land: such an action is governed by the ordinary rules as to the assignment of a chose in action. But where the defendant is sued as an assign of the land burdened by the covenant, the plaintiff can only establish the defendant's liability in equity under the rule in *Tulk v Moxhay*." [16]

The equitable rules under which an express assignment is permissible were crystallised by ROMER LJ in *Re Union of London and Smith's Bank Ltd's Conveyance, Miles v Easter*: [17]

(i) The covenant must have been taken for the benefit of the land of the covenantee and (ii) that land must be indicated with reasonable certainty. This indication need not appear in the conveyance creating the covenant. It is sufficient if in the light of the attendant circumstances the identity of the dominant land is in some other way ascertainable with reasonable certainty. (iii) It must also be retained in whole or part by the plaintiff and (iv) be capable of benefiting from the covenant. (v) The assignment of the covenant and the conveyance of the land to which it relates must be contemporaneous.

Whether the first two requirements were satisfied was neatly raised in *Newton Abbot Co-operative Society Ltd v Williamson and Treadgold Ltd* [18] on the following facts:

The owner of Devonia, in which she carried on the business of an ironmonger, sold a shop on the opposite side of the street to a purchaser who traded there as a grocer. The purchaser covenanted not to trade as an ironmonger at the premises. The conveyance did not define any dominant land for the benefit of which the covenant was taken, but simply described the vendor as "of Devonia".

UPJOHN J held in the first place that the covenant was not a mere covenant in gross. Its objects were not only to protect the vendor personally against competition, but also to enhance the selling value of Devonia if sold to someone intending to trade there as an ironmonger. The learned judge further held that the identity of the dominant land was sufficiently clear. The only reasonable inference to draw from the surrounding circumstances, especially from the propinquity of the two shops, was that the covenant was taken for the benefit not only of the vendor's business, but also of the land that she retained.

Nevertheless, in order to appreciate the limits within which assignment is permissible it is essential to stress that the reason why equity allows a

---

13 *Marquess of Zetland v Driver* [1937] Ch 651; *Roake v Chadha* [1984] 1 WLR 40, [1983] 3 All ER 503; M & B p. 855; p. 625, ante.

14 *Newton Abbot Co-operative Society v Williamson and Treadgold Ltd* [1952] Ch 286, [1952] 1 All ER 279, infra. But see *Federated Homes Ltd v Mill Lodge Properties Ltd*, supra, at 604, at 379, per BRIGHTMAN LJ.

15 P. 611, ante.

16 Preston and Newsom, *Restrictive Covenants* (4th edn), p. 30.

17 [1933] Ch 611 at 631–2; M & B, p. 863.

18 [1952] Ch 286, [1952] 1 All ER 279; M & B, p. 864, approved by WILBERFORCE J in *Marten v Flight Refuelling Ltd* [1962] Ch 115 at 133, [1961] 2 All ER 696. But see (1952) 68 LQR 353 (Sir Lancelot Elphinstone).

restrictive covenant to be enforced against third parties is that the land of the covenantee may be protected, and in particular, that its sale value shall not be diminished.[19] Such a covenant is not an independent entity having its own intrinsic value. It has no *raison d'être* apart from the land for whose protection it was taken. Therefore, as we have already seen, even the covenantee himself cannot enforce the covenant against an assignee of the covenantor after he has disposed of the whole of his dominant land, for it is obvious that he no longer requires protection.[20] This theory, that the maintenance of the value of the covenantee's land is the sole justification for allowing restrictive covenants to run in favour of his successors in title, leads to this result, that the express assignment of the benefit of a covenant is ineffective unless it is contemporaneous with the assignment of the land affected. The covenant has spent its force if the covenantee has not required its aid in disposing of the dominant land.[1]

> But if he has been able to sell any particular part of his property without assigning to the purchaser the benefit of the covenant, there seems no reason why he should at a later date and as an independent transaction be at liberty to confer upon the purchaser such benefit. To hold that he could do so would be to treat the covenant as having been obtained, not only for the purpose of enabling the covenantee to dispose of his land to the best advantage, but also for the purpose of enabling him to dispose of the benefit of the covenant to the best advantage.[2]

Subject to these limitations, however, an express assignment of a covenant to a purchaser of the whole or part of the dominant land made at the time of the purchase is effective.

The benefit of a restrictive covenant is also capable of assignment by operation of law. Thus on the death of the covenantee it passes to his executors and is held by them as bare trustees for the devisee of the dominant land and becomes assignable to him.[3]

There remains to be noticed the question whether the express assignment of the benefit of a restrictive covenant annexes it to the dominant land, so that it will thereafter run automatically with that land without the necessity for any further express assignment. There are judicial dicta which support the view that an express assignment has this effect of annexation,[4] but recent cases are against it. The decision in *Re Pinewood Estate, Farnborough*[5]

---

19 *Chambers v Randall* [1923] 1 Ch 149; *Re Union of London and Smith's Bank Ltd's Conveyance, Miles v Easter* [1933] Ch 611 at 632.
20 P. 617, ante.
 1 *Chambers v Randall*, supra; *Re Union of London and Smith's Bank Ltd's Conveyance, Miles v Easter*, supra; *Re Rutherford's Conveyance* [1938] Ch 396, [1938] 1 All ER 495.
 2 *Re Union of London and Smith's Bank Ltd's Conveyance, Miles v Easter*, supra, at 632, per ROMER LJ.
 3 *Newton Abbott Co-operative Society Ltd v Williamson and Treadgold Ltd* [1952] Ch 286, [1952] 1 All ER 279; M & B p. 864; *Earl of Leicester v Wells-next-the-Sea UDC* [1973] Ch 110, [1972] 3 All ER 77 (special executors of settled land held to be bare trustees of benefit of restrictive covenant for beneficiary under SLA 1925, s. 7 (1)).
 4 *Renals v Cowlishaw* (1878) 9 Ch D 125 at 130–31; *Rogers v Hosegood* [1900] 2 Ch 388 at 408; *Reid v Bickerstaff* [1909] 2 Ch 305 at 320.
 5 [1958] Ch 280, [1957] 2 All ER 517. See the criticism in (1957) CLJ 146 (H. W. R. Wade). See also *Federated Homes Ltd v Mill Lodge Properties Ltd* [1980] 1 WLR 594 at 603, [1980] 1 All ER 371 at 378, where John Mills QC said at first instance: "I am not satisfied or prepared to hold that there is any such thing as 'delayed annexation by assignment' to which the covenantor is not party or privy".

assumes without argument that a chain of assignments is necessary, and that the decision in *Stilwell v Blackman*[6] is inconsistent with the dicta.

(c) Scheme of development (or building scheme)[7]

The third case in which a restrictive covenant is enforceable by and against persons other than the original covenanting parties is when lands are held by their respective owners under a scheme of development.

A scheme of development comes into existence where land is laid out in plots and sold to different purchasers or leased to different lessees, each of whom enters into a restrictive covenant with the common vendor or lessor agreeing that his particular plot shall not be used for certain purposes. In such a case these restrictive covenants are taken because the whole estate is being developed on a definite plan, and it is vital, if the value of each plot is not to be depreciated, that the purchasers or lessees should be prevented from dealing with their land so as to lower the tone of the neighbourhood. When the existence of a scheme of development has been established, the rule is that each purchaser and his assignees can sue or be sued by every other purchaser and his assignees for a breach of the restrictive covenants.[8] In such an action for breach it is immaterial whether the defendant acquired his title before or after the date on which the plaintiff purchased his plot. In other words, the restrictive covenants constitute a special local law for the area over which the scheme extends, and not only the plot-owners, but even the vendor himself, become subject to that law,[9] provided that the area[10] and the obligations to be imposed therein are defined. "They all have a common interest in maintaining the restriction. This community of interest necessarily requires and imports reciprocity of obligation."[11] There thus arises what SIMONDS J has called:

> an equity which is created by circumstances and is independent of contractual obligation.[12]

Pre-eminent among the essentials for the creation of a scheme of development is proof of a common intention that the restrictive covenants

6 [1968] Ch 508, [1967] 3 All ER 514; (1968) 84 LQR at 29–32 (P. V. Baker); M & B, p. 871.
7 "Scheme of development is the genus: building scheme a species": *Brunner v Greenslade* [1971] Ch 993 at 999, [1970] 3 All ER 833 at 836, per MEGARRY J. For recent successful schemes, see *Baxter v Four Oaks Properties Ltd* [1965] Ch 816, [1965] 1 All ER 906; *Re Dolphin's Conveyance* [1970] Ch 654, [1970] 2 All ER 664; M & B, p. 876; *Eagling v Gardner* [1970] 2 All ER 838; *Brunner v Greenslade*, supra; *Texaco Antilles Ltd v Kernochan* [1973] AC 609, [1973] 2 All ER 118; M & B p. 894; *Re 6, 8, 10 and 12 Elm Avenue, New Milton* [1984] 1 WLR 1398, [1984] 3 All ER 632. Cf *Lund v Taylor* (1975) 31 P & CR 167; M & B p. 879, especially STAMP LJ at 176; *Kingsbury v LW Anderson Ltd* (1979) 40 P & CR 136; *Allen v Veranne Builders Ltd* [1988] EGCS 2; *Emile Elias & Co Ltd v Pine Groves Ltd* [1993] 1 WLR 305. This is in marked contrast to the usual fate of schemes during the previous four decades: Preston and Newsom, paras. 2–74 to 2–75.
8 *Spicer v Martin* (1888) 14 App Cas 12; *Renals v Cowlishaw* (1878) 9 Ch D 125; affd (1879) 11 Ch D 866; *Hudson v Cripps* [1896] 1 Ch 265 (lease).
9 *Reid v Bickerstaff* [1909] 2 Ch 305 at 319; *Brunner v Greenslade*, supra at 1004. The scheme may expressly entitle the vendor to dispose of plots free from its restrictions: *Mayner v Payne* [1914] 2 Ch 555.
10 *Lund v Taylor*, supra, where there was no scheme because no area was defined. See also *Harlow v Hartog* (1977) 245 EG 140 (no scheme, due to no estate plan).
11 *Spicer v Martin* (1888) 14 App Cas 12 at 25, per Lord MACNAGHTEN.
12 *Lawrence v South County Freeholds* [1939] Ch 656 at 682; [1939] 2 All ER 503 at 524.

have been taken for the mutual benefit of the respective purchasers.[13] This community of interest and intention may be evidenced by the existence of a deed of mutual covenant to which all the several purchasers are parties,[14] or it may be inferred on the construction of the conveyances of the several parts of the estate.[15] If, however, the necessary intention cannot be derived solely from the formal documents, but extrinsic evidence is also required, a scheme of development may nevertheless come into existence. In these circumstances the conditions formulated by PARKER J in *Elliston v Reacher*[16] must exist before the benefit and the burden of the restrictive covenants can pass to the various purchasers and their assignees:

(a) Both the plaintiff and the defendant to the action for breach of the restrictive covenant must have derived their titles to the land from a common vendor.
(b) Before the sale of the plots to the plaintiff and the defendant, the common vendor must have laid out his estate for sale in lots[17] subject to restrictions which it was intended to impose on all the lots, and which were consistent only with some general scheme of development.[18]
(c) The restrictions were intended by the common vendor to be and were for the benefit of all the lots sold.[19] This intention is gathered from all the circumstances of the case, but if the restrictions are obviously calculated to enhance the value of each lot,[20] the intention is readily inferred.

To a certain extent these three conditions overlap, but the basic requirement is the existence of common regulations, obviously intended to govern the area that is to be developed. As GREENE MR explained:

The material thing I think is that every purchaser ... must know when he buys what are the regulations to which he is subjecting himself, and what are the regulations to which other purchasers on the estate will be called upon to subject themselves. Unless you know that, it is quite impossible in my judgment to draw the necessary inference, whether you refer to it as an agreement or as a community of interest importing reciprocity of obligation.[1]

---

13 *Nottingham Patent Brick and Tile Co v Butler* (1885) 15 QBD 261 at 268, per WILLS J; approved in *White v Bijou Mansions Ltd* [1938] Ch 351 at 361, [1938] 1 All ER 546 at 552. See Preston and Newsom, *Restrictive Covenants* (7th edn), para. 2–53 et seq.
14 *Baxter v Four Oaks Properties Ltd*, supra (where the common vendor had not laid out the estate in lots before the sale); *Price v Bouch* (1986) 53 P & CR 257 (co-operative scheme on part of 53 Victorian tradesmen in Northumberland).
15 *Re Dolphin's Conveyance*, supra (where there was no common vendor and no lotted estate). See (1970) 114 SJ 798 (G. H. Newsom): (1970) 86 LQR 445 (P. V. Baker). For the modification of these covenants under LPA 1925, s. 84, see *Re Farmiloe's Application* (1983) 48 P & CR 317; p. 634, post.
16 [1908] 2 Ch 374 at 385; M & B p. 874; for a case in which all these conditions are considered, see *Eagling v Gardner*, supra.
17 *Lawrence v South County Freeholds Ltd* [1939] Ch 656 at 674.
18 *Willé v St. John* [1910] 1 Ch 84, affd [1910] 1 Ch 325.
19 "It is not necessary that the covenants entered into should benefit only the defined area: ... The mere fact that the covenant is not expressly stated to be for the benefit of the plot holders is in no sense decisive ... I do not think that it is inconsistent with the existence of a scheme of development that the vendor retains his right to exempt part of the [Wildernesse] Estate from stipulations": *Allen v Veranne Builders Ltd* [1988] unreported, supra, per Sir Nicolas BROWNE-WILKINSON V-C. See also *Jamaica Mutual Life Assurance Society v Hillsborough Ltd* [1989] 1 WLR 1101 (no reciprocity: no building scheme).
20 "Enhancement in value ... does not mean merely monetary enhancement, but also enhancement of the ambience in which the residents live": *Allen v Veranne Builders Ltd*, supra.
 1 *White v Bijou Mansions*, supra, at 362, at 552.

(*d*) The original purchasers must have bought their lots on the understanding that the restrictions were to enure for the benefit of the other lots.

(*e*) The geographical area to which the scheme extends must be ascertained with reasonably clear definitiveness.[2]

In order to create a valid scheme, the purchasers of all the land within the area of the scheme must also know what that area is.[3]

The conditions in *Elliston v Reacher* are "a valuable, and perhaps complete guide to what has to be sought in the extrinsic evidence when such evidence is the foundation of the case."[4] This may include parol evidence from the common vendor[5] or his predecessor in title[6] and evidence of what was said and done before the contracts which preceded the conveyances.

The common vendor may reserve the power to waive or vary the restrictive covenants, especially in the case of land of which he has not yet disposed.[7] Furthermore the restrictions which he imposes may vary in detail.[8] But the variation was held to preclude a scheme where covenants imposed on some plots were expressed to be by way of indemnity only, and on others were all by way of absolute covenant.[9]

The subject matter of a scheme generally consists of freehold land which is to be sold in plots to persons who desire to erect houses, but it may equally well comprise houses or a block of flats that have already been built,[10] and leaseholds as well as freeholds.[11] There may also be a sub-scheme within an area which is itself subject to a scheme of development.[12]

Finally we should notice that there is some controversy over the question whether the registration provisions of the Land Charges Act 1972 apply to restrictive covenants under schemes of development. The better view is that they do.[13]

C. SECTION 56 OF THE LAW OF PROPERTY ACT 1925

We have seen how a person may show that he has acquired the benefit of a covenant at law and in equity. We must now consider how far someone may

---

2   *Osborne v Bradley* [1903] 2 Ch 446; *Reid v Bickerstaff* [1909] 2 Ch 305; M & B p. 875; *Torbay Hotel Ltd v Jenkins* [1927] 2 Ch 225; *Lund v Taylor*, supra. See *Jackson v Bishop* (1979) 48 P & CR 57 (developer held liable for breach of covenant of title and negligence where there was a double conveyance due to inaccurate plans of neighbouring plots).

3   *Emile Elias & Co Ltd v Pine Groves Ltd* [1993] 1 WLR 305 at 310, per Lord BROWNE-WILKINSON.

4   (1970) 114 SJ at 800 (G. H. Newsom).

5   *Kelly v Battershell* [1949] 2 All ER 830 at 843.

6   *Kingsbury v L. W. Anderson Ltd* (1979) 40 P & CR 136.

7   *Elliston v Reacher* [1908] 2 Ch 665 at 672; *Pearce v Maryon-Wilson* [1935] Ch 188; *Re Wembley Park Estate Co Ltd's Transfer* [1968] Ch 491 at 497, [1968] 1 All ER 457 at 460.

8   *Collins v Castle* (1887) 36 Ch D 243 at 253; *Elliston v Reacher* [1908] 2 Ch 374 at 384.

9   *Kingsbury v L W Anderson Ltd*, supra.

10   See *Torbay Hotel Ltd v Jenkins*, supra, at 241.

11   See *Spicer v Martin*, supra; *Hudson v Cripps* [1896] 1 Ch 265.

12   See *Knight v Simmonds* [1896] 1 Ch 653; *King v Dickeson* (1889) 40 Ch D 596; *Lawrence v South County Freeholds Ltd*, supra; *Brunner v Greenslade*, supra.

13   (1928) 78 LJ 39 (J.M.L.); (1933) 77 SJ 550; (1950) 20 Conv (NS) 370 (R. G. Rowley); *Emmet on Title*, para. 17–043; Farrand, *Contract and Conveyance* (2nd edn), pp. 420–421; Barnsley, *Conveyancing Law and Practice* (3rd edn), p. 344; Preston & Newsom, paras. 2–80 to 2–83, 3–25.

enforce a covenant by reliance on section 56 of the Law of Property Act 1925 which provides that:[14]

> A person may take an immediate or other interest in land or other property, or the benefit of any condition, right of entry, covenant or agreement over or respecting land or other property, although he may not be named as a party to the conveyance or other instrument.

This section reproduces and extends section 5 of the Real Property Act 1845, which abrogated the technical rule of common law that:

> a grantee or covenantee, though named as such in an indenture under seal expressed to be made inter partes, could not take an immediate interest as grantee nor the benefit of a covenant as covenantee unless named as a party to the indenture.

It is important to notice that this section is not concerned with the *passing* of the benefit of a covenant. It is concerned with the *giving* of the benefit of a covenant, at the time when the covenant is created, to a person other than the covenantee. The section in effect makes the person claiming the benefit of the covenant into an original covenantee, even though he was not named as a party to the deed in which the covenant was created. Once, however, the benefit of a covenant is given to a person by the section, the benefit can then pass to his successors in title by annexation or assignment.

The application of section 56 is not confined to covenants that touch and concern the land,[15] nor is it confined to restrictive covenants in equity. Its application in the latter context may, however, enable an earlier purchaser of a plot of land on an estate, which is not subject to a scheme of development, to enforce a restrictive covenant against a later purchaser of a plot from the common vendor.

Thus, in *Re Ecclesiastical Commissioners for England's Conveyance*:[16]

> in 1887, the purchaser of Blackacre entered into restrictive covenants in favour of the Ecclesiastical Commissioners, the vendors. A separate covenant was also included in the conveyance, providing that the benefit of the covenants should avail the vendors' "assigns, owners for the time being of the land adjoining or adjacent to" Blackacre. Prior to 1887, the Commissioners had sold various freehold plots, situated near Blackacre, to different purchasers and these had passed into other hands by the time of the action.

It was held that the successors in title of the adjacent owners were entitled to enforce the covenants although their respective predecessors in title had not joined in the conveyance of 1887.

The section will not avail a person unless he might have been a party to the deed in question. If he is an ascertainable person at the time of the execution of the deed which purports to grant him an interest in property[17]

---

14 On the section generally, see Cheshire, Fifoot and Furmston, *Law of Contract* (12th edn), pp. 458–461; *Beswick v Beswick* [1968] AC 58, [1967] 2 All ER 1197, especially Lord PEARCE at 93–4, at 1215–6, and Lord UPJOHN at 102–7, at 1221–4; M & B p. 884; (1967) 30 MLR 687 (G. H. Treitel).

15 *Re Ecclesiastical Comrs for England's Conveyance* [1936] Ch 430 at 438; but see *Grant v Edmondson* [1931] 1 Ch 1.

16 [1936] Ch 430; M & B p. 886. See also *Forster v Elvet Colliery Co Ltd* [1908] 1 KB 629; affd sub nom *Dyson v Forster* [1909] AC 98.

17 *Stromdale and Ball Ltd v Burden* [1952] Ch 223, [1952] 1 All ER 59; M & B p. 890; *Drive Yourself Hire Co (London) Ltd v Strutt* [1954] 1 QB 250, [1953] 2 All ER 1475; *Re Foster* [1938] 3 All ER 357 at 365, per CROSSMAN J; *Lyus v Prowsa Developments Ltd* [1982] 1 WLR 1044 at 1049, [1982] 2 All ER 953 at 958, per DILLON J.

or to make a covenant available to him, he and his successors in title are in as good a position as if he had been one of the original parties. On the other hand, a deed is inoperative in so far as it purports to extend the advantage of a covenant to an unascertainable person, such as the *future* owner of specified land.[18] It will, therefore, not enable a later purchaser to enforce a restrictive covenant against an earlier purchaser from a common vendor. In order to succeed, he must prove that the benefit of the covenant has passed to him by annexation, express assignment or under a scheme of development.

D. DISCHARGE AND MODIFICATION OF RESTRICTIVE COVENANTS[19]

(1) SECTION 84 OF THE LAW OF PROPERTY ACT 1925

(a) Position apart from statute

The Law of Property Act 1925 provides for the total extinction of restrictive covenants. Under the law apart from the Act a covenantee (including his assignees) is deprived of his right to enforce the covenant if he has submitted to a long course of usage wholly inconsistent with its continuance, as where he remains inactive for a considerable time while open breaches of the covenant are taking place;[20] if he disregards breaches in such a way as to justify a reasonable person in believing that future breaches will be disregarded;[1] or if the character of the neighbourhood in which the protected property lies is so entirely altered that it would be inequitable and senseless to insist upon the rigorous observance of a covenant that is no longer of any value.[2]

(b) Power to discharge or modify covenants under the Law of Property Act 1925

Section 84 of the Law of Property Act 1925[3] develops this last ground of extinction, and sets up a new method whereby restrictions may be discharged or modified.[4]

---

18 *Kelsey v Dodd* (1881) 52 LJ Ch 34 at 39; *White v Bijou Mansions Ltd* [1937] Ch 610 at 625, [1937] 3 All ER 269 at 277, affd [1938] Ch 351 at 365, [1938] 1 All ER 546 at 554; M & B p. 887. See also *Pinemain Ltd v Welbeck International Ltd* (1984) 272 EG 1166 (benefit of covenant to sue surety on contract of guarantee not within s. 56, since plaintiffs were not identifiable when covenant was made); *Re Distributors and Warehousing Ltd* [1986] 1 EGLR 90, per WALTON J; cf. *Wiles v Banks* (1983) 50 P & CR 80 (plaintiff identifiable).

19 See generally Preston and Newsom, para. 9–16; (1986) 49 MLR 195 (P. Polden), chapter 5.

20 *Gibson v Doeg* (1857) 2 H & N 615; *Hepworth v Pickles* [1900] 1 Ch 108; *Re Summerson* [1900] 1 Ch 112 n.; discussed in *Lloyds Bank Ltd v Jones* [1955] 2 QB 298 at 320–2, [1955] 2 All ER 409 at 422–3. See also *Shaw v Applegate* [1977] 1 WLR 970, [1978] 1 All ER 123 (where an injunction was refused against original covenantor on grounds of acquiescence, but damages were awarded).

1 *Chatsworth Estates Co v Fewell* [1931] 1 Ch 224; M & B p. 892.

2 *Chatsworth Estates Co v Fewell*, supra; see generally, Behan, *Covenants Affecting Land*, pp. 148 et seq; Elphinstone, *Covenants Affecting Land*, pp. 110 et seq; *Westripp v Baldock* [1938] 2 All ER 779; affd [1939] 1 All ER 279; (1966) 5 Melbourne University Law Review, pp. 209–14 (D. Mendes da Costa).

3 As amended by LPA 1969, s. 28. See Law Commission Report on Restrictive Covenants, 1967 (Law Com No. 11), pp. 21–6. Applications made under the section are noted in Current Law and in the Journal of Planning and Environment Law. Some are recorded in P & CR and the EG. Condensed reports of all applications from 1974–1979 appeared in Lands Tribunal Cases.

4 S. 84 (1); see *Richardson v Jackson* [1954] 1 WLR 447, [1954] 1 All ER 437; *Re Kentwood*

The first point to notice is that the Act mainly applies to restrictions imposed on freehold estates. It has no application to leaseholds which are subject to restrictive covenants, except where the lease was originally made for more than 40 years, and 25 years of this term have expired when the question of extinction arises.[5]

It is then provided that any person interested in any such freehold or leasehold land[6] affected by the restrictive covenant,[7] may apply to the Lands Tribunal to have the restriction either wholly or partially discharged, or modified.[8]

In making an order discharging or modifying a restriction the Tribunal may direct the applicant to pay to any person entitled to the benefit of the restriction such sum by way of consideration[9] as it may think it just to award.[10] This must fall under one of the following heads:

(i) a sum to make up for any loss or disadvantage suffered by that person in consequence of the discharge or modification;[11]

(ii) a sum to make up for any effect which the restriction had, at the time when it was imposed, in reducing the consideration then received for the land affected by it.

Before making any order the Tribunal must be satisfied:

(a) that by reason of changes in the character of the property or the neighbourhood[12] or other circumstances of the case[13] which the Lands Tribunal may deem material, the restriction ought to be deemed obsolete; or

---

Properties Ltd's Application [1987] JPL 137 (discretion to modify not exercised where there had been a flagrant, cynical and continuing breach of the covenant). For an unsuccessful application to the European Commission of Human Rights (No 1074/84) on the ground that the Northern Ireland equivalent of section 84 violated the European Convention for the Protection of Human Rights and Fundamental Freedoms, see [1986] Conv 124 (N. Dawson).

5 S. 84 (12), as amended by Landlord and Tenant Act 1954, s. 52. The 25 years is reckoned from the date of the lease, and not from any earlier date at which the term is expressed in the lease to begin: *Earl of Cadogan v Guinness* [1936] Ch 515, [1936] 2 All ER 29.

6 The tribunal should be more reluctant to interfere with leasehold than freehold covenants: *Ridley v Taylor* [1965] 1 WLR 611, [1965] 2 All ER 51; M & B p. 898.

7 It may be personal only: *Shepherd Homes Ltd v Sandham (No. 2)* [1971] 1 WLR 1062, [1971] 2 All ER 1267; *Gilbert v Spoor* [1983] Ch 27, [1982] 2 All ER 576.

8 Lands Tribunal Rules 1975 (S.I. 1975 No. 299); Lands Tribunal (Amendment) Rules 1977 (S.I. 1977 No. 1820); 1981 (S.I. 1981 No. 105); Lands Tribunal (Amendment No. 2) Rules 1981 (S.I. 1981 No. 600); Lands Tribunal (Amendment) Rules 1984 (S.I. 1984 No. 793); 1986 (S.I. 1986 No. 1322); 1990 (S.I. 1990 No. 1382). On the Lands Tribunal generally, see Jones, *The Lands Tribunal* (1982); its address is 48/49 Chancery Lane, London, WC2.

9 See *SJC Construction Co Ltd v Sutton London Borough Council* (1975) 29 P & CR 322, where Stephenson LJ said, *arguendo*, that "consideration" was probably a misprint for "compensation": Preston and Newsom, para. 13–02.

10 LPA 1925, s. 84 (1), as amended by LPA 1969, s. 28 (3). See generally [1976] JPL 18 (W. A. Leach).

11 *SJC Construction Co Ltd v Sutton London Borough Council*, supra ("there is no method prescribed by the Act by which it is to be assessed; it is essentially a question of quantum", per Lord Denning MR at 326).

12 *Keith v Texaco Ltd* (1977) 34 P & CR 249 (coming of oil industry to Aberdeenshire); *Re Bradley Clare Estates Ltd's Application* (1987) 55 P & CR 126; *Re Quaffers Ltd's Application* (1988) 56 P & CR 142 (advent of motorway network).

13 *Re Cox's Application* (1985) 51 P & CR 335 (covenant requiring occupiers of extension of house in East Sussex to be domestic staff employed for service in the house held obsolete); cf. *Re Beechwood Homes Ltd's Application* (1992) 64 P & CR 535 (covenant to prevent cul-de-sac development, involving lopping of trees held not obsolete); *Re Kalsi's Application* (1993) 66 P & CR 313.

(aa) that the continued existence thereof would impede some reasonable user of the land for public or private purposes or, as the case may be, would unless modified so impede such user.[14]

Under this paragraph the Lands Tribunal must be satisfied that the restriction, in impeding the user, either:

(i) does not secure to persons entitled to the benefit of it any practical benefits of substantial value or advantage to them; or
(ii) is contrary to the public interest;

and that money will be an adequate compensation for the loss or disadvantage (if any) which any such person will suffer from the discharge or modification.[15]

(b) that the persons of full age and capacity for the time being or from time to time entitled to the benefit of the restriction, whether in respect of estates in fee simple or any lesser estates or interests in the property to which the benefit of the restriction is annexed, have agreed, either expressly or by implication,[16] by their acts or omissions, to the same being discharged or modified; or
(c) that the proposed discharge or modification will not injure the persons entitled to the benefit of the restriction.[17]

The Lands Tribunal may, however, add further restrictive provisions if it appears to it to be reasonable to do so.[18] This cannot be done unless the applicant accepts them, but, if he does not, the application may be refused.

(c) Scope of changes made by the Law of Property Act 1969

The substantive change made by the Law of Property Act 1969 was to widen the scope of section 84 of the Law of Property Act 1925, and, in particular, to redraft paragraph (aa), so as to enable the Lands Tribunal "to take a broader view of whether the use of land is being unreasonably impeded; and to make clear provision for an award of monetary compensation where the Tribunal thinks that the injury which an objector would suffer by a modification or discharge can be properly compensated in that way."[19] To

---

14 See *Stannard v Issa* [1987] AC 175, where PC construed a similar but not identical paragraph under the Restrictive Covenants (Discharge and Modification) Act (No 2 of 1960) of Jamaica, s. 3 (1).
15 LPA 1925, s. 84 (1A). For the formulation of the questions to be answered by the Lands Tribunal, see *Re Bass Ltd's Application* (1973) 26 P & CR 156.
16 See *Re Memvale's Securities Ltd's Application* (1975) 233 EG 689; *Re Fettishaw's Application (No. 2)* (1973) 27 P & CR 292.
17 *Re Forestmere Properties Ltd's Application* (1980) 41 P & CR 390 ("replacement of one eyesore (Odeon cinema) by another could hardly be said to be an improvement"); *Re Bailey's Application* (1981) 42 P & CR 108 ("quaint rural backwater" not to be changed into riding school with attendant manure and noise including sound of human voice); *Re Livingstones' Application* (1982) 47 P & CR 462 ("eyesore" carport); *Re Severn Trent Water Ltd's Application* (1993) JPL 865 (site for sewage disposal works to become leisure centre).
18 *Re Patten Ltd's Application* (1975) 31 P & CR 180; *Re Dransfield's Application* (1975) 31 P & CR 192; *Re Kershaw's Application* (1975) 31 P & CR 187; *Re Banks Application* (1976) 33 P & CR 138; *Re Forestmere Properties Ltd's Application*, supra; *Re Austin's Application* (1980) 42 P & CR 102; *Re Shah and Shah's Application* (1991) 62 P & CR 450.
19 Law Commission Report on Restrictive Covenants 1967 (Law Com No. 11), p. 23.

enable it to take this broader view the Tribunal must take into account the development plan and any declared or ascertainable pattern for the grant or refusal of planning permissions in the relevant areas, as well as the period at which and context in which the restriction was created or imposed and any other material circumstances.[20]

Since 1969 the new paragraph (*aa*) and the power to award compensation have resulted in an increased number of cases before the Lands Tribunal.[1] Several important criteria have been established for deciding whether a covenant should be modified or discharged. In particular, where the applicant has obtained planning permission for the proposed user, the effect is very persuasive in considering whether that user is reasonable.[2] The proposition that impeding that user is contrary to the public interest may also be aided by a planning permission, but in rather a different way. The question is not whether the proposed user is in the public interest, but whether impeding the proposed user is contrary to it.

> There is here more than a narrow nuance of difference: a planning permission only says, in effect, that a proposal will be allowed; it implies that such a proposal will not be a bad thing, but it does not necessarily imply that it will be positively a good thing.[3]

Consistently with this restrictive approach, the President of the Lands Tribunal said in 1975:[4]

> For an application to succeed on the ground of public interest it must be shown that that interest is so important and immediate as to justify the serious interference with private rights and the sanctity of contract.

An acute shortage of building land in a particular locality does not establish that any restriction which prevents development of land is ipso facto contrary to the public interest;[5] nor does a housing need in the area.[6] In only two situations so far has an application succeeded on the ground of public interest. The first was where there was a scarcity of land available for building development, and, if the restriction were not modified, building

---

20 LPA 1925, s. 84 (1B). See *Re Collins' Application* (1974) 30 P & CR 527.
1 See generally Preston and Newsom, *Restrictive Covenants* (chapters 10–16) [1974] JPL 72, 130; [1975] JPL 644; [1976] JPL 407; [1979] JPL 64; [1981] JPL 551, 656; [1982] JPL 552; [1984] JPL 847 (G. H. Newsom); and for a useful summary of the cases (1979) 129 NLJ 523 (H. W. Wilkinson); M & B pp. 895–906.
2 *Re Beecham Group Ltd's Application* (1980) 41 P & CR 369 (refusal to differ from very "closely reasoned decision" of Secretary of State granting planning permission on appeal from inspector); *Gilbert v Spoor* [1983] Ch 27, [1982] 2 All ER 576 ("the subsection does not make planning decisions decisive", per EVELEIGH LJ at 34, at 581); *Re Martin's Application* (1988) 57 P & CR 119; M & B p. 905.
3 *Re Bass Ltd's Application* (1973) 26 P & CR 156 at 157.
4 *Re Collins' Applications* (1975) 30 P & CR 527 per Douglas Frank QC. See also *Re Mansfield District Council's Application* (1976) 33 P & CR 141 at 143; *Re Brierfield's Application* (1976) 35 P & CR 124; *Re Solarfilms (Sales) Ltd's Application* (1993) 67 P & CR 110.
5 *Re Beardsley's Application* (1972) 25 P & CR 233; *Re Gardner's Application* (1974) JPL 728.
6 *Re New Ideal Homes Ltd's Application* (1978) 36 P & CR 476 (where, however, the covenant was modified on payment by consent of £51,000 compensation because it did not secure practical benefits of substantial value to objecting local authority); *Re Osborn's and Easton's Application* (1978) 38 P & CR 251: *Re Beech's Application* (1990) 59 P & CR 502 (residential enclave in predominantly commercial setting). See also *Re London Borough of Islington's Application* [1986] JPL 214 (covenant forbidding use of land in Islington "except for open space", purchased from Greater London Council who remitted half of the purchase price, discharged on repayment of that half with adjustments for inflation).

work costing £47,000 would have to be demolished. That was to be avoided in "the present economic circumstances of the country".[7]

The second was where modification did not involve the demolition of a building:[8]

> A covenant not to carry on any trade or business in a large house in Worthing was modified to permit use as a community care home for ten psychiatric patients who had been assessed as ready to live independently in the community. The restriction was contrary to the public interest, because government policy was for mental patients to be rehabilitated in the community, and there was a desperate need for such a facility in the area. The restriction did not confer any substantial benefit or advantage because there was already a home for 41 old people which had been built next door in breach of covenant; and planning permission had already been granted.

Further, in considering whether the proposed user secures to the persons entitled to the benefit of the covenant practical benefits of substantial[9] value or advantage,[10] the Lands Tribunal has observed that the words "value or

---

7 *Re SJC Construction Co Ltd's Application* (1974) 28 P & CR 200; affirmed by CA on method of assessing compensation sub nom. *SJC Construction Co Ltd v Sutton London Borough Council* (1975) 29 P & CR 322; *Re Fisher & Gimson (Builders) Ltd's Application* (1992) 65 P & CR 312 (risk of demolition of important housing accommodation against public interest; £6,000 compensation). See also *Re Bradley Clare Estates Ltd's Application* (1987) 55 P & CR 126.

8 *Re Lloyd's and Lloyd's Application* (1993) 66 P & CR 112.

9 On the meaning of substantial, see *Re Gaffney's Application* (1974) 35 P & CR 440; *Re Dransfield's Application* (1975) 31 P & CR 192.

10 *Re John Twiname Ltd's Application* (1972) 23 P & CR 413 at 417–18; *Re Wards Construction (Medway) Ltd's Application* (1973) 25 P & CR 223 at 231 ("even ordinary people not infrequently value space and quiet and light"); *Re Gossip's Application* (1973) 25 P & CR 215 at 220 ("houses built on the application land would overlook the garden and the principal rooms, albeit somewhat screened by a hawthorn, a poor substitute for a covenant"); *Re Ballamy's Application* [1977] JPL 456 (enjoyment of evening sunshine in the sun-lounge); *Re Banks Application*, supra ("direct view of the sea is of immense value"); *Re Bovis Homes Southern Ltd's Application* [1981] JPL 368 (beauty and aesthetic and historic interest of National Trust house and its setting); *Gilbert v Spoor* [1983] Ch 27, [1982] 2 All ER 576 (magnificent view over Tyne Valley from road *adjacent* to objector's land); [1984] Conv 429 (P. Polden); *Re Burr's Application* [1987] JPL 137 (amenities of a high class development); *Stannard v Issa* [1987] AC 175 ("the privacy and quietude of an enclave of single dwellings in large gardens is going to be adversely affected by the introduction on adjoining lands of no less than 40 additional families", per Lord OLIVER OF AYLMERTON at 196); cf *Stockport Metropolitan Borough Council v Alwiyah Developments* (1983) 52 P & CR 278 (loss of bargaining power not a benefit); *Re Bennett's and Tamarlin Ltd's Application* (1987) 54 P & CR 378 (loss of ability to extract money for agreeing to modification of restriction not a benefit); *Re Bushell's Application* (1987) 54 P & CR 386 (particularly fine landscape view at Wimbledon "very unusual so near the centre of London"); *Re Purnell's Application* (1987) 55 P & CR 133 (large garden providing privacy in Orpington, Kent). See also *Re Crest Homes plc's Application* (1983) 48 P & CR 309 (proposal to build 12 houses to replace neglected Edgware Lawn Tennis Club would cause undesirable increase in housing density and change area from semi-rural to urban); *Re Lake's Application* [1984] JPL 887 (proposal to erect split-level house in Lyme Regis would be design out of character with surroundings); *Re Williams' Application* (1987) 55 P & CR 400 (sense of spaciousness; preventing nuisance of building works); *Re Whiting's Application* (1988) 58 P & CR 321 (natural beauty of Howley, Gloucestershire); *Re Tarhale Ltd's Application* (1990) 60 P & CR 368 (preventing intolerable nuisance during construction work); *Re Sheehy's Application* (1991) 63 P & CR 95 (moral obligation undertaken by the St. Aubyn Discretionary Trustees to maintain a scheme of covenants within the Devonport Estate, where cost of administration exceeded total rental income, held to be of practical benefit); *Re Beechwood Homes Ltd's Application* [1994] EGCS 57. See also *Re Edwards' Application* (1983) 47 P & CR 458 (restriction modified to enable house in Mold, North Wales, to be used as a general village store, for "groceries, sweets,

advantage" are not intended to be assessed in terms of pecuniary value only.[11] It takes account of any matters however unusual or personal they may be.[12]

The statutory provisions apply to restrictive covenants entered into either before or after the commencement of the Act, but do not apply where the restriction was imposed on the occasion of a disposition made gratuitously, or for a nominal consideration, for public purposes.[13] Any person aggrieved by the decision of the Tribunal on the ground that it is erroneous in point of law may require that a case be stated for the decision of the Court of Appeal.[14]

(d) Declaration whether restriction binding

In order to meet the case where it may be doubtful whether an effectual restrictive covenant has been imposed on land and if so what persons it now affects, the Act confers jurisdiction upon the court:

(a) to declare whether or not in any particular case any freehold land is, or would in any given event be, affected by a restriction imposed by any instrument; or

(b) to declare what, upon the true construction of any instrument purporting to impose a restriction, is the nature and extent of the restriction thereby imposed and whether the same is, or would in any given event be, enforceable and if so by whom.[15]

(e) Housing Act 1985

If it is proved that a house cannot readily be let as a single tenement but can readily be let if converted into two or more tenements, the Housing Act 1985 empowers the county court to vary any provisions in a lease or any restrictive covenant affecting the lease if these impede the proposed conversion.[16] Such a variation is not permissible unless the converted tenements will be wholly contained within one house.[17]

(f) Town and Country Planning Act 1990

Under section 106, a local planning authority has power to regulate land use

tobacco, cigarettes, cigars, soft drinks, ice cream, newspapers, trinkets, haberdashery, gardening utensils and supplies, tools, nuts and bolts" subject to payment of £500 as compensation to objector for loss of amenity); *Re Shah and Shah's Application* (1991) 62 P & CR 450 (restriction impeding nursing home user so small as to warrant monetary compensation only of £23,000); *Re Hopcraft's Application* (1993) 66 P & CR 475 (pleasant open area to remain open); *Re Kalsi Application* (1993) 66 P & CR 313; *Re Hydeshire's Application* (1993) 67 P & CR 93 (right to build within set limit, provided no one else had done so, not a practical benefit).

11 *Re Bass Ltd's Application*, supra. Loss of bargaining power is not a proper head of compensation: *Stockport Metropolitan Borough Council v Alwiyah Developments* (1983) 52 P & CR 278; *Re Bennett's and Tamarlin Ltd's Application* (1987) 54 P & CR 378 (loss of ability to extract money for agreeing to modification of restriction not a benefit); cf *Re Quaffers Ltd's Application* (1988) 56 P & CR 142 (loss of competition advantage).

12 *Re Matcham's Application* [1981] JPL 431 (house built on tranquil site because of wife's severe migraine).

13 LPA 1925, s. 84 (7).

14 Lands Tribunal Act 1949, s. 3 (4) proviso.

15 LPA 1925, s. 84(2), as amended by LPA 1969, s. 28 (4); *Re Sunnyfield* [1932] 1 Ch 79; *Re Freeman-Thomas Indenture* [1957] 1 All ER 532.

16 S. 610 (1), (2), replacing Housing Act 1957, s. 165. See Preston and Newsom, para. 10–20.

17 *Josephine Trust Ltd v Champagne* [1963] 2 QB 160, [1962] 3 All ER 136.

by agreement.[18] It may enter into an agreement with any person interested in land in their area for the purpose of restricting or regulating the development or use of land, either permanently or during such period as may be prescribed by the agreement. Where such an agreement has been made, the authority is said to hold the benefit of the covenant as custodian of the public interest.[19] Such an agreement may be modified or discharged under the Law of Property Act 1925, section 84.[20]

Under section 237, a local planning authority is authorised, subject to the payment of compensation, to carry out a scheme of development, notwithstanding that it interferes with an easement or infringes a restrictive covenant.[1]

(2) UNITY OF SEISIN

A restrictive covenant will be discharged when a person becomes entitled to both the dominant and servient lands to which it relates.[2] This is similar to the extinguishment of an easement by the unity of ownership and possession.[3] In *Texaco Antilles Ltd v Kernochan*,[4] however, the Privy Council held that, if there is a scheme of development, unity of seisin does not automatically discharge a covenant within the area of unity, and that on severance it revives, unless there is evidence from the circumstances surrounding the severance that the parties intended that it should not do so.

E. LAW REFORM

(1) LAND OBLIGATIONS

The Law Commission Report on the Law of Positive and Restrictive Covenants 1984 recommends a comprehensive reform of the law relating to

18 Replacing TCPA 1971, s. 52. See Current Law Statutes TCPA 1990, s. 106, annotated by M. Grant, paras. 8–299 to 8–302.
19 *Re Abbey Homesteads (Developments) Ltd's Application* [1986] 1 EGLR 24; *Re Martin's Application* (1988) 57 P & CR 119, especially at 125, M & B p. 905, per Fox LJ; *Re Houdret & Co Ltd's Application* (1989) 58 P & CR 310; *Re Jones' and White & Co's Application* (1989) 58 P & CR 512; *Re Quartley's Application* (1989) 58 P & CR 518; *Re Beech's Application* (1990) 59 P & CR 502; [1990] Conv 455 (N. D. M. Parry); *Re Wallace & Co's Application* (1993) 66 P & CR 124; *Re Hopcraft's Application* (1993) 66 P & CR 475 (storage of touring caravans refuse).
20 For successful modifications, see *Re Cox's Application* (1985) 51 P & CR 335; *Re Towner's and Goddard's Application* (1989) 58 P & CR 316 (tennis-court with chain link fencing); *Re Barclays Bank plc's Application* (1990) 60 P & CR 354 (discharge in favour of mortgagee); *Re Poulton's Application* (1992) 65 P & CR 319 (extension of bungalow in Metropolitan Green Belt). *Re O'Reilly's Application* (1993) 66 P & CR 485 (use for car parking only modified to allow erection of six houses on payment of £11,000 compensation); *Re Love & Love's Application* (1993) 67 P & CR 101.
1 *Sutton London Borough Council v Bolton* [1993] 33 EG 91. See Local Government Act 1972, ss. 120 (3), 124 (2).
2 *Re Tiltwood, Sussex* [1978] Ch 269, [1978] 2 All ER 109; (1980) 54 ALJ 156 (G. M. Bates); (1982) 56 ALJ 587 (A. A. Preece); *Re Victoria Recreation Ground, Portslade's Application* (1979) 41 P & CR 119.
3 P. 572, ante.
4 [1973] AC 609, [1973] 2 All ER 118; M & B p. 894; *Brunner v Greenslade* [1971] Ch 993, [1970] 3 All ER 833.

covenants affecting freehold land.[5] It takes as its model the existing law of easements (paras 4.21–4.36; 27.1 (1)).

The reforms proposed should enable obligations, whether restrictive or positive in nature, to run with the benefited and the burdened land so as to be directly enforceable by and against the current owners of each. They should also be such as to cater not only for the simple case of an obligation created between two neighbouring landowners, but also for the more complex needs of property developments (including those involving freehold flats).

In outline the main recommendations are:

(1) There should be a new interest in land, to be known as a Land Obligation (paras 5.2; 27.1(2)).

The Land Obligation should be one of two types.

(a) The neighbour obligation (paras 6.2–6.16; 27.1(3)–(6)) This is to be used where the obligation is imposed on one plot for the benefit of another plot. It can take one of three forms: a restrictive obligation; a positive obligation, which requires either the carrying out of works or the provision of services for the dominant land; and a reciprocal payment obligation, which requires the making of payments for expenditure incurred by a person who carries out a positive covenant, e.g. paying half the cost when the neighbour is under a covenant to repair the boundary fence.

(b) The development obligation (paras 4.29–4.36; 27.1(7)–(11)) This is to be used where an area of land is to be divided into separately owned but inter-dependent units, such as a housing development or a block of flats. This obligation is to be of a necessarily wider scope than the neighbour obligation and it is to be capable of enforcement not only by owners of other parts of the development but also by a manager acting on their behalf, such as an estate agent, a management company or a residents' association.

(2) The development obligation can take the form of a restrictive or of a positive or of a reciprocal payment obligation. It can also require the servient land to be used in a particular way which benefits the whole or part of the development (such as to provide shopping facilities there), and to require payment to a manager for expenditure incurred in performing his functions under the development scheme.

(3) The Land Obligation may be either legal or equitable. To be legal, it must be created by deed, and be equivalent to an estate in fee simple absolute in possession or to a term of years absolute. If it is created in writing or if it is created for any other interest, such as for life, it will be equitable.

In either case, the obligation must be stated to be a Land Obligation, in order to distinguish it from an easement or similar right. The rule against perpetuities will not apply. (paras 27.1(12)–(20).)

(4) The person who enters into the Land Obligation will cease to be subject to it when he has disposed of the land. His liability under the doctrine of

---

5 Law Com No. 127, HC 201. For earlier Reports, see Wilberforce Committee on Positive Covenants 1965 (Cmnd 2719); Law Commission on Restrictive Covenants 1967 (Law Com No. 11) and its Working Paper on Rights Appurtenant to Land 1971 (No. 36); Benson Committee on Legal Services 1979 (Cmnd 7648); Second Report of the Conveyancing Committee: Conveyancing Simplifications 1985, paras 4.52–4.57, 7.21–7.22. See also [1984] JPL 222, 317, 401, 485 (S. B. Edell); 134 NLJ 459, 481 (H. W. Wilkinson); M & B p. 910; [1984] 47 MLR 566 (P. Polden).

privity of contract to the covenantee will end and there will thus be no point in the creation of a chain of indemnity covenants. (paras 11.32–11.34.)

(5) Land Obligations, whether legal or equitable, will be registrable as a new type of Class C Land charge under the Land Charges Act 1972, in the case of unregistered land. In the case of registered land, they will be noted in the dominant and servient titles, and will not be overriding interests under section 70 of the Land Registration Act 1925. (Part IX; paras 27.1.(21)–(23).)

(6) The new scheme will only apply to Land Obligations created after it comes into force. There will thus be three different schemes for covenants affecting freehold land; those created before 1926; those created after 1925 and those under the new scheme. (Part XXIV; paras 27.1.(93)–(101).)

(2) OBSOLETE RESTRICTIVE COVENANTS

The Law Commission, in its Report on Obsolete Restrictive Covenants in 1991,[6] makes proposals to phase out most existing restrictive covenants after the introduction of the Land Obligations scheme envisaged in its Report on the Law of Positive and Restrictive Covenants.

The main proposal is that all restrictive covenants should automatically lapse eighty years after they were first created, but anyone entitled to the benefit of a covenant which was not then obsolete would have the right to replace it with a Land Obligation to the like effect. It would be up to him to take positive action to replace it; failure to do so would involve the automatic lapse of the covenant. A five year period of grace would be allowed for assessing restrictions which are already more than eighty years old.

In 1991 the Government announced that it would introduce commonhold[7] and implement with modifications the 1984 Report on the Law of Positive and Restrictive Covenants.

SECTION III REGISTERED LAND

Under section 40 (1) of the Land Registration Act 1925, a proprietor of registered land may:

> by covenant . . . impose or make binding, so far as the law permits, any obligation or reservation with respect to the building on or other user of the registered land.[8]

This power is made:

> subject to any entry to the contrary on the register, and without prejudice to the rights of persons entitled to overriding interests (if any) and to any incumbrances entered on the register, who may not concur therein.

Subject to this limitation, however, the power to create restrictive covenants and the substantive law relating to the running of the burden and the benefit are similar to those relating to unregistered land.

---

6 Law Com No. 201 (HC 546); M & B pp. 913–917.
7 P. 169, ante.
8 See generally Ruoff and Roper, paras. 35–20 to 35–26; Registered Land Practice Notes (2nd edn), pp. 39–43; Barnsley, *Conveyancing Law and Practice* (3rd edn), pp. 439–443.

(a) Burden of restrictive covenants

Section 50 (1) provides[9] for the entry of a notice of a restrictive covenant or agreement (not being a covenant or agreement made between a lessor and lessee).[10] If the burden of such a covenant is to run with the land of the covenantor, it should be protected by a notice on the charges register of the title to the servient land, otherwise it will be defeated by a registered disposition of that land for valuable consideration.[11] Thus the position of a purchaser of registered land who is affected by notice of a restrictive covenant entered on the register, is similar to that of a purchaser of unregistered land where the restrictive covenant is registered as a land charge under the Land Charges Act 1972.[12] Further, it should be observed that the entry of a notice of the burden of a restrictive covenant merely gives notice[13] and does not mean that the covenant is necessarily enforceable against the servient land.[14]

(b) Benefit of restrictive covenants

The benefit of a covenant is not in practice entered on the register of the title to the dominant land. Unless there is a properly constituted building scheme, it will normally be difficult for any applicant to prove conclusively to the Registrar that he has the benefit of restrictive covenants. There is no provision in the Acts or Rules authorising the Registrar to enter the benefit of covenants on the register of title. If, however, in a particular case, a special request is made, the Registrar will enter a note on the register that a transfer or a conveyance contains covenants which were expressed to be imposed for the benefit of the land in the title.[15]

(c) Positive covenants

The Acts and Rules contain no provision for making entries relating to positive covenants since in this case the burden does not run with the land. In practice, they are often intermixed with restrictive covenants, and where this occurs they are not edited out of the restrictive covenant entry. Furthermore, in order to preserve a record of positive covenants (including indemnity covenants) where they are not referred to on the register by reason of such intermixing, the Land Registry, in most cases where they have been

---

9 See also LRR 1925, rr. 7(c), 212; LRA 1925, s. 40 (3).
10 See Ruoff and Roper, para. 21–19; *Newman v Real Estate Debenture Corpn Ltd and Flower Decorations Ltd* [1940] 1 All ER 131.
11 LRA 1925, ss. 20 (1) (a), (4); 23 (1) (a), (5). See *Hodges v Jones* [1935] Ch 657 at 671, where LUXMOORE J states that a restrictive covenant is not an overriding interest.
12 If the restrictive covenant was protected under LCA 1972 before first registration, it will become unenforceable if no notice is entered on first registration: *Freer v Unwins Ltd* [1976] Ch 288, [1976] 1 All ER 634; p. 789, n. 13, post; (1976) 40 Conv (NS) 304 (F. R. Crane); (1977) 41 Conv (NS) 1; (1976) 35 CLJ 211 (D. Hayton); (1976) 92 LQR 338 (R. J. Smith); (1976) 126 NLJ 523 (S. M. Cretney). See Registered Land Practice Note (2nd edn), p. 42, where Chief Land Registrar states that on first registration he does not normally inquire whether a covenant has become void for non-registration under LCA 1972.
13 LRA 1925, s. 50 (2).
14 Ibid., s. 52; *Cator v Newton and Bates* [1940] 1 KB 415, [1939] 4 All ER 457.
15 Ruoff and Roper, para. 35–20. LRR 1925, r. 3 (2) (c), is unfortunately worded as the Acts and Rules contain no provision for noting the benefit of covenants.

imposed on land after it has been registered, will by way of concession refer to them on the register and sew up a copy in the Land or Charge Certificate.[16]

(d) Discharge and modification

Any release, discharge or modification of a restrictive covenant should be noted on the register.[17] Where the covenant is discharged, modified or dealt with by an order under section 84 of the Law of Property Act 1925, or the court refuses to grant an injunction to enforce it, the entry is either cancelled or reference is made to the order, and a copy is filed at the registry.[18]

SECTION IV COVENANTS AND PLANNING

Tulk v Moxhay[19] was decided in 1848 and the doctrine to which it gave rise was one of the bases for control of land use by private landowners during the suburban expansion of the nineteenth century. Together with leasehold and reciprocal positive freehold covenants, it is fundamental to all private planning. Private planning, however, co-exists side by side with the public control of the use and development of land in the hands of local planning authorities under the principal planning statute, the Town and Country Planning Act of 1990.[20]

It is important to notice that these two methods of control, private and public, are cumulative.[1] A purchaser of land must not only satisfy himself about the existence of private covenants that may bind the land which he is buying, but he must also investigate its planning aspect.

An outline of the public planning law is given in Part IV below.[2]

---

16 This concession is not applied where the document imposing such covenants is for some reason itself sewn up in the Land or Charge Certificate, nor in the case of positive covenants imposed prior to first registration. In the first case the sewn up document can be perused, and in the second the record is preserved in the pre-registration deeds which are returned to the applicant. The concession does not in general extend to the benefit of positive covenants being entered on the title because of practical difficulties and doubts about enforcement: Ruoff and Roper, para 17–51; Ruoff and Pryer, *Land Registration Handbook* (1990), p. 91; M & B p. 906.
17 LRR 1925, r. 212.
18 LRA 1925, s. 50 (3).
19 (1848) 2 Ph 774; M & B p. 833.
20 See Law Commission Report on Restrictive Covenants 1967 (Law Com No. 11), paras 16–19 and on the Law of Positive and Restrictive Covenants 1984 (Law Com No. 127, HC 201), paras 2.5–2.7; M & B pp. 907–909.
 1 See (1964) 28 Conv (NS) 190 (A. R. Mellows).
 2 Pp. 942 et seq, post.

Chapter 20

Rentcharges[1]

SECTION I NATURE OF A RENTCHARGE

(a) Origin and history

We have already seen that a rent payable by a tenant to a landlord is called rent-service because of the tenure which exists between the parties, but that it is called a rentcharge if there is no tenure between the creditor and the debtor from whose land it issues.[2] In former days this lack of tenurial interest between the parties meant that the rent owner had no automatic right at law to distrain upon the land of the debtor for the recovery of arrears, and generally speaking, rentcharges, though of considerable antiquity, were regarded as contrary to the policy of the common law, since the debtor was rendered less able to perform the military service due to his overlord, while the rent owner himself was free from all feudal obligations in respect of the land.[3] It became usual, therefore, for the parties to enter into an express agreement that the creditor should have a power of distress over the debtor's land. A rent supported in this way by a specially reserved power of distress, as distinct from a rent-service where such power existed of common right, was called a rentcharge, since the land liable for payment was charged with a distress.[4] We have seen that there is no longer any necessity to charge the land expressly, for the Law of Property Act 1925, re-enacting the Landlord and Tenant Act 1730, and the Conveyancing Act 1881, confers the right of distress upon all rentacharge owners.[5]

---

1 See generally Preston and Newsom, *Restrictive Covenants Affecting Freehold Land* (8th edn), chapter 7; Easton, *Law of Rentcharges* (2nd edn); Law Commission Report on Rentcharges 1975 (Law Com No. 68) on which the Rentcharges Act 1977 is based.
2 Pp. 421–2, ante.
3 Cruise *Digest*, Tit XXVII. c. i. ss. 1, 7.
4 Co Litt, 144a.
5 LPA 1925, s. 121; p. 423, ante.

A rentcharge is thus an annual sum of money issuing and payable out of land, the due payment of which is secured by a right of distress that is not the result of tenure between the parties but is either expressly reserved or allowed by statute.[6] It is now defined in the Rentcharges Act 1977[7] as:

any annual or other periodic sum charged on or issuing out of land, except

(a) rent reserved by a lease or tenancy, or
(b) any sum by way of interest.

(b) Legal and equitable

A rentcharge is an incorporeal interest that may be limited for all the estates recognized at common law.[8]

Thus it may be limited to a person for an estate in fee simple, in tail, for life, for years or in remainder, but under the Law of Property Act 1925 the interest conferred on the rent owner is a legal interest only where it is in possession and either perpetual or for a term of years absolute.[9] Thus, an annual sum of money granted to a widow for life and charged upon the settled lands by a marriage settlement confers an equitable interest. Furthermore, a rentcharge can only be legal if the proper formalities for its creation have been observed.

(c) Rentcharge on a rentcharge

As the essence of a rentcharge lies in the power of the owner to distrain upon lands, it follows that, strictly speaking, it can issue only out of corporeal hereditaments. A dominant owner, for instance, cannot charge a right of way to which he is entitled, since there is nothing on which the rent owner can distrain, though of course the debtor will be liable for the amount he has agreed to pay.[10] For the same reason at common law a rent cannot be reserved out of a rent,[11] and therefore if A, who is entitled to a rentcharge of £50, grants it to B, but reserves to himself thereout a rentcharge of £25, the reservation is void in the sense that the £25 does not constitute a rentcharge properly so called.

But this rule of the common law has in part been abrogated by the Law of Property Act 1925, which enacts that a rentcharge or annual sum of money (not being a rent-service) may be reserved out of or charged on another rent-charge in the same manner as it could have been charged on land.[12] In such a case the ordinary remedies of distress and entry upon the lands are impossible, and therefore it is provided that where the rent is in arrears for 21 days, the owner of the second rent (£25) shall have power to appoint a receiver of the rent (£50) on which it is charged. The receiver is then entitled

6 See Co Litt, 143*b*, 147*b*.
7 S. 1 (1). This includes an annual sum known by a name other than rentcharge, e.g. chief rent (or chief), fee farm rent and ground rent (a confusing name since it usually means rent payable under a long lease).
8 Cruise *Digest*, Tit. XXVIII. c. ii. ss. 1–3.
9 S. 1 (1)(*b*). A rentcharge, provided that it is not limited to take effect upon the determination of some other interest, is "in possession" not withstanding that its payment is to commence at some time subsequently to its creation: Law of Property (Entailed Interests) Act 1932, s. 2.
10 Co Litt, 47*a*.
11 *Earl of Stafford v Buckley* (1750) 2 Ves Sen 170 at 177.
12 LPA 1925, s. 122. This occurs very rarely in practice.

to acquire the £50 by action, distress or otherwise, and out of this to pay arrears, expenses and his own remuneration.

SECTION II EXAMPLES OF RENTCHARGES

Rentcharges may be created in three main situations:

(a) Sale of land

On the sale of land a vendor, instead of receiving the purchase money in the form of a lump sum, may reserve to himself a legal rentcharge, under which a sum of money is payable annually to himself and his heirs for ever, and, in addition, receive a capital payment. The rentcharge, being legal, binds all subsequent purchasers of the land. This type of transaction occurs mainly in Manchester and other parts of the North West of England, and in the County of Avon, including Bristol, where some 80 per cent of owner-occupied residential property may be subject to rentcharges.[13]

(b) Secured family annuities

In this situation, a rentcharge is created voluntarily or in consideration of marriage or by way of family settlement for the life of any person (or for any shorter but indefinite period, such as widowhood) or for providing sums for the advancement, maintenance or benefit of any persons. In this case the rentcharge is equitable and the land on which the payments are secured becomes settled land under the Settled Land Act 1925,[14] unless it is already settled land or is held upon trust for sale.

(c) Positive covenants

Where, as a result of a property development, there is a distinct grouping of separate freehold houses or where a single building is divided into separate freehold parts, a rentcharge is used as a conveyancing device to enable the burden of positive covenants to run against the unit holder for the time being. As we have seen, it was held in *Austerberry v Corporation of Oldham*[15] that the burden of positive covenants on the sale of land by a freeholder does not run at common law, and neither does it in equity under the doctrine of *Tulk v Moxhay*[16] which is confined to restrictive covenants. In *Austerberry v Corporation of Oldham* LINDLEY LJ expressly mentioned the use of the rentcharge for this purpose.[17]

One scheme in common use for smaller developments has been described as follows:[18]

a rentcharge affecting each unit will be imposed for the benefit of the other units and this rentcharge will be supported by positive covenants to repair, insure, and so on. The purpose of this scheme is not to procure the actual payment of the rentcharge—its amount may be nominal and the rent owners are unlikely to trouble

13 Law Commission Report, para. 16.
14 S. 1 (1)(v), p. 178, ante.
15 (1885) 29 Ch D 750; M & B p. 826; p. 611, ante.
16 (1848) 2 Ph 774; M & B p. 833; p. 614, ante.
17 At 783.
18 Law Commission Report, para. 49; [1988] Conv 99 (S. Bright).

very much whether it is paid or not—but to create a set of positive covenants which are actually designed to preserve the development as a whole but which are directly enforceable because they happen incidentally to support the rentcharge.

The amount of the rentcharge may, however, not be nominal, but considerable, where the object is to provide funds for a management company to look after the maintenance of a large development as a whole.

SECTION III RENTCHARGES ACT 1977

The policy of the Rentcharges Act 1977[19] is to abolish existing rentcharges where possible and to prevent their creation in the future. The creation of a rentcharge under example (a) above is void after 21 August 1977, and an existing rentcharge will be extinguished 60 years after the date of the passing of the Act (i.e. 22 July 2037) or from the date on which it first becomes payable, whichever is the later. [20] Such a rentcharge can cause conveyancing difficulties, especially where the land sold is divided in subsequent sales; the amount of the rentcharge may be very small in relation to the property purchased, and the purchaser may feel that "a liability to pay an annual sum to a former owner who is not necessarily the vendor is repugnant to the concept of freehold ownership". [1]

Rentcharges under the above examples (b) secured family annuities and (c) positive covenants, however, are expressly preserved by the Rentcharges Act,[2] although the conveyancing device of (c) will become unnecessary if the recommendations of the Law Commission are implemented. [3] The Act calls (c) an estate rentcharge and defines it as follows:[4]

A rentcharge created for the purpose

(i) of making covenants to be performed by the owner of the land affected by the rentcharge enforceable by the rent owner against the owner for the time being of the land; or

(ii) of meeting, or contributing towards, the cost of the performance by the rent owner of covenants for the provision of services, the carrying out of maintenance or repairs, the effecting of insurance or the making of any payment by him for the benefit of the land affected by the rentcharge or for the benefit of that or other land.

A rentcharge of more than a nominal amount is not treated as an estate rentcharge unless it represents a reasonable payment for the performance of covenants in (ii) of the definition of an estate rentcharge. [5]

Two other kinds of rentcharge are also preserved by the Act:[6]

(i) a rentcharge under any Act of Parliament providing for the creation of rentcharges in connection with the execution of works on land (whether by way

19 See generally (1977) 127 NLJ 1042 (H. W. Wilkinson).
20 Rentcharges Act 1977, ss. 2 (1), 2 (3).
 1 Law Commission Report, para. 26.
 2 Rentcharges Act 1977, s. 2 (3).
 3 See Law Commission Report on The Law of Positive and Restrictive Covenants 1984 (Law Com No. 127, HC 201).
 4 Rentcharges Act 1977, s. 2 (4).
 5 Ibid., s. 2 (5).
 6 Ibid., s. 2 (3).

of improvements, repairs or otherwise) or the commutation of any obligation to do any such work; and

(ii) a rentcharge by, or in accordance with the requirements of, any order of a court.

Since the year 2037 is sometime in the future and certain kinds of rentcharge may still exist, it is necessary to set out some details of the law apart from the Act.

SECTION IV CREATION OF A RENTCHARGE

A rentcharge may be created by instrument inter vivos, by will, or by statute.

(a) By instrument inter vivos

At common law a rentcharge, if created inter vivos, must be granted by deed.[7] But the equitable principle underlying the doctrine of *Walsh v Lonsdale* applies here just as it does in the case of an agreement to grant a term of years[8] or an easement, so that, where one person has made a contract to grant a rentcharge to another, an equitable rentcharge may be created.[9]

The quantum of the interest in a rentcharge depends upon the words of limitation which are inserted in the deed of grant, and the rule is that such words are construed in exactly the same way as in a grant of corporeal hereditaments. Thus before 1926, in order to pass a perpetual rentcharge it was necessary to convey the rent to the grantee *and his heirs*, or to the grantee *in fee simple*, but the changes which have been effected by the Law of Property Act 1925 in regard to words of limitation sufficient to pass a fee simple estate in land[10] apply to rentcharges, and at the present day the effect of a grant which contains no technical words of limitation is to give the grantee a perpetual rentcharge, or if that is impossible owing to the grantor only having a smaller estate, then to give him a rentcharge for the whole interest possessed by the grantor. This rule is, however, displaced if a contrary intention is shown in the conveyance, and in such a case the size of the grantee's interest will depend upon the intention of the parties.[11]

(b) By will

A rentcharge may be validly created by will, and whether it is so or not depends upon the intention of the testator. If he directs that an annual sum shall be paid to a donee and uses words which show that the money is to be a charge upon the land and not upon his personal property, it is a rentcharge as distinct from an annuity, as for instance where he devises land to A:

subject to and charged and chargeable with the payment of £100 a year to B for 25 years.[12]

---

7 Co Litt, 169a; *Hewlins v Shippam* (1826) 5 B & C 221 at 229.
8 Pp. 377 et seq, ante.
9 *Jackson v Lever* (1792) 3 Bro CC 605.
10 LPA 1925, s. 60; p. 160, ante.
11 S. 60 (1). See Megarry and Wade, *Law of Real Property* (5th edn), p. 823 for an argument that s. 60 may not apply to the creation of rentcharges by deed.
12 *Ramsay v Thorngate* (1849) 16 Sim 575.

Section 28 of the Wills Act 1837[13] only applies to the transfer of an existing rentcharge; it does not apply to the creation of a new one. Thus, if a rentcharge is created by will without any words of limitation, the devisee can take it only for life.[14]

(c) By statute

There are two distinct series of enactments under which an owner of land may carry out certain improvements and arrange that the cost shall be charged upon the land and reimbursed in full, together with interest, by a definite number of annual payments. The chief statute of the first class is the Improvement of Land Act 1864, which allows "landowners" (i.e. anyone except a lessee at a rack rent[15] who is in actual possession of the rents and profits) to borrow money for improvements from certain private land improvement companies.

Money may not be borrowed in this way for every improvement, but only for those specified in the Settled Land Act 1925.[16] No rentcharge can be imposed upon the land until the Secretary of State for the Environment[17] has, on the application of the landowner, satisfied himself that the suggested improvement will permanently increase the yearly value of the land to an extent greater than the annual rentcharge which is contemplated.[18]

If satisfied on this point the Secretary of State issues a provisional order which specifies the sum to be charged upon the land, the rate of interest and the number of years within which it must be paid off. The rate of interest is at the discretion of the Secretary of State,[19] but the period for payments must not exceed 40 years.[20] After the improvements are completed the Secretary of State issues an absolute order imposing the annual sum as a rentcharge upon the fee simple, and this has priority over all existing and future incumbrances affecting the land with the certain specified exceptions.[1] The remedies for its recovery are the same as in the case of other rentcharges,[2] except that the landowner is not personally liable.

The second class of statute is represented by the Settled Land Act 1925, which allows a limited owner to raise money for the purpose of carrying out permanent improvements on the settled land. Prior to 1 January 1926, there was an important difference between the operation of the Improvement of Land Acts and that of the Settled Land Acts in this matter, for, while under the former a tenant for life could raise new money for the purpose, all that the Settled Land Acts did was to authorize the expenditure upon

13 P. 160, ante.
14 *Nichols v Hawkes* (1853) 10 Hare 342.
15 I.e. the full yearly value of the land.
16 P. 189, ante. The improvements specified in the 1864 Act are all covered by those set out in SLA 1925, and the latter are expressly brought within the operation of the earlier Act.
17 Or the Secretary of State for Wales: S.I. 1967 No. 156; S.I. 1970 No. 1681.
18 There are certain improvements which may be allowed although they will not permanently increase the yearly value of the land, i.e. construction of waterworks for the use of residents on the estate (40 & 41 Vict c. 31, s. 5); erection of mansion house under Limited Owners Residence Acts 1870, 1871; planting, under Improvement of Land Act 1864, s. 15; erection or improvement of farmhouse or cottage for use of workers on the land, under Agricultural Credits Act 1923, s. 3 (3).
19 Agricultural Credits Act 1923, s. 3 (1).
20 Improvement of Land Act 1899, s. 1 (1).
 1 Ibid., s. 59.
 2 Infra.

improvements of capital money which happened to be in the hands of the trustees. A tenant for life could not raise new money by mortgage under the Settled Land Acts for carrying out improvements, but this power, as we have seen, has now been expressly conferred upon him by the Settled Land Act 1925.[3]

SECTION V REMEDIES FOR THE RECOVERY OF A RENTCHARGE

The following remedies are available to a rentcharge owner:

(a) Distress

A power to distrain upon the land, out of which the rent issues, is, as we have seen, an implicit incident of a rentcharge, though formerly it had to be specially reserved. Even when the Landlord and Tenant Act 1730 had conferred the power of distress on rent owners, it was the usual practice to insert an express provision to the same effect in all instruments creating rentcharges, but this has ceased to be the practice in the case of instruments coming into effect after 31 December 1881. The Conveyancing Act of that year provides that where any rent (not incident to the relationship of landlord and tenant) is in arrears for 21 days, the person entitled to receive it may enter into and distrain upon the land charged or any part thereof, and dispose of any distrainable objects according to the general law.[4] This remedy is now re-enacted by the Law of Property Act 1925.[5]

(b) Entry upon the land charged

The Law of Property Act 1925 provides that, when a rentcharge is in arrears for 40 days, even though no legal demand has been made for payment, the owner may enter into possession of and hold the land charged or any part thereof and take the income thereof until all arrears and costs and expenses occasioned by the non-payment of the rent are satisfied.[6] The Act, it will be noticed, does not give the owner of the rent a power of entry that will cause a forfeiture of the debtor's interest in the land, as is usual between landlord and tenant, but such a power may be, and generally is, reserved in the instrument of creation.

As we have seen, neither type of power, whether to hold the land until payment or to determine the debtor's interest, is subject to the rule against perpetuities.[7]

(c) Lease to trustees

When a rentcharge is in arrears for 40 days, the person entitled to payment, whether taking possession or not, may by deed lease the whole or part of the land to a trustee for a term of years, with or without impeachment of waste,

3 SLA 1925, s. 71 (1) (ii); p. 189, ante.
4 P. 423, ante.
5 S. 121 (2).
6 S. 121 (3).
7 LPA 1925, s. 121 (6), p. 309, ante (right to enter for purpose of distraint or leasing); PAA 1964, s. 11 (1), p. 326, ante (right to effect forfeiture).

on trust to raise and pay the rent together with all arrears, costs and expenses.[8] The trustee may adopt any *reasonable means*[9] to raise the money, as for instance by the mortgage, assignment or sub-lease of the term vested in him, or by appropriating the income of the land, but he cannot create a *legal* mortgage unless the rentcharge itself is held for a legal estate.

The above three remedies are not enforceable if a contrary intention is expressed in the instrument under which the annual sum arises,[10] and they are subject to the provisions of such instrument. Moreover, when a rentcharge is charged on another rentcharge, the above remedies are excluded and replaced by a right in the rent owner to appoint a receiver of the annual sum charged whenever payment is in arrears for 21 days.[11]

(d) Action for payment

(i) Action of debt It is well settled that an action of debt for the recovery of arrears lies against the *terre tenant*[12] for the time being of the whole or part only of the land charged,[13] provided that he holds a freehold as distinct from a leasehold interest.[14] It is no defence that the profits of the land do not equal in amount the value of the rentcharge. Thus in *Pertwee v Townsend*:[15]

> Lands were charged with the payment of a rentcharge of £80 a year. A certain portion of these lands was acquired by the defendant's predecessor in title, who released the rest of the land from the burden of the charge and imposed it upon the portion so acquired. At the time of the action for the recovery of £80, being one year's arrears, the defendant was able to show that the annual profits of the portion charged, of which he was tenant for life, amounted only to £7.5s., but nevertheless he was held personally liable for the whole £80.

COLLINS J said:[16]

> The defendant holds the land subject to a charge, and he cannot keep the land and refuse to pay the charge. If he does refuse, the remedy against him is personal for the amount of the charge itself.

Although the right to sue runs with the rentcharge and the liability to be sued runs with the land, the benefit of a covenant to pay a rentcharge does not run with the rentcharge so as to entitle an assignee thereof to maintain an action *on the covenant* against the covenantor or his assignee.[17] Thus:

> where A granted a fee simple to B on the terms that A his heirs and assigns should be entitled to a rent issuing out of the land, and the conveyance contained a covenant by B to pay the rent to A his heirs and assigns, it was held that X, to whom A had demised the rent for 1000 years, could not sue B on the covenant.[18]

The technical nature of this rule was demonstrated by LAWRENCE LJ:

> Wherever may be the foundation of the rule, and whether it rests on the broader

8　LPA 1925, s. 121 (4).
9　Ibid.
10　Ibid., s. 121 (5).
11　Ibid., s. 122; p. 646, ante.
12　A *terre tenant* is the person who has the actual possession or occupation of land.
13　*Thomas v Sylvester* (1873) LR 8 QB 368.
14　*Re Herbage Rents* [1896] 2 Ch 811. Distress, however, may be levied on the premises.
15　[1896] 2 QB 129.
16　At 134.
17　*Grant v Edmondson* [1931] 1 Ch 1.
18　*Milnes v Branch* (1816) 5 M & S 411.

principle that (except as between lessor and lessee) no covenant can run with an incorporeal hereditament, or whether it rests on the narrower principle that a covenant to pay a rentcharge is a collateral covenant or a covenant in gross which does not touch or concern the rentcharge, or whether it rests on no principle and is merely arbitrary, I am of opinion that it is too firmly established to be disturbed by this court.[19]

(ii) Apportionment A purchaser of any part of land which is burdened by a rentcharge is liable for the whole of the rent, unless there has been an apportionment. This may be legal where the owner of the rentcharge has formally severed the rent so as to charge part only of it on the land sold, or so as to exonerate the land from the rent. If, however, the owner of the rentcharge is not a party to the severance, the apportionment is equitable, and he is not bound by it. The person affected by the rentcharge remains liable to him for the whole of the rent, with a right of contribution from the other owners of the land.[20]

Under the Rentcharges Act 1977,[1] subject to small exceptions, a rentcharge may be legally apportioned by the Secretary of State for the Environment[2] on the application of any landowner whose land is affected by it. The Secretary of State may make an order, with or without conditions, apportioning the rentcharge between the rentpayer's land and the remaining land affected by the rentcharge. The order is made after a draft apportionment order is served on the person who appears to be the rent owner or his agent, and, subject to their rights of appeal to the Lands Tribunal, the order takes effect after 28 days from the date on which it was made. The effect of the order is to release the applicant's land from any part of the rentcharge not apportioned to it and to release the remaining land from such part (if any) of the rentcharge as is apportioned to the applicant's land.[3]

The Law of Property Act 1925 provides[4] that, where equitable apportionment has been made in a conveyance for valuable consideration, then the apportionment, without prejudice to the rights of the rent owner, shall be binding between the grantor and the grantee under the conveyance and their respective successors in title. If the owner of part of the land fails to pay the rentcharge in accordance with the agreement or fails to perform some covenant, and the owner of the other part is in consequence obliged to pay the charges or damages, the latter may distrain upon the land of the former and may also take the income thereof until he has been satisfied.[5]

19 *Grant v Edmondson* [1931] 1 Ch 1 at 26. See (1931) 47 LQR 380 (W. Strachan).
20 For the problems which arise, see Law Commission Report, paras 12–15, 29–30. In 1982 a consultation paper proposed new arrangements for the apportionment and redemption of rentcharge and ground rents under which they would be primarily operated by the parties themselves: Law Commission Seventeenth Annual Report 1981–1982 (1983 Law Com No. 119), para. 2.105.
 1 Ss. 4–7. Application for apportionment may also be made under Landlord and Tenant Act 1927, s. 20, as amended by Rentcharges Act 1977, s. 17 (1), Sch. 1, para. 3.
 2 Or the Secretary of State for Wales: S.I. 1967 No. 156; S.I. 1970 No. 1681.
 3 Rentcharges Act 1977, s. 7 (4).
 4 S. 190.
 5 S. 190 (2); *Whitham v Bullock* [1939] 2 KB 81, [1939] 2 All ER 310.

SECTION VI   EXTINCTION OF A RENTCHARGE

There are several ways in which a rentcharge may be extinguished and the land freed from liability.

(a) Release

If the rent owner releases the whole of the land charged from any further liability to pay, the rent is extinguished. Indeed, on the somewhat questionable ground that a rent, being entire and issuing out of every part of the land, cannot be thrown upon one particular part not apportioned between several parts, the old rule was that a release of *part* of the land discharged the whole land and produced a total extinguishment of the rent.[6] But the Law of Property Act 1925,[7] re-enacting the Law of Property Amendment Act 1859, provides that the release from a rentcharge of part of the lands charged shall not extinguish the whole rentcharge, but shall only render it unenforceable against the part released. This provision, however, is not to prejudice the rights of the persons who are interested in the unreleased part of the lands unless they concur in or confirm the release. The effect of this enactment is that where the owner of land which is subject to a rentcharge sells the land in separate portions to different persons, and only one portion is released from the charge by the rent owner, the purchaser of the unreleased portions will be liable for the whole rent if they concur in the release, but will be liable only for an apportioned part if they do not concur.[8]

(b) Merger

A rentcharge may also be extinguished by merger.[9] The rigid rule of common law is that, whenever a lesser and a greater estate in the same lands become united in one person in his own right, the lesser estate is merged in the greater and extinguished without regard to the intention of the parties. As we shall see later, however, the equitable view that no merger occurs if it is contrary to the intention of the party in whom the two estates vest now obtains in all courts,[10] and it will suffice to say here that this principle applies to the merger of a rentcharge. Thus, if the absolute owner of a rentcharge also becomes absolute owner in his own right of the land charged, either by grant or by devise, there is prima facie a merger of the rent in the estate because there is no obvious advantage in keeping both the interests alive.[11]

But, on the other hand, if the person who is responsible for the rent mortgages the land charged to the rent owner, there is no merger, since the two interests do not unite in one person in the same right.

(c) Lapse of time

If a rentcharge is not paid for 12 years and no sufficient acknowledgment of the owner's title is made, it is extinguished under the Limitation Act 1980.[12]

---

6 Co Litt 147*b*.
7 S. 70.
8 *Booth v Smith* (1884) 14 QBD 318.
9 As to merger generally, see *Forbes v Moffatt* (1811) 8 Ves 384; Tudor, *Leading Cases on Real Property* (4th edn), p. 244; chapter 27, p. 917, post.
10 Pp. 916–7, post.
11 *Freeman v Edwards* (1848) 2 Exch 732.
12 S. 20 (1), p. 690, post; *Shaw v Crompton* [1910] 2 KB 370.

(d) Statute

Lastly, under the Rentcharges Act 1977,[13] the owner of any land affected by a rentcharge may apply to the Secretary of State for the Environment for a reduction certificate which certifies that the rentcharge has been redeemed.[14] The certificate is issued when the redemption price certified by the Secretary of State has been paid to the rent owner or into court.[15] The price is calculated in accordance with a formula based on the length of time which the rentcharge has still to run.[16] The effect of the certificate is to release the applicant's land from the rentcharge, but it does not affect the rent owner's rights and remedies to recover previous arrears.[17]

This statutory method of redemption does not apply to rentcharges which can still be created, nor to variable rentcharges.[18] It does not, therefore, apply to estate rentcharges,[19] whose attractiveness is thereby enhanced; they had been liable to redemption under the former procedure of the Law of Property Act 1925 for statutory discharge.

SECTION VII REGISTERED LAND

A rentcharge may be created over registered land[20] in the same way as it can over unregistered land. Thus, unless there is some entry on the register to the contrary, the proprietor of registered freehold land may grant a rentcharge in possession, either perpetual or for a term of years absolute in any form which sufficiently refers to the registered land.[1] He may also transfer the fee simple in possession of his registered land or any part of it subject to the reservation thereout of a rentcharge in possession.[2]

Unlike legal easements and profits à prendre, a legal rentcharge is capable of being substantively registered with a separate title.[3] Further, unlike leases, a rentcharge granted for any term of years, no matter how short, may be so registered. As to compulsory registration, the mere fact that the land affected by a rentcharge lies in a compulsory area never makes registration of the rentcharge itself compulsory, since section 120 (1) of the Land Registration Act 1925 in effect exempts from compulsory registration the title to an incorporeal hereditament.[4] However, substantive registration of any rentcharge capable of such registration is always compulsory where the rentcharge issues out of land which is already registered.

13 Replacing the similar but not identical procedure under LPA 1925, s. 191.
14 Rentcharges Act 1977, s. 8 (1); Rentcharges Regulations 1978 (S.I. 1978 No. 16).
15 Ibid., s. 9 (5).
16 Ibid., s. 10 (1).
17 Ibid., s. 10 (3).
18 Ibid., s. 8 (4), (5); p. 648, ante. A rentcharge is variable if the amount of the rentcharge will, or may, vary in accordance with the provisions of the instrument under which it is payable: s. 8 (5).
19 P. 648, ante.
20 See generally Rueff, *Rentcharges in Registered Conveyancing*; Ruoff and Roper, chapter 26, where at para. 26.02 it is said that "no subject receives a more meagre and fragmentary treatment in the Land Registration Acts and Rules than that of rentcharges."
 1 LRA 1925, s. 18 (1) (*b*); LRR 1925, rr. 79, 113.
 2 Ibid., s. 18 (1) (*d*). For rentcharges created by the proprietor of a registered leasehold estate, see LRA 1925, s. 21 (1) (*b*), (*c*).
 3 LRA 1925, s. 3 (xxv); LRR 1925, rr. 50–52.
 4 P. 101, n. 13, ante.

On the other hand a rentcharge for life is not capable of substantive registration, although it may and should be noted as a general equitable charge against the registered title of the land charged;[5] nor can a perpetual or other rentcharge which takes effect under a settlement be registered.

In order to be effective at law, any disposition under which a rentcharge is created, whether by a deed of grant or by a transfer, must, like all other kinds of disposition, be completed by registration.[6] In the case of a rentcharge, there are thus "two processes, namely, the substantive registration of the title to the rentcharge and the entry of notice of the rentcharge as an incumbrance against the title of the landowner ... When a rentcharge is created in favour of the vendor in a transfer of registered land ... the transferor will be registered as the proprietor of the rentcharge under a separate title, and be given a rentcharge.[7] Simultaneously, the transferee is registered as the proprietor of the land, and the rentcharge is noted in the charges register of his title as an incumbrance.[8] In the remarks column of the entry there will be a cross-reference to the rentcharge title."[9]

5 LRA 1925, s. 49 (1) (c); Ruoff and Roper, para. 26.03.
6 Ibid., ss. 19 (2), 22 (2); LRR 1925, rr. 107, 108.
7 LRR 1925, r. 108.
8 LRA 1925, s. 49 (1) (a); LRR 1925, r. 107 (2).
9 LRR 1925, r. 108; Ruoff and Roper, para. 26–17.

Chapter 21

Mortgages[1]

SUMMARY

SECTION I INTRODUCTORY NOTE

A mortgage is a conveyance or other disposition of an interest in property designed to secure the payment of money or the discharge of some other obligation.[2] The party who conveys the property by way of security is called

---

1 See generally Coote, *Law of Mortgages* (9th edn); Cousins, *Law of Mortgage* (1989); Fairest, *Mortgages* (2nd edn); Fisher and Lightwood, *Law of Mortgages* (10th edn); *Snell's Equity* (29th edn), Part IV; Waldock, *Law of Mortgages* (2nd edn); M & B chapter 11; (1978) 94 LQR 571 (P. Jackson).

2 See *Santley v Wilde* [1899] 2 Ch 474, per LINDLEY MR: "A mortgage is a conveyance of land or an assignment of chattels as a security for the payment of a debt or the discharge of some other obligation for which it is given." See also Lawson and Rudden, *Introduction to the Law of Property* (2nd edn), p. 222.

the mortgagor, the lender or obligee who obtains an interest in the property is called the mortgagee, and the debt for which the security is created is termed the mortgage debt. The mortgagee, since he is the grantee of a proprietary interest acquires a real, not merely a personal, security that prevails against the general body of creditors in the event of the mortgagor's bankruptcy. He is not only a creditor of the mortgagor; he is a secured creditor. As long as the mortgaged property remains worth as much as the debt, the mortgagee will receive payment in full; but if it falls in value and becomes worth less than the debt, the mortgagee will only be a secured creditor to the extent of its value, and he must prove in the mortgagor's bankruptcy with the unsecured creditors for the remainder of the debt.

A common feature of our present day society is the purchase of a dwelling-house by an individual; and inseparable from the purchase is the mortgage of that house to a building society or other lender. The political economist refers to a property-owning democracy, and, with more particularity, Lord DIPLOCK refers to:[3]

> a real-property-mortgaged-to-a-building-society-owning democracy.

There may be other reasons why a loan of money is required, as, for instance, where a borrower calculates that he can make more money from the use of borrowed money than the loan will cost him in interest. His capital may be locked up in his business, and he may need a loan in order to expand it.[4] Or a borrower may own one house already and wish to sell it and buy another one instead. If so, he will need a bridging loan for a short period between the purchase of the one house and the sale of the other.

The mortgage industry is big business. The building societies alone made advances of some £20.5 billion in 1991,[5] and the banks, insurance companies and local authorities are also substantial institutional lenders. In 1991 the building societies took 77% of the market.[6]

The law of mortgages which grew up in the eighteenth and nineteenth centuries has had to be adapted to meet twentieth century circumstances:

> Courts of Equity have looked upon a mortgage transaction as one in which the terms were likely to be dictated by the mortgagee. In early days the mortgagor was at a disadvantage in that he was in need of money and must take it on the mortgagee's terms; it was a lender's market. And, while the law followed the maxim "caveat emptor" in the affairs of merchants and trade, equity not surprisingly took a different view in the case of mortgages. The fact that mortgagors were, in the early days, often members of great families and mortgagees were professional money lenders no doubt contributed to some extent to the development. A consideration of the changed position of borrowers and lenders in the capitalist

---

3 *Pettitt v Pettitt* [1970] AC 777 at 824, [1969] 2 All ER 385 at 414. In 1914 ten per cent of houses were owner-occupied; in 1951 this had risen to 29 per cent, and in 1984 to 61 per cent; Central Statistical Office Social Trends. In 1992 there were 24 million dwellings in the United Kingdom, an increase of more than one third since 1961. Between 1961 and 1992 the number of owner occupied dwellings more than doubled to 16 million: 24 (1994 edn), para. 8.1; M & B p. 410.
4 The loan is usually made to the company, but the lender may also insist on a personal guarantee from its directors secured by a charge on their own property.
5 1,492,000 advances were made in 1991, totalling £42,948 million. The total assets of the 110 building societies amounted to £243,979 million: Annual Report of the Building Societies Commission 1991–92, Tables 1 and 2, pp. 56–58. See also Building Society Fact Book (published annually by the Building Societies Association). For building societies as a special type of mortgagee, see pp. 734–6, post.
6 See Clarke, *Mortgage Fraud* (1991); [1993] Conv 181 (H. W. Wilkinson).

society of the present day will suggest that the old cases should be accepted with some reserve. The cases on this subject show a continual struggle between the principle of binding precedent and the requirements of a changing society; they can only be understood with this in mind. Those which were decided about the turn of the present century do not create the principle they apply. That litigation was a challenge to the validity of the principle laid down in earlier centuries, but generally it succeeded only in re-affirming the old principles; it was not until 1914[7] that substantial progress was made.[8]

SECTION II CREATION OF MORTGAGES BEFORE 1926

A. HISTORY OF MORTGAGES BEFORE 1926[9]

If we are to understand the radical alterations that were made by the legislation of 1925 in the methods of creating mortgages, it is necessary to appreciate the principles of the earlier law.

(1) MORTGAGES OF FREEHOLD

(a) At common law

The developed law of mortgages is the joint product of common law, equity and statute. In the earliest days of the common law a mortgage was a mere pledge, which took one of two forms. It might be agreed that the lender should enter into possession of the land, and should take the rents and profits in discharge of both the principal and the interest on the loan. This was called a *vivum vadium*, or living pledge, since it automatically and by its own force discharged the entire debt. But, on the other hand, the arrangement might be that the lender should take the rents and profits of the land in discharge of the interest only, in which case the transaction was called a *mortuum vadium*, a dead pledge, since it did not effect the gradual extinction of the debt.

By the time of Littleton (1402–1481), however, a mortgage had become a species of estate upon condition created by a feoffment defeasible upon condition subsequent.

The land was conveyed in fee simple to the mortgagee on condition that if the loan was repaid upon the day which had been fixed by agreement, the conveyance should be defeated, and the mortgagor be free to re-enter. If repayment was not made on the exact date fixed, then the estate of the mortgagee became absolute, and the mortgagor's interest in the land was extinguished. In the words of Littleton:

> If a feoffment be made upon such condition, that if the feoffor pay to the feoffee at a certain day etc. 40 pounds of money, that then the feoffor may re-enter, etc., in this case the feoffee is called tenant in mortgage, which is as much to say in French as mortgage, and in Latin *mortuum vadium*. And it seemeth that the cause why it is called mortgage is, for that it is doubtful whether the feoffor will pay at the day limited such sum or not, and if he doth not pay, then the land which is put in pledge

---

7 *Kreglinger v New Patagonia Meat and Cold Storage Co Ltd* [1914] AC 25; M & B p. 732; p. 679, post.

8 M & B p. 710.

9 Holdsworth, *History of English Law*, vol. iii. p. 128; Plucknett, *Concise History of the Common Law* (5th edn), pp. 603–9; Simpson, *A History of the Land Law* (2nd edn), pp. 141–143, 242–247.

upon condition for the payment of the money is taken from him for ever, and so dead to him upon condition etc. And if he doth pay the money, then the pledge is dead as to the tenant.[10]

That a feoffor should be bound to repay the loan on the exact day fixed or be precluded for ever from redeeming his property was a hard rule, and:

what made the hardship on the debtor a glaring one was that the debt still remained unpaid and could be recovered from the feoffor notwithstanding that he had actually forfeited the land to his mortgagee.[11]

(b) In equity. Equity of redemption

By the time of Charles I, equity had so fundamentally altered this strict legal view that the law of mortgages was transformed. The form as indicated by Littleton remained, but equity interfered on the general principle that relief should be granted against forfeiture for breach of a penal condition.[12] No longer was redemption to depend upon a strict compliance with the contract. In the view of equity the essential object of a mortgage is to afford security to the lender, and as long as the security remains intact there is no justification for expropriating the property of the mortgagor merely because of his failure to make prompt payment. In the words of Lord NOTTINGHAM:

In natural justice and equity the principal right of the mortgagee is to the money, and his right to the land is only as a security for the money.[13]

Hence the rule ultimately established by courts of equity was that a mortgagor must be allowed to redeem his fee simple despite his failure to make repayment on the appointed day. Time was not to be of the essence of the transaction. This is still the rule, although a mortgage is no longer created by the conveyance of a fee simple estate. The position, then, is this: that upon the date fixed for repayment (which is usually six months after the creation of the mortgage, although in most cases neither mortgagor nor mortgagee intends that the loan shall be repaid on that date) the mortgagor has at common law a contractual right to redeem.

If this date passes without repayment, he obtains a right to redeem in equity.

The equity to redeem, which arises on failure to exercise the contractual right of redemption, must be carefully distinguished from the equitable estate, which, from the first, remains in the mortgagor, and is sometimes referred to as an equity of redemption.[14]

This equity of redemption arises as soon as the mortgage is created, and is an equitable interest owned by the mortgagor. It is an interest in land which may be conveyed, devised or entailed, and it may descend on intestacy or pass as *bona vacantia* to the Crown.[15] It is destructible only by four events,

---

10 Litt s. 332.
11 *Kregliner v New Patagonia Meat and Cold Storage Co Ltd* [1914] AC 25 at 35, per Lord HALDANE.
12 Holdsworth, *History of English Law*, vol. v. p. 330; Turner, *The Equity of Redemption*.
13 *Thornborough v Baker* (1675) 3 Swan 628 at 630. For Lord NOTTINGHAM'S contribution to the development of mortgages, see (1961) 79 Selden Society, pp. 7 et seq (D. E. C. Yale).
14 *Kreglinger v New Patagonia Meat and Cold Storge Co Ltd*, supra, at 48, per Lord PARKER.
15 *Casborne v Scarfe* (1738) 1 Atk 603; *Re Sir Thomas Spencer Wells* [1933] Ch 29; M & B p. 718; Waldock, *Law of Mortgages* (2nd edn), pp. 202 et seq.

namely, its release by the mortgagor, the lapse of time under the Limitation Act 1980,[16] the exercise by the mortgagee of his statutory power of sale,[17] and a foreclosure decree, i.e. a judicial decree that the subject matter of the mortgage shall be vested absolutely in the mortgagee free from any right of redemption.[18]

(c) Position prior to 1926

Up to 1 January 1926, the normal method by which a mortgage of the fee simple was created was for the mortgagor to convey the legal fee simple to the mortgagee together with a covenant to repay the loan in, say, six months' time, with a proviso, however, that if the loan were repaid at such date, the mortgagee would reconvey the legal estate. Outwardly it still seemed as if the mortgagee became absolute owner failing repayment within six months, but essentially, owing to the doctrine of the equity of redemption, the mortgagor was the true owner. Technically he was a mere equitable owner, but in the eyes of equity he was the real owner and, on his repaying the principal and interest with costs to the mortgagee, equity was prepared to grant specific performance of the proviso for reconveyance of the legal estate to him.

A still older method of creating a mortgage, used between the thirteenth and fifteenth centuries and worthy of notice because of its revival by the 1925 legislation, was for the mortgagor to lease his land to the mortgagee for a short term of years. If the debt was not repaid at the end of the lease, the right of the mortgagor was extinguished, and the term was automatically enlarged into a fee simple which vested absolutely in the mortgagee.[19] This method, however, went out of use, mainly because the law in its growing strictness could not countenance this facile mode of enlarging a term of years into a fee. An attempt to resuscitate it was made about the beginning of the nineteenth century, but owing to certain disadvantages, such as the doubt whether the mortgagee was entitled to possession of the title deeds, it failed, and the term of years was used only in family settlements where it was desired to secure money lent for the payment of portions.[20]

(2) MORTGAGES OF LEASEHOLD

If the security offered by the borrower was a leasehold interest, not the fee simple, there were two methods before 1926 by which the mortgage might be created. Usually the mortgagor subleased his term of years to the mortgagee for a period slightly shorter than the remainder of the term. This was the most desirable method, since the sublease did not involve privity of estate between the mortgagee and the superior landlord, and therefore the mortgagee was immune from liability on the covenants contained in the original lease, unless they were negative covenants enforceable under the doctrine of *Tulk v Moxhay*.[1] The alternative method was for the mortgagee to take an assignment of the whole remainder of the term, but in this case he became liable to covenants and conditions under the doctrine of *Spencer's Case*.[2]

16 P. 690, post.
17 P. 695, post.
18 P. 700, post.
19 Holdsworth, *History of English Law*, vol. iii. p. 129.
20 (1925) 60 LJ News 46 (J. M. Lightwood).
 1 Pp. 614 et seq, ante.
 2 Pp. 449 et seq, ante.

(3) EQUITABLE MORTGAGES

In addition to the conveyance of a legal estate, whether a fee simple or a term of years, by way of security, it has long been possible to create an equitable mortgage by the grant of an equitable interest. This is necessarily the method where the borrower himself is an equitable owner, as, for instance, where before 1926 a mortgagor created a second mortgage in the same land: the legal estate had been conveyed to the first mortgagee and what the mortgagor conveyed to the second mortgagee was his equity of redemption. A further example of an equitable mortgage, made by a borrower who is an equitable owner, is where a tenant for life under a strict settlement mortgages his equitable life interest.

On the other hand it is also possible for an equitable mortgage to be created by the owner of a legal estate, as for instance where he agrees to create a legal mortgage; this entitles the lender in equity to enforce specific performance of the promise. Indeed, without the grant even of an equitable interest, an owner may charge his land with the repayment of a loan and so entitle the lender in equity to enforce a sale of the property. These equitable mortgages are considered in more detail later.[3]

B. CHANGES MADE BY THE LEGISLATION OF 1925

The prevailing practice, by which the legal fee simple was conveyed to a mortgagee, presented a difficult problem to the draftsmen of the 1925 legislation. How were they to bring it into line with the principles that they intended to introduce?

The corner-stone of their policy was that the legal fee simple should always be vested in its true owner and that he should be able to convey it free from equitable interests. In the eyes of the law the true owner is the mortgagor. Yet, all that he held before 1926 was an equitable interest, and unless some alteration were made there could be no question of his ability to convey any kind of legal estate during the continuance of the mortgage.

On the other hand it was important to protect the mortgagee in the enjoyment of certain valuable advantages that he derived from his legal ownership. Pre-eminent among these was the priority which, by virtue of the legal fee simple, he obtained over other mortgages created in the same land, for these were necessarily equitable in nature. Moreover, his possession of the title deeds enabled him to control the actions of the mortgagor in his dealings with the land. He also enjoyed the right to take actual possession of the land, and therefore to grant leases; and lastly, when he exercised his power of sale on failure by the mortgagor to repay the loan, he was able to vest the legal estate in the purchaser.[4]

The solution contained in the Law of Property Act 1925 is to revert to the old fifteenth-century method of effecting mortgages by means of a lease for a term of years.

Mortgages by which the legal fee simple is vested in the mortgagee are prohibited, and a mortgagee who requires a legal estate instead of a mere equitable interest is compelled to take either a long term of years or a newly

---

3 P. 668, post.
4 (1925) 60 LJ News 91 (J. M. Lightwood).

invented interest called a *charge by deed expressed to be by way of legal mortgage*. Thus in the first case both parties have legal estates: the mortgagee has a legal term of years absolute, and the mortgagor has a reversionary and legal fee simple, subject to the mortgagee's term. In the case of a charge by way of legal mortgage, however, the mortgagee has the same protection, powers and remedies as if he had taken a legal term of years.

In this way the principle that the legal fee simple should always remain vested in the true owner has been maintained. The mortgagor is owner at law as well as in equity, and the mortgagee has only a right *in alieno solo*. The charge by way of legal mortgage at last provides a method which reflects the reality of the transaction and goes some way towards rebutting Maitland's description of a mortgage deed as one long *suppressio veri* and *suggestio falsi*.[5] We should also notice two important consequences of the changes made by the 1925 legislation. First, the mortgagor's retention of the legal estate means that any second and subsequent mortgages which he creates may be legal. And secondly, the rights of the parties remain unchanged, and in particular, the mortgagor's equity of redemption is still of importance. This, as before 1926, is an equitable proprietary interest and is in value equal to the value of the land less the amount of the debt secured by the mortgage. The mortgagor retains that interest and keeps a legal estate as well. On the other hand, the mortgagee retains all his remedies, and, for instance, may sell and convey the fee simple, if the mortgagor defaults in his obligations.[6]

SECTION III METHODS OF CREATING MORTGAGES AFTER 1925

A. LEGAL MORTGAGES

(1) BY LEASE

(a) Legal mortgage of fee simple

A *legal* mortgage of an estate *in fee simple* must be effected by either:

1. a demise for a term of years absolute, subject to a provision (called a provision for cesser) that the term shall cease if repayment is made on a fixed day; or
2. a charge by deed expressed to be by way of legal mortgage.[7]

(i) Length of lease To confine our attention for the moment to the former method, the Law of Property Act 1925 does not state for what period the lease must be made, but it enacts that if any person in future attempts to create a mortgage by the old method of a transfer of the fee simple, the

5 Maitland *Equity*, p. 182. For a precedent of a mortgage deed, see p. 664, post.
6 P. 696, post. For a mortgagor's action in negligence against (a) his solicitor where he enters into a mortgage as a result of the solicitor's failure to give proper advice, see *Forster v Outred & Co* [1982] 1 WLR 86, [1982] 2 All ER 753; and (b) the mortgagee's valuer on whose negligent report he relied; see *Smith v Eric S Bush* [1990] 1 AC 831, [1989] 2 All ER 514; [1989] Conv 359 (C. Francis); [1989] CLJ 306 (W. V. H. Rogers); (1989) 105 LQR 511 (D. Allen); (1989) 52 MLR 841 (T. Kaye); *Beaumont v Humberts* [1990] 2 EGLR 166; *Roberts v J Hampson & Co* [1990] 1 WLR 94, [1989] 2 All ER 504. On the applicability of the Unfair Contract Terms Act 1977, s. 11(3), see *Smith v Eric S Bush*, supra; *Davies v Parry* [1988] 1 EGLR 147. On the measure of damages against a valuer, see *Swingscastle Ltd v Alastair Gibson* [1991] 2 AC 223, [1991] 2 All ER 353. And generally *Emmet on Title*, para. 1.065; [1989] 18 EG 21; [1990] 03 EG 21 (J. Murdoch).
7 LPA 1925, s. 85 (1).

conveyance shall operate as a lease of the land for 3000 years, without impeachment for waste, but subject to cesser on redemption.[8] There is, of course, no obligation for a mortgage term to be granted for so long a period as this.

(ii) Subsequent mortgages If it is desired to create further *legal* mortgages in the same land, the mortgagor may lease the land to each mortgagee after the first for a term which is usually at least one day longer than the term limited to the immediately preceding mortgagee.[9] If, for instance, the mortgagor raises money first from A, then from B and then from C on the security of Blackacre, there may be:

a lease to A for 3000 years,

a lease to B for 3000 years and one day (subject to A's term), and

a lease to C for 3000 years and two days (subject to the terms of A and B).

The effect in such a case is, as we have seen,[10] that the second and all subsequent mortgagees now take legal interests in the land instead of mere equitable interests as formerly.

At first sight the possession by B of a term of 3000 years and one day, subject to a prior term of 3000 years, does not seem of much value, but when the first term ceases on redemption, B acquires the first right to the land for the residue of the term; and moreover he always has the right, after giving adequate notice, to pay to A what A lent to the mortgagor, and thus to succeed to A's position. In such a case B remains entitled to hold the land under the lease until the advances made both by A and by himself have been paid.

(iii) Precedent of mortgage deed The following is a precedent of a mortgage deed:[11]

Parties.	THIS MORTGAGE is made the first day of January 1994 between A of etc. (hereinafter called the borrower) of the one part and B of etc. (hereinafter called the lender) of the other part.
Recital of title of borrower. Recital of agreement to lend.	Whereas the borrower is the estate owner in respect of the fee simple absolute in possession of the property described in the schedule hereto free from incumbrances. And whereas the lender has agreed to lend to the borrower the sum of £50,000 upon having the repayment thereof together with interest thereon secured in manner hereinafter appearing.
	NOW THIS DEED WITNESSETH as follows:
Covenant for payment of principal and interest.	1. In consideration of the sum of £50,000 now paid by the lender to the borrower (the receipt of which sum the borrower hereby acknowledges) the borrower hereby covenants with the lender that he will pay to the lender on the first day of July next the sum of £50,000 with interest thereon from the date hereof of the rate of £7.64 per cent per annum and if the said sum (hereinafter called the principal money) or any part thereof shall not be paid on the said date will at the date aforesaid pay to the lender (as well after as before any judgment) interest on the principal sum or such part thereof as shall from time to time remain owing by equal half yearly payments on the first of July and the first of January in each year.

8 LPA 1925, s. 85 (2).
9 Ibid, s. 85 (2) (*b*).
10 P. 663, ante.
11 Adapted from *Encyclopaedia of Forms and Precedents* (4th edn), vol. 14, p. 166.

Demise of mortgaged property.

2. For the consideration aforesaid the borrower as beneficial owner hereby demises to the lender all the property specified in the schedule hereto TO HOLD the same unto the lender for the term of 3000 years from the date hereof without impeachment of waste subject to the provision for cesser hereinafter contained.

Proviso for cesser.

3. Provided that if the borrower shall on the first day of July next pay to the lender the principal sum with interest thereon from the date hereof at the rate aforesaid the term hereby created shall cease.

Covenants by borrower.

4. The borrower hereby further covenants with the lender
[Here follow covenants by the borrower to insure and repair buildings etc.]
IN WITNESS ETC.
SCHEDULE

The obvious effect of such a deed is that the mortgagor remains seised in fee simple, while the mortgagee acquires a legal term of years that entitles him, if he so desires, to take possession of the land. Outwardly, indeed, he appears to acquire a term that will necessarily last for 3000 years unless the capital sum is paid on 1 July 1994. Such, of course, is not the true position, for the equity of redemption that arises after that date entitles the mortgagor to procure the cessation of the term by the repayment in full of all that is due by way of principal and interest.

(b) Legal mortgage of leasehold

The next question to examine is how a mortgage is made when the mortgagor holds, not the fee simple, but a term of years. Again, the only possible methods of creating a legal mortgage are by a lease (in this case a sub-lease) for a term of years absolute, or by a legal charge.[12]

Confining ourselves for the moment to a sub-lease,[13] let us suppose that A, the owner in fee simple, has leased his land to T for 99 years, and T wishes to mortgage his tenancy, which has still 70 years to run, to L as security for an advance. The Law of Property Act 1925 provides that T may sublet the premises to L for a period which must be less by at least one day than the term he himself holds.[14] He will therefore grant a sub-lease for, say, 69 years and 355 days, subject to a proviso that the title of L shall cease on the repayment of the loan by T.

If T later wishes to borrow more money from S on the same premises, he must grant him another sub-lease for a period longer by one day than that of L; in fact, however many later mortgagees there may be, they will each take a term one day longer than the immediately preceding term.[15]

The case, then, works out as follows:

A is entitled to the reversion in fee simple;
L is sub-tenant for 69 years and 355 days;
S, subject to the tenancy of L, is sub-tenant for 69 years and 356 days;
T (the mortgagor), subject to the two sub-tenancies, is tenant for 70 years.

If L chooses to take possession, he can do so, and can remain in possession until paid off either by T (the mortgagor) or by S. If L is paid off by T, then

12 LPA 1925, s. 86 (1).
13 For a precedent, see *Encyclopaedia of Forms and Precedents* (4th edn), vol. 14. pp. 421–2.
14 LPA 1925, s. 86 (1).
15 Ibid. 1925, s. 86 (2).

S possesses the same rights until he is paid off by T. If L is paid off by S the latter can take possession and hold it until the advances made both by L and by himself have been paid.

If L sells, as he has a statutory right to do,[16] his conveyance to the purchaser will pass not only his mortgage term of 69 years and 355 days, but also the whole term of 70 years held by the mortgagor, and it will thus extinguish the mortgage terms held by S and any later lender.[17]

Thus, the interest of a subsequent mortgagee, although it amounts to a legal estate, is somewhat precarious security, since it will be destroyed if a prior mortgagee exercises his statutory power of sale or obtains a foreclosure decree.[18] The only remedy then left is to sue the mortgagor upon the personal covenant.

The alternative method before 1926 of creating a mortgage by an assignment of the entire residue of the term to the mortgagee is prohibited, and any purported assignment intended to be by way of mortgage necessarily operates as a sub-lease for a term of years absolute, subject to cesser on redemption.[19]

(c) Sub-mortgage

A mortgage term, whether created by lease or sub-lease, is available as a security to the mortgagee if he himself wishes to raise a loan.

For example, the mortgagee, B, has lent £10,000 to A and has taken a lease of A's fee simple as security. If he now requires £1,000 for his immediate use, it may be inconvenient to enforce his rights against A and to demand repayment in full of £10,000, for perhaps at the moment there is no suitable investment for £9,000. Again, the danger of calling upon A for £1,000 is that he, not having the funds, may be compelled to borrow £10,000 from a third party, X, and to transfer the mortgage to the latter.[20] B, however, may sub-mortgage his own security to C in return for a loan of £1,000. This is effected by an assignment of C of the mortgage debt (i.e. the right to receive £10,000) and by the grant to him of a sub-lease for a period shorter than his own mortgage term, but subject to a right of redemption in B on payment of £1,000.[1] Since a mortgage debt is a chose in action, C should protect himself by giving written notice to A of its assignment.[2]

The effect of this transaction is to put C in the position of B.[3]

Thus, the statutory power of sale is not exercisable by B during the existence of the sub-mortgage,[4] and, therefore, if A defaults in the repayment of the £10,000, C may sell the land by virtue of the original mortgage and transfer a title to the purchaser free from the mortgage and sub-mortgage. Out of the purchase money, he will retain £1,000, pay £9,000 to B and give any surplus to A.

Alternatively, if B defaults in the repayment of £1,000, C may exercise the statutory power of sale incidental to the sub-mortgage. In this case he

16 P. 695, post.
17 LPA 1925, s. 89 (1), p. 696, post.
18 Ibid., s. 89 (2); p. 700, post; Fisher and Lightwood, p. 176.
19 Ibid., s. 86 (2); *Grangeside Properties Ltd v Collingwood's Securities Ltd* [1964] 1 WLR 139, [1964] 1 All ER 143.
20 See Elphinstone, *Introduction to Conveyancing* (7th edn), p. 290.
1 LPA 1925, s. 86 (3); Sch. 1, Part VII, para 4.
2 Ibid., s. 137; pp. 729–31, post.
3 Ibid., s. 88 (5).
4 Said to be doubtful in *Cruse v Nowell* (1856) 25 LJ Ch 709.

transfers to the purchaser the mortgage debt together with the original mortgage term, but of course leaves A's equity of redemption intact. After retaining £1,000, he will pay any surplus to B.[5]

(2) BY A LEGAL CHARGE

The Law of Property Act 1925 provides that a legal mortgage may also be created by

a charge by deed expressed to be by way of legal mortgage.[6]

This invented a simpler and more realistic method of creating a legal mortgage.

(a) Precedent of legal charge

A short precedent of such a charge, which in practice is expanded so as to contain further appropriate covenants by the borrower,[7] is provided by the Law of Property Act 1925.[8]

> THIS LEGAL CHARGE is made the First day of January, 1994, between A of the one part and B of the other part.
> WHEREAS A is seised of the hereditaments hereby charged and described in the schedule hereto for an estate in fee simple in possession free from incumbrances;
> NOW IN CONSIDERATION of the sum of £50,000 now paid by B to A (the receipt whereof A doth hereby acknowledge) this Deed witnesseth as follows:
> 1. A hereby covenants with B to pay on the first day of July next the sum of £50,000 with interest thereon at the rate of 7.64 per cent. per annum.
> 2. A as beneficial owner hereby charges by way of legal mortgage All and Singular the property mentioned in the Schedule hereto with the payment to B of the principal money, interest and other money hereby covenanted to be paid by A.

(b) Effect of charge

The Act does not vest a term of years in the mortgagee,[9] but it provides that he shall have "the same protection, powers and remedies" as if he had taken a lease of a fee simple or a sub-lease of demised premises.[10] In other words, he is in exactly the same position as if the relationship of landlord and tenant existed between him and the mortgagor.[11]

If, for instance, A has charged his term of years in favour of B and later commits a breach of a covenant contained in the lease by reason of which his landlord starts proceedings for the enforcement of his right of re-entry

---

5 For a precedent, see *Encyclopaedia of Forms and Precedents* (4th edn), vol. 14, pp. 777–8.
6 LPA 1925, s. 85.
7 For fuller precedents, see *Encyclopaedia of Forms and Precedents* (4th edn), vol. 14, pp. 170–84, 413–19.
8 Sch. 5, Form No. 1.
9 *Weg Motors Ltd v Hales* [1962] Ch 49, [1961] 3 All ER 181; *Cumberland Court (Brighton) Ltd v Taylor* [1964] Ch 29, [1963] 2 All ER 536; *Thompson v Salah* [1972] 1 All ER 530; *Edwards v Marshall-Lee* (1975) 235 EG 901.
10 LPA 1925, s. 87 (1).
11 *Regent Oil Co Ltd v J A Gregory (Hatch End) Ltd* [1966] Ch 402 at 431, [1965] 3 All ER 673 at 681; M & B p. 715; *Weg Motors Ltd v Hales* [1962] Ch 49 at 77, [1961] 3 All ER 181 at 182 per DONOVAN LJ; M & B p. 716.

under a forfeiture clause, B is entitled to claim relief under section 146 of the Law of Property Act 1925.[12]

This method of creating a mortgage steadily gained popularity since its introduction, and at the present day is adopted by most practitioners in preference to the long lease. Its defect is that it does not contain the proviso for cesser that always figures in the mortgage by demise. This proviso corresponds to the old proviso for redemption, the importance of which lay in fixing the date at which the mortgagor's right to redeem and the mortgagee's right to foreclose came into being. In the mortgage given above on page 664, for instance, the property can neither be redeemed by the mortgagor nor foreclosed by the mortgagee before 1 July 1994[13] and although the right of a legal *chargee* to foreclose probably arises by implication at the date fixed in the covenant for repayment, provided that the mortgagor makes default, yet the matter cannot be regarded as settled until it has been judicially decided. It is safer, therefore, to amplify the statutory form by the insertion of a proviso for redemption or discharge in addition to the covenant for repayment.

(c) Advantages of legal charge

There are three advantages that may be claimed for the legal charge as compared with the mortgage by demise.

First, its form is short and simple and more intelligible to a mortgagor.

Secondly, the legal charge is as appropriate for leaseholds as it is for freeholds, and therefore it provides a simple method of executing a compound mortgage which relates to both these different interests.

Thirdly, a mortgagor with a leasehold interest who holds his term on condition that he will not sub-lease without the consent of his landlord, must clearly obtain this consent if his mortgage takes the form of a sub-demise,[14] but a legal charge, since it does not create an actual legal estate, is presumably not in breach of a covenant against underletting.[15]

(d) Sub-mortgage

If the legal chargee desires to create a sub-mortgage, he cannot do so by means of a sub-lease, since he himself holds no term of years. He must, therefore, assign the mortgage debt to the sub-mortgagee subject to a right of redemption.

B. EQUITABLE MORTGAGES

The statutory provisions that have been noticed so far apply only to a case in which it is desired to create a legal mortgage, and do not affect equitable

---

12 *Grand Junction Co Ltd v Bates* [1954] 2 QB 160, [1954] 2 All ER 358; *Church Comrs for England v Ve-Ri-Best Manufacturing Co Ltd* [1957] 1 QB 238, [1956] 3 All ER 777. See also p. 440, ante.
13 *Williams v Morgan* [1906] 1 Ch 804; *Kreglinger v New Patagonia Meat and Cold Storage Co Ltd* [1914] AC 25 at 48.
14 *Matthews v Smallwood* [1910] 1 Ch 777.
15 *Grand Junction Co Ltd v Bates* [1954] 2 QB 160 at 168, [1954] 2 All ER 385 at 388; M & B p. 715, per UPJOHN J.

mortgages and charges.[16] It always has been, and still is, possible to confer upon a lender an equitable right over the land by way of security, instead of passing a legal estate to him.

The commonest examples of equitable mortgages before 1926 were those which followed a legal mortgage in the same land, but, as we have seen, second and subsequent mortgages may now be created by a long lease or by a charge so as to give each lender a legal estate or interest. The following forms of equitable mortgages, however, still remain.

(1) CONTRACT TO CREATE A LEGAL MORTGAGE

Equity looks on that as done which ought to be done, and therefore if A agrees that, in consideration of money advanced, he will execute a legal mortgage in favour of B, an equitable mortgage is created in favour of B, and he can enforce the execution of a legal mortgage by suing in equity for specific performance.[17] But such a contract does not have this effect unless the money has been actually advanced, for a contract to make a loan, whether executed as a deed or not, can never be specifically enforced by either party.[18] The only remedy is the recovery of damages. As a mortgage of land is an interest in land within the meaning of section 40 of the Law of Property Act 1925, the contract if made before 27 September 1989, is not specifically enforceable unless it is evidenced by a sufficient memorandum or supported by an act of part performance.[19] If made after 26 September 1989, it must comply with the requirements of section 2 of the Law of Property (Miscellaneous Provisions) Act 1989, and be in writing signed by both parties.[20]

Furthermore, an imperfect legal mortgage, as, for instance, where A purports to create a legal mortgage in writing, may be treated by equity as if it were a contract to create a legal mortgage with similar consequences.

(2) DEPOSIT OF TITLE DEEDS

It has been held, since the case of *Russel v Russel*[1] in 1783, that an equitable mortgage is created by the delivery to the lender of the title deeds relating to the borrower's land, provided that it is intended to treat the land as security.

In this particular case there need be no memorandum, since the deposit ranks as an act of part performance before 27 September 1989,[2] and the deposit alone is treated as constituting a contract to execute a legal mortgage.[3] An actual deposit, though essential, is not in itself sufficient. The depositee must go further, and prove by parol or by written evidence that the deposit

16 LPA 1925, s. 117 (1).
17 *Tebb v Hodge* (1869) LR 5 CP 73.
18 *Sichel v Mosenthal* (1862) 30 Beav 371.
19 *Ex parte Leathes* (1833) 3 Deac & Ch 112. As to what constitutes a memorandum or an act of part performance, see pp. 111 et seq, ante.
20 P. 121, ante.
 1 (1783) 1 Bro CC 269. The right to create this kind of equitable mortgage is saved by LPA 1925, s. 13. The mortgagee can retain the deeds until he is paid, but has no separate legal lien: *Re Molton Finance Ltd* [1968] Ch 325, [1967] 3 All ER 843; see also *Capital Finance Co Ltd v Stokes* [1969] 1 Ch 261 at 278, [1968] 3 All ER 625 at 629.
 2 *Bank of New South Wales v O'Connor* (1889) 14 App Cas 273 at 282.
 3 *Carter v Wake* (1877) 4 Ch D 605 at 606, per JESSEL MR.

was intended to be by way of security,[4] for the mere deposit by a customer of his deeds with a bank will not, for instance, constitute the bank an equitable mortgagee in respect of an overdraft.

In practice, however, the borrower usually signs a memorandum executed as a deed contemporaneously with the delivery of the deeds, for such a memorandum makes the transaction a mortgage by deed within the meaning of the Law of Property Act 1925, and entitles the equitable mortgagee to exercise all the powers, including the power of sale, given by the Act.[5] But since an equitable mortgagee cannot convey the legal estate to a purchaser, it is usual to insert a power of attorney or a declaration of trust, or both, in the memorandum, so as to enable the mortgagee to deal with the legal estate.[6]

If the equitable mortgage is created after 26 September 1989, the formalities of section 2 of the Law of Property (Miscellaneous Provisions) Act 1989 do not have to be satisfied. Although the doctrine of part performance ceased to apply under the section, equitable mortgages by deposit are expressly recognised by the 1925 legislation[7] and therefore survive the removal of their original basis.[8]

(3) MORTGAGE OF AN EQUITABLE INTEREST

A mortgage of an equitable interest, such as a life interest arising under a settlement, or a contract for a lease,[9] is itself necessarily equitable. The method of creation corresponds to that employed before 1926 in the case of a legal mortgage of the fee simple, namely, the entire equitable interest is assigned to the mortgagee, subject to a proviso for reassignment on redemption.[10]

The assignment, if not made by will, must be in writing signed by the mortgagor or by his agent thereunto lawfully authorized in writing[11] and the mortgagee should protect himself by giving written notice of it to the owner of the legal estate.[12]

(4) EQUITABLE CHARGE

Another form of equitable security, differing in respect of the remedies it confers from the three forms already described, is the equitable charge. This

4 *Dixon v Muckleston* (1872) 8 Ch App 155; *Re Wallis and Simonds (Builders) Ltd* [1974] 1 WLR 391, [1974] 1 All ER 561; *Thames Guaranty Ltd v Campbell* [1985] QB 210, [1984] 2 All ER 585 (deposit of title deeds (land certificate p. 734, post) to secure a debt by one joint tenant without consent of the other joint tenant not effective to create equitable charge of the jointly owned land; but it may create a charge of the equitable interest of the depositor, if the deposit amounts to an act of severance, p. 217, ante); *First National Securities Ltd v Hegerty* [1985] QB 850, [1984] 3 All ER 641; p. 218, n. 11, ante.
5 Pp. 695 et seq, post.
6 *Encyclopaedia of Forms and Precedents* (4th edn), vol. 14. p. 614.
7 For registered land, LRA 1925, s. 66; for unregistered land, LPA 1925, s. 97. *Emmet on Title*, para. 25.116, says that it is open to argument that the charge created by deposit is "more properly regarded as a *sui generis* equitable charge rather than an agreement to create a charge". If this is correct then its validity is unaffected by the 1989 Act. However the advice is given that as a matter of good practice, lenders should insist on signed writing satisfying s. 2. See also Law Commission Report on Land Mortgages 1991 (Law Com. No. 204, HC 5), para 2.9.
8 *Snell's Equity*, p. 445. See also (1990) 10 LS 341 (L. Bently and P. Coughlan).
9 *Rust v Goodale* [1957] Ch 33, [1956] 3 All ER 373.
10 Waldock, *Law of Mortgages* (2nd edn), pp. 136-9.
11 LPA 1925, s. 53 (1) (c).
12 Ibid., s. 137 (1).

arises where, without any transfer of, or agreement to transfer, ownership or possession, property is appropriated to the discharge of a debt or some other obligation.[13]

In *Matthews v Goodday*[14] KINDERSLEY V-C said:

> With regard to what are called equitable mortgages, my notion is this. Suppose a man signed a written contract, by which he simply agreed that he thereby charged his real estate with £500 to A, what would be the effect of it?
>
> It would be no agreement to give a legal mortgage, but a security by which he equitably charged his lands with payment of a sum of money, and the mode of enforcing it would be by coming into a court of equity to have the money raised by sale or mortgage; that would be the effect of such a simple charge. It is the same thing as if a testator devised an estate to A charged with the payment of a sum of money to B. B's right is not to foreclose A, but to have his charge raised by sale or mortgage of the land . . . But the thing would be distinctly an equitable charge, and not a mortgage nor an agreement to give one. On the other hand the party might agree that, having borrowed a sum of money, he would give a legal mortgage whenever called upon. That agreement might be enforced according to its terms, and the court would decree a legal mortgage to be given, and would also foreclose the mortgage, unless the money was paid.

The remedies of an equitable chargee will be considered later.[15]

C. SUMMARY OF FORMS OF MORTGAGE

If we now glance back at the different kinds of mortgages, we shall find that they may be either legal or equitable, and that the same land may be subjected both to several legal and to several equitable mortgages. For instance the tenant in fee simple of Blackacre may have created the following mortgages upon his land in the following order:

A lease of 500 years to A.
A lease of 500 years and one day to B.
A written agreement charging the land in favour of C.
A lease of 500 years and two days to D.

The first mortgagee, A, may demand the title deeds relating to the property,[16] and in practice usually does so. This is one of the ways of ensuring that subsequent mortgages are put on inquiry as to the existence of a prior mortgage. As we shall see later, failure to enforce this right may entail serious consequences.[17] If A does obtain the deeds, then B and D are called *puisne mortgagees*. A puisne mortgage is defined[18] as:

---

13 *London County and Westminster Bank v Tompkins* [1918] 1 KB 515 at 528.
14 (1861) 31 LJ Ch 282 at 282–3; *Swiss Bank Corpn v Lloyds Bank Ltd* [1982] AC 584 at 594–595, [1980] 2 All ER 419 at 425, per BUCKLEY LJ; [1982] AC 584 at 613, [1981] 2 All ER 449 at 453, per Lord WILBERFORCE; *Thames Guaranty Ltd v Campbell*, supra; *First National Securities Ltd v Hegerty*, supra. Under Charging Orders Act 1979, s. 3 (4), a charge imposed by a charging order has the same effect as "an equitable charge created by the debtor by writing under his hand": *Ladup Ltd v Williams & Glyn's Bank plc* [1985] 1 WLR 851, [1985] 2 All ER 577.
15 P. 708, post.
16 P. 703, post.
17 Pp. 709 et seq, post.
18 LCA 1972, s. 2 (4), Class C (i). Puisne is derived from the old French, *puis* (after) *né* (born); hence a later or subsequent mortgage.

a legal mortgage which is not protected by a deposit of documents relating to the legal estate affected,

and B and D come within the definition, since they have acquired legal estates, but have not obtained possession of the deeds.

On the other hand, C is called a *general equitable chargee*. A general equitable charge is defined[19] as any equitable charge (with a few exceptions):

which (*a*) is not secured by a deposit of documents relating to the legal estate affected; and (*b*) does not arise or affect an interest arising under a trust for sale or a settlement; and (*c*) is not included in any other class of land charge.

The puisne mortgages of B and D and the general equitable charge of C are registrable as land charges under the Land Charges Act 1972, and, as we shall see, registration is of crucial importance in determining the priorities of mortgages.[20]

SECTION IV POSITION AND RIGHTS OF THE MORTGAGOR

A. THE EQUITY OF REDEMPTION

(1) PROTECTION OF THE MORTGAGOR

A mortgagor, as we have seen, is the owner of the equity of redemption.[1] This is fundamental to the law of mortgages. It arises in the case of every conveyance or other transaction relating to property, whether styled a mortgage or not, in which the true intention of the parties is that the subject matter shall be security for a debt or other obligation. Outwardly a transaction may wear the appearance of an absolute conveyance; it may even be deliberately couched in language calculated to give that appearance, yet evidence is admissible to disclose the true intention of the parties.[2] A transaction, for instance, which takes the form of a sale by A to B, with a right in B of repurchase upon payment of a given sum on a day certain may or may not be a mortgage. It is a matter of intention.

The question always is—was the original transaction a bona fide sale with a contract for repurchase, or was it a mortgage under the form of a sale.[3]

If it was the former, there is no right in B to redeem the property after the contract date.

What particularly concerns us here, however, is to notice that equity, in order to ensure that a transaction intended to be by way of mortgage shall afford nothing more than security to the lender, has laid down two important rules concerning, first, the inviolability of the right of redemption; and secondly, the limits within which collateral advantages may be reserved to a mortgagee.

It will be seen, as the cases on these two rules are discussed, that in the 20th century there has been a development from a rigid to a more flexible attitude to the relationship between mortgagor and mortgagee, and an

---

19 LCA 1972, s. 2 (4), Class C (iii).
20 Pp. 719 et seq, post.
1 Pp. 660–1, ante.
2 "No mortgage by any artificial words can be altered, unless by subsequent agreement"; *Jason v Eyres* (1681) 2 Cas in Ch 33.
3 *Williams v Owen* (1840) 5 My & Cr 303 at 306, per Lord COTTENHAM; *Greendon Holdings Ltd v Oragwu* [1989] EGCS 100.

increasing awareness that, unless there is evidence of harsh and unconscionable dealing, a bargain freely entered into between the parties must be kept.

Let us consider these rules separately.

(a) The right of redemption is inviolable

Since the object of a mortgage is merely to provide the mortgagee with a security, any provision which directly or indirectly prevents the recovery by the mortgagor of his property upon performance of the obligation for which the security was created, is repugnant to the very nature of the transaction and therefore void, for when performance is completed there is no longer any need or justification for the retention of the security. As ROMER J said:

> Now there is a principle which I will accept without any qualification ... that on a mortgage you cannot, by contract between the mortgagor and mortgagee, clog, as it is termed, the equity of redemption so as to prevent the mortgagor from redeeming on payment of principal, interest and costs.[4]

This principle is generally expressed in the aphorism, *once a mortgage always a mortgage*.[5] There are two aspects of this rule:

(i) The right to redeem must not be excluded The courts refuse to countenance any provision which unduly restricts, though it does not altogether prevent, the right of redemption. Each of the following cases exemplifies an agreement that was held void as being inconsistent with or repugnant to the true nature of a mortgage transaction.

An agreement that redemption should be available to the mortgagor and *the heirs of his body*, and not to anyone else.[6]

An agreement which renders part of the mortgaged property absolutely irredeemable.[7]

A covenant by the mortgagor that the mortgagee, if he so desired, should be entitled to a conveyance of so much of the mortgaged estate as should equal the value of the loan at twenty years' purchase.[8]

A covenant that if the borrower died before his father the subject matter of the mortgage should belong absolutely to the mortgagee.[9]

In two cases at the beginning of this century the House of Lords considered a provision in a mortgage which gave to the mortgagee an option to purchase the mortgaged property. In *Samuel v Jarrah Timber and Wood Paving Corpn Ltd*,[10] the option was given at the time of the creation of the mortgage and was held to be void; for otherwise the mortgagee by exercising the option could exclude the mortgagor's right of redemption. In *Reeve v Lisle*,[11] however, an option to purchase was held to be valid, where it was given by a subsequent and independent transaction, even though the only consideration

---

4 *Biggs v Hoddinott* [1898] 2 Ch 307 at 314.
5 *Samuel v Jarrah Timber and Wood Paving Corpn Ltd* [1904] AC 323 at 329.
6 *Howard v Harris* (1682) 1 Vern 33; *Salt v Marquess of Northampton* [1892] AC 1.
7 *Davis v Symons* [1934] Ch 442.
8 *Jennings v Ward* (1705) 2 Vern 520, as explained in *Biggs v Hoddinott* [1898] 2 Ch 307 at 315, 323.
9 *Salt v Marquess of Northampton*, supra.
10 [1904] AC 323; M & B p. 718. For searching criticisms of this scholastic attitude, see (1903) 18 LQR 359 (Sir Frederick Pollock); M & B p. 720; (1944) 60 LQR at 191 (G. L. Williams).
11 [1902] AC 461; M & B p. 719. See also *Alec Lobb (Garages) Ltd v Total Oil Great Britain Ltd* [1985] 1 WLR 173, [1985] 1 All ER 303; p. 683, n. 17, post.

was the release of the mortgagor from his obligation to pay the original loan. Lord HALSBURY and Lord MACNAGHTEN, who delivered speeches in both cases, expressed a lack of enthusiasm for their decision in *Samuel v Jarrah Timber and Wood Paving Corpn*. Lord HALSBURY said:[12]

> A perfectly fair bargain made between two parties to it, each of whom was quite sensible of what they were doing, is not to be performed because at the same time a mortgage arrangement was made between them. If a day had intervened between the two parts of the arrangement, the part of the bargain which the appellant claims to be performed would have been perfectly good and capable of being enforced; but a line of authorities going back for more than a century has decided that such an arrangement as that which was here arrived at is contrary to a principle of equity, the sense or reason of which I am not able to appreciate, and very reluctantly I am compelled to acquiesce in the judgments appealed from.

And Lord MACNAGHTEN said[13] of the decision:

> I should not be sorry if your Lordships could see your way to modify it so as to prevent its being used as a means of evading a fair bargain come to between persons dealing at arms' length and negotiating on equal terms. The directors of a trading company in search of financial assistance are certainly in a very different position from that of an impecunious landowner in the toils of a crafty money-lender.

Samuel v Jarrah Timber and Wood Paving Corpn was followed in *Lewis v Frank Love Ltd*[14] where, on the transfer of a mortgage, the mortgagor gave to the transferees an option to purchase. There were separate documents for the transfer and the mortgage, but PLOWMAN J held that the loan and the grant of the option were all part and parcel of one transaction.

The doctrine of *Samuel v Jarrah Timber and Wood Paving Corpn* is due for reconsideration by the House of Lords in view of subsequent developments in other aspects of the equity of redemption.[15]

(ii) The right to redeem may be postponed

1. *Postponement* An important question is whether the postponement for a considerable period of the contractual right to redeem is objectionable as being an unreasonable interference with the rights of the mortgagor. If a mortgage is in essence a mere security, it is arguable that a clause which prolongs the security after the mortgagor is ready and willing to pay all that is due, is one that ought not to be upheld, even though it was accepted by him without objection at the time of the loan. The question was much canvassed by the Court of Appeal in *Knightsbridge Estates Trust Ltd v Byrne*,[16] where the facts were as follows:

12 At 325.
13 At 327.
14 [1961] 1 WLR 261, [1961] 1 All ER 446; (1961) 77 LQR 163 (P.V.B.).
15 See (1985) Real Property Probate and Trust Journal 821 (L. C. Prebble and D. W. Cartwright); (1986–86) 60 St John's Law Review 452 (J. L. Light).
    For legislation in the USA removing the mortgagee's option from the purview of the doctrine of clogs, see Uniform Land Security Interest Act 1986, para. 211; New York General Obligations Law 1986, para. 5.334; California Civil Code (1984), para. 2906; cited 60 St John's Law Review at pp. 492–497.
16 [1939] Ch 441, [1938] 4 All ER 618; M & B p. 724; on appeal, [1940] AC 613, [1940] 2 All ER 401, the House of Lords decided the case on an entirely different ground, namely that the mortgage was a valid debenture under the Companies Act 1929, s. 74 (now 1985, s. 193) and expressed no opinion upon the reasoning of the Court of Appeal.

The Knightsbridge Company had mortgaged their property, consisting of 75 houses, eight shops and a block of flats, to the Prudential Assurance Company in return for a loan of £300,000 at 6½ per cent. The loan was liable to be called in at any time, and the mortgagors, desiring to obtain a reduction in the rate of interest and also to spread the repayment of the principal sum over a long term of years, transferred the mortgage to the Royal Liver Friendly Society. This mortgage was for £310,000 at 5¼ per cent, and at the suggestion of the mortgagors it was agreed that the loan should be repaid in forty years by half-yearly instalments. The mortgagees agreed not to call the money in before the end of this period, provided that the instalments were punctually paid. A few years later the mortgagors sued for a declaration that they were entitled, on giving the usual six months' notice, to redeem the mortgage upon payment of principal, interest and costs.

It was argued for the mortgagors that this suspension for forty years of the contractual right to redeem their property was unreasonable and therefore void. The Court of Appeal, however, upheld the suspension and denied that reasonableness, whether in respect of time or in other respects, is the true criterion of validity in such a case.[17] A contract freely entered into after due deliberation by parties dealing with each other at arms' length is not lightly to be interfered with.

As Sir WILFRID GREENE MR said:

> The resulting agreement was a commercial agreement between two important corporations experienced in such matters, and has none of the features of an oppressive bargain where the borrower is at the mercy of an unscrupulous lender.[18]

A court of equity, indeed, is vigilant in its support of the principle that "redemption is of the very nature and essence of a mortgage",[19] but none the less it does not attempt to reform mortgage transactions.

2. *Illusory right of redemption* A provision, however, which leaves the mortgagor with nothing more than an illusory right of redemption has been held to be void. In *Fairclough v Swan Brewery Co Ltd*,[20] for instance:

> the mortgagor was a tenant of a brewery in Western Australia, with an unexpired lease of seventeen and a half years. The mortgagee prevented redemption until a date six weeks before the lease expired. There was no evidence of oppression.

The Privy Council held that this provision rendered the property substantially irredeemable, and therefore the mortgagor was entitled to redeem at an earlier date.

This decision of the Privy Council is in conflict with an earlier decision of the Court of Appeal, which was not cited to the Council. In *Santley v Wilde*:[1]

> S was the lessee of a theatre, the lease still having ten years to run. In return for a loan for the purpose of carrying on the theatre, S mortgaged the lease to W, and covenanted that she would repay the capital by instalments and also that she would "during the residue of the term, notwithstanding that all principal moneys and interest may have been paid, pay a sum equal to one-third part of the clear net profit rent or rents to be derived" from the lease. There was a provision that the mortgage should determine on payment of the principal sum and interest and "all other the moneys hereinbefore covenanted to be paid". As LINDLEY MR said, W's

---

17 See *Multiservice Bookbinding Ltd v Marden* [1979] Ch 84 at 108, [1978] 2 All ER 489 at 501, p. 677, post.
18 At 455, at 625.
19 *Noakes & Co Ltd v Rice* [1902] AC 24 at 30 per Lord MACNAGHTEN.
20 [1912] AC 565; M & B p. 723. Restraint of trade was also pleaded, at 566.
 1 [1899] 2 Ch 474; M & B p. 721.

"security depended not only on the solvency of the lady but also on the success of the theatre". S claimed a declaration that she was entitled to redeem on payment of principal interest and costs and that the provision for a share of the profits was illegal and void.

The Court of Appeal held that S could not redeem except by observing all the covenants for which her property was given as security, including the profit-sharing covenant. In effect the mortgage was irredeemable until the end of the lease, since only then could the net profits be earned and calculated.

Accordingly, another old rule may come under review in the future, and rather than remorselessly applying the rule in *Fairclough v Swan Brewery Co Ltd* the courts may, in the absence of fraud or oppression, hold the parties to their bargain.

(b) Collateral advantages

A collateral advantage in favour of the mortgagee means something that is granted to him in addition to the return of his loan with interest, as for instance where a mortgagor agrees that for a given number of years he will purchase beer (or oil and petrol) for sale on the premises only from the mortgagee.

The question whether the reservation of such an advantage is valid is rendered difficult by a number of apparently irreconcilable decisions stretching back for more than a century. Indeed, the case law will be unintelligible unless it is realized that the attitude of the courts towards the matter has changed materially in the course of the last hundred years, and that reliance can no longer be placed upon many of the older decisions. Lord HALDANE, in a reference to one of the more modern cases,[2] said:

> In the 17th and 18th centuries a Court of Equity could hardly have so decided, and the judgment illustrates the elastic character of equity jurisdiction and the power of equity judges to mould the rules which they apply in accordance with the exigencies of the time.[3]

In early days the judges frowned upon any attempt by a mortgagee to reap some additional advantage, as is shown by a remark of TREVOR MR in 1705 that:

> a man shall not have interest for his money on a mortgage, and a collateral advantage besides for the loan of it.[4]

In modern times a more realistic and favourable note has been struck, and for this change of heart probably the most significant reason is that at the present day a mortgagor can scarcely be regarded as in need of special protection. In the eye of the novelist, no doubt, he is an impoverished debtor on the brink of ruin, unable to resist the demands of the rapacious lender, and it is perhaps true that the Court of Chancery in its more paternal days tended to take a somewhat similar view of his predicament. In fact, however, the parties to a modern mortgage may be hard-headed businessmen well able to protect their own interests, and in these days, when so much stress is laid upon the sanctity of contracts, it is difficult to appreciate why one of them should be allowed to disregard a bargain freely made, simply because he

2 *Biggs v Hoddinott* [1898] 2 Ch 307; M & B p. 729.
3 *Kreglinger v New Patagonia Meat and Cold Storage Co Ltd* [1914] AC 25 at 38.
4 *Jennings v Ward* (1705) 2 Vern 520.

happens to be a mortgagor. Such maxims as "Once a mortgage, always a mortgage" and "A mortgage cannot be made irredeemable," undoubtedly express an important principle, but to apply them in an unbending and inflexible fashion so as to upset an ordinary commercial transaction would be out of keeping with the times. As Lord PARKER OF WADDINGTON said:[5]

> Such maxims, however convenient, afford little assistance where the court has to deal with a new or doubtful case. They obviously beg the question, always of great importance, whether the particular transaction which the court has to consider is, in fact, a mortgage or not, and if they be acted on without a careful consideration of the equitable considerations on which they are based, can only, like Bacon's idols of the market place, lead to misconception and error.

Despite the judicial uncertainties of the past, the modern law on the subject is clear, though its application to particular cases may be a difficult matter. As we shall see, collateral advantages are no longer struck down simply because they are collateral advantages. They are only invalidated where they are either unfair or unconscionable, or where they unfairly restrict redemption.

(i) The collateral advantage must not be unfair or unconscionable If a contract is oppressive or unconscionable, which is a pure question of fact, it is void not so much because of its association with a mortgage, but because of the general principle of public policy that a contract shall not be used as an engine of oppression. It has repeatedly been affirmed that the courts will set aside "any oppressive bargain, or any advantage exacted from a man under grievous necessity and want of money",[6] and instances are not wanting of where this principle has been applied to a mortgage transaction.[7] In fact, if the mortgagee stands in a fiduciary relationship to the mortgagor, as for instance where he is his trustee, solicitor or spiritual adviser, the burden is on him to prove the fairness of the transaction if it is challenged on the ground of undue influence or unconscionable conduct.[8]

The court will always be astute to invalidate a mortgage which is unfair and unconscionable. Thus, in *Cityland and Property (Holdings) Ltd v Dabrah*:[9]

> the mortgagor was a tenant who was buying the freehold of his house from his landlord and was "obviously of limited means"; he undertook to pay a premium or bonus which represented either no less than 57% of the amount of the loan or interest at 19%.

GOFF J stressed that this was not a "bargain between two large trading concerns" and held that the mortgagor was entitled to redeem by paying the capital sum borrowed with reasonable interest fixed by the court.

In *Multiservice Bookbinding Ltd v Marden*,[10] BROWNE-WILKINSON J emphasised that the mortgagor must show that the bargain was unfair and

5 *Kreglinger v New Patagonia Meat and Cold Storage Co Ltd*, supra, at 53; M & B p. 732.
6 *Barrett v Hartley* (1866) LR 2 Eq 789 at 795, per STUART V-C.
7 *James v Kerr* (1889) 40 Ch D 449. Cf *Horwood v Millar's Timber and Trading Co* [1917] 1 KB 305.
8 Waldock, *Law of Mortgages* (2nd edn), chapter VIII, and cases there cited.
9 [1968] Ch 166, [1967] 2 All ER 639. See also Consumer Credit Act 1974, ss. 137–140, p. 680, post. It would appear that the mortgagor would also have succeeded under these sections.
10 [1979] Ch 84, [1978] 2 All ER 489; M & B p. 737; [1978] Conv 346 (H. W. Wilkinson), 432 (D. W. Williams); and for an economist's view (1981) 131 NLJ 4 (R. A. Bowles). The Consumer Credit Act 1974 was not applicable, since the mortgagor was a body corporate. The rate may be linked to "the base rate of X Bank plc"; see Conv Prec 5–11.

unconscionable and not merely unreasonable and said that "a bargain cannot be unfair and unconscionable unless one of the parties to it has imposed the objectionable terms in a morally reprehensible manner, that is to say, in a way which affects his conscience."[11] In that case:

> the mortgagor was a small but progressive company in need of cash to enable it to expand; it had acted with independent legal advice. The mortgagee was only willing to lend money if he could be safeguarded against a decline in the purchasing power of sterling. The terms of the mortgage were that (i) interest be payable at 2 per cent above bank rate on the full capital sum for the duration of the mortgage (ii) arrears of interest be capitalized after 21 days (thus providing for interest on interest) (iii) the loan be neither called in nor redeemed for 10 years, and (iv) the value of the capital and interest be index-linked to the Swiss franc. When the mortgage became redeemable at the end of ten years in 1976, the total capital repayment had become £87,588 as against £36,000 lent, and the average rate of interest over the ten years would have been 16.01 per cent.

It was held that all the terms of the mortgage were valid. An index-linked money obligation was not contrary to public policy, and the bargain, though hard, was not unfair and unconscionable.[12]

(ii) The collateral advantage must not unfairly restrict redemption We must now turn to the chequered history of collateral advantages. Most of the cases are concerned with an advantage which is to continue *after* redemption. In *Biggs v Hoddinott*,[13] however, where it was designed to cease with redemption, the Court of Appeal had no difficulty in holding it valid. In that case:

> Hoddinott mortgaged his hotel to Biggs, the brewer, in return for an advance of £7654, and agreed that during the continuance of the mortgage he would sell no other beer than that supplied by B. It was mutually agreed that the mortgage should not be redeemable, nor should the loan be repayable, for five years.

The claim of Hoddinott, made two years later, that he was entitled to be released from the solus agreement and to procure beer elsewhere upon repayment of the loan, was rejected.[14]

Where, however, the advantage was designed to continue after redemption, the House of Lords struck it down in two cases. First, in *Noakes & Co Ltd v Rice*,[15] where:

> the tenant of a public-house, under a lease which had 26 years to run, mortgaged the premises as security for a loan and covenanted that for the duration of the lease, whether he had already repaid the mortgage money or not, he would not sell any malt liquors except those provided by the mortgagees. Three years later he claimed a declaration that he should be released from the covenant upon payment of all moneys due under the mortgage.

11 *Boustany v Piggott* [1993] EGCS 85.
12 A building society has power to make an index-linked mortgage: *Nationwide Building Society v Registry of Friendly Societies* [1983] 1 WLR 1226, [1983] 3 All ER 296 (decided under Building Societies Act 1962, ss. 1, 4). See now Building Societies Act 1986, ss. 10 (10), 11 (2).
13 [1898] 2 Ch 307; M & B p. 729; approved by the House of Lords in *Noakes & Co Ltd v Rice* [1902] AC 24; M & B p. 730.
14 There was no appeal from the decision of ROMER J at first instance, that the postponement of the right to redeem for five years was valid; p. 674, ante.
15 [1902] AC 24; M & B p. 730. See also *Morgan v Jeffreys* [1910] 1 Ch 620. The discussions in these two cases could not be justified on the ground that the tie imposed upon the publican was void as being in restraint of trade; see *Esso Petroleum Co Ltd v Harper's Garage (Stourport) Ltd* [1968] AC 269, [1967] 1 All ER 699, p. 683, post.

It was held by the House of Lords that he was entitled to the release he claimed. His right of redemption was hampered in the sense that after attainment of the object for which the security was created he would not be master in his own house—he would not recover his property as it was before the mortgage. "The public-house, which was free when mortgaged, would have been tied to the mortgagee when redeemed."[16]

Secondly, in *Bradley v Carritt*:[17]

the defendant, who owned shares which gave him a controlling interest in a tea company, mortgaged them to the plaintiff, a tea-broker, and in further consideration for the loan, entered into the following contract:

"I agree . . . to use my best endeavours as a shareholder to secure that you or any firm of brokers of which you for the time being shall be a partner shall *always hereafter* have the sale of the company's teas as broker, and in the case of any of the company's teas being sold otherwise than through you or your firm, I personally agree to pay you or your firm the amount of the commission which you or your firm would have earned if the teas had been sold through you or your firm."

The plaintiff was appointed broker; but the defendant repaid the loan, redeemed his shares and transferred them to another mortgagee, X, who succeeded in ousting the plaintiff from his appointment.

The House of Lords, reversing by a majority of 3 to 2 the court of first instance and the Court of Appeal, held that the agreement set out above was void, and that the defendant was not liable for its breach. Lord LINDLEY and Lord SHAND, however, dissented. What weighed with the majority, was that after redemption, the shares would be more or less frozen assets in the hands of the mortgagor, since, unless he showed great vigilance, their sale would almost certainly result in his being liable to the plaintiff for loss of brokerage; they gave him a controlling interest in the tea company, and it was only by retaining them that he could ensure the continued employment of the plaintiff as broker.

In spite of these two decisions, the House of Lords came to a different conclusion in *Kreglinger v New Patagonia Meat and Cold Storage Co Ltd*,[18] where the facts were as follows:

A firm of woolbrokers lent £10,000 to a company which carried on business as meat preservers, the agreement being that the company might pay off the loan at any time by giving a month's notice. The loan was secured, not by an ordinary mortgage, but by an analogous security called a floating charge.[19] It was agreed that for five years from the date of the loan the company would not sell sheepskins to any person other than the lenders, so long as the latter were willing to pay the full market price. It was also agreed that the lenders would not demand repayment before five years had elapsed. The loan was repaid within two and a half years. The point that fell to be decided was whether the option on the sheepskins was enforceable by the lenders after repayment of the loan.

---

16 *Bradley v Carritt* [1903] AC 253 at 277–8, per Lord LINDLEY.
17 [1903] AC 253; M & B p. 731.
18 [1914] AC 25; M & B p. 732.
19 This, through a charge upon the assets for the time being, does not prevent a company from dealing with its property in the ordinary course of business, but it does so when the chargee takes steps, such as by the appointment of a receiver, to crystallize the security. For the characteristics of the charge, see *Re Yorkshire Woolcombers Association Ltd* [1903] 2 Ch 284 at 295, per ROMER J; and for crystallization of a charge, see *Re Woodroffes (Musical Instruments) Ltd* [1986] Ch 366, [1985] 2 All ER 908; *Re Brightlife Ltd* [1987] Ch 200, [1986] 3 All ER 673; (1976) 40 Conv (NS) 397 (J. H. Farrar) [1988] CLJ 213 (E. Ferran); *William Gaskell Group v Highley* [1993] BCC 200. See generally [1994] CLJ 81 (S. Worthington).

The House held unanimously that the lenders were entitled to an injunction restraining the company from selling skins to third parties during the remainder of the five years. While it was true that the company would not be as free in the conduct of their business after repayment of the loan as they were before the grant of the charge, the House of Lords unanimously held that the agreement should be upheld, and that it should continue to bind the mortgagor even though it was to continue after redemption. For Viscount HALDANE LC the matter was one of construction:[20]

> The question in the present case is whether the right to redeem has been interfered with. And this must . . . depend on the answer to a question which is primarily one of fact. What was the true character of the transaction? Did the appellants make a bargain such that the right to redeem was cut down, or did they simply stipulate for a collateral undertaking, outside and clear of the mortgage, which would give them an exclusive option of purchase of the sheepskins of the respondents? The question is in my opinion not whether the two contracts were made at the same moment and evidenced by the same instrument, but whether they were in substance a single and undivided contract or two distinct contracts . . . If your Lordships arrive at the conclusion that the agreement for an option to purchase the respondents' sheepskins was not in substance a fetter on the exercise of their right to redeem, but was in the nature of a collateral bargain the entering into which was a preliminary and separable condition of the loan, the decided cases cease to present any great difficulty.

And their Lordships so concluded. This approach provides the court with a much needed flexibility in the area of collateral advantages and enables it to adapt the earlier strict rules to modern circumstances.

Bradley v Carritt thus represents the high-water mark of the conception of a mortgage as an onerous obligation imposed upon a necessitous borrower, in whose favour the court should therefore intervene.[1] The *Kreglinger* case, on the other hand, reveals a judicial appreciation of a mortgage as a transaction freely concluded by businessmen without colour of oppression, which should therefore form no exception to the maxim *pacta sunt servanda*. This is a more realistic and reasonable approach, and one more compatible with the business conditions of the twentieth century.

In 1914 Lord MERSEY said in the *Kreglinger* case:[2]

> The doctrine itself seems to me to be like an unruly dog, which, if not securely chained to its own kennel, is prone to wander into places where it ought not to be. Its introduction into the present case would give effect to no equity and would defeat justice.

The dog is now under control.

We must now consider three further doctrines for the protection of the mortgagor. The first is statutory, the second equitable and the third common law.

(c) Extortionate credit bargains

Under sections 137–140 of the Consumer Credit Act 1974,[3] the court has power to reopen any credit bargain which it finds extortionate "so as to do

---

20 At 39. See *De Beers Consolidated Mines Ltd v British South Africa Co* [1912] AC 52, M & B p. 740; *Re Petrol Filling Station, Vauxhall Bridge Road* (1968) 20 P & CR 1; M & B p. 741.
1 Waldock, *Law of Mortgages* (2nd edn), chapter VIII.
2 [1914] AC 25 at 46.
3 On the Act generally, see p. 736, post.

justice between the parties". These sections apply to all mortgages, provided that the mortgagor is an individual (including a partnership or other unincorporated body).[4]

Under section 138 (1), a credit bargain is extortionate either if the payments to be made under it are "grossly exorbitant" or if it "otherwise grossly contravenes ordinary principles of fair dealing". The court is required to take into account:

(i)   interest rates prevailing when the bargain was made,
(ii) factors in relation to the debtor, such as his age, experience, business capacity and state of health, and the degree to which he was under financial pressure when he made the bargain,
(iii) the creditor's relationship to the debtor and the degree of risk accepted by him, having regard to the value of the security provided, and
(iv) any other relevant considerations.

The test of extortionate is similar but not identical to that of unconscionability which is the basis of the equitable protection of the mortgagor. There is overlap, and it has been said:

> Under the Act the test is not whether the creditor has acted in a morally reprehensible manner, but whether one or other of the conditions of section 138 (1) is fulfilled, and although it may be thought that if either condition is fulfilled there is likely to be something morally reprehensible about the creditor's conduct, the starting and ending point in determining whether a credit bargain is extortionate must be the words of section 138 (1).[5]

All these matters were considered in *A. Ketley Ltd v Scott*,[6] where the court refused an application to re-open a credit agreement involving a loan of £24,500, secured by a legal charge on a flat, at 12 per cent for three months; this was equal to a rate of interest of 48 per cent per annum. The mortgagor had been advised by his own solicitor, and "judging by his earnings and business experience knew exactly what he was doing".[7]

---

4 Where the mortgagor is a company, the court has power to set aside or vary the terms of any extortionate credit transaction entered into within three years before the day on which the company goes into liquidation or an administration order is made: Insolvency Act 1986, s. 244.
5 *Davies v Direct Loans Ltd* [1986] 1 WLR 823 at 831, per Edward Nugee QC. It is for the creditor to prove that a bargain is not extortionate: s. 171 (7); *Coldunell Ltd v Gallon* [1986] QB 1184, [1986] 1 All ER 429.
6 [1981] ICR 241; 130 NLJ 749; (1979) 8 Anglo-Am 240; (1986) 136 NLJ 796 (H. W. Wilkinson). See also *Castle Phillips v Khan* [1980] CCLR 1; *First National Securities v Bertrand* [1980] CCLR 5, discussed in (1982) 132 NLJ 1041 (R. G. Lawson); *Wills v Wood* (1984) Times, 24 March, where Sir John DONALDSON MR said: "The word is 'extortionate' not 'unwise'. The jurisdiction seems to me to contemplate at least a substantial imbalance in bargaining power of which one party has taken advantage"; *Woodstead Finance Ltd v Petrou* [1986] NLJ Rep 188 (interest of 42.5 per cent per annum for short term loan of £25,000 for six months held to be the normal rate, and therefore not extortionate); *Shahabinia v Gyachi* (1989) unreported (debtor took three loans from creditor for business purposes with flat rates of interest at 78%, 104% and 156%. CA reopened bargain and substituted flat rate of 30% on each loan. "It seems that the word 'extortionate' is to be equated with the words 'harsh and unconscionable' ", per RUSSELL LJ); *Castle Phillips Co Ltd v Wilkinson* [1992] CCLR 83 (rate of interest 3½ times rate charged by a building society; debtor was person of little financial understanding; rate of 20% substituted).
7 See *Castle Phillips Finance Co Ltd v Williams* [1986] CA Transcript 284 unreported, where interest was charged on a short term loan at the rate of 48% per annum; CA, instead of staying an order for possession and remitting the case to the county court to consider whether the bargain was extortionate, referred it to the Director General of Fair Trading to consider the revocation of the lender's licence or any other action under the 1974 Act.

(d) Undue influence

A mortgage may be set aside for undue influence on the part of the mortgagee[8] or of a third party who acts as agent of the mortgagee[9] in exerting influence on the mortgagor.

A typical illustration of third party or "vicarious" undue influence arises where a member of the mortgagor's family acts as the agent of the mortgagee; for example, where the mortgagee entrusts all or substantially all the arrangements for obtaining the execution of the mortgage to a husband or son, who then obtains the wife's or the parent's consent by undue influence.[10]

A mortgage may also be set aside for undue influence by a third party of which the mortgagee has notice.

In *Barclay's Bank plc v O'Brien*[11] the House of Lords considered whether a bank was entitled to enforce against a wife an obligation to secure a debt owed by her husband to the bank, where the wife had been induced to stand as surety for her husband's debt by his undue influence or misrepresentation. Under the ordinary principles of equity, the wife's right to set aside the transaction against her husband would be enforceable against the bank, if either the husband was acting as the bank's agent, or if the bank had actual or constructive notice of the facts giving rise to the equity. *O'Brien* turns on the application of the doctrine of constructive notice.[12] The bank is put on enquiry when a wife stands as surety by two factors:

(i) the transaction is on its face not to the financial advantage of the wife and,

(ii) there is a substantial risk in a transaction of that kind that, in procuring the wife to act as surety, the husband has committed a legal or equitable wrong that entitles the wife to set aside the transaction.[13]

Lord BROWNE-WILKINSON set out guidelines for the future as to what reasonable steps the bank has to take in order to avoid being fixed by constructive notice:[14]

Unless there are special circumstances, a creditor will have taken reasonable steps . . . if the creditor warns the surety (at a meeting not attended by the principal debtor) of the amount of her potential liability and of the risks involved and *advises*

---

8 It is only necessary to prove manifest disadvantage where the undue influence is presumed; it is not necessary where it is actual: *CIBC Mortgages plc v Pitt* [1993] 3 WLR 802, [1993] 4 All ER 433, explaining *National Westminster Bank plc v Morgan*, and overruling *Bank of Credit and Commerce International SA v Aboody* [1990] 1 QB 923, [1992] 4 All ER 955.

9 *National Westminster Bank plc v Morgan* [1985] AC 686, [1985] 1 All ER 821; [1985] Conv 387 (C. J. Barton and P. M. Rank).

10 Agency was proved in *Avon Finance Co Ltd v Bridger* [1985] 2 All ER 281 (mortgagees appointed accountant son to procure charge from old age pensioner parents much less well educated than he); *Kings North Trust Ltd v Bell* [1986] 1 WLR 119, [1986] 1 All ER 423 (mortgagee's solicitors entrusted task of obtaining mortgagor's wife's execution of charge to husband's solicitors). Cf. agency not proved in *Coldunell Ltd v Gallon* [1986] QB 1184, [1986] 1 All ER 429 (son of elderly mortgagors).

11 [1993] 3 WLR 786, [1993] 4 All ER 417; (1993) 143 NLJ 1723 (H. W. Wilkinson); [1994] Conv 141 (M. P. Thompson); [1994] CLJ 21 (M. Dixon); (1994) 110 LQR 167 (J. R. F. Lehane).

12 P. 60, ante.

13 At 798, at 429.

14 At 800, at 431. As to past transactions it depends on the facts of each case whether the bank has taken steps to bring home to the wife the risk she is taking by standing as surety and to advise her to take independent advice.

the surety to take independent legal advice[14a] . . . I would not exclude exceptional cases where a creditor has knowledge of further facts which render the presence of undue influence not only possible but probable. In such cases the creditor to be safe will have to *insist* that the wife is separately advised.

These principles are not limited to transactions involving husband and wife. They also apply to all other cases where there is an emotional relationship between co-habitees.

In *O'Brien* the bank had failed to warn and advise, and the wife was therefore entitled to enforce her equity against the bank. In *CIBC Mortgages plc v Pitt*,[15] however, the result was different. In that case:

the bank made a loan to the husband and wife jointly. The wife established actual undue influence by the husband. The husband was not acting as agent for the bank, and there was nothing to indicate to the bank that this was anything other than a normal advance to husband and wife for their joint benefit.

An unreasonable burden would be placed on banks if it were to be assumed that, whenever husband and wife asked for a joint loan, there was a risk that the wife was being put upon by the husband.

What distinguishes the case of the joint advance from that of the surety is that, in the latter, there is not only the possibility of undue influence having been exercised but also the increased risk of it having in fact been exercised, because at least on its face, the guarantee by a wife of her husband's debts is not for her financial benefit. It is the combination of these two factors that puts the creditor on inquiry.[16]

(e) Restraint of trade

A mortgage is subject to the common law doctrine that invalidates any contract in restraint of trade which places an unreasonable restriction upon the freedom of a man to pursue his trade or profession.[17] This test is unreasonableness and not unconscionability; it takes into account not only the interests of the parties but also the public interest. It may happen, therefore, that a postponement of the right of redemption which is not per se oppressive may nevertheless become so if it is accompanied by an excessive restraint upon the mortgagor's business activities. Thus:

where a garage was mortgaged to suppliers of motor fuels, and the mortgagors covenanted that they would not exercise their right of redemption for twenty-one

14a *Midland Bank plc v Masey* (1994) Times, 23 March CA ("The law does not generally require the creditor to stipulate the nature and extent of the advice," per STEYN LJ); *Midland Bank v Serter* [1994] NPC 29 (wife's guarantee of husband's debts at Lloyds; solicitor acting for both wife and bank held to satisfy requirement of independent adviser; court entitled to assume that solicitor had acted honestly and explained matters properly: *Bank of Baroda v Shah* [1988] 3 All ER 24).

15 [1993] 3 WLR 802, [1993] 4 All ER 433.

16 At 811, at 441.

17 *Esso Petroleum Co Ltd v Harper's Garage (Stourport) Ltd* [1968] AC 269, [1967] 1 All ER 699; *Re Petrol Filling Station, Vauxhall Bridge Road* (1968) 20 P & CR 1; M & B p. 741; *Texaco Ltd v Mulberry Filling Station Ltd* [1972] 1 WLR 814, [1972] 1 All ER 513; *Alec Lobb (Garages) Ltd v Total Oil Great Britain Ltd* [1985] 1 WLR 173, [1985] 1 All ER 303 (trading restraints in sale and 51 year leaseback of part of property entered into between mortgagor and mortgagee after date of mortgage held to be reasonable). See Cheshire, Fifoot and Furmston, *Law of Contract* (12th edn), pp. 397 et seq.; Heydon, *Restraint of Trade Doctrine* (1971), chapters 3, 9. As to the possible impact of Article 85 of the Treaty of Rome on solus agreements, see *Inntrepreneur Estates (GL) Ltd v Boyes* [1993] 47 EG 140; *Inntrepreneur Estates Ltd v Mason* [1993] 45 EG 130; [1994] Conv 150 (T. Frazer).

years and, during the same period, would not buy or sell any fuel other than that supplied by the mortgagees, it was held that the covenant was void as being in restraint of trade, and that the mortgage was redeemable.[18]

(2) ENFORCEMENT OF THE EQUITY OF REDEMPTION

(a) Loss of right of redemption by mortgagor

The right of redemption is lost if any one of the following events occurs:

> The release of the right by the mortgagor to the mortgagee; the lapse of time under the Limitation Act 1980; the sale of the land by the mortgagee under his statutory power; or a foreclosure decree obtained by the mortgagee.

The last two methods are discussed later.[19]

(i) Release of right of redemption by mortgagor Although a provision in the mortgage deed itself giving the mortgagee an option to purchase the land is void as being a clog on the equity,[20] there is nothing to prevent the mortgagor from getting rid of the debt by releasing the equity of redemption to him, provided that it is the result of an independent bargain made subsequently to the mortgage deed.

(ii) Lapse of time As regards lapse of time it is enacted that:

> When a mortgagee of land has been in possession of any of the mortgaged land for a period of twelve years, no action to redeem the land of which the mortgagee has been so in possession shall be brought after the end of that period by the mortgagor or any person claiming through him.[1]

If, however, the mortgagee in possession either receives any sum in respect of principal or interest or signs an acknowledgment of the mortgagor's title, an action to redeem the land may be brought at any time before the expiration of twelve years after the last payment or acknowledgment.[2] An acknowledgment given after the mortgagee has been in possession for twelve years, without receiving a payment in respect of principal or interest, is ineffective.[3]

When a mortgagee has obtained a title to the land free from the mortgage by remaining in possession for twelve years he may by deed enlarge the term of years into a fee simple under the Law of Property Act 1925.[4]

When, as in the ordinary case, a mortgagee does not take possession of the land, the mortgagor can redeem regardless of the lapse of time.

(b) Redemption by mortgagor

Presuming that the mortgagor has not lost his right to redeem the security, he is entitled, under the contract contained in the mortgage deed, to tender the exact amount due,[5] and to claim redemption on the date fixed for repayment. This date is not usually, however, meant to be taken seriously, and if it has elapsed, the mortgagor must give either six months' notice or six months' interest before he can redeem.[6] If a notice so given is not followed

---

18 Ibid.
19 P. 695, post (sale); p. 700, post (foreclosure).
20 P. 673, ante.
 1 Limitation Act 1980, s. 16.
 2 Ibid., ss. 29 (4), 30.
 3 Ibid., s. 17.
 4 LPA 1925, ss. 88 (3), 153; p. 459, ante.
 5 In an action for redemption the mortgagor must pay all that is due in respect of principal and interest, including interest which is statute-barred: *Holmes v Cowcher* [1970] 1 WLR 834, [1970] 1 All ER 1224.
 6 *Cromwell Property Investment Co v Western and Toovey* [1934] Ch 322.

by repayment upon the date notified, he must give a fresh notice of a reasonable length.[7] Where, however, the mortgage is merely temporary, as for instance in the case of an equitable mortgage by deposit of title deeds, the mortgagee is not entitled to six months' notice or interest in lieu. The mortgagor must give him a reasonable time, though it may be short, to look up the deeds.[8]

(i) Reconveyance by endorsed receipt Before 1926, a reconveyance by the mortgagee was necessary to revest the legal estate in the mortgagor upon redemption, but now, when redemption has been effected, there is no need for the mortgagee to execute a deed surrendering the term. A receipt written at the foot of the mortgage deed will be sufficient to extinguish the mortgage, provided that it states the name of the person who pays the money and is executed by the person in whom the mortgage is vested.[9] In the ordinary case of a mortgage by demise this receipt effects a surrender of the term and merges it in the reversion held by the mortgagor.[10] If a person, such as a second mortgagee, to whom the immediate equity of redemption does not belong, pays the money that is due, the benefit of the mortgage passes to him by virtue of the receipt,[11] and thus his incumbrance is kept alive. But of course where there are two mortgages of the same land and the mortgagor pays off the first, the receipt does not transfer the first mortgage term to him so as to enable him to keep it alive against the second mortgagee.[12] Moreover, it is enacted that a mortgage term shall, after repayment of the money, become a satisfied term, and shall cease.[13]

(ii) Disposal of deeds by mortgagee It is the duty of a mortgagee, upon receiving repayment of the loan, to deliver the title deeds to the person who has the best right to them, i.e. the mortgagor if there is only one incumbrance, or the next mortgagee if the land has been subjected to more incumbrances than one.[14] A mortgagee will not, however, incur liability to a later mortgagee for delivering the deeds to the mortgagor, unless he has actual notice of the later mortgage.[15] Mere registration of a mortgage as a land charge under the Land Charges Act 1972[16] does not in this case constitute notice, but nevertheless he is for several reasons well advised to search at the Registry before handing over the deeds to the mortgagor.[17] If the mortgagee has lost the deeds, the mortgagor has an equitable right to compensation on redemption.[18]

(iii) Sale in lieu of redemption The mortgagor may commence proceedings to enforce redemption, and if he is successful, an order will be made directing

---

7 *Cromwell Property Investment Co v Western and Toovey* [1934] Ch 322.
8 *Fitzgerald's Trustee v Mellersh* [1892] 1 Ch 385, per CHITTY J.
9 See *Erewash Borough Council v Taylor* [1979] CLY 1831 (receipt valid in spite of miscalculation of redemption figure by mortgagee).
10 LPA 1925, s. 115 (1). A building society may use either a reconveyance or a special statutory receipt: Building Societies Act 1986, Sch. 4, para. 2.
11 Ibid., s. 115 (2); *Cumberland Court (Brighton) Ltd v Taylor* [1964] Ch 29, [1963] 2 All ER 536.
12 Ibid., s. 115 (3); *Otter v Lord Vaux* (1856) 6 De GM & G 638; *Parkash v Irani Finance Ltd* [1970] Ch 101, [1969] 1 All ER 930.
13 Ibid., s. 116; *Edwards v Marshall-Lee* (1975) 235 EG 901; (1976) 40 Conv (NS) 102.
14 *Re Magneta Time Co Ltd* (1915) 84 LJ Ch 814.
15 LPA 1925, s. 96 (2), as amended by LP (A) A 1926, Schedule.
16 P. 720, post.
17 See (1926) 61 LJ News pp. 431, 471, 488, 519 (T. Cyprian Williams).
18 *Browning v Handiland Group Ltd* (1976) 35 P & CR 345.

the mortgagee to surrender or give a statutory receipt upon receiving payment within six months. But where such proceedings are taken, the mortgagor may have a judgment for sale instead of for redemption, and the court may, on the request either of the mortgagor or of the mortgagee, and despite the dissent of the other party, direct a sale on such terms as it thinks fit.[19]

(iv) Transfer of mortgage Finally, upon payment of the amount due, a mortgagor is entitled to require the mortgagee to transfer the debt and the property to a third person, and the mortgagee unless he is or has been in possession, is bound to comply.[20] This is the procedure adopted where a third person pays the amount of the loan to the mortgagee, and then himself assumes the position of mortgagee.

(3) EFFECT OF DEATH OF MORTGAGOR

On the death of a mortgagor the equity of redemption goes through his personal representatives to the persons entitled on intestacy if he dies without leaving a will, and to his devisee if he leaves a will. Under the law as it existed prior to 1854, such an heir or devisee was entitled to have the mortgage debt paid out of the personal estate of the deceased, and to take the property free from the mortgage burden, but, in accordance with the general principle that he who has the benefit ought to have the burden, this rule was reversed by the Real Estate Charges Acts of 1854, 1867 and 1877. These statutes have now been repealed, although their general tenor is retained, and it is enacted that property, whether land or not, which at the time of the owner's death is charged with the payment of money, whether by way of legal mortgage, equitable charge or otherwise, shall, as between the different persons claiming through the deceased, be primarily liable for the payment of the charge.[1] This rule is not to apply, however, if the deceased has expressed a contrary intention by will, deed or other document, but such intention must be clear and unambiguous, and is not to be implied merely because the deceased has directed that his debts are to be paid out of his personal estate or his residuary estate.[2]

B. RIGHTS OF A MORTGAGOR WHO REMAINS IN POSSESSION

In the eyes of equity the mortgagor remains the true beneficial owner of the property, and as long as he remains in possession he is entitled to appropriate the rents and profits to his own use without any liability to account for them, even though he may be in default in the payment of interest. As we shall see, the mortgagee has the right to enter into possession of the land, independently of any default on the part of the mortgagor,[3] but in normal circumstances the mortgagor remains in possession. Provided that the mortgagee has not given notice of his intention to take possession or to enter into receipt of the rents

19 LPA 1925, s. 91; *Palk v Mortgage Services Funding plc* [1993] Ch 330, [1993] 2 All ER 481, p. 700, post.

20 Ibid., s. 95. The reason for the exception is that a mortgagee, having once been in possession, remains liable to account for the profits that the transferee has, or ought to have, received after the transfer. He should, therefore, never transfer the security without an order of the court: *Hall v Heward* (1886) 32 Ch D 430 at 435.

1 AEA 1925, s. 35 (1).

2 Ibid., s. 35 (1), (2): *Re Neeld* [1962] Ch 643, [1962] 2 All ER 335; *Re Wakefield* [1943] 2 All ER 29.

3 P. 691, post.

and profits, the mortgagor in possession may sue in his own name for the recovery of possession and for the rents and profits. He may bring an action to prevent, or recover damages for, any trespass or other wrong done to the land.[4]

Where a mortgagor retained possession, it was formerly a common practice to include in the mortgage deed a clause by which he *attorned* to the mortgagee, i.e. acknowledged that he held the land as a tenant at will or from year to year of the mortgagee. The chief advantages were that it enabled the mortgagee to pursue the remedies available to a landlord for the recovery of arrears of rent, and also to obtain a summary judgment for possession if the need arose.

These two advantages, however, no longer exist, for the mortgagee cannot distrain upon the premises for arrears unless the attornment clause has been registered as a bill of sale;[5] and a summary judgment is available to him independently of attornment.[6] Nevertheless, an attornment clause is not altogether superfluous, for it enables a covenant by a mortgagor which touches and concerns the land to be enforced against his successors in title.[7]

A mortgagor, *while in actual possession* is given the following statutory powers:

(1) RIGHT TO GRANT VALID LEASES

(a) At common law

At common law a mortgagor is entitled to grant a lease binding between him and the lessee, and his power in this respect has not been affected by statute.[8] But if granted without the concurrence of the mortgagee[9] it confers only a precarious title upon the lessee, since the paramount title of the mortgagee may be asserted against both him and the mortgagor.[10]

(b) By statute

The Conveyancing Act 1881 expanded the power of the mortgagor in this particular by allowing him to grant leases for limited periods which would be binding upon the mortgagee. The present position is governed by the Law of Property Act 1925, which confers upon a mortgagor *in possession* a statutory right to grant the following leases that will be binding upon all incumbrancers:

1. Agricultural or occupation leases for any term not exceeding 21 years, or, if the mortgage was made after 1925, 50 years.
2. Building leases for any term not exceeding 99 years, or, in the case of a mortgage made after 1925, 999 years.[11]

4 LPA 1925, s. 98.
5 *Re Willis, ex parte Kennedy* (1888) 21 QBD 384.
6 RSC Ord. 14, r. 1 (2), Ord. 88. See generally (1969) 22 CLP, pp. 143–6 (E. C. Ryder).
7 *Regent Oil Co Ltd v J A Gregory (Hatch End) Ltd* [1966] Ch 402, [1965] 3 All ER 673, where the covenant was included in a charge by way of legal mortgage. But since the relationship between the parties is in effect that of landlord and tenant, would not the covenant run even in the absence of attornment?; see (1966) 82 LQR 21 (P. V. B.).
8 *Iron Trades Employers' Insurance Association v Union Land and House Investors Ltd* [1937] Ch 313, [1937] 1 All ER 481.
9 The mortgage deed itself may confer leasing powers within defined limits upon the mortgagor: LPA 1925, s. 99 (14).
10 *Corbett v Plowden* (1884) 25 Ch D 678 at 681, per Lord SELBORNE LC.
11 LPA 1925, s. 99 (1), (3).

Such a lease must be made to take effect in possession not later than twelve months after its date; it must reserve the best rent that can reasonably be obtained, and no fine must be taken;[12] it must contain a condition of re-entry in the event of rent being in arrears for 30 days,[13] and the mortgagor is bound to deliver to the mortgagee within one month a counterpart of the lease executed by the lessee.[14]

Thus:

when a mortgagor makes a lease to A for 50 years, the effect is that the mortgagee, though he holds a long term of years, is not entitled to actual possession during the continuance of A's term; but if he is driven to pursue his remedies, he is entitled to receipt of the rent paid by A.

These statutory powers of leasing may be, and in practice frequently are, excluded or abridged by the mortgage deed,[15] but no such exclusion or abridgement is allowed in the case of a mortgage of agricultural land made after 1 March 1948.[16]

(c) Effect of unauthorised lease

If a mortgagor in possession grants a lease which does not satisfy the provisions of the Law of Property Act 1925 or the terms of the mortgage deed, the lease may be binding on both the mortgagor and the tenant under the doctrine of estoppel.[17] Thus the mortgagor may sue or distrain for the rent.[18] The mortgagee, however, is not bound by the lease. As between the lessee and the mortgagee and his successors in title the lease granted by the mortgagor is void,[19] and the lessee is not protected against the mortgagee by the Rent Acts.[20] The mortgagee has an option. He may either treat the lessee as a trespasser or accept him as his own tenant.[1] If, for instance, he demands

12 LPA 1925, s. 99 (5), (6). See, for example, *Rust v Goodale* [1957] Ch 33 at 39, [1956] 3 All ER 373 at 376, where the consideration for a sub-lease was an immediate payment of £2,260 and a rent of £5.
13 Ibid., s. 99 (7). It is doubtful whether this requirement must be satisfied in the case of an oral tenancy: *Pawson v Revell* [1958] 2 QB 360, [1958] 3 All ER 233; *Rhodes v Dalby* [1971] 1 WLR 1325 at 1331–2, [1971] 2 All ER 1144 at 1149–50.
14 Ibid., s. 99 (11). But not in the case of an oral tenancy: *Rhodes v Dalby*, supra. A lease which fails to comply with one or more of these requirements may be validated under s. 152, if it has been made in good faith and if the lessee has entered. It then takes effect in equity as a contract for the grant of a valid lease. See e.g., *Pawson v Revell*, supra.
15 Ibid., s. 99 (13).
16 Agricultural Holdings Act 1986, Sch. 12; see *Pawson v Revell*, supra; *Rhodes v Dalby*, supra.
17 *Cuthbertson v Irving* (1860) 6 H & N 135; *Church of England Building Society v Piskor* [1954] Ch 553, [1954] 2 All ER 85; p. 388, ante.
18 *Trent v Hunt* (1853) 9 Exch 14.
19 *Rust v Goodale* [1957] Ch 33, [1956] 3 All ER 373; cf *Lever Finance Ltd v Needleman's Trustee* [1956] Ch 375, [1956] 2 All ER 378 (mortgagee's assignee estopped from asserting invalidity of lease).
20 *Dudley and District Benefit Building Society v Emerson* [1949] Ch 707, [1949] 2 All ER 252; (contractual tenancy in breach of covenant prohibition held not binding on mortgagee); followed in *Britannia Building Society v Earl* [1990] 1 WLR 422, [1990] 2 All ER 469 (statutory tenancy under Rent Act 1977); *Barclays Bank plc v Tennet* [1984] CA Transcript 242; (1988) 16 LSG 286 (A. Pugh-Thomas); [1990] Conv 450 (S. Bridge); cf. *Appleton v Aspin* [1988] 1 WLR 410, [1988] 1 All ER 904. See also *Quennell v Maltby* [1979] 1 WLR 318, [1979] 1 All ER 658, p. 658, post, for the courts discretion in equity to protect a lessee where possession is sought, but not in good faith to protect the security.
1 *Stroud Building Society v Delamont* [1960] 1 WLR 431 at 434, [1960] 1 All ER 749 at 751; *Chatsworth Properties Ltd v Effiom* [1971] 1 WLR 144, [1971] 1 All ER 604.

that the rent be paid direct to him instead of to the mortgagor, the original tenancy is destroyed and replaced by a yearly tenancy between the mortgagee and the lessee.[2] Moreover, the acceptance of rent without any such demand raises the implication of a yearly tenancy. This implication, however, does not arise merely because the mortgagee, being aware of the lease, allows the tenant to remain in possession.[3]

If a mortgagee refuses to recognize an unauthorized lease, the tenant may redeem the mortgage and thus secure himself against eviction.[4]

(2) RIGHT TO ACCEPT SURRENDERS OF LEASES

Although the statutory powers just mentioned enable a mortgagor to grant a lease out of the mortgagee's term, yet the effect of such a lease is to vest the reversion thereon in the mortgagee, and without the latter's concurrence it would normally be impossible for a mortgagor to accept a surrender of an existing lease with a view to the grant of a new one.[5] The Law of Property Act 1925, therefore, authorizes a mortgagor to accept a surrender of any lease, if, and only if, his object in doing so is to grant a new lease that falls within his statutory powers.[6] Such a surrender, however, is not valid unless a new lease is granted within one month, for a period not shorter than the unexpired term of the surrendered lease, and at a rent not less than the old rent.[7]

A subsequent mortgagee who exercises the statutory powers of leasing and of accepting surrenders exercises them in his capacity as mortgagee and not because he derives his title from the mortgagor.[8] There is therefore, for instance, no obligation on him to deliver a counterpart of the lease to the mortgagor.[9]

SECTION V RIGHTS OF THE MORTGAGEE

A. RIGHTS OF LEGAL MORTGAGEES

We now come to the five remedies which are available to a legal mortgagee for enforcing the payment of what is due to him under the mortgage: the action on the personal covenant to repay the principal with interest; entry into possession of the mortgaged premises; the appointment of a receiver; sale and foreclosure. The first three of these remedies do not involve the realization of the mortgaged property, but as a result of sale and foreclosure the mortgage is terminated.

There are five remedies available to a legal mortgagee.[10] They may all be

---

2 *Taylor v Ellis* [1960] Ch 368 at 375–6, [1960] 1 All ER 549 at 551–2.
3 Ibid.
4 *Tarn v Turner* (1888) 39 Ch D 456.
5 *Robbins v Whyte* [1906] 1 KB 125.
6 LPA 1925, s. 100 (1).
7 Ibid., s. 100 (5).
8 Ibid., ss. 99 (18), 100 (12).
9 Cf *Robbins v Whyte*, supra.
10 A mortgagee may also have an action against a valuer for a negligent valuation which causes him loss: *Corisand Investments Ltd v Druce & Co* (1978) 248 EG 315, 407; *Mount Banking Corpn Ltd v Brian Cooper & Co* [1992] 2 EGLR 142. For a similar action against a surveyor, see *London and South of England Building Society v Stone* (1981) 261 EG 463; *Anglia Hastings and Thanet Building Society v House & Son* (1981) 260 EG 1128.

pursued concurrently as soon as the mortgagor is in default, so that, for instance, the mortgagee at one and the same time may sue upon the personal covenant and begin foreclosure proceedings. They are also cumulative. Thus if the mortgagee exercises his power of sale and the purchase price is less than the mortgage debt, he may sue the mortgagor for the balance on the covenant to pay.[11] Foreclosure, however, puts an end to other remedies; a mortgagee who has foreclosed can only sue on the covenant to pay if he reopens the foreclosure,[12] so that the mortgagor may redeem. If, therefore, the mortgagee sells the mortgaged property after foreclosure, he has put it out of his power to reopen the foreclosure and so can no longer sue the mortgagor[13] or his guarantor on the personal covenant.[14]

(1) ACTION ON THE PERSONAL COVENANT

(a) Personal remedy

A mortgage deed contains an express covenant whereby the mortgagor covenants to repay the principal sum on a definite date, and meanwhile to pay interest at a certain rate per cent. The moment that date has passed, the mortgagee can sue on this personal covenant for the recovery of the principal sum and any interest that may be in arrear, and can have the judgment satisfied out of any property belonging to the mortgagor, though it is not comprised in the mortgage. Further, the mortgagor remains liable on the covenant to the mortgagee, even though he has transferred his interest in the mortgaged property.[15] He usually takes a covenant of indemnity from the transferee.[16]

(b) Effect of lapse of time

An action to recover the principal sum is barred unless it is brought within twelve years from the date when the right to receive the money accrued.[17] This date is that which is fixed by the mortgage deed for repayment, but on each occasion that some part of the principal or interest is paid or a written acknowledgment of his liability to pay is given by the mortgagor, the period of twelve years begins to run afresh.[18] In the case of interest, only six years' arrears are recoverable.[19] Once the mortgagee's right to recover the principal sum is statute barred, he loses his status as a mortgagee. He can no longer sue for possession or for foreclosure, nor can he redeem a prior mortgage.[20]

---

11 *Rudge v Richens* (1873) LR 8 CP 358; *Gordon Grant & Co Ltd v Boos* [1926] AC 781.
12 *Perry v Barker* (1806) 13 Ves 198.
13 *Palmer v Hendrie* (1859) 27 Beav 349. See *Kinnaird v Trollope* (1888) 39 Ch D 636 at 642, per STIRLING LJ; M & B p. 784.
14 *Lloyds and Scottish Trust Ltd v Britten* (1982) 44 P & CR 249.
15 *Kinnaird v Trollope*, supra.
16 A transferee for value is under an implied obligation to indemnify: *Bridgman v Daw* (1891) 40 WR 253.
17 Limitation Act 1980, s. 20 (1).
18 Ibid., ss. 29 (4), 30.
19 Ibid., s. 20 (5)–(7); *Barclays Bank plc v Walters* (1988) Times, 20 October; McGee, *Limitation Periods*, pp. 187–188.
20 *Cotterell v Price* [1960] 1 WLR 1097, [1960] 3 All ER 315.

(2) ENTRY INTO POSSESSION

(a) Right to take possession

A legal mortgagee has the right to enter into possession of the mortgaged property. As HARMAN J said:

> The right of the mortgagee to possession in the absence of some contract has nothing to do with default on the part of the mortgagor. The mortgagee may go into possession before the ink is dry on the mortgage unless there is something in the contract, express or by implication,[1] whereby he has contracted himself out of that right. He has the right because he has a legal term of years in the property.[2]

It is not usual, however, for a mortgagee, despite his legal right, to enter into possession of the mortgaged property, unless he wishes to do so as a preliminary to exercising his statutory power of sale, when the mortgagor is in default. As HARMAN J went on to say:

> An application for possession has become a very fashionable form of relief, because, owing to the conditions now prevailing, if it is desired to realize a security by sale, vacant possession is almost essential.

In other words, entry into possession is a necessary preliminary to sale. It is important for the mortgagee to enter, so that he can evict the mortgagor and offer vacant possession to a purchaser. Otherwise, the property might be difficult to sell, or, if sold, its price might be depressed, if the sale took place with the mortgagor in possession and the purchaser had to evict him after the sale.

(b) Liability of mortgagee to account strictly

It is, in theory at least, possible for a mortgagee to enter into possession to ensure the payment of interest, but a formidable deterrent to this course is the strict supervision which equity exercises over a mortgagee in possession. The rule is that he must get no advantage out of the mortgage beyond the payment of principal, interest and costs, and he is made to account not only for what he has actually received, but also for what he might have received but for his own wilful default or neglect.[3] Thus he is liable for voluntary waste, and again if he allows property to remain vacant which might have been let, he is personally liable to pay an occupation rent.[4] Thus in *White v City of London Brewery Co*:[5]

> Mortgagees, who happened to be brewers, took possession of the mortgaged premises and leased them to a tenant, subject to a restriction that he should take his supply of beer entirely from them. It was held that they must account for the

---

1 See *Esso Petroleum Co Ltd v Alstonbridge Properties Ltd* [1975] 1 WLR 1474 at 1484, [1975] 3 All ER 358 at 367; *Western Bank Ltd v Schindler* [1977] Ch 1, [1976] 2 All ER 393; M & B p. 759.

2 *Four-Maids Ltd v Dudley Marshall (Properties) Ltd* [1957] Ch 317 at 320, [1957] 2 All ER 35 at 36; M & B p. 751. See generally Fisher and Lightwood (10th edn), chapter 19; [1979] Conv 266 (R. J. Smith); [1983] Conv 293 (A. Clarke). See also Report of the Committee on the Enforcement of Judgment Debts 1969 (Cmnd 3909), pp. 355 et seq.

3 *Chaplin v Young* (1864) 33 Beav 330; *White v City of London Brewery Co* (1889) 42 Ch D 237 at 243.

4 *Gaskell v Gosling* (1896) 1 QB 669 at 691.

5 (1889) 42 Ch D 237; M & B p. 752; see also *Hughes v Williams* (1806) 12 Ves 493; (1979) 129 NLJ 334 (H. E. Markson); [1982] Conv 345, at 346–348 (J. E. Stannard).

additional rent that they would have received had they let the premises as a "free" instead of a "tied" house.

(c) Relief of mortgagor

(i) Statutory   If a mortgagee seeks possession he will usually take proceedings in the Chancery Division or the county court.[6] Unless the mortgagee agrees, the court has no jurisdiction to decline the order or to adjourn the hearing. But it may adjourn the application for a short time to enable the mortgagor to pay off the whole of the mortgage debt.[7]

Where, however, a mortgagee brings an action for possession of a *dwelling-house*,[8] wide discretionary powers are given to the court by statute.[9] The court may adjourn the proceedings, or suspend or postpone the possession order:

> if it appears to the court that in the event of its exercising the power the mortgagor is likely to be able within a reasonable period[10] to pay any sums due[11] under the mortgage or to remedy a default consisting of a breach of any other obligation arising under or by virtue of the mortgage.[12]

Where the mortgagor is entitled to pay the principal sum by instalments, or otherwise to defer the payment of it in whole or in part, the court may treat as sums due only those instalments which are actually in arrear, even if the mortgage makes the whole of the balance outstanding payable on any default by the mortgagor.[13] But the court may only exercise its discretion if the mortgagor is likely to be able within a reasonable period also to pay any

---

6 RSC Ord. 88: County Courts Act 1984, s. 21 (1) gives jurisdiction to the County Court where the net annual value for rating does not exceed the county court limit: *P B Frost Ltd v Green* [1978] 1 WLR 949, [1978] 2 All ER 206; *Universal Showcards and Display Manufacturing Ltd v Brunt* (1984) Times, 26 March; County Court (Amendment No. 3) Rules 1993 (S.I. 1993 No. 2175); (1993) 143 NLJ 1762 (R. C. M. Jones). See also Consumer Credit Act 1974, s. 126, p. 737, post.

7 *Birmingham Citizens Permanent Building Society v Caunt* [1962] Ch 883, [1962] 1 All ER 163. A mortgagor's counterclaim or set off against mortgagee for sum exceeding debt is not in itself a reason for an adjournment: *Samuel Keller (Holdings) Ltd v Martins Bank Ltd* [1971] 1 WLR 43, [1970] 3 All ER 950; *Mobil Oil Co Ltd v Rawlinson* (1981) 43 P & CR 221; M & B p. 753; *Citibank Trust Ltd v Ayivor* [1987] 1 WLR 1157, [1987] 3 All ER 241 (right to possession not affected where mortgagor's counterclaim for damages greater than arrears due under mortgage); *First National Bank plc v Syed* [1991] 2 All ER 250; (1991) 141 NLJ 793 (H. W. Wilkinson); (1994) 110 LQR 221 (N. Hickman); *National Westminster Bank plc v Skelton* [1993] 1 WLR 72n; *Ashley Guarantee plc v Zacaria* [1993] 1 WLR 62, [1993] 1 All ER 254.

8 The fact that part of it is used for business purposes does not prevent a house from being a dwelling-house: AJA 1970, s. 39 (2).

9 AJA 1970, s. 37. If the land is outside Greater London or the County Palatine of Lancaster, and if a County Court has jurisdiction (n. 6, supra) the action must be brought in the County Court (ss. 37–8).

10 *Royal Trust Co of Canada v Markham* [1975] 1 WLR 1416, [1975] 3 All ER 433 (an order for suspension must be for a fixed period, and the mortgagor must produce evidence that he is likely to be able to pay); *Target Homes Loans Ltd v Clothier* (1992) 25 HLR 48 (3 months' postponement; mortgagor had better prospect of achieving earlier sale if in possession); [1993] Conv 62 (J. Martin).

11 *Shirlstar Container Transport Ltd v Re-Enforce Trading Co Ltd* [1990] NPC 76 (sums due does not mean sums claimed under the mortgage).

12 AJA 1970, s. 36. The section does not apply to a mortgage which is within the Consumer Credit Act 1974: s. 38A, added by Consumer Credit Act 1974, s. 192, Sch. 4, para 30.

13 AJA 1973, s. 8 (1), reversing the effect of *Halifax Building Society v Clark* [1973] Ch 307, [1973] 2 All ER 33. But the grant of the statutory discretion was unnecessary: *First Middlesbrough Trading and Mortgage Co Ltd v Cunningham* (1974) 28 P & CR 69. See (1973) 37 Conv (NS) 213; (1974) 38 Conv (NS) 1.

further instalments then due.[14] This statutory relief may be given to a mortgagor,[15] whether or not he is in default under the mortgage,[16] and is available in the case of both instalment and endowment mortgages.[17] Where one spouse has defaulted on the mortgage of a dwelling-house, and the mortgagee brings an action for possession, the other spouse may be entitled to be made a party to the action.[18]

(ii) In equity In addition to the statutory relief, equity may have a wide discretion to restrain any unjust use of the right to possession. In *Quennell v Maltby*:[19]

> Q mortgaged his house to a bank. The mortgage deed prohibited the creation of a tenancy without the bank's consent. In breach of that covenant Q let the house to M, who became a statutory tenant protected by the Rent Act. This tenancy was binding on Q but not on the bank.[20] Q, who wanted to sell the house with vacant possession, asked the bank to bring an action for possession against M. On the bank's refusal, Q's wife then paid off the mortgage debt, took a transfer of the mortgage from the bank and claimed possession against M as mortgagee.

The Court of Appeal held that she was not entitled to possession. According to BRIDGE and TEMPLEMAN LJJ, she was to be treated as acting as agent for Q, who, as mortgagor, could not obtain possession. Lord DENNING MR however stated a wider principle:[1]

> The objective is plain. It was not to enforce the security or to obtain repayment or anything of the kind. It was in order to get possession of the house and to overcome the protection of the Rent Acts ... Equity can step in so as to prevent a mortgage, or a transferee from him, from getting possession of a house contrary to the justice of the case. A mortgagee will be restrained from getting possession except when it is sought bona fide and reasonably for the purpose of enforcing the security, and then only subject to such conditions as the court thinks fit to impose.

It is difficult to reconcile this wider principle with previous authority, and it would render unnecessary the protection accorded to the mortgagor by the Administration of Justice Act 1970.

---

14 AJA 1973, s. 8 (2); *Centrax Trustees Ltd v Ross* [1979] 2 All ER 952 (principal to be repaid at indeterminate future date held to be within the section); cf *Habib Bank Ltd v Tailor* [1982] 1 WLR 1218, [1982] 3 All ER 561 (overdraft secured by charge to be repaid on demand in writing held to be not within the section, since there was no agreement as to deferred payment); [1983] Conv 80 (P. H. Kenny); [1982] All ER Rev 117 (P. J. Clarke); [1984] Conv 91 (S. Tromans). In instalment mortgages, the discretionary powers extend to foreclosure actions, whether or not possession is claimed in the same proceedings: s. 8 (3). See *Lord Marples of Wallasey v Holmes* (1975) 31 P & CR 94.

15 Mortgagor and mortgagee includes any person deriving title under the original mortgagor or mortgagee: AJA 1970, s. 39 (1); *Britannia Building Society v Earl* [1990] 1 WLR 422, [1990] 2 All ER 469 (statutory tenant of mortgagor whose tenancy was not binding on mortgagee, p 688, post, was not such a person and court had no jurisdiction to adjourn proceedings); (1990) 140 NLJ 823 (H. W. Wilkinson).

16 *Western Bank Ltd v Schindler* [1977] Ch 1, [1976] 2 All ER 393 (GOFF LJ dubitante); M & B p. 759; (1977) 40 MLR 356 (C. Harpum).

17 *Governor and Co of the Bank of Scotland v Grimes* [1985] QB 1179, [1985] 2 All ER 254; M & B p. 765. AJA 1973, s. 8 is infelicitously drafted and was interpreted "so as to give effect to the general tenor of the language in a purposive way": per Sir John ARNOLD P at 1188, at 258.

18 Matrimonial Homes Act 1983, s. 8, p. 241, ante; LRA 1925, s. 112B.

19 [1979] 1 WLR 318, [1979] 1 All ER 568; M & B p. 755; (1979) 129 NLJ 624 (H. W. Wilkinson); (1979) 38 CLJ 257 (R. A. Pearce).

20 *Dudley and District Benefit Building Society v Emerson* [1949] Ch 707, [1949] 2 All ER 252, p. 688, ante.

 1 [1979] 1 WLR 318 at 322, [1979] 1 All ER 568 at 571.

(3) APPOINTMENT OF A RECEIVER

We have seen that, owing to the strict supervision that the court exercises over a mortgagee, it is undesirable for him to take possession of the land, but, on the other hand, there are cases where it is essential that he should be able to intercept the rents and the profits, and employ them in keeping down the interest. The mortgaged property may have been leased by the mortgagor to third parties under his statutory powers or the property may consist not of land but of a rentcharge, so that there is an annual sum which can be prevented from reaching the mortgagor and can be set against interest. In such cases the most effective procedure is to appoint a receiver of the income of the property.

The mortgage deed may contain special provisions with regard to this matter, and in some cases, as for instance where the property is already let to tenants, it is not uncommon to appoint a receiver from the moment when the mortgage is created. But apart from this a mortgagee has a statutory power of appointing a receiver in the case of every mortgage created by deed,[2] even though he has already gone into possession before the appointment.[3] The appointment and removal of a receiver must be effected in writing.[4]

Although this statutory power arises as soon as the mortgage money has become due, it cannot be exercised until one of those three events that qualify a mortgagee to exercise his power of sale has occurred.[5]

The advantage of such an appointment from the mortgagee's point of view is that the receiver is deemed to be the agent of the mortgagor, and that the sole responsibility for his acts and defaults falls on the latter.[6] The receiver is not entitled to grant leases without the sanction of the court,[7] but he has power to recover the income of the property by action or distress or otherwise, and to give effectual receipts,[8] and he is bound to apply any money received by him in the following order:[9]

1. In discharge of rents, taxes,[9a] rates and outgoings.
2. In keeping down payments that rank before the mortgage.
3. In paying his own commission, fire and other insurance premiums and if so directed in writing by the mortgagee, the cost of repairs. His commission is at a rate not exceeding five per cent on the gross sum received; if no rate is specified, then at five per cent, or at such other rate as the court thinks fit to allow.[10]
4. In payment of the mortgage interest.
5. In discharging the principal sum if so directed in writing by the

2 LPA 1925, s. 101 (1) (iii). *Shamji v Johnson Matthey Bankers Ltd* [1991] BCLC 36 (mortgagee owes no duty of care to mortgagor or guarantor in deciding whether or not to appoint a receiver).
3 *Refuge Assurance Co Ltd v Pearlberg* [1938] Ch 687, [1938] 3 All ER 231.
4 LPA 1925, s. 109 (1) (5).
5 Ibid., s. 109 (1), p. 695, post.
6 Ibid., s. 109 (2). See *Chatsworth Properties Ltd v Effiom* [1971] 1 WLR 144, [1971] 1 All ER 604; *Standard Chartered Bank Ltd v Walker* [1982] 1 WLR 1410, [1982] 3 All ER 938; *American Express International Banking Corpn v Hurley* [1985] 3 All ER 564; p. 699, n. 20, post.
7 *Re Cripps* [1946] Ch 265.
8 LPA 1925, s. 109 (3).
9 Ibid., s. 109 (8).
9a *Sargent v Customs and Excise Comrs* [1993] EGCS 182 (V.A.T.).
10 *Marshall v Cottingham* [1982] Ch 82, [1981] 3 All ER 8.

mortgagee. A breach of this direction renders him liable to an action for an account.[11]

Any residue that remains must be paid to the mortgagor.

(4) SALE[12]

(a) Power of sale

(i) When power arises As soon as the mortgage money has become due, that is, as soon as the date fixed for repayment has passed, the legal mortgagee or chargee has a statutory power, which may be varied or extended by the parties or excluded altogether,[13] to sell the mortgage property *provided that the mortgage has been made by deed*.[14] If the money secured by the mortgage is payable by instalments, the power of sale arises as soon as an instalment is due and unpaid.[15]

(ii) When power exercisable Although the power of sale arises as soon as the mortgage money becomes due, it nevertheless does not become exercisable until *one* of the following events has occurred:

1. Notice requiring payment of the mortgage money has been served on the mortgagor or one of two or more mortgagors, and default has been made in payment of the mortgage money, or of part thereof, for three months after such service.[16]

This notice, which must be in writing,[17] may demand payment either immediately or at the end of three months, and if it is drafted in the latter form, the mortgagee need not wait for a further three months before selling, but can exercise his power after the lapse of three months from the service of notice.[18]

If there are more mortgages than one, the notice should also be served upon the later mortgagees.

2. Some interest under the mortgage is in arrear and unpaid for two months after becoming due.[19]
3. There has been a breach of some provision contained in the mortgage deed or in [the Law of Property Act 1925], and on the part of the mortgagor, or of some person concurring in making the mortgage, to be observed or performed, other than and besides a covenant for payment of the mortgage money or interest thereon.[20]

For instance, if the mortgagor has broken a covenant to keep the premises in repair, the mortgagee can exercise his power of sale immediately, despite the fact that no interest is in arrear and that he has not demanded repayment of the loan.

11 *Leicester Permanent Building Society v Butt* [1943] Ch 308, [1943] 2 All ER 523.
12 See generally Fisher and Lightwood (10th edn), chapter 20; (1976) 73 LSG 92, 654; (1977) 74 LSG 493 (H. E. Markson).
13 *Alliance Building Society v Shave* [1952] Ch 581, [1952] 1 All ER 1033.
14 LPA 1925, s. 101 (1) (i).
15 *Payne v Cardiff RDC* [1932] 1 KB 241; cf *Twentieth Century Banking Corpn Ltd v Wilkinson* [1977] Ch 99, [1976] 3 All ER 361.
16 LPA 1925, s. 103 (i).
17 Ibid., s. 196.
18 *Barker v Illingworth* [1908] 2 Ch 20.
19 LPA 1925, s. 103 (ii).
20 Ibid., s. 103 (iii).

Sections 101–107 of the Law of Property Act 1925 contain detailed provisions dealing with the power of sale.[1] The mortgagee may sell the mortgaged property, or any part thereof, either subject to prior charges or not, and either together or in lots, by public auction or by private contract. He may sell the land either with or apart from the minerals, and may impose either on the sold or on the unsold part of the mortgaged land such conditions or restrictive covenants as seem desirable.[2]

(b) Effect of sale

If a mortgagee realizes his security by exercising the statutory power of sale, the effect is to extinguish the mortgagor's equity of redemption. It is, however, the contract to sell and not the subsequent conveyance that represents the effective exercise of the mortgagee's power; and, providing that there is no impropriety in the sale, the mortgagor's equity is extinguished as soon as the contract of sale is made.[3]

(i) **Fee simple** A mortgagee, although he holds only a term of years or a charge by way of legal mortgage, is given express statutory power to vest the fee simple in the purchaser. The conveyance may be made in the name of the mortgagor as estate owner, and it operates to pass his legal fee simple to the purchaser and to extinguish the mortgage terms vested both in the selling mortgagee and in any subsequent mortgagees.[4] If the person exercising the power of sale is not the first mortgagee, then the purchaser takes the fee simple subject to prior mortgages.

(ii) **Leasehold** Where a term of years has been mortgaged by a sublease, the effect of a sale by the mortgagee is to convey to the purchaser both the mortgage sub-term and the residue of the term vested in the mortgagor.[5] The sub-term is extinguished, since it merges in the mortgagor's reversion which thus passes to the purchaser. The conveyance, however, does not have this effect if the mortgage term does not comprise the whole of the land included in the mortgagor's term, unless the rent and the covenants have been apportioned, or unless the land excluded from the mortgage term bears a rent of no money value.[6] The acquisition of the reversion by the purchaser results in his becoming liable, in his capacity as assignee, upon the covenants contained in the lease from the lessor to the mortgagor. The Act, therefore, provides that if the leave of the court is obtained the sub-term alone may be conveyed to the purchaser to the exclusion of the mortgagor's reversion.[7]

The above provisions also apply where the owner of a charge by way of legal mortgage exercises his power of sale.

---

1 See Consumer Credit Act 1974, s. 126; p. 737, post.
2 LPA 1925, s. 101 (2).
3 *Lord Waring v London and Manchester Assurance Co Ltd* [1935] Ch 310; M & B p. 770; *Property and Bloodstock Ltd v Emerton* [1968] Ch 94, [1967] 3 All ER 321. For the effect of a contract of sale by the mortgagor upon the powers of the mortgagee, see *Duke v Robson* [1973] 1 WLR 267, [1973] 1 All ER 481.
4 LPA 1925, ss. 88 (1), 113.
5 Ibid., s. 89 (1).
6 Ibid., s. 89 (6). "Apportionment" includes an equitable apportionment, i.e. one made without the consent of the lessor: LP (A) A 1926, Sch. amending LPA 1925, s. 89.
7 Ibid., s. 89 (1) (*a*).

(c) Position of purchaser from mortgagee

It is clear, therefore, that there is no difficulty in transferring to a purchaser a valid legal title to the whole interest vested in the mortgagor. Such a purchaser takes the estate freed from all estates, interests and rights to which the mortgage has priority;[8] but if he buys from a second mortgagee he will take the fee simple subject to the term vested in the first mortgagee, and he will himself be deprived of the fee simple if such a first mortgagee exercises his powers of sale or foreclosure. A sale which is made in the professed exercise of the statutory power of sale (and after 1925 every sale made by a mortgagee is deemed so to have been made unless a contrary intention appears) cannot be impeached on the ground that no case has arisen to authorize the sale, or that the power has been improperly exercised. If either of these facts is proved, then the injured person has his remedy against the mortgagee who exercised the power, not against the purchaser.[9]

A purchaser is thus only concerned to see that the power of sale has arisen, and this he can discover merely by examining the mortgage deed. He need not satisfy himself that the power of sale has become exercisable or that it has been properly exercised. If, however, he "becomes aware . . . of any facts showing that the power of sale is not exercisable, or that there is some impropriety in the sale, then, in my judgment, he gets no good title on taking the conveyance".[10]

(d) Application of purchase money

The money received from a purchaser is held by the mortgagee, after any prior mortgages have been paid off, on trust:

First, to pay all expenses incidental to the sale.
Secondly, to pay to himself the principal, interest and costs due under the mortgage, and
Thirdly, to pay the surplus, if any, to the person entitled to the mortgaged property.[11]

The words "person entitled to the mortgaged property" include subsequent mortgagees, and the rule is that where there are several mortgagees interested in the same land, a prior mortgagee holds any surplus proceeds on trust for those later mortgagees of whose incumbrances he has notice.[12] Registration as a land charge now constitutes notice,[13] and therefore if he pays the surplus to the mortgagor he is liable to that extent to the next mortgagee whose

---

8 LPA 1925, s. 104 (1).
9 Ibid., s. 104 (2), (3).
10 *Lord Waring v London and Manchester Assurance Co Ltd* [1935] Ch 310 at 318, per CROSSMAN J. See *Jenkins v Jones* (1860) 2 Giff 99; *Selwyn v Garfit* (1888) 38 Ch D 273; *Bailey v Barnes* [1894] 1 Ch 25; *Price Bros (Somerford) Ltd v J Kelly Homes (Stoke-on-Trent) Ltd* [1975] 1 WLR 1512, [1975] 3 All ER 369; *Northern Developments (Holdings) Ltd v UDT Securities Ltd* [1976] 1 WLR 1230, [1977] 1 All ER 747; *Forsyth v Blundell* (1973) 129 CLR 477; *Pasquarella v National Australia Finance Ltd* [1987] 1 NZLR 312 and generally Emmet, para. 25.048; [1988] Conv 317; [1989] Conv 412 (S. Robinson).
11 LPA 1925, s. 105; *Weld-Blundell v Synott* [1940] 2 KB 107, [1940] 2 All ER 580.
12 *Thorne v Heard and Marsh* [1895] AC 495.
13 LPA 1925, s. 198 (1) as amended by Local Land Charges Act 1975, s. 17, Sch. 1; p. 720, post.

mortgage has been registered.[14] In case of doubt he may pay the money into court.[15]

If, however, the right of redemption of a mortgagor and of persons claiming through him has been extinguished under the Limitation Act 1980 (by reason of the mortgagee having been in possession for 12 years without receiving any sum in respect of principal or interest and without acknowledging the title of the mortgagor), a subsequent mortgagee is not a "person entitled to the mortgaged property". Since the title which he claims through the mortgagor is extinguished, his interest has ceased. Therefore, if the mortgagee sells under his statutory power, he is entitled to retain the whole proceeds, although they may exceed the amount due to him for principal and interest.[16]

(e) Duty of mortgagee exercising power of sale

A mortgagee who exercises his power of sale is not in other respects a trustee for the mortgagor. SALMON LJ in *Cuckmere Brick Co Ltd v Mutual Finance Ltd* said:[17]

> It is well settled that a mortgagee is not a trustee of the power of sale for the mortgagor. Once the power has accrued, the mortgagee is entitled to exercise it for his own purposes whenever he chooses to do so.[18] It matters not that the moment may be unpropitious and that by waiting a higher price could be obtained. He has the right to realise his security by turning it into money when he likes. Nor, in my view, is there anything to prevent a mortgagee from accepting the best bid he can get at an auction, even though the auction is badly attended and the bidding exceptionally low. Provided none of those adverse factors is due to any fault of the mortgagee, he can do as he likes. If the mortgagee's interests, as he sees them, conflict with those of the mortgagor, the mortgagee can give preference to his own interests, which of course he could not do were he a trustee of the power of sale for the mortgagor.

It has even been held that the motive of the mortgagee for selling, such as to spite the mortgagor, is immaterial.[19]

A mortgagee, however, in exercising his power of sale, owes a duty of care

---

14 *West London Commercial Bank v Reliance Building Society* (1884) 27 Ch D 187; affd 29 Ch D 954; *Re Thomson's Mortgage Trusts* [1920] 1 Ch 508. Distinguish the mortgagee's duty with regard to delivery of the title deeds after redemption, for which purpose registration of a later mortgage does not constitute notice; p. 685, ante.

15 TA 1925, s. 63.

16 *Young v Clarey* [1948] Ch 191, [1948] 1 All ER 197.

17 [1971] Ch 949 at 965, [1971] 2 All ER 633 at 643; M & B p. 708.

18 *China and South Sea Bank Ltd v Tan Soon Gin* [1990] 1 AC 536 at 545, [1989] 3 All ER 839 at 842: "The creditor must decide in his own interest if and when he should sell": per Lord TEMPLEMAN; *Countrywide Banking Corpn v Robinson* [1991] 1 NZLR 75; *Cuckmere Brick Co Ltd v Mutual Finance Ltd*, supra; see *Forsyth v Blundell* (1973) 129 CLR 477 at 481, 493. In *Standard Chartered Bank Ltd v Walker*, supra, Lord DENNING MR said at 1415, at 942: "There are several dicta to the effect that the mortgagee can choose his own time for the sale, but I do not think this means that he can sell at the worst possible time. It is at least arguable that, in choosing the time, he must exercise a reasonable degree of care." See also *Predeth v Castle Phillips Finance Co Ltd* [1986] 2 EGLR 144 (where CA accepted the judge's finding that the exercise of reasonable care required mortgagee to expose uninhabitable bungalow at Alton in Hampshire to the market for approximately three months).

19 *Nash v Eads* (1880) 25 SJ 95 (JESSEL MR); *Belton v Bass, Rattcliffe and Gretton Ltd* [1922] 2 Ch 449.

to the mortgagor and to any guarantor of the mortgagor's debt.[20] This duty may be excluded by an appropriate term in the mortgage.[1] The mortgagee must act not only in good faith[2] for the purpose of protecting his security,[3] but also take reasonable care to obtain the true market value of the mortgaged property at the date on which he decides to sell it. Thus, where the price is lower than would have been the case due to his negligence or that of his agent, then he must account to the mortgagor for the difference between that price and the true market value.[4] Moreover, a building society has a statutory duty to take reasonable care to ensure that the price is the best price that can be reasonably obtained[5] but it too can consult its own convenience as regards the time of sale.[6]

The Court of Appeal has recently imposed[7] a novel and restrictive interpretation on the mortgagee's duty of care, in holding that, where the mortgagor is a trustee of the mortgaged property, the mortgagee owes no duty to a beneficiary under the trust of whose interest he has notice. The duty on sale arises solely out of the equitable relationship between mortgagor and mortgagee. As NOURSE LJ said:[8]

> It is both unnecessary and confusing for the duties owed by a mortgagee to the mortgagor and the surety, if there is one, to be expressed in terms of the tort of negligence . . . the duty owed by the mortgagee to the mortgagor was recognised by equity as arising out of the particular relationship between them.

20 *Standard Chartered Bank Ltd v Walker* [1982] 1 WLR 1410, [1982] 3 All ER 938; (1982) 132 NLJ 884 (H. W. Wilkinson); [1982] All ER Rev 39 (D. D. Prentice). See also *American Express International Banking Corpn v Hurley* [1985] 3 All ER 564 (mortgagee responsible for what receiver does as his agent, but not responsible for what he does as mortgagor's agent, unless the mortgagee directs or interferes with receiver's activities).
1 *Bishop v Bonham* [1988] 1 WLR 742. "The exclusion clause must be construed strictly", per SLADE LJ at 752.
2 *Kennedy v De Trafford* [1897] AC 180; *Lord Waring v London and Manchester Assurance Co Ltd* [1935] Ch 310.
3 *Downsview Nominees Ltd v First City Corpn Ltd* [1993] 2 WLR 86 at 98, per Lord TEMPLEMAN.
4 *Cuckmere Brick Co Ltd v Mutual Finance Ltd*, supra (failure to mention planning permission for flats in advertisement for sale of land by auction); *Palmer v Barclays Bank Ltd* (1971) 23 P & CR 30; *Waltham Forest London Borough v Webb* (1974) 232 EG 461; *Johnson v Ribbins* (1975) 235 EG 757; *Bank of Cyprus (London) Ltd v Gill* [1980] 2 Lloyds Rep 51; (1981) 125 NLJ 249 (H. E. Markson); *Norwich General Trust v Grierson* [1984] CLY 2306 (mortgagee held liable for diminution of purchase price due to his negligence in allowing premises to deteriorate between date of taking possession and date of sale); *Garland v Ralph Pay & Ransom* (1984) 271 EG 106, 197 (action by mortgagor against mortgagee's selling agents for negligent marketing technique and valuation); *Predeth v Castle Phillips Finance Co Ltd*, supra (action by mortgagee against surveyor instructed to provide "crash-sale" valuation); [1986] Conv 442 (M. P. Thompson).
5 Building Societies Act 1986, Sch. 4, para 1 (1) (*a*); Building Societies (Supplementary Provisions as to Mortgages) Rules 1986 (SI 1986 No. 2216).
6 *Reliance Permanent Building Society v Harwood-Stamper* [1944] Ch 362, [1944] 2 All ER 75.
7 *Parker-Tweedale v Dunbar Bank plc* [1991] Ch 12, [1990] 2 All ER 577; M & B p. 771; [1990] Conv 431 (L. Bently); HL Appellate Committee refused to appeal: [1991] Ch 12 at 25.
8 At 18, at 582; *Downsview Nominees Ltd v First City Corpn Ltd*, supra; [1993] Conv 401 (R. Grantham). There are dicta to the contrary in *Cuckmere Brick Co Ltd v Mutual Finance Ltd*, supra, and *Standard Chartered Bank Ltd v Walker*, supra. See also *China and South Sea Bank Ltd v Tan Soon Gin* [1990] 1 AC 536, [1989]3 All ER 839; M & B p. 774 (where PC held that no duty was owed by a mortgagee to a surety to sell depreciating mortgaged property; Lord TEMPLEMAN said at 543, at 841: "The Court of Appeal [of Hong Kong] sought to find such a duty in the tort of negligence but the tort of negligence has not yet subsumed all torts and does not supplant the principles of equity or contradict contractual promises or complement the remedy of judicial review or supplement statutory rights").

In any event, the sale must be a genuine sale. A mortgagee cannot sell to himself either alone[9] or with others, nor to a trustee for himself, nor to anyone employed by him to conduct the sale. Such a sale is no sale at all, even though the price fixed is the full value of the property.[10] There is, however, no hard and fast rule that a mortgagee may not sell to a company in which he owns shares; but the onus lies on both the mortgagee and the company to show that the sale was in good faith and that the mortgagee took reasonable precautions to obtain the best price reasonably obtainable at the time.[11]

(f) Discretion of court to order sale at a depressed market price

In *Palk v Mortgage Services Funding plc*:[12]

> a house was mortgaged for £358,587, but could only be sold for £283,000. The mortgagor wished to sell the house, but the mortgagee wished to take possession and to let it on a short-term lease and to sell when the market improved.

The Court of Appeal held that it had a discretion under section 91 (2) of the Law of Property Act 1925,[13] to order a sale at a depressed market price, even against the wishes of the mortgagee.[14] As Sir Donald NICHOLLS V-C said:[15] "It is just and equitable to order a sale because otherwise unfairness and injustice will follow": interest due from the mortgagor will continue to increase and thereby compound his eventual loss.

(5) FORECLOSURE

(a) Foreclosure action[16]

Foreclosure is a judicial procedure by which the mortgagee acquires the land for himself freed from the mortgagor's equity of redemption. We have seen that equity regards the mortgagor's right to redeem the property as inviolable, and that, despite the lapse of the contractual right to redeem, it forbids the mortgagee to appropriate the legal fee simple without making an application to the court. Until the time fixed in the deed for repayment of the loan has arrived, no question of foreclosure can arise, but as soon as that date has passed and the equitable right to redeem has superseded the contractural right, the mortgagee can bring an action in the Chancery Division praying that the mortgagor shall either pay what is due or be foreclosed, that is, deprived altogether of his right to redeem.

---

9 *Williams v Wellingborough Borough Council* [1975] 1 WLR 1327, [1975] 3 All ER 462 ("a see-through dress of a sale", at 1329, at 463, per RUSSELL LJ). The decision itself was reversed by Housing Act 1980, s. 112 for the benefit of existing local authority mortgagees.
10 *Farrar v Farrars Ltd* (1888) 40 Ch D 395 at 409, and authorities cited by LINDLEY LJ.
11 *Tse Kwong Lam v Wong Chit Sen* [1983] 1 WLR 1349, [1983] 3 All ER 54; [1984] Conv 143 (P. Jackson); [1983] All ER Rev 57 (D. D. Prentice).
12 [1993] Ch 330, [1993] 2 All ER 481; [1993] Conv 59 (J. Martin); (1993) 143 NLJ 448 (H. W. Wilkinson).
13 P. 701, post.
14 *Woolley v Colman* (1882) 21 Ch D 169 (sale directed by FRY J who fixed a reserve price sufficient to protect mortgagee).
15 At 422, at 488.
16 See generally Fisher and Lightwood, chapters 21 and 22; (1978) 75 LSG 447; (1979) 129 NLJ 33 (H. E. Markson), 225 (C. M. Pepper); (1981) 260 EG 899 (D. Brahams). On a revival in its popularity as a remedy, see Report of Committee on Enforcement of Judgment Debts 1969 (Cmnd 1309), para 1360; on its rarity, see *Palk v Mortgage Services Funding plc* [1993] 2 WLR 415 at 419, [1993] 2 All ER 481 at 485; and on its commercial use, see *Lloyds and Scottish Trust Ltd v Britten* (1982) 44 P & CR 249.

If the mortgagor does not pay, the court issues what is called an order for *foreclosure nisi*, the effect of which is that the mortgagor loses his property unless he pays upon a certain date (generally six months later) specified by the Master's certificate. The judgment orders that an account shall be taken of what is due to the plaintiff for principal, interest and costs, and directs that if this amount is paid within six months, the mortgage term shall be surrendered to the defendant, but that if default in payment is made, the defendant shall stand absolutely debarred and foreclosed of and from all right, title, interest and equity of redemption in and to the mortgaged premises. The mortgagee then proves in chambers what is due to him for principal, interest and costs, and the Master draws up a certificate of what is due and fixes a day and an hour for repayment (usually six months therefrom). On that day the mortgagee attends, and waits for the mortgagor, and if the latter does not appear, an affidavit is sworn in proof of non-payment either prior to or at the appointed time, and a motion is made for *foreclosure absolute*.

(b) Effect of foreclosure order

The effect of the order absolute is to vest the fee simple absolute (or other whole estate of the mortgagor) in the mortgagee, and to extinguish his mortgage term and all subsequent mortgage terms.[17]

(i) Foreclose down The rights of prior mortgagees are not affected. If there are more mortgagees than one interested in the same land, an order absolute obtained by the first mortgagee forecloses all subsequent incumbrancers, while if (say) the second mortgagee obtains such an order, its effect is to foreclose the third and later mortgagees, but to leave untouched the rights of the first mortgagee. The rule is "foreclose down".[18]

Where there are in this way several mortgagees and the first brings an action for foreclosure, not only the mortgagor, but also each of the subsequent mortgagees must be given an opportunity to redeem, and the ordinary practice is to direct in the order *nisi* that any of the subsequent incumbrancers may repay the amount due to the first man on the date appointed.[19] If subsequent mortgagees are not made parties they are not foreclosed.

(ii) Sale in lieu of foreclosure The court has statutory jurisdiction in a foreclosure action to order a sale instead of a foreclosure on the request of the mortgagee or mortgagor, or of any person interested in the mortgage money or the equity of redemption, notwithstanding the dissent of any other person.[20]

---

17 LPA 1925, ss. 88 (2), 89 (2).
18 From this must be distinguished the maxim "Redeem up, foreclose down". This applies where there are several mortgagees and in a redemption action one of them seeks to redeem a prior mortgage. Thus, if there are five mortgages and the fourth seeks to redeem the second mortgage, he must redeem up i.e. redeem the third as well as the second, and foreclose down, i.e. foreclose the fifth mortgage and the mortgagor. The first mortgage is unaffected. See Waldock, *Law of Mortgages* (2nd edn), p. 337.
19 If subsequent mortgagees request that they may be granted successive periods for repayment, an order to that effect is generally issued: *Platt v Mendel* (1884) 27 Ch D 246.
20 LPA 1925, s. 91 (2); *Silsby v Holliman* [1955] Ch 552, [1955] 2 All ER 373; *Twentieth Century Banking Corpn Ltd v Wilkinson* [1977] Ch 99, [1976] 3 All ER 361. See also *Palk v Mortgage Services Funding plc* [1993] Ch 330, [1993] 2 All ER 481, p. 700, post; *Arab Bank plc v Mercantile Holdings plc* [1994] 2 WLR 307.

(iii) Lapse of time An action for foreclosure is an action to recover land,[1] and must therefore be brought within 12 years from the date upon which the right of recovery accrues.[2] The right accrues at the date fixed for payment of the principal,[3] but there is a fresh accrual, and the 12 years begin to run again, from any payment of principal or interest by the mortgagor or from a written acknowledgment by him of the mortgagee's title.[4]

(c) Revival of equity of redemption

But it must not be thought that a foreclosure absolute irrevocably passes the mortgagor's interest to the mortgagee, although it appears on the surface to do so, for there are certain circumstances in which the foreclosure may be re-opened and the equity of redemption revived. This re-opening takes place if the mortgagee, after obtaining an order absolute, proceeds to sue on the personal covenant,[5] but in addition to this case the court has a discretion to re-open a foreclosure if such relief appears in the special circumstances of the case to be due to the mortgagor. Moreover, the foreclosure may be re-opened against one who has purchased the estate from the mortgagee. It is impossible to lay down a general rule as to when the relief will be granted, for everything turns upon the particular circumstances of each case.

In *Campbell v Holyland*,[6] JESSEL MR enumerated those factors which might influence the court in re-opening the foreclosure: the promptness of the mortgagor's application, his failure to redeem being due to an accident which prevented him from raising the money, the difference between the value of the property and the loan,[7] and any special value which the property had to the parties. Further the court may still re-open the foreclosure, even if the mortgagee has sold the property after the foreclosure absolute; as, for example, where a purchaser bought the property within twenty-four hours after the order and with notice of the fact that it was of much greater value than the amount of the mortgage debt.[8]

(6) FURTHER RIGHTS OF LEGAL MORTGAGEES

(a) Grant and acceptance of surrender of leases

If a mortgagee takes possession of the land with a view to utilizing the profits in satisfaction of the money due to him, he is authorized by statute to grant leases, and to accept surrenders of leases, within the limits made applicable to a mortgagor who is in actual possession.[9] He is also permitted, where the mortgage is made by deed, to cut and sell timber and other trees if they are ripe for cutting and are not planted for shelter or ornament.[10]

---

1 Limitation Act, 1980 s. 20 (4).
2 Ibid., s. 15 (1).
3 *Purnell v Roche* [1927] 2 Ch 142; *Lewis v Plunkett* [1937] Ch 306, [1937] 1 All ER 530.
4 Limitation Act 1980, s. 29; *Harlock v Ashberry* (1882) 19 Ch D 539.
5 *Perry v Barker* (1806) 13 Ves 198; p. 690, ante.
6 (1877) 7 Ch D 166 at 172–5; M & B p. 782.
7 *Lancashire and Yorkshire Reversionary Interest Co Ltd v Crowe* (1970) 114 SJ 435 (foreclosure decree made absolute in respect of mortgage of reversionary interest, and re-opened after the interest fell in possession on death of the tenant for life. The sum due was £3,000, and the fund £6,100).
8 *Campbell v Holyland*, supra.
9 LPA 1925, ss. 99 (2), 100 (2); p. 687, ante.
10 Ibid., s. 101 (1) (iv).

(b) Insurance of the mortgaged property

Where a mortgage is made by deed, the mortgagee has statutory authority to insure the property against loss or damage by fire, and to charge the premiums on the mortgaged property.[11] But the amount of the insurance must not exceed the amount specified in the mortgage deed, or, if no amount is specified, must not exceed two-thirds of the sum it would take to restore the premises in the event of their total destruction. Moreover, the mortgagee does not possess this statutory right where the mortgage deed contains a declaration that no insurance is required, or where an insurance is kept up by the mortgagor according to the mortgage deed, or where that deed contains no provision and the mortgagor himself insures up to the statutory amount.[12] Insurance money, when received, may be applied at the instance of the mortgagee in the discharge of the mortgage debt.[13]

(c) Possession of the title deeds

A legal mortgagee takes a lease or, if he is a chargee, is in the same position as if he had done so, and the ordinary rule is that a leaseholder is not entitled to hold title deeds appertaining to the fee simple of the lessor. But, since the continued possession of the deeds by the mortgagor involves considerable risk to one who has advanced money on the security of the land, it is enacted that a first mortgagee shall have the same right to possession of documents as if his security included the fee simple.[14]

At law the mortgagee becomes the absolute owner of the title deeds, and is therefore under no duty of care in respect of them. He is subject only to pay compensation in equity for their loss on redemption.[15]

(d) Tacking of further advances

We shall see later that a mortgagee who makes a further loan to the mortgagor is allowed, in certain circumstances, to demand that both loans shall be paid out of the land in priority to loans made by other mortgagees, although the latter may have taken their securities before the date of such further loan.[16]

(e) Consolidation

Consolidation is the right of a person who holds two or more mortgages granted by the same mortgagor on different properties to refuse in certain circumstances to be redeemed as to one, unless he is also redeemed as to the other or others.[17]

The mortgages in actual fact are quite separate, having been given on different properties and perhaps at different times, but none the less the mortgagee is allowed in certain cases to consolidate them and treat them as

---

11 LPA 1925, s. 101 (1) (ii).
12 Ibid., s. 108 (1), (2).
13 Ibid., s. 108 (4).
14 Ibid., ss. 85 (1), 86 (1).
15 *Browning v Handiland Group Ltd* (1976) 35 P & CR 345.
16 Pp. 714, 727, post.
17 *Jennings v Jordan* (1881) 6 App Cas 698 at 700; White and Tudor, *Leading Cases in Equity* (9th edn), vol. ii. p. 129. For a criticism of the doctrine, see Waldock, *Law of Mortgages* (2nd edn), pp. 293–5. As to whether the right amounts to a general equitable charge within LCA 1972, s. 2 (4), Class C (iii), see (1948) 92 SJ 736; Wolstenholme and Cherry, vol. 1. p. 189.

one. The right is based upon the doctrine that *he who comes to equity must do equity*; for a mortgagor who is seeking to redeem is in truth asking a favour in the sense that he is petitioning equity for the restoration of his property after the date fixed by the mortgage deed for redemption has passed, and this being so, he must himself be prepared to act equitably.

Suppose, for instance, that:

A has mortgaged Blackacre to B for £10,000 and Whiteacre to B for £10,000. If Blackacre diminishes, while Whiteacre appreciates, in value, it is unethical that A should be allowed to redeem the latter unless he is also prepared to repay the loan of £10,000 on Blackacre. In such a case B can insist that both properties shall be treated as one and redeemed together.

(i) Extension of right This example illustrates the primary meaning and the simplest application of consolidation, but the doctrine has been developed further and extended to cases where the mortgages were originally made to different mortgagees. In such a case if the mortgages ultimately become vested in one person, that is, in one mortgagee, he possesses the right of consolidation.[18] Thus, if:

A mortgages W to B,
A mortgages X and Y to C,
B and C transfer their mortgages to D,

A cannot redeem any one of the properties W, X, Y, unless, if called upon, he pays the amount due on the other two.

But consolidation extends even further than this, and applies to a case where the person who is entitled to redeem is not the original mortgagor, but a transferee of one or more of the equities. There are two different cases to be considered, since the law differs according as the equities of redemption have all become united in one person, or have become separated so that the person claiming to redeem, that is, the person against whom the doctrine of consolidation is invoked, is not the owner of all the equities.

1. *Where all equities transferred to one person* If a person acquires the equities on all the properties, whether as heir, trustee in bankruptcy, purchaser or second mortgagee, the mortgages can in all cases be consolidated against him, even though the mortgage terms did not become vested in one mortgagee until after the person seeking to redeem had obtained the equities.

An illustration may elucidate this statement:[19]

1987 A mortgages U and V to B.
1989 A mortgages W to C.
1990 A mortgages X, Y and Z to D.
1992 A sells the *equities* on U, V, W, X, Y and Z to F.
1994 E acquires all the mortgages from B, C and D.

Here all the mortgages are vested in one person, E, and, although he knew, when he bought out B, C and D, that the equities were not vested in the original mortgagor, he can require F to redeem all the properties or none.

---

18 *Vint v Padgett* (1858) 2 De G & J 611; *Pledge v White* [1896] AC 187; M & B p. 785.
19 *Pledge v White*, supra.

As Lord DAVEY said in *Pledge v White*:[20]

> It appears to me, my Lords, that an assignee of two or more equities of redemption from one mortgagor stands in a widely different position from the assignee of one equity only. He knows, or has the opportunity of knowing, what are the mortgages subject to which he has purchased the property, and he knows they may become united by transfer in one hand. If the doctrine of consolidation be once admitted it appears to me not unreasonable to hold that a person in such a position occupies the place of the mortgagor or assignor to him towards the holders of the mortgages, subject to which he has purchased.

2. *Where equities separated* Turning now to the case where the equities are separated and do not all pass to one person, it will be as well, before stating the general principle, to present an illustration showing how the purchaser of a single equity of redemption may find himself saddled with the burden of redeeming other mortgages of whose very existence he was unaware.

Thus:

> If at different times A mortgages X, Y and Z to B, and then later transfers the fee simple of X to C, who gives full value and knows nothing of the other two properties which have been mortgaged, C, on tendering the amount of the loan due on X, may be unable under the doctrine of consolidation to redeem X unless he also pays what is due on Y and Z.

(ii) Test for application of doctrine Where the mortgage transactions entered into by the original mortgagor are many, and where dealings have taken place both in the equities and in the mortgages, the question whether in any particular case consolidation is enforceable appears at first sight to be both difficult and complicated. But all difficulty disappears if attention is paid to the cardinal rule. This rule covers all cases of separation of equities, and clearly defines the limits within which consolidation is applicable. It may be stated in this way:

> Consolidation is allowed only if, at the date when redemption is sought, all the mortgages, having originally been made by one mortgagor, are vested in one mortgagee and all the equities are vested in one person, or if, *after these two things have once happened, the equities of redemption have become separated.*[1]

If all the mortgages are in one hand and all the equities in another, it is clear that the right of consolidation exists against the mortgagor. It is equally clear that, *once this right has been established in respect of all the properties*, a transferee of one or more of the equities cannot stand in a better position than the mortgagor from whom he took the transfer. The principle of law involved here is that a person who buys an equity of redemption from a mortgagor takes it subject to all liabilities to which it was subject at the time of the sale; one of these is the liability to have certain other mortgages consolidated with it, provided, however, that the consolidation was enforceable against that particular equity *at the time of the purchase*.[2] In the words of Lord SELBORNE:

20 *Pledge v White* [1896] AC 187 at 198; M & B p. 785.
1 Ibid., at 198 per Lord DAVEY.
2 *Cummins v Fletcher* (1880) 14 Ch D 699 at 712; M & B p. 787.

The purchaser of an equity of redemption must take it as it stood at the time of his purchase, subject to all other equities which then affected it in the hands of his vendor, of which the right of the mortgagee to consolidate his charge on that particular property with other charges *then* held by him on other property at the same time redeemable under the same mortgagor was one.[3]

But on no principle of law would it be justifiable to hold the purchaser of an interest bound by equities which were not enforceable against that interest at the time of its sale. It follows from this that the assignee of an equity does not become subject to consolidation in respect of mortgages created *after* the sale to him, nor in respect of mortgages which, though created before that date, became united in one mortgagee afterwards.[4] Suppose, for instance, that the following transactions successively occur:

A mortgages X to B,
A mortgages Y to B,
A sells the equity of redemption in Y to C,
A mortgages Z to B.[5]

When C seeks to redeem his own property Y, he can be compelled by B to redeem X, because, at the time when he bought his equity, the equities on X and Y were vested in one person, and the mortgages were vested in one person. But he cannot be compelled to redeem Z, for the mortgage on it was created only after the sale of the equity on Y to C, so that the right to have Z consolidated with X and Y obviously did not exist at that time.

The holder of an equity of redemption who is compelled under the doctrine of consolidation to redeem some other mortgage steps into the shoes of the mortgagee, and can demand payment from the mortgagor in respect of the mortgage he has had to redeem.

(iii) Mortgages must be by same person No right to consolidation arises if the mortgages were originally made *by* different mortgagors, even though the equities subsequently become united in one hand.[6]

(iv) Reservation of right The right of consolidation does not exist as a matter of course, but only where it is expressly reserved in the various deeds *or in one of them*. When the right is not so reserved, it is enacted that:[7]

A mortgagor seeking to redeem any one mortgage is entitled to do so without paying any money due under any separate mortgage made by him, or by any person through whom he claims, solely on property other than that comprised in the mortgage which he seeks to redeem.

This is a re-enactment of the Conveyancing Act 1881, and it does not apply where all the mortgages were made before 1882. In mortgages made before that date the right of consolidation existed as a matter of course.

B. RIGHTS OF EQUITABLE MORTGAGEES

The remedies of an equitable mortgagee vary according as the security is a mortgage in the strict sense, namely:

3 *Jennings v Jordan* (1881) 6 App Cas 698 at 701.
4 *Harter v Colman* (1882) 19 Ch D 630.
5 *Hughes v Britannia Permanent Benefit Building Society* [1906] 2 Ch 607; M & B p. 787.
6 *Sharp v Rickards* [1909] 1 Ch 109.
7 LPA 1925, s. 93.

a contract to create a legal mortgage,
a deposit of title deeds,
a mortgage of an equitable interest,[8]

or is a mere charge upon property.[9] We will take these two classes separately.

(1) EQUITABLE MORTGAGEE

If the mortgage falls within the first class the general principle is that the remedies available to the lender correspond as nearly as possible with those available to a legal mortgagee.

(a) Foreclosure

Thus the primary remedy of foreclosure applies where a deposit of title deeds with the lender has been accompanied by an agreement by the borrower to give a legal mortgage if required to do so;[10] and the same is true where there has been a deposit without any memorandum, since the law considers that the deposit is evidence of a contract to create a legal mortgage.[11] When such an equitable mortgagee takes foreclosure proceedings to enforce his security, the decree of the court declares that the deposit operated as a mortgage, that in default of payment the mortgagor is trustee of the legal estate for the mortgagee and that he must convey that estate to him.[12]

(b) Sale

The general rule is that foreclosure and not sale is the proper remedy for an equitable mortgagee.[13] But if the mortgage is made in a form which entitles him to require the execution of a mortgage containing a power of sale, he can exercise the statutory power of sale which is given by the Law of Property Act 1925.[14] This statutory power, however, is exercisable only when the mortgage is made by deed, and therefore the proper course is for an equitable mortgagee not to be content with a mere deposit or with a deposit supported by a written memorandum, but to take a memorandum executed as a deed. If this is done he can sell the property subject to the conditions specified by the Act. The memorandum should also give the mortgagee a power of attorney authorizing him, upon exercising the power of sale, to convey the mortgaged property in the name of the mortgagor to the purchaser.[15] This enables the mortgagee, though only an equitable incumbrancer, to convey the legal estate in the property to the purchaser.[16] The same result may be achieved by inserting in the memorandum a declaration of trust, stating that the mortgagor holds the legal estate on trust for the mortgagee and empowering him to appoint someone, including himself, as trustee in place of the mortgagor. The mortgagee can thus vest the legal estate in himself or the purchaser.

8 Pp. 668–71, ante.
9 P. 670, ante.
10 *York Union Banking Co v Artley* (1879) 11 Ch D 205.
11 *Backhouse v Charlton* (1878) 8 Ch D 444; *Carter v Wake* (1877) 4 Ch D 605.
12 *Marshall v Shrewsbury* (1875) 10 Ch App 250 at 254.
13 *James v James* (1873) LR 16 Eq 153.
14 S. 101 (1) (i), p. 695, ante.
15 See Powers of Attorney Act 1971, ss. 4 (1), 5 (3).
16 *Re White Rose Cottage* [1965] Ch 940, [1965] 1 All ER 11; M & B p. 779.

Again, the statutory power of the court to order a sale instead of foreclosure, which we have already noticed, is exercisable in favour of an equitable mortgagee even though he has taken a mere deposit of deeds without a memorandum.[17]

(c) Appointment of receiver

If an equitable mortgage is created by deed, the statutory power of appointing a receiver is available to the mortgagee,[18] but in the absence of a deed the appointment must be made by the court.[19]

(d) Entry into possession

An equitable mortgagee is not entitled to take possession of the land unless the right to do so has been expressly reserved[20] or unless the court makes an order to that effect. Though this is the prevalent view, it has been argued with considerable force that it is justified neither on principle nor on the authorities.[1]

(e) Further rights of equitable mortgagee

An equitable mortgagee can sue the mortgagor personally for recovery of the money lent.

Finally, where an equitable mortgage is created by deposit of title deeds, the mortgagee has the right to retain the deeds under the mortgage until he is paid, but he has no separate legal lien.[2]

(2) EQUITABLE CHARGEE

The second class of equitable security is the charge, which involves no transfer of a legal or equitable interest to the lender, but entitles him to have the debt discharged out of the land. His sole remedies in this respect are to have the charge satisfied by the sale of the land or by the appointment of a receiver under the direction of the court. He has no right to take possession of the land nor may he foreclose. In the words of Lord HATHERLEY:

> Although some of the authorities appear to conflict with each other, it seems, on the whole, to be settled that if there is a charge *simpliciter*, and not a mortgage, or an agreement for a mortgage, then the right of the parties having such a charge is a sale and not foreclosure.[3]

From a mere equitable charge must be distinguished the charge by deed expressed to be by way of legal mortgage introduced by the legislation of 1925, for as we have seen such a chargee has the same remedies as if he held a term of years absolute.[4]

---

17 LPA 1925, s. 91; p. 701, ante.
18 Ibid., s. 101 (1) (ii); p. 694, ante.
19 *Meaden v Sealey* (1849) 6 Hare 620.
20 *Finck v Tranter* [1905] 1 KB 427 at 429; *Barclays Bank Ltd v Bird* [1954] Ch 274 at 280, [1954] 1 All ER 449 at 452.
 1 (1955) 72 LQR 204 (H. W. R. Wade).
 2 *Re Molton Finance Ltd* [1968] Ch 325, [1967] 3 All ER 843. See also *Capital Finance Co Ltd v Stokes* [1969] 1 Ch 261 at 278, [1968] 3 All ER 625, at 629.
 3 *Tennant v Trenchard* (1869) 4 Ch App 537 at 542; *Re Owen* [1894] 3 Ch 220.
 4 P. 667, ante.

SECTION VI PRIORITY OF MORTGAGES[5]

If two or more mortgagees have advanced money on the security of the same land and if the land is of insufficient value when realized to satisfy the claims of all, it is vital to know in what order they are entitled to be paid out of the land. The mortgagor has, let us say, granted separate and successive mortgages on Blackacre to A, B, C and D. Owing to unforeseen circumstances Blackacre has depreciated in value and its sale will produce sufficient money to repay only one or perhaps two of the mortgagees the amount of their advances. This does not mean that mortgagees who fail to get satisfaction out of the land are remediless, for they can of course sue the mortgagor on his personal covenant, but since his other property may be of little value it will be their object to proceed against the land if the law allows them to do so. A knowledge of the former rules that governed this matter, although they are substantially affected by the legislation of 1925, is essential to an understanding of the modern law on this subject; and, as we shall see, there are situations in which they may still be applicable.[6]

The rules for the priority of mortgages, both before 1926 and after 1925, are subject to variation by the mortgagees without the mortgagor's consent, unless the mortgages otherwise provide.[7]

A. PRIORITY OF MORTGAGES BEFORE 1926

(1) THE PRIORITY OF THE LEGAL MORTGAGEE OF LAND

To understand the order in which mortgages ranked for repayment out of the land before 1926 we must recall that under the practice then prevailing it was usual in the case of a mortgage of the fee simple to convey the legal estate in fee simple to the mortgagee. There might be several mortgages of Blackacre, but there could be only one *legal* mortgage, and all the others, whether created before or after the *legal* mortgage, were necessarily equitable in nature.

(a) Where equities are equal the law prevails

The fundamental rule before 1926, based upon the maxim "where the equities are equal the law prevails", was that the mortgagee who held the legal estate ranked, for the purpose of obtaining satisfaction out of the land, before all other mortgagees of whose securities he had no notice at the time when he made his advance.[8] Equity respected the legal title, and it was a rule without exception that a court of equity took away from a purchaser for value without notice nothing that he had honestly acquired.[9] Lord HARDWICKE said:

> As courts of equity break in upon the common law, where necessity and conscience require it, still they allow superior force and strength to a legal title to estates; and therefore where there is a legal title and equity on one side, this court never thought

5 See generally Fisher and Lightwood (10th edn), chapter 24, and for a closely reasoned study [1940] CLJ 243 (R. E. Megarry); Waldock, *Law of Mortgages* (2nd edn), pp. 381–435.
6 Pp. 719 et seq, post.
7 *Cheah Theam Swee v Equiticorp Finance Group Ltd* [1992] 1 AC 472, [1991] 4 All ER 989.
8 *Plumb v Fluitt* (1791) 2 Anst 432.
9 *Health v Crealock* (1874) 10 Ch App 22 at 33.

fit that by reason of a prior equity against a man, who had a legal title, that man should be hurt, and this by reason of that force this court necessarily and rightly allows to the common law and to legal titles.[10]

If therefore a mortgagor granted an equitable mortgage to A and later conveyed the legal estate to B by way of mortgage, the latter had the better right to the land provided that, when he made his own advance, he had no notice of the earlier mortgage to A. The onus lay on him to prove this affirmatively.[11] B, the legal mortgagee, had an even stronger case against mortgagees who obtained their securities at a date *later* than his own, for not only did he alone hold the legal title, but having acquired it first in order of time he could invoke the maxim *qui prior est tempore potior est jure*.

This rule giving priority to the legal mortgagee, however, applied only where the equities were equal, i.e. where the legal mortgagee had as good a moral right as the equitable mortgagees, and in the following cases he was displaced in favour of equitable mortgagees.

(b) Cases where equities are not equal

(i) Where legal mortgagee had notice of earlier mortgage If, at the time when he advanced his money, the legal mortgagee had actual or constructive notice of an earlier incumbrance, he was postponed to the earlier incumbrancer. A legal mortgagee who failed to investigate his mortgagor's title according to the usual practice or who abstained from investigation altogether, was affected with notice of, and therefore postponed to, any earlier mortgage that he would have discovered had he followed the customary practice.[12]

(ii) Where legal mortgagee was negligent with regard to title deeds The obvious duty of a person who acquires a legal estate is to obtain and to keep possession of the title deeds, or, if for some reason this is impossible, to make inquiries for them. Title deeds are the symbol of ownership, and if they are not produced by a mortgagor the suspicion naturally arises that they have been utilized by him in order to vest some right in a third person, and that he is deliberately concealing this transaction from the mortgagee.

There are two indiscretions in this connection that a mortgagee may commit, namely, failure to obtain the deeds at the time of the transaction, and failure to retain deeds of which he has once had possession.

(a) Postponement owing to failure to obtain deeds It was well established before 1926 that a legal mortgagee who made no inquiries whatever for the deeds must be postponed to a prior equitable incumbrancer who had already secured them, and even to a later innocent incumbrancer who was more diligent in getting them into his custody.[13] On the other hand, if he made inquiry and yet failed to obtain them, it depended upon the circumstances whether he was postponed to an earlier equitable incumbrancer in whose possession they were. Postponement was not an automatic result of failure to obtain possession, for it was always held that in addition there must have been some degree of negligence. The cases show a growing severity against the legal mortgagee. At first it was laid down that he must not be postponed unless he had been guilty of fraud in the transaction under which he acquired

10 *Wortley v Birkhead* (1754) 2 Ves Sen 571 at 574.
11 *A-G v Biphosphated Guano Co* (1879) 11 Ch D 327.
12 *Berwick & Co v Price* [1905] 1 Ch 632.
13 *Walker v Linom* [1907] 2 Ch 104; M & B p. 796.

the legal estate, or unless he had shown such wilful negligence as to indicate complicity in the fraud.[14] But a new rule more favourable to an earlier equitable mortgagee was pronounced by the Court of Appeal in 1899 in the case of *Oliver v Hinton*.[15] This may be stated in the words of LINDLEY LJ:

> To deprive a purchaser for value[16] without notice of a prior incumbrance of the protection of the legal estate it is not, in my opinion, essential that he should have been guilty of fraud; it is sufficient that he has been guilty of such gross negligence as would render it unjust to deprive the prior incumbrancer of his priority.[17]

The case related to a purchaser of a legal estate, but the result would have been the same had the person who acquired the legal estate been a mortgagee. The facts were as follows:

> A, the owner of the legal estate, deposited the title deeds with X as security for advances to the value of £400 made by the latter. Some two years later A conveyed the legal estate to the purchaser, P, in consideration of £320. P inquired about the deeds, but was told that they could not be delivered as they related also to some other property. This answer was accepted, and A was not even asked to produce the deeds for inspection. It was held that P, though entirely innocent of fraud or of any complicity in fraud, must be postponed to X.

Epithets such as "gross" are unreliable guides, and the rule as stated by the Court of Appeal left open in each case the question whether the requisite degree of negligence had been shown, but the expression "gross negligence" was described in a later case as meaning something more than mere carelessness. EVE J said:[18]

> It must at least be carelessness of so aggravated a nature as to amount to the neglect of precautions which the ordinary reasonable man would have observed and to indicate an attitude of mental indifference to obvious risks.

1. *Postponement to earlier incumbrancers* If, therefore, a mortgagee had inquired for the title deeds and had been given a reasonable excuse for their non-delivery, he would not be postponed to an earlier equitable mortgage. An extreme case is, perhaps, *Hewitt v Loosemore*,[19] where the defendant, who had taken a legal mortgage of a leasehold interest from a solicitor by way of assignment, failed to obtain possession of the lease, which, as a matter of fact, had already been deposited with the plaintiff. Part of the answer made by the defendant to the bill which the plaintiff brought against him was as follows:

> The defendant . . . was a farmer and unacquainted with legal forms; but upon the said indenture of assignment being handed to him as aforesaid, he inquired of [the mortgagor] whether the lease of the premises ought not to be delivered to him as

---

14 *Hunt v Elmes* (1860) 2 De G F & J 578; *Ratcliffe v Barnard* (1871) 6 Ch App 652; see *Hudston v Viney* [1921] 1 Ch 98 at 103–4; *Northern Counties of England Fire Insurance Co v Whipp* (1884) 26 Ch D 482; M & B p. 792.
15 [1899] 2 Ch 264; M & B p. 791.
16 This includes a mortgagee.
17 It would have been simpler to apply the doctrine of the bona fide purchaser for value without notice and to postpone the later legal mortgagee unless he satisfies that test. See ROMER J at first instance in *Oliver v Hinton* [1899] 2 Ch 264 at 268; and PARKER J in *Walker v Linom* [1907] 2 Ch 104 at 114; M & B p. 796.
18 *Hudston v Viney* [1921] 1 Ch 98 at 104.
19 (1851) 9 Hare 449; M & B p. 790. See also *Agra Bank Ltd v Barry* (1874) LR 7 HL 135.

well; when [the mortgagor] replied that it should, but that, as he was rather busy then, he would look for it and give it to the defendant when he next came to market.

It was held that in the circumstances the plaintiff had failed to make out a sufficient case for postponing the defendant.

2. *Postponement to later incumbrancers* Likewise failure to obtain the deeds might entail postponement of a legal mortgagee to a *later* equitable incumbrancer. Again, however, nothing short of gross negligence was sufficient to produce this result. Thus in *Grierson v National Provincial Bank of England Ltd*:[20]

A mortgagor, having already deposited the deeds with a bank as security for a loan, executed a legal mortgage in favour of the plaintiff. The plaintiff had actual notice of this earlier equitable mortgage, but he neither informed the bank of his legal mortgage, nor instructed them to deliver the deeds to him should the mortgagor repay their loan. The mortgagor later paid off the bank, obtained the deeds and deposited them with the defendant as security for an advance. The defendant was ignorant of the plaintiff's legal mortgage.

It was held that the plaintiff had not been sufficiently negligent to justify his postponement to the defendant.

(b) Postponement due to subsequent negligence It was also the case before 1926 that the conduct of the legal mortgagee in dealing with the title deeds *after* he had obtained them might be such as to justify his postponement to subsequent equitable mortgagees.

In the first place the principle of *Oliver v Hinton* applied, and any conduct on the part of the legal mortgagee in relation to the deeds which would have made it inequitable for him to claim priority over an earlier equitable mortgagee was sufficient to postpone him to a subsequent mortgage the creation of which was due entirely to his own conduct.[1] There need not have been fraudulent conduct, but there must have been gross negligence. Thus in a leading case[2] the priority of the legal mortgagee was not displaced where:

A company took a legal mortgage from its manager, and the manager, having stolen the deeds from a safe to which he had access, used them to create another mortgage in favour of an innocent person.

The following remarks were passed by the court upon the arguments that had been advanced in favour of postponement:

The case was argued as if the legal owner of land owed a duty to all other of Her Majesty's subjects to keep his title deeds secure; as if title deeds were in the eye of the law analogous to fierce dogs or destructive elements, where from the nature of the thing the courts have implied a general duty of safe custody.[3]

In the second place a legal mortgagee was postponed if he constituted the mortgagor his agent with authority to raise more money on the security of the land. This postponement occurred for instance where the mortgagor, having been entrusted with the deeds for the purpose of obtaining a further loan of a given amount, procured one of a greater amount without disclosing

20 [1913] 2 Ch 18.
 1 *Walker v Linom* [1907] 2 Ch 104 at 114; *Northern Counties of England Fire Insurance Co v Whipp*, supra. Cf *Re King's Settlement* [1931] 2 Ch 294.
 2 *Northern Counties of England Fire Insurance Co v Whipp*, supra.
 3 Ibid., at 493.

to the lender the existence of the first mortgage. In such a case the legal mortgagee was postponed on the ground that, having enabled the mortgagor to represent himself as unincumbered owner, he was estopped from asserting that the actual authority had been exceeded.[4]

(2) PRIORITY AS BETWEEN EQUITABLE MORTGAGEES OF LAND

(a) First made, first paid

Where the legal estate was outstanding and a conflict arose between incumbrancers who all held equitable mortgages, the rule was that the several mortgagees must be paid according to their priority of time, *qui prior est tempore potior est jure*.[5]

If, therefore, a mortgagor subjected his land to equitable charges first in favour of A and then in favour of B, or if, after granting a legal mortgage to X, he made subsequent equitable mortgages first to A and then to B, A had the prior right as against B to receive payment out of the land. He had a better and superior equity because it was an earlier equity. This rule was based upon the principle that:

An owner of property, dealing honestly with it, cannot confer upon another a greater interest in that property than he himself has.[6]

All that the mortgagor had to dispose of when he had once made a legal mortgage was the equitable interest, and it had long been the rule that:

Every conveyance of an equitable interest is an innocent conveyance, that is to say, the grant of a person entitled merely in equity passes only that which he is justly entitled to, and no more.[7]

(b) Exceptions

The rule that priority of time gave the better right to payment might, however, be excluded in two cases:

First, where the equities were in other respects not equal.
Secondly, where the doctrine of tacking operated.

(i) Where equities are not equal. Negligence of prior mortgagee In a contest between equitable claimants, the court had to be satisfied that the party with the earlier equity had acted in such a way as to justify his retention of priority over the later incumbrancer.[8] Thus, he lost the protection that was normally due to him if his negligent failure to obtain or to retain the title deeds had misled the later mortgagee into believing that no earlier equity existed. The question as to what degree of negligence sufficed to produce this result scarcely admits of a dogmatic answer, for the judges expressed varying opinions, and one view was that the priority of an equitable mortgage was

---

4 *Perry Herrick v Attwood* (1857) 2 De G & J 21; M & B p. 794; *Northern Counties of England Fire Insurance Co v Whipp*, supra, at 493; *Brocklesby v Temperance Permanent Building Society* [1895] AC 173.
5 *Brace v Duchess of Marlborough* (1728) 2 P Wms 491 at 495; *Willoughby v Willoughby* (1756) 1 Term Rep 763.
6 *West v Williams* [1899] 1 Ch 132 at 143, per LINDLEY MR.
7 *Phillips v Phillips* (1861) 4 De GF & J 208 at 215, per Lord WESTBURY.
8 *National Provincial Bank of England v Jackson* (1886) 33 Ch D 1 at 13, per COTTON LJ.

more easily displaced than that of a legal mortgage.[9] No decision has been found, however, in which the negligence held sufficient to postpone an equitable mortgagee would not also have defeated a legal mortgagee.[10] In the case before 1926 of a legal mortgage to A, followed by equitable mortgages to B and C, the question could arise only exceptionally, since A would normally hold the deeds, but it would arise in an acute form if the only transactions effected by the mortgagor were of an equitable nature. In this connection two rules at least were definitely established.

1. *Failure to obtain deeds* First, if an incumbrancer was entitled to have the deeds as part of his security but did not insist upon his right, he was postponed to a later equitable incumbrancer who obtained them without notice of the earlier equity. This occurred in *Farrand v Yorkshire Banking Co*,[11] where the facts were these:

> The mortgagor agreed to deposit the deeds relating to the mortgaged property with A, but the deposit was never made. A year later he handed the deeds to a bank with which he had made a similar agreement.

It was held that A must be postponed, for it was entirely due to his inactivity that the bank had been defrauded into advancing a second loan.

2. *Failure to retain deeds* Secondly, if an equitable incumbrancer obtained the deeds but later delivered them to the mortgagor, he was postponed to a later lender to whom they had been delivered as security.[12]

> It is an elementary principle that a party coming into equity in such a case is bound to show that he has not been guilty of such a degree of neglect as to enable another party so to deal with that which was the plaintiff's right, as to induce an innocent party to assume that he was dealing with his own.[13]

(ii) Tacking The general rule that equitable mortgagees ranked for payment according to the dates at which they took their mortgages was also liable to be displaced by the operation of the doctrine of tacking, or "the creditor's *tabula in naufragio*" ("the plank in the shipwreck").[14] This doctrine, which is founded on technical and justly suspected reasoning, is an example of the superiority attached by courts of law and of equity to the legal estate. Equitable owners who were equally meritorious in regard to honesty of dealing might compete for the legal estate, and the one who succeeded in obtaining it won the right to rank before an earlier equitable mortgagee despite the maxim *qui prior est tempore potior est jure*. The reason was that, having obtained the legal estate, he could take advantage of that other and more potent maxim "where equities are equal, the legal title prevails".[15]

There were two distinct branches of tacking before 1926, and we must consider these separately.

1. *Where equitable mortgagee acquired legal estate* The first form consisted of joining an equitable mortgage to the legal mortgage in order to squeeze out and gain priority over an intermediate mortgage. If a legal mortgage to A

---

9 *Taylor v Russell* [1891] 1 Ch 8 at 17; affd [1892] AC 244 at 262.
10 See the discussion in Waldock, *Law of Mortgages* (2nd edn), pp. 397–8.
11 (1888) 40 Ch D 182.
12 *Waldron v Sloper* (1852) 1 Drew 193.
13 Ibid. at 200, per KINDERSLEY V-C.
14 *Brace v Duchess of Marlborough* (1728) 2 P Wms 491.
15 *Bailey v Barnes* [1894] 1 Ch 25 at 36, per LINDLEY LJ.

was followed by equitable mortgages first to B and secondly to C, then C would gain priority of payment over B if he paid off A and took a conveyance of his legal estate. C now had the prior right to recover from the land not only the amount which A had advanced on the first mortgage, but also the amount which C himself had advanced to the mortgagor. But he could not tack his own advance to the legal estate and squeeze out B unless he had an equal equity with B; and the equities were not equal unless, *at the time when he made his advance*, he was without notice that B had made an earlier advance.

2. *Where legal mortgagee made further advance* The second form of tacking was available only to a *legal* mortgagee who had made a further advance. It was not available to equitable mortgagees before 1926. If a legal mortgagee, subsequently to his original loan, made a further advance to the mortgagor without at that time having notice of equitable mortgages created after the legal mortgage, he could, by virtue of his ownership of the legal estate, tack the second to the first advance and recover the whole amount due to him in priority to all other incumbrancers.[16]

If, for instance:

The mortgagor made a legal mortgage to A for £2,000, a second mortgage to B, a third mortgage to C, and then a further mortgage to A for £500, A was entitled to be paid £2,500 out of the land before B and C received anything.

But this right did not avail the legal mortgagee if, at the time when he made his further advance, he knew that other persons had already lent money on the security of the land. Thus in *Freeman v Laing*:[17]

Three trustees advanced money jointly on a legal mortgage of land and subsequently made a further advance. At the time of this second advance one alone of the trustees had notice of an intermediate mortgage. It was held that the successors in title of the trustees could not tack the second loan to the first, for since each of them was individually entitled to the entire security, notice to one was notice to all.

An important application of this rule, that notice excluded the right to tack, occurred where land was mortgaged by way of security not only for the original loan, but also for such future advances as might be made. A mortgagee likes to know that he can have recourse to the land in respect of any money he may advance later, and when such further loans are contemplated it has always been customary to provide expressly in the deed that they, equally with the original loan, shall be secured by the land. But it was laid down in *Hopkinson v Rolt*[18] that, notwithstanding such an express provision, the right to tack was excluded by notice of other incumbrances. This principle was carried further by the case of *West v Williams*[19] and made applicable where the legal mortgagee had not (as in *Hopkinson v Rolt*) taken security merely for such further advances as he might *voluntarily* make, but had entered into a binding covenant to make further advances upon the security of the land, if called upon to do so. The fact that he was under a contractual obligation to increase his original loan did not entitle him to

16 *Brace v Duchess of Marlborough*, supra.
17 [1899] 2 Ch 355.
18 (1861) 9 HL Cas 514.
19 [1899] 1 Ch 132.

priority in respect of a further advance made with notice of a later incumbrance.

The doctrine of tacking was abolished in 1874 by the Vendor and Purchaser Act, but as this prejudiced the ability of mortgagors to obtain further advances from first mortgagees, it was restored by the Land Transfer Act of 1875.

(3) PRIORITY BETWEEN ASSIGNEES AND MORTGAGEES OF AN EQUITABLE INTEREST IN PURE PERSONALTY

(a) The rule in *Dearle v Hall*

Priority between mortgagees of pure personalty has been governed since 1823 by the rule in *Dearle v Hall*.[20] This rule, which is of greater importance now than formerly because of its extension by the Law of Property Act 1925, applied whenever successive mortgages or assignments were made of an equitable interest in pure personalty, as distinct from an interest, whether legal or equitable, in freeholds or leaseholds. To make the rule applicable, the mortgagor or assignor must have had an equitable interest in a debt or fund and he must have made two or more successive assignments of that subject matter in favour of different persons.[1] It is chiefly remarkable as being a departure from the fundamental principle that equities are entitled to rank according to the order of time in which they have been created.

The rule laid down that as between mortgagees or assignees of an equitable interest in pure personalty (i.e. excluding leaseholds, but including an interest under a trust for sale[2]) priority depended upon the order in which notice of the mortgages or assignments was received[3] by the legal owner of the personalty (i.e. in most cases by the trustees). However, a later mortgagee or assignee, who had actual or constructive notice of a prior mortgage or assignment at the time when he lent his money, could not gain priority by giving notice first.[4] The head-note to the report of *Dearle v Hall* makes the general position clear:

> A person having a beneficial interest in a sum of money invested in the names of trustees, assigns it for valuable consideration to A, but no notice of the assignment is given to the trustees; afterwards, the same person proposes to sell his interest to B, and B, having made inquiry of the trustees as to the nature of the vendor's title, and the amount of his interest, and receiving no intimation of the existence of any prior incumbrance, completes the purchase, and gives the trustees notice: B has a better equity than A to the possession of the fund, and the assignment to B, though posterior in date, is to be preferred to the assignment to A.

Thus in equitable mortgages of personalty notice to the trustees supplants order of time as the determining factor in the question of priorities.

---

20 (1823) 3 Russ 1; M & B p. 798; *E Pfeiffer Weinkellerei-Weineinkauf GmbH & Co v Arbuthnot Factors Ltd* [1988] 1 WLR 150; *Rhodes v Allied Dunbar Pension Services Ltd* [1987] 1 WLR 1703, [1988] 1 All ER 524; (1989) 9 OJLS 513 (F. Oditah); *Compaq Computer Ltd v Abercorn Group Ltd* [1991] BCC 484; [1992] CLJ 19 (L. S. Sealy).
1 *B S Lyle v Rosher* [1959] 1 WLR 8 at 16, 19, [1958] 3 All ER 597 at 603, 605.
2 *Lee v Howlett* (1856) 2 K & J 531; p. 718, post.
3 *Calisher v Forbes* (1871) 7 Ch App 109.
4 *Spencer v Clarke* (1878) 9 Ch D 137; *Re Holmes* (1885) 29 Ch D 786.

(b) Principle of rule

Although the principle upon which *Dearle v Hall* was decided has been obscured by later cases, it would appear to be simply this, that in order to perfect his title a mortgagee of equitable personalty must do that which in equity is the nearest approach to the delivery of a personal chattel.[5] PLUMER MR explained this as follows:[6]

> They say that they were not bound to give notice to the trustees, for that notice does not form part of the necessary conveyance of an equitable interest. I admit, that, if you mean to rely on contract with the individual, you do not need to give notice; from the moment of the contract, he, with whom you are dealing, is personally bound. But if you mean to go further, and to make your right attach upon the thing which is the subject of the contract, it is necessary to give notice; and, unless notice is given, you do not do that which is essential in all cases of transfer of personal property. The law of England has always been, that personal property passes by delivery of possession; and it is possession which determines the apparent ownership. If, therefore, an individual, who in the way of purchase or mortgage contracts with another for the transfer of his interest, does not divest the vendor or mortgagor of possession, but permits him to remain the ostensible owner as before, he must take the consequences which may ensue from such a mode of dealing.

(c) Rule extended by judicial interpretation

It is in fact the duty of an assignee or mortgagee to affect the conscience of the trustees, for by doing so he acquires a better equity than a prior mortgagee who has failed to act likewise, and where one of two innocent parties must suffer through the fraud of the mortgagor, it certainly should not be the one who has done all in his power to prevent any fraudulent dealing. But this consideration was lost sight of in later years, and instead of the principle being that priority should depend upon the diligence of the claimants in perfecting their title, it was gradually made dependent upon the bare fact of notice, it being held that it was immaterial whether notice was given with the deliberate intention of completing the title or whether it was purely informal or even accidental.[7] The following will serve to illustrate this fact and, at the same time, to state the main rules that have grown up in the application of *Dearle v Hall*.

(i) Notice may be informal It is not necessary, in order to gain priority, that a mortgagee should give express notice to the trustees with the intention of doing all that is possible to perfect his title. In fact it is not necessary that *he* should give notice at all, provided that the trustees have notice. It is enough if he can prove that the mind of the trustee has in some way been brought to an intelligent apprehension of the existence of the incumbrance, so that a reasonable man or an ordinary man of business would regulate his conduct by that knowledge in the execution of the trust.[8] Thus, notice which a trustee obtained from reading a newspaper has been held to be sufficient,[9] and in a later case it was held that where a trustee *before* his appointment acquired

---

5 *Meux v Bell* (1841) 1 Hare 73 at 85; *Foster v Cockerell* (1835) 3 Cl & Fin 456 at 476; but see Lord MACNAGHTEN in *Ward v Duncombe* [1893] AC 369 at 392–3.
6 *Dearle v Hall* (1823) 3 Russ 1 at 22.
7 See (1895) 11 LQR 337 (E. C. C. Firth).
8 *Lloyd v Banks* (1868) 3 Ch App 488 at 490, per Lord CAIRNS.
9 *Lloyd v Banks*, supra.

knowledge of an incumbrance on the trust estate in such a way that when
appointed he would normally act on the information, the priority thereby
attached to the incumbrance was not displaced by an express formal notice
given after his appointment by another incumbrancer.[10]

(ii) Effect of notice not given to *all* trustees The course which a diligent
mortgagee should pursue is to give notice to each trustee, for a failure to do
so may cause his postponement to a later mortgagee who has been more
careful. The two principles relevant to the situation are, first, that a notice
given to one alone of several trustees is effective against later mortgages
created while that one trustee remains in office, but is ineffective against
mortgages created after he vacates office;[11] secondly, that a notice to all
existing trustees remains effective even after they have vacated office. The
result may be appreciated from three examples.

1. A, B and C are the trustees. Mortgagee, X, notifies A only. A later
   mortgagee, Y, notifies A, B and C. A dies.
   ` X ranks before Y, for when Y took his mortgage X's notice to A was
   still effective.[12]
2. A, B and C are the trustees. Mortgagee, X, notifies A only. A dies. A
   later mortgagee, Y, notifies B and C.
   Y ranks before X, since the effectiveness of X's notice ceased with the
   death of the one person to whom he gave it.[13]
3. A, B and C are the trustees. Mortgagee, X, notifies A, B and C. A, B and
   C retire in favour of D, E and F, who are not informed of X's mortgage.
   A later mortgagee, Y, notifies D, E and F.
   X ranks before Y.[14]

(d) Limits of rule

We must finally observe that before 1926 the rule in *Dearle v Hall* was
restricted to the assignment of choses in action, of which an equitable interest
in pure personalty is an example, and to assignments of such interests in real
estate as could reach the hands of the assignor only in the shape of money, as
for instance a beneficial interest given to him by a trust for sale.[15] The rule
did not apply to mortgages or assignments of equitable interests in *land*,
whether freehold or leasehold. Thus in a case where:

> a testator, having bequeathed a leasehold interest to trustees, charged it with the
> payment of an annuity of £45 to his daughter, and the daughter mortgaged the
> annuity first to A and then to B, it was held that A had the prior claim against the
> land, although B alone had given notice to the trustees.[16]

Having thus reviewed the rules which obtained before the legislation of
1925, we are in a position to examine the existing law governing the priorities
between mortgages in general.

10 *Ipswich Permanent Money Club Ltd v Arthy* [1920] 2 Ch 257.
11 *Smith v Smith* (1833) 2 Cr & M 231.
12 *Ward v Duncombe* [1893] AC 369.
13 *Timson v Ramsbottom* (1837) 2 Keen 35; *Re Phillip's Trusts* [1903] 1 Ch 183.
14 *Re Wasdale* [1899] 1 Ch 163.
15 *Lee v Howlett* (1856) 2 K & J 531; *Re Wasdale*, supra; *Ward v Duncombe*, supra.
16 *Wiltshire v Rabbits* (1844) 14 Sim 76.

B. PRIORITY OF MORTGAGES AFTER 1925

The Law of Property Act 1925 and the Land Charges Act 1925[17] introduced a new system for the determination of priorities. The apparent design of this is to fix the priority of a mortgage according to the time of its creation, provided that the mortgagee has taken steps to render the completion of the transaction easily ascertainable by persons who later have dealings with the mortgagor.[18] There are three ways of doing this which vary with the circumstances.

First, by obtaining possession of the title deeds. This will put a later mortgagee upon inquiry and will normally affect him with notice of the earlier incumbrance.

Secondly, if possession of the deeds is unobtainable and if the property given as security is a *legal* estate, by recording the mortgage, whether legal or equitable, in a public register.

Thirdly, if the property given as security is an *equitable* interest in land or pure personalty, by notifying the mortgage to the owner of the legal interest, thereby putting it on record.

Such is the design in outline, but it is not fully worked out by the Acts and we shall see that certain doubts and complexities remain. The paucity of litigation on priorities may suggest that the new system has worked reasonably well, but that may be due more to the considerable rise in the value of land than to the merits of the system.

The modern rules vary not with the nature of the mortgage as under the pre-1926 law, but with the nature of the mortgaged property, and we must therefore consider:

first, legal and equitable mortgages of a *legal estate*; and
secondly, mortgages of an *equitable interest*, whether in land or in personalty.

(1) PRIORITY AS BETWEEN LEGAL AND EQUITABLE MORTGAGEES OF A LEGAL ESTATE

We have seen that before 1926 a legal mortgagee who had not been guilty of gross negligence in respect of the title deeds enjoyed priority over the other mortgagees (necessarily equitable) of the same land of which he had no notice. It is obvious that the introduction of the new method of creating mortgages, under which there may be several *legal* mortgages and not one only as before 1926, precluded the retention of the old rule that the legal estate as such gave priority. Some substitute had to be found. The other rule of the pre-1926 law, that equitable mortgages ranked according to the order of their creation, could scarcely be made universally applicable, since it would render it difficult for a mortgagee to ascertain by inquiry the true state of the mortgagor's commitments. The Acts of 1925, therefore, attempted to introduce a new scheme, the motif of which apparently was that priorities should depend upon the order of registration, though whether in the actual result registration is as important as it was intended to be is, perhaps, a little doubtful.

17 Now replaced by LCA 1972.
18 Waldock, *Law of Mortgages* (2nd edn), pp. 409–10.

(a) Statutory provisions

It is necessary to set out the relevant statutory provisions in order that the matter may be viewed in the right perspective.

(i) Law of Property Act 1925 The Law of Property Act 1925, section 97, provides as follows:

> Every mortgage affecting a legal estate in land made after the commencement of this Act, whether legal or equitable (not being a mortgage protected by the deposit of documents relating to the legal estate affected) shall rank according to its date of registration as a land charge pursuant to the Land Charges Act, 1925.[19]

The same statute, in section 198 (1), provides that registration shall constitute notice:

> The registration of any instrument or matter under the Land Charges Act 1972 or any local land charges register shall be deemed to constitute actual notice of such instrument or matter, and of the fact of such registration, to all persons and for all purposes connected with the land affected, as from the date of registration or other prescribed date and so long as the registration continues in force.[20]

(ii) Land Charges Act 1972. Registrable mortgages The Land Charges Act 1972 contains two relevant sections. Section 2 (4)[1] specifies the two kinds of mortgages that are registrable,[2] namely:

> "Puisne mortgages", i.e. a *legal* mortgage which is not protected by a deposit of documents relating to the legal estate affected (Class C (i)).
> "General equitable charges", i.e. any equitable charge which is not secured by a deposit of documents relating to the legal estate affected, does not arise, or affect an interest arising, under a trust for sale or a settlement, and is not included in any other class of land charge (Class C (iii)).

The Land Charges Act 1972 finally states what the effect shall be of a failure to register. Section 4 (5)[3] provides that a Class C land charge created or arising after 1925 shall:

> be void as against a purchaser of the land charged with it, or of any interest in such land, unless the land charge is registered in the appropriate register before the completion of the purchase.

Section 17 (1) defines "purchaser" as:

> any person (including a mortgagee or lessee) who, for valuable consideration, takes any interest in land or in a charge on land.

A mortgagee does not pay the amount of the loan until the transaction has been completed by the execution of the deed. There is, therefore, a danger that after X, a mortgagee, has searched the register, another mortgage of the same land may have been registered in favour of Y, the effect of which will be to render X's mortgage at the moment of its completion void against Y. X

---

19 Or LCA 1972. See LCA 1972, s. 18 (6).
20 As amended by Local Land Charges Act 1975, s. 17, Sch. 1.
 1 S. 2 (4), Class C (i), (iii), replacing LCA 1925, s. 10 (1).
 2 For registration of charges created by companies, see p. 768, post.
 3 Replacing LCA 1925, s. 13 (2). See *Midland Bank Trust Co Ltd v Green* [1981] AC 513, [1981] 1 All ER 153; p. 766, post.

is, therefore, allowed to protect himself by registering a *priority notice*, giving notice of his contemplated mortgage.[4]

(b) Mortgage accompanied by deeds is not registrable

One outstanding feature, then, of this legislation is that no mortgage, legal or equitable, under which the mortgagee obtains the title deeds, is capable of registration. The principal reason for this exclusion is to avoid the inconvenience that would arise if the efficacy of temporary advances that are so frequently made against a deposit of deeds were to be affected by a failure to register. Section 2 of the Land Charges Act 1972, however, provides that an estate contract shall be registrable as a land charge Class C (iv). An estate contract is a contract by an estate owner to convey or create a legal estate. The normal example is a contract for the sale of a legal fee simple or for the grant of a term of years absolute, but it also includes a contract to create a legal mortgage, i.e. to grant a mortgage term. Further, it would seem to include the equitable mortgage that arises from a deposit of title deeds, for as we have already seen the deposit constitutes an implicit agreement to create a legal mortgage. It has therefore been suggested that an express agreement, accompanied by the title deeds, to create a legal mortgage, and a deposit of title deeds by way of security, are registrable as estate contracts, in spite of the fact that because accompanied by the deeds they are excluded from registration by the paragraph which deals specifically with mortgages.[5] It is submitted, however, that the correctness of this view is at least doubtful. If the sub-section which explicitly defines what mortgages shall be registrable deliberately excludes those that are accompanied by a deposit of documents, it seems inconsistent to permit their registration in their other capacity as estate contracts. The result of doing so would be to render void against a subsequent incumbrancer an unregistered mortgage to which the sub-section concerned with mortgages denies the possibility of registration. Moreover, to put this construction upon the statute would prejudice the commercial practice by which deeds are deposited with bankers to secure a temporary loan, for the result of invalidating against later lenders an arrangement that is often only transient would be to discourage a convenient business transaction. The question can scarcely be answered with assurance until it has come before the courts, and meanwhile the following account is based on the assumption that a mortgage accompanied by a deposit of the deeds is not registrable.

(c) Priorities where no mortgagee obtains deeds

The question of priorities seems comparatively simple to determine against the legislative background if we confine ourselves to a series of mortgage transactions *none of which is accompanied by a delivery of the title deeds*. It depends upon a combination of section 97 of the Law of Property Act 1925 and section 4 (5) of the Land Charges Act 1972, but it would appear that the latter is the dominating enactment. The decisive factor, in other words, is

---

4 LCA 1972, s. 11; for details, see p. 763, post.
5 (1940) CLJ pp. 250–1 (R. E. Megarry); (1962) 26 Conv (NS) pp. 446–449 (R. G. Rowley). Williams, *Contract of Sale of Land*, p. 247; Fairest, *Mortgages* (2nd edn), pp. 133–6; Fisher and Lightwood, *Law of Mortgages* (10th edn), p. 72; Waldock, pp. 425–8. Such mortgages created after 26 September 1989 may be *sui generis*, p. 670, ante.

that a registrable mortgage is void against a later mortgage unless it is registered before completion of the latter transaction.[6] Suppose that:

A takes a mortgage without the title deeds on 1 May.
B takes a mortgage without the title deeds on 10 May.
A registers on 11 May.
B registers on 20 May.
C takes a mortgage without the deeds on 30 May and registers.

The order in which the parties rank, whether their mortgages are legal or equitable, is B-A-C, for A's mortgage, though created before B's was created and registered before B's was registered, was nevertheless not registered upon completion of the second mortgage. It is therefore void under section 4 (5) as against B. It is not of course void as against C, since its registration was effected before completion of C's mortgage on 30 May. Moreover, by virtue of section 198 (1) of the Law of Property Act 1925, C has, but B has not, statutory notice of A's mortgage.

(i) Priority of registration not in itself sufficient It is arguable that in accordance with section 97 of the Law of Property Act 1925 A should rank before B since he was the first to register, but it is difficult to agree that a void charge can be revivified and given precedence over the very charge in relation to which its invalidity has been declared by statute. There can be no renascence of what is void. One of the main objects of registration is to enable a mortgagee to discover the state of the mortgagor's title, but if he is to be displaced by a registration effected after it has been certified to him by the Registrar that no prior charge stands in his way, the object will certainly be frustrated. The truth appears to be that there was a lack of co-ordination in the drafting of section 97 and section 13 (2) of the Land Charges Act 1925 (now replaced by section 4 (5) of the Land Charges Act 1972).[7]

(ii) *Circulus inextricabilis* Subrogation In the example given above priority is not difficult to determine, but this is by no means always true. Suppose, for instance, that, after a mortgage has been granted to X who takes possession of the title deeds, further mortgages of the same land are given in the following order:

A puisne mortgage to A on 1 May to secure £1,000.
A general equitable charge to B on 10 May to secure £1,000.
A puisne mortgage to C on 20 May to secure £2,000.
A registers on 11 May.
C registers on 20 May.
B's charge is not registered.

We know that A's mortgage is statutorily void against B, and that B's mortgage is void against C, but at first sight it seems impossible to arrange all three claimants in order of priority. An objection can be raised to every possible permutation. For instance, the order is not A-B-C, for though A ranks before C he must be postponed to B; neither is it B-A-C, for C is to be preferred to B though not to A; neither is it A-C-B, since A must rank after

6 But for another view, see (1950) 13 MLR 534–5 (A. D. Hargreaves).
7 "Technically LCA 1925 (the predecessor of LCA 1972) was a later statute than LPA 1925, and should prevail in the case of irreconcilable conflict." (Megarry and Wade, *Law of Real Property* (5th edn) p. 1000, n. 97. For a discussion of the question, see [1940] CLJ, pp. 255–6 (R. E. Megarry).

B. If such a case were to arise the court would presumably be driven to base its decision upon the doctrine of subrogation.[8] Subrogation is the process by which one creditor is substituted for another creditor when both have claims against the same debtor.[9] The relevant factors in its application to the present example are that:

B ranks before A,
A ranks before C, and
C ranks before B,

so that any starting point is as arbitrary as any other in this *circulus inextricabilis*. But a solution may be found by transferring to C the right of B to be paid £1,000 before A. C is subrogated to B, *but only to the extent to which B has priority over A*. The actual order of payment will therefore be as follows:

1. C is entitled to a first payment of £1,000.

This is the £1,000 that is due to B in priority to A.

2. A is entitled to the next payment of £1,000.

Theoretically, at any rate, A suffers no injury. His claim is not sustainable until £1,000 has been paid out of the land, and it is no concern of his whether that sum is paid to B or to C.

3. C is entitled to the next payment of £1,000.

This represents the remainder of C's advance, the whole of which is payable before that of B.

4. B is entitled to £1,000 if the proceeds arising from the sale of the land are sufficient.

If the sums advanced were £1,000 by A, £1,000 by B and £600 by C, the order would be this:

1. C: £600.
2. B: £400.
3. A: £1,000.
4. B: £600.[10]

However, it cannot be said that the doctrine of subrogation provides more than a rough and ready method of solving the difficulty. It cannot escape the

8 *Benham v Keane* (1861) 1 John & H 685 at 710–12; *Re Wyatt* [1892] 1 Ch 188 at 208–9; M & B p. 800; cf *Re Weniger's Policy* [1910] 2 Ch 291.
9 White and Tudor's *Leading Cases in Equity* (9th edn), vol. i. pp. 147 et seq.
10 A similar problem may arise under *Dearle v Hall* (1823) 3 Russ 1, p. 716, ante. See, for instance, the illustration given by FRY LJ in *Re Wyatt* [1892] 1 Ch 188 at 208–9; M & B p. 800. There are two trustees of a fund, X and Y. The first incumbrancer, A, notifies X only; the second incumbrancer, B, notifies X and Y; X then dies and the third incumbrancer, C, notifies the surviving trustee, Y. Here A ranks before B (*Ward v Duncombe* [1893] AC 369, p. 718, ante); B before C (ibid); C before A, for A's notice is nullified as against incumbrances created after X's death (*Timson v Ramsbottom* (1837) 2 Keen 35, p. 718, ante). Therefore, says FRY LJ: "The fund would be distributed as follows: First, to the third incumbrancer to the extent of the claim of the first. Secondly, to the second incumbrancer. Thirdly, to the third incumbrancer to the extent to which he might remain unpaid after the money he had received whilst standing in the shoes of the first incumbrancer; see *Benham v Keane* (1861) 1 John & H 685, where a similar problem was similarly solved." See also *Re Woodroffes (Musical Instruments) Ltd* [1986] Ch 366, [1985] 2 All ER 908; [1986] CLJ 25 (L. S. Sealy). See generally (1968) 32 Conv (NS) 325 (W. A. Lee); 71 Yale LJ 53 (G. Gilmore).

criticism of being arbitrary, for it is not obvious why the subrogation should begin with one claimant rather than with another. In the example just given the process might equally well start with B rather than with C. Neither is the justice of the solution obvious. In the first example, B gets nothing until £2,000 has been paid to C and £1,000 to A, and yet he has a prior right to A.

Where the value of the land is insufficient to satisfy all the mortgagees in full, it might be more just to admit the inextricable circle and to decree a payment *pari passu*, i.e. a division of the proceeds among the various claimants in proportion to the respective amounts of their advances.

(d) Priorities where one mortgage protected by deeds

We must now consider the question of priorities where one of the competing mortgages is accompanied by the title deeds, which is, of course, the usual case. The chief problem here is: What is the significance of excluding such a mortgage from the list of registrable incumbrances? Is the implication that in all cases a person who obtains possession of the deeds ranks first? Presumably not, for it must never be forgotten that the governing principles which obtained under the pre-1926 law were not expressly altered by the legislation of 1925. These principles were that:

> A legal was preferred to an equitable mortgage; mortgages ranked in the order of their creation, subject to the preference given to the legal mortgage; but either of these principles might be displaced by negligent conduct with reference to the deeds.

The pre-1926 law, therefore, cannot be ignored altogether, though obviously its application is materially affected by the introduction of the system of registration. Another difficulty is the uncertainty of the statutory expression "protected by a deposit of documents", for a mortgagee may be entitled to this protection if he receives only some of the deeds relating to the legal estate, honestly and reasonably believing that he has received all.[11] Thus a contest may arise between two mortgagees, both of whom are protected by a deposit of documents and neither of whom, because of the deposit, has registered his incumbrance.[12]

The following account of the general question is based upon two hypothetical cases, first, that the mortgage with the deposit of deeds comes first in order of date, secondly that it comes later.[13]

(i) First mortgagee acquires deeds Let us suppose that:

> A takes a mortgage protected by the title deeds;
> B takes a later mortgage, necessarily without the deeds.

We require to ascertain whether the order is A–B, but to do this it is necessary, having regard to the principles of the pre-1926 law which are still to a large extent relevant, to consider the problem according as the parties obtain legal or equitable mortgages.

---

11 *Ratcliffe v Barnard* (1871) 6 Ch App 652; *Dixon v Muckleston* (1872) 8 Ch App 155.
12 For a discussion of this particular case, see [1940] CLJ pp. 249–253 (R. E. Megarry).
13 See the valuable series of articles in (1933) 76 LJ News 83–4, 95, 106–7, 122–3, 131–3 (R. L. Bignell and C. H. H. Wilss).

1. *A's mortgage is legal, B's is equitable* Under the pre-1926 law, as we have seen,[14] the rule in such a case as this was that, by force of the legal estate and also by virtue of the maxim *qui prior est tempore potior est jure*, A ranked first, unless his subsequent negligence with regard to the deeds, as for instance by handing them back to the mortgagor, justified his postponement to B. These rules of the pre-1926 law, which specify the limits within which conduct with regard to deeds causes loss of priority, still hold good, for section 13 of the Law of Property Act 1925 provides that:

> This Act shall not prejudicially affect the right or interest of any person arising out of or consequent on the possession by him of any documents relating to a legal estate in land, nor affect any question arising out of or consequent upon any omission to obtain or any other absence of possession by any person of any documents relating to a legal estate in land.

Presuming that this section is linked to the Land Charges Act by section 97 quoted above,[15] it seems clear that the ranking of A and B still depends upon precisely the same considerations as before 1926. A will rank first unless his fraud or subsequent negligence justifies his postponement.

2. *The mortgages both of A and B are legal* The position could not arise before 1926, when only one legal mortgage of the fee simple was possible. There seems no doubt, however, that A ranks first, since he has the earlier legal estate and also possession of the deeds, though of course if he negligently parts with the deeds and thereby causes the deception of B, he may as in the last case lose his priority.

3. *A's mortgage is equitable, B's is legal* This position arises, for instance, where a mortgage by deposit of deeds is made to A, and later a legal charge is granted to B. Before 1926, B, as the holder of the legal estate, ranked first, unless he had failed to inquire for the deeds or had rested content with an unreasonable excuse for their non-production, or unless he had notice of A's equitable mortgage at the time when he took his own. The question now arises—what constitutes notice of A's mortgage? Certainly not registration, for a mortgagee with the deeds cannot register. The answer is contained in section 199 (1) (ii) of the Law of Property Act 1925. It provides that a purchaser, including a mortgagee,[16] shall not be prejudicially affected by notice of any instrument or matter which is incapable of registration under the Land Charges Act unless:

> (a) it is within his own knowledge, or would have come to his knowledge if such inquiries and inspections had been made as ought reasonably to have been made by him; or
>
> (b) in the same transaction with respect to which a question of notice to the purchaser arises, it has come to the knowledge of his counsel, as such, or of his solicitor or other agent, as such, or would have come to the knowledge of his solicitor or other agent, as such, if such inquiries and inspections had been made as ought reasonably to have been made by the solicitor or other agent.

In other words, the old doctrine of actual or constructive notice is still in force with regard to mortgages that are incapable of registration. Again,

---

14 Pp. 709 et seq, ante.
15 P. 720, ante; *sed quaere*.
16 LPA 1925, s. 205 (1) (xxi).

there is nothing in the legislation of 1925 which deprives the owner of the legal estate of that pre-eminent position which he has always enjoyed.

It would seem, therefore, that in the majority of circumstances B will rank second, for he will have actual notice of A's mortgage if he inquires for the deeds, and constructive notice if he makes no inquiry. Presumably, however, a case like *Hewitt v Loosemore*[17] would still be decided as it was before 1926.

4. *The mortgages both of A and of B are equitable* In this case there has been a deposit of the deeds with A followed by a general equitable charge in favour of B. When there was a contest under the pre-1926 law between equitable incumbrancers, it was the maxim *qui prior est tempore potior est jure* that prevailed. In the circumstances that we are now considering A would have ranked first, unless, by a voluntary redelivery of the deeds to the mortgagor, he had negligently allowed a fraud to be perpetrated on B.[18] There is nothing in the modern legislation to upset the pre-1926 law, and there is little doubt that the maxim *qui prior est tempore potior est jure* is still applicable.[19]

(ii) First mortgagee does not acquire deeds Let us suppose that the following transactions occur:

A takes a puisne mortgage.
B takes a later mortgage, either legal or equitable, and also obtains possession of the deeds.

It is perfectly clear that if A has registered his mortgage before the completion of B's, he will rank first, since section 97 of the Law of Property Act 1925 provides that his mortgage shall rank according to its date of registration, and furthermore section 198 provides that registration under the Land Charges Act shall constitute notice to all persons and for all purposes connected with the land affected. If, however, it was due to A's gross negligence that he failed to obtain the deeds, it is conceivable, but scarcely probable, that despite registration he might, by virtue of section 13 of the Law of Property Act 1925,[20] be postponed to B in accordance with the principles of the pre-1926 law.[1]

It seems equally clear that if A has failed to register his mortgage before the transaction with B is completed, he will in all circumstances be postponed to B. This follows from the enactment that a registrable mortgage shall be void against a purchaser of the land charged, unless it is registered before completion of the purchase.[2] It may be argued, however, that, if A inquired for the deeds in the first place and received a reasonable excuse for their non-delivery, his legal estate, as under the pre-1926 law, will still give him priority by virtue of section 13 of the Law of Property Act 1925.[3]

This seems doubtful. Not only is the mortgage rendered absolutely void against B, but it may also be said that A has been negligent in not taking advantage of the protection that registration would have afforded him.

17 (1851) 9 Hare 449; M & B p. 790; p. 711, ante.
18 P. 712, ante.
19 Cf *Beddoes v Shaw* [1937] Ch 81, [1936] 2 All ER 1108.
20 P. 725, ante.
 1 [1940] CLJ 259 (R. E. Megarry).
 2 LCA 1972, s. 4 (5).
 3 P. 725, ante; (1926) 61 LJ News 398 (J. M. Lightwood), cited and considered (1933) 76 LJ News at 132.

If the facts are altered slightly and we suppose that:

A takes a general equitable charge, and
B takes a later mortgage, either legal or equitable, also obtaining possession of the deeds,

it would seem that the same result ensues. If the charge is registered, A ranks first, otherwise B will be preferred.

(e) Tacking

(i) Partial abolition The doctrine of tacking has been materially affected by the Law of Property Act 1925.[4] One branch of that doctrine has been abolished, the other has been retained. The first branch, which under the pre-1926 law[5] comprised the right of a later mortgagee to buy in the legal estate from the first incumbrancer and to squeeze out an intermediate mortgage, has been abolished.[6] The second branch has been retained, for it is important that a mortgagee should be at liberty to tack further advances to his first loan. In fact, the preservation of this right is essential where a bank takes a mortgage from a client as security for his current account, since a further advance is made whenever his cheque is honoured. It is therefore enacted that in certain cases, which will be given in a moment:

> a prior mortgagee shall have a right to make further advances to rank in priority to subsequent mortgages (whether legal or equitable).[7]

(ii) Tacking of further advances It will be noticed that this enactment does not confine the right to the first mortgagee or to a legal mortgagee, but grants it to any prior mortgagee, legal or equitable, against every later mortgagee. But it is only in the three following cases that the right may be exercised.

1. *When later mortgagees agree*[8] This is an obvious and not an unusual case. After mortgages of Blackacre have been granted to A, B and C, the mortgagor may seek a further advance from B on the same security. B will rank for payment of both his loans before C if he makes an arrangement to that effect with C before advancing further money. C is not likely to agree unless the land is sufficient cover for all the money with which it is charged.

2. *When there is no notice of later mortgages*[9] A mortgagee who has no notice of subsequent mortgages at the time when he makes his further advances may claim priority for both his loans over subsequent mortgagees. This is the same rule as applied before 1926,[10] with this important difference, however, that registration of a later mortgage as a land charge is deemed to constitute *actual* notice of that mortgage.[11] A mortgagee therefore who contemplates a further advance should not make it until he has ascertained by a search at the Land Registry that no later mortgages have been made.

There is, however, an important exception to this rule that the mere

---

4 S. 94. See (1958) 22 Conv (NS) 44 (R. G. Rowley).
5 P. 714, ante.
6 LPA 1925, s. 94 (3). Tacking by purchase of the legal estate survives in other contexts: *McCarthy & Stone Ltd v Julian S Hodge & Co Ltd* [1971] 1 WLR 1547, [1971] 2 All ER 973, p. 60, n. 5, ante.
7 LPA 1925, s. 94 (1).
8 Ibid., s. 94 (1) (*a*).
9 Ibid., s. 94 (1) (*b*).
10 P. 715, ante.
11 LPA 1925, s. 198 (1), as amended by Local Land Charges Act 1975, s. 17, Sch. 1.

registration of a mortgage will prevent a prior mortgagee from tacking later advances. It is enacted that in the case of a mortgage made expressly for securing:

(*a*) a current account, or
(*b*) other further advances,

the mere registration of a subsequent mortgage shall not constitute notice sufficient to deprive the earlier mortgagee of his right to tack. In those two cases the rule is that:

> A mortgagee shall not be deemed to have notice of a mortgage merely by reason that it was registered as a land charge, if it was not so registered at the time when the original mortgage was created or when the last search (if any) by or on behalf of the mortgagee was made, whichever last happened.[12]

Thus registration of a subsequent mortgage constitutes actual notice of that mortgage to a prior incumbrancer and necessarily displaces his right to tack, except where the prior mortgage was taken not merely as security for the original loan, but as security either for the original loan and further advances or for a current account. In either of these cases registration will be notice only if it was in being when the prior mortgage was created (which might of course be before any money was actually advanced by the prior mortgagee, as often happens where a current account is secured), or when the prior mortgagee last made a search at the Land Registry. Failing registration at one of these dates a prior mortgagee will not be deprived of the right to tack unless, at the time of the further advance, he had notice, in the old sense of actual or constructive notice, of the later mortgage.

This exception to the rule that registration is equivalent to actual notice has been made in the interest of bankers, for were the rule unqualified it would be impracticable to take a mortgage as security for a current account. An illustration will make this clear:

> If A mortgages his land to a bank in order to secure an overdraft which at the time of the mortgage is £3,000, and if he subsequently grants a mortgage of the same land to B, notice of which is given to the bank, the rule as laid down in *Hopkinson v Rolt*[13] is that the bank obtains priority only for the amount due from the mortgagor at the time when the second mortgage to B was made. If the overdraft at that moment is £4,000, then £4,000 is the amount with which the land is charged in favour of the bank. When, moreover, A from time to time pays sums into his account, and the overdraft is thus reduced below £4,000, only the reduced amount is recoverable under the mortgage;[14] and although, after notice of the second mortgage, the actual overdraft may be increased as a result of drawings out, the payments or further advances by the bank in respect of these drawings cannot be tacked to the loan as it stood at the time when notice of the second mortgage was received.[15] To fix the mortgage at £4,000 is equitable if the bank has actual notice of the second mortgage, but it would make this side of banking business impossible if mere registration constituted notice, for it would be unsafe to honour the customer's cheques unless on each occasion a search were made at the Land Registry.

Two practical results emerge from this legislation.

First, a mortgage will generally provide expressly that the land shall be

---

12 LPA 1925, s. 94 (2), as amended by LP (A)A 1926, Schedule.
13 (1861) 9 HL Cas 514; p. 715, ante.
14 *Clayton's Case* (1816) 1 Mer 572.
15 *Deeley v Lloyds Bank* [1910] 1 Ch 648, reversed [1912] AC 756.

security for further advances, since this will enable a further advance to be made without a search at the Land Registry; secondly, a mortgagee who searches and discovers the existence of a prior mortgage expressly made to secure a current account or further advances will be careful to notify his mortgage to the prior mortgagee.

3. *When the mortgage imposes an obligation on the mortgagee to make further advances* When the provision in the prior mortgage is not that the land shall be security for any further advances which *may* be made, as in the case (*b*) just considered, but that the mortgagee shall be bound to make further advances if called upon to do so, the new rule is[16] that the doctrine of tacking shall apply to such advances notwithstanding the fact that at the time of making them the prior mortgagee had notice of a later mortgage. The law as laid down in *West v Williams*[17] is therefore reversed.

(2) PRIORITY AS BETWEEN MORTGAGEES OF AN EQUITABLE INTEREST IN LAND
OR PERSONALTY

(a) **Extension of rule in *Dearle v Hall***

We have already seen that under the law before 1926 the priority as between mortgagees of an equitable interest in pure personalty depended, in accordance with the rule in *Dearle v Hall*, upon the order in which the trustees had received notice from the mortgagees, but that this principle did not apply to mortgages of freeholds or of leaseholds.[18] The innovation made by the 1925 legislation is the extension of the rule in *Dearle v Hall* to mortgages of *all* equitable interests, realty being put on the same footing as personalty. This assimilation is accomplished by section 137 (1) of the Law of Property Act 1925:

> The law applicable to dealings with equitable things in action which regulates the priority of competing interests therein, shall, as respects dealings with equitable interests in land, capital money, and securities representing capital money effected after the commencement of this Act, apply to and regulate the priority of competing interests therein.[19]

This extension of the rule to all mortgages and assignments of equitable interests in freeholds and leaseholds is of especial importance owing to the increased number of interests that are necessarily equitable since 1925. Thus, the purchaser or mortgagee of an interest arising under a strict settlement, such as a life interest, an entailed interest or any species of future interest, must protect himself by giving the necessary notice. In effect the priority of mortgages of equitable beneficial interests under strict settlements and trusts for sale is now determined by the same rule.

(b) **Rules regarding notice**

The rules that existed before 1926 with regard to the nature of the notice still hold good,[20] subject to one exception. This is that a notice given otherwise than in writing in respect of any dealing with an equitable interest in real or

16 LPA 1925, s. 94 (1) (*c*).
17 [1899] 1 Ch 132; p. 715, ante.
18 P. 716, ante.
19 For an analysis of the section, see [1993] Conv 22 (J. Howell).
20 Pp. 716, ante.

personal property shall not affect the priority of competing claims of purchasers or mortgagees.[1]

(i) Persons to whom notice must be given The Law of Property Act 1925 contains the following rules with regard to the persons upon whom the written notice must be served.

(1) Where the equitable interest is in settled land or capital money.[2]

Where dealings take place with such an interest, notice must be given to the *trustees of the settlement*. If the interest in question has been created by a derivative settlement (i.e. one by which an interest already settled is resettled), then notice must be given to the trustees of the derivative settlement.

(2) Where the equitable interest is in land held on trust for sale.

In this case notice must be given to the *trustees* for sale.[3]

(3) Where the equitable interest is neither (1) nor (2).[4]

If, for instance, the subject of the transaction is a life annuity charged on land by a tenant in fee simple, it is provided that notice shall be given to the *estate owner*.

It will be remembered that certain complexities had arisen before 1926 with regard to a notice served on a single trustee.[5] The proper course, which, however, is not always adopted, is to serve the notice on each of the trustees and to take a receipt from each, and it is perhaps regrettable that the Act did not made this practice compulsory. No statutory direction has, however, been given, and it therefore appears that in this regard the old decisions continue to represent the law.[6]

(ii) Notice by way of endorsed memorandum To meet any difficulty that may arise in identifying the appropriate person to receive notice, the Act provides that where:

(a) the trustees are not persons to whom a valid notice can be given; or
(b) there are no trustees to whom a valid notice can be given; or
(c) for any other reason a valid notice cannot be served, or cannot be served without unreasonable cost or delay,

the assignee may require that a memorandum of the transaction be endorsed on, or permanently annexed to, the instrument which creates the trust.[7] Such a memorandum, as respects priorities, operates in like manner as if a written notice had been given to trustees. Thus if the land in which the equitable interest exists is subject to a strict settlement, the memorandum will be annexed to the trust instrument; if it is land belonging to an owner who has died intestate, the memorandum will be annexed to the letters of administration. The objection to a memorandum of this nature is that trust instruments may become overladen with endorsements of charges and

1 LPA 1925, s. 137 (3).
2 Ibid., s. 137 (2) (i).
3 Ibid., s. 137 (2) (ii).
4 LPA 1925, s. 137 (2) (iii).
5 P. 718, ante.
6 See (1925) 60 LJ News 264 (J. M. Lightwood); Wolstenholme and Cherry (13th edn), vol. 1 p. 246.
7 LPA 1925, s. 137 (4).

assignments. Therefore an alternative method of registering a notice has been provided.[8]

(iii) Notice to nominated trust corporation It is provided that a settlor when drafting a settlement, or the court at a later date, may nominate a trust corporation to whom notice of dealings affecting real or personal property may be given. Where such a nomination has been made, notice of any dealings with the equitable interest must be given to the trust corporation, and if given to the trustees must be transmitted by them to the corporation. A notice which is not received by the corporation has no effect on priorities.

(iv) Right to production of notice The object of the rule in *Dearle v Hall* is to enable a person to discover by inquiries addressed to the trustees whether the owner of an equitable interest has created any earlier incumbrances. But this object was not always attained under the law before 1926, for since, in the language of LINDLEY LJ:

> it is no part of the duty of a trustee to assist his *cestui que trust* in selling or mortgaging his beneficial interest and in squandering or anticipating his fortune,[9]

it was held that a trustee owed no greater duty to a person who was proposing to deal with a *cesti que trust*.[10] Thus a trustee might refuse to answer inquiries, and even if he gave an answer that contained wrong information, he was not liable for the consequences unless he had been guilty of fraud or had made such a clear and categorical statement that he was estopped from denying its truth.[11] A prospective assignee, however, is given at least this advantage by the Act, that he may demand production of any written notice that has been served on the trustees or their predecessors.[12]

SECTION VII REGISTERED LAND

A mortgage of registered land[13] may be created by registered charge, by unregistered mortgage and by deposit of the land or charge certificate.

(1) REGISTERED CHARGE

(a) Creation

A registered charge is a legal interest which must be created by deed. It may be made by a charge by way of legal mortgage, or it may contain, in the case of freehold land, an express demise, and, in the case of leasehold land, an express subdemise.[14] Otherwise, it will, subject to any contrary provision in

---

8 LPA 1925, s. 138. See also Law Reform Committee 23rd Report (The powers and duties of trustees) 1982 (Cmnd 8733), paras 2.17–2.24.
9 *Low v Bouverie* [1891] 3 Ch 82 at 99.
10 *Burrows v Lock* (1805) 10 Ves 470.
11 Ibid.
12 LPA 1925, s. 137 (8).
13 See generally Ruoff and Roper, chapters 23, 24; Fisher and Lightwood, *Law of Mortgage*, (10th edn), chapter 3.
14 LRA 1925, s. 27 (1), (2); LRR 1925, r. 139 and Schedule substituted by LR (Charges) R 1990 (SI 1990 No. 2613).

the charge,[15] take effect as a charge by way of legal mortgage.[16] In registered land it is not necessary to use the words "by way of legal mortgage" in order to create a legal charge.[17] The land must be described by reference to the register or in some other way that will enable the land to be identified without reference to any other document. A registered charge must not refer to any other interest or charge which (a) would have priority over it and is not registered or protected in the register and (b) is not an overriding interest.

The charge is completed by the Registrar entering on the charges register the chargee as proprietor of the charge.[18] A legal estate does not arise until the charge is registered.[19] A charge certificate is then issued to the chargee, the land certificate being deposited at the registry until the charge is cancelled.[20]

(b) Power of chargee

Subject to any entry on the register or provision in the charge to the contrary, the proprietor of a charge has all the powers conferred by law on the owner of a legal mortgage.[1] Thus he may enter into possession, foreclose and sell. Upon foreclosure the proprietor of the charge is registered as proprietor of the land, and the charge and all incumbrances and entries inferior to it are cancelled. In the same way, a sale will be completed by registration which will transfer the legal estate to the purchaser, once again cancelling the charge and all incumbrances and entries inferior to it. It appears that a right to consolidate may be reserved as in the case of unregistered land.[2]

Covenants are implied, subject to any entry on the register or provision in the charge to the contrary, on the part of the proprietor of the land to pay principal and interest and, where the charge is created on a leasehold, to pay rent, observe covenants and conditions and to indemnify the proprietor of the charge.[3]

(c) Priority of charges

Registered charges rank for priority according to the order in which they are entered on the register, not according to the order in which they are created, unless an entry on the register or a provision in the charge provides otherwise.[4]

(d) Tacking

As regards tacking, section 94 of the Law of Property Act 1925 does not apply to registered land.[5] Tacking is only possible (a) if the registered

---

15 LPA 1925, s. 27 (1).
16 Ibid., s. 25. An equitable charge is not registrable under this section: *Re White Rose Cottage* [1965] Ch 940 at 949, [1965] 1 All ER 11 at 14, per Lord DENNING MR.
17 *Cityland and Property (Holdings) Ltd v Dabrah* [1968] Ch 166, [1967] 2 All ER 639.
18 LRA 1925, s. 26 (1).
19 *Grace Rymer Investments Ltd v Waite* [1958] Ch 831, [1958] 2 All ER 777; M & B p. 809.
20 LRA 1925, ss. 63, 65; LRR 1925, r. 262.
 1 Ibid., s. 34; LRR 1925, r. 140.
 2 Ruoff and Roper, para. 23–41.
 3 LRA 1925, s. 28; LRR 1925, r. 140.
 4 Ibid., s. 29; LRR 1925, r. 140. Priority of certain statutory charges may depend on the order of creation e.g. Housing Act 1985, ss. 201 (3), 230 (3).
 5 P. 727, ante.

proprietor is under an obligation to make further advances or (*b*) where a registered charge is made for securing further advances. In this case the Registrar must, before making any entry on the register which would prejudicially affect the priority of any further advances, give notice by registered post to the proprietor of the charge, who may tack any advances made by him up to the time when he receives or ought to have received the notice in due course of post.[6] In case (*a*) any subsequent registered charge takes effect subject to any further advance made pursuant to the obligation.

(e) Discharge

The discharge of a registered charge can only be effected by notification of the cessation of the charge on the register.[7] The provisions of the Law of Property Act 1925 relating to the discharge of a mortgage of unregistered land do not apply to registered land.[8] There is a prescribed form of discharge, but the Registrar may accept any other proof of satisfaction of a charge which he deems sufficient.[9]

(2) UNREGISTERED MORTGAGE

Subject to any entry to the contrary on the register, a proprietor of registered land may mortgage the land in the same way as if it were unregistered.[10] This takes effect only in equity and needs to be protected as a minor interest, i.e. by a notice under section 49 of the Land Registration Act 1925, if the land certificate can be produced,[11] or is on deposit at the Land Registry;[12] failing that, by a caution under section 54.[13]

It will be recalled that, in unregistered land, priorities of mortgagees or assignments of equitable interests are governed by the rule in *Dearle v Hall* as extended by the Law of Property Act 1925. Until 1987 such priorities in registered land were in some cases governed by the order in which "priority cautions" or "priority inhibitions" had been lodged in the Minor Interests Index.[14] The Index was abolished by the Land Registration Act 1986, and the rule in *Dearle v Hall* now applies in both registered and unregistered land.[15]

---

6 LRA 1925, s. 30 (1), (3), added by LP (A) A, 1926, s. 5; LR (Charges) R 1990, r. 139A (S.I. 1990 No. 2613).
7 Ibid., s. 35; LRR 1925, rr. 151, 267.
8 LPA 1925, s. 115 (10); p. 685, ante.
9 LRR 1925, r. 151, as substituted by LR (Charges) R 1990 (S.I. 1990 No. 2613).
10 LRA 1925, s. 106 as amended by AJA 1977, s. 26 (1); LRR 1925; r. 223.
11 Ibid., ss. 64, 65.
12 It may also have been deposited because of the existence of a prior registered charge.
13 A caution gives scant protection; see LRA 1925, ss. 53–6; p. 803, post. AJA 1977, s. 26 (1) abolished the cumbersome method of protection known as the mortgage caution, as from 30 August 1977. Since then, under s. 26 (2), the Registrar may convert into a registered charge any mortgage so protected.
14 LRA 1925, s. 102; LRR 1925, r. 229.
15 S. 5. For transitional provisions, see s. 5 (2)–(4). The repeal was recommended by the Law Commission Report on Land Registration 1983 (Law Com No. 125), Part V. For the priorities of other minor interests, see p. 804, post; *Re White Rose Cottage* [1965] Ch 940, [1965] 1 All ER 11; M & B p. 779 (equitable mortgage protected by notice of deposit held to have priority over subsequent equitable charge protected by caution); (1966) CLP 26 (E. C. Ryder); *Barclays Bank Ltd v Taylor* [1974] Ch 137, [1973] 1 All ER 752 (unprotected equitable mortgage held to have priority over subsequent estate contract protected by caution); (1977) 93 LQR 687 (R. J. Smith); M & B p. 809; followed in *Mortgage Corpn Ltd v Nationwide*

(3) DEPOSIT OF LAND OR CHARGE CERTIFICATE

The proprietor of registered land or of a registered charge may create a lien by deposit of the land or charge certificate respectively.[16] The lien is similar to a mortgage by deposit of title deeds of unregistered land, and takes effect subject to overriding interests, registered interests and any entries then upon the register. The mortgagee by deposit should give written notice of the deposit to the Registrar, who will enter on the charges register a notice that will operate as a caution.[17] Notices of deposit are often used, especially by banks.[18] The protection they give is threefold; the depositee being in possession of the land certificate can prevent any dealing for which its production is required; purchasers will have notice of the depositee's rights, and the notice operates as a caution.[19] It would appear, however, that the deposit of the land certificate alone is sufficient to give notice to a purchaser.[20] Nevertheless, registration of a notice of deposit would provide greater protection.

SECTION VIII TYPES OF MORTGAGE

Finally, we must notice in broad outline two special types of mortgage.

A. BUILDING SOCIETY MORTGAGES[1]

Building societies are a special kind of mortgagee and have for many years been the main source of finance for the purchase of houses in owner-occupation. They are societies for raising, primarily by the subscriptions of the members, a fund for making to them advances secured on land for their residential use.[2] The Act regulating such societies is the Building Societies Act 1986,[3] which has extended considerably the range of their activities. It makes detailed provisions for the legal framework of building societies and gives responsibility for their supervision to the Building Societies Commission which makes an annual report to Parliament.[4] There are also provisions for the protection of investors under the Building Societies Investment Protection

---

Credit Corpn Ltd [1993] 2 WLR 769 (later mortgage protected by notice); [1993] Conv 227 (J. Martin); *Clark v Chief Land Registrar* [1993] Ch 294, [1993] 2 All ER 936; *Chancery plc v Ketteringham* (1993) Times, 25 November.

16 LRA 1925, s. 66.

17 LRR 1925, r. 239. A lien may also be created by giving a notice of intention to deposit: LRR 1925, rr. 240, 241.

18 The Law Commission Third Report on Land Registration C. Minor Interests 1987 (Law Com No. 158, HC 269), para. 4.81 recommends that the notice of deposit should no longer be available as a method of protection.

19 P. 803, post.

20 *Barclays Bank Ltd v Taylor*, supra.

1 See Wurtzburg and Mills, *Building Society Law* (15th edn), Cousins, *Law of Mortgage*, chapter 9; the Annual Reports of the Chief Registrar of Friendly Societies; Fisher and Lightwood, pp. 204–8.

2 Building Societies Act 1986, s. 5(1).

3 See Building Societies: A New Framework (1984 Cmnd 9316); [1985] Conv 1; [1987] Conv 36 (A. Samuels).

4 Building Societies Act 1986, ss. 1–4, 36–51, Sch. 1. The first chairman is the Chief Registrar of Friendly Societies and the first report was issued in 1987.

Board, if a building society becomes insolvent;[5] and for the appointment of an Ombudsman for the investigation of disputes.[6]

The general method of operation is to borrow money from the general public at interest and then to lend that money at interest by making advances to house purchasers on the security of their houses. The mortgage is usually one of two types; either an instalment or repayment mortgage, that is to say, it is paid off by monthly payments at a rate which covers payment of interest and repayment of capital, so that the capital is paid off over an agreed period of time, for example, 30 years; or an endowment mortgage, that is to say, the money is borrowed from the society and at the same time an endowment assurance policy is taken out; only interest payments are made to the society during the life of the mortgage, the outstanding debt being repaid when the policy matures. The general law of mortgages applies to these transactions. A building society has a statutory power to make advances on terms that the real value of the loan will be repaid to it by adjustments which take account of inflation.[7] There is also a statutory duty on a building society, when selling as a mortgagee, to take reasonable care to ensure that the price is the best price that can reasonably be obtained.[8]

The Building Societies Act removed a number of restrictions on the power of building societies to lend money; in particular, they are no longer limited to lending on first mortgages only, although this remains their traditional and primary activity.[9] Strict limits are placed on the peripheral activities so that at least 90 per cent of total commercial assets must be advanced to individual members of the society secured by a first mortgage of land which is for the residential use of the borrower or a dependant of his (Class 1 advances). Second mortgages, equity mortgages (where the borrower has a share, specified in the mortgage, in the open market value of the property) and loans to corporate bodies may be made, if secured on land (Class 2). Large building societies with total assets of not less than £1 million may make unsecured loans of up to £25,000 to an individual, and of up to £15,000 for the secured purchase of a mobile home (Class 3).[10] Classes 2 and 3 involve riskier forms of lending, and so Class 3 must not be more than 15 per cent of total assets and Classes 2 and 3 combined must not exceed 25 per cent of total assets.[11]

In addition to traditional lending on mortgages for house ownership, building societies are empowered by the Act to offer a wide range of housing and financial services in a competitive market, including banking, insurance, investment, pensions, estate agency, surveying, valuation and conveyancing.[12]

5 Building Societies Act 1986, ss. 24–33, Sch. 5. For an analogy, see the Banking Act 1987 and the Financial Services Act 1986.
6 Ibid., ss. 83–85, Schs. 12–14; (1992) 142 NLJ 1348 (H. W. Wilkinson); *Halifax Building Society v Edell* [1992] Ch 436, [1992] 3 All ER 389 (borrowers' complaints of negligent surveys within ombudsman's jurisdiction).
7 Ibid., s. 10 (10) (*a*). See *Nationwide Building Society v Registry of Friendly Societies* [1983] 1 WLR 1226, [1983] 3 All ER 296; (1984) 134 NLJ 437 (H. Cohen), 513. For index-linking of mortgages generally, see *Multiservice Bookbinding Ltd v Marden* [1979] Ch 84, [1978] 2 All ER 489, p. 737, ante.
8 Ibid. Sch. 4, para 1. See *Reliance Permanent Building Society v Harwood-Stamper* [1944] Ch 362, [1944] 2 All ER 75; p. 698, ante.
9 Ibid., ss. 10–23.
10 Building Societies (Limits on Lending) Order 1992 (S.I. 1992 No. 2931).
11 Building Societies (Limits on Commercial Assets) Order 1988 (S.I. 1988 No. 1142).
12 Building Societies Act 1986, ss. 34–35, Sch. 8. See (1987) 137 NLJ 1113 (M. Boleat).

The expectation is that the package of services offered by building societies and other institutional lenders may become a major factor in reducing the expense and eliminating some of the delay involved in house purchase.

B. CONSUMER CREDIT AGREEMENTS

The Consumer Credit Act 1974[13] establishes a comprehensive code which regulates the supply of credit not exceeding £15,000[14] to an individual.[15] The Act includes provisions on advertising and canvassing; the licensing of credit and hire businesses; all aspects of the agreement; and judicial control over its enforcement.

To come within the Act, a mortgage must constitute a regulated consumer agreement, that is to say, a personal credit agreement by which a creditor provides a debtor with credit not exceeding £15,000.[16] There are, however, exempt agreements,[17] of which the most important are loans made by a building society or local authority for house purchase. Banks are not exempt.

Owing to the financial limit of £15,000, only second mortgages are likely to come within the definition of a regulated consumer agreement. As the Crowther Report, on which the Act is based, said:[18]

> Much of the money borrowed on second mortgage is spent on improvements of various kinds to houses that are used as security. But there is no necessary tie, in most cases, between the loan and the purpose for which it is used—indeed, many of the advertisements emphasise the borrower's freedom to spend it on anything he chooses. Undoubtedly, there are people who have been led by this sort of advertising to endanger the security of their homes for the sake of some unnecessary extravagance.

We can only notice in very general terms the main areas where the law of mortgage is affected.

(a) Creation

If the formalities prescribed by the Act are not complied with,[19] section 65 provides that an agreement which is "improperly-executed" can be enforced against the debtor on an order of the court only.[20]

---

13 See Bennion and Dobson, *Consumer Credit Control* (1976); Guest and Lloyd, *Encyclopaedia of Consumer Credit Law* (1975); Goode, *Consumer Credit Law* (1989); Cousins, chapter 11; Fisher and Lightwood, chapter 10; (1975) 34 CLJ 79 (R. M. Goode); (1975) 39 Conv (NS) 94 (J. E. Adams).
14 Consumer Credit (Increase of Monetary Limits) Order 1983 (S.I. 1983 No. 1878), increasing the amount from £5,000.
15 This includes sole traders and partnerships: s. 189 (1).
16 S. 8.
17 S. 16; as amended by Building Societies Act 1986, Sch. 18, para. 10. Consumer Credit (Exempt Agreements) Order 1989 (S.I. 1989 No. 869); as amended by 1989 (S.I. 1989 Nos 1841 and 2337); 1991 (S.I. 1991 Nos 1393, 1949 and 2844); 1993 (S.I. 1993 No. 2922).
18 (1971) Cmnd 4596, para 2.4.52.
19 Part V of the Act. See also s. 105.
20 The County Court has exclusive jurisdiction: s. 141 (1). See also s. 127, *R v Modupe* (1991) Times, 27 February; *Nissan Finance UK v Lockhart* [1993] CCLR 39.

(b) Rights of mortgagor

We have already discussed the most far-reaching provision for the protection of the mortgagor by which power is given to the court to 're-open' a credit agreement if the credit bargain is extortionate.[1] This power extends to *all* credit bargains, whether regulated, exempt or above the £15,000 limit, other than those in which the debtor is a body corporate.

There are also provisions which protect a debtor under a regulated agreement. These include section 93 which prohibits any term requiring the rate of interest to be increased on default; and section 94 under which the debtor has the right, on giving notice to the creditor, to repay prematurely at any time. Any provision in the agreement which limits his rights in this respect is void.[2] It would seem that if a provision to postpone the contractual right to redeem were included in a regulated agreement it would be void.[3]

(c) Rights of the mortgagee

Consonant with the object of the Act, these are curtailed. A security cannot be enforced by reason of any breach of a regulated agreement by the debtor, until the creditor has served a notice under section 87. This is similar to, but not identical with, the notice required by section 146 of the Law of Property Act 1925 in the case of the forfeiture of a lease.[4] Further, a land mortgage securing a regulated agreement is enforceable by an order of the court only.[5] This is a most important provision, since a mortgagee cannot exercise his rights of taking possession and of sale without such an order. If, however, he sells without an order, it would seem that he can pass a good title to the purchaser.[6]

Finally, under section 113, a creditor shall not derive from the enforcement of the security any greater benefit than he would obtain from enforcement of a regulated agreement, if the security were not provided. This would seem to deny the mortgagee the full benefit of foreclosure.[7]

SECTION IX LAW REFORM

In 1991 the Law Commission recommended that all existing methods of consensually mortgaging or charging interests in land should be abolished and replaced by a new form of mortgage to be used for mortgaging any

---

1 Ss. 137–40. These sections "apply to agreements and transactions whenever made": s. 192 (1), Sch. 3, para. 42; [1989] Conv 164 (L. Bently and C. G. Howells). The County Court has unlimited jurisdiction; s. 139 (5); County Courts (Jurisdiction) Order 1989 (S.I. 1989 No. 724).
2 S. 173 (1).
3 *Knightsbridge Estates Ltd v Byrne* [1939] Ch 441, [1938] 4 All ER 618; p. 674, ante.
4 P. 435, ante.
5 S. 126. For orders which the court can make, see Part IX of the Act; *First National Bank plc v Syed* [1991] 2 All ER 250; *Cedar Holdings Ltd v Thompson* [1993] CCLR 7 (extension of time).
6 S. 177 (2).
7 P. 700, ante; (1975) 39 Conv (NS) 94 at 108.

interest in land whether legal or equitable.[8] "The present complex mortgage structure would be replaced by a new simplified structure." It also proposed a new class of "protected mortgages" by an individual of property which includes a dwelling-house, and wider powers of intervention against unfair mortgages. The rights, remedies and powers of a mortgagee would be exercisable only in good faith for the purpose of protecting or enforcing the security.

The main recommendations are:

(1) CREATION OF MORTGAGES

There are to be only two methods of creating a mortgage: the formal and the informal land mortgage.

   (a) The formal land mortgage would not be valid unless it was created by deed, whether the property mortgaged was a legal estate or an equitable interest. It would require registration under the Land Registration Act 1925 if any part of the mortgagor's title was itself registered; and in the case of unregistered land, it would be registrable as a land charge, Class C(i) under the Land Charges Act 1972.

   (b) The informal land mortgage would not be valid unless it was made by deed or satisfied the requirements of section 2 of the Law of Property (Miscellaneous Provisions) Act 1989 (p. 121, ante). A mortgagee under an informal land mortgage would have no right to enforce the security, nor to take any other action in relation to the mortgaged property, but would have a right to have the mortgage perfected by the grant of a formal land mortgage.

(2) OVERRIDING PROVISIONS

Certain provisions would be overriding in that they cannot be varied or excluded. In particular:

   (a) The mortgagor would have the right to possession unless the mortgagee took possession in order to sell or to prevent a fall in the value of the property.

   (b) The power of sale would only be exercisable if the mortgagor was in arrears or there was an outstanding breach of covenant substantially prejudicing the mortgagee's security or an event had occurred which substantially reduced the mortgagor's ability to meet his financial obligations or which prejudiced the value of the property as security.

   (c) There would be no right of consolidation.

---

8 Land Mortgages 1991 (Law Com No. 204, HC, 5); [1992] Conv 69 (H. W. Wilkinson); (1992) 136 SJ 267, 292 (G. Frost). A summary of the recommendations is contained in Part X of the Report; M & B. pp. 812–819.

   In March 1989 the Law Commission's Conveyancing Standing Committee published a consultation document suggesting the use of a new form of mortgage called a flexi-mortgage as a means of avoiding chains, cutting out delays and defeating gazumping. Its unique feature is that for a limited time it gives the borrower the right to extend the period of the mortgage on a property he is buying and increase the amount he borrows to cover the cost of an overlapping sale and purchase. Payments under his old mortgage are suspended. This allows the house-owner to agree to buy a new property before selling his own by incurring only a small increase in mortgage interest and without increasing his capital repayments. (Law Com No. 190), para. 2.2.

(3) PROTECTED MORTGAGES

A distinction is drawn between commercial and non-commercial mortgages.

> The most important differences lie in the extent to which the law needs to interfere with the parties' freedom of contract. If all provisions have to apply equally to all types of mortgage, it is difficult to reconcile the need to allow maximum flexibility to commercial transactions entered into between parties of equal bargaining power, with the need to provide adequate protection for vulnerable mortgagors who in a wholly free market would have no real choice but to accept whatever terms lenders may choose to dictate. The obvious way of reconciling these conflicting needs is to have a protected class of mortgage. (para. 4.1.)

(a) Definition

A protected mortgage would consist of all formal and informal land mortgages of any interest in land which included a dwelling-house except those where either (i) the mortgagor was a body corporate, or (ii) enforcement of the mortgage would not affect enjoyment of the dwelling-house, or (iii) the dwelling-house was occupied under a service tenancy.

(b) Protection

The main protection afforded to the mortgagor under a protected mortgage would be:

(i) Possession The mortgagee would not be entitled to take possession without serving an enforcement notice in the prescribed form on the mortgagor and obtaining a court order. The court would have power to order that interest payable under the mortgage should cease to accrue after 12 weeks of possession or such other period as the court should decide.

(ii) Sale Similarly, before exercising the power of sale under a formal land mortgage, the mortgagee must serve an enforcement notice and obtain a court order.

If the mortgagee applied to the court for possession or sale, the court would have powers equivalent to those applicable to residential mortgages under the Administration of Justice Acts 1970 and 1973 and the Consumer Credit Act 1974. In addition it would have power to order the debt to be rescheduled.

(iii) Foreclosure There is a general recommendation that the remedy of foreclosure should be abolished and replaced by the power of the mortgagee to sell to himself provided leave of the court is first obtained.

(4) REVISION OF MORTGAGE TERMS

Credit bargains made by land mortgage would be removed from the Consumer Credit Act 1974 and instead be protected under a comprehensive code affecting all land mortgages. Under this:

> the court should have power to set aside or vary any terms of a mortgage "with a view to doing justice between the parties if (a) principles of fair dealing were contravened when the mortgage was granted, or (b) the effect of the terms of the mortgage is that the mortgagee now has rights substantially greater than or different from those necessary to make the property adequate security for the liabilities secured by the mortgage, or (c) the mortgage requires payments to be made which

are exorbitant, or (d) the mortgage includes a postponement of the right to redeem, or a provision intending to impede redemption" (para. 8.5).[9]

This new jurisdiction would be in addition to the court's general powers to set aside on grounds such as fraud, mistake, rectification, estoppel, undue influence, or restraint of trade. The equitable jurisdiction concerned with clogs or fetters on the equity of redemption would be abolished.

9 For a more limited proposal for reform of the Consumer Credit Act provisions, see Unjust
   Credit Transactions: Report by the Director General of Fair Trading (1991); M & B pp. 746–
   747.

Part III

The transfer and extinction of estates and interests

SUMMARY

Part III

It may be said that what we have described so far is the law at rest. Our attention has been directed to the actual rights that can be enjoyed in land. We have taken each estate and interest that is capable of subsisting, either at law or in equity, and have explained by what methods it may be brought into existence and what incidents are applicable to it when it exists. It now remains to treat of the law in motion, that is, to show how estates and interests, once validly created, may be transferred and dealt with generally, and how they may be extinguished.

The principal function of conveyancers as regards real property is to draft appropriate instruments for creating or transferring the landed interests already described, and in connection with this task, to ensure that the person who makes the transfer has an estate or interest that is sufficient to justify the transaction contemplated. Thus, in the case of a conveyance by way of sale of the fee simple, it is essential to see that the vendor has acquired a fee simple estate and is therefore in a position to pass that estate to the purchaser. This preliminary inquiry is known as investigation of title. Again, where the task in question is to draft a will, it is essential to remember, for example, that whatever the testator may desire, it is important not to frame a limitation that offends the rule against perpetuities.

Some of the instruments by which estates and interests may be dealt with have already been described and need little further mention, but it is as well to notice that though it is usual to regard conveyancing as the transfer of rights in property from one person to another, yet frequently an instrument creates rather than transfers a right, as for instance, in the case of the creation of a trust or grant of a mortgage or a lease. Furthermore, all transfers are not necessarily effected by an instrument, but may operate independently of the person whose interest is primarily affected, as for instance, where land passes to a trustee in bankruptcy on the adjudication of its owner as bankrupt.

A. TRANSFER OF ESTATES AND INTERESTS INTER VIVOS

The first point that requires discussion is transfer, which falls naturally into transfer *inter vivos* and transfer upon death.

Transfer *inter vivos* may be either (a) by act of parties, or (b) by act of law, i.e. either due to the deliberate intention of the estate owner or in spite of his intention.

(a) Voluntary transfer

The principal occasions of voluntary transfer by act of parties arise when the land is sold, exchanged or settled.

The main object of the next two chapters (22 and 23), which deal with transfer by act of parties, is to discuss the conveyance of a legal fee simple by way of sale. The general scheme is to show, first, the practice that conveyancers adopt in effecting a conveyance of the legal estate; secondly, the effect of the conveyance upon third party rights.

In the second respect we encounter a difficulty, since not only the details of the conveyance, but more especially its effect upon third party rights, vary with the status of the vendor. We must recall that the legal estate in the entirety of every piece of land is necessarily vested in an *estate owner*. An estate owner is the owner of a legal estate. Every legal estate must have an estate owner. Blackacre may have been subject to a trust, a settlement or a mortgage; it may have been devised to a number of beneficiaries, either in succession or in common; it may have been charged with a variety of incumbrances; but in each case the fee simple absolute in possession is necessarily vested in one person or in a number of persons jointly. Further, every conveyance of the legal estate must be made by the estate owner except where a mortgagee under his power of sale conveys the legal fee simple that is vested in the mortgagor, and even in this case the conveyance may be made in the name of the mortgagor. The possible estate owners are the following:

> Beneficial owners.
> Personal representatives.
> Trustees for sale.
> Tenants for life and statutory owners.
> Mortgagors and mortgagees.
> Bare trustees.[1]

The plan adopted in the following two chapters, therefore, is to begin with a description of a sale by a beneficial owner, i.e. a person entitled to the whole ownership for his own benefit, and then to notice any variation from the law applicable to this transaction that is peculiar to the other estate owners. The main chapter is the first (chapter 22) which deals with the beneficial owner, since it contains a general account of the proof and investigation of title that under the system of unregistered conveyancing is necessary in all cases irrespective of the character of the vendor. This is followed by an account of the different method that must be adopted where the title to the land is registered under the Land Registration Act 1925. The second chapter (chapter 23) treats of personal representatives, for their position raises matters that have not been discussed in the preceding pages. The remaining estate owners—tenants for life, statutory owners, trustees for sale and mortgagors—are grouped together in the same chapter, for to deal with them *in extenso* would involve a considerable repetition.

(b) Involuntary transfer

Involuntary transfer by operation of law arises where the owner of an estate or interest is:

> (i)   sued to judgment for non-payment of a debt, or
> (ii) made bankrupt, or
> (iii) dies insolvent,

1 For definition of bare trustee, see p. 96, n. 18, ante; p. 818, post.

in each of which cases his land is liable to be seized in satisfaction of the debts.

This topic was explained in previous editions of this book, but is omitted in order to save space. Reference should be made to specialist works on bankruptcy.[2]

B. TRANSFER ON DEATH

Turning to transfer on death, testacy and intestacy are dealt with in chapters 24 and 25 respectively.

C. EXTINCTION OF ESTATES AND INTERESTS

The next subject of discussion in this Part is the extinction of estates and interests. Under the modern law a right to land may be extinguished by:

1. forfeiture,
2. lapse of time, or
3. merger.

1. Forfeiture may operate where, for instance, an interest is subjected to a condition subsequent, or where land is leased to a tenant with a condition for forfeiture on non-payment of rent, but, these cases having already been considered in chapters 15 and 16 respectively, the subject of forfeiture will be omitted from the following pages.
2. Lapse of time causes the extinguishment of an interest whose owner remains out of possession, either of the land or of its profits, for the appropriate period designated by the Limitation Act 1980.
3. Where a smaller interest and a larger interest in the same land become united in one person, the doctrine of merger, subject to certain conditions, operates to extinguish the smaller interest.

The discussion of extinction, therefore, is confined to lapse of time and merger in chapters 26 and 27 respectively.

D. INCAPACITIES AND DISABILITIES

Finally attention is given in chapter 28 to those special persons, such as infants, mental patients and corporations, for whom the law has prescribed special rules with respect both to the holding and to the transfer of interests in land.

E. NEGLIGENT CONVEYANCING

A professional adviser, such as a solicitor,[3] or a surveyor or valuer,[4] or estate agent[5] may be liable in negligence. Of the duty which a solicitor owes to his client, OLIVER J said in *Midland Bank Trust Co Ltd v Hett, Stubbs & Kemp*:[6]

---

2 *Muir Hunter on Personal Insolvency.*
3 *Emmet on Title* (9th edn), paras. 1.010–1.011; Kenny, *Conveyancing Practice*, para. 1–019;

The test is what the reasonably competent practitioner would do having regard to the standards normally adopted in his profession.

Further, as MEGARRY V-C said in *Ross v Caunters*:[7]

There is no longer any rule that a solicitor who is negligent in his professional work can be liable only to his clent in contract; he may be liable both to his client and to others for the tort of negligence.

In that case,

solicitors who prepared a will for a testator and sent it to him for execution failed to warn him that the will should not be witnessed by the spouse of a beneficiary.[8] When the testator signed the will, one of the witnesses was the husband of the residuary beneficiary under it. It was held that the beneficiary was entitled to damages against the solicitor for negligence in respect of the loss of the benefits given to her by the will.

Solicitors were also held liable in both tort and contract in *Midland Bank Trust Co Ltd v Hett, Stubbs & Kemp*[9] for failing to advise a client to register an option to purchase as an estate contract under the Land Charges Act 1925 and for failing to register it.

The number of cases in the field of professional negligence is increasing, and reference should be made to specialist works on the subject.[10]

(1986) 136 NLJ 1887, 911 (H. W. Wilkinson). As to the advisability of a solicitor acting for both parties in the same transaction, see *Wills v Wood* (1984) Times, 24 March; *Clark Boyce v Houat* (1993) Times, 7 October (PC held solicitor may so act if he has obtained "informed consent" of both parties) *Emmet on Title*, para. 1.012; Solicitors' Practice Rules 1987, r.6.

4 *Emmet on Title*, para 1.065; *Perry v Sidney Phillips & Son* [1982] 1 WLR 1297, [1982] 3 All ER 705; [1984] Conv 60 (K. Hodkinson); *Hooberman v Salter Rex* [1985] 1 EGLR 144; *Shankie-Williams v Heavey* [1986] 2 EGLR 139 (surveyor instructed for one flat owed no duty of care to potential purchaser of adjoining flat); *Secretary of State for the Environment v Essex, Goodman & Suggitt* [1986] 1 WLR 1432, [1986] 2 All ER 69; *Smith v Eric S. Bush* [1990] 1 AC 831, [1989] 2 All ER 514, p. 663, n. 6, ante; *Sutcliffe v Sayer* [1987] 1 EGLR 155 (no duty on valuer to warn purchaser as to difficulties of resale); *Beaumont v Humberts* [1990] 2 EGLR 166 (valuation of unusual listed Grade II house for insurance reinstatement purposes: differences between all three members of CA); *Watts v Morrow* [1991] 1 WLR 1421, [1991] 4 All ER 937 (detailed examination of basis of damages).

5 *Bradshaw v Press* (1982) 268 EG 565 (failure to check references of tenant; held not liable); *Computastaff Ltd v Ingledew Brown Bennison & Garrett* (1983) 268 EG 906 (estate agent acting for landlord held liable to *tenant* for circulating inaccurate information about property). *McCullagh v Lane Kox & Partners Ltd* [1994] 08 EG 118; *Letgain Ltd v Super Cement Ltd* [1994] 07 EG 192.

6 [1979] Ch 384 at 403, [1978] 3 All ER 571 at 583. The judgment contains a useful analysis of the duty.

7 [1980] Ch 297 at 322, [1979] 3 All ER 580 at 599. Applied in *White v Jones* [1993] 3 WLR 730, [1993] 3 All ER 481 (solicitor, who failed to prepare will for client, held liable in damages to intended beneficiaries; (1993) 109 LQR 344 (J. G. Fleming); (1994) 110 LQR 55 (K. R. Handley); *Kecskemeti v Rubens Rabin & Co* (1992) Times, 31 December; cf. *Clarke v Bruce Lance & Co* [1988] 1 WLR 881, [1988] 1 All ER 364 (solicitors who prepared will did not owe a duty of care to potential devisee when they later acted for testator in an inter vivos transaction which adversely affected his devise); *Hemmens v Wilson Browne* [1993] 4 All ER 826 (solicitor who, by negligent drafting of an inter vivos transaction, failed to give intended beneficiary enforceable rights, held not liable to him, since it remained within power of settlor to remedy situation and the only reason he had not done so was that he had changed his mind). *Preston v Torfaen Borough Council* [1993] NPC 111 (surveyor held not liable to ultimate occupier of house for negligent survey of site prepared for developer).

8 Wills Act 1837, s. 15; p. 837, post.

9 [1979] Ch 384, [1978] 3 All ER 571; p. 766, n. 1, post. Liability in both contract and tort doubted by CA in *Lee v Thompson* [1989] 2 EGLR 151.

10 Jackson and Powell, *Professional Negligence* (3rd edn).

Part III

The transfer and extinction of estates and interests

A. TRANSFER INTER VIVOS BY ESTATE OWNERS

SUMMARY

Chapter 22

Beneficial owners. The sale of land[1]

SUMMARY

There are two quite separate and distinctive methods of conveyancing in operation in England and Wales at the present day; that relating to unregistered land and that relating to registered land. The former is the development of techniques which reach back to medieval times. The system in essence is one whereby the estate owner proves his title to land by showing from deeds and documents in his possession that he derives his title lawfully from some person or persons who have been in peaceful possession for a long period of time. In the nature of things, the title to his estate can never be proved absolutely, for there may have been an interference with the rights of the true owner many years back. However, with the assistance of the Limitation Acts,[2] proof of title during the last fifteen years is, for practical purposes, sufficient; and a purchaser is now required to trace the title back to a good root of title at least fifteen years' old.[3] On completion of the purchase, the deeds are handed over to the purchaser, and he will make title in a similar manner when he decides to sell.

A much more satisfactory system of proof of title is that of registration of the title in a central registry. New countries and states commonly use such a system. The practical difficulties, however, of changing over from a system of unregistered conveyancing to one of registered conveyancing are great. The change involves the recording of all interests in land which need to be placed on the register. In England and Wales, a system of registration of title, introduced in 1862,[4] was superseded by more comprehensive legislation in the Land Registration Act 1925. It provides for registration of title following

---

1 See generally Barnsley, *Conveyancing Law and Practice* (3rd edn); *Williams on Title* (4th edn); *Emmet on Title* (19th edn); Farrand, *Contract and Conveyance* (4th edn); Silverman, *Law Society's Conveyancing Handbook*; Storey, *Conveyancing* (4th edn); Thompson, *Investigation and Proof of Title* (1991).
2 P. 887, ante.
3 LPA 1969, s. 23, p. 751, post.
4 Land Registry Act 1862.

the first conveyance of land after the Act has been made applicable to the district in question; and subsequent conveyancing will be based on the title so registered.

The present decade is one of transition from unregistered to registered conveyancing, from the old to the modern. Compulsory registration of title was extended to the whole of England and Wales as from 1 November 1990.

SECTION I UNREGISTERED CONVEYANCING

A. INVESTIGATION OF TITLE

(1) INTRODUCTORY NOTE

A vendor and a purchaser of land generally desire that a binding[5] contract should be concluded at the earliest possible moment, subject to the purchaser's rights to rescind (in the sense of accepting repudiation[6]) if the vendor cannot show a good unincumbered title. Accordingly the purchaser usually does not investigate the vendor's title before contract.[7] Once a binding contract has been made, however, the procedure to be followed depends upon whether the contract relates to registered or unregistered land. We discuss first the position where land is unregistered.

(a) Delivery of abstract

The vendor is bound to show a good title to the interest that he has contracted to sell, and to this end and with a view to simplifying the purchaser's task, he must at his own expense deliver to the purchaser an abstract of title, that is, a summary of all the documents, such as wills and deeds of conveyance, that have dealt with the interest during the period for which his ownership has to be proved, and of all the events, such as deaths, that have affected the devolution of the ownership during that period. The period is either the 15 years fixed by statute, or that which is prescribed by a special stipulation in the contract of sale, though, as we shall see, the period will be longer than the statutory 15 years if a good root of title cannot otherwise be shown.

(b) Perusal of abstract

The vendor then verifies the abstract by producing evidence of the accuracy of the statements that he has made in the course of setting out his title. After

---

5 For the creation, enforceability and effect of a contract of sale, see chapter 6, p. 107, ante.
6 P. 135, ante.
7 For inquiries which are usually made before contract, see Law Commission Report on "Subject to Contract" Agreements (Law Com No. 65, 1975), pp. 4, 9–13; Aldridge, *Guide to Enquiries before Contract*; Annand and Cain, *Enquiries before Contract* (1986); *Emmet on Title* (19th edn), chapter 1; (1970) 120 NLJ 610, 630; (1973) 123 NLJ 1032; (1985) 135 NLJ 170, 905 (J. E. Adams). See (1992) 108 LQR 2 (C. Harpum), where it is argued that a vendor has an obligation to describe latent defects in title prior to contract.

For valuable Guidance from the Conveyancing Standing Committee of the Law Commission, see its *Preliminary Enquiries: House Purchase—A Practice Recommendation* (1987). The Committee examined and analysed some 75 sets of standard preliminary enquiries now in use. See its Second Report 1986–1987 (Law Com No. 169), para. 2.4.

For the duty of care owed by vendor's solicitor to purchaser when replying to enquiries before contract and subsequent requisitions on title, see *Wilson v Bloomfield* (1979) 123 SJ 860. See also *Computastaff Ltd v Ingledew Brown Bennison & Garrett* (1983) 268 EG 906 (solicitors held liable for failing to check with estate agents discrepancies revealed by answers to preliminary enquiries as to rateable value of premises).

this the purchaser's solicitor, at the expense of the purchaser, peruses the abstract, requisitions (i.e. addresses inquiries to) the vendor about any defects he may observe, satisfies himself that the property described in the contract is identical with that which has been dealt with in the documents abstracted, calls for evidence (such as death certificates) of events material to the title, and finally advises the purchaser whether he can with safety accept the title offered.

(c) Conveyance

The vendor is then obliged to convey the property free from incumbrances, to execute a deed of conveyance and to hand over to the purchaser all the title deeds relating to the property. The expense of preparing the deed of conveyance falls upon the purchaser.

The exact obligations of a vendor may, as we have said, be either specified or unspecified. If they are unspecified, and so left to be implied by law, the vendor is said to sell under an *open contract*. We will now proceed to state the rights and obligations of the parties, first where the contract is open, secondly where it contains the special stipulations generally found in practice.

(2) UNDER AN OPEN CONTRACT

The rights and the duties of the parties under an open contract are as follows:

(a) Duty of vendor to show title for 15 years[8]

Since the obligation of the vendor is to convey to the purchaser the interest that he has agreed to sell, free from incumbrances and competing interests, it follows that he must disclose and verify the state of his title to the land. Save in the rare case where he has been invested with an absolute title by Act of Parliament, he can scarcely show that he is entitled to an interest good against the whole world, for, however long he and his predecessors may have possessed and administered the land, the existence of some adverse claimant, such as a remainderman or reversioner, is always a possibility. But possession is prima facie evidence of seisin in fee and if he shows that he and his predecessors have been in possession for a considerable time, the existence of an earlier and therefore better title is at least improbable. On this assumption, the practical rule was ultimately evolved that proof of the exercise of acts of ownership over the land by the vendor and his predecessors for a period of not less than 60 years was prima facie evidence of his right to convey what he had agreed to sell. "It is a technical rule among conveyancers to approve a possession of sixty years, as a good title to a fee simple."[9] This period was statutorily reduced to 40 years in 1874,[10] to 30 years in 1925,[11] and to 15 years in 1969.[12]

Enjoyment for this period, however, is not conclusive evidence of a good title, and if it appears from the information supplied by the vendor or if it can be shown *ab extra* that the title falls short of what is required by the contract, the purchaser is not bound to complete. Possession by the vendor is

---

8 Barnsley, *Conveyancing Law and Practice* (3rd edn), pp. 250–257.
9 *Barnwell v Harris* (1809) 1 Taunt 430 at 432, per HEATH J.
10 Vendor and Purchaser Act 1874, s. 1.
11 LPA 1925, s. 44 (1).
12 LPA 1969, s. 23.

no doubt evidence of seisin in fee, but nevertheless he must show its origin, for though it is probably attributable to his position as tenant in fee, there is always the possibility that he is a mere tenant for life or years. As Lord ERSKINE once said:[13]

> No person in his senses would take an offer of a purchase from a man, merely because he stood upon the ground.

Even the rule under the Limitation Act 1980, that a person's title to land is extinguished after 12 years' adverse possession by a disseisor, does not in itself enable a disseisor to show a good title by proving possession in himself for even 15 years, since possession for the statutory period does not bar the rights of remaindermen and reversioners entitled to the land upon the determination of the disseisee's interest. He must go further and show what persons were entitled to the land when he took possession and prove that their claims have been barred by his continuance in possession.[14]

The usual way, therefore, in which the vendor proves his title is to produce the deeds or other documents by which the land has been disposed of in the past in order to show that the interest which he has agreed to sell has devolved upon him. Thus, in the normal case, the evidence of his title is documentary and is set out in the abstract of title that he delivers to the purchaser. This abstract must start with what is called a *good root of title*, i.e. a document which deals with the legal estate in the land, which is valid without requiring a reference to any earlier document, which adequately identifies the land, and which contains nothing to cast doubts on the title of the disposing party.

Thus a conveyance by way of sale or of legal mortgage[15] effected at least 15 years ago is a perfect root of title, since it may be presumed that the alienee was satisfied at that time with the state of the alienor's title, and if the intervening dispositions have been satisfactory, the present purchaser will obviously acquire a good title. A *general*, as distinct from a *specific*, devise of land is not a good root of title, since it does not identify the property and therefore does not show that the will passed the ownership of the same land as the vendor has now agreed to sell.

The obligation to begin the abstract with a good root of title may, of course, necessitate going back to some document more than 15 years old. As NORTH J said:[16]

> And when I say a [15] years' title, I mean a title deduced for [15] years, and for so much longer as it is necessary to go back in order to arrive at a point at which the title can properly commence. The title cannot commence in nubibus at the exact point of time which is represented by 365 days multiplied by [15]. It must commence at or before the [15] years with something which is in itself . . . a proper root of title.

There are a few cases in which the period for which title must be shown is longer than 15 years.[17] Thus:

---

13 *Hiern v Mill* (1806) 13 Ves 114 at 122.
14 *Games v Bonnor* (1884) 54 LJ Ch 517; *Scott v Nixon* (1843) 3 Dr & War 388 (Ireland); chapter 27, p. 909, post.
15 Even though a post-1925 mortgage does not take effect as a conveyance of the fee simple; p. 663, ante; Barnsley, *Conveyancing Law and Practice* (3rd edn), p. 254.
16 *Re Cox and Neve's Contract* [1891] 2 Ch 109 at 118.
17 LPA 1925, s. 44 (1). See *Emmet on Title* (19th edn), paras 5.032–5.034.

(*a*) where an advowson is sold, title must be shown for at least 100 years with a list of presentations during that period;[18]
(*b*) upon the sale of a leasehold, an abstract or copy of the lease, however old, must be produced with proof of dealings with the lease from a disposition at least 15 years old,[19] but the purchaser is not entitled to call for the title to the reversion;[20]
(*c*) if the subject matter of the sale is a reversionary interest, an abstract of the instrument which created the interest must be produced, with proof of 15 years' title back from the date of purchase.

(b) Duty of vendor to abstract and produce documents[1]

The vendor must at his own expense abstract and, if under his own control, produce the document which forms the root of his title, and all subsequent documents that affect the legal estate. In addition he must state and prove all facts that have affected the legal estate in the last 15 years.

But there are certain things that must not be abstracted, and certain titles and documents that cannot be called for.

(i) Certain equitable interests not to be abstracted Before 1926, a purchaser who took a conveyance of the legal estate was bound by any equitable interests affecting that estate of which he had notice. If, for instance, the abstract showed that the legal estate was held by the vendor as trustee, then, provided that he was an express trustee for sale, the equitable interests were ipso facto notified to the purchaser. It was necessary for the vendor to abstract the title to the equitable interests, and to obtain the concurrence of the beneficiaries in the conveyance.

But, as we have seen, one of the chief objects of the legislation of 1925 was to enable a purchaser to acquire the legal estate from the estate owner without being required to concern himself with equitable interests enforceable against the land. In general pursuance of this idea the Law of Property Act 1925 provides that in certain cases it shall not be proper to mention equitable interests in the abstract. It does not exclude all such interests, but only those that are overreached by the conveyance. What these are will be stated below.[2] The subsection in question is as follows:[3]

> Where title is shown to a legal estate in land, it shall be deemed not necessary or proper to include in the abstract of title an instrument relating only to interests or powers which will be overreached by the conveyance of the estate to which title is being shown; but nothing in this Part of this Act affects the liability of any person to disclose an equitable interest or power which will not be so overreached, or to furnish an abstract of any instrument creating or affecting the same.

Thus, to take a simple illustration, when a tenant for life contracts to sell settled land, he is not required to abstract the equitable interests of the beneficiaries. These are overreachable and are therefore of no concern to a purchaser.

18 Benefices Act 1898, s. 1; Benefices Act 1898 (Amendment) Measure 1923; Dart, *Vendors and Purchasers of Real Estate* (8th edn), vol. i, p. 292.
19 *Frend v Buckley* (1870) LR 5 QB 213; *Williams v Spargo* [1893] WN 100.
20 LPA 1925, s. 44 (2), (3), (4).
 1 Barnsley, *Conveyancing Law and Practice* (3rd edn), pp. 257–261.
 2 Pp. 814–5, 821–2, post.
 3 LPA 1925, s. 10 (1).

(ii) Freehold title not to be abstracted on sale of leasehold If the subject matter
of the sale is a term of years, the vendor is bound, as we have seen, to abstract
and produce the lease under which he holds the land; but it is enacted that in
an open contract he shall not be required to prove the title to the freehold.[4]
This latter rule applies where a fee simple owner agrees to *grant* a lease.
Thus:

> If A is fee simple owner of the land, and if he agrees to grant a lease to B
> for 99 years, B is not entitled to call for proof of A's title to the fee simple,
> unless he has inserted an express stipulation to that effect in the contract.
> Again, if B agrees later to sell his lease to C, the latter is precluded from
> calling for the title of A.

Similar rules apply to an agreement to sell a leasehold interest that is derived
out of a leasehold interest, or to an agreement to grant such a lease.[5] If, for
example:

> A leases to B and B underleases to C, and C agrees to sell his underlease to
> D, then D is entitled to production of the underlease,[6] but he cannot call
> for the lease to B.

These rules were formerly contained in the Vendor and Purchaser Act
1874, and the Conveyancing Act 1881, and it was held under those statutes
that, failing their express exclusion by the contract, a lessee or a purchaser of
a term of years was bound by equities affecting the legal estate that would
have come to his notice had he expressly required the freehold title to be
disclosed. This was decided in *Patman v Harland*:[7]

> In that case the plantiff sold land to A subject to a restrictive covenant. A sold to B,
> and B leased part of the land to the defendant, who committed a breach of the
> covenant. The defendant had no knowledge of the existence of the restrictive
> covenant, and, in an action brought against her for an injunction, it was argued
> that, as in an open contract she was debarred by the statute from inquiring into the
> title to the freehold out of which her lease was derived, she had no notice, actual or
> constructive, of the restrictive covenant, and therefore was not liable for its breach.

This argument was rejected by the Court of Appeal.

It is now, however, provided that, in contracts made after 1925, a person
who, under the above rules, is not entitled to call for the title to the freehold
or the leasehold reversion shall not be deemed to be affected with notice of
any matter or thing of which, if he had contracted that such a title should be
furnished, he might have had notice.[8] The doctrine of *Patman v Harland* is
therefore abolished in cases where a purchaser of a leasehold interest has no
right to call for the freehold title, though, in the case of registered land, it still
applies to incumbrances which are entered in the register.[9] This statutory
alteration operates, therefore, to the detriment of the owner of the equity,
but the alteration is subject to the qualification that the lessee remains bound

---

4 LPA 1925, s. 44 (2).
5 Ibid., s. 44 (3), (4).
6 *Gosling v Woolf* [1893] 1 QB 39. C is, however, entitled to call for B's lease. This is not
   precluded by s. 44, and, therefore, an under-lessee has constructive notice of the restrictive
   covenants in a lease: *Clements v Welles* (1865) LR 1 Eq 200. See Farrand, *Contract and
   Conveyance* (4th edn), p. 131.
7 (1881) 17 Ch D 353; M & B p. 511. See (1950) 56 LQR 361 (D. W. Logan).
8 LPA 1925, s. 44 (5).
9 *White v Bijou Mansions Ltd* [1937] Ch 610.

by any incumbrances that have been registered under the Land Charges Act 1972.[10]

There is also a more general enactment to the effect that a purchaser shall not be deemed to have notice of any matter or thing of which, if he had investigated the title prior to the beginning of the 15 years' period, he might have had notice, unless he actually makes the investigation.[11]

Purchaser in this connection means one who acquires an interest for money or money's worth, and includes a lessee and a mortgagee.[12] The expression *money's worth* excludes the consideration of marriage.

(c) Obligation of purchaser to bear the cost of producing certain documents

We have seen that one of the duties of a vendor is to produce a perfect abstract of title; it is incidental to this that he must produce at his own expense the documents which go to prove the title. If these are not in his possession, he must arrange for the production of those dated after the period of 15 years began in so far as they are material.[13] But as regards the expense of producing documents, the rule varies according as they are in the possession of the vendor or not.

At common law a vendor was bound to bear the cost of producing documents whether in his own possession or not, but the Conveyancing Act 1881 provided that the expenses of the production and of the inspection of documents *not in the vendor's possession*, the expenses of all journeys incidental thereto, and the expenses of procuring all evidences and information not in the vendor's possession should be borne by the purchaser.[14]

It was held under this section that where the vendor had mortgaged his property, the purchaser must pay the mortgagee's solicitor a fee for producing the deeds relating to the property.[15] This was a harsh application of the rule, and therefore the Law of Property Act 1925, while re-enacting the provisions of the Conveyancing Act, expressly provides that the expense of producing deeds which are in the possession of the vendor's *mortgagee or trustee* shall fall upon the vendor.[16] If, however, the mortgagee retains possession of a document, the purchaser must pay for any copy which he desires to have.

(d) Obligation of purchaser to examine the abstract at his own expense

The perusal of the abstract is carried out by the purchaser's solicitor, whose duty it is to advise whether the vendor has shown a good title to the exact interest that he has agreed to sell. The solicitor must satisfy himself that the abstract exhibits an ordered sequence of all the documents and events which have disposed of or affected the interest during the last 15 years, and if he observes defects or omissions, he must requisition the vendor on the matter. He must compare the abstract with the original deeds which are produced by the vendor's solicitor, and put in requisitions on points of discrepancy.

The solicitor must, for instance, require proper evidence of facts which

---

10 LPA 1925, at 619. See *Shears v Wells* [1936] 1 All ER 832; M & B p. 511; [1956] CLJ pp. 230–4 (H. W. R. Wade).
11 LPA 1925, s. 44 (8).
12 Ibid., s. 205 (1) (*xxi*).
13 *Re Stamford Spalding and Boston Banking Co and Knight's Contract* [1900] 1 Ch 287.
14 S. 3 (6).
15 *Re Willett and Argenti* (1889) 60 LT 735.
16 LPA 1925, s. 45 (4).

affect the interest, ascertain that the abstracted documents bear stamps of the proper value, and inquire concerning the existence of tenancies and easements.

(e) Obligation of purchaser to search registers of incumbrances

One of the first essentials in the investigation of an abstract of title is that a purchaser should search for incumbrances and interests which affect the land to be sold, and which may have been registered by their owners in a public register. This will be seen to be of great importance when we come to examine whether the purchaser of a legal estate takes the estate free from interests charged thereon. There are two main registers to be noticed, namely:

1. a central register[17] kept by the Land Charges Department of the Land Registry at Plymouth, where searches are carried out with the aid of a computer, and
2. the various local land charges registers kept in London by each London borough or the City of London, and elsewhere by each district council.[18]

(i) Land Charges Register

(A) Registrable interests
Under the Land Charges Act 1972, the Registrar of the Land Registry keeps five separate Registers,[19] namely:

(1) a register of pending actions;
(2) a register of annuities;
(3) a register of writs and orders affecting land;
(4) a register of deeds of arrangement affecting land; and
(5) a register of land charges.[20]

We will take these registers separately, and notice what kind of right or interest in land may be registered in each.

1. *Register of pending actions* It is obviously impossible to bring an action relating to land to a successful termination if alienation *pendente lite* is permissible, and therefore, in order that a plaintiff may not lose the fruits of his action, the law provides him with the means of protecting himself. This is afforded by the right to register a pending land action, i.e. any action, information or proceeding which is pending in court, and which relates to land or to any interest in, or charge on, land.[1]

---

17 In 1992–93, there were 197,221 new registrations, rectifications and renewals of land charges, and 3,486,137 searches of the Register: Report on H. M. Land Registry 1991–92, p. 21.
18 Local Land Charges Act 1975, s. 3 (1); p. 767, post.
19 LCA 1972, s. 1. The historical order of the registers, as set out in LCA 1925, s. 1 (1), has been followed. The new order is land charges, pending actions, writs and orders, deeds of arrangement and annuities. See generally Barnsley, *Conveyancing Law and Practice* (3rd edn), pp. 189–196, 333–366. On the history of registration, see *Ministry of Housing and Local Government v Sharp* [1970] 2 QB 223 at 280, [1970] 1 All ER 1009 at 1029, per CROSS LJ.
20 Ibid., s. 1 (1).
 1 Ibid., s. 5 (1), s. 17 (1); see *Taylor v Taylor* [1968] 1 WLR 378, [1968] 1 All ER 843; *Calgary and Edmonton Land Co Ltd v Dobinson* [1974] Ch 102, [1974] 1 All ER 484; *Whittingham v Whittingham* [1979] Fam 9, [1978] 3 All ER 805; *Greenhi Builders Ltd v Allen* [1979] 1 WLR 156, [1978] 3 All ER 1163; *Selim Ltd v Bickenhall Engineering Ltd* [1981] 1 WLR 1318, [1981] 3 All ER 210; *Regan & Blackburn Ltd v Rogers* [1985] 1 WLR 870, [1985] 2 All ER 180; *Sowerby v Sowerby* (1982) 44 P & CR 192; *Haslemere Estates Ltd v Baker* [1982] 1 WLR 1109, [1982] 3 All ER 525; [1983] Conv 69 (J. E. M.); *Perez-Adamson v Perez-Rivas* [1987] Fam 89,

Again, if a creditor wishes to make his debtor's property available for distribution among creditors generally, he may register in the same register the petition in bankruptcy which is the first step in setting bankruptcy proceedings in motion.[2]

If a pending action (i.e. either an action relating to land or a petition in bankruptcy) is registered, the registration remains effective for five years, but it may be renewed for successive periods of five years.[3] A purchaser for value (which word includes a mortgagee or lessee) of any interest in the land takes free from an *unregistered* pending action unless he has express, as distinct from constructive, notice of it.[4] In the case of an unregistered bankruptcy petition, however, this protection avails him only if he is a purchaser of a *legal* estate in good faith for money or money's worth.[5]

2. *Register of annuities* Before 1926 annuities or rentcharges did not affect purchasers of the land upon which they are charged unless they were registered in the Register of Annuities. No annuity can be entered in this Register after 1925, and it will be closed as soon as the annuities registered before 1 January 1926 have been worked off.[6]

Annuities, being interests for life merely, are necessarily equitable in nature after 1925, and they may now be registered as *general equitable charges* in the Register of Land Charges, provided that they do not arise under a settlement or a trust for sale.[7]

3. *Register of writs and orders affecting land* Any writ or order affecting land issued by a court for the purpose of enforcing a judgment or recognisance (e.g. an order of the court charging the land of a judgment debtor with payment of the money due[8]), any order which appoints a receiver[9] or sequestrator of land, any bankruptcy order, whether it is known to affect land or not, and any access order under the Access to Neighbouring Land Act 1992[10] is void against a purchaser for value of the land unless it is registered.[11] The registration remains effective for five years, but it may be renewed for successive periods of five years.[12]

The title of a trustee in bankruptcy, however, is void only against a

---

[1987] 3 All ER 20; [1987] Conv 58 (J. E. Martin); *Kemmis v Kemmis* [1988] 1 WLR 1307; *Willies-Williams v National Trust* (1993) 65 P & CR 359. See generally (1986) 136 NLJ 157 (H. W. Wilkinson).

2 LCA 1972, s. 5 (1).

3 Ibid., s. 5 (1).

4 Ibid., s. 5 (7).

5 Ibid., ss. 5 (8), 6 (5), as amended by Insolvency Act 1985, s. 235, Sch. 8, para. 21 (2) and Sch. 10.

6 LCA 1972, s. 1 (4), Sch. 1.

7 LCA 1972, s. 2 (4), Class C (iii); p. 759, post.

8 Charging Orders Act 1979, s. 3 (3); *Perry v Phoenix Assurance plc* [1988] 1 WLR 940, [1988] 3 All ER 60, M & B p. 297, p. 236, post. A Mareva injunction prohibiting a party from disposing of his assets is not registrable: *Stockler v Fourways Estates Ltd* [1984] 1 WLR 25, [1983] 3 All ER 501.

9 *Clayhope Properties Ltd v Evans* [1986] 1 WLR 1223, [1986] 2 All ER 795 (receivership order made against landlord for specific performance of repairing covenants held registrable). In registered land, this is registrable as a caution under LRA 1925, s. 54.

10 S. 5. See p. 396, n. 6, ante.

11 LCA 1972, s. 6 (1), (4), as amended by Supreme Court Act 1981, s. 152 (1), Sch. 5 and County Courts Act 1984, s. 148 (1), Sch. 2, para. 18.

12 Ibid., s. 8.

purchaser of a legal estate in good faith, for money or money's worth unless the bankruptcy order is registered.[13]

4. *Register of deeds of arrangement affecting land* An insolvent debtor sometimes comes to an arrangement with the general body of his creditors whereby, although he does not pay his debts in full, he obtains a release from the claims of the creditors. As a rule the debtor either compounds with his creditors, or assigns his property to a trustee for distribution among the creditors.

If such an arrangement is reduced to writing, it is called a deed of arrangement whether it is made by deed or not.[14] It is enacted that such an arrangement shall be void against a purchaser for value of the debtor's land unless it is registered in the above Register. Registration ceases to have any effect after five years unless it is renewed.[15]

5. *Register of land charges* The term *land charge* is comprehensive; it includes a number of different rights and interests affecting land. The Land Charges Act 1925, which made considerable additions to this part of the law, divided land charges into five classes, denominated A, B, C, D, and E; a further Class F was added by the Matrimonial Homes Act 1967.[16] The whole has now been consolidated in the Land Charges Act 1972.[17]

Class A[18]

This comprises a rent or a sum of money which is charged upon land, *pursuant to the application of some person*, under the provisions of any Act of Parliament, and with the object of securing money which has been spent on the land under the provisions of such Act. It also comprises a rent or a sum of money charged upon land in accordance with certain sections in, for example:

the Land Drainage Act 1976,[19]
the Agricultural Holdings Act 1986,[20]
the Landlord and Tenant Act 1927.[1]

Thus, if a tenant for life has to pay compensation to an outgoing agricultural tenant, he may obtain an order charging the holding with the repayment of the amount, and may have the charge registered. A land charge of this class is void against a purchaser unless it is registered before the completion of the purchase.[2]

Class B[3]

This comprises a charge on land (not being a local land charge) of any of the kinds described in Class A, provided that it has not been created "pursuant

13 LCA 1972, s. 6 (5) as amended by Insolvency Act 1985, s. 235, Sch. 8, para. 21 (3) and Sch. 10.
14 Deeds of Arrangement Act 1914, s. 1.
15 LCA 1972, s. 7.
16 Now Matrimonial Homes Act 1983; p. 241, ante.
17 See Land Charges Rules 1974 (S.I. 1974 No. 1286); Land Charges (Amendment) Rules 1990 (S.I. 1990 No. 485); Land Charges (Amendment) Rules 1994 (S.I. 1994 No. 287).
18 LCA 1972, s. 2 (2), Class A.
19 S. 26 (6).
20 Ss. 85 (2), (3), 86.
 1 S. 12, Sch. 1, para. 7, as amended by Landlord and Tenant Act 1954, s. 45 and Sch. 7, Pt. I. For other examples, see LCA 1972, s. 2, Sch. 2.
 2 LCA 1972, s. 4 (2).
 3 Ibid., s. 2 (3), Class B as amended by Local Land Charges Act 1975, s. 19, Sch. 2.

to the application of any person", and is imposed automatically by statute. An example is a charge on property recovered or preserved for an assisted litigant arising under the Legal Aid Act 1974, in respect of unpaid contributions to the legal aid fund.[4]

Charges of this class, however, are not important as regards searches in the Land Registry: because they mostly arise under the Public Health Act 1936, and being in the majority of cases of a local nature (as, for instance, those arising in respect of paving expenses) they are *local land charges* and must therefore be registered locally.[5]

Failure to register such a charge (not being a local land charge) at the Land Registry renders it void as against a purchaser for valuable consideration of the land or of any interest therein:

(i) if it arises after 31 December 1925, and has not been registered;
(ii) if it arose before that date and has not been registered within a year from the first conveyance of the charge made after 31 December 1925.[6]

Class C[7]

This class is important in that it creates a system of registration of mortgages of land, and provides for the registration of estate contracts. It comprises four different land charges (not being local land charges), namely:

(i) Puisne mortgage This is a *legal* mortgage not protected by a deposit of documents relating to the legal estate affected.

(ii) Limited owner's charge This is an equitable charge acquired under any statute by a tenant for life or statutory owner by discharging inheritance tax or other liabilities, and to which special priority is given by the statute. Thus a charge may arise under the Finance Act 1986,[8] in favour of a tenant for life who pays inheritance tax in respect of the estate out of which his life interest is carved.

(iii) General equitable charge This is a comprehensive expression that includes all equitable charges that are not assigned to a class of their own (such as estate contracts), and which do not arise or affect an interest arising under a trust for sale or a settlement. In particular it includes an equitable mortgage of a legal estate which is not secured by a deposit of the title deeds, but it also comprises a rentcharge for life and a vendor's lien for unpaid purchase money.[9] To be registrable, the charge must be on land, and not for instance upon the purchase money that will arise from the sale of land.[10]

(iv) Estate contract This is the only item included within Class C which is not in the nature of a mortgage. It is defined as being:[11]

---

4 S. 9.
5 P. 767, post.
6 LCA 1972, s. 4 (5), (7).
7 Ibid., s. 2 (4), Class C, as amended by Local Land Charges Act 1975, s. 17 (1) (*b*).
8 LCA 1972, s. 2 (4), as amended by FA 1975, s. 52, Sch. 12, para. 18 (2); ITA 1984, s. 276, Sch. 8, para. 3 (1) (*a*); FA 1986, s. 100 (1) (*b*). See ITA 1984, ss. 2 (2), 237, 238.
9 See *Uziell-Hamilton v Keen* (1971) 22 P & CR 655; *Property Discount Corpn Ltd v Lyon Group Ltd* [1981] 1 WLR 300 at 313, [1981] 1 All ER 379 at 385.
10 *Georgiades v Edward Wolfe & Co Ltd* [1965] Ch 487, [1964] 3 All ER 433. Report of Committee on Land Charges (1956 Cmnd 9825), para. 13 suggested that Class C (iii) might be abolished, except as regards mortgages.
11 LCA 1972, s. 2 (4), Class C (iv).

a contract by an estate owner or by a person entitled at the date of the contract to have a legal estate conveyed to him to convey or create a legal estate, including a contract conferring either expressly or by statutory implication a valid option of purchase, a right of pre-emption[12] or any other like right.[13]

This in practice means a contract for the sale of a legal fee simple, a contract for the grant of a term of years absolute,[14] or an option to acquire either of these interests.[15] We have already seen that the effect of such a contract is to confer an equitable interest upon the intending purchaser or tenant.[16] The effect of the Land Charges Act is to make it capable of registration.[17]

Class D[18]

This comprises the three following different land charges (not being local land charges):

(i) Inland revenue charge The Commissioners of Inland Revenue may register a charge on the occasion of the transfer of land which gives rise to the liability for inheritance tax under the Finance Act 1986.[19]

(ii) Restrictive covenant This has already been described,[20] and the only remark needed here is that restrictive covenants made between a lessor and a lessee are expressly excluded, and are not capable of registration.

(iii) Equitable easement This is defined as:[1]

any easement right or privilege over or affecting land created or arising on or after 1 January 1926, and being merely an equitable interest.

12 See pp. 127 et seq, ante.
13 *Shiloh Spinners Ltd v Harding* [1973] AC 691 at 719, [1973] 1 All ER 90 at 97.
14 *Sharp v Coates* [1949] 1 KB 285, [1948] 2 All ER 871 (contract by estate owner to convey an estate greater than he was entitled to at the time of the contract). It also includes a contract by which A agrees with B to create a legal estate in favour of such third person as B may nominate: *Turley v Mackay* [1944] Ch 37, [1943] 3 All ER 1; but not a contract by which A agrees that B has the power to accept offers to purchase made by third persons: *Thomas v Rose* [1968] 1 WLR 1797, [1968] 3 All ER 765.
15 *Beesly v Hallwood Estates Ltd* [1960] 1 WLR 549, [1960] 2 All ER 314. The decision was affirmed on another point: [1961] Ch 105, [1961] 1 All ER 90; *Taylors Fashions Ltd v Liverpool Victoria Trustees Ltd* [1982] QB 133n, [1981] 1 All ER 897; and approved in *Phillips v Mobil Oil Co Ltd* [1989] 1 WLR 888, [1989] 3 All ER 97; [1990] Conv 168, 250 (J. Howell); [1989] All ER Rev 193 (P. H. Pettit). A notice to treat served under a compulsory purchase order is not a contract; it may lead to one, and therefore is not registrable: *Capital Investments Ltd v Wednesfield UDC* [1965] Ch 774, [1964] 1 All ER 655. Cf Leasehold Reform Act 1967, s. 5 (5) (notice given by tenant of his desire to acquire the freehold or an extended lease registrable as estate contract); p. 489, ante.
16 P. 124, ante.
17 *Universal Permanent Building Society v Cooke* [1952] Ch 95 at 104, [1951] 2 All ER 893 at 898. See *Barrett v Hilton Developments Ltd* [1975] Ch 237, [1974] 3 All ER 944 (registration against the name of a person who has contracted to purchase the legal estate in land is not sufficient).
18 LCA 1972, s. 2 (5), Class D as amended by Local Land Charges Act 1975, s. 17 (1) (b).
19 Ibid., s. 2 (5), Class D (i), as amended by FA 1975, s. 52, Sch. 12, para. 18 (3) and FA 1986, s. 100 (1) (b). See ITA 1984, s. 237, Sch. 8, para. 3 (1) (b).
20 Pp. 614 et seq, ante.
1 For a discussion of this Class, see *Shiloh Spinners Ltd v Harding* [1973] 1 All ER 90; M & B p. 36 (equitable right of re-entry on breach of contract not registrable as Class D (iii) land charge); (1973) 32 CLJ 218 (P. B. Fairest); p. 530, ante. Report of the Committee on Land Charges (1956 Cmnd 9826), para. 16 suggested that Class D (iii) might be abolished. Law Commission Report on Land Charges affecting Unregistered Land (1969 Law Com No. 18), para. 65, recommended its retention. Registrations in that class were then running at an annual rate of 2,500–3,500; there were 829 registrations during the year ended 31 March 1993: Report on H M Land Registry 1992–93, p. 21.

Thus, an easement held for some smaller interest than a fee simple absolute in possession or for a term of years absolute, or an easement that has been informally created, satisfies this definition and is therefore registrable.

The three charges in Class D are not registrable unless they have arisen after 1925.

Class E

This class comprises annuities created before 1926 and not registered in the Register of Annuities. This register, as we have seen, was closed to new entries as from 1 January 1926, but annuitants who omitted to register before that date may register under Class E.[2]

Class F

This is the right of occupation of a dwelling house given to a spouse by the Matrimonial Homes Act 1967.[3]

(B) Effect of registration

We must now turn to the effect of registration and its mechanics. The effect is contained in section 198 (1) of the Law of Property Act 1925:

> The registration of any instrument or matter in any register kept under the Land Charges Act 1972 or any local land charges register shall be deemed to constitute actual notice of such instrument or matter, and of the fact of such registration, to all persons and for all purposes connected with the land affected, as from the date of registration . . . and so long as the registration continues in force.[4]

As we have seen,[5] this makes a substantial inroad on the doctrine of the bona fide purchaser for value without notice: that doctrine no longer operates in respect of land charges which are registrable.

1. *Registration against name of estate owner* It is important to notice that land charges affecting unregistered land are registered, not against the burdened *land*, as is the case with registered land, but against the *name* of the estate owner of the land at the time when the land charge was created.[6] The name of the estate owner means the name as disclosed by the conveyance.[7] If,

---

2 P. 757, ante.
3 P. 241, ante. Now Matrimonial Homes Act 1983.
4 As amended by Local Land Charges Act 1975, s. 17, Sch. 1. For an exception in the case of tacking, see LPA 1925, s. 198 (2), p. 732, ante. See also s. 96 (2), as amended by LP(A)A 1926, Schedule; p. 701, ante.
5 P. 97, ante.
6 LCA 1972, ss. 3 (1), 17 (1). On the mechanics of the register see *Oak Co-operative Building Society v Blackburn* [1968] Ch 730 at 741, [1968] 2 All ER 117 at 121, per RUSSELL LJ.
7 *Standard Property Investment Plc v British Plastics Federation* (1985) 53 P & CR 25; [1987] Conv 135 (J. E. A.). A person entitled to have the legal estate conveyed to him is not an estate owner: *Barrett v Hilton Developments Ltd* [1975] Ch 237, [1974] 3 All ER 944; *Property Discount Corpn Ltd v Lyon Group Ltd* [1981] 1 WLR 300, [1981] 1 All ER 379.
   The Law Commission recommends that registration of a land charge in the name of an estate owner who has died should be effective notwithstanding his death: Report on Title on Death 1989 (Law Com No. 184, Cm 777), paras. 2.7–2.9: [1990] Conv 70 (H. W. Wilkinson). See Law of Property (Miscellaneous Provisions) Bill 1994 (HL Bill 46), clause 15.

therefore, a purchaser desires to make a complete search at the Land Registry, he will have to discover the names of every owner of a legal estate in the land since 1 January 1926.[8] Even though this may be impossible, he will nevertheless be bound by a registered land charge. This causes difficulty to a purchaser and led to statutory intervention in 1969.[9]

(a) Land charge discovered between contract and completion

As we have seen, a purchaser does not normally investigate the vendor's title before contract.[10] In *Re Forsey and Hollebone's Contract*,[11] Eve J took the view that by virtue of section 198 of the Law of Property Act 1925, a purchaser has notice at the date of the contract of land charges which are then on the register, whether he knows of them or not. The difficulty for a purchaser under an open contract is that at the pre-contract stage he will not normally know the names of all the estate owners, and so he may be compelled to take a conveyance of the land subject to registered land charges which he cannot discover. Section 24 of the Law of Property Act 1969 amends the law so as to ensure that in respect of contracts entered into after 1 January 1970, *as against the vendor*, a purchaser will only be deemed to have notice of those registered land charges of which he has actual or imputed knowledge at the date of the contract.[12] Consequently, a purchaser will no longer be prevented from rescinding the contract on the ground of an undisclosed land charge merely because it has been registered. The owner of the registered land charge, however, remains protected: here registration still constitutes notice to all the world.

Section 24 does not apply to local land charges,[13] and, where they are concerned, the rule in *Forsey and Hollebone's Contract* may still apply. In this case, however, the problem for the purchaser is different. He does not need to know the names of the estate owners; the charges are registered against the land.[14] But the need to search the register before contract rather than at the same time as the other registers, that is to say, shortly before completion, is inconvenient and entails a delay which can put the contract at risk. The correctness of the rule continues to be questioned.[15]

(b) "Old land charge" discovered after completion

In this case a purchaser, who has carried out a full and proper investigation of title, may discover after completion that he is bound by land charges

8 Since January 1889 in respect of Class A land charges.
9 LPA 1969, ss. 24, 25. See generally Report of the Committee on Land Charges 1956 (Cmnd 9825); Law Commission Report on Land Charges affecting Unregistered Land 1969 (Law Com No. 18); (1970) 34 Conv (NS) 4 (F. R. Crane).
10 P. 750, ante.
11 [1927] 2 Ch 379.
12 The parties must not contract out of the section: LPA 1969, s. 24 (2).
13 LRA 1969, s. 24 (1), (3). Nor does it apply to registered land.
14 P. 767, post.
15 *Rignall Developments Ltd v Halil* [1987] 3 WLR 394, [1987] 3 All ER 170 "This part of Eve J's judgment . . . was greeted at the time by conveyancers with consternation and incredulity . . . It has since been subjected to severe criticism by the editors of *Emmet on Title* and other eminent conveyancers.": at 402, at 177 per Millett J; [1987] Conv 291 (C. Harpum); (1987) 137 NLJ 1178 (H. W. Wilkinson). See also *Citytowns Ltd v Bohemian Properties Ltd* [1986] 2 EGLR 256.

registered before the commencement of the vendor's title. He can, of course, stipulate for a list of all estate owners since 1 January 1926,[16] but this may be impracticable. The risk that he may be caught by an "old land charge" is increased by the reduction of the minimum period of investigation of title to 15 years.

The Law of Property Act 1969 preserves the validity of the registered land charge against the purchaser, but provides that where he has suffered loss as a result of its existence he is entitled to compensation.[17] This is payable if (a) his purchase was completed after 1 January 1970, (b) he purchased without actual or imputed knowledge of the land charge and (c) the charge was registered against the name of a person who did not appear as an estate owner in the relevant title.[18] Relevant title means either the statutory period of 15 years under an open contract, or the period of title in fact contracted for, whichever is the longer.[19]

(c) Land charge discovered after grant or assignment of lease

As we have seen, in the case of an open contract for the grant or assignment of a lease or underlease, the lessee or assignee is not entitled to call for the superior reversionary titles.[1] He may, however, be bound by registered land charges affecting those titles, even though he is unable to discover the names of the estate owners which are concealed in those titles. The Law of Property Act 1969 makes no change: the Law Commission is considering the matter in the context of the rule that the reversionary titles may not be called for.[2]

2. *Priority notices* The fact that a charge cannot be registered until it has actually been created occasioned some difficulty after the Land Charges Act 1925 came into operation. The provision of the Act that a charge on land, such as a restrictive covenant, shall be void against a subsequent purchaser of the legal estate for money or money's worth unless it is registered before *completion* of that purchase, produces an *impasse* in certain cases, for it is sometimes impossible to effect registration before completion. A common example of this arises where:

> X agrees to sell Blackacre to Y and takes a restrictive covenant from Y. Y, being unable to find the whole of the purchase money, arranges to mortgage Blackacre to Z. The conveyance from X to Y which creates the restrictive covenant, and the mortgage from Y to Z are in practice completed at the same time, so that it is practically impossible for X to register his restrictive covenant before it is rendered void under the Act by the completion of the purchase in favour of Z.

The Law of Property (Amendment) Act 1926[3] removed this difficulty by providing that any person *intending* to apply for the registration of any *contemplated* charge may register notice of his intention at the Land Registry.

---

16 And perhaps should where he purchases land for development. See (1969) 113 SJ 930 (S. M. Cretney).
17 S. 25. This does not apply to local land charges.
18 S. 25 (1) payable by the Chief Land Registrar out of public funds.
19 S. 25 (10).
1 P. 754, ante.
2 Law Com (1969 No. 18), para 37.
3 S. 4 (1); now LCA 1972, s. 11 (1). See (1977) 74 LSG 136 (P. Freedman).

This notice, which is called a *priority notice*, must be given at least 15 days before the registration is to take effect.[4] When the contemplated charge is actually created and later registered, then, provided that it is registered within 30 days after the priority notice, it takes effect as if registration had been secured at the very moment of its creation.[5]

3. *Official searches* Although a purchaser may search in a register himself, it is usual to obtain an official search. Upon receipt of such a requisition (as it is called) the registrar, after making the search, issues an official certificate, which is conclusive in favour of the purchaser.[6] If another charge is registered by a third person between the time when the certificate is issued and the time when the purchase is completed by the certificate holder, the registration does not affect the latter, provided that he completes his purchase within 15 days of the issue of the certificate.[7]

(C) *Effect of failure to register*

The failure to register a land charge does not affect the original parties to the transaction; as between them it remains valid. The effect as far as third parties are concerned is, however, not uniform. We have already seen the effect in connection with each register, except for land charge, Classes C, D and F. These merit more detailed treatment.

The effect of a failure to register the land charges comprised in Classes C, D, and F is as follows:

(a) Puisne mortgages (C(i))
     Limited owners' charges (C(ii))
     General equitable charges (C(iii))
     Spouse's right of occupation (F)

are void against:

a purchaser of the land charged with it, or of any interest in such land, unless the land charge is registered in the appropriate register before the completion of the purchase.[8]

"Purchaser" is defined in the Land Charges Act 1972 as follows:[9]

Unless the context otherwise requires,—"purchaser" means any person (including a mortgagee or lessee) who, for valuable consideration, takes any interest in land or in a charge on land.

4 LCA 1972, s. 11 (3), (6). Days when the registry is not open to the public are excluded.
5 Ibid., s. 11 (3).
6 Ibid., s. 10 (4). To be effective registration must be in the correct full name of the estate owner. If it is not, a clear certificate as a result of an official search against the correct name will not bind a purchaser. "But if there be registration in what may fairly be described as a version of the full names of the vendor, albeit not a version which is bound to be discovered on a search in the correct full names, we would not hold it a nullity against someone who does not search for all, or who (as here) searches in the wrong name": *Oak Co-operative Building Society v Blackburn* [1968] Ch 730 at 743, [1968] 2 All ER 117 at 122, per RUSSELL LJ; (1968) 31 MLR 705. See too *Du Sautoy v Symes* [1967] Ch 1146, [1967] 1 All ER 25. On liability where an erroneous certificate is issued, see *Ministry of Housing and Local Government v Sharp* [1970] 2 QB 223, [1970] 1 All ER 1009; *Coats Patons (Retail) Ltd v Birmingham Corpn* (1971) 69 LGR 356; *Diligent Finance Co Ltd v Alleyne* (1972) 23 P & CR 346; LCA 1972, s. 10 (6).
7 Ibid., s. 11 (5) (*b*).
8 Ibid., s. 4 (5), (8).
9 Ibid., s. 17 (1).

"Valuable consideration" is widely interpreted and includes the consideration of marriage, and may be inadequate or even nominal.[10]

The effect of the words "any interest" is that a purchaser even of an equitable interest in the land affected takes free from these charges if unregistered, irrespective of whether he has actual notice or not.

(b) Estate contracts (C(iv))
   Restrictive covenants (D(ii))
   Equitable easements (D(iii))

are void against:

> a purchaser for money or money's worth . . . of a legal estate in the land charged with it, unless the land charge is registered in the appropriate register before the completion of the purchase.[11]

(c) Inland Revenue Charge (D(i)) is void against:

> a purchaser in good faith for consideration in money or money's worth other than a nominal consideration and includes a lessee, mortgagee or other person who for such consideration acquires an interest in the property in question.[12]

In this case a very restricted meaning of purchaser is adopted. He must be in good faith; the consideration of marriage is excluded, and so is nominal consideration.

It therefore follows that the four charges in (a) and (b), even if unregistered, bind a purchaser of an equitable interest whether he has notice or not.[13] Again, a purchaser even of a legal estate whose title is supported only by a marriage consideration, cannot rely upon the omission to register.

Subject to these distinctions, the general effect of the non-registration of an interest that is registrable as a land charge is that it is void against a purchaser for value of any interest in the land. It is immaterial that a purchaser has actual knowledge of the unregistered interest, and this is so even if the land is conveyed to him expressly subject to it.[14] As HARMAN J said in *Hollington Bros Ltd v Rhodes*:[15]

> It appears at first glance wrong that a purchaser, who knows perfectly well of rights subject to which he is expressed to take, should be able to ignore them . . . It seems to me, however, that this argument cannot prevail having regard to the words in section 13 (2) of the Land Charges Act 1925[16] . . . The fact is that it was the policy

---

10 *Midland Bank Trust Co Ltd v Green* [1981] AC 513 at 532, [1981] 1 All ER 153 at 159.
11 LCA 1972, s. 4 (6), as amended by FA 1975, s. 52, Sch. 12, para. 18 (5); ITA 1984, s. 276, Sch. 8, para. 3 (2); FA 1986, s. 100 (1) (*b*).
12 FA 1975, s. 51 (1).
13 *McCarthy and Stone Ltd v Julian S Hodge & Co* [1971] 1 WLR 1547, [1972] 2 All ER 973; M & B p. 51 (unregistered estate contract held to have priority over subsequent equitable mortgage).
14 LPA 1925, s. 199 (1) (i).
15 [1951] 2 TLR 691 at 695, [1951] 2 All ER 578 at 580; M & B p. 381; LPA 1925, s. 199 (1) (i). An unregistered registrable interest is not always void and unenforceable owing to lack of registration (e.g. a pending land action: LCA 1972, s. 7) and in such case a purchaser with express notice is bound; p. 756, ante. Such an interest may also be binding (a) by estoppel; *Taylors Fashions Ltd v Liverpool Victoria Trustees Co Ltd* [1982] QB 133n, [1981] 1 All ER 897; M & B p. 563; p. 596, ante; (b) by failure to plead the non-registration when sued: *Balchin v Buckle* (1982) Times, 1 June; M & B p. 52n. 2. As to whether such an interest might be binding under a constructive trust, see (1981) 97 LQR pp. 521–522 (B. Green).
16 Now LCA 1972, s. 4 (6).

of the framers of the 1925 legislation to get rid of equitable rights of this sort unless registered.[17]

The House of Lords adopted a similar approach in *Midland Bank Trust Co Ltd v Green*,[18] when considering the effect of failure to register an estate contract. Lord WILBERFORCE said:[19]

The case is plain. The Act is clear and definite. Intended as it was to provide a simple and understandable system for the protection of title to land, it should not be read down or glossed: to do so would destroy the usefulness of the Act. Any temptation to remould the Act to meet the facts of the present case on the supposition that it is a hard one and that justice requires it, is, for me at least, removed by the consideration that the Act itself provides a simple and effective protection for persons in [the son's] position—viz—by registration.

In that case:

a father granted to his son a 10 year option to purchase the farm of which the son was his tenant. The option was not registered as an estate contract. Later the father, wishing to deprive the son of his option, conveyed the farm, then worth about £40,000 to the mother for £500. When the son found this out, he registered the option and purported to exercise it.

It was held that the mother was a purchaser for money or money's worth and therefore the option was void against her. It was immaterial that she had given inadequate (or even nominal) consideration and might have intended to defeat the unregistered interest. There was no requirement of good faith in the definition of a purchaser in the Land Charges Act, and, even though it existed in other definitions in the 1925 legislation,[20] it should not be imported into that Act. There was no need to psychoanalyse a purchaser.[1]

(D) Summary

In unregistered conveyancing the Land Charges Act 1972 thus plays a major part in enabling a purchaser to discover whether certain rights bind the land or not. The effect of the Act is automatic: if a registrable interest is registered, it binds; if not, in general a purchaser for value of any interest in the land takes free from it. Many of the risks which arise to him from the doctrine of constructive notice have thus been mitigated, but there is still a residual category of equitable interests which are neither registrable nor over-reachable and will therefore bind a purchaser unless he is a bona fide

17 See, however, [1982] Conv 213 (M. Friend and J. Newton) at pp. 215–217; M & B p. 52.
18 Supra.
19 At 528, at 156.
20 LPA 1925, s. 205 (1) (xxi); SLA 1925, s. 117 (1) (xxi); AEA 1925, s. 55 (1) (xviii); LRA 1925, s. 3 (xxi).
1 The "Green saga", which "bids fair to rival in time and money the story of *Jarndyce v Jarndyce*" (see [1980] Ch 590 at 622, [1979] 3 All ER 28 at 32, per Lord DENNING MR), continued. For the liability of the solicitor for failing to advise the son to register the option and for failing to register it, see *Midland Bank Trust Co Ltd v Hett, Stubbs and Kemp* [1979] Ch 384, [1979] 3 All ER 167; and for conspiracy between husband and wife, see *Midland Bank Trust Co Ltd v Green (No. 3)* [1982] Ch 529, [1981] 3 All ER 744. For a full review of all three cases by Sir Peter OLIVER, who tried them at first instance, see *The Green Saga* (1983) Child & Co Oxford Lecture. See also [1981] CLJ 213 (C. Harpum); (1981) 97 LQR 518 (B. Green).

purchaser for value of the legal estate without notice,[2] e.g. a restrictive covenant entered into before 1926,[3] and a licence by estoppel.[4]

Further, the difficulties which are inherent in a system of registration based on a names register are themselves mitigated by the Law of Property Act 1969.

The importance of the Land Charges register will eventually decline now that the system of registration of title under the Land Registration Act 1925 has been extended throughout the country. But its importance will continue for a long time to come. Many freehold and leasehold titles will remain unregistered, since, as we have seen,[5] registration of title occurs only on the first conveyance of the freehold, or on the grant or first assignment of a long lease, and short leases are incapable of registration.

Finally we must mention two registers which are kept in addition to those at the Land Registry.[6]

(ii) Local land charges registers

These are maintained under the Local Land Charges Act 1975[7] by all district councils in England and Wales, and also by London boroughs and the Common Council of the City of London.[8] They differ from those kept at the Land Registry in that the charges are registered against the land and not against the name of the estate owner; they relate both to registered and to unregistered land[9] and are of public rather than a private nature.[10] Local land charges are a heterogeneous collection[11] and include charges for

---

2 P. 59, ante.
3 P. 621, ante.
4 Pp. 595 et seq, ante.
5 P. 100, ante.
6 There are other registers which a purchaser may have to search: (a) Commons and Town and Village Greens under Commons Registration Act 1965, s. 3; p. 567, ante; (b) Agricultural charges under Agricultural Charges Act 1928, s. 5 (charge created by a farmer on his farming stock and other agricultural assets as security for sums advanced to him by a bank); this register is kept at the Land Registry at Plymouth; (c) For other registers maintained by local authorities, see Garner, *Local Land Charges* (11th edn), chapter 10; p. 948, post. On searches generally, see Silverman, *Searches and Enquiries* (2nd edn), especially Parts IV and V, which deal with less usual searches. For the liability of a solicitor who failed to search the Commons Register, see *G and K Ladenbau (UK) Ltd v Crawley and De Reya* [1978] 1 WLR 266, [1978] 1 All ER 682.
7 LLC Rules 1977 (S.I. 1977 No. 985); LLC(A) Rules 1978 (S.I. 1978 No. 1638); 1982 (S.I. 1982 No. 461); 1983 (S.I. 1983 No. 1591); 1986 (S.I. 1986 No. 129); 1987 (S.I. 1987 No. 389); 1989 (S.I. 1989 No. 951); 1990 (S.I. 1990 No. 485); 1992 (S.I. 1992 No. 194). The Act came into force on 1 August 1977 and replaces LCA 1925, s. 15 and other sections set out in LCA 1972, s. 18, Sch. 4. See Law Commission Report on Local Land Charges 1974 (Law Com No. 62, HC 71); Garner, *Local Land Charges* (11th edn), which has a useful table of all local land charges arranged alphabetically (pp. 113–23). See also Aldridge, *Enquiries of Local Authorities*; and the Report of the Law Commission's Conveyancing Standing Committee: Local Authority Enquiries, recommending a ten working days' limit for replies in all routine cases; (1989) 139 NLJ 14.
8 Local Land Charges Act 1975, s. 3 (1). This includes the Inner Temple and the Middle Temple: s. 3 (4).
9 P. 795, post.
10 For an exception, see the notice under the Rights of Light Act 1959, s. 2; p. 555, ante.
11 Local Land Charges Act 1975, ss. 1, 2. A condition or limitation subject to which planning permission is granted is excluded: s. 2 (e); p. 948, post. See the recommendation of the Second Report of the Conveyancing Committee (1985), for a more comprehensive Local Land Charges Register by consolidating the Commons Register with it.

securing money recoverable by local authorities under public health legislation, and prohibitions of or restriction on the user of land imposed by a local authority, Minister of the Crown or a government department.

The Act has made a significant change in the effect of the non-registration of a local land charge. Section 10[12] provides that failure to register such a charge in the local land charges register shall not affect the enforcement of the charge, but that a purchaser[13] shall be entitled to compensation for any loss suffered by him by reason that the charge was not registered, or was not shown as registered by an official search certificate.[14] This follows a recommendation by the Law Commission which observed that the overwhelming majority of local land charges are created in the public interest, and that it is usually inappropriate that lack of registration or non-disclosure in an official certificate of search should affect their enforceability.[15]

(iii) Companies Register

This is a register maintained in Cardiff and in London under the Companies Act 1985 of land charges created by a company for securing money.[16] Registration on this register of a charge created by a company before 1970 or so created at any time as a floating charge, is sufficient in place of registration in the Land Charges Register and has the same effect. A charge created by a company on or after 1 January 1970, other than a floating charge, must be registered at the Land Charges Registry if it is to bind a purchaser.[17] If it is to bind creditors and liquidators it must also be registered in the Companies Charges Register within twenty-one days of its creation.[18]

(f) Duty of vendor to convey the identical property that he has agreed to sell

The vendor must prove that the property which he is able to convey is substantially the same in nature, situation and quantity as that which he has agreed to sell, and it is advisable, when a contract for the sale of land is drafted, to obtain a description of the land from the "parcels" clause of the last conveyance.[19]

If, in the case of an open contract, the property is not identical in quantity

12 As amended by Local Government (Miscellaneous Provisions) Act 1982, s. 34.
13 Local Land Charges Act 1975, s. 10 (3) (*a*) defines a purchaser as a person who, for valuable consideration, acquires any interest in land or the proceeds of sale of land; and this includes a lessee or mortgagee.
14 Under LCA 1925, s. 15, a local land charge was void against a purchaser for money or money's worth of a legal estate in the land affected, unless registered before completion of the purchase.
15 Law Commission Report on Local Land Charges 1974 (Law Com No. 62), para. 90. See also paras 52–4.
16 A company must also keep a register of charges at its registered office: Companies Act 1985, ss. 406–409. See *Buckley on the Companies Act* (14th edn), vol. 1, pp. 238–269; *Gore-Brown on Companies* (43rd edn), paras 18–11 to 18–39; Palmer, *Company Law* (23rd edn), chapter 45.
17 LCA 1972, s. 3 (7), (8), as substituted by Companies Act 1989, s. 107, Sch. 16, para. 1. See *Property Discount Corpn Ltd v Lyon Group Ltd* [1981] 1 WLR 300, [1980] 1 All ER 334 (registration in companies register held sufficient, even though it was not in name of estate owner as required by LCA 1972, s. 3 (1); p. 761, ante; [1982] Conv 43 (D. M. Hare and T. Flanagan).
18 Companies Act 1985, ss. 395–396, as inserted by Companies Act 1989, s. 93. See *Re Molton Finance Ltd* [1968] Ch 325, [1967] 3 All ER 843. For liability in negligence of solicitors in failing to register a charge under Companies Act 1948, s. 95 (now Companies Act 1985, s. 395), see *Re Foster* [1986] BCLC 307.
19 Williams, *Vendor and Purchaser* (4th edn), p. 36; for the "parcels clause", see p. 782, post.

or quality with that agreed to be sold, the vendor cannot compel specific performance of the contract subject to compensation, unless the difference is insignificant and his conduct has been honest.[20]

> If a vendor sues and is in a position to convey substantially what the purchaser has contracted to get, the court will decree specific performance with compensation for any small and immaterial deficiency, provided that the vendor has not, by misrepresentation or otherwise, disentitled himself to his remedy.[1]

Thus, if a contract for sale is made, and investigation of the title shows that the property is subject to restrictive covenants, the vendor cannot force the title on the purchaser subject to compensation,[2] but he can do so, for example, if the sole mistake is that a right of common attached to the land extends only to sheep instead of being, as represented, unlimited.[3]

A purchaser, on the other hand, is in a more favourable position, for as a general rule he is allowed to take all that he can get, and to subject the vendor to a proportionate diminution of the purchase money. But specific performance will not be decreed at the suit of the purchaser if the property which the vendor is in a position to convey is entirely different from that which he agreed to sell, or if the difference is one for which it is impossible to fix pecuniary compensation, or if the effect of decreeing specific performance would be to cause injustice to third parties.[4]

(g) Duty of the purchaser to complete the contract

After the purchaser has investigated the abstract, it is his duty either to accept or to reject the title offered to him. If he takes the latter course, the parties are left to their remedies as specified above.[5] If, however, the purchaser is satisfied with the title, then the contract must be completed in accordance with its terms. Completion of a contract means that the purchaser must at his own expense prepare a proper deed of conveyance which is effectual to pass the interest to be sold and which contains the usual covenants for title by the vendor. He must also tender the price that he has agreed to pay. On the vendor's side completion involves the execution of the conveyance and the delivery of possession of the land to the purchaser.[6]

(h) Duty of vendor to deliver the title deeds[7]

The vendor must deliver to the purchaser all title deeds which relate solely to the property sold, though he may retain such documents where he retains any part of the land to which they relate, or where the document consists of

---

20 *Cox v Convention* (1862) 31 Beav 378; *Re Arnold* (1880) 14 Ch D 270 at 279; p. 135, ante.
 1 *Rutherford v Acton-Adams* [1915] AC 866 at 869–70, per Viscount HALDANE.
 2 Cf *Rudd v Lascelles* [1900] 1 Ch 815.
 3 *Howland v Norris* (1784) 1 Cox Eq Cas 59.
 4 *Willmott v Barber* (1880) 15 Ch D 96; *Rudd v Lascelles*, supra, at 819.
 5 Pp. 129 et seq, ante.
 6 Williams, *Vendor and Purchaser* (4th edn), p. 37; [1991] Conv 15, 81, 185 (D. G. Barnsley). See *Edward Wong Finance Co Ltd v Johnson Stokes & Master* [1984] AC 296, [1984] 2 WLR 1 where PC held purchaser's solicitors liable for negligence in completing sale by payment of purchase price in exchange not for executed documents of title but for an undertaking by vendors' solicitor to forward them within specified period—"completion Hong Kong style".
 7 As to the right to possession of title deeds, see *Clayton v Clayton* [1930] 2 Ch 12.

a trust instrument creating a trust that is still subsisting.[8] Where the documents which are necessary to show a good title remain in the vendor's possession, or where their custody belongs to some person other than the vendor, it is the vendor's duty to give a written acknowledgment of the purchaser's right to their production and to delivery of copies and a written undertaking for their safe custody. The effect of such an acknowledgment is that the purchaser, or persons claiming under him, can, at their own expense, demand to see the documents, or claim to be furnished with copies.[9]

(i) Duty to deliver vacant possession

Lastly, it is an implicit term of a contract of sale that vacant possession shall be given to the purchaser on completion.[10] Therefore a refusal by the purchaser to complete is justified if the land is subject to an unexpired tenancy, or if it has been lawfully requisitioned by a public authority.[11]

(3) CONDITIONS OF SALE UNDER CONTRACTS CONTAINING SPECIAL STIPULATIONS

We have now described in bare outline the nature of the parties' obligations under an open contract. Land, however, is not usually sold in this manner. As we have seen,[12] if the contract is by correspondence, statutory conditions apply; and, in practice, it is usual for the parties to regulate their rights and duties by *special conditions* in the contract of sale. A professionally drawn contract will generally incorporate the terms of Standard Conditions of Sale with variations to meet the particular case. Reference must be made to the standard textbooks on conveyancing for full treatment.[13]

Matters which are commonly the subject of special conditions are:

the root of title and the length of title (although this will be less important as a result of the Law of Property Act 1969);[14]

the date upon which possession is to be given, and the consequences if default is made;

interest to be payable by the purchaser on the purchase price, if the sale is not completed on the stipulated date;

the restriction of the purchaser's remedies for minor misdescriptions; and

planning matters.

---

8 LPA 1925, s. 45 (9).
9 Ibid., s. 64.
10 *Cook v Taylor* [1942] Ch 349, [1942] 2 All ER 85; *Sheikh v O'Connor* [1987] 2 EGLR 269. See Farrand, *Contract and Conveyance* (4th edn), pp. 174–178; [1988] Conv 324, 400 (C. Harpum).
11 *Cook v Taylor*, supra; *James Macara Ltd v Barclay* [1945] KB 148, [1944] 2 All ER 589: cf *Re Winslow Hall Estates Co and United Glass Bottle Manufacturer Ltd's Contract* [1941] Ch 503, [1941] 3 All ER 124; *Hillington Estates Co v Stonefield Estates Ltd* [1952] Ch 627, [1952] 1 All ER 853; *Topfell Ltd v Galley Properties Ltd* [1979] 1 WLR 446, [1979] 2 All ER 388.
12 P. 109, ante.
13 Silverman, *Standard Conditions of Sale* (4th edn); Wilkinson, *Standard Conditions of Sale of Land* (4th edn); [1980] Conv 404 (H. W. Wilkinson); [1982] Conv 85; [1984] Conv 396; *Emmet on Title* (19th edn), paras 2.075 et seq and passim. See also *Conveyancing Lawyer's Conditions of Sale* (1978); (1979) 129 NLJ 286 (H. W. Wilkinson); [1981] Conv 38.
14 P. 751, ante.

B. THE CONVEYANCE

(1) NECESSITY FOR A DEED

(a) Forms of alienation

The appropriate form at the present day for the conveyance of any interest in land is a deed of grant, but this form, though always required for the transfer of incorporeal hereditaments, was not extended to freehold estates in possession until 1845. Before that date the distinction drawn by the law was that freehold estates in possession *lay in livery*, i.e. were transferable by delivery of possession, and that incorporeal interests *lay in grant*, i.e. must be conveyed by deed of grant.[15] The Real Property Act of 1845, however, provided that all corporeal hereditaments should, as regards the conveyance of the immediate freehold thereof, be deemed to lie in grant as well as in livery. This Act did not, however, abolish the old forms of conveyance, and although it led to the general use of a deed of grant as a means of transferring all kinds of landed interests, there were still occasions upon which such forms as the feoffment and the bargain and sale were used.

The Law of Property Act 1925 simplified practice by providing that:[16]

All lands and all interests therein lie in grant and are incapable of being conveyed by livery or livery and seisin, or by feoffment, or by bargain and sale; and a conveyance of an interest in land may operate to pass the possession or right to possession thereof, without actual entry, but subject to all prior rights thereto.

This section, which shows that a grant is the usual method of conveying any interest in land, is followed by another which provides that:[17]

all conveyances of land or of any interest therein are void for the purpose of conveying or creating a legal estate unless made by deed.

This enactment, if unqualified, would cause inconvenience in certain cases, and it is therefore subject to exceptions. These are as follows:[18]

(b) Exceptions to necessity for a deed

(i) **Assents by personal representatives** The land of a deceased person vests in his personal representatives for the purposes of administration, and any devises he may have made are suspended until the administration is completed.[19] Upon such completion the land does not pass automatically to a devisee, but only when the assent of the personal representatives has been given. It is enacted that an assent to the vesting of a legal estate shall be *in writing*, signed by the personal representatives, and shall name the person in whose favour it is given and shall operate to vest in that person the legal estate to which it relates. An assent not in writing or not in favour of a named

---

15 For the history of the forms of alienation, see Holdsworth, *History of English Law*, vol. iii, pp. 217–46; vol. vii, pp. 357–62. See p. 46, n. 4, ante.
16 LPA 1925, s. 51 (1).
17 Ibid., s. 52 (1). For the effect of such a conveyance at law and in equity, see pp. 375 et seq, ante.
18 Ibid., s. 52 (2).
19 Pp. 807 et seq, post.

person is ineffectual to pass a legal estate.[20] An implied assent, i.e. one inferred from conduct, may be effective to pass a title to equitable interests or to *choses in action* and personal chattels.[1]

(ii) Disclaimers by a trustee in bankruptcy When any part of the estate of a bankrupt consists of land which is burdened with onerous covenants and is therefore unsaleable, the trustee in bankruptcy may, by writing, disclaim the property. Such a disclaimer operates to determine the rights and the liabilities of the bankrupt in respect of the property, but it does not affect the rights of third parties. The court may, on the application of any person who is interested in the disclaimed property, make an order vesting the property in him, and the effect of such an order is that the property vests in that person without any conveyance.[2]

(iii) Leases for a term not exceeding three years[3]

(iv) Vesting orders of the court A vesting order is an order made by the court which may operate to vest, convey or create a legal estate in the same way as if a conveyance had been executed by the estate owner.[4] If, for instance, an equitable chargee applies for a sale of the land, the court may make an order vesting the land for a legal estate in the purchaser.[5]

(v) Surrenders by operation of law Surrender is not an instrument, but means that the owner of a smaller estate yields up that estate to the person who is entitled in reversion or remainder to the larger estate in the same lands, as for instance, where the tenant for life of Blackacre surrenders his life interest to the person who is entitled to the fee simple in the land. In such a case the life interest is merged in the fee simple.

Surrenders are either express or implied and when implied they are said to arise by operation of law.

An express surrender is void at law unless it is made by deed, but an implied surrender is effectual without any formality.[6]

(vi) Conveyances taking effect by operation of law[7] Examples of these are grants of probate or of letters of administration and adjudications in bankruptcy.

(vii) Receipts not required to be under seal We have already seen that the legal estate of a mortgagee is re-vested in the mortgagor upon redemption not by a reconveyance under seal, but by an endorsed receipt.[8]

---

20 AEA 1925, s. 36 (1), (4); *Re King's Will Trusts* [1964] Ch 542, [1964] 1 All ER 833; (1964) 28 Conv (NS) 298 (J. F. Garner); (1976) CLP 60 (E. C. Ryder); Farrand, *Contract and Conveyance* (4th edn), p. 106; Barnsley, *Conveyancing Law and Practice* (3rd edn), p. 292. See Law Commission Working Paper on Title on Death 1987 (No. 105), paras 4.19–4.28; Law Commission Report on Title on Death 1989 (Law Com No. 184), paras 1.5–1.6. *Re King's Will Trusts* was not followed in *Mohay v Roche* [1991] 1 IR 560; [1992] Conv 383 (J. A. Dowling).

1 *Re Hodge* [1940] Ch 260; *Re Edward's Will Trusts* [1982] Ch 30, [1981] 2 All ER 941; [1982] Conv 4 (P. W. Smith).

2 Insolvency Act 1986, s. 315; *Eyre v Hall* [1986] 2 EGLR 95.

3 LPA 1925, s. 54 (2); p. 374, ante.

4 Ibid., s. 9.

5 Ibid., s. 90.

6 P. 458, ante.

7 LPA 1925, s. 52 (2) (g).

8 P. 685, ante.

Finally we must consider the formalities necessary for the creation of a trust and for the disposition of an equitable interest. In neither case is a deed required.

(c) Creation of a trust

There are very few rules restricting the mode in which a trust must be created. The trust is the successor of the old use, and for the raising of a use no formalities were necessary. Spoken words were as effectual as written instruments, and according to the preamble to the Statute of Uses bare signs and gestures seem to have been sufficient. The one guiding principle was that effect should be given to the intention of the settlor, no matter how it had been indicated by him. So in general is it with the modern trust.

A trust may be created either by an instrument inter vivos or by will.

If it is created inter vivos and if it relates to land, it must conform to the Law of Property Act 1925, which requires writing.[9]

If it is created by will, then, whether it relates to real or to personal property, the instrument of creation must be made in accordance with the Wills Act 1837, which prescribes the manner in which all wills must be made.[10]

If neither the Law of Property Act 1925 nor the Wills Act 1837 applies, if, that is to say, the trust relates neither to freeholds nor to leaseholds, and if it is not contained in a will, it may be created by word of mouth or by some other indication of intention, and without any kind of formality. A clear oral declaration by the owner of pure personalty that he is a trustee of that property for another person constitutes a valid trust and can be enforced by the volunteer in whose favour it was declared.[11]

But it was found in the case of land that parol declarations of trusts led to disputes and inconveniences, and therefore the Statute of Frauds in 1677 required for the first time that the creation of a trust of real estate should be manifested and proved by some writing signed by the settlor.[12] This provision has now been re-enacted by section 53 (1) (b) of the Law of Property Act 1925 in the following words:

> A declaration of trust respecting any land or any interest therein must be manifested and proved by some writing signed by some person who is able to declare such trust or by his will.

There are several points that should be noticed about this enactment. Thus it is confined to land and does not interfere with the rule that a trust of pure personalty may be constituted by an oral declaration.

It does not require a deed, but only a writing, and even so it does not require that the trust should have been declared by writing in the first place. The statute uses the words "manifested and proved", and it is sufficient if the trust can be proved by some writing signed by the settlor no matter what the date of the writing may have been.[13]

The writing is to be signed by "some person who is able to declare such

9 S. 53 (1) (b), infra.
10 Pp. 835 et seq, post.
11 *Jones v Lock* (1865) 1 Ch App 25; *Richards v Delbridge* (1874) LR 18 Eq 11; *Middleton v Pollock* (1876) 2 Ch D 104; *Paul v Constance* [1977] 1 WLR 527, [1977] 1 All ER 195; M & B, *Trusts and Trustees* (4th edn), pp. 114 et seq.
12 S. 7.
13 *Rochefoucauld v Boustead* [1897] 1 Ch 196 at 206.

trust", that is, the person who is the owner of the property in respect of which the trust is declared.[14] No provision is made for signature by an agent.

The statutory provisions apply only to express trusts, and not to the creation or operation of resulting, implied or constructive trusts.[15]

(d) Disposition of equitable interest

Section 53 (1) (*c*) of the Law of Property Act 1925 provides that:

> a disposition of an equitable interest or trust subsisting at the time of the disposition must be in writing signed by the person disposing of the same, or by his agent thereunto lawfully authorized in writing or by will.

In this context the word "disposition" must be given the wide meaning that it bears in normal usage, and therefore, for instance, an oral direction by a beneficiary to trustees to hold an equitable interest upon new trusts is a disposition that is ineffective for want of writing.[16]

(2) THE GENERAL NATURE OF A DEED[17]

A deed of grant is a formal written instrument which is signed and delivered by the grantor as his act, and in which he expresses an intention to pass an interest to the grantee.

The formalities necessary to constitute a deed at common law have been stated as follows:

> There are but three things of the essence and substance of a deed, that is to say, writing in paper or parchment, sealing and delivery.

Section 1 of the Law of Property (Miscellaneous Provisions) Act 1989[18] prescribes the necessary formalities for deeds executed on and after 31 July 1990 in the following subsections:

> (2) An instrument shall not be a deed unless—
>   (*a*) it makes it clear on its face that it is intended to be a deed by the person making it or, as the case may be, by the parties to it (whether by describing itself as a deed or expressing itself to be executed or signed as a deed or otherwise); and

---

14 *Tierney v Wood* (1854) 19 Beav 330.
15 LPA 1925, s. 53 (2); *Hodgson v Marks* [1971] Ch 892, [1971] 2 All ER 684; *Ottaway v Norman* [1972] Ch 698, [1971] 3 All ER 1235; M & B, *Trusts and Trustees*, (4th edn), p. 148.
16 *Grey v IRC* [1960] AC 1, [1959] 3 All ER 603; *Oughtred v IRC* [1960] AC 206, [1959] 3 All ER 673; *Vandervell v IRC* [1967] 2 AC 291, [1967] 1 All ER 1; *Re Tyler* [1967] 1 WLR 1269, [1967] 3 All ER 389; *Re Danish Bacon Co Ltd Staff Pension Fund Trusts* [1971] 1 WLR 248, [1971] 1 All ER 486; *Re Vandervell's Trusts (No. 2)* [1974] Ch 269, [1974] 1 All ER 47; M & B, *Trusts and Trustees* (4th edn), pp. 48 et seq. See generally H & M, pp. 80 et seq, [1979] Conv 17 (G. Battersby).
17 See generally Barnsley, *Conveyancing Law and Practice* (3rd edn), pp. 393–403.
18 This section is based on Law Commission Report on Deeds and Escrows 1987 (Law Com No. 163, HC 1). It came into force on 31 July 1990 and is not retrospective: Commencement Order 1990 (S.I. 1990 No. 1175); [1990] Conv 1, 90. See Land Registration (Execution of Deeds) Rules 1990 (S.I. 1990 No. 1010); [1990] Conv 85 (D. N. Clarke) 321. See [1991] Lloyd's Maritime and Commercial Law Quarterly 209 (G. Virgo and C. Harpum) for a trenchant criticism of "the recent reforms which have left the law of deeds both more complex and less rational than it was hitherto". A seal is still required for deeds executed by corporations sole, and by corporations aggregate which are not companies within the Companies Act 1985. For precedents, see LR (Execution of Deeds) Rules 1990 (S.I. 1990 No. 1010). See Law Commission Working Paper on Title on Death 1987 (Law Com No. 105), paras 4.19–4.28.

   (*b*) it is validly executed as a deed by that person or, as the case may be, one or more of those parties.
  (3) An instrument is validly executed as a deed by an individual if, and only if—
    (*a*) it is signed[19]—
      (i) by him in the presence of a witness who attests the signature; or
      (ii) at his direction and in his presence and the presence of two witnesses who each attest the signature; and
    (*b*) it is delivered as a deed by him or a person authorised to do so on his behalf.[20]

(a) Writing and sealing

Before 31 July 1990 a deed had to be written on paper or parchment. Section 1 (1) of the Act abolishes any rule of law which restricts the substance on which a deed may be written. Hence a deed may now be written on more durable material than paper, for example, fire- and flood-proof metal.[1]

(b) Sealing

Before 31 July 1990 a deed had to be sealed; that is to say, it had to bear wax, or a wafer, or some other indication of a seal.[2] Section 1 (1) abolishes the requirement of a seal for the valid execution of a deed by an individual.[3]

(c) Attestation

Section 1 makes new and precise attestation provisions for the valid execution of a deed by an individual. The signature must be attested by a witness who is present at the time of the signature. If the deed is not signed by a party, for example, where he is physically incapable of doing so, then it must be signed at his direction and in his presence and there must be *two* witnesses who each attest the signature.

(d) Delivery

Delivery does not mean a mere physical delivery, but a delivery accompanied by words or conduct signifying the grantor's intention to be bound by the provisions in the deed. The most apt and expressive mode of acknowledging this liability is for the grantor to hand the deed over, saying, "I deliver this

---

19 Signing includes making one's mark on the instrument: s. 1 (4).
20 A solicitor who, in the course of a transaction involving the creation or disposition of an interest in land, purports to deliver a deed on behalf of a party is conclusively presumed in favour of a purchaser to be authorised to deliver the deed: s. 1 (5).
1 *Emmet on Title*, para. 18.001.
2 *Stromdale and Ball Ltd v Burden* [1952] Ch 223, [1952] 1 All ER 59; *First National Securities Ltd v Jones* [1978] Ch 109, [1978] 2 All ER 221 (legal charge without wax or wafer, but with attestation clause and signature across printed circle containing letters LS [locus sigilli] held duly executed); (1980) 43 MLR 415 (D. C. Hoath). See also *Commercial Credit Service v Knowles* [1978] CLY 794; *TCB Ltd v Gray* [1986] Ch 621, [1986] 1 All ER 587 (deed not sealed, but grantor estopped from denying that it was).
3 For those within the Companies Act 1985, see s. 36A, as added by Companies Act 1989, s. 130; Report of City of London Law Society, reproduced in Kenny, *Practical Conveyancing*, para. 6071. A deed by a company under the Companies Act 1985 may either be sealed *or* signed by the company either by a director and the secretary or by two directors. It must also be delivered: *Longman v Viscount Chelsea* [1989] 2 EGLR 242, (1991) 141 NLJ 1122 (H. Lewis).

as my deed", but any other words or acts that show an undoubted acknowledgment of immediate liability will suffice.[4]

(e) Escrow

A physical delivery, however, unaccompanied by this express or implied acknowledgment, is insufficient, so that if, for instance, the grantor signs and seals the deed and then delivers it to his solicitor to be dealt with according to instructions to be given later, it does not operate as an immediate grant of the interest.

There are, therefore, two kinds of delivery recognized by the law in this connection, one absolute and the other conditional.[5] If a document is delivered, either to a party to it or to a stranger,[6] with an intimation, express or implied, that it is not to become effective until some condition has been performed, it is called an escrow (or scroll). In such a case the deed is inoperative until the condition is performed, but upon performance it takes effect as a deed without further delivery, and, if necessary, relates back to the time when it was delivered as an escrow.[7] As Lord CROSS OF CHELSEA said:[8]

> On fulfilment of the condition subject to which it was delivered as an escrow, a deed is not taken to relate back to the date of its delivery for all purposes, but only for such purposes as are necessary to give efficacy to the transaction—*ut res magis valeat quam pereat*.[9] Thus the fact that the grantor has died before the condition of an escrow is fulfilled does not entail the consequence that the disposition fails. If and when the condition is fulfilled the doctrine of relation back will save it, but notwithstanding the relation back for that limited purpose the grantee is not entitled to the rents of the property during the period of suspense or to lease it or to serve notices to quit.[10]

A delivery of a deed as an escrow is a final delivery in the sense that it cannot be withdrawn by the grantor before the grantee has had an opportunity to decide whether to fulfil the condition or not. A deed delivered subject to a condition and subject to such a right of withdrawal is not an escrow, but merely an undelivered deed.[11]

A common example of delivery as an escrow occurs where a vendor executes a deed of conveyance and gives it to his solicitor for transference to the purchaser upon payment by the latter of the purchase money. If the sale is not completed in due course, the vendor is released, and the solicitor has no authority to hand over the conveyance.[12] Another example of delivery as

4 *Xenos v Wickham* (1866) LR 2 HL 296 at 312.
5 *Foundling Hospital v Crane* [1911] 2 KB 367 at 377.
6 *London Freehold and Leasehold Property Co v Baron Suffield* [1897] 2 Ch 608 at 621–2.
7 *Vincent v Premo Enterprises (Voucher Sales) Ltd* [1969] 2 QB 609, [1969] 2 All ER 941; *Alan Estates Co Ltd v WG Stores Ltd* [1982] Ch 511, [1981] 3 All ER 481.
8 *Security Trust Co v Royal Bank of Canada* [1976] AC 503 at 517, [1976] 1 All ER 381 at 390; [1982] Conv 409 (P. H. Kenny).
9 *Butler and Baker's Case* (1591) 3 Co Rep. 25a.
10 *Sheppard's Touchstone* (7th edn 1830), p. 60; *Thompson v McCullough* [1947] KB 447, [1947] 1 All ER 265. See also *Terrapin International Ltd v IRC* [1976] 1 WLR 665, [1976] 2 All ER 461; *Venetian Glass Gallery Ltd v Next Properties Ltd* [1989] 2 EGLR 42.
11 *Beesly v Hallwood Estates Ltd* [1961] Ch 105, [1960] 1 All ER 90; *Windsor Refrigeration Co Ltd v Branch Nominees Ltd* [1961] Ch 88, [1960] 2 All ER 568, reversed on a different point [1961] Ch 375, [1961] 1 All ER 277; *D'Silva v Lister House Development Ltd*, supra; *Longman v Viscount Chelsea* (1989) 58 P & CR 189.
12 *Kingston v Ambrian Investment Co Ltd* [1975] 1 WLR 161, [1975] 1 All ER 120; *Glessing v Green* [1975] 1 WLR 863, [1975] 2 All ER 696. As to the time limit for the performance of this condition, see [1975] 39 Conv (NS) 430 (F. R. Crane).

an escrow occurs where a landlord executes a deed creating a lease, and the condition of the escrow is the execution of a counterpart by the tenant.[13]

(f) Deeds poll and indentures

Deeds are either deeds poll or indentures. A deed poll is one which is executed by a party of one part, an indenture is a deed (such as a conveyance by way of sale) to which there are parties of two or more parts.

In ancient days, when deeds were more concise than they are at present, it was usual, when they were made between two parties, to write two copies on the same parchment with some words written in the middle through which the parchment was cut in acute angles or indentations.[14] These two parts were called "counterparts", and, when put together so that the indentations fitted into each other, constituted the complete deed. Hence the name "indenture". Counterparts are not nowadays written on the same parchment, but that which is executed by the grantor of an interest is called the *original*, while that which is executed by the party to whom the interest passes—for example, a lessee—is called the *counterpart*.[15] The custom of indenting deeds gradually died out, and all that the term "indenture" now indicates is that the deed in question involves parties of more than one part. Despite the provision of the Real Property Act 1845 that a deed should have the effect of an indenture although not actually indented, it remained customary to introduce every deed which involved more than one party by the expression *This Indenture*. But even this survival has now gone, for it is enacted[16] that any deed may be described according to the nature of the transaction to be effected, so that now the introductory words are:

This Trust Deed,
This Legal Charge,
This Conveyance,
This Lease,

or a similar appropriate expression.

A deed poll is so called because, unlike an indenture, it was formerly polled (or cut even) at the top.

(g) Conveyance by a person to himself

It is sometimes necessary that an interest shall be conveyed by the grantor to himself jointly with another person, as for instance where a surviving trustee desires to vest the legal estate in himself and a new trustee. At common law this could not be done by one deed, for the effect of a grant by A to A and B was to vest the whole estate in B. The only solution was that A should convey to X, who would then convey to A and B, though an alternative method became available, and in fact general, under the doctrine of uses, for if A conveyed to X *to the use* of himself and B, the effect of the Statute of Uses was to vest an immediate legal estate in A and B jointly. It has been possible, however, since August 1859 in the case of leaseholds, and since 1881 in the case of freeholds, for a person to convey land to himself jointly with another

---

13 *Beesly v Hallwood Estates Ltd*, supra; *Alan Estates Ltd v WG Stores Ltd*, supra (both lease and counterpart executed in escrow).
14 Blackstone, vol. ii, p. 295.
15 Elphinstone, *Introduction to Conveyancing* (7th edn), p. 60.
16 LPA 1925, s. 57.

person by a direct deed of grant, and as the Statute of Uses has been repealed, this is now the only method.[17]

There are also occasions when it is necessary that a person should convey land to himself, as, for example, where personal representatives assent to the land vesting in themselves as trustees for sale.[18] Although, in the example given, the design could be effected in a direct manner under statutory provisions, it remained generally true, prior to 1926, that a conveyance by a person to himself required a grant to uses. It is now provided, however, that:

a person may convey land to or vest land in himself.[19]

This, however, does not enable an owner to grant a tenancy to himself, for a lease, though it falls within the statutory definition of a "conveyance" and no doubt vests a legal estate in the lessee, is essentially a contractual transaction. At the lowest it creates a number of implied obligations and liabilities, a situation that is impossible where only one person is involved. A man cannot contract with himself.[20]

Two or more persons whether trustees or personal representatives or not may convey any property vested in themselves to any one or more of themselves, though if the conveyance amounts to a breach of trust, it is liable to be set aside.[21]

(3) THE MODERN FORM OF A DEED OF CONVEYANCE OF SALE

It will perhaps elucidate the subject if we now set out a simple deed of conveyance,[1] and state and explain the effect of each of its parts. The following is a precedent of a conveyance executed by the owner of a fee simple absolute. The words which form part of the deed are put in heavier type in order to distinguish them from what is added by way of comment or explanation.

(a) Parties

THIS CONVEYANCE is made the 1st day of January 1994 BETWEEN ADAM SMITH of Balliol College, Oxford, Gentleman, (hereinafter called the vendor) of the one part, AND WILLIAM BLACKSTONE of All Souls College, Oxford, Knight (hereinafter called the purchaser) of the other part.

All parties whose intentions are expressed later in the deed must be mentioned, and there are said to be parties of as many "parts" as there are different intentions expressed. Smith intends to transfer the land and receive the purchase money, Blackstone intends to transfer the money and receive

---

17 LPA 1925, s. 72 (1), (2), replacing LP(A)A 1859, s. 21, and Conveyancing Act 1881, s. 50.
18 *Re King's Will Trusts* [1964] Ch 542, [1964] 1 All ER 833.
19 LPA 1925, s. 72 (3).
20 *Rye v Rye* [1962] AC 496, [1962] 1 All ER 146; M & B p. 474; (1962) 78 LQR 175 (P. V. Baker). See Lord RADCLIFFE at 511, at 153: "In effect, putting aside conveyancing forms, a man was able to convey to himself before the 1925 Act. He could, of course, put land in trust for himself by conveying it to a nominee, and, I suppose, if there was any conceivable point in the operation, he could similarly demise land to a nominee." Cf. *Kildrummy (Jersey) Ltd v IRC* [1990] STC 657, where it was held by the Court of Session that land could not be demised to a nominee. *Rye v Rye* was not cited.
21 LPA 1925, s. 72 (4).
 1 An instrument expressed to be supplemental to a previous instrument is deemed to contain a full recital of the previous instrument: LPA 1925, s. 58; *Jashel v Sophie Nursery Products Ltd* (25 February 1993, unreported), CA; [1993] Conv 387 (E. Cooke).

the land, and therefore they are parties of different parts. If Smith and Robinson were selling as trustees for sale, they would be parties of one part.[2]

(b) Recitals

WHEREAS the vendor is seised of the hereditaments intended to be hereby conveyed for an estate in fee simple absolute in possession free from incumbrances and has agreed to sell the same to the purchaser for the sum of £250,000;

Recitals are not a necessary part of a deed, but they are generally inserted in order to indicate the purpose of the deed in which they are contained, and to state the past history of the property conveyed.[3]

Narrative recitals are those which show the nature of the interest that is being transferred, and if the vendor is seised in fee simple (as in our example), they merely state that fact. On the other hand, where a mortgagee sells under his statutory power, the recitals must state that the mortgage was made, and that the mortgage loan remains owing. Again, if it is not obvious why certain persons are parties to the deed, the explanation will be given in the recitals. Thus a conveyance by personal representatives will recite the will, the appointment of the vendors as executors, the death of the testator and the grant of probate.

Introductory recitals are inserted in order to explain the object of the deed— that is, in our example, the transfer from Smith to Blackstone of a fee simple absolute.

Owing to the doctrine of estoppel, great care is necessary in the framing of recitals. Any recital which is precise and unambiguous, and which is clearly intended to bind the person by whom it is made, estops him and all persons claiming through him from denying the truth of the statement. Thus a recital that the vendor is seised in fee simple raises an estoppel. If this statement is untrue, but the vendor at a later date actually acquires the fee simple from the true owner, he is estopped from denying that he was owner at the time of the sale, and the fee simple passes to the purchaser under the doctrine of feeding the estoppel.[4]

The recitals are followed by what is called the *testatum*, which comprises the *operative part* of the deed, i.e. the part by which the object is actually effected.

(c) Testatum

NOW THIS DEED WITNESSETH that in consideration of the sum of £250,000 paid to the vendor by the purchaser (the receipt of which sum the vendor hereby acknowledges) the VENDOR AS BENEFICIAL OWNER

A deed is not void for want of consideration, but it is the invariable practice to state the amount of the purchase money and the fact of its receipt, because the amount of stamp duty payable thereby becomes ascertainable, while a receipt so inserted in the body of a deed is a sufficient discharge to the purchaser without any further receipt being indorsed on the deed.[5] Again, such a receipt is sufficient evidence to a subsequent purchaser of the

2 Elphinstone, *Introduction to Conveyancing* (7th edn), pp. 61–2.
3 See Farrand, *Contract and Conveyance* (4th edn), pp. 242 et seq.
4 P. 388, ante.
5 LPA 1925, s. 67.

payment, provided that he has no notice that the money was not actually paid.[6]

The effect of using the expression "beneficial owner" requires explanation. In former days a deed of conveyance ran to considerable length since it usually contained elaborate covenants for title, the object of which was to render the vendor liable in covenant if a flaw were later discovered in his title. Although titles were traditionally investigated with such care that a purchaser would seldom need to enforce this contractual liability, it was usual before 1882 to set out the appropriate undertakings at length,[7] a practice which, while it militated against simplicity and brevity, increased the profits of solicitors, whose remuneration in those days depended upon the length of the documents they prepared. Since 1881, however, covenants for title need not be expressly stated. If the appropriate words designated by statute[8] are used (and the appropriate words vary according as the grantor conveys freeholds or assigns leaseholds for valuable consideration, or by way of settlement, or as trustee and so on), the effect is that certain covenants for title, also designated by the Act,[9] are implied.

The appropriate words for raising these covenants upon sale of land are "beneficial owner". If the conveyance is for valuable consideration, and if the vendor "conveys and is expressed to convey as beneficial owner", and if in fact he possesses that status,[10] the effect is that the four following covenants are implied:

(i) Covenant that vendor has a good right to convey

This means that the vendor has full power to convey the interest which he has agreed to sell. Hence, if he has agreed to sell 84 acres, and it happens that 150 feet of this area have been acquired by adverse possessors under the Limitation Act 1980,[11] he will be liable under the implied covenant to lose the difference between the value of the property he agreed to sell and that of the property which he is entitled to convey.

(ii) Covenant that purchaser shall have quiet enjoyment

A physical interference with the enjoyment of the land, as, for instance, the exercise of a right of way lawfully acquired by a stranger from the vendor prior to the sale, constitutes a breach of the covenant, though of course in such a case the existence of the easement also constitutes a breach of the covenant that the vendor has a right to convey.

The object of implying this covenant in addition to the covenant that the

---

6 LPA 1925, s. 68.
7 See (1962) 26 Conv (NS) 45 (M. J. Russell).
8 LPA 1925, s. 76.
9 Ibid., Sch. 2. See generally Farrand, *Contract and Conveyance* (4th edn), pp. 258 et seq; Barnsley, *Conveyancing Law and Practice* (3rd edn), chapter 23; (1968) 32 Conv (NS) 123; (1970) 34 Conv (NS) 178 (M. J. Russell). On covenants for title by joint tenants, see (1986) 130 SJ 944, (1987) 131 SJ 51 (M. J. Russell). The Law Commission Report on Implied Covenants for Title 1991 (Law Com No. 199, HC 437) makes recommendations designed to make the covenants clearer, to strengthen the guarantees which they provide and to make them more easily enforceable. See Law of Property (Miscellaneous Provisions) Bill 1994 (HL Bill 46), Part I.
10 *Fay v Miller, Wilkins & Co* [1941] Ch 360 at 362, [1941] 2 All ER 18; *Pilkington v Wood* [1953] Ch 770 at 777, [1953] 2 All ER 810 at 813; *Re Robertson's Application* [1969] 1 WLR 109 at 111–12, [1969] 1 All ER 257 at 258.
11 *Eastwood v Ashton* [1915] AC 900.

vendor has a good right to convey is that the Limitation Act 1980 begins to run from the date of the deed in the latter case, since that is the time at which the breach occurs, but from the date of the interference in the case of a covenant for quiet enjoyment.

(iii) Covenant that the property is free from incumbrances

This means that the property is free from all estates, incumbrances, claims and demands other than those to which the conveyance is expressly made subject.[12]

(iv) Covenant for further assurance

This obliges the vendor to execute assurances and to do everything that is right and possible in order to perfect the conveyance.

It should be noted that the undertakings which have been set out are not four independent and separate covenants, but parts of the one entire contract. They are not absolute, but qualified, since they extend only to the acts and omissions[13] of the vendor and those claiming through him and to the acts and omissions of persons through whom he claims, except those from whom he has taken the property for a money consideration. Thus, a vendor who himself purchased the land for value from X on a previous occasion is not liable under the covenant for quiet enjoyment if X disturbs the possession of the ultimate purchaser.[14]

The benefit of the covenants implied by the Act runs with the land, so that each person in whom the land is vested is entitled to enforce them. Section 76 (6) of the Law of Property Act 1925 provides:[15]

> The benefit of a covenant implied as aforesaid shall be annexed and incident to, and shall go with, the estate or interest of the implied covenantee, and shall be capable of being enforced by every person in whom the estate is, for the whole or any part thereof, from time to time vested.

The covenants may be varied or extended. The different covenants that are implied when the conveyance is by a mortgagor, settlor, trustee, mortgagee and so on, are set out in the second Schedule to the Law of Property Act 1925.[16]

(d) Operative words

HEREBY CONVEYS unto the purchaser

We will now turn to the *operative words* of the conveyance. In old deeds, instead of using the single word *convey*, it was customary *per majorem cautelam* to employ a much more extensive series of words, such as *grant, bargain, sell, aliene, convey, release and confirm*. Since the Real Property Act 1845, however, which enacted that all corporeal hereditaments should lie in

---

12 On exclusion clauses in this context, see [1992] CLJ 263 (C. Harpum).
13 See (1967) 31 Conv (NS) 268 (M. J. Russell).
14 *David v Sabin* [1893] 1 Ch 523; *Stoney v Eastbourne RDC* [1927] 1 Ch 367. "Purchase for value" in this context does not include a conveyance in consideration of marriage: LPA 1925, Sch. 2, Part I.
15 See also s. 77 (5); p. 625, n. 15, ante.
16 For implied covenants in connection with rentcharges, see Rentcharges Act 1977, s. 11 (2), (3), (4). As to the position of mortgages, see (1964) 28 Conv (NS) 205 (A. M. Prichard).

grant, the word *grant* alone has been sufficient to transfer both corporeal and incorporeal interests. This is, however, not essential,[17] and *convey* is the word adopted in the various forms of instrument given in the Law of Property Act 1925.

It sometimes happens that the recitals are inconsistent with the operative words. In this case Lord ESHER stated the law as follows:[18]

> If the recitals are clear and the operative part is ambiguous, the recitals govern the construction. If the recitals are ambiguous, and the operative part is clear, the operative part must prevail. If both the recitals and the operative part are clear, but they are inconsistent with each other, the operative part is to be preferred.

(e) Parcels

ALL and singular the hereditaments known as Blackacre and situate at Kidlington in the County of Oxford and containing 24 acres or thereabouts

The operative words are followed by the *parcels clause*,[19] the object of which is to give a physical description of the property sold: this may be accompanied by a plan, to which reference is made in the clause.[20] A grant operates to pass the rights incidental to the land, such as easements and profits which have become attached thereto. But since rights such as *quasi*-easements which have not become legally appurtenant to the land would not pass without special mention, it was usual, prior to 1882, to insert *general words*, which were framed widely enough to include all rights actually enjoyed by the vendor in respect of the land. Since 1881, however, unless a contrary intention is expressed, such *general words* are implied in every conveyance.[1] Thus a conveyance of land now operates, by virtue of the Law of Property Act 1925, to convey all buildings, erections, fixtures, commons, hedges, ditches, fences, ways, waters, watercourses, liberties, privileges, easements, rights and advantages whatsoever, appertaining or reputed to appertain to the land or any part thereof. An equally wide implication is raised with regard to rights appertaining to buildings.[2]

It was also usual before 1882 to add what was called an *all estate clause* with the object of ensuring that the entire interest of the grantor should be transferred. This was as a matter of fact quite ineffective to transfer anything that would not pass automatically, and it is now omitted in reliance on the enactment that, unless a contrary intention is expressed, every conveyance is

17 LPA 1925, s. 51 (2).
18 *Ex parte Dawes* (1886) 17 QBD 275 at 286; *Re Sassoon* [1933] Ch 858; affd [1935] AC 96.
19 See generally Farrand, *Contract and Conveyance* (4th edn), pp. 280 et seq; Barnsley, *Conveyancing Law and Practice* (3rd edn), pp. 468 et seq.
20 A plan must be construed objectively in its context: *Toplis v Green* [1992] EGCS 20. See *Scarfe v Adams* [1981] 1 All ER 843 at 845, where CUMMING-BRUCE LJ criticizes as "sloppy conveyancing" the use of a 1/2,500 Ordnance Survey map where a large house was being divided into two separate properties; [1981] Conv 257 (M. M. Barrett); *Mayer v Hurr* (1983) 49 P & CR 56 at 59, per DILLON LJ. On boundaries generally, see Aldridge, *Boundaries, Walls and Fences* (7th edn); Sara, *Boundaries and Easements* (1991).
1 LPA 1925, s. 62; p. 534, ante.
2 Ibid., s. 62 (2).

effectual to pass all the estate, right, title, interest, claim, and demand which the conveying parties respectively have in, to, or on the property.[3]

Proceeding now with the precedent, we next arrive at the *habendum clause*.

(f) Habendum

To hold unto the purchaser in fee simple.

The object of this is to define the extent of the interest taken by the purchaser.

Finally comes the *testimonium*, which states that the parties have signed the deed in witness of what it contains, and the *attestation clause*.

(g) Testimonium

In witness whereof the said parties hereto have hereunto set their respective hands the day and year first above written.

(h) Attestation Clause

Signed and delivered[4] by the vendor in the presence of John Roe of 200 St. Aldates Oxford solicitor.

ADAM SMITH

The whole precedent, then, stands as follows:

Parties

THIS CONVEYANCE is made the 1st day of January 1994 BETWEEN ADAM SMITH of Balliol College, Oxford, Gentleman, (hereinafter called the vendor) of the one part, AND WILLIAM BLACKSTONE of All Souls College, Oxford, Knight (hereinafter called the purchaser) of the other part.

Recitals

WHEREAS the vendor is seised of the hereditaments intended to be hereby conveyed for an estate in fee simple absolute in possession free from incumbrances and has agreed to sell the same to the purchaser for the sum of £250,000;

Testatum

NOW THIS DEED WITNESSETH that in consideration of the sum of £250,000 paid to the vendor by the purchaser (the receipt of which sum the vendor hereby acknowledges) the VENDOR AS BENEFICIAL OWNER.

Operative words

HEREBY CONVEYS unto the purchaser.

Parcels

ALL and singular the hereditaments known as Blackacre and situate at Kidlington in the County of Oxford and containing 24 acres or thereabouts,

---

3 LPA 1925, s. 63.
4 Or "Signed as a deed": Land Registration (Execution of Deeds) Rules 1990: Form 19; M & B p. 101.

Habendum

To hold unto the purchaser in fee simple.

Testimonium

In witness whereof the said parties hereto have hereunto set their respective hands the day and year first above written.

Attestation clause

Signed and delivered by the vendor in the presence of John Roe of 200 St. Aldates Oxford solicitor.

ADAM SMITH

SECTION II REGISTERED CONVEYANCING

We have already considered the system of registered conveyancing in outline,[5] and we must now discuss it in more detail.

A. THE MACHINERY OF TRANSFER INTER VIVOS

(1) DUTIES OF VENDOR

The preliminary inquiries and the contract of sale follow the pattern of unregistered conveyancing, but the investigation of the title is radically different. No longer does the vendor need to trace the history of the transactions in which the estate has been involved, for the register is conclusive on the question of ownership.

In lieu of an abstract of title the vendor must supply the purchaser with a copy of the entries and of any filed plans and copies or abstracts of any documents noted on the register.[6] The register is, however, not conclusive as to third party rights and a vendor is therefore required to provide a purchaser with copies, abstracts and evidence of all rights and interests appurtenant to the registered land, as to which the register is not conclusive.[7]

(2) REQUISITIONS AND SEARCHES

Requisitions on title follow the usual form but where the title is absolute or good leasehold, they are limited to overriding interests and other matters in respect of which the register is not conclusive. Possessory or qualified titles will require more careful investigation.[8] Searches must be made of local land charges registers, for local land charges are overriding interests. But it will not be necessary to search the register of land charges under the Land Charges Act 1972, as third party rights which would appear there if the land were unregistered will appear on the register under the Land Registration Act 1925. The main search will therefore be of the register itself. This may be undertaken by an official search with priority. Once a purchaser has

5 Pp. 97 et seq, ante.
6 LRA 1925, s. 76. The register means the register of the individual title only, and not that of the adjoining or all registration land: *A J Dunning & Sons (Shopfitters) Ltd v Sykes & Son (Poole) Ltd* [1987] Ch 287 at 300, [1987] 1 All ER 700 at 706–7; as to conflicts between filed plans and descriptions on the register, see [1979] Conv 316–9, 389–9.
7 Ibid., s. 110.
8 For a detailed treatment of requisitions, see Ruoff and Roper, para. 17–19.

applied for this search, any entry made thereafter during a priority period of 30 working days is postponed to the purchaser's application to register his transfer, provided that he delivers this application to the registry in the proper form before the end of the priority period.[9]

(3) FORM OF TRANSFER

The transfer must be on one of the forms set out in the Rules. It will be deemed to contain the general words implied by section 62 of the Law of Property Act 1925, so far as they are appropriate.[10] The usual covenants for title may be incorporated by inserting the appropriate words whereby a person is expressed to convey "as beneficial owner", "as settlor", "as trustee", etc, as the case may be.[11] The transfer must be by deed in the same way as a conveyance under the Law of Property Act 1925, stamped with the appropriate Inland Revenue Stamp, and sent to the registry together with the land certificate. Registration of the transferee's name completes the transfer and terminates the legal ownership of the transferor; it takes effect as from the day on which a completed application is delivered to the registry.[12]

The simplicity of the form of transfer *inter vivos* is shown from the reproduction below of the form authorised by the Land Registry for the transfer of the whole of a parcel of freehold or leasehold land. It has been completed with the details of the sale of the fee simple of Blackacre similar to those set out in the precedent of the conveyance under the unregistered system on page 783.

H.M. LAND REGISTRY
LAND REGISTRATION ACTS 1925 to 1986

TRANSFER OF WHOLE (*Freehold or Leasehold*)
(Rule 98 or 115, Land Registration Rules 1925)

County and   OXFORDSHIRE
District or London Borough   CHERWELL
Title number   ON 00001
Property   BLACKACRE, KIDLINGTON
Date   1 January 1994   In consideration of   Two hundred and
fifty thousand pounds (£250,000) *receipt of which is acknowledged*

---

9 Land Registration (Official Searches) Rules 1990 (S.I. 1993 No. 3276); Ruoff and Roper, chapter 30. A search may be made by telephone or telex (r. 3 (3)). Such a search is not an official search for the purpose of indemnity under LRA 1925, s. 83 (3), p. 789, post. See Practice Direction H. M. Land Registry: New Telephone Official Search Services: (1992) 142 NLJ 54. For an official search without priority, see rr. 9, 10.
  There were 5,031,795 applications for official search, office copies and other ancillary services made during 1992–1993: Annual Report for 1992–1993, p. 11.
10 LRA 1925, ss. 19 (3), 22 (3); p. 534, ante. See also Ruoff and Roper, para. 6.07.
11 LRA 1925, s. 38 (2): LRR 1925, r. 76. For the usual covenants for title, see pp. 779–81, ante. See Ruoff and Roper, chapter 16; Farrand, *Contract and Conveyance* (4th edn), pp. 275–280; Barnsley (3rd edn), pp. 608–613; [1981] Conv 32 (P. H. Kenny); *Hissett v Reading Roofing Co Ltd* [1969] 1 WLR 1757, [1970] 1 All ER 122; (1970) 34 Conv (NS) 128 (F. R. Crane); *A J Dunning & Sons (Shopfitters) Ltd v Sykes & Son (Poole) Ltd* [1987] Ch 287, [1987] 1 All ER 700; [1987] Conv 214 (A. Sydenham); *Meek v Clarke* [1982] CA Transcript 312, discussed [1989] Conv 18 (D. Partington). For the Law Commission Report on Implied Covenants for Title 1991 (Law Com No. 199, HC 437), see p. 780, n. 9, ante.
12 LRR 1925, rr. 83–85, as substituted by LRR 1978, rr. 8–10.

I,   ADAM SMITH, of BALLIOL COLLEGE,
          OXFORD, GENTLEMAN

as beneficial owner hereby transfer to:

**WILLIAM BLACKSTONE, OF ALL SOULS
COLLEGE, OXFORD, KNIGHT**

---

the land comprised in the title above mentioned
Signed as a deed *or* signed and delivered by the said
    Adam Smith   }   ADAM SMITH
in the presence of
Name   John Roe
Address   200 St. Aldates Oxford
Description or occupation   Solicitor

B. THE TITLE

We have already seen that there are four different classes of title which may be entered on the proprietorship register; absolute, qualified, possessory and good leasehold. We have already described the absolute title, which is available for both freeholds and leaseholds.[13] "Possessory titles are granted in less than one in a hundred applications for first registration in compulsory areas. Qualified titles are virtually unknown. Good leasehold titles are common."[14]

(1) GOOD LEASEHOLD TITLE

The good leasehold title is only available for leaseholds. Where, as frequently happens, a leaseholder cannot produce the title to the reversion, he may be registered as the owner of a good leasehold title. The title to the leasehold interest only is investigated and guaranteed by the Land Registry. This is the same as with an absolute title, with the important exception that registration does not affect or prejudice the enforcement of any estate, right or interest affecting or in derogation of the title of the lessor to grant the lease.[15] The guarantee is similarly limited.

(2) POSSESSORY TITLE

Possessory titles usually arise out of claims by squatters, and also occasionally where a documentary title is lodged, which is too weak for a better kind of title but not deserving of outright rejection. Possessory titles are mainly freeholds, although possessory leaseholds do exist. The guarantee is a limited one, as the registration does not affect or prejudice the enforcement of any estate, right or interest adverse to or in derogation of the title of the first proprietor and subsisting or capable of arising at the time of the first registration.[16] In the case of a freehold or leasehold interest registered with

---

13 P. 102, ante.
14 Ruoff and Pryer, *Land Registration Handbook*, p. 36.
15 LRA 1925, s. 10.
16 Ibid., ss. 6 and 11; *Spectrum Investment Co v Holmes* [1981] 1 WLR 221, [1981] 1 All ER 6; M & B p. 210; p. 914, post.

a possessory title the guarantee covers, therefore, only dealings which take place after the registration and does not extend to the title prior to registration.

(3) QUALIFIED TITLES

Where an application is made to register a freehold with an absolute title and the Registrar comes to the conclusion on examination of the title that it can be established only for a limited period or subject to certain reservations, he may, at the applicant's request, register a qualified title. This title may except from the effect of registration any estate, right or interest arising before a specified date, or arising under a specified instrument, or otherwise described in the register, and has the same effect as an absolute title save for the estate, right or interest excepted.[17] A qualified title may also be registered at the applicant's request in respect of a leasehold when the examination of the title either of the lessor to the reversion, or of the lessee to the leasehold interest, discloses similar problems to those described above. It has the same effect as a good leasehold or absolute title as the case may be, subject to the exception of the specified interests.[18]

(4) CONVERSION OF TITLES

The Act provides for the conversion of inferior titles to absolute or good leasehold titles, and of good leasehold to absolute.[19] Possessory titles, if for no other reason than the effect of the Limitation Act, cannot remain so permanently. For example, the Registrar may and, on application by the proprietor, must convert possessory titles of freehold land to absolute and possessory titles of leasehold to good leasehold, where the land has been registered for at least twelve years and he is satisfied as to the title and that the proprietor is in possession.[20] The Registrar may also convert good leasehold to absolute leasehold titles if he is satisfied as to the title to the freehold and to any intermediate leasehold. He may also convert into absolute (or good leasehold) titles in other cases as set out in section 77.[1]

C. RECTIFICATION AND INDEMNITY[2]

(1) RECTIFICATION OF THE REGISTER

The court has no general discretionary power to rectify the register, but under section 82 of the Land Registration Act 1925, the register may be rectified, inter alia, where the court so orders upon deciding that any person is entitled

---

17 LRA 1925, s. 7.
18 Ibid., s. 12.
19 LRA 1925, s. 77 as substituted by LRA 1986, s. 1., replacing the previous periods of 15 years for freeholds and 10 years for leaseholds.
20 Ibid., s. 77 (2).
 1 For a full discussion, see Ruoff and Roper, chapter 14.
 2 See *Norwich and Peterborough Building Society v Steed* [1993] Ch 116, [1993] 1 All ER 330 for a full examination of the eight statutory grounds; Ruoff and Roper, chapter 40; Farrand, *Contract and Conveyance* (2nd edn), pp. 209–20; Barnsley, *Conveyancing Law and Practice* (3rd edn), chapter 4.

to any estate, right or interest in the land,[3] where an entry has been obtained by fraud,[4] where two or more persons are by mistake registered as proprietors of the same property, where a legal estate has been registered in the name of a person who, if the land had not been registered, would not have been the estate owner,[5] or where, because of any error or omission in the register or because of any entry made under a mistake it would be deemed just to rectify it.[6] In *Chowood Ltd v Lyall (No. 2)*, for example, the register was rectified in favour of a squatter who had acquired title by adverse possession to part of the land registered in the name of the proprietor.[7]

The section, however, protects a *proprietor in possession* by providing that rectification may only take place against him if:

(a) it is to give effect to an overriding interest,[8] or an order of the court,[9] or

(b) he has caused or substantially contributed to the error or omission by fraud or lack of proper care,[10] or

(c) for any other reason, it would be unjust not to rectify the register against him.[11]

The principle which emerges is that a *purchaser* who buys registered land and remains in *possession* of it is guaranteed his possession, and rectification will only be ordered against him in exceptional circumstances.

Where the register is rectified by the removal of the proprietor's name and the substitution of another's name, the effect is to vest the legal estate in the new proprietor;[12] the former proprietor loses his title and, as we shall see, may have a right of indemnity. Section 82 (2) of the Land Registration Act 1925 also provides that the register may be rectified notwithstanding that the

---

3 *Chowood Ltd v Lyall (No 2)* [1930] 2 Ch 156; *Calgary and Edmonton Land Co Ltd v Discount Bank (Overseas) Ltd* [1971] 1 WLR 81, [1971] 1 All ER 551; *Proctor v Kidman* (1986) 51 P & CR 67. See also *Spectrum Investment Co v Holmes* [1981] 1 WLR 221, [1981] 1 All ER 6; M & B p. 210, p. 914, post; *Orakpo v Manson Investments Ltd* [1977] 1 WLR 347, [1977] 1 All ER 666; affd on other grounds [1978] AC 95, [1977] 3 All ER 1.

4 *Argyle Building Society v Hammond* (1984) 49 P & CR 148; M & B p. 165 (transfer void for forgery); [1985] Conv 135 (A. Sydenham); LRA 1925, s. 114; cf. *Norwich and Peterborough Building Society v Steed*, supra (transfer voidable for fraud); (1993) 109 LQR 187 (R. J. Smith); [1992] Conv 293 (C. Davis). See also *Re Leighton's Conveyance* [1936] 1 All ER 667; affd [1937] Ch 149, [1936] 3 All ER 1033 (fraudulent misrepresentation and undue influence).

5 *Chowood Ltd v Lyall (No 2)* [1930] 2 Ch 156.

6 *Re Dances Way, West Town, Hayling Island* [1962] Ch 490, [1962] 2 All ER 42 (notice of adverse easement cancelled). For further powers of rectification under LRR 1925, see r. 13 (clerical errors), r. 14 (registration in error of too much land); r. 131 (where power of disposing of registered land has become vested in some person other than the proprietor), r. 283 (correction of particulars of addresses), r. 284 (corrections of plans), r. 285 (alterations to resolve conflicting descriptions).

7 [1930] 2 Ch 156.

8 *Re Chowood's Registered Land* [1933] Ch 574; M & B p. 173; *Epps v Esso Petroleum Co Ltd* [1973] 1 WLR 1071, [1973] 2 All ER 465; M & B p. 168.

9 As added by AJA 1977, s. 24 (a).

10 As substituted by AJA 1977, s. 24 (b). The original statutory provision had produced the undesirable result of rectification being ordered against a purchaser who innocently put forward a misleading description of property when applying for first registration of his title: *Re 139 High Street Deptford* [1951] Ch 884, [1951] 1 All ER 950. See also *Re Seaview Gardens* [1967] 1 WLR 134, [1966] 3 All ER 935.

11 *Epps v Esso Petroleum Co Ltd*, supra; *Hounslow London Borough Council v Hare* (1990) 24 HLR 9; [1993] Conv 224 (J. Martin).

12 LRA 1925, s. 69 (1).

rectification may affect any estates, rights, charges or interests acquired or protected by registration, or by any entry on the register, or otherwise.[13]

(2) RIGHT OF INDEMNITY

A right of indemnity[14] is available under section 83 to anyone suffering loss by reason of:

(*a*) any rectification of the register,
(*b*) an error or omission on the register which is not rectified,
(*c*) the loss or destruction of any document lodged at the registry for inspection or safe custody, or an error in any official search.

Apart from (*c*), compensation is paid only when someone *suffers loss by reason of* a rectification, or of an error or omission that has been made on the register, which is not to be rectified. Hence, when a purchaser bought registered land on part of which, unknown to the purchaser, a squatter had already established a title by adverse possession and rectification was ordered (because the right was an overriding interest), the purchaser was unable to obtain an indemnity because his loss was not "by reason of the rectification" but had resulted from the purchase itself,[15] i.e. because he had purchased land from a vendor against whom a squatter had already obtained title so that the rectification made him no worse off than before. If, however, a proprietor of registered land claims in good faith under a disposition which is forged and the register is rectified against him, he is deemed to have suffered loss by reason of the rectification.[16] But compensation is never payable if:

the applicant or a person from whom he derives title (otherwise than under a disposition for valuable consideration which is registered or protected on the register) has caused or substantially contributed to the loss by fraud or lack of proper care.[17]

A macabre example of a refusal to rectify leading to a true owner being given indemnity is provided by the case of the acid bath murderer, Haigh.[18] Haigh forged the signature of a registered proprietor, was registered in his name and then, in that name, sold to an innocent purchaser for value. Rectification was not ordered as the purchaser was in possession. But the personal representatives of the real proprietor were compensated in full.

---

13 *Freer v Unwins Ltd* [1976] Ch 288, [1976] 1 All ER 634 (where it was held that the rectification of the register of title to servient land by the entry of a notice of restrictive covenants does not operate retrospectively so as to bind a person taking under a prior registered disposition for valuable consideration). See (1976) 40 Conv (NS) 304 (F. R. Crane); 126 NLJ 523 (S. M. Cretney); Ruoff and Roper, para. 40–15.
14 See *Argyle Building Society v Hammond* (1984) 49 P & CR 148 at 158, per SLADE LJ.
15 *Re Chowood's Registered Land* [1933] Ch 574; M & B p. 173; applied in *Re Boyle's Claim* [1961] 1 WLR 339, [1961] 1 All ER 620.
16 LRA 1925, s. 83 (4).
17 S. 83 (5) (*a*) as amended by Land Registration and Land Charges Act 1971, s. 3. See (1971) 35 Conv (NS) 390.
18 Recounted in Ruoff and Roper (5th edn), p. 71.

(3) LAW REFORM

The Law Commission[19] comments on the present law as follows:

> Defeasibility of title through the existence of section 82 may be regretted in principle, but is compensated for in practice by the possibility of indemnity under section 83. Nevertheless, it is obvious that defeasibility through the ready availability of rectification is productive of future uncertainty and contrary to the raison d'être of registration of title. In the interests of conveyancing simplification, sympathetic attention must be paid to the reasonable expectations of purchasers of registered land who pay the price, take possession and become proprietors in reliance on the register. Accordingly the present provisions restricting the availability of rectification against such proprietors should be reconsidered with a view to possible strengthening.

(a) Rectification

The main recommendation is that there would be no rectification against a registered proprietor if he were a bona fide purchaser for value, who had exercised the standard of care of a prudent purchaser and was in actual occupation, *unless* the rectification is simply the entry of an overriding interest or in favour of a trustee in bankruptcy. The long-stop provision of section 82 (3) (*c*), under which there may be rectification against a proprietor in possession, when "for any other reason, in any particular case, it is considered that it would be unjust not to rectify the register against him", would be repealed, as introducing too great an element of uncertainty into the registration system (paras. 3.6–3.20).

(b) Indemnity

The main recommendation is that, as a result of the recommendations on overriding interests,[20] the indemnity scheme would be extended so that a proprietor against whom an overriding interest is asserted would be able to apply for indemnity, but the Registrar might, as a discretionary condition precedent to paying indemnity, rectify the register by entering the overriding interest in it (para. 3.29).

D. OVERRIDING INTERESTS[1]

(1) DEFINITION

Overriding interests are defined and listed in the Land Registration Act 1925. By section 3 (xvi), unless the context otherwise requires:

> "Overriding interests" mean all the incumbrances, interests, rights, and powers not entered on the register but subject to which registered dispositions are by this Act to take effect . . .

---

19 Third Report on Land Registration B. Rectification and Indemnity 1987 (Law Com No. 158, HC 269), Part III, paras. 3.4–3.5.
20 P. 798, post.
 1 See Ruoff and Roper, chapter 6; Wolstenholme and Cherry, vol. 6, pp. 63–67; Farrand, *Contract and Conveyance* (2nd edn), pp. 184–209; Barnsley, *Conveyancing Law and Practice* (3rd edn), pp. 46–68; Hayton, *Registered Land* (3rd edn), chapter 6; (1961) 24 MLR 136 (G. Dworkin).

By section 70 (1):

> All registered land shall, unless . . . the contrary is expressed on the register, be deemed to be subject to such of the following overriding interests as may be for the time being subsisting in reference thereto . . .

and then follows a list, to which additions have been made by later enactments.[2]

(*a*) Rights of common,[3] drainage rights, customary rights (until extinguished),[4] public rights,[4a] profits à prendre, rights of sheepwalk, rights of way, watercourses, rights of water, and other easements not being equitable easements required to be protected by notice on the register.

As we have seen,[5] equitable easements, although apparently excluded from the paragraph, may be overriding interests by virtue of the incorporation of rule 258 of the Land Registration Rules 1925 into the Land Registration Act 1925.

(*b*) Liability to repair highways by reason of tenure, quit-rents, crown rents, heriots, and other rents and charges (until extinguished) having their origin in tenure;

(*c*) Liability to repair the chancel of any church;[6]

(*d*) Liability in respect of embankments, and sea and river walls;

(*e*) Land tax,[7] tithe rentcharge,[8] payments in lieu of tithe, and charges or annuities payable for the redemption of tithe rentcharges;[9]

(*f*) Subject to the provisions of this Act, rights acquired or in course of being acquired under the Limitation Acts;

As we shall see,[10] when the limitation period has run, the estate of the registered proprietor is not extinguished, as it is under the system of unregistered conveyancing: instead, he holds the land adversely possessed on trust for the adverse possessor.

(*g*) The rights of every person in actual occupation of the land or in receipt of the rents and profits thereof, save where enquiry is made of such person and the rights are not disclosed;[11]

---

2 P. 796, post.

3 By the Commons Registration Act 1965, s. 1 (1), no rights of common over land which is capable of registration under that Act can be registered under the Land Registration Acts; p. 567, ante.

4 See pp. 575–80, ante.

4a *Overseas Investment Services Ltd v Simcobuild Construction Ltd* (1993) Times, 2 November (right to have road constructed under Highways Act 1980, s. 38).

5 P. 581, ante.

6 Law Commission Report on Liability for Chancel Repairs 1985 (Law Com No. 152) recommends that liability should be abolished after 10 years; but, if not abolished promptly, it should be registered in Local Land Charges registers, and failure to register would exonerate a purchaser of the land; (1984) 100 LQR 185 (J. H. Baker). For the liability in unregistered land, see *Hauxton Parochial Church Council v Stevens* [1929] P 240; *Chivers & Sons Ltd v Air Ministry and Queen's College, Cambridge* [1955] Ch 585, [1955] 2 All ER 607.

7 Extinguished by Finance Act 1963, s. 68.

8 Extinguished and replaced by tithe redemption annuities: Tithe Act 1936, s. 13 (11); Finance Act 1962, s. 32.

9 As from 2 October 1977 tithe redemption annuities were extinguished by FA 1977, s. 56.

10 P. 913, post.

11 See *Strand Securities Ltd v Caswell* [1965] Ch 958 at 979–81, [1965] 1 All ER 820 at 826, per Lord DENNING MR; p. 104, ante, and at 984, at 829, per RUSSELL LJ. On the proviso for non-disclosure on enquiry, cf in unregistered land *Midland Bank Ltd v Farmpride Hatcheries Ltd* (1980) 260 EG 493; M & B p. 28; p. 63, ante.

This is an important paragraph which shows that the legislature accepted a compromise in respect of its replacement of the old doctrine of notice by the system of registration. A purchaser should inspect the premises, and he should ask anyone in occupation on what grounds he is there. He will thereby be able to discover the rights and interests of persons in occupation, and it seemed right therefore to subject a purchaser to those rights and interests rather than to let him disregard them because someone had failed to enter them on the register. The paragraph thus operates as a safety-net. Some of these rights may, however, be capable of being protected by notice or caution on the register of the title affected, and if they are, notices or cautions should be applied for by the person entitled. In short, the general policy of the Land Registration Act 1925 is that all claims, rights and interests should be protected by entry on the register as far as possible. This special exception of paragraph (g) is made in the case of the rights of a person in actual occupation. The purchaser should get to know what these rights are, and, on balance, it is better that he should take subject to them, even at the expense of the doctrine of completeness of the register.

(i) Rights within section 70 (1) (g) As we have seen,[12] a contract for the sale or lease[13] of registered land should be protected by notice or caution as a minor interest, but if the purchaser or lessee is let into occupation before formal transfer *and* there is no note on the register of his interest, the mere fact of his occupation turns his minor interest into an overriding one.[14] The paragraph is not confined to the single right to occupy, for it extends to the *rights of those in occupation*. It is the rights of the occupier and not the occupation itself that are crucial. As RUSSELL LJ put it:[15]

> It seems to me that section 70 in all its parts is dealing with rights in reference to land which have the quality of being capable of enduring through different ownerships of the land, according to normal conceptions of title to real property ... It is the rights of such a person which constitute the overriding interest and must be examined, not his occupation.

Thus the deserted wife in occupation of the matrimonial home has no right affecting property entitling her to claim an overriding interest,[16] while the owner of an option to purchase a freehold contained in a lease has, since it "affects the reversion ... and subsists in reference to the registered land".[17]

Other examples of such rights within paragraph (g) are a right of premption;[18] an unpaid vendor's lien where the vendor remains in occupation

---

12 Pp. 513–4, ante.
13 A contract for the grant of a lease (for 21 years or less) is not an overriding interest under LRA 1925, s. 70 (1) (k), as there has been no "grant": *City Permanent Building Society v Miller* [1952] Ch 840, [1952] 2 All ER 621. S. 3 (x), taken by itself, is misleading on this point.
14 *Woolwich Equitable Building Society v Marshall* [1952] Ch 1, [1951] 2 All ER 769; *Mornington Permanent Building Society v Kenway* [1953] Ch 382, [1953] 1 All ER 951.
15 *National Provincial Bank Ltd v Hastings Car Mart Ltd* [1964] Ch 665 at 696, a dissenting judgment which was upheld (with special reference to this passage) in the House of Lords; [1965] AC 1175 at 1226, 1228, 1240 and 1261–2, [1965] 2 All ER 472, at 481, 482, 489 and 503.
16 *National Provincial Bank Ltd v Ainsworth* [1965] AC 1175, [1965] 2 All ER 472; M & B p. 121. See *Eden Park Estates Ltd v Longman* noted in [1982] Conv 239 (payment in advance in respect of rent by tenant to original landlord held not to be overriding interest).
17 *Webb v Pollmount* [1966] Ch 584 at 595–6, 597–9, [1966] 1 All ER 481 at 485, per UNGOED-THOMAS J; M & B p. 128.
18 *Kling v Keston Properties Ltd* (1983) 49 P & CR 212; M & B p. 88.

under a lease back by the purchaser,[19] a right to rectify,[20] and the right of a beneficiary under a bare trust to the fee simple in equity. Thus in *Hodgson v Marks*:[1]

> Mrs. H, an elderly widow, voluntarily transferred the registered title to her house to E, who was her lodger. She intended that the house, though it was in E's name, should remain hers, and she continued to reside there. E then sold it to M who became the registered proprietor and executed a mortgage in favour of a building society. Mrs. H claimed that E held the house as a bare trustee for her, that she was entitled to the beneficial interest in it, and that M and his mortgagee took subject to her rights "as a person in actual occupation" when M became the registered proprietor.

The Court of Appeal held that Mrs H was in actual occupation within the meaning of paragraph (*g*) and ordered rectification of the register in her favour as M had not made any inquiries of Mrs H prior to registration of the transfer to him.[2]

Further, as we have seen, the House of Lords in *Williams and Glyn's Bank Ltd v Boland*[3] held that the beneficial interest of a wife as tenant in common with her husband of the matrimonial home under a statutory trust for sale was an interest which subsists in reference to registered land; and that, being in actual occupation, she had an overriding interest which bound the bank to which her husband had mortgaged the house.

(ii) Actual occupation The paragraph protects the rights of a person in actual occupation. As Lord WILBERFORCE said in *Williams and Glyn's Bank Ltd v Boland*:[4]

> These words are ordinary words of plain English, and, should, in my opinion, be interpreted as such . . . Given occupation, i.e. presence on the land, I do not think that the word "actual" was intended to introduce any additional qualification, certainly not to suggest that possession must be "adverse": it merely emphasises that what is required is physical presence, not some entitlement in law.

The occupation must involve some degree of permanence and continuity which would rule out mere fleeting presence. In *Abbey National Building*

19 *London and Cheshire Insurance Co Ltd v Laplagrene Property Co Ltd* [1971] Ch 499, [1971] 1 All ER 766; M & B p. 145. For the protection of a lien by registration of a caution, see *Woolf Project Management Ltd v Woodtrek Ltd* (1987) 56 P & CR 134.
20 *Blacklocks v JB Developments (Godalming) Ltd* [1982] Ch 183, [1981] 3 All ER 392. But no reference was made to *Smith v Jones* [1954] 1 WLR 1089, [1954] 2 All ER 823; M & B p. 49, where UPJOHN J held that a right to rectify a tenancy agreement would not be enforceable by a tenant against a purchaser of the reversion who had inspected the agreement. See [1983] Conv 169, 257 (J. T. F.), 361 (D. G. Barnsley).
1 [1971] Ch 892, [1971] 2 All ER 684.
2 See (1971) 35 Conv (NS) 255, 268–76 (I. Leeming): Law Commission Working Paper No. 37 (1971), paras. 56–77.
3 [1981] AC 487, [1980] 2 All ER 408; p. 237, ante, where the facts of the case are set out; *Emmet on Title*, para. 5.200; [1980] Conv 361; [1981] Conv 84 (J. Martin); (1979) 95 LQR 501; (1982) 97 LQR 12 (R. J. Smith); (1980) 130 NLJ 896 (R. L. Deech); *City of London Building Society v Flegg* [1988] AC 54, [1987] 3 All ER 435; M & B p. 281, p. 818, post (equitable interests of parents as tenants in common arising from contribution to purchase price of house registered in names of their daughter and son-in-law held to be overreachable by payment to two trustees, even though the parents were in actual occupation). Cf *Winkworth v Edward Baron Development Co Ltd* [1986] 1 WLR 1512, [1987] 1 All ER 114. A beneficial interest under a strict settlement is not capable of being an overriding interest: p. 202, ante.
4 At 504–5, at 412.

Society v Cann,[5] the House of Lords held that there was no actual occupation where carpets were laid out and furniture moved into a dwelling-house with the vendor's consent. As Lord OLIVER OF AYLMERTON said:[6]

> These were acts of a preparatory character carried out by the courtesy of the vendor prior to completion.

Similarly, in *Epps v Esso Petroleum Co Ltd*, the parking of a car at night on an undefined strip of land did not suffice;[7] and in *Strand Securities Ltd v Caswell*,[8] it was held that the tenant of a flat was not in actual occupation, even though the tenant and members of his family used it as a London rendezvous, and he had a key to the flat which contained some of his furniture.[9]

The nature and state of the property may also be relevant. In *Lloyds Bank plc v Rosset*,[10] the Court of Appeal held that, in the case of a semi-derelict farmhouse:

> there was physical presence on the property by the wife and her agent of the nature, and the extent, that one would expect of an occupier having regard to the then state of the property, namely, the presence involved in actively carrying out the renovation necessary to make the house fit for residential use.

A person may be in actual occupation through the agency of another, such as his caretaker or employee, but not through his gratuitous licensee acting on his own account.[11] On the other hand, it has been suggested that "physical presence" does not connote continued and uninterrupted presence: "such a notion would be absurd". Nor is the requisite presence negatived by repeated and regular absence. Thus a wife would be in actual occupation of a matrimonial home where she spent virtually some part of every day in order to discharge her duties as housewife and mother, but where she did not usually sleep.[12]

Finally, it should be noticed that the date for deciding when there is actual occupation is the date of completion of the purchase, when the transferee hands over the purchase money in return for the land certificate. It is not the

---

5 [1991] 1 AC 56, [1990] 1 All ER 1085; M & B p. 143; (1990) 106 LQR 32, 545 (R. J. Smith); [1990] CLJ 397 (A. J. Oakley); (1990) 87 LSG 19–24, 34–19 (M. Beaumont, junior counsel for Mrs Cann); [1991] Conv 116 (S. Baughen), 155 (P. T. Evans).
6 At 94, at 1101.
7 [1973] 1 WLR 1071, [1973] 2 All ER 465; M & B p. 168. Cf *Celsteel Ltd v Alton House Holdings Ltd* [1985] 1 WLR 204, [1985] 2 All ER 562, M & B p. 702 (lessee exercising right of way to garage held to be in actual occupation).
8 [1965] Ch 958, [1965] 1 All ER 820; M & B p. 141.
9 In *Chhokar v Chhokar* [1984] FLR 313; M & B p. 145, furniture was held to be relevant.
10 [1989] Ch 350, [1988] 3 All ER 915; M & B p. 138; [1988] Conv 453 (M. P. Thompson); [1989] CLJ 180 (P. G. McHugh); [1988] All ER Rev 163 (P. J. Clarke); (1988) 104 LQR 507 (R. J. Smith); [1989] Conv 342 (P. Sparkes). HL reversed CA on the ground that Mrs Rossett had no beneficial interest under a trust; no views were expressed on the question of her actual occupation: [1991] 1 AC 107, [1990] 1 All ER 1111; M & B p. 130.
11 See *Strand Securities Ltd v Caswell*, supra.
12 *Kingsnorth Finance Co Ltd v Tizard* [1986] 1 WLR 783 at 788, [1986] 2 All ER 54 at 59 per Judge John FINLAY QC; M & B p. 144; [1987] CLJ 28 (P. C. McHugh); [1986] Conv 283 (M. P. Thompson). This was a case on unregistered land. See also *Chhokar v Chhokar*, supra (wife evicted by fraudulent purchaser of matrimonial home from husband held to be in actual occupation).

later date when the transferee is registered as proprietor.[13] If, however, there has been an overriding interest on the relevant date, it is not lost if its holder subsequently goes out of occupation.[14]

(iii) Section 70 (1) (g) and the doctrine of *Hunt v Luck* Paragraph (*g*), as we have seen, carries the doctrine of *Hunt v Luck*[15] forward into registered land. It may, however, be wider than the doctrine in two ways. First it protects not only the rights of every person in actual occupation of the land, but also those of every person in receipt of the rents and profits thereof.[16] In this context, receipt means the actual receipt of rent from a tenant, and not the mere right to receive it.[17] Secondly, it is clear from *Williams and Glyn's Bank Ltd v Boland* that the actual occupation need not be such as to give constructive notice to a purchaser.[18] This emphasises the crucial importance of the inspection and inquiries which a purchaser must make in respect of overriding interests which will bind him whether he knows about them or not and however extensive his enquiry may be.[19]

As we have seen, the doctrine of *Hunt v Luck* applies where a person is in possession of unregistered land together with the vendor.[20] The position is similar in registered land, where the House of Lords adopted a literal construction of paragraph (*g*) in *Williams and Glyn's Bank Ltd v Boland*,[1] and held that the presence of the vendor in occupation does not exclude the possibility of occupation by others. As the expression "*any* person" suggests, two persons can be in actual occupation by themselves jointly or each of them severally. The House of Lords further rejected an argument that where a wife lives in the matrimonial home with her husband it is the husband alone who is in actual occupation of it.[2]

We must now discuss the remaining overriding interests:

(*h*) In the case of a possessory, qualified, or good leasehold title,[3] all estates, rights, interests, and powers excepted from the effect of registration.

These three classes of title may be converted[4] and on a conversion this overriding interest determines to the extent resulting from the conversion.

13 *Abbey National Building Society v Cann*, supra. The date for all other overriding interests is the date of registration. Lord BRIDGE OF HARWICH also held that the relevant date for para (*g*) is that of completion, but by a different route. For him the date for all overriding interests is that of completion, except for para (*i*) (rights under local land charges).
14 *London and Cheshire Insurance Co Ltd v Laplagrene Property Co Ltd* [1971] Ch 499, [1971] 1 All ER 766; M & B p. 141.
15 P. 104, ante.
16 *Strand Securities Ltd v Caswell*, supra.
17 *E S Schwab & Co Ltd v McCarthy* (1975) 31 P & CR 196.
18 [1981] AC 487 at 504, 511, [1980] 2 All ER 408 at 412. See *Hodgson v Marks*, supra at 932, at 688, per RUSSELL LJ.
19 See *Kling v Keston Properties Ltd* (1983) 49 P & CR 212 at 221–222, per VINELOTT J. For a suggested method of enquiry, see [1980] Conv 85, 311. See also (1980) 124 NLJ 651, 670 (P. W. Smith).
20 P. 63, ante.
 1 Supra. So too in *Hodgson v Marks*, supra, where CA held that Mrs H, who resided in the house together with E, the vendor, was in actual occupation.
 2 This argument was adopted in *Caunce v Caunce* [1969] 1 WLR 286, [1969] 1 All ER 722; M & B p. 297; pp. 63, 243, ante, the counterpart of *Williams and Glyn's Bank Ltd v Boland* in unregistered land; the case was disapproved by HL at 505, 511, at 413, 418 and not followed in *Kingsnorth Finance Co Ltd v Tizard* [1986] 1 WLR 783, [1986] 2 All ER 54, p. 64, n. 10, ante.
 3 P. 786, ante.
 4 LRA 1925, s. 77, as amended by LRA 1986, s. 1, p. 787, ante.

(*i*) Rights under local land charges unless and until registered or protected on the register in the prescribed manner.[5]

This is a very important category of overriding interests. Local land charges have the same meaning as they have in the Local Land Charges Act 1975 and that Act applies to both unregistered and registered land. A purchaser must therefore search in the local authority's register whether or not the land is registered.

The Registrar comments as follows on the failure to require the entry of all local land charges on the register at the Land Registry:[6]

> Just as it would be impracticable to set out a summary of the material facts relating to them on the deeds and documents used in unregistered conveyancing, so there is at present no machinery for entering them on the register of title at the Land Registry save in particular cases.

(*j*) Rights of fishing and sporting, seignorial and manorial rights of all descriptions (until extinguished), and franchises.[7]

(*k*) Leases granted for a term not exceeding twenty-one years.[8]

This paragraph does not include a contract for the grant of a lease for 21 years or less, as there has been no grant. It does not, however, require that the lease takes effect in possession.[9]

(2) OVERRIDING INTERESTS UNDER LATER LEGISLATION

The following overriding interests have been added:

(a) All coal and mines of coal and associated interests and ancillary rights which are vested in the British Coal Corporation.[10]

(b) Rights, privileges and appurtenances appertaining or reputed to appertain to land or demised, occupied or enjoyed therewith or reputed or known as part or parcel of or appurtenant thereto, which adversely affect registered land.[11]

Further, it should be noted that certain rights are declared by statute *not* to be overriding interests; a spouse's right of occupation under the Matrimonial Homes Act 1983, the right of a tenant arising from a notice under the Leasehold Reform Act 1967 of his desire to acquire the freehold or an extended lease, and the rights conferred by or under an access order under the Access to Neighbouring Land Act 1992.[12] The right of a secure tenant under Part V of the Housing Act 1985 to acquire the freehold or to be granted

---

5 I.e. on the register at the Land Registry.
6 Ruoff and Roper, para. 6.23. A local land charge to secure money must be registered as a registered charge at the Land Registry before it can be entered against registered land: LRA 1925, s. 59(2).
7 *Morris v Dimes* (1834) 1 Ad & El 654; *Wyld v Silver* [1963] Ch 243, [1962] 3 All ER 309; *Gloucestershire County Council v Farrow* [1985] 1 WLR 741, [1985] 1 All ER 878; Law Commission Third Report on Land Registration (Law Com No. 158, HC 269), Appendix F.
8 As amended by LRA 1986, s. 4 (1). Previously gratuitous leases or leases granted for a premium were excluded; existing such leases are overriding transitionally: s. 4 (4).
9 P. 792, n. 13, ante. Paragraph (*l*) specifies certain rights to mines and minerals existing before 1926.
10 Coal Act 1938, s. 41; Coal Industry Nationalisation Act 1946, ss. 5, 8, Sch. 1; Coal Industry Act 1987, s. 1.
11 LRR 1925, r. 258; *Celsteel Ltd v Alton House Holdings Ltd* [1985] 1 WLR 204, [1985] 2 All ER 562; M & B p. 702; p. 582, ante.
12 Matrimonial Homes Act 1983, s. 8 (3) (*b*), replacing Matrimonial Homes Act 1967, s. 2 (7); Leasehold Reform Act 1967, s. 5 (5); Access to Neighbouring Land Act 1992, s. 5 (5). See p. 396, n. 6, ante. And also excluded by implication is an interest under a strict settlement: LRA 1925, s. 86 (2), p. 202, n. 13, ante.

a lease is declared by statute not to be an overriding interest under paragraph (*k*).[13]

(3) CRITICISM OF OVERRIDING INTERESTS

The effect of overriding interests is, as we have seen, to bind a transferee from a registered proprietor, whether he knows about them or not. They thus detract from the principle that the register should be a mirror of the title, and so it is important that they should be able to justify their existence as a separate category within the system of registered conveyancing. A balance has to be struck between the protection of the person enjoying the interest and the inconvenience to a purchaser. Sympathy for the latter leads to a plea for as complete an abolition of the category as is feasible.

Criticism of overriding interests must, however, be tempered by four considerations. Firstly, the category cannot be abandoned completely, however desirable it is that the register should be a complete mirror of the title. It is impossible to enter on the register rights arising under the Limitation Act 1980, or easements and profits being acquired by prescription. Secondly, as we have seen, the legislature has decided as a matter of policy that protection should be accorded to the rights of a person in actual occupation, even if he has failed to register his interests. This is most desirable in those situations where the holder of the right might not consult a solicitor and therefore be unaware of the need for entry on the register, e.g. a contract for a lease. This is the opposite to the Draconian policy of the Land Charges Act 1972 for unregistered conveyancing.[14] "The rule for registered land is much more reasonable, for possession is the strongest possible title to security."[15] Thirdly, it is impracticable to require the registration of all short tenancies. Fourthly, overriding interests appear frequently on the register, and if they do they are not regarded as overriding.[16] The Registrar has a mandatory duty to enter a notice on first registration of "any easement, right, privilege, or benefit created by an instrument" which appears on the title and adversely affects the land.[17] He also has a discretion to enter on the register a notice that the land is free from or subject to certain overriding interests.[18] As the Registrar writes:

> The plain fact is . . . that there are mandatory provisions requiring most overriding interests to be entered on the register, which operate either on first registration,[19] or on a dealing with registered land,[20] or at any time on proof of their being furnished,[1] and so ensure that, save for squatters' rights,[2] which cannot be recorded, or rights of occupiers or lessees, which are discoverable, under the rule in *Hunt v*

---

13 Housing Act 1985, s. 154 (7), as added by LRA 1986, s. 2 (4), p. 487, ante.
14 This aspect of the LCA 1925 may have been due to an error on the part of the draftsman of the 1925 legislation: (1977) 41 Conv NS p. 419, n. 31 (C. Harpum); [1982] Conv, pp. 215–217 (M. Friend and J. Newton); M & B p. 52.
15 (1956) CLJ 228 (H. W. R. Wade).
16 *Webb v Pollmount Ltd* [1966] Ch 584 at 594, [1966] 1 All ER 481 at 484, per UNGOED-THOMAS J; LRA 1925, s. 3 (xvi).
17 LRA 1925, s. 70 (2). *Re Dances Way, West Town, Hayling Island* [1962] Ch 490 at 508, [1962] 2 All ER 42 at 52, per DIPLOCK LJ; p. 580, ante.
18 Ibid., s. 70 (1), (3); LRR 1925, rr. 194, 197, 198, 250, 252, 254.
19 LRA 1925, s. 70 (2).
20 Ibid., ss. 19 (2), 22 (2).
 1 Ibid., s. 70 (3). This is in fact discretionary only.
 2 Ibid., s. 70 (1) (*f*).

Luck,[3] from a proper inspection and inquiry, or local land charges which obviously must be recorded locally,[4] they are all entered on the register.[5]

(4) LAW REFORM

(a) Developments after *Boland*

Since the decision in *Williams and Glyn's Bank Ltd v Boland*, institutional lenders naturally sought ways in which to avoid the consequence of being bound by such an overriding interest as arose from actual occupation in that case. They had to make more careful inquiries of the mortgagor[6] and of the property, and, if they discovered an actual occupant who had a beneficial interest in the property, they resorted to forms of consent or waiver to be signed by the occupant. But difficulties still exist. The waiver may be invalid, if there is undue influence on the part of the lender or of an agent acting on his behalf; and he may owe a duty of care to the occupant to explain the transaction and be liable if loss is caused by his failure to discharge that duty.[7]

Another possibility is to insist on the appointment of an additional trustee (there was only one trustee in *Boland*) so that the mortgage money can be paid to two trustees, thereby overreaching the beneficial interest of the occupant and attaching it to the equity of redemption in the hands of the mortgagor and the money paid to him.[8]

On the other hand, if the occupant knows that the property is being acquired by the registered proprietor with the aid of a mortgage, the occupant's interest may not bind the mortgagee, either by virtue of estoppel,[9] or by virtue of an imputed intention that his interest is subject to the rights of the mortgagee.[10]

(b) Law Commission Report 1987

In 1987 the Law Commission made important recommendations about overriding interests.[11] It proposes to adopt two principles; with the first being subject to the second:

3 [1902] 1 Ch 428.
4 LRA 1925, s. 70 (1) (*i*). See p. 767, ante.
5 (1969) 32 MLR at 129 (T. B. F. Ruoff). There is, on general principle, a duty to declare any overriding interest that is not obvious.
6 "Reliance on the true ipse dixit of the vendor will not suffice": *Hodgson v Marks* [1971] Ch 892 at 932, [1971] 2 All ER 684 at 688, per RUSSELL LJ.
7 See pp. 682–3, ante.
8 *City of London Building Society v Flegg* [1988] AC 54, [1987] 3 All ER 435, p. 818, post.
9 *Spiro v Lintern* [1973] 1 WLR 1002, [1973] 3 All ER 319; *Emmet on Title*, para. 11.031.
10 *Bristol and West Building Society v Henning* [1985] 1 WLR 778, [1985] 2 All ER 606; *Paddington Building Society v Mendelsohn* (1985) 50 P & CR 244; [1986] Conv 57 (M. P. Thompson); *Abbey National Building Society v Cann* [1991] 1 AC 56, [1990] 1 All ER 1085 at 94, at 7101; *Equity and Law Home Loans Ltd v Prestridge* [1992] 1 WLR 137, [1992] 1 All ER 909. And the mortgage itself may be invalid if the registered proprietor has no power to create it.
11 Third Report on Land Registration (Law Com No. 158, HC 269), which contains a valuable and critical account of the existing law. Its recommendations are summarised in paras. 2.105–2.108. For an earlier recommendation, see The Implications of *Williams and Glyn's Bank Ltd v Boland* 1982 (Law Com No. 115, Comnd 8636) favouring the purchaser, and for draft proposals treating overriding interests and rectification and indemnity as interconnected topics, see the summary in para. 2.7, n. 36 of the 1987 Report.

(1) In the interests of certainty and of simplifying conveyancing, the class of right which may bind a purchaser otherwise than as the result of an entry on the register should be as narrow as possible but

(2) Interests should be overriding where protection against purchasers is needed, yet it is either not reasonable to expect or not sensible to require any entry on the register.

The welfare of the conveyancer, or rather his client, is our first but not our paramount consideration. However, particularly perturbed by thoughts of honest and careful purchasers suffering losses because of principle (2), we propose that the ordinary indemnity provisions should become available for claims occasioned by overriding interests.

In outline the proposals are as follows:

(a) The Law Commission first examines the list of overriding interests and recommends that it be redrafted and curtailed. Only the following should remain:

   (i) Legal easements and profits à prendre. Paragraph (*a*) of section 70 (1) should be redrafted so as to exclude superfluous wording and equitable easements and profits. (paras. 2.25–2.35.)

   (ii) Rights acquired by adverse possession. (paras. 2.36–2.37.)

   (iii) Leases for 21 years or less. Para. (*k*) should cover rights having reference to the subject matter of a lease granted (i.e. not a contract for a lease) for a continuous term not exceeding 21 years taking effect in possession either immediately or within one month. (para. 2.38–2.53.)

   (iv) Rights of persons in actual occupation of land. Paragraph (*g*) should exclude the receipt of rents and profits, and also the proviso as being superfluous, but should include rights under strict settlements. (paras. 2.54–2.70.)

   (v) Customary rights. These should be removed from para. (*a*) and become a separate category. (para. 2.75.)

(b) The following three amendments should apply to all these five categories:

   (i) They should be expressly subject to a general provision regarding fraud or estoppel.

   (ii) Their relevant date should be not registration, but completion of a disposition.

   (iii) The indemnity scheme should be extended to the retained overriding interests. The registered proprietor's claim should not succeed in full or perhaps at all if he has contributed to the loss suffered due to lack of proper care on his part. (paras. 2.74–2.78.) The availability of indemnity would go some way to enabling an acceptable balance to be achieved between competing innocent interests. (paras. 2.10–2.14.)

(c) A new category of general burdens as a class of rights over registered land should be recognised. These rights should bind registered proprietors as existing overriding interests, but not attract the indemnity recommendation. The remaining paragraphs of section 70 (1) would fall into this category, i.e. public rights, chancel repairs liability, local land charges, mineral rights and franchises. (paras. 2.15, 2.79–2.81, 2.94, 2.100–2.102.)

E. MINOR INTERESTS

(1) DEFINITION

Minor interests are defined by section 3 (xv) of the Land Registration Act 1925 as follows:

"Minor interests" mean the interests not capable of being disposed of or created by registered dispositions and capable of being overridden (whether or not a purchaser has notice thereof) by the proprietors unless protected as provided by this Act, and all rights and interests which are not registered or protected on the register and are not overriding interests, and include:

(*a*) in the case of land held on trust for sale, all interests and powers which are under the Law of Property Act, 1925, capable of being overridden by the trustees for sale, whether or not such interests and powers are so protected; and

(*b*) in the case of settled land, all interests and powers which are under the Settled Land Act, 1925, and the Law of Property Act, 1925, or either of them, capable of being overridden by the tenant for life or statutory owner, whether or not such interests and powers are so protected as aforesaid.

This definition is complex, by being both exclusionary and inclusionary in its terms, and must be read in conjunction with section 2 of the Land Registration Act 1925. Once it is laid down in that section that the only estates which can be registered are "estates capable of subsisting as legal estates", then it follows that they must be excluded from the definition of minor interests and that "all other interests in registered land (except overriding interests . . .) shall take effect in equity as minor interests". Minor interests therefore are a residual category of interests within the system of registered land.

The definition prefaces the two classes (*a*) and (*b*) with the word "include". There is thus no finite list as there is in unregistered land. Any interest, right or claim may be entered on the register in the appropriate manner, but the validity of the entry may be challenged later.

There are two main classes of minor interests:

(a) those which are capable of being overridden[12] by registered dispositions for valuable consideration, whether or not they are protected by an entry on the register. This class includes those interests which are overreachable under the Law of Property Act 1925, and the Settled Land Act 1925, in unregistered conveyancing, i.e. the equitable interests of beneficiaries under a trust for sale or a strict settlement.

(b) All other minor interests. The most important examples in this class are those interests which in unregistered conveyancing are registrable as land charges under the Land Charges Act 1972.[13] Interests in this class must be protected by an entry on the register, if they are not to be overridden by a

---

12 See *City of London Building Society v Flegg* [1988] AC 54 at 85, [1987] All ER 435 at 449, where Lord OLIVER OF AYLMERTON says: "Plainly here 'overridden' is used as embracing interests which can be overreached under the provisions of section 2 of the Law of Property Act".

13 The provisions of the Land Charges Act 1972 are excluded from registered conveyancing: LRA 1925, s. 59. If an option to renew a lease is void for non-registration under LCA 1972, s. 4 (6), it cannot be revived by subsequent first registration under LRA 1925, s. 9 and the entry on the charges register of the lease containing the option: *Kitney v MEPC* [1977] 1 WLR 981, [1978] 1 All ER 595. For a chart showing the registration machinery which replaces that of the Land Charges Act, see Ruoff and Roper, para. 7–08; M & B pp. 154–155.

registered disposition for valuable consideration. Furthermore, as in unregistered conveyancing, actual notice of what should be protected in the register, but is not so protected, is immaterial.[14]

It is important to notice that in neither class will interests be overridden by any disposition made without valuable consideration, and in this case, it is immaterial whether or not they have been entered on the register.[15]

(2) PROTECTION OF MINOR INTERESTS

Minor interests may be protected on the register in four different ways, namely, by the entry of a notice, a restriction, a caution or an inhibition.[16]

(a) Notice

A notice may be entered on the charges register[17] to protect any of a number of lesser interests and rights affecting the land.[18] It will only protect an interest that is valid and effective independently of the register for, unlike registration of title, a notice is incapable of converting an invalid interest into a potentially valid one. Nor does entry of a covenant guarantee that it will run with land.[19] A notice may also be entered of a claim to a right or interest.[20] A notice of such a claim includes notice of claim to rights appurtenant to a title as well as to those binding it. It is sometimes used to indicate that the proprietor of a title claims an appurtenant right, the title to which can neither be guaranteed nor rejected out of hand. But subject to

---

14 *Hodges v Jones* [1935] Ch 657 at 671, per LUXMOORE J. LRA 1925, s. 59 (6), as amended by FA 1975, s. 52, Sch. 12, para. 5; ITA 1984, s. 226, Sch. 8, para. 1; *De Lusignan v Johnson* (1973) 230 EG 499.

See, however, two decisions at first instance, where the constructive trust was used to avoid the consequences of failure to register a right as a minor interest, but which have been much criticized: (a) *Peffer v Rigg* [1977] 1 WLR 285, [1978] 3 All ER 745; M & B p. 160, where GRAHAM J treated a transferee under s. 20 (1) and a purchaser, defined in s. 3 (xxi) as "bona fide purchaser for value", as synonymous, and held that, where an ex-wife purchased a house from her former husband, with actual knowledge that he held it on trust for himself and her brother-in-law, she was not a bona fide transferee under s. 20 (1), and therefore was bound by the trust. He also held that she was a constructive trustee of the house: (1977) 41 Conv (NS) 207 (F. R. Crane); (1977) 93 LQR 341 (R. J. Smith); [1977] CLJ 227 (D. J. Hayton); (1977) 40 MLR 602 (S. Anderson); [1978] Conv 52 (J. Martin). (b) *Lyus v Prowsa Developments Ltd* [1982] 1 WLR 1044, [1982] 2 All ER 953; M & B p. 160, where a purchaser, who agreed to take part of a building estate expressly "subject to and with the benefit of" an existing contract for the sale of one plot, was held bound by that contract under a constructive trust, on the ground that the LRA was not to be used as an instrument of fraud. For criticism, see (1983) 46 MLR 96 (P. H. Kenny); [1982] All ER Rev (P. J. Clarke); [1983] CLJ 54 (C. J. Harpum); [1983] Conv 64 (P. Jackson); (1983) 133 NLJ 798 (C. T. Emery and B. Smythe); cf (1984) 47 MLR 476 (P. Bennett); [1985] CLJ 280 (M. P. Thompson). See also *Du Boulay v Raggett* (1988) 58 P & CR 138; *Emmet on Title*, para. 20.020. On constructive trusts and registered land generally, see Oakley, *Constructive Trusts* (2nd edn), chapter 2; H & M chapter 12; pp. 592–5, ante.

15 LRA 1925, ss. 20 (4), 23 (5).

16 See generally (1958) 22 Conv (NS) 14 (F. R. Crane); (1953) 17 Conv (NS) 105 (T. B. F. Ruoff). For mortgages, see pp. 731, ante.

17 LRR 1925, r. 7.

18 LRA 1925, ss. 52, 59, and LRR 1925, r. 190. For the residual character of notices, see particularly s. 49 (1) as amended by Charging Orders Act 1979, s. 3 (3).

19 *Cator v Newton and Bates* [1940] 1 KB 415, [1939] 4 All ER 457; LRA 1925, s. 52; p. 643, ante (entry that freehold land is subject to positive covenant does not make that covenant enforceable against third party). See also *Kitney v MEPC Ltd* [1977] 1 WLR 981, [1978] 1 All ER 595; p. 800, n. 13, ante.

20 LRA 1925, s. 52 (2).

these reservations, entry by way of a notice gives protection to and information about important rights adverse to land like easements,[1] covenants, long leases[2] and estate contracts. Noting of adverse interests is quite separate, of course, from the registration of leaseholds and of the benefit of easements in the property register; though there will frequently be cross references. For instance, registration of a lease will always be accompanied by a note of it on the title out of which it is carved.[3]

Notice on the register has, in general, the same function that registration in the Land Charges Register has in unregistered conveyancing. Subsequent dispositions of the land are subject to those interests capable of affecting a transferee as are the subject of a notice, while purchasers for valuable consideration take free of interests requiring a notice for protection if they are not so protected,[4] unless they are also overriding interests, or are protected in some other way, e.g. by a caution.

The availability of protection by way of a notice does not exclude protection under other parts of the registration machinery. Thus, an option in a lease to purchase the freehold can both be protected by a notice and, independently of the register, may constitute an overriding interest;[5] again, a deposit of a land certificate as security for a loan can be the subject of protection in several different ways.[6]

A notice is a particularly good method of protecting an interest or right, as, assuming the right or interest itself to be valid, all dispositions by the proprietor of the land take effect subject to the right or interest (unless it is capable of being overridden by the disposition independently of the Land Registration Act 1925).[7] The weakness of a notice lies in that, in order to secure its entry, the applicant must, except in the case of a notice of a lease at a rent without taking a fine, lodge the land certificate of the title concerned,[8] unless it is already deposited at the Land Registry because of the existence of a prior registered charge.[9] Notices thus can usually be entered only with the co-operation of the owner of the land affected.

---

1 The Registrar must enter on the register all adverse easements shown to exist in the documents produced at the time of first registration: s. 70 (2). Thereafter, adverse easements may be entered by him, in his discretion: LRR 1925, r. 41 (1). See generally *Re Dances Way, West Town, Hayling Island* [1962] Ch 490, [1962] 2 All ER 42.
2 Leases for a term not exceeding 21 years are overriding interests: LRA 1925, s. 70 (1) (*k*), as amended by LRA 1986, s. 4 (1); and, despite the generous wording of LRA 1925, s. 70 (3), they never appear on the register, but are protected only as overriding interests. See LRA 1925, ss. 19 (2), 48 (1). Generally on the subject of leases and underleases, see *Strand Securities Ltd v Caswell* [1965] Ch 958, [1965] 1 All ER 820; pp. 513–4 et seq, ante.
3 Lease includes underlease: s. 3 (x). Accordingly, underleases are properly noted on the title of the head-lease.
4 LRA 1925, ss. 20, 23, 48, 50, 52 (1), 101; *White v Bijou Mansions* [1937] Ch 610, [1937] 3 All ER 269.
5 *Webb v Pollmount Ltd* [1966] Ch 584, [1966] 1 All ER 481; M & B p. 792, interpreting LRA 1925, s. 59 (1). Again, LRA 1925, s. 48 makes provision for notice, on the superior title, of leases that do not constitute overriding interests *as such* (i.e., leases for more than 21 years), but in fact most lessees and lessors can claim the protection given to an overriding interest under s. 70 (1) (*g*): see p. 792, ante.
6 *Re White Rose Cottage* [1965] Ch 940, [1965] 1 All ER 11; M & B p. 156, especially per Lord DENNING MR, at 949–50, at 14–15; p. 734, ante.
7 LRA 1925, s. 52 (1).
8 Ibid., s. 64 (1) (*c*) as amended by FA 1975, s. 52, Sch. 12, para. 5.
9 Ibid., s. 65.

(b) Restriction

A restriction is an entry which prevents dealings in registered land until certain specified conditions or requirements have been complied with.[10] Its object is thus to record, on the proprietorship register,[11] any impediment to the proprietor's freedom of disposal. A restriction can in effect only be entered on the register with the concurrence of the proprietor or at the instance of the Registrar and, once entered, no transaction will be permitted except in conformity with its terms, although the Registrar must not enter any restriction which be considers to be "unreasonable or calculated to cause inconvenience". As we have seen,[12] restrictions at the instance of the Registrar are employed, inter alia, to give effect to strict settlements and trusts for sale of registered land and the entry of such restrictions is obligatory. The rules on the production of the land certificate are the same as in the case of notices.

(c) Caution

(i) Caution against dealings A caution against dealings, unlike a notice or a restriction, is a hostile act, and is used to protect interests in land (or a charge) registered in the name of another person. Production of the land or charge certificate is not necessary, nor is the concurrence of the proprietor of the land or charge. If the caution is against the land, it is entered in the proprietorship register; if against the charge, in the charges register.[13] Cautions can be "warned off" by the registered proprietor, in which case notice is served by the Registrar on the cautioner, and if the cautioner consents or does not object within the time specified in the notice, the caution is cancelled. If the cautioner objects, and cannot resolve his objection by agreement with the registered proprietor, the dispute is adjudicated on by the Registrar or the court.[14]

---

10 LRA 1925, s. 58.
11 LRR 1925, r. 6. Or on the charges register when interests in a registered charge are to be protected.
12 Pp. 202, 209, ante.
13 LRA 1925, s. 54; LRR 1925, rr. 6, 7. *Re White Rose Cottage* [1965] Ch 940, [1965] 1 All ER 11 (equitable charge), p. 733, ante; *Parkash v Irani Finance Ltd* [1970] Ch 101, [1969] 1 All ER 930 (charging order), p. 804, n. 16, post; *Elias v Mitchell* [1972] Ch 652, [1972] 2 All ER 153 (equitable tenant in common under trust for sale), p. 243, ante; cf. *Myton Ltd v Schwab-Morris* [1974] 1 WLR 331, [1974] 1 All ER 326.
14 For the court's exercise of its jurisdiction to order the vacation of cautions, see *Rawlplug Co Ltd v Kamvale Properties Ltd* (1968) 20 P & CR 32; *Calgary and Edmonton Land Co Ltd v Discount Bank (Overseas) Ltd* [1971] 1 WLR 81, [1971] 1 All ER 551; *Clearbrook Property Holdings Ltd v Verrier* [1974] 1 WLR 243, [1973] 3 All ER 614; *Tiverton Estates Ltd v Wearwell* [1975] Ch 146 at 161, 171, [1974] 1 All ER 209 at 219, 228; *Lester v Burgess* (1973) 26 P & CR 536 (a useful analysis of the jurisdiction by GOULDING J); *Price Bros (Somerford) Ltd v J Kelly Homes (Stoke-on-Trent) Ltd* [1975] 1 WLR 1512, [1975] 3 All ER 369; *Calgary and Edmonton Land Co Ltd v Dobinson* [1974] Ch 102, [1974] 1 All ER 484; *Norman v Hardy* [1974] 1 WLR 1048, [1974] 1 All ER 1170; (1974) 38 Conv (NS) 208 (F. R. Crane); *Northern Developments (Holdings) Ltd v UDT Securities Ltd* [1976] 1 WLR 1230, [1977] 1 All ER 747; (1976) 41 Conv (NS) 173 (F. R. Crane); *Sowerby v Sowerby* (1982) 44 P & CR 192; *Alpenstow Ltd v Regalian Properties plc* [1985] 1 WLR 721, [1985] 2 All ER 545; *Hynes v Vaughan* (1985) 50 P & CR 444; *Chancery Land Developments Ltd v Wades Stores Ltd* (1986) 53 P & CR 306; *Tucker v Hutchinson* (1987) 54 P & CR 106; *Carlton v Halestrap* (1988) 4 BCC 538; *Woolf Project Management Ltd v Woodtrek Ltd* (1987) 56 P & CR 134; *Cabra Estates plc v Glendower Investments Ltd* [1992] EGCS 137; *Willies-Williams v National Trust* (1993) 65 P & CR 359.

If the caution is not "warned off" or withdrawn by the cautioner, it remains on the register, and the Registrar may not register any dealing or notice of deposit affecting the land (or the charge, if the caution is against the charge) until he has served notice on the cautioner. After such notice has been served, it operates as though it were a "warning-off" notice.

(ii) Caution against first registration In order to protect an interest in land not yet registered, a caution against first registration may be lodged. The Registrar will serve notice on the cautioner, who may then oppose the application for first registration in manner similar to that in which a cautioner against dealings may oppose the registration of a dealing or notice of deposit.

The provisions of the Acts and Rules relating to cautions against dealings and against first registration are complex,[15] but the following observations may be made:

(i) Cautions give no priority or protection other than a right to object. The objection may or may not succeed. A caution against dealings is thus much inferior to a notice, and should therefore be applied for only where application for a notice will fail because the land certificate is not available for lodging, or is not already on deposit.

(ii) If there is no successful objection to a caution against dealings, it seems that a purchaser takes subject to an interest which is protected by the entry.[16] But the entry does not affect priorities as between two competing equitable interests. Apart from statutory provision,[17] a caution does not give a later equitable interest priority over an earlier one. Thus in *Barclays Bank Ltd v Taylor*,[18] an equitable mortgage by deposit of the land certificate, even though it was not itself protected by a notice of the deposit,[19] was held by the Court of Appeal to have priority over a subsequent estate contract which was protected by a caution. As RUSSELL LJ said:[20]

> We ask ourselves what provision is there in the Act which reverses the ordinary rule that as between equities . . . priority is governed by the time sequence? [After answering this question in the negative, his Lordship continued:] The caution lodged on behalf of the purchasers had no effect whatsoever by itself on priorities: it simply conferred on the cautioners the right to be given notice of any dealing proposed to be registered.

(iii) A caution against dealings will not be accepted by the Registrar if the

---

Notice of an appeal from an order of the court vacating a caution is registrable under LRR 1925, r. 301: *Belcourt v Belcourt* [1989] 1 WLR 195, [1989] 2 All ER 34.

For the liability of a solicitor in negligence for failing to ensure that a notice under Matrimonial Homes Act 1967 was cancelled, see *Holmes v Kennard H & Son* (1984) 49 P & CR 202; p. 241, ante.

15 For a full discussion see Ruoff and Roper, chapters 13 and 36.
16 *Parkash v Irani Finance Ltd* [1970] Ch 101, [1969] 1 All ER 930; M & B p. 157.
17 LRA 1925, s. 102 (2); p. 733, ante.
18 [1974] Ch 137, [1973] 1 All ER 752; M & B p. 809; (1973) 89 LQR 170 (P. V. B.). For a detailed discussion of priorities of minor interests, see (1971) 35 Conv (NS) 100, 168; (1974) 124 NLJ 634 (S. Robinson); (1976) CLP 26 at 37, et seq (D. J. Hayton); [1977] 93 LQR 541 (R. J. Smith), referring to "a fog of obscure and conflicting detail"; *Clark v Chief Land Registrar* [1993] Ch 294, [1993] 2 All ER 936.
19 For the creation of mortgages in registered land, see pp. 731 et seq, ante.
20 At 146, at 757.

cautioner's interest is already registered or protected by a notice or restriction, unless the Registrar specifically consents.[1]

(iv) The cautioner's interest, unless it is in a charge, must be in "land". This includes an interest under a trust for sale of the land.[2]

(v) If a person lodges a caution without reasonable cause, he is liable to pay compensation to those who have sustained damage as a result.[3]

(iv) In addition to cautions against dealings and against first registration, cautions against the conversion of a registered title to a higher class can be lodged. This form of caution is extremely rare.[4]

(d) Inhibition

An inhibition is also hostile, and is entered on the application of a person interested.[5] Such an entry prevents any dealings with the registered land, either generally or for a given time or until the occurrence of a specified event. This is an extreme step to take and should be considered only in exceptional circumstances, as, for instance, where it is suspected that there has been or is likely to be a fraudulent dealing. Inhibitions are very rarely encountered, except for the bankruptcy inhibition automatically entered by the Registrar.[6]

(3) LAW REFORM

The Law Commission has made a number of recommendations for the reform of minor interests.[7] The two most important are:

(a) All transferees and other purchasers who wish to take free from unprotected minor interests should take in good faith and for valuable consideration, thus bringing the Land Registration Act 1925 into line with the Law of Property Act 1925 and the Settled Land Act 1925 which both define purchaser as necessarily involving good faith.[8] The burden of proof should be on the minor interest holder to show absence of good faith on the part of the transferee. Actual knowledge of the interest is not deemed to be bad faith. (paras. 4.14–4.18.)

---

1 LRA 1925, s. 54; as amended by LRA 1986, s. 5 (5) (*a*).
2 *Elias v Mitchell* [1972] Ch 652, [1972] 2 All ER 153 (equitable tenant in common under trust for sale), p. 241, ante; cf *Lynton International Ltd v Noble* (1991) 63 P & CR 452 (contractual right to share in proceeds of sale). See Ruoff and Roper, para. 36–13.
3 LRA 1925, s. 56 (3); *Clearbook Property Holdings Ltd v Verrier* [1974] 1 WLR 243, [1973] 3 All ER 614; *Tucker v Hutchinson* (1987) 54 P & CR 106; (1987) 131 SJ 798 (P. M. Rank). And on the firm line which the court will take against misuse of the caution, see *Rawlplug Co Ltd v Kamvale Properties Ltd* (1968) 20 P & CR 32 at 40, per MEGARRY J. There is no similar provision for notices: *Watts v Waller* [1973] QB 153 at 169, [1972] 3 All ER 257 at 264.
4 See Ruoff and Roper, paras. 14–09, 36–14.
5 LRA 1925, s. 57. The court, or the Registrar, must agree to its entry.
6 Ibid., s. 61.
7 Third Report on Land Registration C. Minor Interests 1987 (Law Com No. 158, HC 269) Part IV. See in particular its critique of the machinery of protection in Appendix E.
8 It would be out of line with LCA 1925 (referred to by LPA 1925, s. 199) where good faith is not made an element. See *Midland Bank Trust Co Ltd v Green* [1981] AC 513, [1981] 1 All ER 153; M & B p. 40, p. 766, ante. Cf *Peffer v Rigg* [1977] 1 WLR 285, [1978] 3 All ER 745; M & B p. 160; *Lyus v Prowsa Developments Ltd* [1982] 1 WLR 1044, [1982] 2 All ER 953, M & B p. 160; p. 801, n. 14, ante.

(b) The priority of minor interests inter se should be governed by the order of their entry on the register, whether created later in time or not, subject to any agreement or statutory provision to the contrary.[9] This order of registration rule is only liable to be upset where there has been fraud or estoppel on the part of an earlier protected interest holder. (paras. 4.94–4.104)

9 Cf *Barclays Bank Ltd v Taylor* [1974] Ch 137, [1973] 1 All ER 752; M & B p. 809; p. 804, ante.

Chapter 23

Other estate owners

SUMMARY

SECTION I PERSONAL REPRESENTATIVES

A. FUNCTIONS AND POWERS

The next class of estate owner consists of personal representatives, i.e. the persons, whether executors or administrators, to whom the property of a deceased owner passes. The functions and powers of those persons are described later,[1] but certain matters must be anticipated. Under the Administration of Estates Act 1925, all the property of a deceased person, real as well as personal, with the exception of life interests, joint tenancies, entailed interests unless disposed of by the deceased's will and interests of a corporator sole in the corporation property, becomes vested in his personal representatives.[2] Their duties are to pay the debts of the deceased and all expenses and dues arising on his death out of the property, and then to distribute the residue among the beneficiaries under the will or among those entitled in the case of intestacy. Both at common law and by statute they have exceedingly wide powers of disposition over the property.[3]

1 Pp. 843 et seq, post.
2 Ss. 1 (1), 3 (1), (3), (4), (5).
3 P. 843, post.

Thus a conveyance by personal representatives of the legal estate may become necessary in two types of cases; first where, in order to raise money for the payment of debts, they convey to a purchaser in the ordinary course of administration; secondly, where they transfer the land to a beneficiary. Amongst the powers of disposal conferred upon them are included:

> All the powers, discretions and duties conferred or imposed by law on trustees holding land upon an effectual trust for sale (including power to overreach equitable interests and powers as if the same affected the proceeds of sale).[4]

Thus personal representatives have all the powers of trustees for sale, and therefore, all the powers of a tenant for life and trustees under the Settled Land Act 1925.[5]

B. TRANSFERS BY PERSONAL REPRESENTATIVES

(1) TRANSFER TO BENEFICIARY BY ASSENT

(a) Form of assent

The transfer of land to a beneficiary is effected in practice, not by a conveyance by deed, but by an *assent*, i.e. a document in writing that operates to vest the estate or interest in the person entitled.[6] Prior to 1926 an assent was valid if it was oral or even if it could be inferred from conduct,[7] but, as we have already seen, this is no longer true where the interest to be transferred is a *legal estate*.[8]

The beneficiary, in order to protect himself against a later conveyance of the same land by the personal representative, usually requires that notice of the assent be endorsed on the probate copy of the will or letters of administration, i.e. on the official documents which certify that the representative is entitled to act as such.[9] Even so, a beneficiary in whose favour an assent has been made is not secure, for an unpaid creditor of the deceased may enforce payment by following the property into the hands of a devisee, except one who takes in consideration of money or marriage.[10] When this course is taken, the court, notwithstanding the assent, may declare a beneficiary to be a trustee of the land for a creditor, or may order a sale or other transaction to be carried out in order to satisfy the rights of the persons interested, or may make a vesting order with a view to the execution of a conveyance.[11]

(b) Overreaching powers

The statutory provision that personal representatives shall have the overreaching powers of trustees holding land "upon an effectual trust for sale",[12] shows that the overreaching effect of their conveyance is normally

---

4 AEA 1925, s. 39 (1) (ii).
5 SLA 1925, s. 28 (1), pp. 185, 205, ante.
6 AEA 1925, s. 36 (1), (2). Until then the beneficiary has no more than a right to have the estate duly administered: *Passant v Jackson* [1986] STC 164 at 167.
7 E.g. *Wise v Whitburn* [1924] 1 Ch 460.
8 P. 771, ante.
9 AEA 1925, s. 36 (5).
10 Ibid., s. 38 (1); *Salih v Atchi* [1961] AC 778.
11 Ibid., s. 38 (2).
12 Ibid., s. 39 (1) (i), (ii).

that of a conveyance made by ordinary trustees for sale,[13] and also, if the occasion arises, that of a conveyance made by approved trustees under an *ad hoc* trust for sale.[14] Thus, even equities charged on the land prior to the death of the deceased may be overreached. No approval by the court is necessary; neither is it necessary, as it is in the case of trustees for sale, that there should be at least two personal representatives.[15]

(c) Subsequent conveyance by beneficiary

The assent plays an important part when the beneficiary in whose favour it has been made conveys the legal estate to a purchaser, since it acts as a "curtain" to keep the equities off the title. The Administration of Estates Act 1925[16] provides that the assent shall, in favour of a purchaser for money or money's worth, be sufficient evidence that the beneficiary is entitled to have the legal estate conveyed to him, unless notice of a previous assent or conveyance has been endorsed on the probate copy or letters of administration. It has been held, however, that an assent will not avail a purchaser if his investigation of title discloses that the person in whose favour it was given was not entitled to the legal estate.[17] The first duty, then, of the purchaser is to inspect the probate copy, for in the normal case he will find there an endorsement of an assent in favour of the beneficiary. Thus, the last two links in the title made by a beneficiary are the probate copy or letters of administration and the assent. The assent is a transfer of the legal title, showing its passing from the deceased through the personal representative to the beneficiary: it then operates as a "curtain" in the sense that the purchaser need not investigate the will (which operates only in equity) in order to ascertain whether the assent has been given in favour of the proper beneficiary. The beneficial interests under a will, like those arising under a settlement or a trust for sale, are thus kept off the title to land, the legal estate in which has passed to a beneficiary by virtue of an assent.

(2) TRANSFER TO PURCHASER BY CONVEYANCE

Another section of the Act comes into play when the personal representatives themselves convey to a purchaser. The danger here is that the legal estate may already have been passed to a beneficiary under the will, but it is provided that a written statement by a personal representative that he has not given or made an assent or conveyance in respect of a legal estate, shall, in favour of a purchaser for money or money's worth, be sufficient evidence that no previous assent or conveyance has been given, unless notice of such has been endorsed on the probate or administration.[18] A purchaser who obtains this written statement acquires a good title to the legal estate, subject, however, to one exception, for it is provided that the statement shall not be conclusive against an earlier purchaser for money or money's worth who has taken a conveyance either from the personal representative or from a beneficiary in whose favour an assent has been given. If, therefore, A takes a conveyance for value of a legal estate from a personal representative without

13 Pp. 817, post.
14 Pp. 820, post.
15 LPA 1925, s. 27 (2).
16 S. 36 (7), (11).
17 *Re Duce and Boots Cash Chemists (Southern) Ltd's Contract* [1937] Ch 642.
18 AEA 1925, s. 36 (6), (11).

having the fact endorsed on the probate, and B later takes a conveyance from the personal representative of the same estate, relying upon the written but untrue statement that no previous conveyance has been made, it would seem that B obtains no protection from the statute.

The revocation of the probate or administration after a conveyance has been made by a personal representative does not affect the title of the purchaser.[19] If, for instance, probate of a will dated 1992 is granted to an executor, A, and subsequently a different will dated 1994 is discovered, the grant of probate to A will be revoked and a new one made to the executor appointed by the 1994 will. All conveyances, however, of any interest in real or personal estate made by A *virtute officii* in favour of a purchaser remain valid.

C. SETTLED LAND

As we shall see, general personal representatives give way to special personal representatives in respect of property which the deceased held as tenant for life under a settlement.[20] In such a case, after paying taxes due on the death the special executors or administrators execute a vesting assent by which they transfer the legal estate to the next tenant for life. The vesting assent and the special probate or letters of administration, since they are documents passing the legal estate, will appear on the title if the tenant for life subsequently exercises his power of sale.

It has been held, however, in *Re Bridgett and Hayes' Contract*,[1] that if the settlement ceases on the death of the tenant for life there is no necessity for a special grant of probate or administration. In that case:

> By a will which took effect before 1926 land was devised to A for life, and if (as happened) she should die without leaving children, to trustees upon trust for sale. A died in 1926 and a general grant of probate of her will was made to the executor, X. X made a contract to sell the land.

It was held that a special grant of probate to the trustees was unnecessary, and that X could make a good title to the land under his general grant.

The statute requires a special grant of probate in the case of "settled land". "Settled land", however, means land which continues to be settled after the death of the testator. In the instant case the land ceased to be settled on the death of A and became subject to a trust for sale. The provisions relating to special grants do not apply to trusts for sale. Therefore, the land was vested in X, to whom a general grant of A's property had been made, and X, by virtue of his executorship under the grant, could make title.

19 AEA 1925, s. 37; confirming *Hewson v Shelley* [1914] 2 Ch 13. "Purchaser" means a lessee, mortgagee or other person who in good faith acquires an interest in property for valuable consideration, and "valuable consideration" includes marriage, but does not include a nominal consideration in money: ss. 55 (1) (xviii).
20 Infra.
1 [1928] Ch 163; M & B p. 336; followed in *Re Bordass's Estate* [1929] P 107; *Re Birch's Estate* [1929] P 164.

D. REGISTERED LAND

Personal representatives of a sole registered proprietor or of the survivor of two or more joint proprietors are entitled to be registered as proprietors in place of the deceased proprietor on the production to the Registrar of the grant of probate or letters of administration.[2] There is, however, an alternative procedure which is more frequently adopted, for the personal representatives need not themselves be registered but may have the land transferred direct to the devisee, legatee or purchaser, who will be registered in place of the deceased proprietor on production of the instrument of assent or transfer together with the grant of probate or letters of administration.[3] Although this latter alternative procedure saves some trouble, it is undesirable, as, pending the lodging of the transfer or assent, the register is necessarily kept out of date, and notice served by the Land Registry on the deceased proprietor could well go astray.

Rule 170 (5) of the Land Registration Rules 1925, dealing with transfer or assent by personal representatives,[4] provides that:

> it shall not be the duty of the Registrar nor shall he be entitled to consider or to call for any information concerning the reason why any transfer is made, or as to the terms of the will, and, whether he has notice or not of its contents, he shall be entitled to assume that the personal representative is acting (whether by transfer, assent or appropriation or vesting assent) correctly and within his powers.

This rule shows the extent to which the curtain principle applies to registered land.

SECTION II TENANTS FOR LIFE AND STATUTORY OWNERS

In the earlier part of the book we discussed the evolution and framework of the strict settlement.[5] On the conveyancing side three further topics require consideration in more detail: the vesting of the legal estate in each new tenant for life as and when he becomes entitled to possession; the termination of the settlement; and the statutory simplification of a conveyance of settled land.

A. VESTING OF LEGAL ESTATE

The scheme of the Act, as we have already noticed, is that the legal estate shall be vested from time to time in each new tenant for life as and when he becomes entitled to possession. Let us take the different circumstances that may arise and observe how this procedure operates.

(a) Death of tenant for life

Let us suppose that under a settlement lands stand limited to H for life and then, after certain interests in favour of the other members of H's family, to

---

2 LRA 1925, s. 41; LRR 1925, r. 168.
3 Ibid., s. 37; LRR 1925, r. 170.
4 Assents must be in Form 57 in the case of land settled by the deceased's will, and in Form 56 in all other cases. Transfers by personal representatives are in the usual form of transfer: LRR 1925, r. 170 (1), (3).
5 Pp. 67 et seq, ante; 175 et seq., ante.

his son, S, for life. When H dies the legal estate devolves upon his special personal representatives, i.e. the trustees of the settlement, and not upon his general personal representatives whose task it is to administer his non-settled property.[6] Upon the death of H the special personal representatives come under an obligation to convey the legal estate to S. This may be done either by a vesting deed or by a vesting assent, which contains the particulars set out above at page 180.[7]

(b) Infant tenant for life reaches full age

An infant cannot be an estate owner,[8] and if he becomes entitled to a tenancy for life under a settlement the statutory powers are exercisable by the trustees, to whom, in their capacity as *statutory owners*,[9] the legal estate must be conveyed. It is their duty, however, upon the attainment by the infant of his majority, to convey the legal estate to him by a vesting deed or a vesting assent.[10]

(c) Tenant for life deprived of statutory powers

Where, for example, there is a limitation to A for life with a limitation over to X and Y on *protective trusts* (i.e. trusts which give certain powers to X and Y if A becomes bankrupt or attempts to part with his life interest in favour of his creditors),[11] A is bound to convey the legal estate to X and Y as statutory owners upon the occurrence of an event bringing the trusts into operation.[12]

(d) Person of full age becomes absolutely entitled

If a person of full age becomes absolutely entitled to the land, e.g. where there is a limitation to A for life with remainder to X in fee simple and A dies, the settlement comes to an end and the land is no longer settled. There is no room for *special* personal representatives and the legal estate must be conveyed by A's general personal representatives to X, the absolute owner.[13]

B. TERMINATION OF SETTLEMENT

A settlement comes to an end if all equitable interests have ceased and if there can be no further occasion to exercise the statutory powers, provided that the person entitled to the legal estate is of full age.[14] When this occurs it is essential that the person beneficially entitled should have a document showing his right to deal freely with the land, and it is therefore provided that he may require the trustees to execute a deed of discharge declaring that

---

6 AEA 1925, s. 22 (1); pp. 843 et seq, post.
7 SLA 1925, s. 7 (1), Sch. 1, Form No. 5.
8 P. 921, post.
9 P. 185, ante. Wide powers of management are conferred by SLA 1925, s. 102 upon the trustees during a minority; see pp. 926, post.
10 SLA 1925, s. 7 (2), (3); s. 19 (3).
11 P. 357, ante.
12 SLA 1925, s. 7 (4).
13 Ibid., s. 7 (5); *Re Bridgett and Hayes' Contract* [1928] Ch 163; M & B p. 336; p. 810, ante; *Re Bordass's Estate* [1929] P 107.
14 SLA 1925, s. 3; LP(A)A 1926, Sch.

the land is free from the trusts.[15] The termination of a settlement, however, most frequently occurs on the death of a tenant for life, as for example when he dies leaving no widow, but an only son who bars the entail limited to him by the settlement. In this case there is no need for a deed of discharge. It is sufficient if the personal representatives of the tenant for life vest the legal estate in the son by an absolute vesting assent, i.e. one which does not nominate trustees.[16]

C. SIMPLIFICATION OF CONVEYANCING

(1) POSITION OF PURCHASER

Taking the normal case, and presuming that the legal estate has been vested in the tenant for life by virtue of a vesting deed, it is worth our while to notice how the sale of the settled land to a purchaser is expedited and simplified, as compared with the practice prevailing before 1926. The main object of reducing the rights of the various beneficiaries to the status of equitable interests is to keep those rights off the title to the legal estate and to relieve a purchaser from the responsibility of seeing that they are not prejudiced by the sale. The fate of the equitable interests is to be no concern of the purchaser. His one concern is that the title to the *legal* estate shall be proved. He must, therefore, investigate the title down to the first vesting deed, i.e. he must require the vendor to prove that the person who purported to vest the legal estate in the estate owner by the principal vesting deed was entitled to do so, though of course if land remains settled for a generation or two the time will come when title is made by the production of a series of vesting deeds or assents. But the former practice of abstracting the beneficial limitations is forbidden. The trust instrument is not disclosed; it is not allowed to appear on the title; and with a few exceptions[17] the purchaser is not entitled to call for it or to make it the subject of interrogatories. Moreover, once satisfied that the vesting deed was executed by a party competent to execute it, "a purchaser of a legal estate in settled land" must take it at its face value and make the following assumptions:

> That the estate owner named in the vesting deed is the tenant for life or statutory owner and entitled to exercise the statutory powers.
> That the trustees named in the deed are the properly constituted trustees.
> That the settlements contained in the deed in accordance with the requirements of the Settled Land Act 1925 are correct.
> That a later deed appointing new trustees is correct.[18]

This is a distinct simplification of the practice that obtained before 1926. Before that date, as we have seen,[19] a purchaser was compelled to investigate the whole settlement, including resettlements, so as to satisfy himself that the land was settled land within the meaning of the Settled Land Act 1882, that the vendor was tenant for life within the same meaning, and that there were

---

15 SLA 1925, s. 17 (1).
16 Ibid., s. 110 (5).
17 Ibid., s. 110 (2) (*a*), (*b*), (*c*), (*d*). For example, where a settlement inter vivos has not been created by the proper method or where there is a pre-1926 settlement, whether made inter vivos or by will. See *Emmet on Title*, paras. 22.050–22.051.
18 SLA 1925, s. 110 (2); but the proviso to the section contains exceptions.
19 Pp. 75–6, ante.

proper trustees of the settlement. But all these facts are now certified by the vesting deed, for this short document guarantees the fundamental matters concerning which inquiries had formerly to be made. The purchaser is secure in taking a conveyance of the legal estate from the person by whom the vesting deed asserts that this estate is held; he can presume, in reliance on the same deed, that the Settled Land Act powers apply to the property; and, provided that he pays the purchase money to the certified trustees,[20] he can ignore the equitable rights of the beneficiaries.

(2) OVERREACHABLE INTERESTS

In other words, the conveyance by the tenant for life overreaches the equitable interests of the beneficiaries and also certain other interests, i.e., makes them enforceable against the money in the hands of the trustees, and no longer against the land. More precisely, the position in this respect is as follows:

The conveyance by the tenant for life passes to the purchaser a title to the legal estate discharged from the following:

(i)   All legal or equitable estates, interests and charges arising *under* the settlement.[1]

(ii) Limited owner's charges,[2] general equitable charges[3] and certain annuities.[4]

These three interests are overreached even though they have been registered as land charges and even though they were created prior to the settlement.[5] The reason is that they lose nothing in value or protection by their conversion into claims against the purchase money.

On the other hand the conveyance by the tenant for life does *not* overreach the following:

(i)   Legal estates and charges by way of legal mortgage having priority to the settlement.[6]

(ii) Legal estates and charges by way of legal mortgage to secure money which has been actually raised before the date of the conveyance.[7]

An example is a mortgage created before the conveyance by which money has been raised for the payment of portions.

(iii) Terms of years, easements and profits granted for money or money's worth under the settlement.[8]

(iv) Estate contracts, restrictive covenants and equitable easements created after 1925,[9] if registered as land charges.[10]

20 P. 815, post.
1 SLA 1925, s. 72 (2).
2 P. 759, ante.
3 P. 759, ante.
4 I.e., under LCA 1972, s. 1 (4), Sch 1. "Annuity" is here limited to annuities for one or more life or lives created after 25 April 1855, and before 1 January 1926. The register in which they might formerly have been entered was closed as from 1 January 1926. All annuities created after 1925 are registrable as general equitable charges.
5 SLA 1925, s. 72 (3); see (1934) 77 LJ News 3, 21, 39, 57 (J.M.L.).
6 Ibid., s. 72 (2) (i).
7 Ibid., s. 72 (2) (ii). See *Re Mundy and Roper's Contract* [1899] 1 Ch 275 at 289, per CHITTY LJ.
8 Ibid., s. 72 (2) (iii) (a).
9 Pp. 759, 760, ante.
10 SLA 1925, s. 72 (2) (iii) (a), (b).

(v) Restrictive covenants and equitable easements created before 1926, but only if the purchaser has actual or constructive notice of them.[11]

(vi) Estate contracts created before 1926 if the purchaser has actual or constructive notice of them, or if they are capable of registration and have been registered. Such a contract becomes capable of registration upon its assignment after 1925.[12]

For the overreaching provisions to apply, it is essential that upon a sale of the land by the tenant for life or the statutory owner, the purchase money is paid either to the trustees or into court;[13] moreover, except where the trusteeship is held by a trust corporation,[14] there must be at least two trustees to whom this payment is made.[15]

(3) FAULTY CONVEYANCES

If the machinery of the Settled Land Act 1925 is observed, then not only is conveyancing simplified in favour of a purchaser, but also adequate protection is accorded to the beneficial interests of the settlement. We have seen how the Act makes provision for failure to use the machinery at all,[16] and we must now consider some of the problems that arise where the statutory machinery is used but nevertheless mistakes occur in its use.

In the first place, section 5 (3) of the Settled Land Act 1925 provides that a vesting deed shall not be invalidated by reason only of any error in any of the statements or particulars required to be contained in it. This must be read in conjunction with section 110 (2) which, as we have seen,[17] provides that a purchaser of a legal estate in settled land shall not be entitled to call for the trust instrument, but, instead, must assume that certain particulars stated in

11 P. 813, ante.
12 LCA 1972, s. 4 (7).
13 SLA 1925, s. 18 (1) (b).
14 Ibid., s. 117 (1) (xxx). "Trust corporation" means, "The Public Trustee or a corporation either appointed by the court in any particular case to be a trustee or entitled by rules made under sub-s. (3) of s. 4 of the Public Trustee Act 1906, to act as custodian trustee."
    Corporations which are entitled under the Public Trustee Rules 1912, r. 30, as substituted by the Public Trustee (Custodian Trustee) Rules 1975 (S.I. 1975 No. 1189, as amended by S.I. 1976 No. 836; S.I. 1981 No. 358; S.I. 1984 No. 109; S.I. 1985 No. 132; S.I. 1987 No. 1891), include "any corporation constituted under the law of the United Kingdom and empowered by its constitution to undertake trust business and having one or more places of business there", and being a registered company "having a capital (in stock or shares) for the time being issued of not less than £250,000, of which not less than £100,000 has been paid up in cash".
    The definition was extended by LP(A)A 1926, s. 3 to include the "Treasury Solicitor, the Official Solicitor, and any person holding any other official position prescribed by the Lord Chancellor, and, in relation to the property of a bankrupt and property subject to a deed of arrangement, includes the trustee in bankruptcy and the trustee under the deed respectively, and, in relation to charitable, ecclesiastical and public trusts, also includes any local or public authority so prescribed, and any other corporation constituted under the laws of the United Kingdom or any part thereof which satisfies the Lord Chancellor that it undertakes the administration of any such trusts without remuneration, or that by its constitution it is required to apply the whole of its net income after payment of outgoings for charitable, ecclesiastical or public purposes, and is prohibited from distributing, directly or indirectly, any part thereof by way of profits amongst any of its members, and is authorised by him to act in relation to such trusts as a trust corporation". See also LPA 1925, s. 205 (1) (xxviii); TA 1925, s. 68 (18); AEA 1925, s. 55 (1) (xxvi); Supreme Court Act 1981, s. 128.
15 Ibid., s. 18 (1) (c).
16 Pp. 182–3, ante.
17 Pp. 813–4, ante.

the vesting deed are true. There are, however, exceptional cases in which a purchaser must examine the trust instrument and satisfy himself that the statements in the vesting deed are true. In these cases, of course, section 5 (3) will not avail him.

In the second place a purchaser may take a conveyance of settled land under the mistaken impression that the vendor is still a tenant for life, whereas in fact he is no longer so. What is the position if a testator leaves Blackacre by will to W, his widow, for her life or until re-marriage, remainder to X in fee simple; W then re-marries and, as tenant for life, purports to sell Blackacre to Y who pays the purchase money to the trustees of the settlement? It is probable that Y obtains the legal estate from W, but the question then arises whether he can rely on section 110 (2) and defeat a claim to the legal fee simple by X. To do this Y must show that he is "a purchaser of a legal estate in the settled land" and he can only do this if "settled land" means "land which appears to be settled land but is not".[18]

The converse situation, where a purchaser takes a conveyance from a vendor under the mistaken impression that the vendor is an absolute owner in fee simple when he is in fact a tenant for life of settled land, however, has been the subject of two inconsistent judicial decisions at first instance. The solution to this problem depends on how far reliance can be placed on section 110 (1), which reads as follows:

> On a sale, exchange, lease, mortgage, charge, or other disposition, a purchaser dealing in good faith with a tenant for life or statutory owner shall, as against all parties entitled under the settlement, be conclusively taken to have given the best price, consideration, or rent, as the case may require, that could reasonably be obtained by the tenant for life or statutory owner, and to have complied with all the requisitions of this Act.

In *Weston v Henshaw*[19] X, a tenant for life, suppressed the settlement and purported to grant a legal mortgage to Y as security for advances made to him personally, professing to be absolute and beneficial owner of the fee simple. The question was whether the mortgage to Y was void against the beneficiaries under the settlement. DANCKWERTS J held that the mortgage was void because it was not a transaction authorised under section 18 (1) (a).[20] He rejected an argument that Y was protected under section 110 (1); admittedly Y was in good faith and had complied with all the requirements of the Act, but nevertheless the section could only be relied upon where Y knows X to be a tenant for life and deals with him on that footing.

In *Re Morgan's Lease*,[1] however, UNGOED-THOMAS J took the opposite view:

> There is, in the section, no express provision limiting its benefit to a purchaser who knows that the person with whom he is dealing is a tenant for life. On its face it reads as free of limitation and as applicable to a person without such knowledge as to a person who has it. There is a limitation, namely that the purchaser must act in good faith; but that limitation reads as applicable to a purchaser with such knowledge as without. Thus my conclusion is that section 110 applies whether or not the purchaser knows that the other party to the transaction is tenant for life.[2]

---

18 For the problem and its detailed analysis, see Megarry and Wade, *Law of Real Property* (5th edn), p. 335; M & B p. 338; [1984] Conv 354 (P. A. Stone); [1985] Conv 377 (R. Warrington).
19 [1950] Ch 510; M & B p. 311.
20 *Bevan v Johnston* [1990] 2 EGLR 33; [1991] Conv 601 (J. Hill).
1   [1972] Ch 1, [1971] 2 All ER 235; M & B p. 312.
2   At 9, at 242; *Mogridge v Clapp* [1892] 3 Ch 382.

This interpretation of section 110 (1) seems preferable. *Weston v Henshaw* appears to be the only decision in unregistered land which is an exception to the immunity of the bona fide purchaser for value of the legal estate without notice.[3]

SECTION III TRUSTEES FOR SALE

The definition of a trust for sale and the powers of the trustees for sale have already been discussed.[4] It remains to consider the investigation of title when the land is sold, and the overreaching effect of the conveyance to the purchaser.

A. PROOF OF TITLE

What has been said above about the proof and investigation of title in the case of a sale by a person beneficially entitled in his own right to a fee simple estate applies equally to trustees for sale.[5] Failing a special stipulation, they must show by reference to a good root of title at least 15 years old that the creator of the trust was entitled to vest the legal estate in them. There are, however, certain statutory provisions designed to protect the purchaser and to facilitate dealings with the land. We have already noticed those that relate to the postponement of sale[6] and the requirement of consents.[7]

If the beneficiaries are all of full age and have become absolutely entitled under the limitations of the settlement, they may terminate the trust and direct the trustees not to sell the land. Theoretically, this confronts a purchaser with a difficulty, for how does he know that such a direction has not been given to the trustees? It is, therefore, enacted that, so far as regards the safety and protection of the purchaser, the trust is to be deemed to be subsisting until the land has been conveyed to, or under the direction of, the persons interested in the proceeds of sale.[8] In other words, the purchaser is safe in taking a conveyance from the trustees until the beneficiaries, being absolutely entitled and of full age, have terminated the trust by taking a conveyance to themselves.[9]

B. OVERREACHING

(1) THE PRINCIPLE

As we have already seen, a virtue long possessed by the trust for sale is that upon the sale of the land the equitable interests of the beneficiaries are kept

---

3 See (1971) 87 LQR 338 (D. W. Elliott); (1973) 36 MLR, p. 28 (R. H. Maudsley).
4 Pp. 203–9, ante.
5 Pp. 749 et seq, ante.
6 P. 205, ante.
7 P. 207, ante.
8 LPA 1925, s. 23; re-enacting Conveyancing Act 1911, s. 10. Law Reform Committee 23rd Report (The powers and duties of trustees) 1982 (Cmnd 8733), paras 5.5–6, recommends that specific machinery be provided for the termination of a trust for sale of land corresponding to AEA 1925, s. 36 (7); p. 809, ante.
9 For a difficulty in joint tenancy, see p. 232, ante.

off the title to the legal estate and are not disclosed to the purchaser.[10] The conveyance by the trustees overreaches the beneficial interests that arise *under* the trust for sale. By the equitable doctrine of conversion the beneficial interests are in the proceeds of sale from the moment that the trust for sale comes into operation; by the conveyance the interests are transferred from notional to actual money. To be more precise, the purchaser acquires a title to the legal estate, unaffected by the trusts that have been declared of the proceeds of sale and of the rents and profits until sale, even though the trusts have been declared by the same instrument as that which creates the trust for sale.[11] He does not enjoy this immunity, however, unless he pays the purchase money to at least two trustees or to a trust corporation, if one has been appointed.[12]

(2) BARE TRUSTS

The principle of overreaching, however, does not apply where there is a conveyance by bare trustees. Thus in *Hodgson v Marks*,[13] where the owner of a house voluntarily transferred the legal estate to her lodger, on the understanding that she retained the beneficial ownership, and he then sold the house to a purchaser, there was no question of her interest being overreached. A bare trust is not a trust for sale. The difficulty to a purchaser is a serious one, and the Law Commission has recommended that the principle of overreaching should extend to conveyances by bare trustees.[14]

(3) BENEFICIARIES IN OCCUPATION

In registered land payment to at least two trustees or to a trust corporation overreaches the beneficial interests under a trust for sale, even though the beneficiaries are in actual occupation.

In *City of London Building Society v Flegg*:[15]

Mr. and Mrs. M-B purchased Bleak House and were registered as proprietors. The house was conveyed to them upon trust for sale as beneficial joint tenants, with an express declaration that the trustees should have all the powers of mortgaging of an absolute owner. Part of the purchase price was provided by Mr. and Mrs. F (the parents of Mrs. M-B) who thereby became beneficial tenants in common in respect of their contribution; their interests were not entered on the register. Mr. and Mrs. M-B raised their part of the purchase price on mortgage with the consent of Mr. and Mrs. F. Later, without telling Mr. and Mrs. F, they mortgaged Bleak House by way of second and third charges, and finally they mortgaged it to the Building Society for £37,500, again without the knowledge of Mr. and Mrs. F, using the proceeds to repay the three earlier loans. At all material times Mr. and Mrs. F were in actual occupation of the house. When Mr. and Mrs. M-B defaulted and were made bankrupt, the Building Society sued for possession. The House of Lords held that the society succeeded; the payment of the mortgage money had been made to

10 Pp. 76, ante.
11 LPA 1925, ss. 2 (1), 27 (1); TA 1925; s. 14 (1); p. 74, ante. Although it is better to execute two deeds on the creation of a trust for sale, there is no necessity for this.
12 Ibid., s. 27 (2). For a definition of trust corporation see LPA 1925, s. 205 (1) (xxviii), as extended by LP(A)A 1926, s. 3; p. 815, n. 14, ante.
13 [1971] Ch 892, [1971] 2 All ER 684.
14 Report on Overreaching: Beneficiaries in Occupation 1989 (Law Com No. 158), paras. 2.17, 3.10, 4.27.
15 [1988] AC 54, [1987] 3 All ER 435; [1987] All ER Rev 149 (P. J. Clarke); (1988) 51 MLR 365 (S. Gardner); [1988] Conv 108 (M. P. Thompson), 141 (P. Sparkes).

two trustees, thereby overreaching the equitable interests of Mr. and Mrs. F, whose interests were transferred to the equity of redemption vested in Mr. and Mrs. M-B and to the £37,500 received by them.

Mr and Mrs F claimed that, by virtue of their actual occupation, they were entitled to an overriding interest under section 70 (1) (g), of the Land Registration Act 1925[16] and that this prevented the overreaching of their interests, unless they had given their consent. In rejecting this argument Lord TEMPLEMAN said:[17]

> The interests of the respondents cannot at one and the same time be overreached and overridden and at the same time be overriding interests . . . There must be a combination of an interest which justifies continuing occupation plus actual occupation to constitute an overriding interest. Actual occupation is not an interest in itself.

And Lord OLIVER OF AYLMERTON said:[18]

> Section 70 (1) (g) protects only the rights in reference to the land of the occupier whatever they are at the material time—in the instant case the right to enjoy in specie the rents and profits of the land held in trust for him. Once the beneficiary's rights have been shifted from the land to capital monies in the hands of the trustees, there is no longer an interest in the land to which the occupation can be referred or which it can protect. If the trustees sell in accordance with the statutory provisions and so overreach the beneficial interests in reference to the land, nothing remains to which a right of occupation can attach and the same result must, in my judgment, follow vis-à-vis a chargee by way of legal mortgage so long as the transaction is carried out in the manner prescribed by the Law of Property Act 1925, overreaching the beneficial interests by subordinating them to the estate of the chargee which is not longer 'affected' by them so as to become subject to them on registration pursuant to section 20 (1) of the Land Registration Act 1925. In the instant case, therefore, I would, for my part, hold that the charge created in favour of the appellants overreached the beneficial interests of the respondents and that there is nothing in section 70 (1) (g) of the Land Registration Act 1925 or in *Boland's* case which has the effect of preserving against the appellants any rights of the respondents to occupy the land by virtue of their beneficial interests in the equity of redemption which remains vested in the trustees.

Any other decision would have undermined the main object of the doctrine of overreaching whereby a compromise is effected between on the one hand the interests of the public in securing that land held in trust is freely marketable and, on the other hand, the interests of the beneficiaries in preserving their rights under the trusts.[19]

If, however, the mortgage moneys had been paid to only *one* trustee, as in *Williams & Glyn's Bank Ltd v Boland*,[20] then the interests of Mr and Mrs F would not have been overreached, and the overriding interests geared to

---

16 P. 791, ante.
17 At 73, 74, at 440, 441.
18 At 91, at 453.
19 Similarly in unregistered land, the possession of Mr and Mrs F would not have prevented their interests from being overreached; per Lord OLIVER OF AYLMERTON at 84, at 448. See Law Commission Report on Overreaching: Beneficiaries in Occupation 1989 (Law Com No. 188), which recommends that there should be no overreaching without the consent of every occupying beneficiary of full age irrespective of registration. This would in effect reverse the decision in *City of London Building Society v Flegg*; [1990] CLJ 277 at pp. 311–333 (C. Harpum); (1988) OJLS 367 (S. Gardner).
20 [1981] AC 487, [1980] 2 All ER 408, M & B p. 122.

actual occupation would have given them an effective defence against the society's claim for possession.

It was further held that their interests were not affected by section 14 of the Law of Property Act 1925, which says:

> This Part of this Act [Part I] shall not prejudicially affect the interest of any person in possession or in actual occupation of land to which he may be entitled in right of such possession or occupation.

The overreaching provisions are to be found in Part I. As Lord TEMPLEMAN said:

> Section 14 is not apt to confer on a tenant in common of land held on trust for sale, who happens to be in occupation, rights which are different from and superior to the rights of tenants in common, who are not in occupation on the date when the interests of all tenants in common are overreached by a sale or mortgage by trustees for sale.[1]

Finally, we must notice that the extent of overreaching in the case of a trust for sale would appear to be less than that accorded to a purchaser from a tenant for life under the Settled Land Act 1925.[2] There is no power to overreach any interests which arise prior to the trust for sale.[3]

SECTION IV   APPROVED TRUSTEES

The overreaching effect of a conveyance either by trustees for sale or by a tenant for life under a settlement is limited in the sense that it does not extend to equitable interests that were in existence before the creation of the trust or settlement.[4] If, for instance, a fee simple owner charges his land with the payment of a sum of money, and later subjects it to a trust for sale, the normal rule is that a purchaser from the trustees takes the legal estate burdened by the equitable charge.

A. AD HOC TRUST FOR SALE

The Law of Property Act 1925 introduced what is variously called an *ad hoc*, or a *special* or an *approved* trust for sale which enables the trustees to overreach even prior interests.[5] Whether it is of this special nature depends entirely upon the character of the trustees. They must be either:

---

1 At 72, at 439. See Lord OLIVER OF AYLMERTON at 80, at 445, where he says: "The ambit of section 14 is a matter which has puzzled conveyancers ever since the Law of Property Act was enacted . . . What section 14 does not do, on any analysis, is to enlarge or add to whatever interest it is that the occupant has in right of his occupation." He then agreed with Wolstenholme and Cherry (13th edn), vol. i. p. 69, that s. 14 was designed to preserve the principle of *Hunt v Luck* [1902] 1 Ch 428; p. 63, ante. See [1982] Conv 213 (M. Friend and J. Newton); M & B p. 52.

2 P. 814, ante.

3 Apart from the creation of an *ad hoc* trust for sale. See *Emmet on Title* (19th edn), para. 5.177; Megarry and Wade, *Law of Real Property* (5th edn), p. 404, n. 64, citing *Re Ryder and Steadman's Contract* [1927] 2 Ch 62 at 82.

4 Except in three cases under SLA 1925, s. 72 (2), (3); p. 775, ante.

5 LPA 1925, s. 2 (2).

(a) two or more individuals approved or appointed by the court or the successors in office of the individuals so approved or appointed; or
(b) a trust corporation.[6]

B. AD HOC SETTLEMENT

An alternative open to an estate owner whose land is already subject to an equitable interest is to create an *ad hoc* settlement under the Settled Land Act. If he executes a vesting deed, declaring the legal estate to be vested in him upon trust to give effect to equitable interests to which it is subject, and if at the same time he names as trustees either a trust corporation or two persons appointed or approved by the court,[7] the result is that the land becomes settled land and he acquires the statutory powers of a tenant for life, including the power of sale.[8]

C. OVERREACHABLE INTERESTS

The *ad hoc* trust for sale and the *ad hoc* settlement are similar in their effects. The land will be conveyed by the estate owner—by the trustees in the one case, by the tenant for life in the other—and, though the equitable charge will be overreached by the conveyance to the purchaser, it will be the duty of the trustees to see that it is paid out of the proceeds of sale to which it has now become attached.

Neither device, however, is of great practical use, for the number of equitable interests capable of being overreached is severely limited. It is enacted that a conveyance, whether under the trust for sale or under the settlement, shall not affect the following interests:[9]

(i) Equitable interests protected by a deposit of documents, relating to the legal estate affected e.g., where title deeds are deposited with a bank to secure an overdraft.
(ii) Certain equitable interests that cannot be represented in terms of money, namely,

   (a) restrictive covenants;
   (b) equitable easements
   (c) estate contracts.[10]

These three interests, however, if created after 1925, will be void as against a purchaser of the legal estate for money or money's worth, unless they are registered under the Land Charges Act 1972. If they were created before 1926, they do not bind a purchaser unless he has actual or constructive notice of them.[11]

---

6 Defined p. 815, n. 14, ante.
7 SLA 1925, s. 21.
8 Ibid., s. 21 (1) (*a*).
9 LPA 1925, s. 2 (3); SLA 1925, s. 21 (2).
10 Pp. 759, ante.
11 LPA 1925, s. 2 (5).

(iii) Any equitable interest that has been registered in accordance with the Land Charges Act 1972,[12] *except*

    (a) certain annuities;[13]
    (b) limited owner's charges;[14] and
    (c) general equitable charges.[15]

Registration of these three interests does not prevent them from being overreached, since they are adequately protected if enforceable against the money instead of against the land.

Thus, if land held by a beneficial owner in his own right, i.e., land that is subject neither to a trust for sale nor a settlement, is burdened with the payment of, for instance, a general equitable charge which impedes the transfer of an absolute title to a purchaser, there are four possible methods of clearing off the incumbrances, namely:

(i)   The creation of an *ad hoc* trust for sale.
(ii) The creation of an *ad hoc* settlement.
(iii) A conveyance of the land to the purchaser by the beneficial owner with the concurrence of the incumbrancer.
(iv) An application for leave to pay into court a sum of money in discharge of the incumbrance.[16]

SECTION V MORTGAGORS AND MORTGAGEES

It will be recalled that in a mortgage of a legal fee simple, the mortgagor remains the estate owner of the legal fee simple, but nevertheless the mortgagee is entitled by virtue of his power of sale to convey it to a purchaser.[17]

The rules concerning proof of title by a beneficial owner apply to a sale by a mortgagee. He must satisfy the purchaser in the usual manner that the legal estate is vested in the mortgagor. The purchaser, however, although he must investigate the title to the legal estate, is not concerned to inquire whether a case has arisen to authorize the sale or whether notice has been given by the mortgagee to the mortgagor.[18]

---

12 P. 756, ante.
13 I.e., annuities created and registered before 1926; p. 757, ante.
14 P. 759, ante.
15 P. 759, ante.
16 LPA 1925, s. 50.
17 P. 677, ante.
18 P. 695, ante.

Part III

The transfer and extinction of estates and interests

B. TRANSFER ON DEATH

We now pass to the law of succession. It is usual and advisable to make a will giving directions as to the devolution of property on death. The contents of a will may range from the home-made laconic "I leave everything to my wife"[1] to a document of several pages drawn up with professional advice.[2]

A person, however, may not make a will. If so, he dies intestate and his estate is distributed according to the rules of a statutory code. The value of most intestate estates is small; a striking example of a substantial one was that of Lord Ashton who died intestate in 1930 worth £10 million.[3] Although a person may choose deliberately not to make a will, the majority of intestacies arise "through a combination of procrastination and the not uncommon belief that 'there's no hurry: I'm not going to die tomorrow', coupled, all too often, with an ignorance of the law regarding intestacy".[4]

---

1 Cf *Re Wynn* [1984] 1 WLR 237, [1983] 3 All ER 310; p. 876, n. 19, post. ("I wish that all I possess is not given to my husband").
2 Legal aid is available for professionally drawn wills: Legal Aid Act 1974, s. 2 (1) (*b*).
3 *Re Ashton* (1934) 78 SJ 803; cited Sherrin and Bonehill, *Law and Practice of Intestate Succession* (1987) at p. 1.
4 *Re Leach* [1984] FLR 590 at 602 per Michael WHEELER QC (sitting as a Deputy High Court Judge).

SUMMARY

Chapter 24

Testacy[1]

SUMMARY

---

1 See generally *Jarman on Wills* (8th edn); *Theobald on Wills* (15th edn); *Williams on Wills* (6th edn); Mellows, *The Law of Succession* (4th edn); Miller, *The Machinery of Succession*; Parry and Clark, *The Law of Succession* (9th edn).

SECTION I GENERAL NATURE OF A WILL

A. A WILL IS REVOCABLE

A will is a declaration made by a testator, in the form required by law, of what he desires to be done after his death. It may define his desires with regard to several matters, such as the manner in which his funeral shall be conducted, the appointment of guardians for his children and the like, but we are concerned to examine a will only in so far as it operates as a disposition of property. There is a clear distinction between a will and a deed. As BACON V-C said:[2]

> A deed is a contract by which the owner of property gives a certain destination to it then and thenceforth for ever, and he parts with all his power over it. A will is an instrument which is not to take effect till the death of the testator.

Thus a settlement, created *inter vivos*, is an instrument by which a settlor may make a disposition of beneficial interests to persons by way of succession. Unless expressly stated to the contrary, this is irrevocable. A will, on the other hand, is always revocable notwithstanding the strongest expressions to the contrary that it may contain. Thus, if a person makes a disposition by will in fulfilment of a contract to leave certain property to another, the power of revocation remains open to him, though if the contract is made for consideration and, in the case of land, satisfies the formality requirements for contracts for the sale or other disposition of an interest in land[3] he or his executors will be liable for breach of contract.[4] If he puts such testamentary disposition out of his power by conveying the property in his lifetime to a third person, he is, personally and at once, liable in damages; if he dies possessed of the property, but without having made the disposition he agreed to make, the court, although it does not set the will aside, may order the property to be conveyed to the promisee.[5]

B. A WILL IS AMBULATORY

So a will has no effect, either upon the testator's property or in any other regard, until death, but when that event occurs the will takes effect as a disposition of property. Its essential characteristic is that it is ambulatory, a fact which is clear if we again contrast the case of a settlement. The effect upon the beneficial enjoyment by A is exactly the same where A devises Blackacre to B in fee simple as where he settles it upon himself for life with remainder to B in fee simple, but in the former case B is entitled to nothing until the death of A, while in the latter he immediately becomes entitled to a vested interest in remainder.[6]

A devise of land before the Wills Act 1837 was treated very differently from a bequest of personalty. It was regarded as a species of posthumous conveyance, and therefore acquired several attributes of a conveyance. Thus, since it is impossible for a man to convey what he has not got, every devise

---

2 *Olivant v Wright* (1875) 1 Ch D 346 at 650.
3 Pp. 108 et seq, ante.
4 See *Wakeham v Mackenzie* [1968] 1 WLR 1175, [1968] 2 All ER 783; M & B p. 72.
5 *Synge v Synge* [1894] 1 QB 466; *Schaefer v Schuhmann* [1972] AC 572, [1972] 1 All ER 621.
  See also Inheritance (Provision for Family and Dependants) Act 1975, s. 11; p. 827, post.
6 *Jarman on Wills* (8th edn), p. 26.

was necessarily specific, i.e. it was capable of passing only specific property owned by the testator at the time of the will. It did not pass land that he acquired later, or land that he disposed of after the will, notwithstanding that he later re-acquired it. Even a residuary devise was specific. Hence:

> if T, seised of Blackacre and Whiteacre, devised Blackacre to A and the residue of his land to B and the gift of Blackacre failed owing to the death of A before T, Blackacre did not pass to B, for the gift to him of the residue was nothing more than a gift of the specific Whiteacre under the denomination "residue".[7]

On the other hand, it was well established that a bequest of personalty included all the personalty belonging to the testator at the time of his death. It spoke from his death, not from its execution.

Real estate, however, was put on the same footing as personalty in this respect by the following section of the Wills Act 1837:

> Every will shall be construed, with reference to the real estate and personal estate comprised in it, to speak and take effect as if it had been executed immediately before the death of the testator, unless a contrary intention shall appear by the will.[8]

A further section provides that a residuary devise shall include devises that have lapsed or become void.[9]

Consequently, if the subject matter of a devise is described generically, it may be increased or diminished after the will is made, and whether the testator has parted with land that he owned at the time of the will or has acquired more land subsequently, his devise will pass what he actually owns at his death. Thus a will is ambulatory in the sense that it may pass property coming to the testator after its execution.

C. CODICIL

Although, strictly speaking, a will consists of all the properly executed writings in which a person has expressed his intentions, it is usual to contrast it with a codicil. A codicil is part of a person's will, and must be executed in precisely the same manner, but whereas the will is the principal, the codicil is the accessory instrument. It is in effect a supplementary instrument by which a testator alters or adds to his will.

SECTION II PROVISION FOR FAMILY AND DEPENDANTS[10]

In most European countries testamentary freedom has been restricted by the rule that the members of a testator's family are entitled to a definite

---

7 Hayes, *Introduction to Conveyancing*, vol. i. pp. 343–4; on the subject generally, see Digby, *History of the Law of Real Property*, p. 385.
8 S. 24.
9 S. 25.
10 Ross, *Inheritance Act Claims: Law and Practice* (1993), which contains a brief description of every case decided under the Inheritance (Family Provision) Act 1938, and the Inheritance (Provision for Family and Dependants) Act 1975; Maurice, *Family Provision on Death* (6th edn); Martyn, *Family Provision: Law and Practice* (2nd edn); Tyler's *Family Provision* (2nd edn). Martyn and Tyler both contain notes of cases not to be found in the Law Reports, but Tyler Appendix A has the transcripts of many of them. See also Cretney and Masson, *Principles of Family Law* (5th edn), chapter 23.

proportion of his estate. A similar rule obtained in England in early days with regard to wills of personalty, but it has long disappeared and for many years an English testator has been free to confer a princely endowment upon a prostitute or a charity and to leave his family penniless.[11] In 1938, however, the Inheritance (Family Provision) Act introduced a new principle by empowering the court to vary a will at the instance of the testator's surviving spouse and children.

In 1952 the Act was extended to cases of intestacy,[12] and in 1958 a former spouse of the deceased was first given the right to apply for provision from the deceased's estate.[13] In 1975 this piecemeal legislation was repealed, and a single code enacted to empower the court to make provision from the estate of a deceased person for his or her family and dependants. The Inheritance (Provision for Family and Dependants) Act 1975[14] applies to any person dying domiciled in England and Wales[15] on or after 1 April 1976.[16]

A. APPLICANTS FOR PROVISION

(a) The list

The Act enables the court[17] to modify either the will or the rules of distribution on intestacy,[18] if it is satisfied that reasonable financial provision has not been made for one of the following persons set out in section 1 (1):

    (a) the wife or husband of the deceased;[19]

11 In the case of the fee simple and the estate tail, a widow might be fortunate enough to obtain her third by way of dower, but in practice she was generally deprived of this by the device of uses to bar dower and since 1833 she has in this respect been entirely in her husband's power; p. 874, post.
12 Intestates' Estates Act 1952. It was further amended by the Family Provision Act 1966, the Family Law Reform Act 1969, and the Law Reform (Miscellaneous Provisions) Act 1970.
13 Matrimonial Causes (Property and Maintenance) Act 1958, ss. 3–6. These provisions were replaced by Matrimonial Causes Act 1965, ss. 26–8, which were amended by the statutes in n. 12 and also by the Divorce Reform Act 1969 and the Matrimonial Proceedings and Property Act 1970.
14 See Law Commission Family Law Second Report on Family Property: Family Provision on Death (Law Com No. 61, 1974). For the earlier legislation, see Wolstenholme and Cherry, vol. 5.
15 For criticism of this limitation, see (1946) 62 LQR 170, 178–9 (J. H. C. Morris). See also Law Com No. 61, paras 258–62. Inheritance (Provision for Family and Dependants) (Northern Ireland) Order 1979 (S.I. 1979 No. 924) contains corresponding provisions for Northern Ireland.
16 Inheritance (Provision for Family and Dependants) Act 1975, ss. 1 (1), 27 (3).
17 Applications in the High Court may be made to the Chancery or Family Division; the County Court has jurisdiction where the net estate does not exceed £30,000 at the date of death: County Courts Act 1984, s. 32; County Courts Jurisdiction (Inheritance—Provision for Family and Dependants) Order 1981 (S.I. 1981 No. 1636).
18 See e.g. *Re Coventry* [1980] Ch 461, [1979] 3 All ER 815; *Re Kirby* (1981) 11 Fam Law 210; *Re Wood* [1982] LS Gaz R 774; *Re Callaghan* [1985] Fam 1, [1984] 3 All ER 790; *Re Leach* [1986] Ch 226, [1985] 2 All ER 754; *Harrington v Gill* (1983) 4 FLR 265.
19 Including a person who in good faith entered into a void marriage with the deceased (which was not dissolved or annulled during the deceased's lifetime) and who did not enter into a later marriage during the deceased's lifetime: s. 25 (4); and a wife of a polygamous marriage: *Re Sehota* [1978] 1 WLR 1506, [1978] 3 All ER 585; *Re Crawford* (1983) 4 FLR 273.

(b) a former wife or former husband of the deceased[20] who has not remarried;[1]

(c) a child[2] of the deceased;[3]

(d) any person (not being a child of the deceased) who, in the case of any marriage to which the deceased was at any time a party, was treated by the deceased as a child of the family in relation to that marriage;

(e) any person (not being a person included in the foregoing paragraphs of this subsection) who immediately before the death of the deceased was being maintained, either wholly or partly, by the deceased.[4]

(b) Paragraph (*d*)

In *Re Leach*,[5] SLADE LJ set out the considerations for deciding whether a step-child comes within this paragraph, saying:

> The legislature cannot have contemplated that the mere display of affection, kindness or hospitality by a step-parent towards a step-child will by itself involve the treatment by the step-parent of the step-child as a child of the family in relation to the marriage. Something more is needed. . . . I can see no reason why even an adult person may not be capable of qualifying provided that the deceased has, *as wife or husband* (or widow or widower) under the relevant marriage, expressly or impliedly, assumed the position of a parent towards the applicant, with the attendant *responsibilities and privileges* of that relationship. If things take their natural course, the privileges of the quasi-parent may well increase and the responsibilities may well diminish as the years go by.

20 Since 1984 persons whose marriages have been ended abroad are equally eligible to apply: Matrimonial and Family Proceedings Act 1984, s. 25.

1 Including a spouse who is judicially separated from the deceased at the date of death: *Re Fullard* [1982] Fam 42, [1981] 2 All ER 796 (divorced wife).

2 Child includes an illegitimate child and a child *en ventre sa mère*: Inheritance (Provision for Family and Dependants) Act 1975, s. 25 (1); and an adopted child: see Adoption Act 1976, s. 39. But not a child adopted after the death of the deceased: *Re Collins* [1990] Fam 56, [1990] 2 All ER 47; *Whyte v Ticehurst* [1986] Fam 64, [1986] 2 All ER 158.

3 *Re Coventry* [1980] Ch 461, [1979] 3 All ER 815 (award refused to adult son of deceased in good health and paid employment); *Re Christie* [1979] Ch 168, [1979] 1 All ER 546 (award granted to adult son); *Re Dennis* [1981] 2 All ER 140 (award refused to spendthrift son aged 38); *Re Debenham* [1986] 1 FLR 404 (award granted to 58 year-old married epileptic daughter); *Williams v Johns* [1988] Fam Law 257 (award refused to troublesome able-bodied daughter aged 43); [1989] Conv 446 (J. E. M.).

4 *CA v CC* (1978) Times, 18 November (£5,000 for testator's de facto wife and half share of remainder of estate for their son); *Malone v Harrison* [1979] 1 WLR 1353 (£19,000 for testator's part-time mistress); (1980) 96 LQR 165 (M. W. Bryan); *Re Beaumont* [1980] Ch 444, [1980] 1 All ER 266 (no award for man living with testatrix widow as man and wife); *Re Wilkinson* [1978] Fam 22, [1978] 1 All ER 221 (application by 61 year old arthritic who had lived with her sister allowed to proceed); *Re Viner* [1978] CLY 3091 (£2,000 for 71 year-old widow from deceased brother's estate); *Jelley v Iliffe* [1981] Fam 128, [1981] 2 All ER 29 (application by widower who had lived with his brother-in-law's widow allowed to proceed); *Kourgey v Lusher* (1983) 4 FLR 65 (application by mistress, for whose maintenance deceased abandoned general responsibility before his death, failed); *Re Dymott* [1980] CA Transcript 942 ("the norm of the relationship was not one of dependance": per ORMROD LJ); *Re Kirby* (1982) 11 Fam Law 210 (association over 35 years akin to marriage in all but formality).

5 [1986] Ch 226 at 235, 237, [1985] 2 All ER 754 at 760, 762 (55 year-old spinster succeeded against deceased step-mother's estate even though she had never lived with nor been maintained by her; but the step-mother had intended to make a will in her favour, and most of the step-mother's estate had come from the step-daughter's father); criticised (1986) 83 LSG 93 (R. D. Oughton); *Re Callaghan* [1985] Fam 1, [1984] 3 All ER 790 (47 year-old married step-son succeeded against deceased step-father's estate).

(c) Paragraph (*e*)

Section 1 (3) contains a definition of the words "being maintained" where they appear in paragraph (*e*):

> a person shall be treated as being maintained by the deceased, either wholly or partly, as the case may be, if the deceased, other than for full valuable consideration, was making a substantial contribution in money or money's worth towards the reasonable needs of that person.

This paragraph was a new addition by the 1975 Act to the list of applicants, and has been called "the mistresses' charter".[6] It has received detailed interpretation by the courts.[7]

(i) Paragraph (*e*) and section 1 (3) The definition in section 1 (3) is exhaustive; to qualify within paragraph (*e*), an applicant must satisfy section 1 (3) as if before the words "*if the deceased*" the draftsman has inserted the word "only".[8]

(ii) Immediately before the death These words refer to the general and settled basis of arrangement for maintenance subsisting at the time of death. So that if, for example, the deceased had been making regular payments to the support of an old friend the claim would not be defeated if those payments ceased during a terminal illness because the deceased was too ill to make them.[9]

(iii) Assumed responsibility If the deceased has in fact maintained the applicant, this raises a presumption that he has assumed responsibility for the maintenance.[10] This presumption may be rebutted by circumstances including a disclaimer of any intention to maintain.

(iv) Striking the balance This was explained by GRIFFITHS LJ as follows:[11]

> Section 1 (3) requires the court to balance the benefits received by the applicant from the deceased against those provided by the applicant to the deceased. In striking the balance the phrase "for full valuable consideration" is not to be construed as being limited to benefits provided under a contract. Only if the balance comes down heavily in favour of the applicant will it be shown that the deceased was "making a substantial contribution in money or money's worth towards the reasonable needs" of the applicant. In striking this balance the court must use common sense and remember that the object of Parliament in creating this extra class of persons who may claim benefit from an estate was to provide relief for persons of whom it could truly be said that they were wholly or partially dependent on the deceased. It cannot be an exact exercise of evaluating services in pounds and pence. By way of example if a man was living with a woman as his wife providing the house and all the money for their living expenses she would clearly be dependent upon him, and it would not be right to deprive her of her claim by arguing that she was in fact performing the services that a housekeeper would perform and it would cost more to employ a housekeeper than was spent on her and indeed perhaps more than the deceased had available to spend upon her. Each case will have to be looked

---

6 (1975) HC Deb vol. 898, col 175.

7 *Re Beaumont*, supra; *Re Wilkinson*, supra; *Jelley v Iliffe*, supra.

8 Otherwise a hotel guest might be able to claim aginst the estate of the deceased proprietor: *Re Beaumont*, supra, at 450 at 270, per MEGARRY V-C.

9 *Jelly v Iliffe*, supra, at 141, at 38, per GRIFFITHS LJ.

10 The opposite view was taken by MEGARRY V-C in *Re Beaumont* supra, 457–8, at 275.

11 *Jelley v Iliffe*, supra, at 141, at 38; *Harrington v Gill* (1983) 4 FLR 265 (balance between claims of mistress of deceased and his daughter).

at carefully on its own facts to see whether common sense leads to the conclusion
that the applicant can fairly be regarded as a dependant.[12]

B. REASONABLE FINANCIAL PROVISION

(a) The test

We must now consider how the court decides whether "reasonable financial
provision" has been made for an applicant by the deceased's will or by the
rules of intestacy, and, if not, how it exercises its discretion in making an
order.

The Act draws a new distinction between an applicant who is a surviving
spouse and all other applicants. In the case of the former, reasonable financial
provision means:

> such financial provision as it would be reasonable in all the circumstances of the
> case for a husband or wife to receive, whether or not that provision is required for
> his or her maintenance.

For other applicants, its meaning is limited to:

> such financial provision as it would be reasonable in all the circumstances of the
> case for the applicant to receive for his maintenance.[13]

The test is thus not subjective but objective. It is not whether the deceased
stands convicted of unreasonableness, but whether the provision in fact
made is reasonable.[14] As OLIVER J said in *Re Coventry*:[15]

> In order to enable the court to interfere with and reform those dispositions it must
> be shown, not that the deceased acted unreasonably, but that, looked at objectively,
> his disposition or lack of disposition produces an unreasonable result in that it does
> not make any or any greater provision for the applicant—and that means, in the
> case of an applicant other than a spouse, for that applicant's maintenance. It clearly
> cannot be enough to say that the circumstances are such that if the deceased had
> made a particular provision for the applicant, that would not have been an
> unreasonable thing for him to do and therefore it now ought to be done. The court
> has no carte blanche to reform the deceased's dispositions or those which statute
> makes of his estate to accord with what the court itself might have thought would
> be sensible if it had been in the deceased's position.

(b) Statutory guidelines

(i) All applications Section 3 (1) of the Act sets out guidelines to which the
court must have regard in determining all applications for financial provision.
It must consider the following matters, based on facts known to it at the date

---

12 *Bishop v Plumley* [1991] 1 WLR 582, [1991] 1 All ER 236; [1991] All ER Rev 195 (S. M.
Cretney), 340 (C. H. Sherrin); [1993] Conv 270 (F. Bates). The Law Commission Report on
Distribution on Intestacy 1989 (Law Com No. 187, 60) paras. 59–60 recommends that
cohabitants should be able to apply for reasonable financial provision without having to
show dependance.
13 Inheritance (Provision for Family and Dependants) Act 1975, s. 1 (2).
14 *Re Goodwin* [1969] 1 Ch 283 at 288, [1968] 3 All ER 12 at 75, per MEGARRY J; *Millward v
Shenton* [1972] 1 WLR 711, [1972] 2 All ER 1025 (1938 Act).
15 [1980] Ch 461 at 474, [1979] 2 All ER 408 at 418. This statement was approved by CA. See
also *Re Christie*, supra, doubted by GOFF LJ in *Re Coventry* [1980] Ch 461 at 490, [1979] 3 All
ER 815 at 824.

of the hearing; the financial resources and needs of the applicant,[16] of any other applicant and of any beneficiary of the estate; any obligations and responsibilities of the deceased to any applicant or beneficiary; the size and nature of the net estate; any physical or mental disability of any applicant or beneficiary; and any other matter, including the conduct of the applicant[17] or any other person,[18] which in the circumstances of the case the court may consider relevant.[19] The Court of Appeal has held that it could not take into account legally unenforceable assurances by other beneficiaries under a will that they were not going to insist on their legal rights.[20]

(ii) Particular applications Section 3 also sets out the following *additional* matters which must be considered for each category of applicant:

Spouses Where the applicant is a surviving spouse under section 1 (1) (*a*) or a former spouse under (*b*), the age of the applicant and the duration of the marriage; the contribution made by the applicant to the welfare of the family of the deceased; and, in the case of a surviving spouse, the provision which the applicant might reasonably have expected to receive if, when the deceased died, the marriage had been ended by divorce, and not by death.[1]

Children Where the applicant is a child under (*c*) or a child of the family under (*d*), the manner in which the applicant was being, or in which he might expect to be, educated or trained; and also, in the case of a child of the family, whether the deceased had assumed any responsibility for the applicant's maintenance and, if so, the extent to which and the basis upon which the deceased assumed responsibility and the length of time for which the deceased discharged that responsibility; whether in assuming and discharging that responsibility the deceased did so knowing that the applicant

---

16 The life style previously enjoyed by a widow is relevant: *Re Besterman*; *Re Bunning* supra. On the relevance of the availability of state aid, see *Re Wood* (1982) 79 LSG 774; *Re Collins* [1990] Fam 56, [1990] 2 All ER 47 (receipt of security benefits irrelevant). See also *Re E* [1966] 2 All ER 44.

17 *Re Snoek* (1983) 13 Fam Law 18 ("atrocious and vicious behaviour"); *Williams v Johns* [1988] 2 FLR 475 (stormy conduct of adopted daughter).

18 *Re Dawkins* [1986] 2 FLR 360 (deceased left widow life interest in former matrimonial home, but before he died he sold it to their daughter for £100; his estate was insolvent; widow granted £10,000 payable from proceeds of sale).

19 *Re Fullard* [1982] Fam 42, [1981] 2 All ER 796 (divorce and terms of financial settlement made on divorce); *Whiting v Whiting* [1988] 1 WLR 565, [1988] 2 All ER 275; [1989] Conv 444 (J. E. M.). See s. 15 (as substituted by Matrimonial and Family Proceedings Act 1984, s. 8 (1)); s. 15A, as added by s. 25 (3).

20 *Rajabally v Rajabally* [1987] Fam Law 314.

1 Inheritance (Provision for Family and Dependants) Act 1975, s. 3 (2); *Re Besterman* [1984] Ch 458, [1984] 2 All ER 656 (out of an estate of £1.37 million deceased left his wife £3,500 per annum, representing one sixth of his assets, and the residue mainly to Oxford University for research on Voltaire and Rousseau; widow's share increased to one quarter of assets); *Re Bunning* [1984] Ch 480, [1984] 3 All ER 1 (out of an estate of £237,000, deceased left nothing to his widow, from whom he had separated four years before his death, and residue mainly to Cambridge University for research on cats and dogs; widow granted £60,000). See also *Re Rowlands* [1984] Fam Law 280; *Stead v Stead* [1985] Fam Law 154; *Stephens v Stephens* (1 July 1985, unreported). For a comprehensive review, see (1986) 102 LQR 445 (J. G. Miller); *Kusminow v Barclays Bank Trust Co Ltd* [1989] Fam Law 66; [1989] Conv 445 (J. E. M.) (widow would have got half of family assets on a divorce, in view of long marriage and her hard work); *Moody v Stevenson* [1992] Ch 486, [1992] 2 All ER 524 where WAITE J refers, at 498, at 533, to "the mental gymnastics which the test is liable to impose on the court"; *Jessop v Jessop* [1992] 1 FLR 591; [1992] Conv 442 (J. Martin).

was not his own child; and the liability of any other person to maintain the applicant.[2]

Other dependants Where the applicant is a dependant under (*e*), the extent to which and the basis upon which the deceased assumed responsibility for the maintenance of the applicant, and the length of time for which the deceased discharged that responsibility.[3]

C. COURT ORDERS

If the court is satisfied, on an application being made to it, that the will of the deceased or the law relating to intestacy, or the combination of the will and that law, does not make reasonable financial provision for the applicant, it may make an order for such provision to be made out of the net estate.[4] The court may treat the severable share of a joint tenancy as part of the net estate at its value immediately before death.[5]

The court may make an order for periodical payments, or for a lump sum,[6] or for both. It may also make an order for the transfer or settlement of any property;[7] for the acquisition of property for the applicant or for settlement for his benefit; and for the variation of a marriage settlement. The court has wide powers to allocate the burden of the award between beneficiaries.[8]

(a) Interim orders

If it appears that the applicant is in immediate need of financial assistance but that it is not yet possible to determine what order should be made, and if there is available property to meet the need of the applicant, the court may make an interim order for the payment to him of such sums and at such intervals as appear reasonable.[9]

(b) Limit of time for application

An application for an order must be made within six months from the date on which representation is first taken out,[10] but the court may permit a later application.[11]

2 Inheritance (Provision for Family and Dependants) Act 1975, s. 3 (3).
3 Ibid., s. 3 (4); *Re Beaumont*, supra. See *Malone v Harrison*, supra, for the operation of s. 3 (1), (4).
4 Ibid., s. 2. A grant of probate or letters of administration are necessary before an application can be made: *Re McBroom* [1992] 2 FLR 49. See also ss. 8, 10. A claim under the Act does not survive to the personal representative: *Re R* [1986] Fam Law 58 (former wife of deceased); *Whyte v Ticehurst* [1986] Fam 64, [1986] 2 All ER 158 (widow of deceased).
5 Ibid., s. 9; *Powell v Osbourne* [1993] Fam Law 287; *Jessop v Jessop*, supra.
6 This may be made payable by instalments, s. 7 (1); *Re Callaghan* [1985] Fam 1, [1984] 3 All ER 790; *Re Leach* [1986] Ch 226, [1985] 2 All ER 754; *Re Besterman* [1984] Ch 458, [1984] 2 All ER 656.
7 See *Harrington v Gill* (1983) 4 FLR 265.
8 Inheritance (Provision for Family and Dependants) Act 1975, s. 2 (4).
9 Ibid., s. 5.
10 I.e. the date of effective or valid representation: *Re Freeman* [1984] 1 WLR 1419, [1984] 3 All ER 906 (probate revoked and letters of administration granted).
11 Inheritance (Provision for Family and Dependants) Act 1975, s. 4.

In *Re Salmon*,[12] MEGARRY V-C identified guidelines for the exercise of this jurisdiction. The discretion of the court, though unfettered, is to be exercised judicially and in accordance with what is just and proper, and the onus is on the applicant to establish sufficient grounds for taking the case out of the time limit. It is material to consider how promptly and in what circumstances the extension is sought; whether any negotiations have been commenced within the time limit; whether the estate has been distributed before any claim has been made or notified, and, lastly, whether or not the applicant will have redress against anyone else, as, for example, against a solicitor who may have been responsible for the delay. A further guideline was added in *Re Dennis*;[13] whether the applicant had an arguable case by reference to the same factors as are considered in deciding whether to give leave to defend in proceedings for summary judgment.[14]

(c) Variation of orders

The court has power to vary any order made for periodical payments,[15] but orders for lump sum payments or for transfer of property are final and not subject to later variation.[16]

(d) Joint tenancy

The court also has power to make an order concerning the deceased's severable share of any property of which he was a beneficial joint tenant immediately before his death. It may order that it shall be treated as part of the net estate to such extent as appears to be just in all the circumstances.[17] In the absence of this power, the court would be unable to make an order for provision out of such property, since on the death of one joint tenant the beneficial ownership is held by the surviving joint tenant.[18] This is important where husband and wife are beneficial joint tenants of the matrimonial home.[19]

(e) Power to counter evasion

Further the Act gives the court important powers to counter evasion of its provisions. Where the deceased makes an inter vivos disposition less than six years before his death, otherwise than for full valuable consideration being given by the donee, and with the intention of defeating an application for financial provision under the Act, the court may order the donee to provide property or money from which a claim for provision may be

---

12 [1981] Ch 167, [1980] 3 All ER 532 (5½ months' delay; bulk of estate distributed; application refused); *Re Dennis* [1981] 2 All ER 140 (19 months' delay; estate not distributed; application refused). See also *Re Ruttie* [1970] 1 WLR 89, [1969] 3 All ER 1633; *Re Gonin* [1979] Ch 16, [1977] 2 All ER 720; *Escritt v Escritt* (1981) 131 NLJ 1266; *Re Adams* [1981] CA Transcript 299; s. 9 (1).
13 [1981] 2 All ER 140.
14 RSC Ord. 14.
15 Inheritance (Provision for Family and Dependants) Act 1975, s. 6.
16 Except in the case of instalments, when the amount, number and date of payments may be varied. Ibid., s. 7 (2).
17 Inheritance (Provision for Family and Dependants) Act 1975, s. 9. See [1980] Conv 60 (S. Farren); *Kourgey v Lusher* (1983) 4 FLR 65; *Re Crawford* (1983) 4 FLR 273.
18 P. 215, ante.
19 P. 238, ante.

satisfied.[20] Similar provisions apply, mutatis mutandis, where the deceased enters at any time into a contract to leave property by will, or undertakes that his personal representatives will transfer property out of his estate.[1]

SECTION III FORMALITIES OF WILLS

The formalities essential to the creation of a valid will are prescribed by section 9 of the Wills Act 1837[2] as substituted with amendments by the Administration of Justice Act 1982.[3] The new section applies where a testator dies on or after 1 January 1983, and is in the following words:

No will shall be valid unless—

(a) it is in writing, and signed by the testator, or by some other person in his presence and by his direction; and

(b) it appears that the testator intended by his signature to give effect to the will; and

(c) the signature is made or acknowledged by the testator in the presence of two or more witnesses present at the same time; and

(d) each witness either—

(i) attests and signs the will; or

(ii) acknowledges his signature,

in the presence of the testator (but not necessarily in the presence of any other witness),

but no form of attestation shall be necessary.

The essentials, then, are these:

(1) writing,

(2) signature of the testator, either made or acknowledged in the presence of the witnesses, and

(3) attestation by the witnesses.

A. CREATION OF WILL

(1) WRITING

A will must be in writing. It may be typed, printed or photographed,[4] either in whole or in part. It does not have to be in any particular form. It is sufficient that the instrument, however irregular in form or artificial in

---

20 Inheritance (Provision for Family and Dependants) Act 1975, ss. 10, 12. See *Clifford v Tanner* [1987] CLY 3881.

1 Ibid., ss. 11, 12, 13. Ss. 10 and 11 do not apply to dispositions or contracts made before 1 April 1976, s. 11 (6).

2 In a survey during a period of three months in 1978, 93 out of 40,664 wills admitted to probate were rejected for failing to satisfy s. 9 (testator's signature incorrectly placed 8; less than two witnesses 34; witnesses not present at same time 20; not signed in testator's presence 19; other reasons (including 9 not signed by testator) 12). Of these 93 wills, at least 89 were home-made.

For formalities where wills are made abroad, see Wills Act 1963; Cheshire and North, *Private International Law* (12th edn), pp. 839 et seq.

3 S. 17. This follows the recommendations of the Law Reform Committee 22nd Report on the Making and Revocation of Wills 1980 (Cmnd 7902). On this and other changes made by AJA 1982, see [1983] Conv 21 (A. Samuels); [1984] CLP 115 (J. B. Clark).

4 Interpretation Act 1978, s. 5, Sch 1.

expression, discloses the intention of the maker respecting the posthumous destination of his property.[5] Blanks in a will which is printed or typed may be filled in ordinary writing, either in ink or in pencil. If two wills are found, one in pencil and the other in ink, it may be inferred that the one in pencil is merely deliberative, and the one in ink the final version.[6] Where a will appeared to have been first written in pencil and then inked over, only the words in pencil were admitted to probate.[7]

(2) SIGNATURE

The testator must sign the will either by writing his name at its end in the normal fashion or by adding some mark or phrase intended to represent his name. Thus, the signature may be represented, for instance, by a rubber stamp or by the impress of an ink-smudged thumb,[8] or by some such phrase as "your loving mother".[9] Alternatively he may procure some person to sign on his behalf in his presence and under his direction.

The Act of 1837 required that the signature should be *at the foot or end* of the will, but as the courts construed this strictly and refused to admit a signature unless it was so placed that nothing could be written between it and the last words of the will, the law was altered by the Wills Act Amendment Act 1852. This provided that a signature was valid if it was:

> so placed at or after, or following, or under, or beside, or opposite to the end of the will, that it shall be apparent on the face of the will that the testator intended to give effect by such his signature to the writing signed as his will.[10]

The courts put a liberal construction on this enactment. They ignored the numbered order of a three page will, where the testator had signed on page one only;[11] they admitted a signature in the margin[12] and on the envelope containing the will.[13]

Where a testator dies after 1982, the new section 9 abolished the rule that the signature must appear at the foot or end of the will, and instead provides that it must appear that "the testator intended by his signature to give effect to the will". The original section 9 did not contain any such express wording, but it is clear that such a requirement was also essential under the previous law, as can be seen from the wording of the Wills Act Amendment Act 1852 set out in the paragraph above, and from the "envelope cases". This may be illustrated by *Re Beadle*[14] which was decided in 1973. In that case:

> the testatrix signed her will in the top right hand corner and also wrote her name on the envelope in which the will was enclosed. GOFF J held that she had not intended her name on the envelope to be a signature but merely to be a label

5 *Re Berger* [1990] Ch 118 at 133, [1989] 1 All ER 591 at 602, per Sir Denys BUCKLEY. It may be made in any language.
6 *Rymes v Clarkson* (1809) 1 Phillim 22.
7 *Re Bellamy* (1866) 14 WR 501; *Re Adams* (1872) LR 2 P & D 367.
8 *Re Finn* (1935) 52 TLR 153. See *Re Chalcraft* [1948] P 222, [1948] 1 All ER 700 (testatrix too ill to write more than "E. Chal"; held valid); *Re Colling* [1972] 1 WLR 1440, [1972] 3 All ER 729.
9 *Re Cook* [1960] 1 WLR 353, [1960] 1 All ER 689.
10 S. 1; *Re Little* [1960] 1 WLR 495, [1960] 1 All ER 387.
11 *Re Smith* [1931] P 225; cf *Royle v Harris* [1895] P 163.
12 *Re Usborne* (1909) 25 TLR 519; *Re Roberts* [1934] P 102.
13 *Re Mann* [1942] P 146, [1942] 2 All ER 193; (1943) 59 LQR 20 (R.E.M.); cf *Re Bean* [1944] P 83, [1944] 2 All ER 348.
14 [1974] 1 WLR 417, [1974] 1 All ER 493.

identifying the document when placed with her other papers. The signature on the will, being at the top and not at the bottom, was invalid, and therefore so was the will.

Under the new section 9, the signature on the will would have been valid, but not that on the envelope.

Where a will is signed before the dispositive provisions have been written, affirmative evidence is necessary to show that the testator intended to give effect to the provisions. In *Wood v Smith*:[15]

the testator made a handwritten will which began "My Will by Percy Winterbone". He did not sign again at the end of the will, pointing out to the witnesses that he had already signed it. The Court of Appeal held that, by writing his name and the dispositive provisions in one single operation, the testator had provided the necessary evidence, and accordingly the will had been duly executed.

(3) ATTESTATION

(a) Mode of attestation

The testator must sign, or acknowledge his signature, in the simultaneous presence of the witnesses, i.e. both the witnesses must be present at the moment of signature or acknowledgment by the testator,[16] and finally they must attest and sign the will in his presence. Under the original section 9 of the Wills Act, witnesses, unlike the testator, cannot acknowledge their signatures. But the new section 9 provides that where the testator dies after 1982, a witness may acknowledge his signature "in the presence of the testator (but not necessarily in the presence of any other witness)".[17] Although not specifically required by the statute, the usual practice is for the witnesses to attest in the presence of each other and to record the fact in the following attestation clause, which records that all the statutory requirements have been observed:

Signed by the said testator as his last will in the presence of us, present at the same time, who in his presence and at his request and in the presence of each other have hereunto subscribed our names as witnesses.

If this clause is omitted, probate will not be granted unless it is proved by an affidavit of one of the witnesses or by some other satisfactory evidence that the statutory requirements have been observed.[18] Such evidence, however, is not conclusive.[19]

(b) Effect of gift to witness

The Wills Act 1837 also provides that if any beneficial interest is given to a witness or to the spouse of a witness who is married at the time of the

---

15 [1993] Ch 90, [1991] 3 All ER 556; [1992] Conv 438 (J. E. Martin); [1992] All ER Rev 398 (C. H. Sherrin).

16 *Re Groffman* [1969] 1 WLR 733, [1969] 2 All ER 108; *Re Colling* [1972] 1 WLR 1440, [1972] 3 All ER 729.

17 Thus reversing *Re Colling*, supra (when testator acknowledged his signature, one witness had already subscribed and did not subscribe again although he acknowledged his earlier signature; probate refused).

18 Non-Contentious Probate Rules, 1987 (S.I. 1987 No. 2024), r. 12; *Re Selby-Bigge* [1950] 1 All ER 1009. A blind person is incapable of witnessing a will: *Re Gibson* [1949] P 434, [1949] 2 All ER 90.

19 *Re Vere-Wardale* [1949] P 395, [1949] 2 All ER 250.

attestation, the attestation is valid and effective, but the gift is void.[20] An attesting witness is not excluded as a beneficiary under this enactment unless he is interested under the will at the time of attestation. He may retain any benefit that accrues to him later.[1] Again, the gift to him is void only if it is contained in the very document that he has attested, not, for instance, where he is a beneficiary under a secret trust,[2] nor where his attestation is confined to a codicil that merely confirms the will under which he claims.[3]

The Wills Act 1968 modifies the law in one respect. Where a testator dies after 30 May 1968, the attestation by a beneficiary or his or her spouse shall be disregarded if the will is duly executed without his attestation; that is to say, where there are at least two witnesses who are not themselves beneficiaries as well.

(4) INTERNATIONAL WILLS

The Administration of Justice Act 1982[4] gives legislative effect in the United Kingdom to the Convention Providing a Uniform Law on the Form of an International Will. This is an alternative to a will under the Wills Act 1837, and is useful where a testator has assets in more than one of the signatory countries. The formalities of such a will are similar to those of section 9 of the Wills Act, but in addition it must be acknowledged before "a person authorised to act in connection with international wills". If the formalities are complied with, such a will is valid as regards form, irrespective of the place where it is made, of the location of the assets, and of the nationality, domicile or residence of the testator.

B. ALTERATIONS IN WILL

Section 21 of the Wills Act provides that:

> No obliteration, interlineation or other alteration made in any will after the execution thereof shall be valid and have any effect, except so far as the words or effect of the will before such alteration shall not be apparent, unless such alteration shall be executed in like manner as herein-before is required for the execution of the will.

The section further provides that signatures of the testator and the witnesses may be made in the margin or some other part of the will opposite or near to the alteration, or at the foot or end of or opposite to a memorandum referring to such alteration, and written at the end or some other part of the will. Initials suffice for a signature.[5]

The effect of an unattested alteration depends on whether the original

---

20 The section does not apply to the privileged will described infra: *Re Limond* [1915] 2 Ch 240; *Re Finnemore* [1991] 1 WLR 793, [1992] 1 All ER 800. In *Ross v Caunters* [1980] Ch 297, [1979] 3 All ER 580 a solicitor was held liable in negligence to a beneficiary for failing to warn a testator that the will should not have been witnessed by the beneficiary's husband. See *Seale v Perry* [1982] VR 193; (1983) 99 LQR 346 (P. Cane), and, for a history and criticism of this rule, (1984) 100 LQR 453 (D. E. C. Yale).
1 *Re Royce's Will Trusts* [1959] Ch 626, [1959] 3 All ER 278.
2 *Re Young* [1951] Ch 344, [1950] 2 All ER 1040. As to secret trusts, see H & M, chapter 5.
3 *Re Trotter* [1899] 1 Ch 764.
4 Ss. 27, 28, Sch. 2.
5 *Re Blewitt* (1880) 5 PD 116; *Re White* [1991] Ch 1, [1990] 3 All ER 1 (testator failed to sign the alterations or the will again); [1991] Conv 136 (J. E. Martin).

obliterated words are apparent within the meaning of the section. If they are, then probate will contain those original words. If they are not, probate is granted in blank, i.e. without the original words. The words are apparent if on inspection of the will they can be read with the naked eye, assisted by any natural means such as by holding the will up to the light, or by the use of a magnifying glass.[6] Resort cannot, however, be had to any physical interference with the will, such as by removing paper pasted over the words,[7] or by using chemicals;[8] nor can the words be deciphered by infra-red photography.[9] As ORMEROD J said in *Re Itter*:[10]

> If the words of the document can be read by looking at the document itself, then I think that they are apparent within the meaning of the section, however elaborate may be the devices used to assist the eye and however skilled the eye which is being used; but if they can only be read by creating a new document, as in this case by producing a photograph of the original writing, then I cannot find that the words are apparent. They may be discoverable ... but that is not the word used in the section.

Where the original words have been made "non-apparent" by the obliteration, the alteration, although it is unattested, is rendered valid by the section. There is *pro tanto* destruction of the will, and the will is in part revoked by the alteration.[11]

The doctrine of dependent relative revocation may be applied to an alteration.[12] If it can be proved that the testator intended to revoke the obliterated words only if the substituted words could have effect, then the doctrine may apply, with the result that the obliterated words are unrevoked and can then be deciphered by any means, including infra-red photography.[13]

C. PRIVILEGED WILLS

(1) SOLDIERS, SAILORS AND AIRMEN

At common law no particular form was required for wills, which in the case of pure personalty might even be nuncupative. This was altered by the Statute of Frauds, which, besides placing such restrictions upon the nuncupative will that it fell into disuse, required a will of *land* to be in writing and attested by three or four credible witnesses. It provided, however, in section 22 that soldiers' wills with regard to their "movables, wages and personal estates" might still be made in the informal manner hitherto recognized as sufficient.

This indulgence was continued by section 11 of the Wills Act 1837, which provided that:

6 *Ffinch v Combe* [1894] P 191; *Re Adams* [1990] Ch 601, [1990] 2 All ER 97.
7 *Re Horsford* (1874) LR 3 P & D 211. See *Re Gilbert* [1893] P 183 (where the court allowed removal of paper in order to discover whether anything amounting to revocation was underneath it).
8 *Ffinch v Combe*, supra, at 193.
9 *Re Itter* [1950] P 130, [1950] 1 All ER 68.
10 At 132, at 69.
11 For revocation by destruction under Wills Act 1837, s. 20, see pp. 861, post.
12 P. 862, post.
13 *Re Itter*, supra (amounts of legacies obliterated and new amounts substituted by unattested slips of paper pasted over the figures but revocation intended only on substitution of new amounts; slips could be removed and infra-red photography used for discovery of original amounts).

any soldier being in actual military service or any mariner or seaman being at sea

might dispose of his *personal estate* (an expression which has been held to include personal property over which there is a general or special power of appointment),[14] as he might have done before the passing of the Act. Such a will is privileged in the sense that the usual statutory formalities are not essential for its making or revocation,[15] and it is valid even though the testator is under the age of 18 years.[16] But for spoken words to constitute a nuncupative will, they must have been intended by the deceased to operate as a disposition of his property.[17] They must not merely inform his hearers of what he proposes to do,[18] but must be intended to guide them in carrying out his wishes.[19]

The Wills (Soldiers and Sailors) Act 1918 extended the privilege by providing that it should apply to wills of realty in England or Ireland[20] and that the expression "soldier" should include a member of the Air Force.[1] In the result there are two classes of privileged testators: first, any soldier or airman who is *in actual military service* at the time of making his will, or any member of the naval or marine forces of the Crown who at that time "is so circumstanced that if he were a soldier he would be *in actual military service* within the meaning of" section 11 of the Wills Act 1837;[2] secondly, any member of the naval or marine forces of the Crown or any member of the merchant marine who is *at sea* at the time of making his will.

The difficulty experienced by the courts has been to determine the meaning of the two expressions *in actual military service*[3] and *at sea*.

(2) IN ACTUAL MILITARY SERVICE

The statutory privilege has existed for over 300 years and it is not surprising that with the gradual change in the nature of war the courts, in construing the expression "in actual military service", have at different times laid the emphasis upon different factors. Until comparatively recent times, the instinct of the courts was to construe the expression in the light of Roman law from which the rule in the Statute of Frauds had admittedly been copied.[4] An English soldier was not to be privileged unless a Roman legionary, placed in like circumstances, would have been regarded as *in expeditione*. According to this test, which has now, however, been discarded,[5] the will of a soldier

---

14 *Re Earl of Chichester's Will Trusts* [1946] Ch 289, [1946] 1 All ER 722.
15 *Re Gossage* [1921] P 194; Family Law Reform Act 1969, s. 3 (4).
16 Wills (Soldiers & Sailors) Act 1918, s. 1, confirming *Re Wernher* [1918] 2 Ch 82; Family Law Reform Act 1969, s. 3 (1).
17 *Re Jones* [1981] Fam 7, [1981] 1 All ER 1 ("if I don't make it, make sure Anne gets all my stuff").
18 *Re Knibbs* [1962] 1 WLR 852, [1962] 2 All ER 829 ("if anything ever happens to me, Iris will get anything I have got").
19 *Re Stable* [1919] P 7 ("if anything happens to me, and I stop a bullet, everything of mine will be yours"); *Re Spicer* [1949] P 441, [1949] 2 All ER 659; *Re Jones*, supra.
20 S. 3.
1 S. 5 (2).
2 Wills (Soldiers & Sailors) Act 1918, s. 2.
3 See (1949) 12 MLR 183 (D. C. Potter).
4 The eminent civilian, Sir Leoline Jenkins, was responsible for it.
5 *Re Booth* [1926] P 118 at 136; *Re Wingham* [1949] P 187, [1948] 2 All ER 908.

made while he was quartered in barracks even in time of war would not be privileged.[6] In the first half of the nineteenth century, the Ecclesiastical Courts, which had exclusive jurisdiction in probate until 1857, further insisted that the testator should be *inops consilii* at the time of making the will, and on this ground it was held in one case that the privilege did not apply to an officer stationed in Bombay, whose unit had been ordered to proceed to attack the citadel of Jodhpur and who made his will two days before setting out.[7]

In the course of the Boer War and of the First World War the conception of actual military service was broadened in the sense that emphasis was now laid upon whether the testator had taken some active step towards engaging in hostilities, as for example by going into barracks preparatory to being drafted to the seat of war.[8] The decisions during the Second World War went further in the same direction and showed so marked a tendency to extend the class of privileged testators as to evoke the criticism that the mere wearing of uniform in time of war is equivalent to being in actual military service.[9] The authorities, indeed, seem to justify the statement that not only the fighting troops, but also men and women, such as doctors, nurses and chaplains, who are:

actually serving with the Armed Forces in connexion with military operations which are or have been taking place or are believed to be imminent

are in actual military service within the meaning of the Wills Act.[10]

The statute is satisfied in that respect, for instance, if at the time of making the will and while war is impending or in progress, the testator or testatrix is an airman undergoing training in Saskatchewan,[11] an artillery officer under orders to rejoin his battery just before the outbreak of war,[12] a soldier quartered at a camp in England though not under orders to proceed to the scene of fighting,[13] a member of the Women's Auxiliary Air Force in charge of a depot in Gloucestershire,[14] a person on duty as a member of the Home Guard,[15] or a serviceman under 21 of the British Army of the Rhine stationed in Germany nine years after the cessation of hostilities.[16] The test of actual military service was further extended, where a soldier was killed on military patrol in Northern Ireland, even though:

the enemy was not a uniformed force engaged in regular warfare, or even an insurgent force organised upon conventional military lines, but rather a conjuration of clandestine assassins and arsonists.[17]

6 *Drummond v Parish* (1843) 3 Curt 522.
7 *Bowles v Jackson* (1854) 1 Spinks 294.
8 *Re Hiscock* [1901] P 78.
9 (1949) 12 MLR, at p. 188 (D. C. Potter).
10 *Re Wingham* [1949] P 187 at 196, [1948] 2 All ER 908 at 913, per DENNING LJ.
11 *Re Wingham*, supra.
12 *Re Rippon* [1943] P 61, [1943] 1 All ER 676.
13 *Re Spark* [1941] P 115, [1941] 2 All ER 782.
14 *Re Rowson* [1944] 2 All ER 36.
15 *Blyth v Lord Advocate* [1945] AC 32, [1944] 2 All ER 375.
16 *Re Colman* [1958] 1 WLR 457, [1958] 2 All ER 35.
17 *Re Jones* [1981] Fam 7 at 13, [1981] 1 All ER 1 at 5, per ARNOLD P; following *Re Anderson* (1953) 75 WNNSW 334 (Australian contingent operating against terrorists in Malaya). See also *Re Berry* [1955] NZLR 1003 (Korea); (1981) 13 NLJ 659 (R. D. Mackay).

(3) AT SEA

A mariner in the Royal Navy or in the merchant service, though not in actual military service, is entitled to the statutory privilege even in time of peace, subject to the condition that he is *at sea* at the time of making his will. The expression "*at sea*" has been liberally construed and is considerably wider than "on the sea".[18] Thus the condition was held to be satisfied where at the critical moment the testator was the mate of a gunnery vessel permanently moored in Portsmouth Harbour,[19] a woman living in lodgings until the next sailing of the *Lusitania* on which she was employed as a typist,[20] and an officer of a tanker under orders to rejoin his ship at Sunderland within the next three days.[1]

D. LOSS AND DEPOSIT OF WILL

(a) Loss

The contents of a private document must, if possible, be proved by primary evidence, that is, by production of the document itself, but they may be proved by secondary evidence, as for instance by oral testimony, when the document has been lost. Such extrinsic evidence is admissible in the case of a will that has been lost or destroyed *sine animo revocandi*.[2]

Declarations, written or oral, made by a testator, both before and after the execution of his will, are, in the event of its loss, admissible as secondary evidence of its contents. The contents of a lost will may be proved by the evidence of a single witness, though interested, whose veracity and competency are unimpeached. When the contents of a lost will are not completely proved, probate will be granted to the extent to which they are proved.[3]

The standard of proof required is the ordinary standard of proof in civil cases, namely, a reasonable balance of probabilities, and not proof beyond all reasonable doubt.[4]

(b) Deposit and registration

A testator may avoid the danger of his will not being found at his death by depositing it during his lifetime at the Principal Registry of the Family Division.[5] Few wills are so deposited.[6] Such a will can be withdrawn, and

---

18 The authorities are fully discussed in *Re Newland* [1952] P 71, [1952] 1 All ER 841.
19 *Re M'Murdo* (1868) LR 1 P & D 540.
20 *Re Sarah Hale* [1915] 2 IR 362.
 1 *Re Wilson* [1952] P 92, [1952] 1 All ER 852; *Re Newland* [1952] P 71, [1952] 1 All ER 841; *Re Rapley* [1983] 1 WLR 1069, [1983] 3 All ER 248 (indentured apprentice who had not yet received orders to join his ship).
 2 *Re Webb* [1964] 1 WLR 509, [1964] 2 All ER 91. As to the position where loss effects a revocation of the will, see p. 864, post.
 3 Taken verbatim from the headnote to *Sugden v Lord St Leonards* (1876) 1 PD 154. See too Civil Evidence Act 1968, s. 2.
 4 *Re Wipperman* [1955] P 59, [1953] 1 All ER 764, per PEARCE J explaining a dictum of Lord HERSCHELL in *Woodward v Goulstone* (1886) 11 App Cas 469; *Re Yelland* (1975) 119 SJ 562 (will proved by daughter's recollection of its contents). Cf *Re Macgillivray* [1946] 2 All ER 301.
 5 Supreme Court Act 1981, s. 126; Wills (Deposit for Safe Custody) Regulations 1978 (S.I. 1978 No. 1724); (1975) 72 LSG 96 (R. Gillis).
 6 79 were deposited in 1975.

there are regulations which provide for the procedure on the death of the testator.[7]

The Administration of Justice Act 1982 extended this system of voluntary deposit. It provides that specified registering authorities (the Principal Registry of the Family Division in the case of England and Wales) shall provide and maintain safe and convenient depositaries for the custody of the wills (including international wills) of living persons, and for their registration.[8]

SECTION IV PERSONAL REPRESENTATIVES AND THEIR DUTIES AND POWERS[9]

A. APPOINTMENT OF EXECUTORS

We have already seen that the property of a testator does not go directly to the beneficiaries under the will, but devolves upon his personal representatives for the purposes of administration.[10] Personal representatives are either executors or administrators. An executor is a person who is appointed by the testator for the purpose of carrying the provisions of his will into effect. If no such appointment is made, or if the appointment fails, for instance, by the death, renunciation, infancy or lunacy of the executor, the court makes a grant of administration *cum testamento annexo*.[11] The order of priority of right to such a grant is based on the beneficial claims under the will, the residuary legatee or devisee having the first right.[12]

If a last surviving executor proves the will of X, and dies testate without having completed his office, then *his* executor steps into his place and becomes the excecutor of X.

> An executor of a sole or last surviving executor of a testator is the executor of that testator.[13]

But if such last surviving executor dies intestate, his administrator does not become executor of the will of X,[14] and in such a case it is necessary for the court to appoint another person to administer such property as is still unadministered. This is called administration *de bonis non*.

While any legal proceeding that concerns the validity of a will is pending, the court may appoint an administrator *pendente lite*, who has all the powers of a general administrator except that he cannot distribute the residue among those entitled.[15]

---

7 Wills (Deposit for Safe Custody) Regulations 1978, supra, regs. 8, 9.
8 Ss. 23–25.
9 See generally *Williams, Mortimer and Sunnucks on Executors, Administrators and Probate*; Rossdale, *Probate and the Administration of Estates* (1991).
10 P. 843, ante.
11 Supreme Court Act 1981, s. 119.
12 Non-Contentious Probate Rules 1987, r. 20.
13 AEA 1925, s. 7 (1).
14 Ibid., s. 7 (3).
15 Supreme Court Act 1981, s. 117; RSC Ord 76, r. 15.

B. THEIR DUTY TO OBTAIN PROBATE

(1) JURISDICTION TO GRANT PROBATE

The first duty of an executor is to prove the will in court. The jurisdiction to grant and revoke probates, which was formerly vested in the ecclesiastical courts, was transferred in 1858 to the Court of Probate.[16] When the Supreme Court of Judicature was set up under the Judicature Act 1873, the jurisdiction was vested in the Probate, Divorce and Admiralty Division of the High Court of Justice. Under the redistribution of business among the divisions of the High Court on 1 October 1971 by the Administration of Justice Act 1970, this Division was renamed the Family Division. Non-contentious or common form probate business remains with the Family Division, and all other probate business is assigned to the Chancery Division.[17]

The proof of a will may be either in common or in solemn form.

(a) Probate in common form

Probate in common form is granted, not by the court itself, but by the principal registry of the Family Division in London or by a district probate registry,[18] and such a grant has effect over the estate of the deceased in all parts of England.[19] The executor must swear an oath before a Commissioner of Oaths, in which he states his belief that the instrument he submits for probate is the true and last will of the testator, and in which he declares the gross value of the real and personal estate. If the will is correct in form and contains the attestation clause which has been given above, probate is granted on the oath of the executor alone.[20]

(b) Probate in solemn form

Probate in solemn form, which is an action before the court in the Chancery Division, is necessary where the validity of the will is doubtful, or where there is a likelihood that it may be opposed. The action may be brought by the executor, a person who contests the will, or a "person interested", i.e. a widow or widower, a legatee or devisee and the persons who would be entitled to take on intestacy. A creditor is not a "person interested".

(c) Delay

The cases support the view that the court will never strike out an action to revoke a grant of probate or letters of administration on the mere ground of

---

16 Court of Probate Act 1857.
17 Supreme Court Act 1981, s. 61 (1), Sch. 1.
18 District Probate Registries Order 1982 (S.I. 1982 No. 379). There are 11 such registries; all except one have one or more sub-registries attached.
19 Supreme Court Act 1981, ss. 105, 106. The County Court has jurisdiction in contentious matters, where the value of the net estate is less than £30,000; County Courts Act 1984, s. 32; County Courts Jurisdiction Order 1981 (S.I. 1981 No. 1123). In the case of small estates, where the value of the net estate is less than £1,000 and that of the gross estate less than £3,000, an application for grant of representation may be made through an authorized officer of customs and excise: Small Estates (Representation) Act 1961, s. 1 (1). As to cases where property may be disposed of on death without representation, see Administration of Estates (Small Payments) Act 1965; this is subject to a limit of £5,000 (S.I. 1984 No. 539).
20 P. 837, ante.

delay in instituting it, unless it is satisfied that the claim is otherwise frivolous or vexatious or is for other reasons an abuse of the process of the court.[1]

(2) TITLE OF EXECUTOR

A will, after it has been proved, is kept in the Registry of the court, and a copy, together with a certificate that the will has been proved, is given to the executor. The contents of the will then become open to public inspection[2] and may be seen by any member of the public at Somerset House in London. The copy and the certificate are called the probate of the will, and they are conclusive as to the validity both of the testamentary dispositions and of the right of the executor to perform his duties. But an executor derives his title from the will and not from the grant of probate, and therefore the general rule is that he may do all such things and perform all such duties upon the death of the deceased as fall within the province of an executor.[3]

(3) EXECUTOR *DE SON TORT*

If a person without obtaining a grant of probate takes upon himself to meddle with the property of a deceased person in such a way as to indicate that he assumes the rights of an executor, he is said to be an executor *de son tort*.[4] Section 28 of the Administration of Estates Act 1925 provides that if any person, to the defrauding of creditors or without full valuable consideration, obtains, receives or holds any real or personal estate of a deceased person or releases any debt due to the estate, he shall be liable as an executor *de son tort* to the extent of the estate in his hands or of the debt released, after deducting:

(1) any debt for valuable consideration and without fraud due to him from the deceased, and

(2) any payment made by him which might properly be made by a personal representative.

C. THEIR DUTY TO ADMINISTER THE ESTATE

It is not within the scope of this book to give an exhaustive account of an executor's duties, and only a *résumé* will be attempted.

(i) Inventory An executor should make an inventory and account of the real and personal estate of the deceased, and he may be compelled, upon an

1 *Re Flynn* [1982] 1 WLR 310, [1982] 1 All ER 882. See *Re Coghlan* [1948] 2 All ER 68 (claim to establish will 54 years after death of testator).

2 Supreme Court Act 1981, s. 125. A method of avoiding the prying eye is to use the device of a secret trust. See H & M, chapter 8; *Snell's Equity* (29th edn), pp. 108–113; Miller, *Machinery of Succession*, pp. 210–215.

3 He cannot obtain relief from the court without first proving his title by obtaining a grant of probate: *Chetty v Chetty* [1916] 1 AC 603; *Re Crowhurst Park* [1974] 1 WLR 583, [1974] 1 All ER 991.

4 An executor named in the will who intermeddles before probate is not a wrongdoer: *Sykes v Sykes* (1870) LR 5 CP 113 at 117, per BOVILL CJ. He may pay debts and legacies, but he will not enjoy the statutory protection afforded to an executor who is acting under a grant of probate: AEA 1925, s. 27. See also *Re Clore* [1982] Ch 456, [1982] 3 All ER 419.

application to the court by a person interested in the estate of the testator, to exhibit the inventory on oath.[5]

(ii) Realization of estate His next duty is to collect all the estate of the deceased, to realize investments which it is undesirable to keep, to recover loans which are protected merely by personal security, to call in money lent on mortgage if it is required for some testamentary purpose. For these purposes all causes of action vested in the deceased survive to the personal representative, except in the case of defamation.[6]

(iii) Power to dispose of estate in order to pay debts Having collected and obtained control over the assets, the executor must next pay the debts of the deceased. We have already seen what this duty is in this respect. In order that this may be effectually performed, the Administration of Estates Act 1925, after providing that the real as well as the personal estate of the deceased shall vest in the personal representatives, enacts that they shall have the same power to dispose of and deal with the land as they formerly possessed in respect of personal property.[7] Personal representatives always had complete power of alienation over personal property, and since the Land Transfer Act 1897 they have been in the same position as regards land.

Thus they can sell, mortgage or partition the land,[8] and they are now empowered by statute to grant a lease for a term of years absolute (with or without impeachment of waste) to trustees upon trust for raising any sum of money for which the land is liable, and also to grant a rentcharge for giving effect to any annual sum for which the land is liable.

(iv) Disposition of land But a sale of land by executors differs, in its method, from a sale of personalty. One executor may sell pure personalty without the concurrence of his co-executors, but it is enacted that a conveyance of land shall not be made without the concurrence of all the proving executors, unless an order of the court is obtained.[9]

(v) Representatives trustees for sale In order that personal representatives may have full powers of management while they are dealing with the property of the deceased, it is provided that in addition to having power to raise money by mortgage they shall be in the position of trustees for sale as regards both the ability to overreach equitable interests and the right to exercise the powers conferred by statute upon trustees for sale.[10] These powers are those which are conferred upon a tenant for life under the Settled Land Act 1925,

---

5 AEA 1925, s. 25, as replaced by AEA 1971, s. 9. The court may replace executors, who have shown a lack of urgency in the administration of the estate, by an administrator *ad colligenda bona*: *Re Clore*, supra; Supreme Court of Judicature (Consolidation) Act 1925, s. 162 (1) (*b*), now Supreme Court Act 1981, s. 116 (1), p. 858, post. See also AJA 1985, s. 50.
6 Law Reform (Miscellaneous Provisions) Act 1934, s. 1, as amended by Law Reform (Miscellaneous Provisions) Act 1970, ss. 4, 5; AJA 1982, s. 2. A claim for bereavement under Fatal Accidents Act 1976, s. 1A does not survive for the benefit of a person's estate on his death: LR (Miscellaneous Provisions) Act 1934, s. 1 (1A), as amended by AJA 1982, s. 4 (1). See also p. 833, n. 4, ante.
7 S. 2.
8 *Re Kemnal and Still's Contract* [1923] 1 Ch 293.
9 AEA 1925, s. 2 (2). See *Fountain Forestry Ltd v Edwards* [1975] Ch 1, [1974] 2 All ER 280 as to contracts by a single personal representative. The Law Commission recommends that all personal representatives should be required to join in any contract or conveyance to sell the land of a deceased owner: Report on Title on Death 1989 (Law Com No. 184, Cm 777), paras. 2.13–2.19; [1990] Conv 71 (H. W. Wilkinson). See Law of Property (Miscellaneous Provisions) Bill (HL, Bill 46), clause 16.
10 Ibid., s. 39, p. 205, ante.

in addition to the powers given by the Trustee Act 1925 and the Law of Property Act 1925.[11]

(vi) Distribution of estate After the debts have been paid, the duty of the executor is to distribute the residue among those persons who are beneficially entitled under the will. He normally does this within the executor's year, which is one year from the date of the testator's death. Before he does this, however, he should protect himself against claims of which he may not be aware by publishing advertisements in accordance with the directions of the Trustee Act 1925.[12] This provides that, with a view to the conveyance of real or personal property to beneficiaries, either trustees or personal representatives may give notice by advertisement in the *Gazette* and a newspaper circulating in the district where the land is situated, requiring persons to give particulars of any claim they may have against the estate of the deceased. At the expiration of the time fixed by the notice (which must not be less than two months) the personal representatives may convey the property to the beneficiaries, and they are not liable to any person of whose claim they had no notice at the time of the conveyance.

(vii) Right to follow property But the creditors may follow the property even after it has been conveyed to beneficiaries. Notwithstanding such a conveyance, a creditor or other person interested in the property may apply to the court, and the court may declare a beneficiary to be a trustee of the land for the creditor, or may order a different conveyance to be made or may make a vesting order.[13] This power to follow the property does not, however, exist where the conveyance is made not to a beneficiary, but to a purchaser in the ordinary way of administration.[14] In such a case the purchaser receives ample protection.[15] Thus all conveyances of *any interest* in real or personal property made to a purchaser, either by an executor who has proved the will or by the administrator of a person who had died intestate, are valid notwithstanding a subsequent revocation or variation of the probate or administration.[16]

SECTION V PARTICULAR RULES

A. FAILURE OF GIFTS BY LAPSE

(1) COMMORIENTES

A lapse occurs where the donee predeceases the testator, and a preliminary point to notice is that it may be difficult to decide whether this has been the sequence of events if both have been the victims of a common calamity, as for instance where they have both been killed in the same motor car accident. The common law rule in such a case is that the representatives of the donee who claims under the will must prove that in fact he survived the testator.

11 LPA 1925, s. 28, p. 205, ante.
12 TA 1925, s. 27; as amended by LP (A)A 1926, Sch.; *Re Aldhous* [1955] 1 WLR 459, [1955] 2 All ER 80.
13 AEA 1925, s. 38.
14 Ibid., s. 38.
15 Ibid., s. 36 (6), (7), (8).
16 Ibid., s. 37, extending *Hewson v Shelley* [1914] 2 Ch 13.

Otherwise the claim fails.[17] This rule was altered by section 184 of the Law of Property Act 1925:

> In all cases where, after the commencement of this Act, two or more persons have died in circumstances rendering it uncertain which of them survived the other or others, such deaths shall (subject to any order of the court), for all purposes affecting the title to property, be presumed to have occurred in order of seniority, and accordingly the younger shall be deemed to have survived the elder.[18]

It was thought that this section had finally solved the question, but in *Hickman v Peacey*,[19] where four persons had been killed by the explosion of a bomb, it was contended that the common law rule still prevailed if the deaths were simultaneous. If, it was argued, two persons have died simultaneously, it is not "uncertain which of them survived the other". For the section to apply the deaths must have been consecutive. This argument, which inter alia ignores the virtual impossibility of two human beings ceasing to breathe at exactly the same moment of time, was rejected by a bare majority of the House of Lords, and the simple rule laid down that unless it is possible to say for certain which of the persons died first, the younger is presumed to have survived.

In other words, the section is not excluded unless there is clear evidence that one person survived the other.[20] In one case, for instance:

> a man aged twenty-nine, left all his property to his wife, aged twenty-six, with a gift over to his nephew in the event of her death "preceding or coinciding" with his own. A month later the husband and wife set sail on a ship which sank with all on board, only one body being found. It was held that the words "coinciding with" were not intended to denote two deaths occurring on the same occasion from the same cause, but two deaths coincident in point of time, i.e. so close to each other that the normal man would describe them as simultaneous. There was no evidence as to the order of their occurrence, and therefore the wife was presumed to have survived her husband.[1]

(2) LAPSE

(a) **Meaning of lapse**

Once it is proved that the donee under a will died before his testator, the rule is that the gift lapses and ceases to take effect.[2] This is so despite the addition to the gift of words of limitation such as to the donee and his heirs or to him and his executors.[3] It is usual to provide against the event, but to render this effective something more is required than a mere declaration that the gift shall not lapse. There must be a further gift limited to take effect upon the premature death of the first donee, as for example by a provision that:

> the devise to A shall not lapse if he predeceases the testator but shall take effect in favour of his eldest surviving son.[4]

17 *Wing v Angrave* (1860) 8 HL Cas 183.
18 For its modification as between spouses if one of them dies intestate, see IEA 1952, s. 1 (4) p. 876, post.
19 [1945] AC 304, [1945] 2 All ER 215.
20 *Re Bate* [1947] 2 All ER 418.
 1 *Re Rowland* [1963] Ch 1, [1962] 2 All ER 837 (Lord DENNING MR dissenting); (1962) 26 MLR 353 (M. Albery).
 2 For the explanation, see *Re Harvey's Estate* [1893] 1 Ch 567 at 570.
 3 *Elliott v Davenport* (1705) 1 P Wms 83; *Browne v Hope* (1872) LR 14 Eq 343.
 4 *Re Greenwood* [1912] 1 Ch 392; *Re Ladd* [1932] 2 Ch 219.

(b) Statutory exceptions

The Wills Act 1837 provides that no lapse shall occur in the following two cases, unless there is a contrary intention:

(i) The exceptions 1. *Gift of entailed interest* Section 32 provides that, where a person, to whom realty or personalty has been left by will in tail, dies in the lifetime of the testator leaving issue capable of inheriting under the entail, and any such issue shall be living at the death of the testator, the gift does not lapse, but takes effect as if the death of such person had happened immediately after the testator's death.[5]

2. *Gift to testator's issue* Section 33 provides that a devise or bequest to the child or other issue of the testator for an interest not determinable at or before the death of the donee does not lapse if the donee predeceases the testator leaving issue alive at the testator's death, but takes effect as if the death of the donee had happened immediately after the testator's death.[6]

The second exception does not apply where the gift to the issue of the testator is a class gift, for the essence of such a gift is that it is made to a fluctuating class of objects who are to be ascertained at the death of the testator.[7] Hence, if there is a devise to the children of A, or to the children of A equally, the entire property vests in those children who survive the testator irrespective of prior deaths.[8] Nor does the exception apply to an appointment by will under a special power.[9]

(ii) Operation of exceptions The Wills Act, it will be noticed, fictitiously prolongs the life of the donee until immediately after the death of the testator. The sole purpose of this, however, is to amplify the preceding words and to leave no manner of doubt that the gift is to be effective despite the premature death in fact of the donee. His life is not deemed to have been prolonged for any other purpose. The estate that he himself may have left is, indeed, posthumously increased by virtue of his ancestor's will, but this increase falls to be administered with the rest of his estate according to the circumstances as they existed at the time of his actual death.[10] The significance of this may be seen from a hypothetical case:

> The testator, T, devises Blackacre to his son, X, in fee simple. X predeceases T but is survived by his own son Y.

In this case, if X died intestate, the ascertainment of the persons entitled to the additional property, Blackacre, will depend upon the circumstances existing at the time of his death, not at the moment immediately after T's death; it follows that it will vest in his trustee in bankruptcy if he dies a bankrupt or fall into the residue,[11] for, although the survival of Y prevents

---

5 LPA 1925, s. 130 (1).
6 Wills Act 1837, s. 33. Issue includes legitimated issue: *Re Brodie* [1967] Ch 818, [1967] 2 All ER 97; and, where the testator dies after 1969, illegitimate issue: Family Law Reform Act 1969, s. 16.
7 P. 296, ante.
8 *Olney v Bates* (1855) 3 Drew 319; *Re Harvey's Estate* [1893] 1 Ch 567.
9 *Holyland v Lewin* (1884) 26 Ch D 266. Cf *Eccles v Cheyne* (1856) 2 K & J 676 (general power).
10 *Re Basioli* [1953] Ch 367, [1953] 1 All ER 301; where all the authorities are collected.
11 *Johnson v Johnson* (1843) 3 Hare 157.

the lapse of the gift, there is no provision that what has been given to X shall pass beneficially to Y. Y will only take, however, if he is entitled under X's will or intestacy. Again, since Blackacre is deemed to have belonged to X at his death, it follows that it will vest in his trustee in bankruptcy if he dies a bankrupt.[12]

A new section 33 was substituted by the Administration of Justice Act 1982[13] applicable where the testator dies after 1982. Unless there is a contrary intention in the will the new section applies where the gift is made to individual children or other issue and also where there is a class gift.

In the first case the gift takes effect as a gift to the issue directly, and the issue take in equal shares per stirpes. Accordingly the will of the deceased child or other issue no longer affects the devolution of the property. In our example, neither X nor his trustee in bankruptcy can take.

In the second case, when there is a class gift to the children or other issue, the new section 33 provides that the gift includes the issue of a deceased member of the class who are living at the death of the testator.

In both cases, a child or other issue, who is en ventre sa mère at the death of the testator and born alive thereafter, is deemed to have been living at that death, so as to bring the new section into operation. Further, the illegitimacy of any person is to be disregarded.

(c) Destination of lapsed property

Where neither of the exceptions applies, the destination of lapsed property depends upon whether the will contains a residuary gift. If so, the property passes to the residuary devisee or legatee according as it is realty or personalty;[14] otherwise it enures for the benefit of those persons entitled on intestacy.

(3) MURDER OR MANSLAUGHTER OF TESTATOR

A person who is guilty of the murder or manslaughter of the testator cannot benefit under the will,[15] or the intestacy of his victim.[16] This rule applies in cases of diminished responsibility,[17] but not of insanity.[18] In the case of manslaughter it may only apply where there has been deliberate, intentional and unlawful violence or threats of violence.[19] The effect of the rule is that the gift goes as if the killer died immediately before the testator;[20] and that

---

12 *Re Pearson* [1920] 1 Ch 247.
13 S. 19.
14 Wills Act 1837, s. 25.
15 *Re Hall* [1914] P 1 (manslaughter: will).
16 *Re Crippen* [1911] P 108; *Re Sigsworth* [1935] Ch 89 (murder: intestacy).
17 *Re Giles* [1972] Ch 544, [1971] 3 All ER 1141 (wife killed husband with single blow from domestic chamber pot).
18 *Re Pitts* [1931] 1 Ch 546.
19 *Re K* [1985] Ch 85 at 96, 98, [1985] 1 All ER 403 at 412, 413 per VINELOTT J; affd [1986] Ch 180, [1985] 2 All ER 833, where the point was not raised; *Gray v Barr* [1970] 2 QB 626, [1970] 2 All ER 702; *R v Chief National Insurance Comr, ex p Connor* [1981] QB 758, [1981] 1 All ER 769 applied; *Re H* [1990] 1 FLR 441 (forfeiture rule held not to apply where killing not deliberate); *Davitt v Titcumb* [1990] Ch 110, [1989] 3 All ER 417 (one tenant in common unable to profit indirectly from his murder of the other tenant in common where a joint life insurance policy was used by their building society to pay off the mortgage); [1991] Conv 48 (J. E. Martin).
20 In some cases, there may be a constructive trust. See H & M pp. 320–323.

no application can be made for financial provision under the Inheritance (Provision for Family and Dependants) Act 1975.[1]

Under the Forfeiture Act 1982[2] the court may make an order modifying the effect of the rule, except where there has been a conviction for murder. The application must be made within three months of the conviction, and the court must be satisfied that, having regard to the conduct of the offender and of the deceased and to such other circumstances as appear to it to be material, the justice of the case requires the effect of the rule to be so modified.[3] The Act expressly provides that the rule no longer precludes an application for financial provision under the 1975 Act.[4]

B. EFFECT OF A GENERAL DEVISE OF LAND

A devise of land is either specific or general.

A specific devise is a gift by will of a particular part of the testator's real estate and identified by a sufficient description, as for instance a gift of "my farm Blackacre" or of "all my lands in the parish of X".

A general devise is a gift of land which does not specify any particular part, but is couched in generic terms, as for instance a gift of "all my freehold lands".

(1) LEASEHOLDS

The rule before the Wills Act 1837 was that if a testator had both freeholds and leaseholds and made a devise of all his "land", the devise operated to pass only the freeholds.[5] If, however, he had leaseholds only, then they passed under the general gift. This rule was altered by that Act, which provides that a devise of land described in a general manner shall be construed to include the leasehold as well as the freehold interests unless a contrary intention appears in the will.[6] This enactment does not apply to entailed interests, which, despite the power of testamentary disposition given by the Law of Property Act 1925 to a tenant in tail in possession, are not caught by a general devise.[7]

(2) PROPERTY SUBJECT TO GENERAL POWER OF APPOINTMENT

Similarly, the rule before the Wills Act 1837 was that a general devise of land did not operate to pass land over which the testator had a power of appointment, unless he had no land other than that which was subject to the power.[8] This rule was altered by section 27, which provides that a general devise of land shall include estates over which a testator has "power to appoint in any manner he may think proper", and shall operate as an

---

1 *Re Royse* [1985] Ch 22, [1984] 3 All ER 339.
2 (1983) 46 MLR 66 (P. H. Kenny).
3 The relief can be total: *Re K*, supra (relief granted to loyal wife who having suffered repeated violence from her husband, killed him with a 12 bore shot gun which he had kept loaded for shooting rabbits; it went off when she was threatening him. She was convicted of manslaughter and put on probation for two years); [1985] All ER Rev 273 (C. H. Sherrin).
4 S. 3 (1), (2). See *Re Royse*, supra; [1984] All ER Rev 270 (C. H. Sherrin).
5 Carson, *Real Property Statutes* (3rd edn), p. 526.
6 Wills Act 1837, s. 26.
7 P. 263, ante.
8 Hawkins and Ryder, *Construction of Wills*, pp. 27 et seq.

execution of such power, unless a contrary intention shall appear by the will.[9] A similar rule is prescribed for a general bequest of personalty. The Act, it will be noticed, does not refer to a general as distinct from a special power, but to one which the donee may exercise without restriction. The power vested in the testator may not be "special" in the sense that it is exercisable in favour only of defined objects,[10] yet, if it in any manner limits his choice, as where it is exercisable in favour of any person in the world except himself[11] or his wife,[12] he cannot be described as entitled to appoint "in any manner he may think proper", and therefore section 27 is inapplicable.

It is a difficult question in practice to decide whether a general gift operates as an exercise of a special power of appointment. It is no doubt true:

> that in order to exercise a special power there must be a sufficient expression or indication of intention in the will or other instrument alleged to exercise it; and that either a reference to the power or a reference to the property subject to the power constitutes in general a sufficient indication for the purpose,[13]

but the problem is to determine whether the testator's language is sufficiently precise where he has referred neither to the power nor to its subject matter.[14]

C. EFFECT OF A GIFT OVER ON FAILURE OF ISSUE

(1) BEFORE 1837

The natural meaning of a devise of realty:

> to A, but if he shall die without issue, then to B,

is that A is to take a fee simple, which, if he has no children or other issue *at the time of his death*, is to go over to B. Before 1837, however, the courts construed such expressions as:

> die without issue; or
> die without leaving issue,

as meaning an indefinite failure of issue, i.e. that the estate given to A was to endure until his issue failed, no matter how long it might be before the failure occurred. The effect of this construction was that A took an estate tail by implication, with remainder to B and his heirs.[15] A could, therefore, bar the entail and so defeat both his issue and the remaindermen.

(2) WILLS ACT 1837

In order, therefore, to assimilate the legal and the natural meaning of the expression it was provided by the Wills Act 1837 that the words "die without issue" or "die without leaving issue", or any other words which import a failure of the issue of a person either at his death or at some indefinite time,

---

9 Wills Act 1837, s. 27; *Re Thirlwell* [1958] Ch 146, [1957] 3 All ER 465.
10 P. 299, ante.
11 *Re Park* [1932] 1 Ch 580; *Re Jones* [1945] Ch 105.
12 *Re Byron's Settlement* [1891] 3 Ch 474; cf *Re Harvey* [1950] 1 All ER 491, where the excepted appointee did not and could not exist.
13 *Re Ackerley* [1913] 1 Ch 510 at 515, per SARGANT J, adapting similar language used by BUCKLEY J in *Re Weston's Settlement* [1906] 2 Ch 620 at 624.
14 See *Re Knight* [1957] Ch 441, [1957] 2 All ER 252, and cases there cited.
15 A similar gift of personalty was construed to give A the absolute ownership since personalty was not entailable before 1926.

shall be construed to mean a want or failure in his lifetime, and not an indefinite failure.[16]

The effect of this enactment, which applies to gifts both of realty and personalty, if taken alone, is that in the example given above B becomes entitled to take the fee simple if A dies leaving no issue. But as this would mean that A could never know during his lifetime whether the fee simple given to him by the will was absolute or not, because of the possibility that his existing children might predecease him and so entitle B to take, further statutory alterations have been made.

(3) CONVEYANCING ACT 1882

The Conveyancing Act 1882,[17] enacted in the case of instruments coming into operation after 31 December 1882, that where there is a person entitled to land for an estate in fee, or for a term of years absolute, or for term of life *with an executory limitation over on failure of his issue* whether within a specified time or not, such executory limitation shall be void and become incapable of taking effect as soon as there is living any issue who has attained the age of 21 years. It will be noticed that this enactment applies only to land and that its operation is restricted to the interests specifically mentioned. It is still the governing enactment with regard to instruments coming into operation between 31 December 1882 and 31 December 1925.

(4) LAW OF PROPERTY ACT 1925

In furtherance of the general principle of assimilation it is now enacted for instruments coming into operation after 31 December 1925 that where there is a person entitled to:

   (a) an equitable interest in land for an estate in fee simple or for any less interest not being an entailed interest, or

   (b) any interest in other property, not being an entailed interest,

a gift over on failure of issue shall be void as soon as there is living any issue who has attained the age of 18 years.[18] This rule applies to deeds as well as to wills, and to all interests in property, whether real or personal, with the exception of entailed interests. The reason for excepting an entailed interest is that the gift over can, in any event, be defeated by disentailment. The reason for confining the rule to an *equitable* fee simple is that, under the modern law, a fee simple subject to a gift over cannot subsist as a legal estate, but is necessarily equitable.[19]

SECTION VI CONSTRUCTION OF WILLS

A. GENERAL RULE

The duty of a court which is called upon to construe a will is first to discover what was the intention of the testator as expressed by his will, and then to give effect to that intention. The fundamental rule is that the intention of a testator must be obeyed, however informal the language may be by which it

16 Wills Act 1837, s. 29.
17 S. 10.
18 LPA 1925, s. 134, as amended by Family Law Reform Act 1969, s. 1 (3), Sch. 1.
19 Ibid., s. 1 (1), (3). The land, being subject to a gift over, becomes settled land.

has been expressed;[20] but, though this principle has been asserted with vehemence from the earliest times, and has on various occasions been referred to as *the pole star, the sovereign guide,* and *the cardinal rule,* it is important to remember that in ascertaining intention the court considers the writing alone. It does not indulge in conjecture. It attributes to the written words their ordinary grammatical meaning, it gives to technical words, such as "heir", their technical meaning, and does not allow itself to be influenced by the probability that such could not have been the meaning intended by the testator.[1] For one thing, the facts known to the testator may not be before the court;[2] for another, it would be futile to require a will to be in writing if the clearly written wishes of the testator were to be open to revision after his death.

Although the primary rule is that the words in a will must normally be given their natural meaning—"the strict, plain, common meaning of the words themselves"[3]—the court may construe words in some special sense, if it is clear from the will itself that they are so used. In *Perrin v Morgan,*[4] the testatrix in a home-made will left "all moneys of which I die possessed". The strict legal meaning of money is cash and debts due, but the House of Lords held that the phrase included stocks and shares and personal property generally. As Viscount SIMON LC said:[5]

> The word "money" may be used to cover the whole of an individual's personal property—sometimes, indeed, all of a person's property, whether real or personal. "What has he done with his money?" may well be an inquiry as to the general contents of a rich man's will. Horace's satire at the expense of the fortune-hunter who attached himself to childless Roman matrons, has its modern equivalent in the saying: "It's her money he's after."

In some cases the court may invoke the "dictionary principle", where the testator has shown in his will that he has used a word in a particular sense and has in effect supplied his own dictionary; for example, he has included a definition clause in his will.[6]

B. EXTRINSIC EVIDENCE

Extrinsic evidence (i.e. evidence from outside the will itself) is in general inadmissible to contradict, add to or vary what the testator wrote.[7] There are, however, exceptions to this principle.

---

20 A statutory exception to this rule has been made by LPA 1925, s. 130, which provides that an entailed interest can be created only by formal words of limitation; p. 252, ante.
1 *Boyes v Cook* (1880) 14 Ch D 53.
2 *Ralph v Carrick* (1879) 11 Ch D 873 at 878.
3 *Shore v Wilson* (1842) 9 Cl & Fin 355 at 565.
4 [1943] AC 399, [1943] 1 All ER 187. On this judicial tendency toward a more liberal construction of wills, see [1976] 40 Conv NS 66 (C. H. Sherrin).
5 At 407, at 190. See also *Re Barnes' Will Trusts* [1972] 1 WLR 587, [1972] 2 All ER 639; *Re Gammon* [1986] CLY 3547 (money included freehold house).
6 *Hill v Crook* (1873) LR 6 HL 265 at 285; *Re Davidson* [1949] Ch 670, [1949] 2 All ER 551; *Re Cook* [1948] Ch 212 at 216, [1948] 1 All ER 231 at 233, where HARMAN J said: "Testators can make black mean white if they make the dictionary sufficiently clear."
7 *Earl of Newburgh v Countess of Newburgh* (1820) 5 Madd 364.

(1) WHERE THE TESTATOR DIES BEFORE 1983

(a) Addition or omission of words

If it is clear on the face of the will that he has not accurately or completely expressed his intention, the court will add words, provided that no person applying common sense can have any doubt what in fact he intended.[8] Similarly, it will omit words which have come in by inadvertence or misunderstanding, if their omission gives effect to the intention of the testator. Thus:

> where a solicitor drew up a codicil revoking the whole of clause 7 of the testator's will, but the revocation was only intended to apply to clause 7 (iv), the codicil was admitted to probate with the omission of the numeral 7.[9]

(b) Surrounding circumstances

Again, the words used by a testator refer to facts and circumstances within his knowledge concerning his property and the persons mentioned in his will, and therefore it would often be impossible to fulfil his intention unless extrinsic evidence were admissible. "You may place yourself, so to speak, in the testator's armchair, and consider the circumstances by which he was surrounded when he made his will to assist you in arriving at his intention."[10] As has been said: "When seated there, however, the court is not entitled to make a fresh will for the testator merely because it strongly suspects that he did not mean what he has plainly said."[11] In other words, "the function of a court of construction is not to declare the actual subjective intention of the testator, but the objective intention as expressed in his language."[12]

> Thus if a testator devises the house he lives in, or his farm called Blackacre, or the lands which he purchased of A, parol evidence must be adduced to show what house was occupied by the testator, what farm is called Blackacre, or what lands were purchased of A; such evidence being essential for the purpose of ascertaining the actual subject of disposition. The distinction obviously is that, although evidence *dehors* the will is not admissible to show that the testator used his terms of description in any peculiar or extraordinary sense, yet it may be adduced to ascertain what the description properly comprehends.[13]

Other cases where extrinsic evidence is admitted for the same reason occur where a testator uses nicknames in the will, or expressions which, though bearing a definite meaning in ordinary language, are used in a peculiar sense by persons of the class to which the testator belonged or in the locality where he dwelt.[14]

---

8 *Re Whitrick* [1957] 1 WLR 884, [1957] 2 All ER 467; and authorities there cited.
9 *Re Morris* [1971] P 62, [1970] 1 All ER 1057; *Re Phelan* [1972] Fam 33 (revocation clauses omitted); *Re Reynette-James* [1976] 1 WLR 161, [1975] 3 All ER 1037 (where typist omitted words which significantly altered construction of clause in will, held that the gift in that clause was to be omitted from probate).
10 *Boyes v Cook* (1880) 14 Ch D 53 at 56, per JAMES LJ.
11 *Perrin v Morgan* [1943] AC 399 at 420, [1943] 1 All ER 187 at 197, per Lord ROMER.
12 (1963) 26 MLR, p. 357 (M. Albery).
13 *Jarman on Wills* (8th edn), p. 522.
14 Ibid., p. 515.

(c) Equivocation

Further, parol evidence is admissible to explain an equivocation. The word *equivocation* in this connection means that although the devise is on the face of it perfect and intelligible, yet an ambiguity arises making it hard to determine which of two persons or things the testator meant to denote, since the words of the will point equally well to either. An early instance of such a latent ambiguity was where:[15]

> a testator devised one house to George Gord the son of George Gord, a second to George Gord the son of John Gord, and a third to "George Gord the son of Gord". It was held that evidence of the testator's declarations were admissible to show that he intended by this last description to indicate George Gord the son of George Gord.

(d) Limits to admissibility of extrinsic evidence

But although extrinsic evidence is admissible in such cases, it is never admitted to prove that words which are perfectly clear in themselves were intended by the testator to bear some different meaning. If a will bears a definite construction it cannot have another different construction imposed upon it by extrinsic evidence, for there is a fundamental distinction between evidence which is simply explanatory of the words of a will and evidence which is designed to prove intention itself as an independent fact.[16] This was explained by Lord CAVE in the following manner:[17]

> No doubt a court, called upon to construe a will, is entitled to know the facts which the testator knew, and to use that knowledge for the purpose of resolving doubts as to the identity of persons or things mentioned in the will, or of assigning a meaning to expressions which otherwise would have no adequate or intelligible sense....
>
> But it is quite another thing to say that when a testator has used an unambiguous expression such as *"my brothers and sisters"*, extrinsic evidence can be adduced to show that he must have intended the expression to refer to brothers and sisters already born. That would be to use the facts, not as evidence of identity, but as evidence of intention; and such a use of them would be contrary to settled principles of construction.

(2) WHERE A TESTATOR DIES AFTER 1982

(a) Interpretation of wills

Section 21 of the Administration of Justice Act 1982 sets out a comprehensive list of the circumstances in which extrinsic evidence is admissible to assist in the interpretation of the will of a testator who dies after 1982. Such evidence, *including evidence of the testator's intention*, may be admitted in three situations:

> (*a*) in so far as any part of the will is meaningless;
> (*b*) in so far as the language used in any part of it is ambiguous on the face of it;
> (*c*) in so far as evidence, other than evidence of the testator's intention, shows that

---

15 *Doe d Gord v Needs* (1836) 2 M & W 129; *Re Jackson* [1933] Ch 237. But see *Re Mayo* [1901] 1 Ch 404.
16 *Re Grainger* [1900] 2 Ch 756 at 763–4, per RIGBY LJ; reversed sub nom *Higgins v Dawson* [1902] AC 1 at 10.
17 *Ward v Van der Loeff* [1924] AC 653 at 663–4; p. 295, ante.

the language used in any part of it is ambiguous in the light of the surrounding circumstances.

The section is an extension of the previous rules in that direct evidence of the testator's intention was never admissible in the circumstances of paragraphs (*a*) and (*b*), and only sometimes admissible in those of paragraph (*c*).[18]

In *Re Williams*[19] the court took a rather broad view of what is meant by ambiguity for the purposes of the section. In that case:

> the testatrix made a short home-made will seven days before she died. In it she listed twenty-five names in three groups without words of gift or any indication as to what proportion of her estate they were to receive. The question arose as to whether a letter written by the testatrix to her solicitors on the day before she made her will was admissible to assist in its interpretation.

It was held that the will was ambiguous on the face of it and that the letter was admissible. In fact the letter provided no such assistance, and it was held that the estate should be divided equally between all 25.

NICHOLLS J said:[20]

> The evidence may assist by showing which of two or more possible meanings a testator was attaching to a particular word or phrase. "My effects" and "my money" are obvious examples. That meaning may be one which, without recourse to the extrinsic evidence, would not really have been apparent at all. So long as that meaning is one which the word or phrase read in its context is capable of bearing, then the court may conclude that, assisted by the extrinsic evidence, that is its correct construction. But if, however liberal may be the approach of the court, the meaning is one which the word or phrase cannot bear, I do not see how in carrying out a process of construction—or interpretation, to use the word employed in section 21—the court can declare that meaning to be the meaning of the word or phrase. Such a conclusion, varying or contradicting the language used, would amount to rewriting part of the will, and that is a result to be achieved, if at all, under the rectification provisions in section 20. . . . Again, if extrinsic evidence shows that a testator was unclear, or undecided, on what he meant by the ambiguous word or phrase, I do not see how that can require or enable the court to reject the word or phrase altogether if the court is able to construe the word or phrase without the aid of extrinsic evidence.

The words "clerical error" mean an error made in the process of recording the intended words of a testator in the drafting or transcription of a will. They have been held to include the omission by a solicitor to reproduce in a will a power of appointment from an earlier will.[1]

(b) Rectification of wills

As we have seen, the equitable doctrine of rectification applies to non-testamentary documents.[2] Section 20 of the Administration of Justice Act 1982 introduced a limited statutory power to rectify a will, where a testator

---

18 See the useful account in *Williams on Wills*, pp. 492–495.
19 [1985] 1 WLR 905, [1985] 1 All ER 964, *Williams on Wills*, p. 494, n. (n) suggests that the provisions might be "meaningless" within para (*a*); [1985] All ER Rev 270 (C. H. Sherrin).
20 At 911, at 969.
1 *Wordingham v Royal Exchange Trust Co Ltd* [1992] Ch 412, [1992] 3 All ER 204; [1992] All ER Rev 401 (C. H. Sherrin).
2 P. 138, ante.

dies after 1982. The court must be satisfied that the will fails to carry out the testator's intentions, in consequence:

(*a*) of a clerical error;[3] or

(*b*) of a failure to understand his instructions.

Application must be made within six months from the date on which representation was first taken out, unless the court permits an extension of time. Protection is given to the personal representatives by providing that after the end of the six months they can distribute without taking into account the possibility that the court might extend this time limit, but this provision does not prejudice any power to recover assets by reason of the court's order.

C. CLASS GIFTS. RULES OF CONVENIENCE

Where there is a gift to a class, e.g. to the children of X, certain rules of construction have been established for the ascertainment of the class.[4] The object of the rules, which are sometimes known as the rule in *Andrews v Partington*,[5] is to enable the donees to know their shares and the executors to distribute the estate at the earliest possible moment.[6] We have already seen their operation in the context of the rule against perpetuities,[7] but it is important to understand that their primary purpose is to facilitate the distribution of the estate and that it is only incidentally that they may save a gift from invalidity under that rule. Thus, in the case of a gift to the children of X, prima facie all those in existence at the death of the testator take, so that those who predecease the testator and those who are born after his death are excluded. If, however, no child of A is alive at the testator's death the class remains open and all after-born children will be included.[8] Further, where there is a gift to X for life, then to such of X's children who shall attain the age of 21, the class closes at the death of X, or when the eldest child becomes 21, whichever event happens last.[9] If, however, there are no children alive when X dies, the class closes when the eldest child becomes 21, and after-born children are excluded.[10] Finally, it must be noticed that these rules are rules of construction only. They may be excluded by the testator's express direction or where they are inconsistent with the context of his will, and it seems that the courts are becoming less reluctant to find that inconsistency.[11]

---

3 This is not limited to the error of a clerk. "A testator writing out or typing his own will can make a clerical error just as much as someone else writing out or typing a will for him": per NICHOLLS J in *Re Williams*, supra, at 912, at 969.

4 For a full and valuable account of the technical class-closing rules, see (1954) 70 LQR 61 (J. H. C. Morris); Morris and Leach, *The Rule against Perpetuities* (2nd edn, and Supplement), pp. 109 et seq; [1958] CLJ 39 (S. J. Bailey); *Theobald on Wills* (11th edn), chapter 32; Maudsley, *Modern Law of Perpetuities*, pp. 17–25.

5 (1791) 3 Bro CC 401.

6 The rules apply to all forms of property, and to settlements as well as to wills.

7 Pp. 288–9, ante.

8 *Weld v Bradbury* (1715) 2 Vern 705; *Re Ransome* [1957] Ch 348 at 359, per UPJOHN J.

9 *Re Emmet's Estate* (1880) 13 Ch D 484.

10 *Re Bleckly* [1951] Ch 740, [1951] 1 All ER 1064.

11 See the cases cited, p. 298, n. 12, ante.

D. STATUTORY MEANING OF CHILD

Finally, we may notice that legislation has changed the long established rule of construction that "the description 'child', 'son', 'issue', every word of that species must be taken prima facie to mean legitimate child, son or issue".[12]

Firstly, section 15 of the Family Law Reform Act 1969 provides that in the case of dispositions made after 1969 reference to any child or other relation shall, unless a contrary intention appears, include a reference to any illegitimate child and to any person related through an illegitimate person. And there are similar provisions relating to legitimated[13] and adopted persons.[14]

Secondly, the Family Law Reform Act 1987[15] provides that, in the case of dispositions made after 3 April 1988, references to any relationship between two persons shall, unless the contrary intention appears, be construed in accordance with the general principle of the Act that it is immaterial whether or not a person's parents have or had been married to each other at any time.[16] This effectively means that, for example:

> a gift to the testator's son will extend to the illegitimate son, and that a gift to his grandchild will extend to any child of his own child, irrespective of whether the testator or his child have themselves been married.

SECTION VII REVOCATION OF WILLS

A will is revoked in any of the following ways:

A. SUBSEQUENT MARRIAGE OF TESTATOR

Marriage, since it raises a moral obligation to provide for the new family, requires a reconsideration of any testamentary gifts that may have already been made by either party. At common law, subsequent marriage revoked the will of a woman, but not that of a man, since in any event his wife was adequately provided for under the law of dower.

It is enacted, however, by section 18 (1) of the Wills Act 1837 that a will made by a man or a woman shall be revoked by his or her marriage.[17] There are two exceptions to this rule.

(i) Power of appointment The first derives from the postulate that it is useless to invalidate a prior will if in the result no benefit will accrue to the testator's family. The Act, therefore, provides that the testamentary exercise of a

12 *Wilkinson v Adam* (1813) 1 Ves & B 422, per Lord ELDON LC.
13 See Legitimacy Act 1976, s. 5 (2).
14 Adoption Act 1976, s. 39.
15 S. 1 (1). See Law Commission Reports: Illegitimacy 1982 (Law Com No. 118, HC 98); Illegitimacy (Second Report) 1986 (Law Com No. 157, Cmnd 9913); [1988] Conv 410 (G. Miller).
16 The Act extends to entailed interests: s. 19 (2); but not to titles of honour: s. 19 (4). Succession to the throne is also unaffected by the Act.
17 Wills Act 1837, s. 18 (replaced as regards wills made after 1982 by AJA 1982, s. 18). And this is so even if the marriage is voidable for lack of consent under Matrimonial Causes Act 1973, s. 12: *Re Roberts* [1978] 1 WLR 653, [1978] 3 All ER 225.

power of appointment shall not be revoked by the testator's subsequent marriage, unless the property if unappointed would go to his heir, executor, administrator or the persons entitled on intestacy.[18]

(ii) Contemplation of marriage Secondly, the Law of Property Act 1925 provides[19] that a will expressed to be made *in contemplation of marriage* shall not be revoked by the solemnization of the marriage contemplated.[20] To escape revocation, however, the will must be expressed to be made in contemplation of marriage to a particular person, and moreover it must be followed by the solemnization of that marriage.[1]

The will must contain an expression which sufficiently shows that the will as a whole[2] was made in contemplation of the particular marriage solemnized. This may be in express terms, but the section is satisfied if the will as a whole is made in favour of "my fiancée" X,[3] or, probably, of "my wife" Y.[4]

If the will is made after 1982,[5] it need only appear from the will that the testator was "expecting to be married to a particular person" and that he intended that the will, or a particular disposition in it, should not be revoked by the marriage. Section 18 also provides that, where there is a particular disposition in the will, that disposition is not revoked, nor is any other disposition in the will, unless it appears from the will that the testator intended the disposition to be revoked by the marriage.

B. DISSOLUTION OR ANNULMENT OF MARRIAGE OF TESTATOR

Under the Wills Act 1837 the dissolution or annulment of the testator's marriage had no effect on his will. Section 18A[6] now provides that, where a testator dies after 1982, the dissolution or annulment causes the lapse of any devise or bequest to the former spouse, unless the will shows a contrary intention. Where a life interest to the former spouse so lapses, any remainder is accelerated. In *Re Sinclair*[7] the Court of Appeal held that the word "lapse"

---

18 Ibid. *Re Gilligan* [1950] P 32. The language of this exception in the original s. 18 is outdated, referring to "heir, customary heir" and "Statutes of Distribution". See AEA 1925, s. 50(1); p. 875, post.
19 S. 177 (1).
20 *Pilot v Gainfort* [1931] P 103.
1 *Sallis v Jones* [1936] P 43; *Re Langston* [1953] P 100, [1953] 1 All ER 928.
2 And not merely parts of it: *Re Coleman* [1976] Ch 1, [1975] 1 All ER 675.
3 *Re Langston*, supra; *Re Coleman*, supra, where the authorities are reviewed by MEGARRY J. See also (1975) 39 Conv (NS) 121 (R. J. Edwards and B. F. J. Langstaff).
4 *Pilot v Gainfort* [1931] P 103; criticised in *Re Coleman*, supra.
5 S. 18, as substituted by AJA 1982, s. 18; based on the recommendations of the Law Reform Committee 22nd Report on The Making and Revocation of Wills 1980 (Cmnd 7902), paras 3.13–3.18.
6 Inserted by AJA 1982, s. 18; based on the recommendations of the Law Reform Committee 22nd Report, supra, para. 3.26–3.38. The lapse does not prejudice an application by the former spouse under the Inheritance (Provision for Family and Dependants) Act 1975, p. 827, ante.
7 [1985] Ch 446, [1985] 1 All ER 1066; reversing *Re Cherrington* [1984] 1 WLR 772, [1984] 2 All ER 285. The Law Commission has recommended that, subject to any contrary intention, any property devised or bequested to the former spouse should pass as if the former spouse had pre-deceased the testator. The former spouse is deemed to have died on the date when the marriage was dissolved or annulled: The Effect of Divorce on Wills 1993 (Law Com No. 217, Cm 2322).

meant simply "fail", and did not have its technical meaning of "failure by reason of the death of the legatee during the lifetime of the testator".[8] In that case:

the testator made a will in 1958, leaving property to his wife, but, if she failed to survive him, then to Imperial Cancer Research. A divorce took place in 1962. The testator died in 1983, survived by his wife. It was held that the property did not pass to the charity, but went on intestacy. The wife had in fact survived the testator, and section 18A could not be construed as a deeming provision directing that the other provisions of the will should take effect as if she had died in the testator's lifetime.

C. LATER WILL OR CODICIL

A will may be revoked by a later will or codicil, provided that the later instrument observes the formalities required by law for the execution of a valid will.[9]

(1) EXPRESS REVOCATION

A will or a codicil may revoke a prior will either by an express clause of revocation or by disposing of property in a manner inconsistent with a previous devise. The first method requires no comment, except that there is no technical rule as to the words necessary to operate as a revocation or as to the extent of the revocation, the question being simply one of intention.[10] The usual practice is, however, for a testator to use the simple formula:

I hereby revoke all former wills, codicils and testamentary instruments made by me, and declare this to be my last will.

(2) IMPLIED REVOCATION

As regards a later disposition of property inconsistent with one made in a prior will, we must note that the mere use of the words "last will" does not necessarily revoke a former will.[11] A will may consist of several independent instruments executed at different times, and where a testator expresses his intention in several instruments without having executed an express clause of revocation, the earlier instruments are revoked by implication in so far, but only in so far, as they are inconsistent with the later ones.

The mere fact of making a subsequent testamentary paper does not work a total revocation of a prior one, unless the latter expressly or in effect revokes the former, or the two be incapable of standing together; for though it be a maxim . . . that no man can die with two testaments, yet any number of instruments, whatever be their relative date, or in whatever form they may be (so as they be all clearly testamentary), may be admitted to probate, as together containing the last will of the deceased.[12]

8 See e.g. Wills Act 1837, ss. 32, 33; p. 849, ante.
9 Wills Act 1837, s. 20.
10 *Cotterell v Cotterell* (1872) LR 2 P & D 397 at 399; *Lowthorpe-Lutwidge v Lowthorpe-Lutwidge* [1935] P 151.
11 *Simpson v Foxon* [1907] P 54.
12 *Williams on Executors and Administrators* (5th edn), p. 140, adopted *Lemage v Goodban* (1865) LR 1 P & D 57 at 62; *Re Plant* [1952] Ch 298, [1952] 1 All ER 78 n. See Williams, Mortimer and Sunnucks, *Executors, Administrators and Probate* p. 194.

If, for instance:

a testator, having devised Blackacre to A in fee, by a subsequent will devises it to B in fee, the former devise is obviously revoked; but if he devises Blackacre to C in fee and then, by codicil, devises it to the first son of D who shall attain the age of 21 years, the first devise is revoked only to the extent necessary to give effect to the executory interest, so that C will take the fee simple until the son of D attains the required age.[13]

(3) DOCTRINE OF DEPENDENT RELATIVE REVOCATION

If, however, a subsequent and inconsistent gift, which, if valid, would override a prior gift, fails by reason of the rule against perpetuities or for any other reason, it does not operate as a revocation unless an independent and clear intention to revoke is expressed.[14] This is known as the doctrine of dependent relative revocation.[15]

The revocation is relative to the new gift, and if the gift fails the revocation fails also, unless the testator clearly shows in the later instrument that he intends in any event to revoke the earlier will.[16]

In other words, the revocation of the prior gift is conditional on the effectiveness of its substitute. This doctrine applies even where there is an express clause of revocation in the later instrument, for at bottom the question is always one of intention, but in this case a heavy burden lies upon those who allege that what was expressly prescribed was intended to be conditional upon the validity of the substituted gift.[17]

If the court is satisfied that such was the testator's intention, it may in certain circumstances spell one composite will out of the two that he has executed. This solution was reached on the following facts:

By the earlier will the testatrix appointed X executor, made certain bequests and left the residue of her estate to X absolutely. By the later will, she revoked all previous wills, appointed X executor, made certain bequests which were entirely inconsistent with those contained in the earlier will, and then left the residuary clause incomplete so that in fact the residue was undisposed of.

It was held that she had inserted the revocation clause in the mistaken belief that she had disposed of the whole of her estate, and that therefore the later will, omitting the revocation clause, and the earlier will, omitting the bequests, must both be admitted to probate as together constituting the true last will of the testatrix.[18]

13 *Duffield v Duffield* (1829) 1 Dow Cl 268; cf. *Re Baker* [1929] 1 Ch 668; *Re Pearson* [1963] 1 WLR 1358, [1963] 3 All ER 763.
14 *Ward v Van der Loeff* [1924] AC 653; p. 295, ante; (the revocation of the gift in the will was held to be related to and dependent on the validity of the gift in the codicil. That was void for perpetuity, and the gift in the will therefore was not revoked); *Re Robinson* [1930] 2 Ch 332; *Re Hawksley's Settlement* [1934] Ch 384 at 400–1; *Re Hope Brown* [1942] P 136, [1942] 2 All ER 176.
15 See *Re Hope Brown*, supra, at 138 where LANGTON J said "The name of this doctrine seems to me to be somewhat overloaded with polysyllables ... The whole matter can be quite simply expressed by the word 'conditional'".
16 *Ward v Van der Loeff*, supra, at 656, per JENKINS KC arguendo. See (1955) 71 LQR 374 (F. H. Newark).
17 *Re Murray* [1956] 1 WLR 605, [1956] 2 All ER 353.
18 *Re Cocke* [1960] 1 WLR 491, [1960] 2 All ER 289.

D. INSTRUMENT OF REVOCATION

The Wills Act 1837 provides that revocation may be effected not only by a later will or codicil duly executed, but also "by *some writing* declaring an intention to revoke" a will. A writing, however, is ineffectual to cause revocation unless it is executed in accordance with the formalities prescribed by the Act.[19]

Such a writing may be, for example, by a codicil,[20] a memorandum on the will,[1] a letter,[2] or a declaration of intention to revoke.[3]

E. DESTRUCTION *ANIMO REVOCANDI*

Section 20 of the Wills Act 1837 provides that a will may be revoked:

> by the burning, tearing, or otherwise destroying the same by the testator, or by some person in his presence and by his direction, with the intention of revoking the same.

(1) PHYSICAL DESTRUCTION

It will be seen that two distinct things must occur if a will is to be revoked by destruction. There must be the physical act of destruction[4] and the mental act of the intention to revoke.

> All the destroying in the world without intention will not revoke a will, nor all the intention in the world without destroying: there must be the two.[5]

Again, the act of destruction, if not carried out by the testator, must be carried out in his presence by some person acting under his direction.[6] Destruction without intention, intention without destruction, destruction with intention but carried out in the absence of the testator, none of these is operative to produce revocation.

Thus in one case:

> a testator drew his pen through parts of his will, wrote on the back of it "this will is revoked" and threw it into the waste-paper basket. A servant later rescued it and placed it on the table where it was found seven years later at the testator's death.

The will was admitted to probate. It had not been revoked by a signed and attested writing, neither had it been physically destroyed. Indeed, had the servant burnt the contents of the basket, there would have been no destruction within the meaning of the Act.[7] If the testator destroys part of a will, that

---

19 Wills Act 1837, s. 20.
20 *Brenchley v Still* (1850) 2 Rob Eccl 162.
1 *Re Hicks* (1869) LR 1 P & D 683.
2 *Re Durance* (1872) LR 2 P & D 406 (letter to brother); *Re Spracklan's Estate* [1938] 2 All ER 345 (letter to bank manager).
3 *Toomer v Sobinska* [1907] P 106.
4 The test for destruction by obliteration under s. 20 is the same as that for revocation of part of a will under s. 21; p. 838, ante: *Re Adams* [1990] Ch 601, [1990] 2 All ER 97 (signatures of testatrix and witnesses impossible to read having been heavily scored out by ballpoint pen).
5 *Cheese v Lovejoy* (1877) 2 PD 251 at 253.
6 *Re Dadds* (1857) Dea Sw 290.
7 *Cheese v Lovejoy*, supra; *Stephens v Taprell* (1840) 2 Curt 458 (writing cancellation across will held not to be revocation).

part only will be revoked,[8] unless the mutilation is such as to raise an inference that it was done *animo revocandi* of the whole will.[9]

(2) INTENTION TO REVOKE

The physical act of destruction is in itself inconclusive, and it may be necessary to show whether it was accompanied by the *animus revocandi* or not. For this purpose extrinsic evidence is admissible. Thus, if a testator has destroyed a will in a fit of drunkenness[10] or of insanity[11] or under the mistaken impression that it is useless,[12] parol evidence of his declarations, his capacity or his conduct may be adduced in order to show that the necessary intention to revoke was wanting.

Where a will has been traced to the possession of the testator but cannot be found at his death, there is a presumption that the will was destroyed by the testator with the intention of revoking it.[13] The presumption, however, may be rebutted by evidence of non-revocation.[14]

(3) DOCTRINE OF DEPENDENT RELATIVE REVOCATION

The doctrine of dependent relative revocation is also applicable[15] where a testator destroys his will *animo revocandi*. His intention to revoke may be conditional and not absolute. He may, for example, intend to revoke his will only if he executes a new will, in which case the old will remains valid even if the new will is never executed. Whether the intention to revoke is conditional or absolute is a question of fact to be decided upon all the evidence. The mere intention of a testator to make a new will at the time when he destroys his existing will is not sufficient in itself to raise the inference that revocation of the old will was intended to be conditional on the subsequent execution of a new will.[16]

The doctrine also operates where the act of destruction is conditional upon an assumption that is in fact false,[17] as for example that a new will is valid;[18] that the effect is to revive a former will;[19] or that the beneficiary under the destroyed will is entitled to equal benefits if the testator dies intestate.[20]

> If the truth of a particular fact is a condition of the destruction, and the facts turns out not to be true, there is no revocation.[1]

8 *Re Woodward* (1871) LR 2 P & D 206 (seven or eight lines excised from will written on seven sheets); *Re Everest* [1975] Fam 44, [1975] 1 All ER 672 (lower half of first page cut away).
9 *Leonard v Leonard* [1902] P 243 (first two out of five sheets destroyed).
10 *Re Brassington* [1902] P 1.
11 *Re Hine* [1893] P 282.
12 *Beardsley v Lacey* (1897) 78 LT 25; *Re Southerden's Estate* [1925] P 177.
13 *Welch v Phillips* (1836) 1 Moo PCC 299 at 232, per Lord WENSLEYDALE.
14 *Re Davies* (1978) Times, 23 May; *Re Dickson* (1984) 81 LSG 3012.
15 P 862, ante. For an exhaustive review of the doctrine, see *Re Finnemore* [1991] 1 WLR 793, [1992] 1 All ER 800 (revocation clause treated as distributive (i.e. relative absolutely to some dispositions, but conditionally to others)); [1992] All ER Rev 399 (C. H. Sherrin).
16 *Re Jones* [1976] Ch 200, [1976] 1 All ER 593.
17 *Re Feis* [1964] Ch 106, [1963] 3 All ER 303.
18 *Onions v Tyrer* (1716) 1 P Wms 343 at 345.
19 *Powell v Powell* (1866) LR 1 P & D 209; *Re Bridgewater* [1965] 1 WLR 416, [1965] 1 All ER 717.
20 *Re Southerden's Estate* [1925] P 177. See *Re Jones*, supra, at 209, at 599; *Re Carey* (1977) 121 SJ 173 (where testator destroyed will under erroneous belief that he no longer had anything to leave and conditional on that belief).
1 Ibid., at 184, per WARRINGTON LJ.

F. REVOCATION OF PRIVILEGED WILL

The will of a soldier, sailor or airman may be revoked by an informal act, expressing an intention to revoke, provided that the conditions at the time of revocation are the same as those required for the validation of such a will. In particular the strict rules for revocation by destruction do not apply. For instance:

> a soldier before proceeding to South Africa on active service left his will with his fiancée, but in consequence of certain statements made as to her conduct wrote from that country instructing her to hand the will to his sister, which she did. Later, in accordance with his written request, the sister burnt the will and it was held that this was a sufficient revocation notwithstanding that the destruction did not take place in the testator's presence.[2]

G. REVIVAL OF WILL

It is provided by the Wills Act 1837 that a will which has been revoked cannot be revived unless the testator re-executes it with the proper formalities, or unless he executes a codicil showing an intention to revive the will.[3] The object of this enactment was to abolish implied revivals, for under the law prior to 1837 a revoked will was presumed to be revived if the will which effected the revocation was itself later revoked. Now, however, the intention to revive the revoked will must appear on the face of the later instrument, either by express words referring to a will as revoked and importing an intention to revive the same, or by some expression conveying to the mind of the court with reasonable certainty the existence of the intention.[4]

2 *Re Gossage* [1921] P 194.
3 Wills Act 1837, s. 22.
4 *Re Steele's Goods* (1868) LR 1 P & D 575; *Goldie v Adam* [1938] P 85, [1938] 1 All ER 586; *Re Davis's Estate* [1952] P 279, [1952] 2 All ER 509; *Re Pearson* [1963] 1 WLR 1358, [1963] 3 All ER 763. The doctrine of dependent relative revocation may also apply in the case of revival; see (1981) 125 SJ 351 (S. M.).

Chapter 25

Intestacy[1]

SUMMARY

SECTION I APPOINTMENT OF THE ADMINISTRATOR AND HIS GENERAL POWERS

A. GRANT OF ADMINISTRATION

When a person dies testate having appointed executors in his will, the estate is administered, as we have seen, by the executors. If, however, he dies intestate, or, though testate, fails to appoint executors, it is necessary to make application to the court for the appointment of personal representatives. When the court does this, it is said to grant administration, or more fully, to grant letters of administration, and the personal representative to whom the grant is made is called an administrator.

The property of the deceased, both real and personal, passes to an administrator upon his appointment by the court to the same extent as it passes to an executor, but in the interval between the death of the deceased and the appointment of an administrator both the real and personal estate of the deceased vests in the Probate Judge, i.e. the President of the Family Division of the High Court until administration is granted.[2]

---

1 See generally Sherrin and Bonehill, *Law and Practice of Intestate Succession*; Williams, Mortimer and Sunnucks, *Executors, Administrators and Probate*; Miller, *The Machinery of Succession*, chapter 5.
2 AEA 1925, ss. 9, 55 (1) (xv), as amended by Administration of Justice Act 1970, s. 1, Sch. 2, para. 5. See *Wirral Borough Council v Smith* (1982) 43 P & CR 312; *Practice Direction* [1965] 1 WLR 1237, [1965] 3 All ER 230.
  The Law Commission recommends that the Public Trustee should replace the President of the Family Division: Law Commission Report on Title on Death 1989 (Law Com No. 184), para. 2.24–2.26: [1990] Conv 72 (H. W. Wilkinson). See Law of Property (Miscellaneous Provisions) Bill (HL Bill 46), clauses 14 and 19.

B. WHO MAY BE APPOINTED ADMINISTRATORS

The first question that requires consideration is this: To what persons will the court grant letters of administration? The Non-Contentious Probate Rules 1987 set out a list of persons who are entitled to the grant, in order of priority;[3] but the court may appoint as an administrator such a person as it thinks fit, if by reason of any special circumstances it appears to the court to be necessary or expedient;[4] for example, where the estate is insolvent, or where land has been settled by the intestate in his lifetime. In the latter case the grant of administration might be given to the trustees of the settlement if they were willing to act.[5]

Representation is not to be granted to more than four persons in regard to the same property, and where any beneficiary is an infant, or a life interest arises, administration must be granted either to a trust corporation (with or without an individual) or to not less than two individuals, unless it appears to the court to be expedient in all the circumstances to appoint an individual as sole administrator.[6]

The court may limit its grant in any way it thinks fit.[7] For instance, it may grant representation in respect of the realty separately from the personalty, or in respect of a trust estate alone, or in respect of the realty alone if there is no personal estate.

C. TITLE OF ADMINISTRATOR

An administrator, unlike an executor, derives his title solely from the grant of letters, and until he receives the grant he is not entitled to deal with the estate of the deceased. But in order that no wrong may go without a remedy, it has been the rule from the earliest times that the administrator's title upon his appointment relates back to the death of the intestate, so that he may maintain trespass against a wrongdoer who has interfered with the estate of the deceased between the death and the grant of administration.[8] Although this rule is more often of importance in the case of goods, it applies equally to wrongs committed against land.[9]

The death of an administrator before the administration has begun or been

3 Non-Contenious Probate Rules 1987 (S.I. 1987 No. 2024) r. 22. The order in priority of rights to a grant of administration is as follows: (1) husband or wife; (2) children or other issue of deceased taking *per stirpes*; (3) father or mother; (4) brothers and sisters of the whole blood, or the issue of the whole blood taking *per stirpes*; (5) brothers and sisters of the half blood, or the issue of deceased brothers and sisters of the half blood taking *per stirpes*; (6) grand-parents; (7) uncles and aunts of the whole blood, or the issue of deceased uncles and aunts of the whole blood taking *per stirpes*; (8) uncles and aunts of the half blood, or the issue of deceased uncles and aunts of the half blood taking *per stirpes*; (9) the Crown; (10) creditors.
4 Supreme Court Act 1981, s. 116, replacing the more detailed provisions of Supreme Court of Judicature (Consolidation) Act 1925, s. 162. For the power of the court to appoint substitutes for, or to remove, personal representatives, see AJA 1985, s. 50.
5 See also *Re Edwards-Taylor's Goods* [1951] P 24, [1950] 2 All ER 446.
6 Supreme Court Act 1981, s. 114.
7 Ibid., s. 113, replacing the more detailed provisions of Supreme Court of Judicature (Consolidation) Act 1925, s. 155.
8 *Tharpe v Stallwood* (1843) 12 LJ CP 241.
9 *Re Pryse* [1904] P 301.

completed necessitates the appointment of another person, for the office does not devolve on death as does that of an executor.[10]

D. POWERS OF ADMINISTRATOR

An administrator, as we have said, has the same powers with regard to the administration of the estate as are possessed by executors, but a new departure was made by the Administration of Estates Act 1925, by vesting in him a statutory trust for sale. This is required because the property of the intestate is usually distributable in shares among the beneficial successors, and it has the added advantage of enabling the administrator to make an overreaching conveyance of land. It is expressly enacted that upon the death of a person intestate his real and personal estate shall be held by his personal representatives:

(a) as to the real estate upon trust to sell the same; and
(b) as to the personal estate upon trust to call in, sell and convert into money such part thereof as may not consist of money.[11]

The administrator, however, has full power to postpone the sale for such period as he may think proper. He is not to sell any reversionary interest until it falls into possession unless there is some special reason to justify the sale, neither is he to sell personal chattels unless they are required for purposes of administration owing to a deficiency of other assets, or unless there is some other special reason for the sale.[12]

The Administration of Estates Act defines personal chattels as meaning:[13]

carriages, horses,[14] stable furniture and effects (not used for business purposes),[15] motor cars and accessories (not used for business purposes), garden effects, domestic animals, plate, plated articles, linen, china, glass, books, pictures, prints, furniture,[1] jewellery,[2] articles of household or personal use[3] or ornament, musical and scientific instruments and apparatus, wines, liquors and consumable stores, but do not include any chattels used at the death of the intestate for business purposes nor money or securities for money.

E. RESIDUARY ESTATE OF INTESTATE

The administrator must use the money arising from the sale, and also any ready money that the intestate may have left, in discharging the funeral, testamentary and administration expenses, and the debts due from the

10 P. 843, ante.
11 AEA 1925, s. 33 (1).
12 Ibid.
13 Ibid., s. 55 (1) (x).
14 *Re Hutchinson* [1955] Ch 255, [1955] 1 All ER 689.
15 For meaning of "business", see *Re Ogilby* [1942] Ch 288, [1942] 1 All ER 524.
 1 *Re Crispin's Will Trusts* [1975] Ch 245, [1974] 3 All ER 772 (long case and bracket clocks).
 2 *Re Whitby* [1944] Ch 210, [1944] 1 All ER 299.
 3 *Re Reynolds' Will Trusts* [1966] 1 WLR 19, [1965] 3 All ER 686 (stamp collection kept as a hobby); (1966) 82 LQR 18 (R.E.M.); cf *Re Collin's Will Trusts* [1971] 1 WLR 37, [1971] 1 All ER 283; *Re Chaplin* [1950] Ch 507, [1950] 2 All ER 155 (small yacht used for family purposes); *Re Crispin's Will Trusts*, supra (clocks and watches worth £50,000).

estate.[4] During the minority of any person beneficially entitled and pending the final distribution of the estate the administrator may invest in authorised securities[5] so much of the money as is not required for the payment of debts.[6]

After all the debts have been paid, the residue of the money arising from sale and any investments which may have been made, and any property which may have been retained unsold, are together called *the residuary estate of the intestate*.[7] It is this estate that is distributed among the persons who are entitled to succeed to the property of the intestate.

SECTION II DISTRIBUTION OF THE RESIDUARY ESTATE OF THE INTESTATE

A. INTRODUCTORY NOTE

(1) ASSIMILATION OF REAL TO PERSONAL PROPERTY

A far-reaching reform of the law governing the beneficial distribution of the property of an intestate dying after 1925 was effected by the Administration of Estates Act 1925. Before 1926 the destination of the property varied according as it consisted of freehold estates of inheritance or of leaseholds and chattels personal. The rules of descent relating to the fee simple and the fee tail depended partly upon the common law and partly upon statute; the rules by which leaseholds and chattels personal were distributed depended entirely upon statutes, the chief of which were the Statutes of Distribution of 1670 and 1685. The Administration of Estates Act 1925, however, abolished the law of descent so far as it related to the fee simple, and introduced a new scheme of distribution which applies both to realty and to personalty. This scheme is not the same as that laid down for chattels by the Statutes of Distribution. Those statutes have been swept away, and a fresh start has been made.

(2) PRE-1926 RULES MAY STILL APPLY

Unfortunately, however, there are four situations where the canons of descent in respect of the fee simple that prevailed before 1926 may still be applicable.

(a) Old titles

The investigation of title upon the sale of land may disclose the intestacy of a former owner. The vendor or some predecessor in title may have claimed the estate as heir of that intestate, and it will therefore be necessary for the purchaser to ascertain who was entitled under the old rules to succeed to the estate, and to satisfy himself that the right person did succeed.

(b) Entailed interests

Secondly, the persons who are entitled to succeed to an entailed interest which has neither been barred nor devised by its owner must be ascertained according to the old rules of descent.[8]

---

4 AEA 1925, s. 33 (2).
5 See Trustee Investments Act 1961, which greatly increased the range of investments previously authorised by the Trustee Act 1925 and is now inadequate; p. 200, ante.
6 AEA 1925, s. 33 (3).
7 Ibid., s. 33 (4).
8 Pp. 249–50, ante.

(c) Heirs taking by purchase

Thirdly, section 132 of the Law of Property Act 1925 provides as follows:

A limitation of real or personal property in favour of the heir, either general or special, of a deceased person which, if limited in respect of freehold land before the commencement of this Act, would have conferred on the heir an estate in the land by purchase, shall operate to confer a corresponding equitable interest in the property on the person who would, if the general law in force immediately before such commencement had remained unaffected, have answered the description of the heir, either general or special, of the deceased in respect of his freehold land, either at the death of the deceased or at the time named in the limitation, as the case may require.

The object of this provision is clear. A testator who has no wish to die intestate, yet who desires that his land shall go to the person who will be his heir-at-law, may make a will devising his land to his heir. The effect of this is that the heir, when ascertained according to the rules of intestate succession, takes the land as devisee, i.e. as a purchaser and not by title of descent.[9] A will in these terms before 1926 was convenient and reasonable, for in every case but one the heir was a single person. The legislation of 1925, however, abolished heirship except for entailed interests, and introduced a system under which the fee simple is sold and the proceeds distributed among near relatives. The effect of the present enactment is, therefore, that a testator who is so minded may still devise land to his heir, and that if he does so the devisee shall be ascertained according to the old law of descent. When ascertained he takes the fee simple in the case of inheritable freeholds, and the absolute ownership of personalty.

(d) Mental patient's property

Fourthly, it is provided that in certain cases the property of a person suffering from mental disorder, within the meaning of the Mental Health Act 1983 who dies intestate shall descend according to the old rules.[10]

B. THE DESCENT OF THE FEE SIMPLE BEFORE 1926

(1) DESCENT MUST BE TRACED FROM THE LAST PURCHASER[11]

This rule obliges us to look for the heir of the person who last took the land otherwise than by descent on intestacy, escheat,[12] partition[13] or enclosure;[14] in other words, by act of parties (i.e. where he took the land by buying it or by having it given or devised to him), and not by operation of law.[15] This law persisted till 1926, save only for a modification in 1859 by the Law of Property (Amendment) Act,[16] which provided that if there are no heirs of

9 Inheritance Act 1833, ss. 3, 4. See *Re Bourke's Will Trusts* [1980] 1 WLR 539, [1980] 1 All ER 219.
10 AEA 1925, s. 51 (2), as amended by the Mental Health Act 1959, s. 149(2), Sch. 8. See *Re Gates* [1930] 1 Ch 199; *Re Sirett* [1969] 1 WLR 60, [1968] 3 All ER 186.
11 Inheritance Act 1833, ss. 1, 2.
12 P. 17, ante.
13 P. 219, ante.
14 P. 573, ante.
15 P. 158, ante.
16 S. 19.

the last purchaser, the descent shall be traced from the person who was last *entitled* to the land, although he may not have been a *purchaser*. If, for instance:

> a purchaser dies intestate leaving a widow and one son, but no other relative, the son becomes *entitled* by descent to take the land. If the son dies intestate and a bachelor, the land would, apart from this statutory rule, escheat to the Crown. But since the statute permits the heir of the person last entitled (that is, the son) to take, the land may go to the son's mother, because, although she is not of the blood of her husband, the last purchaser, she *is* of the blood of the son.[17]

(2) MALES HAVE A PRIOR RIGHT TO FEMALES

The fee simple passes in the first place to the lineal descendants of the purchaser, and the male are preferred to the female descendants.

(3) PRIMOGENITURE

Under the rule of primogeniture, the eldest male takes to the exclusion of all other males in equal degree. Females in equal degree, however, take equally as coparceners. If, for instance, the intestate dies leaving two sons and two daughters, the eldest son takes the whole of the land. If, however, there are no male descendants, then the female descendants who are in equal degree share the land equally as coparceners.[18]

(4) REPRESENTATION

The lineal descendants of the purchaser represent him in that they stand in the same place as he himself would have done. Thus the lineal descendants of a deceased child who, had he lived, would have been heir, stand in the place of that child. If, for instance, the purchaser has two sons and dies leaving his younger son alone alive, the estate will pass to the eldest son of his deceased elder son and not to his living younger son.

(5) LINEAL ANCESTORS TAKE AFTER LINEAL DESCENDANTS[19]

The rule prior to the Inheritance Act 1833 was that a fief could not ascend, but that Act provides that if there are no lineal descendants of the purchaser, or if they have all failed, the estate shall go to the nearest lineal ancestor.

(6) THE PATERNAL ANCESTORS ARE PREFERRED TO THE MATERNAL[20]

(a) Male paternal ancestors

The effect of this rule and the preceding one is that if there are no lineal descendants of the purchaser, the land will go to the nearest male ancestor or, if he is dead leaving issue, then to the issue representing the ancestor under (4). Thus the nearest lineal ancestor is the father of the intestate, or, if the father is dead, the eldest son of the father. A father therefore is a nearer

---

17 See also *Bradley v McAtamney* [1936] NI 74.
18 P. 222, ante. This rule was varied by the local customs of gavelkind and borough-English; p. 24, ante.
19 Inheritance Act 1833, s. 6.
20 Ibid., ss. 7, 8.

heir than a brother. But in searching for the heir among the paternal ancestors and their issue, the rule is that preference must be given to the whole blood as against the half blood.[1]

(b) Half blood on male side

Before the Inheritance Act 1833 the half blood were excluded altogether, but that Act provided that where the common ancestor is a male (i.e. where a man has married two wives), a relative by half blood ranks next after a relative in the same degree of the whole blood and his or her issue. If, for instance,

the father of a purchaser who dies without descendants married Emma and had by her the purchaser and a sister Julia, and then married Arabella, by whom he had John, the effect of the statutory rule is that, while Julia and her issue take first, the estate passes to John if they fail.

If the purchaser's father is dead and the father's issue non-existent or extinct, recourse is next had to the father's father and his issue, and so on up through the male *paternal* ancestors; and when the males in this class are exhausted they are followed by the females.

(c) Female paternal ancestors

If there is no reasonable likelihood of ascertaining that there are descendants from the male paternal ancestors still alive,[2] then the next persons who are entitled, and who must be sought for, are the female paternal ancestors and their descendants.[3] But the search for the heir within this class is not the same as in the case of the male paternal ancestors. We have seen that after the purchaser's descendants are exhausted, we go to the male paternal ancestors, and that we start with the father and work upwards. In other words, we go from the father to the grandfather and then to the great-grandfather and so on. But the Inheritance Act provides that in dealing with the female paternal ancestors we start with the mother of the remotest male *paternal* ancestor known and her descendants.

Suppose, for instance, that the purchaser's father, grandfather and great-grandfather are dead, and their descendants extinct. The next person whose descendants are entitled is the great-great-grandfather. If, however, he is not known, then we take the last paternal ancestor who *is* known, i.e. the great-grandfather, and look for the descendants of his mother.

That is the meaning of the enactment that:[4]

Where there shall be a failure of male paternal ancestors of the person from whom the descent is to be traced and their descendants, the mother of his more remote male paternal ancestor, or her descendants, shall be the heir or heirs of such person, in preference to the mother of a less remote male paternal ancestor, or her descendants.

If there are no descendants of the great-grandfather's mother, the next

1 Inheritance Act 1833, s. 9.
2 *Greaves v Greenwood* (1877) 2 Ex D 289.
3 Inheritance Act 1833, s. 7.
4 Ibid., s. 8. For this curious rule, said to be justified by feudal principles, but which has given rise to no decision, see Blackstone, vol. ii. p. 238.

persons entitled are the descendants of the grandfather's mother, then the grandmother and her descendants, and lastly the mother and her descendants.

(d) Male and female maternal ancestors

Having exhausted the male and female paternal ancestors, the next step is to start with the mother and work up the male and down the female line, as in the case of the father.

When the person entitled to succeed is a female ancestor who is dead, the estate will descend to her issue as representing her.

If, for instance:

the only ancestor with issue is the purchaser's mother, and she is dead having left a child by another husband than the father of the purchaser, that child will be entitled to take. The child, of course, is a relative of the half blood to the purchaser.

We have seen that where the common ancestor is a male, the relatives of the half blood take after the relatives of the same degree of the whole blood. Where, however, as in the present case, the common ancestor is a female, i.e. where the purchaser's *mother* has married twice, it is enacted that the relatives of the half blood shall take next after the female ancestor.[5]

(7) CURTESY AND DOWER

It must be remembered that the above rules of descent were subject, under the old law, to the respective rights of a surviving husband and a surviving wife. If a wife died intestate, the husband was entitled, in certain circumstances, to an estate by the curtesy in her freeholds of inheritance. This species of estate has already been discussed.[6]

Similarly, when a husband died having at some time been solely seised of a fee simple or an estate tail, his surviving wife became entitled by way of dower to a life estate in one-third of the land.[7] In order to establish this right, however, she must have been able to show:

(a) that issue capable of inheriting the land *might* have been born, and
(b) that she had not been expressly deprived of the right to her one-third.

(a) Birth of heritable issue possible

As regards the first point, she must have shown that she herself might have had a child capable of inheriting the land out of which she claimed dower. Thus:

if land was settled on a husband and his heirs begotten on the body of X, X was dowable even though the husband died childless, but if X died and the husband married Y, the latter had no claim to dower, for she could never have had children capable of inheriting the land in accordance with the terms of the original limitation.

---

5 Inheritance Act 1833, s. 9.
6 P. 250, ante.
7 For the customary rule in gavelkind, see p. 24, ante.

(b) Dower not barred

As to the second point, the rule after the Dower Act 1833 was that a husband could deprive his wife either expressly or by implication of her right to dower, and the law was that no such right existed if the husband had disposed of the estate by deed or will;[8] if he expressly stated in a deed or will that she was not to have dower;[9] if he devised to her other land out of which she was not dowable;[10] or if, as for instance under a settlement, she accepted a jointure. Thus in effect it was only where a husband died intestate actually seised of an unbarred interest in tail or of a fee simple estate that a question of dower arose.

C. THE MODERN RULES OF DISTRIBUTION

The Administration of Estates Act 1925 prepared the way for new rules of distribution by abolishing with regard to the real and personal estate of persons dying on or after 1 January 1926, all the former rules of descent and distribution. Moreover, it abolished the husband's curtesy, the widow's dower, and all customary modes of descent, such as gavelkind and borough-English, that formerly obtained in any part of the country. Escheat, whether to the Crown or to a mesne lord,[11] was also abolished and replaced by the right of the Crown to take all undistributed property as *bona vacantia*.[12]

On the death of a person intestate, his estate, as we have seen, is held by his personal representatives upon trust:

(a) to sell the real estate, and

(b) to sell such part of the personal estate as does not consist of money,

with power to postpone the sale for so long as may seem fit.[13]

The Act then provided that the residuary estate (i.e. the residue, after payment of debts, of the proceeds of sale and any investments by which they are represented, including any part of the estate still unsold)[14] should be distributed according to certain rules which varied according as the intestate left or did not leave a surviving spouse. Where a surviving spouse is left, however, these rules have been radically altered by the Intestates' Estates Act 1952, as amended by the Family Provision Act 1966 and the Family Provision (Intestate Succession) Order 1987.[15] In 1969 the Family Law Reform Act amended the law with respect to illegitimate children. The present position where the intestate died on or after 1 March 1994 is as follows.

---

8 Dower Act 1833, s. 4.

9 Ibid., s. 6.

10 Ibid., s. 7.

11 See *Re Lowe's Will Trusts* [1973] 1 WLR 882, [1973] 2 All ER 1136.

12 AEA 1925, s. 45. Certain of the old rules still apply to the entailed interest; p. 250, ante. Curtesy is still possible in the case of an entailed interest not disposed of by will.

13 Ibid., s. 33 (1); p. 869, ante.

14 Ibid., s. 33 (4). The residuary estate is confined to assets, succession of which is regulated by English law: *Re Collens* [1986] Ch 505, [1986] 1 All ER 611; [1988] Conv 30 (G. Miller).

15 S.I. 1987 No. 799.

(1) WHERE THE INTESTATE LEAVES A SURVIVING SPOUSE

If it is uncertain which spouse survived the other the statutory rule that the younger spouse survived the elder[16] does not apply. The estate of each is distributed separately.[17] If a spouse dies intestate after a decree of judicial separation and whilst the separation is still continuing, his or her estate devolves as if the other spouse were dead.[18]

(a) Intestate leaves issue

If the intestate also leaves issue, the surviving spouse takes:[19]

  (i) all the personal chattels absolutely;[20]
 (ii) a fixed net sum of £125,000[1] (or such larger sum as may from time to time be fixed by the Lord Chancellor), with interest thereon at the rate of 6 per cent,[2] from the date of death;[3]
(iii) a life interest in half of the residuary estate.

The other half of the residuary estate and the reversion on the life interest is held upon the statutory trusts for the issue.[4]

(b) No issue, but a parent or brother or sister

If the intestate leaves no issue, but leaves one or more of the following, namely, a parent, a brother or sister of the whole blood or issue of such brother or sister, the surviving spouse takes:

  (i) the personal chattels absolutely;
 (ii) £200,000[5] (or such larger sum as may from time to time be fixed by the Lord Chancellor), with interest at 6 per cent from the date of death;
(iii) one-half of the residuary estate absolutely.

The other half of the residue goes to the parents absolutely or, if there is no surviving parent, to the brothers and sisters or their issue upon the statutory trusts.[6]

16 P. 847, ante.
17 AEA 1925, s. 46 (3), added by IEA 1952.
18 Matrimonial Causes Act 1973, s. 18 (2), replacing Matrimonial Proceedings and Property Act 1970, s. 40.
19 In *Re Wynn* [1984] 1 WLR 237, [1983] 3 All ER 310, a surviving spouse was excluded from benefit under his wife's intestacy by a single provision in her will that "I wish that all I possess is not given to my husband".
20 For definition, see p. 869, ante.
 1 Family Provision (Intestate Succession) Order 1993 (S.I. 1993 No. 2906), art 2 (*a*).
 2 Intestate Succession (Interest and Capitalisation) Order 1977 (Amendment) Order 1983 (S.I. 1983 No. 1374), art 2.
 3 AEA 1925, s. 46 (1) (i), as amended by IEA 1952, s. 1; Family Provision Act 1966, s. 1 (1) (*a*), and AJA 1977, s. 28 (1).
 4 Ibid., s. 46 (1) (i), as amended by IEA 1952, s. 1 (2), Family Provision Act 1966, s. 1 and AJA 1977, s. 28 (1). For the rights of the issue, see pp. 877 et seq., post.
 5 Family Provision (Intestate Succession) Order 1993, supra, art 2 (*b*).
 6 AEA 1925, s. 46 (1) (i), as amended by IEA 1952, s. 1, by Family Provision Act 1966, s. 1 (i) (*a*) and by AJA 1977, s. 28 (1) (*a*).

(c) No issue, parents or brothers or sisters

If the intestate leaves no issue, no parents, and no brothers or sisters of the whole blood or their issue, the surviving spouse takes the whole residuary estate absolutely to the exclusion of all other relatives.[7] Thus where there is a surviving spouse, the brothers and sisters of the half-blood are entirely excluded.

(d) Subsidiary rules

There are several subsidiary rules to be noticed.

(i) Redemption of life interest We have seen that where the intestate leaves issue, the surviving spouse takes a life interest in one-half of what is left of the estate after deduction of the personal chattels and £125,000. The existence of this life interest precludes a final distribution of the estate, and in most cases the survivor prefers to receive a lump sum. The Act, therefore, provides that if the surviving spouse so elects the personal representatives must redeem the life interest by paying its capital value to the tenant for life.[8] Thus the initiative lies with the surviving spouse, but the election must be made within twelve months from the date on which representation is first taken out, unless the court extends the period on the ground that it will operate unfairly.[9] Once made, it cannot be revoked without the consent of the personal representatives.[10] Owing to the difficulty of valuing reversionary interests, it is provided that a demand for redemption can be made only in respect of property to which the intestate was entitled in possession.[11]

(ii) Rights of surviving spouse in matrimonial home The Administration of Estates Act 1925 empowers a personal representative to appropriate any part of the estate of the deceased in its actual condition or state of investment in or towards satisfaction of any share or interest in the estate to which a beneficiary may be entitled.[12] Thus, for example, an investment held by the intestate at the time of his death may be allocated to his widow in part satisfaction of her right to £125,000. The consent of any beneficiary who is absolutely and beneficially entitled in possession must first be obtained.[13]

This power of appropriation has been extended to include the matrimonial home. The Intestates' Estates Act 1952 provides that:

> where the residuary estate of the intestate comprises an interest in a dwelling-house in which the surviving husband or wife was resident at the time of the intestate's death, the surviving husband or wife may require the personal representative to appropriate the said interest in the dwelling-house in or towards satisfaction of any

---

7 AEA 1925, s. 46 (1) (i) as substituted by IEA 1952, s. 1 (2).
8 Ibid., s. 47A added by IEA 1952, Sch. 1. For rules upon which the capital value must be calculated, see s. 47A (3A), (3B), as added by AJA 1977, s. 28 (2), (3); Intestate Succession (Interest and Capitalisation) Order 1977 (Amendment) Order 1983 (S.I. 1983 No. 1374), art 2.
9 Ibid., s. 47A (5).
10 Ibid., s. 47A (6).
11 Ibid., s. 47A (3).
12 Ibid., s. 41.
13 Ibid., s. 41 (1) (ii) (*a*).

absolute interest of the surviving husband or wife in the real and personal estate of the intestate.[14]

This right is personal to the survivor and is not exercisable after his or her death.[15] If the house is worth more than the interest to which the survivor is entitled, it may be appropriated upon payment in cash of the balance.[16]

(iii) Meaning of "dwelling-house" The expression "dwelling-house" includes part of a building that at the time of the intestate's death was used as a separate dwelling.[17] In the following four cases, however, the right of the survivor is not exercisable unless an application is made to the court and the court is satisfied that the appropriation is not likely to diminish the value of assets in the residuary estate (other than the interest in the dwelling-house) or to make them more difficult to dispose of, namely where:[18]

(a) the dwelling-house forms part of a building and an interest in the whole of the building is comprised in the residuary estate; or
(b) the dwelling-house is held with agricultural land and an interest in the agricultural land is comprised in the residuary estate; or
(c) the whole or a part of the dwelling-house was at the time of the intestate's death used as a hotel or lodging house; or
(d) a part of the dwelling-house was at the time of the intestate's death used for purposes other than domestic purposes.

There is no right to the appropriation if the house was held by the intestate on a lease due to end within two years of his or her death or on a lease, such as one from year to year, that the landlord can determine by a notice given within two years after the death.[19]

(iv) Time limit for claim The right must be claimed within twelve months after representation has first been taken out[20] and it must be exercised by a written notification to the personal representatives, or, where there are two or more representatives of whom one is the claimant, to all of them.[1] During this period of twelve months the house may not be sold without the written consent of the surviving spouse, unless there is an insufficiency of assets for the payment of debts.[2] If a sale is effected in violation of this prohibition, however, no right against the purchaser is conferred upon the surviving spouse.[3]

The requirement of a written notice to the representatives is expressly excluded where the surviving spouse is the sole personal representative, for a person can scarcely demand of himself that he shall effect a certain transaction for his own benefit.[4] Unfortunately, however, it is not clear whether a surviving spouse who is also the sole personal representative can exercise

---

14 IEA 1952, s. 5, Sch. 2, para. 1 (1). Although this power of appropriation is exercisable only in satisfaction of an "absolute interest", the latter expression includes a life interest which the survivor has elected to have redeemed; para. 1 (4). The date for valuation is that of appropriation, not death: *Re Collins* [1975] 1 WLR 309, [1975] 1 All ER 321.
15 Ibid., s. 5, Sch. 2, para. 3 (1) (*b*).
16 Ibid., para. 5 (2); *Re Phelps* [1980] Ch 275, [1979] 3 All ER 373.
17 Ibid., para. 1 (5).
18 Ibid., para. 2.
19 Ibid., para. 1 (2).
20 Ibid., para. 3 (1) (*a*).
 1 Ibid., Sch. 2, para. 3 (1) (*c*).
 2 Ibid., para. 4 (1).
 3 Ibid., para. 4 (5).
 4 Ibid., para. 3 (1) (*c*).

this right of appropriation under the Act of 1952. It may be that his only course is to proceed under section 41 of the Administration of Estates Act 1925.[5]

(2) WHERE THE INTESTATE LEAVES NO SURVIVING SPOUSE

The rules for the distribution of the residuary estate in this event are laid down by the Administration of Estates Act 1925, and are unaffected by the Intestates' Estates Act of 1952.

They prescribe that the estate shall be distributed among the relatives of the deceased according to the following scheme:

(a) Intestate leaves issue. Statutory trusts

If the intestate leaves issue the residuary estate is held on the *statutory trusts* for the issue.[6]

The word "issue" means the lineal descendants of the intestate. Under this rule the beneficiaries are the surviving children and the descendants of children who predeceased the intestate. Such descendants represent the deceased child and take among themselves the exact share that the child would have taken had he survived the intestate. This taking by representation is called taking *per stirpes*—according to the roots.

> All the branches inherit the same share that their root, whom they represent, would have done.[7]

If, for instance, the intestate is survived by two children and by four grandchildren, the offspring of a daughter who predeceased him, the children each take one-third of the estate and the remaining third is divisible equally between the four grandchildren.

(b) No issue, but parents

If the intestate leaves no issue but is survived by a parent or parents, his father and mother take the whole estate absolutely in equal shares.[8] If only one parent survives, that parent takes absolutely.[9]

(c) No issue or parents

If the intestate leaves no issue or parent, the following persons "living at the death of the intestate" are entitled in the following order:[10]

    (i) his brothers and sisters of the whole blood, on the statutory trusts; failing these

   (ii) his brothers and sisters of the half-blood, on the statutory trusts; failing these

  (iii) his grandparents, if more than one, in equal shares; failing these

  (iv) his uncles and aunts of the whole blood, on the statutory trusts; failing these

---

5 P. 877, ante; see (1925) 16 Conv (NS), pp. 417–419 (G. B. Graham).
6 AEA 1925, s. 46 (1) (ii); p. 881, post.
7 Blackstone, vol. ii. p. 217.
8 AEA 1925, s. 46 (1) (iii).
9 Ibid., s. 46 (1) (iv).
10 Ibid., s. 46 (1) (v). See *Re Scott* [1975] 1 WLR 1260, [1975] 2 All ER 1033.

(v) his uncles and aunts of the half-blood, on the statutory trusts.

If the deceased leaves none of the relatives just enumerated and no issue or surviving spouse, his estate belongs to the Crown or to the Duchy of Lancaster or Duke of Cornwall, as the case may be, as *bona vacantia* and in lieu of any right to escheat.

The Crown or Duchy etc. may however, provide out of the estate for dependants of the intestate, whether kindred or not, and other persons for whom he might reasonably have been expected to make provision.[11]

The words "living at the death of the intestate" in the opening statement of the enumeration do not exclude the issue of a brother, sister, uncle or aunt who predeceased him, for under the doctrine of representation they take the share that their parent would have taken had he survived the intestate.[12]

The list of beneficiaries, it will be noticed, does not include distant relatives. Since the oldest ancestor entitled is the grandparent, the claimant must at least have descended from him or her, and it follows that the most remote relative entitled to a share is a first cousin and his issue, i.e. first cousins once, twice or further removed. Thus, second cousins are excluded.

(3) CAPACITY TO TAKE UNDER AN INTESTACY

In addition to legitimate relations the following may take under these provisions:

(a) Adopted

Adopted children are deemed to be the children of their adopting and not their natural parents; and members of the adopting family may take under the intestacy of an adopted child.[13]

(b) Legitimated

Similarly where a child is legitimated by the subsequent marriage of his or her parents the rules of distribution apply as if the child had been born legitimate.[14]

(c) Illegitimate

Where death occurs after 1969 and before 4 April 1988 the Family Law Reform Act 1969[15] provides that an illegitimate child shall be entitled to share in the intestacy of both his parents equally with their legitimate issue. Both parents are equally entitled to share in his intestacy. On the other hand the Act does not abolish the distinction between legitimate and illegitimate birth for the purposes of intestacy. An illegitimate child may not take under the intestacy of collaterals or of ancestors more remote than parents. Nor may any person take under the intestacy of an illegitimate if he dies without leaving issue, a surviving spouse or either parent. For the purposes of

---

11 See generally Ing, *Bona Vacantia*, chapter 10; [1987] LSG 18 (D. A. Chatterton).
12 AEA 1925, s. 47 (1) (i), (3).
13 Adoption Act 1976, s. 39.
14 Legitimacy Act 1976, s. 5.
15 S. 14. It does not apply to or affect the right of any person to take any entailed property: s. 14 (5).

distribution an illegitimate child is presumed not to have been survived by his father, unless the contrary is shown.

Where death occurs after 3 April 1988, the effect of the Family Law Reform Act 1987 is that entitlement to succeed on intestacy now depends entirely on blood (or adoptive) relationship.[16] It is immaterial whether a claimant, or anyone through whom his relationship is deduced, is legitimate or illegitimate. However, in order to facilitate administration of the estate, there is a rebuttable presumption that the father of an illegitimate person predeceased him.[17]

(4) THE STATUTORY TRUSTS

Whenever the property is distributable among a class of persons the members of which may be indefinite in number and some of them under age, the Act provides that it shall be held for them on the *statutory trusts*.[18] This is so in the case of issue, brothers, sisters, uncles and aunts, but not in the case of parents or grandparents.

(a) Statutory trusts for the issue

The statutory trusts for the issue mean that the property is held in trust in equal shares for the children of the intestate alive at his death who attain the age of eighteen or who, whether male or female, marry under that age. Thus the children take *per capita*. But if a child predeceases the intestate leaving issue alive at the death of the intestate, such issue as attain eighteen or marry represent their parent and take his share *per stirpes*.[19]

(i) Position during infancy of beneficiary

The result is that an infant, whether a child or more remote issue, takes only a contingent share that will not vest until marriage or the attainment of majority. In the meantime, however, the personal representatives may, at their sole discretion, apply the whole or part of the income of the property to which the infant is contingently entitled for or towards his maintenance, education or benefit.[20] They may also apply the capital for his advancement or benefit[1] to an amount not exceeding one-half of his presumptive share, but this must be brought into account when he becomes entitled to a vested interest at his majority or marriage.[2] Subject to the exercise of these powers, the personal representatives must accumulate the income at compound interest and hold the accumulation in trust for the infant.[3] The personal representatives may also permit any infant contingently entitled to have the use and enjoyment of any personal chattels in such manner and subject to such conditions (if any) as they may consider reasonable, and without being liable to account for any consequential loss.[4]

---

16 S. 18 (1) Family Law Reform Act 1987, s. 18 (1).
17 Ibid., s. 18 (2).
18 Unfortunately the same expression is used by LPA 1925, in the entirely different context of tenancies in common and joint tenancies, see p. 226, ante.
19 AEA 1925, s. 47 (1), as amended by Family Law Reform Act 1969, s. 3 (2). Where the intestate died before 1970, the age remains 21.
20 Ibid., s. 47 (1) (ii); TA 1925, s. 31 (1).
 1 *Pilkington v IRC* [1964] AC 612, [1962] 3 All ER 622.
 2 TA 1925, s. 32 (1).
 3 Ibid., s. 31 (2).
 4 AEA 1925, s. 47 (1) (iv), as added by IEA 1952, s. 4 and Sch. 1.

(ii) Statutory trusts illustrated The operation of the statutory trusts may be elucidated by a simple illustration. Suppose the following facts:

The intestate had four sons, A to D. At his death, A and B are alive.

C is dead, but he is survived by two children, C1 and C2 both over 18 years of age.

D and his son D1 are dead, but D1 left two daughters D2 and D3 who are alive at the intestate's death, but are still infants and unmarried.

The residuary estate, therefore, is divided into fourths. A and B each take one-fourth; C1 and C2 represent their father, C, and share equally the fourth that would have accrued to him had he lived; the infants, D2 and D3, being issue of D, are equally, but contingently, entitled to the remaining fourth part. If one of them dies in infancy and still unmarried, her share passes to her sister. While their shares remain contingent, the income may be spent on their maintenance or education and up to one-half of the capital may be employed for their advancement or benefit.

(iii) Hotchpot The distribution of the property among the issue, however, is subject to what is called the *hotchpot rule*, which is designed to ensure equality of distribution. The rule, failing a contrary intention, is that any money or property which the intestate in his lifetime has paid to or settled on, or covenanted to pay to or settle on, a child, either by way of advancement or in view of marriage, shall be brought into account and deducted from the share which is payable to that child or to that child's issue under the intestacy.[5] If the advance was made directly to a grandchild (or remoter issue) it is not taken into account if that grandchild becomes entitled to share in the intestacy as representing his deceased parent.

No absolute test can be laid down as to what constitutes an advancement for the purposes of the rule, but its broad meaning is a gift intended to make a permanent provision for the child—an intention that is more readily inferred if the sum is substantial and if it has been paid at an early stage in the life of the child.[6] It does not include casual payments or money given to relieve a child from some temporary embarrassment. JESSEL MR dealt with the matter in these words:

I have always understood that an advancement by way of portion is something given by the parent to establish the child in life, or to make what is called a provision for him. . . . You may make the provision by way of marriage portion on the marriage of the child. You may make it on putting him into a profession or business in a variety of ways; you may pay for a commission, you may buy him the goodwill of a business and give him stock in trade; all these things I understand to be portions or provisions. Again, if in the absence of evidence you find a father giving a large sum to a child in one payment, there is a presumption that that is intended to start him in life or make a provision for him; but if a small sum is so given you may require evidence to show the purpose.[7]

In the case from which these words are quoted it was held that the payment of the admission fee to an Inn of Court was an advancement, but that the price of an outfit and the passage money of a military officer who was going with his regiment to India, the payment of debts incurred by an officer in the

5 AEA 1925, s. 47 (1) (iii). See (1961) 25 Conv (NS) 469 (J. T. Farrand).
6 *Re Hayward* [1957] Ch 528, [1957] 2 All ER 474; (1957) 73 LQR 21, 302 (R. E. M.); *Hardy v Shaw* [1976] Ch 82, [1975] 2 All ER 1052.
7 *Taylor v Taylor* (1875) LR 20 Eq 155 at 157.

army, and sums given to a clergyman towards his housekeeping expenses were not advancements.

(b) Statutory trusts for classes other than issue

The statutory trusts for brothers, sisters, uncles and aunts are the same as those applicable to issue, except that the hotchpot rule is excluded.[8]

If, for instance, the intestate dies unmarried leaving no parents, but survived by a brother and a nephew, the son of a deceased brother, his estate will be divided equally between these two survivors, and any advancement that he may have made in his lifetime to his deceased brother will not be deducted from the nephew's share.

(5) PARTIAL INTESTACY

The above rules apply to a case of partial intestacy, which occurs where a person leaves a will disposing only of part of his property. In these circumstances the property that is undisposed of is distributed among the persons in the manner and order applicable to a case of total intestacy. There is a distinction, however, between a total and partial intestacy with regard to the hotchpot rule. The position is this:

First, the value of any beneficial interest, other than a bequest of chattels, left by the will to the surviving spouse must be set off against the sum of £125,000 or £200,000 (as the case may be)[9] payable to that spouse under the partial intestacy.[10]

Secondly, children must account for beneficial interests given to them by the will as well as for advancements made to them in the lifetime of the deceased.[11]

Thirdly, remoter issue must account for beneficial interests left to them by the will and for advancements made to children through whom they claim, but not for advancements made to them personally by the deceased in his lifetime.[12]

The term "beneficial interest" includes a life or a lesser interest[13] and also an interest given by the testamentary exercise of a general power of appointment, but not of a special power.[14]

D. LAW REFORM

In 1989 the Law Commission recommended that the surviving spouse should receive the whole estate which is not disposed of by will, but that otherwise

8 AEA 1925, s. 47 (3), added by IEA 1952, Sch. 1.
9 P. 876, ante.
10 AEA 1925, s. 49 (1) (*aa*), added by IEA 1952, s. 3 (2).
11 Ibid., s. 49 (1) (*a*).
12 Ibid., ss. 47 (1) (iii), 49 (1) (*a*).
13 *Re Young* [1951] Ch 185; *Re Morton* [1956] Ch 644, [1956] 3 All ER 259; *Re Grover's Will Trusts* [1971] Ch 168, [1970] 1 All ER 1185. See also *Re Bowen-Buscarlet's Will Trusts* [1972] Ch 463, [1971] 3 All ER 636; (1973) 26 CLP 208 (E. C. Ryder).
14 AEA 1925, s. 49, added by IEA 1952, s. 3 (3). It includes interests in foreign property: *Re Osoba* [1978] 1 WLR 791 at 796–797, [1978] 2 All ER 1099 at 1104, per MEGARRY V-C; [1979] 1 WLR 247 at 255, [1979] 2 All ER 393 at 400, per GOFF LJ.

the basic structure of the rules for distribution should remain with only minor changes.[15] These are that:

(i) the statutory hotchpot rule affecting issue should be repealed
(ii) the statutory hotchpot rules affecting issue and spouses upon partial intestacy should be repealed and
(iii) a spouse should only inherit under the intestacy rules if he or she survived the intestate for fourteen days.

The Law Commission also recommended that cohabitants should be provided for, not under the intestacy rules, but where appropriate under the Inheritance (Provision for Family and Dependants) Act 1975. In 1993 the Government announced that it would accept most of the proposed changes, except for the recommendation that a surviving spouse should in all circumstances receive the whole estate.

---

15 Report on Distribution on Intestacy 1989 (Law Com. No. 187); [1990] Conv 358 (R. Kerridge).

Part III

The transfer and extinction of estates and interests

C. EXTINCTION OF ESTATES AND INTERESTS

SUMMARY

Chapter 26

Extinction under the Limitation Act 1980

SECTION I INTRODUCTORY NOTE

Most systems of law have realized the necessity of fixing some definite period of time within which persons who have been unlawfully dispossessed of their land must pursue their claims. It is, no doubt, an injustice that after this period has elapsed the wrongdoer should be allowed to retain the land against the person whom he has ousted, but it would be an even greater injustice to the world at large if the latter were allowed after any interval of time, however long, to commence proceedings for recovery of possession. If A, having ejected B, is allowed to remain in long and undisturbed possession of the land, the impression will grow that his title is superior to B's, and the public should be allowed to deal safely with him on that footing. As Lord St. Leonards remarked:[1]

All statutes of limitation have for their object the prevention of the rearing up of

---

1 *Dundee Harbour Trustees v Dougall* (1852) 1 Macq 317. See too *R B Policies at Lloyd's v Butler* [1950] 1 KB 76 at 81, [1949] 2 All ER 226 at 229; [1985] Conv 272 (M. Dockray).

claims at great distances of time when evidences are lost; and in all well-regulated countries the quieting of possession is held an important point of policy.

(a) Limitation and prescription

The effect of a person remaining in possession of the land of another for the period of time fixed by law varies in different countries and in different ages. Thus the effect of *usucapio* in Roman Law was to confer a positive title to the land upon a person who had remained in possession for a certain time. Under the Statutes of Limitation which were in force in England prior to 1833 the effect of remaining in possession for the prescribed period was to bar only the remedy of the person dispossessed, not his right. His *title* remained intact, and if he came lawfully into possession of the land again, his title might prevail against the possessor.[2] Under the statutes that have been in force since 1833[3] the effect of remaining in possession for the statutory period of 12 years is still merely negative, but now in the sense that the right as well as the remedy of the person dispossessed is extinguished. The *usucapio* of Roman Law exemplified what is sometimes called acquisitive prescription in the sense that possession of another's land for a given period conferred a positive title upon the occupier, or squatter as he is familiarly described, but English law has never adopted this theory in its treatment of corporeal hereditaments and chattels, though it has done so in the case of easements and profits.

(b) The modern Acts

The English law relating to the period within which an action for the recovery of land must be brought was recast and simplified by the Real Property Limitation Act of 1833; was consolidated and amended by the Limitation Act 1939; and, after further amendment by the Limitation Amendment Act 1980, was again consolidated by the Limitation Act 1980. Originally the period was fixed at the discretion of individual judges. Later, certain dates (such as the first coronation of Henry II) were chosen from time to time by the legislature. Then in 1623 the Limitation Act introduced the modern principle that actions must be brought within a fixed number of years. But even so the state of the law was unsatisfactory owing to the variety of remedies that lay for the recovery of land, and to the fact that the period of limitation varied according to the nature of the remedy adopted. An account of the old law must, however, be sought in works on legal history.[4] We confine ourselves to describing the law as it has been established by the Limitation Act 1980.[5]

2 Lightwood, *Possession of Land*, p. 153. See *Buckinghamshire County Council v Moran* [1990] Ch 623 at 644, [1989] 2 All ER 225 at 238, per NOURSE LJ.

3 Real Property Limitation Act 1833; Real Property Limitation Act 1874; Limitation Act 1939; Limitation Amendment Act 1980; Limitation Act 1980, as amended by Latent Damage Act 1986.

4 See especially Hayes, *Introduction to Conveyancing*, vol. i. pp. 222 et seq; Holdsworth, *History of English Law*, vol. iv. p. 484; vol. vii. pp. 29 et seq; Simpson, *A History of the Land Law*, (2nd edn), pp. 151–155.

5 This is based on the Law Reform Committee 21st Report (Final Report on Limitations of Actions) 1977 (Cmnd 6923), which contains a valuable discussion of all aspects of limitation. The Act came into force on 1 May 1981. For transitional provisions, see s. 40 (1), Sch. 2. See the annotation in Current Law Statutes 1980 (D. Morgan); and generally Franks, *Limitation of Actions*; McGee, *Limitation Periods* (1990); Preston and Newsom, *Limitation of Actions*

SECTION II PERIOD OF LIMITATION FOR ACTIONS TO RECOVER LAND

No action can be brought to recover any land after the expiration of 12 years from the date on which the *right of action accrued* to the plaintiff,[6] or to the person through whom he claims.[7] This limitation applies to a foreclosure action.[8]

Land is defined in wide terms. It includes:[9]

corporeal hereditaments, tithes[10] and rentcharges and any legal or equitable estate or interest therein, including an interest in the proceeds of the sale of land held upon trust for sale, but except as provided above in this definition does not include any incorporeal hereditament.

It will be observed that although land held upon trust for sale is deemed to be money under the doctrine of conversion,[11] yet the interests of the beneficiaries in the proceeds of sale are regarded as interests in land for the purposes of limitation.

There are certain exceptional cases in which the ordinary period of 12 years is increased.

(a) Actions by the Crown

The Crown Suits Act 1769, generally called the *Nullum Tempus* Act, altered the ancient rule that Statutes of Limitations do not bind the Crown and prescribed a period of 60 years in the case of an action to recover land. This period is now 30 years,[12] and there is a general provision that the "Act shall apply to proceedings by or against the Crown in like manner as it applies to proceedings between subjects."[13] An action to recover land brought *against* the Crown, however, is subject to the 12 years' period.

(b) Action by corporation sole

An action to recover land by a spiritual or an eleemosynary corporation sole, such as a bishop, dean or master of a hospital, must be brought within 30 years after the date on which the right of action accrued to the corporation or to the person through whom the corporation claims.[14] The ordinary period

(4th edn); Prime and Scanlon, *Modern Law of Limitation* (1993); Redmond-Cooper, *Limitation of Actions* (1992); Josling, *Periods of Limitation* (6th edn).

6 After a judgment for possession has been obtained in an action begun in due time, the successful plaintiff has 12 years from the date of judgment: *BP Properties Ltd v Buckler* (1987) 55 P & CR 337.

7 Limitation Act 1980, s. 15 (1). An appointee under a special power is not deemed to claim through the appointor: s. 38 (6).

8 Ibid., s. 20 (4).

9 Ibid., s. 38 (1).

10 P. 92, n. 19, ante.

11 P. 235, ante.

12 Limitation Act 1980, s. 15 (7), Sch. 1, para. 10. It remains 60 years where foreshore is owned by the Crown: para. 11; *Secretary of State for Foreign and Commonwealth Affairs v Tomlin* (1990) Times, 4 December (former embassy of Government of Cambodia in St John's Wood, London).

13 Ibid., s. 37 (1). This applies to proceedings by or against the Duke of Cornwall or the Duchy of Lancaster.

14 Ibid., s. 15 (7), Sch. 1, para. 10.

of 12 years applies in the case of a corporation aggregate, such as one of the colleges of Oxford or Cambridge.

In the case of the Crown or a spiritual or eleemosynary corporation the position with regard to *claiming through a person* may be illustrated by examples:

> The Crown purchases from A in 1994 land which is in the wrongful possession of a third party, X.

If a right of action to recover the land from the wrongful possessor accrued to A more than 12 years before 1994, A's title is extinguished and the Crown acquires nothing. If, however, A's right of action accrued less than 12 years before 1994, say in 1989, then the Crown can sue the wrongdoer at any time within 30 years after 1989.[15]

The reverse case arises where a person claims through the Crown or a corporation sole after a cause of action has already accrued, as for example where:

> In 1994 the Crown conveys to A land which has been in the wrongful possession of X since 1974.

The statutory rule here is that A's remedy against X is barred either 30 years after 1974, when the cause of action accrued to the Crown, or 12 years after the cause of action accrued to himself, *whichever period expires first*.[16] The cause of action accrued to A by virtue of the conveyance of 1994, but nevertheless his remedy is barred in 2004.

(c) Advowsons

No patron may bring an action to enforce a right to present to or bestow any ecclesiastical benefice after the period during which three successive incumbencies have been held adversely to the right, or 60 years of adverse possession, whichever is the longer, with a maximum of 100 years.[17]

SECTION III THE DATE FROM WHICH TIME BEGINS TO RUN

A. THE GENERAL RULE

(1) ACCRUAL OF RIGHT OF ACTION

Time begins to run against a plaintiff only from the date on which the right of action accrued to him or to the person through whom he claims. In the case of land, as distinct from other cases such as contract or tort, the Act lays down specific rules fixing the date at which in varying circumstances this accrual occurs.[18] It deals separately with present interests, future interests, settled land, land held on trust for sale, tenancies and forfeiture or breach of condition.

---

15 Limitation Act 1980, s. 15 (7), Sch. 1, paras. 10, 13.
16 Ibid., para. 12.
17 Ibid., s. 25.
18 For accrual in negligence cases in respect of latent damage to property, see the Latent Damage Act 1986, which is based on the recommendations of the Law Reform Committee 24th Report on Latent Damage (1984 Cmnd 9390); McGee, *Limitation Periods*, chapter 6; (1991) 54 MLR 345 (N. J. Mullany).

(2) ADVERSE POSSESSION

Before dealing with these different cases, however, it is necessary to notice an overriding provision of the greatest importance. This is that time does not begin to run from the specified dates unless there is some person in adverse possession of the land. It does not run merely because the land is vacant.[19] There must be both absence of possession by the plaintiff and adverse possession by the defendant.

This rule, founded on the obvious reason that a right of action cannot accrue unless there is somebody against whom it can be asserted, was well established after the Real Property Limitation Act 1833, in the case where an *actual possessor* left possession vacant, though there was some doubt whether it applied where the land of a deceased owner remained vacant owing to the failure of the person entitled thereto to take possession. All doubts are now dispelled, for each statutory rule fixing the date at which the right of action accrues is subject to the overriding condition that there must be some person in possession of the land in whose favour time can run. This condition is enacted in the following words:[20]

No right of action to recover land shall be treated as accruing unless the land is in the possession of some person in whose favour the period of limitation can run (referred to below in this paragraph as "adverse possession"); and where . . . any such right of action is treated as accruing on a certain date and no person is in adverse possession on that date, the right of action shall not be treated as accruing unless and until adverse possession is taken of the land.[1]

(3) SUCCESSIVE ADVERSE POSSESSORS

This general principle may be illustrated by the case where the adverse possessor (let us call him X) fails for one reason or another to occupy for the

---

19 *M'Donnell v M'Kinty* (1847) 10 ILR 514; *Smith v Lloyd* (1854) 9 Exch 562.

20 Limitation Act 1980, s. 15 (6), Sch. 1, para 8 (1). "Adverse possession" bore a technical meaning before the Real Property Limitation Act 1833. Before that date wrongful possession did not ripen into a claim to bar the owner's remedy unless there had been ouster of the seisin in one of five ways (for which see Carson, *Real Property Statutes*, notes to RPLA 1833, s. 2). Moreover, possession where possible was referred to a lawful title, and there were several cases where possession obviously held without title was held not to be "adverse". For instance, possession of a younger brother was possession of the heir; possession of one co-parcener, joint tenant or tenant in common was the possession of all, unless an intention to claim the whole was expressed; tenant for years continued to hold for lessor after the lease ended; if a squatter was entitled to an interest in the land less in extent than that which he claimed under the statute, his possession was referred to his lawful title; see *Lightwood on Possession*, pp. 159 et seq. Lord St. LEONARDS described the effect of the 1833 Act in these words: "It is perfectly settled that adverse possession is no longer necessary in the sense in which it was formerly used, but that mere possession may be and is sufficient under many circumstances to give a title adversely": *Dean of Ely v Bliss* (1842) 2 De GM & G at 476–7. The effect of the Act was "to substitute for a period of adverse possession in the old sense a simple period of time calculated from the accrual of the right of action": Preston and Newsom (3rd edn), p. 87. So "adverse possession" is now a useful expression to describe the possession of those against whom a right of action has accrued to the owner. See generally Smith's *Leading Cases* (12th edn), vol. ii. pp. 667 et seq; *Lightwood on Possession*, pp. 159 et seq, pp. 180–1; Holdsworth, *History of English Law*, vol. vii. pp. 69–72, 78–9. See *Paradise Beach and Transportation Co Ltd v Price-Robinson* [1968] AC 1072, [1968] 1 All ER 530.

1 *Moses v Lovegrove* [1952] 2 QB 533, [1952] 1 All ER 1279. The mere fact that the premises become subject to the Rent Acts, so that possession cannot be recovered without a court order, does not prevent the tenant's possession from being adverse. See too *Hughes v Griffin* [1969] 1 WLR 23, [1969] 1 All ER 460.

full period of 12 years. In this connection there are four possible situations which must be considered separately.

(a) X dies or transfers his interest to another person before the lapse of 12 years

The principle obtaining here is that since possession is prima facie evidence of seisin in fee, X holds a transmissible interest in the land. The time during which he has possessed is available to his successor in title, and therefore a purchaser or devisee who immediately follows him into possession and holds for the remainder of the 12 years acquires as good a right to the land as if he himself had been in possession for the whole period.[2]

(b) Possession is abandoned by X and is not retaken by another person

After this abandonment the dispossessed person is in the same position as if he had never been deprived of possession by X. There is no one whom he can now sue. There is no need for him to perform some act or ceremony in order to rehabilitate himself. The former possession of X, as Lord MACNAGHTEN said, is not available to "some casual interloper or lucky vagrant".[3] This rule is now statutory:

> Where a right of action to recover land has accrued and after its accrual, before the right is barred, the land ceases to be in adverse possession, the right of action shall no longer be treated as having accrued and no fresh right of action shall be treated as accruing unless and until the land is again taken into adverse possession.[4]

(c) Possession is abandoned by X and after an interval of time is taken by Y

It follows from what was said by Lord MACNAGHTEN and from what is now enacted, that in this case the time during which X has occupied is not available to Y, for during a distinct and definite period there was no person against whom the person ousted by X could bring an action for the recovery of the land. Y is not a successor in title of X, and his intrusion causes a fresh right of action to accrue in favour of the person dispossessed by X.

(d) X loses possession and is followed by a succession of trespassers each claiming adversely to the others

Here there is no distinct interval of time during which the possession is vacant. X, for instance, ejects V, Y ejects X, Z ejects Y, and is in actual possession when the statutory period of 12 years has run from the time of V's ejectment. Who is entitled to succeed in an action to recover the land?[5] Objection may be taken to the title of each of these persons, for V has been out of possession for more than 12 years, and yet none of the trespassers has been in possession for that period. Nevertheless, V is barred.

---

2 *Asher v Whitlock* (1865) LR 1 QB 1; M & B 203; *Mount Carmel Investments Ltd v Peter Thurlow Ltd* [1988] 1 WLR 1078, [1988] 3 All ER 129.

3 *Trustees, Executors and Agency Co Ltd v Short* (1888) 13 App Cas 793 at 798; explained by PARKER J in *Samuel Johnson and Sons Ltd v Brock* [1907] 2 Ch 533 at 538; (1956) 19 MLR p. 22, n. 11 (A. D. Hargreaves).

4 Limitation Act 1980, s. 15 (6), Sch. 1, para. 8 (2).

5 See Pollock and Wright, *Possession in the Common Law*, pp. 95 et seq; Lightwood, *Possession of Land*, pp. 275 et seq.

A continuous adverse possession for the statutory period, though by a succession of persons not claiming under one another, does, in my opinion, bar the true owner.[6]

As for the trespassers, something might be said by the moralist for the earliest possessor, also for the one who has possessed for the longest period, and again for the latest possessor,[7] but it is clear that these conflicting claims must be decided in accordance with the general principle that possession is evidence of title.[8] X, while in possession, is ejected by Y. His possession, therefore, entitles him to recover the land from the wrongdoer, Y. If he takes no proceedings, then Y, upon being ejected by Z, may recover upon the strength of his existing possession.

Possession being once admitted to be a root of title, every possession must create a title which, as against all subsequent intruders, has all the incidents and advantages of a true title.[9]

We are now in a position to deal with the accrual of the cause of action in the different cases described by the statute.

B. ACCRUAL OF RIGHTS OF ACTION

(1) PRESENT INTERESTS

Time does not begin to run against a person in present possession of land until possession has been taken by another person. The Act states the rule in this way:[10]

Where the person bringing an action to recover land, or some person through whom he claims, has been in possession of the land, and has while entitled to the land been dispossessed or discontinued his possession, the right of action shall be treated as having accrued on the date of the dispossession or discontinuance.

(a) Discontinuance or dispossession

The language of the above paragraph is not altogether happy, for it might be thought that a mere abandonment of possession is sufficient to set time running. This is not so, however, for the factor common to dispossession and discontinuance is entry upon the land by a stranger.[11]

In *Treloar v Nute*, Sir John PENNYCUICK said:[12]

The person claiming by possession must show either (1) discontinuance by the paper owner followed by possession or (2) dispossession (or as it is sometimes called "ouster") of the paper owner. Clearly, possession concurrent with the paper owner is insufficient. On the other hand, where the person claiming by possession establishes possession in the full sense of exclusive possession, that by itself connotes absence of possession on the part of the paper owner and I doubt if there is any real difference in the concept of taking possession and the concept of

6 *Willis v Earl Howe* [1893] 2 Ch 545 at 553, per KAY LJ.
7 *Dixon v Gayfere (No 1)* (1853) 17 Beav 421 at 430, per Lord ROMILLY.
8 *Asher v Whitlock* (1865) LR 1 QB 1 at 6; M & B p.203; approved *Perry v Clissold* [1907] AC 73; Pollock and Wright, p. 98.
9 Pollock and Wright, p. 95.
10 LA 1980, s. 15 (6), Sch. 1, para. 1.
11 Preston and Newsom (3rd edn), p. 99. See *Rains v Buxton* (1880) 14 Ch D 537, per FRY J; *Tecbild Ltd v Chamberlain* (1969) 20 P & CR 633.
12 [1976] 1 WLR 1295 at 1300, [1977] 1 All ER 230 at 234.

dispossession except in the special type of case where the owner, although not technically in possession, has some purpose to which he intends to put the land in the future.

(i) Adverse possession Leaving aside for the moment the "special type of case", the question whether there is adverse possession does not always admit of a ready answer. The test was well put by Lord O'HAGAN:[13]

As to possession, it must be considered in every case with reference to the peculiar circumstances. The acts, implying possession in one case, may be wholly inadequate to prove it in another. The character and value of the property, the suitable and natural mode of using it, the course of conduct which the proprietor might reasonably be expected to follow with a due regard to his own interests—all these things, greatly varying as they must, under various conditions, are to be taken into account in determining the sufficiency of a possession.

Some cases, of course, may be obvious, as for instance, where a stranger occupies the house of another or encloses and cultivates a strip of his neighbour's land.[14] It must be a very exceptional case in which enclosure will not demonstrate the relevant adverse possession required for a possessory title;[15] but enclosure is not necessarily conclusive.[16] And cultivation without fencing may amount to adverse possession.[17]

---

13 *Lord Advocate v Lord Lovat* (1880) 5 App Cas 273 at 288; cited in *Treloar v Nute*, supra, at 1299, at 233.
14 *Marshall v Taylor* [1895] 1 Ch 641.
15 *George Wimpey & Co Ltd v Sohn* [1967] Ch 487 at 512, [1966] 1 All ER 232 at 241, per RUSSELL LJ.
16 Ibid. (where the stranger had an easement over the land in question). See also *Littledale v Liverpool College* [1900] 1 Ch 19; *Hughes v Cork* [1994] EGCS 25.
17 *Seddon v Smith* (1877) 36 LT 168. See also *Tecbild Ltd v Chamberlain*, supra (playing by children and tethering of ponies held to be acts too trivial for adverse possession); *Basildon District Council v Manning* (1975) 237 EG 879 (erecting fence and dumping poultry manure held not to be adverse possession); *Red House Farms (Thorndon) Ltd v Catchpole* (1976) 244 EG 295 (shooting over marshy ground held to be adverse possession); *Treloar v Nute*, supra (grazing of two cows and a yearling, storing timber and stone and filling in a gully held to be adverse possession); *Hyde v Pearce* [1982] 1 All ER 1029 (continued occupation by purchaser, after termination of licence to occupy pending completion, held not to be adverse possession since "he had at no time made it clear that he was no longer bound by the contract of sale"); cf. *Bridges v Mees* [1957] Ch 475, [1957] 2 All ER 577 (contracting purchaser having equitable ownership held adverse possession); [1982] Conv 383 (J.E.M.); 46 MLR 89 (M. Dockray); *Bills v Fernandez-Gonzalez* (1981) 132 NLJ 60 (compost pens, bonfires, free-ranging chickens and planting trees and shrubs, together with adjoining owner's walking along line of fence for purposes of *his* garden, held not to be adverse possession); *Williams v Usherwood* (1983) 45 P & CR 235 (enclosure of land by fence, parking of three cars in enclosed curtilage of private dwelling house and paving of driveway with decorative crazy-paving stones held to be adverse possession); [1983] Conv 398 (M. Dockray); 134 NLJ 144 (H. Wilkinson); *Dear v Woods* [1984] CA Transcript 318 (playing of children, single perambulation by male plaintiff and laying of tar macadam on strip half the width of a brick held not to be adverse possession; this note was cited by Sir David CAIRNS as containing examples of trivial acts that will not suffice); *Boosey v Davis* (1987) 55 P & CR 83 (grazing of goats, cutting down of scrub and erection of secondary wire mesh fence held not to be adverse possession); *Buckinghamshire County Council v Moran* [1990] Ch 623, [1989] 2 All ER 225, M & B p. 184 (placing of new lock and chain on access gate held to be adverse possession); *Marsden v Miller* (1992) 64 P & CR 239 (erection of fence for 24 hours held not to be adverse possession by person having no documentary title against another such person); *Wilson v Martin's Executors* [1993] 24 EG 119 (walking boundary, cutting chestnuts for repair of fence, clearing fallen timber for firewood, repairing wire fence and cutting trees for sale held not to be adverse possession).

(ii) Intention to possess Not only must the stranger establish factual possession; he must also show that he has the requisite intention to possess (*animus possidendi*) to the exclusion of all other persons, including the true owner.[18] What is required for this purpose is not an intention to own or even an intention to acquire ownership but an intention to possess.[19] In *Powell v McFarlane*[20] SLADE J's elaboration of the requirement of intention shows how heavy the burden of proof is on a stranger whose alleged possession originates in a trespass:

> An owner or other person with the right to possession of land will be readily assumed to have the requisite intention to possess, unless the contrary is clearly proved. This, in my judgment, is why the slightest acts done by or on behalf of an owner in possession will be found to negative discontinuance of possession. The position, however, is quite different from a case where the question is whether a trespasser has acquired possession. In such a situation the courts will, in my judgment, require clear and affirmative evidence that the trespasser, claiming that he has acquired possession, not only had the requisite intention to possess, but made such intention clear to the world. If his acts are open to more than one interpretation and he has not made it perfectly plain to the world at large by his actions or words that he has intended to exclude the owner as best he can, the courts will treat him as not having had the requisite *animus possidendi* and consequently as not having dispossessed the owner.[1]

In the absence of concealed fraud,[2] it is irrelevant that the true owner is ignorant that he has been dispossessed. As SLADE J said:[3]

> In view of the drastic results of a change of possession, a person seeking to dispossess an owner must at least make his intentions sufficiently clear so that the owner, if present at the land, would clearly appreciate that the claimant is not merely a persistent trespasser, but is actually seeking to dispossess him.[4]

(iii) Intention of true owner Difficulties have arisen in the special type of case to which Sir John PENNYCUICK referred, i.e. where the owner of a strip of land who has no immediate use for it, retains it for some specific purpose in the future, and meanwhile some other person has physical possession of it. Until recently the owner was not treated as dispossessed. In *Leigh v Jack*,[5]

---

18 *Littledale v Liverpool College*, supra, at 23, per LINDLEY MR.
19 *Buckinghamshire County Council v Moran* [1990] Ch 623 at 642, [1989] 2 All ER 225 at 238, per SLADE, LJ; *Bladder v Phillips* [1991] EGCS 109 (cleaning of ditch at defendant's request ("thinking it was my ditch") held not to be adverse possession); *Ellett-Brown v Tallishire Ltd* (29 March 1990, unreported), CA (clipping of hedge, filling in ditch, planting of daffodils and building of brick pillar to serve as gatepost held not to be adverse possession).
20 (1977) 38 P & CR 452; M & B p. 181 (infant who at age of 14 began to graze the cow Kashla, otherwise known as Ted's cow, held not to have requisite intent); (1980) 96 LQR 333 (P. Jackson); [1982] Conv 256, 345 (M. Dockray).
 1 *Morrice v Evans* (1989) Times, 27 February (claimant accepted an assertion by the true owner of a right to restrict the claimant's activities on the land); *Pavledes v Ryesbridge Properties Ltd* (1989) 58 P & CR 459 (claimant of land for car-parking asked the true owner "to do its duty as the person entitled to possession to keep out trespassers"); *R v Secretary of State for the Environment, ex p Davies* (1990) 61 P & CR 487 (claimant described herself as "having adopted the travelling way of life", and offered to pay rent to the true owner).
 2 P. 910, post.
 3 *Powell v McFarlane*, supra, at 480.
 4 *Wilson v Martin's Executors* [1993] 24 EG 119.
 5 (1879) 5 Ex D 264.

for instance, where a stranger deposited heavy factory materials on a strip of land which the owner intended to dedicate as a highway at a future date, it was held that there was neither discontinuance nor dispossession. As BRAMWELL LJ said:[6]

> In order to defeat a title by dispossessing the former owner, acts must be done which are inconsistent with his enjoyment of the soil for the purposes for which he intended to use it: that is not the case here, where the intention of the plaintiff and her predecessor in title was not either to build upon or to cultivate the land, but to devote it at some future time to public purposes.

Since *Buckinghamshire County Council v Moran*[7] this special type of case no longer establishes a separate rule based on the owner's intended use, whereby a stranger is prevented from establishing his claim under the Limitation Act. The intention of the dispossessed owner may, however, be indirectly relevant.

> If an intention on the part of the true owner to use the land for a particular purpose at some future date is known to the squatter, then his knowledge may affect the quality of his own intention, reducing it below that which is required to constitute adverse possession. To say that is only to emphasise that it is adverse possession on which everything depends.[8]

(iv) Implied licence If the owner gives permission to a stranger to commit the acts of possession upon which he seeks to rely, then the latter cannot succeed, because time does not run in favour of a licensee.[9] The reliance in some earlier cases on a doctrine of an implied or hypothetical licence[10] has been rejected by the Limitation Act 1980. The doctrine was explained by SLADE J as follows:[11]

> Very broadly ... it would appear that in any case where the acts of an intruder, however continuous and far-reaching, do not substantially interfere with any present or future plans which the owners may have for the use of unbuilt land, the court will not treat the intruder as having dispossessed the owner for the purpose of the Limitation Act 1939 because it will treat him as having been there under some implied or hypothetical licence.

The Limitation Act 1980 has rejected this doctrine while preserving the possibility of a licence being implied where the actual facts of the case warrant it:[12]

> For the purpose of determining whether a person occupying any land is in adverse possession of the land it shall not be assumed by implication of law that his occupation is by permission of the person entitled to the land merely by virtue of

6 At 273.
7 Supra; M & B p. 184; [1990] CLJ 23 (C. Harpum); [1989] Conv 211 (G. McCormack); [1989] All ER Rev 176 (P. J. Clarke).
8 At 645, at 239, per NOURSE LJ; *Pulleyn v Hall Aggregates (Thames Valley) Ltd* (1992) 65 P & CR 276 (squatter's claim failed).
9 *BP Properties Ltd v Buckler* [1987] 2 EGLR 168.
10 *Wallis's Cayton Bay Holiday Camp Ltd v Shell-Mex and BP Ltd*, supra, at 103, at 580, per Lord DENNING MR; *Gray v Wykeham-Martin and Goode* [1977] Bar Library Transcript No. 10A (where there had first been an express licence); *Powell v McFarlane*, supra. The contrary approach along traditional lines was demonstrated in *Treloar v Nute*, supra. See (1980) 77 LSG 270 (P. A. Kay).
11 *Powell v McFarlane*, supra, at 484.
12 S. 15 (6), Sch. 1, para. 8 (4), replacing Limitation Amendment Act 1980, s. 4.

the fact that his occupation is not inconsistent with the latter's present or future enjoyment of the land.

This provision shall not be taken as prejudicing a finding to the effect that a person's occupation of any land is by implied permission of the person entitled to the land in any case where such a finding is justified on the actual facts of the case.

(b) Deceased person in possession at death

When A, the person entitled to land, dies while still in possession, and a stranger seizes possession after his death, time begins to run from the date of his death, not from the wrongful seizure, against those who claim under his will or upon his intestacy.[13] The same rule applies to a rentcharge created by will or taking effect upon death.[14]

(c) Grant of present interest

Where an interest in possession has been granted to A, or where the land has been charged in his favour with the payment of a rentcharge, and he has not taken possession or has not received the rent, time begins to run against him from the date of the grant.[15]

So far as a rentcharge is concerned this rule meets the case where the rent payer has never made a payment of the money due.

Where, however, he wrongfully makes payment to a stranger,[16] the statutory rule is that time shall begin to run against the owner of the rentcharge from "the date of the last receipt of rent" by him.[17] The result of this is to reduce the limitation period of 12 years, for normally a right of action would accrue and time would begin to run, not from the last receipt of rent, but from the date when the rent again became due.

If, for example, the rent is payable annually on 29 September and payment is duly made on that date in 1993, no *right of action or of distraint* accrues until 29 September 1994.

Nevertheless time begins to run under the statute on 29 September 1993, so that in effect the period of limitation is reduced to 11 years.[18]

(2) FUTURE INTERESTS

(a) Alternative periods

The date upon which time begins to run against the owner of a future interest depends upon whether the person entitled to the preceding estate was in possession when it came to an end. Suppose, for instance, that there is a:

grant to A for life, remainder to B in fee simple,

and that B fails to take possession on the death of A. In such a case the statute enacts alternative rules.

13 Limitation Act 1980, s. 15 (6), Sch. 1, para. 2.
14 Ibid.
15 Ibid., para. 3.
16 See generally Preston and Newsom, para. 6.6.4.
17 Limitation Act 1980, s. 38 (8).
18 *Owen v De Beauvoir* (1847) 16 M & W 547.

(i) If A dies while still possessed of the land, B's right of action accrues upon the determination of the life interest, i.e. he must sue within 12 years from the death of A.[19]

(ii) If A is not in possession at death, e.g. where he has been dispossessed by a stranger, B has the longer of two alternative periods within which he may bring his action, namely, 12 years from the time when the cause of action accrued to A, or six years from the death of A.[20]

This second rule does not apply where the preceding estate is a term of years absolute.[1] Thus time does not begin to run against a landlord until the lease determines, even though the tenant may have been ejected before that date.[2]

(b) Entailed interest

Neither rule applies to an interest limited after an entailed interest which is capable of being barred by the tenant in tail.[3] In this case the remainderman "claims through" the tenant in tail, so that if time has commenced running against the latter it continues to run against the remainderman, and does not start afresh upon the determination of the entail.

(c) Settlement made by person out of possession

Future interests created by a settlor after time has commenced to run against him are subject to a different rule. The second case given above contemplates that *after* the settlement in favour of B has been made, a right of action accrues to A, the owner of the preceding estate, against an adverse possessor. In those circumstances, as we have seen, B may recover the land within six years from the death of A, though it may be more than 12 years since A was wrongfully dispossessed. But if time once begins to run against a settlor, no *subsequent* alteration in his title, e.g. by the later creation of future interests, will prevent the bar from operating after the lapse of 12 years. The persons deriving title from the settlor cannot be in a better position than he is:[4]

> Thus, if A, seised in fee in possession, were dispossessed by X, and were afterwards to settle the estate upon B for life, remainder to C in fee, the time would run from the dispossession, in the same manner as if no such settlement had been made.[5]

(d) Same person entitled to successive interests

Where a person is entitled to successive interests in land, one present, the other future, the general principle is that, if his present interest is barred, the bar shall extend also to his future right.[6] Thus if land stands limited:

> to A for life, remainder to B for life, remainder to A in fee simple,

---

19 Limitation Act 1980, s. 15 (6), Sch. 1, para. 4.
20 Ibid., s. 15 (2). The corresponding periods are 30 years and 12 years where the Crown or a spiritual or eleemosynary corporation is entitled to the future interest: s. 15 (6), Sch. 1, para. 13.
 1 Ibid.
 2 P. 907, post.
 3 Limitation Act 1980, s. 15 (3).
 4 Ibid., s. 15 (4).
 5 Hayes, *Introduction to Conveyancing*, vol. i. p. 257.
 6 Limitation Act 1980, s. 15 (5).

and A is dispossessed for 12 years, he and those claiming under him lose the right to recover both the life interest and the fee simple in remainder. The right to recover the fee simple, however, is not barred if, to quote the words of the Act, "possession has been recovered by a person entitled to an intermediate estate or interest".[7] If, for instance, in the example just given, B were to recover possession after A had been dispossessed for 12 years, a right of recovery in respect of the fee simple would accrue to A and those claiming under him, upon the death of B.

(3) FORFEITURE OR BREACH OF CONDITION

A right of action to recover land by virtue of a forfeiture or breach of condition accrues on the date on which the forfeiture was incurred or the condition broken. If, however, a reversioner or remainderman fails to take advantage of the forfeiture or breach of condition he still retains the right of recovery that accrues to him when his estate falls into possession.[8] So if A, lessee for years, subject to a condition of re-entry, breaks the condition, the time runs against the reversioner in respect of his right of entry for the breach from its occurrence; but a bar to such right of entry will not affect his right to enter on the expiration of the lease by effluxion of time.[9]

(4) SETTLED LAND AND LAND HELD ON TRUST

Equitable interests in land, such as a life interest under a settlement and equitable interests in the proceeds of sale of land held upon trust for sale, are land within the meaning of the Limitation Act 1980.[10] In general, the provisions of the Act apply to these interests in like manner as they apply to legal estates, and the right to sue for the recovery of the land is deemed to accrue to the person entitled in possession on the date on which it would accrue if his interest were a legal estate.[11] Where such equitable interests exist the legal estate will, according to the circumstances, be vested in a tenant for life or statutory owner, or in personal representatives or in trustees for sale, all of whom are trustees for the purposes of the Act.[12]

There are two circumstances in which the beneficiaries entitled to the equitable interests may be affected by wrongful possession:

(i) The trustee in possession may disregard the rights of the beneficiaries.
(ii) A stranger may seize possession and hold it adversely to the beneficiaries.

(a) Adverse possession by trustee

The first case raises no difficulty, for a trustee cannot obtain a title to the land by adverse possession against the beneficiaries. It is expressly enacted that no period of limitation shall apply to an action brought by a beneficiary:

(*a*) in respect of any fraud or fraudulent breach of trust to which the trustee was a party or privy; or

7 Limitation Act 1980, s. 15 (5).
8 Ibid., s. 15 (6), Sch. 1, para. 7.
9 Hayes, *Introduction to Conveyancing*, vol. i. p. 252.
10 Limitation Act 1980, s. 38 (1).
11 Ibid., s. 18 (1).
12 Ibid., s. 38 (1).

(*b*) to recover from the trustee trust property or the proceeds of trust property in the possession of the trustee or previously received by the trustee and converted to his use.[13]

Thus, if a person, who is in possession of land as trustee for A and B, pays the whole of the profits to A, time does not run against B.[14] Even a notional receipt of property may come within this enactment. Thus, a trustee who remains in occupation of trust land for his own benefit is deemed to have received profits belonging to the beneficiaries, since in the circumstances he is chargeable with an occupation rent. Therefore, he can never escape liability for payment of this by pleading lapse of time, unless, indeed, under the equitable doctrine of laches, a beneficiary has been so tardy in bringing his action that it would be practically unjust to grant him relief.[15]

(i) Tenancies in common The statutory provision (*b*) has an important effect upon tenancies in common. Where land is limited to A and B as tenants in common in fee simple, the beneficiaries become, as we have seen,[16] joint tenants and trustees of the legal estate upon trust to sell the land and to give effect to their own beneficial interests. If, therefore, A appropriates the whole of the rents and profits to himself for many years, he does not acquire a title against B, for, since the land is in his possession as trustee, time does not run in his favour.[17]

Where the claim is not comprised in provisions (*a*) and (*b*), as for instance where it concerns an unauthorized investment, the beneficiary must sue the trustee six years from the accrual of his cause of action.[18]

(ii) Relief for trustee–beneficiary In one case a trustee who is *also a beneficiary* under the trust is entitled to some relief from the effect of these provisions. If he distributes the trust property amongst himself and e.g. A and B, two other beneficiaries under the trust, and then another beneficiary C appears more than six years after the distribution, under these provisions C would be able to claim from the trustee the full amount of the share of the trust property to which he would have been entitled if all the beneficiaries had claimed in time. The law was amended in 1980 to limit the liability of a trustee who has acted honestly and reasonably in making the distribution: he has to pay to C only the excess over his, the trustee's, proper share.[19]

(b) Adverse possession by stranger

As regards (ii), that is to say, where a stranger seizes possession, the rule stated above, that the statutory provisions apply to equitable interests as well as to legal estates, if it stood alone, would mean that 12 years' possession held by the stranger adversely to the trustee would extinguish the legal estate and bar the remedy of the beneficiaries. This, however, is not so. It is provided

13 Limitation Act 1980, s. 21 (1).
14 *Knight v Bowyer* (1858) 2 De G & J 421; see Preston and Newsom (3rd edn), pp. 148, 169.
15 *Re Howlett* [1949] Ch 767, [1949] 2 All ER 490; p. 903, post.
16 P. 225, ante.
17 *Re Landi* [1939] Ch 828; *Re Milking Pail Farm Trusts* [1940] Ch 996; Preston and Newsom (3rd edn), pp. 149–51. See (1941) 57 LQR 26 (R.E.M.); (1971) 35 Conv (NS) 6 (G. Battersby).
18 Limitation Act 1980, s. 21 (3). The section does not apply to an action by the Attorney-General to enforce a charitable trust, because there is no relevant beneficiary: *A-G v Cocke* [1988] Ch 414, [1988] 2 All ER 391.
19 Ibid., s. 21, replacing Limitation Amendment Act 1980, s. 5.

by another section that[20] where possession of land has been held for 12 years adversely to the trustee (i.e. adversely to a tenant for life or statutory owner of settled land, or to trustees for sale), the legal estate shall not be extinguished so long as the right of a beneficiary to recover the land has not accrued or has not been barred.

Thus the legal estate is not extinguished until the right of action of the *beneficiary* is barred. There is a further provision that a statutory owner or a trustee may sue for the recovery of the land on behalf of a beneficiary whose title to the equitable interest has not been barred.[1] By way of illustration:

> Suppose that land is settled upon A for life with remainder to B in fee simple, and that a stranger seizes the land in A's lifetime and remains in adverse possession for twelve years.

In these circumstances the *beneficial* life interest of A is extinguished, with the result that the adverse possessor acquires an equitable interest *pur autre vie*. Nevertheless the *legal fee simple*, held by A under the provisions of the Settled Land Act 1925, remains intact, and therefore B, as the owner of a future interest, will be able to enforce his right of action when it accrues to him upon the death of A. When that event occurs, the representatives of A, upon whom his legal fee simple devolves, may recover the land on behalf of B.[2]

(c) Adverse possession by beneficiary

The only case remaining for consideration is where a *beneficiary* claims title by virtue of adverse possession for 12 years. Under the law as it stood before the Limitation Act 1939, such a person, although he was ordinarily regarded as tenant at will of the trustee, acquired a title by 12 years' possession if he occupied the land to the exclusion of the trustees and the other beneficiaries.[3] Now, however, his possession cannot be adverse to these persons, for it is enacted that during his occupation of the land time shall not run against a tenant for life, statutory owner, trustee or beneficiary.[4]

(5) TENANCIES

(a) Recovery of possession from the tenant

The right of action of a lessor to recover the land from the tenant accrues when the lease determines by effluxion of time.[5] He must, therefore, sue within 12 years from this date. The mere fact that he has received no rent for many years does not affect his right to recover the land within this period.[6]

(i) Encroachment If a tenant avails himself of the opportunity afforded him by his tenancy to encroach on other land (whether belonging to the lessor or to a third party), he is presumed to have done so for the benefit of his lessor. But this presumption may be rebutted by showing that there are circumstances pointing to an intention to take the land for his own benefit exclusively.

20 Limitation Act 1980, s. 18 (2), (3).
1 Ibid., s. 18 (4).
2 See generally Preston and Newsom (3rd edn), pp. 143–6.
3 *Burroughs v M'Creight* (1844) 1 Jo & Lat 290 (Ireland).
4 Limitation Act 1980, s. 15 (6), Sch. 1, para. 9. But see Preston and Newsom (3rd edn), p. 148.
5 Ibid., para. 4.
6 *Doe d Davy v Oxenham* (1840) 7 M & W 131.

Although a tenant may thus acquire a title by adverse possession over other land, he must give it up to the lessor at the end of his lease.[7]

(ii) Forfeiture If the lease contains a clause providing for the forfeiture of the premises upon non-payment of the rent, and if the rent is not paid within the stipulated period, the landlord acquires by virtue of this clause a right to recover the land during the continuance of the tenancy.[8] This right accrues to him, as we have seen, when the forfeiture is incurred,[9] but the fact that he fails to enforce it does not affect his right to recover the land within 12 years after the determination of the term. Moreover, his failure to enforce one forfeiture does not prejudice him with regard to the future. A fresh right of re-entry accrues to him on each occasion that the tenant defaults in payment.[10]

(b) Recovery of possession from a stranger

If a stranger enters upon land which is held by lease, time begins to run in his favour against the *tenant* from the moment when the latter is dispossessed; but it does not begin to run against the *landlord* until the end of the lease, for it is only then that the landlord's right of action arises. The landlord must sue within the next 12 years, even though the existing lease is renewed in favour of the lessee while the stranger is still in possession.[11]

But since the receipt of rent is the only fact that symbolizes the landlord's title to the land, and since an adverse receipt by a stranger is really tantamount to dispossession, it is enacted that:[12]

Where—

  (a) any person is in possession of land by virtue of a lease in writing by which a rent of not less than ten pounds a year is reserved; and
  (b) the rent is received by some person wrongfully claiming to be entitled to the land in reversion immediately expectant on the determination of the lease; and
  (c) no rent is subsequently received by the person rightfully so entitled;

the right of action to recover the land of the person rightfully so entitled shall be treated as having accrued on the date when the rent was first received by the person wrongfully claiming to be so entitled and not on the date of the determination of the lease.

Thus, if the rent is wrongfully received by a stranger for 12 years, both the right of action and the title of the landlord are irretrievably barred, but if before the 12 years have elapsed rent is once more received by him, his right of action revives. If the lease is not in writing or if the annual rent is less than ten pounds, adverse receipt of the rent does not set time running against the landlord.

---

7 *Kingsmill v Millard* (1855) 11 Exch 313; *Whitmore v Humphries* (1871) LR 7 CP 1; *Smirk v Lyndale Developments Ltd* [1975] Ch 317, [1975] 1 All ER 690; M & B p. 195; *Kensington Pension Developments Ltd v Royal Garden Hotel (Oddenino's) Ltd* [1990] 2 EGLR 117.
8 P. 427, ante.
9 P. 899, ante.
10 *Barratt v Richardson and Cresswell* [1930] 1 KB 686.
11 *Ecclesiastical Commrs of England and Wales v Rowe* (1880) 5 App Cas 736; *Gray v Wykeham-Martin and Goode* [1977] Bar Library Transcript 10A; M & B p. 197.
12 Limitation Act 1980, s. 15 (6), Sch. 1, para. 6. Limitation Amendment Act 1980, s. 3 (2) had substituted ten pounds for twenty shillings.

(c) Tenancies

Tenancies at will and from year to year have received special treatment.

(i) Tenancy at will Time begins to run against the lessor from the determination of the tenancy.[13] The landlord may determine the tenancy either by demanding possession or by exercising some act of ownership on the land which is inconsistent with the right of the tenant.

Until the rule was abolished in 1980,[14] in the absence of determination, time began to run against the lessor at the end of one year from the beginning of the tenancy.[15] If, therefore, the lessor did nothing that constituted a positive determination, his title was extinguished in thirteen years from the commencement of the tenancy.

This rule was confined to a tenancy at will properly so called. If, for instance, A were given exclusive occupation of the land of B for an indefinite period and the circumstances showed that all that was intended was that he should have a personal privilege with no interest in the land, he was not a tenant at will, but a licensee, and time did not run against B while the licence subsisted.[16]

A tenancy at will and a licence are in this respect now on the same footing.

(ii) Tenancy from year to year In the case of a tenancy from year to year or other period *without a lease in writing*,[17] the right of the lessor to recover the land accrues either at the end of the first of such years or other period, or at the last receipt of rent, whichever shall last occur.[18] If the tenant remains in possession without paying rent for twelve years after the right of action has arisen, and without giving a written acknowledgment of the lessor's title, the cause of action is effectually barred,[19] and subsequent acknowledgment or payment of rent does not start time running afresh.[20]

If the lease is in writing the present rule does not apply, and the lessor's right of action accrues when he determines the tenancy by notice to quit.

(iii) Tenancy at sufferance In the case of a tenancy at sufferance, time runs from the beginning of the tenancy.

C. THE DOCTRINE OF LACHES

Despite the general rule that the provisions of the Limitation Act apply to equitable interests in land,[1] there are certain cases in which an equitable claim is unaffected by the statutory bars just discussed. Thus, as we have seen, a claim by a beneficiary to recover trust property retained by a trustee or to recover damages from a fraudulent trustee is subject to no period of

---

13 Limitation Act 1980, ss. 17, 29 (5), (6).
14 Limitation Amendment Act 1980, ss. 3 (1), 13 (2), Sch. 2.
15 Limitation Act 1939, s. 9 (1).
16 *Cobb v Lane* [1952] 1 All ER 1199; *Hughes v Griffin* [1969] 1 WLR 23, [1969] 1 All ER 460; *Heslop v Burns* [1974] 1 WLR 1241, [1974] 3 All ER 406; p. 382, ante.
17 The possession by the tenant of a rent book does not covert an oral into a written lease: *Moses v Lovegrove* [1952] 2 QB 533, [1952] 1 All ER 1279.
18 Limitation Act 1980, s. 15 (6), Sch. 1, para. 5 (1).
19 *Hayward v Challoner* [1968] 1 QB 107, [1967] 3 All ER 122, M & B p. 194; *Jessamine Investment Co v Schwarz* [1978] QB 264, [1976] 3 All ER 521.
20 *Nicholson v England* [1926] 2 KB 93.
1 Limitation Act 1980, s. 18 (1).

limitation.[2] Again, the statutory bars do not apply to any claim for specific performance, an injunction or other equitable relief, except in so far as they may be applied by analogy to the Act.[3]

Nevertheless, whenever a plaintiff seeks to enforce an equitable right to which no statute of limitation applies or to obtain a form of relief unknown to the common law, courts of equity have always required him to prosecute his claim with due diligence. In pursuance of the maxim—*vigilantibus non dormientibus aequitas solverit*—they discourage what is called *laches*, a word that signifies the negligent failure of a plaintiff to take proceedings for the enforcement of his claim within a reasonable time after he has become aware of his rights.[4] But the application of the doctrine of laches has always depended upon whether or not the suit in equity corresponds to an action at law that is within a statute of limitation.

If the equitable claim is substantially similar to a legal right that is subject to a statutory bar, the courts act by analogy to the statute and enforce the same bar upon the equitable right of action.[5] Thus an action by a widow for the assignment to her of specific land in satisfaction of her right to dower, which lay in Chancery before the abolition of dower, would fail unless she started proceedings within the statutory period prescribed for an action of ejectment.[6] The court, however, will not adopt the analogous statutory bar if the equitable claim has been deliberately omitted from the Act as a matter of policy. Relevant examples are the right of a mortgagor to redeem a mortgage of personalty,[7] or of a beneficiary to recover trust property retained by a trustee.

This principle of analogous application is now of much diminished importance, for the legislation of the nineteenth century, fortified by the Limitation Act 1980, has imposed a statutory bar upon most equitable claims.

If there is no corresponding claim or remedy at common law, or if, despite such correspondence, the equitable claim has been omitted from the statutory limitation as a matter of policy, equity applies its own test of unreasonable delay. Mere delay is seldom sufficient to constitute laches. It must be considered in the light of the circumstances:

> A defence based on staleness of demand renders it necessary to consider the time which has elapsed and the balance of justice and injustice in affording or refusing relief.[8]

At bottom, the inquiry is whether the reasonable inference from the delay and the attendant circumstances is that the plaintiff has acquiesced in the violation of his right, once it has become known to him, and thereby has in effect waived his claim against the defendant.[9] A further factor is whether

2 Limitation Act 1980, s. 21 (1); p 899, ante.
3 Ibid., s. 36 (1).
4 For a detailed discussion, see Brunyate, *Limitation of Actions in Equity*, pp. 185 et seq; Preston and Newsom (3rd edn), pp. 256–64; *Snell's Principles of Equity* (29th edn), pp. 33–36.
5 *Knox v Gye* (1872) LR 5 HL 656 at 674, per Lord WESTBURY.
6 *Williams v Thomas* [1909] 1 Ch 713.
7 Waldock, *Law of Mortgages* (2nd edn), p. 199. An action to foreclose a mortgage of personalty is barred by the Limitation Act after twelve years, but not an action to redeem such a mortgage.
8 *Re Sharpe* [1892] 1 Ch 154 at 168, per LINDLEY LJ.
9 *Lindsay Petroleum Co v Hurd* (1874) LR 5 PC 221 at 239; approved in *Erlanger v New Sombrero Phosphate Co* (1878) 3 App Cas 1218 at 1279; *Habib Bank Ltd v Habib Bank A-G Zurich* [1981] 2 All ER 650 at 665.

the defendant has altered his position to his prejudice in the belief that the claim has been abandoned.[10]

Such will be the nature of the inquiry if laches is pleaded as a defence to an action by a beneficiary to recover property retained by a trustee;[11] by a mortgagor, to redeem a mortgage of pure personalty;[12] or by a mortgagee, to foreclose an equitable mortgage of an advowson.[13]

The doctrine of laches, which is of ancient origin, is preserved by the following provision of the Limitation Act 1980:

> Nothing in this Act shall affect any equitable jurisdiction to refuse relief on the ground of acquiescence or otherwise.[14]

SECTION IV THE NATURE OF THE TITLE ACQUIRED UNDER THE LIMITATION ACT 1980

A. TITLE TO LAND

It is necessary to consider what effect the expiration of the statutory period produces upon the title to the land.

What is the effect upon the legal position, first, of the person dispossessed,[15] secondly of the person who has held adverse possession for 12 years?

(1) TITLE OF PERSON DISPOSSESSED

When time has run against a claimant, the effect in every case, no matter whether his claim is founded on tort, breach of contract, dispossession of land or some other wrong, is to bar his *remedy*. As a general rule, however, his *right* is not barred. He is precluded by the extinction of his remedy from a resort to legal proceedings, but he is free to enforce his still existent right by any other method that may be available. Before 1833 this was the effect of adverse possession of land for the required period, but the Real Property Limitation Act of that year provided that at the end of the statutory period the right, as well as the remedy, of the dispossessed owner should be extinguished.[16] This rule is retained by the Limitation Act 1980 in a section which runs as follows:[17]

> At the expiration of the period prescribed by this Act for any person to bring an action to recover land (including a redemption action) the title of that person to the land shall be extinguished.

10 *Allcard v Skinner* (1887) 36 Ch D 145 at 192, per BOWEN LJ.
11 See e.g. *Baker v Read* (1854) 18 Beav 398; *Re Jarvis* [1958] 1 WLR 815, [1958] 2 All ER 336.
12 *Weld v Petre* [1929] 1 Ch 33.
13 *Brooks v Muckleston* [1909] 2 Ch 519. Such an action of foreclosure is subject to no statutory bar, since an advowson, an incorporeal interest, is not land within the meaning of the Limitation Act 1980. Cf an action to enforce an advowson which is barred after the expiration of the relevant period prescribed by the Limitation Act 1980, s. 25; p. 890, ante.
14 S. 36 (2).
15 For the remedies against a squatter before the statutory period expires, see Webber, *Possession Proceedings* (3rd edn.); *Possession of Business Premises*.
16 S. 34.
17 S. 17. Similarly for an action to enforce an advowson: s. 25 (3). The extinguishment of title also extinguishes the rights to claim rent and mesne profits during the period of adverse possession: *Mount Carmel Investments Ltd v Peter Thurlow Ltd* [1988] 1 WLR 1078, [1988] 3 All ER 129.

There are, however, two exceptions.

First, in the case of settled land and land held on trust for sale, as we have already seen, the title of the trustee to the legal estate is not extinguished until all the beneficiaries have been barred.[18]

Secondly, where a person registered as owner under the Land Registration Act 1925 is dispossessed for 12 years, his title is not forthwith extinguished, but he is deemed to hold the land upon trust for the adverse possessor.[19] The register may be rectified in favour of the latter if he makes application to that end, but no rectification will prejudice any other person interested in the land whose right has not been extinguished by lapse of time.[20]

In considering the extent to which the *status quo ante* of the parties is affected by the statutory extinguishment of the right of action, we will deal first with the former possessor and then with the squatter.

The dispossessed person and those who claim through him lose the title to possession that he could previously have enforced against the squatter. To that extent, his title is finally destroyed and there is no method by which it can be revived, not even by a written acknowledgment given by the squatter.[1]

But the restricted effect of the extinguishment must be realized. It extinguishes nothing more than the title of the dispossessed *against the squatter*.[2] Thus, the dispossession of a lessee does not destroy his lease. His title against the lessor remains good, so that, for instance, he is entitled to resume possession if the land is vacated by the squatter. Likewise, the lessor remains entitled to sue the lessee on the covenants or indeed to re-enter the land for a forfeiture committed by the squatter if the lease contains a proviso for forfeiture.[3]

A fortiori, the titles of third parties who have enforceable interests in the land, such as those entitled to the benefit of a restrictive covenant, are unaffected by the adverse possession of the land, for no remedy accrues to them until *their* rights have been infringed.[4]

(2) TITLE OF SQUATTER

It follows from what has been said, that the sole, though substantial, privilege acquired by a squatter is immunity from interference by the person dispossessed. In other words, the statutory effect of 12 years' adverse possession is merely negative; not, as Baron PARKE once said,[5] "to make a parliamentary conveyance to the person in possession". This judicial heresy has long been exploded and it is now recognised that we must not confound the negative effect of the statute with the positive effect of a conveyance.[6]

---

18 P. 900, ante.
19 LRA 1925, s. 75 (1).
20 Ibid., s. 75 (2), (3); p. 913, post.
 1 *Nicholson v England* [1926] 2 KB 93.
 2 *Fairweather v St Marylebone Property Co Ltd* [1963] AC 510 at 539, [1962] 2 All ER 288 at 293, per Lord RADCLIFFE.
 3 Ibid., at 545, at 297, per Lord DENNING. See also *Jessamine Investment Co v Schwarz* [1978] QB 264, [1976] 3 All ER 521 (sub-lessee, protected as statutory tenant under Rent Act 1968, acquired title by adverse possession against his immediate lessor. Held (1) title of immediate lessor not extinguished as against the freeholder until head-lease expired: (2) when it did expire, sub-lessee still protected against freeholder under the Rent Act).
 4 *Re Nisbet and Potts' Contract* [1905] 1 Ch 391; M & B p. 208; p. 620, ante.
 5 *Doe d Jukes v Sumner* (1845) 14 M & W 39 at 42.
 6 Hayes, *Introduction to Conveyancing*, vol. i. p. 269.

There is no transfer, statutory or otherwise, to the squatter of the very title held by the dispossessed person. As Lord RADCLIFFE said:

> He is not at any stage of his possession a successor to the title of the man he has dispossessed. He comes in and remains in always by right of possession, which in due course becomes incapable of disturbance as time exhausts the one or more periods allowed by statute for successful intervention. His title, therefore, is never derived through but arises always in spite of the dispossessed owner.[7]

Thus if a man ejects a tenant for years and remains in possession for the statutory period, he cannot be sued for breach of a repairing covenant contained in the lease, for there has been no transfer to him of the tenant's estate.[8] Again, any right enjoyed by the dispossessed person that is based upon an implied grant, such as a way of necessity, will not avail an adverse possessor, for the doctrine of implication cannot be imported into a statutory provision that is purely negative.[9]

(a) Dispossession of lessee

The decision of the House of Lords in *Fairweather v St. Marylebone Property Co Ltd*,[10] is a further illustration of the rule that there is no transfer to a squatter of an interest commensurate with that held by the person dispossessed. The facts relevant to the present inquiry may be stated in a much simplified form as follows:

> A house and garden containing a shed were leased by X to Y for 99 years. The shed was occupied by a neighbour, Z, for more than twelve years adversely to Y. While the lease was still running, Y surrendered it to the freeholder, X.
>
> The question was whether, X, *qua* freeholder, could resume possession immediately or whether he had no such right until the lease determined by effluxion of time.

The majority of the House of Lords, overruling *Walter v Yalden*,[11] gave judgment for X. Despite the title acquired by the squatter against Y the lessee, the relationship between X and Y still continued with all its implications, including the right of Y to retain possession as against X. By surrendering the lease, Y had abandoned the right to possession, with the result that his tenancy had merged in the freehold and had disappeared. Therefore, the landlord could recover the shed on the strength of his own right to immediate possession of the freehold.[12]

The earlier decision of *Taylor v Twinberrow*[13] was approved. In that case, the facts were in effect as follows:

> X, a yearly tenant, allowed Y to occupy a cottage for more than thirteen years as a

---

7 *Fairweather v St Marylebone Property Co Ltd* [1963] AC 510 at 535, [1962] 2 All ER 288 at 291.
8 *Tichborne v Weir* (1892) 67 LT 735; M & B p. 208; p. 456, ante.
9 *Wilkes v Greenway* (1890) 6 TLR 449; similarly in registered land, *Palace Court Garages (Hampstead) Ltd v Steiner* (1958) 108 LJ 274.
10 [1963] AC 510, [1962] 2 All ER 288; M & B p. 204.
11 [1902] 2 KB 304.
12 Lord MORRIS dissented. He took the view that the tenant could not surrender what he had not himself got, namely, a right to immediate possession. *Nemo dat quod non habet*. For a criticism of the decision, see (1962) 78 LQR 541 (H. W. R. Wade). For a discussion of the difficulty of terminology in this context, see (1964) 80 LQR 63 (B. Rudden). See also (1973) 37 Conv (NS) 85 (J. A. Omotola).
13 [1930] 2 KB 16.

tenant at will. X then bought the fee simple, with the result that the yearly tenancy was determined by its merger in the freehold. It was argued that the title acquired by Y was commensurate with that lost by X and that therefore he was entitled to the half a year's notice to quit appropriate to a yearly tenancy.

This argument was fallacious. All that the squatter had acquired was a title to possession indefeasible by the yearly tenant. With the disappearance of the yearly tenancy, the former yearly tenant had become the freeholder, and as such he had an immediate right to recover possession.

One effect of these decisions is that the lessor and lessee can combine to defeat the squatter. If the lessor accepts a surrender of the term, he is then able to grant a new lease to the tenant.[14]

(b) Subsequent improvement of title

Nevertheless, despite the negative operation of the Limitation Act, the title to possession acquired by a squatter against the person dispossessed may ultimately ripen into a title to the fee simple. As COZENS–HARDY MR said:

> Whenever you find a person in possession of property, that possession is prima facie evidence of ownership in fee, and that prima facie evidence becomes absolute once you have extinguished the right of every other person to challenge it.[15]

In other words, a squatter, though a wrongdoer, acquires by virtue of his possession a new independent title to the fee simple which prevails against all persons except those who can rely on an earlier and therefore a better title. Moreover, it is a title that will prevail against those with better titles if they fail to assert their rights within the period prescribed by the Limitation Act. Thus, a title originally defeasible may in course of time become indefeasible.[16]

For instance:

> X dispossesses W, the fee simple owner of Blackacre, and remains in possession for eight years when he himself is dispossessed by Y.

As between X and Y, X's is the earlier and therefore the stronger title of the two, but he must assert it against the weaker within the statutory period. If Y is allowed to remain in possession for 12 years without being challenged either by W or by X, his title to possession of the fee simple becomes indefeasible. It rests on the infirmity of the right of others to eject him.[17]

Again, if some lesser title than that to the fee simple is destroyed, as when a lessee is ejected, the squatter may still be challenged by the lessor, the freeholder. So, if the lease terminates by effluxion of time or becomes forfeitable for breach of condition,[18] the freeholder's right to recover possession accrues and prevails over that of the squatter. Relatively to the tenant, the squatter's right is the stronger; relatively to the freeholder, it is the weaker. But if the freeholder does not pursue his remedy within six years from the end of the lease, the squatter's title to the fee simple becomes indefeasible.

---

14 *Fairweather v St Marylebone Property Co Ltd* [1963] AC 510 at 547, [1962] 2 All ER 288 at 299, per Lord DENNING.
15 *Re Atkinson and Horsell's Contract* [1912] 2 Ch 1 at 9.
16 *St Marylebone Property Co Ltd v Fairweather* [1962] 1 QB 498 at 513, [1961] 3 All ER 560 at 567, per HOLROYD PEARCE LJ.
17 Darby and Bosanquet, *Statutes of Limitation* (2nd edn), p. 493, adopted by BOWEN LJ in *Tichborne v Weir* (1892) 67 LT 735.
18 *Tickner v Buzzacott* [1965] Ch 426, [1965] 1 All ER 131.

B. PROOF OF TITLE

A consequence of the negative effect of the Limitation Act 1980 is that as
between vendor and purchaser a title based on adverse possession alone for
the limitation period or longer is not necessarily a good title. The claims of a
reversioner or a remainderman may have yet to be extinguished;[19] the
reversion may be on a 99 year lease; the remainderman's interest may not
vest in possession for over 100 years.[20] But if a vendor can establish that the
flaw in an otherwise good title is one that can be cured by the running of time
in his favour under the Act, he can force a purchaser to take the title.[1] Proof
that rival claims have been extinguished by the lapse of time may be very
difficult, and in practice a purchaser often agrees to accept an imperfect
title.[2]

SECTION V CIRCUMSTANCES IN WHICH THE STATUTORY PERIOD IS EXTENDED

In three cases, namely:

1. where the person entitled to recover land is under a disability;
2. where there has been fraud or deliberate concealment of a cause of action; and
3. where a person seeks relief from the consequences of a mistake;

the period of 12 years within which an action must normally be brought is
lengthened.

A. DISABILITY

A person is deemed to be under a disability for the purposes of the Act while
he is an infant or of unsound mind.[3]

If, on the date when a right of action for the recovery of land accrues, the
person to whom it has accrued is under a disability, the action may be
brought at any time within six years from the removal of the disability or
from his death, whichever event first occurs, notwithstanding that the period
of limitation has expired.[4] No action, however, to recover land or money
charged on land may be brought after the expiration of 30 years from the
date on which the right accrued.[5] A disability which begins *after* the accrual

19 Limitation Act 1980, ss. 15, 18.
20 *Cadell v Palmer* (1833) 1 Cl & Fin 372; vesting postponed for over 100 years (note to *Re Villar* [1928] Ch 471 at 478); p. 292, ante.
 1 *Re Atkinson's and Horsell's Contract* [1912] 2 Ch 1; *Re Spencer and Hauser's Contract* [1928] Ch 598; distinguished in *George Wimpey & Co Ltd v Sohn* [1967] Ch 487, [1966] 1 All ER 232.
 2 M & B p. 179; Farrand, *Contract and Conveyance* (4th edn), pp. 108–109.
 3 Limitation Act 1980, s. 38 (2), (3), (4); *Kirby v Leather* [1965] 2 QB 367, [1965] 2 All ER 441. If a cause of action arose before 1 January 1970, the change from 21 to 18 years for the age of majority does not affect the time for bringing actions: Family Law Reform Act 1969, s. 1 (4), Sch. 3, para 8.
 4 Ibid., s. 28 (1).
 5 Ibid., s. 28 (4).

of a right of action does not prevent time from continuing to run against the disabled person.[6]

If before the cessation of one disability another one supervenes, time does not begin to run until both have ceased.[7] For instance:

A dispossesses B, an infant six years of age. When 15 years old B becomes of unsound mind, and is still in this state upon the attainment of his majority. Time does not begin to run until he recovers his sanity.

If the person entitled to the right of action dies while still under a disability, his successor in title must sue within six years even though he himself is under a disability.[8]

B. FRAUD OR DELIBERATE CONCEALMENT OF RIGHT OF ACTION

Section 32 (1) of the Limitation Act 1980 provides that where:

(a) the action is based upon the fraud of the defendant; or
(b) any fact relevant to the plaintiff's right of action has been deliberately concealed from him by the defendant

time shall not begin to run until the plaintiff has discovered the fraud or concealment, or could with reasonable diligence have discovered it.[9] The defendant includes the defendant's agent and any person through whom the defendant claims and his agent.[10]

The section, however, provides that the enactment shall not enable a person to recover the land or its value from a purchaser for valuable consideration who was not a party to the fraud or to the concealment, and who at the time of the purchase did not know and had no reason to believe that the fraud or concealment had taken place.[11]

"Fraud" in paragraph (a) bears its usual meaning,[12] but deliberate concealment in paragraph (b) is more difficult. It is presumably intended to take account of the restrictive interpretation placed by the courts on the words "concealed fraud" which occurred in the corresponding section of the Limitation Act 1939.[13] The word "deliberate" is not defined, but section 32 (2) provides that:

deliberate commission of a breach of duty in circumstances in which it is unlikely

6 Limitation Act 1980, s. 28 (1), (2).
7 *Borrows v Ellison* (1871) LR 6 Exch 128.
8 Limitation Act 1980, s. 28 (3).
9 *Peco Arts Inc v Hazlitt Gallery Ltd* [1983] 1 WLR 1315 at 1323, [1983] 3 All ER 193 at 199 (drawing Études Pour le Bain by Ingres).
10 *Eddis v Chichester Constable* [1969] 2 Ch 345, [1969] 2 All ER 747 (painting attributed to Caravaggio).
11 Limitation Act 1980, s. 32 (3), (4).
12 See *Beaman v ARTS Ltd* [1949] 1 KB 550 at 558, [1949] 1 All ER 465 at 467, per Lord GREENE.
13 S. 26. See *Applegate v Moss* [1971] 1 QB 406 at 413, [1971] 1 All ER 747 at 750, per Lord DENNING; *Clark v Woor* [1965] 1 WLR 650 at 654, [1965] 2 All ER 352 at 356; *King v Victor Parsons & Co* [1973] 1 WLR 29 at 33, [1973] 1 All ER 206 at 209; *Tito v Waddell (No 2)* [1977] Ch 106 at 224-5, [1977] 3 All ER 129 at 244-5; *Lewisham London Borough v Leslie & Co Ltd* (1978) 250 EG 1289; *Bartlett v Barclays Bank Trust Co Ltd* [1980] Ch 515 at 537, [1980] 1 All ER 139 at 154-155.

to be discovered for some time amounts to deliberate concealment of the facts involved in that breach of duty.

Deliberate concealment is clearly less than fraud, and in essence:

> denotes conduct by the defendant or his agent such that it would be "against conscience" for him to avail himself of the lapse of time.[14]

Thus, wrongfully to enter land without the knowledge of the owner would not constitute deliberate concealment.[15] It would, however, be deliberate concealment in the context of adverse possession where a person, knowing that the land belongs to X, conceals from X the circumstances which confer the right upon him, and thus enables himself to enter and hold.[16] Examples are the destruction of title deeds,[17] the intentional concealment of a voluntary conveyance to the plaintiff,[18] the passing off of an illegitimate son as the eldest legitimate son,[19] the procuring of a conveyance from a person of unsound mind,[20] and where a builder covers up what he knows to be rubbishy foundations and does not tell the owner anything about it.[1]

C. MISTAKE

Similar provisions apply:

> where the action is for relief from the consequences of a mistake.[2]

The relief, however, is only available "where the mistake is an essential ingredient of the cause of action",[3] as for instance where the action is to recover money paid under a mistake. There is no general rule that a mistake prevents time from running under the Act.

SECTION VI THE METHODS BY WHICH TIME MAY BE PREVENTED FROM RUNNING

Time which has begun to run under the Act is stopped, either when the owner asserts his right or when his right is admitted by the adverse possessor.

A. ASSERTION OF OWNER'S RIGHT

Assertion of right occurs when the owner takes legal proceedings or makes an effective entry onto the land.

---

14 *Applegate v Moss*, supra, at 413, at 750, per Lord Denning; *Westlake v Bracknell District Council* [1987] 1 EGLR 161; *Johnson v Chief Constable of Surrey* (1992) Times, 23 November; *Sheldon v RHM Outhwaite (Underwriting Agencies) Ltd* (1993) Times, 8 December (deliberate concealment after cause of action held to prevent time from running).
15 *Rains v Buxton* (1880) 14 Ch D 537.
16 *Petre v Petre* (1853) 1 Drew 371 at 397, per Kindersley V-C.
17 *Lawrance v Lord Norreys* (1890) 15 App Cas 210.
18 *Re McCallum* [1901] 1 Ch 143.
19 *Vane v Vane* (1873) 8 Ch App 383.
20 *Lewis v Thomas* (1843) 3 Hare 26.
 1 *Applegate v Moss*, supra; *King v Victor Parsons & Co*, supra.
 2 Limitation Act 1980, s. 32 (1) (c).
 3 *Phillips-Higgins v Harper* [1954] 1 QB 411 at 419, [1954] 1 All ER 116 at 119, per Pearson J.

B. ADMISSION OF OWNER'S RIGHT

An admission of the right of the person entitled occurs when the adverse possessor acknowledges the right, or, if the right is to the payment of money, where he makes a part payment.

(1) ACKNOWLEDGMENT

Where a right of action to recover land or an advowson or to foreclose a mortgage has already accrued to X and his title is later acknowledged by the person in possession, his right is treated as having accrued on and not before the date of the acknowledgment.[4] The effect is that the owner's right of action recommences, not only against the person who makes the admission, but also against all later possessors, and remains effective until there has been adverse possession for a further period of 12 years.[5] An acknowledgment, however, has no effect if it is given after the period of limitation has run its full course.[6]

Every acknowledgment must be in writing and signed by the person by whom it is made.[7] It must be made to the person whose title or claim is being acknowledged or to his agent.[8] Any written statement is sufficient that implicitly recognizes the title of the person to whom it is made, as for instance an offer by a squatter to purchase the land from the freeholder;[9] or a request for further time within which to pay made by the possessor of land in response to a demand for rent.[10]

(2) PART PAYMENT

If, after a right of foreclosure or other cause of action has accrued to a mortgagee, the possessor of the land or the person liable for the mortgage debt makes any payment of principal or interest, there is a fresh accrual of the right of action from the date of payment.[11]

Where a right of action has accrued to recover any debt or other liquidated pecuniary claim, as for instance rent due under a lease, and the person liable acknowledges the claim or makes any payment in respect thereof, the right is treated as accruing on and not before the date of the acknowledgment or payment.[12] A payment of part only of rent does not, however, enable the remainder then due to be recovered more than six years after it became due.[13] An acknowledgment to be effective for this purpose must admit the

---

4 Limitation Act 1980, s. 29 (1), (2) (*a*).
5 Ibid., s. 31 (1).
6 *Sanders v Sanders* (1881) 19 Ch D 373.
7 Limitation Act 1980, s. 29 (1). See *Browne v Perry* [1991] 1 WLR 1297 at 1301, per Lord TEMPLEMAN.
8 Ibid., s. 29 (2).
9 *Edginton v Clark* [1964] 1 QB 367, [1963] 3 All ER 468 (letter to owner's agent offering to purchase land held to be effective acknowledgment); *Re Compania de Electricidad de la Provincia de Buenos Aires Ltd* [1980] Ch 146, [1978] 3 All ER 668 (balance sheet effective acknowledgment if received by creditor).
10 *Fursdon v Clogg* (1842) 10 M & W 572.
11 Limitation Act 1980, s. 29 (3).
12 Ibid., s. 29 (5).
13 Ibid., s. 29 (6).

existence of the debt, but it need not state its precise amount, provided that this is ascertainable by extrinsic evidence.[14]

(3) PERSONS BOUND BY ACKNOWLEDGMENT AND PART PAYMENT

There is a distinction between acknowledgment and part payment with regard to the persons upon whom they are binding. An acknowledgment binds only the acknowledgor and his successors,[15] i.e. persons who claim through him, such as a trustee in bankruptcy or an executor.[16] A part payment of a debt or other liquidated money claim, on the other hand, binds all persons liable in respect thereof,[17] for since they derive advantage from the payment it is only just that they should share the disadvantage of a fresh accrual of a right of action to the creditor. Thus a part payment of rent by a tenant revives the landlord's right of action against a surety.[18]

(4) ACKNOWLEDGMENT OR PART PAYMENT AFTER TIME HAS RUN

No acknowledgment or part payment can revive any right to recover land if it is made after the full period of limitation has run. The reason is that the effect of the Limitation Act is to bar not only the remedy of an owner for recovering the land but also his right to it;[19] and, since the right as well as the remedy is barred, there is nothing left to acknowledge. Where, however, the remedy alone is barred, e.g. in the case of an action for the payment of a debt, the rule used to be that an acknowledgment or part payment was effective even if given after the period had elapsed.[20] This rule was changed in the Limitation Act 1980, where it was enacted[1] that:

> a current period of limitation may be repeatedly extended by further acknowledgments or payments, but a right of action, once barred by this Act, shall not be revived by any subsequent acknowledgment or payment.

SECTION VII REGISTERED LAND

The Limitation Act 1980 applies to registered land, and a title to a registered estate may be acquired by adverse possession.[2] There is, however, one important difference which springs from the mechanics of registration. When a squatter acquires a legal title to unregistered land by adverse possession, the former owner's estate is automatically extinguished. With registered land, however, there is no automatic extinction of the proprietor's title but it is deemed to be held by the proprietor on trust for the squatter, though without prejudice to the rights of any other person interested in the

---

14 *Dungate v Dungate* [1965] 1 WLR 1477, [1965] 3 All ER 393, explaining *Good v Parry* [1963] 2 QB 418, [1963] 2 All ER 59; *Surrendra Overseas Ltd v Government of Sri Lanka* [1977] 1 WLR 565, [1977] 2 All ER 481; *Kamouh v Associated Electrical Industries International Ltd* [1980] QB 199; *Re Overmark Smith Warden Ltd* [1982] 1 WLR 1195, [1982] 3 All ER 513.
15 Limitation Act 1980, s. 31 (6).
16 Ibid., s. 31 (9).
17 Ibid., s. 31 (7).
18 *Re Powers* (1885) 30 Ch D 291; *Re Frisby* (1889) 43 Ch D 106.
19 P. 905, ante.
20 See Limitation Act 1939, s. 25 (5), (6).
1 S. 29 (7), replacing Limitation Amendment Act 1980, s. 6. A squatter may be estopped from asserting his title: *Colchester Borough Council v Smith* [1991] Ch 448, [1991] 1 All ER 29.
2 See generally Ruoff and Roper, chapter 32.

land whose estate or interest is not extinguished by the Act of 1980. Anyone claiming to have acquired a title to registered land under the Limitation Act may apply to be registered as proprietor and he may be registered with an absolute, good leasehold, qualified or possessory title, as the case may be, but his estate will be a completely new one and the registration will be treated as that of a first proprietor.[3]

In *Spectrum Investment Co v Holmes*[4] the question arose whether the rule in *Fairweather v St Marylebone Property Co Ltd*[5] applied to registered land:

> In 1902 a registered freeholder granted a registered lease of a house to T. In 1968 H acquired a title by adverse possession against D, a registered assignee of T, under the Limitation Act 1939. H applied for and obtained registration as proprietor of the leasehold interest with possessory title, and the title under which D was registered was closed. In 1975 D "woke up" and purported to surrender the lease to S the freeholder's successor in title, who was then the registered proprietor with absolute title to the freehold. S then claimed possession against H, the registered squatter.

BROWNE-WILKINSON J held that the rule in *Fairweather* did not apply to registered land. Since D's title had been closed, D was no longer the registered proprietor of the lease, and was therefore unable to surrender it. In any event the surrender itself was invalid as not having been effected by a registered disposition.[6]

It would seem to follow that in the case of registered land the freeholder and the tenant can together defeat the squatter's title by surrender at any time *before* he obtains registration of his possessory title. The difference between registered and unregistered land only occurs *after* the squatter has been registered.

Rights acquired or in course of being acquired under the Limitation Act are overriding interests,[7] and therefore a registered purchaser for value can never be in a better position than his predecessor in title and must take subject to the rights of the squatter.[8] The purchaser's registered title even if absolute may be rectified in favour of the squatter,[9] but the purchaser will not be entitled to an indemnity, as he has only lost thereby a valueless asset, i.e. a title barred by adverse possession on the part of the squatter.[10]

---

3 LRA 1925, s. 75; *Fairweather v St Marylebone Property Co Ltd* [1963] AC 510 at 541, 548, [1962] 2 All ER 288 at 295, 299; *Spectrum Investment Co v Holmes* [1981] 1 WLR 221 at 229, [1981] 1 All ER 6 at 13; (1981) 131 NLJ 718 (P. F. Smith); 774 (E. G. Nugee); [1981] Conv 155 (R. E. Annand); [1982] Conv 201 (P. H. Kenny).

4 [1981] 1 WLR 221, [1981] 1 All ER 6; M & B p. 210.

5 [1963] AC 510, [1962] 2 All ER 288; p. 907, ante.

6 LRA 1925, ss. 21, 22, 69 (4). D's claim to rectification of the register to enable her to execute a valid surrender was rejected. H was properly registered under the mandatory requirements of s. 75 (3). See also *Mount Carmel Investments Ltd v Peter Thurlow Ltd* [1988] 1 WLR 1078 at 1089, [1988] 3 All ER 129 at 137 (original squatter forged a long lease from the registered freeholder and assigned it to another squatter).

7 Ibid., s. 70 (1) (*f*); *Bridges v Mees* [1957] Ch 475, [1957] 2 All ER 577.

8 *Bridges v Mees*, supra.

9 *Chowood v Lyall (No. 2)* [1930] 2 Ch 156.

10 See *Re Chowood's Registered Land* [1933] Ch 574; M & B p. 173.

Chapter 27

Merger

SUMMARY

The term *merger* means that, where a lesser and a greater estate in the same land come together and vest, without any intermediate estate, in the same person and in the same right, the lesser is immediately annihilated by operation of law. It is said to be "merged", i.e. sunk or drowned, in the greater estate.[1]

For example:

If land is limited to A for life, remainder to B in fee simple, merger will result from any event which produces the union in one person of the life interest and the remainder in fee. Thus if A conveys his life interest to B, or if B conveys his remainder to A, there is in each case a merger. Again, a term of years may merge in a life interest, and an estate *pur autre vie* may merge in the interest held by a tenant for his own life.

SECTION I AT COMMON LAW

At common law the doctrine of merger has nothing to do with the intention of the parties, and provided that certain essentials are satisfied, the effect is automatically to annihilate the smaller estate.

The essentials are that the estates shall unite in the same person without any intervening estate, and that the person in whom they unite shall hold them both in the same right.

To illustrate the first essential, if A, who is tenant for life, with remainder to B for life, remainder to C in fee, purchases and takes a conveyance of C's fee, the intervening life interest of B, since it is vested, excludes the possibility of merger.

As regards the second essential, if an executor takes, under the Administration of Estates Act 1925, a term of years which belonged to the testator, and then purchases the reversion in fee on his own behalf, the term which the executor holds for the purposes of administration does not merge in the fee which he owns beneficially.[2]

---

1 Blackstone, vol. 11, p. 177; Cruise, *Digest* Tit. xxxix, s. 1.
2 *Chambers v Kingham* (1878) 10 Ch D 743.

A. ENTAILED INTEREST

The exception to the doctrine of merger at common law is that an entailed interest does not merge in the fee simple in reversion or remainder, for the intention of the Statute *De Donis* is that such an interest shall descend to the issue of the tenant in tail. If, for instance, where lands are limited to A in tail, remainder to B in fee simple, A were able by a purchase of the reversion in fee to extinguish his entailed interest under the doctrine of merger, a simple method of defeating the issue would be thrown open. It has therefore been the rule since the sixteenth century that in such a case no merger results.[3]

B. TERM OF YEARS

One effect of the common law doctrine was that the merger of a term of years in the reversion destroyed the covenants contained in any sub-lease that has been carved out of the term.

Suppose, for instance, that A, seised in fee, leased the land to T who sub-leased it to S. If T were to surrender his interest to A, the covenants contained in the sub-lease would become unenforceable, since the reversion to which they were formerly attached no longer existed.[4]

To remedy this, it was enacted in effect by the Real Property Act 1845,[5] in a section reproduced in the Law of Property Act 1925,[6] that where the reversion on a lease is destroyed by surrender or merger, the next vested interest in the land shall be deemed to be the reversion for the purpose of preserving the incidents and obligations of the defunct reversion. Thus, in the example given above, the covenants entered into between T and S are enforceable by and against A and S respectively.

SECTION II IN EQUITY

Equity has taken a different view of merger. At common law merger results automatically from the union of two estates in the circumstances we have mentioned, and intention does not affect the result. But equity looks to the intention and to the duties of the parties. If an intention is expressly declared to the effect that the lesser estate shall be kept alive, there is no difficulty;[7] but even in the absence of such an express declaration equity will presume an intention against merger if it is clearly advantageous to the person in whom the estates are united, or if it is consistent with his duty, that the lesser interest shall not be destroyed.[8] This view now prevails, for it was enacted by the Judicature Act 1873 that there should be no merger by operation of law of any estate the beneficial interest in which would not be deemed to be merged or extinguished in equity.[9]

3 *Wiscot's Case* (1599) 2 Co Rep 60*b*, 61*a*.
4 *Webb v Russell* (1789) 3 Term Rep 393.
5 S. 9; *Bromley Park Garden Estates Ltd v George* [1991] 2 EGLR 95.
6 S. 139; *Electricity Supply Nominees Ltd v Thorn EMI Retail Ltd* [1991] 2 EGLR 46 at 48, per Fox LJ.
7 *Golden Lion Hotel (Hunstanton) Ltd v Carter* [1965] 1 WLR 1189, [1965] 3 All ER 506.
8 *Ingle v Vaughan Jenkins* [1900] 2 Ch 368; *Re Fletcher* [1917] 1 Ch 339.
9 S. 25(4); reproduced in LPA 1925, s. 185.

In *Snow v Boycott*, for instance:[10]

land was limited to A for life, remainder to B for life. A, being too old to manage the property, conveyed the land to B for the rest of her life to the use that B should pay her £400 a year out of the profits. The effect of this was that an estate *pur autre vie* and an estate for his own life vested in B, so that at common law the estate *pur autre vie* was destroyed by merger. B died in the lifetime of A, and the question arose whether A's life estate had been destroyed so as to let in the estates which were limited to take effect after B's life estate. It was held that there was no merger in *equity*, and therefore no such destruction, for the parties could not have intended to create an interest *pur autre vie* in order that it should be immediately swallowed up in an existing life interest and thereby lost.

In another case:

X, the first tenant for life under a settlement, agreed to let three acres of the land for 99 years to Y, the second tenant for life, at an annual ground rent of £9, in consideration that Y would erect thereon a house at a cost of £1,500. After the house had been erected, X died, with the result that at common law Y's term of years was merged in the life interest to which he now became entitled.

On the death of Y, the remainderman contended that Y's executor was prevented by this merger from claiming any further leasehold interest in the land. The contention failed. The court's one concern is the benefit of the person in whom the two interests unite, and in the instant circumstances it was obviously to the advantage of Y that the term of years should be kept separate from the life interest.[11]

---

10 [1892] 3 Ch 110.
11 *Ingle v Vaughan Jenkins* [1900] 2 Ch 368.

Part III

The transfer and extinction of estates and interests

D. INCAPACITIES AND DISABILITIES WITH REGARD TO THE HOLDING AND TRANSFER OF ESTATES AND INTERESTS

SUMMARY

Chapter 28

Incapacities and disabilities

SECTION I INFANTS

An infant[1] is a person, whether male or female, who has not attained full age. After 1 January 1970, a person attains full age at the first moment of the eighteenth anniversary of his birth.[2] Hitherto the age of majority had been the first moment of the day preceding the twenty-first anniversary.[3]

---

1 Or a minor: Family Law Reform Act 1969, s. 12. Limitation Act 1980, s. 38 (2), continues to use infant.
2 Persons of 18 or over, but under 21 attained full age on that date: Family Law Reform Act 1969, ss. 1 (1), 9. See Report of the Committee on the Age of Majority (the Latey Report) 1967 (Cmnd 3342); (1979) 120 NLJ 144 (S. M. Cretney). S. 1 (2) provides that for the "construction of 'full age', 'infant', 'infancy', 'minor', 'minority' and similar expressions" in any statutory provision, whenever passed or made, the references shall be deemed to be references to the age of majority as amended by the Act. Where, however, a statutory provision refers to a specified age, s. 1 (3), Sch. 1, sets out those statutes in which references to 21 are changed to 18. S. 1 (4), Sch. 2 excepts certain statutes from s. 1 (2) e.g. the Regency Acts 1937–1953; Representation of the People Act 1969, now 1983. For changes in fiscal legislation, see FA 1969, s. 16, and, in the age of franchise, Representation of the People Act 1983, s. 1. In the case of private transactions the Act is not retrospective, e.g. "to X on

Our task in the present chapter is to deal with three aspects of infancy, namely:

1.   the acquisition by an infant of interests in land;
2.   the alienation by an infant of interests in land; and
3.   the management of an infant's property.

A. ACQUISITION BY INFANT OF INTERESTS IN LAND

In accordance with the fundamental principle of the legislation of 1925, an infant can never hold a *legal estate* in land.[4] He cannot be an estate owner. This restriction, which is imposed in the interests of a simplified system of conveyancing, does not mean that he cannot hold and enjoy beneficially an equitable interest[5] and there is nothing to prevent land being transferred to him by way of gift, sale, settlement or lease. In such a case, the statutory policy is to treat the land as settled land, and during the infancy to vest the legal estate in trustees whose identity will depend upon whether the infant comes to his interest as grantee, devisee, heir on intestacy, beneficiary under a settlement, mortgagee, or trustee of the land for the benefit of another person.

(1) GRANT INTER VIVOS TO INFANT

It is enacted that a conveyance of a legal estate in land to an infant alone, or to two or more persons jointly, both or all of whom are infants, for his or their own benefit, shall operate only as an agreement for valuable consideration to execute a settlement in his or their favour.[6] This means that the grantor must as soon as possible execute a principle vesting deed and a trust instrument,[7] meanwhile holding the land in trust for the infant. In this case, however, the legal estate will be transferred by the vesting deed not to the infant as tenant for life, but to the trustees when they are appointed, who then become the statutory owners.[8]

If a legal estate is conveyed to an infant jointly with one or more other persons of full age, the person or persons of full age take the legal estate on trust for sale.[9] In this case the persons of full age hold upon the statutory trusts applicable to a joint tenancy, i.e. upon trust to sell the land and to hold the proceeds and the profits until sale for the benefit of themselves and the infant.[10] If, however, life interests are given, there is a settlement and the adults are tenants for life under the Settled Land Act 1925.[11]

---

attaining his majority", if made in a will or settlement before 1970, X takes at 21; if made after 1968, X takes at 18.

3 See Report of the Committee on the Age of Majority (1967) Cmnd 3342, paras. 37–42; *Re Shurey* [1918] 1 Ch 263.
4 LPA 1925, s. 1 (6).
5 Ibid., s. 19 (1); SLA 1925, ss. 26 (6), 27 (2).
6 Ibid., s. 19 (1); SLA 1925, s. 27 (1). This is registrable as an estate contract under LCA 1972; p. 759, ante. On the grant of a lease to an infant, see Law Commission Report on Minors' Contracts 1984 (Law Com No. 134, 494), paras. 5.13–5.16, explaining supposed difficulties.
7 Pp. 179 et seq, ante. Or he may execute a confirmatory conveyance to the infant after the infant attains majority: *Darvell v Basildon Development Corpn* (1969) 211 EG 33 at 37.
8 P. 185, ante.
9 LPA 1925, s. 19 (2).
10 Ibid., s. 35.
11 S. 19 (3).

(2) DEVISE TO INFANT

In the case of a devise to an infant the legal estate vests at first in the personal representatives of the deceased by virtue of the Administration of Estates Act 1925, but in considering the ultimate destination of the legal estate we must distinguish between a devise of an absolute interest, and a devise by way of settlement in which trustees of the settlement have been appointed.

Where the land is devised to the infant for an estate in fee simple or for a term of years absolute, or where it is settled upon him for life and no trustees are appointed, the personal representatives can retain the land until the infant attains his majority, and until that time they possess all the powers of a tenant for life under a settlement,[12] and also the powers of trustees for sale.[13] If, however, they do not desire to retain the land, they may appoint trustees to be trustees of the land for the purposes of the Settled Land Act and for the purposes of the statutory provisions relating to the management of land during a minority.[14]

Where the land is devised by way of settlement to an infant for a limited interest and the testator has appointed trustees of the settlement, the Act directs that the personal representatives shall, when their administration duties are completed, transfer the legal estate to the trustees if they are required to do so.[15]

(3) DESCENT OF LAND TO INFANT

(a) Fee simple

In the case of deaths occurring after 1925 it is impossible for an infant to become entitled to a fee simple estate by descent. The rules of primogeniture do not apply and the residuary estate of the intestate, as we have seen,[16] is held by the administrator upon trust to sell and to divide the proceeds among the relatives entitled under the Administration of Estates Act 1925. If an infant is the sole relative so entitled, he will become entitled absolutely to the fee simple when he either marries or attains his majority. But as we have seen, an infant cannot hold a legal estate in land, and therefore, the land remains settled land until he attains his majority.[17]

(b) Entailed interest

The old law of descent, however, still applies to the entailed interest, but if the heir is an infant the legal estate must be vested in the trustees of the settlement until he attains his majority. If money is required during his minority for his maintenance, education or benefit, the court if necessary may make an order under the Trustee Act 1925,[18] appointing a person to execute a disentailing assurance which will bar the issue and remaindermen as completely as if it were effected by the infant after attaining his majority.[19]

12 SLA 1925, s. 26 (1).
13 AEA 1925, s. 39 (1).
14 Ibid., s. 42.
15 SLA 1925, ss. 6, 26.
16 Pp. 875 et seq, ante.
17 AEA 1925, s. 47, p. 880, ante.
18 TA 1925, s. 53.
19 *Re Gower's Settlement* [1934] Ch 365.

(4) SETTLEMENT OF LAND IN FAVOUR OF INFANT

A person who desires to settle land in favour of an infant has an alternative, for he may create either a settlement under the Settled Land Act 1925 or a trust for sale.

In the case of a settlement, the statutory powers of a tenant for life and the trustees of a settlement, together with any additional powers that may be conferred by the settlement, become exercisable by the trustees,[20] who, in their capacity as "statutory owners",[1] are entitled to have the legal estate transferred to them by a vesting deed. If the settlor adopts the method of a trust for sale, the trustees not only obtain the legal estate but they also possess all the statutory powers under the Settled Land Act 1925, so long as the land remains unsold.[2]

If a tenant for life under an existing settlement is succeeded by an infant tenant for life, the latter is not entitled to the legal estate until he attains his majority. In the meantime the legal estate and the statutory powers will be held by the trustees of the settlement.[3]

Where an infant becomes absolutely entitled under a settlement, as, for example, where there is a grant or a devise:

> to A for life, remainder to B (an infant) in fee simple, and A dies during the minority of B,

the settlement continues until B attains his majority,[4] the legal estate in the meantime being vested in the trustees of the settlement. In a case such as this, statutory provision is made to meet the contingency of the infant dying under age, for it is enacted that unless he marries before reaching his majority he shall be deemed to have had an entailed interest at the time of his death.[5] In other words, the fee simple of the infant B, in the above example, though potentially absolute,[6] is cut down to an entail until he marries or reaches eighteen. Therefore, if he is an unmarried infant at his death, the estate will revert to the settlor if the settlement was by deed, or will pass to the residuary devisee in the case of a testamentary settlement, for an infant cannot make a valid will, and if unmarried cannot have heirs capable of taking the estate tail. It is better that there should be this reversion to the settlor, rather than that the estate should enure for the benefit of some distant relative of the infant, which would be the result if he were to die owning an absolute interest.

(5) MORTGAGE TO INFANT

It is expressly enacted that a legal estate cannot be conveyed to an infant by way of mortgage. A grant of a legal mortgage of land to an infant merely operates as an agreement for valuable consideration that the grantor will execute a proper conveyance when the infant attains full age, and that in the

---

20 SLA 1925, s. 26 (1) (*b*).
1 Ibid., s. 117 (1) (xxvi).
2 LPA 1925, s. 28 (1).
3 SLA 1925, s. 26 (1).
4 Ibid., s. 3 (*b*).
5 AEA 1925, s. 51 (3).
6 *Re Taylor* [1931] 2 Ch 242 at 246.

meantime he will hold the beneficial interest on trust for the infant.[7] If, however, the conveyance is made to the infant and to another person of full age, it operates as if the infant had not been named, though of course his beneficial interest is not prejudiced.[8]

(6) CONVEYANCE TO INFANT AS TRUSTEE

An infant cannot be appointed a trustee.[9] A conveyance which purports to convey land to an infant as trustee does not transfer the legal estate, but operates as a declaration of trust in favour of the beneficiaries designated.[10] In such a case the person who is empowered to the trust instrument to appoint new trustees may make a new appointment,[11] or, if there is no such person, the court may do so.[12]

We have already seen that the legal estate cannot pass to an infant who is appointed executor by the will of a testator.[13]

B. ACQUISITION AND ALIENATION OF EQUITABLE INTERESTS IN LAND BY INFANT

(1) CONVEYANCE TO INFANT

An equitable interest, as distinct from a legal estate, may be effectively transferred to an infant, but since the ownership of an interest in land may occasionally prove to be more of a burden than a benefit, especially in the case of a leasehold containing onerous covenants, the long established rule is that the transfer is voidable at the option of the infant, either on attaining his majority or within a reasonable time thereafter.[14] In the event of his death his personal representatives may exercise the same power within a reasonable time.[15] But repudiation must not be unduly delayed. Thus where an infant bought land at a price payable by instalments, and continued to pay them for some time after he reached full age, it was held that his procrastination had defeated his right of avoidance and that he must pay the instalments which remained due.[16]

(2) CONVEYANCE BY INFANT

An infant cannot make an irrevocable disposition of his interest, for the rule is that any disposition is voidable and can be repudiated by him during his

---

7 LPA 1925, s. 19 (6). The infant's interest is registrable as an estate contract under LCA 1972; p. 759, ante.
8 Ibid., s. 19 (6).
9 Ibid., s. 20.
10 Ibid., s. 19 (4).
11 TA 1925, s. 36.
12 Ibid., s. 41.
13 Supreme Court Act 1981, s. 118. Nor can an infant be an administrator: *Re Manuel* (1849) 13 Jur 664.
14 *Ketsey's Case* (1613) Cro Jac 320.
15 Blackstone, vol. 11, p. 292; *North Western Rly Co v McMichael* (1850) 5 Exch 114 at 123.
16 *Whittingham v Murdy* (1889) 60 LT 956; *Davies v Benyon-Harris* (1931) 47 TLR 424 (lease). If the infant repudiates the lease, he cannot recover rent already paid: *Valentini v Canali* (1889) 24 QBD 166.

minority or within a reasonable time after he attains full age.[17] So the disability is not absolute. It goes no further than is necessary for the protection of the infant. It leaves him the power to act during infancy, but in order that he may have protection, it permits him to avoid the transaction when he comes of age if he finds it right and proper to do so.[18] The tendency of the courts, however, is to regard very slight acts, such as the receipt of rent in the case of a lease, as amounting to a ratification of the conveyance.[19]

(3) WILL OF INFANT

An infant cannot make a will, either of real or of personal property,[20] unless he is a person entitled to the privileges granted by the Wills Act 1837,[1] and the Wills (Soldiers and Sailors) Act 1918.[2]

(4) SETTLEMENT BY INFANT

In accordance with the principle applicable to alienation in general, a settlement made by an infant in contemplation of marriage is voidable, but it becomes binding upon him or her unless it is repudiated within a reasonable time after the attainment of majority.[3] The reasonable time is calculated from the attainment of majority, and not, as was once thought, from the moment when the property falls into possession.[4] If, for instance, an infant settles a reversionary interest, consisting of a fee simple estate which will come to him on the death of his mother, he will lose his right to repudiate unless he takes the necessary steps soon after he reaches full age, notwithstanding that it may be many years before possession of the land becomes available by the death of his mother.

His ignorance of the right of repudiation does not absolve him from the obligation to take steps within a reasonable time.[5]

C. MANAGEMENT OF INFANT'S PROPERTY

(1) POWERS OF TRUSTEES

Land to which an infant is beneficially entitled, either absolutely or as tenant for life, is, as we have seen, deemed to be settled land. This involves the existence of trustees, and wide powers of management have been conferred upon them by statute. Thus they have all the ordinary powers conferred on a tenant for life and upon settlement trustees by the Settled Land Act 1925.[6] They may enter into and continue in possession of the land on behalf of the

---

17 Co Litt 171b. The Infant Settlements Act 1855, which enabled a male infant over 20 and a female infant over 17 to make a binding marriage settlement of property with the consent of the Chancery Division, was repealed by the Family Law Reform Act 1969, s. 11 (a) as from 1 January 1970, "except in relation to anything done before" that date.
18 *Burnaby v Equitable Reversionary Interest Society* (1885) 28 Ch D 416 at 424.
19 *Slator v Brady* (1863) 14 ICLR 61.
20 Wills Act 1837, s. 7.
 1 S. 11, p. 839, ante.
 2 S. 3 (1); pp. 839–42, ante.
 3 *Edwards v Carter* [1893] AC 360.
 4 *Carnell v Harrison* [1916] 1 Ch 328.
 5 *Carnell v Harrison*, supra.
 6 SLA 1925, s. 26; pp. 185 et seq, ante.

infant, and if they do, they are directed to manage or superintend the management of the land, with full power, inter alia:

1.   to fell timber in the usual course for sale or for repairs;
2.   to erect, pull down, rebuild and repair buildings;
3.   to work mines which have usually been worked;
4.   to drain or otherwise improve the land;
5.   to deal generally with the land in a proper and due course of management. [7]

These powers are also exercisable, subject to any prior interests or charges, where an infant is contingently entitled to land. [8]

(2) APPLICATION OF SURPLUS INCOME

As regards the use which must be made of surplus income during the minority, it is provided [9] that the trustees may, at their sole discretion, apply a reasonable part of the income of the property for the maintenance, education or benefit of the infant, notwithstanding that some other fund may be applicable to those purposes, or that some other person, such as a parent, may be legally bound to provide for the infant's maintenance or education. But in deciding whether income shall be used for such purposes, the trustees must have regard to the age and requirements of the infant and to the circumstances of the case in general. In particular they must, in spite of the latitude allowed them, take into account whether some other fund may be used for the purpose.

The residue of the income is to be accumulated by way of compound interest, and the accumulations are to be paid over to the infant when he attains eighteen years or marries under that age, provided that his interest is vested. [10] If the infant has a merely contingent interest, or if he dies under eighteen years of age and without having married, the accumulations must be added to capital. [11] Where land to which an infant is entitled is subject to a trust for sale, the trustees are empowered to use the capital to an amount not exceeding one-half of his presumptive or vested share for his advancement or benefit. [12]

D. REGISTERED LAND

As with unregistered land, an infant cannot be an estate owner, [13] and, consequently, he cannot be registered as a proprietor. [14] If he is so registered, the register may be rectified, [15] so as to give effect to the legal position as it would be in unregistered conveyancing, [16] and until rectification has been

---

7   SLA 1925, s. 102.
8   Ibid., s. 102 (5).
9   TA 1925, s. 31 (1).
10 Reduced from 21 years by Family Law Reform Act 1969, s. 1, Sch. 3, para. 5, in respect of dispositions coming into effect after 1969.
11 TA 1925, s. 31 (2).
12 Ibid., s. 32.
13 LRA 1925, s. 3 (iv). See generally Ruoff and Roper, para 10–05, 31–14.
14 Ibid., s. 2 (1).
15 Ibid., s. 82 (1) (g).
16 Ruoff and Roper, para. 10–05.

effected, the position can be safeguarded by entering a restriction to prevent all dealings with the land.

Section 111 of the Land Registration Act 1925 provides that no purported disposition in favour of an infant, whether by deed or will, shall entitle the infant to be registered as proprietor until he attains full age, but in the meantime shall operate only as a declaration binding on the proprietor or personal representative that the registered land is to be held on trust to give effect to minor interests in favour of the infant corresponding, as nearly as may be, to the interests which the disposition purports to transfer or create. The disposition or a copy or extract from it must be deposited at the Land Registry and must unless and until the tenants for life, statutory owners, personal representatives or trustees for sale are registered as proprietors, be protected by means of a restriction or otherwise on the register. If a disposition is made to an infant jointly with another person of full age, that person will, during the minority, be entitled to be registered as proprietor and the infant may not be registered until he attains full age. The beneficial interest of the infant should be protected by the entry of an appropriate restriction.

SECTION II MARRIED WOMEN

Married women have at last emerged from that bondage which formerly characterized their status. The history of their proprietary disabilities forms an illuminating chapter in the growth of English law.

(1) COMMON LAW

At common law husband and wife are one person.[17] The general result of this merger of the wife's status in that of her husband was that he became absolute owner of her personal chattels, he might dispose of her leaseholds and take the proceeds, and he had the sole right of controlling and managing her freehold estates. If she predeceased him, he became absolutely entitled to any personal property of which she died possessed, and to a life estate by curtesy in her freehold estates of inheritance provided that a child had been born.[18] Again, a man could not make a grant to his wife directly or enter into a covenant with her, for to allow either of these things would have been to suppose her separate existence. In short, the effect of marriage at common law was to make an man complete master of his wife's property and to deprive her of contractual capacity.

(2) EQUITY

Gradually, however, and quite apart from legislation, wives were placed by the courts of equity in an even more favourable position than men or unmarried women, a result that was due to the invention by the Court of

---

17 For a history of the rule, see *Midland Bank Trust Co Ltd v Green (No. 3)* [1979] Ch 496 at 512 et seq, [1979] 2 All ER 193 at 206 et seq, where OLIVER J traces its origin to Genesis chapter 2, verse 24 and then refers to chapter 3, verses 12–13: "The common law was a trifle selective in its application of biblical doctrine. Adam after all was treated as a competent witness against Eve and his evidence was accepted and acted upon." For the "Green saga", see p. 766, ante. The decision was affirmed [1982] Ch 529, [1981] 3 All ER 744, where Sir George BAKER refers at 542, at 751, to "the erudite and so felicitously so expressed judgment of OLIVER J".

18 P. 250, ante.

Chancery of the doctrine of *equitable separate estate*. If property was given to a married women by words which indicated either expressly or by implication that she was to enjoy it *for her sole and separate use*, equity removed that property from the control of the husband by regarding him as trustee, and conferred upon the wife full powers of enjoyment and disposition. But equity went even further than this, for, perceiving the danger that a husband might over-persuade his wife to sell her separate property and hand the proceeds to him, it permitted the insertion in marriage settlements of what was known as a *restraint upon anticipation*. The effect of such a restraint was that a woman, while possessing full enjoyment of the income, was prevented during her coverture from alienating or charging the corpus of the property. She could devise, but could not sell or mortgage it.

(3) STATUTE

The next step in the emancipation of married women came with the enactment from 1870 onwards of various Married Women's Property Acts.[19] The principle of these was not to let the existence of separate property depend upon the intention of the donor, but to provide that in all cases property of married women should be separate property. Thus the intervention of the court of equity was no longer needed, for all property belonging to a married woman became her *statutory separate property* over which she had sole control and power of disposition.

The final stage in the emancipation of married women came with the Law Reform (Married Women and Tortfeasors) Act 1935. This provides that so far as concerns the acquisition, holding and disposition of any property a married woman shall be in the same position as if she were a *feme sole*. This Act also forbade the imposition of restraints upon anticipation after 1935, while preserving those already in existence, but in 1949 all restrictions upon anticipation or alienation, whether already imposed or not, were totally abolished.[20] Thus in future any restriction which it is proposed to place upon the enjoyment of property by a married women must take the form of a protective trust, which is the only form of restriction applicable to a man or a *feme sole*.[1]

The position of a married woman has, indeed, been improved in a more positive sense by a statute which entitles her to a half share in any property acquired out of money given to her for household expenses.[2]

We have already discussed the rights of ownership and occupation which a husband and wife may have in the matrimonial home.[3]

SECTION III PERSONS MENTALLY DISORDERED

A. MENTAL HEALTH ACT 1983

(1) JURISDICTION

The law relating to mentally incompetent persons, originally styled "lunatics" by the legislature, then "persons of unsound mind" and now "mental

19 See Dicey, *Law and Opinion in England* (2nd edn), pp. 371–395.
20 Married Women (Restraint upon Anticipation) Act 1949.
 1 P. 337, ante.
 2 Married Women's Property Act 1964, s. 1. See Bromley, *Family Law* (8th edn), pp. 572–573.
 3 Pp. 238 et seq, ante.

patients", was codified and radically altered by the Mental Health Act 1959. It is now consolidated in the Mental Health Act 1983.[4] There is no longer any distinction between lunatics *so found* and lunatics *not so found*, for the former practice under which, after a formal inquiry ("inquisition"), a patient could be declared to be of unsound mind and the management of his property be entrusted to a person called a "committee" has been abolished. Moreover, there are no longer different categories of patients, but only one, namely, a person who is suffering from "mental disorder" as defined by the Act.[5] The jurisdiction relating to the property of a patient is vested in the Lord Chancellor and one or more judges of the Chancery Division, called "nominated judges", whose functions are usually exercised by the Master or a nominated officer of the Court of Protection or by the Public Trustee,[6] subject to an appeal to a nominated judge.[7] When exercising the statutory powers of management, such a person is referred to as "the judge".[8]

(2) POWERS OF JUDGE

This jurisdiction is exercisable where, after considering medical evidence, the judge is satisifed that a person is incapable by reason of mental disorder of managing and administering his property and affairs,[9] though in a case of emergency the judge may exercise his powers pending the determination of mental incapacity.[10] The jurisdiction is very wide.

> The general scheme of the new code is to confer on the judge a wide power in general terms to do anything expedient for the benefit of the patient or members of his family or other persons for whom he might be expected to provide, followed by certain express powers which are to be without prejudice to the overriding general power. In fact, it is difficult to think of any power which the judge would want to exercise which is not to be found in the specific powers.[11]

Thus, in pursuance of his specific powers, the judge may make such orders as he thinks fit for the sale, exchange, charging or other disposition of the patient's property,[12] and for the acquisition, settlement or gift of any property.[13] In the case of any such settlement, the judge has power to vary it, if any material fact was not disclosed when the settlement was made or if there has been any substantial change in circumstances.[14]

Since 1969 the judge has had power to direct or authorize the execution of

---

4 See Court of Protection Rules 1984 (S.I. 1984 No. 2035), and generally Heywood and Massey, *Court of Protection Practice* (12th edn 1991).
5 Mental Health Act 1983, s. 94 (2); *Re D (J)* [1982] Ch 237 at 246, [1982] 2 All ER 37 at 44.
6 Public Trustee and Administration of Funds Act 1986, s. 2.
7 This is not in fact a court, but an office of the Supreme Court: Supreme Court Act 1981, ss. 88, 89 (1), Sch. 2.
8 Mental Health Act 1983, ss. 93, 105, 112.
9 Ibid., s. 94.
10 Ibid., s. 98.
11 (1960) 23 MLR 421, 423 (R. Jennings). The general powers are set out in ss. 95, 96.
12 Mental Health Act 1983, s. 96 (1) (*b*).
13 Ibid., s. 96 (1) (*c*), (*d*). See e.g. *Re DML* [1965] Ch 1133, [1965] 2 All ER 129; *Re L(WJG)* [1966] Ch 135, [1965] 3 All ER 865; *Re CMG* [1970] Ch 574, [1970] 2 All ER 740.
14 Ibid., s. 96 (3); *Re CHWT* [1978] Ch 67, [1978] 1 All ER 210. A settlement made by a settlor before becoming a mental patient may be varied under the Variation of Trusts Act 1958: *Re CL* [1969] 1 Ch 587, [1968] 1 All ER 1104. See *Practice Note* [1983] 1 WLR 1077.

a will or codicil, provided that the patient is of full age and the judge has reason to believe that the patient is incapable of making a valid will himself.[15]

In *Re D(J)* MEGARRY V-C set out the principles to be followed in making a will for a patient:[16]

The first ... is that it is to be assumed that the patient is having a brief lucid interval at the time when the will is made. The second is that during the lucid interval the patient has a full knowledge of the past, and a full realisation that as soon as the will is executed he or she will relapse into the acute mental state that previously existed, with the prognosis as it actually is ... The third proposition is that it is the actual patient who has to be considered and not a hypothetical patient. One is not concerned with the patient on the Clapham omnibus ... If I may adapt Dr. Johnson's words ... the court is to do for the patient what the patient would fairly do for himself, if he could ... Fourth, I think that during the hypothetical lucid interval the patient is to be envisaged as being advised by competent solicitors ... Fifth, in all normal circumstances the patient is to be envisaged as taking a broad brush to the claims on his bounty, rather than an accountant's pen. There will be nothing like a balance sheet or profit and loss account.

The judge may also appoint as receiver a specified person or the holder of a specified office and may authorize him to do all such things in relation to the property of a patient as he himself is empowered to do by the Act.[17]

The paramount consideration of the judge in his exercise of these powers is the interest of the patient, even though this may mean changing the nature of his property to the detriment of those who would otherwise have been entitled to it on his death. The Act, therefore, includes provisions designed to preserve the interests of such persons. It provides in effect that where any of the patient's property has been disposed of by sale, exchange, charging or other disposition or where money has been spent on the purchase of property, then the proprietary rights of the persons entitled under his will or intestacy shall attach to that property in its new form. If the property was real property, any property representing it shall so long as it remains part of his estate be treated as real property.[18]

As regards conveyances of property, it is enacted that when a legal estate in land (whether settled or not) is vested in a person suffering from a mental disorder, the judge may order his receiver or some other authorized person to make all requisite dispositions for conveying or creating a legal estate on his behalf.[19] Again, if land is vested in such a person on trust for sale, a new trustee must be appointed in his place.[20]

As regards the descent of land on intestacy, the rule under the

15 Mental Health Act 1983, ss. 96 (1) (*e*), 97, replacing AJA 1969, ss. 17, 18, which substituted special formalities for those of the Wills Act 1837, s. 9; p. 835, ante; (1970) 34 Conv (NS) 150 (D. G. Hunt and M. E. Reed); *Re HMF* [1976] Ch 33, [1975] 2 All ER 795; *Re Davey* [1981] 1 WLR 164, [1980] 3 All ER 342. From September 1980 to July 1981 there were some 90 applications for wills: *Re D (J)*, supra, at 253, at 50.

16 [1982] Ch 237 at 243; [1982] 2 All ER 37 at 42; *Re C* [1991] 3 All ER 866 (patient mentally disabled from birth who had never enjoyed a rational mind: HOFFMANN J held that "the court must assume that she would have been a normal decent person, acting in accordance with contemporary standards of morality"); [1991] All ER Rev 340 (C. H. Sherrin). See also CROSS J in *Re L (WJG)*, supra, at 145, at 872 (the making of a settlement). On the exercise of a power of appointment, see *Re B* [1987] 1 WLR 552, [1987] 2 All ER 206.

17 Mental Health Act 1983, s. 99.

18 Ibid., s. 101 (1).

19 LPA 1925, s. 22 (1), as substituted by Mental Health Act 1959, s. 149 (1), Sch. 7, Part 1 and amended by Mental Health Act 1983, s. 148, Sch. 4, para. 5.

20 Ibid.

Administration of Estates Act 1925 is that, where a person of unsound mind was alive on 1 January 1926 and was before that date entitled to a beneficial interest in freehold property, such interest shall in the event of his intestacy descend according to the old canons of descent applicable to freeholds of inheritance before 1926.[1]

(3) PATIENT'S INCAPACITY

Finally we must notice that, once a receiver has been appointed, the patient loses all legal capacity to exercise any powers of disposition *inter vivos* over his property. Any attempted disposition is void.[2] He can, however, make a will during a lucid interval.[3] The explanation for the difference was stated in *Re Beaney* as follows:[4]

> A patient cannot, even during a lucid interval, make a valid disposition of his property inter vivos, since that would raise a conflict with the court's control of his affairs. The case of a will is different. A patient can make a valid will during a lucid interval. That is because a will does not take effect until death, at which time the Court of Protection has no further concern for his affairs. There is therefore no conflict of control.

If no receiver has been appointed, a disposition made during mental incapacity in voidable at the instance of the person making it, if the other party knows or ought to know of the incapacity.[5]

(4) POWER OF ATTORNEY

In order to avoid the subsequent necessity and expense of an application to the Court of Protection, a person may decide to grant a power of attorney to manage his affairs during mental incapacity. At common law a power of attorney is automatically revoked when the donor becomes mentally incapable. The Enduring Powers of Attorney Act 1985,[6] however, establishes a procedure for the creation of an enduring power which will continue to be effective notwithstanding the incapacity of the donor. Certain statutory conditions must be complied with; for example, the power must be in a prescribed form, executed by both donor and donee, and be registered with the Court of Protection in the event of the actual or impending mental

1 AEA 1925, s. 51 (2); p. 871, ante. See *Re Gates* [1930] 1 Ch 199; *Re Sirett* [1969] 1 WLR 60, [1968] 3 All ER 186.
2 *Re Walker* [1905] 1 Ch 160; *Re Marshall* [1920] 1 Ch 284. No change was made in the rules by the Mental Health Acts 1959 and 1983.
3 *Re Walker's Estate* (1912) 28 TLR 466.
4 [1978] 1 WLR 770 at 772, [1978] 2 All ER 595 at 600 per NOURSE QC (giving judgment). The case discusses the mental capacity required of a donor who is not a mental patient under the Act.
5 *Molton v Camroux* (1849) 4 Exch 17; *Beaver v M'Donnell* (1854) 9 Exch 309; *Imperial Loan Co v Stone* [1892] 1 QB 599; *Hart v O'Connor* [1985] AC 1000, [1985] 2 All ER 880; [1986] Conv 178 (A. H. Hudson).
6 Based on the Law Commission Report: The Incapacitated Principal 1983 (Law Com No. 122, Cmnd 8977). See (1986) 136 NLJ 375 (H. W. Wilkinson), and, generally, Cretney, *Enduring Powers of Attorney* (3rd edn). For problems which have arisen in the operation of the Act, see (1986) 43 LSG 3566, (1987) 16 SLG 1219 (P. D. Lewis); (1990) 134 SJ 971; (1991) SJ 135 (R. T. Oerton); Survey by Bristol University on the operation of the Act, summarised in (1991) 141 NLJ 933; Law Commission Consultation Paper: Mentally Incapacitated Adults and Decision-taking 1993 (Law Com No. 128).
  Ordinary powers of attorney under the Powers of Attorney Act 1971 are not affected by the 1985 Act.

incapacity of the donor.[7] Notice of the intention to register must first be given to the donor and to certain of his relatives who may then make objections.[8]

An enduring power of attorney is validly created if the donor is capable of understanding the nature and effect of the power, notwithstanding that, at the time of its execution, he was incapable by reason of mental disorder of managing his property and affairs.[9]

B. REGISTERED LAND

Where the proprietor of registered land or a registered charge is suffering from mental disorder, his receiver may exercise, in the name and behalf of the patient, all the powers which he could have exercised for himself if free from disability. In practice no restriction is entered on the register, unless the receiver expressly asks for one, or is himself registered as the proprietor.[10]

SECTION IV CORPORATIONS

A. NATURE OF CORPORATIONS

One of the reasons for the existence of corporations is the principle of law that rights of property can be vested only in definite persons. It frequently occurs that a body of persons desires to hold and enjoy land, but apart from the case where a fluctuating class of persons acquires rights in the nature of easements by the method known as custom,[11] there are only two methods by which effect can be given to the desire. Either the land must be vested in trustees upon trust to hold and manage the land for the benefit of the proposed beneficiaries,[12] or else the indefinite body of persons must be turned into a definite, though artificial, person called a corporation; and this must be done by Royal Charter or by the authority of Parliament, whether in a special statute of by incorporation under the Companies Act 1985. The effect of this latter method is that the corporation becomes in the eye of the law a separate person, distinct from the member of which it is formed, and capable of acquiring, holding and alienating land.

Thus the modern limited liability company is not, like a partnership, a mere collection or aggregate of the shareholders, but is a metaphysical entity, a legal *persona* with many of the rights and powers of a human person.

B. CLASSIFICATION OF CORPORATIONS

Corporations may be classified in several ways. The main classification is into aggregate and sole.

---

7 Ss. 2, 4; Court of Protection (Enduring Powers of Attorney) Rules 1986 (S.I. 1986 No. 127); Enduring Powers of Attorney (Prescribed Form) Regulations 1987 (S.I. 1987 No. 1612).
8 S. 4 (3), Sch. 1.
9 *Re K* [1988] 1 All ER 358.
10 LRA 1925, s. 111 (5), as amended by Mental Health Act 1959, s. 149 (1), Sch. 7 and Mental Health Act 1983, s. 148, Sch. 4, para. 6. See Ruoff and Roper, para. 10–06.
11 Pp. 575 et seq, ante.
12 On the holding of property by unincorporated associations, see Warburton, *Unincorporated Associations*, chapter 5; Conv. Prec. 15–14.

(a) Aggregate and sole

A corporation aggregate is a collection of several persons who are united together into one body and who are followed by a perpetual succession of members, so that the corporation is capable of existing for ever.[13] Examples are:

> the head and fellows of a college,
> the dean and chapter of a cathedral,
> the mayor and corporation of a city,
> a limited liability company incorporated under the Companies Act 1985,
> national corporations, such as the BBC and the British Railways Board.

A corporation sole consists of a single person occupying a particular office and each and several of the persons in perpetuity who succeed him in that office, as, for instance, the vicar of a parish, the Secretary of State for the Environment and the Public Trustee.

(b) Ecclesiastical and lay

Another division of corporations is into ecclesiastical and lay.

Ecclesiastical corporations are those which exist for upholding religion and perpetuating the rights of the Church, such as bishops, parsons, and deans and chapters, and the abbot and monks of an earlier age.

Lay corporations may be either trading or non-trading corporations.

Trading corporations are those which have been incorporated by charter, by special Act of Parliament or under the provisions of the Companies Act 1985, and whose main object is trade.

Non-trading corporations are those which have no concern with commerce, but which exist either for the better government of a town or district, such as urban district councils and municipal corporations, or for eleemosynary purposes, such as St. Thomas's Hospital and the colleges of Oxford and Cambridge.

C. METHODS OF CREATION

A corporation can in general exist only if it has been formed under the authority of the State, and the two methods of creation in use at the present day are by charter from the Crown or by the authority of Parliament. If, for instance, a town wishes to become a borough, application must be made for a charter; while persons who wish to form themselves into a trading corporation must either secure the passing of a private Act of Parliament or take advantage of the Companies Act 1985, which contains provisions enabling companies to be formed without the necessity of a special statute.

But in addition to those that are incorporated by charter or by statute, corporations may also exist by common law and prescription.

Examples of common law corporations are a parson, a bishop, and the Crown. Corporations by prescription are those which have existed so long that the law presumes that they received from the Crown a grant or charter that has been lost.[14]

13 Blackstone, vol. 1, p. 469.
14 *Re Free Fishermen of Faversham* (1887) 36 Ch D 329; p. 579, ante.

D. DOCTRINE OF ULTRA VIRES

Statutory corporations are subject to the *ultra vires* doctrine.[15] At common law a corporation that has been created by charter has power to deal with its property and to bind itself by contract to the same extent as a private person, and even if the charter imposes some direction which would have the effect of limiting its natural capacity, the legal power of the corporation is not affected, though the direction may be enforced by the Attorney-General.[16]

But the case of a statutory corporation is very different. Such a body exists for certain purposes which are defined in the statute to which it owes its origin, and the powers of a statutory corporation are limited to those which are reasonably necessary to the realization of the purposes for which it is incorporated. The corporation possesses its own constitution (called, in the case of a trading company, the memorandum of association), which has statutory effect. Anything that the constitution authorizes, either expressly or by implication, can be done, but what is not so authorized is *ultra vires* and cannot be done.

The doctrine may be rendered ineffective by the drafting of the terms of the memorandum of association in very wide and general terms;[17] and as a result of substantial changes made by the European Communities Act 1972,[18] and the Companies Act 1989,[19] the doctrine is now restricted to the internal management of the company. Third parties who deal with a company are no longer bound to make enquiries about its capacity or the authority of its directors; and:

> the validity of an act done by a company shall not be called into question on the ground of lack of capacity by reason of anything in the company's memorandum.

However, as a matter of internal management, if the directors act ultra vires, a shareholder may be able to restrain them by injunction, if he acts in time, and the company itself may have an action against the directors.

E. CAPACITY TO DEAL WITH LAND

Corporations, whether aggregate or sole, have the same capacity as natural persons to acquire, hold and dispose of land. Where land is registered and the powers of alienation are limited in a way that would affect a purchaser if it were unregistered, an entry, usually in the form of a restriction, must be made on the register.[20]

---

15 See Cheshire Fifoot and Furmston, *Law of Contract* (12th edn), pp. 443–447.
16 *Baroness Wenlock v River Dee Co* (1883) 36 Ch D 675 at 684, per BOWEN LJ.
17 See *Bell Houses Ltd v City Wall Properties Ltd* [1966] 2 QB 656, [1966] 2 All ER 674; *Re Introductions Ltd* [1969] 1 All ER 887, where HARMAN LJ said at 888: "The little man starting a grocery business usually combines groceries with the power to bridge the Zambezi."
18 S. 9 (1).
19 Companies Act 1985, ss. 35, 35A and 35B; as amended and inserted by Companies Act 1989, s. 108; (1990) 140 NLJ 709 (M. Stamp). Substantial recommendations for reform were made by the Cohen Committee in 1945 (Cmnd 6659, para. 12) and by the Jenkins Committee in 1962 (Cmnd 1249, paras. 35–42); and its abolition was recommended by the Prentice Report in 1986.
20 LRR 1925, r. 123 (4). See generally Ruoff and Roper, paras. 10–13 to 10–16 and chapter 30.

(a) Abolition of technicalities

The Law of Property Act 1925 has removed certain conveyancing difficulties. There were rules at common law that leaseholds could not be granted to a corporation *sole* in such a way as to make them vest in the successive holders of the office; and that a grant of land to a corporation sole made at a time when the office was vacant was void. If leaseholds were granted to a parson *qua* parson, and he died before the term had run out, his personal representatives and not his successor in the office became entitled to the residue of the lease.[1]

It is now, however, enacted[2] that where any property or *any interest* therein is or has been vested in a corporation sole, whether before or after 1926, it shall pass to the successors from time to time of such corporation. Again, it is enacted[3] that where property is granted to a corporation sole during a vacancy of the office, or to a corporation aggregate during a vacancy of the headship, the property shall, notwithstanding such vacancy, vest in the successor of the corporation sole, or in the corporation aggregate, as the case may be.

(b) Words of limitation

Again, the rule formerly was that, unless a grant was made to a corporation sole *and his successors*, the grant operated to confer a life estate upon the actual holder of the office in his natural capacity; but now, as we have already seen, a conveyance of freehold land to a corporation sole by his corporate designation even without the word "successors" passes to the corporation the fee simple or other the whole interest which the grantor has power to convey in such land, unless a contrary intention appears in the conveyance.[4]

(c) Dissolution of corporation

The rule at common law is that when a corporation is dissolved, any land which it may have held does not escheat to the Crown, but reverts to the original donor,[5] but after 1925 when a legal estate determines for this reason, the court is empowered to vest a corresponding estate in the person who would have been entitled to the estate had it not determined.[6] This power is apparently meant to be used when the corporation has been holding land as a trustee.

(d) Repeal of law of mortmain

Until 1 January 1961, when the Charities Act 1960 came into force, the long established rule was that no land could be assured to or for the benefit of, or acquired by or on behalf of, any corporation unless the corporation was authorized, either by some statute or by a licence from the Crown, to hold land. If land was transferred by way of gift, sale, mortgage, settlement or devise to a corporation which had no such authority, the land was liable to

---

1 Co Litt 46*b*.
2 LPA 1925, s. 180 (1).
3 Ibid., s. 180 (2).
4 P. 160, ante.
5 Co Litt 13*b*; Blackstone, vol. 1, pp. 484–5; *Hastings Corpn v Letton* [1908] 1 KB 378; *Re Woking UDC* [1914] 1 Ch 300 at 310.
6 LPA 1925, s. 181.

be forfeited to the Crown.[7] The explanation of this disability lies far back in history and is to be found in the exigencies of the feudal system.[8]

With the progress of time the restrictions imposed by the Mortmain and Charitable Uses Act 1891 had become of little significance, for the vast majority of corporations were for one reason or another exempt from the necessity to obtain a licence from the Crown. The subject, however, requires no further elaboration, for the Act was repealed by the Charities Act 1960,[9] and thus the law of mortmain is now defunct.

SECTION V   CHARITIES

A. DISPOSITION OF LAND TO A CHARITY

The right of a charity to acquire land was severely restricted by the Mortmain and Charitable Uses Acts of 1888 and 1891, which dealt separately with assurances *inter vivos* and devises. Subject to many exceptions, the statutory rule broadly speaking was that an assurance of land *inter vivos* was void unless it was irrevocable and gave the charity the right to take immediate possession; and, if not made for valuable consideration, unless it was executed at least twelve months before the death of the alienor.

On the other hand, charitable devises, which generally speaking were not permitted until 1891, were declared to be valid by the Act of that year, subject however to the proviso that the land must be sold within one year from the testator's death unless the High Court or the Charity Commissioners decided otherwise.[10]

These restrictions, however, have now disappeared with the repeal of the Acts of 1888 and 1891 by the Charities Act 1960.[11]

B. DISPOSITION OF LAND BY A CHARITY

All land which is vested in trustees for charitable, ecclesiastical or public purposes is deemed to be settled land under the Settled Land Act 1925, and the trustees have all the powers conferred by that Act on a tenant for life and on the trustees of the settlement, subject to obtaining any consents or orders required apart from the Act.[12] The land does not, however, become settled land for all purposes; for instance, a conveyance to a charity does not have to be made by a vesting deed and a trust instrument, and a sole trustee may receive capital money if the trust deed for the charity allows him to do so.[13]

These wide powers are subject to important restrictions.

(a) Restriction on disposition

(i) Before 1993 The freedom of charities to alienate or deal with their land has long been restricted by a series of Charitable Trusts Acts and then by the

7 Mortmain and Charitable Uses Act 1888, s. 1.
8 See Simpson, *A History of the Land Law* (2nd edn), pp. 53–56, 183–184.
9 S. 38.
10 Mortmain and Charitable Uses Act 1891, s. 5.
11 S. 38.
12 SLA 1925, s. 29, as amended by Charities Act 1960, Sch. 7.
13 *Re Booth and Southend-on-Sea Co's Contract* [1927] 1 Ch 579.

Charities Act 1960. The latter, replacing the former statutes, provides that no property forming part of the permanent endowment[14] of a charity shall, without an order of the court or of the Charity Commissioners, be mortgaged or charged by way of security for the repayment of money borrowed, nor, in the case of land in England or Wales, be sold, leased or otherwise disposed of.[15] Similar restrictions apply to land which is or has at any time been occupied for the purposes of a charity, even though it does not form part of the permanent endowment; but if a transaction in respect of such land is entered into without the required order, it will nevertheless be valid in favour of a person who in good faith acquires an interest in or charge on the land for money or money's worth.[16] An order, however, is not required for a charity to grant a lease for a term ending not more than 22 years after it is granted, provided that it is not granted wholly or partly in consideration of a fine.[17]

(ii) After 1992 The Charities Act 1992 made important changes.[18] The distinction between permanent endowment property and charity occupied property has been abolished, and the trustees of a charity may sell, lease or otherwise dispose of its land without an order of the court or of the Charity Commissioners, provided that certain procedural steps are taken.

In the case of a sale or lease, the trustees must take advice from a qualified surveyor, and, having considered that advice, decide that the terms are the best that can reasonably be obtained for the charity, and normally advertise the proposed transaction.[19] In the case of a mortgage, the trustees must take advice on its necessity, its terms and the charity's ability to repay on those terms.[20]

(b) Exempt charities

The restrictions upon disposition do not affect exempt charities, a list of which is given in the Act.[1] The list includes, inter alia, the universities of Oxford, Cambridge, London and Durham; the colleges and halls in Oxford, Cambridge and Durham; any university or similar institution declared by an Order in Council to be an exempt charity,[2] the British Museum and the Church Commissioners.

---

14 I.e. property held subject to a restriction on the expenditure of capital: Charities Act 1960, s. 45 (3).

15 Charities Act 1960, s. 29(1); *Michael Richards Properties Ltd v Corpn of Wardens of St Saviour's Parish, Southwark* [1975] 3 All ER 416 (contract for sale of charity land made expressly subject to approval of Charity Commissioners held valid); *Haslemere Estates Ltd v Baker* [1982] 1 WLR 1109, [1982] 3 All ER 525; *Hounslow London Borough Council v Hare* (1990) 24 HLR 9; [1993] Conv 224 (J. Martin).

16 Ibid., s. 29 (2).

17 Ibid., s. 29 (3) (*b*).

18 Sections 32–37; now Charities Act 1993, ss. 36–40; Charities (Qualified Surveyors' Reports) Regulations 1992 (S.I. 1992 No. 2980); LR Charities Rules 1992 (S.I. 1992 No. 3005).

19 Advertisement is not necessary for a lease of seven years or less (other than one granted wholly or partly in consideration of a fine): ibid., s. 32 (5).

20 Sections 34–37; now Charities Act 1993, ss. 38–40.

1 Charities Act 1960, s. 29 (4), Sch. 2, now Charities Act 1993, ss. 3, 96, Sch. 2.

2 Further universities were added by Exempt Charities Order 1962 (S.I. 1962 No. 1343); 1965 (S.I. 1965 No. 1715); 1966 (S.I. 1966 No. 1460); 1967 (S.I. 1967 No. 821) and 1969 (S.I. 1969 No. 1469) (the Open University); 1978 (S.I. 1978 No. 453); 1982 (S.I. 1982 No. 1661); 1983 (S.I. 1983 No. 1516); 1984 (S.I. 1984 No. 1976); 1987 (S.I. 1987 No. 1823); 1989 (S.I. 1989 No. 2394). For a list, see Ruoff and Roper, para 33–24.

(c) Registered land

In the case of registered land, the managing trustees of the charity, or, if there are no managing trustees and the land is vested in a corporation, the corporation, will be the registered proprietors, unless the legal estate is vested in the Official Custodian for Charities,[3] who will then be registered as proprietor, notwithstanding that the powers of disposition are vested in the managing trustees.[4] Further, if consent is required for dealing with the land, then a restriction must be entered on the register.[5] It is upon the Registrar "that the responsibility falls for reproducing on the register the facts of ownership and the limitations on the power of disposition which exist in the case of charity land."[6]

Purchasers of registered charity land need to see that the terms of any restriction on the register have been complied with, but if they do this it is not incumbent on them to give the registered title of a charity the same complex and detailed consideration that they would in the case of unregistered charity land.

3 A public official in whom the property of a charity may be vested as a custodian trustee: Charities Act 1960, ss. 3, 17 (1).
4 LRA 1925, s. 98; LRR 1925, r. 60; now Charities Act 1993, s. 2, 18 (1), 22 (1).
5 LRR 1925, rr. 123 (2), 124.
6 Ruoff and Roper, para 33.01; see generally chapter 33.

Part IV

Planning law

SUMMARY

Chapter 29

Planning control[1]

SUMMARY

SECTION I THE LEGAL BASIS OF PLANNING

A. PRIVATE AND PUBLIC PLANNING CONTROL

(1) PLANNING OBJECTIVES

The aims of "planning control" are not identical with those of "planning".
Planning control is negative: its purpose is to prevent changes on land which
are thought to be objectionable. Planning is positive: its purpose is to
encourage the improvement of land from the standpoint of amenity and
convenience, though not necessarily of profit. These aims are subjective, and
will be tolerable only if a sufficient measure of agreement about them exists
among the public at large or the people who will be affected.

The planning legislation now in force suggests that those aims remain
acceptable to public opinion, though not necessarily to all individuals.
Common law and equity have also developed a body of law relevant to the
objectives of both "planning" and of "planning control". There is the positive
development of land which all owners and occupiers may carry out within
the framework and protection of the law—the building and engineering
projects, the mining and quarrying and other forms of land exploitation,
which give us our present towns and villages, farms and factories—subject
to the familiar restraints on activities which unjustifiably affect other persons
either directly or indirectly. There are also those obligations by which the use
and development of land is regulated between private owners, or public

---

1 See generally *Butterworths Planning Law Handbook* which contains the text of the statutes
and statutory instruments referred to in the following pages. See also *Encyclopedia of Planning
Law and Practice*; Heap, *An Outline of Planning Law* (10th edn); McCauslan, *Land, Law and
Planning*; Telling and Duxbury, *Planning Law and Procedure* (9th edn).

bodies acting in the same way as private owners, namely building and letting schemes comprising restrictive and leasehold covenants.[2]

(2) ORIGINS OF PUBLIC PLANNING

The objectives of private planning and control by these methods are fundamentally the same as the objectives of public planning and control, but the decisions are taken largely with private ends in view, not public ones. This is very natural. The spacious squares and crescents might please the public, but these were intended primarily to please the prospective residents who would be induced to buy or rent them. Many matters of public interest might not be dealt with completely or at all: sanitation and new main roads, prevention or removal of slums, containment of industry and commerce, preservation of the countryside and open space. The conclusion drawn from this, perhaps grudgingly, was that a body of *public* land law must be brought into existence beside the already developed body of private land law concerned with these objectives, and that it could only be achieved by statute. The immense variety of private local Acts, the general Acts governing public health and housing, waterworks and tramways and innumerable other public matters affecting land, which Parliament enacted during the nineteenth century, dealt in detail with specific kinds of land use. A generalized procedure for acquiring land for these various purposes, with recourse to compulsion if neccessary, was evolved at the same time. Eventually it came to be accepted that there should be a generalized public control of land use as well. The first planning statute was passed in 1909,[3] though it only applied to "town" planning, and planning on the fringes of existing towns at that. Planning control, which was still potential rather than actual, later came to be extended more generally over towns, and then over the countryside also.[4] Finally, in 1943, the general extent of control became actual instead of potential and the modern planning era opened.[5]

Private planning law is as extensive as ever it was, and the development of case law means that in theory and principle it is still growing.[6] In effect, what we now have are two general planning systems in law: one private, one public. The latter, however, seems to have stolen much of the thunder once belonging to the former, and with it this chapter is concerned.

2 And to a lesser extent reciprocal positive freehold covenants and also easements; pp. 517, 610, ante.

3 Housing, Town Planning, &c Act 1909.

4 Hence "*town and country*" planning, though it might be thought less cumbersome to speak now simply of "planning", or "land planning". Under TCPA 1932 it depended largely on the initiative of local authorities whether or not a "planning scheme" would be devised in each particular case.

5 TCP (Interim Development) Act 1943. "Interim development" was originally development of any land begun *between* the decision to prepare a planning scheme and its coming into force; this needed official approval if it were to rank for compensation in the event of being overridden later by the requirements of the plan. The Act of 1943 applied this control everywhere.

6 The unwary developer who thinks that because he has a planning permission he can ignore a restrictive covenant may receive a shock. But LPA 1969, s. 28, requires the Lands Tribunal to "take into account the development plan and any declared or ascertainable pattern for the grant or refusal of planning permissions" when deciding whether a restrictive covenant should be discharged or modified; p. 637, ante. For development plans, see p. 946, post.

B. THE PUBLIC PLANNING SYSTEM

(1) ADMINISTRATION

The system described in this chapter is that which exists in England and Wales. Parallel arrangements exist in Scotland, and, in a more modified form in Northern Ireland. The principal planning statute in England and Wales, which consolidates the previous statutes from the Town and Country Planning Act 1947 onwards, is the Town and Country Planning Act 1990.[7]

Planning control is administered by a system of authorities, central and local. The central authority is now the Department of the Environment.[8] The Secretary of State for the Environment does not usually administer planning control directly; but appeals are made to him from decisions of local planning authorities and he has the power to "call in" applications from them for decision at first instance.[9] A mass of statutory detail, including some matters of fundamental importance, is contained in subordinate legislation, the Acts having entrusted him with wide powers of making orders and regulations. He also may make certain orders on his own initiative[10] and exercises a co-ordinating function by issuing circulars which give guidance and advice to local planning authorities.

Detailed administration is the task of the local planning authorities. These are county councils as "county planning authorities", concerned chiefly with broad policy matters, and district councils as "district planning authorities", concerned normally with the routine business of planning control. This dual system reflects the "two-tier" structure of local government in the non-metropolitan or "shire" counties of England and Wales, the upper tier being the counties and the lower tier the districts into which they are divided. A single tier system exists in the areas which are the six metropolitan counties[11] and Greater London. Here the metropolitan district and London Borough Councils and the City of London Corporation are the local authorities and consequently the local planning authorities.[12] There are, however, proposals

---

7 The Act is supplemented by the Planning (Listed Buildings and Conservation Areas) Act 1990, the Planning (Hazardous Substances) Act 1990 and the Planning (Consequential Provisions) Act 1990. There have been further refinements introduced by the Planning and Compensation Act 1991, many of them in the form of additional inserted sections such as TCPA 1990, s. 54A.

8 Successor to the Ministry of Town and Country Planning (whose existence was begun by the Minister of Town and Country Planning Act 1943), the Ministry of Local Government and Planning (1951) and the Ministry of Housing and Local Government (1951–1970). The duty of the Minister of Town and Country Planning was one of "securing consistency and continuity in framing and execution of a national policy with respect to the use and development of land throughout England and Wales" (1943 Act, s. 1, repealed by the Secretary of State for the Environment Order 1970, S.I. 1970 No. 1681, and not replaced). There are separate statutes for planning control in Scotland and Northern Ireland.

9 See p. 957, post.

10 TCPA 1990, ss. 100, 104 (revocation and discontinuance).

11 West Midlands; Greater Manchester; Merseyside; South Yorkshire; West Yorkshire; Tyne and Wear.

12 For the system of local planning authorities generally, see TCPA 1990, Part I, as amended. The Secretary of State may authorise the setting up of joint planning boards, and has done so for the Lake District and Peak District National Parks. The 1990 Act refers to a planning function entrusted to a county council as a "county matter"; this expression covers (a) mineral development generally, (b) development *partly* within a National Park and (c) any operations prescribed by regulations: Sch. 1. A county council is thus a "mineral planning authority" as is any authority in Greater London and the six metropolitan counties. Apart from this, a limited role as local planning authority is for some purposes bestowed on the

for further radical changes in local government which in due course will change the system of local planning authorities.

Planners' work at all levels is facilitated by a series of Development Control Policy Notes, issued from 1969 onwards, and of Planning Policy Guidance Notes, issued from 1988 onwards. These are produced, with necessary revisions, by the Department of the Environment, and concentrate on practical policy matters.

(2) PLANS

(a) The concept of the development plan

These authorities must not make their decisions at random. They are required to make, and constantly revise, "development plans" for their area; and planning decisions should always be made with the appropriate development plan in mind even if for sound reasons they deviate from it.[13] The original system[14] of development plans was discredited by its delays, which were caused by the requirements that the Minister must approve all plans, in every detail, before they could become effective. Since 1968 it has gradually been replaced by a system of "structure plans" and "local plans". This new system, however, has been partly overtaken by a still newer system of "unitary development plans", which in essence heralds a return to the system of undivided (or "old") development plans introduced in 1947.

(b) Structure plans and local plans

The system which began in 1968,[15] consists of two kinds of plan, to match the "two-tier system" of county and district planning authorities in the non-metropolitan counties (but not, of course, the six metropolitan counties and Greater London). First comes the structure plan, to formulate "general policies in respect of the development and use of land" which the county planning authority will already have made and will under the current legislation have a duty to update. This is done by alteration or by replacement.[16] Formal proposals have to be adopted.[17] Then come the local

Broads Authority (Norfolk and Suffolk Broads), enterprise zone authorities, urban development corporations and housing action trusts: TCPA 1990, ss. 5–8. The Leasehold Reform, Housing and Urban Development Act 1993, Part III, creates a new body, the Urban Regeneration Agency, which may be designated as a local planning authority in specified areas.

13 TCPA 1990, s. 70(2) requires local planning authorities to "have regard to the provisions of the development plan, so far as material to the application" for planning permission in any particular case. S. 54A provides that, when they do, "the determination shall be made in accordance with the plan, unless material considerations indicate otherwise."

14 Ibid., Sch. 2 (Part III) continues "any old development plan" in force if necessary; but, if newer plans have also come into force, they prevail pro tanto, and local plans covering particular areas replace the "old development plans" for those areas completely. "Old" plans are pre-1968 plans.

15 TCPA 1968, Part I, now re-enacted in TCPA 1990, Part II, Chapter II (ss 29–54), as amended.

16 TCPA 1990, ss. 31–32, and they must consult various prescribed bodies and "consider any representations made" as a result, in accordance with regulations, before deciding finally on the contents of the plan: s. 33.

17 Ibid., s. 35. County planning authorities prepare these proposals on their own initiative or at the direction of the Secretary of State: s. 32; or he may call in the proposals and approve them with or without modifications or reject them: s. 35A. Before adopting the proposals the authority must hold an "examination in public" which will "be conducted by a person or

plans, which may provide in detail for the area covered by the structure plan.[18]

The essence of a structure or local or old-style plan is a written statement. In addition, a local plan "shall contain a map illustrating each of the detailed policies", but a structure plan may only be illustrated by diagrams.[19] The prerequisite for all these plans is a survey, which it is "the duty of the local planning authority to institute ... in so far as they have not already done so".[20]

(c) Unitary plans

Unitary development plans are to be produced, from dates to be appointed by the Secretary of State, by local planning authorities in Greater London and the metropolitan counties, where there is only one "tier" of authorities because of the abolition of the GLC and metropolitan county councils. Such plans "shall comprise two parts", Part I being a written statement of detailed proposals plus a map, a "reasoned justification", and "diagrams, illustrations or other descriptive or explanatory matter". The two written statements "shall be in general conformity" with one another.[1]

(d) Purpose of development plans

The legal effect of development plans is largely indirect, in that their main function is to guide authorities in making policy decisions. There are exceptions to this, notably the requirement to consider development plans when compulsory purchase compensation is claimed on the basis that it includes "development value",[2] and also the right to serve certain kinds of "blight notice".[3]

persons appointed by the Secretary of State" (i.e. an inspector), at which objectors may or may not be given a hearing: s. 35B.
18 TCPA 1990, ss. 36–46. District planning authorities must prepare, and make proposals for, local plans embodying "detailed policies for the development and use of land in their area" and follow consultation and adoption procedures similar to those for structure plan proposals. The Secretary of State may "call in" proposals for local plans or give directions for their alteration. There is to be one general local plan for each district, plus one "minerals local plan" and one "waste local plan". Local plans may specify "action areas" (see p. 980, notes 16, 17, post).
19 Ibid., ss. 31, 36. The Secretary of State may specify "other matters" to be included.
20 Ibid., s. 30. Planning staffs of local authorities continually review the state of development of their areas, so that plans may be as up-to-date as possible. The legal validity of a development plan can only be challenged in the courts on the ground that substantially or procedurally it is *ultra vires*, and only within six weeks: ibid., ss. 284, 287. In *South Western Regional Health Authority v Avon County Council* (1991) 62 P & CR 629, the inclusion of land in a local plan in contradiction of the structure plan was successfully challenged in this way.
1 Ibid., Part II, Chapter I (ss. 10–28), as amended. The authority "shall keep under review the matters which may be expected to affect the development of their area" and "may, if they think fit, institute a survey or surveys. . . ." When preparing their unitary development plan they must consult the public; and when they have prepared it they must publicise it, for examination and the making of objections, which must be considered at "a local inquiry or other hearing" conducted by an inspector appointed by the Secretary of State or by themselves. They may then adopt it if they wish with or without modifications, subject to the Secretary of State's power to direct changes, or to "call in" the plan to deal with it himself.
2 The point is decided in many cases by seeing how the land is "zoned" in the current plan. See p. 976, post.
3 The occasion for a "blight notice" in many cases is an indication in the current plan that land will be required for some project of public development—roads being the most notorious example. See p. 981, post.

(3) PUBLIC INTEREST AND PUBLIC RECORDS IN PLANNING

A distinction is sometimes drawn between "negative" and "positive" planning, though it does not appear explicitly in the statutes. The former refers to the control exercised by planning authorities in the public interest over the development projects of others, and what is said here concerning "planning control" deals with it. The latter relates to planning authorities' own projects; and, in as much as it normally involves the acquisition of land for the carrying out of development in the public interest, it is dealt with later under "compulsory purchase in planning".[4]

A brief mention may be made here of registers which local planning authorities are required to keep for public inspection. In addition to registers of local land charges, which include various orders, agreements and notices relevant to planning and compulsory purchase,[5] there are registers kept specifically for planning. Thus there are registers of planning applications, of applications for consent to display advertisements and of caravan site licences; and there are also lists of buildings of special architectural or historic interest.[6] Prospective purchasers and their solicitors should always consult these registers and lists in appropriate circumstances, just as they normally apply for an official search of the local land charges registers.

C. PLANNING AND THE COURTS

(1) PLANNING DISPUTES

(a) Settlement of disputes

Planning disputes most commonly arise between local planning authorities and developers, or between acquiring authorities and owners; and the rules of planning law, like practically all law, are framed with the basic purpose of giving guidance towards the settlement of disputes. If the assessment of compensation is in issue the dispute should be settled by the Lands Tribunal,[7] but if not the Secretary of State should normally settle it. But any dispute may have to be settled by the courts if it turns on a point of law.

(b) Law, fact and policy

The best way to understand the theory which underlies the system is to add, to the two judicial elements of law and fact, a third element, policy.[8] The Secretary of State is entitled to reach a decision on a general basis of law, fact and policy, or any of them, but his paramount concern, as the central planning authority, is with policy, so long as he ascertains the facts and complies with the law. Indeed he is normally empowered to substitute his

---

4 See p. 980, post.
5 E.g. enforcement notices, revocation and discontinuance orders, planning agreements, tree preservation orders, lists of buildings of special interest and notices of compulsory purchase orders if general vesting declarations are to be made. See Local Land Charges Act 1975; p. 767, ante.
6 TCPA 1990, s. 69; Planning (Listed Buildings and Conservation Areas) Act 1990, ss. 1–2; Caravan Sites and Control of Development Act 1960, s. 25; Town and Country Planning (Control of Advertisement) Regulations 1992 (S.I. 1992 No. 666), reg. 21.
7 See Lands Tribunal Act 1949; pp. 971, 975–6, post.
8 Usually referred to by the courts as "discretion," to indicate that it lies outside their control so long as its exercise is *intra vires*.

own policy decision purely and simply for that of the local planning authority. Thus an "appeal" to the Secretary of State is to be understood in an administrative rather than a judicial sense.[9]

However, even statutory branches of law are developed by judicial interpretation, and there is a constant flow of planning cases into the law reports. These cases come before the courts whenever a dispute throws up a pure issue of law which the parties are prepared to pursue separately from disputes of fact or policy. The courts interpret the statutes, in principle and in detail, as confining them to such issues, and it is submitted that this is entirely right. The public authorities are inevitably the experts on policy, subject to Parliament and the electorate. The courts are the experts on the law.[10] Thus a court will sometimes say, for example, "the ground . . . stated by the Minister is not a valid ground at all and accordingly in my judgment this decision will have to be quashed";[11] or, "the Minister erred in law . . . In my judgment this case must go back to the Minister with the opinion of this court".[12] On the other hand the courts frequently speak in terms like these: "Having come to the conclusion that it is impossible to say that the Minister erred in law, I would dismiss the appeal".[13] But the courts must not alter a decision on policy grounds, even if they are "surprised" by a policy decision.[14]

(c) Restrictions on recourse to the courts

There are restrictions on recourse to the courts in that many, but not all, decisions of the Secretary of State (as distinct from those of other authorities) can only be challenged by application within six weeks to the High Court; and even so the court can only quash such decisions on the ground that they are "not within the powers of [the relevant Act], or that the interests of the applicant have been substantially prejudiced" by some procedural default.[15]

This restriction on recourse to the courts applies to a dispute over the validity of a decision in detail, that is to say, which assumes that it is valid in principle. The right to challenge the existence of a decision on the ground that it is invalid in principle and so a nullity seems not to be restricted; otherwise "the court may accept and could not even inquire whether a purported determination was a forged or inaccurate order . . .", which would be absurd. "A more reasonable and logical construction is that . . . Parliament

---

9 See *Stringer v Minister of Housing and Local Government* [1970] 1 WLR 1281, [1971] 1 All ER 65.
10 *Certiorari* will lie to quash a decision of a planning authority for *ultra vires* conduct, e.g. "error of law on the face of a record": *R v Hillingdon London Borough Council, ex parte Royco Homes Ltd* [1974] QB 720, [1974] 2 All ER 643.
11 *R v Minister of Housing and Local Government, ex parte Chichester RDC* [1960] 1 WLR 587 at 589, [1960] 2 All ER 407 at 410, per Lord PARKER CJ. See p. 955, n 13, post.
12 *Birmingham Corpn v Minister of Housing and Local Government and Habib Ullah* [1964] 1 QB 178 at 190, [1963] 3 All ER 668 at 676, per Lord PARKER CJ.
13 *Cheshire County Council v Woodward* [1962] 2 QB 126 at 135, [1962] 1 All ER 517 at 519, per Lord PARKER CJ.
14 *Bendles Motors Ltd v Bristol Corpn* [1963] 1 WLR 247 at 252, [1963] 1 All ER 578 at 581, per Lord PARKER CJ.
15 See, e.g. TCPA 1990, s. 288; see also s. 284. These provisions were considered by HL in *Griffiths v Secretary of State for the Environment* [1983] 2 AC 51, [1983] 1 All ER 439. Procedural misconduct by a planning authority may however give rise to private law liability, e.g. in negligence: *Davy v Spelthorne Borough Council* [1984] AC 262, [1983] 3 All ER 278, in which a landowner was misled in respect of his statutory rights.

meant a real determination, not a purported determination."[16] Again, "the courts' supervisory duty is to see that [the authority] makes the authorised inquiry according to natural justice and arrives at a decision, whether right or wrong . . . they will not intervene merely because it has or may have come to the wrong answer, provided that this is an answer that lies within its jurisdiction".[17]

In a case, where it was alleged that a purported planning permission was invalid in principle, the court said, "the validity of the so-called permission being a matter completely outside the jurisdiction of the Minister, there could be no conceivable reason for the [developers] not being able, if they so desired, to proceed in the courts for a declaration as to the validity of the permission".[18]

(2) LEGAL CONTROL OF PROCEDURE

(a) Natural justice

The reference to "natural justice" leads to the next point, that the Secretary of State's decisions, taken remotely from each locality concerned, are usually reached on the basis of first granting a hearing to objectors. Many of the statutory provisions require him to "afford . . . an opportunity of appearing before, and being heard by, a person appointed by the Secretary of State for the purpose"[19] (i.e an inspector) to objectors, appellants, claimants or "persons aggrieved". It is settled that such proceedings must not be conducted in defiance of "natural justice", which comes down to two basic rules, namely that the person presiding must not be biased and that both sides are given a proper hearing on the points at issue.[20] A proceeding of this kind, although held as part of an *administrative* process, is often said to be "quasi-judicial" even though the rest of the process is not; so that the final decision emerging from that process can be quashed by the courts if "natural justice" is not observed. The quashing will be on an issue of law, never of fact or policy.

16 *Anisminic Ltd v Foreign Compensation Commission* [1969] 2 AC 147 at 199, [1969] 1 All ER 208 at 237, per Lord PEARCE. Contrast *R v Secretary of State for the Environment, ex parte Ostler* [1977] QB 122, [1976] 3 All ER 90. And see *Co-operative Retail Services Ltd v Taff-Ely Borough Council* (1979) 39 P & CR 223; p. 955, n. 13, post.
17 Ibid., at 195, at 223. The decision questioned in this case was a determination by the Foreign Compensation Commission which, as provided by the Foreign Compensation Act 1950, s. 4(4), "shall not be called in question in any court of law". This is not a planning case, but the underlying principle is fully relevant to planning law.
18 *Edgwarebury Park Investments Ltd v Minister of Housing and Local Government* [1963] 2 QB 408 at 417, [1963] 1 All ER 124 at 129, per Lord PARKER CJ. The distinction between invalidity in detail and in principle (a "nullity") has been re-emphasized by HL in *London and Clydesdale Estates Ltd v Aberdeen District Council* [1980] 1 WLR 182, [1979] 3 All ER 876.
19 See, e.g. TCPA 1990, ss. 77(5), (6), 79(2), (3), 98(2)–(5), 103(3)–(6), 140(3), (4).
20 See *R v Sussex Justices, ex parte McCarthy* [1924] 1 KB 256, for the first rule ("justice should not only be done, but should manifestly and undoubtedly be seen to be done"); and *Errington v Minister of Health* [1935] 1 KB 249, for the second rule. A person affected by an official decision must be given "a fair crack of the whip": *Fairmount Investments Ltd v Secretary of State for the Environment* [1976] 1 WLR 1255 at 1266, [1976] 2 All ER 865 at 874, per Lord RUSSELL OF KILLOWEN. See also *Steeples v Derbyshire County Council* [1985] 1 WLR 256, [1984] 3 All ER 468. There is no such thing as a "technical" breach of natural justice: *George v Secretary of State for the Environment* (1979) 38 P & CR 609.

(b) Inquiries Procedure Rules

Recently some of these inquiries have been subjected to safeguards additional to the rules of "natural justice". These are planning appeal and planning enforcement appeal inquiries[1] and compulsory purchase order inquiries. The various sets of Inquiries Procedure Rules[2] governing these inquiries prescribe time limits, and what notice shall be given to the parties concerned, and above all that there shall be written submissions made in advance by the authority, stating the contentions on which they intend to rely. Another important provision is that, although the Secretary of State has full discretion to make his eventual decision, so that he may reject any or all of the recommendations made by the inspector in his report, nevertheless he must hear any further representations if he should disagree on any finding of fact (not policy) or consider any new issues or evidence of fact; and in the latter two cases he must re-open the inquiry if asked to do so.[3]

SECTION II PUBLIC CONTROL OF LAND USE

A. THE DEVELOPMENT PROCESS

(1) NATURE OF DEVELOPMENT

(a) General definition

The definition of "development" is the basic concept of planning law. Section 55(1) of the Town and Country Planning Act 1990 defines it as meaning "the carrying out of building, engineering, mining[4] or other operations in, on, over or under land, or the making of any material change in the use of any buildings or other land". Thus there will be development either if an "operation" is carried out, or if a "material change of use" is brought about. Often a project involves development because there will be one or more operations and a material change of use as well.[5]

(b) Use Classes

Section 55 lists specified matters which either are or are not "development". The latter include "in the case of buildings or other land which are used for a

---

1 Enforcement appeals were not covered until 1982. See n. 2, intra.
2 See Compulsory Purchase by Non-Ministerial Acquiring Authorities (Inquiries Procedure) Rules 1990 (S.I. 1990 No. 512); Compulsory Purchase by Ministers (Inquiries Procedure) Rules 1967 (S.I. 1967 No. 720); TCP (Enforcement) (Inquiries Procedure) Rules 1992 (S.I. 1992 No. 1903); TCP (Inquiries Procedure) Rules 1992 (S.I. 1992 No. 2038); TCP Appeals (Determination by Inspectors) (Inquiries Procedure) Rules 1992 (S.I. 1992 No. 2039).
3 One or two requirements govern conduct of the inquiry itself, but by and large the inspector is not bound by rules of evidence and procedure which must be observed in court. Disagreement on policy is not of course disagreement on fact: see *Lord Luke of Pavenham v Minister of Housing and Local Government* [1968] 1 QB 172, [1967] 2 All ER 1066. Where issues wider than those of pure planning are at stake, the Secretary of State may replace an ordinary inquiry by a "planning inquiry commission", which will involve a more elaborate procedure altogether. See TCPA 1990, s. 101.
4 The specialised nature of mining development and control involves peculiarities which, though included in TCPA 1990, cannot be discussed here for lack of space. See *Thomas David (Porthcawl) Ltd v Penybont RDC* [1972] 1 WLR 1526, [1972] 3 All ER 1092.
5 E.g. if a field used for agriculture is developed by building a house on it. For expansion of a building below ground, see TCPA 1990, s. 55(2)(*a*). For interpretation generally, see s. 336. Construction of a building must not be confused with its use: *Western Fish Products Ltd v Penwith District Council* [1981] 2 All ER 204.

purpose of any class specified in an order made by the Minister under this section, the use thereof for any other purpose of the same class".[6] For the purposes of this provision, with effect from 1 June 1987 sixteen "use classes" are listed in the Town and Country Planning (Use Classes) Order 1987,[7] and any change within a "use class" is not development at all,[8] or in other words not "material".[9]

(2) DEVELOPMENT IN PARTICULAR CASES

(a) "Fact and degree"

Whether any work amounts to an "operation" or whether any change of use is "material" is a "question of fact and degree"[10] in the circumstances of each particular case. Building a model village as a permanent structure has been held to involve an "operation"[11] but not placing a mobile hopper and conveyor in a coal-merchant's yard.[12] Placing an egg-vending machine on the roadside of a farm has been held to involve a material change of use;[13] but not altering part of a railway station yard from a coal depot to a transit depot for crated motor vehicles.[14] In all four cases the court merely declined to invalidate a finding already made. The burden of proof, in other words, rests on that party who alleges that a finding in relation to development is *ultra vires*.

(b) Special aspects of development

Ownership of land, or of things placed on land, is irrelevant to planning except in special circumstances:[15] what matters is the nature of what is done on or to the land. Some ancillary questions which may be relevant are:

---

6 TCPA 1990, s. 55(2)(*f*). It is not use but change of use which is in question.
7 S.I. 1987 No. 764. The "use classes" are grouped as follows: Part A, Classes A1–3; Part B, Classes B1–8; Part C, Classes C1–3; Part D, Classes D1–2. The previous Use Classes Order (S.I. 1972 No. 1385) contained a straight list of 18 classes.
8 Except under a planning permission granted subject to a condition that no change of use occurs, even within the same use class: see *Kingston-upon-Thames Royal London Borough Council v Secretary of State for the Environment* [1973] 1 WLR 1549, [1974] 1 All ER 193.
9 For the attitude of the House of Lords to this, see *Newbury District Council v Secretary of State for the Environment* [1981] AC 578, [1980] 1 All ER 73. Any change of use other than a change within the limits of the same use class may or may not be "development"; i.e. it is an open question to be decided by applying the principles contained in TCPA 1990, s. 55.
10 Per GLYN-JONES J in *Marshall v Nottingham Corpn* [1960] 1 WLR 707, [1960] 1 All ER 659, quoted by Lord PARKER CJ in *East Barnet UDC v British Transport Commission* [1962] 2 QB 484 at 491, [1961] 3 All ER 878 at 885. Use for agriculture or forestry of land and buildings occupied therewith is not development, despite any change in use: TCPA 1990, s. 55(2)(*e*). But see *Belmont Farm v Minister of Housing and Local Government* (1962) 13 P & CR 417.
11 *Buckinghamshire County Council v Callingham* [1952] 2 QB 515, [1952] 1 All ER 1166.
12 *Cheshire County Council v Woodward* [1962] 2 QB 126, [1962] 1 All ER 517.
13 *Hidderley v Warwickshire County Council* (1963) 14 P & CR 134. So has a change from bed-sitters to hotel accommodation: *Mayflower Cambridge v Secretary of State for the Environment* (1975) 30 P & CR 28. "What really has to be considered is the character of the use of the land, not the particular purpose of a particular occupier"; *Westminster City Council v Great Portland Estates plc* [1985] AC 661 at 669, [1984] 3 All ER 744 at 949 per Lord SCARMAN.
14 *East Barnet UDC v British Transport Commission* [1962] 2 QB 484, [1961] 3 All ER 878.
15 See (1960) JPL 436. Also irrelevant is the question whether a public body or a private firm is carrying out a particular use of premises: *Rael-Brook Ltd v Minister of Housing and Local Government* [1967] 2 QB 65, [1967] 1 All ER 262.

(i) actual area involved;[16] (ii) whether there are multiple uses on a given area of land and whether these are of equal importance,[17] or are major and minor uses,[18] or are confined to separate parts of the premises,[19] or are intermittent, alternating or recurring.[20] Problems have arisen over whether demolition is an "operation", and whether the abandonment or the intensification of a use is a "material change".[1]

B. CONTROL OF DEVELOPMENT

(1) PLANNING PERMISSION GENERALLY

(a) Planning permission and development orders

Section 57 of the Town and Country Planning Act 1990 states that planning permission is "required" for carrying out development (subject to certain special exceptions).[2] Section 59 empowers the Secretary of State to make "development orders", for the purpose (among others) of actually granting permission, on a general and automatic basis, for certain forms of development. The Town and Country Planning General Development Order 1988,[3] widely known as the "GDO", currently (as amended) gives such permission for thirty-one classes of development which it carefully specifies. Apart from this there are other sections in the 1990 Act under which planning permission is "deemed" to be granted.[4]

16 The relevant "planning unit" is normally the total area of land occupied, e.g. house conservatory and curtilage, not the conservatory in isolation: *Wood v Secretary of State for the Environment* [1973] 1 WLR 707, [1973] 2 All ER 404. See *Jennings Motors Ltd v Secretary of State for the Environment* [1982] QB 541, [1982] 1 All ER 471; *Tyack v Secretary of State for the Environment* [1989] 1 WLR 1392.

17 *Marshall v Nottingham Corpn* [1960] 1 WLR 707, [1960] 1 All ER 659.

18 *Mansi v Elstree UDC* (1964) 16 P & CR 153; *Vickers-Armstrong Ltd v Central Land Board* (1957) 9 P & CR 33.

19 *Hartnell v Minister of Housing and Local Government* [1965] AC 1134, [1965] 1 All ER 490.

20 *Webber v Minister of Housing and Local Government* [1968] 1 WLR 29, [1967] 3 All ER 981.

1 The Planning and Compensation Act 1991, s. 13, reversing the effect of *Cambridge City Council v Secretary of State for the Environment* (1992) 90 LGR 275, provides that demolition is now included in the definition of "development" as being within the meaning of "building operations" (a nice paradox); but the Secretary of State can give general or specific directions excluding various kinds of demolition from "development" and in addition to that has given automatic permission in most other cases by means of the GDO: see n. 3, infra. Abandonment of any use of land is hardly likely to be held to constitute development, but resumption of use after abandonment is another matter. See *Hartley v Minister of Housing and Local Government* [1970] 1 QB 413, [1969] 3 All ER 1658; and *Fyson v Buckingham County Council* [1958] 1 WLR 634, [1958] 2 All ER 286. A planning permission, however, cannot be abandoned; see p. 956, n. 1, post. For intensification, see *Birmingham Corpn v Minister of Housing and Local Government* [1964] 1 QB 178, [1963] 3 All ER 668.

2 Omitted here for reasons of space. They relate to temporary and intermittent uses, and lack of use, dating back to 1948, and also to resumption of uses after temporary planning permissions or enforcement notices. See *LTSS Print and Supply Services Ltd v Hackney London Borough Council* [1976] QB 663, [1976] 1 All ER 311; *Young v Secretary of State for the Environment* [1983] 2 AC 662, [1983] 2 All ER 1105.

3 S.I. 1988 No. 1813, as amended by S.I. 1988 No. 2091, S.I. 1989 No. 603, S.I. 1990 Nos. 457 and 2032, and S.I. 1991 Nos. 1536, 2268 and 2805. The 31 classes of development automatically permitted are set out in Sch. 2 of the Order.

4 See ss. 58(2), 90 and 222; pp. 958–9, post.

(b) Simplified planning zones

Sections 82–87 and Schedule 7 of the Town and Country Planning Act 1990[5] require local planning authorities to consider making simplified planning zone schemes, and the Secretary of State may direct them to do so. A scheme resembles a development order, in that it automatically grants planning permission for specified classes of development, with or without conditions, in the whole or part of a zone.

(c) Detailed and outline applications

The GDO prescribes the procedure for making applications to the district planning authority for planning permission. If a building is to be erected, an application may be made for "outline" permission, which means for approval in principle. If this is refused no time and expense need be wasted on detailed plans. If it is granted, separate application will need to be made for details to be approved—"reserved matters".[6]

(d) How to apply for planning permission

Any person may apply for planning permission; but unless no one but the applicant owns a freehold or a leasehold with at least seven years to run in the property, he must notify all who do and any farm tenants as well, either directly or, if that is not possible, by local press publicity. There are also certain classes of controversial development which must be publicised.[7] Persons notified by these methods may "make representations" which the authority must take into account.

If the proposed development comes within certain categories in accordance with EC Council Directive 85/337, as being especially likely to have harmful environmental effects, for example, pollution, planning permission must not be granted unless an "environmental statement" has been submitted in due form describing "the likely significant effects, direct and indirect, on the environment", and taken into consideration.[8]

(e) Determinations and planning obligations

A more tentative approach may be made by a prospective developer who is not certain whether his project amounts to "development" at all, by requesting the authority (in writing) to "determine that question".[9] Again, it is possible for "a person interested in land" to make an agreement with the

---

5 A simplified planning zone scheme will last for ten years. National Parks, conservation areas and other special amenity land are excluded from these provisions.

6 GDO arts. 7, 8. A local planning authority must abide by "outline" permission when considering the applications regarding the "reserved matters"; see *Heron Corpn Ltd v Manchester City Council* [1978] 1 WLR 937, [1978] 3 All ER 1240.

7 TCPA 1990, ss. 65–68; GDO arts. 12–12c. TCPA 1990, s. 303 authorises the Secretary of State to make regulations for the charging of fees for planning applications: see TCP (Fees for Applications and Deemed Applications) Regs. 1989 (S.I. 1989 No. 193). But there is no lawful authority to charge fees for the giving of advice to applicants: *McCarthy & Stone Developments Ltd v Richmond-upon-Thames London Borough Council* [1992] 2 AC 48, [1991] 4 All ER 897.

8 TCP (Assessment of Environmental Effects) Regs. 1988 (S.I. 1988 No. 1199) made under European Communities Act 1972.

9 And also to say if an application for planning permission "is required": s. 64. Appeal lies to the Secretary of State, and thence, on a point of law, to the High Court: s. 290.

authority to create a planning obligation (enforceable against him or persons deriving title under him) regulating development of that land on a more general basis than for a normal planning permission.[10]

(f) Grant or refusal of planning permission

On receiving an application the district planning authority must consult other authorities and government departments, as appropriate,[11] and comply with directions given by the Secretary of State; and they must also "have regard to the provisions of the development plan".[12] Within eight weeks they must notify their decision to the applicant.[13] They may grant permission[14] unconditionally, or "subject to such conditions as they think fit", or refuse it.[15] The possibility that a project could be regulated under some other statutory procedure does not preclude a refusal of planning

10 TCPA 1990, ss. 106–106B. These were originally known as "planning agreements", enforceable as restrictive covenants and subject to LPA 1925, s. 84, p. 634, ante. The Planning and Compensation Act 1991, s. 12 has now recast s. 106 in such a way as to convert them into "planning obligations". These must be entered into by deed, "by agreement or otherwise", in respect of particular land, and may be positive or negative (i.e. by requiring or restricting development, or by any other uses or operations). "Any person interested in land" in the area of a local planning authority may enter into a planning obligation, which also binds anyone deriving title from that person. It is enforceable by injunction and is registrable as a local land charge. If the local planning authority subsequently declines to modify or discharge a "planning obligation", appeal lies to the Secretary of State, and *not* to the Lands Tribunal.
11 Applications relating to "county matters" are to be referred to the county planning authority; p. 945, ante.
12 TCPA 1990, ss. 62, 70–71; GDO, arts. 14–20. To "have regard to" the development plan does not mean that there is any duty to conform strictly with its details: *Enfield London Borough v Secretary of State for the Environment* (1974) 233 EG 53; "other material considerations" (s. 70(2)) must also be taken into account: see *South Oxfordshire District Council v Secretary of State for the Environment* [1981] 1 All ER 954. But to "have regard to the development plan means that the decision shall be made in accordance with the plan, unless material conditions indicate otherwise" (s. 54A).
13 GDO, arts. 23, 24. It must be the authority's decision, not that of an official acting on his own initiative: *Co-operative Retail Services Ltd v Taff-Ely Borough Council* (1979) 39 P & CR 223. But they can delegate: Local Government Act 1972, s. 101.
14 A person with the benefit of a planning permission has the choice either to make use of it or to continue as before. If he chooses the former he cannot complain of being made to forgo the latter. In *Petticoat Lane Rentals Ltd v Secretary of State for the Environment* [1971] 1 WLR 1112, [1971] 2 All ER 793, permission was given, and acted on, to build upon a derelict site. An attempt to continue the previous use of the site for market trading (the new building being raised on pillars) was held to be a breach of planning control. Planning permission may be retrospective: TCPA 1990, s. 63.
15 TCPA 1990, s. 70 (1) (*a*), (*b*). Reasons must be given for refusals or conditional grants of planning permission: GDO, art. 25. Decisions will be communicated by officials, who must not exceed their authority. But they have an implied authority to allow trivial variations of permission: *Lever Finance Ltd v City of Westminster London Borough Council* [1971] 1 QB 222, [1970] 3 All ER 496. An authority may be estopped from denying a permission given in excess of an officer's powers, though not if the recipient suffers no detriment from the denial: *Norfolk County Council v Secretary of State for the Environment* [1973] 1 WLR 1400, [1973] 3 All ER 673. Estoppel is not in principle to be used to hamper authorities in carrying out their functions in the public interest; see *Western Fish Products Ltd v Penwith District Council* [1981] 2 All ER 204, p. 951, n. 5, ante; but issue estoppel (res judicata) is relevant: see *Thrasyvoulou v Secretary of State for the Environment* [1990] 2 AC 273, [1990] 1 All ER 65. See also TCPA 1990, s. 76 (provision for the disabled).

permission, even if that other procedure might carry with it a right to compensation.[16]

(g) Conditional planning permissions

Planning conditions are subject to a test of validity both in principle and in detail. That is to say they must "fairly and reasonably relate to the permitted development"[17] and they must be reasonable in respect of their detailed terms. A condition that cottages to be built must only be occupied by "persons whose employment or latest employment is or was employment in agriculture" seems to have satisfied both tests.[18] A condition that a project of industrial development on a site next to a dangerously congested main road must include the provision of a special access road, and that this access road should be made available to members of the public visiting adjoining premises, seems to have satisfied the first test but not the second.[19]

(h) Time limits for development

Conditions which may be valid include those which require a new use to cease after a stated time and thus give rise to temporary planning permissions;[20] but permissions are normally permanent and "enure for the benefit of the land".[1] Other time conditions, which are so frequent as to be virtually standard-form conditions, specify the time within which development must take place, or at least begin. There is a statutory three-year deadline in "outline" permissions for seeking approval for all details or "reserved matters",[2] followed by a two-year deadline for starting development

---

16 *Westminster Bank Ltd v Beverley Borough Council* [1971] AC 508, [1970] 1 All ER 734. In 1954 the Government went so far as to say that authorities choosing procedures which entitle landowners to compensation would be *penalized* for so doing; see per Viscount DILHORNE at 534, at 743. And see TCPA 1990, s. 335.

17 *Pyx Granite Co Ltd v Minister of Housing and Local Government* [1958] 1 QB 554 at 572, [1958] 1 All ER 625 at 633, per Lord DENNING. This case concerned quarrying in the Malvern Hills. TCPA 1990, Sch. 5, now makes comprehensive provision for "restoration" and "aftercare" conditions included in planning permissions for mining operations.

An applicant may by a condition be required to do or to refrain from doing something on other land, provided that it is owned or controlled by him, not otherwise: *Pedgrift v Oxfordshire County Council* (1991) 63 P & CR 246.

18 *Fawcett Properties Ltd v Buckinghamshire County Council* [1961] AC 636, [1960] 3 All ER 503.

19 *Hall and Co Ltd v Shoreham UDC* [1964] 1 WLR 240, [1964] 1 All ER 1. If an invalidated condition is trivial the planning permission will survive shorn of it, but if it is not trivial the permission falls with it: *Kent County Council v Kingsway Investments (Kent) Ltd* [1971] AC 72, [1970] 1 All ER 70, per Lord MORRIS OF BORTH-Y-GEST. Yet this question would seem to be one of planning policy, not law, and should therefore be remitted to the appropriate authority to decide. Planning permissions, however conditional, ought to be regarded *as a whole*. An altered permission is a different permission, except perhaps in respect of trivial variations: see *Lever Finance Ltd v City of Westminster London Borough Council* [1971] 1 QB 222, [1970] 3 All ER 496. The court may remit a case to a planning authority; see *Birmingham Corpn v Minister of Housing and Local Government* [1964] 1 QB 178, [1963] 3 All ER 668.

20 TCPA 1990, s. 72. Planning permissions "granted for a limited period" (ibid.) are not necessarily the same as those granted subject to "limitations". See *Cynon Valley Borough Council v Secretary of State for the Environment* (1987) 53 P & CR 68.

1 Ibid., s. 75. Therefore they cannot be abandoned: *Pioneer Aggregates (UK) Ltd v Secretary of State for the Environment* [1985] AC 132, [1984] 2 All ER 358.

2 Thus in cases of "outline" permissions applicants may submit as many detailed proposals in respect of the "reserved matters" as they wish, so long as they do so within the three-year period: *Kingsway Investments Ltd v Kent County Council* [1969] 2 QB 332 at 607 [1969] 1 All ER 601 at 607, per DENNING MR.

after final approval; alternatively there is an overall five-year deadline for starting development, if longer,[3] as well as a five-year deadline for starting development under ordinary as distinct from "outline" permissions.[4] The authority, however, can vary any of these periods. There is, moreover, an additional control, by "completion notice". Where any of the above deadlines applies and development has duly begun in the time specified but has not been completed in that time, the local planning authority may serve a "completion notice", subject to confirmation by the Secretary of State (with or without amendments) specifying a time, not less than a year, by which development must be complete or else the permission "will cease to have effect".[5]

(2) PLANNING CONTROL IN SPECIAL CASES

(a) "Called in" applications and appeals

If he so wishes, the Secretary of State may direct that a planning application be "called in" (as it is usually termed), that is, referred to him instead of decided by the local planning authority.[6] Such cases, however, are as rare as appeals are frequent. Appeals to the Secretary of State against a refusal of permission, or a grant made subject to conditions, or a failure to give any decision within the appropriate time limit, must be made in writing within six months of the adverse decision or of the expiry of the time limit.[7] He may allow or dismiss the appeal or reverse or vary any part of the permission, and his decision is as free as if he were deciding at first instance. The procedure is now governed by statutory rules, which have already been discussed, and a hearing must be given if it is asked for.[8]

The Secretary of State's decision in such a case, or that made by an inspector on his behalf, is "final" and cannot be challenged in a court except in the circumstances described earlier.[9]

(b) Revocation, modification and discontinuance orders

Planning permission can be revoked or modified.[10] The authorities which do this must pay compensation for any abortive expenditure and for any depreciation in relation to development value which, having come into

3 TCPA 1990, s. 92.
4 Ibid., s. 91.
5 Ibid., s. 94.
6 Ibid., s. 77; GDO art. 22. The proposed development will probably be controversial.
7 Ibid., ss. 78–9; GDO art. 26. The time limit of eight weeks (GDO arts. 23, 24; see p. 955, n. 13, ante) is merely to facilitate appeals; it is not mandatory, and a decision given later (there are many such) will not be automatically invalidated: *James v Secretary of State for Wales* [1968] AC 409, [1966] 3 All ER 964.
8 The inspector, who presides over the hearing or inquiry afforded in connection with a decision to be made by the Secretary of State, may be allowed in prescribed cases to make the decision himself instead of merely reporting back: TCPA 1990, Sch. 6. This may make for quicker results in routine cases. See TCP (Determination of Appeals by Appointed Persons) (Prescribed Classes) Regs. 1981, S.I. 1981 No. 804 and TCP (Appeals) (Written Representations Procedure) Regs. 1987, S.I. 1987 No. 701. The public are normally entitled to be present at inquiries: TCPA 1990, s. 321.
9 See p. 949, ante. Such challenges are in fact quite common. An instructive example is *French Kier Developments Ltd v Secretary of State for the Environment* [1977] 1 All ER 296, in which the decision was quashed for obscurity and mishandling of evidence.
10 TCPA 1990, s. 97. The recipient is entitled to prior notice and a hearing. For the compensation payable, see p. 984, n. 19, post: ss. 107–113.

existence by virtue of the permission, disappears because of the revocation or modification. Revocation or modification orders must be confirmed by the Secretary of State except in uncontested cases.[11] If permission is given automatically by the GDO it may *in effect* be revoked or modified, if by an "article 4 direction" under the GDO it is partly or wholly withdrawn and a specific application is then made which is refused or only granted subject to conditions.[12]

In so far as authorized development has actually taken place, even if only in part, revocation or modification orders and "article 4 directions" are ineffective.[13] To put an end to any actual development or "established use" of land (except of course where it is the necessary consequence of acting on a planning permission that this should happen) requires a discontinuance order, which must be confirmed by the Secretary of State *a fortiori*.[14] Compensation must be paid for loss of development value and abortive expenditure and also the cost of removal or demolition.[15] As compliance involves physical action there is also an enforcement procedure in cases of recalcitrance, similar in essentials to ordinary enforcement of planning control.[16]

(c) Industrial and office development, and use for advertisements

Permission for industrial and office development used to be subject to additional control exercised by the Secretary of State; but this is no longer the case, and planning permission for such development must be sought in the ordinary way. But if the use of any property for the display of advertisements in accordance with advertisement regulations involves development, planning permission is deemed to be granted for it automatically.[17]

(d) Land belonging to the Crown and other public authorities

Public authorities are subject to planning control with certain reservations. The most far-reaching concerns the Crown, to which planning control does not apply at all, though as a matter of practice the relevant government departments do normally consult local planning authorities when proposing to develop land. Government departments responsible for Crown land can

11 TCPA 1990, ss. 98–9. The Secretary of State may himself make an order, which will have the same consequences as if the relevant local planning authority had made it itself: s. 100.

12 GDO, art. 4. The Secretary of State must normally make or confirm such directions (art. 5), except for some temporary ones which the local planning authority may make: see *Thanet District Council v Ninedrive Ltd* [1978] 1 All ER 703; but there is no provision for any prior notice or hearing. Or the development order itself might be partly or wholly withdrawn. For compensation, see p. 984, n. 19, post; TCPA 1990, ss. 107–112. See also GDO art. 6 (directions restricting certain kinds of permitted mineral development).

13 An "article 4 direction" was held to be ineffective when permitted development under the GDO had been carried out in *Cole v Somerset County Council* [1957] 1 QB 23, [1956] 3 All ER 531.

14 TCPA 1990, s. 102. See *Parkes v Secretary of State for the Environment* [1978] 1 WLR 1308, [1979] 1 All ER 211. The recipient is entitled to prior notice and a hearing.

15 Ibid., s. 115. See p. 984, n. 19, post.

16 Ibid., s. 189. For ordinary enforcement procedure, see pp. 959–62, post.

17 Ibid., s. 222; see p. 966, n. 3, post. The special system of control for office development (TCPA 1971, ss. 73–86) was terminated by Control of Office Development (Cessation) Order 1979 (S.I. 1979 No. 908). The special system of control for industrial development (TCPA 1971, ss. 66–72) was repealed by the Housing and Planning Act 1986; see ss. 48 (1) (*b*), 49 (2) and Sch. 12, Part III.

seek planning decisions, or authorise anyone else to seek them, for the benefit of persons or bodies other than the Crown ("private interests") to whom that land may be transferred or leased.[18]

Ordinary local authorities, however, have no such immunity, except that when any project which involves expenditure requires the approval of a government department such approval may also be expressed to confer "deemed" planning permission, with or without conditions, if needed.[19] This rule applies to "statutory undertakers" as well, that is, the nationalized industries and public utility authorities; but with them there is also another factor, the difference between their "operational" and non-operational land (the latter being offices, houses, investment property and any other land which is not the site of their operating functions). "Operational" land has the benefit of one or two special rules in planning law, for example in regard to compensation for restrictions on development.[20] As for local *planning* authorities, separate regulations are prescribed, whereby they are "deemed" to have planning permission from the Secretary of State (unless he requires a specific application) for any development they propose to carry out.[1]

(e) Enterprise zones

Finally, reference should be made to "enterprise zones". The Secretary of State is empowered to approve schemes designating these zones which are prepared by local authorities or new town or urban development corporations at his invitation. Planning permission is automatically granted for various kinds of development specified in each scheme; it may in some cases be "outline" permission.[2]

C. BREACH OF PLANNING CONTROL

(1) ENFORCEMENT PROCEDURE

(a) Enforcement notices and breach of condition notices

It is not a criminal offence to develop land without planning permission. If this happens the local planning authority should first consider whether it would be "expedient" to impose sanctions, "having regard" to the development plan and to any other material considerations.[3] If it would, they may issue an "enforcement notice".[4] It must specify the "breach of planning

---

18 TCPA 1990, ss. 299–302. It should be noted that the Act does not provide for the Crown to be bound, and so the Crown needs no planning permission: *Ministry of Agriculture, Fisheries and Food v Jenkins* [1963] 2 QB 317, [1963] 2 All ER 147; but agreements with local planning authorities may be made, subject to the approval of the Treasury, concerning the use of Crown Land: see TCPA 1990, ss. 296–298.
19 Ibid., ss. 58, 90. Planning authorities can stop up highways: ibid., Part X.
20 Ibid., ss. 279–282.
1 Ibid., s. 316; TCP General Regulations 1992, S.I. No. 1492.
2 Local Government, Planning and Land Act 1980, s. 179; TCPA 1990, ss. 88–89. There are fiscal benefits also.
3 TCPA 1990, s. 172 (1). It would be vindictive to impose sanctions for unauthorized development if permission would have been granted in response to a proper application.
4 Ibid., s. 172(1)–(3). Copies of it must be served (a) within 28 days of issue, and (b) at least 28 days before the date on which the notice states that it will take effect, on the owner and occupier of the land and on any other person whose interest in the land is in the authority's opinion "materially affected". Caravan dwellers may be "occupiers": *Stevens v Bromley London Borough Council* [1972] Ch 400, [1972] 1 All ER 712.

control" complained of, the steps required to remedy it, the date when it is to take effect, and the time allowed for compliance.[5] "Breach of planning control" occurs when development takes place either without the necessary permission or in disregard of conditions or limitations contained in a permission.[6]

There is also what amounts to a limitation period, in that, if the "breach of planning control" comprises either a *change of use* to a single dwelling-house or any kind of operation, the time limit for serving an enforcement notice is restricted to four years,[7] and in other cases to ten years.

(b) Planning contravention notices

A local planning authority to whom "it appears . . . that there may have been a breach of planning control" may serve a "planning contravention notice" on the owner or occupier of the land in question, or on the person carrying out operations thereon, requiring the recipient to furnish specified information which will enable the authority to decide what action (if any) to take by way of enforcement. Failure to comply within 21 days is a criminal offence, punishable by a fine up to level 3 on the standard scale; the giving of false information either knowingly or recklessly is punishable by a fine up to level 5 on the standard scale.[8]

(c) Stop notices

The period specified in the enforcement notice before it takes effect is intended to allow for making an appeal, and the notice is "of no effect" while any appeal is going forward.[9] This may encourage a recalcitrant developer to press on with his activities in the meantime, in the hope of creating a *fait accompli*. Local planning authorities therefore have the additional power, during this period, to serve a "stop notice" prohibiting any activity which is "specified in the enforcement notice as an activity which the local planning authority requires to cease, and any activity carried out as part of that activity or associated with that activity".[10]

---

5 TCPA 1990, s. 173. S. 187A makes similar provision in respect of "breach of condition notices" (served where planning conditions are not complied with).
6 Ibid., s. 171A. For the relevance of this to purchase notices, see p. 981, n. 19, post. Breaches of planning control on Crown Land by private individuals or corporations can be dealt with by a "special enforcement notice": s. 294.
7 Ibid., s. 171B.
8 Ibid., ss. 171C–D.
9 Ibid., ss. 174–175. It may be withdrawn or varied before it "takes effect": s. 173A.
10 Ibid., ss. 183–184. A stop notice cannot prohibit use of any building as a dwelling nor any use which began more than four years previously. It must take effect on a specified date three to 28 days ahead. Contravention is an offence punishable by a fine up to £20,000 in summary proceedings or without a specified limit on indictment and the fine should take into account "any financial benefit which has accrued or is likely to accrue" to the offender (s. 187); but it is a defence to prove that the accused did not know or could not reasonably be expected to have known of the stop notice. But a stop notice may in effect turn out to be unjustified, and the authority will be liable then to pay compensation for loss caused thereby (s. 186).

(2) LEGAL CONTROL OF ENFORCEMENT

(a) Appeals

Appeals may be made against an enforcement notice by a person having an interest in the land or a relevant occupier (i.e. a licensee) within the time specified before it is to take effect.[11] It must be made in writing to the Secretary of State, and may be on one or more of eight specified grounds: (*a*) permission ought to be granted or a condition or limitation ought to be discharged; (*b*) the alleged breach did not take place; (*c*) the facts do not disclose any "breach of planning control"; (*d*) the breach occurred more than four or ten years ago, as the case may be, whichever limitation period applies; (*e*) the breach occurred before 1964; (*f*) copies were not served on the proper parties; (*g*) the specified steps for compliance are excessive; (*h*) the specified time for compliance is too short. The Secretary of State must arrange a hearing or inquiry before an inspector, if either side requires it; and he may uphold, vary or quash the enforcement notice and also grant planning permission if appropriate. He may "correct any defect, error or misdescription" in the notice, or vary its terms, "if he is satisfied that the correction or variation will not cause injustice to the appellant or the local planning authority.[12] Judicial comment on all this is as follows: "an enforcement notice is no longer to be defeated on technical grounds. The Minister . . . can correct errors so long as, having regard to the merits of the case, the correction can be made without injustice. No informality, defect or error is a material one unless it is such as to produce injustice". That was said in the course of a judgment in which it was held to be at most an immaterial misrecital for an enforcement notice to allege development "without permission" when in fact a brief temporary permission existed under the GDO. "The notice was plain enough and nobody was deceived by it."[13]

(b) Enforcement and the courts

Further appeal from the Secretary of State's decision on an enforcement notice lies to the High Court on a point of law.[14] Except by this procedure, no one may challenge the validity of an enforcement notice in legal

---

11 TCPA 1990, s. 174. The burden of proof lies on the appellant: *Nelsovil Ltd v Minister of Housing and Local Government* [1962] 1 WLR 404, [1962] 1 All ER 423. Ss. 191–196 enact that a conclusive presumption that there is no breach of planning control may be achieved by means of a "certificate of lawfulness of existing use or development", or a "certificate of lawfulness of proposed use or development". The certificate is obtainable from the local planning authority (penalties for supplying false information for the purpose being a fine up to £5,000 on summary conviction or without a specified limit on indictment, with the addition of imprisonment for up to two years for conviction on indictment). An appeal lies to the Secretary of State, whose decision is "final" (see p. 957, n. 9, ante).

12 Ibid., ss. 175–177. Although the notice of appeal must be given within the time specified (p. 959, n. 4, ante) the grounds of appeal may be notified later: *Howard v Secretary of State for the Environment* [1973] QB 481, [1974] 1 All ER 644. The TCP (Enforcement Notices and Appeals) Regulations 1981 (S.I. 1981 No. 1742) provide that the appellant must deliver a statement specifying the grounds on which he is appealing against the notice and stating briefly the facts on which he proposes to rely in support of each of those grounds (reg. 5) within 28 days of the Secretary of State requiring him to do so. For Inquiries Procedure Rules, see p. 951, n. 2, ante.

13 *Miller-Mead v Minister of Housing and Local Government* [1963] 2 QB 196 at 221, [1963] 1 All ER 459 at 468, per Lord DENNING.

14 TCPA 1990, s. 289. The Rules of the Supreme Court, Ord. 94, r. 12, impose a time limit of 28 days. See *Button v Jenkins* [1975] 3 All ER 585.

proceedings on any of the eight grounds specified above.[15] Conversely, a challenge on any other ground can only be made in the courts, for example, the omission of a procedural requirement, such as specifying the date on which the notice shall take effect.[16] A breach of planning control is not a criminal offence, but disregard of an enforcement notice is.[17] On prosecution for failure to carry out *works* it is specially provided that an owner who has transferred his interest to a subsequent owner can bring the latter before the court. On prosecution for failure to discontinue a *use* or to comply with any condition or limitation, the accused can in certain circumstances challenge the enforcement notice, even on the eight grounds specified above.[18]

(c) Enforcement default powers

In addition to prosecution after failure to comply with an effective enforcement notice within the time specified in it, the authority also have the power, after that time, to enter on the land and carry out the steps prescribed by the notice, other than discontinuance of any use, and recover from the owner the net cost reasonably so incurred. He may in turn recover from the true culprit, if different, his reasonable expenditure on compliance.[19]

D. AMENITY AND SAFETY

(1) MEANING OF AMENITY AND SAFETY

The other major aim of planning law apart from the control of development is the protection of amenity and safety. These aims are closely linked in practice; but the basic concepts are distinct. There is no statutory definition of amenity or safety; but amenity "appears to mean pleasant circumstances, features, advantages";[20] and the standpoint seems to be that of the general public rather than of particular persons.

The subject matter of the provisions governing amenity comprises trees, buildings of special interest, advertisements, caravan sites and unsightly land. The subject matter of the provisions concerning safety comprises advertisements and "hazardous substances".

15 TCPA 1990, s. 285. But this is subject to the special exception mentioned below; s. 285(2); n. 18, infra. If enforcement proceedings are defied with impunity, the authority can seek an injunction; see s. 187B, and also *Runnymede Borough Council v Ball* [1986] 1 WLR 353, [1986] 1 All ER 629; *A-G v Bastow* [1957] 1 QB 514, [1957] 1 All ER 497; *Kent County Council v Batchelor (No 2)* [1979] 1 WLR 213, [1978] 3 All ER 980 (tree preservation order, see p. 963, post); *Westminster City Council v Jones* (1981) 80 LGR 241. On the general principle of injunctions to protect the public interest, see *Stoke-on-Trent City Council v B & Q (Retail) Ltd* [1984] AC 754, [1984] 2 All ER 332.
16 See *Burgess v Jarvis and Sevenoaks RDC* [1952] 2 QB 41, [1952] 1 All ER 592. An omission to allege and prove the time for compliance will vitiate a subsequent prosecution (see n. 17, post): *Maltedge v Wokingham District Council* (1992) 64 P & CR 487.
17 TCPA 1990, s. 179. The penalties on conviction are the same as for failure to comply with a stop notice; p. 960, n. 10, ante). Failure to comply with a breach of condition notice (p. 960, n. 5, ante) is an offence punishable on summary conviction by a fine up to level 3 on the standard scale: s. 187A(12).
18 Provided that no copy was served on him, his interest in the land dates back before the time for service, and he could not reasonably have known of it: TCPA 1990, s. 285(2) (amended).
19 TCPA 1990, s. 178. A subsequent planning permission will cause an enforcement notice to lapse; but mere compliance with the notice will not, because of the possibility that offending development may recur after compliance: ss. 180–181.
20 *Re Ellis and Ruislip-Northwood UDC* [1920] 1 KB 343 at 370, per SCRUTTON LJ.

The consolidating Acts of 1990 have distributed these provisions three ways. Trees, advertisements and unsightly land are included in the Town and Country Planning Act, Part VIII. Buildings of special interest are in a separate statute, the Planning (Listed Buildings and Conservation Areas) Act 1990. Hazardous substances are also in a separate statute, the Planning (Hazardous Substances) Act 1990. Caravan sites however, remain in separate statutes, as before.

(2) TREES

To grow or cut trees is not of itself development.[1] But local planning authorities are specifically empowered, "in the interests of amenity", to make "tree preservation orders" (TPOs) for specified "trees, groups of trees or woodlands", restricting interference with the trees except with the consent of the local planning authority. Trees may, however, be cut if necessary to comply with any statutory requirements or because of any nuisance; and there are provisions governing replanting.[2] Unauthorized interference with any protected tree calculated to destroy it is a criminal offence.[3]

A TPO is made and confirmed by the local planning authority or the Secretary of State after considering any objections from owners and occupiers of the relevant land, though, if necessary, a provisional TPO taking immediate effect can be made for up to six months.[4] Regulations are prescribed governing the procedure for making TPOs, and their content. Standard provisions in TPOs lay down essentially the same procedure for applying for consents to interfere with protected trees as exists for making planning applications.[5]

(3) SPECIAL BUILDINGS

(a) Conservation areas

"Amenity" is not expressly mentioned in relation to buildings of special interest, which are now governed by the Planning (Listed Buildings and Conservation Areas) Act 1990. Part II of that Act[6] refers to "areas of special architectural or historic interest, the character or appearance of which it is desirable to preserve or enhance", and requires local planning authorities to determine where such areas exist and designate them as "Conservation

---

1 Either might be part of a "material" change of use, and conditions in planning permissions commonly require the preservation or planting of trees. TCPA 1990, s. 197 requires "the imposition of conditions, for the preservation or planting of trees", in planning permissions, as far as is reasonably possible.

2 TCPA 1990, ss. 198, 206. *County* planning authorities can only make TPOs in connection with grants by them of planning permissions, or for land not wholly situated within a single district, or for land in which they hold an interest, or for land in a National Park; Sch. 1, para. 13. For Crown Land see s. 300. Control from the standpoint of commercial timber production is imposed by the Forestry Act 1967, as amended.

3 Penalties on conviction are the same as for failure to comply with an enforcement or stop notice: p. 960, n. 10, ante: TCPA 1990, s. 210. But if the offence is "otherwise" (i.e. less destructive) the maximum fine is level 4 on the standard scale: s. 210(4). "Radical" injury is equivalent to destruction: *Barnet London Borough Council v Eastern Electricity Board* [1973] 1 WLR 430, [1973] 2 All ER 319. Ignorance of the existence of the TPO is not a defence: *Maidstone Borough Council v Mortimer* [1980] 3 All ER 552. For compensation for loss incurred because of tree preservation restrictions, see ss. 203–205; p. 984, n. 19, post.

4 TCPA 1990, ss. 198–202.

5 TCP (Tree Preservation Order) Regs. 1969, S.I. 1969 No. 17, as amended by 1981 S.I. 1981 No. 14, which contain a "Model" TPO.

6 Ss. 69–80.

Areas". When one of these areas has been designated, "special attention shall be paid to the desirability of preserving or enhancing the character or appearance of that area" by exercising appropriate powers to preserve amenities under planning legislation, and also by publicizing planning applications for development which in the authority's opinion would affect that character or appearance.[7] All trees in conservation areas are protected in the same way as if subject to a TPO.[8]

(b) Buildings of special interest

The phrase "special architectural or historic interest" applies chiefly to buildings, although trees and other objects may affect their character and appearance. The Secretary of State has the duty of compiling or approving lists of such buildings, after suitable consultations, and supplying local authorities with copies of the lists relating to their areas.[9] Such authorities must notify owners and occupiers of buildings included in (or removed from) these lists.[10] The Secretary of State may, when considering any building for inclusion in a list, take into account the relationship of its exterior with any group of buildings to which it belongs and also "the desirability of preserving . . . a man-made object or structure fixed to the building or forming part of the land and comprised within the curtilage of the building".[11] If a building is not "listed" the local planning authority may give it temporary protection by a "building preservation notice" while they try to persuade the Secretary of State to list it.[12]

(c) Control of listed buildings

Except when for the time being a "listed building" is an ecclesiastical building used for ecclesiastical purposes[13] or an ancient monument (when no doubt it will be adequately protected by either Church or State), it is a criminal offence to cause such a building to be demolished, or altered "in any manner which would affect its character as a building of special architectural or historic interest", without first obtaining and complying with a "listed building consent" from the local planning authority or the Secretary of State, unless works have to be done as a matter of urgency. A consent may be

---

7 Planning (Listed Buildings and Conservation Areas) Act 1990, ss. 69–76; note especially s. 74 which prohibits demolition generally in a conservation area without a listed building consent granted in accordance with Part I, Chapter II of the Act; p. 956, n. 16, post, and imposes on local planning authorities a duty to formulate and publicise proposals for enhancing conservation areas. As to planning applications in conservation areas, see *South Lakeland District Council v Secretary of State for the Environment* [1992] 2 AC 141, [1992] 1 All ER 573.

8 TCPA 1990, ss. 211–214.

9 A developer can apply to the Secretary of State for a certificate that he does not intend to list a building which it is planned to alter or demolish: Planning (Listed Buildings and Conservation Areas) Act 1990, s. 6.

10 Ibid., s. 2. Ancient monuments, however, have a special code of protection under the Ancient Monuments and Archaeological Areas Act 1979. See *Hoveringham Gravels Ltd v Secretary of State for the Environment* [1975] QB 754, [1975] 2 All ER 931 and also the National Heritage Act 1983.

11 Ibid., s. 1.

12 Ibid., s. 3. If they fail, they may have to pay compensation: s. 29.

13 Ibid., s. 60. This exemption ceases to apply in cases of impending demolition; see *A-G v Howard United Reformed Church Trustees, Bedford* [1975] QB 41, [1975] 3 All ER 273. The Secretary of State may make an order specifying ecclesiastical buildings in respect of which the exemption is to be restricted or excluded: s. 60(5), (6).

granted subject to conditions, contravention of which is also a criminal offence;[14] and it is normally effective for five years.[15]

The procedure for applying for listed building consents, and for appeals and revocations, is laid down on lines very similar to the procedure in ordinary cases of planning permission for development; and so is the procedure for listed building enforcement notices and purchase notices.[16] Compensation is payable for depreciation or loss caused by revocation or modification of listed building consents or by the service of building preservation notices.[17] If an owner fails to keep a listed building in proper repair, a local authority or the Secretary of State may first serve a "repairs notice" and, if this is not complied with after two months, may then compulsorily purchase the property.[18] Local authorities can, on seven days' notice to the owner, carry out urgent works at his expense to preserve any unoccupied building, or part of a building, which is listed.[19]

(4) ADVERTISEMENTS, CARAVAN SITES AND UNSIGHTLY LAND

(a) **Advertisements**

Control of the display of advertisements is provided for, in the interests of amenity and safety, but not censorship.[20] The details of this control are laid down in regulations.[1] The use of any land for the display of advertisements requires in general an application to the local planning authority for consent, which in normal cases is for periods of five years. Appeal lies to the Secretary of State. There are several categories of display in which consent is "deemed" to be given, including the majority of advertisements of a routine nature and purpose; but "areas of special control" may be declared where restrictions are greater. If however the authority "consider it expedient to do so in the interests of amenity or public safety" they may serve a "discontinuance

---

14 TCPA 1990, ss. 7–9.17. The penalty on conviction for either offence is imprisonment up to six months or a fine up to £20,000, or both, in summary proceedings, and imprisonment up to two years or a fine without a specified limit, or both, on indictment; and the fine should be fixed in the light of any financial benefit enjoyed by the offender. See *R v Wells Street Metropolitan Stipendiary Magistrates, ex parte Westminster City Council* [1986] 1 WLR 1046, [1986] 3 All ER 4 as to the absolute nature of the offence. Acts intended to cause damage to a listed building are, unless authorised, punishable on summary conviction by a fine up to level 3 on the standard scale, with a further daily fine (up to one tenth of level 3) for failing to take steps to prevent further damage thereafter: s. 59.

15 Ibid., s. 18. Application may be made to vary or discharge conditions: s. 19. S. 14 provides that applications for listed building consent in Greater London shall first be referred to the Historic Buildings and Monuments Commission for England.

16 Ibid., ss. 10–26, 32–46. For planning compensation generally, see pp. 983–4, post. For purchase notices, see pp. 980–1, post.

17 Ibid., ss. 28–31.

18 Ibid., ss. 47–51. If the owner does comply with the repairs notice he may apply to the magistrates to stay compulsory purchase proceedings. But if he has deliberately allowed the building to become derelict not only will the compulsory purchase take place, but he will be entitled only to "minimum compensation", excluding any element of value whatever in respect of the possibility of demolition or alteration. This procedure should be considered as an alternative to a dangerous structure orders under the Building Act 1984, s. 77(1)(a), or the London Buildings Act (Amendment) Act 1939, ss. 65, 69(1). For compulsory purchase of land generally, see chapter 30, p. 969, post.

19 Ibid., ss. 54–55. The Secretary of State (to whom an appeal lies within 28 days) may himself carry out such works for buildings in Wales and may authorise the Historic Buildings and Monuments Commission (n. 15, ante) to do so for buildings in England.

20 Ibid., s. 220.

1 TCP (Control of Advertisements) Regs. 1992, S.I. 1992 No. 666.

notice" to terminate the "deemed" consent of most kinds of advertisement enjoying such consent; but there is a right of appeal to the Secretary of State. Contravention of the regulations is a criminal offence.[2] Consent under the regulations is "deemed" to convey planning permission also, should any development be involved.[3]

(b) Caravan sites

The control of caravan sites, in the context of planning law, may be regarded as a question of amenity, even though "amenity" is only referred to very incidentally in the legislation. The purpose of control is, in detail, very much a question of public health, and there is authority for the view that control for purposes of public health must not be exercised for purposes of amenity.[4] But there can be little doubt in practice that, although control is concerned with health and safety on the caravan site itself, it preserves amenity for the neighbourhood of the site.

Until 1960 disputes over the establishment of caravan sites were largely ordinary planning disputes, turning on the question of whether there was a "material" change of use in a given case, i.e. development requiring planning permission.[5] Since 1960 the question of development still arises, and planning permission must still be sought for it; but the detailed control of the use of the site is governed by a system of "site licences", obtainable from the local authority.[6] "There are two authorities which have power to control caravan sites. On the other hand, there is the planning authority . . . On the other hand, there is the site authority . . . The planning authority ought to direct their attention to matters in *outline*, leaving the site authority to deal with all matters of *detail*. Thus the planning authority should ask themselves this broad question: Ought this field to be used as a caravan site at all? If 'Yes', they should grant planning permission for it, without going into details as to number of caravans and the like, or imposing any conditions in that regard." Nevertheless—"Many considerations relate both to planning and to site . . . In all these matters there is a large overlap, where a condition can properly be based both on planning considerations and also on site considerations."[7]

It is the "occupier" of land who must apply for a site licence, which must be granted if the applicant has the benefit of a specific planning permission, and withheld if he has not; and it must last as long as that permission lasts,

2 Punishable summarily by a fine up to level 3 on the standard scale, while continuance after conviction is a further offence punishable by a daily fine up to one tenth of level 3 on the standard scale: TCPA 1990, s. 224. Prima facie the owner of the land or the vendor of the goods advertised will be liable: see *John v Reveille Newspaper Ltd* (1955) 5 P & CR 95.
3 TCPA 1990, s. 222. See also s. 223 and TCP (Control of Advertisements) Regs. 1992, reg. 17; p. 984, n. 19, post, for compensation payable in certain special cases.
4 *Pilling v Abergele UDC* [1950] 1 KB 636, [1950] 1 All ER 76.
5 "Intensification" of the use of land for caravans by means of a gradual increase in numbers was one problem: *Guildford RDC v Fortescue* [1959] 2 QB 112, [1959] 2 All ER 111. Seasonal change of use is a problem which has also arisen: *Webber v Minister of Housing and Local Government* [1968] 1 WLR 29, [1967] 3 All ER 981. For movement of caravans from one field to the next, see *Morel v Dudley* (1961) 178 EG 335. For the availability of an injunction as the ultimate deterrent, at the suit of the Attorney-General, see *A-G v Bastow* [1957] 1 QB 514, [1957] 1 All ER 497.
6 Caravan Sites and Control of Development Act 1960, s. 3.
7 *Esdell Caravan Parks Ltd v Hemel Hempstead RDC* [1966] 1 QB 895 at 922, [1965] 3 All ER 737 at 741, per Lord DENNING MR. It follows that a condition in a site licence based solely on planning considerations is *ultra vires*. See also *Wyre Forest District Council v Secretary of State for the Environment* [1990] 2 AC 357, [1990] 1 All ER 780 (the meaning of "caravan").

perpetually in a normal case.[8] The practical question, therefore, is what conditions a site licence shall contain. They are "such conditions as the authority may think it necessary or desirable to impose", with particular reference to six main kinds of purpose.[9] Appeal may be made to a magistrates' court against the imposition of any conditions, or a decision or refusal to vary them at any time after imposition, on the ground that as imposed or varied they are "unduly burdensome".[10]

There are several categories of use of land for caravans which are exempted from control, and also additional powers conferred on local authorities in special cases.[11] Caravan sites for gypsies are provided by county and London borough councils.[12]

(c) Unsightly land

There is also the question of unsightly land: neglected sites, rubbish dumps and the like. Local planning authorities are empowered to deal with any land in their area the condition of which is such that "the amenity of a part of their area, or of any adjoining area, is adversely affected" thereby.[13] A notice is served on the owner and occupier specifying steps to be taken to remedy the state of the land. As with enforcement notices, two time limits must also be specified: a period (of 28 days or more) before the notice takes effect, and the time for compliance.[14]

Appeal lies, at any time before the notice takes effect, to a magistrates' court on any of the following grounds: (*a*) the condition of the land is not injurious to amenity; (*b*) the condition of the land reasonably results from a use or operation not contravening planning control; (*c*) the specified steps for compliance are excessive; (*d*) the specified time for compliance is too short. The magistrates may uphold, quash or vary the notice, and "correct any informality, defect or error" if it is not material.[15]

---

8 Caravan Sites (etc.) Act 1960, s. 4. For the meaning of "occupier" and "caravan site", see s. 1(3), (4). Use of land as a caravan site without a site licence is an offence: s. 1(1), (2); unless the local authority have failed to grant one within 2 months: s. 3 (4), (6). Contravention of the terms of a licence is also an offence, punishable on the third occasion by revoking the licence: s. 9. For transfer of licences to new owners, see. s. 10.

9 Ibid., s. 5. The list of purposes is not exhaustive, but any terms unconnected with health, safety or amenity will almost certainly be *ultra vires*: *Mixnam's Properties Ltd v Chertsey UDC* [1965] AC 735, [1964] 2 All ER 627. Agreements between owners and occupiers of such sites are now regulated by the Mobile Homes Act 1983.

10 Ibid., ss. 7, 8.

11 Ibid., Sch. 1, and ss. 23, 24.

12 Under Caravan Sites Act 1968, as amended by Local Government, Planning and Land Act 1980, Part XVII. See Department of the Environment Consultation Paper: Reform of the Caravan Sites Act 1968; [1993] Conv 39, 111 (G. Holgate).

13 For a site to which this control in its original form was held not to apply, see *Stephens v Cuckfield RDC* [1960] 2 QB 373, [1960] 2 All ER 716; but the decision might have been different under the present form of control.

14 TCPA 1990, s. 215. The "condition" of land is not to be regarded in isolation from its use: *Britt v Buckinghamshire County Council* [1964] 1 QB 77, [1963] 2 All ER 175. Failure to comply is a summary offence punishable by a fine up to level 3 on the standard scale while continuance after conviction is a further offence punishable by a daily fine up to level 3 on the standard scale: s. 216.

15 Ibid., s. 217. There is a further right of appeal to the Crown Court: s. 218. The notice is suspended while an appeal is going forward.

The authority may also, in default of compliance with an effective notice within the specified period, enter on the land and carry out the steps prescribed by it and recover the net cost reasonably so incurred from the owner. The owner or occupier may recover from the

(5) HAZARDOUS SUBSTANCES

An additional set of controls over the use of land has been introduced into planning law in regard to the placing on any premises of substances such as dangerous chemicals. The purpose of this control is to protect safety, and to a lesser extent amenity. It is additional to existing controls upon the handling of such substances, in that its emphasis relates to the *land* as distinct from the *substances* themselves; but nevertheless it has been derived from those controls, specifically the Health and Safety at Work etc Act 1974. "Hazardous substances" are defined in the Notification of Installations Handling Hazardous Substances Regulations 1982.[16] On 1 May 1984 the Use Classes Order and the GDO were amended[17] so as to withdraw generally from the scope of those orders any use of premises involving a "notifiable quantity" of any "hazardous substance", as defined in the above Regulations of 1982 (apart from certain limited types of permission preserved in the GDO).

The Planning (Hazardous Substances) Act 1990 enacts for England and Wales a new code, whereby the presence of a hazardous substance on, over or under land requires the consent of the hazardous substances authority but not if "the aggregate quantity of the substance . . . is less than the controlled quantity".[18] The Secretary of State is empowered by the Planning (Hazardous Substances) Act 1990[19] to define "hazardous substances" afresh by specifying them in regulations, together with "the controlled quantity of any such substance" (as distinct from the "notifiable quantity" referred to above).

Control of land, the use of which involves hazardous substances is to be exercised whenever they are present in an appreciable amount ("controlled quantity"). The Act requires applications for "hazardous substances consents" to be made to "hazardous substances authorities" which are, by and large, the local planning authorities, including county councils where sites used for mineral workings or waste disposal are involved and in most National Parks, as well as certain urban development corporations and housing trusts. Central government is also involved because the "appropriate ministers" are the authorities for the "operational land" of "statutory undertakers". The system of consents (with or without conditions), plus revocations, appeals, enforcement, etc., is broadly similar to planning control, and in fact was previously integrated with it; the purpose of the separation is to free this system of control from being tied to the concept of "development" as against *safety* which is the true consideration. Regulations to be made will prescribe "appropriate consultations" to take place with the Health and Safety Executive of the Health and Safety Commission.

true culprit, if different from themselves, their reasonable expenditure on compliance: s. 219. Powers of control over dumping of refuse and abandonment of vehicles are given to local authorities by the Refuse Disposal (Amenity) Act 1978.

16 S.I. 1982 No. 1357. Note that the Radioactive Substances Act 1960 enacts the "duty of public and local authorities not to take account of any radioactivity in performing their functions". That Act was amended by Part V of the Environmental Protection Act 1990, which empowers the Secretary of State for the Environment to appoint inspectors to enforce safety requirements.

17 By 1983, S.I. 1983 Nos. 1614 and 1615 respectively. See pp. 951, 953, ante, for the Use Classes Order and the GDO.

18 Planning (Hazardous Substances) Act 1990, s. 4.

19 The Act came into force on 1 June 1992, subject to some amendments by the Environment Protection Act 1990. See also the Planning (Hazardous Substances) Regulations 1992 (S.I. 1992 No. 656) and DoE Circular 11/92.

Chapter 30

Compulsory purchase and compensation[1]

SUMMARY

SECTION I THE GENERAL LAW OF COMPULSORY PURCHASE

A. BACKGROUND OF COMPULSORY PURCHASE

(1) ORIGINS

(a) Early forms of compulsory purchase

Compulsory purchase of land is considerably older than planning control. In the eighteenth century it commonly took the form of inclosures, whereby various owners' rights in land were transformed compulsorily, either by redistribution or by expropriation, the compulsion being sanctioned by statute. Such statutes were private local Acts, and these specified the actual land to be dealt with in each case. Vast numbers of such Acts, at great expense, were procured during the century 1750–1850, differing (on the whole) only in respect of the particular land to which they related.

In the early nineteenth century similar local initiatives brought about the promotion, by municipal corporations or other groups of persons, of various forms of public works and "improvements" such as water-works and gas-works. At the same time canal and railway undertakings were being promoted. The result was another stream of private local Acts for these purposes.

(b) Procedure standardized

Eventually the idea dawned that a general statute could be passed to standardize the repetitive grant of powers, and the Lands Clauses Consolidation Act 1845 duly provided a procedural code for compulsory purchase and compensation, though not for the actual choice of land required. It became customary for statutes to authorize compulsory purchase

---

1 See generally *Encyclopedia of Compulsory Purchase and Compensation*; Davies, *Compulsory Purchase and Compensation* (4th edn); Denyer-Green, *Law of Compulsory Purchase and Compensation* (3rd edn).

on the basis that particular land was to be selected when required and the necessary authorization for its compulsory purchase given by a "provisional order", made by a Minister on the acquiring body's behalf and submitted to Parliament (with a batch of other such orders) in a Provisional Order Bill.[2] In the twentieth century the "compulsory purchase order" was devised instead, the difference being that for this submission to Parliament is not normally necessary.[3]

The development of the law governing compensation is quite recent. Until the First World War Parliament assumed that compensation was solely a question of evidence (expert or otherwise)[4] and left the courts to evolve the rules necessary to settle disputes. But eventually, in the Acquisition of Land (Assessment of Compensation) Act 1919, Parliament devised its own set of rules for assessment of the "market value" of land. Later still, the introduction of planning control gave rise to difficulties in deciding whether "market value" should comprise any "development value" over and above "existing use value" in particular cases, and the statutory rules governing "market value" had to be made more elaborate as a result.

(2) THE MODERN SYSTEM

(a) Compulsory purchase statutes

The position now is that compulsory purchase of land normally brings into play four main sets of statutory provisions, as follows. First, there is the authorizing Act. No longer is this normally a private local Act, but instead in most cases a public general Act authorizing a public body or class of public bodies (e.g. county councils)[5] to carry out some specified function; and going on to state (*a*) whether such a body may acquire land for the purpose, (*b*) whether they may buy it compulsorily, (*c*) whether they may obtain power to do this by compulsory purchase order (CPO) specifying the land required, and (*d*) if so what procedure is to be followed when making the CPO. There is now a standardized procedure laid down by the Acquisition of Land Act 1981. Second, therefore, is the Act of 1981, in accordance with which the CPO will be made in the majority of cases. Third is the Compulsory Purchase Act 1965, which has to all intents and purposes replaced the Act of 1845 and governs the actual procedure for acquisition after the CPO has sanctioned

---

2 Procedure could be separately prescribed by each Act, but was later largely standardized; it is now rarely used.

3 Compulsory purchase orders must sometimes be laid before each House of Parliament before they come into effect, though this does not involve the sequence of stages needed for legislation and is therefore not the same as "provisional order" procedure. See Statutory Orders (Special Procedure) Acts 1945 and 1965 for this "special parliamentary procedure", as it is called. The Acquisition of Land Act 1981, Part III, requires this procedure to be used when taking National Trust land, open space land or, in some cases, land held by public bodies.

4 Elaborate provisions for assessment *procedure* (not principles) were laid down in Lands Clauses Consolidation Act 1845, ss. 22–68.

5 The typical acquiring authority nowadays is a local authority; but government departments, "statutory undertakers" and other public bodies are also acquiring authorities in many circumstances. As for *disposal* of land (sale, lease, exchange, appropriation to a different purpose), see Local Government Act 1972, ss. 120–3 and TCPA 1959, ss. 23, 26, both as amended by Local Government, Planning and Land Act 1980, Sch. 23. See also *London and Westcliff Properties Ltd v Minister of Housing and Local Government* [1961] 1 WLR 519, [1961] 1 All ER 610; *Laverstoke Property Co Ltd v Peterborough Corpn* [1972] 1 WLR 1400, [1972] 3 All ER 678.

it.[6] Fourth is the Land Compensation Act 1961, which contains the current rules for assessing compensation in so far as it relates directly to land values.

(b) Lands Tribunal and the courts

Disputes over compulsory purchase fall broadly into two main cases, depending on whether or not they relate to the assessment of compensation. If they do (and also in one or two special cases to be mentioned below) they must be brought before the Lands Tribunal, a specialized body staffed by valuers and lawyers. Otherwise they should normally be brought before the High Court. Appeal lies to the Court of Appeal not only from the High Court but also from the Lands Tribunal (though on a point of law only, by way of case stated, and within six weeks of the Tribunal's decision).[7]

B. COMPULSORY PURCHASE PROCEDURE

(1) COMPULSORY PURCHASE ORDERS

Any acquiring authority, who are empowered by the appropriate authorizing Act to select and acquire compulsorily the particular land they need by making a CPO, must normally do so by following the procedure laid down in the Acquisition of Land Act 1981, Parts I, II and III. This involves making the order in draft, and submitting it to a "confirming authority", which will be the appropriate Minister or Secretary of State unless of course he himself is acquiring the land. In all cases there must be prior press publicity and notification to the owners and occupiers of the land, and the hearing of objections by an inspector from the Ministry or Department concerned. Statutory inquiries procedure rules for hearings and inquiries are in force, closely parallel to those discussed above in relation to planning appeals.[8] The order may be confirmed, with or without modifications, or rejected. If confirmed it takes effect when the acquiring authority publish a notice in similar manner to the notice of the draft order and serve it on the owners and occupiers concerned. The order cannot be challenged (except possibly on the ground of invalidity) apart from the standard procedure for appeal to the High Court within six weeks on the ground of *ultra vires* or a procedural defect substantially prejudicing the appellant.[9]

---

6 In most cases the statutes which apply to the various stages of a compulsory purchase will be public general Acts, and particular land will be mentioned not in them but in the CPOs and other procedural instruments made under them. For a rare exception, see the Public Offices (Site) Act 1947 (a parcel of land near Westminster Abbey, specified in the Act by reference to a plan).

7 Lands Tribunal Act 1949, s. 3 (4); Rules of Supreme Court (Revision) 1965, Sch. 1, Ord. 61; Lands Tribunal Rules 1975, S.I. 1975 No. 299, as amended by S.I. 1977 No. 1820, S.I. 1981 Nos. 105 and 600, and S.I. 1984 No. 793.

8 P. 951, n. 2, ante. And see *Sunley Homes v Secretary of State for the Environment* (1974) 233 EG 519 (facts distinguished from opinions). In a few cases, e.g. the New Towns Act 1981, Schs. 4 and 5, a separate procedure is laid down for the making of CPOs, which takes the place of the normal procedure under the Acquisition of Land Act 1981, though the differences are not great.

9 1981 Act, Part IV. On this, cf pp. 949, n. 15, ante. For examples of *ultra vires* orders, see *London and Westcliff Properties Ltd v Minister of Housing and Local Government* [1961] 1 WLR 519, [1961] 1 All ER 610 (urban redevelopment), and *Webb v Minister of Housing and Local Government* [1965] 1 WLR 755, [1965] 2 All ER 193 (coast protection). For a challenge which failed, see *R v Secretary of State for Transport, ex p de Rothschild* [1989] 1 All ER 933 (disagreement over alternative sites). See (1971) 35 Conv (NS) 316 (K. Davies). For

(2) COMPULSORY PURCHASE CONVEYANCING

(a) Notices to treat

The CPO will lapse, in relation to any of the land comprised in it, unless it is acted on within three years.[10] When the authority wish to act on the order they must serve a "notice to treat" on the persons with interests in the land to be acquired, requiring them to submit details of their interests and their claims for compensation.[11] When the compensation is agreed in each case, it and the notice to treat together amount to an enforceable contract for the sale of the land.[12] This is then subject to completion by the execution of a conveyance in the same way as a private land transaction.[13]

(b) General vesting declarations

There is, however, an alternative procedure at the authority's option whereby the two stages comprising respectively the notice to treat and the conveyance are telescoped into one stage. This is the "general vesting declaration". The authority must notify the owners and occupiers concerned, in the same notice as that which states that the CPO is in force (or in a separate, later notice), that they intend to proceed in this manner by making a vesting declaration not less than two months ahead. This, when made, will by unilateral action vest the title to the land in the authority on a date not less than 28 days after notification to the owners concerned; and it will by and large have the same consequences as if a notice to treat were served.[14]

(c) Interests acquired

Freeholds and leaseholds, both legal and equitable,[15] are capable of compulsory acquisition. Leaseholds with a year or less to run, including

procedural details, forms etc., see Compulsory Purchase of Land Regulations 1982, S.I. 1982 No. 6.

10 CPA 1965, s. 4. This is taken to mean that a "notice to treat" must be served within that period: see *Grice v Dudley Corpn* [1958] Ch 329, [1957] 2 All ER 673.

11 Ibid., s. 5, as amended by the Planning and Compensation Act 1991, s. 67. The notice to treat will, unless superseded by a general vesting declaration, expire three years after it has been served, unless it has been acted on by (a) entry on the land, or (b) settlement of the compensation, or (c) reference of any dispute over the assessment of compensation to the Lands Tribunal. If the notice expires, the acquiring authority must notify the persons on whom it has been served and compensate them for any consequential loss. Details should be submitted, or negotiations begun, within 21 days, failing which, or in default of agreement, the case goes to the Lands Tribunal: CPA 1965, s. 6.

12 *Simpson's Motor Sales (London) Ltd v Hendon Corpn* [1964] AC 1088, [1963] 2 All ER 484.

13 The costs, including stamp duty, are borne by the acquiring authority: CPA 1965, s. 23. Local Government, Planning and Land Act 1980, Part X empowers the Secretary of State to compile a register of land acquired by public authorities which he considers to be under-used, with a view to its compulsory disposal.

14 Compulsory Purchase (Vesting Declarations) Act 1981. The notice which states that this procedure is to be used must be registered as a local land charge. The procedure will not affect leasehold tenants with a year or less to run, including periodic tenants, nor those with such longer periods to run as may be specified by the acquiring authority; though notices to treat may subsequently be served.

15 "Land" is usually defined in the appropriate authorizing Act. Equitable freeholds and leaseholds include estate contracts, under which the benefit has already passed to the purchaser: *Hillingdon Estates Co v Stonefield Estates Ltd* [1952] Ch 627, [1952] 1 All ER 853. Options are included in the rule: *Oppenheimer v Minister of Transport* [1942] 1 KB 242, [1941] 3 All ER 485. The same applies to equitable leases: *Blamires v Bradford Corpn* [1964] Ch 585, [1964] 2 All ER 603. In this context, failure to register the estate contract as a land charge is

periodic tenancies, are not subject to acquisition and compensation but allowed to run out, after the due service of notice to quit if necessary, unless possession is needed in a hurry, in which case it can be taken subject to payment of compensation for the loss caused.[16] An authority cannot normally, without clear statutory authorization, take rights over land in the limited form of an easement or other right less than full possession (even a stratum of land or building above or beneath the surface).[17] But if they acquire a dominant tenement they acquire the easements appurtenant to it, as in private conveyancing; and if they acquire a servient tenement they either allow the easements and other servitudes over it to subsist without interference or else pay compensation for "injurious affection" to the dominant land if they do so interfere.[18]

(d) Partial acquisitions

If part only of an owner's land is to be acquired, this is "severance". The owner of "any house, building or manufactory" or of "a park or garden belonging to a house" can require the authority to take all or none; but the authority can counter this by saying that to take part only will not cause any "material detriment", and any such dispute is to be settled by the Lands Tribunal.[19] Similar rules now apply to farms.[20]

(e) Delay and entry

Unjustifiable delay by the authority after service of a notice to treat may amount to abandonment of the acquisition.[1] As for making actual entry on

immaterial. An authority can acquire freeholds and leave leaseholds, or even vice versa; but see *London and Westcliff Properties Ltd v Minister of Housing and Local Government* [1961] 1 WLR 519, [1961] 1 All ER 610.

16 CPA 1965, s. 20; *Newham London Borough Council v Benjamin* [1968] 1 WLR 694, [1968] 1 All ER 1195. This procedure applies whether notices to treat or general vesting declarations are being used for the interests in reversion.

17 This was in issue when a compulsory purchase order for part of the Centre Point building in London was quashed in *Sovmots Investments Ltd v Secretary of State for the Environment* [1979] AC 144, [1977] 2 All ER 385. For the taking of strata of land, see *Metropolitan Rly Co v Fowler* [1893] AC 416; *City and South London Rly Co v United Parishes of St. Mary Woolnoth and St. Mary Woolchurch Haw* [1905] AC 1.

18 This is "injurious affection arising on land not taken from the claimant": see p. 978, post. See e.g. *Eagle v Charing Cross Rly Co* (1867) LR 2 CP 638 (easement of light) and *Re Simeon and Isle of Wight RDC* [1937] Ch 525, [1937] 3 All ER 149 (restrictive covenant not to interfere with percolating water). The same principle seems to be applicable in cases of appropriation of land, as well as acquisition: *Dowty Boulton Paul Ltd v Wolverhampton Corpn (No. 2)* [1976] Ch 13, [1973] 2 All ER 491. But see *Earl of Leicester v Wells-next-the-Sea UDC* [1973] Ch 110, [1972] 3 All ER 77.

19 CPA 1965, s. 8 (1), and Land Compensation Act 1973, s. 58. The right to make the acquiring authority take all the land in such a case seems to apply even if the CPO itself relates only to the part of the land the authority require; see *Genders v LCC* [1915] 1 Ch 1. The Compulsory Purchase (Vesting Declarations) Act 1981 applies similar rules to general vesting declarations. On the meaning of "material detriment", see *Ravenseft Properties Ltd v London Borough of Hillingdon* (1968) 20 P & CR 483.

20 Land Compensation Act 1973, ss. 53–7. The test is whether the rest of the farm unit cannot be reasonably farmed even with any other available land.

1 *Grice v Dudley Corpn* [1958] Ch 329, [1957] 2 All ER 673. But delay was held not to amount to abandonment in *Simpson's Motor Sales (London) Ltd v Hendon Corpn* [1964] AC 1088, [1963] 2 All ER 484 (the owners themselves being at least partly responsible for it). Most causes of delay will now be resolved by the expiry of the notice to treat as described on p. 972, n. 11, ante.

the land, the authority is not normally entitled to do this until completion and the payment of compensation, unless, after service of notice to treat, they serve a "notice of entry" on both owners and occupiers; and entry before payment of compensation entitles a claimant to receive interest on the compensation to be paid.[2]

(f) Acquisition by agreement and third party rights

Many acquisitions by authorities are made by agreement.[3] Obligations owed to third parties, as in restrictive covenants, do not normally involve the expropriated owner in liability, and the third party should seek his remedy against the authority if there is any breach in such a case.[4] On the other hand an owner must not increase the authority's liability to compensation by creating new tenancies and other rights in the land or carrying out works on it after service of the notice to treat, which are "not reasonably necessary".[5]

C. COMPULSORY PURCHASE COMPENSATION

(1) EXTENT OF COMPENSATION

The acquiring authority must compensate the expropriated owner for the land taken, by way of purchase price, and for any depreciation of land retained by him, as well as for "all damage directly consequent on the taking".[6]

(2) PURCHASE PRICE

(a) "Market value"

The basis of compensation for the taking or depreciation of land is "market value", namely "the amount which the land *if sold in the open market by a willing seller* might be expected to realize". "Special suitability or adaptability" of the land which depends solely on "a purpose to which it could be applied only in pursuance of statutory powers, or for which there is no market apart from the requirements of any authority possessing compulsory purchase

---

2 CPA 1965, s. 11 (1). The period of notice must be at least 14 days. For land taken "piecemeal", see *Chilton v Telford Development Corpn* [1987] 1 WLR 872, [1987] 3 All ER 992. For interests conveyed by a general vesting declaration notices of entry are not needed, but interest must still be paid in respect of advance entry. For interest, the rate of which is prescribed by the Treasury from time to time and which fluctuates in accordance with interest rates generally, see Land Compensation Act 1961, s. 32.

3 See CPA 1965, s. 3; *Munton v Greater London Council* [1976] 1 WLR 649, [1976] 2 All ER 815; *Duttons Brewery Ltd v Leeds City Council* (1981) 43 P & CR 160. Authorities are usually wise to obtain a CPO first, in case negotiations break down. Agreement does not abrogate the *ultra vires* rule; such acquisitions are still governed by the appropriate authorizing Act. The selling owner may himself be vulnerable in law, if he is in the position of a trustee, and may, therefore, apply to the Lands Tribunal to certify that a sale by agreement is "at the best price that can reasonably be obtained": Land Compensation Act 1961, s. 35.

4 See *Baily v De Crespigny* (1869) LR 4 QB 180. But see *Matthey v Curling* [1922] 2 AC 180.

5 Acquisition of Land Act 1981, Part V. Assignments, however, are in order: *Cardiff Corpn v Cook* [1923] 2 Ch 115.

6 *Harvey v Crawley Development Corpn* [1957] 1 QB 485 at 492, [1957] 1 All ER 504 at 506, per DENNING LJ.

powers", must be disregarded.[7] There must be no addition to nor deduction from market value purely on the ground that the purchase is compulsory, nor any addition specifically on account of the project to be carried out by the acquiring authority.[8] An increase in the value of adjoining land of the owner not taken by the authority, if it results from the compulsory acquisition, must be "set off" against compensation.[9]

If the property has been developed and used for a purpose which has no effective market value, such as a church, then the Lands Tribunal may order that compensation "be assessed on the basis of the reasonable cost of equivalent reinstatement", if "satisfied that reinstatement in some other place is bona fide intended".[10] This requires a finding that the present use of the land is for a purpose for which there is "no general demand or market".[11]

These intricate legal rules are intended for the guidance of valuers rather than lawyers. Valuers engaged in the assessment of the compensation are required, subject to such guidance, to reach a figure which will put the expropriated owner in a position as near as reasonably possible to that in which he would find himself if there had been no compulsory acquisition and he had sold his land in an ordinary private sale.[12]

7 Land Compensation Act 1961, s. 5. Any restrictions burdening the land must be taken into account in the valuation: *Abbey Homesteads (Developments) Ltd v Northamptonshire County Council* (1992) 64 P & CR 377. But unauthorised uses must not: *Hughes v Doncaster Metropolitan Borough Council* [1991] 1 AC 382, [1991] 1 All ER 295. For "sitting tenants", see *Lambe v Secretary of State for War* [1955] 2 QB 612, [1955] 2 All ER 386. Disregard of "special suitability" used to extend additionally to "the special needs of a particular purchaser" until the repeal of those words by the Planning and Compensation Act 1991, s. 70 and Sch. 15. Business and farm tenants are to be compensated on expropriation on the footing that the value of their statutory security of tenure is to be taken into account; and this is reflected also in their landlords' compensation: Land Compensation Act 1973, ss. 47–8.

8 Ibid., ss. 5, 9; *Pointe Gourde Quarrying and Transport Co Ltd v Sub-Intendent of Crown Lands* [1947] AC 565; *Wilson v Liverpool Corpn* [1971] 1 WLR 302, [1971] 1 All ER 628; *Jelson Ltd v Blaby District Council* [1977] 1 WLR 1020, [1978] 1 All ER 548; *Birmingham District Council v Morris and Jacombs Ltd* (1976) 33 P & CR 27; *Melwood Units Pty Ltd v Main Roads Comr* [1979] AC 426, [1979] 1 All ER 161. The so-called "*Pointe Gourde* rule" cannot be fully reconciled with the "willing seller" rule which is the true basis for assessing compensation, and raises doubts whether the law on compensation is fully consistent with the principle of market value.

9 Ibid., s. 7. There must be no artificial additions to or reductions from the price of the land taken, on the assumption that it might *not* have been taken, which are attributable to the authority's development to be carried out on the rest of the land taken, if that is unlikely to have been carried out in circumstances other than those of the acquisition itself: s. 6 and Sch. 1 (as amended by New Towns Act 1966 and Local Government, Planning and Land Act 1980, s. 145 and Sch. 25). See also s. 8, and *Davy v Leeds Corpn* [1965] 1 WLR 445, [1965] 1 All ER 753.

10 Ibid., s. 5, rule 5; *Birmingham Corpn v West Midland Baptist (Trust) Association (Inc)* [1970] AC 874, [1969] 3 All ER 172; *Zoar Independent Church Trustees v Rochester Corpn* [1975] QB 246, [1974] 3 All ER 5.

11 In *Harrison & Hetherington Ltd v Cumbria County Council* (1985) 50 P & CR 396, HL held that these words applied to land used for a livestock market. *Sed quaere.*

12 "... the sum to be ascertained is in essence one sum, namely, the proper price or compensation payable in all the circumstances of the case": *Horn v Sunderland Corpn* [1941] 2 KB 26 at 34, [1941] 1 All ER 480 at 486, per GREENE MR. For purchases by agreement, p. 974, n. 3, ante. For particular applications of the general principle, see *Hertfordshire County Council v Ozanne* [1991] 1 WLR 105, [1991] 1 All ER 769 ("ransom strip"); *Stokes v Cambridge Corpn* (1961) 13 P & CR 77 (inadequate access).

(b) Market demand and planning control

Market value, however, has in any case two distinct main elements: "existing use value" and "prospective development value".[13] Since development is not lawful without planning permission, the absence of permission will inhibit purchasers from paying any amount over and above "existing use" value, whether the land is built on or vacant in its present state of development. Before the days of planning control, "prospective development value" over and above "existing use value" depended on market demand; and this is still true. "It is not planning permission by itself which increases value. It is planning permission coupled with demand."[14]

Assessing the existence of demand is essentially a question of valuers' expert evidence; though of course the Lands Tribunal is better qualified than a court to pronounce on such evidence. Assessing the availability of planning permission, however, calls for special statutory rules, because there are many cases where planning permission is refused purely because proposed development, which is otherwise acceptable, is ruled out by the impending compulsory purchase, which in turn will often be for the purpose of a public works project with little or no market value.

(c) Planning assumptions

"Assumptions as to planning permission" are therefore, for compensation purposes *only*, authorized by statute. The most useful of these turn on the allocation or "zoning" in the current development plan of areas of land which include the owner's property for uses which command a lucrative development value: residential, commercial or industrial. There may be a range of such uses.[15] But permission can only be assumed if it is also reasonable to do so in relation to the particular physical or planning circumstances of the land itself.[16]

---

13 The latter completely excludes the cost of development, including the developer's profit; any actual development carried out will add yet another item to the eventual total cost of land. "Prospective development value" is the amount (if any) which the market adds to "existing use value" when, for example, a field is in demand as a building plot, but no steps have yet been taken to carry out building works on it, or a house is in demand for office use but has not so far been converted. It is "development potential", not development.

14 *Viscount Camrose v Basingstoke Corpn* [1966] 1 WLR 1100 at 1106, [1966] 3 All ER 161 at 164, per Lord DENNING MR. See also *Myers v Milton Keynes Development Corpn* [1974] 1 WLR 696, [1974] 2 All ER 1096.

15 See Land Compensation Act 1961, ss. 14–16. Planning permission can be assumed (under s. 15) for the development which the acquiring authority itself intends to carry out. It can also be assumed for (a) development consisting of rebuilding works, subject to certain constraints on floor space, "so long as the cubic content of the original building is not substantially exceeded", and so long as that building existed on 1 July 1948, or, if not, "was in existence at a material date" thereafter, or was demolished between 7 January 1937 and 1 July 1948, and (b) for converting a single dwelling-house into two or more separate dwelling-houses: TCPA 1990, Sch. 3 as amended by Planning and Compensation Act 1991. But these assumptions will rarely be as beneficial to claimants as those based on "zoning"; nor will any assumption as to planning permission be beneficial to a claimant unless market demand for development can be proved in addition.

16 See *Margate Corpn v Devotwill Investments Ltd* [1970] 3 All ER 864; *Provincial Properties (London) Ltd v Caterham and Warlingham UDC* [1972] 1 QB 453, [1972] 1 All ER 60. If land being acquired includes a listed building, a listed building consent will be assumed for any works of alteration, but not demolition (unless in connection with development within the terms of TCPA 1990, Sch. 3; see n. 15, supra.); Planning (Listed Buildings and Conservation Areas) Act 1990, s. 49.

Whether or not the development plan is found to "zone" the land in this way the owner (or the authority) can apply to the local planning authority for a "certificate of appropriate alternative development" in relation to the particular circumstances of the land. Appeal lies to the Secretary of State; and from him in turn lies the usual limited right of appeal within six weeks to the High Court. The cost of applying for that certificate will be included in the compensation, if the applicant is successful in claiming development value by this means.[17]

(d) Subsequent development

If, within ten years after a compulsory acquisition, any subsequent planning permission is granted which adds to the development value of the land acquired, that additional value may be claimed by the expropriated owner from the acquiring authority, calculated on the basis of values at the time of the acquisition from him.[18]

(3) DEPRECIATION AND DISTURBANCE

(a) Severance and injurious affection

In addition to purchase price compensation there is compensation for depreciation of land retained. This is usually termed "severance" if it relates to the *pro rata* reduction in value of the land retained over and above its reduction in size.[19] If, however, it refers to depreciation caused by what is done on the land taken, it is termed "injurious affection".[20] The latter is closely analogous to damages in tort for private nuisance,[1] though it may well include loss not compensatable in tort.[2] But if what is done goes beyond what is authorized by the statutory powers of the acquiring authority, then it

---

17 Land Compensation Act 1961, ss. 17–22, as amended by Local Government, Planning and Land Act 1980, s. 121 and the Planning and Compensation Act 1991, s. 65. S. 70 and Sch. 15 provide that an assumption which is upheld in a certificate of appropriate alternative development must be taken into account when considering an assumption based on the development plan even if they conflict. See *London & Clydeside Estates Ltd v Aberdeen District Council* [1980] 1 WLR 182, [1979] 3 All ER 876 in regard to the giving of reasons and information.

18 Land Compensation Act 1961, Part IV, inserted by the Planning and Compensation Act 1991, s. 66 and Sch. 14. There are various special cases specified in these provisions where the right to additional compensation is excluded. The time of the acquisition is in normal cases to be taken as the date of the notice to treat.

19 As a result of that reduction (i.e taking part of the owner's land and leaving part). See *Holt v Gas Light and Coke Co* (1872) LR 7 QB 728; *Palmer and Harvey Ltd v Ipswich Corpn* (1953) 4 P & CR 5. But note that CPA 1965, s. 7, speaks of "severing ... or *otherwise* injuriously affecting ..." "Injurious affection" is in fact the Victorian term for "depreciation", in which sense it strictly *includes* "severance".

20 The depreciation need not be caused *entirely* by what is done on the land taken as distinct from other land, provided that it is at least *partly* so caused: Land Compensation Act 1973, s. 44.

1 Land "retained" by an owner may be considered for severance and injurious affection compensation even if not immediately contiguous with the land taken: *Cowper Essex v Acton Local Board* (1889) 14 App Cas 153, and even if enjoyed under a different interest, such as an option: *Oppenheimer v Minister of Transport* [1942] 1 KB 242, [1941] 3 All ER 485.

2 E.g. loss of privacy. The leading case is *Duke of Buccleuch v Metropolitan Board of Works* (1872) LR 5 HL 418. The depreciation must be compensated *in full* as a straightforward matter of valuation on a "before and after" basis.

will in any case be unlawful and so compensatable (if at all) in tort and not as "injurious affection".[3]

(b) Injurious affection when no land is taken from the claimant

It is also possible to obtain compensation for "injurious affection" when *no* land has been acquired from the claimant. Here it is necessary to prove four things: (*a*) the loss is caused by acts authorized by statute, (*b*) it would be actionable in private law if it were not so authorised, (*c*) it is strictly a depreciation in land value, and (*d*) it arises from the carrying out of works on the compulsorily acquired land and not from its subsequent use.[4] But depreciation caused by the *use* of public works, including highways and aerodromes, is in many cases now compensatable under Part I of the Land Compensation Act 1973, if attributable to "physical factors".[5] The claim period of six years starts to run from one year after the use begins.[6]

(c) Disturbance and related matters

Another head of compensation is "disturbance", which is not strictly land value but "must . . . refer to the fact of having to vacate the premises".[7] Thus it may include the loss of business profits and goodwill, removal expenses and the cost of acquiring new premises.[8] It has been held that to claim for

3 Including where the authority "have statutory powers which they . . . exercise in a manner hurtful to third parties" when they could have done so "in a manner innocuous to third parties", this being a perverse choice amounting to negligence: *Logan Navigation Co v Lambeg Bleaching etc. Co* [1927] AC 226, per Lord ATKINSON. Stopping up a highway does not, *per se*, normally give a right to compensation: see *Jolliffe v Exeter Corpn* [1967] 1 WLR 993, [1967] 2 All ER 1099.

4 *Metropolitan Board of Works v McCarthy* (1874) LR 7 HL 243. See also *Ricket v Metropolitan Rly Co* (1867) LR 2 HL 175; *Argyle Motors (Birkenhead) Ltd v Birkenhead Corpn* [1975] AC 99, [1974] 1 All ER 201; *Wrotham Park Settled Estates v Hertsmere Borough Council* [1993] 33 RVR 56; *Re Simeon and Isle of Wight Rural District Council* [1937] Ch 525, [1937] 3 All ER 149.

5 These are: noise, vibration, smell, fumes, smoke, artificial lighting, and solid or liquid discharge. See *Hickmott v Dorset County Council* (1977) 35 P & CR 195; *Marchant v Secretary of State for Transport* [1979] RVR 113.

6 Limitation Act 1980, s. 9; Land Compensation Act 1973, s. 3, as amended by Local Government, Planning and Land Act 1980, ss. 112, 113.

7 *Lee v Minister of Transport* [1966] 1 QB 111 at 122, [1965] 2 All ER 986 at 989, per DAVIES LJ. It is regarded as part of the price of the land, and is therefore only payable to a claimant who is *expropriated* and so entitled to a market value purchase price as well as being dispossessed. This excludes those tenants who, though dispossessed (by notice to quit or by effluxion of time), are not expropriated and landlords who, though expropriated, are not dispossessed. But expropriated landowners not in occupation can now claim *expenses* of obtaining alternative property in UK, as if claiming disturbance compensation, provided that they do so within one year from the date of entry: Planning and Compensation Act 1991, s. 70 and Sch. 17, inserting a new s. 10A in the Land Compensation Act 1961. A dispossessed licensee as such will get nothing: *Woolfson v Strathclyde Regional Council* (1978) 39 P & CR 521 (other than a company having the same directors as a related company which *is* being expropriated: *DHN Food Distributors Ltd v Tower Hamlets London Borough Council* [1976] 1 WLR 852, [1976] 3 All ER 462). As to costs incurred in advance, see *Prasad v Wolverhampton Borough Council* [1983] Ch 333, [1983] 2 All ER 140.

8 *Harvey v Crawley Development Corpn* [1957] 1 QB 485, [1957] 1 All ER 504. The additional capital cost of buying dearer property, however, is "value for money", and not compensatable. It is not the same as compensation on the basis of "equivalent reinstatement". See the judgment of DENNING LJ. The cost of preparing the compensation claim itself may be included in the claim (*London County Council v Tobin* [1959] 1 WLR 354, [1959] 1 All ER 649) but as "any other matter", not "disturbance": *Lee v Minister of Transport*, supra; Land Compensation Act 1961, s. 5 (6). On goodwill, see Land Compensation Act 1973, s. 46 (claimants aged over 60) and *Bailey v Derby Corpn* [1965] 1 WLR 213, [1965] 1 All ER 443.

"disturbance" an owner must forgo "prospective development value" in his purchase price compensation; that is to say, his "true loss" is whichever is the higher: "existing use" plus "prospective development" or "existing use" plus "disturbance".[9]

Since disturbance *compensation* is (illogically) supposed to be an integral part of land value[10] it is not payable where the acquiring body, having expropriated the landlord, displace a short-term tenant by *notice to quit* or by effluxion of time. In such cases the Land Compensation Act 1973[11] provides for "disturbance payments" (removal expenses, business losses) by the acquiring body to the tenant.[12]

(d) Assessment of compensation

A claimant "must once for all make one claim for all damages which can be reasonably foreseen".[13] The date of the notice to treat fixes the interests which may be acquired, but not compensation, which must be assessed as at the time of making the assessment, or of taking possession (if earlier), or of the beginning of "equivalent reinstatement".[14]

---

9 *Horn v Sunderland Corpn* [1941] 2 KB 26, [1941] 1 All ER 480. In a private sale to a developer a vendor would expect to sacrifice all the profits arising from the existing use in order to secure the additional value which the prospect of development would put on to the market price of the land. But even a vendor selling purely at the "existing use" value would not expect to get his removal expenses paid by the purchaser; so to this extent "disturbance" compensation may be a bonus.

10 See *IRC v Glasgow & South Western Rly Co* (1887) 12 App Cas. 315. It is therefore part of a capital sum, though some may represent lost *income* (e.g. profits). On the taxation complexities arising out of this, see *Stoke-on-Trent City Council v Wood Mitchell & Co Ltd* [1980] 1 WLR 254, [1979] 2 All ER 65, and Taxation of Chargeable Gains Act 1992, s. 245. On the relevance of grants, see *Palatine Graphic Arts Co Ltd v Liverpool City Council* [1986] QB 335, [1986] 1 All ER 366.

11 Ss. 37–8. See *R v Islington London Borough Council, ex p Knight* [1984] 1 WLR 205, [1984] 1 All ER 154. See also ss. 29–33 ("home loss payments"), ss. 34–6 ("farm loss payments") and ss. 39–43 (rehousing displaced residents). These provisions are as amended by the Planning and Compensation Act 1991, ss. 68–70 and Sch. 17. *Home* loss payments are obtainable by claimants who are displaced from their homes by compulsory purchase, provided that they have occupied them for a year by virtue of freehold or leasehold ownership; a tenant for less than three years is entitled to £1,500, but a tenant or owner for three years or more is entitled to 10 per cent of the market value of his interest (but not less than £1,500 nor more than £15,000) and a deserted spouse can claim in place of the deserter. *Farm* loss payments are payable to farmers who have held a yearly tenancy or greater interest in their farm and are displaced by compulsory purchase of "the whole or a sufficient part" of it, the claimable amount being based on the average profit from the farm; but it is a necessary pre-condition that the claimant is moving to another farm elsewhere in Great Britain.

12 Farm tenants are separately catered for: ss. 59, 61. Farm and business tenants enjoying statutory security of tenure have compensation rights against their *landlords*.

13 *Chamberlain v West End of London etc. Rly Co* (1863) 2 B & S 617, per ERLE CJ. If a claim is not submitted within 21 days of service of the notice to treat (or the general vesting declaration; see p. 972, n. 14, ante) the dispute is referable to the Lands Tribunal: CPA 1965, s. 6. Unreasonable delay in submitting a claim will lead to an order to pay the authority's costs incurred through the delay; and if either side refuses an unconditional offer by the other, which is then kept secret (a "sealed offer") and turns out to be more favourable than the Tribunal's award, the costs of the other side incurred through the delay thereby caused will also have to be paid: Land Compensation Act 1961, s. 4. See *Pepys v London Transport Executive* [1975] 1 WLR 234, [1975] 1 All ER 748.

14 *Birmingham Corpn v West Midland Baptist (Trust) Association (Inc)* [1970] AC 874, [1969] 3 All ER 172. For advance payments, see Land Compensation Act 1973, ss. 52 and 52A, as amended and added by Planning and Compensation Act 1991, s. 63 (up to 90 per cent of the estimated amount, with subsequent adjustments for insufficient and excessive payments, and yearly payments of accrued interest on unpaid balances exceeding £1,000).

SECTION II COMPULSORY PURCHASE AND COMPENSATION IN PLANNING

A. COMPULSORY PURCHASE IN PLANNING

(1) ACQUISITION "FOR PLANNING PURPOSES"

The planning statutes are themselves the authorizing Acts for certain kinds of compulsory purchase of land. Thus they authorize acquisition "in connection with development and for other planning purposes".[15] This means land required "in order to secure the carrying out of one or more of the following activities, namely, development, redevelopment and improvement", or "required for a purpose which it is necessary to achieve in the interests of the proper planning of an area in which the land is situated":[16] in other words, "positive planning". Local authorities in general have this power in respect of land in their areas, subject to the standard compulsory purchase procedure. They can themselves develop land so acquired, with the Secretary of State's consent. More usually they dispose of the land with his consent in specified cases "in such manner and subject to such conditions as may appear to them to be expedient".[17]

(2) INVERSE COMPULSORY PURCHASE

(a) Varieties of compulsory purchase instigated by owners

Another aspect of compulsory purchase in planning is "inverse compulsory purchase", of which there are two species: purchase notices and "blight notices". The owners supply the compulsion in these cases, not the acquiring authorities.[18] A purchase notice is served in consequence of an adverse planning decision; but a blight notice is served in consequence of adverse planning proposals.

(b) Purchase notices

If planning permission is in a particular case refused, or granted subject to conditions, so that as a result "the land has become incapable of reasonably

---

15 Acquisition of land "for planning purposes" can perhaps be said to occur also under e.g. New Towns Act 1981, National Parks and Access to the Countryside Act 1949, Countryside Act 1968, Wild Life and Countryside Act 1981, Land Compensation Act 1973 Part II, Local Government, Planning and Land Act 1980 Part XVI ("urban development corporations") and Leasehold Reform, Housing and Urban Development Act 1993 Part III (Urban Regeneration Agency). Local authorities can also make grants or loans to encourage improved use of land in declining "inner city areas", with central government assistance: Inner Urban Areas Act 1978.

16 TCPA 1990, s. 226. A local plan may be prepared for an "action area" chosen for "comprehensive treatment, by development, redevelopment or improvement". See s. 12 (8); p. 947, n. 18, ante.

17 Ibid., ss. 232–246. This is what happens to bring about "urban renewal", meaning town-centre redevelopment in most cases. "Action areas" will normally be prescribed for such "positive planning" in future (see n. 16, supra). See s. 227 for acquisitions by agreement; and s. 228 for compulsory acquisition by the Secretary of State of "land necessary for the public service".

18 Ibid., Part VI. No CPO is required, and an effective notice is the equivalent of a notice to treat, so that all that remains to be done is to assess the compensation by the usual procedure: ss. 139, 143 (purchase notices); 154, 160 (blight notices). Compensation for purchase notices will largely be concerned with prospective development value, for blight notices with existing use value, though not exclusively so in either case.

beneficial use in its existing state", then an owner may serve a purchase notice on the local borough or district council.[19] If the council are unwilling to accept it they must normally refer it to the Secretary of State who must then exercise his own judgment as to whether the notice is justifiable and ought to be upheld.[20] He must not uphold it merely on the ground that "the land in its existing state and with its existing permissions is substantially less useful to the server", since that is true of nearly all planning refusals.[1] The land[2] must in fact be virtually useless to justify a purchase notice.

(c) "Blight notices"

A "blight notice" is served on the "appropriate authority", meaning a prospective acquiring authority.[3] There are four principal requirements: (1) the owner's land must be "blighted land"; (2) the server must hold a "qualifying interest"; (3) he must have made genuine but unsuccessful attempts to sell for a reasonable price on the open market; and (4) the authority must in fact intend to acquire the land.[4] Within two months the authority concerned may serve a counter-notice alleging that any of the above requirements has not been met. The claimant then has two more months in which to refer the dispute to the Lands Tribunal, before whom the burden of proof is on the authority if they deny an intention to acquire any or all of the land but on the claimant in other cases.[5]

The categories of blighted land all relate to planning proposals by public bodies which envisage compulsory acquisition by one or more public authorities. For example, land may be indicated as being required for the

19 TCPA 1990, s. 137. The procedure can also be used in consequence of the service of revocation and discontinuance orders, etc., see p. 957, ante. On the relevance of breaches of planning control to the meaning of "incapable of reasonable beneficial use", see *Balco Transport Services Ltd v Secretary of State for the Environment (No. 2)* [1986] 1 WLR 88, [1985] 3 All ER 689.

20 Ibid., ss. 141–143. If he considers the notice unjustified, he must reject it; if justified, confirm it. But in the latter case he has discretion to arrange for permission to be given for some alternative development, or for an alternative body to acquire the land.

1 *R v Minister of Housing and Local Government, ex p Chichester RDC* [1960] 1 WLR 587, [1960] 2 All ER 407. But see TCPA 1990, s. 142 (reversing *Adams and Wade Ltd v Minister of Housing and Local Government* (1965) 18 P & CR 60). For the meaning of "owner", see *London Corpn v Cusack-Smith* [1955] AC 337, [1955] 1 All ER 302, and TCPA 1990, s. 336 (1).

2 *All* the land affected: *Smart and Courtenay Dale Ltd v Dover RDC* (1972) 23 P & CR 408.

3 TCPA 1990, s. 169 ("the government department, local authority or other body or person by whom . . . the land is liable to be acquired"). There may be more than one such authority: *R v Secretary of State for the Environment, ex p Bournemouth Borough Council* [1987] 1 EGLR 198.

4 Ibid., ss. 149–151. Land is "blighted" if it comes within any of 23 categories set out in Sch. 13. A "qualifying interest" is a freehold or leasehold of 3 years or more: s. 168 (3), by virtue of which the claimant is an occupier (subject to an annual value limit for rating, if the property is not residential, of £18,000 under the TCP (Blight Provisions) Order 1990 (S.I. 1990 No. 465), and occupation must have lasted for 6 months up to the date of service of the blight notice or to an earlier date (not more than 12 months previously). If a claimant dies after service of a blight notice, it continues for the benefit of his personal representatives; and in some circumstances a mortgagee can serve a notice: TCPA 1990, ss. 161–162.

5 Ibid., ss. 151–153. The authority may in some cases deny that it intends to acquire the land at all and in other cases deny that it intends to acquire it during the next 15 years: s. 151 (4). See *Bolton Corpn v Owen* [1962] 1 QB 470, [1962] 1 All ER 101. In *Mancini v Coventry City Council* (1982) 44 P & CR 114, CA doubted the proposition that an objection on the ground that the authority do not intend to acquire the land is "not well-founded" if undue hardship results to the claimant.

functions of a public[6] body in a local plan or, failing that, in a structure plan or, failing that, indicated in any development plan as required for a highway; or as land in or beside the line of a trunk or special road,[7] or sufficiently indicated in writing by the Secretary of State to the local planning authority as required for such a road, or selected for a highway by a resolution of a local highway authority; or as land covered by a CPO which has not yet been acted upon, or else subject to compulsory purchase by virtue of a special enactment.[8]

B. BETTERMENT AND PLANNING COMPENSATION

(1) NEW AND OLD MEANINGS OF BETTERMENT

In discussing "market value" compensation above, "existing use value" was distinguished from "prospective development value", and the latter shown to depend on there being both market demand and planning permission for development. "Prospective development value" is synonymous with "betterment" in its current meaning, although formerly "betterment" seems to have meant the increase in the *overall* market value of land by reason of beneficial public works on other land nearby. Either way, the meaning is a purely financial one.

The switch in meaning was the result of the Uthwatt Report of 1942.[9] The new meaning has held the field since then, and with it has arisen the view that "betterment", unlike "existing use" value or the actual cost of development, has not been earned by the owner who realizes it. In a sense, only the community as a whole can be said to have "earned" the prospective development value of land.

(2) PUBLIC APPROPRIATION OF BETTERMENT

(a) Development charges

If "betterment" accrues, therefore, is the community entitled to take all or any of it? The Town and Country Planning Act 1947 went on the assumption that the community was entitled to take all of it, since it could not thenceforth come into existence without a planning permission. The Act imposed a "development charge" which appropriated to a new government body, the Central Land Board, all "betterment" (i.e. development value) accruing as the result of any grant of planning permission. At the same time it was decided that all owners to whom such betterment had already accrued by the time of the Act's commencement should receive once-for-all compensation for the loss of it.[10] This was to have been paid in 1953 out of a special £300

6 Land "zoned" for housing in a development plan is *not* thereby indicated as required for the local council as housing authority, since at that stage the question is still open whether private housing development may be permitted there: *Bolton Corpn v Owen, supra.*

7 As indicated in an operative scheme or order under the Highways Act 1980.

8 TCPA 1990, Sch. 13. As regards the rateable value limit, see p. 781, ante; *Essex County Council v Essex Incorporated Congregational Church Union* [1963] AC 808, [1963] 1 All ER 326. If a farm is only within the "specified descriptions" as to part of its area, the rest can be included in the blight notice provided that it is not reasonably capable of being farmed on its own or with any other available land: ibid., ss. 158–159.

9 Final Report of the Expert Committee on Compensation and Betterment 1942 (Cmd 6386).

10 TCPA 1947, Part IV. The compensation was to be "once-for-all", but development charges would be imposed every time permission was granted. Commencement occurred on 1 July 1948, the "appointed day".

million fund; but as from 1952 development charges were abolished and the compensation proposals halted.[11] The "established claims" on the fund, however, were soon to be made use of in a peculiar manner.[12]

(b) Capital gains tax, betterment levy and development land tax

In 1965 betterment came within the scope of capital gains tax[13] at 30 per cent, after being untaxed for thirteen years. The Land Commission Act 1967 replaced this charge on betterment by a separate "betterment levy" initially set at 40 per cent,[14] and set up the Land Commission to collect it. This was abolished in 1971: but betterment reverted to being taxed as a capital gain, which in 1974 became treated for tax purposes as if it were income.[15] In 1976 this "development gains tax" was superseded by "development land tax", which was set at 60 per cent (initially 80 per cent), subject to various exemptions, but was repealed by the Finance Act 1985, for disposals of land on and after 19 March 1985.[16] Betterment has thus for the third time become taxable as a capital gain.

(3) PLANNING COMPENSATION

(a) Loss of development value

The converse of appropriating "betterment" to the community is awarding compensation to owners who are deprived of it by the community, not in the sense that market demand is prevented from arising for the development of particular land but in the sense that development itself is prevented by planning restrictions. It might be thought that, as a principle of State policy, it would be logical to decide either that if there is 100 per cent betterment levy there should be no planning compensation, or that there should be 100 per cent compensation if there is no levy. In practice the policy applied has not been so simple, nor so logical.

The Town and Country Planning Act 1947 adopted the principle that, since "betterment" would be taxed at 100 per cent, there should be no compensation other than a once-for-all award to owners of land which already enjoyed development value before the "appointed day" when the Act came into force (1 July 1948). This logical but Draconian principle was jettisoned in 1952. There then followed a period of confusion in which those landowners who obtained planning permission retained the development value which then accrued, whereas those who did not were not compensated in lieu except in some limited classes of case.

These classes have now been abolished by section 31 of the Planning and Compensation Act 1991, subject to certain exceptions. Before section 31 came into force it was true to say that to obtain planning compensation for loss of development value caused by refusals of permission (or grants of

11 TCPA 1953.
12 This was in order to justify paying compensation for planning restrictions provided that the land affected was subject to an "unexpended balance of established development value" (UXB) derived from an "established claim". This limited entitlement to compensation survived until the Planning and Compensation Act 1991, s. 31 abolished it: infra.
13 Finance Act 1965.
14 Land Commission Act 1967, ss. 27–8; Betterment Levy (Prescribed Rate) Order 1967, S.I. 1967 No. 544.
15 Land Commission (Dissolution) Act 1971; Finance Act 1971, s. 55; Finance Act 1974, s. 38.
16 Development Land Tax Act 1976, s. 1 (80%); Finance Act (No. 2) 1979, s. 24 (60%); Finance Act 1985, s. 93 (abolition).

permission subject to onerous conditions) was the exception and not the rule.[17] Thereafter such compensation ceased to be obtainable at all.[18]

(b) Entitlement to planning compensation today

Restrictions on development imposed by way of revocation, modification or discontinuance orders, since they are in effect regarded as interference with the enjoyment of development value previously conceded to an owner by the grant of planning permission, are fully compensatable by the local planning authority.[19]

Disputes are to be referred to the Lands Tribunal,[20] with the usual limited right of appeal to the Court of Appeal.[1] In addition to loss of development value, compensation may have to include abortive expenditure.[2]

---

17 TCPA 1990, ss. 114, 119–136, repeating the substance of provisions dating back to TCPA 1954, under which compensation was payable for restrictions on development: (a) within TCPA 1990, Part II, Sch. 3, or (b) not within Sch. 3, but relating to land with a UXB; p. 983, n. 12, ante.

18 But TCPA 1990, Sch. 3, as amended by Planning and Compensation Act 1991, Sch. 6, para. 40, retains two categories of such compensation which are obtainable in cases not of planning refusals but of compulsory purchase: p. 976, n. 15, ante.

19 TCPA 1990, ss. 107–113, 115; pp. 957–8, ante. An example can be seen in *Blow v Norfolk County Council* [1967] 1 WLR 1280, [1966] 3 All ER 579 (discontinuance order). For tree preservation orders and certain special cases of advertisements, see ss. 203–205, 223, and TCP (Control of Advertisements) Regs. 1992, reg. 17. See also *Bollans v Surrey County Council* (1968) 20 P & CR 745 (tree preservation). For listed buildings and building preservation notices, see Planning (Listed Buildings and Conservation Areas) Act 1990, ss. 28–31; p. 965, n. 17, ante.

20 TCPA 1990, ss. 118–119. Market value is to be calculated "so far as applicable and subject to any necessary modifications" in accordance with the rules in Land Compensation Act 1961, s. 5; but see *Canterbury City Council v Colley* [1993] AC 401, [1993] 1 All ER 591.

1 P. 971, n. 7, ante.

2 See *Pennine Raceway Ltd v Kirklees Metropolitan Borough Council* [1983] QB 382, [1982] 3 All ER 628.

Index